U-V Volume 20

The World Book Encyclopedia

WORLD
BOOK

a Scott Fetzer company
Chicago
www.worldbookonline.com

The World Book Encyclopedia

World Book, Inc.
233 North Michigan Avenue
Chicago, IL 60601
U.S.A.

http://www.worldbook.com

About the cover design

The encyclopedia is available in both traditional and SPINESCAPE® bindings. The SPINESCAPE® design for the 2009 edition—*The Diversity of Life*—pictures endangered and vulnerable animals. These species, all threatened with extinction, include the whale shark and elkhorn coral of the oceans, the Karner blue butterfly and whooping crane of North America, the cheetah of Africa, and the snow leopard, orangutan, Asian elephant, giant panda, and Bactrian camel of Asia. *The Diversity of Life* underscores the importance of protecting the variety of animal life for future generations.

© SeaPics.com; © Franklin Viola, Animals Animals; © Ken Cole, Animals Animals; © age fotostock/SuperStock; © JupiterImages/Creatas/Alamy Images; © Hanne & Jens Eriksen, Nature Picture Library; © Anup Shah, Taxi/Getty Images; © Lockwood & Dattatri, Nature Picture Library; © Thomas & Pat Leeson, Photo Researchers; © Tom Mangelsen, Minden Pictures; © Gertrud & Helmut Denzau, Nature Picture Library

Library of Congress Cataloging-in-Publication Data

The World Book encyclopedia.
    p. cm.
    Includes index.
    Summary: "A 22-volume, highly illustrated, A-Z general encyclopedia for all ages, featuring sections on how to use World Book, other research aids, pronunciation key, a student guide to better writing, speaking, and research skills, and comprehensive index"--Provided by publisher.
    ISBN 978-0-7166-0109-8
    1. Encyclopedias and dictionaries. I. World Book, Inc.
AE5.W55 2009
031--dc22

                    2008028060

Printed in the United States of America

08 5 4 3 2 1

Printed on acid-free recycled paper with a minimum of 20 percent post-consumer recovered fiber.

Uu

U is the 21st letter of our alphabet. It came from a letter which the Semitic peoples of Syria and Palestine called *waw. Waw* was also the source of the letters F, V, W, and Y. The word *waw* meant *hook,* and was represented by a symbol of a tenthook. The symbol was probably borrowed from an Egyptian *hieroglyphic* (picture symbol). The Greeks borrowed the letter from the Phoenicians and gave it a Y shape. The Romans, when they adopted the letter, dropped its bottom stroke and wrote it as V. They used it for the vowel sound, *u,* and the consonant sound, *v.* About A.D. 900, people began to write *u* in the middle of a word and *v* at the beginning. During the Renaissance, it became customary among the people to use *u* as a vowel and *v* as a consonant. See **Alphabet.**

Uses. *U* or *u* is about the 12th most frequently used letter in books, newspapers, and other printed material in English. As an abbreviation on report cards, *u* means *unsatisfactory.* In geographic names, it may mean *united, union,* or *upper.* It often stands for *university.* In chemistry, *U* is the symbol for the element *uranium.*

Pronunciation. *U* is a vowel, and has many sounds in English. The sound we associate with its name, *you,* is really a diphthong. It is made by linking two separate sounds pronounced continuously. A person forms this sound by rounding the lips, with the tip of the tongue below the lower teeth, and raising the back of the tongue. Other sounds of *u* are those in *sun, duty, presume, bull,* and *fur.* A silent *u* may occur after *g,* as in *guard* and *guess.* See **Pronunciation.**

Marianne Cooley

Development of the letter U

The ancient Egyptians used this symbol of a supporting pole about 3000 B.C. The Semites adapted the symbol and named it *waw,* their word for *hook.*

The Phoenicians, about 1000 B.C., made a letter like a hook.

The Greeks added the letter *upsilon* to their alphabet about 600 B.C.

The Romans, about A.D. 114, used the letter V for both U and V sounds.

Medieval scholars began writing U for a vowel and V for a consonant.

The small letter u was used in spelling some words as early as the A.D. 500's. It did not come into regular use as a vowel until the 1500's.

A.D. 500   1500   Today

Special ways of expressing the letter U

International Morse Code

Braille

International Flag Code

Semaphore Code

Sign Language Alphabet

Common forms of the letter U

Handwritten letters vary from person to person. *Manuscript* (printed) letters, *left,* have simple curves and straight lines. Cursive letters, *right,* have flowing lines.

Roman letters have small finishing strokes called *serifs* that extend from the main strokes. The type face shown above is Baskerville. The italic form appears at the right.

Sans-serif letters are also called *gothic letters.* They have no serifs. The type face shown above is called Futura. The italic form of Futura appears at the right.

Computer letters have special shapes. Computers can "read" these letters either optically or by means of the magnetic ink with which the letters may be printed.

U-boat. See Submarine (World Wars I and II); **World War II** (The Battle of the Atlantic).

U Thant. See Thant, U.

U2, a rock group from Ireland, is one of the most popular bands in rock music history. The group consists of Bono, the lead singer; the Edge, who plays guitar; Adam Clayton, the bassist; and Larry Mullen, Jr., the drummer.

U2 has maintained its international popularity since the 1980's while remaining one of the most adventurous bands in rock music. The group has incorporated strong pacifist, Christian, and political themes into its music since its early years, and its influence has extended beyond the music world. Bono, in particular, has become a spokesman for such causes as aid for impoverished African nations and banning nuclear weapons.

U2 was organized in Dublin in 1976 as a group named Feedback. They changed their name to the Hype before finally taking the name U2 in 1978. The band recorded its first album, *Boy*, in 1980. U2 gained its first major recognition with the album *War* (1983), which dealt with many political subjects, such as religious strife in Northern Ireland. The band's 1987 album, *The Joshua Tree*, was a hit. It included two number-one songs, "With or Without You" and "I Still Haven't Found What I'm Looking For."

In the 1990's and early 2000's, U2 consolidated its position in rock music with exciting concerts and such albums as *Achtung Baby* (1991), *Zooropa* (1993), *Pop* (1997), *All That You Can't Leave Behind* (2000), and *How to Dismantle an Atomic Bomb* (2004). Bono continued to gain attention beyond his music performances with his political activism. He met with world leaders, including Pope John Paul II, British Prime Minister Tony Blair, and United States Presidents Bill Clinton and George W. Bush.

Bono, whose real name is Paul David Hewson, was born on May 10, 1960. He and Mullen, born on Oct. 31, 1961, are both natives of Dublin, Ireland. The Edge, whose real name is David Evans, was born in Barking, London, England, on Aug. 8, 1961. Clayton was born in Chinnor, Oxfordshire, England, on March 13, 1960. *U2 by U2* (2006) is a collection of pictures, documents, and interviews with members of the band.   William McKeen

See also **Rock music** (picture: Rock music).

U.A.R. See United Arab Republic.

UAV. See Unmanned aerial vehicle.

Ubangi River, *yoo BANG gee,* is the chief northern tributary of the Congo River in Africa. For location, see the map in the article **Congo** (Kinshasa). The Ubangi— also spelled *Oubangui*—is formed by the union of the Mbomou and Uele rivers, and it empties into the Congo near Lake Tumba in Congo (Kinshasa). With its main headstream, the Mbomou, the Ubangi River is about 1,400 miles (2,250 kilometers) in length. For about 700 miles (1,100 kilometers), the Ubangi forms the boundary separating Congo (Kinshasa) from Congo (Brazzaville) on the west, and from the Central African Republic on the northwest. The southern part of the river is navigable throughout the year.

French colonists established the city of Bangui on the Ubangi River in 1889. In 1894, Bangui became part of the newly created territory of Ubangi-Shari, part of a federation of colonies known as French Equatorial Africa. The Ubangi River formed part of the border between French Equatorial Africa and the Belgian Congo, now Congo (Kinshasa). In 1960, Ubangi-Shari gained independence as the Central African Republic.   Vernon Domingo

See also **Bangui; Central African Republic; French Equatorial Africa.**

Uccello, *oo CHEHL oh,* **Paolo,** *PAH oh loh* (1397-1475), was an Italian Renaissance painter. Uccello's decorative works emphasize patterns of color and simplified forms.

The Battle of San Romano (about 1456-1460), a tempera painting on wood panel; Uffizi Gallery, Florence, Italy (SCALA/Art Resource)

An Uccello painting shows the artist's fascination with perspective and his decorative style. This work is one of three scenes Uccello painted to commemorate Florence's defeat of Siena in 1432.

His paintings also show his fascination with perspective.

Uccello's best-known works are three scenes called *The Battle of San Romano* (about 1456-1460). Despite the violence of the subject, the paintings have an ornamental, theatrical appearance. A detail of one of the paintings is reproduced in this article. Uccello's other significant works include several *frescoes* (paintings on wet plaster). Among his important frescoes are the portrait *Sir John Hawkwood* (1436) and the Biblical scenes *The Sacrifice of Noah, The Drunkenness of Noah,* and *The Flood* (all 1447-1448).

Uccello was born in Florence. His given and family name was Paolo di Dono, but he was nicknamed Uccello. He was fond of birds, and *uccello* is an Italian word meaning *bird*. Little is known of his early life. During the late 1420's, Uccello worked on the mosaics in the Basilica of Saint Mark in Venice. Two frescoes dating from about 1431 are thought to be his earliest surviving works. He died on Dec. 10, 1475.   Vernon Hyde Minor

UFO. See **Unidentified flying object.**

Uganda, *yoo GAN duh* or *oo GAHN dah,* is a thickly populated country in east-central Africa. Uganda's people belong to several ethnic groups. English is Uganda's official language, but the people speak many African languages. Kampala is Uganda's capital and largest city.

Uganda has magnificent scenery, including snow-capped mountains, thick tropical forests, semidesert areas, and many lakes. Part of Lake Victoria, the world's second largest freshwater lake, lies in the country. Many wild animals roam the vast national parks.

For almost 70 years, the United Kingdom governed the territory as the Uganda Protectorate. Uganda won independence in 1962.

Government. A president, who is elected by the people, heads the government of Uganda. The president appoints a cabinet, which helps carry out the operations of government. A single-house Parliament makes the country's laws. Both the president and the members of Parliament serve five-year terms.

People. Ugandans belong to more than 20 ethnic groups, nearly all of which have their own language. The country has no language that is understood by everyone. The Ganda, also called the Baganda, are the largest and wealthiest group. They live in central and southern Uganda. Their political and social organization is one of the most highly developed in central Africa. Until 1967, the Ganda had their own *kabaka* (king) and *Lukiko* (parliament).

Most Ganda are farmers. Women do much of the farm work. The Ganda live in houses with corrugated iron roofs and walls of cement, cinder block, or mud.

Like the Ganda, three other ethnic groups in southern Uganda had their own kings until 1967. Most of the people are farmers. But the Karamojong in the northeast and several other ethnic groups in the drier parts of the north lead wandering lives as herders. Karamojong men mat their hair with colored clay in elaborate patterns.

Many Ugandans practice traditional African religions. But about two-thirds are Christians. A small minority are Muslims. More than half the people can read and write. Makerere University is in Kampala.

Land. Most of Uganda is a plateau about 4,000 feet (1,200 meters) above sea level. Thick forests grow in the south. Most of the north is *savanna* (grassland with low

Facts in brief

Capital: Kampala.
Official language: English.
Area: 93,065 mi² (241,038 km²).
Population: *Estimated 2008 population*—30,730,000; density, 330 per mi² (127 per km²); distribution, 88 percent rural, 12 percent urban. *2002 census*—24,442,084.
Chief products: bananas, cassava, coffee, corn, cotton, millet, potatoes, sugar, tea, tobacco.
National anthem: "Uganda."
Flag: A white-crested crane is centered on horizontal stripes of black (for Africa), yellow (sunshine), and red (brotherhood). See **Flag** (picture: Flags of Africa).
Money: *Basic unit*—Ugandan shilling.

trees), but some northeastern areas are semidesert.

Highlands rise near the east and west borders. In the east, Mount Elgon towers 14,178 feet (4,321 meters). Margherita Peak rises 16,763 feet (5,109 meters) in the Ruwenzori Range in the southwest. The Great Rift Valley lies just east of the western highlands and contains Lakes Albert, Edward, and George. The headwaters of the White Nile drain Uganda (see **Nile River**).

The equator crosses southern Uganda. But because of the high altitude, temperatures are mild. In most areas, the temperature seldom goes above 85 °F (29 °C) at midday, or below 60 °F (16 °C) at night. Most of Uganda receives over 40 inches (100 centimeters) of rain a year.

Economy. Most Ugandans are farmers, and much of the country's industry and exports are related to agriculture. The chief food crops include bananas, cassava, corn, millet, and potatoes. Coffee, cotton, sugar cane, tea, and tobacco are raised mostly for export.

Uganda has rich deposits of many minerals, including clay, copper, and limestone. In addition to processing agricultural products, Uganda also manufactures cement and other construction materials, consumer goods, and textiles. Most of the roads are unpaved. Cargo and passenger ships operate on Lakes Albert, Kyoga, and Victoria, and on the Albert Nile. Uganda has an international airport at Entebbe.

© David Keith Jones, Images of Africa Photobank/Alamy Images

Kampala, the capital of Uganda, is also the country's chief commercial center. The city sits on a series of hills. It is connected by railroad to Mombasa, Kenya's main port.

Uganda

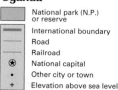

National park (N.P.) or reserve

International boundary

Road

Railroad

⊛ National capital

• Other city or town

+ Elevation above sea level

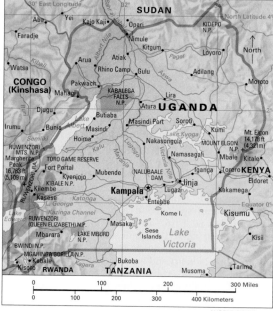

WORLD BOOK maps

History. By A.D. 100, the people in parts of what is now Uganda had developed agriculture and the use of iron. Later, they organized a form of government headed by chiefs. Several local kingdoms developed after 1300. The most important was Bunyoro-Kitara.

Arab traders came to the area about 1850. By then, the Ganda had formed a rich and powerful kingdom called Buganda. It had a large army and a highly developed government. British explorers and missionaries arrived in Uganda in the 1860's and 1870's. The United Kingdom made Buganda a British protectorate in 1894. Buganda then helped the British conquer nearby territory.

Uganda attained its present boundaries in 1926. Cash crops, such as coffee and cotton, became the basis for its economy. After World War II (1939-1945), Africans' role in governing Uganda increased. A movement for Bugandan independence caused trouble in the 1950's between the kabaka of Buganda and the British.

On Oct. 9, 1962, Uganda became independent. Milton Obote, a member of a northern ethnic group, became prime minister. Buganda got special powers and was more independent of the central government than the other kingdoms. In October 1963, Sir Edward Mutesa II, the kabaka of Buganda, was elected president. But differences arose between the kabaka and Obote. In 1966, Obote dismissed Mutesa and announced a new constitution that made Obote president. Mutesa fled when troops attacked his palace. Another constitution was

adopted in 1967. It made Uganda a republic and abolished its traditional kingdoms, including Buganda.

In 1967, Uganda, Kenya, and Tanzania formed the East African Community to promote trade among the three nations. But the organization fell apart in 1977.

The Uganda Army overthrew Obote in 1971 and set up a military government. Major General Idi Amin Dada, commander of the armed forces, headed the new government as president. In 1972, Amin ordered an estimated 40,000 to 50,000 Asians who had been living in Uganda to leave the country. Many Asians had not become Ugandan citizens, but owned numerous businesses in Uganda. Amin ruled Uganda as a dictator. Thousands of Ugandans who disagreed with his policies were killed.

In 1978, a border dispute led to fighting between Uganda and Tanzania. In 1979, Tanzanian troops, aided by Ugandans who opposed Amin, defeated Uganda's army and overthrew Amin's government. The Ugandans who opposed Amin took control of the government. In December 1980, elections for a new civilian government were held. Obote, who had been living in exile, returned to Uganda. His political party won the most seats in the National Assembly, and he became president again. Opponents of Obote charged his supporters with election fraud and began a guerrilla war to oust Obote.

In July 1985, military leaders overthrew Obote. They dissolved the National Assembly and took control of the government. General Tito Okello became president. But the National Resistance Movement (NRM), led by Yoweri Museveni, began a military campaign to overthrow Okello. NRM troops captured Kampala in January 1986. Museveni became president. In March, all activities of political parties were suspended. By the end of 1986, Museveni had restored peace to most of Uganda. But fighting between government forces and rebel groups continued in some areas, especially the north. The largest rebel group, the Lord's Resistance Army (LRA), seeks to replace Uganda's nonreligious government with a Christian one. The LRA has carried out thousands of murders, rapes, and child kidnappings. In 1995, Uganda adopted a new constitution. Elections for a president and a new Parliament were held in 1996. Museveni was elected president. He was reelected in 2001 and 2006.

Several cults sprang up in Uganda in the 1990's. In 2000, hundreds of members of a cult called the Movement for the Restoration of the Ten Commandments of God died in a church fire in Uganda. Police determined that the fire had been set intentionally. They also found hundreds of other cult members' bodies in mass graves.

In 1999, Uganda, Kenya, and Tanzania signed a treaty to reestablish the East African Community, which aims to promote economic and political cooperation. It was formally launched in 2001. In a 2005 referendum, Ugandans voted to restore multiparty democracy, which had been suspended in 1986.

In 2006, the Ugandan government and the LRA rebel group signed a cease-fire agreement. The two sides were scheduled to sign a permanent peace agreement in 2008, but the LRA leader remained in hiding and did not sign.   John A. Rowe

Related articles in *World Book* include:

Amin Dada, Idi	Kampala	Lake Victoria
Entebbe	Lake Albert	Nile River
Ganda	Lake Edward	Obote, Milton

© Havlicek, ZEFA

Kiev, Ukraine's capital and largest city, lies along the Dnieper River, *foreground,* in north-central Ukraine. The city has many attractive parks and high-rise apartment and office buildings, and it is a major transportation and manufacturing center.

Ukraine

Ukraine, *yoo KRAYN,* is a country in eastern Europe. It is Europe's second largest country in area. Only Russia, Ukraine's neighbor to the east, has more land. Ukraine's capital and largest city is Kiev (Kyiv in Ukrainian).

About four-fifths of the country's people are ethnic Ukrainians, a Slavic nationality group that has its own customs and language. Russians are the second largest group and make up about a sixth of Ukraine's population. The country is famous for its vast plains called *steppes.* The steppes are covered with fertile black soil, which has made Ukraine one of the world's leading farming regions.

During the A.D. 800's, Kiev became the center of a Slavic state called Kievan Rus. In the 1300's, most of Ukraine came under Polish and Lithuanian control. Ukrainian soldiers called Cossacks freed Ukraine from Polish rule in the mid-1600's.

During the late 1700's, nearly all of Ukraine came under Russian control. In 1917, revolutionaries known as Bolsheviks (later called Communists) seized control of Russia. Ukraine became an independent country the following year, but it soon came under Russian rule. In 1922, Ukraine became one of the four original republics of the Soviet Union, and it became known as the Ukrainian Soviet Socialist Republic. For many decades, the Soviet Union forced Ukrainians to use the Russian language and favored the Russian culture over the Ukrainian culture. Many Ukrainians began protesting the restrictions in the 1960's.

In 1991, following an upheaval in the Soviet govern-

Facts in brief

Capital: Kiev.
Official language: Ukrainian.
Official name: Ukrayina (Ukraine).
Area: 233,090 mi² (603,700 km²). *Greatest distances*—north-south, 550 mi (885 km); east-west, 830 mi (1,335 km). *Coastline*—1,800 mi (2,900 km).
Elevation: *Highest*—Mount Hoverla, 6,762 ft (2,061 m) above sea level. *Lowest*—sea level along the coast of the Black Sea.
Population: *Estimated 2008 population*—46,060,000; density, 198 per mi² (76 per km²); distribution, 68 percent urban, 32 percent rural. *2001 census*—48,457,102.
Chief products: *Agriculture*—barley, beef and dairy cattle, chickens, corn, hogs, potatoes, sugar beets, sunflowers, tobacco, wheat. *Manufacturing*—chemical fertilizers, clothing, iron and steel, machinery, military equipment, processed foods, refrigerators, shoes, television sets, transportation equipment, washing machines. *Mining*—coal, iron ore, manganese, natural gas, salt.
Money: *Basic unit*—hryvnia. One hundred kopiyka equal one hryvnia.

Jaroslaw Bilocerkowycz, the contributor of this article, is Associate Professor of Political Science at the University of Dayton.

ment, Ukraine declared its political independence. Late that year, it became recognized as an independent country after the breakup of the Soviet Union.

Government

National government. Ukraine has a democratic political system. The country's government has an executive branch, which includes a president and a prime minister; and a legislative branch, which consists of a national parliament.

The president is commander in chief of the military and can issue orders called *edicts* in some matters without the approval of the parliament. The people of Ukraine elect the president to a five-year term. Ukrainians 18 years old or older may vote.

The prime minister heads a cabinet. The parliament names the prime minister, who then selects Cabinet members. Cabinet ministers have responsibility for such areas as foreign affairs and the economy.

Ukraine's parliament, called the Supreme Council, is the nation's lawmaking body. It has 450 members, who serve five-year terms. They are chosen under a system called *proportional representation*. This system gives a political party a share of seats in the parliament according to the party's share of the total votes cast in an election. To qualify, a party needs to receive at least 3 percent of the vote.

Local government. Ukraine is divided into 24 political units called *oblasts*. Kiev and the city of Sevastopol also have their own municipal governments, with a status like that of the oblasts. The Crimea, a peninsula in southern Ukraine, has special status as an *autonomous* (self-governing) republic. It has greater control over its internal affairs than do the oblasts or the municipalities.

Politics. The Yulia Tymoshenko Bloc and Our Ukraine–People's Self-Defense are the two major political groups in Ukraine that favor economic reform, closer ties with Western nations, and less reliance on Russia. The Party of Regions backs some economic reform but favors close ties with Russia. It receives support from Ukraine's Russian minority. The Communist Party favors government control of the economy and union with Russia. Its support has declined sharply during the early 2000's. The Socialist Party is more moderate than the Communist Party.

Courts. Ukraine's highest court is the Supreme Court. A Constitutional Court decides questions about the constitutionality of laws. Ukraine also has regional and district courts.

Armed forces. Ukraine has an army, an air force, and a small navy. About 200,000 troops serve in the three divisions. Ukraine also has paramilitary forces, including a border guard and a coast guard.

People

Ancestry. The majority of the people of Ukraine belong to the Ukrainian ethnic group. Russians make up the country's second largest ethnic group. Other groups include Belarusians, Bulgarians, Crimean Tatars, and Moldovans. Government leaders have encouraged cooperation among ethnic groups. Independent Ukraine has tried to accommodate the cultural concerns of its ethnic minority groups.

Most Ukrainians are of East Slavic ancestry. In the

Symbols of Ukraine. The Ukrainian flag was adopted in 1992. The flag's blue stripe symbolizes the sky, and its yellow stripe represents the wheat fields of Ukraine. The coat of arms, dating from the late 900's, features a *trident* (three-pointed spear).

WORLD BOOK map

Ukraine is a large country in eastern Europe, second only to Russia in area. It borders seven countries and the Black Sea.

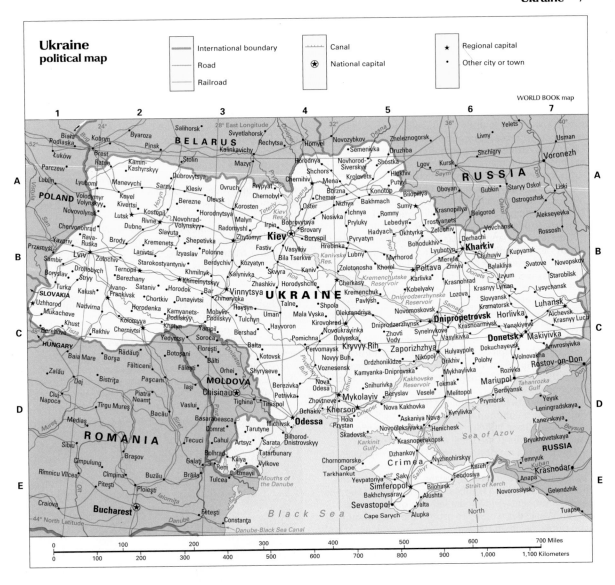

Ukraine map index

A.D. 800's, the East Slavs included the ancestors of the Ukrainians, the Belarusians, and the Russians. The three groups became separate states in the centuries that followed. Ukrainians are proud of their nationality and preserve many of its traditions.

Language. Ukrainian is the official language of Ukraine. From the 1930's to the 1980's, during the period when Ukraine was part of the Soviet Union, the Soviets forced Ukrainians to use the Russian language in government, schools, and newspapers and television. Many Ukrainians resented this policy. But decades of the Soviet policy caused many Ukrainians to know the Russian language better than Ukrainian. In the late 1980's and early 1990's, a growing number of ethnic Ukrainians and non-Ukrainians began studying the Ukrainian language. The government allows ethnic minorities to use their own languages in schools and other local affairs.

The Ukrainian language has several regional dialects, which vary according to a region's history and the influence of other cultures on the region. Ukrainian dialects spoken by west Ukrainians, for example, show some Polish influence. Dialects from eastern Ukraine reflect more Russian traits.

Way of life

City life. About two-thirds of the people live in cities. Kiev, Ukraine's capital and largest city, is an attractive city known for its treelined boulevards. Other large cities in Ukraine include Dnipropetrovsk, Donetsk, Kharkiv, Lviv, and Odessa.

High-rise apartment buildings from the period of Soviet rule are a common sight in Ukrainian cities. However, many of these buildings were poorly constructed, and the apartments are small and overcrowded.

Pollution is a major problem in Ukraine, especially in its cities. The quality of air and water has been damaged by factory smoke and other wastes, particularly in the heavily industrialized Donbas region of eastern Ukraine. An environmental movement led by a group called Green World has worked to protect the environment and public health in Ukraine.

Ukraine faces growing unemployment as it moves toward a free market economy, which permits people to engage in economic activities largely free from government control. Poor economic conditions have contributed to a growing crime rate.

Rural life. About a third of Ukraine's population lives in rural areas. Most rural Ukrainians work on farms or in the timber industry, or they make small handicrafts. Western Ukraine is heavily rural. The standard of living in the countryside is generally lower than that in the cities. Small homes are common. Rural Ukrainians have strong ties to their families and farms. However, many young people have left the countryside to live and work in the cities.

Clothing. Ukrainians generally wear clothing similar to that worn in western Europe and North America. But on special occasions, they may wear traditional peasant costumes. These costumes feature white blouses and shirts decorated with colorful embroidery.

Food and drink. The Ukrainian diet includes chicken, fish, and such pork products as ham, sausage, and bacon. Ukrainians also eat large amounts of potatoes, cooked buckwheat mush called *kasha,* sour rye bread,

and sweetened breads. Popular drinks include tea, coffee, cocoa, a special soured milk drink, honey liqueur, and vodka with pepper.

Traditional Ukrainian dishes include *varenyky, borsch,* and *holubtsi.* Varenyky consists of boiled dumplings filled with potatoes, sauerkraut, cheese, plums, or blueberries. The dumplings may be eaten with sour cream, fried onions, or bacon bits. Borsch is a soup made of beets, cabbage, and meat. It is served with sour rye bread and sour cream. Holubtsi are stuffed cabbage rolls filled with rice, buckwheat, and meat.

Recreation. Ukrainians enjoy many sports, including basketball, ice hockey, skating, soccer, swimming, track and field, and volleyball. Soccer is by far the most popular team sport in Ukraine. Dynamo Kiev has ranked as one of Europe's top soccer teams for decades.

Ukrainians also enjoy music, and many of them perform in choruses and folk dance groups. Chess is a popular game. Many Ukrainians vacation by camping in the Carpathian Mountains. Ukrainians also travel to the Black Sea coast for its warm weather and mineral springs.

Religion. Ukrainians remained a strongly religious people despite decades of religious restrictions under Soviet rule. About three-quarters of Ukraine's religious believers are Orthodox Christians. Other groups include Ukrainian Catholics, Protestants, Jews, and Muslims.

Most Orthodox Christians live in eastern and central Ukraine. They belong to one of three Orthodox groups. The Ukrainian Orthodox Church of the Kiev *Patriarchate*

© Peter Turnley, Black Star

Marketplaces in Ukrainian cities offer shoppers a wide variety of fruits, vegetables, and other foods. At Kiev's central market, *shown here,* workers in white coats serve customers.

AP/Wide World

Ukrainian Easter eggs, known as *pysanky,* feature colorful, intricate designs. Artists draw designs in wax on the eggs before dipping them in a deep-colored dye.

(District), established in 1992, has the most followers. The Ukrainian Orthodox Church of the Moscow Patriarchate has the most parishes. The Ukrainian *Autocephalous* (Independent) Orthodox Church has been a strong supporter of Ukrainian independence. The Soviet dictator Joseph Stalin banned the Autocephalous Orthodox Church in 1930, but it regained legal status in 1990.

About 6 percent of Ukraine's people are Ukrainian Catholics, also known as Uniates or "Greek" Catholics. They practice Eastern Orthodox forms of worship but recognize the authority of the Roman Catholic pope. The church is strongest in western Ukraine.

Education. Ukrainian law requires children to attend school for 12 years, from the ages of about 6 to 18. After the ninth grade, students may continue a general academic program or enroll in technical or trade schools.

Ukraine has more than 900 schools of higher education. The largest and best-known universities include Ivan Franko National University of Lviv, National University of Kyiv-Mohyla Academy, Odessa I. I. Mechnikov National University, National Taras Shevchenko University of Kyiv, and V. N. Karazin Kharkiv National University.

The arts. Ukrainians are well known for their folk arts and crafts. *Pysanky*—Ukrainian Easter eggs decorated with colorful designs—are world famous. Craftworkers in the Hutsul region of the Carpathian Mountains make woodcarvings with striking inlaid designs.

Ukrainian music often features a stringed instrument called the *bandura.* In a popular Ukrainian folk dance called the *hopak,* male dancers compete against each other in performing acrobatic leaps.

The poet Taras Shevchenko, who wrote during the mid-1800's, is the country's most famous cultural and national figure. He urged Ukrainians to struggle for social equality and freedom from oppression by the Russian czars. His *Kobzar* (1840), a collection of poems, dealt with Ukrainian historical themes and made Ukrainian a popular language for poetry and books. Other notable Ukrainian writers include Ivan Franko and Lesia Ukrain-

ka, who both died in 1916. Franko was a journalist who wrote novels, poems, and plays. Ukrainka was a poet.

The land

Ukraine lies in eastern Europe, north of the Black Sea and the Sea of Azov. The country consists mainly of a flat, fertile plain. About a third of the land is suitable for growing crops. Ukraine can be divided into six main land regions: (1) the Dnieper-Prypyat Lowland, (2) the Northern Ukrainian Upland, (3) the Central Plateau, (4) the Eastern Carpathian Mountains, (5) the Coastal Plain, and (6) the Crimean Mountains.

The Dnieper-Prypyat Lowland lies in northern Ukraine. Forests once blanketed all of the lowland but now cover only about a fourth of its area. Farmers use much of the region's land as pasture for dairy cattle. The eastern lowland includes the Dnieper River basin and the city of Kiev. The Prypyat River drains the western lowland, which has many marshes and forests of pine and oak.

The Northern Ukrainian Upland consists of a low plateau in the northeastern part of Ukraine. Farmers in the region grow wheat and sugar beets and raise livestock. Large deposits of natural gas lie to the south of the city of Kharkiv.

The Central Plateau extends from eastern to western Ukraine, and it is part of the Great European Plain. Rich, black soils called *chernozem* and sufficient rain make the region Ukraine's most productive farmland.

The Donets Basin, often called the Donbas, lies in the eastern part of the plateau. This area is Ukraine's leading industrial region and has large coal deposits. The area includes the cities of Donetsk, Horlivka, and Luhansk.

The Eastern Carpathian Mountains are in western Ukraine. Ukraine's highest peak, Mount Hoverla, rises 6,762 feet (2,061 meters). Farming in the river valleys, raising livestock, and logging are major economic activities in the region. The mountains have deposits of oil and natural gas.

The Coastal Plain extends along the coasts of the Black Sea and the Sea of Azov and includes most of the

Natalie Sluzar

Ukraine has rich farmland and has historically been called the *breadbasket of Europe.* After Ukraine gained independence in 1991, government control of the farms began to give way to private ownership.

Crimean Peninsula. Its coastline has cliffs and many shallow lagoons. The region receives less rain than other parts of Ukraine and sometimes suffers from droughts. The Dnieper River flows through the central plain. Farmers use its water to irrigate crops.

The Crimean Mountains rise in the southern part of the Crimean Peninsula. The mountains climb gradually from the north but slope steeply to the Black Sea in the south. The highest point in the Crimean Mountains, a peak called Roman-Kosh, stands 5,069 feet (1,545 meters) above sea level.

Rivers and lakes. The Dnieper River is Ukraine's longest river. It flows through the country from the north to the Black Sea. It is 1,420 miles (2,285 kilometers) long and ranks as Europe's third longest waterway. Only the Volga and Danube rivers are longer. Ships travel along most of the Dnieper's length. Ukraine's second longest river, the Dniester (Dnister in Ukrainian), measures 845 miles (1,360 kilometers). It flows through western Ukraine from the Carpathian Mountains to the Black Sea. Other major waterways include the Pivdennyy Buh, Desna, Prypyat, and Donets rivers. Ukraine has about 3,000 lakes.

Climate

Most of Ukraine has cold winters and warm summers, which favor growing crops. Eastern Ukraine is slightly colder in winter and warmer in summer than western Ukraine. Temperatures in Kharkiv in eastern Ukraine average about 19 °F (–7 °C) in January and 68 °F (20 °C) in July. Temperatures in Lviv in the west average about 25 °F (–4 °C) in January and 64 °F (18 °C) in July.

Precipitation ranges from about 30 inches (76 centimeters) a year in the north to about 9 inches (23 centimeters) in the south. Rainfall is highest in June and July. In the Carpathian and Crimean mountains, weather is colder and wetter at higher elevations. The southern coast of Crimea has warmer weather and less rainfall.

Economy

Ukraine has a developed economy with strong industry and agriculture. However, the nation lacks modern technology and equipment in its factories and on its farms. About a fourth of Ukraine's people work in industry, and about a fifth work in agriculture. Most other Ukrainians have jobs in such service industries as education and health care.

Manufacturing. Ukraine's heavy industries produce iron and steel and such machines as tractors, machine tools, and mining equipment. The machine industry accounts for much of Ukraine's industrial output. Ukraine also produces airplanes, automobiles, buses, locomotives and railway cars, ships, and trucks. Many of Ukraine's heavy industries are in the Donbas region of

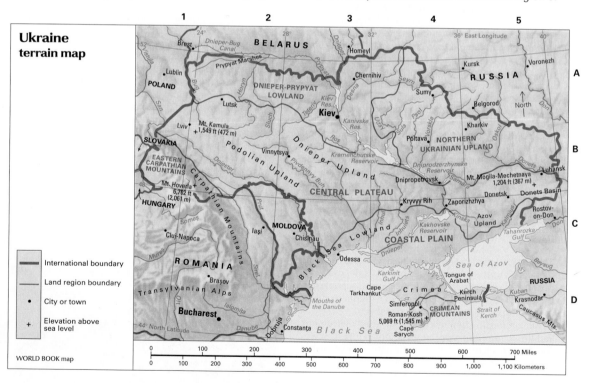

Physical features

Azov Upland	C 5	Dnieper River	C 4	Kakhovske Reservoir	C 4	Mount Mogila-Mechetnaya	B 5	Samara River	B 4
Black Sea	D 3	Dnieper Upland	B 3	Kalmius River	C 5			Sea of Azov	D 5
Black Sea Lowland	C 3	Dniester River	B 2	Kanivske Reservoir	B 3	Oskol River	B 5	Seym River	A 4
Bug River	A 1	Dniprodzerzhynske Reservoir	B 4	Karkinit Gulf	D 4	Pivdennyy Buh River	B 2	Sluch River	B 2
Cape Sarych	D 4			Kerch Peninsula	D 4	Podolian Upland	B 2	Strait of Kerch	D 5
Cape Tarkhankut	D 3	Donets Basin (Donbas)	C 5	Kinska River	C 4	Prypyat River	A 2	Sula River	B 4
Carpathian Mountains	C 1	Donets River	B 5	Kremenchutske Reservoir	B 3	Prypyat Marshes	A 2	Tahanrozka Gulf	C 5
Danube River	D 2	Horyn River	A 2	Mount Hoverla	C 1	Psol River	B 4	Teteriv River	B 2
Desna River	A 3	Inhul River	C 3	Mount Kamula	B 1	Roman-Kosh (mountain)	D 4	Tongue of Arabat	D 4
		Inhulets River	C 4			Ros River	B 3	Uday River	B 3
								Vorskla River	B 4

Sandy beaches and warm weather make Yalta a favorite vacation spot for Ukrainians. The city lies on the southern coast of the Crimean Peninsula along the Black Sea.

eastern Ukraine, near mines that supply raw materials. Ukraine also manufactures chemical fertilizers; such processed foods as meat, refined sugar, and wine; and consumer goods, including clothes, refrigerators, shoes, television sets, and washing machines.

Ukraine has a strong defense industry. During Soviet rule, defense factories accounted for approximately a fourth of Ukraine's industrial output. Independent Ukraine produces some military equipment for export. But it plans to convert some defense factories to manufacture other products.

Agriculture. Because of its agricultural production, Ukraine became known as the *breadbasket of Europe.* Its moderate climate and rich soils have made the country one of the world's most productive farming regions.

Until the late 1990's, most farms in Ukraine were owned and controlled by the government. They included *state farms* and *collective farms.* State farms were managed entirely by the government, which paid wages to farmworkers. Collective farms were owned and managed in part by the workers, who received wages as well as a share in farm profits.

Between 1991 and 2001, Ukraine gradually converted all of its state and collective farms into various forms of privately owned farms. Large corporations purchased some farms. Other farms are *cooperative farms.* A cooperative farm is owned and managed entirely by a group of farmers, who divide the profits equally. Many farmworkers who received land when the collective farms were broken up leased their land to one of the larger groups. The number of individual farmers who own and work their land has been growing, however.

Ukraine ranks as a leading producer of sugar beets, and it is also a major producer and exporter of wheat. Other important crops include barley, cabbages, corn, potatoes, sunflowers, tobacco, and tomatoes. Ukrainian farmers also raise beef and dairy cattle, chickens, and hogs. Near cities, farmers often grow fruits and vegetables to sell at markets.

Service industries account for more than half of Ukraine's economic production and employ more than half of the country's workers. The country's chief service industries include education, health care, scientific research and engineering, transportation, and trade.

Mining. Ukraine is a leading producer of manganese, which is used in making steel. Coal is another important mined product. Huge coal deposits lie in the Donbas, the center of Ukraine's heavy industry. Ukraine also mines aluminum, iron ore, natural gas, nickel, salt, titanium, and uranium.

Fishing. Ukrainian fishing fleets operate mainly in the Antarctic and Indian oceans, and in the Black Sea and the Sea of Azov. Ukrainians also fish in the country's rivers and lakes. Ocean fleets catch mackerel and tuna. River fishing is most important on the Dnieper and lower Danube rivers. The chief commercial fish from seas and rivers include bream, carp, perch, pike, and trout.

Energy sources. Coal, natural gas, and petroleum have long been Ukraine's major sources of electric power. The country also has hydroelectric plants, mainly on the Dnieper River. Ukraine imports much natural gas and petroleum from Russia and Turkmenistan.

During the 1980's, nuclear power plants began providing an important new source of energy. Today, these plants produce much of Ukraine's electric power. Many Ukrainians, however, oppose the use of nuclear energy because of an accident at the Chernobyl nuclear power plant in north-central Ukraine in 1986. The accident caused the release of large amounts of radioactive material into the atmosphere.

Trade. Ukraine's chief exports include chemicals, food products, fuels, iron and steel, and machinery. The country imports chemicals, machinery, natural gas, oil, vehicles, and wood products. Ukraine's major trading partners include China, Germany, Italy, Poland, Russia, Turkey, Turkmenistan, and the United States. In 2008, Ukraine joined the World Trade Organization, a group that promotes international trade.

Transportation and communication. Ukraine has a well-developed transportation system. Most of the system is owned by the government. Almost all of Ukraine's roads are paved. Buses and taxis are common in larger cities. Kiev and Kharkiv have subway systems. A large railroad network connects major cities and industrial centers. Ukraine has several airports. Its chief international airport is at Boryspil, near Kiev. The country's major ports include Illichivsk, Kerch, Kherson, Mariupol, Mykolayiv, Odessa, Sevastopol, and Yalta.

Most of Ukraine's newspapers are privately owned. Leading daily papers include *Fakty i Kommentarii, Segodnya, Silski Visti,* and *Vecherniye Vesti.* Many people in Kiev and other cities have access to the Internet.

History

Early days. People have lived in the Ukraine region for thousands of years. One of the earliest cultures was

ITAR-Tass from Sovfoto

A combine harvests wheat on a farm in the Khmelnitskiy region of Ukraine. The region lies in the Central Plateau, which has the country's most productive farmland.

ITAR-Tass from Sovfoto

A natural gas pipeline links Ukraine with gas fields in Siberia in northern Russia. Ukraine uses natural gas to generate electric power for homes and industry.

that of the Trypillians, who lived in southwestern Ukraine from about 4000 to 2000 B.C. The Trypillians raised crops for a living, decorated pottery, and made drills for boring holes in wood and stone.

By about 1500 B.C., nomadic herders occupied the region. They included a warlike, horse-riding people called the Cimmerians. The Scythians, a people from central Asia, conquered the Cimmerians about 700 B.C. Between 700 and 600 B.C., Greeks started colonies on the northern coast of the Black Sea. But the Scythians controlled most of the region until about 200 B.C., when they fell to a group called the Sarmatians. The region was invaded by Germanic tribes from the west in A.D. 270 and by the Huns, an Asian people, in 375.

Kievan Rus. During the A.D. 800's, a Slavic civilization called Rus grew up at Kiev and at other points along river routes between the Baltic Sea and the Black Sea. The region around Kiev, called Kievan Rus, became the first

Important dates in Ukraine

A.D. 800's East Slavs established the state of Kievan Rus.
c. 988 Vladimir I made Christianity the state religion of Ukraine.
1240 The Mongols destroyed Kiev and conquered Ukraine.
1569 Ukraine came under Polish control.
mid-1600's A Ukrainian Cossack began a revolt that eventually freed Ukraine from Polish rule.
1790's Russia gained control of most of Ukraine.
1918 Ukraine became an independent country after a revolution in Russia in 1917. But Communist Russia regained control of most of Ukraine by 1920.
1922 Ukraine became one of the four original republics of the Soviet Union.
1932-1933 Millions of Ukrainians died from a famine after Soviet authorities took food from their homes.
1941-1945 The Ukrainian Insurgent Army fought for Ukrainian independence against German and Soviet forces in World War II. It continued fighting the Soviets until the early 1950's.
1960's Ukrainians began a protest movement against Soviet rule. Soviet authorities imprisoned thousands of protesters.
1991 The Ukrainian parliament declared Ukraine an independent country. The Soviet Union was dissolved.
1996 Ukraine adopted a new constitution.

of the East Slavic states. The city of Kiev was its capital. Scandinavian merchant-warriors called Varangians (also known as Vikings) played a part in organizing the East Slavic tribes into Kievan Rus. Oleg, a Varangian, became its first ruler in 882. During the 900's, other states recognized Kiev's leadership.

Vladimir I (Volodymyr in Ukrainian), the ruler of the Russian principality of Novgorod, conquered Kievan Rus in 980. Under his rule, the state became a political, economic, and cultural power in Europe. About 988, Vladimir became a Christian and made Christianity the state religion. Before the East Slavs became Christians, they had worshiped idols and nature spirits. In 1240, Mongol tribes known as Tatars swept across the Ukrainian plains from the east and conquered the region.

Lithuanian and Polish rule. After the fall of Kievan Rus, several *principalities* (regions ruled by princes) developed in the Ukraine region. The state of Galicia-Volhynia grew in importance in what is now western Ukraine. In the 1300's, however, Poland took control of Galicia. Lithuania seized Volhynia and later, Kiev. Under Polish and Lithuanian rule, Ukrainian peasants were bound to the land as *serfs,* farmworkers who were not free to leave the land they worked. By 1569, Poland ruled all of the region.

Many discontented peasants joined bands of independent soldiers that became known as Cossacks. They occupied the territory that lay between the Poles and the Tatars. In the mid-1600's, a Cossack named Bohdan Khmelnitsky led an uprising that freed Ukraine from Polish control. In 1654, Khmelnitsky formed an alliance with the *czar* (emperor) of Russia against Poland.

Russian rule. Ukraine was divided between Poland and Russia in 1667. Poland gained control of lands west of the Dnieper River. Ukrainian lands east of the Dnieper had self-rule but came under Russian protection. By 1764, Russia abolished Ukrainian self-rule. In the 1790's, Russia gained control of all of Ukraine except Galicia, which Austria ruled from 1772 until 1918.

Russia favored its language and culture over those of

the Ukrainians and other peoples. From 1863 to 1905, it banned publications in Ukrainian. The Austrians, however, allowed the Ukrainians greater freedom than did the Russians. As a result, Galicia became a major center of Ukrainian culture during the 1800's.

Soviet rule. In 1917, revolutionaries known as Bolsheviks (later called Communists) overthrew the czar of Russia and seized control of the government. In 1918, the Ukrainians formed an independent country called the Ukrainian People's Republic. However, Communist Russia had superior military power and seized eastern and central Ukraine by 1920. The rest of Ukraine came under Polish, Czechoslovak, and Romanian control.

In 1922, Ukraine became one of the four original republics of the Soviet Union. In the 1920's, the Soviet government encouraged Ukrainian culture and use of the Ukrainian language to weaken opposition to the Communist system. By the 1930's, however, the Soviet dictator Joseph Stalin began a program that imposed the Russian language and culture on the Ukrainian people.

In the late 1920's and early 1930's, the Communist government took over privately owned farms in Ukraine and combined them into larger, state-run farms. This program, called *collectivization,* brought great hardship to the people of Ukraine. Several hundred thousand Ukrainian farmers resisted the seizure of their land and were sent to prison labor camps in Siberia or Soviet Central Asia. In 1932 and 1933, the Soviet government seized grain and food from people's homes, causing a major famine. Between 5 million and 7 ½ million Ukrainians died of starvation.

World War II. Nazi Germany occupied Ukraine from mid-1941 to mid-1944, during World War II. About 5 million Ukrainian civilians, including 600,000 Ukrainian Jews, were killed during the war. The Ukrainian Insurgent Army, a force of about 40,000 soldiers, fought both Germany and the Soviet Union for Ukrainian independence. The force continued fighting the Soviets until the early 1950's.

By the end of World War II in 1945, the Soviet Union had taken control of many parts of Ukraine that had belonged to Poland, Czechoslovakia, and Romania. That year, Soviet Ukraine became one of the original members of the United Nations. In 1954, Russia transferred control of the Crimea to Ukraine.

Protest movements. Many Ukrainians opposed Soviet Russian rule and the limits on Ukrainian culture. In the 1960's, a protest movement developed to advance human rights and the rights of the Ukrainian people. Although thousands of protesters were arrested, the movement continued during the 1970's and 1980's.

The Chernobyl disaster. In 1986, an explosion and fire at the nuclear power plant in Chernobyl (also spelled Chornobyl), near Kiev, released large amounts of radioactive material into the atmosphere. Soviet officials reported that 31 people died as a result of the explosion and its aftermath, and about 200 were seriously injured. The disaster led to increased rates of cancer and other illnesses among the cleanup workers and residents in parts of Ukraine, Belarus, and Russia. Health experts estimate that about 4,000 people will die from radiation exposure caused by the accident.

Independence. During the period of Soviet rule, the government owned most of Ukraine's factories, farms, and businesses. By the 1980's, many government-owned farms and factories operated inefficiently and wasted resources. The economy slumped, and the Soviet government struggled to meet demands for consumer goods. During the late 1980's, the government took steps to increase private ownership of economic activities. A Ukrainian nationalist movement began to gain strength, as Ukrainians demanded more control over their government, economy, and culture.

In 1990, Ukraine's parliament passed a declaration of *state sovereignty.* This declaration stated that Ukraine would follow its own laws if they came into conflict with those of the Soviet Union.

In August 1991, hard-line Communists failed in an attempt to overthrow the reform-minded Soviet president, Mikhail S. Gorbachev. The failed coup renewed demands for self-rule among the Soviet republics, including Ukraine. Soon afterward, Ukraine's parliament declared Ukraine independent, and several other republics made similar declarations.

On Dec. 1, 1991, over 90 percent of Ukrainians voted in favor of independence. Leonid M. Kravchuk, a former Communist official who became a Ukrainian nationalist and a democrat, was elected president. On December 25, the Soviet Union was formally dissolved.

After gaining independence, Ukraine began to change its economy to one based on a free market. At the time, most factories, farms, and businesses were still owned by the government.

Ukraine and Russia argued over many issues, including how much of the Soviet national debt each country should assume and how the Soviet Navy's Black Sea fleet should be divided. In May 1992, Russia's Supreme Soviet voted to declare the Soviet government's 1954 grant of Crimea to Ukraine an illegal act. Ukraine opposed this decision.

AP/Wide World

The Orange Revolution of 2004 was an important step toward democracy in Ukraine. After a disputed election, supporters of democratic reformer Viktor Yushchenko took to the streets of Kiev. Yushchenko eventually won the presidency in a second runoff election.

In 1992, Ukraine and two other former Soviet republics with nuclear weapons—Belarus and Kazakhstan—agreed to eliminate all nuclear weapons on their territories within seven years. The three countries also agreed to become parties to the Treaty on the Non-Proliferation of Nuclear Weapons, a United Nations agreement that forbids the spread of nuclear weapons. Ukraine ratified the treaty in 1994. In 1996, Ukraine completed the transfer of its short- and long-range Soviet nuclear weapons to Russia for destruction.

In 1994, Leonid D. Kuchma was elected to succeed Kravchuk as Ukraine's president. Kuchma continued the efforts toward economic reform.

After several years of debate, Ukraine's parliament passed a new constitution in 1996. It was the country's first constitution since Ukraine became independent of Soviet rule.

In 1997, Ukraine and Russia signed an agreement on the division of the Black Sea fleet. Ukraine kept about a fifth of the fleet. Russia leased from Ukraine docking space for its ships at the port of Sevastopol in Crimea.

Political changes. Kuchma was reelected president in 1999. In 2000, scandal erupted when Kuchma was linked to the murder of a journalist who had published reports critical of the government. Elections in 2002 split the parliament between reformers, Communists, and Kuchma's supporters.

Ukraine underwent a major shift toward democratic government in late 2004. The shift became known as the Orange Revolution, after the campaign color of the leading democratic political party. The Orange Revolution was sparked by accusations of government interference and unfair voting practices during that year's presidential election. After a vote in October, the two leading candidates, Viktor Yanukovych and Viktor Yushchenko, faced each other in a runoff election in November. Yanukovych was declared the winner, but Yushchenko's supporters and international observers disputed the results. Some 1 million Ukrainians protested peacefully in Kiev. Many stayed in tents for several weeks in the winter cold. In December, Ukraine's Supreme Court *annulled* (canceled) the results of the runoff election and called for a new one to be held. Yushchenko, the democratic reformer, won the second runoff election and took office in January 2005. However, Yushchenko faced opposition in the parliament after Yanukovych's Party of Regions joined with the Communist and Socialist parties to form a majority.

In 2006, Yushchenko's rival Yanukovych became prime minister after his coalition won a majority of the votes in parliamentary elections. Yushchenko and Yanukovych repeatedly clashed over policies and power. After new parliamentary elections in 2007, Yanukovych was replaced as prime minister by Yulia Tymoshenko, who had sided with Yushchenko in the Orange Revolution.

Jaroslaw Bilocerkowycz

Related articles in *World Book* include:

Paul Robert Perry

The ukulele looks somewhat like a small guitar. It is played by strumming the four strings with the fingers.

Ukulele, *YOO kuh LAY lee,* is a four-stringed musical instrument that is related to the guitar. A player strums the ukulele with the fingers of one hand. With the fingers of the other hand, the player picks out chords on the finger board along the neck of the instrument. Most written ukulele music consists of chord symbols that indicate finger positions instead of notes. Therefore, the player need not know how to read music. The ukulele was developed from a small guitar brought to Hawaii by the Portuguese in the late 1800's. The ukulele is used mainly to accompany folk and popular singing.　André P. Larson

Ulaanbaatar, *OO lahn BAH tawr* (pop. 515,000), also spelled Ulan Bator, is the capital and largest city of Mongolia. It is also Mongolia's center of culture and industry. The city lies in the northeastern part of the country (see **Mongolia** [map]).

Large government buildings line Ulaanbaatar's central square. The city has a university, a national theater, and several museums. Its manufactured products include furniture, cast iron, paper, pharmaceutical products, soap, and textiles. Meat packing is also an important industry in the city.

In 1639, a Lamaist monastery was built on the site of what is now Ulaanbaatar. Lamaism is a form of Buddhism. A settlement grew up around the monastery, and it became an important trade center. The city was called Urga until 1924, when Mongolia became an independent republic. It was then named Ulaanbaatar by Sühbaatar, the leader of the fight for independence (see **Mongolia** [History]).　Andrew C. Hess

Ulcer, *UHL suhr,* is an open sore in the skin or mucous membrane. During the development of an ulcer, part of the surface tissue breaks down and dies, leaving a raw, inflamed area that heals slowly.

Probably the best-known kinds of ulcers are *peptic ulcers,* which occur in the digestive system. There are two main types of peptic ulcers. *Duodenal ulcers* form in the duodenum, the upper part of the small intestine. *Gastric ulcers* develop in the stomach. During digestion and at certain other times, the stomachs of most people produce hydrochloric acid and an enzyme called *pepsin.* These powerful digestive juices can eat through the lining of the stomach and duodenum. Normally, mucous secretions protect the stomach and duodenum from the effects of digestive juices. Secretions of bicarbonate into the duodenum also neutralize these juices.

Most people who have peptic ulcers are also infected with *Helicobacter pylori,* a bacterium in the stomach. Scientists believe that *H. pylori* is associated with the development of ulcers, but they are uncertain exactly how. The bacterium may cause an increase in stomach acid, or it may produce a toxin that harms the stomach lining. *H. pylori* infection occurs worldwide, but it is most common in developing countries. In the United States, the bacterium infects 10 to 20 percent of people under age 30 and more than 50 percent of people over age 60.

Other agents that increase the risk of getting ulcers include aspirin and nonsteroidal anti-inflammatory drugs. These widely used medications can inhibit function of *prostaglandins,* chemical compounds found throughout the body. Prostaglandins in the stomach control the production of stomach acid.

Most peptic ulcers cause pain in the upper abdomen. The pain usually occurs when the stomach is empty, either between meals or at night. Medications that neutralize stomach acid or suppress its secretion relieve the pain temporarily. Eating may also ease the pain. If *H. pylori* is present, doctors may prescribe antibiotics. People can reduce the risk of ulcers by eliminating cigarette smoking and the consumption of alcoholic beverages.

Patients with peptic ulcers may develop such complications as blockage of the stomach or duodenum, internal bleeding, and perforation of the stomach wall. These conditions usually require surgery.

Other kinds of ulcers include *chronic leg ulcers,* which may result from poor blood circulation caused by diabetes, hardening of the arteries, or varicose veins. *Decubitus ulcers,* commonly called *bedsores,* afflict many patients who are confined to bed or a wheelchair. Ulcers also occur in the mouth, in the wall of the bladder, and on the eyes.   James L. Franklin

See also **Antacid; Bedsore; Inflammatory bowel disease; Stomach** (Peptic ulcers).

Ulster. See **Northern Ireland.**

Ulster Unionist Party (UUP) is one of the leading political parties in Northern Ireland, a division of the United Kingdom. Ulster is another name for the northern part of Ireland, and *unionist* means that the party seeks to maintain Northern Ireland's union with the United Kingdom. The party's central organization is known as the Ulster Unionist Council.

The UUP has played a key role in efforts to end decades of conflict between Protestants and Roman Catholics in Northern Ireland. About half the people of Northern Ireland are Protestants, as are most people of the rest of the United Kingdom. Most of the other half of Northern Ireland's population is Catholic, as are most people in the Republic of Ireland. In general, Protestants want Northern Ireland to remain in the United Kingdom, and Catholics want it to become part of the Irish Republic. The dispute has led to decades of violence.

The UUP was founded in 1905, when all of Ireland was part of the United Kingdom. The party's founders and earliest members included Protestant members of the British Parliament who represented Ireland. They formed the UUP to fight a plan for Ireland called *home rule.* Under this plan, Ireland would have remained part of the United Kingdom, but it would have had its own parliament for domestic affairs. Protestants, who feared that such a parliament would be a move toward unity with Catholics in the south, opposed the plan.

In 1921, the Anglo-Irish Treaty established the Irish Free State in the south but preserved Northern Ireland as a part of the United Kingdom. The UUP accepted the treaty, and the party dominated Northern Ireland's politics from the beginning. But many Catholics rejected the division of Ireland and demanded complete independence for a single, united Irish republic. The new government made little effort to win the loyalty of Catholics, and tensions continued for years as Catholics claimed discrimination and civil rights violations by Protestants.

In the late 1960's, the conflict became more violent. In 1972, the United Kingdom suspended Northern Ireland's local government and began to rule directly from London. A key breakthrough came in 1998, when the UUP and Sinn Féin, a Catholic-dominated political party, both supported the Good Friday agreement. Under its terms, Northern Ireland regained local government. For more details, see **Northern Ireland** (History).   Paul E. Gallis

Ultima Thule. See **Thule.**

Ultramicroscope is an instrument that allows a person to see objects much smaller than those that can be seen under an ordinary microscope. Scientists use this

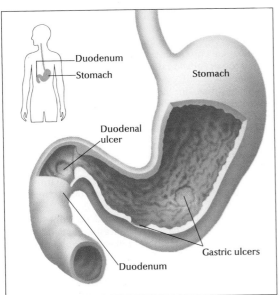

WORLD BOOK illustrations by Leonard E. Morgan

Peptic ulcers are open sores in the digestive system. There are two main types of peptic ulcers. *Duodenal ulcers* form in the duodenum, the upper part of the small intestine. *Gastric ulcers* develop in the stomach. Both types result from the erosive action of two digestive juices, hydrochloric acid and pepsin.

microscope to study such *colloidal particles* as fog drops, smoke particles, and paint pigments that float in liquids or gases (see **Colloid**). Objects as small as 5 *millimicrometers* in diameter can be seen with an ultramicroscope. One millimicrometer equals 1 billionth of a meter, or $\frac{1}{25,400,000}$ of an inch.

The ultramicroscope consists of a compound microscope and a high-intensity light system. In most cases, the strong light originates from an arc lamp. The light is focused into a thin beam and directed at the particles from the side of the microscope. As the beam passes through the particles, it produces a cone of light because of the light-scattering effect of the particles. This is called the *Tyndall effect.* The particles are observed by the light they scatter. They are viewed against a black background and appear as tiny bright dots of light, without structural detail. The first ultramicroscope was designed in 1903 by two German scientists, Richard Zsigmondy and Henry Siedentopf.   John B. Sharkey

See also **Microscope.**

Ultrasound is sound that is too high-pitched for human beings to hear. But many animals can hear and produce ultrasound. They use it to locate obstacles and to detect the movement of their prey. Scientists and engineers have invented ultrasound devices, especially for medical and industrial uses.

The pitch of a sound depends upon the *frequency* of *vibration* of the sound wave. Frequency is the number of cycles of vibration per second. Higher-pitched sounds have higher frequencies than do lower-pitched sounds. Scientists measure frequencies in *hertz.* One hertz is one cycle per second. The highest frequency that a human being can hear depends upon the person's age and other factors. Scientists commonly classify sounds with frequencies higher than 20,000 hertz as ultrasound.

Animal uses of ultrasound. Bats, dolphins, and other animals use ultrasound to locate objects in the dark and to determine the motion of prey. In *echolocation,* the animal sends out *pulses* (short bursts) of ultrasound. The pulses reflect from objects, producing echoes. The animal hears the echoes and uses them to determine the direction and distance to the reflecting object.

To determine motion, animals use echolocation and a change in the frequency of waves known as the *Doppler effect.* This change occurs due to relative motion between the source of the waves and the object that reflects the waves—in this case, the hunted animal.

Some hunted animals—for example, the mantid, or praying mantis—can also hear ultrasound. Thus, these animals can use their hearing to avoid capture by animals that are using echolocation to try to catch them.

Ultrasound devices. People have invented various devices that produce ultrasound. One simple device, an ultrasonic whistle, can produce ultrasound in air. Dogs can hear ultrasound, and so people use such whistles to call their dogs. Complex devices called *ultrasonic transducers* send ultrasound into liquids and solids and receive echoes of the ultrasound. These devices convert electric energy into ultrasound and vice versa. Ultrasonic transducers are made of materials, such as quartz and some ceramics, that are *piezoelectric* (pronounced *pee AY zoh ih LEHK trihk).* This kind of material vibrates when an electric voltage is applied to it and produces a voltage when a sound wave causes it to vibrate.

Medical uses. Ultrasound can produce images of almost all regions of the human body. It can produce two-dimensional or three-dimensional images that represent "slices" through the internal structures of the body. Physicians can use such images to detect and evaluate cancer and other conditions or to check the development of a *fetus* (unborn baby). The imaging instruments range from large, sophisticated machines to simple, battery-powered units. The images can be sent electronically to hospital computer systems and to consulting physicians at other locations. Instruments that use the Doppler effect help physicians detect and evaluate abnormalities that alter blood flow in the heart and blood vessels. Simpler Doppler instruments monitor the heartbeat of fetuses during pregnancy and labor.

More powerful ultrasound beams are used in several medical treatments, including stimulation of wound healing and deep heating as part of physical therapy. *High-intensity focused ultrasound* (HIFU) generates heat inside the body that can remove excess tissue from an enlarged prostate gland, destroy cancerous tumors, or stop an internal flow of blood. A *lithotripter* uses high-intensity pulses of ultrasound to break up kidney stones.

Other uses. Devices that use ultrasound include burglar alarms, automatic door openers, instruments that detect flaws in metal parts, machines that weld plastic, tools that cut metal, and cleaning instruments that loosen dust and other contaminants from delicate electronic components. Underwater *sonar* (*so*und *n*avigation *a*nd *r*anging) devices operate much like radar to measure distances to the ocean floor, detect submarines, and even locate schools of fish.   Frederick W. Kremkau

See also **Pregnancy** (picture: An ultrasound examination); **Sonar.**

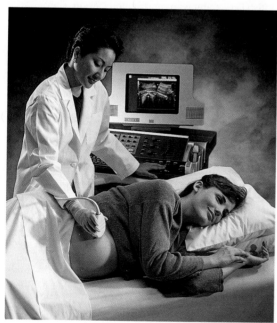

Advanced Technology Laboratories

An ultrasound examination can produce images of the inner structures of the human body. One of the most common uses of ultrasound by physicians is to check growth of an unborn baby.

Ultraviolet rays are an invisible form of light. They lie just beyond the violet end of the visible spectrum. The sun is the major natural source of ultraviolet rays. Lightning, or any other electric spark in the air, also emits ultraviolet rays. The rays can be produced artificially by passing an electric current through a gas or vapor, such as mercury vapor. Ultraviolet rays can cause sunburn. Overexposure can cause skin cancer. However, ultraviolet rays destroy harmful organisms and have other useful effects.

Ultraviolet rays have shorter wavelengths than visible light has. A wavelength, the distance between the crests of two waves, is often measured in units called *nanometers.* A nanometer (nm) is a billionth of a meter, or $1/_{25,400,000}$ inch. Wavelengths of visible light range from about 400 to 700 nm. Scientists working in different fields use different numbers for the shortest wavelength of ultraviolet rays. Astronomers typically use a figure of 10 nm, while the World Meteorological Organization (WMO), a specialized agency of the United Nations, uses 100 nm. Scientists separate ultraviolet rays into three categories—known as *UVA, UVB,* and *UVC*—according to wavelength. The WMO uses a range of 100 to 280 nm for UVC, 280 to 320 nm for UVB, and 320 to 400 nm for UVA. See **Electromagnetic waves** (diagram: The electromagnetic spectrum).

The wavelength of ultraviolet rays determines whether a material they shine on absorbs the rays or transmits them. For example, only ultraviolet rays with large wavelengths can pass through ordinary window glass. The glass absorbs rays with shorter wavelengths, though they can pass through other materials.

Uses of ultraviolet rays. Ultraviolet rays with wavelengths shorter than 300 nm are effective in killing bacteria and viruses. Hospitals use germicidal lamps that produce these short rays to sterilize surgical instruments, water, and the air in operating rooms. Many food and drug companies use germicidal lamps to disinfect various types of products and their containers.

Direct exposure to ultraviolet rays with wavelengths shorter than 320 nm produces vitamin D in the body. Physicians once used sun lamps that produced these rays to prevent and treat rickets, a bone disease caused by the lack of vitamin D. The lamps are used today to treat some skin disorders, such as acne and psoriasis.

Some instruments use ultraviolet rays to identify the chemical composition of unknown materials. Medical researchers use such instruments to analyze substances in the human body, including amino acids and proteins. The electronics industry uses ultraviolet rays in manufacturing integrated circuits.

Harmful effects. The sun's shortest ultraviolet rays—those with wavelengths below about 320 nm—are particularly harmful to living things. Overexposure to these rays can cause painful eye irritation or eye inflammation. High-quality sunglasses protect the eyes. Overexposure to ultraviolet rays also can cause a painful burn. *Melanin,* brown-black pigment in the skin, and sunscreen lotions provide some protection against sunburn.

Exposure to the sun's ultraviolet rays over a long period can cause skin cancer and other changes in human cells. Such exposure also can damage or kill plants. *Ozone,* a form of oxygen in Earth's upper atmosphere, absorbs most of the sun's ultraviolet radiation. Without the ozone layer, ultraviolet rays would probably destroy most plant and animal life. See **Ozone**.

Scientific research. Ultraviolet rays originate within the atoms of all elements. Scientists learn about the makeup and energy levels of atoms by studying the rays. Experts also learn about distant stars and galaxies by analyzing the ultraviolet rays that they give off.

Much research has focused on the role of ultraviolet rays in chemical reactions that break down Earth's protective ozone layer. As the ozone layer breaks down, it becomes less effective as a barrier against harmful ultraviolet rays. Experiments indicate that bees, butterflies, and other insects can see ultraviolet light. The reflection of ultraviolet rays off wings reveals patterns that help insects identify mates.   James J. Chisholm

See also **Telescope** (Other telescopes).

Uluru, also known as Ayers Rock, is a giant outcrop of rock in the Northern Territory of Australia. It rises abruptly 1,100 feet (335 meters) from the sand dune plains, about 280 miles (450 kilometers) southwest of Alice Springs. The rock is more than 1 ½ miles (2.4 kilometers) long and 1 mile (1.6 kilometers) wide. It measures 5 miles (8 kilometers) around its base.

The rock's coarse sandstone glows red during sunrise and sunset. Uluru consists of beds of *arkose* (sandstone containing feldspar minerals) that date back to the Cambrian Period, about 543 million to 490 million years ago. Similar rock lies at shallow depths under the sand plain surrounding Uluru. The erosion that formed Uluru probably started in the Cretaceous Period, from about 145 million to 65 million years ago.

Uluru is a place of spiritual significance for its traditional owners, the Anangu people, an Australian Aboriginal group. Uluru has many sacred sites and caves decorated with rock art. The first European to see Uluru was the English explorer Ernest Giles in 1872. The explorer William Gosse visited it in 1873. He named it *Ayers Rock* after Sir Henry Ayers, who was then the premier of South Australia.

In 1985, Australia's government legally returned the land where Uluru stands to the Anangu. The Anangu then turned over the management of Uluru (now Uluru-Kata Tjuta) National Park to the Australian government on a 99-year lease. The Uluru-Kata Tjuta National Park is listed as a World Heritage Site because of its unique environmental and cultural significance.   Kate Darian-Smith

See also **Australia** (picture: Uluru); **Seven Natural Wonders of the World** (picture: Uluru).

Ulysses, *yoo LIHS eez,* was king of Ithaca and a brave and cunning hero in Greek mythology. His name is *Odysseus* in Greek and *Ulysses* in Latin. Ulysses was especially noted for his cleverness. In early Greek writings, he also was generous and noble. Some later Greek writers portrayed him as a sly, deceitful trickster.

Most of the stories about Ulysses tell about his life during and after the Trojan War, a conflict between Greece and the city of Troy. Ulysses is a major character in the *Iliad* and the hero of the *Odyssey,* the two great epics attributed to the Greek poet Homer. The *Iliad* deals with events that occurred in the last year of the Trojan War. The *Odyssey* describes Ulysses's adventures as he returns home after the Trojan War.

The Trojan War. Ulysses was the son of Laertes, the king of Ithaca, and Anticleia. But just before her marriage to Laertes, Anticleia had been seduced by Sisyphus, the king of Corinth. Some Greeks believed that Sisyphus was Ulysses's father.

Ulysses married Penelope, the daughter of Icarius, the king of Sparta. Soon after the birth of their son, Telemachus, a group of Greek leaders tried to recruit Ulysses to fight Troy. But Ulysses did not want to go to war. To avoid joining the army, Ulysses pretended to be insane. He yoked an ox and a donkey to a plow and then sowed his fields with salt. Palamedes, a member of the group, suspected that Ulysses was faking insanity. Palamedes took Telemachus and put him in the path of Ulysses's plow. Ulysses turned the plow aside to protect the baby and thus proved that he was sane.

Ulysses reluctantly agreed to sail with the Greek army for Troy, but he never forgave Palamedes. After the Greeks arrived at Troy, Ulysses tricked them into believing that Palamedes was a traitor. The Greek soldiers then killed Palamedes.

During the Trojan War, Ulysses was a valiant fighter and a wise counselor to the Greek leaders. He went on dangerous missions to spy on the Trojan forces. The Greeks honored him by giving him the armor of Achilles, the greatest Greek warrior, after Achilles's death.

Return to Ithaca. The Greeks finally defeated the Trojans after 10 years of fighting, and Ulysses set sail for Ithaca. During his return voyage, he visited the land of *Cyclopes* (one-eyed giants). Ulysses was captured by Polyphemus, a Cyclops, but he escaped after blinding the Cyclops with a heated stake. Polyphemus prayed for revenge to his father, the sea god Poseidon. Poseidon then tried to make Ulysses's return home as difficult as possible. With some help from the goddess Athena, Ulysses finally reached home after 10 years of wandering and many thrilling adventures. See **Odyssey.**

During Ulysses's long absence, several noblemen had moved into his palace. The men claimed that Ulysses must have died, and they demanded that Penelope marry one of them. Penelope finally agreed to marry the man who could string Ulysses's huge bow and shoot an arrow through 12 axes.

Ulysses arrived at the palace the day before the archery contest, disguised as a beggar. Penelope allowed him to enter the contest. He was the only one who could perform the feat. After revealing his identity, he killed the noblemen with the help of Athena, Telemachus, and loyal servants. He then was reunited with his wife.

Cynthia W. Shelmerdine

See also **Penelope; Trojan War.**

Umbilical cord, *uhm BIHL uh kuhl,* is a ropelike structure that connects a developing baby to the *placenta* during pregnancy (see **Placenta**). The cord contains two arteries and one vein. The arteries carry blood containing waste products from the developing baby to the placenta. The vein carries blood containing oxygen and food substances obtained from the mother's blood back to the baby. When the baby is born, the doctor carefully cuts the umbilical cord about 2 inches (5 centimeters) from the baby's abdomen. The baby's lungs, liver, and other organs then take over the functions performed by the placenta and the mother. The remaining stump of the umbilical cord falls off within 7 to 10 days, leaving the navel, also called the *umbilicus,* which remains throughout life.　Gerald B. Merenstein

See also **Baby** (picture: Seconds after birth); **Childbirth.**

Umbrella is a device that protects people from rain and sun. It consists of a circular piece of fabric stretched on a frame attached to a central handle. The frame can be folded when it is not needed.

Umbrellas were originally used as sunshades. In many cultures, they were a symbol of rank. In ancient Egypt and Babylonia, for example, only royalty and nobility were permitted to have umbrellas.

Umbrellas were first widely used against rain during the 1700's, when heavy umbrellas made of wood and oil-cloth became common in Europe. During the 1800's, light, decorative sunshades called *parasols* became fashionable among women throughout Europe and the United States. Many of these umbrellas had whalebone or metal frames and fine silk coverings edged with lace and fringe. They were popular until about the 1920's.

Today, umbrellas are used primarily as protection against rain or snow. Most umbrellas are made with metal or plastic frames and covered with plain or patterned fabric or clear plastic. They come in a wide variety of colors. Many umbrellas fold up to fit in purses and briefcases.　Lois M. Gurel

Umbrellabird is the name of three species of birds that live in the tropical forests of Central and South America. Male umbrellabirds have an umbrellalike crest of feathers that spread over the head. Males also have a growth of skin, called a *wattle,* that hangs down from the neck. In two species, the wattle is covered with feathers. Male umbrellabirds display the crest and wattle to attract a mate. The crest and the wattle are relatively undeveloped in females. An umbrellabird is about the size of a crow and has black feathers.　David M. Niles

WORLD BOOK illustration by Trevor Boyer, Linden Artists Ltd.

Umbrellabird

Scientific classification. Umbrellabirds belong to the cotinga family, Cotingidae. They form the genus *Cephalopterus.*

UN. See **United Nations.**

Un-American Activities Committee was an investigating committee of the United States House of Representatives. It investigated the threat of *subversion* (overthrowing the government) by groups in the United States and recommended legislation to the House.

The House Committee on Un-American Activities (HUAC) grew from a special investigating committee established in 1938. It became a *standing* (permanent) committee in 1945. In 1969, the House changed the committee's name to the Committee on Internal Security. The House abolished the committee in 1975.

The committee's main interest was to search for Communist influence inside and outside the government. After World War II ended in 1945, many people viewed such investigations as a contribution to the struggle against world Communism. President Harry S. Truman established a loyalty-security program in 1947 after it was discovered that some Communists had held jobs within the government before and during the war. The committee also investigated the activities of other radical or extremist groups.

The committee received attention in 1947 for its hearings on the influence of Communism in the motion-picture industry. But it gained its greatest fame in 1948 during its investigation of Communists in the Department of State. Its hearings led to the perjury trial and conviction of Alger Hiss, a former high official of the department (see **Hiss, Alger**). Representative Richard M. Nixon, a committee member, played a key role in the investigation (see **Nixon, Richard M.** [U.S. representative]).

After the Hiss case, the Un-American Activities Committee looked into suspected Communist influence in almost all areas of life. Committees in the U.S. Senate and in state legislatures also investigated Communist influence. As a result, public employees and a number of employees in private industries had to take loyalty oaths. Persons accused of Communist associations were *blacklisted* (denied employment) by some firms.

The committee's critics charged that it often abused its investigative power and violated the constitutional rights of witnesses. They maintained that people labeled as subversives should have the right to cross-examine their accusers. Others believed that the discovery of conspirators should be the responsibility of the police, the FBI, and the courts. Decisions by the Supreme Court of the United States in the 1950's and 1960's curbed the committee's activities. For example, the court ruled that witnesses may refuse to answer any questions unrelated to the matter under investigation.   Harvey Glickman

Unamuno, *oo nuh MOO noh,* **Miguel de,** *mee GEHL deh* (1864-1936), was a Spanish philosophical essayist, poet, novelist, and dramatist. The leading humanist of modern Spain, he argued that the individual—not civilization, society, or culture—was "the subject and supreme object of all thought."

Unamuno's best-known work, *The Tragic Sense of Life* (1913), examines the conflict between faith and reason from the Renaissance to the 1900's. In this book, the author evaluates the significance of will, the desire for immortality, and the search for love in human history. Unamuno's study of Spanish culture in *Concerning Traditionalism* (1895) helped stimulate the Spanish intellectual revival known as the Generation of 1898. His finest poem is the long meditation called *The Christ of Velázquez* (1920). His best novel, *Mist* (1914), examines the mysteries of human existence. The novel *Saint Emmanuel Bueno, Martyr* (1931) portrays the agony of a priest who doubts the existence of life after death.

Miguel de Unamuno y Jugo was born in Bilbao on Sept. 29, 1864. He was appointed professor of Greek at the University of Salamanca in 1891 and rector of the university in 1900. In addition to his many books, Unamuno wrote more than 3,000 short essays and articles. A bold political critic, he incurred the hostility of four successive Spanish governments. He died on Dec. 31, 1936.
       David Thatcher Gies

Uncas, *UHNG kuhs* (1588?-1683?), was a chief of the Mohegan Indians in Connecticut during colonial times. He became noted for his assistance to the English settlers, and his name has been perpetuated in the character Uncas in James Fenimore Cooper's book, *The Last of the Mohicans* (see **Mohegan Indians**).

Uncas, serving his tribe's interests, joined the English in a war against the Pequot Indians in 1637. The English settlements along the Connecticut River probably owed their survival to the help of Uncas. Uncas defeated the Narragansett tribe in 1643, and five years later fought the Mohawk, Narragansett, and other tribes.

A monument to Uncas was erected by the citizens of Norwich, Connecticut, in 1847. Another monument to him stands on the site of the home of James Fenimore Cooper, at Cooperstown, New York.   John W. Ifkovic

Uncle Sam is a figure that symbolizes the United States. The term originated as an unfriendly nickname for the U.S. government during the War of 1812.

The term "Uncle Sam" was used as early as 1813. That year, a Troy, New York, newspaper stated that it apparently had arisen because of the initials "U.S." on government wagons. In 1816, the nickname appeared in a book title, *The Adventures of Uncle Sam*. It was later asserted that the term had its origin in a specific person—Samuel "Uncle Sam" Wilson of Troy, New York, who supplied the Army with "U.S."-stamped barrels of provisions.

The costume of Uncle Sam, decorated with stars and stripes, originated in cartoons of the 1830's and 1840's. But the figure did not assume its present form until after the American Civil War (1861-1865). In 1961, Congress passed a resolution saluting Wilson as the person who inspired America's national symbol.   Reginald Horsman

See also **Brother Jonathan.**

Granger Collection

Uncle Sam has appeared in several forms in different periods of United States history. In the poster shown, which was painted by James Montgomery Flagg, Uncle Sam urges men to enlist in the U.S. Army during World War I (1914-1918).

Uncle Tom's Cabin is a famous antislavery novel by the American author Harriet Beecher Stowe. It first appeared as a serial in the abolitionist magazine *National Era* in 1851 and 1852. The novel was published as a book later in 1852 and quickly became a best seller in the United States and the United Kingdom.

Stowe wrote *Uncle Tom's Cabin* to criticize slavery, which she considered a national sin. She hoped that her novel would help bring slavery to an early and peaceful end. However, the book increased the hostility of many Northerners toward the South. Southerners, on the other hand, considered Stowe's description of slavery inaccurate. They called the book an insult and an injustice. Historians believe that the bitter feelings aroused by Stowe's book helped cause the American Civil War (1861-1865).

The chief character in *Uncle Tom's Cabin* is Uncle Tom, a dignified old black slave. The story describes Tom's experiences with three slaveholders. Two of them—George Shelby and Augustine St. Clare—treat Tom kindly. But the third, Simon Legree, abuses Tom and has him brutally beaten for refusing to tell where two escaped slaves are hiding. Tom dies from the beating. A subplot of the novel tells about the family of slaves—George and Eliza and their baby—who flee to freedom in Canada.

The novel presents a realistic account of American life 10 years before the Civil War. Stowe created a vivid picture of Southern life, with Tom being sold from one slaveowner to another. *Uncle Tom's Cabin* also describes the upper Midwest as seen by George and Eliza as they flee northward into Canada.

After the Civil War, *Uncle Tom's Cabin* became known chiefly through abridgments of the novel and by plays based on the book. However, these versions distorted the original story and characters. The term "Uncle Tom" came to stand for a black man who, for selfish reasons or through fear, adopts a humble manner to gain favor with whites. But the novel portrayed Tom as a brave man who dies rather than betray two fellow slaves. Few people realized that Simon Legree, the cruel villain, was a Northerner, and that Augustine St. Clare, a Southerner, recognized the evils of slavery.   John Clendenning

See also **Stowe, Harriet Beecher.**

Unconscious, in psychology, is a term used to describe such mental processes as thoughts, ideas, and feelings that go on in people's minds without their being aware of them. Many people commonly refer to the *unconscious* as the *subconscious*. The existence of mental processes that are active in the mind without being conscious was first studied scientifically by the French neurologist Jean Martin Charcot and his pupils in the 1800's. They studied the unconscious by means of hypnosis. Soon after, doctors realized many mentally ill people, such as those with hysteria, were influenced by unconscious thoughts and feelings.

The doctor who first realized clearly the importance of unconscious thoughts and feelings in human psychology was Sigmund Freud of Austria. He developed the method of *psychoanalysis* for treating mentally ill patients. This method also serves as a way of learning what goes on unconsciously in a patient's mind. With psychoanalysis, Freud proved that unconscious thoughts and feelings not only produce the symptoms of many types of mental illness, but that they are also of basic importance in the way the minds of normal people work. This knowledge has enabled doctors to make great advances in the treatment of the mentally ill.   Allen Frances

Related articles in *World Book* include:

Freud, Sigmund   Hypnotism   Hysteria

Jung, Carl G.   Phobia   Psychotherapy
Neurosis   Psychoanalysis   Subliminal

Underground, in political terms, is a secretly conducted movement to overthrow the government or the military occupation forces of a country. Underground tactics have been used since early history, but reached a high point of activity during World War II (1939-1945). Since then, Communist organizations have worked underground in attempts to overthrow many governments.

Adolf Hitler used an underground group called the *fifth column,* especially in the early stages of World War II (see **Fifth column**). German agents worked inside various countries before and during the German invasions of those countries. The agents used espionage, propaganda, and sabotage to aid the German cause and destroy the invaded country's morale.

But once the Germans had conquered a country, the underground of that country's patriots hampered German operations. Underground workers sprang up in France, Belgium, the Netherlands, Denmark, Norway, Yugoslavia, occupied areas of the Soviet Union, and other conquered areas. They plagued the Germans by blowing up railroad trains and bridges, sabotaging factories, distributing illegal newspapers, rescuing marooned Allied servicemen, and gathering valuable military information.   Stephen Goode

See also **Guerrilla warfare; Maquis; Partisans; World War II** (Resistance groups).

Underground railroad was an informal system that helped slaves escape to the Northern States and Canada during the mid-1800's. The system was neither underground nor a railroad. It was called the underground railroad because of the swift, secret way in which the slaves escaped. The slaves traveled by whatever means they could, moving almost entirely at night and hiding during the day. The fugitives and the people who aided them used many railroad terms as code words. For example, hiding places were called *stations,* and people who helped the runaways were known as *conductors.*

The underground railroad had no formal organization. Free blacks and some whites in both the South and the North provided the runaways with food, clothing, directions, and places to hide. Some Southern slaves also helped fugitives escape. In the North, many Quakers and other white abolitionists furnished hiding places and helped slaves move from one refuge to the next.

The term *underground railroad* was first used about 1830. From then until 1860, the system helped thousands of slaves escape. Some settled in the North, but there they could be captured and returned to slavery. Therefore, many fled to Canada, especially after Congress passed a strict fugitive slave law in 1850. The major haven for runaways in Canada was southern Ontario.

The most heavily traveled routes of the underground railroad ran through Ohio, Indiana, and western Pennsylvania. Large numbers of fugitives followed these routes and reached Canada by way of Detroit or Niagara Falls, New York. Others sailed across Lake Erie to Ontario from such ports as Erie, Pennsylvania, and Sandusky, Ohio. In the East, the chief center of the underground railroad was southeastern Pennsylvania. Many runaway slaves followed routes from that area through New England to Quebec.

A few people became famous for their work with the

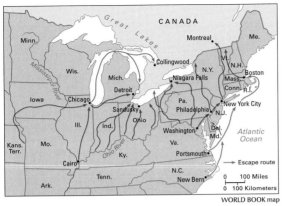

WORLD BOOK map

The underground railroad was a network of escape routes used by slaves during the mid-1800's. It led from the slave states—shown in dark gray—to the free states and Canada.

underground railroad. Levi Coffin, a Quaker who was called the "president of the underground railroad," helped more than 3,000 slaves escape. His home in Newport (now Fountain City), Indiana, was on three major escape routes. The most famous black leader of the underground railroad was Harriet Tubman, a runaway slave herself. She returned to the South 19 times and helped about 300 blacks escape to freedom.

The underground railroad showed the determination of blacks and many whites to end slavery in the United States. The underground railroad's operations angered many Southerners and contributed to the hostility between North and South that led to the American Civil War (1861-1865).   David Herbert Donald

See also **Abolition movement; Compromise of 1850; Fugitive Slave Laws; Tubman, Harriet.**

Additional resources

Bordewich, Fergus M. *Bound for Canaan.* Amistad, 2005.
Hansen, Joyce, and McGowan, Gary. *Freedom Roads.* Cricket Bks., 2004. Younger readers.

Underwriting is a term first used in England in the 1600's. *Underwriters* (insurers) wrote their names at the bottom of proposed insurance contracts covering a ship and its cargo. They indicated in this way their willingness to assume part of the risk. Today, every insurance company has an underwriting department which is important to the success of the company. Underwriting experts must determine the premium rates for various kinds of insurance policies and the amount and degree of risk to be assumed for each policy.

Underwriters also examine all applications for insurance to guard against bad risks and to prevent the company from assuming too many of the same kinds of risks. For example, a fire insurance underwriter may find that several suspicious fires have occurred in the building to be insured. On the basis of this finding, the underwriter may decide the risk is bad.

In finance, the term *underwriting* has another meaning. It is an agreement to purchase a corporation stock or bond issue.   Dan R. Anderson

See also **Insurance** (Careers in the industry); **Lloyd's.**

Undset, *OON seht,* **Sigrid,** *SIHG rihd* (1882-1949), a Norwegian author, won the 1928 Nobel Prize in litera-

ture. *Kristin Lavransdatter* (1920-1922), her major work, is an epic trilogy of life in Norway during the Middle Ages. It consists of the novels *The Bridal Wreath, The Mistress of Husaby,* and *The Cross.* The novels tell the story of Kristin—her childhood, stormy marriage, and dedication to Christian service after the death of her husband. The displacement of heathen customs by Christian ideals in medieval Norway is dealt with in a second but less impressive epic, *The Master of Hestviken* (1925-1927). The series consists of *The Axe, The Snake Pit, In the Wilderness,* and *The Son Avenger.*

Undset was born on May 20, 1882, in Kalundborg, Denmark. She was the daughter of Ingvald Undset, a distinguished Norwegian archaeologist. Her father awakened in her a strong interest in the Middle Ages. After he died, Undset gave up plans for a career as a painter and went to work in an Oslo business office. While working there from 1899 to 1909, she gathered impressions that she used in her early realistic stories of lower middle-class life.

Jenny (1911), her first novel to attract widespread attention, deals with the sexual problems of a female artist. Undset wrote other novels about life in her time. They include *The Wild Orchid* (1929) and *The Burning Bush* (1930), stories of a man's conversion to Roman Catholicism. They reflect Undset's own conversion to Catholicism in 1924. Undset took refuge in the United States from 1940 to 1945, while the Nazis occupied Norway. She lectured and wrote while in the United States. She died on June 10, 1949.   Niels Ingwersen

Undulant fever. See Brucellosis.

Unemployment is the condition of a person who is out of work and actively looking for a job. Unemployment contributes to numerous problems for jobless individuals, their families, and society as a whole. For the individual, it causes a loss of income and, in many cases, emotional distress or a loss of self-respect. For society, it indicates lost production and may lead to increased levels of homelessness, criminal activity, and antisocial behavior. Unemployment is commonly measured by a statistic called an *unemployment rate.* An unemployment rate is the percentage of jobless individuals in a community's total *labor force*—that is, in the segment of the population that is willing and able to be employed. Business executives, economists, and government officials use unemployment rates as indications of economic health.

Before the 1900's, people commonly believed that unemployment resulted from laziness or other flaws in character. Today, most people realize that women and men may be out of work through no fault of their own.

How people become unemployed

People become unemployed in a number of ways. Many people are dismissed from their jobs, by either being *laid off* or being *fired.* Workers may be laid off if companies reorganize or close down, or if employers need to reduce payroll costs. Layoffs are common during economic downturns, and they are sometimes temporary in nature. Firings are usually permanent, and they are typically the result of employee misconduct, poor job performance, or disagreements in the workplace. Workers who have been fired usually remain unemployed longer than workers who have been laid off.

Unemployment rate in selected countries

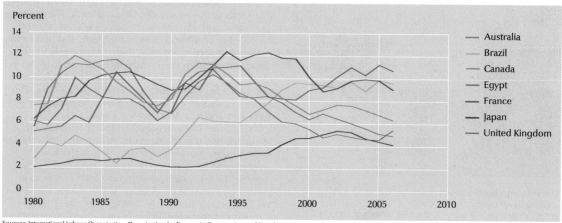

Sources: International Labour Organization; Organisation for Economic Co-operation and Development; national statistics agencies.

In many cases, workers leave their jobs voluntarily. Some leave because they are unhappy with their wages or working conditions, or because they feel there are better opportunities elsewhere. However, most people who leave jobs voluntarily do not become unemployed, because they arrange for new jobs before leaving.

Some unemployed individuals are new to the labor force and have not yet found jobs. People entering the labor force for the first time often include graduating students, students searching for work while still attending school, and former homemakers seeking their first jobs. Some people who have left the labor force—possibly to pursue advanced education or to care for children—become unemployed as they reenter the labor force at a later date.

Types of unemployment

Many economists classify unemployment into three categories, according to the basic causes. These categories are (1) frictional, (2) structural, and (3) cyclical.

Frictional unemployment exists in efficiently operating labor markets, even when jobs are plentiful. The frictionally unemployed category includes people who are between jobs, because they either quit their old jobs or were laid off or fired. It also includes individuals entering the labor force who have started searching but have not yet found jobs. Such unemployment arises because of regular changes in a free market economy and the time required for people to find new jobs.

Seasonal unemployment, a type of frictional unemployment, occurs in industries that lay off workers during certain seasons each year. In some areas, for instance, construction workers are often between jobs during periods of severe weather, and workers in resort areas are often out of work during the off-season.

Structural unemployment exists when there is a mismatch between the individuals seeking work and the jobs that are available. For example, coal miners may be seeking work at the same time there is a shortage of salespeople. Structural unemployment also includes people in the wrong location to fill available jobs. There may be layoffs in one region while there are numerous job openings in another.

Structural unemployment may also result from technological change and the development of new products, machinery, and manufacturing methods. Such developments may lead to increased demand for new and different skills and reduced demand for traditional skills. For example, the percentage of clerical and professional workers in the labor force has risen sharply since 1900. Meanwhile, the number of jobs in coal mining, railroading, and other traditional industries has declined. Structural unemployment caused by technological change is sometimes called *technological unemployment.*

Cyclical unemployment, sometimes called *deficient demand unemployment,* results from downturns in the economy. When many goods and services remain unsold, many industries reduce production and lay off employees. They often do this instead of attempting to maintain existing production levels and reducing prices and wages. An especially severe period of high cyclical unemployment occurred during the Great Depression, a worldwide economic slump of the 1930's.

Government and unemployment

Governments throughout the world have attempted a variety of strategies to control unemployment. They have also established programs and policies that seek to address the societal problems associated with joblessness. Studies of unemployment greatly influence social and economic policies at various levels of government.

Measuring unemployment. The specific methods for measuring unemployment vary from country to country. Unemployment totals generally do not include people who are not seeking work because of age, illness, or a mental or physical disability. Nor do they include people who are not seeking work because they are attending school, homemaking, uninterested in working, or discouraged by their job search. Such people are instead classified as *out of the labor force* rather than unemployed.

In the United States, the Census Bureau in the U.S. Department of Commerce collects and tabulates unemployment statistics. The Bureau of Labor Statistics in the U.S. Department of Labor then analyzes and publishes the data. The Bureau of Labor Statistics reports the unemployment rate for each month. The annual U.S. unemployment rate represents the average of the monthly figures for a year. Statistics Canada, the statistical agency of the Canadian government, compiles unemployment statistics in Canada. National Statistics performs similar functions in the United Kingdom, and the Australian Bureau of Statistics does so in Australia. The International Labour Organization (ILO), a specialized agency of the United Nations (UN), regularly reports world employment and unemployment statistics.

Programs and policies. Many governments operate *unemployment insurance* (UI) programs. Payments from unemployment insurance help ease the loss of income for people who have lost a job and are looking for work. Many industrial nations—including the United States, Canada, and the United Kingdom—have government-sponsored unemployment insurance systems.

Certain types of government policies seek to address specific categories of unemployment. To combat frictional unemployment, for example, many governments have public employment agencies that inform unemployed workers of suitable job openings. To address structural unemployment, some governments offer programs that train people in skills required for available jobs. Other programs rehabilitate workers who need special assistance.

Governments may also seek to control unemployment through *fiscal policy* and *monetary policy.* Fiscal policy refers to a government's taxing and spending programs. Monetary policy involves decisions that influence the money supply, the availability of loans, and interest rates. Fiscal and monetary policies can help create new jobs by making more money available for employers to hire workers. However, such efforts may also lead to budget deficits and severe *inflation* (price increases).

Some people have suggested that the government should become the *employer of last resort* if industry cannot employ the nation's total labor force. The U.S.

government experimented with the idea in the 1930's, when government agencies, such as Federal Emergency Relief Administration (FERA) and the Works Progress Administration (WPA), provided temporary work relief jobs for the unemployed. But since the end of the Depression, such policies have received little support.

Unemployment levels throughout the world

Unemployment rates vary greatly from country to country. The rates also vary for different groups within a country. For instance, in many countries, unemployment rates tend to be significantly higher for teenage workers than for adults. Similarly, unskilled people generally experience significantly higher levels of unemployment than highly trained workers. In some countries, unemployment rates are higher for certain racial and ethnic minority groups.

Countries throughout the world experienced historic levels of unemployment during the Great Depression. In Canada, Germany, and the United Kingdom, unemployed people accounted for approximately 13 to 27 percent of the labor force. In the United States, the unemployment rate reached nearly 25 percent. In most countries, unemployment rates decreased significantly after 1940. The unemployment rate in the United States ranged from about 4 to 6 percent through most of the late 1900's and early 2000's. Unemployment rates in Australia, Canada, the United Kingdom, and most western European countries generally ranged from 4 to 10 percent in the early 2000's.

Some countries have traditionally maintained low levels of unemployment. Unemployment rates in Norway and Iceland, for instance, were less than 5 percent through the late 1900's and early 2000's. Japan has also had traditionally low unemployment rates. However, a period of extremely slow economic growth in Japan during the late 1900's and early 2000's caused the Japanese rates to rise significantly.   Price V. Fishback

Employment and unemployment in the United States*

Number of employed and unemployed

Millions of people

Unemployment rate

Percent

Year	Civilian labor force		Unemployment rate (%)
	Employed	Unemployed	
1900	26,956,000	1,420,000	5.0
1905	30,918,000	1,381,000	4.3
1910	34,559,000	2,150,000	5.9
1915	36,223,000	3,377,000	8.5
1920	39,208,000	2,132,000	5.2
1925	43,716,000	1,453,000	3.2
1930	44,183,000	4,340,000	8.9
1935	41,673,000	10,610,000	20.3
1940	47,520,000	8,120,000	14.6
1945	52,820,000	1,040,000	1.9
1950	58,918,000	3,288,000	5.3
1955	62,170,000	2,852,000	4.4
1960	65,778,000	3,852,000	5.5
1965	71,088,000	3,366,000	4.5
1970	78,678,000	4,093,000	4.9
1975	85,846,000	7,929,000	8.5
1980	99,303,000	7,637,000	7.1
1985	107,150,000	8,312,000	7.2
1990	118,793,000	7,047,000	5.6
1995	124,900,000	7,404,000	5.6
2000	136,891,000	5,692,000	4.0
2002	136,485,000	8,378,000	5.8
2005	141,730,000	7,591,000	5.1
2006	144,427,000	7,001,000	4.6
2007	146,047,000	7,078,000	4.6

*Based on a sample of households throughout the country: for 1900-1946, people 14 years old and older; after 1946, people 16 years old and older.
Sources: U.S. Bureau of Labor Statistics; U.S. Census Bureau.

Related articles in *World Book* include:

Automation (Automation and
  jobs)
Careers
Depression
Employment agency
Employment Service,
  United States

Great Depression
National Alliance of Business
Outsourcing
Poverty
Recession
Unemployment insurance
Welfare

Additional resources

Alpern, Michele. *The Effects of Job Loss on the Family.* Chelsea
  Hse., 2002. Younger readers.
Folsom, Franklin. *Impatient Armies of the Poor: The Story of Collective Action of the Unemployed, 1808-1942.* Univ. Pr. of Colo.,
  1991.
Lange, Thomas, ed. *Unemployment in Theory and Practice.* Edward Elgar, 1998.
St. Pierre, Stephanie. *Everything You Need to Know When a Par-
  ent Is Out of Work.* 3rd ed. Rosen Pub. Group, 1997.

Unemployment insurance is a means of protecting
workers who are out of work and looking for employment. These unemployed workers receive cash payments, usually each week for a limited period. Besides
aiding individual workers, unemployment insurance
may help limit slumps in business activity by enabling
unemployed people to buy goods and services. Such
purchases help preserve existing jobs. Most industrial
nations have government-sponsored unemployment
insurance systems.

The first known unemployment insurance plan was
adopted in Baisle Town (now Basel), Switzerland, in
1789. In 1911, the United Kingdom set up an unemployment insurance system that required the participation of
workers and employers.

In 1932, Wisconsin adopted the first unemployment
insurance law in the United States. A federal-state unemployment insurance plan was established by the Social
Security Act of 1935. By 1937, all the states had unemployment insurance laws that met the requirements of
the Social Security Act. Canada adopted an unemployment insurance program in 1940.

United States plan. The states administer the U.S.
unemployment insurance system and determine the
benefits. However, federal law requires that the states
maintain a system that meets certain standards.

Unemployment insurance is financed chiefly by payroll taxes on employers. Both the federal and the state
governments levy unemployment taxes.

Unemployment insurance taxes. The Federal Unemployment Tax Act levies a payroll tax on businesses that
(1) employ one or more workers for a minimum number
of weeks in a year or (2) have a quarterly payroll of a certain minimum amount. The money received by the U.S.
government is used for state and federal administrative
expenses, for paying extended benefits during a recession, and for loans to states that have exhausted their
funds for paying benefits.

The states collect an unemployment insurance tax
from employers. Employees contribute a small amount
in a few states. Unemployment taxes collected by the
states go into a state fund for paying benefits to workers.

Coverage and benefits. Unemployment insurance
protection covers most workers in industry and commerce and includes civilian federal employees. Some
state systems cover more workers than the federal law
requires. Railroad workers have their own system.

Each state has different benefit provisions. The unemployed worker typically must apply at state offices both
for benefit payments and for help finding work. All
states require workers to be able to work and to be
available for work in order to qualify. Most states require unemployment insurance recipients to actively
seek work. A worker must also have done a certain
amount of covered work in a preceding period, usually
a year. Most states have a short waiting period before
benefits are payable, and a maximum period during
which unemployed workers may collect benefits. Some
states pay extra benefits to unemployment insurance
recipients with dependents.

Canadian plan. Canada's federal government administers the Canadian unemployment insurance program.
The program applies in all provinces and territories and
covers nearly all Canadian workers. People must work a
minimum number of hours before they become eligible
for benefits. Under the plan, some unemployed workers
receive extra benefits if they are sick, pregnant, or have
children. Employers and workers pay special taxes to finance the Canadian plan. The program is administered
by a federal agency called Human Resources Development Canada.   Paul L. Burgess

See also **Social security; Unemployment; Welfare.**

UNESCO is a specialized agency of the United Nations
(UN). Its full name is United Nations Educational, Scientific and Cultural Organization. Countries that belong to
UNESCO agree to contribute to peace and security by
cooperating in the areas of education, science, and culture. Almost all countries—and nearly all UN members—
belong to UNESCO. Countries that belong to UNESCO
provide most of the agency's funds. UNESCO was founded in 1945 and has headquarters in Paris.

UNESCO seeks to increase respect for justice, law,
human rights, and fundamental freedoms for all people.
The agency carries out programs to promote these aims
only at the request of its members. Many of the agency's
decisions can be carried out only if the governments of
member nations take action in their own countries.

UNESCO tries to increase the flow of ideas among the
peoples of the world. It stresses the development and
quality of education, the sharing of cultures, and the
increase and peaceful use of scientific knowledge. The
organization encourages artists, scientists, students, and
teachers to travel, study, and work in other countries.
UNESCO focuses on the use of the social sciences to
help solve such problems as discrimination and violence. UNESCO also works with other UN agencies to
help developing countries.

About 500 private international associations called
nongovernmental organizations (NGO's) consult with
UNESCO. The NGO's help plan and carry out programs
in which they take a special interest.

What UNESCO does

Education. UNESCO considers learning important for
economic development and for peace. It helps countries
in their efforts to improve education at all levels. The
agency sponsors programs to train teachers, build
courses of study, and carry out research in education.
UNESCO has started literacy programs. It also sponsors
permanent and mobile libraries.

Science. UNESCO also considers science and technology as important tools for peace and development. The agency promotes international scientific cooperation and encourages basic scientific research and the application of scientific findings. UNESCO distributes scientific information, sponsors training courses, and organizes science conferences and seminars. It operates scientific centers in Africa, Asia, and Latin America. It helped establish the CERN (European Organization for Nuclear Research), which performs research on the peaceful uses of nuclear energy.

UNESCO contributes to the growth of knowledge in the social sciences by sponsoring research and teaching programs. It promotes the application of the social sciences to solving practical problems. Among its social science concerns are race relations, economic development, and the status of women.

Culture. UNESCO encourages international cooperation to protect different cultures and to develop and share an appreciation of them. The agency advises governments on how to restore and preserve national monuments. In addition, it sponsors exhibits and other efforts to acquaint the public with works of art, literature, and music.

Members of the organization stress the rights to inform and to be informed. UNESCO has programs in all major areas of mass communication—including books, films, newspapers, radio, and television. It provides technical aid to developing nations for communications systems.

How UNESCO is organized

The General Conference consists of delegates who are appointed by the member nations. It meets every two years. The conference decides on UNESCO policies and programs. It also approves the budget and passes staff regulations. The conference selects the Executive Board and appoints the director-general of UNESCO. In addition, it admits new members to UNESCO and prepares conventions and recommendations for approval by the member nations. Most conference meetings take place in Paris.

The Executive Board has 51 members. These members are elected to four-year terms and may be reelected. The Executive Board meets in regular session at least twice a year. The board supervises UNESCO programs, prepares the General Conference agenda, recommends new member nations, and nominates the director-general.

The Secretariat administers UNESCO's programs. People from most member nations work in the Secretariat. These people include administrators, general service personnel, and various specialists. Some of these people work at UNESCO headquarters. Others work in the field.

The director-general, the chief administrative officer of UNESCO, appoints and directs the Secretariat. This executive officer also makes regular reports on UNESCO activities to member nations and the Executive Board, and submits work plans and budget estimates to the board. The director-general is elected to a six-year term and may be reelected.

The national commissions of the member nations advise their governments. They also assist the delegations to the General Conference. Most commission members come from national organizations interested in education, science, and culture.

History

The United Nations Charter was signed in San Francisco during June 1945. In November of that year, the United Nations Conference for the Establishment of an Educational and Cultural Organization met in London. Scientists persuaded the planners to add a reference to science in the title of the proposed agency. Government representatives of 44 nations drew up the Constitution of UNESCO, and UNESCO officially came into existence on Nov. 4, 1946. By that date, 20 governments had ratified the Constitution.

As UNESCO has grown, it has become increasingly difficult for its members to agree on priorities. New members—especially newly independent states—have had new ideas about how UNESCO should use its resources. Both decisions and decision-making procedures have become more controversial. As a result, UNESCO has not always received the support it needs to accomplish its goals.

Four nations have withdrawn from UNESCO since its founding. In 1956, South Africa left the organization when its government accused UNESCO of interfering in the country's racial problems. South Africa rejoined UNESCO in 1994. The United States withdrew in 1984 and the United Kingdom in 1985 because of what their governments viewed as UNESCO's anti-Western bias, its efforts to restrict press freedom, and its wasteful management methods. The United Kingdom rejoined the organization in 1997. The United States rejoined in 2003. Singapore left UNESCO in 1985 because its government felt that the country was expected to make too large a contribution to the UNESCO budget.   James P. Sewell

See also **Huxley, Sir Julian Sorell; Library** (International library programs); **United Nations.**

Ungulate, *UHNG gyuh liht* or *UHNG gyuh layt,* is any mammal whose toes end in hoofs. The name comes from the Latin word *ungula,* meaning *hoof.* Scientists di-

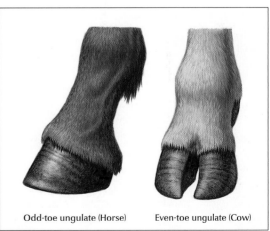

Odd-toe ungulate (Horse)   Even-toe ungulate (Cow)

WORLD BOOK illustrations by John D. Dawson

Ungulates are hoofed mammals that may be divided into two groups, those that have odd-toed hoofs and those that have even-toed hoofs. A horse's odd-toed hoof, *above left,* has only one toe. A cow's even-toed hoof, *above right,* has two toes.

vide ungulates into two groups, *odd-toed ungulates* and *even-toed ungulates.* Odd-toed ungulates include horses, which have one toe on each foot, and rhinoceroses, with three. Even-toed ungulates include deer, with two toes per foot, and pigs, with four. Ungulates are the only horned mammals, but not all ungulates have horns. All ungulates are *herbivores* (animals that eat chiefly plants). Elephants, the largest land animals, are ungulates.

Valerius Geist

Related articles in *World Book* include:

Alpaca	Dromedary	Karakul
Antelope	Elephant	Llama
Babirusa	Giraffe	Musk ox
Bighorn	Goat	Okapi
Boar, Wild	Guanaco	Peccary
Buffalo	Herbivore	Rhinoceros
Camel	Hippopotamus	Ruminant
Caribou	Hog	Sheep
Cashmere	Horn	Vicuña
goat	Horse	Wart hog
Cattle	Ibex	Yak
Deer		

UNICEF, *YOO nuh sehf,* is the commonly used name for the United Nations (UN) agency officially called the United Nations Children's Fund. The name comes from the agency's original title—United Nations International Children's Emergency Fund.

UNICEF aids children in over 150 countries by assisting governments in such areas as health care, nutrition, water supply and sanitation, education, and services for pregnant women and women with young children. In addition, the agency provides relief supplies in emergencies.

UNICEF works to protect the rights of every child as expressed in the Convention on the Rights of the Child. This convention, adopted by the UN General Assembly in 1989, includes the rights to health care, proper nutrition, education, freedom of expression, and protection from unfair treatment. The agency was created in 1946 to help children in Europe after World War II. In 1965, UNICEF received the Nobel Peace Prize for its accomplishments.

AP/Wide World

UNICEF promotes the health and well-being of young people throughout the world. This infant is receiving a polio vaccination as part of a UNICEF immunization program in Afghanistan.

UNICEF depends entirely on voluntary contributions. Most of its income comes from governments.

Critically reviewed by UNICEF

Unicorn is a legendary, one-horned animal described in ancient and medieval literature. Although there is no evidence that such an animal ever lived, many people believed in unicorns.

About 2,400 years ago, a Greek physician named Ctesias wrote about a strange animal said to live in India. This animal resembled a wild ass and had a white body, blue eyes, and a single horn on its forehead.

In early Christian legends, the unicorn was as small as a goat but so fierce that no hunter could capture him by force. The only way to catch a unicorn was to send a maiden alone into the forest. When the unicorn found the maiden, he would rest his head in her lap and fall asleep.

Detail of a tapestry (1490-1500); Musée de Cluny, Paris (French Government Tourist Office)

The unicorn is a legendary animal. Many European paintings and tapestries featured images of unicorns. This tapestry is part of a famous set called *The Lady with the Unicorn.*

During the Middle Ages, stories about unicorns became increasingly popular. Many medieval paintings and tapestries featured images of these animals. Nobles purchased objects believed to be unicorn horns for extremely high prices. Most of these objects were the tusks of walruses or of unusual whales called narwhals. Today, the unicorn remains a popular character in fantasy literature. Carl Lindahl

See also **Tapestry** (picture).

Unicycle is a vehicle with a seat and frame mounted above a single wheel. The rider causes the unicycle to move forward or backward by rotating two pedals with the feet. Unicycles are ridden by children and adults and are used primarily for recreation. People often juggle objects or perform other stunts while riding unicycles.

Unicycles first appeared in the late 1800's as part of circus acts and similar entertainments. These early models were handcrafted by their riders. In the mid-1900's, several bicycle companies began manufacturing unicycles in the United States for sale to the general public. Today, some bicycle stores sell models in standard sizes with seats as high as 6 feet (1.8 meters) above the

Schwinn Bicycle Company

A unicycle, *center,* has only one wheel and no handlebars. Riders steer with their feet and by shifting their weight.

ground. Unicycles more than 6 feet high and specialty unicycles must still be handmade.

Critically reviewed by the Unicycling Society of America, Inc.

Unidentified flying object (UFO) is a light or object in the air that has no obvious explanation. Some people believe UFO's are spaceships from other planets. However, investigators discover ordinary explanations for most UFO sightings, largely because most witnesses are generally reliable individuals. UFO hoaxes are rare.

Many reported UFO's are actually bright planets, stars, or meteors. People have reported aircraft, missiles, satellites, birds, insect swarms, and weather balloons as UFO's. Unusual weather conditions also can create optical illusions that are reported as UFO's.

Investigators can explain all but a small percentage of UFO reports. The remainder may be due to an unknown phenomenon or merely to limitations in human perception, memory, and research. Most scientists believe that there is not enough reliable evidence to connect these sightings with life from other planets.

Some UFO's are called *flying saucers.* This term was coined by the press in 1947 to describe a sighting by Kenneth Arnold, a civilian pilot, who reported unknown objects speeding through the air.

Beginning in 1952, the United States Air Force, in a program called Project Blue Book, investigated over 12,000 UFO reports to determine whether UFO's were a potential threat to national security. In addition, from 1966 to 1968, the Air Force sponsored an independent study of UFO's by scientists at the University of Colorado. The Colorado scientists advised the Air Force that further study of UFO's was not likely to produce useful information concerning a security threat. As a result, the Air Force ended Project Blue Book in 1969.

Nevertheless, many people throughout the world continue to believe that UFO's are spacecraft from other planets. Accounts of encounters with alien visitors have appeared in many books, newspaper articles, motion pictures, and TV programs. Some people have even reported that they have been abducted by aliens.

But even believers in alien encounters disagree over certain famous cases. Particularly controversial is the use of hypnosis to obtain previously unremembered, or perhaps imaginary, information.   James Oberg

See also **Extraterrestrial intelligence; Roswell.**

Additional resources

Clark, Jerome. *The UFO Encyclopedia.* 2 vols. 2nd ed. Omni-graphics, 1998.
Elfman, Eric. *Almanac of Alien Encounters.* Random Hse., 2001. Younger readers.
Lewis, James R. *UFOs and Popular Culture.* ABC-CLIO, 2000.
Randles, Jenny. *UFOs and How to See Them.* Sterling Pub., 1992.

UNIDO. See **United Nations Industrial Development Organization.**

Uniform Code of Military Justice is a set of laws that establishes a military justice system in the United States. The laws apply to all members of the U.S. armed forces. The code prohibits certain conduct as criminal and provides for a system of courts and judges to try military members accused of violating the laws. It also outlines the procedures to be followed in these cases.

The code's list of crimes includes such offenses as murder, rape, and robbery. It also includes typically military offenses, such as desertion, disobedience of an order, and disrespect to a superior officer. In addition, the code bans any other conduct that may be damaging to good order and discipline or that may bring discredit on the armed forces. Such conduct includes bribery, adultery, and negligent homicide. The courts outlined by the code include (1) trial courts, called *courts-martial;* (2) one intermediate appellate court for each branch of the armed forces, called a *court of military review;* and (3) a top military appellate court, called the United States Court of Appeals for the Armed Forces.

Robert C. Mueller

See also **Court-martial; Court of Appeals for the Armed Forces, United States.**

Union, Act of, in Canadian history, united the colonies of Upper Canada and Lower Canada. These colonies occupied much of what is now Ontario and Quebec. The British Parliament passed the act in 1840, and it took effect in 1841. Upper and Lower Canada had been created in 1791 out of the province of Quebec, which Britain gained from France in 1763. The colonies were created to provide separate governments for the chiefly British Ontario region and the mainly French Quebec region. However, political unrest in the 1830's led to calls for the colonies to be reunited.

The Act of Union provided for a single governor of the united province, which was called the Province of Canada, and a legislative council of at least 20 members appointed by the governor. The former colonies elected 42 members each to a legislative assembly. The Act of Union made English the only official language of the legislature, but French was added in 1848. The act did not result in stable government, but it encouraged economic development and paved the way for the creation of the Dominion of Canada in 1867.   J. M. Bumsted

Union, Labor. See **Labor movement; Labor union.**

Union Jack is the name sometimes used for the national flag of the United Kingdom, officially called the British Union Flag. The United States Jack has been called a union jack. See also **Flag** (picture: Historical flags of the world).

The rise of the Soviet Union began in the early 1900's. The *Bolsheviks* (later called Communists) overthrew the Russian government in 1917. The Bolshevik leader V. I. Lenin, *above,* headed the new government, which established the Union of Soviet Socialist Republics in 1922.

U.S.S.R.

Union of Soviet Socialist Republics (U.S.S.R.), also called the Soviet Union, was the world's first and most powerful Communist country. It existed from 1922 to 1991. In 1991, the Communist Party lost power, and the Soviet Union broke up into a number of independent states.

From the mid-1940's to the late 1980's, the Soviet Union was one of the two world superpowers. The other was the United States. Intense rivalry between these two countries shaped much of the history of this period.

Before its breakup, the Soviet Union was the largest country in the world in area. It covered more than half of Europe and nearly two-fifths of Asia. The Soviet Union had the third largest population in the world, after China and India.

The Soviet Union was officially created in 1922 when Russia joined with three other territories under the

The contributor of this article is James R. Millar, Professor of International Affairs and Director of the Institute for European, Russian, and Eurasian Studies at George Washington University.

name *Union of Soviet Socialist Republics.* These became the first of the country's 15 *union republics.* The other republics were created and added between 1922 and 1940. The union republics were Armenia, Azerbaijan, Byelorussia (now Belarus), Estonia, Georgia, Kazakhstan, Kirghiz (now Kyrgyzstan), Latvia, Lithuania, Moldavia (now Moldova), Russia, Tadzhikistan (also spelled Tajikistan), Turkmenistan, Ukraine, and Uzbekistan.

Each republic had its own government, but these governments were strictly under the control of the Communist central government. In 1991, the Communists fell from power after a failed attempt by conservative Communist officials to overthrow Soviet President Mikhail S. Gorbachev. Shortly after the attempted take-over, most of the republics declared their independence. All but Georgia and the three Baltic republics of Estonia, Latvia, and Lithuania formed a loose confederation called the Commonwealth of Independent States. The Soviet Union ceased to exist.

At its height, the Soviet Union was an industrial giant, ranking second after the United States in total production. For years, it led all other countries in space exploration. Its armed forces were the largest in the world, and its nuclear arsenal was second only to that of the United States. However, many Soviet families lived in crowded conditions because there was not enough

AP/Wide World

The fall of the Soviet Union came in 1991 after the Communists lost power. A jubilant crowd in Moscow, *shown here,* displayed the banner of the Russian republic in celebration.

housing. There were often shortages of meat, shoes, and many other goods. The Communist leaders controlled the country's government, economy, educational system, and communications media. They restricted religious practices and punished those who opposed their policies.

Government

The Communist Party. For almost its entire history, the Soviet Union was dominated by the Communist Party. The Communist Party tolerated no other political party. At the time of the country's breakup, about 16 million people—about 6 per cent of the Soviet population—were members of the Communist Party.

The Communist Party structure was like a pyramid. At the bottom of the pyramid were about 440,000 local groups called *primary party organizations.* They were set up throughout the U.S.S.R. in such places as factories, farms, government offices, and schools. The primary party organizations, formerly called *cells,* were responsible for local political and economic life. They rewarded party members for productivity at work or for living according to Communist teachings. They also disciplined members for neglecting their duties.

Just above the primary party organizations were the district party organizations. The district organizations

operated under the regional party organizations, which, in turn, reported to the republic party organizations.

At the top of the Communist Party pyramid were the party congresses, which met periodically—usually every five years. Thousands of delegates from party organizations throughout the country attended these congresses. Each congress elected a Central Committee to handle its work. The Central Committee, in turn, elected a Politburo (Political Bureau) and a Secretariat. In actual practice, the Politburo and the Secretariat selected their own members and those of the Central Committee.

The Politburo was the most powerful body in the Soviet Union. It set all important policies. The Secretariat managed the daily work of the Communist Party. The general secretary, or chairman, of the Central Committee headed the Politburo and the Secretariat and was the most powerful person in the U.S.S.R.

A Soviet citizen who wanted to join the Communist Party would enter at the lowest level, applying to join a primary party organization. A candidate had to be at least 18 years old and had to be recommended by three members of the primary party organization. Both the primary and district party organizations had to approve the applicant. The candidate then was required to wait a year before being approved as a full member. The process was designed to permit only those who were most loyal to Communist ideals to join the party.

National government. The main body of the official Soviet central government was a two-house federal parliament called the Supreme Soviet of the U.S.S.R. *Soviet* is a Russian word meaning *council.* The two houses were the Soviet of the Union and the Soviet of Nationalities. The members of each house were called *deputies.* The number of deputies to the Soviet of the Union from each republic depended on population. Each republic—and certain other political units within the Soviet Union—sent a fixed number of deputies to the Soviet of Nationalities. Almost all the members of the Supreme Soviet of the U.S.S.R. were Communist Party members.

The formal duties of the Supreme Soviet were to write laws and supervise the administration of the government. But for most of the country's history, the parliament met only twice a year for a week or less. It passed without question all proposed laws, which came from the Communist Party's leaders. The chairman of the Supreme Soviet served as head of state, legislative leader, and commander of the armed forces.

The Soviet government included two other important bodies. These were the Presidium of the Supreme Soviet and the Council of Ministers. The members of both bodies were officially elected by the Supreme Soviet. But they were actually chosen by Communist Party leaders. The Presidium handled legislative matters. The Council of Ministers was the highest executive body of the government, with primary responsibility for the economy.

The Committee on State Security, known as the *KGB,* was an agency of the Council of Ministers. It was the government's political police system and had offices and agents throughout the Soviet Union.

Local government. In addition to the union republics, the Soviet Union included various autonomous republics, autonomous regions, and autonomous areas. *Autonomous* means *self-governing,* but the autono-

The Supreme Soviet was the parliament of the Soviet government. It met twice a year to pass laws proposed by Communist Party leaders.

Rudi Frey, *Time* Magazine

The republics of the U.S.S.R.   The U.S.S.R. covered more than half of Europe and nearly two-fifths of Asia. This map shows the country's 15 republics and the dates when they became republics. The country dissolved in 1991. The republics are now independent nations.

WORLD BOOK map

Soviet military power paraded through Red Square in Moscow in annual May Day celebrations. The Soviet armed forces had about 4 million members and ranked as the largest in the world.

AP/Wide World

mous republics, regions, and areas actually had little control over their own affairs. The political structure of the union republics and the autonomous republics was much like that of the entire country. Each republic was governed by a supreme soviet with a presidium, and a council of ministers. Each one also had its own constitution. The lower levels of local government, from autonomous regions to small districts, had soviets of people's deputies.

Armed forces of the U.S.S.R. were the largest in the world. At the time of its breakup, the Soviet Union had a total of about 4 million people in its army, navy, and air force.

People

The population of the Soviet Union consisted of more than 100 ethnic groups. The Soviet republics were set up on the basis of ethnic groups and carried their names. For example, Georgians lived mainly in the Georgian Soviet Socialist Republic (now the independent nation of Georgia), and Armenians were centered in the Armenian Soviet Socialist Republic (now independent Armenia).

Slavic ethnic groups made up about 70 per cent of the total Soviet population. The Russians, the largest Slavic group, made up about half of the country's population. They lived throughout the country and held an excessively large share of leadership positions in the various governments. The Ukrainians were the second largest Slavic group, and the Belarusians (then called *Byelorussians*) were the third largest. In 1991, the Ukrainians and Belarusians formed their own independent nations.

Turkic peoples ranked second in number to Slavic peoples in the Soviet Union. The largest Turkic groups included the Uzbeks, the Kazakhs, the Kyrgyz (then spelled *Kirghiz*) people, and the Turkmen. These four Turkic groups also formed their own independent nations. Other ethnic groups who gained nationhood included the Tajiks (then spelled *Tadzhiks*) and the

Moldovans, whom the Soviets called *Moldavians.*

Minority groups in the Soviet Union included Finno-Ugric peoples and Germans. Many small Siberian groups, related to Native Americans of the Far North, made their homes in the Arctic.

Each nationality in the Soviet Union tried to preserve its own language and culture. But a number of government policies were aimed at merging groups into one common culture, based on Russian. The Russian language was used everywhere. Languages once written in the Roman or Arabic alphabets had to use the Cyrillic alphabet of the Russian language. Those who supported the single-culture idea were given many top political and economic positions. Their privileged status caused friction with minority ethnic groups.

Ethnic differences also led to conflicts between non-Russian groups. In the late 1980's, for example, violence broke out between Armenians and Azerbaijanis. The Armenians demanded that Nagorno-Karabakh, a district of Azerbaijan largely populated by Armenians, be made part of Armenia.

Jews, who were listed as a nationality group by the Soviet census, faced widespread discrimination in the Soviet Union. During most of the 1900's, the government discouraged the practice of Judaism and Jewish customs, and it restricted Jewish emigration.

Way of life

Personal freedom. For much of Soviet history, especially during the 1930's, the people lived in fear. The secret police arrested millions of citizens suspected of anti-Communist views or activities. The victims were shot or sent to prison camps. In the late 1980's, the government began to grant the people greater freedom. It allowed criticism of the Soviet system. Also, the works of writers whose views had been officially condemned were permitted to be read openly.

Until 1990, the Communists restricted religious practices. They were officially *atheists* (people who believe there is no God). They looked on religion as an anti-Communist force. Religious worship survived in the Soviet Union, however, and the restrictions gradually decreased. In 1990, the government promised freedom of religion.

Privileged classes. The early Communists hoped to achieve a *classless society*—a society with neither rich nor poor people. The government took over all privately owned factories, farms, and other means of production. It abolished income from real estate and other private property. The government provided such benefits as free medical and hospital care. The goal, as stated by Karl Marx, the German philosopher whose ideas formed the basis of Communism, was, "From each according to his abilities, to each according to his needs." In theory, everyone would serve society in the best way possible, and no one would have any special claims.

The Communists failed to achieve a classless society. The old classes that possessed special rights based on inherited rank and wealth disappeared. However, new groups with special rights developed under the Soviet system. These groups included top officials of the Communist Party and the government, and also some professional people, including certain favored artists, engineers, scientists, and sports figures. They received automobiles, comfortable apartments and *dachas* (country homes), and other luxuries most Soviet citizens did not have.

City life. By 1990, about two-thirds of the Soviet people lived in urban areas. Cities were crowded, and most families lived in small and poorly maintained but cheap apartments. Housing shortages forced some families to share space and kitchen or bathroom facilities with other families.

Because the government kept prices artificially low, there were frequent shortages of meat, shoes, soap, and many other goods. Shoppers often had to spend much time looking for what they wanted. They often had to wait in line for hours for quality or imported goods.

Rural life. Living conditions in the rural areas of the Soviet Union were poorer than in the cities. In rural vil-

© Dieter Blum from Peter Arnold

Modern apartment buildings were built by the government in cities throughout the Soviet Union in an effort to reduce a shortage of housing in the nation's urban areas.

lages, many people lived in small log huts or in community apartments. Many of the families had no gas, plumbing, or running water, and some did not have electricity. There were fewer stores in the villages, and stores carried a smaller variety of goods.

Most people in rural areas traditionally worked on huge government-controlled farms. Farmers were allowed to cultivate small plots of land for private use and to keep a few animals. Farmers could sell dairy products, meat, and vegetables produced on this land for private income. These private plots produced about one-fourth of the total value of agricultural production in the U.S.S.R.

Education. During the early 1900's, Russia was largely a country of poor, uneducated peasants. After the Communists seized control, they strongly promoted

Reuters/Bettmann

Long lines of shoppers, such as those waiting to buy sausage, *left,* became common in the Soviet Union because of frequent shortages of meat and many other consumer goods.

education. Highly trained managers and workers were needed to build up the country. To meet this need, the government expanded its schools and made major improvements in education. The schools stressed science and technology. Soviet achievements in these fields were among the highest in the world.

Soviet children had to attend school for 11 years, from the age of 6 to 17. Education was free. In addition to schoolwork, students were graded on classroom behavior and leadership in group activities, both in class and after school.

The Soviet Union had many schools for gifted children, who were chosen by examination. These schools, beginning in the first grade, provided extra instruction in the arts, languages, or mathematics and science.

After ninth grade, many students attended technical or trade schools. These schools trained young people to be skilled technicians and workers in agriculture, engineering, industry, and other fields. The Soviet Union also had about 70 universities and more than 800 technical institutes and other schools of higher education.

Science and technology. The government established many research institutions and employed hundreds of thousands of scientists, engineers, and technicians. These specialists made it possible for the Soviet Union to become an industrial and military power. Soviet scientists developed new processes and new technology for industries and new weapons for defense. In addition, their work enabled the U.S.S.R. to lead the world in space exploration. In 1957, the Soviet Union launched Sputnik 1, the first artificial satellite. In 1961, Soviet air force officer Yuri A. Gagarin orbited the earth and became the first person to travel in space.

The arts. For most of the history of the Soviet Union, the Communist Party attempted to control all artistic expression. The government permitted only an art style called *socialist realism,* which emphasized the goals and benefits of Soviet socialism. Such writers as Boris Pasternak and Alexander Solzhenitsyn were disciplined for criticizing Communism. The publication of most of their works was prohibited in the Soviet Union for years. In the late 1980's, however, the Soviet government began

Novosti from Sovfoto

Soviet cosmonaut Yuri A. Gagarin became the first person to travel in space when he orbited the earth on April 12, 1961. From the mid-1950's through the 1970's, the Soviet Union and the United States competed for leadership in space exploration.

to allow artists much greater freedom in their work.

Even under the strict controls, a number of Soviet artists made noteworthy achievements. Pasternak and Solzhenitsyn won the Nobel Prize for literature. Director Sergei Eisenstein became famous for his methods of film editing. The music of composers Aram Khachaturian, Sergei Prokofiev, and Dimitri Shostakovich received worldwide attention. The Moscow Art Theater, founded in 1898, remained the most respected theater company in the Soviet Union. The Bolshoi Theater Ballet and the Kirov Ballet continued to earn international fame for the brilliant technical skill and dramatic dancing of their performers.

Economy

The Soviet Union developed the world's largest centrally planned economy. Until the mid-1980's, the Soviet Union ranked second after the United States in production of goods and services. The government owned the country's banks, factories, land, mines, and transportation systems. It planned and controlled the production, distribution, and pricing of all important goods.

Beginning in 1928, the Soviet economy grew rapidly under a series of plans emphasizing industrialization. But improvements in living conditions lagged behind the growth of the economy. The country's participation in World War II (1939-1945) caused a major economic setback. The standard of living rose rapidly between 1953 and 1975. But it then stopped improving and remained stalled far below that of the United States.

In the late 1980's, the Soviet leadership began a major reform of the economy called *perestroika* (pronounced *PEHR uh STROY kuh*) in an attempt to promote innovation, to increase efficiency, and to respond to consumer wants. The reform called for state enterprises to be more independent from central control and authorized private cooperative businesses run by individuals and families. Perestroika also included plans for the Soviet

AP/Wide World

Sports received strong support from the Soviet government. Soviet gymnast Olga Korbut, *above,* won two gold medals in the 1976 Summer Olympics.

Union to become more competitive in international trade. In spite of these efforts, economic problems continued until the Soviet Union was dissolved.

Manufacturing. During the 1920's, the U.S.S.R. was mainly a farming country. But it had been developing its industry since the late 1800's, and under Communism it became an industrial giant. Only the United States outranked the Soviet Union in the value of manufactured products.

In 1928, the Soviet Communist leaders began the first of a series of *five-year plans* to promote industry. Each plan set up investment programs and production goals for a five-year period. At first, the government chiefly developed factories that produced heavy-industry products, including chemicals, construction materials, machine tools, and steel. Heavy industry, especially steelmaking, expanded rapidly. But housing construction and the production of consumer goods lagged seriously right to the end.

The Soviet government had widespread control over the operation of individual factories. Government agencies told factory managers which products to make, how many items of each to produce, and where to sell them. The government took about three-fifths of the factories' profits in taxes. The factories used the remaining profits to improve production and for bonuses to managers and workers.

Agriculture. The U.S.S.R. had more farmland than any other country in the world. Its farmland covered more than $2\frac{1}{4}$ million square miles (5.8 million square kilometers), over a fourth of the entire country. The Soviet Union was one of the world's two leading crop-producing countries. The United States was the other leader. The U.S.S.R. had more than twice as much farmland as the United States, but U.S. farmland is generally more fertile. In addition, much of the farmland in what was the Soviet Union lies near the Arctic Circle, where growing seasons are short, or in regions of light rainfall. Many Soviet government farm production plans were impractical and interfered with the farm manager's job of mak-

Novosti from Sovfoto

Heavy industry, such as steelmaking, *shown here,* helped the U.S.S.R. become an industrial giant. In the late 1980's, the Soviet Union produced more steel than any other nation.

ing the best use of the land and workers.

In the 1980's, about two-thirds of the farmland in the U.S.S.R. consisted of some 22,000 *sovkhozy* (state farms). These huge farms averaged about 42,000 acres (17,000 hectares) in size. The state farms were operated like government factories, and the farmworkers received wages.

About a third of the farmland in the U.S.S.R. consisted of some 26,000 *kolkhozy* (collective farms), which were

Novosti Press

The leading farmworkers on a state farm received an award for a good harvest from the Communist Party. The Soviet government owned and operated huge state farms, and it paid wages to the people who worked on these farms.

controlled by the government but managed in part by the farmers. These farms averaged about 16,000 acres (6,500 hectares). In general, a collective farm supported about 500 households. The collective farmers were paid wages and a share of the production and profits. Families on collective farms could farm small plots for themselves and sell their products privately.

Foreign trade played only a small part in the Soviet economy because the country's policy was to be self-sufficient. The Soviet Union's enormous natural resources provided almost all the important raw materials needed. No other country had so much farmland, so many mineral deposits or forests, or so many possible sources of hydroelectric power as the Soviet Union had.

The country's major exports were lumber and wood products, machinery, natural gas, petroleum, and steel. Its main imports were consumer goods—including grain—and industrial equipment. Most of the Soviet Union's trade was with the countries of Eastern Europe, including Bulgaria, Czechoslovakia, Hungary, and Poland. The Soviet Union's chief trading partners outside of Eastern Europe were Cuba, Finland, France, Germany, Italy, and Japan.

History

This section traces the major developments of the history of the Soviet Union, from the country's founding in 1922 until its breakup in 1991. The section begins with the revolution of 1917, which led to Communist rule in Russia. For the history of Russia before 1917 and after 1991, see **Russia** (History).

Background of the revolution. Since the mid-1500's, Russia had been ruled by leaders called *czars.* Under the czars, the country remained far behind the industrial progress made in Western Europe. Most of the people were poor, uneducated peasants. They farmed the land with the same kinds of simple hand tools their ancestors had used. Through the years, revolts against the harsh rule of the czars had occasionally broken out, but these revolts were not successful.

In the late 1890's, discontented Russians formed several political organizations. One group, the *Marxists,* followed the socialist teachings of Karl Marx, a German social philosopher. The Marxists established the Russian Social Democratic Labor Party. The *Bolsheviks* (later called Communists) made up a group within that party. The Bolshevik leader was Vladimir I. Ulyanov, who used the name V. I. Lenin.

After an economic depression began in Russia in 1900, a number of student protests, peasant revolts, and worker strikes broke out. In 1905, two uprisings were crushed by government troops, but the revolutionary movement continued to gain strength underground. The uprisings forced the czar to establish a fully elected lawmaking body, the Duma.

The February Revolution. World War I began in 1914. Germany declared war on Russia in August of that year. During the war, Russia had enormous losses, and the people suffered severe shortages of food, fuel, and housing. Untrained Russian troops behind the fighting lines feared being sent to the front, where they might be killed.

Early in March 1917, the people revolted. (The month was February in the old Russian calendar, which was re-placed in 1918.) Riots and strikes over shortages of bread and coal grew more violent in the Russian capital, Petrograd. (The city of Petrograd was known as St. Petersburg until 1914, was renamed Leningrad in 1924, and again became St. Petersburg in 1991.) Troops were called in to halt the uprising, but they joined it instead. The people of Petrograd turned to the Duma for leadership. Czar Nicholas II ordered the Duma to dissolve itself, but the parliament ignored his command. The Duma established a *provisional* (temporary) government. Nicholas had lost all of his political support, and he gave up the throne on March 15. Nicholas and his family were then imprisoned. Bolshevik revolutionaries killed them in July 1918.

A Soviet of Workers' and Soldiers' Deputies was formed in Petrograd in March 1917. The soviet was a rival of the provisional government. Many similar soviets were set up throughout Russia. In April, Lenin demanded "all power to the soviets," and, in July, armed workers and soldiers tried to seize power in Petrograd. They failed. Lenin fled to Finland. Some of his followers escaped or were jailed. Others were driven underground. Later that month, Alexander F. Kerensky, a socialist, became premier.

The October Revolution. General Lavr Kornilov, the army commander in chief, planned to seize power from Kerensky. But the local soviets throughout Russia rallied behind Kerensky. So did the Bolsheviks. The general advanced on Petrograd in September 1917, but his group broke up before reaching the city. After this episode, the soviets became more radical. Many army units supported the Bolsheviks.

Lenin returned from Finland in October and convinced the Bolsheviks that they should try to seize power. He hoped a revolution would set off other socialist revolts in Western countries. Lenin's most capable assistant, Leon Trotsky, helped him plan the take-over. On November 7 (October 25 in the old Russian calendar), the armed workers took over important points in Petrograd. After a bloody struggle in Moscow, the Bolsheviks controlled that city by November 15.

The Bolsheviks formed a new Russian government, headed by Lenin. The peasants had already seized much farmland from Russian nobles and the czarist state. For a time, Lenin endorsed these land seizures. He permitted workers to control the factories and to play important roles in the local soviets. But after a civil war broke out between the Bolsheviks and their opponents, the government tightened control and forced the peasants to give the government most of their products. The government also took over Russian industries and set up central management bureaus to control them. The Cheka, a secret police force, was established.

After the Bolsheviks seized the government, Russia withdrew from World War I and began peace talks with Germany. In March 1918, Russia signed the Treaty of Brest-Litovsk with Germany. Under the treaty, Russia gave up large areas, including the Baltic states, Finland, Ukraine, and the part of Poland that had been ruled by Russia. After the war, Armenia and Georgia set up independent republics.

In 1918, the Bolsheviks moved the Russian capital back to Moscow, which had been the center of government until Czar Peter I made St. Petersburg the capital in

1712. The Bolsheviks also changed the name of their Russian Social Democratic Labor Party to the Russian Communist Party. They later changed the name to the Communist Party of the Soviet Union. They organized the Red Army, which was named for the color of the Communist flag. The Communists themselves were called *Reds.*

Civil war. From 1918 to 1920, Russia was torn by war between the Communists and the anti-Communists, called *Whites.* The peasants believed they would lose their lands to their old landlords if the Whites won, and so they generally supported the Reds. The Whites were aided by troops from Britain, France, Japan, the United States, and other countries that opposed the Communist government. But these nations helped little because they were unwilling to fight another war after World War I. The Whites were poorly organized, and the Reds defeated them.

After the civil war, the Red Army invaded Georgia, Ukraine, and eastern Armenia, and helped put down nationalist independence movements in Belarus (then called Byelorussia) and central Asia. Communist rule was gradually established in these areas.

In 1920, Poland invaded Ukraine in an attempt to expel the Communists. The Red Army drove the invaders out and nearly reached Warsaw, Poland's capital. But the Polish troops, with help from France, finally defeated the Red Army. A treaty signed in 1921 gave Poland the western parts of Byelorussia and Ukraine.

The New Economic Policy. By 1921, seven years of war, revolution, civil war, famine, and invasion had exhausted Russia. Millions of people had died. Agricultural and industrial production had fallen disastrously. About $1\frac{1}{2}$ million Russians, many of them skilled and educated, had left the country. The people's discontent broke out in new peasant uprisings, in workers' strikes, and in a sailors' revolt at the Kronstadt naval base near Petrograd. Bolshevik leaders had to compromise to protect their revolution.

In 1921, Lenin established a compromise called the New Economic Policy (NEP) to strengthen the country. Small industries and retail trade were allowed to operate under their own control. The peasants no longer had to give most of their farm products to the government. The government kept control of the most important segments of the economy—banking, heavy industry, the transportation system, and foreign trade. The economy recovered steadily under the NEP.

Formation of the U.S.S.R. In December 1922, the Communist government established the Union of Soviet Socialist Republics (U.S.S.R.). Byelorussia, Transcaucasia, and Ukraine joined with Russia to make up the union's first four republics.

During the 1920's, three other union republics were established—Tadzhikistan (now spelled Tajikistan), Turkmenistan, and Uzbekistan. In 1936, Transcaucasia was divided into Azerbaijan, Armenia, and Georgia. Kazakhstan and Kirghiz (now called Kyrgyzstan) also became union republics in 1936.

Stalin gains power. Lenin became seriously ill in 1922. A struggle for power developed among members of the Politburo. Leon Trotsky ranked after Lenin in power. But the next two most important members of the Politburo—Lev Kamenev and Grigori Zinoviev—joined

Important dates in the U.S.S.R.

1917 A revolution overthrew Czar Nicholas II in March. The Bolsheviks (later called Communists) seized power in November, led by V. I. Lenin.
1918-1920 The Communists defeated their anti-Communist opponents in a civil war.
1922 The U.S.S.R. was established. Joseph Stalin became general secretary of the Communist Party and began his rise to power as dictator.
1930's Millions of Soviet citizens died from a famine and the Great Purge. The famine was caused by a government policy that forced peasants onto state-owned farms. The Great Purge was Stalin's campaign to kill or imprison his opponents.
1941-1945 The Soviet Union fought on the side of the victorious Allies during World War II. The country suffered heavy casualties.
Late 1940's The Soviet Union set up the Iron Curtain to cut off contacts between Communist and Western nations. The Cold War developed.
1953 Stalin died, and Nikita S. Khrushchev became head of the Communist Party.
1956 Khrushchev announced a policy of peaceful coexistence with the West. He also criticized Stalin's rule by terror, and Soviet life became freer.
1957 The U.S.S.R. launched Sputnik 1, the first spacecraft to circle the earth.
1958 Khrushchev became premier of the Soviet Union.
1961 Yuri A. Gagarin, a Soviet air force officer, became the first person to orbit the earth.
1962 The U.S.S.R. set up missile bases in Cuba and then removed them under pressure from the United States.
1964 High-ranking Communists forced Khrushchev to retire. He was replaced by Leonid I. Brezhnev as head of the Communist Party.
1979-1989 Soviet troops fought in Afghanistan to support a pro-Communist Afghan government against rebels.
1982 Brezhnev died.
1985 Mikhail S. Gorbachev became Communist Party head. He began to introduce new policies of openness and economic reform.
1989 The first contested elections in Soviet history were held.
1991 Communist rule ended, and the republics declared their independence. The Soviet Union was dissolved.

forces to oppose Trotsky. They chose Joseph Stalin to be their partner, greatly strengthening his position as general secretary of the party.

Stalin's influence in the party grew rapidly. As general secretary, he had the support of the local party secretaries, whose careers were dependent on his approval. Stalin defeated his rivals one by one. Trotsky lost power in 1925. Stalin then helped to expel from the party his own former partners, Kamenev and Zinoviev. Stalin's economic program, the First Five-Year Plan, was introduced in 1928. By 1929, Stalin had become dictator of the Soviet Union.

Stalin's policies. The First Five-Year Plan had two major goals. First, most private enterprises would be taken over by the government. The NEP compromise would end. Second, the production of such heavy-industry products as chemicals, construction materials, machine tools, and steel would be expanded rapidly under highly centralized control.

A crisis in grain deliveries to the cities threatened to sink the First Five-Year Plan. Stalin forced the peasants into collective farms called *kolkhozy*, where they had to give most of their products to the government at low prices. These products were needed to supply raw materials to industry, to feed the people of the growing

Joseph Stalin, *center,* one of the cruelest rulers in history, was dictator of the U.S.S.R. from 1929 to 1953.

AP/Wide World

manufacturing centers, and to pay for imported machinery. The peasants opposed being forced to join collective farms, and destroyed much of their livestock and crops in protest. As punishment, Stalin had millions of peasants killed or exiled to prison labor camps in Siberia and the Aral-Caspian Lowland during the early 1930's.

In 1932 and 1933, a famine killed 5 million to 7 million people in Ukraine and in the Volga and Kuban regions of western Russia. The famine resulted from a government policy that forcibly took food from the farmers. Farm production lagged and the people's diets suffered, but Soviet industries expanded rapidly.

Many Soviet citizens opposed Stalin's policies during the mid-1930's. In order to crush opposition, Stalin began a program of terror that was called the Great Purge. Secret police, the forerunners of the KGB, arrested millions of people. Neighbors and even family members spied on one another. Fear spread throughout the country. Stalin eliminated all real or suspected threats to his power by having the prisoners shot or sent to labor camps.

Adolf Hitler had become dictator of Germany in 1933, and one of his stated goals was to destroy Communism. But Hitler did not want enemies toward both the west and the east. In August 1939, the Soviet Union and Germany signed a *nonaggression pact,* an agreement that neither nation would attack the other. The two countries agreed secretly to divide Poland between themselves.

World War II began when Hitler's troops invaded Poland from the west on Sept. 1, 1939. Two days later, France and Britain declared war on Germany. Soviet troops invaded Poland from the east on Sept. 17, 1939, and soon occupied eastern Poland. On November 30, the U.S.S.R. attacked Finland. The Soviet Union had won much Finnish territory by March 1940, when Finland had to agree to a peace treaty.

In June 1940, the Red Army moved into Bessarabia (then part of Romania) and the Baltic countries of Estonia, Latvia, and Lithuania, which had become independent after the fall of the czar. In August 1940, the Baltic countries became separate republics of the Soviet Union, and most of Bessarabia became part of the new Moldavian Soviet Socialist Republic (now Moldova).

On June 22, 1941, a huge German force invaded the U.S.S.R. German warplanes destroyed much of the Soviet air force, and Hitler's tanks drove deep into Soviet territory. In September, the Germans captured Kiev and attacked Leningrad. By December, the Germans came close to Moscow. The attack on Leningrad lasted until January 1944, when the Germans were finally driven off.

Britain and the other Western Allies welcomed the U.S.S.R. as a partner in the war against Germany. Britain, Canada, and the United States began shipping supplies to the Soviet Union. The United States joined the Allies in December 1941, after the Japanese attack on Pearl Harbor.

By early 1942, the Red Army had driven the Germans back from the Moscow area and some other battlegrounds. The five-month Battle of Stalingrad (now Volgograd), which began in late August 1942, was a major turning point in the war. By the time the Germans surrendered, about 300,000 of their troops had been killed or captured.

After the victory at Stalingrad, the Red Army advanced steadily across Eastern Europe and into eastern Germany. As the Red Army swept across Eastern Europe, they freed many countries from German control, including Czechoslovakia, Hungary, Poland, and Romania. In April 1945, Soviet troops began to attack Berlin. The city fell to the Red Army on May 2. Germany surrendered to the Allies on May 7. The war in Europe was over.

Results of the war. About $7\frac{1}{2}$ million Soviet troops were killed in World War II, and about 5 million were wounded. Another 3 million troops were captured and died in German prison camps. No other country suffered so many military casualties. Also, millions of Soviet civilians died, whole regions of the U.S.S.R. lay in ruins, and much of the Soviet economy was shattered.

In February 1945, Stalin had met with President Franklin D. Roosevelt of the United States and Prime Minister Winston Churchill of Britain at Yalta in the Crimea. At this conference, Stalin promised to help in the war against Japan. On August 6, the United States dropped on Japan the first atomic bomb used in warfare. Two days later, the U.S.S.R. declared war on Japan and invaded Japanese-held Manchuria and Korea. Soviet troops occupied Manchuria for eight months and took

ITAR-Tass from Sovfoto

Soviet troops halted the eastward advance of Nazi German forces at the Battle of Stalingrad in 1942 and 1943, during World War II. The battle marked a major turning point in the war.

nearly a billion dollars' worth of industrial machinery from the region. Japan's surrender to the Allies on Sept. 2, 1945, marked the end of World War II.

Beginnings of the Cold War. During World War II, Stalin had promised Roosevelt and Churchill to help promote freedom throughout the world. After the war, however, the Soviet Union cooperated with the Allies only in continuing an agreement to occupy the eastern zone of Germany and a sector of Berlin. East-West relations in Germany became tense. The U.S.S.R. set up a Communist police state in its zone and blocked Western efforts to unite Germany.

Red Army units remained in the Eastern European countries that they had freed from German control during the war. These units helped Communist governments take power in these nations.

The Communists in Eastern European countries formed what seemed to be *coalition* governments. In such governments, two or more political parties share power. But the Communists, supported by the Soviet Union, seized important government positions and held the real power. Their strength grew, and they did not permit free elections. By early 1948, Bulgaria, Czechoslovakia, Hungary, Poland, and Romania had become *Soviet satellites* (countries controlled by the Soviet Union). The U.S.S.R. also influenced Communist governments in Albania and Yugoslavia.

In addition, the U.S.S.R. controlled its East German occupation zone, which surrounded West Berlin. The Soviet Union promised the Western powers freedom to move through East Germany to West Berlin. But in June 1948, Soviet troops blocked all land and water routes to West Berlin. The Western powers then flew food and other supplies to West Berlin daily. The blockade ended in May 1949.

The U.S.S.R. cut off nearly all contacts between its satellites and the West. Its barriers against communication, trade, and travel came to be known as the Iron Curtain. Distrust grew between East and West. The Cold War, a struggle between the two sides for international influence and allies, spread through Europe and many other regions of the world.

The rise of Khrushchev. Rapid Soviet industrialization resumed after World War II under new five-year

plans. Restrictions on the peasants, which had been loosened during the war, again became severe. Rebuilding heavy industry took priority over producing consumer goods. The collective farms were reorganized and enlarged. Stalin also began a new wave of political arrests and executions. Then, on March 5, 1953, he died after a stroke.

No one leader immediately replaced Stalin. A *collective leadership* of several men ruled. For almost two years, Georgi M. Malenkov held the major leadership position as premier, or chairman of the Council of Ministers. During this period, a struggle for power developed among Malenkov and other leading Communists. Nikita S. Khrushchev became the Communist Party head in September 1953. Khrushchev outmaneuvered Malenkov, who was forced to resign in 1955. Nikolai A. Bulganin became premier, but Khrushchev held the real power. Khrushchev defeated his rivals and forced his enemies to lose all positions of power. In 1958, Khrushchev became premier as well as Communist Party leader.

At the 20th Communist Party Congress in 1956, Khrushchev openly criticized Stalin to disgrace his rivals and began a program to dishonor the former leader. He accused Stalin of murdering innocent people and of faulty leadership. Buildings, cities, and towns that had been named for Stalin were renamed. In addition, pictures and statues of Stalin were destroyed.

Khrushchev's policies differed greatly from Stalin's. The secret police did not spread terror, and the government allowed somewhat freer political discussion. Writers, painters, scientists, and scholars were permitted greater freedom of expression. The workweek was shortened to about 40 hours, and workers were allowed to quit or change jobs. Khrushchev also sought to raise the people's standard of living through greater production of clothing, food, appliances, and other consumer goods.

Soviet relations with the West improved after Stalin's death. Unlike other Communist leaders, Khrushchev denied that war with the West was necessary for Communism to triumph. In 1956, Khrushchev announced a policy of *peaceful coexistence.* He described it as a means

UPI/Bettmann

Fidel Castro, *left,* declared Cuba to be Communist and began to receive Soviet support. Castro is shown above signing an agreement with Soviet leader Nikita Khrushchev.

of avoiding war while competing with the West in technology and economic development. Khrushchev eased restrictions on communication, trade, and travel across the Iron Curtain. He made friendly visits to several Western countries, including the United States. But the U.S.S.R. still tried to expand its influence by encouraging revolts, riots, and strikes in non-Communist countries.

China's Communist government believed war with the West was necessary and criticized the "soft" Soviet policy. China also wanted Soviet aid. The dispute between the two Communist powers peaked at the 22nd Communist Party Congress in Moscow in 1961. The Chinese premier, Zhou Enlai, suddenly returned to China. Only Albania supported China.

Under Khrushchev, the Soviet Union began to spend huge sums on space exploration. In 1957, Soviet scientists launched Sputnik 1, the first spacecraft to circle the earth. In 1961, Yuri A. Gagarin, a Soviet air force officer, became the first person to orbit the earth.

Relations with the United States. In 1960, an American U-2 plane was shot down over Soviet territory. The pilot confessed he had been spying, and President Dwight D. Eisenhower admitted that U.S. planes had been taking photographs over the Soviet Union for four years. Khrushchev demanded an apology, but Eisenhower refused. Khrushchev then walked out of a conference with Eisenhower and French and British leaders.

Another crisis occurred in 1962. The United States learned that the Soviet Union had missile bases in Cuba. These bases could have launched nuclear attacks against the United States or other parts of the Western Hemisphere. President John F. Kennedy ordered a naval *quarantine* (blockade) of Cuba and demanded the removal of all the missiles and bases. The Soviets removed their missiles in exchange for the withdrawal of U.S. nuclear missiles from Turkey and Kennedy's promise that the United States would not invade Cuba.

In 1963, the U.S.S.R., the United States, and Britain signed a treaty prohibiting all nuclear weapons tests except those conducted underground. Also in 1963, the Soviet Union and the United States set up a direct teletype connection called the *hot line* between Moscow and Washington, D.C. They hoped it would help prevent any misunderstanding from leading to war.

Brezhnev comes to power. Although Khrushchev improved Soviet relations with the West, many of his other policies failed. Farm output lagged, and in 1963 the U.S.S.R. began to buy wheat from the West. Economic growth slowed down, and people criticized the many poorly made products. Also, the split with China and the retreat in Cuba drew criticism. In 1964, a conspiracy among the highest-ranking Communists led to the overthrow of Khrushchev. Khrushchev was replaced by Leonid I. Brezhnev as Communist Party head and Aleksei N. Kosygin as premier.

The new leaders took power amid worsening Soviet relations with a number of countries. In Eastern Europe, several Soviet satellite countries sought to lessen Soviet control and follow their own policies. For example, the government of Czechoslovakia began a reform movement to give the people more freedom. In 1968, Soviet troops invaded Czechoslovakia and crushed this movement. In 1969, fighting broke out between the Soviet Union and China over a disputed border region.

In Africa, however, Soviet influence expanded during the 1970's. The Soviet Union supplied military equipment and advisers to Communist groups that sought to gain, or keep, control of African lands.

Like Khrushchev, Brezhnev and Kosygin tried to step up the production of consumer goods and the construction of housing. The Soviet economy made important gains, though it never met government goals. The rate of growth of Soviet industrial production began to decline. Also, agricultural production suffered from planning problems and a series of disastrous harvests. As a result, the U.S.S.R. continued to import grain from the West.

During the early 1970's, Brezhnev's power increased at Kosygin's expense. By the mid-1970's, Brezhnev was dominant.

Détente. Brezhnev pursued a policy of friendlier relations with the West. This easing of tensions between East and West became known as *détente* (pronounced *day TAHNT*). Brezhnev sought détente chiefly to improve the Soviet Union's economic and military position. For example, the country needed advanced Western technology to tap natural resources in Siberia. Increased trade with the West offered a way to pay for imported grain and technology.

Soviet trade with the West greatly expanded in the period of détente. The United States agreed to supply the U.S.S.R. with wheat. West German firms agreed to build a pipeline to carry natural gas from Siberia to Western Europe. In all, Soviet foreign trade increased about fivefold from 1970 to 1980. Soviet industry, however, continued to lag.

In 1972, the Soviet Union and the United States signed two agreements to limit nuclear arms. These agreements resulted from a series of meetings called the Strategic Arms Limitation Talks (SALT). In 1975, the leaders of the Soviet Union and many other countries agreed to honor such basic human rights as freedom of thought and freedom of religion. This pledge, called the Final Act, was one of several agreements known as the Helsinki Accords.

AP/Wide World

Arms agreements eased Cold War tensions. Soviet leader Leonid I. Brezhnev, *right,* and U.S. President Richard M. Nixon shook hands after signing a nuclear weapons treaty in 1974.

During détente, Western ideas entered the Soviet Union along with Western goods and technology. Some of these ideas challenged the Soviet government's level of control over the lives of its citizens. In Ukraine, Georgia, and the Baltic republics, local leaders sought greater control over cultural and economic matters. Some groups, such as Jews and Germans, demanded and received the right to emigrate. Soviet writers and other intellectuals protested government violations of the people's rights.

The Soviet government arrested many of its critics. It sentenced some of them to prison or to mental hospitals. Other were sent to live in remote areas, and a few were expelled from the country.

The collapse of détente began during the late 1970's. United States President Jimmy Carter strongly supported human rights. Under Carter, U.S. relations with the Soviet Union and other countries that violated their citizens' human rights became strained. In late 1979 and early 1980, Soviet troops invaded Afghanistan to try to keep that country's pro-Communist government in power. Governments around the world condemned the invasion. The United States protested the invasion by limiting shipments of wheat to the U.S.S.R. and by boycotting the 1980 Summer Olympic Games held in Moscow.

Soviet-U.S. relations worsened in 1981. That year, U.S.

Soviet influence in Eastern Europe

By the late 1940's, the Soviet Union had occupied East Germany and helped set up Communist governments in Poland, Czechoslovakia, Hungary, Romania, and Bulgaria. It also influenced Communist Yugoslavia and Albania. Communist rule ended in most of these countries in the late 1980's and early 1990's.

WORLD BOOK map

President Ronald Reagan called for a U.S. military build-up to match an expansion of Soviet arms under Brezhnev. Soviet leaders feared that this build-up would give the United States a military advantage. They also realized that the U.S.S.R. could not compete with the U.S. economy.

The rise of Gorbachev. The older generation of Soviet leaders, who had been trained under Stalin, had nearly died out by the mid-1980's. Kosygin resigned in 1980 because of ill health and died a few months later. Brezhnev died in 1982. He was succeeded as head of the Communist Party by Yuri V. Andropov. Andropov died in 1984. Konstantin U. Chernenko replaced Andropov, but he died in March 1985.

Mikhail S. Gorbachev then became head of the Communist Party. At age 54, Gorbachev became the first member of a new generation of Soviet leaders to head the country.

Gorbachev's reforms. Under Gorbachev, the Soviet Union changed rapidly. Gorbachev sought to improve economic performance by means of the policy of *perestroika.* He wanted to restructure the economy to stimulate growth and increase efficiency in Soviet industry. The reforms failed and even made things worse. Shortages increased. Inflation grew, and hoarding became widespread.

The most striking change was a new policy of openness called *glasnost* (pronounced *GLAHS nawst*). Gorbachev introduced *glasnost* to help win popular support for his policies and overcome resistance to *perestroika* in the Communist Party and the Soviet government. *Glasnost* made it possible to discuss political and social issues critically and with more freedom than ever before in the Soviet Union. In addition, a new freedom of expression in literature and the arts developed, and books by opponents of Communism became available in stores.

The Soviet Communist Party resisted Gorbachev's reforms. Therefore, Gorbachev promoted a reduction in the role of the Communist Party. In March 1989, the Soviet Union held its first contested elections in history. These elections, to the newly created Congress of People's Deputies, resulted in the defeat of many top Communist Party officials and several top generals. The Communist Party's role was further reduced in March 1990, when the Soviet government voted to permit the creation of non-Communist political parties in the Soviet Union.

Under Gorbachev, the Soviet Union's relations with the West improved. In 1987, Gorbachev and Reagan signed a treaty that was the first of a series of agreements to reduce the size of U.S. and Soviet nuclear forces. Between May 1988 and February 1989, Soviet troops withdrew from Afghanistan.

In March 1990, the Soviet government created the office of president of the U.S.S.R. The president became the head of the country's central government and the most powerful person in the Soviet Union. Previously, the head of the Communist Party had held the most power in thr country. The Congress of People's Deputies elected Gorbachev to serve as the first president of the U.S.S.R.

Threats to unity. Soviet control over Eastern Europe ended in 1989. Popular support for reform unseated

AP/Wide World

Mikhail S. Gorbachev, the last leader of the Soviet Union, is shown above after his televised resignation on Dec. 25, 1991. The existence of the Soviet Union ended with the resignation.

most of the Communist parties that had controlled Eastern European countries.

Powerful popular movements in many regions of the Soviet Union had long demanded greater freedom from the central government. Such movements began to gain strength during the late 1980's, particularly in the Baltic republics of Estonia, Latvia, and Lithuania. In 1990, Lithuania declared independence, and Estonia and Latvia called for a gradual separation from the Soviet Union. By the end of 1990, all 15 republics had declared that laws passed by their legislatures took precedence over laws passed by the central government.

To prevent further disintegration, Gorbachev proposed a union treaty designed to satisfy demands by the republics for more control over their affairs. In July 1991, Gorbachev and the leaders of 10 republics reached agreement on a treaty that would give the republics a large amount of independence. The treaty was to be signed by five of the republics on August 20.

On August 19, before the treaty could be signed, conservative officials of the Communist Party staged a *coup* (attempted overthrow) against Gorbachev's government. The coup leaders imprisoned Gorbachev and his family in their vacation home. The president of the Russian republic, Boris N. Yeltsin, led opposition to the coup, which collapsed on August 21. Yeltsin's role in defying the coup increased his power and prestige both at home and abroad.

After the coup, Gorbachev returned to the office of president but never regained full power. He then resigned as head of the Communist Party. Also, the Supreme Soviet suspended all Communist Party activities for an indefinite period.

The breakup of the Soviet Union. The collapse of the coup renewed demands by the republics for a greater amount of control over their own affairs. By November, 13 of the 15 republics—all except Russia and Kazakhstan—had declared independence. However, 11 of the republics—all but the Baltic republics and Georgia—had agreed to remain part of a new, loose confederation of self-governing states. Many of the republics, however, viewed this confederation as only a temporary arrangement.

The Congress of People's Deputies formed a *transitional* (temporary) government that would maintain the

unity of the country until a new union treaty could be written. The transitional government recognized the independence of the Baltic republics in September 1991.

The final blow to Soviet unity came in December. On December 8, Yeltsin and the presidents of Belarus and Ukraine met in Minsk, Belarus. The leaders announced that they had formed a new, loose confederation called the Commonwealth of Independent States. They declared that the Soviet Union had ceased to exist and invited the remaining republics to join the commonwealth. Most soon did so. On December 25, Gorbachev resigned as Soviet president, and the Soviet Union was formally dissolved.

In 1993, 12 leaders of the 1991 failed coup against Gorbachev went on trial. The Russian government had charged them with treason and plotting to seize power. In February 1994, the Russian parliament granted amnesty to the coup leaders and freed them.

James R. Millar

Related articles in *World Book* include:

Biographies

E. Education   G. The arts
F. Science and technology
IV. Economy
A. Manufacturing   C. Foreign trade
B. Agriculture
V. History

Questions

Who planned the October Revolution of 1917?
Which nationality groups made up the largest percentage of the total Soviet population?
What were *glasnost* and *perestroika*?
What were the major goals of Stalin's First Five-Year Plan?
Why did the Soviet Union break apart?
Who was the Soviet Union's first president?
Why did the Communists restrict religious practices?
What was the Soviet Union's most powerful government body?
What Soviet achievement started the space age?

Additional resources

Level I

Dowswell, Paul. *The Russian Revolution*. Raintree, 2004.
Gottfried, Ted. *The Rise and Fall of the Soviet Union*. 4 vols. 21st Century Bks., 2002-2003.
Matthews, John R. *The Rise and Fall of the Soviet Union*. Lucent Bks., 2000.
Ross, Stewart. *The Collapse of Communism*. Heinemann, 2004.

Level II

Eaton, Katherine B. *Daily Life in the Soviet Union*. Greenwood, 2004.
Kort, Michael G. *The Handbook of the Former Soviet Union*. Millbrook, 1997. *The Soviet Colossus*. 5th ed. Sharpe, 2001.
Streissguth, Thomas, ed. *The Rise of the Soviet Union*. Greenhaven, 2002.

Union Pacific Railroad. See Credit Mobilier of America; Western frontier life in America (Improvements in transportation).

Union Party. See Republican Party (The American Civil War).

Union shop is a form of security given to a union in a collective-bargaining agreement. An employer formally recognizes a union as the sole bargaining agent for a specific group of employees. All these employees must belong to the union, or must join it within a specified period, usually 30 or 60 days following the signing of the contract or of their employment, whichever is later. Usually they must remain members as long as the contract or its union shop provision lasts, or they will lose their jobs. See also **Closed shop; Labor movement** (What labor unions do); **Open shop.**   Daniel Quinn Mills

Unions, Labor. See Labor movement; Labor union.

Unit, in measurement, is a quantity adopted as the standard by which any other quantity of the same kind is measured. The standard units of measure in science, commerce, and industry have been tabulated in groups called *tables of denominate numbers*. There are units of money, length, time, surface, volume, and weight, among other things.   Richard S. Davis

See also **Denominate number; Metric system; Weights and measures.**

Unit rule, in the United States, was a voting rule permitted by the Democratic Party at its presidential nominating conventions from 1860 until 1968. The rule permitted the entire vote of a state delegation to be cast for one candidate, even though a minority of the delegation members favored another candidate. The national convention did not require the unit rule, but it enforced state instructions to delegates to vote as a unit. The prac-tice was abolished at the 1968 Democratic National Convention. The Republican Party has never used the unit rule.   Charles O. Jones

Unitarian Universalist Association is a religious denomination formed in 1961 to consolidate the American Unitarian Association and the Universalist Church of America. The association's members are local, self-governing congregations and fellowships. The association is organized under a Board of Trustees chosen by a General Assembly.

This denomination developed from protests against the doctrine of the Trinity held by orthodox Christians. It supports complete freedom of belief by its members. The denomination is historically centered in New England, especially Boston, but today it exists in urban areas across the United States. The association is also affiliated with similar groups in Europe and Asia. Headquarters are in Boston. For more information, see **Unitarians.**

Critically reviewed by the Unitarian Universalist Association

Unitarians believe in the unity of God, rather than in the doctrine of the Trinity as found in the historic creeds of the Christian church. In addition, the term *Unitarians* extends to religious groups dating from the 1500's to the present who rejected not only the doctrine of the Trinity, but also creeds as the basis for religious authority.

History. Early supporters of Unitarianism on the continent of Europe were Francis David (1510-1579) in Transylvania, then part of Hungary; and Faustus Socinus (1539-1604), leader of the Minor Reformed Church in Poland. In England, Unitarian views were advanced by John Biddle (1615-1662). But the main development of English Unitarianism came during the 1700's, when many churches that had previously been Presbyterian became Unitarian. The British and Foreign Unitarian Association was formed in 1825.

In America, Unitarianism developed during the 1700's within the Congregational churches in New England. The movement reacted against Calvinistic doctrines that emphasized human sinfulness, as well as the Trinity. Unitarians argued that such doctrines were inconsistent with the Bible and contrary to reason.

The dispute in the United States between the liberals (Unitarians) and orthodox Congregationalists became so bitter after 1805 that many churches divided, especially in New England during the first third of the 1800's. The Unitarians organized as a separate religious body. The most prominent supporter of the Unitarians in this period was a Boston clergyman, William Ellery Channing. His sermon "Unitarian Christianity" (1819) was widely accepted as a good statement of their position. The American Unitarian Association was organized in 1825.

Channing believed in Christianity as a divinely inspired religion proved by the miracles of Jesus. Younger Unitarian ministers soon began to argue that religious truth should be based on universal religious experiences rather than on the record of historical events. In addition, these ministers believed that religious truth and inspiration could be found in traditions other than Christianity.

Such ideas were expressed by the American writer and philosopher Ralph Waldo Emerson in his "Divinity School Address" (1838), and by the American clergyman and social reformer Theodore Parker in his sermon "The Transient and Permanent in Christianity" (1841). These two addresses expressed a new point of view in philosophy and religion. This view was called *transcendentalism* because it stated that people may have an experience of reality that *transcends* (goes beyond) the experience of the senses.

Transcendentalism had a lasting effect on Unitarianism, especially in making it more receptive to religious ideas drawn from non-Christian sources. Since that time, two views have emerged in the denomination. One emphasizes liberal religion strongly attached to the Christian tradition. The other refuses to accept any such limits and often argues that the modern mind, under the impact of science, has moved beyond Christianity altogether. See **Transcendentalism.**

Organization. In 1865, the Unitarian churches in the United States founded a national conference. In 1925, this organization was absorbed into the American Unitarian Association. In 1961, the American Unitarian Association merged with the Universalist Church of America to form the Unitarian Universalist Association.

The Unitarian Universalist denomination is organized on the basis of congregational church government. That is, the local church exerts basic authority. The local church strongly emphasizes individual freedom of belief and democratic participation in church affairs. Regional and national organizations provide leadership and services for the local churches but do not control them.

Unitarianism's original area of strength was based in New England. Today, Unitarian Universalist churches are found in many other parts of the United States and Canada. Most of these churches are in urban areas, and many are in university communities.   Henry Warner Bowden

See also **Emerson, Ralph Waldo; Parker, Theodore; Unitarian Universalist Association.**

Unitas, Johnny (1933-2002), was one of the greatest quarterbacks in National Football League (NFL) history. He was noted for his daring play selection and passing accuracy. During his 18 seasons in the NFL, Unitas completed 2,830 passes in 5,186 attempts for 40,239 yards and 290 touchdowns. He passed for more than 300 yards in 26 games. Unitas holds an NFL record for throwing at least one touchdown pass in 47 consecutive games.

John Constantine Unitas was born on May 7, 1933, in Pittsburgh. He attended the University of Louisville and, after graduating in 1955, was drafted by the Pittsburgh Steelers in the ninth round. The Steelers released him before the football season began.

Unitas played semiprofessional football for a season before he signed with the Baltimore Colts in 1956. He became the starting quarterback in the fourth game that season after the regular quarterback was injured. He played for the Colts through the 1972-1973 season, leading them to the league championship in 1958 and 1959. Unitas played the 1973-1974 season with the San Diego Chargers before retiring in 1974.

During his career, Unitas was an all-NFL selection at quarterback five times, was the NFL player of the year three times, and was selected to the Pro Bowl 10 times. He was elected to the Pro Football Hall of Fame in 1979. Unitas died on Sept. 11, 2002.   Carlton Stowers

UNITE HERE is a North American labor union that represents workers in the clothing, hotel, restaurant, and food service industries. The organization seeks to improve working conditions, wages, and benefits for

workers throughout the United States and Canada. It has headquarters in New York City. UNITE HERE is affiliated with the Change to Win labor federation.

Members of UNITE HERE work in textile mills; in laundries and dry cleaning shops; in retail stores; at airport concession stands; and in motels, hotels, restaurants, cafeterias, casinos, and bars. The majority of UNITE HERE members are women. For membership, see **Labor movement** (table).

UNITE HERE was formed in 2004 by a merger of two unions: the Union of Needletrades, Industrial and Textile Employees (UNITE) and the Hotel Employees and Restaurant Employees International Union (HERE). UNITE was formed in 1995 by a merger between the International Ladies' Garment Workers' Union and the Amalgamated Clothing and Textile Workers Union. HERE was established by members of cooks' and waiters' unions in 1891.   Critically reviewed by UNITE HERE

United Arab Emirates is a federation of seven independent Arab states in southwestern Asia. These states lie along the eastern coast of the Arabian Peninsula, at the south end of the Persian Gulf. From west to east, they are Abu Dhabi, Dubai (also spelled Dubayy), Ash Shariqah, Ajman, Umm al Qaywayn, Ras al Khaymah, and Al Fujayrah. Each state's capital city has the same name as the state.

The city of Abu Dhabi is the federation's capital and second largest city. Dubai, the largest city, is an important port and commercial center.

In the early 1800's, the United Kingdom began to protect the states from attack by outsiders. It also guarded ships near their coastlines against pirate attacks. By the early 1900's, the United Kingdom had taken control of the states' foreign affairs and guaranteed their independence. Known as the Trucial States, they remained under British protection until 1971, when they gained full independence. That year, six states formed the United Arab Emirates (UAE). The state of Ras al Khaymah joined the union in 1972.

Before the mid-1900's, when oil was discovered, most people earned a living by fishing and pearl fishing, herding camels, trading, or date farming. Oil brought sudden wealth to the region and led to the development of modern industries and cities. Many people left their traditional ways of life and took jobs in the oil industry and other modern fields. By the 1970's, the United Arab

Facts in brief

Capital: Abu Dhabi.
Official language: Arabic.
Area: 32,278 mi² (83,600 km²). *Greatest distances*—north-south, 250 mi (402 km); east-west, 350 mi (563 km). *Coastline*—483 mi (777 km).
Elevation: *Highest*—Jabal Yibir, 5,010 ft (1,527 m) above sea level. *Lowest*—Salamiyah, a salt flat slightly below sea level.
Population: *Estimated 2008 population*—4,724,000; density, 146 per mi² (57 per km²); distribution, 77 percent urban, 23 percent rural. *2004 official government estimate*—4,320,000.
Chief products: *Agriculture*—dates, livestock, melons, tomatoes. *Mining*—natural gas, petroleum.
Flag: The flag has a vertical red stripe and horizontal stripes of green, white, and black. It was adopted in 1971. See **Flag** (picture: Flags of Asia and the Pacific).
Money: *Basic unit*—Emirati dirham. One hundred fils equal one dirham.

United Arab Emirates

▬▬▬	International boundary
───	Road
┼─┼─┼	Oil pipeline
▭▭▭	Salt flat
⊛	National capital
•	Other city or town

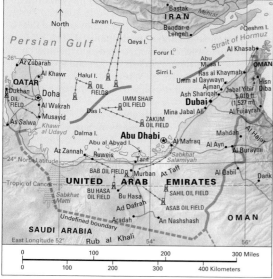

WORLD BOOK maps

try and other economic activities has enabled the UAE to construct apartment buildings, schools, hospitals, and roads to meet the needs of the growing population.

Citizens of the UAE prefer traditional Arab clothes. Many immigrants wear the clothing of their country of origin. Arabic is the official language, but English is widely used. About 90 percent of people 15 years of age or older can read and write.

Land and climate. Swamps and marshes cover much of the UAE's northern coast. The inland area is mostly desert with some water wells and oases. The largest oasis, Al Buraymi, lies both in the UAE and in Oman, the country's neighbor to the east. Hills and mountains cover much of the eastern part of the UAE.

The UAE has a hot climate with little rainfall. The humidity is often high along the coast, but the inland desert regions are dry. The mountainous areas are generally cooler and receive more rainfall than the rest of the country. Summer temperatures in the UAE average more than 90 °F (32 °C) and often reach as high as 120 °F (49 °C). Temperatures are cooler from about November to April, but still seldom drop below 60 °F (16 °C). The country receives an average of less than 5 inches (13 centimeters) of rain a year.

Economy. The economy of the UAE depends largely on the production and export of petroleum. Abu Dhabi is the largest oil producer, followed by Dubai. Much of the petroleum is exported in crude form, but some of it is refined in the country. The UAE is a member of the Organization of the Petroleum Exporting Countries (OPEC) and the Organization of Arab Petroleum Exporting Countries (OAPEC). Other important sources of income for the UAE include natural gas production and trading and banking activities. Dubai is a center for finance, real estate, tourism, and trade.

Less than 1 percent of the land of the UAE is suitable

Emirates had one of the highest *per capita* (per person) incomes in the world.

Government. Each of the seven states of the UAE is called an *emirate* and is ruled by an *emir* (prince), commonly called a *sheik.* Each emir controls his state's political and economic affairs. The federal government controls foreign affairs and defense and plays a large role in the country's economic and social development.

The seven emirs form the Supreme Council of Rulers. The council elects a president, who serves as chief executive and head of state of the UAE. The president appoints a prime minister and a Council of Ministers. The Council of Ministers supervises various federal government departments. The emirs appoint 20 representatives to the federal legislature, called the Federal National Council (FNC). Voters chosen by each emir elect another 20 FNC members.

People. The citizens of the UAE belong to Arab tribes that have long inhabited the region. But most of the people who live in the UAE are not citizens of the country. Instead, the population consists largely of people who came from other Arab countries and from such countries as Bangladesh, India, Iran, Pakistan, and the Philippines. Most of these people came to work in the oil and construction industries and in commerce.

The tribes of the UAE have similar traditions, but rivalries among them have made it difficult to establish a unified nation. In addition, the rapid increase in population since the 1960's has brought other challenges, including housing shortages. However, money from the oil indus-

© A.C. Waltham, Alamy

Abu Dhabi is the capital of the United Arab Emirates. This picture shows a vegetable *suq* (outdoor market) in front of a *mosque* (Muslim house of worship) in the city.

Jill Brown, Shostal

Oil pipelines cross desert regions in the United Arab Emirates (UAE). The oil industry provides jobs for thousands of people from the UAE and from several neighboring Arab countries.

for raising crops. Farmers in the desert oases and the hilly regions of the eastern UAE grow dates, melons, tomatoes, and other crops. Desert nomads tend herds of camels, goats, and sheep. People who live in the coastal areas catch fish, shrimp, and other seafood products.

Dubai, Abu Dhabi, and Ash Shariqah are the chief ports of the UAE. In addition to oil, the country exports natural gas and small amounts of dates and fish. Leading imports include building supplies, clothing, food products, household goods, and machinery.

Roads link the major cities and towns of the UAE. The country has four international airports. Several of the states operate radio stations, and Abu Dhabi and Dubai have television stations.

History. People have lived in what is now the United Arab Emirates for thousands of years. Arab chiefs gradually gained control of the region. The Arab groups adopted Islam, the Muslim religion, in the A.D. 600's.

The Persian Gulf region is part of a major world trade route. Beginning in the 1500's, various European nations established trading posts in the area. The British became the strongest European power in the Persian Gulf region. During the 1700's, the Arab states that now make up the UAE began to develop. At first, Ras al Khaymah and Ash Shariqah were the strongest states. Their strength came partly from their naval power and partly from the wealth they obtained from such activities as pearl fishing and trading.

In the late 1700's and early 1800's, Ras al Khaymah and Ash Shariqah fought many wars with other gulf states for control of the region's trade. The British aided the rivals of Ras al Khaymah and Ash Shariqah. In 1820, after destroying the city of Ras al Khaymah, the British forced all the states in the region to sign a truce forbidding warfare at sea and outlawing the slave trade. Two other truces were signed in 1835 and 1853, and the region became known as the *Trucial States* because of the truces.

By the early 1900's, Abu Dhabi and Dubai had become the leading states. However, the United Kingdom had

taken control of the states' foreign affairs in agreements signed in 1892. The United Kingdom guaranteed them protection from attack by outsiders. The states' rulers continued to handle internal matters.

In the mid-1900's, foreign oil companies began to drill for oil in the Trucial States. In 1958, oil was discovered in Abu Dhabi, and the state began to export crude oil in 1962. Large oil deposits were found in Dubai in 1966. Oil production began in Ash Shariqah in 1974. Money from oil production enabled Abu Dhabi, Dubai, and Ash Shariqah to begin to develop into modern states. Other states later began to produce some oil. But they continued to rely chiefly on agriculture and fishing as the basis of their economies.

On Nov. 30, 1971, Iran invaded and occupied the islands of Greater and Lesser Tunb and half of Abu Musa Island. At the time, these islands were governed by the emirates of Ras al Khaymah and Ash Shariqah. In 1992, Iran gained control of the rest of Abu Musa. The UAE still claims these islands.

In December 1971, the Trucial States gained full independence from the United Kingdom. In spite of traditional rivalries, all the states except Ras al Khaymah came together and formed the United Arab Emirates on Dec. 2, 1971. Sheik Zayid bin Sultan al-Nahyan of Abu Dhabi became the first president of the UAE. That same year, the UAE became a member of the Arab League and the United Nations. Ras al Khaymah joined the UAE in February 1972.

Under the Provisional Constitution adopted by the UAE in 1971, each emir continued to handle the internal affairs of his state. But the rulers agreed to share their resources and work for the economic development of all the states. The UAE's economy boomed in the 1970's as oil production increased. In addition, natural gas deposits were discovered in Ash Shariqah. But in the 1980's, worldwide oil prices fell, causing difficulties for the UAE's economy.

In 1981, the UAE, Kuwait, Bahrain, Qatar, Saudi Arabia, and Oman formed the Gulf Cooperation Council (GCC). The members of the GCC work together in such matters as defense and economic projects.

Iraq invaded Kuwait in August 1990. In early 1991, the UAE and the other GCC members participated in the allied air and ground offensive that liberated Kuwait. In 2003, the UAE supported the United States-led invasion of Iraq.

In 2004, Sheik Zayid died. He was succeeded as president by his son, Sheik Khalifa bin Zayid al-Nahyan. In December 2006, the UAE held legislative elections for the first time. The voters, chosen by the emirs, elected half of the Federal National Council members.   Imad Harb

Related articles in *World Book* include:
Abu Dhabi
Arabs
Dubai
Gulf Cooperation Council
Middle East
Organization of the Petroleum Exporting Countries

United Arab Republic (U.A.R.) was a union of two independent Middle Eastern countries, Egypt and Syria. President Gamal Abdel Nasser of Egypt and Shukri al-Kuwatly of Syria proclaimed the union on Feb. 1, 1958. Nasser was chosen as the union's president. Syrian rebels ended it on Sept. 29, 1961, setting up an independent government for Syria. Egypt continued to use the name United Arab Republic until 1971, when the country changed its official name to the Arab Republic of Egypt.

The U.A.R. had a centralized government, with Cairo as the capital. Egypt and Syria became provinces, with provincial capitals at Cairo for Egypt and Damascus for Syria.

Before World War I (1914-1918), most of the Middle East was part of the Ottoman Empire. But the United Kingdom had gained control of Egypt in 1882, and kept it until 1922, when it granted Egypt nominal independence. After World War I, the Middle East was carved into a number of political divisions. Syria, along with Lebanon, became a League of Nations mandate of France, which controlled them until after World War II (1939-1945).

Following World War II, many Arabs wanted to be united under a single government. Nasser came into power in Egypt during the 1950's, and he became the leader of the Arab unity movement. Many Arab leaders were suspicious of the West and turned to the Soviet Union for assistance. Nasser accepted Soviet aid, although he suppressed Communism within Egypt. The Communists also gained great power in Syria. The desire for Arab unity, the fear of Communist influence in Syria, and Nasser's ambition all contributed to the formation of the United Arab Republic.

Nasser regarded the union of Egypt and Syria as the first step toward uniting all the Arab states. On March 8, 1958, Yemen agreed to form a federation with the U.A.R. The union was called the United Arab States and had Hodeida (now Al Hudaydah), Yemen, as its permanent seat. The United Arab States was not a true federation. Yemen kept its own membership in the United Nations and had separate relations with other countries. Nasser dissolved the United Arab States in December 1961. He declared that the federation was no longer of any value.

Nasser made clear that the U.A.R. would be neutral in world affairs. In 1959, he accused the Soviet Union of trying to interfere with the republic's internal affairs. At the same time, he improved relations with the West.

The government introduced many reforms in both provinces. But many Syrians began to feel that Nasser was raising the level of living in Egypt only by lowering it in Syria. Finally, late in 1961, Syrian officers in the U.A.R. army carried out an almost bloodless revolt and proclaimed an independent Syria, ending the existence of the U.A.R.   Robert L. Tignor

Related articles in *World Book* include:

Egypt	Nasser, Gamal Abdel
Gulf Cooperation Council	Syria
Iraq	Yemen

United Automobile Workers (UAW) is one of the largest labor unions of the United States. It has over 950 local unions throughout the country. The union's official name is International Union, United Automobile, Aerospace and Agricultural Implement Workers of America.

The UAW's membership includes workers employed in the manufacture or assembly of cars, automotive parts, aircraft, aerospace products, agricultural implements, electronic products, and household appliances, or in allied metalworking trades. Other UAW members work in banking and insurance businesses, hospitals, le-

gal services, local government, and universities.

The union was founded in Detroit in 1935. It was an early, important member of the Congress of Industrial Organizations (CIO). The UAW was part of the CIO merger with the American Federation of Labor (AFL) in 1955. The UAW withdrew from the AFL-CIO in 1968 but rejoined it in 1981. National headquarters are in Detroit. For membership, see **Labor movement** (table).

Critically reviewed by the United Automobile Workers

See also **Bieber, Owen Frederick; Reuther, Walter P.; Woodcock, Leonard.**

United Church of Canada is the largest Protestant church in Canada. It was established in 1925 by the union of the Methodist Church, Canada; the Congregational Union of Canada; and most of the Presbyterian Church in Canada. A fourth denomination, the Canada Conference of the Evangelical United Brethren Church, joined the union in 1968. The United Church has more than 3 million members and followers.

Doctrine and organization. In 1924, the Canadian Parliament passed the United Church of Canada Act. This act, which became effective on June 10, 1925, formally established the United Church.

A constitution called the *Basis of Union* sets forth the administration, legal procedures, and organization of the United Church. The Basis of Union also includes 20 *Articles of Faith* that state the church's Biblically based doctrine. The United Church is organized regionally in administrative units called, from smallest to largest, congregations, presbyteries, and conferences. At the national level, a General Council meets every three years. It has doctrinal authority over the entire church.

The United Church has a presbyterian form of government—that is, the clergy and laity share equal responsibility for setting church policy and for administration. The presbyteries, conferences, and General Council are all governed by bodies made up equally of clergy and laity. All clergy of the United Church are called ministers and have equal rank. Both men and women (since 1936) may be ministers. Since 1988, church policy has explicitly stated that sexual orientation is not a barrier to either church membership or eligibility to be a minister.

Activities and services. The United Church is affiliated with 13 theological colleges and programs, and 6 other universities and colleges. In addition, it runs study resource centers and centers for continuing education and secondary schools. The church also has five training centers that prepare the laity for leadership positions in the church. The church produces much of its own educational and resource material, and it publishes a monthly periodical called the *United Church Observer*.

In addition to its educational activities, the United Church manages several hospitals and, largely through local congregations, provides accommodation for senior adults. Through its regional conferences and presbyteries, the church also supports hundreds of local outreach ministries and social service agencies. A Mission and Service Fund, administered by the national church office, finances this mission.

The United Church is liberal in its theological point of view. It believes in conversion to the teachings of Jesus Christ and commitment to correcting social evil and injustice. The church tries to guide the thinking of its membership on these matters and to speak broadly to

Canadian society. Through a wide network of global partners, the church addresses many international justice concerns. The church's national offices are in Toronto. Critically reviewed by the United Church of Canada

United Church of Christ is a Protestant religious denomination. It was formed in 1957 by the union of the Congregational Christian Churches and the Evangelical and Reformed Church. The United Church of Christ has a *general synod* (central body) that directs business affairs, elects church officers, and performs other duties related to church operations. However, individual congregations have the right to govern themselves.

In 1931, the Congregational churches merged with a union of three small church groups that all used the name Christian to form the Congregational Christian Churches. The Evangelical and Reformed Church was formed in 1934 by the union of two American churches of German background. The United Church of Christ has about 1,400,000 members. Headquarters are in Cleveland, Ohio. Critically reviewed by the United Church of Christ

See also **Congregationalists**; **National Association of Congregational Christian Churches**.

United Colonies of New England. See **New England Confederation**.

United Empire Loyalists were American colonists who moved to British colonies in Canada during and after the Revolutionary War in America (1775-1783). They remained loyal to the British and left the American Colonies to escape persecution by people who supported the war. Many of the Loyalists also were drawn to Canada by offers of free land. About 40,000 Loyalists moved to Canada. Loyalists settled mainly in the western parts of the colonies of Nova Scotia and Quebec.

The Loyalists greatly influenced Canada's cultural and political development. Many of the Loyalists brought their English heritage into areas that had been dominated by people with French traditions. In addition, the French-speaking population quickly lost its status as the overwhelming majority group. Soon, the Loyalists began to demand more authority over their local affairs. These demands led to the creation of the colony of New Brunswick in 1784 and the colony of Upper Canada in 1791. William Morgan Fowler, Jr.

See also **Canada, History of** (The United Empire Loyalists); **New Brunswick** (British settlement); **Ontario** (Early settlement).

United Farm Workers of America is a well-known union of farm laborers. The union, commonly called the UFW, is active in many parts of the United States, especially in California and Florida and in the Northeast. It seeks job security and higher wages for migrant workers and other farm laborers and works to improve their living and working conditions.

Cesar E. Chavez, a leading spokesman for Mexican American farmworkers, founded the National Farm Workers Association in 1962. Chavez received help from cofounder Dolores Huerta, a farmworker activist. The association and another union merged in 1966 to form the United Farm Workers Organizing Committee. This committee became the UFW in 1972. In its efforts to organize farm laborers and obtain union contracts for them, the UFW often urged consumers to boycott farm products produced by nonunion workers. These boycotts brought national attention to the farm labor movement

and were supported by many church and student groups, by members of various minority groups, and by other unions. The UFW joined the labor organization Change to Win in 2005. In 2006, the union ended its affiliation with the American Federation of Labor and Congress of Industrial Organizations (AFL-CIO).

The UFW's headquarters are in Keene, California, near Bakersfield. For membership, see **Labor movement** (table: Important U.S. labor unions). Critically reviewed by the United Farm Workers of America

See also **Chavez, Cesar E.**; **Huerta, Dolores F.**

United Food and Commercial Workers International Union is one of the largest unions in the United States. Most of the union's members are butchers, canners, meat packers, supermarket employees, or other workers in the food industry. The union, usually called the UFCW, also represents clerks of department stores, drugstores, and shoe stores; employees of hospitals and nursing homes; workers in the fur, leather, and shoe industries; and other employees. It is affiliated with the Change to Win labor federation.

The United Food and Commercial Workers International Union was formed in 1979 by the merger of the Amalgamated Meat Cutters and Butcher Workmen of North America with the Retail Clerks International Union. UFCW headquarters are in Washington, D.C. For membership, see **Labor movement** (table).

Critically reviewed by the United Food and Commercial Workers International Union

United Jewish Communities is a Jewish humanitarian organization with headquarters in New York City. Commonly called the UJC, the organization raises funds to support health, cultural, and human services for Jewish people worldwide. The UJC is the umbrella organization for hundreds of Jewish federations and independent communities throughout the United States and Canada. The UJC distributes funds in more than 60 countries to assist in community building and to support social programs. The organization was created in 1999, when the United Jewish Appeal merged with the United Israel Appeal and the Council of Jewish Federations.

Critically reviewed by the United Jewish Communities

United Kennel Club (UKC) is the second largest dog registry in the United States. It recognizes more than 300 breeds of purebred dogs and registers about 250,000 dogs each year. The UKC registers more kinds of breeds than any other registry in the United States. Only the American Kennel Club (AKC) registers more dogs.

The UKC maintains ownership records and *pedigrees* (records of a purebred dog's ancestors). It issues *P.A.D. pedigrees,* which list up to seven generations of a dog's ancestors and their performance records. The UKC and the AKC classify some breeds of dogs differently. For example, the AKC registers a dog breed called the American Staffordshire terrier. But the UKC registers it as the American pit bull terrier.

The UKC administers dog shows that emphasize performance tests, such as hunting or obedience trials. It was the first registry to allow mixed-breed dogs to participate in its obedience trials. The UKC publishes three magazines—*Bloodlines, Hunting Retriever,* and *Coonhound Bloodlines.* The registry was founded in 1898. Its headquarters are in Kalamazoo, Michigan.

Critically reviewed by the United Kennel Club

London, England

© Adrian Greeman, The Stock Market

Northern Ireland Tourist Board

Belfast, Northern Ireland

© Dave G. Houser

Edinburgh, Scotland

Aerofilms

Cardiff, Wales

The capitals of the United Kingdom's four divisions include London, which is also the country's capital and government headquarters; Belfast, a center of industry; Edinburgh, a cultural and educational center; and Cardiff, an economic and cultural hub.

United Kingdom

United Kingdom is a country in northwestern Europe. It consists of four main political units—England, Scotland, and Wales, which make up the island of Great Britain, and Northern Ireland, which occupies the northeastern part of the island of Ireland. The nation's official

The contributors of this article are Peter R. Mounfield, Senior Lecturer in Geography at the University of Leicester; Anthony Sutcliffe, Special Professor in the Department of History at the University of Nottingham; and Brendan O'Leary, Professor of Political Science, Stanley I. Sheer Endowed Term Chair in the Social Sciences, and Director of the Solomon Asch Center for the Study of Ethnopolitical Conflict, University of Pennsylvania.

name is the United Kingdom of Great Britain and Northern Ireland. When people refer to the country, most shorten its name to the United Kingdom, the U.K., or Britain. London is the capital of the United Kingdom and its largest city.

More than 75 countries are larger in area than the United Kingdom, and the country has only about 1 percent of the world's people. But the United Kingdom has a rich history. The British started the Industrial Revolution, a period of rapid industrialization that began in the 1700's. They founded the largest empire in history. They have produced some of the world's greatest scientists, explorers, artists, and political leaders.

The landscape of the United Kingdom varies dramatically. Northern Scotland is a wild, windswept region, broken by long arms of the sea that reach far inland.

Much of Northern Ireland has low mountains and rolling fields. Wales is famous for its rugged mountains and deep, green valleys. Most of England is covered by rolling plains, laid out in a patchwork of fields and meadows. The coastline is a shifting scene of steep cliffs, golden beaches, jagged rocks, and fishing towns tucked in sheltered bays. The United Kingdom has magnificent old castles and modern nuclear laboratories, snug villages and sprawling cities, and ancient universities and new factories.

The English Channel separates the island of Great Britain from France. This narrow stretch of water helped shape the character and history of the British people. It helped protect Britain from invasion and gave the people a feeling of security. In 1066, a group of descendants of the Vikings called the Normans sailed across the channel from northwestern France and conquered England. After the Norman Conquest, no enemy ever again crossed the channel and invaded the country.

Cut off from the rest of Europe by the sea and secure from invasion, the British developed their own character and way of life. They came to respect privacy and to value old traditions. They developed a dry wit, a love for personal freedom, and a high degree of self-criticism. The British have shown themselves at their best—brave and united—in times of crisis. Their courage against German bombs and overwhelming odds during World War II (1939-1945) won the admiration of the world.

The history of Britain is the story of how a small country became the world's most powerful nation—and then declined. In the 1700's, the Industrial Revolution made Britain the world's richest manufacturing country. The British ruled the seas and were the world's greatest traders. By 1900, they had an empire that covered about a fourth of the world's land and included about a fourth of its people. The British spread their way of life throughout their empire.

Then came the 1900's—and the shock of two crippling world wars. The British Empire began to break up as Britain's colonies sought independence. Britain faced one economic crisis after another. Today, the United Kingdom is still a leading industrial and trading nation. But it is no longer the world power it once was.

This article describes the United Kingdom's people, geography, and economy and its history since 1707, when England and Wales first officially united with Scotland. For detailed information on each division, see **England; Northern Ireland; Scotland;** and **Wales.**

For population and other key statistics, see the *United Kingdom in brief* feature in this article.

Government

National government. The United Kingdom is a constitutional monarchy. The monarch, Queen Elizabeth II, is the head of state, but the *prime minister* and a cabinet of senior politicians govern the country. The prime minister is the head of the government. Parliament is the chief lawmaking body.

The constitution of the United Kingdom is not one document, as are the constitutions of many other countries. Some parts of the constitution are laws passed by Parliament. Other parts come from *common law,* a body of laws and judgments based on traditional customs and beliefs. There are also many unwritten *constitutional conventions*—ideas and practices developed through the years, such as the cabinet system of government.

The one unalterable principle of the British constitution is that Parliament has supreme lawmaking authority on all matters. Parliament even has authority to make constitutional changes in the same manner in which it makes normal laws. Most countries with constitutions require special measures to change their constitutions.

The monarchy in Britain can be traced back about 1,200 years, although its role has changed significantly. The monarch must approve all bills passed by Parliament before they can become laws. However, no monarch has rejected a bill since the early 1700's.

The prime minister is usually the leader of the political party that has the most seats in the House of Commons. After each general election, the monarch ceremonially appoints the prime minister and asks him or her to form a government. The prime minister then picks a special group of about 20 ministers to make up the Cabinet. The prime minister also makes appointments to many other ministerial offices.

The Cabinet directs the general conduct of the government. The prime minister and Cabinet control what new laws and what amendments to existing laws will be introduced to Parliament. The prime minister chairs the Cabinet. Ministers who head the most important government departments are always included in the Cabinet. These departments include the Treasury, the Home Office, the Foreign and Commonwealth Office, the Department of Health, and the Ministry of Defence.

The largest political party in the House of Commons that opposes the party in power is called *Her* (or *His) Majesty's Opposition.* The head of that party is the *leader of the opposition.* The opposition has the duty of criticizing the government in power and standing ready to set up a new government. For this reason, the leading members of the opposition party are popularly referred to as the *Shadow Cabinet.*

Parliament makes the laws of the United Kingdom. A *bill* (proposed law) must be approved by both houses of Parliament to become law. The British Parliament has been called the *Mother of Parliaments* because many of the world's legislatures have copied features from it.

The House of Commons, often called simply the Commons, is by far the more powerful of Parliament's two houses. The House of Commons has 646 members, elected from the four main political units that make up the United Kingdom. Each member represents a district called a *constituency.* A member does not have to live in the constituency he or she represents. Members are chosen in a general election, in which the whole nation votes. A general election must be held at least every five years. However, an election may be called anytime by the prime minister. Almost all citizens 18 years old or older may vote. Those who cannot vote include *peers* (members of the nobility) and the mentally ill.

The House of Lords, often called the Lords, has little power. It can delay, but not defeat, any bill that the Com-

© Alpha from Globe Photos

Queen Elizabeth II reviews her troops in an annual ceremony. She has ruled as the United Kingdom's monarch since the death of her father, King George VI, in 1952.

mons is determined to pass. The House of Lords has about 750 members. Ninety-two members are drawn from the kingdom's dukes, earls, countesses, and other *hereditary peers and peeresses*. Hereditary peers and peeresses are members of the nobility who have inherited their titles. The 2 archbishops and 24 of the bishops of the Church of England have seats in the House of Lords. The remaining members are *life peers and peeresses*, given the rank of baron or baroness in honor of some outstanding accomplishment. Their titles do not descend to their children. Among the life peers are about 12 peers who were appointed as *law lords* to handle legal matters that come to Parliament.

Membership in the European Union—an organization that promotes political and economic cooperation among member states—requires the United Kingdom to adopt certain European laws. The British Parliament can-

not significantly change these laws, but the British judicial system enforces them. This arrangement gives British courts more power than they have had in the past. European Union laws also fill in some of the gaps in the British constitution.

Regional government. In referendums held in 1997, Welsh voters approved plans for a 60-member assembly for Wales, and the Scots voted to accept plans calling for the election of 129 representatives to a Scottish parliament. These legislative bodies met for the first time in 1999. They have control in certain domestic affairs.

A 1998 political settlement in Northern Ireland created three new political bodies: the Northern Ireland Assembly, the North-South Ministerial Council, and the British-Irish Council. These groups began meeting in 1999.

The Northern Ireland assembly has responsibility for many domestic matters. The voters of Northern Ireland

British Information Service

The House of Commons is the more powerful of the two houses of the British Parliament. The prime minister and Cabinet members sit on the front bench on one side of the chamber, *at left in photo*. The leading members of the largest opposition party sit on the front bench on the other side.

United Kingdom in brief

Capital: London.
Official language: English.
Official name: United Kingdom of Great Britain and Northern Ireland.
National anthem: "God Save the Queen" (or "King").
Largest cities: (2001 census)

London (7,172,036)	Sheffield (513,234)
Birmingham (977,091)	Bradford (467,668)
Leeds (715,404)	Edinburgh (448,624)
Glasgow (577,869)	Liverpool (439,476)

United Kingdom's flag is known as the *British Union Flag* or the *Union Jack.* It was officially adopted in 1801.

Royal arms date from 1837 in their present form. The shield bears symbols of England, Ireland, and Scotland.

Land and climate

Land: The United Kingdom lies in northwestern Europe. It includes the island of Great Britain and the northeastern part of the island of Ireland. France lies south across the English Channel; the Republic of Ireland west across the Irish Sea; and Belgium, the Netherlands, Germany, Denmark, and Norway east across the North Sea. Most of the land is flat or rolling. There are rugged sections in northern Scotland, in Wales, and in northern, central, and far southwestern England.

WORLD BOOK map

Area: 93,784 mi² (242,900 km²). *Greatest distances*—north-south, about 600 mi (970 km); east-west, about 300 mi (480 km). *Coastline*—2,521 mi (4,057 km).
Elevation: *Highest*—Ben Nevis, 4,406 ft (1,343 m) above sea level. *Lowest*—Great Holme Fen, near the River Ouse in Cambridgeshire, 9 ft (2.7 m) below sea level.
Climate: Summers mild—daytime highs about 73 °F (23 °C) in the south, about 65 °F (18 °C) in Scotland. Cool winters—nighttime temperatures drop nearly to freezing, but rarely much below, except in the Scottish Highlands. Precipitation moderate, generally higher in the west.

Government

Form of government: Constitutional monarchy. In practice, a parliamentary democracy.
Head of state: Monarch (queen or king). The monarch acts in largely ceremonial roles as head of the executive and judicial branches.
Head of government: Prime minister, usually the head of the majority party in the House of Commons.
Legislature: Parliament of two houses: House of Commons has 646 members, elected by the people; House of Lords has about 750 members. House of Commons is much more powerful than House of Lords.
Executive: Prime minister and Cabinet.
Political units: England, Scotland, Wales, Northern Ireland, united under one government. Each unit has its own divisions of local government.

People

Population: *Estimated 2008 population*—60,590,000. *2001 census*—58,789,194.
Population density: 646 per mi² (249 per km²).
Distribution: 89 percent urban, 11 percent rural.
Major ethnic/national groups: 95 percent of mostly British or Irish descent. About 5 percent recent immigrants or their descendants. Immigrants mostly from former British colonies.
Major religions: About 50 percent Church of England, 10 percent Roman Catholic, 4 percent Church of Scotland; also several other Protestant denominations, Muslims, Hindus, Jews.

Population trend

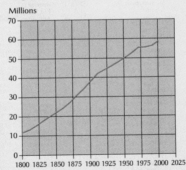

Millions

Year	Population
1801	11,944,000
1811	13,368,000
1821	15,472,000
1831	17,835,000
1841	20,183,000
1851	22,259,000
1861	24,525,000
1871	27,431,000
1881	31,015,000
1891	34,264,000
1901	38,327,000
1911	42,082,000
1921	44,027,000
1931	46,038,000
1951	50,225,000
1961	52,709,000
1971	55,515,000
1981	55,638,000
1991	56,467,000
2001	58,789,194

Economy

Chief products: *Agriculture*—barley, beef and dairy cattle, chickens and eggs, hogs, potatoes, rapeseed, sheep, sugar beets, wheat. *Manufacturing*—aerospace equipment, chemicals and pharmaceuticals, electrical and electronic products, foods and beverages, machinery, motor vehicles, printed materials, ships, steel, textiles and clothing. *Mining*—coal, natural gas, petroleum. *Fishing industry*—cod, crabs, haddock, herring, mackerel, whiting.
Money: *Basic unit*—British pound. One hundred pence equal one pound.
International trade: *Major exports*—aerospace equipment, chemicals and pharmaceuticals, foods and beverages, machinery, motor vehicles, petroleum. *Major imports*—chemicals, clothing, foods (especially fruit, meat, vegetables), machinery, metals, motor vehicles, paper and newsprint, petroleum products, textiles. *Major trading partners*—Belgium, France, Germany, Ireland, Netherlands, Spain, United States.

United Kingdom map index

Political divisions

Name	Population	Area In mi²	Area In km²	Capital
England	49,138,831	50,352	130,410	London
Northern Ireland	1,685,267	5,467	14,160	Belfast
Scotland	5,062,011	29,767	77,097	Edinburgh
Wales	2,903,085	8,015	20,758	Cardiff

Cities, towns, and local government areas*

Name	Population	Map key
Aberdeen	212,125	B 4
Aberystwyth		G 3
Allerdale†	93,493	E 4
Amlwch		F 3
Antrim†	48,366	E 2
Arbroath (Angus District)	108,400	C 4
Ards†	73,244	E 2
Armagh	54,263	E 2
Arnold (Gedling District)†	111,776	G 5
Ashford	91,000	I 7
Aylesbury [Vale]	165,749	H 5
Ayr		D 3
Ballantrae		D 3
Ballycastle		D 2
Ballymena	58,610	E 2
Banbridge†	41,392	E 2
Banbury		H 5
Banff		B 4
Barnsley	218,062	F 5
Barnstaple		I 3
Barrow-in-Furness	71,979	F 4
Barry (Vale of Glamorgan)†‡	119,293	H 4
Basildon	165,661	H 6
Basingstoke [and Deane]	152,583	I 5
Bath [and North East Somerset]‡	169,045	H 4
Bedford [Borough]	147,913	H 6
Belfast	277,391	E 2
Belford		D 5
Benfleet (Castle Point District)†	86,614	H 6
Birkenhead (Wirral District)	312,289	F 4
Birmingham	977,091 §2,555,596	G 5
Blackburn [with Darwen]‡	137,471	F 4
Blackpool‡	142,284	F 4
Blaenau Gwent†‡	70,058	H 4
Blyth [Valley]	81,265	D 5
Bognor Regis (Arun District)†	140,787	I 6
Bolton	261,035	F 4
Boston	55,739	G 6
Bournemouth‡	163,441	I 5
Bracknell [Forest]†‡	109,606	H 5
Bradford	467,668	F 5
Braemar		B 4
Braintree	132,171	H 7
Breckland†	121,422	G 7
Brentwood	68,426	H 6
Bridgend†‡	128,650	H 3
Bridlington		F 5
Brighton [and Hove]‡	247,820	I 6
Bristol‡	380,615	H 4
Broadland†	118,497	G 7
Brodick		D 3
Bromsgrove	87,846	G 4
Broxtowe†	107,572	F 5
Burnley†	89,541	F 4
Bury†	180,612	F 4
Bury St. Edmunds (St. Edmundsbury District)	98,179	G 7
Caernarfon		G 3
Caerphilly†‡	169,521	H 3
Camborne (Carrick District)†	87,861	J 2
Cambridge	108,879	H 6
Cannock [Chase]	92,127	G 5
Canterbury	135,287	H 7
Cardiff‡	305,340	H 4
Cardigan		H 3
Carlisle	100,734	E 4
Carmarthen (Carmarthenshire)‡	173,635	H 3
Carrickfergus†	37,659	E 2
Castlereagh†	66,488	E 4
Ceredigion†‡	75,384	H 3
Charnwood†	153,461	G 5
Chelmsford	157,053	H 6
Cheltenham	110,025	H 5
Cherwell†	131,792	G 5
Chester	118,207	G 4
Chesterfield	98,852	F 5
Chichester	106,445	I 5
Chiltern†	89,226	H 6
Chorley†	100,449	F 4
Christchurch	44,869	I 5
Clacton-on-Sea (Tendring District)	138,555	H 7
Colchester	155,794	H 7
Coleraine	56,315	D 2
Colwyn Bay		F 3
Conwy†‡	109,597	G 3
Cookstown	32,581	E 1
Corby	53,177	G 5
Coventry	300,844	G 5
Craigavon†	80,671	D 4
Crawley	99,754	I 6
Crewe [and Nantwich]	111,006	F 4
Cumnock		D 3
Cunninghame†	137,094	D 2
Cwmbran (Torfaen)‡	90,967	H 4
Dacorum†	137,807	H 6
Darlington‡	97,822	E 5
Dartford†	85,911	H 6
Denbighshire†‡	93,092	G 4
Derby‡	221,716	G 5
Derwentside†	85,065	E 5
Doncaster	286,865	F 5
Dorchester		I 4
Douglas		E 3
Dover	104,490	I 7
Down†	63,828	E 2
Dudley	305,164	G 4
Dumbarton		D 3
Dumfries [and Galloway]	147,765	E 3
Dunbar		D 4
Dundee	145,663	C 4
Dunfermline		C 4
Dungannon	47,735	E 1
Duns		D 4
Dunstable (South Bedfordshire District)†	112,627	H 6
Durham	87,725	E 5
Dunvegan		B 2
Easington†	93,981	E 5
East Hertfordshire†	128,922	H 6
East Kilbride		D 3
East Riding of Yorkshire†‡	314,076	F 5
Eastbourne	89,667	I 6
Eastleigh†	116,177	I 5
Edinburgh	448,624	D 4
Ellesmere Port [and Neston]†	81,671	F 4
Epping [Forest]	120,888	H 6
Epsom [and Ewell]†	67,075	H 6
Erewash†	110,091	F 5
Esher (Elmbridge District)†	121,911	H 5
Exeter	111,078	I 4
Falkirk†	145,191	D 4
Fareham†	107,969	I 5
Fenland†	83,523	G 7
Fermanagh†	57,527	E 1
Flintshire†‡	148,565	G 4
Folkestone (Shepway District)	96,241	I 7
Galashiels		D 4
Gateshead	191,151	E 5
Gillingham		H 5
Glasgow	577,869	D 3
Glastonbury		I 4
Gloucester	109,888	H 4
Gosport	76,414	I 5
Grantham (South Kesteven District)	124,788	G 6
Gravesend (Gravesham District)†	95,703	H 6
Great Gimsby, see Grimsby		
Great Malvern (Malvern Hills District)	72,196	H 4
Great Yarmouth	90,813	G 7
Greenock (Inverclyde District)	84,203	D 3
Grimsby		F 6
Guildford	129,717	I 6
Gwynedd†‡	116,838	G 3
Halifax (Calderdale District)	192,396	F 5
Halton†‡	118,215	F 4
Hamilton		D 3
Harlow	78,899	H 6
Harrogate	151,339	F 5
Hartlepool‡	88,629	E 5
Hastings	85,027	I 6
Havant†	116,857	I 5
Haverhill		H 6
Helmsdale		A 4
Henley-on-Thames		H 5
Hereford		H 4
Herefordshire†‡	174,844	H 4
High Wycombe		H 5
Hinckley [and Bosworth]†	100,138	G 5
Hitchin (North Hertfordshire District)†	116,911	H 6
Horsham	122,078	I 6
Huddersfield (Kirklees District)	388,576	F 5
Hull (Kingston upon Hull)‡	243,595	F 6
Huntingdon (Huntingdonshire)	156,950	G 6
Inverness	44,084	B 3
Inverurie		B 4
Ipswich	117,074	H 7
Isle of Anglesey†‡	66,828	F 3
Isle of Wight‡	174,844	I 5
Kerrier†	92,536	J 2
Kettering	81,842	G 5
Kilmarnock [and Loudoun]		D 3
King's Lynn [and West Norfolk]	135,341	G 6
Kingston upon Hull, see Hull		
Kinross		C 4
Kirkcaldy		C 4
Kirkwall		E 7
Knowsley†	150,468	H 5
Kyle of Lochalsh		B 2
Lancaster	133,914	F 4
Larne	30,832	E 2
Leeds	715,404 §2,079,217	F 5
Leicester‡	279,923	G 5
Leominster		H 4
Lerwick		D 7
Lichfield	93,237	G 5
Limavady†	32,422	E 1
Lincoln	85,616	F 6
Lisburn	108,694	E 2
Liverpool	439,476 §1,362,034	F 4
Llandovery		H 3
Llanelli		H 3
Lockerbie		E 4
London (Greater London)	7,172,036	H 6
Londonderry		E 1
Louth		G 6
Lowestoft (Waveny District)	112,342	G 7
Ludlow		G 4
Luton‡	184,390	H 6
Lymington (New Forest District)	169,329	I 5
Macclesfield	150,144	F 5
Maidstone	138,959	H 6
Mallaig		B 2
Manchester	392,819 §2,482,352	F 4
Mansfield	98,095	G 5
Margate (Thanet District)	126,712	H 7
Matlock (Amber Valley District)†	116,475	G 5
Merthyr Tydfil‡	55,983	H 4
Mid Sussex†	127,383	H 6
Middlesbrough‡	134,847	E 5
Milford Haven		H 2
Milton Keynes‡	207,063	H 5
Monmouthshire†‡	84,879	H 4
Montrose		C 4
Newark-upon-Trent		G 5
Newcastle-under-Lyme	122,040	G 4
Newcastle upon Tyne	259,573 §1,075,979	E 5
Newport‡	137,017	H 4
Newport		I 5
Newry [and Morne]	87,058	E 2
Newtown St. Boswell		D 4
Newtownabbey	79,995	E 2
North Down†	76,323	E 2
North East Lincolnshire†‡	157,983	F 6
North Lincolnshire†‡	152,839	F 5
North Somerset†‡	188,556	I 4
North Tyneside†	191,663	E 5
Northallerton		E 5
Northampton	194,477	H 5
Norwich	121,553	G 7
Nottingham‡	266,995	G 5
Nuneaton [and Bedworth]	119,147	G 5
Oldham	217,393	F 5
Omagh	47,952	E 1
Oxford	134,248	H 5
Paisley (Renfrewshire District)	172,867	D 3
Pembrokeshire†‡	112,901	H 3
Perth [and Kinross]	134,949	C 4
Peterborough‡	156,060	G 6
Peterhead		B 5
Plymouth‡	240,718	I 3
Poole‡	138,299	I 5
Port Talbot (Neath Port Talbot)‡	134,471	H 3
Portsmouth‡	186,704	I 5
Potters Bar (Hertsmere District)	94,457	H 6
Powys†‡	126,344	G 4
Preston†	129,642	F 4
Reading‡	143,124	H 5
Redcar and Cleveland†‡	139,141	C 5
Redditch	78,813	H 6
Reigate [and Banstead]	126,519	I 6
Restormel†	95,547	J 2
Rhondda [Rhondda, Cynon, Taff]†‡	231,952	H 4
Rochdale†	205,233	F 4
Rochester [Medway]†‡	249,502	H 6
Rotherham	248,176	F 5
Rugby	87,449	G 5
Rutland†‡	34,560	G 5
St. Albans	128,982	H 6
St. Andrews		C 4
St. Helens	176,845	F 4
St. Peter Port		J 1
St. Helier		J 1
Salford†	216,119	F 4
Salisbury	114,614	I 5
Sandwell†	282,901	G 5
Scarborough	106,233	E 6
Seaham (Easington District)†	93,981	E 5
Sedgefield†	87,206	E 5
Sevenoaks	109,297	I 6
Sheffield	513,234 §1,266,337	F 5
Shrewsbury [and Atcham]	95,896	G 4
Slough‡	119,070	H 6
Solihull	199,521	G 5
South Gloucestershire†‡	245,644	H 4
South Lakeland†	102,306	E 4
South Oxfordshire†	128,177	H 5
South Shields (South Tyneside District)	152,785	E 5
Southampton‡	217,478	I 5
Southend-on-Sea‡	160,256	H 7
Southport (Sefton District)	282,956	F 4
Southwold		G 7
Spalding		G 6
Spelthorne†	90,414	H 6
Stafford	120,653	G 5
Stevenage	79,724	H 6
Stirling	86,212	C 3
Stamford		G 6
Stockport	284,544	F 4
Stockton-on-Tees‡	178,405	E 5
Stoke-on-Trent‡	240,643	G 4
Stonehaven		C 4
Stornoway		A 2
Stourie		A 3
Strabane	38,248	E 1
Stranraer		E 2
Stratford-upon-Avon	111,474	H 5
Stroud	107,899	H 4
Sunderland	280,807	E 5
Sutton in Ashfield (Ashfield District)	111,482	F 5
Swale	122,802	H 6
Swansea‡	223,293	H 3
Swindon‡	180,061	H 5
Tain		B 3
Tameside†	213,045	H 6
Tamworth	74,531	G 5
Tarbert		A 2
Taunton (Deane)	102,304	I 4
Teignbridge†	120,967	I 4
Telford [and the Wrekin]‡	158,285	G 4
Test Valley†	109,760	H 6
Thurrock†‡	143,042	H 6
Thurso		A 4
Tobermory		C 2
Tonbridge [and Malling]	107,560	I 6
Torbay‡	129,702	I 4
Trafford†	210,135	F 5
Truro		J 2
Tunbridge Wells	104,030	I 6
Vale of White Horse†	115,632	H 6
Vale Royal†	122,081	F 4
Wakefield	315,173	F 5
Walsall	253,502	G 5
Warrington‡	191,084	F 4
Warwick	125,962	G 5
Watford	79,729	H 6
Waverly†	115,639	H 6
Wealden†	140,021	H 6
Wellingborough	72,530	G 5
Welshpool		G 4
Welwyn Garden City (Welwyn Hatfield District)	97,546	H 6
West Berkshire†‡	144,445	H 5
West Dunbartonshire†	93,378	D 3
Weston-super Mare		H 4
Weymouth [and Portland]	63,665	I 4
Whitchurch		G 4
Wick		A 4
Wigan	301,417	F 4
Winchester	107,213	I 5
Windsor [and Maidenhead]‡	133,606	H 5
Woking	89,836	H 6
Wokingham†‡	150,257	H 5
Wolverhampton	236,573	G 4
Worcester	93,358	H 4
Worksop (Bassetlaw District)†	107,701	F 5
Worthing	97,540	I 6
Wrexham‡	128,477	G 4
Wychavon†	112,949	H 5
Wyre†	105,584	F 4
Wyre Forest†	96,945	G 5
York‡	181,131	F 5

* Populations are for districts, which may include some rural area as well as the city or town.
The government of the United Kingdom does not report populations for individual cities and towns.
† Does not appear on map; key shows general location.
‡ Unitary authority.
§ Population of metropolitan area, including suburbs.
Source: 2001 census.

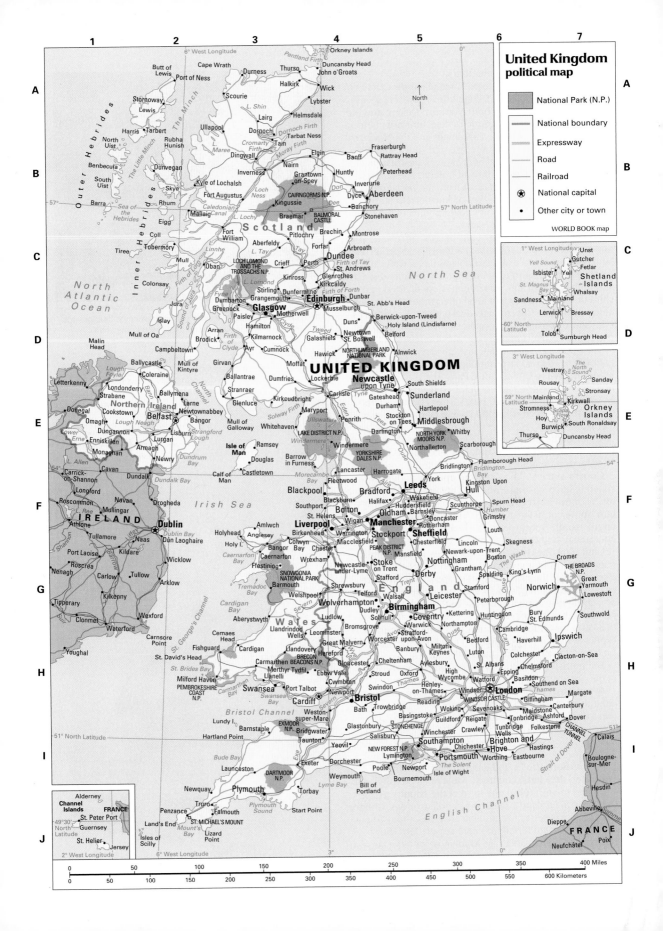

elect the Assembly's 108 members.

The North-South Ministerial Council handles affairs of the entire island of Ireland. It includes representatives from the governments of both Northern Ireland and the Republic of Ireland. The council's decisions are subject to the approval of the Irish Parliament and the Northern Ireland Assembly.

The British-Irish Council addresses issues of concern to all of the United Kingdom and Ireland. The council brings together representatives from the parliaments of both countries; the assemblies of Northern Ireland, Scotland, and Wales; and the governments of the Channel Islands and the Isle of Man.

Local government. The units of local government in Scotland and Wales are unitary authorities. Northern Ireland is divided into districts. England has various administrative units, including counties, metropolitan districts, and unitary authorities. The counties are divided into shire districts. Each unit of local government has its own elected council. The councils deal with such matters as education, housing, refuse collection, and roads. Local governments may collect taxes, but about half of their income comes from the national government.

Politics. The two largest political parties in the United Kingdom are the Conservative Party and the Labour Party. The Conservative Party developed from the Tory Party, which began in the late 1600's. The Labour Party began in 1900. A third party, the Liberal Democrats, was formed in 1988.

Other parties in the United Kingdom include nationalist parties in Northern Ireland, Scotland, and Wales. They favor independence from the United Kingdom.

Courts of the United Kingdom operate under three separate legal systems—one for England and Wales, one for Northern Ireland, and one for Scotland. In each system, some courts hear only criminal cases and other courts handle only civil cases. Decisions made by lower courts may be appealed to higher courts.

Until 2009, the House of Lords serves as the highest court of appeal for civil cases in all three legal systems. It also serves as the highest court of appeal for criminal cases, except in Scotland. In Scotland, people convicted of a crime may appeal their case to the High Court of Justiciary, but they have no further appeal to the Lords. In 2009, a new Supreme Court of the United Kingdom is expected to begin operations. At that time, the judicial function of the House of Lords will end.

The monarch appoints all British judges on the advice of the government. Judges serve until retirement.

Armed forces of the United Kingdom are made up of volunteers. About 215,000 volunteers serve in the nation's army, navy, and air force.

People

Population. The United Kingdom is more thickly populated than most countries. Most of its people live in cities and towns. About one-third of the country's residents live in England's seven metropolitan areas. Greater London, the largest metropolitan area, has about 10 percent of the United Kingdom's total population. The six other metropolitan areas are as follows, with the largest city of each area shown in parentheses: Greater Manchester (Manchester), Merseyside (Liverpool), South

Robert Harding Picture Library

The United Kingdom's people represent many ethnic groups. Most people live in urban areas, as do these Londoners.

Population density

The most densely populated areas in the United Kingdom are southeastern England and the industrial regions of central England. The Highlands of Scotland have the fewest people.

WORLD BOOK map

Persons per mi²	Persons per km²
More than 500	More than 200
250 to 500	100 to 200
125 to 250	50 to 100
12 to 125	5 to 50
Less than 12	Less than 5

Yorkshire (Sheffield), Tyne and Wear (Newcastle upon Tyne), West Midlands (Birmingham), and West Yorkshire (Leeds).

More than four-fifths of the population of the United Kingdom live in England. London and England as a whole have great influence over the rest of the United Kingdom because of their large populations.

Ancestry. Celtic-speaking people lived in what is now Britain by the mid-600's B.C. Over the next 1,700 years, the land was invaded by the Romans, Angles, Saxons, Jutes, Danes, and Normans. Most of the British are descendants of these early peoples.

Since the 1950's, many immigrants have come to Britain from countries that belong to the Commonwealth. The Commonwealth is an association of countries and other political units that were once part of the British Empire. Many immigrants have come from Commonwealth countries in Asia and the West Indies. Most of the newcomers have settled in cities and towns already facing housing shortages. In the early 1960's, the British government began restricting immigration.

Language. English is the official language of the United Kingdom and is spoken throughout most of the country. English developed chiefly from the language of the Anglo-Saxon and Norman invaders.

Less than a fifth of the people of Wales speak both English and Welsh, a language that developed from one of the languages of the Celts. A few people of Wales speak only Welsh. Thousands of people in Scotland speak the Scottish form of Gaelic, which is another Celtic language. The Irish form of Gaelic is spoken by a small number of people in Northern Ireland.

Way of life

City life. A number of the United Kingdom's important cities grew rapidly in the 1700's and early 1800's, during the Industrial Revolution. But today, many of those cities—including London, Birmingham, Liverpool, Manchester, and Leeds—are in decline. They are faced with such problems as falling employment, rising crime, and poor housing. They are losing population as people move from the inner cities into the suburbs and beyond. Greater London's population, for example, peaked in 1939 and has been falling ever since.

The industries that supported the growth of the large cities have declined or disappeared. New industries, such as electronics, have developed outside the cities, many near *motorways* (expressways) or near research establishments and universities.

The British government in 1988 launched an urban renewal program called Action for Cities. The purpose of the program is to revive the inner cities by means of new housing and new development. The government also established areas called *enterprise zones* to attract new businesses to inner cities. Businesses within enterprise zones receive tax cuts and other advantages. However, people continue to move away from the inner cities to find jobs, and these areas do not attract enough private investment. The cost of such basic services as street lighting and road repair is increasingly falling upon fewer people. And many of these people are the members of society who can least afford such costs— the elderly, single-parent families, the poorly paid, and the unemployed.

Rural life. At one time, the rural areas of the United Kingdom were devoted mainly to farming. But the availability of convenient transportation enables people to work in a city and live in the countryside. In many rural communities, full-time farmers are outnumbered by retired people, commuters, and workers who serve the needs of tourists.

The attractiveness and variety of rural Britain is one of the tourist industry's prime assets. These qualities also attract many retired people. In some rural areas, more than a fifth of the population is over retirement age. These areas include the counties of Cornwall, Devon, Dorset, East and West Sussex, and the Isle of Wight; the Scottish Borders; and parts of rural Wales.

Food and drink. Most British cooking is simple. A typical meal includes roast beef, mutton, or pork with potatoes and one or more other vegetables. Since the 1960's, the British have increased their consumption of poultry, fresh fruit, and frozen vegetables. Consumption of lamb, beef, veal, bread, potatoes, eggs, butter, and sugar has fallen.

Pizza houses, Chinese restaurants, and hamburger places that offer *takeaway* and *fast food* have grown in popularity. They rival the shops offering *fish and chips,* a popular meal of fried fish and French fried potatoes. The traditional Sunday midday meal of roast beef and *Yorkshire pudding,* a battercake baked in meat fat, is still a family favorite, however.

The British diet tends to be high in fat, salt, and sugar and low in fiber. These eating habits can contribute to a variety of health problems, including heart disease. The country has a high level of heart disease, especially in northern Britain. There is evidence, however, that health considerations have begun to influence food consumption. People are drinking more low-fat milk instead of whole milk and eating more whole grain bread, which has more fiber than white bread.

Tea with milk and sugar is the most popular hot beverage. Beer, including ale and lager, is the favorite alcoholic drink. A high proportion of beer drinking takes place in *pubs* (public houses), which provide a focus of social life for many people.

Recreation. The British love the outdoors. They flock to Blackpool, Brighton and Hove, and other seaside resorts on vacation. Several million vacationers visit Spain, France, and other countries. Other vacationers prefer mountain climbing or walking in Wales or in the beautiful Lake District of northwestern England. Still others enjoy automobile or bicycle trips through the country.

The British also spend much time in their gardens. About half of the families in the United Kingdom have a garden.

The British are enthusiastic sports fans. The most popular spectator sport by far is soccer, which the British also call *football.* During the football season, thousands of fans jam the stadiums every Saturday. Cricket has been popular in England for hundreds of years. It is played with bats and a ball and two 11-player teams.

Gardens are popular throughout the United Kingdom, and gardening is a favorite pastime. This formal garden is the Royal National Rose Society's garden at Chiswell Green, St. Albans, in England.

© Eric Crichton, Bruce Coleman Ltd.

Schools, universities, and almost all towns and villages have cricket teams. Other popular sports include archery, *bowls* (a sport similar to bowling), golf, hockey, horseback riding, horse racing, rugby football, sailing, and tennis.

Religion. The United Kingdom has two *established* (national) churches. They are the Church of England, which is episcopal (governed by bishops), and the Church of Scotland, which is presbyterian (governed by councils of ministers and elders). The monarch must belong to the Church of England and is its worldly head. The spiritual head of the English Church is the archbishop of Canterbury.

The Church of England has about 25 million members, and the Church of Scotland has about $2\frac{1}{2}$ million members. Other Protestant churches have a total of about 5 million members. The country has about $5\frac{1}{2}$ million Roman Catholics. About 3 million people in the United Kingdom belong to other faiths. Approximately

17 million people are nonreligious.

Education. Each division of the United Kingdom has its own system of public education. Each system is run by its own department of education, which works closely with local elected education authorities. The four systems differ in many ways. Traditionally, teachers throughout the United Kingdom have had much freedom in selecting the courses they teach and in developing their own teaching methods. However, teachers are being increasingly guided by a national curriculum.

Most British children are required by law to begin school at the age of 5 and continue until they are 16. Children in Northern Ireland must begin school at the age of 4. Generally, students attend elementary school until they are 11 years old, and then they go on to high school. There are several types of high schools. Some students attend *grammar schools,* which provide a college preparatory education. Some attend schools that stress a more general, technical, or vocational educa-

© Sidler/*Figaro* Magazine from Gamma/Liaison

Students at Eton take exams. Eton is a boarding school for boys. It is one of England's best-known *public schools,* which are actually private schools. Private schools, called *independent schools,* are supported by fees and private donations. However, most schools in the United Kingdom are free.

Horse racing is a popular spectator sport in the United Kingdom. Races take place nearly every day, except most Sundays. The Royal Ascot race meeting, *shown here,* is held every June. This fashionable event is usually attended by some of the royal family.

© Cynthia Matthews, The Stock Market

tion. Most students attend *comprehensive schools,* which provide all types of high school education.

Most schools in the state system are free. About 95 percent of all schoolchildren attend elementary schools and high schools supported by public funds. The rest go to *independent schools.*

The independent schools are private schools supported by fees paid by parents and by private gifts of money. There are several types of independent schools. The best known are the English *public schools,* which provide a high school education. Although they are private schools, they are called public because the earliest of these schools were established for the children of the middle classes. Traditionally, these schools have emphasized discipline, the building of character, and scholarship. The reputation of some of these schools, such as Eton, Harrow, and Winchester, is extremely high. The leading public schools stress preparation for Oxford or Cambridge, which are the United Kingdom's

oldest and most honored universities.

Oxford University was founded in the 1100's, and Cambridge University was established in the 1200's. They have a greater reputation than other universities because of their age, traditions, and high standards of scholarship. The United Kingdom has about 75 other universities. The University of London is the United Kingdom's largest traditional university. The Open University has more students, but it has no regular classrooms. Instruction is carried out through radio, television, correspondence, audiotapes, and videocassettes.

Museums and libraries. The United Kingdom has about 2,500 museums and art galleries. The largest collections are owned by about 20 national museums and art galleries, most of which are in London. The world-famous British Museum, in London, is noted for its collections in archaeology and many other fields. The National Gallery and the Tate Britain gallery, also in London, have some of the world's greatest paintings.

© Richard Steedman, The Stock Market

Golf is played throughout the United Kingdom. The Scots probably developed the game as we know it. The Old Course at St. Andrews, Scotland, *shown here,* is one of the world's oldest and most famous golf courses.

Soccer, also called *football* in the United Kingdom, is by far the country's most popular spectator sport. The players in this match represent rival teams of Glasgow, Scotland.

The United Kingdom's public library system serves people throughout the country. The nation's largest library, the British Library, has about 18 million volumes. The national libraries of Scotland and Wales have about 5 million volumes each. Other important libraries include Oxford's Bodleian Library and the Cambridge University Library.

The arts. The government encourages and supports the arts in the United Kingdom chiefly through agencies called arts councils. There is an arts council for England, Scotland, and Wales and another one for Northern Ireland. Each council receives a government grant and, in turn, makes grants to help pay for musical, theatrical, and other artistic activities. Many local areas have their own arts councils to coordinate and finance local artistic activities.

The United Kingdom is one of the world's major centers for theater. Visitors come from all parts of the world to see British theater productions. About 50 theaters operate in the central London district known as the West End. The Royal National Theatre performs at its three stages on London's South Bank. The Royal Shakespeare Company is based at Stratford-upon-Avon and also performs at the Barbican Centre in London. The English Stage Company at the Royal Court Theatre in London performs the works of talented new playwrights. Notable regional theaters include the Bristol Old Vic, the Festival Theatre in Chichester, the Lyric Theatre in Belfast, and the Royal Lyceum in Edinburgh.

The United Kingdom has 11 principal professional symphony orchestras and several smaller orchestras. Five of the principal orchestras have their headquarters in London. The best-known orchestras outside London include the Hallé Orchestra of Manchester and the City of Birmingham Symphony Orchestra.

The most famous British arts festival is the Edinburgh International Festival, which was founded in 1947. It is held every August. Its program includes operas, concerts, ballets, and plays. The Cheltenham Festival, held in July, specializes in music by contemporary British composers. A summer drama festival takes place in Chichester. Glyndebourne, near Brighton and Hove, has an annual summer opera festival of international fame.

The land

The United Kingdom covers a large island called Great Britain, part of the island of Ireland, and thousands of small islands. The island group is sometimes called the British Isles. England, Scotland, and Wales occupy the island of Great Britain. Northern Ireland occupies the northeastern part of the island of Ireland. The inde-

Walkers in Wales rest in Snowdonia National Park. The park's mountain ranges and dramatic scenery attract vacationers. Many British people spend their vacations mountain climbing or hiking.

pendent Republic of Ireland occupies the rest of the island of Ireland.

The island of Great Britain is the eighth largest island in the world. It covers 84,550 square miles (218,980 square kilometers). The North Sea on the east and the English Channel on the south separate the island from the mainland of Europe. The island of Ireland lies to the west, across the Irish Sea. The island of Great Britain is separated from mainland Europe by only about 20 miles (32 kilometers) of water at the closest point. Most of the coastline of Great Britain is so broken by deep bays and inlets that no point on the island is more than 75 miles (121 kilometers) from the sea.

The United Kingdom can be divided into eight main land regions. Seven of them occupy the island of Great Britain. They are (1) the Scottish Highlands, (2) the Central Lowlands, (3) the Southern Uplands, (4) the Pennines, (5) Wales, (6) the Southwest Peninsula, and (7) the English Lowlands. Northern Ireland makes up the eighth region.

The Scottish Highlands cover the northern two-thirds of Scotland. They are a region of mountain ranges, plateaus, and deep valleys. The highest point in the United Kingdom, 4,406-foot (1,343-meter) Ben Nevis, rises in the Highlands. Many bays cut into the region's Atlantic Ocean and North Sea coasts. Some narrow bays, called *sea lochs,* are flanked by steep mountain slopes and reach far inland. Most of the Highlands is a *moor*—an area of coarse grasses, a few small trees, and low evergreen shrubs called *heather.* The soil of this rugged, windswept region is thin and poor. Few people live there. Most of them raise sheep, or they fish in the seas.

The Central Lowlands lie south of the Scottish Highlands, in the valleys of the Rivers Clyde, Forth, and Tay. This region is a gently rolling plain. It has Scotland's best farmland and its richest coal deposits. Most of the Scottish people live there, and most of Scotland's industry is in the Lowlands.

The Southern Uplands rise gently south of the Central Lowlands. This is a region of rounded, rolling hills. Sheep graze on the short grass that covers much of the hills. Their fleece goes to Scotland's woolen mills in the region's Tweed Valley. In the south, the Uplands rise to the Cheviot Hills, which form the border between Scotland and England.

The Pennines are a region of rounded uplands that extend from the Scottish border about halfway down the length of England. They are also known as the *Pennine Chain* or *Pennine Hills,* and they are often called the *backbone of England.* They are rich in coal. West of the Pennines lies the Lake District, a scenic area of clear, quiet lakes and low mountains. The Lake District is one of England's most famous recreation areas.

Wales lies southwest of the Pennines. It is separated from the Pennines by a narrow strip of the English Lowlands. The Cambrian Mountains cover most of Wales. These mountains are especially rugged and beautiful in the north and are more rounded in central Wales. Southern Wales is largely a plateau deeply cut by river valleys. Most of the people live on the narrow coastal plains or in the deep, green river valleys. These are the best areas for crop farming and raising dairy cattle. The rest of the land is too steep for raising crops and is used mostly for grazing sheep and some beef cattle. Wales

has large deposits of coal in the south, though most of its mines have been closed. Much of the industry of Wales is centered in the large coastal towns.

The Southwest Peninsula lies south of Wales, across the Bristol Channel. It is a plateau whose surface is broken by great masses of granite. Near much of the coast, the plateau ends sharply in magnificent cliffs that tower above the sea. Tiny fishing villages lie in sheltered bays along the coast. The region has mild winters and summers that are not too dry. This climate helps make agriculture important in the fertile lowland areas. Farmers grow vegetables and raise dairy cattle.

The peninsula was once famous for its tin and copper mines, but most of these metals have been worked out. More important today is the region's fine white china clay, used to make pottery. The Southwest Peninsula's beauty and pleasant climate attract many artists and retired people and thousands of vacationers every year.

The English Lowlands cover all of England south of the Pennines and east of Wales and the Southwest Peninsula. This region has most of the United Kingdom's farmable land, industry, and people. The Lowlands consist chiefly of broad, gently rolling plains, broken here and there by low hills and ridges. Much of the land is a patchwork of fields and meadows, bordered by tall hedges, stone fences, or rows of trees.

A grassy plain called the Midlands lies in the center of the English Lowlands, just south of the Pennines. Parts of the Midlands extend along the western and eastern

Fritz Henle, Photo Researchers

The Scottish Highlands are a wild, desolate region. They have some of Britain's most magnificent scenery—sparkling lakes, heather-covered mountains, and deep valleys.

Physical features

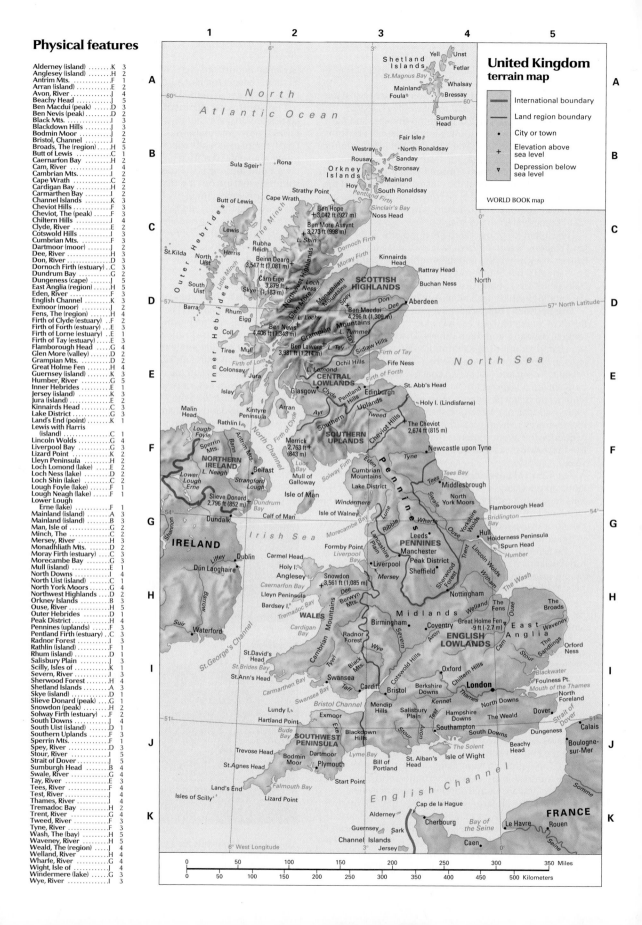

The English Lowlands are chiefly a region of broad, rolling plains, broken by low hills. This region has most of the United Kingdom's farmable land and industry, and most of the country's people live there. The Lowlands county of Shropshire, *shown here,* lies along England's border with Wales.

© Ben Osborne, Tony Stone Images

borders of the Pennines. The Midlands are the industrial heart of the United Kingdom. Birmingham and the surrounding communities form the country's chief manufacturing center.

South of the Midlands, a series of hills and valleys crosses the land to the valley of the River Thames. London, the United Kingdom's capital and great commercial and cultural center, stands on the Thames. Most of the land north of the Thames and up to a bay of the North Sea called The Wash is low and flat. This area has some of the country's richest farmland. A great plain called The Fens borders The Wash. In The Fens, near Ely, is the lowest point on the island of Great Britain. It ranges from sea level to 15 feet (4.6 meters) below sea level, depending on the tide of the North Sea.

South of the Thames, low chalk hills and valleys cross the land. Where the hills reach the sea, they form great white cliffs. The most famous cliffs are near Dover. On clear days, people in Calais, France, can look across the Strait of Dover and see the white cliffs of Dover gleaming in the sun.

Northern Ireland is a region of low mountains, deep valleys, and fertile lowlands. The land is lowest near the center and rises to its greatest heights near the north and south coasts. The chief natural resources are rich fields and pastures, and most of the land is used for crop farming or grazing.

Rivers and lakes. Britain's longest rivers are the Thames and the Severn. The Thames is 210 miles (340 kilometers) long. The Severn is nearly the same length. Many British rivers have drowned, or sunken, mouths called *estuaries,* up which the ocean tides flow. These rivers include the Clyde and Forth of Scotland; the Humber, Mersey, and Thames of England; and the Severn of England and Wales. The estuaries of these rivers make excellent harbors. Bristol, Hull, Liverpool, London, Southampton, and other cities on or near estuaries are important ports.

Lough Neagh (pronounced *lahk NAY)* in Northern Ireland is the largest lake in the British Isles. It is about 18 miles (29 kilometers) long and up to 15 miles (24 kilometers) wide. The lake covers about 150 square miles (388

square kilometers). Loch Lomond in Scotland is the largest lake on the island of Great Britain. The lake is 23 miles (37 kilometers) long and 5 miles (8 kilometers) wide at its widest point. England's biggest lakes are in the Lake District. The largest, Windermere, is about 10 miles (16 kilometers) long and up to 1 mile (1.6 kilometers) wide.

Climate

The United Kingdom has a mild climate, even though it lies as far north as bitterly cold Labrador. Winter temperatures rarely drop as low as 10 °F (−12 °C), and summer temperatures seldom rise above 90 °F (32 °C). The climate is influenced by the Gulf Stream, a warm ocean current that sweeps up from the equator and flows past the islands of Great Britain and Ireland. Steady southwest winds blow across this current and bring warmth in winter. In summer, the ocean is cooler than the land. Winds over the ocean come to Britain as refreshing breezes.

© Rosemary Evans, Tony Stone Images

Brixham, near Torbay, and other Southwest Peninsula towns have a mild climate that keeps their ports ice-free. Britain's climate is influenced by the Gulf Stream, a warm ocean current.

The sea winds also bring plentiful rain. The heaviest rains fall in the highland areas of western Scotland. Some of these areas get 150 to 200 inches (380 to 510 centimeters) a year. Less than 20 inches (51 centimeters) of rain falls yearly in some parts of southeastern England. The United Kingdom has rain throughout the year, and rarely is any section of the country dry for as long as three weeks. Much of the rain comes in light, but steady, drizzles.

Mild fogs hang over parts of the country from time to time. But the famous "pea soup" fogs of London and other big cities seldom occur any more. These thick, heavy fogs were caused chiefly by smoke and other pollution released into the air by factories, automobiles, and homes where coal was burned for heat. Antipollution laws have helped make such fogs much less severe than they once were.

Average monthly weather

	London						Edinburgh				
	Temperatures				Days of rain or snow		Temperatures				Days of rain or snow
	°F		°C				°F		°C		
	High	Low	High	Low			High	Low	High	Low	
Jan.	44	35	7	2	17	Jan.	43	35	6	2	18
Feb.	45	35	7	2	13	Feb.	43	35	6	2	15
Mar.	51	37	11	3	11	Mar.	47	36	8	2	15
Apr.	56	40	13	4	14	Apr.	50	39	10	4	16
May	63	45	17	7	13	May	55	43	13	6	15
June	69	51	21	11	11	June	62	48	17	9	15
July	73	55	23	13	13	July	65	52	18	11	17
Aug.	72	54	22	12	13	Aug.	64	52	18	11	17
Sept.	67	51	19	11	13	Sept.	60	48	16	9	16
Oct.	58	44	14	7	14	Oct.	53	44	12	7	18
Nov.	49	39	9	4	16	Nov.	47	39	8	4	18
Dec.	45	36	7	2	16	Dec.	44	36	7	2	17

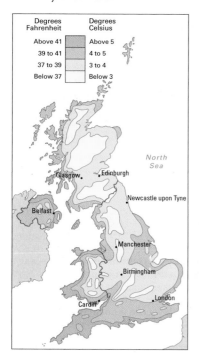

Degrees Fahrenheit / Degrees Celsius

Above 41 / Above 5
39 to 41 / 4 to 5
37 to 39 / 3 to 4
Below 37 / Below 3

Degrees Fahrenheit / Degrees Celsius

Above 61 / Above 16
59 to 61 / 15 to 16
55 to 59 / 13 to 15
Below 55 / Below 13

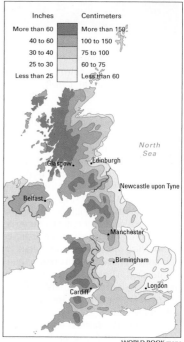

Inches / Centimeters

More than 60 / More than 150
40 to 60 / 100 to 150
30 to 40 / 75 to 100
25 to 30 / 60 to 75
Less than 25 / Less than 60

WORLD BOOK maps

Average January temperatures
Northern Ireland and the south and west of Britain have milder winters. Upland areas have the coldest weather.

Average July temperatures
The south, particularly the southeast, has warmer summer temperatures than Scotland and the north of England.

Average yearly precipitation
The western upland areas of the United Kingdom receive the most precipitation. Southeastern England gets the least.

Economy

The United Kingdom is an important manufacturing and trading nation. In fact, it can survive only by manufacturing and trading. The country's farms produce only about three-fifths of the food needed by the people. Except for coal, natural gas, and oil, the United Kingdom has few natural resources. The country must import about two-fifths of its food and many of the raw materials it needs for manufacturing.

Service industries account for about 75 percent of the United Kingdom's *gross domestic product* (GDP). The GDP is the total value of goods and services pro-

duced within the country annually. About 80 percent of British workers are employed in service industries. The country's service industries are concentrated in and near its largest cities, especially London.

Finance, insurance, real estate, and business services contributes a larger portion of the United Kingdom's GDP than any other service industry group. Most of the country's financial companies operate in London, one of the world's leading financial cities. Major financial institutions there include the Bank of England, the United Kingdom's national bank; the London Stock Exchange;

The United Kingdom's gross domestic product

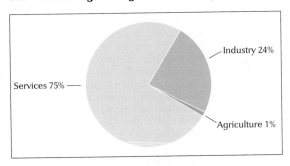

The United Kingdom's gross domestic product (GDP) was $2,377,000,000,000 in United States dollars in 2006. The GDP is the total value of goods and services produced within a country in a year. *Services* include community, government, and personal services; finance, insurance, real estate, and business services; trade, restaurants, and hotels; and transportation and communication. *Industry* includes construction, manufacturing, and mining and utilities. *Agriculture* includes agriculture, forestry, and fishing.

Production and workers by economic activities

Economic activities	Percent of GDP* produced	Employed workers	
		Number of persons	Percent of total
Finance, insurance, real estate, & business services	29	6,392,000	20
Community, government, & personal services	23	9,996,000	32
Trade, restaurants, & hotels	15	7,063,000	22
Manufacturing	13	3,287,000	10
Transportation & communication	7	1,883,000	6
Construction	6	2,177,000	7
Mining & utilities	5	170,000	1
Agriculture, forestry, & fishing	1	440,000	1
Total†	100	31,408,000	100

*GDP = gross domestic product, the total value of goods and services produced in a year.
†Figures do not add up to 100 percent due to rounding.
Figures are for 2006.
Source: United Kingdom Office for National Statistics.

and Lloyd's of London insurance organization. Britain has many firms that offer such business services as accounting, advertising, data processing, and engineering.

Community, government, and personal services ranks second among the service industries of Britain in terms of the GDP. This group employs more people than any other industry in the country. It includes such activities as education, health care and social work, legal services, and military operations.

Trade, restaurants, and hotels ranks next among the service industries. Aberdeen and London are major centers of petroleum distribution. Leeds is the chief center for the wholesale trade of clothing. Tourist activities in Britain, especially in the London area, provide important income to restaurants, hotels, and retail shops. Tourists spend over $30 billion yearly in the United Kingdom. Britain's other service industries, transportation and communication, are discussed later in this section.

Manufacturing. The United Kingdom is a leading industrial nation. Most British industries are in central England, the London area, the Scottish Central Lowlands, the Newcastle upon Tyne area, and southern Wales. Early factories were near the coal fields because coal powered the steam engines that moved the machinery. Today, the use of electric power, oil, and gas has enabled many new industries to develop far from the coal fields, especially in southern England.

Britain ranks as an important steel-producing country. It exports about half of its finished steel. The rest is used in Britain to make hundreds of products. Much steel is used in the manufacture of automobiles, buses, trucks, and motorcycles. The United Kingdom also produces heavy machinery for industry, farming, and mining. The country is one of the world's largest producers of tractors. Other products include cranes, earth movers, road graders, harvesters, and drilling machines. British factories also make railway equipment, household appliances, and machine tools. The city of Sheffield is famous for its high-quality knives and hand tools.

BAE Systems is one of the world's largest defense and

© Kevin Morris, AllStock

A marching band passes the gates of Buckingham Palace, the home of the monarch. The parade of the palace guards in their colorful uniforms attracts many tourists. Tourism is an important service industry throughout the United Kingdom.

aerospace companies. It supplies the armed forces of the United Kingdom, the United States, and other countries with a wide range of products, including military aircraft, missiles, and land warfare systems.

A growing percentage of the United Kingdom's manufactured goods consists of sophisticated electronic equipment. Much of this equipment is exported. Factories make such items as cable television gear, data processing equipment, fiber-optic communications systems, and radar devices, as well as undersea telephone cables.

The chemical industry in the United Kingdom produces a variety of products—from industrial chemicals to plastics and soap. The United Kingdom is one of the largest exporters of *pharmaceuticals* (medicinal drugs). The country's pottery industry is centered in Stoke-on-

Trent. Outstanding names in British pottery include Worcester, Spode, and Wedgwood.

The United Kingdom is one of the world's chief centers of printing and publishing. British companies print paper money and postage stamps for many countries. Books published in the United Kingdom are exported to countries throughout the world.

The Industrial Revolution began in the British textile industry. The United Kingdom remains an important producer of cotton and wool. British manufacturers also make synthetic fibers and fabrics. The east Midlands region of England is a center for the production of lace and knitwear. Cotton and wool are produced in northern England. Scotland produces knitwear and is famous for its fine woolen products. Northern Ireland has a

Economy of the United Kingdom

This map shows the economic uses of land in the United Kingdom. In addition, it indicates the country's main farm products and its most important fishing products. Major manufacturing centers are also shown. The United Kingdom's most important livestock are beef and dairy cattle, hogs, poultry, and sheep. The country's main crops are barley, potatoes, rapeseed, sugar beets, and wheat.

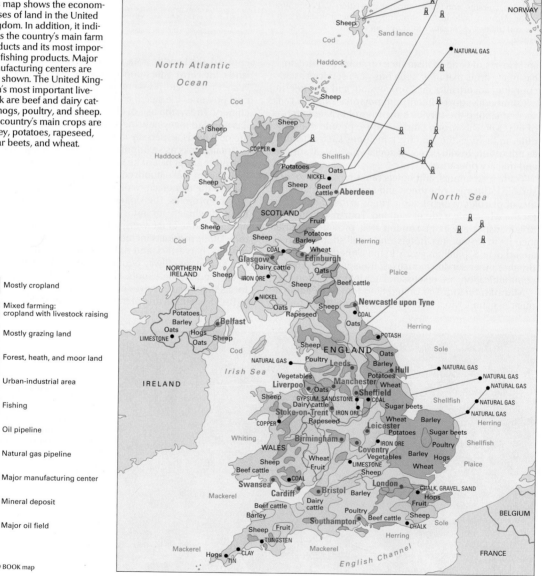

WORLD BOOK map

worldwide reputation for its linen goods.

Britain has one of Europe's largest clothing industries. The biggest centers are Leeds, Leicester, London, and Manchester. British clothing has long been famous for its quality. But today, Britain imports more clothing than it exports because many countries with lower labor costs can produce clothing more cheaply than the British can.

Processing of foods and beverages ranks as one of Britain's major industries. Most processed foods and beverages are consumed in Britain. But some are exported. Scotch whisky has a large world market. Other British industries manufacture bricks and cement, furniture, glassware, leather goods, and paper.

Agriculture. Britain produces approximately three-fifths of its food supply and imports the rest. The imports include avocados, bananas, citrus fruits, peppers, pineapples, and other items that cannot be easily grown in Britain's climate.

Farmland covers about three-fourths of the United Kingdom's land area. The nation has about 275,000 farms. About three-fifths of the country's farms are less than 50 acres (20 hectares). About half of the people who operate or work on farms do so on a part-time basis.

Many British farmers practice *mixed farming*—that is, they raise a variety of crops and animals. Methods of mixed farming vary from farm to farm. In the rough highlands of Scotland, Wales, and western England, grass grows much better than farm crops. There, farmers use most of their land for grazing. The land in southern and eastern England is drier and flatter, and it is more easily worked. Farmers in eastern England use most of their land for raising crops.

Britain's most important crops are barley, potatoes, rapeseed, sugar beets, and wheat. Farmers in southern and eastern England grow almost all the country's rapeseed, sugar beets, and wheat and most of its barley. Potatoes are grown throughout the United Kingdom. Farmers in southern England grow most of Britain's fruits and garden vegetables. One of the most productive regions is the county of Kent in southeastern England. It is called the *Garden of England* and is famous for the beautiful blossoms of its apple and cherry orchards in springtime. Farmers in Kent also grow hops, which are used in making beer.

Sheep are one of Britain's chief livestock. Farmers in almost every part of the country raise sheep for meat and wool. British farmers also raise beef cattle, dairy cattle, and hogs. Chickens are raised mainly in special mass-production plants.

Mining. The United Kingdom is the largest producer of petroleum and natural gas in the European Union. These fuels account for about 90 percent of the value of total mineral production in the country.

Petroleum is Britain's most valuable mineral. British oil wells produce about 700 million barrels of petroleum a year. In the past, the country had to import petroleum to meet its needs. But during the 1970's, Britain began producing petroleum from wells in the North Sea. Today, Britain's oil wells provide nearly all the petroleum that the country uses and also supply petroleum for export.

Britain obtains natural gas from deposits below the North Sea. These deposits provide enough gas to meet most of the country's needs.

The United Kingdom's largest coal-mining regions lie near the River Trent in central England and in North Yorkshire. Coal from these areas is an important fuel source for the country's electric power plants. Britain's other important minerals include chalk, clays, fluorspar, gypsum, potash, salt, and sand and gravel. The Southwest Peninsula has fine china clay, used in making pottery. Southeastern England has large deposits of chalk, used for cement.

Fishing. The United Kingdom is an important fishing nation. The British fishing industry supplies about 720,000 tons (650,000 metric tons) of fish yearly. More than half of this catch comes from the waters west of Scotland and from the northern North Sea. The principal catches include cod, haddock, herring, mackerel, plaice, and whiting. Large catches of crabs and other shellfish are also brought in. The main fishing ports are on the east coast and in the southwestern part of the island of Great Britain.

Fish farms in the United Kingdom produce salmon, trout, and shellfish. Scotland is especially known for its salmon farms.

Energy sources. Fuel-burning plants provide about 75 percent of Britain's electric power. Nuclear energy

© Bruce Coleman Ltd.

Fishing is an important industry in the United Kingdom, which is one of Europe's most productive fishing nations. This fishing boat empties a catch of shellfish at a Scottish port.

provides most of the remaining electric power. In 1956, the United Kingdom opened the world's first large-scale nuclear power station at Calder Hall, Cumbria, in northwestern England. Natural gas fields under the North Sea provide most of the country's natural gas needs. Petroleum deposits off the coast of Scotland supply enough oil to meet the United Kingdom's needs.

International trade. The United Kingdom ranks as a leading trading nation. The country once imported chiefly raw materials and exported mostly manufactured products. However, manufactured goods now account for most of the country's imports and exports.

The United Kingdom exports aerospace equipment, chemicals and pharmaceuticals, foods and beverages, machinery, motor vehicles, petroleum, and scientific and medical equipment. The country's imports include alcoholic beverages, chemicals, clothing, foods (especially fruit, meat, and vegetables), machinery, metals, motor vehicles, paper and newsprint, petroleum products, and textiles.

Most of the United Kingdom's trade is with other developed countries, especially other members of an organization known as the European Union. France, Germany, and the United States are the United Kingdom's leading customers and suppliers. Other major trade partners include Belgium, China, Ireland, Italy, Japan, the Netherlands, Spain, and Sweden.

The value of the United Kingdom's imports of goods usually exceeds the value of its exports. British banks and insurance companies make up part of the difference by selling their services to people and firms in other lands. Another important source of income is the spending by the more than 25 million tourists who visit the United Kingdom each year. The British merchant fleet also brings in money by carrying cargoes for other countries.

Transportation. Roads and railways carry most passenger and freight traffic within the United Kingdom. A system of high-speed motorways links major cities and towns. Bus systems provide local and intercity transportation. *Lorries* (trucks) carry about 80 percent of the inland freight.

An extensive rail network crisscrosses the United Kingdom. The railroads provide high-speed passenger service, as well as freight hauling.

The United Kingdom has a large merchant fleet. The ships in the fleet carry British-made goods to ports throughout the world and bring back needed imports. In addition, British ships carry freight for other countries. There are about 90 ports of commercial significance throughout the United Kingdom. About 75 percent of the country's international trade comes through these ports.

The inland waterways of the United Kingdom are used to carry freight, as well as for recreational boating. The Thames, which flows through London, is the United Kingdom's busiest river and one of the world's busiest.

Ferry services connect coastal and island communities in the United Kingdom. *Hovercraft* (vehicles that ride over water on a cushion of air) carry passengers mainly across the English Channel between England and France. In 1987, work began on a railroad tunnel to link the United Kingdom and France beneath the channel. This railroad tunnel opened in 1994.

© ZEFA

A North Sea oil rig helps produce petroleum, the United Kingdom's most valuable mineral. Oil wells in the North Sea yield enough petroleum for the country's needs and for export.

British Airways, the largest airline in the United Kingdom, operates flights to all parts of the world. Smaller airlines provide service within the United Kingdom and to other countries. Heathrow Airport, one of the busiest airports in the world, is near London. The United Kingdom also has large airports at Gatwick and Stansted, both near London, and at Birmingham, Edinburgh, Glasgow, and Manchester.

Communication. The United Kingdom has about 100 daily newspapers. About 10 of these dailies have nationwide circulation. Their main offices are in London. *The Sun,* the *Daily Mail,* and the *Daily Mirror* have the largest circulations. The country's most influential papers include *The Times, The Guardian, The Daily Telegraph,* and *The Independent.*

The British Broadcasting Corporation (BBC), a public corporation, provides commercial-free radio and television service. The BBC is financed chiefly by yearly licenses that people must buy to own a television set. Numerous commercial radio and television stations also broadcast throughout the country.

The British Post Office provides many services in addition to handling mail. For example, people can draw pensions and family allowances and also bank their savings at the country's post offices.

In 1707, the Parliament of the Kingdom of England and Wales and the Parliament of the Kingdom of Scotland each passed the Act of Union. This act joined the two kingdoms under one government as a "united kingdom of Great Britain," now called the United Kingdom.

By 1707, the English Parliament had won a controlling influence over the monarchy, and the Tory and Whig political parties had developed. England controlled the seas and possessed the beginnings of an empire. For the history of the area before 1707, see the articles **England; Scotland; Wales.**

The beginning of cabinet government. Queen Anne, the first British monarch, died in 1714. Her second cousin George, a German prince, was her closest Protestant relative and became king. British law prohibited a Roman Catholic from being monarch. George I did not speak English well. He chose his council of ministers from the Whig Party and seldom attended council meetings. His chief minister, Sir Robert Walpole, took control of the council—and the British cabinet system of government began to develop. Walpole is considered Britain's first prime minister. George I's son became king in 1727. George II was also a German and, like his father, left much authority to his Cabinet.

George III succeeded his grandfather George II in 1760 and reigned until 1820. George III was born in England. He wanted to regain some of the king's powers and tried to build up his following in Parliament. But after the Revolutionary War in America broke out in 1775, Parliament began to lose faith in the king's policies. A sickness that made George appear to be mentally ill further weakened his influence. Since George's reign, no monarch has had such a direct role in the activities of the British government.

The growing empire. In the late 1600's, England and France had begun to challenge each other for commercial and colonial control of North America. Troops, traders, and settlers of both nations battled in the New World. British and French trading companies also competed for control in India. In Europe, Britain had fought France in a series of wars. But none of these conflicts had settled the rivalry between the two countries. Another war was inevitable.

The Seven Years' War began in Europe in 1756. It had already begun in North America in 1754, when British and French troops clashed. In America, the war was called the French and Indian War. In Europe, Britain and its ally, Prussia, fought France and its allies, Austria and Russia. Prussia did most of the fighting in Europe, while Britain battled France in North America and India. The war ended in 1763 in a brilliant triumph for Britain. France lost almost all its territories in North America and India. Britain won Canada and all French possessions east of the Mississippi River.

The Revolutionary War in America cost Britain the most valuable part of its empire—the American Colonies. One of the war's main causes was taxation. The colonists insisted that Britain had no right to tax them without their consent. King George III and his Tory advisers disagreed. Britain sent troops to support its authority, and the colonists met force with force. As the war dragged on, Parliament increasingly urged George to give up. The king refused. He feared that if Britain lost the colonies, it would become a second-rate power.

Britain did lose the war, and in 1783 it recognized the independence of the American Colonies. But Britain did not become a second-rate power. It soon had a more prosperous trade with the independent United States than it ever had with the American Colonies.

The Industrial Revolution began in Britain in the 1700's. It made Britain the world's richest country. The revolution started in the cotton textile industry and spread to mining, transportation, and other fields. Before the revolution, people had worked at home, spinning cotton into yarn and weaving the yarn into cloth. Machines gradually replaced hand labor, and the factory system developed. At first, water wheels and horses on treadmills powered the machines. By the late 1700's, steam engines provided much of the power. Steam engines needed coal, and coal mining expanded to meet the demand. Coal was also needed to smelt iron ore. Factory towns sprang up around the coal fields. Better transportation was needed, and an era of road and canal building began. In the early 1800's, steam railways started operating.

The Industrial Revolution was one part of a general economic revolution that swept over Britain. Agriculture improved as small farms were combined into larger units and scientific farming methods were introduced. The industrial and agricultural improvements, in turn, stimulated trade. The need for larger amounts of cash led to the growth of banks and joint-stock companies, businesses owned in shares by stockholders.

Important dates in the United Kingdom

1707 The Act of Union united England and Wales with Scotland.

1756-1763 As a result of the Seven Years' War, Britain won control of France's North American empire.

1775-1783 Britain lost its American Colonies in the Revolutionary War in America.

1793-1815 Britain defeated France in the Napoleonic Wars.

1801 The kingdoms of Ireland and Great Britain joined to form the United Kingdom of Great Britain and Ireland (U.K.).

1832 The first Reform Act gave most men of the middle class the right to vote.

1837-1901 Under Queen Victoria, the U.K. became the world's richest country, and the British Empire reached its height.

1914-1918 The United Kingdom and the other Allies defeated Germany and the other Central Powers in World War I.

1931 The Commonwealth of Nations was established.

1939-1945 The United Kingdom and the other Allies defeated Germany, Italy, and Japan in World War II.

1947-1949 India, Pakistan, and Ceylon (now Sri Lanka) became independent members of the Commonwealth of Nations. Burma (now Myanmar) and the Republic of Ireland left the Commonwealth.

1973 The U.K. became a member of the European Community, an economic organization now part of the European Union.

1982 British forces defeated Argentine forces in battles for control of the Falkland Islands.

1991 British troops took part in the Persian Gulf War of 1991.

1994 A railroad tunnel opened under the English Channel between the United Kingdom and France.

1997 Scotland and Wales voted to set up their own legislatures.

1998 Peace talks on Northern Ireland ended in an agreement that included plans for a legislative assembly for Northern Ireland.

2001 The U.K. joined the United States and other countries in a worldwide campaign against terrorism. British troops took part in military strikes in Afghanistan led by the United States.

2003- British troops took part in the Iraq War.

The Napoleonic Wars. The French Revolution began in 1789. At first, many British approved the revolution as a triumph of liberty for the French people. But they changed their mind after the revolution grew more violent. Then the new French government seized Belgium and threatened the Netherlands. Britain protested. In 1793, Britain and France again went to war.

Britain feared a strong power in Europe. Its foreign policy was based on keeping the balance of power so that no European nation could control the others. To maintain this balance, Britain often aided weak countries and formed various alliances. By keeping the balance of power, Britain protected its own freedom, trade, and sea power. In addition, Britain's rulers—like those of other European countries—feared the democratic ideas of the French revolutionaries.

Beginning in 1799, Napoleon Bonaparte, a man of endless ambitions, led the French. At the height of his glory in 1812, Napoleon controlled most of Europe. In 1803, he began a plan to invade Britain. But in 1805, Admiral Horatio Nelson of Britain won a great victory over the French and Spanish fleets at Trafalgar, off the southern coast of Spain. The Battle of Trafalgar crushed Napoleon's naval power and ended all his hopes of invading Britain. Napoleon next tried to defeat Britain by striking at its dependence on trade. He ordered all countries under his control to close their markets to Britain. Britain struck back with a naval blockade of France and its allies. But British interference with United States shipping brought on the War of 1812 between Britain and the United States. Napoleon was finally defeated in 1815 in the Battle of Waterloo.

Troubles with Ireland flared up during the Napoleonic Wars. The English had governed Ireland for centuries, but the Irish hated English rule. Most of the people in Ireland were Roman Catholics, and most of the English were Protestants. In 1798, the Irish rebelled. British leaders then decided to make Ireland part of Britain. The Act of Union, passed in 1800, ended Ireland's Parliament and created the United Kingdom of Great Britain and Ireland. The act became effective in 1801. But Catholic men, as well as women of any religion, could not serve in the British Parliament or hold

public offices. Catholic men won these rights in 1829. Women did not gain full political rights until 1928.

The era of reform. Social, economic, and political reform had been needed in Britain for many years. After the Napoleonic Wars, the people's demands for reform became so strong that Parliament had to act.

Britain's criminal laws badly needed reforming. People convicted of crimes were whipped or given other brutal public punishment. Dreadful conditions existed in prisons. About 200 offenses—even stealing a rabbit—were punishable by death. During the 1820's, many of these abuses were corrected.

In 1824, Parliament struck down the laws forbidding workers to form trade unions. In 1833, it passed the Factory Act. This act provided that no child under 9 years of age could work in a factory, and no one under 18 could work more than 12 hours a day.

But the most burning issue was for Parliament to reform itself. Great landowners controlled most seats in Parliament, and few citizens had the right to vote. Some members of Parliament represented districts that had few or no voters. On the other hand, many districts with large populations had little or no representation.

In 1830, the Whig Party came to power. The Whigs had promised parliamentary reform. In 1831, they introduced a reform bill in Parliament. The Tories fiercely opposed it. The struggle over the bill became so great that people rioted and revolution almost broke out. Parliament finally passed the bill, which became the Reform Act of 1832.

The Reform Act of 1832 redistributed the seats in the House of Commons. Property qualifications to vote were lowered, so that most men of the middle class received the right to vote. In addition, the act made the right to vote a matter of national law, rather than of local custom. Yet only about 15 percent of Britain's adult males could vote because the act ignored the working class.

The Victorian Age. In 1837, an 18-year-old woman named Victoria became queen. She reigned for 63 years, until 1901—the longest reign in British history. This period is called the Victorian Age. During this period, the British Empire reached its height. It included about a quarter of the world's land and about a quarter

The Mansell Collection

A British tea plantation in the 1870's in India showed how the British way of life spread throughout the British Empire. The empire reached its height during the reign of Queen Victoria, from 1837 to 1901. At its peak, the empire included about a fourth of the world's land and a fourth of the world's people.

of the world's people. Wealth poured into Britain from its colonies. British industry continued to expand, and the country was called the *workshop of the world*. Railways and canals covered Britain, and telephone and telegraph lines linked the big cities. Literature and science flourished.

Establishment of free trade. The Victorian Age began during hard times. Farmers had poor harvests, and a depression swept across Britain. Many people blamed their troubles on the Corn Laws, which taxed imports of grain (called *corn* in Britain). The taxes protected landowners by helping keep foreign grain out of Britain. But the taxes also raised the price of bread.

In 1841, Sir Robert Peel, a Tory, became prime minister. Like many other government leaders, Peel came to believe that restrictions on trade hurt the economy. He ended all export duties and ended or reduced import duties on hundreds of items. But the Corn Laws remained. Peel did not repeal these laws because many members of his party strongly favored them. Then, in 1845 and 1846, the potato crop failed in Ireland. In addition, the English had a bad wheat harvest. Peel felt he had to repeal the Corn Laws and let foreign wheat come into Britain. In 1846, he did so—and split his party and ended his career. But Britain prospered under free trade as never before.

Political confusion followed Peel's fall from power and lasted until about 1865. Tories who agreed with Peel's free trade policy were called *Peelites*. They refused to work with the members of their party who favored tariffs. The Whigs were also split into a liberal and a conservative group. During this period, many shifts in politics occurred. Finally, the Peelites joined the Whigs in forming a new party, the Liberal Party. Meanwhile, the Tory Party became known as the Conservative Party.

The outstanding statesman of the period was Viscount Palmerston. Palmerston served as foreign minister almost continuously from 1830 to 1851 and as home secretary from 1852 to 1855. He was prime minister from 1855 to 1858 and from 1859 to 1865. Palmerston cared mostly about defending Britain's colonies, stopping Russian expansion, and restoring good relations with France. During the 1830's, he supported Belgium in its revolt against the Netherlands. In the 1840's, he forced China to open its ports to British trade and acquired Hong Kong. From 1854 to 1856, he led Britain in the Crimean War against Russia.

Although Palmerston supported political reform in other countries, he promoted only minor reforms in Britain. In spite of his conflicting policies, he was very popular, which helped keep the political situation confused. After Palmerston's death in 1865, a strong two-party system was born with the battle between two political giants—William Gladstone, a Liberal, and Benjamin Disraeli, a Conservative.

Gladstone and Disraeli had much in common. Both came from wealthy families and were well educated, hard working, and courageous. They were also bitter rivals. Their brilliant debates in Parliament made them the centers of political storms. Gladstone and Disraeli alternated as prime minister from 1868 to 1885. Their rivalry began over the Reform Act of 1867.

In 1866, Gladstone introduced a reform bill to give more people the right to vote. His bill was defeated. Disraeli knew that a bill had to be passed because of public pressure. In 1867, he introduced his own bill, which Parliament passed. The Reform Act of 1867 nearly doubled the number of voters by giving the vote to many small farmers and city workers. Disraeli hoped the new voters would gratefully elect Conservatives in the next election. Instead, they voted overwhelmingly in 1868 for Liberals. Gladstone became prime minister.

Gladstone's first term, which lasted until 1874, brought some of the most liberal reforms of the 1800's. Under the Irish Church Act of 1869, the Irish no longer had to pay taxes to the Church of England, which had few Irish members. The Education Act of 1870 set up locally elected school boards, which could require children to attend school until the age of 13. In 1870, the civil service system was improved by making tests the basis for employment. Government officials could no longer simply give civil service jobs to friends or relatives. In 1872, the secret ballot was introduced. Gladstone angered various groups with each of these reforms and lost the election of 1874.

Disraeli then served as prime minister until 1880. British imperialism reached its height under Disraeli, who tried to extend Britain's control over its colonies and over other countries. In 1875, he bought a controlling interest in the Suez Canal from Egypt's ruler. In 1876, he declared Queen Victoria empress of India. At the Congress of Berlin in 1878, Disraeli helped block Russian expansion in the Balkans, a region in southeastern Europe, and he won Cyprus for Britain. British people of all classes watched proudly as Britain expanded its influence in China, the Middle East, and Africa.

Disraeli also desired social reforms to help the working class. But his party, which included many wealthy people, supported only minor reforms. In the election campaign of 1880, Gladstone attacked Disraeli's imperialistic policies. The election brought the Liberals—and Gladstone—back to power. Disraeli died the next year.

Gladstone's second term as prime minister lasted until 1885. It produced the Reform Act of 1884, which gave the vote to almost all adult males. Gladstone served twice more as prime minister—in 1886 and from 1892 to 1894. He shattered his party and went down to defeat during his third and fourth terms because he supported more *home rule* (self-government) for Ireland. The Irish question split the Liberal Party into *Gladstonian Liberals,* who supported home rule, and *Liberal Unionists,* who opposed it. The Unionists later combined forces with the Conservatives.

At the turn of the century, Britain fought the Anglo-Boer War of 1899-1902 in South Africa. The war was costly, and general worldwide reaction against it left Britain isolated. The nation had followed a foreign policy of *splendid isolation.* But with the rise of Germany in the late 1800's, Britain began to feel that it needed allies. In 1902, it made an alliance with Japan. In 1904, Britain signed a treaty of friendship, the *Entente Cordiale,* with France. This agreement became the *Triple Entente* in 1907, when Russia joined.

In 1906, the Liberal Party won a great election victory. The Liberals then put through a sweeping reform program to aid the working class. In 1909, the Liberals introduced a budget calling for sharply increased taxes. The House of Lords rejected the budget. A political struggle followed over the veto power of the Lords. The struggle ended in 1911, when the Lords agreed to a bill that allowed them to delay—but not to veto—bills passed by the House of Commons.

World War I began in 1914. The Allies—Britain, France, the United States, and other countries—fought the Central Powers—Germany, Austria-Hungary, the Ottoman Empire, and Bulgaria. The war was caused chiefly by political and economic rivalry among the various nations. Part of this rivalry was between Britain and Germany. German industry was growing rapidly, and Germany also had built a powerful navy.

Britain entered the war on Aug. 4, 1914, after German troops invaded neutral Belgium on their way to attack France. The fighting lasted until 1918, when the Allies finally defeated Germany.

David Lloyd George, a Liberal, served as prime minister during the second half of the war. He helped write the Treaty of Versailles, which officially ended the war with Germany. The treaty set up the League of Nations, a forerunner of the United Nations, and gave Britain control over German colonies in Africa. The Treaty of Sèvres, signed with the Ottoman Empire, gave Britain control over some of the Ottomans' possessions in the Middle East.

The war had a shattering effect on Britain. About 750,000 members of the British armed forces died. German submarines sank almost 8 million short tons (7 million metric tons) of British shipping. The war also created severe economic problems for Britain and shook its position as a world power.

Postwar problems. British industry thrived briefly after World War I, but the prosperous times ended in 1920. During the war, Britain's factories produced war goods, and the country lost some of its markets to competitors. Two of Britain's best customers before the war—Germany and Russia—could not afford its goods after the war. In addition, the United States and Japan had taken much of its export business. With the decline in foreign trade, a depression swept Britain.

Meanwhile, the Irish question had become explosive. In 1919, Irish leaders declared Ireland independent. Bitter fighting followed between the Irish rebels and a special British police force called the Black and Tans. In 1921, southern Ireland agreed to become a British *dominion.* That is, it would be a self-governing member of the British Empire, while maintaining its allegiance to the Crown. The new dominion was called the Irish Free State. Most of the people of northern Ireland were Protestants, and they did not want to be part of the Roman Catholic Irish Free State. Northern Ireland remained in the United Kingdom, which was renamed the United Kingdom of Great Britain and Northern Ireland.

The rise of the Labour Party. In January 1924, a new party, the Labour Party, came to power under James Ramsay MacDonald. The party represented socialist groups and trade unions. It began to develop in the late 1800's and gathered strength through the years. While the Labour Party grew stronger, the Liberal Party declined. Many voters could see little difference between Conservatives and Liberals. They saw the Labour Party, with its socialist aims, as an alternative to the Conservative Party. The Labour Party held office only until November 1924. It lacked a majority in the House of Commons and needed the Liberal Party's support. The Liberals soon withdrew their support. The Conservatives, under Stanley Baldwin, then held control of the government until 1929.

In the 1929 elections, the Labour Party became the largest party for the first time. MacDonald returned as prime minister. A few months later, the worldwide Great Depression began. In 1931, MacDonald formed a government of Labour, Conservative, and Liberal leaders to deal with the emergency. The government raised taxes, abandoned free trade, and cut its own spending. But by 1932, about 3 million British workers had no job.

"Peace in our time." In 1933, in the depth of the Great Depression, Adolf Hitler and his Nazi Party won control of Germany. Germany began to rearm, but few leaders in Britain, or elsewhere, saw the danger.

Meantime, Britain faced an unusual problem at home. King George V died in 1936, and his oldest son became King Edward VIII. Edward wanted to marry an American divorcée, Wallis Warfield Simpson. The government, the Church of England, and many British people objected. Edward then gave up the throne to marry "the woman I love." His brother became king as George VI.

Neville Chamberlain, a Conservative, became prime minister in 1937. In 1938, Hitler seized Austria and then demanded part of Czechoslovakia. Chamberlain and Premier Édouard Daladier of France flew to Munich, Germany, to confer with Hitler. They gave in to Hitler's demands after the German dictator said he would seek no more territory. Chamberlain returned to Britain and said: "I believe it is peace in our time." But he met sharp attacks in the House of Commons. Winston Churchill, a Conservative, called the Munich Agreement "a disaster of the first magnitude."

World War II. In March 1939, Germany seized the rest of Czechoslovakia. On September 1, Germany invaded Poland and World War II began. Two days later, Britain and France declared war on Germany. In April 1940, German troops invaded Denmark and Norway. Chamberlain resigned on May 10, and Churchill became prime minister. That same day, Germany attacked Belgium, Luxembourg, and the Netherlands and advanced toward France.

Churchill told the British people he had nothing to offer but "blood, toil, tears, and sweat" to win "victory at all costs." Germany conquered France in June, and Britain stood alone against the Nazi war machine.

Britain prepared for invasion, and Churchill urged the British people to make this "their finest hour." He inspired them to heights of courage, unity, and sacrifice. Hundreds of German planes bombed Britain nightly. German submarines tried to cut Britain's lifeline by torpedoing ships bringing food and other supplies to the island country. Severe rationing limited each person's share of food, clothing, coal, and oil. The British refused to be beaten, and Hitler gave up his invasion plans.

In June 1941, Germany invaded the Soviet Union. In December, Japan attacked Pearl Harbor, in Hawaii, and the United States entered the war. Britain, the United States, the Soviet Union, and the other Allies finally defeated Germany and Japan in 1945. Near the end of the war, Britain helped establish the United Nations.

About 360,000 British servicemen, servicewomen, and civilians died in the war. Great sections of London and other cities had been destroyed by German bombs. The war had shattered the United Kingdom's economy. The United States and the Soviet Union came out of the war as the world's most powerful nations.

The welfare state. The Labour Party won a landslide victory in 1945. The party had campaigned on a socialistic program. Clement Attlee became prime minister, and the Labour Party stayed in power until 1951. During those six years, the United Kingdom became a *welfare state.* Its social security system was expanded to provide welfare for the people "from the cradle to the grave." The Labour government also *nationalized* key industries by putting them under public control. The nationalized industries included the Bank of England, the coal mines, the iron and steel industry, railways, and trucking.

Although the Labour government struggled to restore the economy, conditions improved little. Rationing and other wartime controls continued. The United Kingdom borrowed heavily from the United States.

Decline of the empire. World War II sealed the fate of the British Empire, though the United Kingdom had begun loosening control over its empire earlier. In 1931, the United Kingdom granted independence within the empire to Australia, Canada, the Irish Free State, New Zealand, Newfoundland, and South Africa. They became the first members of the Commonwealth of Nations, an association of countries and dependencies (now called overseas territories) that succeeded the empire.

After World War II, the peoples of Africa and Asia increased their demands for independence. The United Kingdom could no longer keep control of its colonies. In 1947, India and Pakistan became independent nations within the Commonwealth. In 1948, Ceylon (now Sri Lanka) became an independent Commonwealth country. That same year, Burma (now Myanmar) achieved independence—and left the Commonwealth. In 1949, the Irish Free State declared itself the independent Republic of Ireland and also left the Commonwealth. That same year, Newfoundland became a province of Canada. South Africa left the Commonwealth from 1961 to 1994 because the United Kingdom had criticized its racial policies. Blacks made up a majority of the population in South Africa, but whites controlled the government. Also, the South African government had an official policy of racial segregation called *apartheid.* South Africa rejoined the Commonwealth when it ended its apartheid and gave blacks greater voice in the government.

Since the early 1950's, many more British possessions have become independent nations. They include Brunei, Cyprus, Ghana, Kenya, Malaysia, Malta, Nigeria, Papua New Guinea, Solomon Islands, Sudan, Trinidad and Tobago, and Uganda. In 1965, Rhodesia (now Zimbabwe) declared its independence from the United Kingdom. There, as in South Africa, whites controlled the government even though blacks made up a majority of the population. The United Kingdom had refused to grant Rhodesia independence until blacks were given a greater voice in the government. In 1980, after a long struggle for more power, blacks gained control of the government, and the United Kingdom recognized Rhodesia's independence. Rhodesia's name was changed to Zimbabwe. Generally, the British Empire was disbanded in an orderly way. Most independent countries stayed in the Commonwealth.

European unity. While the British Empire was breaking up during the postwar years, other European nations united in economic and political organizations. The United Kingdom was reluctant to join them. Throughout history, the United Kingdom had preferred to stay out of European affairs—except to keep the balance of power in Europe. By joining the new organizations, the United Kingdom feared it might lose some of its independ-

The British Empire The British colonial empire spanned two eras. England held the American Colonies from the early 1600's until the 1770's. The other great colonial expansion was in the 1800's and the early 1900's. The map also shows those areas that are overseas territories of the United Kingdom today.

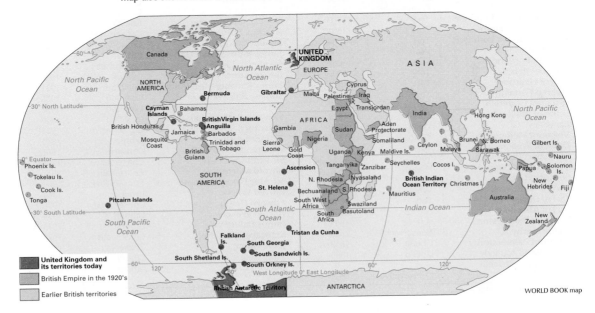

WORLD BOOK map

ence and felt it would also be turning its back on the Commonwealth. In the 1950's, the United Kingdom refused to join the European Coal and Steel Community and the European Atomic Energy Community (Euratom). Most important, it did not join the European Economic Community (EEC). This association, sometimes called the European Common Market, was set up by France and five other nations. After the EEC showed signs of succeeding, the United Kingdom set up the European Free Trade Association (EFTA) with six other nations. But EFTA was only a mild success, and the United Kingdom later regretted its refusal to join the EEC.

After World War II, the United Kingdom's foreign policy was closely allied with the United States. The United Kingdom joined the North Atlantic Treaty Organization—a defense alliance of European and North American nations—and fought in the Korean War (1950-1953).

In July 1956, Egypt nationalized the Suez Canal, which was owned mainly by the British and French. In October, Israel invaded Egypt, its enemy. The United Kingdom and France then attacked Egypt in an attempt to retake the canal. Pressure from the United States, the Soviet Union, and the United Nations forced the United Kingdom, France, and Israel to withdraw from Egypt.

Economic recovery—and collapse. A Conservative government had returned to power in 1951 under Win-

British monarchs*

House of Stuart		House of Saxe-Coburg-Gotha	
Anne	1702-1714	Edward VII	1901-1910
House of Hanover		George V	1910-1917
George I	1714-1727	**House of Windsor†**	
George II	1727-1760		
George III	1760-1820	George V	1917-1936
George IV	1820-1830	Edward VIII	1936
William IV	1830-1837	George VI	1936-1952
Victoria	1837-1901	Elizabeth II	1952-

*For the rulers of England before 1702, see **England** (table).
†Changed from House of Saxe-Coburg and Gotha during World War I.
Each monarch has a biography in *World Book*.

ston Churchill. The Conservatives accepted most of the changes the Labour Party had made. By 1955, rationing and most other wartime controls had ended. Industry was thriving, jobs were plentiful, and wages were good. Churchill retired in 1955, and Sir Anthony Eden succeeded him as prime minister. Eden resigned in 1957. He had been greatly criticized for his decision that the United Kingdom join France in trying to seize the Suez Canal in 1956. Harold Macmillan succeeded Eden.

The British economy continued to expand until the early 1960's. Hoping to improve the economy, the United Kingdom applied for membership in the EEC. By joining the EEC, Macmillan hoped that the United Kingdom

British prime ministers

Name	Party	Took office		Name	Party	Took office
* Sir Robert Walpole	Whig	1721		* Benjamin Disraeli	Conservative	1868
Earl of Wilmington	Whig	1742		* W. E. Gladstone	Liberal	1868
Henry Pelham	Whig	1743		* Benjamin Disraeli	Conservative	1874
Duke of Newcastle	Whig	1754		* W. E. Gladstone	Liberal	1880
Duke of Devonshire	Whig	1756		* Marquess of Salisbury	Conservative	1885
Duke of Newcastle	Whig	1757		* W. E. Gladstone	Liberal	1886
Earl of Bute	Tory	1762		* Marquess of Salisbury	Conservative	1886
George Grenville	Whig	1763		* W. E. Gladstone	Liberal	1892
Marquess of Rockingham	Whig	1765		Earl of Rosebery	Liberal	1894
* William Pitt, Earl of Chatham	Whig	1766		* Marquess of Salisbury	Conservative	1895
Duke of Grafton	Whig	1768		* A. J. Balfour	Conservative	1902
* Lord North	Tory	1770		* Sir Henry	Liberal	1905
Marquess of Rockingham	Whig	1782		Campbell-Bannerman		
Earl of Shelburne	Whig	1782		* H. H. Asquith	Liberal	1908
Duke of Portland	Coalition	1783		* H. H. Asquith	Coalition	1915
* William Pitt, the Younger	Tory	1783		* David Lloyd George	Coalition	1916
Henry Addington	Tory	1801		* Andrew Bonar Law	Conservative	1922
* William Pitt, the Younger	Tory	1804		* Stanley Baldwin	Conservative	1923
Lord Grenville	Whig	1806		* James Ramsay MacDonald	Labour	1924
Duke of Portland	Tory	1807		* Stanley Baldwin	Conservative	1924
Spencer Perceval	Tory	1809		* James Ramsay MacDonald	Labour	1929
Earl of Liverpool	Tory	1812		* James Ramsay MacDonald	Coalition	1931
George Canning	Tory	1827		* Stanley Baldwin	Coalition	1935
Viscount Goderich	Tory	1827		* Neville Chamberlain	Coalition	1937
* Duke of Wellington	Tory	1828		* Winston S. Churchill	Coalition	1940
Earl Grey	Whig	1830		* Winston S. Churchill	Conservative	1945
Viscount Melbourne	Whig	1834		* Clement Attlee	Labour	1945
* Duke of Wellington	Tory	1834		* Winston S. Churchill	Conservative	1951
* Sir Robert Peel	Tory	1834		* Sir Anthony Eden	Conservative	1955
Viscount Melbourne	Whig	1835		* Harold Macmillan	Conservative	1957
* Sir Robert Peel	Tory	1841		* Sir Alec Douglas-Home	Conservative	1963
* Lord John Russell	Whig	1846		* Harold Wilson	Labour	1964
Earl of Derby	Tory	1852		* Edward Heath	Conservative	1970
Earl of Aberdeen	Peelite	1852		* Harold Wilson	Labour	1974
* Viscount Palmerston	Liberal	1855		* James Callaghan	Labour	1976
Earl of Derby	Conservative	1858		* Margaret Thatcher	Conservative	1979
* Viscount Palmerston	Liberal	1859		* John Major	Conservative	1990
* Earl Russell (formerly Lord John Russell)	Liberal	1865		* Tony Blair	Labour	1997
Earl of Derby	Conservative	1866		* Gordon Brown	Labour	2007

*Has a separate biography in *World Book*.

would be able to expand its export trade. But in January 1963, Britain's application was rejected, largely because of opposition from French President Charles de Gaulle. The rejection was a defeat for Macmillan. That year, the government was shaken by a scandal involving the secretary for war, John Profumo. The 1964 election brought the Labour Party back to power under Harold Wilson.

Wilson faced mounting economic problems. Britain was importing far more goods than it was exporting, and its industrial growth rate was too slow. Britain's financial reserves shrank, and the nation had to borrow more and more money from other countries and international agencies. In 1966, the government began an *austerity* program by raising taxes and putting a ceiling on wages and prices. The EEC, the European Coal and Steel Community, and Euratom merged their executive agencies in 1967 and became known as the European Community (EC). That year, Britain was again rejected for membership in the EC. The government devalued the pound in response to the serious economic situation.

In the 1970 elections, the Conservative Party regained control of the government. Edward Heath became prime minister. In 1971, agreement was reached on terms for Britain's entry into the EC. Britain joined the EC in 1973. But continuing inflation, fuel shortages, strikes, and other matters caused serious problems for the government. Elections in 1974 brought the Labour Party back to power, and Harold Wilson again became prime minister. Wilson retired in 1976. James Callaghan succeeded him as prime minister and Labour Party leader.

Long-standing conflicts between Catholics and Protestants in Northern Ireland became a serious problem for Britain during the late 1960's and the 1970's. In 1969, Britain began sending troops to Northern Ireland to try to stop riots there. But the violence continued. The unstable situation caused a series of political crises in Northern Ireland during the 1970's. Britain established direct rule over the region, while attempts were made to form a stable government in which Catholics and Protestants shared power.

Many people in Scotland and some in Wales demanded complete independence from Britain. Many others believed Scotland and Wales should have their own legislatures. Still others favored no changes in the relations between Scotland and Wales and the rest of the United Kingdom. In 1979, the British government allowed the people of Scotland and Wales to vote on the question of whether they should have their own legislatures. The voters in both areas failed to approve the establishment of the legislatures.

Thatcher. Elections in 1979 returned the Conservatives to power. Conservative Party leader Margaret Thatcher replaced Callaghan as prime minister. She became the first woman ever to hold the office. She served as prime minister for the next $11\frac{1}{2}$ years, longer than any other person in the 1900's.

As prime minister, Thatcher worked to reduce government involvement in the economy. For example, the government sold its interests in many industries to private citizens and businesses. It also sold thousands of public-housing units to their tenants, promoting home ownership. In addition, direct taxes were reduced.

In 1982, Thatcher won praise for her decisive handling of a conflict with Argentina. Since 1833, Britain has ruled the Falkland Islands, which lie about 320 miles (515 kilometers) east of the southern coast of Argentina. But Argentina has long claimed ownership of the islands. In April 1982, Argentine troops invaded and occupied the Falklands. The United Kingdom then sent troops, ships, and planes. British and Argentine forces fought air, sea, and land battles for control of the islands. The Argentine forces surrendered to the United Kingdom in June 1982.

In 1985, Thatcher and Prime Minister Garret FitzGerald of Ireland signed the Anglo-Irish Agreement, an agreement that established an advisory conference for Northern Ireland. The conference, consisting of officials of the United Kingdom and Ireland, gave Ireland an advisory role in Northern Ireland's government.

By the mid-1980's, the United Kingdom's productivity had improved, but unemployment, inflation, and other economic problems continued. During the late 1980's, unemployment declined, but inflation began to rise. Roads, hospitals, and schools were deteriorating through lack of public investment. The number of homeless people was increasing. In 1990, the economy entered a recession. Unemployment rose.

Thatcher resigned as Conservative Party leader and prime minister in 1990. She had been under growing pressure from her own party to do so. Her party was divided over two issues—Thatcher's reluctance to seek further economic and political union with the European Community and her support of a new household tax.

John Major succeeded Thatcher as party leader and prime minister. He had been serving as chancellor of the exchequer, the United Kingdom's chief financial officer. As prime minister, Major abandoned the household tax. He also sent British troops to fight as part of a U.S.-led coalition against Iraq in the Persian Gulf War of 1991.

In addition, Major negotiated with the European Community for closer union. In 1993, the United Kingdom and the other EC countries formed the European Union (EU) to increase their economic and political cooperation. Many people accused Major of failing to protect British interests as he sought closer ties with the EU. Disagreements over the EU caused divisions within the Conservative Party and weakened Major's government.

© Bassignac/Deville/Gaillard from Gamma/Liaison

French and British tunnel workers met beneath the English Channel in 1990, three years after construction of the railroad tunnel began. The tunnel opened in 1994.

However, gradual economic growth continued during the middle and late 1990's. Recovery from the economic recession had begun in mid-1992.

Political changes. In 1997 elections, the Labour Party defeated the Conservatives by a landslide. Labour leader Tony Blair became prime minister. He called for referendums to be held in Scotland and Wales to allow these areas to vote on whether or not they wanted their own legislatures. In September 1997, Scotland and Wales approved the plans. Also in September 1997, the first negotiations began that included all parties involved in the Northern Ireland conflict. The talks concluded in an agreement in April 1998. The agreement was put to referendums in Northern Ireland and Ireland, and the voters supported it.

The agreement committed all parties to using peaceful means to resolve political differences. It called for the creation of three bodies: (1) a legislative assembly for Northern Ireland, (2) a North-South Ministerial Council with representatives from Northern Ireland and Ireland, and (3) a British-Irish Council that would include representatives from the Irish parliament as well as the various legislative assemblies of the United Kingdom. After several months of negotiations, full implementation of the agreement began at the end of 1999.

Also in 1999, elections were held in Scotland for members of the new Scottish parliament, and in Wales for members of the new Welsh assembly. Both legislative bodies convened shortly after the elections.

Recent developments. In elections in 2001, the Labour Party again won control of the government. Blair retained his seat as prime minister.

On Sept. 11, 2001, after the elections, many British citizens died with thousands of other people in terrorist attacks in the United States. In response, the United States, the United Kingdom, and many other countries launched a campaign against terrorism. The campaign included military strikes in Afghanistan, the country that served as a base for the terrorist group suspected of carrying out the attacks. Blair played a key role in building international support for the campaign.

The Northern Ireland peace plan brought some stability to Northern Ireland in the early 2000's. The plan called for the disarmament of the Irish Republican Army (IRA), which had sought to unite Northern Ireland with Ireland. Disagreements over IRA disarmament and other matters led the United Kingdom to suspend the power-sharing government several times.

A coalition led by the United States attacked Iraq in March 2003, launching the Iraq War. Blair supported the U.S action despite strong public opposition at home to the war. The United Kingdom sent tens of thousands of troops to the region to take part in the fighting. For more information, see **Iraq War.**

In elections in May 2005, the Labour Party again won control of the government. Blair continued as prime minister.

Terrorist bombs exploded on three subway trains and a bus on July 7, 2005, in London, killing more than 50 people and injuring about 700. An official investigation determined that four suicide bombers with ties to radical Islamists had carried out the attacks.

On July 28, the IRA announced that it would stop using violence to achieve its goal of a united Ireland. In

AP/Wide World

Supporters greet Tony Blair after he first became prime minister. In May 1997 elections, Blair's Labour Party defeated the Conservatives by a landslide. Behind Blair is his wife, Cherie.

response, the United Kingdom began to reduce the number of troops it had stationed in Northern Ireland. In 2007, a new power-sharing government began in Northern Ireland.

Blair resigned as prime minister in June 2007. Gordon Brown was named to replace him as prime minister and Labour Party leader.

Peter R. Mounfield, Anthony Sutcliffe, and Brendan O'Leary

Related articles in *World Book.* See England; Northern Ireland; Scotland; and Wales and their lists of *Related articles.* See also the following articles:

Monarchs

See the table *British monarchs* with this article.

Prime ministers

See the table *British prime ministers* with this article.

Other political leaders

Astor, Lady	Fox, Charles James
Beaverbrook, Lord	Grey, Earl
Bondfield, Margaret Grace	Hastings, Warren
Bryce, James	Heseltine, Michael R. D.
Burke, Edmund	Kinnock, Neil Gordon
Castlereagh, Viscount	Philip, Prince
Charles, Prince	Pitt, William
Clive, Robert	Webb, Sidney and Beatrice
Cobden, Richard	Wilberforce, William

Military leaders

Alexander of Tunis, Earl	Kitchener, Horatio H.
Allenby, Lord	Lawrence, T. E.
Carleton, Sir Guy	Montgomery, Bernard L.
Cornwallis, Charles	Mountbatten, Louis
Gordon, Charles G.	Nelson, Horatio
Haig, Douglas	Simcoe, John Graves
Howe, Richard	Wellington, Duke of
Howe, William	Wolfe, James
Jellicoe, John R.	

Government

Cabinet	Nobility
Conservative Party	Order in Council
Constitution	Parliament
House of Commons	Privy Council
House of Lords	Royal Household of the
Labour Party	United Kingdom
Magna Carta	White paper
Ministry	

History

Anglo-Boer Wars
Balaklava, Battle of
Balfour
  Declaration
Bering Sea
  controversy
Black Hole of
  Calcutta
Chartism
Cold War
Colonialism
Corn Laws
Crimean War
Fabian Society

French and Indian
  wars
French Revolution
Ghent, Treaty of
Great Depression
  (Effects in
  Europe)
Great Irish Famine
Indian Rebellion
Industrial
  Revolution
Ireland (History)
Korean War

League of Nations
Louisbourg
Revolutionary War
  in America
Seven Years' War
Succession wars
Suez Canal
Tory Party
Trafalgar, Battle of
War of 1812
Waterloo, Battle of
World War I
World War II

Treaties and agreements

Berlin, Congress of
Clayton-Bulwer Treaty
Colombo Plan
Europe, Council of
European Union
Ghent, Treaty of
Hay-Pauncefote Treaty
Jay Treaty
Locarno Conference
London, Treaties of
Munich Agreement

North Atlantic Treaty
  Organization
Sèvres, Treaty of
Southeast Asia Treaty Organi-
  zation
Versailles, Treaty of
Vienna, Congress of
Washington, Treaty of
Webster-Ashburton
  Treaty
Western European Union

Other related articles

Air force (The
  British air force;
  World War II)
Army (The British
  Army)
Bank of England
BP
British America
British Broadcast-
  ing Corporation
British-Irish Coun-
  cil
British Isles
British Museum
Channel Tunnel
Clothing (pictures)

Commonwealth of
  Nations
Cricket
Crown
Diana, Princess of
  Wales
English Channel
English language
English literature
Falkland Islands
Flag (picture: His-
  torical flags of
  the world)
Furniture
Gaelic language
God Save the
  Queen

Great Britain
John Bull
Lloyd's
Medicine (The
  United
  Kingdom)
Navy (Major
  navies of the
  world)
North-South Min-
  isterial Council
Postal services
  (The creation of
  the Penny Post)
Victoria Day
Wellcome Trust
William, Prince

Outline

I. **Government**
  A. National government
  B. Regional government
  C. Local government
  D. Politics
  E. Courts
  F. Armed forces
II. **People**
  A. Population
  B. Ancestry
  C. Language
III. **Way of life**
  A. City life
  B. Rural life
  C. Food and drink
  D. Recreation
  E. Religion
  F. Education
  G. Museums and libraries
  H. The arts
IV. **The land**
  A. The Scottish Highlands
  B. The Central Lowlands
  C. The Southern Uplands
  D. The Pennines
  E. Wales
  F. The Southwest Peninsula
  G. The English Lowlands
  H. Northern Ireland
  I. Rivers and lakes
V. **Climate**
VI. **Economy**
  A. Service industries
  B. Manufacturing
  C. Agriculture
  D. Mining
  E. Fishing
  F. Energy sources
  G. International trade
  H. Transportation
  I. Communication
VII. **History**

Questions

What are the four political divisions of the United Kingdom?
What is by far the most popular spectator sport in the United Kingdom?
Why does the United Kingdom have a mild climate, even though it lies as far north as Labrador?
What is Her (or His) Majesty's Opposition?
How large was the British Empire at its height?
Why is the British Parliament called the *Mother of Parliaments?*
Who inspired the British people to courage, unity, and sacrifice during World War II?
What is the largest lake in the United Kingdom?
In which British industry did the Industrial Revolution begin?
Who was the first woman to hold the office of prime minister of the United Kingdom?

Additional resources

Baedeker's Great Britain. 4th ed. Automobile Assn., 2000.
Cannon, John A., ed. *The Oxford Companion to British History.* Oxford, 1997.
Encyclopedia of Britain. Helicon, 1999.
Innes, Brian. *United Kingdom.* Raintree Steck-Vaughn, 2002. Younger readers.
Leapman, Michael, and others. *Portrait of Britain.* D K Pub., 1999.
Office for National Statistics. *Britain: The Official Yearbook of the United Kingdom.* Her Majesty's Stationery Office, published annually.

United Methodist Church is the largest Methodist denomination in the United States. It was formed in 1968 through a union of the Methodist Church and the Evangelical United Brethren Church. The church has approximately 10 million members, with about 8 million living in the United States. The denomination has about 36,000 churches. It supports 13 seminaries and more than 100 colleges and universities. It has more than 2,000 mission workers in over 60 countries. The church has 49 bishops supervising administration in the United States.

The United Methodist Church takes an active stand on social, economic, and political issues. It works for world peace, justice for all, and an end to all discrimination. Only the church's General Conference has the authority to speak for it. The General Conference consists of about 1,000 delegates and meets every four years.

Critically reviewed by the United Methodist Church

See also **Methodists.**

United Mine Workers of America (UMW) is an industrial trade union that represents workers in many of the coal mines and coal-processing industries of the United States. It also has local unions in Canada.

The UMW was organized in Columbus, Ohio, in 1890. It belonged to the American Federation of Labor (AFL) until 1936. The UMW helped form the Congress of Industrial Organizations (CIO) in 1935 but withdrew in 1942. It reaffiliated with the AFL in 1946 but withdrew again in 1947. The UMW remained independent until 1989. Then it joined the AFL-CIO, which had been formed by the merging of the AFL and the CIO in 1955.

The UMW won fame under John Mitchell in the early 1900's. John L. Lewis served as union president from 1919 until 1960. Under Lewis, the union experienced its greatest growth and obtained many benefits for its members. The UMW has headquarters in Washington, D.C.

Critically reviewed by the United Mine Workers of America

See also **Coal** (Mineworkers); **Labor movement** (table: Important U.S. labor unions); **Lewis, John L.; Roosevelt, Theodore** (Friend of labor); **West Virginia** (Labor developments).

United Nations Headquarters consists of several buildings along the East River in New York City. The tall Secretariat Building, *center,* has become a well-known symbol of the UN. Other UN buildings include the General Assembly Building, *left,* and the Dag Hammarskjöld Library, *right.*

United Nations

United Nations (UN) is an organization of nations that works for world peace and security and the betterment of humanity. Almost all of the world's independent countries belong to the UN. Each member nation sends representatives to UN Headquarters in New York City, where they discuss and try to solve problems.

The United Nations has two main goals: peace and human dignity. If fighting between two or more countries breaks out anywhere, the UN may be asked to try to stop it. After the fighting stops, the UN may help work out ways to keep it from starting again. But the UN tries above all to deal with problems and disputes before they lead to fighting. It seeks the causes of war and tries to find ways to eliminate them.

The United Nations has met with both success and failure in its work. It has been able to keep some disputes from developing into major wars. The organization has also helped people in numerous parts of the world gain their freedom and better their way of life. The UN works to defend human rights and to provide

Richard E. Rupp, the contributor of this article, is Associate Professor of Political Science at Purdue University Calumet. The photographs in the article are used through the courtesy of the United Nations unless otherwise credited.

aid for countries or groups of people in need around the world. For many years, however, disagreements among UN member nations prevented the organization from operating effectively. Since the mid-1980's, greater cooperation among members has enabled the UN to attempt missions in more and more countries. But these missions have added to the UN's financial troubles.

The United Nations was established on Oct. 24, 1945, shortly after World War II. As the war drew to an end, the nations that opposed Germany, Italy, and Japan decided that such a war must never happen again. Representatives of these nations met in San Francisco in April 1945 and worked out a plan for an organization to help keep world peace. This plan was described in a document called the Charter of the United Nations. In June 1945, 50 nations signed it. They were the first UN members. Since then, over 140 other nations have joined.

In some ways, the UN resembles the League of Nations, which was organized after World War I (see **League of Nations**). Many of the nations that founded the UN had also founded the League. Like the League, the UN was established to help keep peace between nations. The main organs of the UN are much like those of the League. But the UN differs from the League in two main ways. First, all the great military powers except Communist China were UN members from the beginning, and Communist China gained membership in 1971. By contrast, several powerful countries, including the United States, either did not join the League or withdrew from it. Second, the UN's concern with economic and social problems gives it broader responsibilities than the League had.

The six major organs of the United Nations carry on the work of the organization. These organs are (1) General Assembly, (2) Security Council, (3) Secretariat, (4) Economic and Social Council, (5) International Court of Justice, and (6) Trusteeship Council. A variety of specialized agencies related to the UN deal with such problems as communications, food and agriculture, health, and labor.

UN Headquarters consist of several buildings along the East River in New York City. The three main build-

The United Nations flag has a map of the world surrounded by a wreath of olive branches. The branches symbolize peace.

Members of the United Nations

The UN has 192 members. In this table, charter members of the UN do not have dates after their names. Other nations are listed with the years they became UN members.

Afghanistan (1946)
Albania (1955)
Algeria (1962)
Andorra (1993)
Angola (1976)
Antigua and
    Barbuda (1981)
Argentina
Armenia (1992)
Australia
Austria (1955)
Azerbaijan (1992)
Bahamas (1973)
Bahrain (1971)
Bangladesh (1974)
Barbados (1966)
Belarus*
Belgium
Belize (1981)
Benin (1960)
Bhutan (1971)
Bolivia
Bosnia-Herzegovina (1992)
Botswana (1966)
Brazil
Brunei (1984)
Bulgaria (1955)
Burkina Faso (1960)
Burundi (1962)
Cambodia (1955)
Cameroon (1960)
Canada
Cape Verde (1975)
Central African Republic (1960)
Chad (1960)
Chile
China[†]
Colombia
Comoros (1975)
Congo (Brazzaville) (1960)
Congo (Kinshasa) (1960)
Costa Rica
Côte d'Ivoire (1960)
Croatia (1992)
Cuba
Cyprus (1960)
Czech Republic (1993)
Denmark
Djibouti (1977)

Dominica (1978)
Dominican Republic
East Timor (2002)
Ecuador
Egypt
El Salvador
Equatorial Guinea (1968)
Eritrea (1993)
Estonia (1991)
Ethiopia
Fiji (1970)
Finland (1955)
France
Gabon (1960)
Gambia (1965)
Georgia (1992)
Germany (1973)[‡]
Ghana (1957)
Greece
Grenada (1974)
Guatemala
Guinea (1958)
Guinea-Bissau (1974)
Guyana (1966)
Haiti
Honduras
Hungary (1955)
Iceland (1946)
India
Indonesia (1950)
Iran
Iraq
Ireland (1955)
Israel (1949)
Italy (1955)
Jamaica (1962)
Japan (1956)
Jordan (1955)
Kazakhstan (1992)
Kenya (1963)
Kiribati (1999)
Korea, North (1991)
Korea, South (1991)
Kuwait (1963)
Kyrgyzstan (1992)
Laos (1955)
Latvia (1991)
Lebanon
Lesotho (1966)

Liberia
Libya (1955)
Liechtenstein (1990)
Lithuania (1991)
Luxembourg
Macedonia (1993)[§]
Madagascar (1960)
Malawi (1964)
Malaysia (1957)
Maldives (1965)
Mali (1960)
Malta (1964)
Marshall Islands (1991)
Mauritania (1961)
Mauritius (1968)
Mexico
Micronesia, Federated
    States of (1991)
Moldova (1992)
Monaco (1993)
Mongolia (1961)
Montenegro (2006)[‡‡]
Morocco (1956)
Mozambique (1975)
Myanmar (1948)
Namibia (1990)
Nauru (1999)
Nepal (1955)
Netherlands
New Zealand
Nicaragua
Niger (1960)
Nigeria (1960)
Norway
Oman (1971)
Pakistan (1947)
Palau (1994)
Panama
Papua New Guinea (1975)
Paraguay
Peru
Philippines
Poland
Portugal (1955)
Qatar (1971)
Romania (1955)
Russia[#]
Rwanda (1962)
St. Kitts and Nevis (1983)

St. Lucia (1979)
St. Vincent and
    the Grenadines (1980)
Samoa (1976)
San Marino (1992)
São Tomé and Príncipe (1975)
Saudi Arabia
Senegal (1960)
Serbia[‡‡]
Seychelles (1976)
Sierra Leone (1961)
Singapore (1965)
Slovakia (1993)
Slovenia (1992)
Solomon Islands (1978)
Somalia (1960)
South Africa
Spain (1955)
Sri Lanka (1955)
Sudan (1956)
Suriname (1975)
Swaziland (1968)
Sweden (1946)
Switzerland (2002)
Syria
Tajikistan (1992)
Tanzania (1961)
Thailand (1946)
Togo (1960)
Tonga (1999)
Trinidad and Tobago (1962)
Tunisia (1956)
Turkey
Turkmenistan (1992)
Tuvalu (2000)
Uganda (1962)
Ukraine**
United Arab
    Emirates (1971)
United Kingdom (Britain)
United States
Uruguay
Uzbekistan (1992)
Vanuatu (1981)
Venezuela
Vietnam (1977)
Yemen (1990)[††]
Zambia (1964)
Zimbabwe (1980)

* Called the Byelorussian Soviet Socialist Republic until 1991.
† Nationalist China (Taiwan) held a seat in the UN until October 1971, when the General
   Assembly voted to expel Nationalist China and admit Communist China.
‡ East Germany and West Germany each held seats from 1973 until 1990, when German
   unification occurred.
§ Also called the Former Yugoslav Republic of Macedonia (FYROM).

Source: United Nations.

Assumed the seat of the Union of Soviet Socialist Republics (U.S.S.R.) when that country
   was dissolved in 1991. The U.S.S.R. was a charter member of the UN.
** Called the Ukrainian Soviet Socialist Republic until 1991.
†† In 1990, Yemen (Sanaa), which became a member in 1947, and Yemen (Aden), a member
   since 1967, merged to form Yemen.
‡‡ In 1992, Montenegro and Serbia formed a new, smaller Yugoslavia. The old Yugoslavia
   had been a UN charter member. In 2006, Serbia and Montenegro became independent
   countries. Serbia retained the existing seat. Montenegro gained separate membership.

ings are the General Assembly Building, the Secretariat Building, and the Conference Building. The flags of all the members fly in front of UN Headquarters.

The charter

The Charter of the United Nations is the constitution of the UN. It includes the plan used for organizing the UN and the rules by which the UN is governed. UN members agree to carry out the requirements of the charter. The charter has 19 chapters divided into 111 articles that explain the *purposes* (goals), *principles* (basic beliefs), and operating methods of the UN.

Purposes and principles. The charter lists four purposes and seven principles of the United Nations. The first purpose is to preserve world peace and security. The second purpose is to encourage nations to be just in their actions toward one another. The third is to help nations cooperate in trying to solve their problems. The fourth purpose is to serve as an agency through which nations can work toward these goals.

The first principle of the United Nations is that all members have equal rights. Second, all members are expected to carry out their duties under the charter. Third, they agree to the principle of settling their disputes peacefully. Fourth, they agree not to use force or the threat of force against other nations, except in self-defense. Fifth, members agree to help the UN in every action it takes to carry out the purposes of the charter. Sixth, the UN agrees to act on the principle that non-member states have the same duties as member states to preserve world peace and security. And seventh, the UN accepts the principle of not interfering in the actions of a member nation within its own borders. But these actions must not hurt other nations.

Membership requirements. The first members of the United Nations were the nations that signed the charter in 1945. Since then, many other nations have requested to join the organization. The charter states that membership in the UN is open to all "peace-loving states" that are "able and willing" to carry out the duties required by the charter. Both the Security Council and the General Assembly must approve applications for membership. A member nation that violates the charter may be suspended or even expelled from the UN.

The six major UN organs. The charter sets up the six main organs of the UN and explains the duties, powers, and operating methods of each. The General Assembly is the only major organ in which all UN members are represented. The charter permits the Assembly to discuss any question of importance to the UN and to recommend action to be taken by the members or by other UN organs. The Security Council has the major responsibility in the UN for keeping the peace. The charter gives the Council special powers to carry out this responsibility. The Secretariat has the job of helping all the other organs do their work as efficiently as possible. The charter gives the *Economic and Social Council* several duties, such as advancing human rights and helping people to better their way of life. The International Court of Justice handles international legal disputes. The charter established the Trusteeship Council to watch over and assist a number of small territories that were not self-governing at the time that the UN was founded.

The United Nations has established many other agencies, committees, and commissions since the charter was written. But the six main organs are the only UN bodies that operate under rules included in the charter.

Amending the charter. The UN charter sets forth the rules for changing the charter. Amendments may be proposed in either of two ways. The General Assembly may propose an amendment if two-thirds of all its members agree to do so. Or two-thirds of the General Assembly members and any nine members of the Security Council may call a General Conference to discuss making changes in the charter. As in the General Assembly, a two-thirds vote of a General Conference is required to propose an amendment. A proposed amendment does not go into effect until it has been approved by two-thirds of all members of the United Nations, including the five permanent members of the Security Council.

The charter called for the 10th yearly session of the General Assembly to make plans for a General Conference if one had not already taken place. In 1955, the Assembly took up the question and appointed a planning committee. The committee has met from time to time and has reported to the General Assembly. But the Assembly has taken no further action.

The General Assembly

The General Assembly is the only major organ of the United Nations in which all members are represented.

The preamble to the Charter of the United Nations

A preamble of about 200 words precedes the chapters of the charter and expresses the guiding spirit of the organization. Jan Christiaan Smuts of South Africa is credited with drafting the preamble (see **Smuts, Jan C.**). The complete preamble states:

"We the peoples of the United Nations determined

to save succeeding generations from the scourge of war, which twice in our lifetime has brought untold sorrow to mankind, and

to reaffirm faith in fundamental human rights, in the dignity and worth of the human person, in the equal rights of men and women and of nations large and small, and

to establish conditions under which justice and respect for the obligations arising from treaties and other sources of international law can be maintained, and

to promote social progress and better standards of life in larger freedom,

and for these ends

to practice tolerance and live together in peace with one another as good neighbors, and

to unite our strength to maintain international peace and security, and

to ensure, by the acceptance of principles and the institution of methods, that armed force shall not be used, save in the common interest, and

to employ international machinery for the promotion of the economic and social advancement of all peoples,

have resolved to combine our efforts to accomplish these aims.

Accordingly, our respective Governments, through representatives assembled in the city of San Francisco, who have exhibited their full powers found to be in good and due form, have agreed to the present Charter of the United Nations and do hereby establish an international organization to be known as the United Nations."

The United Nations system

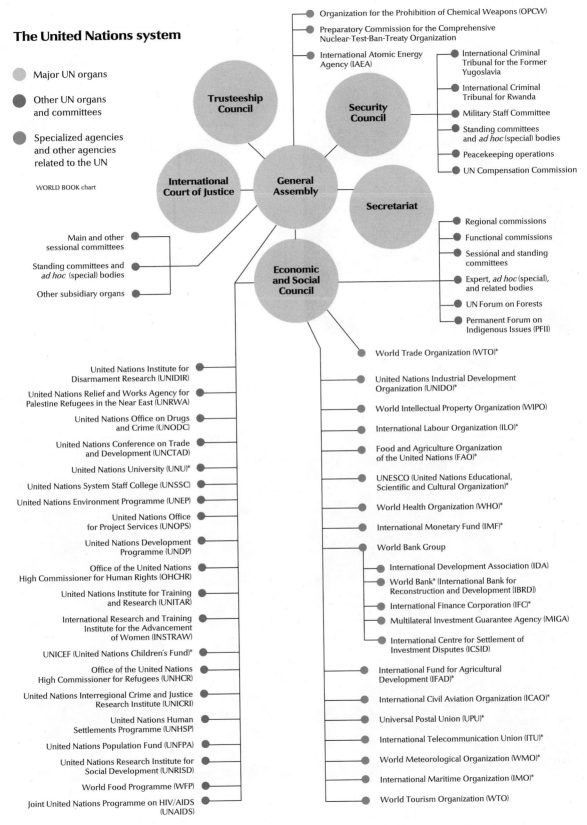

Major UN organs

Other UN organs
and committees

Specialized agencies
and other agencies
related to the UN

WORLD BOOK chart

Trusteeship Council

Security Council

International Court of Justice

General Assembly

Secretariat

Economic and Social Council

Organization for the Prohibition of Chemical Weapons (OPCW)

Preparatory Commission for the Comprehensive Nuclear-Test-Ban-Treaty Organization

International Atomic Energy Agency (IAEA)

International Criminal Tribunal for the Former Yugoslavia

International Criminal Tribunal for Rwanda

Military Staff Committee

Standing committees and *ad hoc* (special) bodies

Peacekeeping operations

UN Compensation Commission

Regional commissions

Functional commissions

Sessional and standing committees

Expert, *ad hoc* (special), and related bodies

UN Forum on Forests

Permanent Forum on Indigenous Issues (PFII)

Main and other sessional committees

Standing committees and *ad hoc* (special) bodies

Other subsidiary organs

United Nations Institute for Disarmament Research (UNIDIR)

United Nations Relief and Works Agency for Palestine Refugees in the Near East (UNRWA)

United Nations Office on Drugs and Crime (UNODC)

United Nations Conference on Trade and Development (UNCTAD)

United Nations University (UNU)*

United Nations System Staff College (UNSSC)

United Nations Environment Programme (UNEP)

United Nations Office for Project Services (UNOPS)

United Nations Development Programme (UNDP)

Office of the United Nations High Commissioner for Human Rights (OHCHR)

United Nations Institute for Training and Research (UNITAR)

International Research and Training Institute for the Advancement of Women (INSTRAW)

UNICEF (United Nations Children's Fund)*

Office of the United Nations High Commissioner for Refugees (UNHCR)

United Nations Interregional Crime and Justice Research Institute (UNICRI)

United Nations Human Settlements Programme (UNHSP)

United Nations Population Fund (UNFPA)

United Nations Research Institute for Social Development (UNRISD)

World Food Programme (WFP)

Joint United Nations Programme on HIV/AIDS (UNAIDS)

World Trade Organization (WTO)*

United Nations Industrial Development Organization (UNIDO)*

World Intellectual Property Organization (WIPO)

International Labour Organization (ILO)*

Food and Agriculture Organization of the United Nations (FAO)*

UNESCO (United Nations Educational, Scientific and Cultural Organization)*

World Health Organization (WHO)*

International Monetary Fund (IMF)*

World Bank Group

International Development Association (IDA)

World Bank* (International Bank for Reconstruction and Development [IBRD])

International Finance Corporation (IFC)*

Multilateral Investment Guarantee Agency (MIGA)

International Centre for Settlement of Investment Disputes (ICSID)

International Fund for Agricultural Development (IFAD)*

International Civil Aviation Organization (ICAO)*

Universal Postal Union (UPU)*

International Telecommunication Union (ITU)*

World Meteorological Organization (WMO)*

International Maritime Organization (IMO)*

World Tourism Organization (WTO)

*Has a separate article in *World Book*.

Superstock

UN Headquarters buildings, *foreground above,* are identified in the diagram at the right. The Secretariat Building houses the administrative offices of the UN. Millions of people have taken guided tours of the UN, which are conducted in 20 languages.

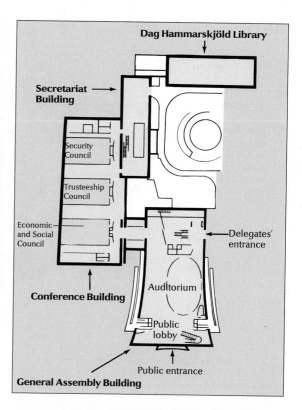

Dag Hammarskjöld Library

Secretariat Building

Security Council

Trusteeship Council

Economic and Social Council

Delegates' entrance

Auditorium

Conference Building

Public lobby

Public entrance

General Assembly Building

Frank Wen, Shostal

The General Assembly Building lobby has displays donated by UN members such as the artificial satellite, *center right,* and the statue in the foreground. The ramp in the background leads to the auditorium, where the General Assembly meets.

WORLD BOOK photo by Dan Budnik

A statue representing peace, called "Let Us Beat Swords into Plowshares," expresses the UN's main goals. The title is a quotation from Isaiah 2:4 in the Old Testament of the Bible. The statue stands in the grounds of the UN Headquarters.

The General Assembly meets to discuss such matters as the UN budget and peacekeeping efforts.

Each member may send five delegates, five alternate delegates, and as many advisers as it wishes. However, each member nation has only one vote.

The General Assembly elects a new president and a number of vice presidents at the beginning of each annual session. The president's main duty is to lead the Assembly's discussions and direct its work.

Powers. The Assembly is responsible in some way for every other UN organ. It elects or takes part in electing the members of the other major organs, and it directs the operations of some UN bodies. The Assembly also controls the UN's budget.

The General Assembly may discuss any question that concerns the work of the UN. It reaches decisions through a vote of its members. As a result of such a vote, the Assembly may suggest actions to be taken by other UN bodies or by member nations. According to the charter, the only decisions of the General Assembly that UN members must obey are votes on the UN budget. All other decisions made by the General Assembly are simply recommendations.

The General Assembly's responsibility for keeping the peace is second only to the similar responsibility of the Security Council. The kind of peacekeeping action that the Assembly can take has been strengthened since the charter was written. In the early years of the UN, sharp disagreements in the Security Council prevented the Council from acting in many cases. In 1950, the General Assembly approved a *resolution* (formal statement) called "Uniting for Peace." This resolution gave the Assembly the power to step in whenever peace is threatened and the Security Council has failed to act. In such an emergency, the Assembly can recommend actions for the UN, including the use of armed force.

Meetings and voting. The General Assembly holds one *regular session* each year, beginning on the third Tuesday in September and lasting about three months. A *special session* may be called if either the Security Council or a majority of member states requests it. Several special sessions have been called to discuss such matters as peacekeeping and finances. The "Uniting for Peace" resolution in 1950 set up a system for calling an *emergency special session* of the General Assembly. Such a meeting can be called on 24 hours' notice if peace is threatened and the Security Council has not acted. Any nine members of the Security Council or a majority of UN members may call an emergency special session. Such sessions have been held for situations in the Middle East, Hungary, and other parts of the world.

In September 2000, the General Assembly held its 55th session, which it called the Millennium Assembly. Over 150 government leaders met at the UN Headquarters to discuss the role of the UN and the challenges it faces. The meeting was the largest gathering of world leaders ever assembled.

Most questions that are voted on in the General Assembly are decided by a simple majority vote. Some subjects that the charter calls "important questions" need a two-thirds majority vote. These topics include peace and security and the election of new UN members. A simple majority vote of the Assembly may also make any other question an "important" one.

Committees. The UN Charter permits the Assembly to create as many committees as it needs to help carry on its work. The Assembly has set up seven main committees—the First, Second, Third, Fourth, Fifth, and Sixth committees, and the Special Political Committee. Every Assembly member—thus, every UN member—may have a representative on all these committees.

The First Committee discusses political and security questions and arms control. The Special Political Committee assists the First Committee. The Second Committee deals with economic and financial questions, the Third with social and cultural matters, and the Fourth with problems of countries that are not self-governing. The Fifth Committee handles administrative and budget matters, and the Sixth handles questions of law. Each committee studies problems assigned to it and makes recommendations to the Assembly.

The Assembly has also set up other committees. They help organize and conduct each Assembly session, advise the Second and Fifth committees on financial and budget matters, or deal with problems involving nuclear energy, colonialism, and peacekeeping.

The Security Council

The UN Charter makes the Security Council responsible for keeping the peace. Until 1965, the Council had 11 members. Since then, it has had 15 members, of which 5 are permanent. The permanent members are China, France, Russia, the United Kingdom, and the United States. Russia's seat on the Council was held by the Soviet Union until 1991, when the Soviet Union broke apart. The 10 nonpermanent members of the Council are elected to two-year terms by the General Assembly. Each member of the Security Council has one delegate on the Council. Several nations of the UN support expanding the number of permanent Security Council members to reflect the UN's global membership.

Powers. The Security Council has the power to decide what action the UN should take to settle international disputes. The charter states that the Council's decisions are made in the name of all UN members, who must accept them and carry them out. The Council encourages the peaceful settlement of disputes by calling on the opposing sides to work out a solution. Or the Council may ask the sides to accept a settlement worked out by other nations, individuals, or groups.

The Council itself may investigate a dispute and suggest ways of settling it. For example, the Council may call on UN members to stop trading with a country that is endangering peace and security. It may also ask the members to cut off communications with such a state, or to end contacts with its government. If such actions are not effective, the Security Council may ask UN members to furnish military forces to settle the dispute. The *Working for peace and security* section of this article describes some actions taken by the Security Council.

The Security Council also has several other important powers. It must approve all applications for membership in the UN. It selects a candidate for secretary-general. And it can recommend plans for arms control.

Meetings and committees. Security Council meetings may be called to consider any situation serious enough to lead to war. Such a situation can be brought to the Council's attention by any UN member—and in certain cases by nonmembers—by the secretary-general or by any major UN organ. The delegates must be able to attend a meeting as soon as it is called.

The Council makes its own rules for conducting its meetings. In the early years of the UN, it became a custom for the representative of a different nation to serve as president each month. The representatives take turns, in the order that their country's name appears in the English alphabet. UN members that are not members of the Council—and even nations that are not UN members—may be invited to take part in debates that affect them. But these nations have no vote.

The Council may set up as many committees as it needs. The charter calls only for a Military Staff Committee, which is made up of military representatives of the five permanent members. Other committees have been appointed from time to time, especially to help the Council organize its work and to consider applications for UN membership.

Voting in the Security Council differs from that in any other UN organ. The Council can take action on some questions if any nine members vote in favor of the action. But on many other questions, the Council can act only if nine members—including all five permanent members—agree to do so. A "no" vote by any permanent member defeats such a question, no matter how many other members vote in favor of it. This special voting right of the permanent members is called a *veto.*

Almost any decision of the Council can be vetoed, but the Council has never established what kinds of decisions cannot be vetoed. Through the years, a few customs concerning the veto have developed. For example, a permanent member usually does not veto a decision about what subjects the Council should discuss, or

Meetings of the Security Council are held in a special chamber in the Conference Building. Delegates and their assistants sit at the semicircular table. Interpreters and other UN employees sit at the long table in the center.

Trygve Lie

Dag Hammarskjöld

U Thant

Kurt Waldheim

Javier Pérez de Cuéllar

Boutros Boutros-Ghali

Kofi Annan

The first seven UN secretaries-general were Trygve Lie of Norway, who served from 1946 to 1953; Dag Hammarskjöld of Sweden, 1953 to 1961; U Thant of Burma (Myanmar), 1961 to 1971; Kurt Waldheim of Austria, 1972 to 1981; Javier Pérez de Cuéllar of Peru, 1982 to 1991; Boutros Boutros-Ghali of Egypt, 1992 to 1996; and Kofi Annan of Ghana, 1997 to 2006.

about when the Council should adjourn. But a permanent member sometimes vetoes a decision about the order in which subjects are to be discussed. If a permanent member decides not to vote or is absent at the time of voting, its action is not considered a veto.

For many years, the use of the veto in the Security Council prevented the United Nations from dealing with a number of major problems. The Soviet Union, until shortly before it was dissolved in 1991, used the veto over 100 times, much more than any of the other four permanent members. The United States used the veto for the first time in March 1970. It vetoed a Security Council resolution requiring UN members to cut off communications with Rhodesia (now Zimbabwe).

The Secretariat

The Secretariat manages the day-to-day business of the United Nations. Its main job is to provide services for all the other UN organs. The Secretariat is made up of the secretary-general and other administrators assisted by clerks, secretaries, and specialists.

The secretary-general has broader powers than any other United Nations official. The secretary-general is the chief administrator of the UN and reports to the General Assembly each year on the organization's problems and accomplishments. The secretary-general advises governments and uses the influence of the office to help solve many problems. Most important, the secretary-general has power to advise the Security Council of any situation that might threaten world peace.

The secretary-general is nominated by the Security Council and appointed by the General Assembly to a five-year term. All five permanent members of the Security Council must agree on a candidate before that person can be nominated. The Security Council then makes a recommendation to the General Assembly. A majority vote of the General Assembly appoints a secretary-general. The secretary-general is assisted by a deputy secretary-general.

Eight men have served as secretary-general. Their names, nationalities, and years of service are (1) Trygve Lie of Norway, 1946 to 1953; (2) Dag

Eskinder Debebe, UN/DPI Photo
Ban Ki-moon of South Korea became the eighth secretary-general of the UN in 2007.

Hammarskjöld of Sweden, 1953 to 1961; (3) U Thant of Burma (now Myanmar), 1961 to 1971; (4) Kurt Waldheim of Austria, 1972 to 1981; (5) Javier Pérez de Cuéllar of Peru, 1982 to 1991; (6) Boutros Boutros-Ghali of Egypt, 1992 to 1996; (7) Kofi Annan of Ghana, 1997 to 2006; and (8) Ban Ki-moon of South Korea, who became secretary-general in 2007. For more information on these men, see their separate biographies in *World Book*.

In 1960, the Soviet Union demanded that the UN appoint three people to serve together as secretary-general. They wanted one representative for Communist members, another for Western nations, and a third for *uncommitted* nations—that is, nations that supported neither side. The Soviets called their proposed triple leadership a *troika. Troika* is a Russian word meaning *a group of three*. Their demand was rejected. But after U Thant took office in 1961, he appointed undersecretaries from Communist, Western, and uncommitted nations.

Other employees. The Secretariat has several thousand employees working at UN Headquarters. Thousands more work at the UN's European headquarters in Geneva, Switzerland, or in special UN missions and agencies throughout the world.

The secretary-general appoints and organizes the staff of the Secretariat. The charter instructs the secretary-general to choose staff members from as many different member nations as possible. Employees include accountants, economists, lawyers, mathematicians, translators, and writers. Every UN member country may fill at least six Secretariat jobs if it can provide qualified individuals. Employees who work for the Secretariat are not allowed to take orders from any member nation.

Other main organs

The Economic and Social Council. The United Nations is the first international organization with a major organ devoted to improving the way people live. The Economic and Social Council works to encourage higher standards of living, better health, cultural and educational cooperation among nations, and observance of human rights. It makes recommendations in these areas to the General Assembly, individual nations, and the UN's specialized agencies. For example, the Council recommends to the General Assembly the economic and social projects it considers worthy of UN support. The Assembly then may grant funds for these projects.

The Economic and Social Council is responsible for working with the specialized agencies. In addition to making recommendations to them, the Council communicates recommendations from the agencies to the General Assembly. The Council also cooperates with more than 100 other organizations throughout the world, including the Red Cross and labor unions.

The Council has 54 member nations. Each year, the General Assembly elects 18 members to serve for three years. The Council meets at least twice a year. Each member has one vote, and decisions are made by a simple majority. The Council may allow any UN member or specialized agency to take part in discussions of concern to them. But only Council members may vote.

The Council has several commissions that assist it. Some deal with the economic and social issues of specific regions, such as Africa, Asia, Europe, and Latin America. Other commissions deal with such issues as criminal justice, narcotics, and women's rights. Other bodies that assist the Council include the governing boards of the United Nations Children's Fund (UNICEF) and the United Nations Development Programme.

The International Court of Justice deals with the legal problems of the United Nations. The court has 15 judges, each appointed to a nine-year term. The Security Council and the General Assembly, voting independently, select the judges. No two judges may come from the same country, and the world's major civilizations and legal traditions must be represented. The court traditionally includes one judge from each of the permanent members of the Security Council. It elects a president and vice president to three-year terms. Headquarters are at The Hague in the Netherlands.

Any UN member may bring a case before the court. The court has helped settle disputes between various countries, including the United Kingdom and Norway, Belgium and the Netherlands, and Honduras and Nicaragua. These disputes have concerned fishing rights and the ownership of border territory. The General Assembly and the Security Council have also permitted nonmember states to have cases heard by the court. An individual cannot bring a case to the court unless his or her government sponsors it.

No nation can be forced to bring its disputes before the International Court of Justice. Many governments have declared that they will seek court rulings in certain types of disputes. The United States and other nations have said they will decide for themselves what cases to bring before the court. Any nation that seeks a ruling from the court must agree to accept the court's decision. The court makes its decisions by majority vote.

The International Court gives advisory opinions to the General Assembly upon request. The Assembly also has permitted the Security Council, the Economic and Social Council, the Trusteeship Council, and the specialized agencies to request such opinions.

The Trusteeship Council was designed to help territories that were not self-governing at the end of World War II (1939-1945). The Council suspended its operations in 1994, after the last of the territories gained independence. However, the Council still exists under the UN Charter.

Some of the territories the Council was designed to help were colonies of Italy and Japan. Others were German colonies that had become *mandates* of the League of Nations after World War I (see **Mandated territory**). The UN Charter made the Trusteeship Council responsible for all these territories and for any others that nations might choose to entrust to it. Such areas were called *trust territories.* The Council worked to help the trust territories become self-governing or independent.

There were originally 11 trust territories. The UN accepted one or more member nations as *trustees* for

Former UN trust territories

This table lists the 11 original trust areas, their trustees, and the dates their status as trust territories ended.

Name	Trustee	Status
Cameroons	United Kingdom	Became parts of Cameroon and Nigeria, 1961
Cameroons	France	Independent as Cameroon, 1960
Nauru	Australia	Independent, 1968
New Guinea	Australia	Became part of Papua New Guinea, 1975
Pacific Islands	United States	Independent as Palau, 1994*
Ruanda-Urundi	Belgium	Independent as Rwanda and Burundi, 1962
Somaliland	Italy	Independent as Somalia, 1960
Tanganyika	United Kingdom	Independent, 1961
Togoland	France	Independent as Togo, 1960
Togoland	United Kingdom	Became part of Ghana, 1957
Western Samoa	New Zealand	Independent, 1962

*Palau was the last remaining part of the Trust Territory of the Pacific Islands. For information on the other parts and when they separated from the territory, see **Pacific Islands, Trust Territory of the.**

each territory. The trustee countries governed the trust territories under the direction of the UN. The Trusteeship Council was made up of representatives of the trustee nations and of all permanent members of the Security Council that did not govern trust territories. The Trusteeship Council met at least once every year.

Specialized agencies

The specialized agencies are self-governing international organizations related to the UN. They deal with such worldwide problems as agriculture, communications, living and working conditions, and health. Some of the agencies are older than the UN itself.

Each agency has its own organization, membership, and rules, and each has signed an agreement with the UN. The agency agrees to consider recommendations made by the UN and to report back on steps it takes to carry them out. The Economic and Social Council has the responsibility of helping the UN and the specialized agencies work together effectively.

Each specialized agency was set up to deal with a problem involving the cooperation of many nations. Some of the agencies were established to deal with

Irrigation and land development projects receive funds from the Food and Agriculture Organization (FAO), a specialized agency of the United Nations. As part of an FAO program, these workers are rebuilding an irrigation canal in Sumatra.

Specialized agencies of the United Nations

Food and Agriculture Organization of the United Nations (FAO)

Helps improve the production of farms, forests, and fishing waters.

International Civil Aviation Organization (ICAO)

Works for greater safety in air service and for standard international flying regulations.

International Development Association (IDA)

Works with the World Bank. It lends money on easier terms than does the World Bank or the International Finance Corporation.

International Finance Corporation (IFC)

Works with the World Bank. It encourages smaller, private developments. It mostly lends money for large governmental projects.

International Fund for Agricultural Development (IFAD)

Finances projects to increase food production in developing countries.

International Labour Organization (ILO)

Helps improve working and living conditions throughout the world.

International Maritime Organization (IMO)

Encourages cooperation in shipping practices and regulations.

International Monetary Fund (IMF)

Helps adjust differences between the money systems used by various countries, making it easier for nations to trade with one another.

International Telecommunication Union (ITU)

Helps nations cooperate to solve problems dealing with radio, telephone, telegraph, and satellite communications.

UNESCO (United Nations Educational, Scientific and Cultural Organization)

Encourages educational, scientific, and cultural progress to increase understanding among nations.

United Nations Industrial Development Organization (UNIDO)

Organizes and funds industrialization projects for developing countries.

Universal Postal Union (UPU)

Works for international cooperation in the delivery of mail.

World Bank

Officially called the International Bank for Reconstruction and Development (IBRD). It lends money to help countries with such projects as dams, power plants, and railroads.

World Health Organization (WHO)

The world's principal agency for dealing with health problems.

World Intellectual Property Organization (WIPO)

Works for international cooperation to protect artistic and literary works, inventions, and trademarks against copying.

World Meteorological Organization (WMO)

Encourages nations to cooperate in weather forecasting.

problems of transportation or communication between countries. Others were set up to help countries that had suffered greatly as a result of war or that had recently become independent. These agencies may provide loans, educational assistance, or other types of aid.

See the *Related articles* at the end of this article for a list of the specialized agencies that have separate articles in *World Book.*

The members at work

Delegations. Each nation has its own rules for appointing delegates to the UN. In the United States, the president nominates the delegates. The nominees are subject to approval by the Senate. In Canada, the prime minister and the Cabinet choose the delegates. The delegation of each country has a *head delegate* who is that nation's official representative at the United Nations. Most countries call their head delegate an ambassador.

Most UN members keep a permanent *mission* of one or more representatives at UN Headquarters. A permanent mission is helpful for taking part in long-term projects and for keeping up with current developments.

Breaking the language barrier. United Nations delegates speak dozens of languages. But when conducting official business, the UN uses only six languages—Arabic, Chinese, English, French, Russian, and Spanish. Delegates may address the General Assembly in any language if they provide a translation into one of the official languages. Interpreters instantly translate the words into the other official languages. The delegates wear earphones to listen to the translation they choose.

Groups with common interests. As UN membership has grown, most nations with similar interests have banded together. The African nations have their own group, as do the Arab countries and the Asian lands. Many Latin American nations make up another group. All these groups meet regularly for various reasons—for example, to decide on a plan of action or to agree on candidates in a UN election. Canada and the other members of the Commonwealth of Nations meet together regularly for discussion but seldom vote as a group. A few nations, including Israel and the United States, do not meet or vote regularly with any group.

Publications and information services. The UN provides information about its work to member nations and to the public. Each major UN organ, as well as numerous UN agencies, issues documents that give a complete account of its work. These documents give UN members information that helps them carry out their duties. The UN also issues many publications of interest to the public. The *UN Chronicle,* for example, describes

Heads of United States and Canadian delegations to the UN

Heads of United States delegations

Name	Served
Warren R. Austin	1947-1953
Henry Cabot Lodge	1953-1960
James J. Wadsworth*	1960-1961
Adlai E. Stevenson	1961-1965
Arthur J. Goldberg	1965-1968
George Ball**	1968
James R. Wiggins	1968-1969
Charles W. Yost	1969-1971
George H. W. Bush	1971-1973
John A. Scali	1973-1975
Daniel Patrick Moynihan	1975-1976
William W. Scranton	1976-1977
Andrew J. Young, Jr.	1977-1979
Donald F. McHenry	1979-1981
Jeane J. Kirkpatrick	1981-1985
Vernon A. Walters	1985-1989
Thomas R. Pickering	1989-1992
Edward J. Perkins	1992-1993
Madeleine K. Albright	1993-1997
Bill Richardson	1997-1998
A. Peter Burleigh*	1998-1999
Richard C. Holbrooke	1999-2001
John D. Negroponte	2001-2004
John C. Danforth	2004-2005
Anne W. Patterson*	2005
John R. Bolton	2005-2006
Zalmay Khalilzad	2007-

*Acting head.   **Resigned the day after his nomination was confirmed by the Senate.

Heads of Canadian delegations

Name	Served
Andrew G. L. McNaughton	1948-1950
R. G. Riddell	1950-1951
E. Herbert Norman*	1951
D. M. Johnson	1951-1955
R. A. Mackay	1955-1958
C. S. A. Ritchie	1958-1962
Paul Tremblay	1962-1966
George Ignatieff	1966-1968
Yvon Beaulne	1969-1972
Saul Rae	1972-1976
William H. Barton	1976-1980
Michel Dupuy	1980-1981
Gerard Pelletier	1981-1984
Stephen Lewis	1984-1988
Yves Fortier	1988-1992
Louise Frechette	1992-1994
Robert Fowler	1995-2000
Paul Heinbecker	2000-2004
Allan Rock	2004-2006
John McNee	2006-

*Served as acting head from March to September. Not considered an official head by the UN.

Shostal

The Economic and Social Council works to improve the standard of living in UN member nations.

work done by the UN. Booklets deal with such subjects as economic development, human rights, or statistics. Many UN publications are issued in several or all of its six official languages. The UN maintains a Web site with information about the organization.

The UN has a Department of Public Information, which is part of the Secretariat. One of its duties is to direct UN information offices in a number of cities throughout the world. Each office provides information about the UN to people in nearby regions.

Working for progress

An increasingly important goal of the United Nations is to help make the world a better, safer place in which to live. One way the UN works toward this goal is by providing various types of aid for countries and different groups of people. The UN also works for progress in many other fields, including human rights, peaceful uses of nuclear energy, and pollution control.

Economic and technical aid consists of grants, loans, training programs, and other means of helping nations develop their resources, production, and trade. After World War II, the International Bank and the International Monetary Fund gave financial assistance to war-torn countries. But the amount of aid they could give was small compared with the amount needed. Most western European countries depended on the United States to help them recover from the war.

As more and more poor countries joined the UN, the organization began to help them. The resources of these countries are either undeveloped or have been developing slowly. Many such nations have become independent since World War II.

The UN dedicated the period from 1961 through 1970 as the first United Nations Development Decade. The UN's goal during this period was to help the developing countries increase their national income by 5 percent each year. Developed nations were asked to donate 1 percent of their yearly national income to the program.

The first Development Decade did not meet all its goals, but some progress was made. The International Bank increased the number and size of its loans for the construction of roads, factories, and similar projects. In 1964, the UN held a Conference on Trade and Development (UNCTAD). The main aim of this conference was to encourage international trade, especially between the rich, developed countries and the poor, less developed ones. The conference set up a Trade and Development Board, and itself became a permanent organ of the General Assembly. UNCTAD decides on courses of UN action concerning trade and development. The Trade and Development Board carries out UNCTAD's decisions. The board meets at least twice a year to consider such matters as improving international shipping or helping poor countries find markets for their products.

In 1965, the UN combined its technical aid programs to form the United Nations Development Programme (UNDP). The UNDP helps nations make studies of their unused natural resources so they can find ways to use them. For example, it suggests ways for nations to make their farms, mines, and water resources more productive. It also helps people learn the skills needed to develop their country's resources. The UN has helped people learn to manage, as well as work in, industries that will benefit their countries. In 1966, the General Assembly set up the United Nations Industrial Development Organization (UNIDO) to encourage industrialization in developing countries.

During the late 1900's, the United Nations increased its efforts to expand international trade and to provide

Afghan refugees are one of the many groups of people in various parts of the world that receive UN aid. UN agencies also provide loans and other assistance for developing countries.

economic and technical assistance. It also worked to help developing countries regulate population growth, and to promote world disarmament.

Aid to refugees. The United Nations aids refugees by protecting their legal rights, providing them with food and shelter, and finding them new homes. The UN has declared that the legal rights of refugees include the right to a job, to an education, and to freedom of religion. During World War II, 44 governments cooperated in setting up the United Nations Relief and Rehabilitation Administration (UNRRA) to conduct war relief. After the UN was created, UNRRA was replaced by the International Refugee Organization (IRO), a specialized agency. By 1951, the worst of the problems caused by the war were over and the IRO was discontinued.

In 1951, the General Assembly set up the Office of the United Nations High Commissioner for Refugees. The agency's main duty is to protect the rights of refugees in foreign countries. The office has a small fund raised by voluntary contributions. But in general, it must work through governments and private agencies.

The UN has a special agency to assist Palestinian refugees—the United Nations Relief and Works Agency for Palestine Refugees in the Near East (UNRWA). The General Assembly set up the agency to help the hundreds of thousands of Palestinians who were made homeless by the 1948 war between Israel and Arab countries. UNRWA originally provided food, shelters, medical care, and other services. Today, educational programs and health care have become the major focus of UNRWA's work.

Aid to children. The General Assembly established the United Nations Children's Fund (UNICEF) in 1946 to provide clothing, food, and medical supplies for child victims of World War II. The emergency caused by the war ended by the early 1950's, but UNICEF had become so popular that the General Assembly made it permanent in 1953. Today, UNICEF provides aid for child development and care, family planning, and job training. In 1989, UNICEF set up the Convention on the Rights of the Child, which seeks special protection for children throughout the world.

Most of UNICEF's funds come from donations by governments. The United States Committee for UNICEF raises several million dollars yearly. See **UNICEF.**

Human rights. In 1946, the United Nations set up the Commission on Human Rights as part of the Economic and Social Council. The commission wrote the Universal Declaration of Human Rights, which all members of the General Assembly approved in 1948. This declaration expressed the hope that people would learn to respect the rights and dignity of others. Parts of the declaration have been included in the constitutions of El Salvador, Haiti, Indonesia, Jordan, Libya, Puerto Rico, and Syria.

Racial problems have received more attention than any others brought before the UN. These problems— and those of colonialism and economic development— are the main concern of the Asian and African delegates, who make up a majority in the UN. In 1965, the General Assembly approved a treaty called the International Convention on the Elimination of All Forms of Racial Discrimination. The treaty went into effect in 1969, after the governments of 27 nations had approved it. Similar UN treaties deal with slavery, the rights of refugees, and the crime of *genocide* (extermination of an entire national, racial, or religious group).

In 1998, 120 UN member nations voted to approve a treaty calling for the establishment of the International Criminal Court. This UN court is designed to prosecute genocide, war crimes, and crimes against humanity. The court began operations in 2003.

In 2006, the General Assembly voted to eliminate the

UNICEF aids children by assisting countries in such areas as education, health care, and sanitation and water supply. The UNICEF workers shown in this photograph are drilling a water well for a village in Sierra Leone.

UN agencies provide training programs and other economic aid to industries in developing countries. Dairy workers in Chile, *shown here,* are learning about powdered milk production.

Commission on Human Rights and replace it with a new Human Rights Council. The new council meets regularly throughout the year to address human rights issues.

Peaceful uses of nuclear energy. In 1953, President Dwight D. Eisenhower of the United States suggested that governments contribute nuclear materials to an international agency. This agency would use such materials to help develop peaceful uses of nuclear energy.

In 1957, the UN set up the agency that Eisenhower had suggested. The International Atomic Energy Agency (IAEA) is separate from the UN but works with it. The agency tries to ensure that no nuclear materials held or supplied by its member nations are used for making weapons. It has placed controls on its members' nuclear materials and conducts inspections of nuclear facilities each year. A treaty prohibiting the spread of nuclear weapons took effect in 1970. The IAEA is responsible for inspections that make sure the treaty is not broken.

The IAEA cooperates with many other agencies to encourage the sharing of nuclear information. It also encourages research and experiments dealing with nuclear fuels, nuclear medicine, *desalination* (removing the salt) of seawater, and other uses of nuclear energy. Money for IAEA projects comes from dues paid by member nations and from voluntary contributions.

Controlling the environment. The UN has called attention to air and water pollution and other dangers that threaten the environment. In 1968, the General Assembly passed a resolution pledging the UN to work for solutions to problems concerning the environment.

The UN Conference on Human Environment met in 1972 to discuss how UN members could jointly protect the environment. As a result of the conference, the General Assembly established the UN Environment Programme in 1972. The program encourages international cooperation to fight pollution and preserve Earth's natural resources. In 1992, representatives of UN member nations met in Rio de Janeiro, Brazil, for the United Nations Conference on Environment and Development. At this conference, also known as the Earth Summit, UN members signed agreements on the prevention of global warming, the preservation of forests and endangered species, and other issues. In 2002, representatives met again, at the UN's World Summit on Sustainable Development in Johannesburg, South Africa.

Fighting hunger has always been a major goal of the UN. The Food and Agriculture Organization of the United Nations (FAO), a specialized agency, was established in 1945. The agency works to improve the production and distribution of food and other agricultural products. The World Food Programme began in 1962 as a joint project of the UN and FAO. It provides emergency food aid and other assistance to developing countries.

In the 1970's, the production of food in many countries fell behind population growth. As a result, large numbers of people suffered from severe malnutrition. In 1974, the UN World Food Conference met in Rome to discuss the food shortage. The conference set up a new UN agency, the World Food Council. The council coordinates the delivery of food to less developed nations. It also accumulates world food reserves for use in time of famine. The council works through the FAO, the United Nations Development Programme (UNDP), UNICEF, and other agencies. The Rome conference also created an international warning system to detect future shortages.

In some cases, the UN has delivered food and medicine to war-torn countries to relieve civilians of shortages. It has also sent troops to protect such deliveries.

Disaster relief. The UN works to help communities prepare for and recover from earthquakes, floods, landslides, and other natural disasters. The organization seeks to prevent injury, sickness, and loss of life; minimize environmental damage; and address economic concerns relating to destructive events.

In late 2004, a series of large ocean waves called a *tsunami* caused massive destruction in many coastal areas of Asia and Africa bordering the Indian Ocean. Over 200,000 people were killed, and millions more were left homeless. Following the disaster, the UN began coordinating relief and reconstruction efforts in the region. After Hurricane Katrina struck the United States Gulf Coast in 2005, UN agencies provided support to victims in the region.

Working for peace and security

The most important goals of the United Nations include world peace and security. The UN has helped end a number of conflicts around the world through the negotiation of cease-fires and peace agreements. After the fighting stops, the UN may engage in keeping the peace by sending peacekeeping forces to the region. It may also help the warring groups find ways to prevent the

A warehouse for storing food is being constructed by villagers in central Africa with aid from the United Nations Development Programme (UNDP). This program helps nations develop their human and natural resources.

fighting from starting again. In addition, the UN may try to restore order to a country in which civil war has broken out. Such action is sometimes called *peacemaking* instead of *peacekeeping*. The United Nations also has sought to promote world peace and security by sponsoring arms control agreements and treaties on the peaceful use of outer space and the seabed.

Peacekeeping operations encourage the peaceful settlement of disputes and try to end fighting throughout the world. There are two types of UN peacekeeping operations—observer missions and peacekeeping forces. The UN Security Council establishes peacekeeping operations, defines their mission, and dispatches the observer mission or peacekeeping force to the problem region. Any of the five permanent Security Council members—China, France, Russia, the United Kingdom, and the United States—can veto any decision on peacekeeping operations.

Observer missions consist of a group of military officers, usually unarmed. The UN sends such a mission to monitor an international situation that threatens the peace. The observers' functions may be to watch and report to the United Nations on the maintenance of a cease-fire, to investigate reported violations of an international agreement, or to do whatever they can to ease friction in a tense situation.

Peacekeeping forces consist of lightly armed troops. The United Nations sends such forces to deal with an international dispute if both sides in the conflict agree to have them come. The UN may also send peacekeepers if such action seems to be the only way to end hostilities. UN peacekeepers may create and patrol buffer zones between opposing forces, encourage peace negotiations, monitor cease-fire agreements, or help enforce peace treaties.

Because the UN has no army, UN member nations voluntarily provide troops and equipment for each peacekeeping force. Canada and the island nation of Fiji have taken part in almost every peacekeeping operation since the UN was founded. Other leading contributors of troops include Bangladesh, Brazil, India, and Pakistan.

© J. Bleibtreu, UN/DPI

Disarming land mines is a job done by UN peacekeeping forces. The peacekeepers shown here, *in blue caps,* are teaching a Cambodian soldier how to disarm a mine in Cambodia.

Destroying weapons, UN peacekeeping troops in Honduras help maintain peace in 1990, after a civil war in neighboring Nicaragua. The peacekeepers, *wearing blue caps,* are cutting up guns surrendered by the Nicaraguan rebels known as *contras.*

© Steen Johansen, UN/DPI

Peacekeeping soldiers wear their own national uniforms. They also wear blue hats or blue helmets and the United Nations insignia to identify them as UN peacekeepers. Peacekeeping forces are allowed to use their weapons only for self-defense. They are required to remain completely impartial at all times and to avoid any action that might affect the claims or the positions of the parties in a dispute.

The first UN peacekeeping operation was an observer mission called the United Nations Truce Supervision Organization (UNTSO). The mission was established in 1948 to supervise a truce between Arab countries and Israel in the first Arab-Israeli war. UNTSO's activities have changed over the years, but it remains in the Middle East, where it works to keep the peace.

The first UN peacekeeping force was established in 1956 during a dispute over the Suez Canal. Fighting had broken out after Egypt blocked Israeli ships from the canal and seized the canal from its British and French owners. Israel, France, and the United Kingdom attacked Egypt in response. The UN arranged a cease-fire and sent a peacekeeping force called the United Nations Emergency Force (UNEF) to guard the borders between Egypt and Israel. The UNEF completed its mission in 1967, but conflict between Arabs and Israelis continued.

Over the years, the UN has helped arrange several cease-fires to stop the fighting in the Middle East. The organization also has sent other peacekeeping forces to the Middle East and other parts of the world. For example, the UN Disengagement Observer Force has supervised Syrian and Israeli troops in the disputed area of the Golan Heights since 1974. The UN Interim Force in Lebanon has served in that country since 1978. The Interim Force helped end fighting between Israel and Lebanon in 2006. The UN Organization Mission in the Democratic Republic of the Congo has sought to reduce hostilities between government and rebel groups since 1999.

In 1988, UN peacekeeping forces were awarded the Nobel Peace Prize for helping control military conflict in the Middle East and other areas. The UN won the Nobel Peace Prize again in 2001 for its continued efforts to build peace and security. For more information, see **Arab-Israeli conflict; Middle East.**

Military actions. The UN has used force to punish aggression in two major international conflicts, the Korean War and the Persian Gulf War of 1991.

The Korean War (1950-1953) marked the first time a world organization ever took part in fighting a war. In this conflict, UN troops prevented Communist armies of North Korea from taking over South Korea.

The war grew out of the Cold War tensions that existed between Communist countries and non-Communist countries. At the end of World War II in 1945, Communist troops from the Soviet Union occupied Korea north of the 38th parallel, and United States troops occupied it to the south. In 1947, the UN appointed a commission to find ways to unite the country and form a national government. The northern part of Korea refused to take part in this plan. But elections were held in the southern part, and the Republic of Korea was set up there. In 1948, the General Assembly declared that the government of the Republic of Korea (South Korea) was the only legal government in Korea.

On June 25, 1950, troops from Communist-ruled North Korea invaded South Korea. The UN called the invasion a violation of international peace and demanded that the Communists withdraw from South Korea. The Security Council agreed on what it called a "police action." It voted to ask members of the UN to send troops to assist South Korea. The Soviet Union could not veto the Council's action because it had temporarily withdrawn its delegate to protest Nationalist China's membership on the Council.

On July 7, 1950, the Council formed a UN military command under the leadership of the United States. Of the 60 UN members, 16 sent troops to Korea and 41 sent supplies. But the United States contributed about 90 percent of all the troops and supplies. In October 1950, Chinese Communist forces entered the war. The Security Council met to discuss the situation, but the Soviet delegate had returned and vetoed any attempt of the Council to act. The war ended on July 27, 1953, when North Korea and the UN signed a cease-fire agreement. By then, the Communist troops had been expelled from almost all of the area south of the 38th parallel.

The Persian Gulf War of 1991. In 1991, a military coalition of UN members expelled Iraq from Kuwait, an oil-rich country on Iraq's southern border. Iraq had invaded and occupied Kuwait in August 1990. The economies of many Western countries depended on oil from Kuwait and from neighboring Saudi Arabia, which many Westerners feared Iraq would invade next.

Soon after Iraq invaded Kuwait, the UN Security Council demanded that Iraq withdraw its forces. The Council also called on all countries to end their trade with Iraq until Iraq withdrew from Kuwait. As a result, trade with Iraq declined sharply.

In November 1990, the Security Council authorized UN member nations to "use all necessary means" to expel Iraq from Kuwait if Iraq did not withdraw by Jan. 15, 1991. Iraq did not remove its armed forces by this deadline. On January 17, air forces of UN members started bombing Iraqi military targets in Iraq and Kuwait. UN members that sent troops included the United States, Canada, and several Western European and Arab countries. Ground forces invaded Kuwait and Iraq on February 24. On February 28, all military operations ended. On April 6, Iraq agreed to comply with UN resolutions.

The end of the Cold War. From the late 1940's to the 1980's, many UN efforts to achieve world peace focused on easing Cold War tensions. The Cold War was a struggle for international power between Communist nations, led by the Soviet Union, and non-Communist nations, led by the United States. The Korean War, for example, resulted largely from Cold War friction.

In the late 1980's and early 1990's, several Communist governments in Eastern Europe collapsed because the Soviet Union did not use its military forces to back them up. The Soviet Union then broke apart, and the Cold War ended. As a result, the UN shifted much of its attention to other international conflicts. The ending of Cold

War tensions also led to greater cooperation among UN member nations and enabled the UN to expand its peacekeeping operations. In the 1990's, for example, UN peacekeeping forces supervised elections in many parts of the world, including Cambodia, Eritrea, Namibia, and Nicaragua. They also distributed food and other humanitarian aid in Bosnia, Rwanda, and Somalia. In the early 2000's, approximately 15 peacekeeping operations remained active, most of them in the Middle East, Africa, and Europe.

Arms control. The UN Charter mentions only briefly the need for arms control. But the charter was written before the nuclear age began. By 1949, both the Soviet Union and the United States had atomic bombs. They agreed that controls were needed for such weapons but could not agree on what kind. The UN studied the problem, and the General Assembly issued many appeals for nations to reduce their arms production.

In 1961, the Soviet Union and the United States agreed on a plan to establish a disarmament committee. The UN approved the plan, and an 18-nation committee was set up. More nations were added in 1969. In 1979, the number was increased to 40, and the Committee on Disarmament became an official UN organ.

The Cuban missile crisis of 1962 persuaded both the Soviet Union and the United States to work harder for control of nuclear weapons. During that crisis, the world stood on the brink of nuclear war (see **Cuban missile crisis**). In 1963, three nations with nuclear weapons—the Soviet Union, the United Kingdom, and the United States—along with most other UN members, signed a treaty outlawing nuclear tests in the atmosphere, in outer space, and underwater—but not underground. The Soviet Union, the United Kingdom, and the United States also agreed not to put such weapons in orbit.

In 1968, the UN approved a *nonproliferation treaty.* This treaty prohibits the nuclear powers that signed and ratified it—originally the United Kingdom, the Soviet Union, and the United States—from giving nuclear weapons to nations that do not already have them. The treaty went into effect in 1970. China and France signed the treaty in 1992. After the Soviet Union was dissolved in 1991, the former Soviet republics with nuclear weapons signed the treaty—Russia in 1992, Belarus and

Christopher Morris, Black Star

UN vehicles carry peacekeeping troops who are monitoring a cease-fire in Croatia. Fighting broke out in Croatia in 1991 after Croatia declared its independence from Yugoslavia.

UPI/Bettmann

Palestinian leader Yasir Arafat addressed the UN in 1974 during a debate on the status of the Palestinian people. After the debate, the UN recognized the Palestinians' right to nationhood.

Kazakhstan in 1993, and Ukraine in 1994. In 1971, the General Assembly approved a treaty banning the production and stockpiling of biological weapons. The treaty took effect in 1975. In 1993, more than 120 countries signed a UN-sponsored treaty banning the manufacture, use, transfer, and stockpiling of chemical weapons. The treaty went into effect in 1997.

In 1996, the UN approved the Comprehensive Nuclear Test Ban Treaty, which was designed to end the testing of nuclear weapons. To officially go into effect, the pact had to be ratified by the legislatures of all countries that had *nuclear reactors* (devices for producing nuclear energy). Two of those countries—India and Pakistan—opposed the treaty. However, the countries that approved the pact were expected to abide by it even if India and Pakistan did not ratify it.

In the years following the Persian Gulf War of 1991, the UN sent teams of inspectors to Iraq to investigate suspected weapons sites. The searches were aimed at ensuring that Iraq did not possess *weapons of mass destruction*—that is, biological, chemical, or nuclear weapons. The UN inspectors left Iraq in 1998, after the Iraqi government had failed to cooperate with the inspectors. In 2002, the UN Security Council passed a resolution calling for the return of weapons inspectors to Iraq. The inspectors returned to Iraq later that year. However, they left in early 2003, when the United States and its allies began military action to disarm Iraq. See **Iraq War.**

Fighting terrorism. In September 2001, the Security Council adopted a resolution requiring all member nations to take steps against international terrorism. The resolution ordered nations to restrict the funding, training, and movement of terrorists and to cooperate with one another in antiterrorist campaigns and investigations. Both the Security Council and the General Assembly stressed that governments that sponsor, assist, or protect terrorist groups will be punished. The UN's ac-

tions came in response to terrorist attacks on the World Trade Center in New York City and on the Pentagon Building near Washington, D.C., earlier that month.

Other UN efforts to fight terrorism have included the 1963 Convention on Offences and Certain Other Acts Committed on Board Aircraft, the 1997 International Convention for the Suppression of Terrorist Bombings, and the 1999 International Convention for the Suppression of the Financing of Terrorism.

The UN itself has at times been the target of terrorist violence. Numerous civilian staff members and officials have been killed or taken hostage in the line of work. In 2003, a terrorist bombing killed more than 20 people, including a senior UN official, at a UN facility in Baghdad, Iraq.

Peaceful uses of outer space and the seabed. In 1958, the UN secretary-general asked all nations to agree not to claim territory in outer space. The General Assembly stated in 1963 that outer space should benefit all people and no nation could claim any of it. In 1967, more than 90 countries signed a treaty reflecting these aims.

The question of uses of the seabed came before the General Assembly for the first time in 1967. The Assembly noted that new inventions allowed nations to use the seabed as a source of valuable minerals and in other new ways. The Assembly appointed a permanent 42-nation committee to study the problem. The committee agreed that a large area of the seabed should be beyond the control of individual nations and should be used only for the benefit of all people. In 1971, the UN created a treaty barring the testing or use of nuclear weapons from the seabed beyond a 12-nautical-mile coastal zone. The treaty took effect in 1972. In 1982, a UN conference adopted the Law of the Sea Treaty Convention, a treaty that covered many uses of the ocean. The pact took effect in 1994.

Working for self-government

Another major goal of the United Nations is to help peoples and territories gain self-government and independence from colonial rule. The organization also works to assist former territories in the development of free political institutions.

After World War II ended in 1945, the European nations that controlled most colonies in Africa and Asia lacked the resources to continue ruling their colonies. Demands for self-government had been growing among colonial peoples, and many people throughout the world had come to oppose colonialism as unjust. In 1960, the UN General Assembly adopted a resolution called the Declaration on the Granting of Independence to Colonial Countries and Peoples. The resolution declared that "immediate steps shall be taken ... to transfer all powers" to the peoples in colonies "to enable them to enjoy complete independence and freedom."

From 1950 to 1980, more than 45 African colonies gained their freedom. Most European colonies in Asia and the Middle East also became self-governing. The formation of so many new nations led to a big increase in the membership of the UN. Seventeen newly independent nations, 16 of them African, joined the UN in 1960.

Much of the work of ending colonial rule was carried out by the UN Trusteeship Council. From 1945 to 1994,

Important dates in UN history

1945 (Oct. 24) The UN was established when the required number of nations approved the Charter of the United Nations.

1946 The first session of the General Assembly took place in London.

1948 (June) The first UN observer mission, the UN Truce Supervision Organization, was established and sent to the Middle East to monitor a truce between Arab countries and Israel.

1948 (Dec. 10) The UN approved the Universal Declaration of Human Rights, which asserts that all people are equal in dignity and rights, and have the right to life, liberty, and security.

1950 The UN became the first world organization to use force to stop aggression when it sent troops to prevent Communist North Korea from taking over South Korea in the Korean War.

1954 The Office of the United Nations High Commissioner for Refugees was awarded the Nobel Peace Prize for providing protection for millions of refugees.

1956 (November) The General Assembly established the first UN peacekeeping force, the United Nations Emergency Force, to find a peaceful solution to a dispute over the Suez Canal.

1965 UNICEF was awarded the Nobel Peace Prize for its aid to children.

1968 The General Assembly endorsed the Treaty on the Non-Proliferation of Nuclear Weapons, a pact designed to stop the spread of such weapons. The treaty took effect in 1970.

1972 The first UN Environment Conference was held in Stock-holm, Sweden. The conference led to the establishment of the UN Environment Programme to encourage international cooperation to fight pollution and preserve natural resources.

1981 The Office of the United Nations High Commissioner for Refugees was again awarded the Nobel Peace Prize.

1987 UN efforts led to the signing of the first global environmental protection treaty, a pact known as the Montreal Protocol on Substances That Deplete the Ozone Layer. The treaty took effect in 1989.

1988 UN peacekeeping forces were awarded the Nobel Peace Prize for helping control military conflicts in the Middle East and other parts of the world.

1991 The UN, for the second time in its history, used force to stop aggression when it sent troops to expel Iraq from Kuwait in the Persian Gulf War of 1991.

1994 The UN Convention on the Law of the Sea, which covered many uses of the ocean, took effect after 60 nations ratified it.

2000 The 55th General Assembly session, called the Millennium Assembly, became the largest gathering of world leaders ever assembled.

2001 The UN and its secretary-general, Kofi Annan, were awarded the Nobel Peace Prize.

2003 UN Security Council members disagreed over the issue of invading Iraq. The United States moved toward war despite the disagreement among the Security Council members.

the Trusteeship Council helped 11 territories gain self-government, either as independent nations or by voluntarily becoming part of an independent nation. The council suspended its operations in 1994 after Palau, the last of the territories, became self-governing and joined the United Nations. For more information, see the section *The Trusteeship Council* earlier in this article.

The campaign to secure Namibian independence ranks as the UN's most extensive effort to free a former colony. In 1966, the General Assembly voted to end South Africa's administration of Namibia. However, South Africa refused to let a UN council enter the region. The South West Africa People's Organization (SWAPO), a black Namibian political group, tried to persuade South Africa to grant Namibia independence. In the mid-1960's, it began using guerrilla tactics. In 1989, the UN approved a plan calling for Namibia's full independence. Later that year, the UN sent a peacekeeping force to the region. South Africa withdrew its troops from Namibia by November 1989. In 1990, Namibia gained independence after holding UN-supervised elections. The UN withdrew its peacekeeping force in 1991.

The UN has also worked to establish an independent state for native Palestinians in the region of Palestine. In 1974, the General Assembly adopted a resolution recognizing the right of Palestinians, including those in Israel, to nationhood. See **Palestine.**

In 1999, the UN created an interim administration for East Timor to help its people prepare for full independence. The administration provided security, helped develop civil and social services, and coordinated and delivered humanitarian aid. East Timor became independent in 2002. See **East Timor; Timor.**

The founding of the UN

Early in World War II, the representatives of nine European governments fled to London. Nazi Germany had conquered much of Europe and had driven these leaders from their homelands. Representatives of the United Kingdom and the Commonwealth nations met in London with leaders of Belgium, Czechoslovakia, France, Greece, Luxembourg, the Netherlands, Norway, Poland, and Yugoslavia. On June 12, 1941, all these nations signed a declaration pledging to work for a free world, where people could live in peace and security. This pledge, usually called the Inter-Allied Declaration, was the first step toward building the UN.

The Atlantic Charter followed the Inter-Allied Declaration by two months. It was signed by President Franklin D. Roosevelt of the United States and Prime Minister Winston Churchill of the United Kingdom. The Atlantic Charter expressed their hope for a world where all people could live free from fear and need. It also expressed their intention to seek eventual disarmament and economic cooperation. See **Atlantic Charter.**

On Jan. 1, 1942, representatives of 26 nations signed the Declaration by United Nations. This was the first official use of the words *United Nations.* The declaration approved the aims of the Atlantic Charter and was later signed by 21 other nations.

On Oct. 30, 1943, representatives of the United Kingdom, China, the Soviet Union, and the United States signed the Moscow Declaration on General Security. This declaration approved the idea of establishing an international organization for preserving world peace. A month later, Roosevelt, Churchill, and Premier Joseph Stalin of the Soviet Union met at Tehran, Iran. The three men declared that they recognized the responsibility of all the United Nations to achieve lasting peace. See **Tehran Conference.**

The Dumbarton Oaks Conference. In 1944, representatives of China, the Soviet Union, the United Kingdom, and the United States held meetings at the Dumbarton Oaks estate in Washington, D.C., and made a plan for a peacekeeping organization. The plan's main feature was a Security Council on which the United Kingdom, China, France, the Soviet Union, and the United States would be permanently represented. The issue of voting rights and procedures within the Council remained unsettled, however. See **Dumbarton Oaks.**

In February 1945, Roosevelt, Churchill, and Stalin met at Yalta in the Crimea. At this meeting, they agreed that some minor actions of the Security Council could not be vetoed by the permanent members. The three leaders announced that a conference of United Nations would open in San Francisco on April 25, 1945. This conference would use the plan worked out at the Dumbarton Oaks Conference to help prepare a charter for the UN.

The San Francisco Conference. Delegates from 50 nations met in San Francisco for the United Nations Conference on International Organization. The conference opened on April 25, 1945, 13 days after the death of Roosevelt and 12 days before the surrender of Germany. Victory over Japan was still four months away.

At the conference, some major disagreements arose between the Big Three (the United Kingdom, the Soviet Union, and the United States) and the smaller, less powerful nations. The Big Three believed they could guarantee future peace only if they continued to cooperate as they had during the war. They insisted that the Charter of the United Nations should give them the power to veto actions of the Security Council. The smaller nations opposed the veto power but could not defeat it. They did succeed in adding to the importance of such UN organs as the General Assembly and the Economic and Social Council. In these bodies, responsibilities could be shared more equally than in the Security Council. Such efforts by smaller nations helped create an organization that had far-reaching powers and responsibilities.

On June 26, 1945, all 50 nations present at the conference voted to accept the charter. Poland had been unable to attend but later signed the charter as an original member. The charter then had to be approved by the governments of the five permanent members of the Security Council and of a majority of the other nations that signed it. It went into effect on Oct. 24, 1945, a date celebrated every year as United Nations Day.

Building UN Headquarters. The first session of the General Assembly opened in London early in 1946. The delegates took up the question of where the permanent headquarters of the United Nations should be. They considered invitations from various countries and finally agreed that the headquarters should be in the United States. On Dec. 14, 1946, the Assembly accepted a gift of $8 ½ million from John D. Rockefeller, Jr., of the United States to buy 18 acres (7 hectares) of land along the East River in New York City. The city itself donated additional land in the area. In 1947, the General Assembly approved plans for the headquarters buildings. The next year, the U.S. Congress approved an interest-free loan of $65 million for their construction. The buildings were completed in the fall of 1952.

Continuing problems

Finances. Every UN member must pay a share of the organization's daily expenses. The amount each member pays depends on its ability to pay. However, the UN has been weakened by the failure of many of its members to pay their share.

Membership questions. Most nations are members of the United Nations. The question of membership for Communist China came up at every General Assembly session from 1950 to 1971. In 1971, the Assembly voted to expel Nationalist China and admit Communist China to the UN.

In 1992, the UN suspended Yugoslavia's participation in the General Assembly and in the Economic and Social Council after most Yugoslav republics had declared their independence. All the independent republics have been admitted to the UN as separate nations. Under new government, Yugoslavia rejoined the UN in 2000. In 2003, Yugoslavia changed its name to Serbia and Montenegro. In 2006, the two parts of the country—Serbia and Montenegro—separated into independent countries. Serbia retained the existing UN seat. Montenegro gained separate membership.

Nations join the UN for various reasons. Membership gives some nations a place in the international community that they might not otherwise have. It enables small nations to bring their problems to public attention and to take part in UN programs of economic and technical assistance. But the presence of many small nations in the UN has also created some problems. In the General Assembly, the vote of the smallest state counts the same as the vote of the largest. Some nations have suggested that small countries be given less than a full vote.

Only one nation—Indonesia—has ever withdrawn from the UN. But it rejoined the UN less than two years

United Nations

The signing of the Charter of the UN took place on June 26, 1945. President Harry S. Truman, *far left,* stood by as Secretary of State Edward R. Stettinius, Jr., signed for the United States.

later. Most nations realize the importance of international effort in dealing with certain kinds of economic and social problems. Above all, members understand that UN efforts toward peacekeeping and peacemaking can help prevent a third world war.

Policy disagreements. In some cases, disagreements among members may affect the UN's ability to work toward peace. In 2002 and 2003, for instance, members of the UN Security Council debated whether military action was necessary to confront Iraq's suspected possession of banned weapons. The United States and the United Kingdom supported military action, while France, Germany, and Russia argued for more time to seek a diplomatic solution to the problem. The sides were unable to reach an agreement, and the United States and the United Kingdom led a military campaign against Iraq without the Council's backing. United States President George W. Bush argued that the Security Council had "not lived up to its responsibilities" in disarming Iraq.

In 2004, the UN received criticism for its handling of an "oil-for-food" program in Iraq. Under this program, which lasted from 1996 to 2003, money from Iraqi oil sales was to be used, with UN supervision, to buy food and medicine for Iraqi civilians. However, investigations later revealed that Saddam Hussein, then president of Iraq, was able to abuse the program and profit illegally from oil sales. Some critics claimed that several UN officials also abused the program.

Supporters and critics of the UN have long debated on reforms that would improve the effectiveness of the institution. Secretary-General Kofi Annan was a major advocate of reform. His recommendations were made in a 2004 report called "A More Secure World: Our Shared Responsibility." Annan's suggestions continue to play a role in UN debates. Richard E. Rupp

Related articles in *World Book* include:

Biographies

Albright, Madeleine Korbel
Annan, Kofi Atta
Ban Ki-moon
Boutros-Ghali, Boutros
Bunche, Ralph J.
Hammarskjöld, Dag
Lie, Trygve
Pandit, Vijaya L.
Pearson, Lester B.
Pérez de Cuéllar, Javier
Richardson, Bill
Smuts, Jan C.
Spaak, Paul-Henri
Thant, U
Waldheim, Kurt

Specialized agencies

Food and Agriculture Organization
International Civil Aviation Organization
International Development Association
International Finance Corporation
International Fund for Agricultural Development
International Labour Organization
International Maritime Organization
International Monetary Fund
International Telecommunication Union
Postal Union, Universal
UNESCO
United Nations Human Rights Council
United Nations Industrial Development Organization
World Bank
World Health Organization
World Meteorological Organization

Other related articles

Cold War
Cuban missile crisis
Human Rights, Universal Declaration of
International Atomic Energy Agency
International Court of Justice
International Criminal Court
Korean War
Law of the Sea Convention
League of Nations
Nuclear Nonproliferation Treaty
San Francisco Conference
UNICEF
United Nations University

Outline

I. **The charter**
A. Purposes and principles
B. Membership requirements
C. The six major UN organs
D. Amending the charter

II. **The General Assembly**
A. Powers
B. Meetings and voting
C. Committees

III. **The Security Council**
A. Powers
B. Meetings and committees
C. Voting

IV. **The Secretariat**
A. The secretary-general
B. Other employees

V. **Other main organs**
A. The Economic and Social Council
B. The International Court of Justice
C. The Trusteeship Council

VI. **Specialized agencies**

VII. **The members at work**
A. Delegations
B. Breaking the language barrier
C. Groups with common interests
D. Publications and information services

VIII. **Working for progress**
A. Economic and technical aid
B. Aid to refugees
C. Aid to children
D. Human rights
E. Peaceful uses of nuclear energy
F. Controlling the environment
G. Fighting hunger
H. Disaster relief

IX. **Working for peace and security**
A. Peacekeeping operations
B. Military actions
C. The end of the Cold War
D. Arms control
E. Fighting terrorism
F. Peaceful uses of outer space and the seabed

X. **Working for self-government**

XI. **The founding of the UN**
A. The Atlantic Charter
B. The Dumbarton Oaks Conference
C. The San Francisco Conference
D. Building UN Headquarters

XII. **Continuing problems**
A. Finances
B. Membership questions
C. Policy disagreements

Additional resources

Level I
Melvern, Linda. *United Nations.* Watts, 2001.
Patterson, Charles. *The Oxford 50th Anniversary Book of the United Nations.* Oxford, 1995.
Ross, Stewart. *United Nations.* Raintree, 2004.

Level II
Baehr, Peter R., and Gordenker, Leon. *The United Nations: Reality and Ideal.* 4th ed. Palgrave, 2005.
Fomerand, Jacques. *Historical Dictionary of the United Nations.* Rev. ed. Scarecrow, 2007.
Osmanczyk, Edmund J. *Encyclopedia of the United Nations and International Agreements.* Ed. By Anthony Mango. 4 vols. 3rd ed. Routledge, 2003.

The United Nations Web site at http://www.un.org presents additional information on the organization's activities.

United Nations Children's Fund. See UNICEF.

United Nations Educational, Scientific and Cultural Organization. See UNESCO.

United Nations Human Rights Council is a group within the United Nations (UN) that works to protect the rights and freedoms of all people. The council encourages worldwide respect for human rights and seeks to address situations where rights are violated. It also reviews the human-rights records of all UN members. The Human Rights Council consists of 47 member countries, which are elected by the UN General Assembly. The council meets in Geneva, Switzerland, regularly throughout the year.

From 1946 to 2006, the chief UN body responsible for safeguarding human rights was the UN Commission on Human Rights. The commission met annually and prepared recommendations and guidelines for the protection of rights and freedoms. However, by the early 2000's, many people believed that the commission lacked credibility and needed reform. Critics charged that certain members of the commission—such as Libya and Sudan—had poor human-rights records themselves. In March 2006, the UN General Assembly voted to replace the commission with the Human Rights Council. The council held its first meetings in June 2006.

Richard E. Rupp

United Nations Industrial Development Organization (UNIDO) is a specialized agency of the United Nations (UN) that promotes industrialization in developing countries. Most of the countries that belong to the United Nations are also members of UNIDO. UNIDO programs provide developing countries with assistance in such areas as industrial training and planning and in promoting lasting industrial development. In addition, the agency encourages investment in, and the transfer of technology to, developing countries. UNIDO was created in 1966 as part of the UN Secretariat. The agency became a specialized agency in 1986. Its headquarters are in Vienna, Austria.

Critically reviewed by the United Nations Industrial Development Organization

United Nations University is a worldwide research and advanced training institution established by the United Nations (UN). Unlike a traditional university, it has no campus, students, or faculty, and it does not grant degrees. Rather, the United Nations University is a central planning agency for networks of cooperating institutions and scholars.

The United Nations University promotes joint study and the exchange of knowledge to solve global problems. The university organizes and coordinates research, training, and information services worldwide. It has two main program areas: peace and governance and environmental and sustainable development.

The UN General Assembly chartered the United Nations University in 1973, and it began operations in 1975. The university chooses its own programs and the institutions and individuals through which it works. It receives most of its funds from a permanent endowment established by voluntary contributions from members of the United Nations. The university has headquarters in Tokyo.

P. A. McGinley

United Negro College Fund, usually called the UNCF, is a nonprofit fund-raising organization. Its membership consists of about 40 historically black colleges and universities in the United States. The UNCF raises money to help operate the schools, all of which are private. In addition, it provides other services to the colleges and universities, including educational and administrative counseling.

The organization was founded in 1944 by Frederick D. Patterson, president of Tuskegee Institute (now Tuskegee University). The UNCF receives contributions from corporations, foundations, and individuals. Headquarters are in Fairfax, Virginia.

Critically reviewed by the UNCF

United Parcel Service, Inc., is the world's largest package delivery company. The company, popularly known as UPS, operates throughout the United States and in more than 200 other countries and territories. It offers transportation of packages of all sizes by air, ground, and sea. The company also manages the *supply chains* of other businesses, performing such tasks as warehousing and managing transportation to bring products or services to market. United Parcel Service has headquarters in Atlanta.

In 1907, two teenagers named James Casey and Claude Ryan borrowed $100 and started a messenger service for businesses in Seattle. The firm later began delivering packages. In 1919, it was named United Parcel Service. By the early 1950's, the company was delivering for retail stores in more than a dozen metropolitan areas. Since 1952, UPS has been a *common carrier,* offering pickup and delivery service for both businesses and individuals.

Critically reviewed by United Parcel Service, Inc.

United Press International (UPI) is a privately owned worldwide news service. The service distributes news, photographs, and videotape to thousands of clients. Its clients include newspapers, radio and television stations, news magazines, cable television outlets, and Internet sites in many countries.

United Press Associations was formed in 1907 by Edward Wyllis Scripps. In the 1930's, United Press established a network of news bureaus throughout the world. In 1958, United Press merged with International News Service to form United Press International.

The E. W. Scripps Company sold United Press International in 1982 to Media News Corporation. In 1984, the British news agency Reuters (now Thomson Reuters) purchased UPI's foreign photo service. At around the same time, UPI, which had been experiencing financial problems, filed for reorganization under United States bankruptcy laws. The company was sold several times in the 1980's and 1990's. In 2000, the service was purchased by News World Communications, Inc., a newspaper publisher based in Washington, D.C., that is owned by the Unification Church. The size of UPI's operation has been much reduced from earlier times.

Maurine H. Beasley

United Service Organizations (USO) is a civilian nonprofit organization that serves the members of the United States armed forces and their families. It provides community information, family services, recreational activities, cultural programs, and celebrity entertainment. The USO offers its services worldwide in such locations as airport centers, fleet centers, and family and community centers. Volunteers help run the USO, which operates entirely on private contributions. The USO was founded in 1941 at the request of President Franklin D. Roosevelt. Its world headquarters are in Washington, D.C.

Critically reviewed by United Service Organizations

© Tom Bean, The Stock Market

Farms in the Midwest produce enormous quantities of corn, wheat, and other crops; and also dairy products and livestock. Flat, fertile land covers much of the central part of the United States.

© Ric Ergenbright

Scenic cityscapes in the United States attract visitors from throughout the world. In the picture shown here, the Golden Gate Bridge frames the San Francisco skyline.

United States

United States of America is the third largest country in the world in population, and it is the fourth largest country in area. China and India are the only countries with more people. Only Russia, Canada, and China have larger areas. The United States covers the entire midsection of North America, stretching from the Atlantic Ocean in the east to the Pacific Ocean in the west. It also includes Alaska, in the northwest corner of North America; and Hawaii, far out in the Pacific. The United States is often called the *U.S.,* *U.S.A.,* or *America.*

The land of the United States is as varied as it is vast. It ranges from the warm beaches of Florida and Hawaii to the frozen northlands of Alaska, and from the level Midwestern prairies to the snow-capped Rocky Mountains. This huge and beautiful country is rich in natural resources. It has great stretches of some of the most fertile soil on earth, a plentiful water supply and excellent water routes, and large stretches of forests. Huge deposits of valuable minerals, including coal, natural gas, and petroleum, lie underground.

The contributor of this article is Teresa A. Sullivan, Vice President and Graduate Dean, and Professor of Sociology and Law, at the University of Texas at Austin.

Economically, the United States is one of the world's most highly developed and productive nations. No other country equals the United States in the production of goods and services. Its people enjoy one of the world's highest standards of living.

Until the 1500's, most of what is now the United States was thinly populated forests and prairies. Small groups of Indians lived scattered over the land between the Atlantic and Pacific. Inuit (also called Eskimos) inhabited what is now Alaska, and Polynesians lived in Hawaii. People in Europe saw in this vast "new world" a chance to build new and better lives. Small groups of Spaniards settled in what is now the southeastern and western United States in the 1500's. People from England and some other European countries began settling along and near the East Coast during the 1600's. In 1776, colonists in the East established an independent nation based on freedom and economic opportunity. Through the years, large numbers of Europeans continued to settle in the United States. People from almost every other part of the world also settled in the country. Except for black Africans brought in as slaves, these immigrants came seeking the rights and the opportunities that had become part of the American way of life. As a result of this immigration, the United States today has one of the world's most varied populations. It has been called "a nation of immigrants."

The vast space and resources of the land, the ideals of

© David Ball, The Stock Market

The Statue of Liberty is a symbol of the United States and one of the country's most famous sites. The huge copper sculpture stands on Liberty Island in New York Harbor.

© John Running, Black Star

Yellowstone National Park and other national parks are among America's favorite vacationlands. Yellowstone, located chiefly in Wyoming, is home to buffaloes and other wild animals.

freedom and economic opportunity, and hard work by the people all helped build the United States into the economic giant it is today. The Americans—as the people are commonly called—also made major contributions in such fields as technology, science, and medicine. Americans developed the mass production system of manufacturing, the electric light bulb, the telephone, polio vaccine, and the transistor. They also created the skyscraper and such new art forms as jazz and musical comedy.

At times, the U.S. economy has run into difficulty. Even so, it remains one of the most productive systems ever developed. In some cases, groups of Americans have suffered socially and economically from discrimination. But the country's laws have helped many people overcome discrimination and achieve better lives.

This article discusses the nation's regions, people, way of life, land, climate, and economy. For government and history information, see **United States, Government of the,** and **United States, History of the.**

The nation

Political divisions. The United States consists of 50 states and the District of Columbia. The District of Columbia is a piece of land set aside by the federal government for the nation's capital, Washington, D.C. For a list of the states, see the table in this article titled *Facts in brief about the states.*

In area, population, and economic output, some of the states are comparable to many nations. The United States has a federal system of government, which gives the states many powers that national governments have in most other countries. For example, the states have broad control over public education and the establishment of civil and criminal laws.

Regions. The states of the United States, excluding Alaska and Hawaii, are often divided into seven major regions. Each region is made up of states that have similarities in geography, climate, economy, traditions, and history. The regions are (1) New England, (2) the Middle Atlantic States, (3) the Southern States, (4) the Midwestern States, (5) the Rocky Mountain States, (6) the Southwestern States, and (7) the Pacific Coast States. For a list of the states in each region, see the table titled *Regions of the United States* in this article. The map that accompanies the table shows the location of each of these regions.

New England is a small region in the northeast corner of the country that is known for charming rural villages, picturesque fishing harbors, and colorful autumn scenery. It was the nation's first industrial center, and manufacturing is still a leading source of income. Industrial cities dot southern New England. Much of the land is too hilly or rocky to grow crops. But New England produces large amounts of dairy and poultry products and is famous for its maple syrup. Many tourists visit the region to see its historic sites—especially those from colonial times—and to enjoy its natural beauty.

United States in brief

Capital: Washington, D.C.
Language: English spoken throughout the country, but does not have official status. Spanish second most common language.
Official name: United States of America.
Motto: *In God We Trust,* adopted on July 30, 1956.
National anthem: "The Star-Spangled Banner," adopted on March 3, 1931.
Flag: Adopted on June 14, 1777.
Bird: Bald eagle, adopted on June 20, 1782.
Flower: Rose, adopted on Oct. 7, 1986.
Largest cities:

New York City (8,008,278)	Philadelphia (1,517,550)
Los Angeles (3,694,820)	Phoenix (1,321,045)
Chicago (2,896,016)	San Diego (1,223,400)
Houston (1,953,631)	Dallas (1,188,580)

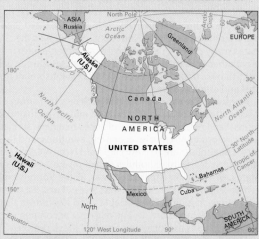

Symbols of the United States include the American flag and the Great Seal. The eagle holds an olive branch and arrows, symbolizing a desire for peace but the ability to wage war.

Land and climate

Land: Lies in North America. Includes Alaska and Hawaii. Borders Canada and Mexico. Pacific and Atlantic oceans.
Area: 3,615,276 mi² (9,363,520 km²), including 78,937 mi² (204,447 km²) of inland water but excluding 60,053 mi² (155,535 km²) of Great Lakes and Lake St. Clair and 42,529 mi² (110,148 km²) of coastal water. *Greatest distances ex-*

cluding Alaska and Hawaii—east-west, 2,807 mi (4,517 km); north-south, 1,598 mi (2,572 km). *Greatest distances in Alaska*—north-south, about 1,350 mi (2,150 km); east-west, about 2,350 mi (3,800 km). *Greatest distance in Hawaii*—northwest-southeast, about 1,500 mi (2,400 km). *Extreme points including Alaska and Hawaii*—northernmost, Point Barrow, Alaska; southernmost, Ka Lae, Hawaii; easternmost, West Quoddy Head, Maine; westernmost, Cape Wrangell, Attu Island, Alaska. *Coastline*—4,993 mi (8,035 km), excluding Alaska and Hawaii; 12,383 mi (19,929 km), including Alaska and Hawaii.

Elevation: *Highest*—Mount McKinley in Alaska, 20,320 ft (6,194 m) above sea level. *Lowest*—In Death Valley in California, 282 ft (86 m) below sea level.
Physical features: *Longest river*—Missouri, 2,565 mi (4,130 km). *Largest lake within the United States*—Michigan, 22,300 mi² (57,757 km²). *Largest island*—island of Hawaii, 4,038 mi² (10,458 km²).

Government

Form of government: Republic.
Head of state and head of government: President.
Legislature: Congress of two houses—the House of Representatives (435 members) and the Senate (100 members).
Executive: President, assisted by an appointed Cabinet.
Judiciary: Highest court is the Supreme Court of the United States.
Political subdivisions: 50 states.
For details, see United States, Government of the.

People

Population: *Estimated 2008 population*—304,848,000; *2000 census*—281,421,906.
Population density: 84 per mi² (33 per km²).
Distribution: 80 percent urban, 20 percent rural.
Major ethnic/national groups: About 75 percent white, 13 percent of Hispanic origin (who may also be white, black, or American Indian), 12 percent black, 4 percent of Asian descent, 1 percent American Indian.
Major religions: About 50 percent Protestant, 40 percent Roman Catholic, 2 percent Eastern Orthodox, 2 percent Jewish, 2 percent Mormon, 2 percent Muslim.

Population trend

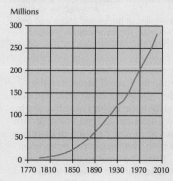

Millions

Year	Population
1790	3,929,214
1810	7,239,881
1830	12,866,020
1850	23,191,876
1870	39,818,449
1890	62,974,714
1910	91,972,266
1930	122,775,046
1950	150,697,361
1970	203,302,031
1990	248,709,873
2000	281,421,906

Economy

Chief products: *Agriculture*—beef cattle, *broilers* (young, tender chickens), corn, cotton, dairy products, greenhouse and nursery products, hogs, soybeans, wheat. *Fishing industry*—crabs, salmon, shrimp. *Manufacturing*—chemicals, computer and electronic products, fabricated metal products, food products, machinery, paper products, plastics and rubber products, transportation equipment. *Mining*—coal, natural gas, petroleum.
Money: *Basic unit*—United States dollar. One hundred cents equal one dollar.
Foreign trade: *Major exported goods*—chemical elements and compounds, including plastic materials; food crops and live animals; machinery and transportation equipment; manufactured articles; metals and paper. *Major imported goods*—chemical products; iron, steel, and other metals; fuels and lubricants; machinery and transportation equipment; manufactured articles; paper and newsprint. *Main trading partners*—Canada, China, Japan, and Mexico.

A New England village covered with snow lies among low hills in Vermont. Such tiny, picturesque settlements are common in the northeastern corner of the United States. English Puritans settled the region during the 1600's.

© Tom Pantages

Regions of the United States

This map shows the location of the seven regions of the continental United States that are discussed in this section. The table with the map lists the states within each region.

New England
Connecticut, Maine, Massachusetts, New Hampshire, Rhode Island, Vermont

Middle Atlantic States
New Jersey, New York, Pennsylvania

Southern States
Alabama, Arkansas, Delaware, Florida, Georgia, Kentucky, Louisiana, Maryland, Mississippi, North Carolina, South Carolina, Tennessee, Virginia, West Virginia

Midwestern States
Illinois, Indiana, Iowa, Kansas, Michigan, Minnesota, Missouri, Nebraska, North Dakota, Ohio, South Dakota, Wisconsin

Rocky Mountain States
Colorado, Idaho, Montana, Nevada, Utah, Wyoming

Southwestern States
Arizona*, New Mexico*, Oklahoma, Texas

Pacific Coast States
California, Oregon, Washington

*Arizona and New Mexico are often grouped with the Rocky Mountain States.

Many New Englanders, especially in the rural north, are descendants of English Puritans who settled the region during the 1600's. The more densely populated southern section of New England has people of many backgrounds, including African, Irish, Italian, and French Canadian. The southern section includes Boston, New England's largest city by far.

The Middle Atlantic States Region stretches inland from the Atlantic Ocean southwest of New England. Deepwater harbors help make the region a major center of international trade. The busiest harbor is at New York City, the largest city in the United States. Factories in and near such Middle Atlantic cities as—in order of size—New York City, Philadelphia, Pittsburgh, Buffalo, and Newark produce a wide variety of goods. Coal mining

Main outlying areas of the United States

Name	Acquired	Status
American Samoa	*	Unorganized unincorporated territory
Baker Island and Jarvis Island	1856	Unincorporated territory
Guam	1898	Organized unincorporated territory
Howland Island	1856	Unincorporated possession
Johnston Island and Sand Island	1858	Unincorporated territory
Kingman Reef	1922	Unincorporated territory
Midway Island	1867	Unincorporated territory
Northern Mariana Islands	1947	Commonwealth
Palmyra Island	1898	Unincorporated possession
Puerto Rico	1898	Commonwealth
Virgin Islands of the United States	1917	Organized unincorporated territory
Wake Island	1898	Unincorporated possession

*Acquired in stages between 1900 and 1925.

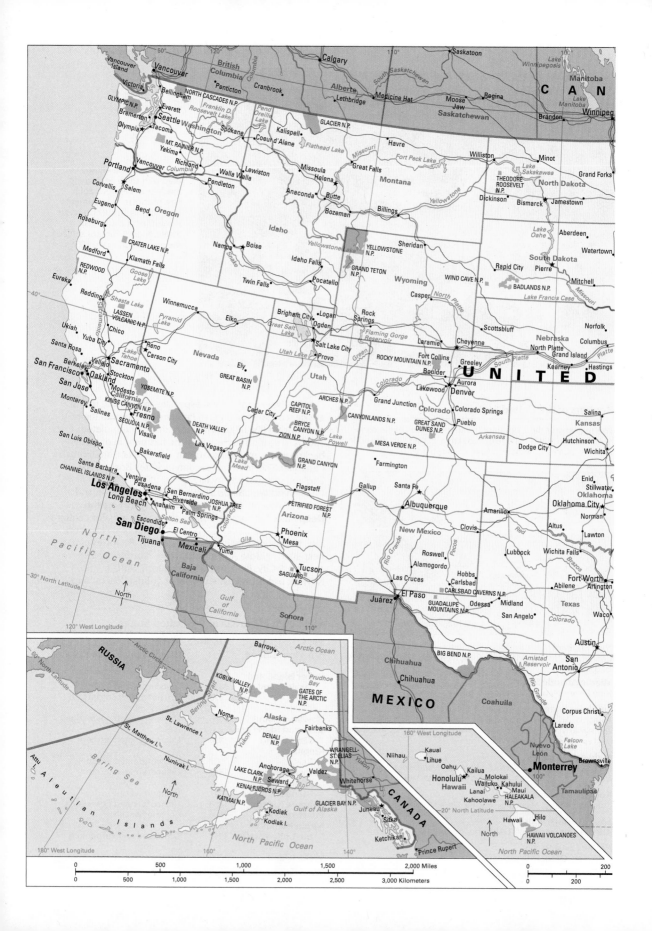

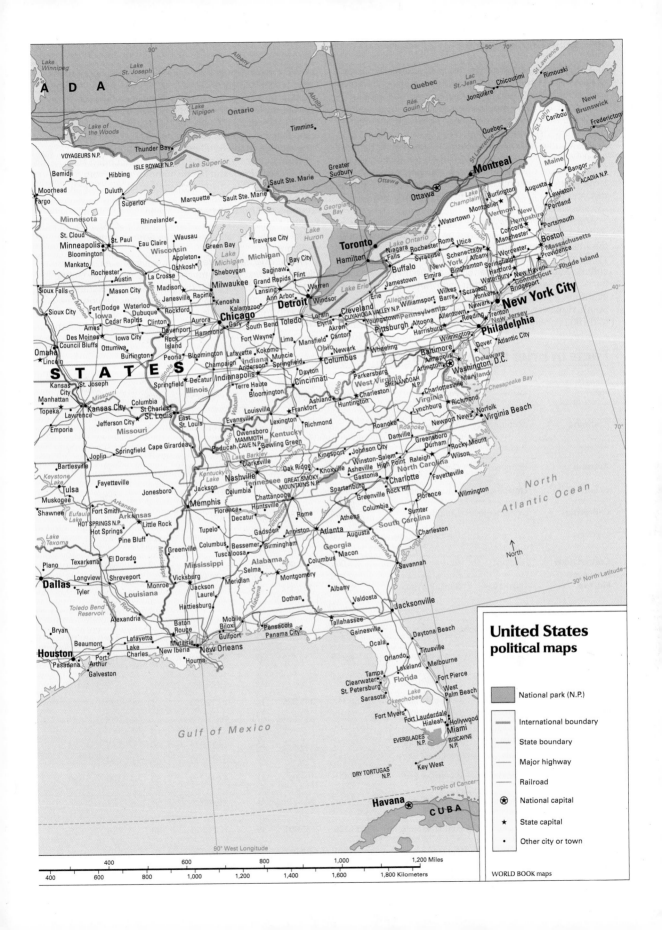

and related industries are important economic activities in the western part of the Middle Atlantic States Region. Farms dot hillsides and fertile plains in various parts of the region. Forested mountains, sandy seashores, scenic lakes and rivers, historic sites, and big-city attractions draw many visitors to the region.

The Middle Atlantic States Region ranks as the nation's most densely populated area. Its urban population includes people of varied European backgrounds, and large groups of people of African American, Latin American, and Asian ancestry. Many of the region's rural dwellers are of British descent.

The Southern States Region is an area of rolling hills, mountains, and plains bordered by broad beaches along the Atlantic Ocean and the Gulf of Mexico. Until the mid-1900's, the region's economy was based heavily on agriculture. Such warm-weather crops as sugar cane, rice, tobacco, and—especially—cotton contributed greatly to the economy. Agriculture has retained importance in the South. However, an industrial boom that began in the mid-1900's greatly increased manufacturing and im-

proved the balance of the region's economy. Tourists flock to coastal resorts in the South—especially in winter, when temperatures are usually relatively mild. Jacksonville is the largest city of the region. Baltimore, Memphis, Washington, D.C., Nashville, Charlotte, and New Orleans rank next in size. Washington, D.C., is not part of a state, but it is in the Southern States Region.

Large numbers of Southerners are descended from early English, Irish, and Scottish immigrants. From the 1600's to the 1800's, many Africans were brought to the region to work on plantations as slaves. Today, large numbers of African Americans live in the Southern States Region. Many Southerners have a strong sense of regional loyalty and take pride in the South's history and traditions.

The Midwestern States Region is a vast area of generally flat land that covers much of the center of the United States. The Midwest is famous for its large stretches of fertile soil. Farms in the Midwestern States Region produce enormous quantities of corn, wheat, and other crops; and also dairy products and livestock. In addition,

Facts in brief about the states

State	Capital	Popular name	Area (mi²)	(km²)	Rank in area	Population*	Rank in pop.*	Population density* (mi²)	(km²)
Alabama	Montgomery	The Heart of Dixie	51,718	133,950	29	4,447,100	23	82	33
Alaska	Juneau	Last Frontier	587,878	1,522,596	1	626,932	48	1.07	0.41
Arizona	Phoenix	Grand Canyon State	114,007	295,276	6	5,130,632	20	45	17
Arkansas	Little Rock	Natural State	53,183	137,742	27	2,673,400	33	50	19
California	Sacramento	Golden State	158,648	410,896	3	33,871,648	1	214	82
Colorado	Denver	Centennial State	104,100	269,618	8	4,301,261	24	41	16
Connecticut	Hartford	Constitution State	5,006	12,966	48	3,405,565	29	680	263
Delaware	Dover	First State	2,026	5,246	49	783,600	45	387	149
Florida	Tallahassee	Sunshine State	58,681	151,982	22	15,982,378	4	272	105
Georgia	Atlanta	Empire State of the South	58,930	152,627	21	8,186,453	10	139	54
Hawaii	Honolulu	Aloha State	6,459	16,729	47	1,211,537	42	188	72
Idaho	Boise	Gem State	83,574	216,456	13	1,293,953	39	15	6
Illinois	Springfield	Land of Lincoln	56,343	145,928	24	12,419,293	5	220	85
Indiana	Indianapolis	Hoosier State	36,185	93,720	38	6,080,485	14	168	65
Iowa	Des Moines	Hawkeye State	56,276	145,754	25	2,926,324	30	52	20
Kansas	Topeka	Sunflower State	82,282	213,110	14	2,688,418	32	33	13
Kentucky	Frankfort	Bluegrass State	40,411	104,665	37	4,041,769	25	100	39
Louisiana	Baton Rouge	Pelican State	47,717	123,586	31	4,468,976	22	94	36
Maine	Augusta	Pine Tree State	33,128	85,801	39	1,274,923	40	38	15
Maryland	Annapolis	Old Line State	10,455	27,077	42	5,296,486	19	507	196

*2000 census figures.

the Midwest has a number of large industrial cities. The cities include, in order of size, Chicago, Detroit, Indianapolis, Columbus, Milwaukee, and Cleveland.

The Mississippi River system, the Great Lakes, and many railroads give the region an excellent transportation network. Lakes and rivers—some of which are set among rolling hills and rugged bluffs—provide numerous recreation areas.

The Midwestern States Region has a varied population. Its rural areas include large groups of descendants of settlers from England, Germany, Norway, Scotland, Sweden, and eastern and southern Europe. The region's urban population includes many descendants of people who came from northern, southern, and eastern Europe. Other large ethnic groups in the cities include African Americans, Mexican Americans, and Asian Americans.

The Rocky Mountain States Region lies west of the Midwest. It is named for the rugged, majestic Rocky Mountains, which cut through it. The region also has areas of deserts, plains, and plateaus. Although much of it is a thinly populated wilderness, some of its cities and towns are among the nation's fastest-growing areas. Denver and Las Vegas rank as the region's largest cities.

Rich deposits of gold, silver, and other metals first attracted settlers to the Rocky Mountain States Region. Mining remains an important economic activity, but such services as health care, hotels, and data processing are now the chief sources of income. Cattle and other livestock graze on dry, grassy ranges, and farmers grow a variety of crops in the Rocky Mountain States Region. Many tourists visit the region to enjoy its scenic beauty and numerous ski resorts.

The population of the Rocky Mountain States Region includes people of European descent, African Americans, Mexican Americans, and American Indians. Mormons, whose ancestors founded a religious community in Utah in the 1800's, form an important cultural group in the Rocky Mountain States Region.

The Southwestern States Region spreads over a vast area that is sometimes called the "wide open spaces." There, cattle graze on huge ranches, and vast fields of cotton and other crops soak up rays of blazing sunshine.

State abbreviation	State bird	State flower	State tree	State song	Admitted to the Union†	Order of admission	Members of Congress Senate	House
AL	Yellow-hammer	Camellia	Southern longleaf pine	"Alabama"	1819	22	2	7
AK	Willow ptarmigan	Forget-me-not	Sitka spruce	"Alaska's Flag"	1959	49	2	1
AZ	Cactus wren	Saguaro cactus blossom	Paloverde	"Arizona"; "Arizona March Song"	1912	48	2	8
AR	Mockingbird	Apple blossom	Pine	"Arkansas"; "Oh, Arkansas"	1836	25	2	4
CA	California quail	Golden poppy	California redwood	"I Love You, California"	1850	31	2	53
CO	Lark bunting	White and lavender columbine	Colorado blue spruce	"Where the Columbines Grow"; "Rocky Mountain High."	1876	38	2	7
CT	American robin	Mountain laurel	Charter oak	"Yankee Doodle"	1788	5	2	5
DE	Blue hen chicken	Peach blossom	American holly	"Our Delaware"	1787	1	2	1
FL	Mockingbird	Orange blossom	Sabal palm	"Old Folks at Home" ("Swanee River"); "Florida (Where the Sawgrass Meets the Sky)"	1845	27	2	25
GA	Brown thrasher	Cherokee rose	Live oak	"Georgia on My Mind"	1788	4	2	13
HI	Nene (Hawaiian goose)	Yellow hibiscus	Kukui	"Hawaii Ponoi" (Hawaii's Own)	1959	50	2	2
ID	Mountain bluebird	Syringa	Western white pine	"Here We Have Idaho"	1890	43	2	2
IL	Cardinal	Violet	White oak	"Illinois"	1818	21	2	19
IN	Cardinal	Peony	Tulip-poplar (yellow-poplar)	"On the Banks of the Wabash, Far Away"	1816	19	2	9
IA	Eastern goldfinch	Wild rose	Oak	"The Song of Iowa"	1846	29	2	5
KS	Western meadowlark	Native sunflower	Cottonwood	"Home on the Range"	1861	34	2	4
KY	Cardinal	Goldenrod	Tulip-poplar (yellow-poplar)	"My Old Kentucky Home"	1792	15	2	6
LA	Eastern brown pelican	Magnolia	Baldcypress	"Give Me Louisiana"; "You Are My Sunshine"	1812	18	2	7
ME	Chickadee	White pine cone and tassel	White pine	"State of Maine Song"	1820	23	2	2
MD	Baltimore oriole	Black-eyed Susan	White oak	"Maryland, My Maryland"	1788	7	2	8

†The 13 colonies became the original states of the Union on July 4, 1776, when they formed the United States of America. Traditionally, however, the date of admission to the Union for these states is considered to be the year the state ratified the U.S. Constitution.

Facts in brief about the states

State	Capital	Popular name	Area (mi²)	Area (km²)	Rank in area	Population*	Rank in pop.*	Population density* (mi²)	Population density* (km²)
Massachusetts	Boston	Bay State	8,262	21,398	45	6,349,097	13	768	297
Michigan	Lansing	Wolverine State	58,513	151,548	23	9,938,444	8	170	66
Minnesota	St. Paul	Gopher State	84,397	218,587	12	4,919,479	21	58	23
Mississippi	Jackson	Magnolia State	47,698	123,537	32	2,844,658	31	60	23
Missouri	Jefferson City	Show Me State	69,709	180,546	19	5,595,211	17	80	31
Montana	Helena	Treasure State	147,047	380,849	4	902,195	44	6	2
Nebraska	Lincoln	Cornhusker State	77,359	200,358	15	1,711,263	38	22	9
Nevada	Carson City	Silver State	110,567	286,367	7	1,998,257	35	18	7
New Hampshire	Concord	Granite State	9,283	24,044	44	1,235,786	41	133	51
New Jersey	Trenton	Garden State	7,790	20,175	46	8,414,350	9	1,080	417
New Mexico	Santa Fe	Land of Enchantment	121,599	314,939	5	1,819,046	36	15	6
New York	Albany	Empire State	49,112	127,200	30	18,976,457	3	386	149
North Carolina	Raleigh	Tar Heel State	52,672	136,421	28	8,049,313	11	153	59
North Dakota	Bismarck	Flickertail State	70,704	183,123	17	642,200	47	9	4
Ohio	Columbus	Buckeye State	41,328	107,040	35	11,353,140	7	275	106
Oklahoma	Oklahoma City	Sooner State	69,903	181,048	18	3,450,654	27	49	19
Oregon	Salem	Beaver State	97,052	251,365	10	3,421,399	28	35	14
Pennsylvania	Harrisburg	Keystone State	45,310	117,351	33	12,281,054	6	271	105
Rhode Island	Providence	Ocean State	1,213	3,142	50	1,048,319	43	864	334
South Carolina	Columbia	Palmetto State	31,117	80,593	40	4,012,012	26	129	50
South Dakota	Pierre	Mount Rushmore State	77,122	199,744	16	754,844	46	10	4
Tennessee	Nashville	Volunteer State	42,146	109,158	34	5,689,283	16	135	52
Texas	Austin	Lone Star State	266,874	691,201	2	20,851,820	2	78	30
Utah	Salt Lake City	Beehive State	84,905	219,902	11	2,233,169	34	26	10
Vermont	Montpelier	Green Mountain State	9,615	24,903	43	608,827	49	63	24
Virginia	Richmond	Old Dominion	40,598	105,149	36	7,078,515	12	174	67
Washington	Olympia	Evergreen State	68,126	176,446	20	5,894,121	15	87	33
West Virginia	Charleston	Mountain State	24,231	62,759	41	1,808,344	37	75	29
Wisconsin	Madison	Badger State	56,145	145,414	26	5,363,675	18	96	37
Wyoming	Cheyenne	Equality State	97,818	253,349	9	493,782	50	5	2

*2000 census figures.

State abbreviation	State bird	State flower	State tree	State song	Admitted to the Union†	Order of admission	Members of Congress Senate	House
MA	Black-capped chickadee	Mayflower	American elm	"All Hail to Massachusetts"	1788	6	2	10
MI	Robin	Apple blossom	White pine	"My Michigan"	1837	26	2	15
MN	Loon	Pink and white lady's-slipper	Norway, or red, pine	"Hail! Minnesota"	1858	32	2	8
MS	Mockingbird	Magnolia	Magnolia	"Go Mis-sis-sip-pi"	1817	20	2	4
MO	Native bluebird	White hawthorn blossom	Flowering dogwood	"Missouri Waltz"	1821	24	2	9
MT	Western meadowlark	Bitter root	Ponderosa pine	"Montana"	1889	41	2	1
NE	Western meadowlark	Goldenrod	Cottonwood	"Beautiful Nebraska"	1867	37	2	3
NV	Mountain bluebird†	Sagebrush†	Single-leaf piñon and bristlecone pine	"Home Means Nevada"	1864	36	2	3
NH	Purple finch	Purple lilac	White birch	"Old New Hampshire"	1788	9	2	2
NJ	Eastern goldfinch	Common meadow violet	Red oak	None	1787	3	2	13
NM	Greater roadrunner	Yucca flower	Piñon, or nut pine	"O, Fair New Mexico"	1912	47	2	3
NY	Bluebird	Rose	Sugar maple	"I Love New York"	1788	11	2	29
NC	Cardinal	Dogwood	Pine	"The Old North State"	1789	12	2	13
ND	Western meadowlark	Wild prairie rose	American elm	"North Dakota Hymn"	1889	39	2	1
OH	Red cardinal	Scarlet carnation	Buckeye	"Beautiful Ohio"	1803	17	2	18
OK	Scissor-tailed flycatcher	Rose	Redbud	"Oklahoma!"	1907	46	2	5
OR	Western meadowlark	Oregon grape	Douglas-fir	"Oregon, My Oregon"	1859	33	2	5
PA	Ruffed grouse	Mountain laurel	Hemlock	"Pennsylvania"	1787	2	2	19
RI	Rhode Island Red Hen	Violet	Red maple	"Rhode Island's It for Me"	1790	13	2	2
SC	Carolina wren	Yellow jessamine	Sabal palmetto	"Carolina"; "South Carolina on My Mind"	1788	8	2	6
SD	Chinese ring-necked pheasant	Pasqueflower	Black Hills spruce	"Hail, South Dakota"	1889	40	2	1
TN	Mockingbird	Iris	Tulip-poplar (yellow-poplar)	"My Homeland, Tennessee"; "My Tennessee"; "Rocky Top"; "The Tennessee Waltz"; "When It's Iris Time in Tennessee"	1796	16	2	9
TX	Mockingbird	Bluebonnet	Pecan	"Texas, Our Texas"	1845	28	2	32
UT	California sea gull	Sego lily	Blue spruce	"Utah, This Is the Place"	1896	45	2	3
VT	Hermit thrush	Red clover	Sugar maple	"These Green Mountains"	1791	14	2	1
VA	Northern cardinal	American dogwood	American dogwood	None§	1788	10	2	11
WA	American goldfinch	Coast rhododendron	Western hemlock	"Washington, My Home"	1889	42	2	9
WV	Cardinal	Rhododendron	Sugar maple	"The West Virginia Hills"; "This Is My West Virginia"; "West Virginia, My Home Sweet Home"	1863	35	2	3
WI	Robin	Wood violet	Sugar maple	"On, Wisconsin!"	1848	30	2	8
WY	Meadowlark	Indian paintbrush	Plains cottonwood	"Wyoming"	1890	44	2	1

†The 13 colonies became the original states of the Union on July 4, 1776, when they formed the United States of America. Traditionally, however, the date of admission to the Union for these states is considered to be the year the state ratified the Constitution.

§In its 1997 regular session, the Virginia legislature retired the state song "Carry Me Back to Old Virginia."

However, petroleum has brought the region most of its wealth. The region has large deposits of petroleum and natural gas, as well as various other minerals. In the 1900's, refineries and petrochemical factories led the way to industrialization in the Southwest.

The industrialization has helped bring about much urban growth in the Southwestern States Region. The region includes many of the nation's fastest-growing cities. Its largest cities are, in order of size, Houston, Phoenix, Dallas, San Antonio, Austin, El Paso, Fort Worth, and Tucson. The region also has many retirement communities. Tourist attractions in the Southwest include huge, unspoiled areas of incredible natural beauty, such as the Grand Canyon and the Painted Desert.

Many cultures come together in the Southwest. The population includes people of various European backgrounds, as well as African Americans, Mexican Americans, and American Indians.

The Pacific Coast States Region, which borders the Pacific Ocean, is known for its dense forests, rugged mountains, and dramatic ocean shore. The scenic beauty and relatively mild climate encourage an outdoor lifestyle enjoyed by both residents and tourists.

© Shrout & Shrout

A Southern mansion in Alabama dates from 1853. Originally a private home, it is now a museum and a reminder of the architecture of the South before the American Civil War (1861-1865).

Fertile valleys in the Pacific Coast States Region produce a large part of the nation's fruits, nuts, vegetables, and wine grapes. The region also has abundant timber, minerals, and fish. Much manufacturing takes place in its large cities, which include—in order of size—Los Angeles, San Diego, San Jose, San Francisco, and Seattle.

The discovery of gold and the opening of the Oregon Territory in the mid-1800's brought a stream of settlers to the Pacific Coast. New residents, many drawn by the area's booming computer industry, have continued to pour in ever since. Today, the population includes people of European, African American, and Mexican American ancestry. The region also has more people of Asian ancestry than any other part of the United States, and a large number of American Indians.

Outlying areas. The United States has possession of various island territories in the Caribbean Sea and the Pacific Ocean. Some of them, such as Guam and the Virgin Islands, have a large degree of self-government. Puerto Rico, one of the areas, is a commonwealth associated with the United States that has been given wide powers of self-rule by the U.S. Congress. American Samoa, Guam, the Northern Mariana Islands, Puerto Rico, and the Virgin Islands each send to Congress a nonvoting delegate. See the table titled *Main outlying areas of the United States* in this article.

People

Population. The U.S. Census Bureau reported that in 2000 the country had a population of 281,421,906. Figures from the 1990 census had put the population of the United States at 248,709,873.

Whites make up about 75 percent of the country's population. African Americans account for about 12 percent of the population. About 3 ½ percent of the population is of Asian descent. American Indians make up about 1 percent of the population. Other groups combine to make up the remaining 8 ½ percent.

The U.S. population includes many Hispanic people, such as people of Mexican, Puerto Rican, or Cuban descent. Hispanics consist mainly of whites, but they also include some blacks and American Indians. Hispanics make up about 13 percent of the U.S. population.

About 51 percent of the people in the United States

© Michael Philip Manheim

Giant cactuses of the Southwest symbolize the "wide open spaces" of the region. The Southwest has huge, unspoiled areas of natural beauty that attract many tourists.

are females. The United States has one of the highest life expectancies of any country—74.9 years. Since 1945, the part of the U.S. population that is over 65 years old has increased from 8 percent to $12\frac{1}{2}$ percent. Improvements in medical care have been the main reason for the increase. The over-65 population of the United States will continue to grow at a rapid rate as advances in medicine continue and as the large numbers of people born during the "baby boom" grow older. The baby boom was a period of high birth rate that occurred in the United States from 1946 to 1964.

Approximately 90 percent of the total population was born in the United States. The largest foreign-born groups are, in order of size, Mexicans, Germans, Canadians, Italians, Cubans, and Filipinos. The population density in the United States varies widely from place to place. See the map in this section of the article for the density throughout the country.

Ancestry. The United States has one of the world's most varied populations in terms of ancestry. The population includes descendants of people from almost every part of the world.

The first people to live in what is now the United States were American Indians, Inuit (also called Eskimos), and Hawaiians. The Indians and Inuit are descended from peoples who migrated to North America from Asia thousands of years ago. The ancestors of the Hawaiians were

Polynesians who sailed to what is now Hawaii from other Pacific islands about 2,000 years ago.

Most white Americans trace their ancestry to Europe. Some Spaniards settled in what is now the United States during the 1500's. European settlement increased sharply during the 1600's. At first, most of the settlers came from England. But America soon attracted many immigrants from other nations of northern and western Europe, including France, Germany, Ireland, the Netherlands, and Scotland; and the Scandinavian lands of Denmark, Norway, and Sweden. Until the late 1800's, northern and western Europe provided most of the immigrants. Then, large waves of people began arriving from southern and eastern European nations, including Austria-Hungary, Greece, Italy, Poland, and Russia.

Most Hispanic Americans are people who immigrated—or whose ancestors immigrated—to the United States from Latin America. A small percentage of them trace their ancestry directly back to Spain. Some have mainly Spanish ancestry. Others have mixed Spanish and Indian or black ancestry.

Most African Americans are descendants of Africans who were brought to the United States as slaves during the 1600's, 1700's, and 1800's and forced to work on plantations. See **Slavery** (Slavery in the United States).

Since the 1800's, the United States has attracted immigrants from Asia. Most Asian Americans trace their an-

Population density and centers of population   This map shows the population density throughout the United States. Population density is the average number of persons who live on each square mile or square kilometer in an area. The map also shows how the country's center of population moved westward between 1790 and 2000.

WORLD BOOK map

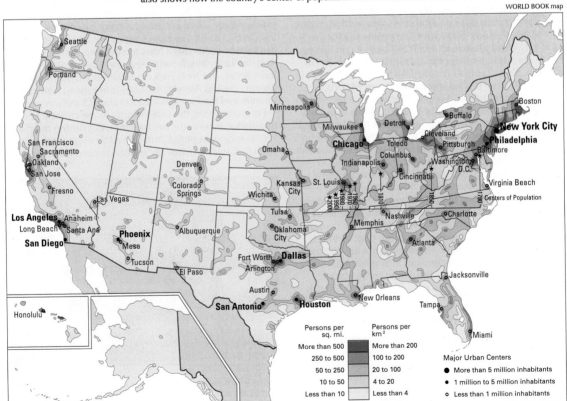

cestry to China, India, Indochina, Japan, Korea, or the Philippines. For more details on the flow of people into the United States through the years, see **Immigration**.

The United States has often been called a *melting pot.* This term refers to the idea that the country is a place where people from many lands have come together and formed a unified culture. Americans have many things in common. For example, the vast majority of them speak English, and people throughout the country dress similarly and eat many of the same kinds of foods. Public education, mass communication, and other influences have helped shape a common identity.

But in other ways, U.S. society is an example of *cultural pluralism.* That is, large numbers of its people have retained features of the cultures of their ancestors. Many Americans take special pride in their origins. They preserve traditions—and in some cases the languages—of their ancestors. In many cities, people of different national or ethnic origins live in separate neighborhoods, and shops and restaurants reflect their cultural heritages. Ethnic festivals, parades, and other events emphasize the country's cultural pluralism.

Language. The United States has never had an official language, but English has always been the chief language spoken there. Immigrants from England, Scotland, and Ireland—who included the nation's founders—spoke English. Many immigrants from other lands who spoke little or no English also came to the United States. They learned at least enough English to be able to communicate with other Americans. Their children learned English in school. The immigrants' children generally spoke both English and their ethnic language, and in many families the immigrants' grandchildren spoke only English.

Today, Spanish is the second most common language in the United States. The region that is now the southwestern United States was colonized by Spain in the 1500's. As a result, many people from that region speak Spanish. Since the 1950's, many Spanish-speaking people have immigrated to the United States from Mexico, Cuba, and other places. Many of these people learned English. But others speak only Spanish. This is especially true in Spanish-speaking neighborhoods that developed in cities. Some people feel that special efforts should be made to provide education and other services in Spanish for people who speak only Spanish.

Many people believe every American should know English. They point out that it is difficult to get a job outside Spanish-speaking neighborhoods without a knowledge of English. They also argue that a language shared by everyone is an important unifying force for a country. Many states have passed laws declaring English to be their only official language. These laws provide that the government must offer its services in English, and need not do so in any other language. But in some places, public documents and signs are written in both English and Spanish.

Way of life

For census purposes, the United States is divided into *urban areas* and *rural areas.* An urban area, as defined by the U.S. Census Bureau, is a community with 2,500 or more people. A rural area is a community with fewer than 2,500 people. In 1790, the year of the first census, about 95 percent of the country's people lived in rural

areas, and only about 5 percent were urban dwellers. Over time, these percentages changed steadily and dramatically. Today, about 80 percent of all the people live in urban areas. Only about 20 percent live in rural areas.

Several factors contributed to the dramatic population shift from the countryside to urban areas. Through the years, Americans greatly improved agricultural methods and equipment. From the 1800's onward, farm work has become more and more efficient, farm production has soared, and fewer and fewer people have been needed to work on the country's farms. At the same time, an industrial boom has created large numbers of new jobs in the country's urban areas. As a result of these economic changes, a steady flow of people from rural to urban areas has taken place. Also, large numbers of immigrants—many of whom had been farmers in their homelands—found jobs in cities and settled there when they reached the United States. In addition, the variety of job choices and recreational, educational, and cultural opportunities in cities attracted many rural people, especially the young. Large numbers of rural people left home to seek employment and excitement in cities.

Urban life. Urban areas, which range from giant cities surrounded by suburbs to small towns, dot the U.S. landscape. Although urban areas cover about 3 percent of the land, about four-fifths of the people live in them. New York City, with about 8 million people, is the largest U.S. city by far. Los Angeles has about 3⅔ million people. Nearly 3 million people live in Chicago. Six other U.S. cities—Houston, Philadelphia, Phoenix, San Diego, Dallas, and San Antonio—each have over 1 million people.

Networks of suburbs surround many U.S. cities. The central cities and their suburbs form units called metropolitan areas. There are about 360 metropolitan areas in the United States. The three largest are, in order of size, the New York-Northern New Jersey-Long Island, Los Angeles-Long Beach-Santa Ana, and Chicago-Naperville-Joliet areas. The New York area has more than 18 million people, the Los Angeles area has more than 12 million people, and the Chicago area has about 9 million people.

For many years, the vast majority of the country's urban population lived in the central cities. But during the mid-1900's, suburban population soared throughout the United States, while central city growth slowed down or de-

© Nick Gunderson, Tony Stone Images

Urban areas dot the U.S. landscape and are home to three-fourths of the population. St. Louis, *shown here,* lies along the Mississippi River. Its Gateway Arch is a major tourist attraction.

© John Launois, Black Star

African American communities are part of many cities in the United States. Most cities in the country include neighborhoods in which almost all the residents belong to the same ethnic or nationality group.

WORLD BOOK photo by Joseph A. Erhardt

Hispanic neighborhoods can be found in urban areas throughout the United States. Most Hispanic Americans are of Mexican, Puerto Rican, or Cuban descent.

creased. In 1970, for the first time, more Americans lived in suburbs than in central cities.

The Northeast and Midwest have long had most of the

The 50 largest cities in the United States*

1.	New York City	8,008,278	
2.	Los Angeles	3,694,820	
3.	Chicago	2,896,016	
4.	Houston	1,953,631	
5.	Philadelphia	1,517,550	
6.	Phoenix	1,321,045	
7.	San Diego	1,223,400	
8.	Dallas	1,188,580	
9.	San Antonio	1,144,646	
10.	Detroit	951,270	
11.	San Jose	894,943	
12.	Indianapolis	791,926	
13.	San Francisco	776,733	
14.	Jacksonville, FL	735,617	
15.	Columbus, OH	711,470	
16.	Austin, TX	656,562	
17.	Baltimore	651,145	
18.	Memphis	650,100	
19.	Milwaukee	596,974	
20.	Boston	589,141	
21.	Washington, D.C.	572,059	
22.	El Paso	563,662	
23.	Seattle	563,374	
24.	Denver	554,636	
25.	Nashville	545,524	
26.	Charlotte, NC	540,828	
27.	Fort Worth, TX	534,694	
28.	Portland, OR	529,121	
29.	Oklahoma City, OK	506,132	
30.	Tucson, AZ	486,699	
31.	New Orleans, LA	484,674	
32.	Las Vegas, NV	478,434	
33.	Cleveland, OH	478,403	
34.	Long Beach, CA	461,522	
35.	Albuquerque, NM	448,607	
36.	Kansas City, MO	441,545	
37.	Fresno, CA	427,652	
38.	Virginia Beach, VA	425,257	
39.	Atlanta, GA	416,474	
40.	Sacramento, CA	407,018	
41.	Oakland, CA	399,484	
42.	Mesa, AZ	396,375	
43.	Tulsa, OK	393,049	
44.	Omaha, NE	390,007	
45.	Minneapolis, MN	382,618	
46.	Honolulu, HI	371,657	
47.	Miami, FL	362,470	
48.	Colorado Springs, CO	360,890	
49.	St. Louis, MO	348,189	
50.	Wichita, KS	344,284	

*In 2003, Louisville, Kentucky, merged with Jefferson County, Kentucky, and now has a population of 693,604 based on 2000 census figures. Source: 2000 census.

nation's largest urban areas. But during the 1900's, other parts of the country experienced dramatic urban growth. Since the early 1900's, many California urban communities—especially Los Angeles—have grown tremendously. Since the mid-1900's, the populations of many more urban areas in the West, and in the South and Southwest, have soared. Such metropolitan areas as Atlanta, Dallas, Denver, Houston, and Phoenix grew rapidly. Large numbers of people were attracted to the West, South, and Southwest by jobs created by new industries. Also, many

© David R. Frazier

A suburban street is lined with comfortable single-family homes. Suburbs surround many U.S. cities. Large numbers of suburban residents commute to jobs in the city.

of the fastest-growing communities have warm, sunny climates, which helped attract many of the newcomers. Parts of the South, Southwest, and West are sometimes called the *Sun Belt* because they have such climates.

Urban economies provide jobs for a great variety of workers, including office and factory workers, bankers, doctors, firefighters, medical personnel, police officers, teachers, trash collectors, and construction and transportation workers. Urban life also has many other attractive features. Because urban areas have large populations, they generally offer a wide variety of specialized services and shops. Urban dwellers can take advantage of an assortment of restaurants, recreation facilities, and places of entertainment. Because of such facilities as art galleries, museums, libraries, theaters, and concert halls, many cities are important cultural centers. These and other features make urban areas exciting and interesting places to live for many people.

The people of most U.S. urban areas represent a variety of ethnic backgrounds. Most cities include neighborhoods in which almost all the people belong to the same ethnic or nationality group. The people of large urban areas are also divided economically. Urban society includes extremely wealthy and extremely poor people, and a huge middle class. The wealthy live in luxurious apartments or condominiums, or in large, comfortable single-family houses. Middle-class housing also includes apartments, condominiums, and single-family houses. In general, the housing of the middle class is comfortable, though not as luxurious as that of the wealthy. In contrast, large numbers of urban poor people live in substandard housing. They rent crowded, small apartments or run-down single-family houses.

In addition to substandard housing, urban areas have a number of other unpleasant features. Such features include high crime rates, racial and ethnic friction, noisy surroundings, pollution, and traffic jams. See **City** (City problems).

Rural life. About 97 percent of all the land of the United States is classified as rural. But much of the rural land is uninhabited or only thinly inhabited. About 20 percent of all Americans live in rural areas.

© Terry Farmer, Tony Stone Images

Farmers exhibit livestock at an exposition at the State Fairgrounds in Des Moines, Iowa. Only a small percentage of the rural people of the United States work on farms.

Farms provide the economic basis of the nation's rural areas. However, only about 8 percent of the country's rural people work on farms. Many other rural people own or work in businesses related to agriculture, such as grain and feed stores and warehouses. Mining and related activities and light industries also employ many rural people. Still other rural Americans work as teachers, police officers, salesclerks, or in other occupations. Many farmers hold other jobs for part of the year to add to their incomes.

American farmers of today lead vastly different lives from those of their grandparents. Machines have eliminated much backbreaking farm work. Farmers use machines to help them plow, plant seeds, harvest crops, and deliver their products to market. Many farms have conveyor systems so that the farmer no longer has to shovel feed to farm animals. Milking machines make morning and evening chores easier. In the home, farm families may have all the comforts and conveniences of city people. In the 1900's, the automobile, telephone, radio, television, and computer brought U.S. farm families into close contact with the rest of the world.

The steady decline in the percentage of the country's rural population has slowed since 1970. Although many people continued to move away from rural areas, others chose to move into rural towns and farm communities. Many of the newcomers wanted to escape the overcrowding, pollution, crime, and other problems that are part of life in urban areas and to take advantage of benefits of country living. Rural areas have lower crime rates and less pollution than urban areas. They are also far less noisy and crowded.

Because of their small populations, rural communities collect less tax revenues than urban communities do, and they generally cannot provide the variety of services that urban areas can. For example, rural communities have cultural and recreational facilities that are more limited than those available in urban areas. For many rural Americans, social life centers around family gatherings, church and school activities, special interest clubs, and such events as state and county fairs.

Rural areas generally have less diversified economies than urban areas. Because there are fewer jobs and a smaller variety of jobs to choose from, rural communities may experience more widespread economic hardships than urban communities. A single economic downturn—a drop in farm prices, for example, or the closing of a mine—can cause economic hardship for an entire rural area.

The nation's rural areas, like its urban areas, have wealthy, middle class, and poor people. For the most part, however, the gaps between economic classes are not as large in rural areas as in urban areas. Most rural Americans live in single-family houses. The majority of the houses are comfortable and in good condition. But some people, including many who live in parts of Appalachia—in the eastern United States—and other pockets of rural poverty, have run-down houses and can afford few luxuries.

Education has been an important factor in the economic development of the United States and in the achievement of a high standard of living for most Americans. It has also contributed to the enjoyment of life for many people. Americans are among the best-educated

Chicago Academy of Fine Woodworking (WORLD BOOK photo)

Adult education is an important part of the U.S. educational system. Millions of adults take courses every year. In the class shown here, the teacher is giving lessons in woodworking.

© Felicia Hunt-Taylor, Charles H. Wright Museum of African American History, Detroit, MI

Museums throughout the country display a variety of articles. The *field cradle* shown here was used outdoors by an African American slave mother to hold her baby while she worked.

people in the world. Schools, libraries, museums, and other educational institutions in the country provide learning opportunities for people of all ages.

Schools. During the early history of the United States, most schools were privately owned. Church groups owned and operated many of them. In the early 1800's, the idea of free public schools began to gain widespread support in the country. State and local governments took the responsibility for establishing public school systems. By 1918, every state had laws requiring children to attend school until they reached a certain age or completed a certain grade. Today, about 75 percent of the nation's elementary and high schools, and about 45 percent of its institutions of higher learning, are public schools. The rest are private schools run by religious organizations or private groups.

Many American children begin their schooling before enrolling in first grade. About 35 percent of all the children aged 3 and 4 attend nursery schools, and about 95 percent of all 5-year-olds attend kindergarten. More than 99 percent of all U.S. children complete elementary school, and about 75 percent of them graduate from high school. Approximately 60 percent of the high school graduates go on to colleges or universities. About 20 percent of the country's adults complete at least four years of higher education.

Adult education is an important part of the school system in the United States. Millions of adults take courses at universities, colleges, vocational schools, recreation centers, or other institutions. Many adults continue their schooling to improve their job skills or to get training for a new job. Others attend classes simply to develop new

hobbies or to find out more about topics that interest them. A growing number of part-time and full-time college and university students are men and women who have held jobs or raised families and are returning to school to get a degree.

Public schools in the United States are supported mainly by taxation. Private schools get their operating funds chiefly from tuition and contributions of private citizens. The nation's schools, like its private businesses, have always had to deal with financial problems. Rapidly rising material and salary costs have increased the financial problems of the schools. Some public and private schools have cut back on programs and reduced their faculties to try to keep expenses in line with revenues. Colleges and universities have sharply increased their tuition and fee charges.

Schools in the United States face a number of other problems. Many schools, particularly in large cities, have run-down buildings, inadequate supplies, and overcrowded conditions. A far higher percentage of young people in these areas drop out of school than in other areas. Some people claim that schools in their areas fail to provide students with the skills to obtain and hold jobs. Schools with large numbers of students from other countries face the problem of educating some children who speak little or no English. See **Education**.

Libraries provide the American people with access to books, periodicals, pamphlets, and other printed matter. In addition, many libraries offer compact discs, videotapes, and other multimedia materials; Internet access; research services; lectures; and educational exhibits.

There are thousands of public libraries in the United

States. They range from one-room libraries in small towns to huge city libraries and their branches. There are also thousands of university and college libraries in the United States, as well as thousands of libraries in elementary schools and high schools.

The nation's library system also includes large numbers of private research libraries and special libraries with collections limited to certain fields of knowledge. In addition, many government agencies and businesses operate their own libraries. Three of the government's many libraries are considered national libraries because of their large and varied collections and because of the many services they provide. They are the Library of Congress, the National Agricultural Library of the Department of Agriculture, and the National Library of Medicine of the Department of Health and Human Services. See **Library.**

Museums. There are thousands of museums in the United States. They include museums of art, history, natural history, and science. In addition, a number of historic houses and villages are classed as museums. The collections of many of the nation's museums are devoted to a single topic of interest, such as the history of baseball or railroads. Some museums have huge collections of items from many parts of the world. Others feature exhibits of local interest. In addition to exhibits, many U.S. museums offer classes, lectures, films, field trips, and other educational services. The most famous museums in the United States include the Metropolitan Museum of Art in New York City, the Museum of Science and Industry in Chicago, and the Smithsonian Institution in Washington, D.C. See **Museum.**

Religion. More than 60 percent of all the American people are members of an organized religious group. Among them, about 50 percent are Protestants, and about 40 percent are Roman Catholics. Jews, Mormons, Muslims, and members of Eastern Orthodox Churches each make up about 2 percent of the total. Relatively small numbers of Americans belong to other faiths, such as Buddhism and Hinduism. Roman Catholics make up the largest single religious denomination in the United States. About 65 million Americans are Roman Catholics. The country's largest Protestant groups are, in order of size, Baptists, Methodists, Pentecostals, Lutherans, and Presbyterians.

Religion has played an important role in the history of the United States. Many people came to the American Colonies to escape religious persecution in other lands. The early colonists included Puritans in New England, Roman Catholics in Maryland, and Quakers in Pennsylvania. The early Americans made religious freedom one of the country's basic laws. The First Amendment to the Constitution of the United States, which was adopted in 1791, guarantees every American freedom of religion. It also provides that no religious group be given official recognition as a state church. These provisions were intended to prevent persecution of religious minorities and the favoring of one church over another. Religious freedom was one of the reasons immigrants continued to flock to the United States through the years.

Although all religious groups in the United States enjoy freedom, Christian traditions have had a stronger influence on American life than those of any other faith. For example, most offices, factories, and other places of em-

© Archie Lieberman

Religion plays an important role in the lives of millions of Americans. The country's churches provide people with moral guidance and places for worship. Many churches also serve as centers for social gatherings, such as a church picnic, *shown here.*

ployment are closed on Sunday, the Sabbath of most Christians. The influence of Christianity results from the fact that a majority of the people are Christians.

Throughout the country's history, religion has influenced everyday life in a number of ways. For example, in colonial America many religious rules were enforced by local governments. Some of the laws that prohibited activities on Sunday still exist.

Today, religion has relatively less influence in the everyday lives of most Americans. But churches and other religious organizations continue to play important roles in American life. Their chief functions are to provide moral guidance and places for worship. However, religious groups also operate many elementary and secondary schools, colleges, universities, hospitals, and nursing homes. They provide aid for refugees, the poor, the elderly, orphans, and other persons in need. Social gatherings are held at many churches. Some religious groups take active roles in discussing such issues as birth control and rights for minorities and women.

Recreation. Most Americans have a great deal of leisure time, and they spend it in a variety of ways. They pursue hobbies, take part in sports, attend sporting and cultural events, watch movies and television, listen to music, and read books and magazines. They visit museums, beaches, parks, and zoos. They take weekend and vacation trips, eat at restaurants, go on picnics, and entertain friends at home. These and other activities contribute to the richness and diversity of American life.

Sports rank as a leading American pastime. Millions of Americans enjoy watching such sports events as automobile races, horse races, and baseball, basketball, and football games—either in person or on television. Many Americans, especially children and other young people, play baseball, basketball, football, and soccer. People of most ages participate in such sports as bicycle riding,

Baseball games and other sports events attract many spectators. Turner Field in Atlanta, Georgia, *shown here,* is the stadium where the Atlanta Braves of the National League play baseball.

boating, bowling, fishing, golf, hiking, hunting, running, skiing, softball, swimming, and tennis.

Motion pictures, plays, concerts, operas, and dance performances attract large audiences in the United States. Americans find entertainment at home, as well. Almost all American homes have a television set. On the average, a set is in use in each home for about seven hours a day.

Hobbies occupy much of the leisure time of many Americans. Large numbers of people enjoy raising flower or vegetable gardens or indoor plants. Other popular hobbies include stamp collecting, coin collecting, and photography. In the last half of the 1900's, interest in such crafts hobbies as needlepoint, quilting, weaving,

The Boston Marathon is an annual footrace that attracts thousands of runners. Many Americans enjoy using their leisure time to participate in sports activities.

pottery making, and woodworking increased sharply.

Most Americans spend part of their leisure time traveling. Many take annual vacations, as well as occasional one-day excursions or weekend trips. Some have vacation homes near lakes or seashores, in the mountains, or in other recreation areas. Others own motor homes or trailers, which provide living and sleeping quarters during trips. Some people enjoy camping in tents. Others prefer to stay in hotels or motels while on trips.

Food. Americans eat a wide variety of foods. A typical dinner consists of meat and potatoes, plus a lettuce salad or a vegetable, and sometimes rolls or bread. Favorite dinner meats include beef steaks, ground beef dishes, chicken, ham, and turkey. Fish, shellfish, and such dishes as pizza and spaghetti also serve as main courses.

For lunch, many Americans eat a sandwich, such as a hamburger or a hot dog. Other favorite sandwiches include those made with meat or sliced sausage, cheese, peanut butter, and chicken or tuna salad.

Some Americans enjoy a hearty breakfast of eggs or pancakes served with bacon or sausage. Others prefer a light breakfast of toast or a pastry, or cereal with milk and fruit. Orange juice accompanies many breakfasts.

Cake, cookies, pie, and ice cream are eaten as desserts and snacks. Other snack foods include chocolate candy, potato or corn chips, and such fruits as bananas, apples, oranges, and grapes.

Beverages are drunk with meals and also at other times for refreshment. Consumption of soft drinks, especially cola, exceeds that of any other beverage. Americans also drink much coffee, milk, and beer, and smaller amounts of fruit juices, tea, and wine.

Americans eat out often. *Fast-food* restaurants have wide popularity. They offer a limited variety of foods, all of which are served within a few minutes. Common fast-food items include hamburgers and other sandwiches, fried chicken, and French fried potatoes. Many Americans also enjoy the cooking of other countries. Chinese, French, Italian, and Mexican restaurants have long been popular. In recent years, Americans have also begun to enjoy the cuisines of India, Japan, Thailand, the Middle East, and many other areas.

Some regions of the United States have distinctive food specialties. For information on such foods, see **Hawaii** (People); **Louisiana** (People); **Pennsylvania Dutch.**

The arts

European colonists arrived in America during the early 1600's, bringing European art traditions with them. But within a few years, colonists were building houses that probably rank as the first major American

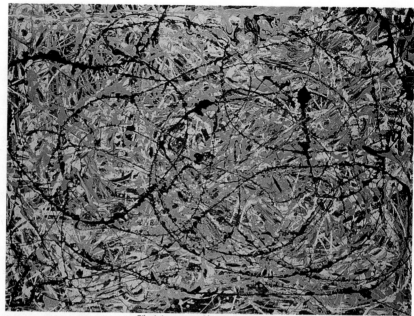

Oil painting on canvas (about 1947); National Gallery of Modern Art, Rome, Italy © Artists Rights Society (ARS), New York (Giraudon/Art Resource)

American abstract art is illustrated by Jackson Pollock's *Watery Path, shown here.* Pollock was the best known of the Abstract Expressionist painters, who favored the use of untraditional materials applied in new ways. Pollack dripped paint onto his canvases as they lay on the floor.

Oil painting on canvas (1773); the Historical Society of Pennsylvania

Paintings of colonial America include many portraits. John Singleton Copley's portrait of soldier and politician Thomas Mifflin and his wife, *shown here,* illustrates Copley's ability to capture the human character of colonial leaders. Copley is generally considered the greatest portrait painter of the colonial period.

Museum of the American Indian, New York City, Heye Foundation

Artwork of Native Americans includes handsome pottery, rich woven materials, and many other beautiful objects. The Hopi Indians of Arizona carve wooden figures called kachina dolls, such as the one shown here. Kachinas represent messengers sent by the gods and are used to teach children about the spirits.

Winslow Homer's *Breezing Up* shows three boys and an adult sailing. The painting reflects two of the artist's main themes, vivid and dramatic images of the sea and nostalgic scenes of childhood.

Skyscrapers began to be built by U.S. architects in the last half of the 1800's. They first appeared in Chicago and New York City. Today, Sears Tower, *shown here,* dominates the Chicago skyline.

Residential architecture in the Prairie style was a specialty of Frank Lloyd Wright. Wright was one of America's most influential and most imaginative architects. His distinctive homes emphasize horizontal lines and natural materials that harmonize with the landscape. Fallingwater, *shown here,* was completed in 1937 at Bear Run, Pennsylvania, near Uniontown. It shows Wright's ability to blend a structure with its natural setting.

Jazz is a kind of popular music that originated in the United States beginning in the late 1800's. One of the key elements of jazz is *improvisation*—the ability to create music spontaneously. Louis Armstrong, standing in the center of the group in this photo, was the first great jazz soloist.

King Oliver's Creole Jazz Band; Ramsey Archive

Country music has a wide following. It combines elements of folk music, the blues, religious music, and popular songs. It developed in the southern United States during the 1800's. Country music singer LeAnn Rimes, *holding the microphone,* began her rise to fame as a teen-ager in the mid-1990's.

Rock music originated in the United States in the early 1950's. Elvis Presley, *playing the guitar,* became rock music's first and best-known superstar. He helped make rock the country's leading type of popular music in the last half of the 1900's.

© Mitchell Layton, Retna

© Sean Shaver

© 1937 Walt Disney Productions

Animated films have been popular since the early 1900's. Film producer Walt Disney created many memorable examples, including *Snow White and the Seven Dwarfs* (1937), *shown here.*

Everett Collection

Motion pictures are an influential art form in the United States. The American Civil War drama *Gone with the Wind* (1939), *shown here,* is one of the country's award-winning films.

Martha Swope © Time Inc.

Dancing in the United States often explores American subjects. The famous dancer and dance composer Martha Graham created *Appalachian Spring* (1944), *shown here,* a ballet that celebrates the courage and dignity of American pioneers during the early 1800's.

© Eileen Darby

Modern American drama includes the work of such playwrights as Arthur Miller. *Death of a Salesman,* shown here in its original New York production in 1949, is generally considered Miller's masterpiece.

© Michael Cooper

Musicals are an important part of American theater. Although they vary in style and subject matter, most musicals today employ large casts and elaborate sets. *Ragtime* (1996), *shown here,* offers a panoramic look at the United States at the beginning of the 1900's.

works of art. During the 1700's, American craftworkers began to produce outstanding examples of furniture, sculpture, and silverwork. By the mid-1700's, colonial painters were creating excellent portraits.

The first important American literature appeared in the early 1800's with the works of such authors as Washington Irving and James Fenimore Cooper. During the late 1800's, American architects began designing skyscrapers that revolutionized urban architecture throughout the world. Two uniquely American art forms, jazz and musical comedy, developed during the late 1800's and early 1900's. In the early 1900's, the United States gained international leadership in the new art forms of motion pictures and modern dancing.

Today, American architects, authors, composers, painters, and sculptors have achieved worldwide recognition and influence. Many of them have shown a keen interest in developing new styles, new ways of expressing themselves, and even new forms of art.

The land

The United States, excluding Alaska and Hawaii, can be divided into seven major land regions. The regions are: (1) the Appalachian Highlands; (2) the Coastal Lowlands; (3) the Interior Plains; (4) the Ozark-Ouachita Highlands; (5) the Rocky Mountains; (6) the Western Plateaus, Basins, and Ranges; and (7) the Pacific Ranges and Lowlands. For a discussion of the land regions of Alaska and the islands of Hawaii, see the articles on those states.

The Appalachian Highlands extend from the northern tip of Maine southwestward to Alabama. This rugged region has many mountain ranges.

The White Mountains and the Green Mountains of

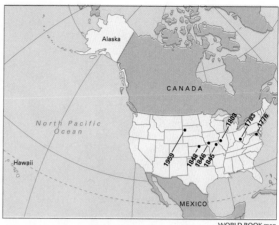

WORLD BOOK map

The geographic center of the United States has moved westward as the country added new territory. Since 1959, when Alaska and Hawaii were added, the center has been in South Dakota.

northern New England are old mountains, worn down but craggy in some places. Southern New England consists mostly of hilly land. New England's chief river is the Connecticut. The Adirondack Upland of northern New York includes mountains and many beautiful lakes.

From central New York southward, the Appalachian Highlands has three main subdivisions. They are, from east to west: the Blue Ridge Mountains Area, the Ridge and Valley Region, and the Appalachian Plateau.

The Blue Ridge Mountains Area consists of some of the oldest mountains in the country. The Blue Ridge

© Kunio Owaki, The Stock Market

The Appalachian Highlands make up a rugged region that extends along the eastern part of the United States from the northern tip of Maine to Alabama. The region has many scenic areas that attract visitors, such as Glade Creek in Babcock State Park, West Virginia, *shown here.*

Mountains themselves are a narrow chain that stretches from southeastern Pennsylvania to northeastern Georgia. The Great Smoky Mountains of Tennessee and North Carolina are also part of this area. The Hudson Highlands of New York and New Jersey form a northern extension of the area. Several mighty rivers, including the Delaware, Hudson, Potomac, and Susquehanna, cut through the mountains to form *water gaps.* The gaps provide low, level land for highways and railroads.

The Ridge and Valley Region consists of the Great Valley in the east and a series of alternating ridges and valleys in the west. The rolling Great Valley is actually a series of valleys, including the Cumberland, Lebanon, and Lehigh valleys in Pennsylvania; the Shenandoah Valley in Virginia; the Valley of East Tennessee; the Rome Valley in Georgia; and the Great Valley of Alabama. The region has some forests, but other wooded areas have been cleared to take advantage of fertile soil and relatively level land for farming. About 50 dams on the Tennessee River and its branches in the southern Great Valley provide flood control and hydroelectric power.

The Appalachian Plateau extends from New York to Alabama. Glaciers covered the northern plateau during the most recent ice age, which ended about 11,500 years ago, and carved out natural features, including the Finger Lakes in New York. Deep, narrow river valleys cut through the plateau in some areas, creating steep, rugged terrain. Deposits of coal, iron ore, oil, and other minerals lie beneath the surface, and many people in the region work in mining. Parts of the region have good farmland. But thin, rocky soil covers much of the plateau, and the steep hillsides are badly eroded.

The Coastal Lowlands extend from southeastern Maine, across the eastern and southern United States, to

The Interior Plains have fertile soil that is ideal for growing crops. The area, America's vast heartland, includes many wheat-growing areas, such as the part of Kansas shown here.

The Coastal Lowlands extend from New England to Texas. Florida's Everglades National Park, *shown here,* in the southernmost lowlands, includes this swamp with baldcypress trees.

eastern Texas. Forests of hickory, oak, pine, and other trees are common throughout the lowlands. The region has three subdivisions: (1) the Piedmont, (2) the Atlantic Coastal Plain, and (3) the Gulf Coastal Plain.

The Piedmont is a slightly elevated rolling plain that separates the Blue Ridge Mountains from the Atlantic Coastal Plain. It stretches from southern New York to Alabama. The eastern boundary of the Piedmont is called the *Fall Line.* Rivers that reach the Fall Line tumble down from the Piedmont to the lower coastal plains in a series of falls and rapids. In the early days of settlement of the eastern United States, boats traveling inland on coastal rivers stopped at the Fall Line and unloaded their cargoes. The rapids prevented the boats from traveling farther. They also provided water power for early industries. As a result, many cities grew up along the Fall Line. Tobacco is a leading agricultural product of the Piedmont, and the region also has many orchards and dairy farms. See **Piedmont Region; Fall line.**

The Atlantic Coastal Plain extends eastward from the Piedmont to the Atlantic Ocean. It ranges from a narrow strip of land in New England to a broad belt that covers much of North and South Carolina, Georgia, and Florida. In colonial times, the broad southern part of the plain encouraged the development of huge plantations for growing cotton. Cotton is still grown there. Other farm products include vegetables, citrus fruits, peanuts, and tobacco. In New England, where the plain narrows to a

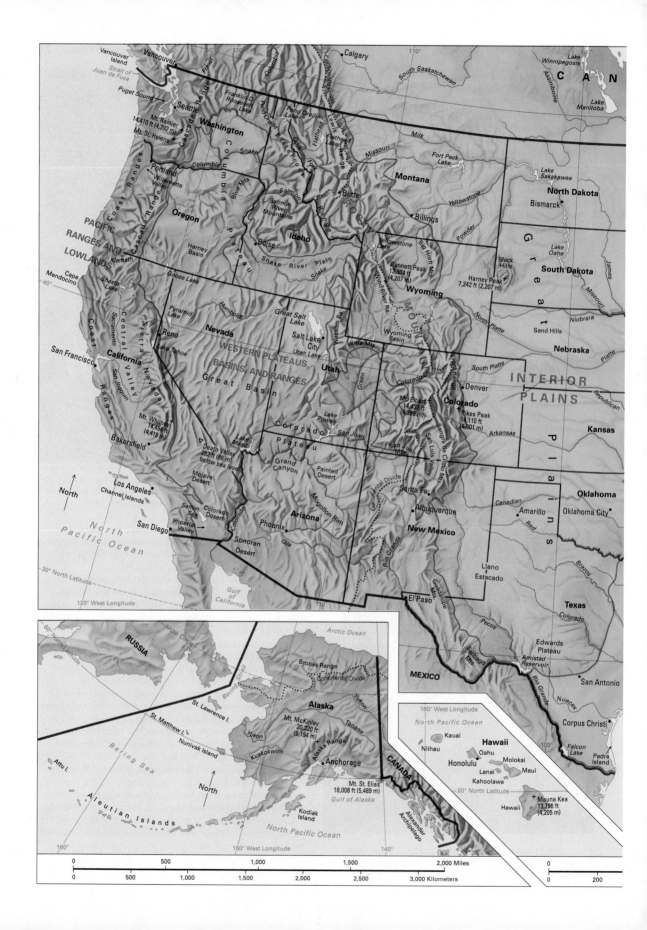

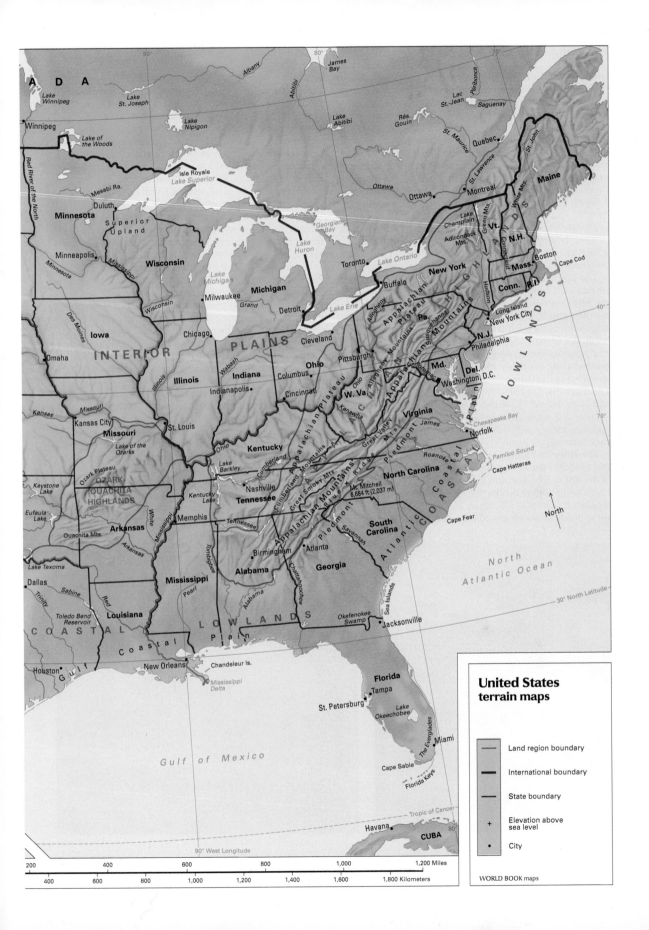

ADA

Lake Winnipeg
Winnipeg
Red River of the North
Lake of the Woods

Lake St. Joseph

Albany

Abitibi

James Bay

Lake Nipigon

Lake Abitibi

Rés. Gouin

Péribonca

Lac St.-Jean

Saguenay

St. Maurice

Quebec

St. John

Isle Royale
Lake Superior

Mesabi Ra.

Duluth

Minnesota

Minneapolis

Superior Upland

Wisconsin

Mississippi

Milwaukee

Lake Michigan

Michigan

Grand

Lake Huron

Georgian Bay

Ottawa

Ottawa

Montreal

Lake Champlain

Adirondack Mts.

White Mts.

Green Mts.

Maine

Vt.

N.H.

Connecticut

Mass.

Boston

Cape Cod

Toronto

Lake Ontario

New York

R.I.

Conn.

Minnesota

Iowa

Des Moines

INTERIOR   PLAINS

Chicago

Buffalo

Allegheny

Appalachian Plateau

Susquehanna

Hudson

Long Island

New York City

40°

Omaha

Illinois

Wabash

Indiana

Cleveland

Pittsburgh

Allegheny Mountains

Pa.

N.J.

Philadelphia

Kansas

Missouri

Kansas City

Missouri

St. Louis

Illinois

Ohio

Columbus

Cincinnati

Ohio

W. Va.

Kanawha

Appalachian Plateau

Appalachian

Potomac

Md.

Del.

Washington, D.C.

70°

Virginia

James

Great Valley

Blue Ridge Mts.

Piedmont Mts.

Chesapeake Bay

Norfolk

Keystone Lake

Ozark Plateau

OZARK-OUACHITA HIGHLANDS

Lake of the Ozarks

Kentucky

Lake Barkley

Ohio

Cumberland

Appalachian Mountains

Cumberland Mts.

Great Smoky Mts.

Mt. Mitchell 6,684 ft (2,037 m)

Roanoke

Pamlico Sound

Cape Hatteras

North Carolina

ATLANTIC   COASTAL   PLAIN

Eufaula Lake

Ouachita Mts.

Arkansas

White

Mississippi

Memphis

Nashville

Kentucky Lake

Tennessee

Tennessee

Blue Ridge

Piedmont

South Carolina

Cape Fear

North

Dallas

Trinity

Sabine

Red

Toledo Bend Reservoir

Lake Texoma

Mississippi

Arkansas

Pearl

Tombigbee

Alabama

Mississippi

Birmingham

Alabama

Appalachian Mountains

Atlanta

Chattahoochee

Georgia

Savannah

Piedmont

Sea Islands

North Atlantic Ocean

30° North Latitude

Houston

COASTAL

Gulf

New Orleans

Coastal   Plain

LOWLANDS

Chandeleur Is.

Mississippi Delta

Okefenokee Swamp

Jacksonville

Florida

Tampa

St. Petersburg

Lake Okeechobee

Florida

The Everglades

Miami

Gulf   of   Mexico

Cape Sable

Florida Keys

United States terrain maps

	Land region boundary
	International boundary
	State boundary
+	Elevation above sea level
•	City

WORLD BOOK maps

Tropic of Cancer

Havana

CUBA

80°

90° West Longitude

200   400   600   800   1,000   1,200 Miles

400   600   800   1,000   1,200   1,400   1,600   1,800 Kilometers

90°

80°

70°

width of about 10 miles (16 kilometers) in some places, farming has always been less important. Many New Englanders turned to manufacturing, fishing, or shipping instead of farming.

Numerous rivers cross the plain and flow into the Atlantic Ocean. They include the Delaware, Hudson, James, Potomac, Roanoke, Savannah, and Susquehanna. Bays cut deeply into the plain in some areas, creating excellent natural harbors. They include Cape Cod Bay, Boston Bay, Chesapeake Bay, Delaware Bay, and Long Island Sound.

Many resort areas flourish around the beautiful sandy beaches and offshore islands that line much of the Atlantic shore from New England to Florida. In some inland regions, swamps and other wetlands cover large areas where trees and grasses rise up from shallow waters and tangled vines and roots form masses of vegetation.

The Gulf Coastal Plain borders the Gulf of Mexico from Florida to southern Texas. Numerous rivers—including the Alabama, Mississippi, Rio Grande, and Trinity—cross the plain and flow into the Gulf. The Mississippi, which originates in the Interior Plains to the north, is the most important of these rivers. Barges carrying cargoes from many parts of the country travel along the river. Soil deposited along the banks of the Mississippi and other rivers in the Gulf Coastal Plain creates fertile farmland. The plain also has belts of hilly forests and grazing land, and large deposits of petroleum and natural gas lie beneath it and in the offshore Gulf waters. The Gulf Coastal Plain has many sandy beaches, swamps, bays, and offshore islands.

The Interior Plains occupy a huge expanse of land that stretches from the Appalachian Highlands in the east to the Rocky Mountains in the west. Glaciers covered much of the region during the Ice Age. They stripped the topsoil from parts of Michigan, Minnesota, and Wisconsin and carved out thousands of lakes. Today, much of

this area is heavily forested. Farther south—in parts of Illinois, Indiana, Iowa, and Ohio—the glaciers flattened the land and deposited rich soil ideal for growing crops. The plains slope gradually upward from east to west and get progressively drier.

The western part of the region, called the Great Plains, has vast grasslands where livestock graze. It also has large areas of fertile soil that yield corn, wheat, and other crops. Few trees grow on the Great Plains. Some rugged hills, including the Black Hills of South Dakota and Wyoming, rise up out of the plains.

Deposits of iron ore and coal provide raw materials for many manufacturing industries in the eastern part of the Interior Plains. Important deposits of petroleum and metal ores lie in the western part.

Glaciers carved out the five Great Lakes in the Interior Plains. The lakes—Erie, Huron, Michigan, Ontario, and Superior—are the largest group of freshwater lakes in the world. The lakes provide a vital transportation route for shipping the agricultural and industrial products of the Interior Plains. The Mississippi River is the region's other great waterway. The Mississippi and its many branches, including the Missouri and Ohio rivers, form a river system that reaches into all parts of the Interior Plains.

The Ozark-Ouachita Highlands rise up between the Interior Plains and Coastal Lowlands. The highlands form a scenic landscape in southern Missouri, northwest Arkansas, and eastern Oklahoma. The region is named for the Ozark Plateau and the Ouachita (pronounced *WAWSH ih tah)* Mountains. Rivers and streams have cut deep gorges through the rugged highland terrain. The highlands include forested hills, artificial lakes, and many underground caves and gushing springs. Much of the region has poor soil for farming, but fertile land lies along the river valleys. Deposits of coal, iron ore, and other

© David Muench

The Rocky Mountains, west of the Interior Plains, soar to heights of more than 14,000 feet (4,270 meters) above sea level. The majestic scene above is in Colorado.

© David Muench

Desert areas cover much of the Western Plateaus, Basins, and Ranges land region, west of the Rockies. The land shown above is in the Nevada portion of the Great Basin, a part of the land region.

The Pacific Coast forms the western border of the Pacific Ranges and Lowlands region, which extends from Canada to Mexico. Rugged rock formations line parts of the coast, including the California area shown here.

© Jerry Howard, Stock, Boston

minerals are valuable natural resources of the highlands.

The Rocky Mountains form the largest mountain system in North America. They extend from northern Alaska, through Canada and the western United States to northern New Mexico. Many peaks of the Rockies are more than 14,000 feet (4,270 meters) high. The *Continental Divide,* also called the *Great Divide,* passes through the mountains. It is an imaginary line that separates streams that flow into the Pacific Ocean from those that flow into the Atlantic, the Gulf of Mexico, and the Arctic Ocean. Many important rivers, including the Colorado, Missouri, and Rio Grande, begin in the Rockies.

Forests cover the lower mountain slopes. The *timber line* marks the elevation above which trees cannot grow. Grasses, mosses, and lichens grow above the line. Bighorn sheep, elk, deer, bears, mountain lions, and other animals live in the mountains. Lakes and streams add to the region's spectacular beauty.

Lumbering and mining are important industries in the Rockies. The mountains are a storehouse of such metals as copper, gold, lead, silver, and zinc. The region also has large deposits of oil and natural gas. Mountain meadows provide grazing land for beef and dairy cattle, and valleys are used for growing crops.

For many years, the Rockies formed a major barrier to transportation across the United States. In the 1860's, the nation's first transcontinental rail line was built, passing through the Rocky Mountain region at the Wyoming Basin. Today, other railroads and highways cut through tunnels and passes in the mountains, and airplanes fly over the mountains.

The Western Plateaus, Basins, and Ranges lie west of the Rocky Mountains. This region extends from Washington south to the Mexican border. It is the driest part of the United States. Parts of it are deserts with little plant

life. But the region has some forested mountains, and some fertile areas where rivers provide irrigation water necessary for growing crops. In other areas, livestock graze on huge stretches of dry land.

The Columbia Plateau occupies the northernmost part of the region. It has fertile volcanic soil, formed by lava that flowed out of giant cracks in the earth thousands of years ago. The Colorado Plateau lies in the southern part of the region. It has some of the nation's most unusual landforms, including natural bridges and arches of solid rock and huge, flat-topped rock formations. The plateau's spectacular river gorges, including the Grand Canyon, rank among the world's great natural wonders.

The Basin and Range part of the region is a vast area of mountains and desert lowlands between the Columbia and Colorado plateaus. It includes Death Valley in California. Part of Death Valley lies 282 feet (86 meters) below sea level and is the lowest place in the United States. The Great Basin is an area within the larger Basin and Range area. Great Salt Lake is the largest of many shallow, salty lakes in the Great Basin. Bathers cannot sink in Great Salt Lake because the high salt content provides great buoyancy, enabling swimmers to float with ease. Near the lake is the Great Salt Lake Desert, which includes a large, hard, flat bed of salt.

The Pacific Ranges and Lowlands stretch across western Washington and Oregon and most of California. The region's eastern boundary is formed by the Cascade Mountains in the north and by the Sierra Nevada in the south. Volcanic activity formed the Cascades. Two of the Cascades—Lassen Peak in California and Mount St. Helens in Washington—are active volcanoes. Some of the range's highest peaks have glaciers and permanent snowfields. Evergreen forests cover the lower slopes and provide the raw materials for lumber and paper products industries. The Sierra Nevada are granite mountains, dotted with lakes and waterfalls.

Broad, fertile valleys lie west of the Cascade and Sierra Nevada mountains. They include the Puget Sound Lowland of Washington, the Willamette (pronounced *wih LAM iht*) Valley of Oregon, and the Central Valley of California. Valley farms produce large amounts of fruits and vegetables.

West of the valleys, the Coast Ranges line the Pacific shore. In many places, they rise up abruptly from the ocean, creating craggy walls of rock. In other areas, the mountains lie behind sandy coastal plains. Deep bays that jut into the coast include Puget Sound, Columbia River Bay, San Francisco Bay, and San Diego Bay.

The San Andreas Fault runs through the Coast Ranges in California. It is a break in Earth's rocky outer shell, along which movements of the rock have taken place. Giant redwood trees grow on the mountains in northern California. Set among the Coast Ranges are a number of rich agricultural valleys that produce much of the nation's wine grapes and other fruit, and lettuce.

Climate

The climate of the United States varies greatly from place to place. Average annual temperatures range from 10 °F (–12 °C) in Barrow, Alaska, to 76 °F (24 °C) in Death Valley, California. The highest temperature ever recorded in the country was 134 °F (57 °C). It was registered at Death Valley on July 10, 1913. The lowest recorded temperature was –80 °F (–62 °C). It was registered at Prospect Creek, Alaska, near Barrow, on Jan. 23, 1971.

Precipitation varies from a yearly average of about 2

© David Muench

Death Valley, California, the country's driest place, receives about 2 inches (5 centimeters) of precipitation yearly. It recorded the highest U.S. temperature ever, 134 °F (57 °C).

© David Muench

Waimea Canyon, Hawaii, was formed by water from Mount Waialeale, the wettest place in the United States. The mountain receives about 460 inches (1,170 centimeters) of rain a year.

© Galen Rowell, Corbis

Barrow, Alaska, has the lowest average annual temperature in the United States, 10 °F (–12 °C). Prospect Creek, near Barrow, recorded the lowest U.S. temperature ever, –80 °F (–62 °C).

Average January temperatures

The southern and far western parts of the United States have milder winters than the rest of the country. This map shows how average January temperatures generally decrease from south to north.

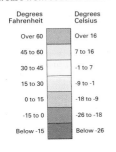

Degrees Fahrenheit	Degrees Celsius
Over 60	Over 16
45 to 60	7 to 16
30 to 45	-1 to 7
15 to 30	-9 to -1
0 to 15	-18 to -9
-15 to 0	-26 to -18
Below -15	Below -26

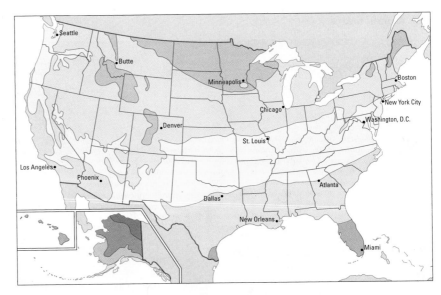

Average July temperatures

Average July temperatures in most of the United States are in the range of 75 to 90 °F (24 to 32 °C) or 60 to 75 °F (16 to 24 °C). Temperatures are lower in most of Alaska and higher in the Southwest desert.

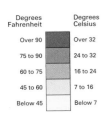

Degrees Fahrenheit	Degrees Celsius
Over 90	Over 32
75 to 90	24 to 32
60 to 75	16 to 24
45 to 60	7 to 16
Below 45	Below 7

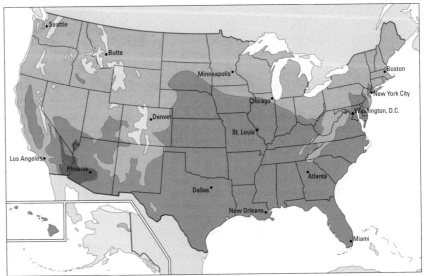

Average yearly precipitation

The amount of yearly precipitation in the United States generally increases from west to east . But some areas along the west coast and in Alaska and Hawaii receive the most precipitation.

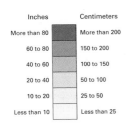

Inches	Centimeters
More than 80	More than 200
60 to 80	150 to 200
40 to 60	100 to 150
20 to 40	50 to 100
10 to 20	25 to 50
Less than 10	Less than 25

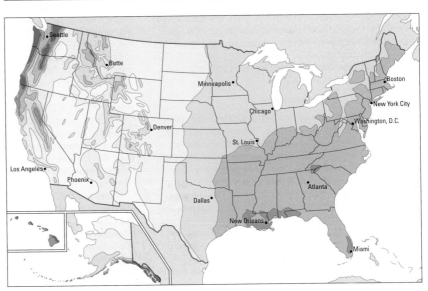

WORLD BOOK maps

The United States economy is the world's largest in terms of economic production. The huge warehouse shown here stores grain before it is shipped to distant markets. Barges, railroad cars, trucks, and other transportation facilities are used to transport products.

© Cameramann Int'l.

inches (5 centimeters) at Death Valley to about 460 inches (1,170 centimeters) at Mount Waialeale (pronounced *wy AH lay AH lay)* in Hawaii. In general, however, most parts of the United States have seasonal changes in temperature and moderate precipitation. The Midwest, the Middle Atlantic States, and New England experience warm summers and cold, snowy winters. In the South, summers are long and hot, and winters are mild. Along the Pacific Coast, and in some other areas near large bodies of water, the climate is relatively mild all year. Mountains also affect the climate. In the West, for example, the mountainous areas are cooler and wetter than the neighboring plains and plateaus. Parts of the West and Southwest have a desert climate.

The moderate climate in much of the United States has encouraged widespread population settlement. It has also helped make possible the production of a great variety of agricultural goods.

See **North America** (Climate). See also the section on *Climate* in each state article.

Economy

The United States ranks first in the world in the total value of its economic production. The nation's *gross domestic product*—the value of all the goods and services produced within a country in a year—was over $11 ½ trillion in 2004. This was more than twice as large as the gross domestic product of Japan, which ranked second.

The U.S. economy is based largely on a *free enterprise system.* In such a system, individuals and companies are free to make their own economic decisions. Individuals and companies own the raw materials, equipment, factories, and other items necessary for production, and they decide how best to use them to earn a profit.

Even though the U.S. economy is based on free enter-

prise, the government has placed regulations on economic practices through the years. It has passed antitrust laws, which are designed to keep one company or a few firms from controlling entire industries. Such control, called a monopoly, does away with competition and enables controlling companies to charge high prices and reduce the quality of goods. Government regulations help protect consumers from unsafe merchandise. They also help protect workers from unsafe working conditions and unreasonably low wages. The government has also enacted regulations designed to reduce environmental pollution.

Some people argue that the government interferes in the economy too much, while others say it should do more. Despite government involvement, the United States still has one of the least regulated economies in the world. See **Capitalism; Monopoly and competition.**

Despite its overall strength, the United States economy faces problems from time to time. The problems include *recessions* (mild business slumps), *depressions* (severe business slumps), and *inflation* (rising prices). See **Depression; Great Depression; Inflation; Recession.**

Natural resources. The United States has a vast array of natural resources including a moderate climate, fertile soils, and plentiful minerals, water, forests, and fish. However, the United States uses more than it has and must import some raw materials to provide for the needs of its citizens.

Minerals. The United States has large deposits of coal, iron ore, natural gas, and petroleum, which are vital to the country's industrial strength. Its many other important mined products include copper, gold, lead, limestone, phosphates, silver, sulfur, and zinc. To meet its needs, however, the United States must import additional amounts of iron ore, petroleum, and other materials.

© John Running, Stock, Boston

Forests are one of the many natural resources that support the United States economy. Logs from forests are used for lumber and in making paper and other valuable products.

Soils. The United States has vast expanses of fertile soil that is well suited to growing crops. The most fertile soils include the dark soils of the Interior Plains and the *alluvial* (water-deposited) soils along the lower Mississippi River Valley and other smaller river valleys. Rich, wind-blown soil called *loess* covers parts of eastern Washington and the southern Interior Plains.

Water. Lakes, rivers, and underground deposits supply water for households, farms, and industries in the United States. The nation uses about 400 billion gallons (1,500 billion liters) of water daily. Households use only about 10 percent of this total. The vast majority of the rest is used to irrigate farms and to operate steam power plants.

Forests cover nearly a third of the United States, and they yield many valuable products. About a fourth of the nation's lumber comes from forests in the Pacific Northwest. Forests in the South supply lumber, wood pulp—which is used to make paper—and nearly all the pitch, rosin, turpentine, and wood tar produced in the United States. The Appalachian Mountains and parts of the Great Lakes area have fine hardwood forests. Hickory, maple, oak, and other hardwood trees cut from these forests provide quality woods for the manufacture of furniture.

Fish. Americans who fish for a living catch almost 5 million tons (4.5 million metric tons) of sea products annually. The greatest quantities are taken from the Pacific Ocean, which supplies cod, crabs, halibut, pollock, salmon, tuna, and other fish. Leading catches from the Gulf of Mexico include crabs, menhaden, oysters, and shrimp. The Atlantic yields flounder, herring, menhaden, and other fish; and such shellfish as clams, crabs, lobsters, oysters, and scallops.

Service industries account for the largest portion of the U.S. gross domestic product and employ a majority of the country's workers. This industry group includes a wide variety of businesses that provide services rather than producing goods.

Finance, insurance, and real estate play an important part in the nation's economy. Banks finance much of the economic activity in the United States by making loans to both individuals and businesses. American banks loan billions of dollars annually. Most of the bank loans go to individuals to help finance the purchase of automobiles, houses, or other major items. Bank loans to businesses provide an important source of money for *capital expansion*—the construction of new factories and the purchase of new equipment. As a business expands, it hires more workers.

These workers, in turn, produce more goods and services. In this way, the nation's level of employment and its economic output both increase.

Other important types of financial institutions include commodity and security exchanges. Commodities are basic goods, such as grains and precious metals. Securities are certificates of investment, such as stocks and bonds.

Gross domestic product of the United States

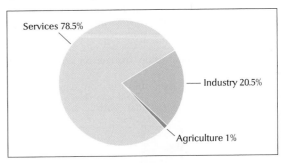

The gross domestic product (GDP) is the total value of goods and services produced within a country in a year. The GDP measures a nation's economic performance and can also be used to compare the economic output and growth of countries. The U.S. GDP was $11,655,300,000,000 in 2004.

Production and workers by economic activities

Economic activities	Percent of GDP produced	Employed workers	
		Number of people	Percent of total
Finance, insurance, & real estate	23	16,351,700	10
Community, business, & personal services	21	54,554,600	32
Trade, restaurants, & hotels	15	36,349,200	21
Government	12	23,725,000	14
Manufacturing	12	14,905,800	9
Transportation & communication	7	8,963,700	5
Construction	5	10,302,500	6
Utilities	2	590,100	*
Agriculture	1	3,964,200	2
Mining	1	775,900	*
Total†	100	170,482,700	100

*Less than one-half of 1 percent. †Figures do not add up to 100 percent due to rounding. Figures are for 2004; employment figures include full- and part-time workers.
Source: U.S. Bureau of Economic Analysis.

The prices of commodities and securities are determined by the buying and selling that takes place at exchanges. The New York Stock Exchange is the nation's largest security exchange. The CME Group in Chicago is the world's largest commodity exchange.

The United States has the world's largest private insurance industry. The country has thousands of insurance companies. Real estate is important to the economy because of the large sums of money involved in the buying and selling of property.

Community, business, and personal services employ more people than the businesses that make up any other U.S. industry. Businesses within this group include engineering companies, information technology companies, law firms, private health care, private research laboratories, and repair shops.

Trade, restaurants, and hotels play major roles in the American economy. Wholesale trade, which includes international trade, takes place when a buyer purchases goods directly from a producer. The goods may then be sold to other businesses for resale to consumers. Retail trade involves selling products to the final consumer. Automobile dealerships, department stores, and grocery stores are examples of retail trade establishments. Restaurants and hotels greatly benefit from the tens of millions of tourists from other countries who visit the United States annually.

International trade provides markets for surplus agricultural goods and many raw materials and manufactured goods produced in the United States. The nation imports goods that it lacks entirely or that producers do not supply in sufficient quantities. It also imports goods produced by foreign companies that compete with U.S. firms. Traditionally, the value of U.S. exports has exceeded, or been about the same as, the value of U.S. imports. But since the mid-1960's, the value of imports has usually been much higher than the value of exports.

Important U.S. exports include (1) machinery and transportation equipment, such as aircraft, computers, electric power equipment, industrial machinery, and motor vehicles and parts; (2) chemical elements and compounds, including plastic materials; (3) manufactured articles, especially scientific measuring equipment; (4) basic manufactures, such as metals and paper; (5) food crops and live animals; and (6) crude materials, including textile fibers and metal ores.

The leading U.S. imports are (1) machinery and transportation equipment, such as automobiles and auto parts, office machines, and telecommunications equipment; (2) manufactured articles, such as clothing, shoes, and toys; (3) fuels and lubricants, especially petroleum; (4) basic manufactures, such as iron, steel, and other metals, and paper and newsprint; and (5) chemical products.

Canada, China, Japan, and Mexico are the country's chief trading partners. Other major trading partners include France, Germany, Malaysia, South Korea, and the

United States land use   This map shows major land uses in the United States, and also offshore fishing areas. Labels on the map identify chief products of various areas. The label size generally indicates product importance. Other labels on the map locate major manufacturing centers in the country.

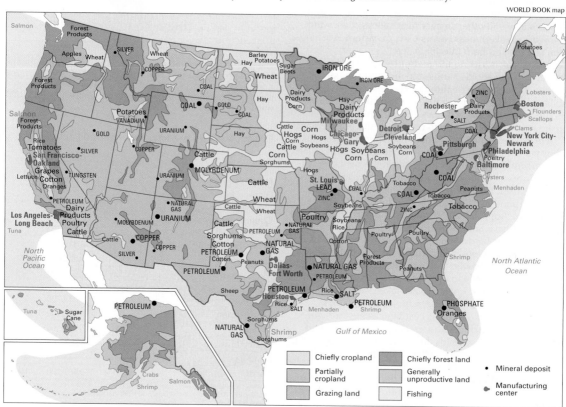

WORLD BOOK map

© Gail Mooney, Corbis

Service industries are those economic activities that provide services rather than goods. They include such retail establishments as the food market shown here. The majority of United States workers are employed in service industries.

© James R. Holland, Stock, Boston

The construction industry provides jobs for many Americans. Workers help put up a high-rise building in the center of a city, *shown here.*

United Kingdom. The North American Free Trade Agreement, which took effect in 1994, eliminated trade barriers among Mexico, Canada, and the United States.

Government services play a major role in the economy. Federal, state, and local governments employ many U.S. workers. Many government employees are directly involved in making public policies. Others—including police officers, postal workers, teachers, and trash collectors—provide public services.

Federal, state, and local governments buy a fifth of all the goods and services produced in the nation. These purchases range from paper clips to office buildings. The federal government is the nation's largest single buyer of goods and services. Its agencies, including the military, buy billions of dollars worth of equipment from private companies. In addition, federal grants finance much of the nation's research activity. State governments spend most of their income on education, health care and hospitals, highways, and public welfare. Local governments spend over a third of their income on education, and less for police and fire protection, hospitals, streets, sanitation and sewerage, and parks.

In addition to its roles as an employer and purchaser of goods and services, government influences the economy by providing income to certain groups of people. For example, the federal government makes Social Security payments to retired people and people with disabilities. Federal, state, and local governments provide welfare assistance to the needy. Such government programs are the only source of income for some Americans.

Transportation and communication are also important to the economy. More information on transportation and communication appears later in this section.

Manufacturing is an important economic activity in the United States both in terms of employment and the gross domestic product. The value of American manufactured goods is greater than that of any other country. Factories in the United States turn out a tremendous variety of *producer goods,* such as sheet metal and printing presses; and *consumer goods,* such as cars, clothing, and TV sets. The leading categories of U.S. products are, in order of value, chemicals, transportation equipment, food products, computer and electronic products, fabricated metal products, machinery, plastics and rubber products, paper products, primary metal products, beverage and tobacco products, petroleum and coal products, nonmetallic mineral products, printed materials, and electrical equipment and appliances.

The Midwest and Northeast have long been major U.S. centers of manufacturing. Since the mid-1900's, the country's fastest-growing manufacturing areas have been on the West Coast, in the Southwest, and in the South. Today, California ranks first among the states in the value of its manufactured goods, followed by Texas, Ohio, Illinois, Pennsylvania, Michigan, North Carolina, and Indiana. Manufacturers in California produce aircraft, aerospace equipment, chemicals, computers and electronic components, food products, and many other goods.

Midwestern factories turn out much of the nation's iron and steel, automobiles, and other heavy industrial products. The Northeast has many clothing factories, food-processing companies, printing plants, and manufacturers of electronic equipment. Petroleum refineries and petrochemical industries account for much of the manufacturing activity in Texas and other states bordering the Gulf of Mexico. Atlanta, Dallas-Fort Worth, Seattle, and Wichita are important centers for the manufacture of aircraft and related equipment.

The Boeing Company

Manufacturing is an important economic activity in the United States. The country's factories turn out an enormous variety of products. Transportation equipment—including airplanes, such as the Boeing 777 jetliner shown here—ranks among the leading categories of United States products.

Through the years, Americans have developed manufacturing processes that have greatly increased productivity. During the early 1900's, United States automobile firms introduced the moving assembly line and identical interchangeable parts for cars. These innovations led to mass production, in which large numbers of goods could be produced in less time and at a lower cost than ever before. Beginning in the mid-1900's, U.S. industries turned increasingly to *automation*—the use of machines that operate with little human help. American inventors and engineers developed computers to bring automation to an even higher level. Today, computers operate machines, handle accounting, and perform many other important functions in industries. See **Manufacturing.**

Construction consists of activities involved in building and maintaining residences, business offices, storage warehouses, and other structures. This industry employs such workers as architects, engineers, contractors, bricklayers, carpenters, electricians, plumbers, roofers, ironworkers, and plasterers.

Agriculture accounts for only a small part of the U.S. gross domestic product. Yet the United States is a world leader in agriculture production. The country's farms turn out as much food as the nation needs, with enough left over to export food to other countries. Food exports account for about one-fifth of U.S. farm income.

Michigan Apple Committee

Agriculture accounts for only a small part of the U.S. economy. But farms produce enough for the nation's needs as well as for export. The farmer shown here is checking his apple crop.

IBM Corporation

Computers are an important United States product. The workers in this "clean room" are completely covered to protect sensitive electronic equipment that is in the process of development.

Beef cattle rank as the most valuable product of American farms. Millions of beef cattle are raised on huge ranches in the western United States. The South and Midwest also produce large numbers of beef cattle. Other leading farm products, in order of value, include dairy products, *broilers* (young, tender chickens), corn, soybeans, greenhouse and nursery products, hogs, wheat, and cotton. United States farms also produce large amounts of almonds, eggs, grapes, hay, lettuce, oranges, potatoes, tomatoes, and turkeys.

Farmers throughout the country raise dairy cattle for milk and other products. Much of the dairy production is concentrated in a belt that extends from Minnesota through New York. Midwestern states account for much of the nation's corn, hog, and soybean production. The nation's chief wheat-growing region stretches across the Great Plains. The South raises most of the broilers. California, Texas, and a few other states in the South and Southwest raise almost all the country's cotton. Farms in various areas also produce poultry, eggs, and crops of fruits, vegetables, nuts, and grains.

The United States has played a major role in the modernization of agriculture. During the 1800's, American inventors developed the first successful harvesting machine and steel plow. United States scientists have contributed to the development of improved plant varieties and livestock breeds, as well as agricultural chemicals for fertilizer and pest control.

The use of modern farm machinery and agricultural methods has helped make U.S. farms the most efficient in the world. But it has also contributed to rapidly rising production costs. Many farmers who have been unable to meet these rising costs have been forced to quit farming and sell their land. Since 1925, the number of farms in the United States has decreased from approximately 6,500,000 to about 2,100,000. At the same time, average farm size increased from about 143 acres (58 hectares) to about 470 acres (190 hectares). Some of the largest farms in the United States are owned by corporations. But more than 90 percent of all the farms are owned by individuals or partnerships made up of members of farm families. See **Agriculture; Farm and farming.**

Mining. The United States ranks among the leading countries in the value of its mine production. The chief mined products of the United States are, in order of value, natural gas, petroleum, and coal. The United States ranks second, after Russia, in the production of natural gas. It is third to Saudi Arabia and Russia in petroleum production. The United States also ranks second in coal—after China. Most coal deposits lie in the Interior Plains and the Appalachian Highlands. Major deposits of petroleum and natural gas occur in Alaska, California, Louisiana, New Mexico, Oklahoma, and Texas. Other important mined products include cement, clays, copper, gold, granite, iron ore, limestone, phosphate rock, salt, sand and gravel, sulfur, traprock, and zinc.

Although mining accounts for a small share of the total U.S. economic output, it has been a key to the growth of other parts of the economy. Coal and iron ore, for example, are needed to make steel. Steel, in turn, is used to make automobiles, buildings, bridges, and many other goods. Coal is also a fuel for electric power plants. Refineries turn petroleum into gasoline; fuel oil for heating and industrial power; and petrochemicals used in plastics, paint, drugs, fertilizers, and synthetic fabrics. Limestone, granite, and traprock are crushed for use in construction materials. Sand and gravel are also used in construction. Sulfur and phosphates are used to make fertilizer. See **Mining.**

Energy sources. The farms, factories, households, and motor vehicles of the United States consume vast amounts of energy annually. Various sources are used to generate the energy. Petroleum provides about 40 percent. It is the source of most of the energy used to power motor vehicles, and it heats millions of houses and factories. Coal and natural gas each generate about 25 percent of the energy used. Coal's major uses are in the production of electric power and steel. The electric power lights buildings and powers factory and farm machinery. Many industries use natural gas for heat and power, and millions of households burn it for heat, cooking, and drying laundry. Nuclear power plants generate just under 10 percent of the country's energy. Hydroelectric plants provide less than 5 percent.

Since the mid-1900's, the cost of energy—especially petroleum—has risen sharply. The rising cost became a major contributor to inflation in the United States and other countries. For more details, see **Energy supply.**

Transportation. A sprawling transportation network spreads out over the United States. The country has millions of miles or kilometers of streets, roads, and highways. The federal interstate highway system provides a network of more than 46,000 miles (74,000 kilometers) of highways. The United States has an average of more than 75 motor vehicles for every 100 people. Americans use cars for most of their personal travel. Trucks carry nearly 30 percent of the freight in the United States. See **Automobile; Road; Truck.**

Railroads rank as the leading freight carriers in the United States, handling over 35 percent of the freight. But they account for less than 1 percent of all passenger traffic. See **Railroad.**

Airlines handle about 10 percent of all United States passenger traffic, but less than one-half of 1 percent of the freight traffic. Five of the 10 busiest airports in the

The U.S. interstate highway system

This map shows the interstate highway system that spreads out across the United States. East-west routes have even numbers, and north-south routes have odd numbers. The lowest numbered routes are in the southern and western parts of the country.

WORLD BOOK map

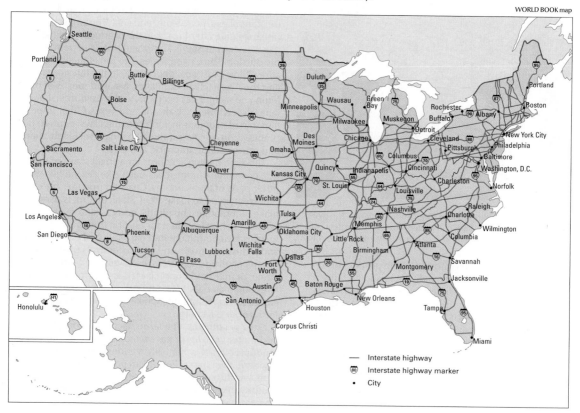

— Interstate highway
(80) Interstate highway marker
• City

world are in the United States. See **Airport; Aviation.**

Nearly 15 percent of the freight traffic within the United States travels on waterways. The Mississippi River system handles about 50 percent of this freight. Ships and barges traveling on the Mississippi and its branches, including the Arkansas, Missouri, and Ohio rivers, can reach deep into the country's interior. The Great Lakes form the nation's other major inland waterway. The St. Lawrence Seaway links the lakes with the Atlantic Ocean. See **Inland waterway.**

The United States has many major ports. A port west of New Orleans ranks as the nation's busiest port, followed by the ports of Houston and New York City. See **Port.**

The nation has a vast network of pipelines that carries crude oil, petroleum products, and natural gas. Pipelines account for about 20 percent of the total freight handled in the United States. See **Pipeline.**

Communication. Private corporations operate the publishing and broadcasting industries in the United States. The First Amendment of the Constitution guarantees freedom of the press and speech. These guarantees allow newspapers and broadcasters to operate without government censorship. Laws prohibit the publishing or broadcasting of libelous, obscene, and treasonous materials. But, for the most part, the government interferes little in the operation of the communication industry. The free exchange of ideas and information is a vital part of

the democratic heritage of the United States.

Publishers in the United States issue about 1,500 daily newspapers, which have a total circulation of about 54 million copies. The nation also has thousands of weekly and semiweekly newspapers. The newspapers provide information on local, national, and international events. Many also include such special features as opinion columns, articles on health and fashion, and comic strips and crossword puzzles.

In the United States, most newspapers serve a local region. But *The Wall Street Journal, USA Today, The New York Times,* and *The Christian Science Monitor* circulate to most of the country. *USA Today,* a nationwide general interest newspaper, has the largest circulation among U.S. papers. See **Newspaper.**

There are thousands of radio and television stations and also thousands of cable TV systems in the United States. Radio and TV provide the public with entertainment, news, and public interest programs. In the United States, both national networks and local stations produce and broadcast programs. Almost every American household has at least one TV set and one or more radios, and about two-thirds of households subscribe to cable television. See **Radio; Television.**   Teresa A. Sullivan

Related articles in *World Book.* See **United States, Government of the;** and **United States, History of the,** and their lists of *Related articles.* See also the separate article on each state and its *Related articles.* Additional related articles include:

Education

Education
School
Universities and colleges

National parks and monuments

See **National Park System** (tables: National parks; National monuments).

Outlying areas

American Samoa
Caroline Islands
Guam
Line Islands
Mariana Islands
Marshall Islands
Midway Island
Northern Mariana Islands, Commonwealth of
Puerto Rico
Virgin Islands, United States
Wake Island

Physical features

See **Dam; Lake; Mountain; River;** and their *Related articles.*

Social and cultural life

American literature
Architecture
Book
Christmas
Dance
Drama
Easter
Holiday
Library
Motion picture
Museum
Music
Painting
Recreation
Religion
Sculpture
Theater

Other related articles

African Americans
Air Force, United States
Army, United States
Asian Americans
Census
Citizenship
City
Clothing
Coast Guard, United States
Conservation
Farm and farming
Flag
Food
Hispanic Americans
Housing
Immigration
Indian, American
Marine Corps, United States
Minority group
Money
Navy, United States
Rand Corporation
Segregation
Transportation

Outline

I. The nation
   A. Political divisions
   B. Regions
   C. Outlying areas
II. People
   A. Population
   B. Ancestry
   C. Language
III. Way of life
   A. Urban life
   B. Rural life
   C. Education
   D Religion
   E. Recreation
   F. Food
IV. The arts
V. The land
   A. The Appalachian Highlands
   B. The Coastal Lowlands
   C. The Interior Plains
   D. The Ozark-Ouachita Highlands
   E. The Rocky Mountains
   F. The Western Plateaus, Basins, and Ranges
   G. The Pacific Ranges and Lowlands
VI. Climate
VII. Economy
   A. Natural resources
   B. Service industries
   C. Manufacturing
   D. Construction
   E. Agriculture
   F. Mining
   G. Energy sources
   H. Transportation
   I. Communication

Questions

How does the United States rank among the countries of the world in population and area?
Why is the country called a *melting pot?*
What are the country's main land regions?
How does mineral production contribute to other parts of the American economy?
What are some leading farm products in the United States?
What are some of the reasons why the United States changed from a rural nation to an urban nation?
Where is the lowest land in the United States?
What are some problems faced by schools in the United States?
What are the major religions in the United States?
What are some desirable and undesirable features of U.S. urban life and rural life?

Additional resources

Level I

De Capua, Sarah. *Becoming a Citizen.* Children's Pr., 2002.
Hintz, Martin. *United States of America.* Children's Pr., 2004.
Hopkins, Lee B., comp. *My America: A Poetry Atlas of the United States.* Simon & Schuster, 2000.
Leacock, Elspeth, and Buckley, Susan. *Journeys in Time: A New Atlas of American History.* Houghton, 2001. *Places in Time: A New Atlas of American History.* 2001.
Rubel, David. *Scholastic Atlas of the United States.* Rev. ed. Scholastic, 2003.

Level II

Haskell, Barbara. *The American Century: Art and Culture, 1900-1950.* Norton, 1999.
Hudson, John C. *Across This Land: A Regional Geography of the United States and Canada.* Johns Hopkins, 2002.
Pendergast, Tom and Sara, eds. *St. James Encyclopedia of Popular Culture.* 5 vols. St. James Pr., 2000.
Phillips, Lisa, and Haskell, Barbara. *The American Century: Art and Culture, 1950-2000.* Norton, 1999.
Rasmussen, R. Kent. *The Fifty States.* Salem Pr., 2000.
Smolan, Rick, and Cohen, D. E., eds. *America 24/7.* DK Pub., 2003. A book of photographs.
U.S. Bureau of the Census. *Statistical Abstract of the United States.* U.S. Government Printing Office, published annually.

The United States government has its headquarters in Washington, D.C. The United States Capitol in that city, *shown here,* is where Congress meets to make the nation's laws.

United States government

United States, Government of the. The government of the United States represents, serves, and protects the American people at home and abroad. Because the United States is a nation of great wealth and military strength, the actions of its government affect all parts of the world.

The Constitution of the United States establishes the basic structure of the U.S. government. The Constitution creates a *federal system,* in which political power is divided between the national government and the governments of each state. The national government is sometimes called the *federal* government. The Constitution also creates three separate branches of government—legislative, executive, and judicial—to share the work of creating, enforcing, and interpreting the laws of the nation. The branches are represented by Congress, the president, and the Supreme Court of the United States.

The national government of the United States is the country's largest government system. It employs more than 2 ⅔ million civilian workers and approximately 1 ⅓ million military personnel. Each year, it collects about $2 ¾ trillion in taxes from American citizens and corporations to help finance its work.

From the United States capital in Washington, D.C., the national government conducts thousands of activities that affect the lives of Americans. It helps fund many state government services, including job training, welfare payments, roads, and health care. It manages a Social Security program that provides a pension plan and other benefits to the nation's retired or disabled workers. It sets standards for programs to aid poor, aged, or disabled people. It tests food and drugs for purity and safety, conducts research on such diseases as AIDS and cancer, and sets standards to control pollution. It con-

Roger H. Davidson, the contributor of this article, is Professor of Government and Politics Emeritus at the University of Maryland and coauthor of Congress and Its Members.

ducts and coordinates space exploration. It oversees air travel, forecasts the weather, and runs hospitals for veterans. It maintains national parks, forests, historic sites, and museums.

The national government also deals with the governments of other nations. It works in dozens of international organizations that promote cooperation among nations. Many of these organizations are associated with the United Nations. The government also operates numerous diplomatic and military posts around the world.

This article provides a broad overview of the system of national government in the United States. Separate *World Book* articles give detailed information on many of the topics discussed. For a list of these articles, see the *Related articles* at the end of this article.

Principles of American government

Constitutional authority. The national government gets its authority from the American people through a written document—the Constitution of the United States. The Constitution defines the goals of the national government and what it can and cannot do.

According to the Constitution, the national government's purpose is to "establish justice, insure domestic tranquility, provide for the common defense, promote the general welfare, and secure the blessings of liberty. ..." The Constitution grants the national government strong powers to work toward these goals. The government has direct authority over all citizens. It can collect taxes and pay debts, borrow money, negotiate with other governments, regulate trade between the states and with other countries, create armed forces, and declare war. It can also create and enforce all laws that are "necessary and proper" to carry out its constitutional goals and powers.

The Constitution also limits the authority of the government. It forbids certain laws and actions. The Bill of Rights in the Constitution describes certain basic freedoms and rights of all Americans and forbids the gov-

Cameramann International, Ltd.

The Supreme Court Building is where Supreme Court justices meet to interpret the laws that govern the nation.

Karen A. McCormack

The White House is the official residence of the president of the United States and also the place where the president works.

ernment to violate those rights. For example, the government must respect the people's freedoms of speech, religion, press, and peaceful assembly.

American citizens can change the Constitution. An amendment may be proposed by Congress or by a national convention called by Congress. The amendment becomes part of the Constitution after being *ratified* (approved) by the legislatures of three-fourths of the states or by conventions in three-fourths of the states. There have been 27 amendments to the Constitution.

Separation of powers. Three separate branches share the powers of the United States government. Each branch has both *expressed powers*—those specifically listed in the Constitution—and *implied powers*—those reasonably suggested by its expressed powers. In general, the legislative branch makes the nation's laws, the executive branch enforces the laws, and the judicial branch interprets the laws if questions arise.

A system of *checks and balances* makes sure that each branch acts only within its constitutional limits. Each branch has some powers that curb, or check, those of the other two. This prevents any single government group or official from becoming too powerful.

The Constitution ensures that the branches remain separate by forbidding members of Congress from serving in another branch. In addition, executive and judicial officials may not serve in Congress. The Constitution provides that the vice president officially preside over the Senate, one of the two bodies of Congress. However, the Senate presidency is mostly a ceremonial role, and the vice president rarely appears in Congress.

Federalism is the division of powers between a national or central government and local authorities. The Constitution divides powers between the national and state governments. In addition, the states share and divide powers with such local political subdivisions as counties, cities, and towns.

The national, or federal, government can exercise only those powers that are listed in the Constitution or implied by the Constitution. The states, or the people, retain all powers not denied them, or not given to the national government, by the Constitution. The federal

and state governments have some *concurrent* powers—that is, they both have authority to do some things. Concurrent powers include the right to tax, spend, and borrow money.

Each state has its own constitution, its own laws, and its own legislative, executive, and judicial branches. In general, state laws and activities must not conflict with the U.S. Constitution, acts of Congress, or U.S. treaties. The states take the lead in such areas as education , public safety, and consumer and environmental protection. Through the years, however, the role of the federal government has increased in these and other state government activities.

Representative democracy. The United States government relies on the consent of the people. The peo-

Symbols of the United States include the American flag and the Great Seal. The eagle holds an olive branch and arrows, symbolizing a desire for peace but the ability to wage war. The reverse side bears the Eye of Providence, representing God, and a pyramid dated 1776.

ple elect a certain number of their fellow citizens to represent them in making laws and in other matters. Federal, state, and local laws regulate elections.

Political parties play an important role in elections. They select candidates to run for public office, provide opposition to the party in power, and raise funds to conduct election campaigns. They also inform voters about public affairs and about problems they believe need government action.

The United States has a *two-party system*—that is, it has two major political parties, the Democratic and the Republican. Members of these two parties hold almost all the offices in the national and state governments.

Minor political parties in the United States rarely elect candidates to government offices. These parties serve chiefly to express discontent over problems that the major parties may have neglected. Often, one or both of the major parties moves toward solving such a problem. Then the third party may disappear or be absorbed by a major party.

The legislative branch

Congress creates, abolishes, and changes federal laws, which govern the nation. Congressional lawmakers also play an important role in establishing *public policy*—what the government does or says in response to political issues.

Organization. Congress consists of two chambers—the Senate and the House of Representatives. The two chambers have about equal power. Voters in each state elect the members of each chamber, or *house*. The Senate has 100 members, 2 from each state, who serve six-year terms. About a third of the seats come up for election every two years. The House of Representatives, usually called simply the House, has 435 members. House members, or *representatives,* serve two-year terms. The number of representatives from each state is based on the state's population. Each state has at least one representative. The Senate and House meet in separate wings of the Capitol in Washington, D.C.

Elections are held in November of even-numbered years. The members start each two-year Congress the following January. Beginning with the First Congress (1789-1791), each Congress has been numbered.

The legislative branch includes several agencies that provide Congress with information and services. For example, the Government Accountability Office *audits* (closely examines) the financial records of various departments and agencies of the federal government and reports its findings to Congress. Other support agencies of Congress include the Congressional Budget Office, the Congressional Research Service of the Library of Congress, and the Government Printing Office.

In addition, each senator and representative has a personal staff to advise him or her on issues, answer mail from voters, handle publicity, and help in other ways. There are also staffs that assist committees in Congress and *aides* (assistants) for each house.

Functions. Making laws is the main job of Congress. During each two-year Congress, senators and representatives introduce up to 10,000 bills. In that period, Congress passes, and the president signs into law, about 600 bills.

Congress makes laws on all kinds of matters. Some laws are major policy decisions, such as taxing and spending measures. Others deal with administrative details, such as employee benefits or the purchase of land. Still others are *commemorative* laws, which honor a group, person, or event. In 1914, for example, Congress honored mothers with a law that declared the second Sunday in May as Mother's Day. All of these laws are called *public laws* if they apply to people in general. Congress also passes a few *private laws* that apply to specific individuals, such as immigration cases.

Congress does more than make laws. It investigates the actions of the executive branch and makes sure the laws are carried out. Congress also reviews the election, qualifications, and ethical behavior of its own members. It can remove federal officials from office, including members of Congress, for serious offenses. The House brings *impeachment* (misconduct) charges against an official, and the Senate tries the official.

Each chamber of Congress has some independent duties. The Senate approves or rejects the people that the president appoints to certain high-level federal positions. It also approves or rejects treaties that the president makes. All legislation that deals with taxes or spending must start in the House.

In addition, senators and representatives spend much time serving their *constituents*—the people who elected them. They answer individuals' questions or requests, meet with visitors, and inform the public of issues. They often travel to their home states to appear at public events, study area problems, and talk with voters and local officials. In addition, legislators, usually with the help of their parties, conduct their own election campaigns, including fund-raising.

Committee system. Congress does much of its work through committees. The House has 20 *standing* (permanent) committees, each with authority over bills in a certain area, such as agriculture or banking. The Senate has 16 standing committees. Most standing committees have subcommittees to handle particular topics. In addition, each house may form *select committees* or *special committees* for investigations or other special purposes. *Joint committees*—made up of members from both the House and the Senate—handle mainly research and administrative details. Most legislators serve on several committees and subcommittees.

When committees or subcommittees study bills, they may hear testimony from experts and other interested people. Committees work out amendments to the bills and other details and recommend bills to the full House or Senate for passage.

Party leadership has an important influence on Congress. Democratic and Republican members of Congress choose official party leaders for each house. Party leaders plan the legislative strategy of the party, communicate their party's position on issues to other members, and encourage members to vote along party lines. When voting on major legislation, senators and representatives weigh their party loyalty against their own judgment or the interests of their constituents. On less important bills, legislators usually vote according to their party's position.

In each house, the *majority party*—that is, the party with the most members—chooses one of its members to lead the entire chamber. The House chooses a *speaker,*

Government of the United States

The chart on this page shows the basic structure of the government of the United States. The U.S. Constitution creates three separate branches—legislative, executive, and judicial—to share government powers. In general, the legislative branch makes the nation's laws, the executive branch carries out the laws, and the judicial branch interprets the laws.

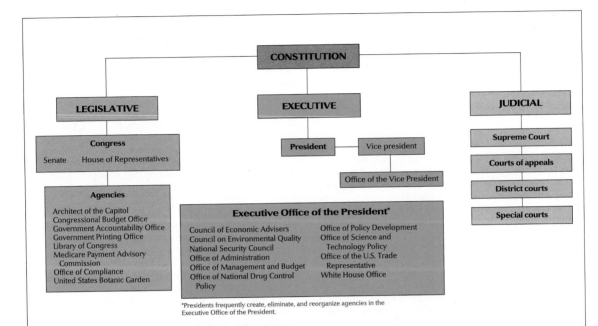

CONSTITUTION

LEGISLATIVE

Congress

Senate   House of Representatives

Agencies

Architect of the Capitol
Congressional Budget Office
Government Accountability Office
Government Printing Office
Library of Congress
Medicare Payment Advisory Commission
Office of Compliance
United States Botanic Garden

EXECUTIVE

President   **Vice president**

Office of the Vice President

Executive Office of the President*

Council of Economic Advisers
Council on Environmental Quality
National Security Council
Office of Administration
Office of Management and Budget
Office of National Drug Control Policy

Office of Policy Development
Office of Science and Technology Policy
Office of the U.S. Trade Representative
White House Office

*Presidents frequently create, eliminate, and reorganize agencies in the Executive Office of the President.

JUDICIAL

Supreme Court

Courts of appeals

District courts

Special courts

Executive departments†

Department of Agriculture

Department of Commerce

Department of Defense

Department of Education

Department of Energy

Department of Health and Human Services

Department of Homeland Security

Department of Housing and Urban Development

Department of the Interior

Department of Justice

Department of Labor

Department of State

Department of Transportation

Department of the Treasury

Department of Veterans Affairs

†There is a separate *World Book* article on each executive department. The articles are listed under their key word, as in **Agriculture, Department of.**

Independent agencies‡

The executive branch includes about 80 agencies that are not part of an executive department. This chart lists some of the best-known independent agencies.

Central Intelligence Agency

Commission on Civil Rights

Consumer Product Safety Commission

Environmental Protection Agency

Equal Employment Opportunity Commission

Export-Import Bank of the United States

Federal Communications Commission

Federal Deposit Insurance Corporation

Federal Election Commission

Federal Maritime Commission

Federal Mediation and Conciliation Service

Federal Reserve System

Federal Trade Commission

General Services Administration

International Trade Commission

National Aeronautics and Space Administration

National Archives and Records Administration

National Foundation on the Arts and the Humanities

National Labor Relations Board

National Mediation Board

National Science Foundation

Nuclear Regulatory Commission

Peace Corps

Railroad Retirement Board

Securities and Exchange Commission

Small Business Administration

Social Security Administration

Tennessee Valley Authority

United States Postal Service

‡There is a separate *World Book* article on each of the independent agencies listed.

and the Senate chooses a *president pro tempore* (temporary president) to serve in the vice president's absence. In addition, majority-party members head congressional committees.

Each party in the House and Senate also elects a *floor leader* and an assistant leader called a *whip.* The floor leaders, known as *majority leaders* or *minority leaders* depending on their party, and the whips work for passage of their party's legislative program.

In the House, the majority party has strong control over the agenda. The Speaker and the majority leader schedule the House's business and coordinate the committees' work on bills. House debate rules are formal and rigid, designed to let the majority have its way.

In the Senate, a smaller and less formal body, the majority party has less control. Debate rules allow senators opposed to a bill to make *filibusters*—long speeches or other tactics designed to slow down or block the legislative process or force the bill's sponsors to compromise on its content or abandon the bill.

The lawmaking process weeds out bills that lack sufficient support. At every stage in the process, a bill's backers must bargain for the support of their fellow lawmakers. A bill is debated by one or more committees and, if approved, by the full House or Senate. Both houses must approve a bill in exactly the same form before it is sent to the president. If they adopt different versions of a bill, a *conference committee,* made up of committee leaders from both houses, may be formed to work out the differences.

For a detailed description of the lawmaking process, see the chart *How a bill becomes a law in the United States* in this article. See also **Congress of the United States** (How Congress makes laws).

The executive branch

The executive branch carries out federal laws. It also creates and enforces regulations based on the laws. The president heads the executive branch. Fifteen executive departments and about 80 agencies handle the daily work of administering federal laws and programs.

The presidency. The president is elected to serve a four-year term. The 22nd Amendment to the Constitution, approved in 1951, provides that no one can be elected to the presidency more than twice.

A nationwide presidential election is held every four years in November. The people of each state elect delegates to the Electoral College. The delegates, or *electors,* then choose the president and vice president based on the popular votes in the states they represent. If no candidate receives a majority of Electoral College votes, the House elects the president and the Senate selects the vice president. If the president dies, is removed from office, or becomes unable to perform the duties of office, the vice president takes over the presidency until the next election. The president lives in the White House in Washington, D.C., and has offices there.

The president has many roles and duties. As chief executive, the president enforces federal laws, directs the preparation of the federal budget, and appoints many high-ranking officials. As commander in chief of the armed forces, the president directs foreign and national security affairs. As chief diplomat, the president negotiates treaties with other countries. As legislative leader,

the president recommends laws to Congress and works to win their passage. The president may veto bills approved by Congress. The threat of a veto can influence the way Congress develops a bill.

Congress has the power to restrain most of the president's powers. Congress must approve the federal budget and the president's legislative plans. It can override a president's veto by a vote of a two-thirds majority of the members present in each house. In addition, all treaties and high-level appointments by the president require Senate approval.

For many Americans and people around the world, the president represents the United States government. Presidents can use their visibility in the news media to focus attention on their programs and to create public support for their policies. However, their visibility is a double-edged sword. People often blame presidents for problems, such as an economic depression or a foreign crisis, that the president may not have caused and can do little to solve.

The Executive Office of the President consists of a number of staff agencies that provide the president with information, ideas, and advice on a wide range of issues. One agency, the Office of Management and Budget (OMB), helps plan the federal budget. The OMB also advises the president on proposed laws and regulations, shaping its recommendations to promote the president's goals. Another key unit, the White House Office, includes the president's personal aides, policy advisers, speechwriters, and lawyers.

Executive departments and agencies carry out laws and create and enforce detailed regulations based on laws. Congress creates departments and agencies to deal with particular matters. It controls the basic structure and authority of each. The Office of Management and Budget and Congress control the funding of departments and agencies. Presidents cannot create, eliminate, or reorganize departments or agencies without the approval of Congress.

Executive departments are vast organizations that conduct a wide range of government activities. Each is divided into bureaus, divisions, offices, or other units. The president, with the approval of the Senate, appoints the head of each department. The department heads form the president's Cabinet, an informal advisory group that helps the president.

Independent agencies. The executive branch includes dozens of agencies that perform government functions. These agencies are called *independent agencies* because they are not part of an executive department. Some independent agencies, such as the National Aeronautics and Space Administration and the Peace Corps, carry out programs or provide services. Others, called *regulatory agencies* or *regulatory commissions,* enforce laws dealing with aspects of American economic life. For example, the Federal Trade Commission works to protect consumers from unfair trade practices.

Government corporations are independent agencies that are organized in ways similar to businesses. They conduct commercial activities, perform services, or raise funds for the public. For example, the Tennessee Valley Authority works to develop the natural resources of the Tennessee Valley. The U.S. Postal Service provides mail services.

Control of departments and agencies. Except for high-level officials appointed by the president, executive departments and independent agencies are made up of permanent staffs of civil service workers. They establish their own ways of carrying out programs and policies. Departments and agencies may be influenced by powerful interest groups. For example, the Forest Service, a division of the Department of Agriculture, manages the national forests. It must juggle the often-conflicting needs of such groups as campers, environmentalists, ranchers, and logging companies. In addition, departments and agencies must cooperate with Congress, especially with the committees that write their laws and approve funds for their programs.

Because of these influences, presidents may find it difficult to push departments and agencies and their programs in new directions. To have an effect, presidents may find it necessary to create wide public support for their policies. They can also influence departments and agencies by shaping the federal budget to reflect their goals and by making sure their policies are reflected in new regulations.

The judicial branch

The judicial branch interprets the nation's laws. It is made up of a system of federal courts and judges. The Supreme Court of the United States is the highest court in the nation.

Authority of the courts. Federal courts settle disputes among citizens involving the Constitution or federal laws, and disputes between citizens and the federal government. They also hear cases involving treaties or *maritime* (sea) laws. In addition, federal courts may decide certain cases between individuals or groups from different states, and cases involving other countries or their citizens.

The courts' most important power is *judicial review*—that is, their authority to overturn laws they judge unconstitutional. Any court in the United States can declare laws or the actions of public officials illegal if they

---

How a bill becomes law in the United States

The drawings on this page and the next three pages show how federal laws are enacted in the United States. Thousands of bills are introduced during each Congress, which lasts two years, and hundreds become law. All bills not enacted by the end of the two-year period are killed.

WORLD BOOK illustrations by David Cunningham

Ideas for new laws come from many sources. The president, members of Congress, and other government officials may propose laws. Suggestions also come from individual citizens; special-interest groups, such as farmers, industry, and labor; newspaper editorials; and public protests. Congressional committees, in addition to lawyers who represent special-interest groups, actually write most bills. Specialists called *legislative counsels* in both the Senate and House of Representatives also help prepare many bills for congressional action.

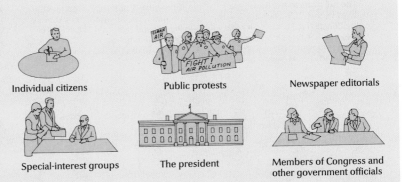

Individual citizens

Public protests

Newspaper editorials

Special-interest groups

The president

Members of Congress and other government officials

Each bill must be sponsored by a member of the House or Senate. Any number of senators or representatives may co-sponsor a bill. A bill may originate in either house of Congress unless it deals with taxes or spending. The Constitution provides that all revenue bills must be introduced in the House. By tradition, spending bills begin there also. This practice came from England.

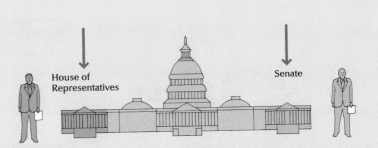

House of Representatives

Senate

Continues on the next page.

How a bill moves through Congress

The drawings on this page and the next show the normal path of a bill introduced in the House of Representatives. The process is the same for a bill introduced in the Senate, except that the House action comes after the Senate action. A bill may die at almost any stage of the process if no action is taken on it. A majority of the bills introduced in Congress fail and never become law.

Introduction in the House. A sponsor introduces a bill by giving it to the clerk of the House or placing it in a box called the *hopper.* The clerk reads the title of the bill into the *Congressional Record* in a procedure called the *first reading.* The Government Printing Office prints the bill and distributes copies.

Assignment to committee. The Speaker of the House assigns the bill to a committee for study. The House has 20 *standing* (permanent) committees, each with jurisdiction over bills in a certain area.

The bill goes to the Senate to await its turn. Bills normally reach the Senate floor in the order that they come from committee. But if a bill is urgent, the leaders of the majority party might push it ahead.

Committee action. The committee or one of its subcommittees studies the bill and may hold hearings. The committee may approve the bill as it stands, revise the bill, or table it.

Assignment to committee. The presiding officer of the Senate assigns the proposed law to a committee for study. The Senate has 16 standing committees.

The Senate considers the bill. Senators can debate a bill indefinitely, unless they vote or agree to limit discussion. When there is no further debate, the Senate votes. Most bills must have a simple majority to pass.

A conference committee made up of members of both houses works out any differences between the House and Senate versions of the bill. The revised bill is sent back to both houses for their final approval.

The committee studies the bill and hears testimony from experts and other interested people. In many cases, a subcommittee conducts the study. The committee may release the bill with a recommendation to pass it, revise the bill and release it, or lay it aside so that the House cannot vote on it. Releasing the bill is called *reporting it out,* and laying it aside is called *tabling.*

The bill goes on a *calendar,* a list of bills awaiting action. The Rules Committee may call for quick action on the bill, limit debate, and limit or prohibit amendments. Undisputed bills may be passed by unanimous consent, or by a two-thirds vote if members agree to suspend the rules.

Introduction in the Senate. To introduce a bill, a senator must be recognized by the presiding officer and announce the introduction of the bill. A bill that has passed either house of Congress is sometimes called an *act,* but the term usually means legislation that has passed both houses and become law.

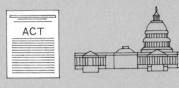

Consideration by the House begins with a second reading of the bill, the only complete reading in most cases. A third reading, by title only, comes after any amendments have been added. In most cases, if the bill passes by a *simple majority* (at least one more than half the votes), it goes to the Senate.

The bill is printed by the Government Printing Office in a process called *enrolling.* The clerk of the house of Congress that originated the bill certifies the final version.

The speaker of the House signs the enrolled bill, and then the vice president signs it. Finally, Congress sends the proposed new legislation to the White House for consideration by the president.

Action by the president

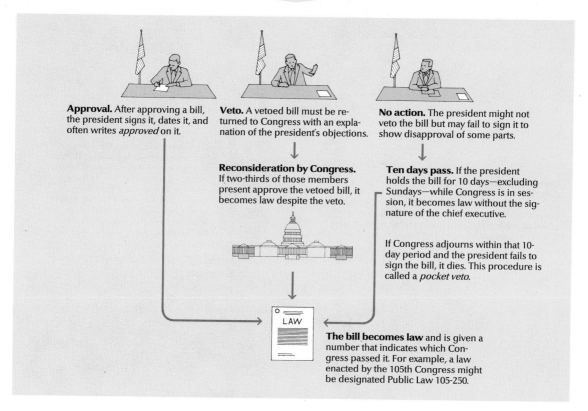

A bill passed by Congress goes to the president, who has 10 days—not including Sundays—to sign or veto it. The president may also let a bill become law by letting 10 days pass without acting.

Approval. After approving a bill, the president signs it, dates it, and often writes *approved* on it.

Veto. A vetoed bill must be returned to Congress with an explanation of the president's objections.

No action. The president might not veto the bill but may fail to sign it to show disapproval of some parts.

Reconsideration by Congress. If two-thirds of those members present approve the vetoed bill, it becomes law despite the veto.

Ten days pass. If the president holds the bill for 10 days—excluding Sundays—while Congress is in session, it becomes law without the signature of the chief executive.

If Congress adjourns within that 10-day period and the president fails to sign the bill, it dies. This procedure is called a *pocket veto*.

The bill becomes law and is given a number that indicates which Congress passed it. For example, a law enacted by the 105th Congress might be designated Public Law 105-250.

conflict with the U.S. Constitution. The Supreme Court, however, is the final authority on such matters. Judicial review provides an important check on the executive and legislative branches, as well as on state and local governments. The Supreme Court first established the power of judicial review in the famous case of *Marbury v. Madison* (1803), which struck down part of an act of Congress. Since then, the court has overturned all or parts of more than 125 federal laws and more than 1,000 state laws.

Lower court system. The Constitution gives Congress the job of creating a system of lower courts. In 1789, Congress passed the Judiciary Act, which established the federal court system. Today, the system includes both *trial courts,* which conduct the first hearing of a case, and *appellate courts,* which review a trial court's decision at the request of the losing party. Most federal courts hear a wide variety of cases. Several spe-

cialized courts deal only with particular matters.

District courts are trial courts with general federal jurisdiction. There are 94 district courts in the United States and its possessions. Each state has at least one. Most federal cases begin in a district court.

Courts of appeals are appellate courts that review district court decisions on matters of law. A court of appeals can change a ruling if it decides the lower court incorrectly applied the law to the case. Courts of appeals also hear appeals of decisions made by federal agencies. The United States is divided into 12 judicial areas called *circuits,* each of which has one court of appeals. A 13th court, the United States Court of Appeals for the Federal Circuit, has nationwide jurisdiction.

Special courts. The federal court system includes several courts that deal with particular matters. For example, the United States Court of Federal Claims hears cases involving claims against the federal government. The

Court of International Trade settles disputes over imports. The United States Tax Court handles conflicts between taxpayers and the Internal Revenue Service. The Court of Appeals for the Armed Forces hears appeals from rulings by *courts-martial* (military courts).

The Supreme Court, the nation's highest court, is mainly an appellate court. It can review appeals from federal appellate courts and, in certain cases, appeals directly from district courts. It can also review appeals from the highest court in each state, providing the case involves an important federal question. In certain cases, the Supreme Court is a trial court. It tries disputes involving diplomats from other countries or conflicts between states.

The Supreme Court has a chief justice and eight associate justices. Four justices must agree to hear a case. At least six justices hear the cases chosen and decide each case by a majority vote. In the event of a tie, the lower court decision stands. The Supreme Court meets regularly in the Supreme Court Building in Washington, D.C.

Caseload. The court receives thousands of appeals each year, but it can choose which ones it will hear. Each year, it hears about 100 cases. Justices select cases that raise important questions about the government system or the rights of Americans. For example, the court hears many cases about the First Amendment guarantees of free speech and religion and about the Fourteenth Amendment's declaration that all citizens are entitled to equal protection under the law. Justices may choose a case because it involves a question that two or more lower appellate courts have decided differently.

Effects of decisions. A Supreme Court decision has great importance. Once the court rules on a constitutional question, all other courts throughout the United States are required to follow the decision in similar cases. In this way, the Supreme Court helps guarantee legal equality to all Americans.

Supreme Court decisions are not always carried out. The court must rely on the executive and legislative branches, as well as state and local officials, to enforce its decisions. Government officials may be slow to act on rulings with which they disagree. For example, the court ruled in the 1954 case of *Brown v. Board of Education of Topeka* that public school segregation was unconstitutional. But many Southern communities moved slowly in desegregating their schools after that landmark decision. Congress or state legislatures can pass laws that bypass the Supreme Court's ruling. If a ruling is extremely unpopular, the Constitution itself can be amended to override the court's decision.

Judges. The president appoints all federal judges with the approval of the Senate. Most federal judges may remain in office for life. This lifetime appointment protects them from political control and helps ensure their independence from the other branches of government. However, Congress can remove judges from office through impeachment for corruption or other abuses of office.

Because of the importance of Supreme Court decisions, the political opinions of each justice are of great public interest. Presidents generally nominate individuals to the Supreme Court who share their views on important issues. Before approving each nomination, the Senate carefully examines the nominee's qualifications.

Supreme Court nominees with extreme views on key issues usually face fierce opposition.

Growth of the federal government

Background. The American Colonies won their independence from Britain (now also called the United Kingdom) in the American Revolution (1775-1783). They founded the first national government of the United States in 1781 under a document called the Articles of Confederation. Under the Articles, however, the states kept much of their independence. The national government could not collect taxes, regulate trade, or force states to fulfill their obligations. Such leaders as George Washington, Benjamin Franklin, James Madison, and Alexander Hamilton feared that the weak national government would collapse. This concern about the Articles of Confederation led to the Constitutional Convention of 1787 in Philadelphia.

The state delegates at the convention wanted a strong national government but feared that it would not respect the independence of the states and the liberties of the people. In framing the Constitution, they used ideas from the constitutions of New York, Massachusetts, and other states. The delegates also drew on political theories set forth by philosophers of the 1600's and 1700's. Such thinkers as England's John Locke and France's Baron Montesquieu, for example, had urged separate governmental branches as a way to prevent tyranny.

The delegates created a bold new system of government—the Constitution of the United States. The document went into effect on June 21, 1788, when New Hampshire became the ninth state to ratify it. The first 10 amendments, called the Bill of Rights, were ratified in 1791. The Constitution is the oldest written national charter still in force. It establishes a broad framework of government, flexible enough to change as the nation changes. Through the years, government leaders have worked out the details as required by economic, political, and social conditions.

Early years. The federal government was tiny when it began operating in 1789. That year, Congress created the first three executive departments—Foreign Affairs (later the Department of State), Treasury, and War—and the office of the attorney general. Only a few hundred clerks served the departments and Congress.

Alexander Hamilton, the nation's first secretary of the treasury, strongly influenced the early development of the U.S. government. He believed the Constitution should be interpreted loosely to give the federal government broad power. Hamilton pushed bills through Congress that helped pay the nation's debt from the American Revolution. He also launched plans that provided for such internal improvements as roads and canals, and aided the nation's struggling new industries.

In 1803, the United States almost doubled its area in a transaction with France known as the Louisiana Purchase. The government sold much of the new land to canal and railroad companies, greatly enriching its Treasury. During the mid-1800's, the United States gained control of Texas, California, and other lands, extending its boundaries westward to the Pacific Ocean. Because of revenue from land sales, as well as taxes on imported goods, the government often collected more money than it spent during the 1800's.

The rise of big government. The size and role of the government grew as the United States expanded westward and became an industrial nation. Certain crises and events caused major spurts of government growth.

The American Civil War (1861-1865) led to a great increase in the U.S. government's size. The war forced the government to build up its military forces. The government also had to increase its administrative activities to arm, transport, feed, and clothe the troops. After the war, the government required record keeping and paperwork on a scale never before achieved to process pensions for war veterans.

During the late 1800's and early 1900's, federal regulations increased as the government began to actively supervise the marketplace. For example, the government passed laws curbing the power of *trusts,* large business organizations that limited competition. New laws were created to set railroad rates, improve workplace conditions, and ensure the purity of food and drugs. In addition, the government began to set aside national parks and forests, help farmers grow crops more effectively, and train students for vocational trades.

During the 1930's, the Great Depression caused the government to greatly increase its role in supervising the economy. Under the New Deal programs of President Franklin D. Roosevelt, Congress established many agencies to regulate and influence financial, business, agricultural, and industrial practices. Congress also passed laws to provide jobless benefits and old-age pensions, known as Social Security. In addition, the government spent billions of dollars on relief and on public works projects to create jobs. Citizens built thousands of schools, hospitals, and other public facilities.

After the Great Depression, the government continued to sponsor public works. For example, the Army Corps of Engineers and the Tennessee Valley Authority dammed rivers to provide flood control and electric power. The interstate highway program, started in 1956, was one of the largest public works projects in history.

During the 1960's, the federal government expanded again. It passed strong new civil rights laws and began to set environmental standards. It also increased its role in matters that were once handled only by state and local governments, such as education, job training, health care, and transportation.

Responding to world events. During the 1900's, the activities of the federal government spread throughout the world. Both World War I (1914-1918) and World War II (1939-1945) thrust the United States into vast multinational military campaigns in other countries.

Cold War tensions greatly influenced the federal government's foreign policy and spending for many years. The Cold War was a struggle for international power between Communist nations, led by the Soviet Union, and non-Communist nations, led by the United States. During the Cold War, which began after World War II, the United States government kept its armed forces in a state of military readiness and invested in a massive build-up of nuclear weapons. It also provided billions of dollars in aid to many non-Communist nations. The United States fought two wars, the Korean War (1950-1953) and the Vietnam War (1957-1975), in an effort to stop the spread of Communism in Asia.

During the late 1980's and the early 1990's, Communist rule collapsed in most countries, and the Cold War ended. In 1991, the Soviet Union broke apart. As a result, the U.S. government shifted much of its attention from foreign affairs to domestic issues, especially the economy.

After terrorist attacks in the United States in 2001, the elimination of international terrorist networks and the prevention of future attacks became central goals of the U.S. government. The U.S. government increased security at government buildings, high-profile events, and other likely terrorist targets. It also assembled an emergency government operation—sometimes called a "shadow government"—that could meet in a secret location in the event of a major attack on the government facilities in Washington, D.C.

Domestic challenges. Since the early 1990's, a long list of national problems has demanded the U.S. government's attention. Many of the nation's industries have struggled to compete with industries in other countries. Many measures of educational achievement are not as high as they once were. In addition, Americans have been concerned about racial conflict, crime, drug abuse, and poverty, especially in the nation's cities.

Current issues in U.S. government

Current issues in United States government include debates over how much the federal government should do, how effective it is, and how democratic it is.

How much should the federal government do? People disagree on what the federal government should do about the nation's problems, and whether it has been doing too much or too little. In general, people with *liberal* political views call for the government to increase its efforts to solve economic and social problems. Those with *conservative* views believe economic and social problems are best solved when government interference is kept to a minimum. But they want the government to promote traditional values.

How effective is the government? The complex system of checks and balances between the executive and legislative branches makes it difficult for government officials to take quick action. Power is constantly shifting between the president and Congress. Strong presidents can use their position to arouse widespread public support for their plans and thus push them through Congress. The president assumes a dominant role during a crisis, especially a war or a severe economic depression, when the nation wants a strong leader. But in the absence of a crisis, the president must bargain and compromise with Congress.

In a *divided government*—when one political party wins the presidency and another controls Congress— bargaining may be especially difficult. For example, the president may want to lower taxes. But if the majority party in Congress plans to increase tax-funded social programs, Congress may reject the proposed tax cut.

Even when one political party controls both branches, *factions* (groups) within the party can stall government action. Elected officials also may be influenced by many powerful special-interest groups who constantly strive for policies that benefit their members. Achieving clear-cut results or sweeping reforms under such a system is usually difficult and sometimes impossible.

How democratic is the government? Some people feel that certain features of the national government system are undemocratic and block majority rule. For example, the indirect election of the president by the Electoral College has resulted in some candidates winning with only a minority of the popular vote. Other features sometimes considered undemocratic include the appointment—rather than the election—of federal judges and the equal representation of each state in the Senate. In addition, many people believe the expense of election campaigns gives wealthy donors an unfair degree of influence on public officials.

Since the federal government began in 1789, Americans have disagreed on how their government should operate and how much it should do. Historians, political scientists, and other experts agree that no system of government can be perfect. Citizens have a right—and even a duty—to ask how their government is doing and to work to improve the system.   Roger H. Davidson

Related articles in *World Book.* See **Constitution of the United States; Government;** and **United States, History of the** and their lists of *Related articles.* See also the following articles:

Legislative branch

Congress of the United States
Government Accountability Office
Government Printing Office
House of Representatives
Library of Congress
Senate

Executive branch

Economic Advisers, Council of
Management and Budget, Office of
National Security Council
President of the United States
Vice president of the United States

Executive departments and agencies

See the chart *Government of the United States* in this article.

Judicial branch

Court
Court-martial
Court of appeals
Court of Appeals for the Armed Forces, United States
Court of claims
Court of International Trade, United States
District court
Judicial review
Marbury v. Madison
Supreme Court of the United States

Symbols of government

American's Creed
Columbia
E Pluribus Unum
Flag
Great Seal of the United States
Liberty Bell
Pledge of Allegiance
Star-Spangled Banner
Statue of Liberty
Uncle Sam

Other related articles

Articles of Confederation
Bill of rights
City government
Civil service
Continental Congress
County
Declaration of Independence
Democracy
Electoral College
Executive order
Federalism
Foreign Service
Government regulation
Hoover Commission
Initiative and referendum
Law
Local government
Locke, John
Montesquieu
National debt
Naturalization
Political action committee
Political party
Presidential succession
Public lands
Social security
Spoils system
State government
States' rights
Taxation
Term limits
Territory
United States capitals
Veto

Voice of America
Voting
Washington, D.C.
White House

Outline

I. Principles of American government
  A. Constitutional authority
  B. Separation of powers
  C. Federalism
  D. Representative democracy

II. The legislative branch
  A. Organization
  B. Functions
  C. Committee system
  D. Party leadership
  E. The lawmaking process

III. The executive branch
  A. The presidency
  B. The Executive Office of the President
  C. Executive departments and agencies
  D. Control of departments and agencies

IV. The judicial branch
  A. Authority of the courts
  B. Lower court system
  C. The Supreme Court
  D. Judges

V. Growth of the federal government
  A. Background
  B. Early years
  C. The rise of big government
  D. Responding to world events
  E. Domestic challenges

VI. Current issues in U.S. government
  A. How much should the federal government do?
  B. How effective is the government?
  C. How democratic is the government?

Questions

What are the three branches of the United States government?
How does each branch of the government exercise its powers of checks and balances?
What is the source of the United States government's authority?
What are the two major political parties in the United States?
How did the American Civil War enlarge the United States government?
How is the president of the United States elected?
Who appoints nearly all federal judges?
What is *judicial review?* Why is it important?
What types of courts make up the federal court system?
What are some features of the national government system that may be considered undemocratic?

Additional resources

Level I

Anderson, Dale. *Forming a New American Government.* World Almanac Lib., 2006.
Friedman, Mark. *Government: How Local, State, and Federal Government Works.* Child's World, 2005.
Giddens-White, Bryon. *Our Government.* 4 vols. Heinemann Lib., 2006.
Horn, Geoffrey M. *The Bill of Rights and Other Amendments.* World Almanac Lib., 2004. *Political Parties, Interest Groups, and the Media.* 2004.
Patrick, John J., and others. *The Oxford Guide to the United States Government.* Oxford, 2001.

Level II

Brudney, Kent M., and Weber, M. E. *Critical Thinking and American Government.* 3rd ed. Thomson Wadsworth, 2007.
Curry, James A., and others. *Constitutional Government.* 6th ed. Kendall-Hunt, 2006.
Schmidt, Steffen W., and others. *American Government and Politics Today.* 13th ed. Thomson Wadsworth, 2007.
Welch, Susan, and others. *Understanding American Government.* 11th ed. Thomson Wadsworth, 2008.
Woll, Peter. *American Government: Readings and Cases.* 17th ed. Pearson Longman, 2008.

© Joseph Sohm, ChromoSohm/Corbis

A colorful celebration at the United States Capitol in 1987 marks the 200th anniversary of the signing of the Constitution of the United States, which established the basic structure of the United States government and defined the rights and liberties of the American people.

United States, History of the

United States, History of the. The history of the United States is a story about the lives of many groups of people. It includes accounts of conquest and struggle, mistreatment and resistance, creativity, bold action, and courage on the part of millions of people. The men and women who came to America and built the new nation called the United States had many reasons for their actions. Some wanted to get rich. Others wanted to improve people's lives. Still others wanted religious or other freedoms, or simply wanted to be left alone. Many found inventive ways to adapt to conditions they did not expect.

The United States has always been a place of diversity and variation. The first people to live in North America—now known as Indians or Native Americans—arrived thousands of years ago. Long before the arrival of the Europeans and Africans in the 1600's, these peoples had established many different societies. Hundreds of separate Indian groups spoke different languages, practiced their own religions, and pursued various economic activities. The groups maintained complex trading and diplomatic networks, some spanning the continent. The Europeans and Africans were similarly diverse, as were the Asians who began to arrive in the 1800's.

Spain had started to colonize parts of North America in the 1400's and 1500's, mainly by sending soldiers and missionaries to enslave Indians and convert them to Christianity. In the 1600's, England (which later became part of Great Britain and later still part of the United Kingdom) began sending settlers. These colonists took land from the Indians and, in many places, imported Africans as slave laborers. The British colonies expanded along the eastern coast of North America, eventually stretching from present-day Maine to Georgia. The settlers found British rule agreeable until conflicts in the 1760's and 1770's drove them to declare their independence from Britain. They established the United States of America in 1776. At the start, the survival of the new nation was in doubt. The colonists had to defeat the mighty British Empire in the Revolutionary War in America (1775-1783) to establish their claim to independence.

The American people dedicated their new nation to the principles of democracy, freedom, equality, and opportunity. From the start, these promises attracted people from other countries. Millions of immigrants, most of them from Europe, poured into the United States. At the same time, the slave trade brought millions of Africans against their will. Waves of white settlers invaded the lands of Indian groups as they moved westward.

Rapid population growth, resulting from immigration and natural increase, was accompanied by rapid economic growth. Wherever they went, American settlers cut down forests and plowed vast stretches of prairie to establish farms. They found minerals and other valuable resources, and built towns nearby. Cities grew along the main transportation routes, and business and industry prospered. This rapid expansion made the United States one of the largest nations in the world in both size and population.

The United States has often been divided, largely because it has been so diverse. Americans have often found themselves separated by race, religion, and other differences. In the North, most states abolished slavery during and after the Revolutionary War. In the South, slavery expanded. In the West, settlers and Indians fought bitter wars when Indians resisted expansion into their lands. In the 1860's—less than 100 years after the Revolutionary War—the very survival of the United States was threatened. Eleven Southern states withdrew from the Union and tried to establish an independent nation. The American Civil War (1861-1865) between the North and South followed. The North won the war, and the nation survived, though hundreds of thousands of people died in the fighting.

The economic growth of the United States, though rapid, has not always been smooth. At times, depressions brought the economy to a standstill. The worst depression struck in the 1930's. Huge numbers of Americans lost their jobs and homes and fell into poverty.

In the 1900's, the United States became one of the world's strongest military powers. As such, it took a more active role in the world. This role led the United States into two world wars and a series of other conflicts. The Vietnam War (1957-1975) was the first foreign war in which U.S. combat forces failed to achieve their goals. After the war, many Americans questioned what the country's role should be in world affairs. They asked the same question again after terrorists from the Middle East attacked New York City and Washington, D.C., in 2001.

In the early 2000's, the United States faced numerous challenges. These challenges included the existence of poverty amid great wealth; continuing racial, ethnic, and religious discrimination; and pollution of the environment. The threat of terrorism heightened disputes over national security and the protection of civil liberties. Nevertheless, Americans held a deep pride in their country, and most believed it could overcome these challenges.

America before colonial times

For thousands of years, Indians were the only inhabitants of the Western Hemisphere. Most historians believe the first groups were hunters who came to North America from Asia at least 15,000 years ago by crossing a narrow strip of land that then linked Siberia to Alaska. After the land bridge sank underwater, people crossed the Bering Strait by boat. The migrants spread southward and eastward across North and South America. By A.D. 1000, ancestors of the Inuit—another Asian people —lived in what is now northern Alaska. The Inuit spread eastward across the Arctic but remained in the Far North, near the Arctic Circle.

The Vikings were probably the first Europeans to reach America. A band of these seafarers explored and temporarily settled part of the east coast of North America about 1,000 years ago. But serious exploration and settlement of America by Europeans did not begin for another 500 years, until 1492. Then, the Italian navigator Christopher Columbus sailed westward from Spain, seeking a short sea route to Asia. He found, instead, a vast New World. After Columbus, European explorers, soldiers, and settlers flocked to America.

The first Americans. Scholars do not know how many Indians lived in the Americas in the 1400's, when Europeans reached what they called the New World. Many experts believe there were from 30 million to 75 million Indians living in all of North and South America, with about 1 million to 5 million in what is now the United States. But some estimates run as high as 118 million for the Americas, including more than 15 million in the United States.

The American Indians formed hundreds of cultures, with many different languages and ways of life. Some groups, including the Aztec, Inca, and Maya in the south, established advanced civilizations. They erected cities with huge, magnificent buildings. They also accumulated gold, jewels, and other riches. North of Mexico, most American Indians lived in small villages and relied on hunting or farming. The main crops were corn, beans, and squash. In the dry Southwest, the Anasazi built large towns and vast irrigation systems. In the wetter and cooler climate of what is now the Midwest, the Mississippians also built large towns and complex cultures. The fortified city of Cahokia, in present-day Illinois, may have had a population of 10,000 to 20,000 at its peak. In the 1500's, Spanish explorers visited flourishing Mississippian towns in present-day Alabama, Georgia, and Oklahoma.

In the Northeast, from Canada to North Carolina, most Indians spoke either the Iroquoian or Algonquian languages. The Iroquois lived in permanent villages and combined farming with hunting and gathering wild plants. They had great military power. By the early

---

About this article

The contributors of this article are Robin L. Einhorn, Professor of History at the University of California, Berkeley, and Bruce J. Schulman, Professor of History at Boston University. The article traces the history of the United States from its beginning to the present day. The outline below shows the major sections of the article. World Book *also has many individual articles on important events and people in United States history. Cross-references within this article and in the Related articles section refer readers to other* World Book *articles for details on key topics.*

Article outline:

1600's, five Iroquois nations had founded the Iroquois League, a diplomatic arrangement that increased their strength.

The Algonquian peoples were spread over a large area but were less powerful. Some Algonquian lived in permanent villages and mixed farming with fishing, hunting, and gathering. Others had more mobile life-styles. The Algonquian were divided into many tribes. One of their largest organizations was the Powhatan Confederacy in Virginia. Under the Algonquian leader Powhatan, this confederacy had united more than 30 tribes with about 15,000 people by 1607, when the first Europeans reached their land.

European discoveries. About A.D. 1000, a Norse people called the Vikings, who had settled in Greenland, became the first white people to reach the North American mainland. Led by Leif Eriksson, they sailed to what is now the Canadian province of Newfoundland and Labrador and explored the area. But they did not establish permanent settlements.

By the time of Columbus's voyage in 1492, most Europeans did not know that the Viking expeditions had taken place, nor that the Western Hemisphere even existed. The Italian trader Marco Polo's *Description of the World* (1298) had described fabulous wealth and advanced technologies in the Far East. Inspired by such reports,

Europeans became interested in finding a short sea route to China, Japan, and India.

Columbus, an Italian navigator, believed he could find a short route to the East by sailing west. Financed by the Spanish king and queen, he set sail westward from Spain on Aug. 3, 1492. Columbus reached land on October 12 and assumed he had arrived in the Far East. Actually, he landed on an island in the Bahamas, just east of the North American mainland. He explored other Caribbean islands, still thinking he was in Asia. Leaving a crew on the island of Hispaniola, he returned to Spain and published a widely read account of his voyage. In 1493, Columbus returned to Hispaniola with a large army. Over the next few years, he conquered and enslaved the Taíno Indians. The Taíno were a subgroup of the Arawak, who lived on most of the islands of the West Indies. Many Indians died from exposure to European diseases. The Arawak population of about 300,000 in 1492 fell to about 500 in 1548. Steep population drops—resulting from war, enslavement, and especially epidemics of European diseases—also struck other Indian peoples across the Americas.

Columbus died in 1506. He still believed he had sailed to an unknown land in the Far East. Other Europeans called this land the New World and honored Columbus as its discoverer. Europeans also called it America, after

European explorers from several countries made voyages to America during the 1500's. This scene shows the French explorer Jean Ribaut and his crew approaching the Florida coast in 1562. Friendly Indians gathered along the shore to greet the newcomers.

The French Arrive in Florida (1591), an engraving by Theodore de Bry based on a painting by Jacques le Moyne; Library of Congress

the Italian explorer Amerigo Vespucci, who claimed to have explored the land in 1497. However, many scholars have questioned Vespucci's claims of discovery.

Exploration and early settlement. The discovery of America caused great excitement in Europe. To many Europeans, the New World offered opportunities for wealth, power, and adventure. European rulers and merchants wanted to gain control of the hemisphere's resources to add to their wealth. Rulers also sought New World territory to increase their power. Christian missionaries wanted to spread their religion to the Indians. Explorers saw the New World as a place to seek adventure, fame, and fortune. Before long, Europeans from several countries sailed across the Atlantic Ocean to explore America and set up trading posts and colonies. For details, see **Exploration.**

The Europeans often treated Indians cruelly. But even when they were friendly, their arrival was disastrous for the Indians, who had never encountered many diseases that were common in Europe. Horrifying epidemics of smallpox, influenza, and other illnesses wiped out Indian populations across the Americas.

The Spanish and Portuguese. During the 1500's, the Spanish and Portuguese spread out over the southern part of the Western Hemisphere in search of gold, silver, and jewels. The Spaniards conquered the Inca of Peru, Maya of Central America, and Aztec of Mexico. The Portuguese gained control of the Guaraní and other groups in what is now Brazil. By 1600, Spain and Portugal controlled most of the Western Hemisphere from Mexico southward.

Also during the 1500's, Spaniards moved into what is now the southeastern and western United States. They did not discover riches there, but they took control of Florida and the land west of the Mississippi River. In 1526, the Spanish founded San Miguel de Gualdape, the first European settlement in the present-day United States. Historians believe the colony stood on the coast of what is now South Carolina or Georgia. The Spanish soon abandoned it because of disease or bad weather. In 1565, they founded St. Augustine, Florida, the oldest

permanent European settlement in what is now the United States. They also founded missions and other settlements in the West and South. See **Mission life in America; Spain** (The Spanish Empire).

*The English and French b*egan exploring eastern North America around 1500. At first, both nations sent only explorers and fur traders. But after 1600, they began founding permanent settlements. The French settlements were chiefly in what is now Canada, but also in the territory from the Great Lakes to Louisiana. The English settlements included the 13 colonies that formed the United States in 1776.

For years, Britain and France struggled for control of Canada and the land between the Appalachian Mountains and Mississippi River. They also competed with each other for trade with the Indians.

Impact on Indians. Because the early explorers spread diseases that caused huge epidemics among the Indians, the settlers who followed often moved onto lands that were sparsely populated. Some found cleared fields and recently abandoned towns that helped them recognize the best places to settle.

Kevin L. Martin

An Acoma Indian village is one of the oldest continuously inhabited settlements in the United States. The village, on a *mesa* (flat-topped hill) in New Mexico, probably dates from the 1300's. Long before European settlement, Indians developed complex societies in many parts of the Americas.

Jamestown, established in 1607 in what is now Virginia, was the first permanent settlement by English colonists in America. A triangular fort, *far left,* protected the settlement.

Many Indians traded with the early European settlers and helped them survive in the wilderness. At first, the Indians did not realize how great a threat the Europeans were, mainly because the newcomers seemed unable even to feed themselves. As growing numbers of settlers pushed westward, Indians realized that they presented a grave threat, and whites and Indians became enemies. Even so, they maintained economic and diplomatic links.

Contact with the Europeans changed Indian life in many ways. Trade with the Europeans, who wanted furs and deerskins to export to Europe, caused Indians to hunt and trap many more animals than before. Once they exhausted local supplies of beaver and other animals, they invaded the territories of other tribes, causing wars between groups of Indians. Trade with the Europeans also led many Indians to replace their traditional technologies with imported ironwork, cloth, and guns. This switch made the Indians dependent on trade with Europeans. Disease was the most devastating European import into the Indian world. However, large supplies of cheap alcohol from European traders also brought harm to many Indians.

The American Colonies (1607-1753)

The first English attempt to establish a colony in what is now the United States took place in 1585. Sir Walter Raleigh sent settlers to Roanoke Island, off the coast of North Carolina. But this attempt at colonization failed (see **Lost Colony**).

In 1607, a band of about 100 English colonists reached the coast near Chesapeake Bay. They founded Jamestown, the first permanent English settlement in North America (see **Jamestown**). During the next 150 years, a steady stream of colonists arrived and settled near the coast. Most were British, but they also included people from France, Germany, Ireland, and other countries. Many were Africans who were kidnapped from their homes and brought to the colonies as slaves.

The earliest colonists faced great hardship and danger. They suffered from lack of food and from disease. Sometimes, the colonists maintained peace and trade

An oil painting on canvas (about 1919) by Jean Leon Gerome Ferris; Smithsonian Institution, Washington, D.C. (Corbis/Bettmann)

The Pilgrims founded Plymouth Colony in what is now Massachusetts in 1620. Indians who helped the Pilgrims were invited to a Thanksgiving feast in 1621, *shown here.*

with the Indians. Other times, they fought fierce wars with them. Soon, however, the colonies prospered. They established small family farms and large slave-labor plantations; built towns, roads, and churches; and began many small industries. Their populations grew, and their wealth increased.

The colonists developed political practices and social beliefs that have had a major influence on the history of the United States. Some established democratic governments. Most placed a high value on individual liberty and respected hard work as a means of getting ahead. Many had the unsupported belief that white Europeans were superior to Indians and Africans. As a result, they felt they had the right to take Indian land by violence and to force African labor through slavery.

In the early 1600's, the English king began granting *charters,* documents bestowing the right to establish colonies in America. The charters went to companies of merchants and to individuals called *proprietors.* The merchant companies and proprietors were responsible for recruiting people to settle in America and, at first, for governing them. By the mid-1700's, most of the settlements had been formed into 13 colonies. Each had a governor and a legislature, but was under the ultimate control of the British government.

The Thirteen Colonies stretched from what is now Maine in the north to Georgia in the south. They included the New England Colonies of Massachusetts, Connecticut, Rhode Island, and New Hampshire; the Middle Colonies of New York, New Jersey, Pennsylvania, and Delaware; and the Southern Colonies of Virginia, Maryland, North Carolina, South Carolina, and Georgia. (Some historians classify Virginia and Maryland, which lie along Chesapeake Bay, as Chesapeake Colonies.)

Virginia and Maryland were among the earliest British colonies. They were established for different reasons, but they developed in much the same way.

Virginia was the largest of the Thirteen Colonies. It began with the Jamestown settlement of 1607. The Virginia Company of London (later shortened to Virginia Company), an organization of English merchants, sent settlers to America hoping they would find gold and other riches. But the settlers found no riches and faced great hardships. Captain John Smith played a major role in helping the colony survive its early days, mainly by forcing the colonists to grow food. In 1612, some Jamestown colonists began growing tobacco, which the Virginia Company sold in Europe. Virginia prospered as tobacco production increased in response to rising European demand. English settlers came in droves and established new farms and settlements.

Maryland was founded by the Calverts, a family of wealthy Roman Catholics. Catholics were persecuted in England, and the Calverts wanted a place where they could have religious freedom. In 1632, Cecilius Calvert became proprietor of the Maryland area. Colonists, led by Cecilius's brother, Leonard Calvert, established the first Maryland settlement in 1634. The Maryland settlers also raised tobacco. As production increased, their colony prospered.

The settlers of Virginia and Maryland made important strides toward self-government and individual rights. The Virginians appealed to the Virginia Company for a voice in their local government. The company wanted

Facts in brief (1607-1753)

First permanent settlement, each colony
Virginia (1607), Massachusetts (1620), New Hampshire (1623), New York (1624), Connecticut (1633), Maryland (1634), Rhode Island (1636), Delaware (1638), Pennsylvania (1643), North Carolina (about 1653), New Jersey (1660), South Carolina (1670), Georgia (1733).

Important dates
1607 About 100 colonists founded Jamestown, the first permanent English settlement in North America.

1619 Virginia established the House of Burgesses, the first representative legislature in America.

1620 The Pilgrims founded Plymouth Colony, the second permanent English settlement in North America.

1624 The Dutch began the settlement of New Netherland.

1636 Harvard—the first college in the colonies—was founded.

1638 People from Sweden established the settlement of New Sweden.

1647 Massachusetts established the first colonial public school system.

1649 Maryland passed the first religious toleration act in North America.

1664 England took control of New Netherland and New Sweden.

1672 The Boston Post Road was completed, linking Boston and New York City.

1704 *The Boston News-Letter,* the first successful colonial newspaper, began publication.

1752 Benjamin Franklin proved that lightning is an electric spark.

Population growth and change

Total population, about 100
1607 | Rural, 100%

Total population, 1,328,000
1753 | Rural, 98%

Urban, 2%

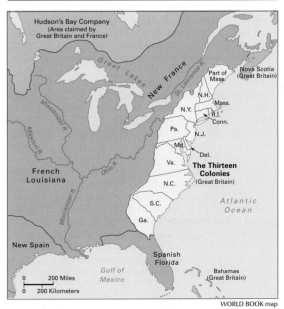

WORLD BOOK map

The Thirteen Colonies stretched along the eastern coast of North America. French territory lay to the north and west of the colonies, and Spanish territory lay to the south.

Penn's Treaty with the Indians (1771), an oil painting on canvas by Benjamin West; Pennsylvania Academy of the Fine Arts, Philadelphia

William Penn, *arms extended,* made his first treaty with the Indians in 1682. His fair dealings with the Native Americans helped the colony of Pennsylvania grow and prosper. Many Indians traded with the early settlers and helped them survive in the wilderness.

to attract newcomers to its colony, and so it agreed. In 1619, it established the House of Burgesses, the first representative legislature in America. Maryland attracted both Catholic and Protestant settlers. In 1649, the Calverts granted religious freedom to people of both faiths. This grant was the first law in North America calling for religious toleration.

Virginia and Maryland also began a practice that violated individual rights—slavery. By the 1680's, planters in both colonies had begun to buy African slaves and force the Africans to work on their lands.

New England. Puritans, originally financed by English merchants, founded the New England Colonies. Puritans were English Protestants who faced persecution because of their opposition to the Church of England, their homeland's official church. See **Puritans.**

In 1620, a group of Separatists (Puritans who had separated from the Church of England) and other colonists settled in New England. Called Pilgrims, they founded Plymouth Colony, the second permanent English settlement in North America. Between 1628 and 1630, Puritans founded the Massachusetts Bay Colony at what are now Salem and Boston. Plymouth became part of Massachusetts Bay Colony in 1691. See **Massachusetts Bay Colony; Plymouth Colony.**

Settlers spreading out from Massachusetts founded the other New England Colonies. Connecticut was first settled in 1633 and became a colony in 1636. Colonists

took up residence in Rhode Island in 1636, and Rhode Island became a colony in 1647. New Hampshire, first settled in 1623, became a colony in 1680. Important Puritan leaders included governors William Bradford of Plymouth and John Winthrop of Massachusetts, and Roger Williams, the founder of Rhode Island.

Life in New England centered on towns organized around churches. Each family farmed its own plot of land, but they all lived close together in a town so they could walk to church. Most of the New England colonists farmed for a living. But they also developed a thriving shipping business and started many small industries, including fishing, lumbering, and crafts. There were few African slaves in New England.

The Puritans of New England did not tolerate religious dissent, but they made important contributions to democracy in America. In 1620, the Pilgrims established the Mayflower Compact, an agreement among the adult males to provide "just and equal laws" for all (see **Mayflower Compact**). The Puritans created a democratic political system in which all the officials were elected. At town meetings, most male adults could participate in decisions.

The Middle Colonies. Soon after English settlement began, the Dutch founded New Netherland, a trading post and colony that included what are now New York and northern New Jersey. They started a settlement in New York in 1624 and in New Jersey in 1660. In 1638, the

Detail of *Baltimore in 1752* (about 1807), an aquatint by Daniel Bowley based on a drawing by John Moale; Maryland Historical Society, Baltimore

Baltimore, Maryland, *shown here,* began as a cluster of houses and other buildings along the banks of the Patapsco River. Colonists fished in the river, *left foreground,* and grew tobacco in a large field, *far right.* Maryland, Virginia, and other colonies grew tobacco for export to England.

Swedes established New Sweden, a settlement in present-day Delaware and southern New Jersey. The Dutch claimed New Sweden in 1655. In 1664, the English took over New Netherland and New Sweden.

King Charles II of England gave the New York and New Jersey territory to his brother, James, Duke of York. Friends of the duke founded huge farming estates in New York along the Hudson River. New York City developed from the Dutch city of New Amsterdam. It became a shipping and trading center. The Duke of York gave New Jersey to two of his friends. They allowed much po-

litical and religious freedom, and New Jersey attracted many settlers.

Swedes established a small settlement in what is now Pennsylvania in 1643. In 1681, a wealthy Englishman named William Penn received a charter that made him the proprietor of Pennsylvania. Penn was a member of the Quakers, a religious group that was persecuted in many countries (see **Quakers**). At Penn's urging, Quakers and other settlers who sought freedom flocked to Pennsylvania. Penn carefully planned settlements in his colony, and Pennsylvania thrived. Philadelphia became

Library of Congress

New York Public Library, Arents Collection

The industrious colonists worked hard to establish communities in the wilderness. A Northern colonist, *left,* shaves a board to size for a house he is building. Slaves on a Southern plantation, *right,* pack tobacco for shipment to Europe as plantation owners look on.

Detail of *Raising the Liberty Pole*, an engraving by John McRae (Granger Collection)

Joyful celebrations followed the signing of the Declaration of Independence on July 4, 1776. The scene above shows colonists raising a liberty pole to mark the occasion. At the right, colonial army officers sign up a volunteer for service in the war for independence against Great Britain.

the largest city in colonial America. Penn also became proprietor of the Delaware region.

Most settlers in the Middle Colonies were farmers, whose main crop was wheat. The colonies developed thriving commerce and small industries. They had more slaves than New England had, but far fewer than the South. The Middle Colonies contributed to democracy and religious freedom in America. Adult white males could vote for most officials. Most colonists were Protestants but belonged to many different churches.

North Carolina, South Carolina, and Georgia. About 1650, colonists from Virginia established a settlement in northern Carolina, the land between Virginia and Florida. In 1663, King Charles II gave Carolina to eight of his nobles. He called them *lords proprietors* (ruling landlords). Carolina soon attracted English settlers, French Protestants called Huguenots, and Americans from other colonies. In 1712, the northern two-thirds of the region was divided into two colonies, North Carolina and South Carolina. Much of North Carolina consisted of small farms. Many African slaves also labored in the colony on tobacco plantations and in for-

est industries. In South Carolina, wealthy landowners purchased slaves to work the large plantations where they grew rice and *indigo.* Indigo is a plant that produces blue dye for coloring textiles. South Carolina was the only colony that had more blacks than whites.

Few European settlers came to the southern one-third of Carolina until 1733. Then James Oglethorpe, a British social reformer, founded Georgia there. Oglethorpe hoped Georgia would become a colony of small farms. The colony's charter banned the importation of Africans so that neither slavery nor plantations would develop. But Georgia later changed the law to allow settlers to bring in slaves, and plantations flourished.

Life in colonial America. Reports of the economic success and religious and political freedom of the early colonists attracted a steady flow of settlers. Through immigration and natural increase, and the slave trade from Africa, the colonial population rose to 1 ⅓ million. The colonies drew newcomers from almost every country of western Europe. Despite the varied backgrounds of the early settlers, the white Americans of the mid-1700's had, as one writer said, "melted into a new race of men."

The slave trade brought in so many Africans that, by the 1750's, blacks made up one-fifth of the population.

Why the colonists came. A person who came to America faced hardship and danger. But the New World also offered the opportunity for a fresh start. As a result, many people were eager to become colonists. Some Europeans came seeking religious freedom. In addition to Puritans, Catholics, Quakers, and Huguenots, they included Jews and members of German Protestant sects.

Many Europeans became colonists for economic reasons. Some were well-to-do but saw America as a place where they could become rich. Many poor Europeans came to America as *indentured servants.* An indentured servant agreed to work for another person, called a *master.* In return, the master paid for the servant's transportation across the Atlantic and provided food, clothing, and shelter. Most agreements between servants and masters lasted from four to seven years, after which the servants were freed.

Others who came to America had no choice in the matter. A few were convicts from overcrowded English jails. Most were Africans captured in intertribal warfare or kidnapped, and then sold to European traders. The convicts and slaves were sold into service in America.

At first, black slaves had the same legal status as white indentured servants. But by about 1660, colonies began to enact laws that became known as *slave codes,* which stripped the Africans of basic human rights. All the American Colonies had slaves, but slavery became more common in the South than in the North. The South had plantations that required enormous labor, and their owners found it profitable to buy slaves to do the work. By the 1750's, African American slaves accounted for 2 percent of the population in Massachusetts and Pennsylvania, 40 percent in Virginia, and 60 percent in South Carolina.

Economic and social opportunity. The earliest colonists struggled to produce enough food to stay alive. But before long, America had a thriving economy. Planters and their slaves grew large crops of indigo, rice, and tobacco. Small farmers raised livestock and such crops as wheat and corn. Many colonists fished and hunted. Some cut lumber from forests to make barrels, ships, and other products. The colonists used part of what they produced, but they exported large quantities of goods. They traded chiefly with Britain and the British colonies of the West Indies. The colonies exported fish, indigo, lumber, rice, tobacco, and wheat. They imported manufactured goods, especially clothing, furniture, and metal utensils from Britain. Their other major imports were sugar, tea, and African slaves. The colonies traded with the French, Dutch, and Spanish as well.

Colonial America, like Europe, had both wealthy upper-class and poor lower-class people. But in Europe, traditions designed to keep wealth concentrated among the upper classes made it difficult for anyone to achieve economic and social advancement. America had few such traditions. New waves of immigrants arrived all the time, and advancement was possible for most people. Land became more plentiful and easy to obtain as settlers took more of it from the Indians. There were also many opportunities to start businesses. Many indentured servants acquired land or worked in a trade after their period of service ended. Some former servants or their sons became well-to-do merchants or landowners.

The colonies had a great need for professional people, such as lawyers, doctors, schoolteachers, and members of the clergy. Women were excluded from these careers and many other jobs. However, the professions were open to most white men because they required less specialized training than they do today.

Facts in brief (1754-1783)

Important dates

1763	The French and Indian War, which had begun in 1754, ended with Britain controlling almost all French lands in eastern North America.
1763	Britain stationed a standing army in North America and prohibited colonists from settling west of the Appalachian Mountains.
1765	The British Parliament passed the Stamp Act of 1765, taxing newspapers, legal documents, and various other written materials in the colonies.
1770	British troops killed American civilians in an event that became known as the Boston Massacre.
1773	Colonists staged the Boston Tea Party, dumping British tea into Boston Harbor.
1774	The Coercive Acts—which Americans called the Intolerable Acts—closed Boston Harbor and included other steps to punish the colonists.
1774	The First Continental Congress met to consider action against the British.
1775	The Revolutionary War between the colonists and the British began.
1776	The colonists adopted the Declaration of Independence and formed the United States of America.
1777	The French entered the war on the side of the United States.
1781	The Americans defeated the British at Yorktown, Virginia, in the last major battle of the Revolutionary War.
1783	The Treaty of Paris officially ended the Revolutionary War.

Population growth and change

Manuscript Division, New York Public Library

Rare Book Division, New York Public Library; Astor, Lenox, and Tilden Foundation

The Stamp Act, passed by Parliament in 1765, required colonists to buy stamps as a tax on various written materials. A tax stamp appears at the left. A colonial illustrator drew a skull and crossbones—a symbol of death—*right,* to protest the law.

Total population, 1,360,000

1754 | Rural, 98% | Urban, 2%

Total population, 3,125,000

1783 | Rural, 96% |

Urban, 4%

Colonial government. The colonists lived under British rule. Voters elected their own colonial legislatures, but the British king appointed governors and other top officials in most colonies. The British also passed many laws to regulate trade in ways that helped Britain and only sometimes helped the colonies. But the colonists often ignored British laws they disliked. The British found it hard to enforce laws across the Atlantic Ocean. The tightening of British control over the colonists after they had grown self-reliant led to a clash between the Americans and the British in the late 1700's. For more information on life in the American Colonies, see **Colonial life in America.**

The movement for independence (1754-1783)

Relations between the American Colonies and Britain began to break down during the 1760's. Suddenly, Britain tried to tighten its control over the colonies. Its leaders passed laws that taxed the colonists and restricted their freedoms. The colonists had become accustomed to governing themselves. As a result, they resented what they saw as British interference in their internal affairs. Friction between the Americans and British mounted until, in 1775, the Revolutionary War broke out. During the war—on July 4, 1776—the colonists declared their independence. In 1783, they defeated the British and made their claim to independence stick.

The French and Indian War. Britain and France had struggled for control of eastern North America throughout the colonial period. As their settlements moved inland, both nations claimed the vast territory between the Appalachian Mountains and the Mississippi River. This struggle led to the French and Indian War (1754-1763), which the British won. Under the Treaty of Paris of 1763, Britain gained control of (1) almost all French territory in what is now Canada and (2) all French territory east of the Mississippi except New Orleans. Britain also received Florida from Spain in 1763. As a result, the British controlled almost all of North America from the Atlantic to the Mississippi.

The French and Indian War was a turning point in American history. It triggered a series of British policy changes that eventually led to the movement for colonial independence. See **French and Indian wars** (The French and Indian War).

Policy changes. The French and Indian War created problems for Britain. It led to a huge Indian uprising in America in 1763, as colonists moved west into the territory Britain won from France. The uprising became known as Pontiac's Rebellion, or Pontiac's War. Also, Britain spent so much money fighting the French and Indian War that its national debt had nearly doubled. George III, who had become king in 1760, instructed Parliament to solve these problems. Parliament began passing laws that taxed the American colonists, restricted their freedom, or both.

In 1763, Parliament voted to station a standing army in North America to defend the colonists against the Indians. Two years later, in the Quartering Act, it required the colonists to help pay for this army by providing the troops with living quarters and supplies. In addition, Britain sought to keep peace with the Indians. In the Proclamation of 1763, it prohibited the American colonists from settling west of the Appalachian Mountains,

thus reserving that land for the Indians.

King George and Parliament believed the time had come for the colonists to start obeying trade regulations and paying their share of the cost of maintaining the British Empire. For that reason, in 1764, Parliament passed the Sugar Act. This law provided for the collection of taxes on molasses brought into the colonies. The Sugar Act also gave British officials the right to search the property of people suspected of violating the law. The Stamp Act of 1765 extended to the colonies the traditional English tax on newspapers, legal documents, and various other written materials (see **Stamp Act**).

Colonial reaction. The colonists opposed the new British policies. They claimed that the British government had no right to restrict their settlement or deny their freedom in any other way. They also opposed British taxes. The colonists were not represented in Parliament. Therefore, they argued, Britain had no right to tax them. The colonists expressed this belief in the slogan, "Taxation Without Representation Is Tyranny."

To protest the new laws, colonists organized a boycott of British goods. Men joined secret clubs called Sons of Liberty that used threats of violence to prevent enforcement of the laws (see **Sons of Liberty**). Women made items for themselves and their families to avoid purchasing British goods. For example, they created and wore homespun garments instead of clothing imported from Britain. In 1765, representatives of nine colonies met in the Stamp Act Congress to consider joint action against Britain. The colonial boycott and other acts of resistance were successful. In 1766, Parliament repealed the Stamp Act. But at the same time, in the Declaratory Act, it insisted that Britain had the right to make laws for the colonies.

Renewed conflict. The repeal of the Stamp Act eased tensions between the Americans and the British only briefly. In 1767, Parliament passed the Townshend Acts, which taxed lead, paint, paper, and tea imported into the colonies. Colonists responded with renewed protests and another boycott of British goods.

As tensions between the Americans and British grew, Britain sent troops into Boston and New York City. The sight of British troops in their streets aroused the colonists' anger. On March 5, 1770, a crowd of Boston civilians taunted and attacked a small group of soldiers. The troops fired on the civilians, killing three people and wounding eight others, two of whom died later. This incident, the Boston Massacre, shocked Americans and disturbed the British. See **Boston Massacre.**

In 1770, Parliament repealed all provisions of the Townshend Acts except one, the tax on tea. Three years later, in the Tea Act, Parliament reduced the tax on tea sold by the East India Company, a British firm, and gave the company's agents a monopoly on local tea sales in the colonies. The colonists saw these actions as taxing them and hurting American shopkeepers to benefit a big British company. Americans vowed not to drink tea, and mobs frightened the agents who tried to sell it. On Dec. 16, 1773, a group of colonists dramatized their opposition in the Boston Tea Party. Dressed as Indians, they boarded the East India Company's ships and threw its tea into Boston Harbor. See **Boston Tea Party.**

Angered by the Boston Tea Party, Parliament passed laws in 1774 to punish the colonists. Britain called these

The **Revolutionary War in America** began on April 19, 1775, on the village green in Lexington, Massachusetts, *shown here*. British troops, *in red coats,* defeated the Americans in the war's first battle. But later in the day, colonists at nearby Concord drove the British back.

Detail of *The Battle of Lexington, April 19th, 1775* (1775), an engraving by Amos Doolittle; Connecticut Historical Society, Hartford

laws the Coercive Acts. Americans called them the Intolerable Acts. The laws included provisions that closed the port of Boston, suspended democratic government in Massachusetts, and required the colonists to house and feed British soldiers.

The First Continental Congress. The Coercive Acts stirred colonial anger more than ever. On Sept. 5, 1774, delegates from 12 colonies met in the First Continental Congress in Philadelphia. The delegates were cautious men who disliked lawlessness and still hoped for a settlement with the British government. They reaffirmed American loyalty to Britain and agreed that Parliament could direct colonial foreign affairs. However, the dele-

gates called for a boycott of all trade with Britain until Parliament repealed certain laws and taxes, especially the Coercive Acts. King George shattered hope for reconciliation by insisting that the colonies submit to British rule or be crushed. See **Continental Congress.**

The Revolutionary War begins. On April 19, 1775, British troops tried to seize the military supplies of the Massachusetts militia. This action led to the start of the Revolutionary War. Colonists—first at Lexington, and then at Concord, Massachusetts—took up arms and inflicted numerous casualties on the British. Word of their success spread, and hope grew for victory over Britain. Colonial leaders met in the Second Continental Con-

Congress Voting Independence (begun late 1700's), an oil painting on canvas by Robert Edge Pine and Edward Savage; Historical Society of Pennsylvania, Philadelphia

The vote for independence from Great Britain took place on July 2, 1776. On July 4, the Second Continental Congress adopted the Declaration of Independence, and the United States of America was born.

Scene at the Signing of the Constitution of the United States (1940), an oil painting on canvas by Howard Chandler Christy, U.S. Capitol, Washington, D.C. (Granger Collection)

The signing of the Constitution ranks among the most important events in American history. The delegates to the Constitutional Convention signed the document in 1787. The Constitution was *ratified* (approved) in 1788 and has served as the basic law of the United States ever since.

gress on May 10, 1775, to prepare for war. The Congress organized the Continental Army and, on June 15, chose George Washington of Virginia as its commander in chief.

King George officially declared the colonies in rebellion on Aug. 23, 1775. He warned the Americans to end their rebellion or face certain defeat. But the threat had little effect on the colonists' determination. Some Americans, called Loyalists, remained true to Britain, but a growing number of Americans supported the fight for independence. Many who had been unsure were convinced by Thomas Paine's pamphlet *Common Sense* (1776). Paine called for complete independence from Britain and the creation of a strong federal union.

The Declaration of Independence. On July 4, 1776, the Second Continental Congress adopted the Declaration of Independence and formed the United States of America. Drafted by Thomas Jefferson of Virginia, the Declaration was a sweeping indictment of King George and the British Parliament. It also set forth certain principles that were basic to the revolutionary cause. It says all men are created equal and are endowed by their Creator with *inalienable rights*—that is, rights which cannot be taken away—to life, liberty, and the pursuit of happiness. Governments exist to protect those rights and derive their powers from the consent of the governed. The Declaration also says that when a government ceases to preserve those rights, it is the people's duty to change the government, or abolish it and form a new one.

American victory. In the Revolutionary War, the Americans faced the world's most powerful empire. They lacked a well-trained army, a navy, military sup-

plies, and money. But they had the advantage of fighting on their home territory. The British, on the other hand, had well-trained and well-equipped troops and officers, a powerful navy, and Indian allies who wanted to prevent Americans from taking more of their lands. But the British were fighting far from home.

Foreign aid helped the American cause. France and other European nations who opposed Britain loaned money to the United States. In 1777, France entered the war on the American side. Its army and navy ultimately helped the United States win the war.

The Revolutionary War raged on through the 1770's. Then, on Oct. 19, 1781, American and French troops won a decisive victory at the Battle of Yorktown in Virginia. Thousands of British soldiers surrendered. Within months, the British government decided to seek peace. Two years of peace negotiations and occasional fighting followed. Finally, on Sept. 3, 1783, the Americans and the British signed the Treaty of Paris. The treaty officially ended the Revolutionary War, with British recognition of American independence. For a detailed account of the war, see **Revolutionary War in America.**

Forming a new nation (1784-1819)

As a result of the Treaty of Paris of 1783, the new nation controlled all of North America from the Atlantic to the Mississippi between Canada and Florida. Canada remained British territory. Britain returned Florida to Spain, and Spain continued to control the area west of the Mississippi. The original Thirteen Colonies made up the first 13 states of the United States, which was only a loose confederation of states at first.

Establishing a government. Americans began setting up a new system of government as soon as they declared their independence. Each of the new states had its own constitution before the Revolutionary War ended. The constitutions gave the people certain liberties, usually including freedom of speech, religion, and the press. In 1777, the Second Continental Congress designed a weak federal government under the Articles of Confederation. By the time the states finished ratifying the Articles in 1781, some Americans already thought the nation needed a stronger federal government.

The Articles of Confederation. Under the Articles of Confederation, the federal government consisted of Congress. There was no president or federal court system. Congress organized the Revolutionary War effort and managed foreign diplomacy. But the Articles did not allow Congress to collect taxes, regulate foreign trade, or direct the activities of the states.

Under the Articles, each state worked independently for its own ends. Congress could make recommendations but could not enforce them. Yet the new nation faced problems that demanded a strong federal government. The United States had piled up a huge debt during the Revolutionary War. Because Congress could not collect taxes, the nation could not pay the interest on this debt to achieve a sound financial footing. Congress could not even pay the salaries of the Continental Army. It had no power to regulate the nation's trade.

Some states issued their own paper money, causing sharp changes in the value of currency and economic chaos. In 1786 and 1787, this chaos led to Shays's Rebellion in Massachusetts. Rebels led by Daniel Shays, a former army officer, shut down the state courts to stop them from hearing debt cases. Shays's Rebellion scared many Americans and dramatized the weaknesses of the Articles of Confederation. See **Articles of Confederation; Shays's Rebellion.**

Writing the Constitution. In 1787, delegates from every state except Rhode Island met in Philadelphia's Independence Hall to consider amendments to the Articles of Confederation. Rhode Island did not take part because its leaders worried about outside interference in the state's affairs. The convention decided not to draft amendments to the Articles. Instead, the delegates wrote an entirely new Constitution for the United States.

The delegates debated long and hard over the provisions of the Constitution. Some of them wanted a document that gave much power to the federal government. Others wanted to protect the power of the states and called for a weak central government. Delegates from large states said their states should have greater representation in Congress than the small states. But small-state delegates demanded equal representation in Congress. Delegates from the Southern States insisted that slaves be counted in determining the representation of each state in Congress. Northern delegates answered that because slaves could not vote, counting them would give white Southerners an unfair advantage.

The delegates finally reached an agreement on a new Constitution on Sept. 17, 1787. The authors worked out a system of government that satisfied the opposing views of the delegates to the convention. At the same time, they created a system that was flexible enough to continue in its basic form to the present day.

Facts in brief (1784-1819)

Presidents   (with political parties and dates of service)
George Washington, no political party, 1789-1797
John Adams, Federalist, 1797-1801
Thomas Jefferson, Democratic-Republican, 1801-1809
James Madison, Democratic-Republican, 1809-1817
James Monroe, Democratic-Republican, 1817-1825

States in the Union
The 13 states that ratified the Constitution:
Delaware (1787), Pennsylvania (1787), New Jersey (1787), Georgia (1788), Connecticut (1788), Massachusetts (1788), Maryland (1788), South Carolina (1788), New Hampshire (1788), Virginia (1788), New York (1788), North Carolina (1789), Rhode Island (1790).
New states added through 1819:
Vermont (1791), Kentucky (1792), Tennessee (1796), Ohio (1803), Louisiana (1812), Indiana (1816), Mississippi (1817), Illinois (1818), Alabama (1819).

Important dates
1787   The Founding Fathers wrote the Constitution.
1790's   The first U.S. political parties developed.
1791   Ten amendments called the Bill of Rights added further guarantees of individual freedom to the Constitution.
1793   Eli Whitney developed a toothed cotton gin.
1800   Washington, D.C., became the national capital.
1803   The Louisiana Purchase almost doubled the size of the United States.
1811   Work began on the National Road, which—when completed—linked the East and the Midwest.
1812-1815 The United States and the United Kingdom fought the War of 1812.
1814   Francis Scott Key wrote "The Star-Spangled Banner."

Population growth and change
Total population, 3,240,000
1784 Rural, 96%   Urban, 4%

Total population, 9,358,000
1819 Rural, 93%
                                        Urban, 7%

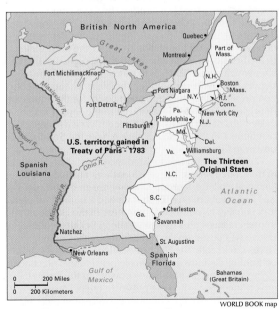

WORLD BOOK map

The United States after the revolution extended from the Atlantic Ocean to the Mississippi River. British territory lay to the north, and Spanish territory lay to the west and south.

George Washington, *standing at the end,* became the first president of the United States in 1789. The other men in the picture are the members of his first Cabinet—*left to right,* Henry Knox, Thomas Jefferson, Edmund Randolph, and Alexander Hamilton.

Chicago Historical Society

The men who wrote the Constitution included some of the most famous and important figures in American history. Among them were George Washington and James Madison of Virginia, Alexander Hamilton of New York, and Benjamin Franklin of Pennsylvania. The authors of the Constitution, along with such other early leaders as Thomas Jefferson of Virginia, won lasting fame as the Founding Fathers of the United States.

Provisions of the Constitution. The Constitution established a two-house legislature, consisting of a House of Representatives and a Senate. In the House, representation was based on population to satisfy the large states. In the Senate, each state had two seats, regardless of its size, which pleased the small states. In a compromise between the Northern and Southern states, the Constitution provided that the population count for the House of Representatives would include all free people plus three-fifths of the slaves. The three-fifths clause caused resentment in the North because it gave the South extra power in Congress.

The Constitution also created the office of president of the United States. The president was elected by an Electoral College, a group of men chosen by the states (see **Electoral College**). Each state had a number of electors equal to its number of members in the House of Representatives plus its two senators. Because the House was based on the three-fifths clause and no slaves could vote, the Electoral College effectively granted Southern whites extra votes in presidential elections.

The Constitution gave many powers to the federal government, including the power to collect taxes and regulate trade. But the document also reserved certain powers for the states. The Constitution provided for three branches of the federal government: (1) the executive, headed by the president; (2) the legislative, made

up of the two houses of Congress; and (3) the judicial, consisting of the federal courts. The authors of the Constitution created a system of checks and balances among the three branches of government. Each branch received specified powers and duties to ensure that the other branches did not have too much power.

Adopting the Constitution. Before the Constitution became law, it needed *ratification* (approval) by nine states. Some Americans opposed the Constitution, and a fierce debate broke out. Hamilton, Madison, and John Jay responded to criticism of the document in a series of 85 newspaper essays published in 1787 and 1788. Called *The Federalist,* the essays gained much support for the Constitution (see **Federalist, The**). On June 21, 1788, New Hampshire became the ninth state to ratify.

The Bill of Rights. Much opposition to the Constitution stemmed from fears that it did not guarantee enough individual rights. In response, 10 amendments called the Bill of Rights were added. The Bill of Rights became part of the Constitution on Dec. 15, 1791. Among other things, it guaranteed freedom of speech, religion, and the press; and the rights to trial by jury and peaceful assembly. For more details, see **Bill of Rights; Constitution of the United States.**

Setting up the government. In 1789, the Electoral College unanimously chose George Washington to serve as the first president. It reelected him unanimously in 1792. Local voters elected members of the House of Representatives, as they do today. But state legislatures chose the members of the Senate, a practice that continued until the early 1900's. The government went into operation in 1789, with its temporary capital in New York City. The capital moved to Philadelphia in 1790, and to Washington, D.C., in 1800.

Financial problems plagued the new government.

The national debt piled up during the Revolutionary War threatened the financial health of the United States. Americans split over how to deal with the financial problems. One group, led by Secretary of the Treasury Alexander Hamilton, wanted the federal government to take vigorous action to pay off the debt and foster economic growth. Another group, headed by Secretary of State Thomas Jefferson, wanted the government to proceed more cautiously on the debt and opposed government participation in economic affairs.

Hamilton proposed that the federal government increase *tariffs* (taxes on imports) and that it tax certain products made in the United States, such as liquor. The government would use the money to pay its own debts and those of the states. The government would also use the funds for ongoing expenses and internal improvements, such as roads and bridges. Hamilton proposed a national bank, an agency that would be authorized to issue currency and perform other financial services for the federal government.

Jefferson and his followers, who included many Southerners, denounced Hamilton's plans. But Jefferson later agreed to support some of Hamilton's proposals. In return, Hamilton agreed to support a shift of the national capital to the South. Congress approved the financial plan and moved the capital to Washington, D.C. Jefferson continued to oppose the bank proposal. However, in 1791, Congress chartered a national bank to handle the government's finances for 20 years (see **Bank of the United States**).

The new tax program led to an uprising called the Whiskey Rebellion. In 1794, farmers in Pennsylvania who made whiskey refused to pay the liquor tax. President Washington sent in troops who ended the rebellion. Washington's action did much to establish the federal government's authority to enforce its laws within the states. See **Whiskey Rebellion**.

Problems in foreign affairs. The new government faced serious problems in foreign affairs. In 1793, France went to war against Britain and Spain. Americans were grateful to France for its help in the Revolutionary War, but they also wanted to reestablish trade with Britain and its colonies in the West Indies. Americans disagreed over which side to support. Jefferson and his followers wanted to back France. Hamilton and his group favored Britain.

President Washington insisted that the United States remain neutral in the European war. He rejected French demands for support, and he also sent diplomats to Britain and Spain to clear up problems with those countries. Chief Justice John Jay, acting for Washington, negotiated the Jay Treaty with Britain in 1794. The treaty included a trade agreement and a British promise to remove troops still stationed on U.S. territory. In 1795, Thomas Pinckney negotiated the Pinckney Treaty, or Treaty of San Lorenzo, with Spain. This treaty settled a dispute with Spain over the Florida border. Spain also granted the United States free use of the Mississippi River. See **Jay Treaty; Pinckney Treaty**.

In 1796, Washington refused to seek a third term as president, in part because he thought staying too long would make him resemble a king. John Adams of Massachusetts succeeded Washington in 1797. At about that time, French warships began attacking U.S. merchant vessels. Adams, like Washington, hoped to use diplomacy to solve foreign problems. He sent diplomats to France to try to end the attacks. But three agents of the French government insulted the diplomats by demanding a bribe. The identity of the agents was not revealed. They were called X, Y, and Z, and the incident became known as the XYZ Affair. Reports of the French action created uproar in the United States. But Adams was determined to keep peace. In 1799, he again sent diplomats to France. This time, the United States and France reached a peaceful settlement. See **XYZ Affair**.

Establishing political parties. Washington and many other American leaders opposed political parties, believing that they caused disagreement and ill will. But in the 1790's, the disputes over government policies led to the establishment of two parties. Hamilton and his followers, chiefly Northerners, formed the Federalist Party. The Federalist Party favored a strong federal government and generally backed Britain in international disputes. Jefferson and his followers, chiefly Southerners, created the Democratic-Republican Party, also known as the Republican Party. It had no relation to today's Republican Party. The Democratic-Republicans wanted a weak central government and generally sided with France in foreign disputes. See **Democratic-Republican Party; Federalist Party**.

The Alien and Sedition Acts. It took a while for Americans to accept the idea that taking strong political positions was a normal part of democratic politics. The Federalists and Democratic-Republicans could not believe their opponents had the country's best interests at heart. After the XYZ Affair, for example, the Federalist Party denounced the Democratic-Republicans for their support of France. The Federalists had a majority in Congress. They set out to silence their critics, including Democratic-Republicans and foreigners living in the United States. In 1798, Congress passed the Alien and Sedition Acts, with the approval of President Adams, who was also a Federalist. These laws made it a crime for anyone to criticize the president or Congress, and subjected foreigners to unequal treatment.

These attacks on freedom caused a nationwide outcry. The protests included the Kentucky and Virginia Resolutions. The resolutions were statements by the Kentucky and Virginia state legislatures that challenged the constitutionality of the Alien and Sedition Acts. The most offensive parts soon expired or were repealed. But the Alien and Sedition Acts gave the Federalists the reputation as a party that restricted freedom. See **Alien and Sedition Acts; Kentucky and Virginia Resolutions**.

The Jeffersonian triumph. Public reaction to the Alien and Sedition Acts helped Jefferson defeat John Adams to win election as president in 1800. Supporters of Jefferson called his election a triumph for his political philosophy, which became known as Jeffersonian democracy. Jefferson envisioned the United States as a nation of small farmers. In his ideal society, the people would lead simple but productive lives and direct their own affairs. As a result, the need for government would decline. Jefferson hoped that slavery would eventually die out but doubted that the government could do anything to restrict it. Despite his views, Jefferson took actions as president that expanded both slavery and the role of the government.

A ceremony in New Orleans celebrated the Louisiana Purchase of 1803. The United States bought an enormous area called the Louisiana Territory from France for about $15 million.

The Louisiana Purchase, the first major action of Jefferson's presidency, almost doubled the size of the United States. It also led, ultimately, to the westward expansion of slavery. In 1801, Jefferson learned that France had taken over from Spain a large area between the Mississippi River and the Rocky Mountains called Louisiana. After France failed to crush a slave revolution in Haiti, the French ruler, Napoleon I, abandoned his plans to exert influence in the Western Hemisphere. He decid-

ed to sell Louisiana to the United States. Jefferson arranged to buy it for about $15 million in 1803. The Constitution did not authorize the government to buy foreign territory. Jefferson agreed that he had created a new power.

The Louisiana Purchase added 827,987 square miles (2,144,476 square kilometers) of territory to the United States. The first states to be carved out of the Louisiana Purchase were Louisiana (1812), Missouri (1821), and Arkansas (1836). All three were slave states.

The power of the federal government increased during Jefferson's presidency as a result of rulings by the Supreme Court. John Marshall had become chief justice of the United States in 1801. Under Marshall, the court became a leading force in American society. In 1803, in the case of *Marbury v. Madison,* the Supreme Court asserted its right to rule on the constitutionality of federal laws (see **Marbury v. Madison**). From then to Marshall's death in 1835, the court reviewed about 50 cases that involved constitutional issues.

Marshall's court expanded the power of the federal government. For example, in the case of *McCulloch v. Maryland* (1819), it ruled that Congress has implied powers in addition to the powers specified in the Constitution. The Supreme Court also said that federal authority prevails over state authority when the two come into conflict (see **McCulloch v. Maryland**).

Jefferson's foreign policy. In 1803, Britain, by then known as the United Kingdom, went to war again with France. Both nations began seizing U.S. merchant ships. The British also captured U.S. seamen and forced them into the British Navy. Jefferson again expanded the government's powers, this time to protect U.S. shipping. At his request, Congress passed laws designed to end British and French interference. The Embargo Act of 1807 made it illegal for American goods to be exported to foreign countries. The embargo threatened to ruin the nation's economy, and the law was repealed in 1809. The Non-Intercourse Act of 1809 prohibited Americans from trading with the United Kingdom or France. But the

The Louisiana Purchase nearly doubled the size of the United States. The buying of the Louisiana Territory, a vast area between the Mississippi River and the Rocky Mountains, led to the further exploration of the American West.

← Lewis and Clark expedition

— Treaty line

— State or territorial boundary

☐ United States in 1803

0   500 Miles

0   500 Kilometers

WORLD BOOK map

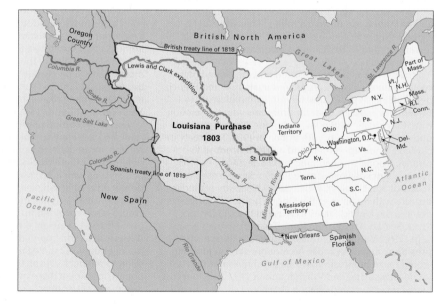

Capture of the City of Washington (1815), an anonymous engraving;
Anne S. K. Brown Military Collection, Brown University Library, Providence, RI

British troops captured Washington, D.C., in 1814—during the War of 1812. The British set fire to
the United States Capitol, the White House, and other government buildings in the city.

warring nations still interfered with U.S. trade.

The War of 1812. James Madison succeeded Jefferson as president in 1809. France soon promised to end its interference with U.S. shipping, but the United Kingdom did not. Additionally, in the Ohio River Valley, the Shawnee chief Tecumseh helped unite Indian tribes to try to stop westward expansion by white settlers. Americans believed that the British were supplying the Indians. For these reasons, many Americans demanded war against the United Kingdom. They were led by members of Congress from the West and South called War Hawks. The War Hawks included Henry Clay of Kentucky and John C. Calhoun of South Carolina. Other Americans, especially New Englanders, opposed the War Hawks' demand. But on June 18, 1812, at Madison's request, Congress declared war on the United Kingdom, and the War of 1812 began.

The two sides struggled to gain an advantage in the war. The United Kingdom was busy fighting the French in Europe, and the United States was poorly prepared for war. United States forces killed Tecumseh in a battle in Canada in 1813 and won a naval victory on Lake Erie near Detroit, but the Americans also suffered major setbacks. On Aug. 24, 1814, the British captured Washington, D.C., and burned the White House and other government buildings. Eventually, U.S. troops drove back the British.

Neither side won the War of 1812. The Treaty of Ghent, signed in 1814 and *ratified* (approved) in 1815, ended the war. See **War of 1812.**

Decline of the Federalists. In 1814 and early 1815, New England Federalist leaders who opposed the War of 1812 held a meeting called the Hartford Convention. They were angry about the war and Southern domination of the federal government. They demanded seven amendments to the Constitution, including one removing the three-fifths clause and another making it harder for Congress to declare war. Opponents charged that they threatened the *secession* (withdrawal) of the New England States from the Union. The Federalists never recovered from this charge or their opposition to the War of 1812. Democratic-Republicans called them disloyal, and the Federalist Party broke up as a national organization after 1816. The breakup left no party to oppose the Democratic-Republicans. The Democratic-Republican candidate for president in 1820, James Monroe of Virginia, ran unopposed. See **Hartford Convention.**

The Era of Good Feeling. A spirit of nationalism swept through the nation following the War of 1812. The war increased feelings of self-confidence. The defeat of Tecumseh made it easier for settlers to move west. Peace in Europe led to expanded trade and allowed Americans to concentrate on their own affairs. The nation acquired new territory, and new states entered the Union. The economy prospered. Historians sometimes call the period from 1815 to the early 1820's the Era of Good Feeling because of its relative peace, unity, and optimism about the future.

The American System. After the War of 1812, Henry Clay and other nationalists said the government should

Detail of *Fairview Inn* (1889), a water color on paper by Thomas C. Ruckle; Maryland Historical Society, Baltimore

The National Road was a transportation route in early America. When completed, it stretched from Maryland to Illinois. A steady stream of pioneers moved westward along the road. Inns, like this one near the National Road, provided resting and eating stops for travelers.

actively foster the economy's growth. They proposed a set of measures called the American System. They said the government should raise tariffs to protect American manufacturers from foreign competition so that industries would grow and employ more people. The government should spend the tariff revenues on transportation projects and other internal improvements to help farmers ship their crops to market and knit the country together. A national bank should regulate the nation's currency and take care of the government's finances.

Congress soon put the American System into practice. In 1816, it enacted a high tariff and chartered the second Bank of the United States. The federal government also increased its funding of internal improvement projects, the most important of which was the National Road. Begun in 1811, the road stretched from Maryland to Illinois when completed. It became an important route for the shipment of goods and the movement of settlers westward.

Other transportation improvements included the development of the steamboat. In 1807, the American inventor Robert Fulton demonstrated the first commercially successful steamboat, the *Clermont.* The steamboat soon became the fastest way to ship goods and carry passengers by river.

The state governments as well as the federal government financed transportation improvements. The states built many canals to connect natural waterways. The Erie Canal, the most important, was built by New York state. Completed in 1825, it connected Albany, on the Hudson River, to Buffalo, on Lake Erie. It led to the growth of farms and towns across New York. By establishing a water route from New York City to the Great Lakes, the Erie Canal made it profitable for settlers to start farms in the Midwest. Canal boats carried manufactured goods from east to west and farm produce from west to east. See **Erie Canal.**

A national culture. Americans had patterned their culture largely after European civilization. Architects, painters, and writers tended to imitate European mod-

els. In the early 1800's, however, the writer Ralph Waldo Emerson and other thinkers called for an art and culture based on uniquely American experiences. Architects began to design simple houses that blended into their surroundings. Craftworkers built sturdy furniture that was suited to frontier life, yet elegantly simple. The nation's literature also flourished when it began to reflect American experiences. The writings of Washington Irving, a leading early author, helped gain respect for American literature.

Cotton and slavery. In the 1700's, the main crops in the South were tobacco and rice. In the 1800's, however, cotton became the region's leading crop. In 1793, the American inventor Eli Whitney devised the cotton gin, a machine that separated cotton fiber from the seeds as fast as 50 people could by hand. This machine helped cause a boom in cotton production across the South (see **Cotton gin**). Cotton planters, who used African American slaves to work their fields, poured into the new states of Louisiana, Alabama, and Mississippi. In 1819, the United States acquired Florida in a treaty with Spain, and cotton growers also went there. New Orleans, Louisiana, prospered as the nation's leading slave market. Slaveowners farther east in Virginia, Maryland, and other states sold hundreds of thousands of slaves into what was soon known as the Cotton Kingdom. Slave traders and owners often separated African American families by selling children, parents, and other relatives away from each other.

The Missouri crisis. The Era of Good Feeling did not mean an end to all the country's political disputes. The westward expansion of slavery caused a bitter fight between Northerners and Southerners in Congress from 1819 to 1821. By 1819, every Northern state had outlawed slavery. But the plantation system had spread throughout the South, and the economy of the Southern States depended on slave labor. The question of whether to encourage or limit the westward expansion of slavery became a hotly disputed political issue. Through the years, the United States had kept a balance between the number of free states, where slavery was prohibited, and slave states, where it was allowed. This balance meant that both sides had the same number of members in the U.S. Senate. By 1819, there were 11 free states and 11 slave states.

When the Territory of Missouri applied for admission to the Union as a slave state, most Northern members of Congress insisted that it enter as a free state instead. Either way, the balance in the Senate between free and slave states would be upset. After almost two years of angry debates, Congress worked out the Missouri Compromise, which temporarily maintained the balance. Massachusetts agreed to give up the northern part of its territory. This area became the state of Maine, and entered the Union as a free state in 1820. In 1821, Missouri entered as a slave state, and so there were 12 free and 12 slave states.

The Missouri Compromise also had another important provision. It provided that slavery would be "forever prohibited" in all territory gained from the Louisiana Purchase that was north of Missouri's southern border, except for Missouri itself. See **Missouri Compromise.**

Expansion (1820-1849)

From the 1820's to the 1850's, the United States grew greatly in land, population, and wealth. Thousands of settlers moved westward into new states and territories. Immigration from Europe brought hundreds of thousands of newcomers. British, Irish, German, and Scandinavian immigrants settled in Eastern cities and across the West. In the 1850's, Chinese immigrants also began to arrive on the West Coast. The federal government made more land available to white settlers through the policy of Indian removal, in which the U.S. Army forced Indians to leave their lands in both Eastern and Western states. In the South, the cotton industry grew so rapidly that cotton accounted for half the value of all U.S. exports. Meanwhile, in the Northeast, the nation's first large factories appeared. Some of the factory workers

Facts in brief (1820-1849)

Presidents (with political parties and dates of service)
James Monroe, Democratic-Republican, 1817-1825
John Quincy Adams, Democratic-Republican/National Republican, 1825-1829
Andrew Jackson, Democrat, 1829-1837
Martin Van Buren, Democrat, 1837-1841
William H. Harrison, Whig, 1841
John Tyler, Whig, 1841-1845
James K. Polk, Democrat, 1845-1849
Zachary Taylor, Whig, 1849-1850

States in the Union
Number at start of period: 22
Number at end of period: 30
States added during the period:
Maine (1820), Missouri (1821), Arkansas (1836), Michigan (1837), Florida (1845), Texas (1845), Iowa (1846), Wisconsin (1848).

Important dates

1820	The Missouri Compromise ended a slavery dispute.
1823	The Monroe Doctrine warned Europeans against interference in Western Hemisphere affairs.
1825	The Erie Canal opened, providing a water route between the Atlantic Ocean and the Great Lakes.
1830	The *Tom Thumb,* the nation's first commercial steam locomotive, operated in Baltimore.
1832	South Carolina threatened secession over a tariff.
1834	Cyrus McCormick patented the reaper.
1837	Samuel F. B. Morse demonstrated the first successful telegraph in the United States.
1846	The United Kingdom ceded the southern part of the Oregon Country to the United States.
1848	Victory in the Mexican War gave the United States vast new territory in the West.
1848	The Gold Rush began in California.

Population growth and change

Total population, 9,638,453
1820 Rural, 93% Urban, 7%

Total population, 22,488,000
1849 Rural, 85% Urban, 15%

Prairie Scene: Mirage (1837), a water color by Alfred Jacob Miller; Walters Art Gallery, Baltimore

Americans moved westward by the thousands during the early 1800's. Hardy pioneers piled their belongings into covered wagons and set out to find new homes in the West. The push westward continued until the nation stretched from coast to coast.

The Lewis and Clark expedition, which lasted from 1804 to 1806, mapped much of the vast northwestern wilderness. The explorers traveled almost 7,700 miles (12,400 kilometers) from St. Louis, Missouri, to the Pacific Ocean. Meriwether Lewis and William Clark, *far left,* obtained valuable information from Indians they met.

Detail of a mural (1938) by Barry Faulkner and F. H. Schwarz in the State Capitol, Salem, OR; Oregon State Highway Department

were women and children, and many were immigrants.

The United States moves west. By 1820, Americans had established settlements as far west as the Mississippi River. By the 1830's, they had pushed the frontier across the river, into Iowa, Missouri, Arkansas, and eastern Texas. The land beyond, called the Great Plains, was dry and treeless, and it seemed to be poor farmland. But explorers, traders, and others who had journeyed farther west told of rich land and forests beyond the Rocky Mountains. In the 1840's, large numbers of settlers made the long journey across the Great Plains to the Far West.

The Western settlers included Easterners from both the North and South. Many other settlers came from Europe. Some people went west in search of religious freedom. The best known of these were the Mormons, who settled in Utah in 1847. African Americans often went west against their will, as slaves.

Most of the settlers became farmers who owned their own plots. But urban life also moved westward with the frontier. Bustling towns and cities grew up in the West. There, traders in farm equipment and other supplies carried on a brisk business. The towns had banks, churches, hotels, and stores. The townspeople included craftworkers, doctors, lawyers, government officials,

Expansion in the mid-1800's extended the nation westward to the Pacific Ocean. The Oregon Country was ceded to the United States by the United Kingdom. The rest of the new territory came from Mexico.

Pioneer trail
State or territorial boundary
U.S. area in mid-1800's

0 — 500 Miles
0 — 500 Kilometers

WORLD BOOK map

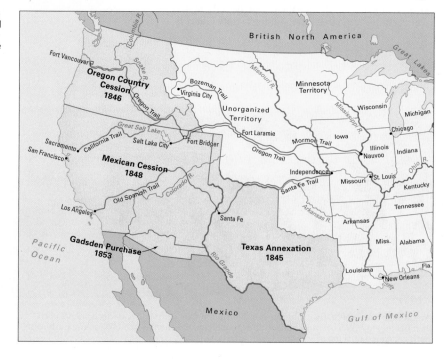

A pioneer homestead in Missouri consisted of a log cabin in a clearing and a plot of farmland. The farmer cleared timber from the surrounding forest to build a house and to burn as fuel.

Settlement of Immigrants in Missouri (about 1850), a lithograph by E. Sachse; Missouri Historical Society, St. Louis

schoolteachers, and members of the clergy.

Westward expansion of the United States gave rise to changes in American politics. It revived conflict over slavery because Congress had to decide whether to allow slavery into new states and territories. Western settlers joined up with Easterners who wanted the government to improve the country's transportation system with new roads, canals, and railroads. For more details, see **Westward movement in America.**

The Monroe Doctrine. The United States maintained peaceful relations with Europe during the era of expansion. But as Mexico and the nations of Central and South America won independence from Spain in the 1820's, Americans worried that Europeans might interfere. In 1823, President James Monroe issued the Monroe Doctrine, a statement warning European countries not to interfere with the nations in the Western Hemisphere (see **Monroe Doctrine**).

Manifest destiny. Some settlers moved beyond the western boundary of United States territory. They flocked to Texas, California, and other lands belonging to Mexico. Americans also settled in the Oregon Country, a large territory between California and Alaska claimed by both the United Kingdom and the United States. By then, many Americans had come to believe that westward expansion was the *manifest destiny* of the United States—that is, the clear future of the nation. According to the belief of manifest destiny, the United States had the right to take all of North America. For many, manifest destiny justified the idea that white Americans were superior to Indians and Mexicans. Stirred by this belief, Americans demanded control of the Oregon Country and much of Mexico.

The conflicting claim with the United Kingdom over Oregon was settled fairly easily. The British decided the effort needed to hold on to all of Oregon was not worth-

while. In 1846, they turned over to the United States the part of Oregon south of the 49th parallel, except Vancouver Island. See **Oregon Territory.**

The struggle over Mexican territory was more complicated. It began in Texas in 1835, when American settlers, who had been invited to settle there by the Mexican government, revolted against Mexican rule. In 1836, these settlers proclaimed Texas an independent republic. Nine years later, the United States annexed Texas and made it a state, despite Mexico's opposition.

The Mexican War. The United States gained additional Mexican territory in the Mexican War. In 1846, President James K. Polk sent General Zachary Taylor to occupy land near the Rio Grande that both the United States and Mexico claimed. Fighting broke out between Taylor's troops and Mexican soldiers. On May 13, 1846, at Polk's request, Congress declared war on Mexico. The United States quickly defeated its neighbor. The Treaty of Guadalupe Hidalgo, signed on Feb. 2, 1848, officially ended the war. The treaty gave the United States a vast stretch of land from Texas west to the Pacific and north to Oregon. The nation then extended from coast to coast. See **Mexican War.**

In 1853, in the Gadsden Purchase, the United States bought from Mexico the strip of land on the southern edge of Arizona and New Mexico. Although many Indians disagreed, the United States now claimed to own all the territory of its present states except Alaska (purchased from Russia in 1867) and Hawaii (annexed in 1898). See **Gadsden Purchase.**

Economic growth. Expansion into the rich interior of the continent enabled the United States to become the world's leading agricultural nation. Southern cotton was in great demand as a raw material for textile mills in Europe and the northeastern United States. Planters, slaves, and family farmers in the South as far west as

River traffic encouraged development of the Western lands. St. Louis, *left,* was a gateway to the West and a main port of Mississippi River steamboats during the first half of the 1800's.

Detail of an oil painting on canvas of the steamboat *Yellowstone* (1832-1833) by George Catlin; Smithsonian American Art Museum, Washington, D.C. (© Art Resource)

Texas raised cotton to supply the mills. Many planters in Kentucky and Tennessee prospered by growing tobacco and hemp, used for making rope. Midwesterners and Westerners produced large crops of corn and wheat, and also raised livestock. New machines boosted the output of U.S. farms. Eli Whitney's cotton gin had already transformed Southern agriculture. The reaper, patented by the American inventor Cyrus McCormick in 1834, allowed Northern farmers to harvest grain much quicker than before.

The discovery of minerals in the West also boosted the economy. The most famous mineral strike took place in 1848, when gold was discovered at Sutter's Mill in California. See **Forty-Niners; Gold rush.**

The period also marked the beginning of large-scale manufacturing in the United States. Previously, most manufacturing was done by craftworkers at home or in small shops. However, in the early 1800's, businesses began to erect factories with machinery that enabled them to produce goods more rapidly and cheaply.

Advances in transportation and communications contributed to the economic growth of the United States. New or improved roads, such as the National Road in the East and the Oregon and Santa Fe trails in the West, eased the difficulty of traveling and shipping goods by land. The increased use of steamboats and the construction of canals improved water transportation. The steam-powered railroad soon rivaled steamboats and canal boats. By 1850, about 9,000 miles (14,500 kilometers) of railroad lines were in operation.

In 1837, the American inventor Samuel F. B. Morse demonstrated the first successful telegraph in the United States. The telegraph gave businesses the fastest means of communication yet known.

The election of 1824 destroyed the one-party rule of the Era of Good Feeling. Four Democratic-Republicans sought to succeed James Monroe as president. Andrew Jackson received the most electoral votes, and John

Detail of *A Cotton Plantation on the Mississippi* (1884), a Currier and Ives lithograph based on a painting by W. A. Walker; Museum of the City of New York

A cotton plantation on the Mississippi River is typical of the many plantations that sprang up throughout the South in the 1800's. Cotton became so important to the Southern economy that people called the crop "King Cotton." Many white planters used black slaves to work in their fields.

The Camden and Amboy Railroad with the Engine "Planet" in 1834 (1904), an oil painting on canvas by Edward Lamson Henry; Graham Gallery, New York City

Railroads and steamboats became important means of transportation during the early to middle 1800's. In this scene, New Jersey travelers transfer from a steamboat, *background,* to a train. A stagecoach and a carriage—two other means of transportation—appear at the right.

Quincy Adams came in second. But nobody won a majority, and the House of Representatives had to select the new president. The House chose Adams. Embittered, Jackson and his followers formed a separate wing of the Democratic-Republican Party, which soon developed into the Democratic Party.

The rise of Andrew Jackson. Historians often call the 1830's and 1840's the Age of Jackson, after Andrew Jackson of Tennessee, the most influential political leader of the era. Jackson, a rich slaveholder and a general in the War of 1812, was famous for success in battles against Indians and the British. He created a new kind of politics in which appeals to the "common man" drew enthusiastic mass support. By the 1820's, most white men had gained the right to vote, as states abolished requirements that voters own land. Yet most states barred African American men and all women from voting. Even so, high turnouts at elections—up to 80 percent of the men who were eligible to vote—made U.S. politics more democratic than ever before.

Jackson ran for president for a second time in 1828. He appealed for support from Western farmers and Eastern city laborers and craftworkers. His reputation as a war hero and Indian fighter made him popular. He promised to end what he called a "monopoly" of government by the rich and to protect the interests of the "common man." Jackson was elected by wide margins in 1828 and again in 1832.

Jackson as president. When Jackson became president, he fired many federal officials and gave their jobs to his supporters. He called this policy "rotation in office" and said it was democratic because it allowed more men to hold federal positions. His opponents called it the "spoils system" and said it was corrupt because it distributed federal jobs to reward men for their party loyalty instead of their qualifications.

One of Jackson's main crusades as president involved the second Bank of the United States. The bank held the government's deposits and regulated the nation's money supply by controlling how much currency was issued. Jackson thought that the bank favored the wealthy

and that it was unfair for one bank to have a monopoly on holding the government's money. In 1832, Congress voted to recharter the bank, but Jackson vetoed the bill. He soon withdrew the government's money from the bank, and the bank later collapsed.

Another great issue of Jackson's administration involved tariffs and *nullification* (action by a state to cancel a federal law). In 1828, Congress passed a bill that placed high tariffs on goods imported to the United States. The South believed the bill favored Northern manufacturing interests and denounced it as a "tariff of abominations." Speaking for South Carolina, John C. Calhoun (then the vice president) claimed that any state could *nullify* (declare invalid) a federal law it deemed unconstitutional. In 1832, Congress lowered tariffs somewhat, but not enough to please South Carolina. South Carolina declared the tariff act "null and void" and threatened to secede from the Union if federal officials tried to collect tariffs in the state. This action created a constitutional crisis. Jackson believed in states' rights, but he also thought the Union must be preserved. In 1833, he persuaded Congress to pass a *force bill,* a law that allowed him to use the armed forces to collect tariffs. But Congress lowered tariffs to a point acceptable to South Carolina, and the nullification crisis faded away.

Politics after Jackson. Jackson's influence on politics continued after he left office. As the undisputed leader of the Democrats, Jackson chose Martin Van Buren to be the party's candidate in the 1836 presidential election. Jackson's opponents had formed the Whig Party four years earlier. In an effort to attract Jackson's followers, most Whigs supported William Henry Harrison against Van Buren. Harrison, like Jackson, had won fame as an Indian fighter. But American voters, loyal to Jackson, elected Van Buren.

A depression called the Panic of 1837 crippled the U.S. economy shortly after Van Buren took office. The presidential election of 1840 again matched Van Buren and Harrison. In their campaign, the Whigs blamed Van Buren's economic policies for the depression. They also promoted Harrison as a war hero and associated him with hard cider, the log cabin, and other symbols of the frontier. This time, Harrison won the election.

Immigration. The United States had always been made up mainly of immigrants. But from 1845 through 1860, more than 100,000 immigrants arrived in the country every year. Most came to find opportunities in the growing U.S. economy. A majority settled in the North because slavery reduced the opportunities available to free workers in the South. The immigrants made major contributions to the economic growth of the United States. They came from many countries, but the largest numbers were from Ireland and Germany.

Irish men and women had been coming to the United States since the 1600's, many as indentured servants. In the mid-1840's, a famine in Ireland caused mass starvation. Huge numbers of Irish used meager savings to leave Ireland on ships bound for North America. Some Irish landlords paid for their tenants' passage on these vessels. Relatives already in America sent others ticket money. Having paid fares enabled Irish famine refugees to cross the Atlantic Ocean without selling themselves into servitude.

Irish immigrants often settled in such Eastern cities as Boston and New York City, though some also moved to the West. They worked on the canals and railroads, on the docks, in the new factories, and as domestic servants. The Irish faced great discrimination in the United States, in part because they were poor and Catholic.

German immigrants had been coming to America in large numbers since the early 1700's. In the 1840's and 1850's, many came because it was easier to buy farms in the growing West than in Europe. Some Germans settled in Eastern cities, but many built farms in the Midwest or moved to such cities as St. Louis, Chicago, and Milwaukee. Most big American cities had robust German communities in the 1800's, with German-language newspapers, athletic clubs, and other institutions. Some had heavily German industries, such as breweries.

Indian removal. As settlers moved westward, they took over huge tracts of land that belonged to Indians. Fighting often broke out between the settlers and Indians, and the U.S. government sent soldiers to battle the Indians. United States soldiers also fought two wars in Florida against the Seminole. The United States won most of these so-called Indian wars (see **Indian wars**).

The Cherokee, Creek, Choctaw, and Chickasaw still held onto their lands in the Southeast. At the urging of President Jackson, Congress passed the Removal Act of 1830. The idea of Indian removal was that tribes in the East would trade their lands for other lands in the West. The United States would guarantee that the Indians could keep the new lands "forever."

The Indians of the Southeast developed several strategies to prevent whites from taking their lands. In what is now Georgia, for example, the Cherokee nation established a strong tribal government that included a written constitution. The Cherokee constitution forbade individual Cherokees to sell land to Americans. These actions enraged whites in Georgia, who wanted this land. The Georgia legislature declared Indian laws void and be-

Detail of *The Trail of Tears* (1942), an oil painting on canvas by Robert Lindneux; Woolaroc Museum, Bartlesville, Okla.

The Trail of Tears was the forced removal of Cherokee Indians from their homelands in Georgia to territory west of the Mississippi River. About 4,000 Cherokee died on the journey. The government forced thousands of Eastern Indians to move during the 1830's as whites took over their land.

gan distributing the Cherokee land to whites. The Cherokee appealed these actions to the Supreme Court of the United States. In the 1831 case of *Cherokee Nation v. Georgia,* the court refused to strike down Georgia's laws. A year later, however, in *Worcester v. Georgia,* the Supreme Court decided that Cherokee law, rather than Georgia law, applied on Cherokee land. President Jackson supported Georgia and refused to enforce the court's decision.

In 1835, some Cherokee signed a treaty agreeing to removal, though most of the tribe's members and its leader, John Ross, objected. In 1838, the U.S. Army rounded up the Cherokee and forced them to march to Oklahoma. About 4,000 Cherokee died on what became known as the Trail of Tears. The government also relocated the Creek, Choctaw, and Chickasaw, whose lands were mainly in Alabama and Mississippi, as well as some Indians from Ohio and other Northern areas.

Cultural changes. After 1820, the wilderness seemed less and less hostile to Americans. Increasingly, writers and artists glorified the frontier and nature. The public eagerly read the novels of James Fenimore Cooper, which described Indians and pioneers as pure of heart and noble in deeds. Ralph Waldo Emerson and other American philosophers praised nature as a source of truth and beauty for all.

Developments in printing spread art and information to more people than ever before. A new printing process called *lithography* enabled artists to produce many copies of their works cheaply. The popular lithographs of Nathaniel Currier and James Merritt Ives depicted everyday American scenes, often in a sentimental style. Faster printing presses and cheaper paper reduced the cost of newspapers. After 1835, many newspaper publishers lowered the cost of their papers to one cent, a price even poor people could afford.

The spoken word remained an important means of mass communication. Large numbers of people attended gatherings where political candidates and famous lawyers, writers, and members of the clergy made speeches. Improved transportation, especially by rail, made it easier for speakers to travel across the country.

City people flocked to theaters to see plays and other forms of entertainment. P. T. Barnum, the most famous showman of the time, fascinated the public by exhibiting midgets, "fat ladies," and other unusual attractions. Blackface minstrel shows were especially popular. In these shows, white performers blackened their faces to impersonate blacks. The shows reinforced scornful images of blacks that lasted long after the shows had disappeared. The American songwriter Stephen Foster wrote some of his most famous songs for minstrel shows. See **Barnum, P. T.; Minstrel show.**

Social reform. A wave of Protestant religious revivalism had swept the United States in the 1820's and 1830's. Church membership shot up. Churches and other reform groups set up charities to aid the poor. Many people joined social reform movements to improve society. People concerned about the extent of alcohol use urged *temperance*—that is, the reduction or elimination of the use of alcoholic beverages. In the mid-1800's, prohibitionists pressed states to outlaw the sale of liquor. Women's participation in activities outside the home became more socially acceptable, especially in the North.

An American teacher named Dorothea Dix and other reformers campaigned to improve the dismal conditions in prisons and "insane asylums," as mental hospitals were called. Workers joined labor unions to pressure employers to raise wages, to improve working conditions, and to reduce the workday to 10 hours from the usual 12 to 14 hours. Reformers also worked for better education, women's rights, and the abolition of slavery.

Better education. In the early 1800's, most good schools in the United States were expensive private schools. Poor children went to second-rate "pauper," or "charity," schools, or did not go at all. African American children were not allowed to attend most schools in the North, and in the South it was a crime to teach slaves to read. Prudence Crandall, a Connecticut educator, set up a school for African American girls, but she was forced to close it. Slaves sometimes found whites who taught them to read and write. Others managed to teach themselves. But racial discrimination in education persisted.

Poor whites made more progress than blacks did in gaining opportunities for education. During the 1830's, Horace Mann of Massachusetts and other reformers began demanding better education and public schools open to both the rich and poor. States started establishing public school systems, more children enrolled, and students attended longer. Colleges began training teachers for a more standardized system of public education. As a result, schoolchildren throughout the country received much the same lessons. For example, many studied the McGuffey Readers to learn to read. These books taught patriotism and morality as well as reading.

Women's rights. In the 1800's, American women had few rights. There were almost no colleges for women, and most professional careers were closed to them. A married woman could not own property. Instead, any property she had belonged to her husband. Women could not vote in most elections. Many Americans believed in the idea of "separate spheres." This idea held that women's sphere was the home and men's area of activity was the larger world outside the home.

As women participated in the reform movements of the period, they began to realize that they could work to improve their own situations. A women's rights movement developed after 1820. In 1833, the Oberlin Collegiate Institute (now Oberlin College) opened as the first coeducational college in the United States. In 1848, New York passed a law allowing women to keep control of their property after marriage. Also in 1848, two reformers named Lucretia Mott and Elizabeth Cady Stanton organized a Women's Rights Convention that met in Seneca Falls, New York. The convention issued the first formal appeal for woman *suffrage* (the right to vote).

The abolition movement was the most intense and controversial reform activity of the period. Since colonial times, some Americans, called *abolitionists,* had demanded an end to slavery. By the early 1800's, the Northern States had begun to outlaw the practice. But the plantation system had spread across the South. Southern whites depended on slavery, got rich from it, and had no intention of allowing anyone to abolish it.

The westward expansion of slavery had already caused bitter political conflicts. In the 1820's and 1830's, abolitionists began to demand an end to slavery in the South. In 1821, Benjamin Lundy, a Quaker editor, called

Stump Speaking (1854), hand-colored engraving by Louis Adolphe Gautier after George Caleb Bingham's oil painting; private collection (Art Resource)

Political candidates traveled far and wide to bring their messages to frontier audiences. Speeches from platforms like the one shown here became known as *stump speeches.*

for gradual abolition in a journal called *The Genius of Universal Emancipation.* William Lloyd Garrison, a fiery Boston journalist, went much further. Garrison demanded the immediate and unconditional abolition of slavery throughout the United States. He founded *The Liberator,* a leading abolitionist journal, in 1831. Some African Americans who had gained their freedom became important speakers for the abolition movement. They included Frederick Douglass and Sojourner Truth. See **Abolition movement.**

Also in 1831, Nat Turner led the largest slave rebellion of the period. Turner was a slave and a preacher in Southampton County, Virginia. He and his followers killed 60 whites before the Virginia militia arrived. The militia captured and hanged 20 rebels, including Turner. Then, local whites killed about 100 blacks who likely had not taken part in the rebellion (see **Turner, Nat**). The radical abolitionists in the North and rebellious slaves in the South terrified Southern whites. Southern legislatures passed laws to tighten white control over African Americans. Some even made it a crime to criticize slavery.

The growing strength of the abolition movement made Southerners fear that the federal government would outlaw slavery. Southerners had always argued that slavery was necessary to the plantation economy.

Now, they stressed the unsupported belief that blacks were inferior to whites, and therefore fit only to be slaves. Even many Southern whites who owned no slaves took comfort in the belief that they were superior to blacks. Southern whites also knew that many Northerners, even those who disapproved of slavery, shared their beliefs about blacks.

The nation divided (1850-1869)

The long dispute between the North and South over the expansion of slavery came to a head after the Mexican War ended in 1848. The vast new area the United States acquired in the West in the 1840's created a problem Americans could not avoid. It was obvious that the new land would be split up into territories, and then into states. Southerners argued against any restraints on slavery in the new territories and states. Northerners wanted the federal government to ban slavery in the newly acquired lands. Some politicians tried to compromise by proposing the rule of *popular sovereignty.* Under this rule, the people of the territories and states would decide for themselves whether to allow slavery.

Members of Congress represented various views about slavery. John C. Calhoun, then a senator from South Carolina, expressed the views of Americans who believed in the right to own slaves. Senator William H. Seward of New York spoke for people with antislavery beliefs. He said the government could not expand slavery because moral law, a higher law than the Constitution, favored freedom. Senator Henry Clay of Kentucky represented Americans who held views between those of Calhoun and Seward. Clay urged the North and South to compromise because the alternative was the end of the Union.

California applied for admission as a free state in 1849. The application triggered a huge debate because it would upset the balance of free and slave states. Southerners recognized that the faster growth of the Northern population meant that Northerners would control the House of Representatives. Southerners insisted on maintaining their power in the Senate by blocking the admission of new free states. They threatened a civil war if Congress admitted California without slavery.

The Compromise of 1850. Clay and others brought about a compromise to admit California. They won approval of the Compromise of 1850, a series of laws that made concessions to both the North and South. Measures designed to satisfy the North included the admission of California as a free state and the abolition of the slave trade, but not slavery itself, in Washington, D.C. As part of the compromise, Congress created the territories of New Mexico and Utah under the rule of popular sovereignty. This meant that when these territories became states, their voters would decide whether or not to allow slavery.

To satisfy the South, Congress enacted the Fugitive Slave Act to stop Northerners from helping slaves who escaped into Northern states. It required federal marshals to capture suspected fugitives and return them to the South. The Fugitive Slave Act enraged Northerners, as they watched the federal government enforce slavery everywhere in the country. The American author Harriet Beecher Stowe wrote the novel *Uncle Tom's Cabin* (1851-1852) in protest against the Fugitive Slave Act. This powerful work about the horrors of slavery soon be-

The Old Print Shop, Inc., New York City

The Compromise of 1850 temporarily cooled the heated dispute over slavery. Henry Clay, *center,* led the effort in Congress to pass the compromise, which made concessions to both sides.

came one of the most widely read books in the United States. See **Compromise of 1850; Uncle Tom's Cabin.**

The Kansas-Nebraska Act. The Compromise of 1850 did not solve the problem of the expansion of slavery into the West. In the early 1850's, Congress began considering the creation of new territories in the area roughly between Missouri and present-day Idaho. Again, there was bitter debate over whether the new territories should ban or allow slavery. Those who called for a ban cited the Missouri Compromise to back their position. The land under consideration was part of the area where the Compromise had "forever prohibit-

Detail of *The Slave Auction* (1862), an oil painting on canvas by Eyre Crowe; Kennedy Galleries, Inc., New York City

Slaves were sold at public auctions in the South. Pictures of blacks being sold like merchandise stirred much resentment in the North against slavery.

ed" slavery. But in 1854, Congress passed the Kansas-Nebraska Act, a law that allowed slavery to spread into this area. The act created two territories west of Missouri—Kansas and Nebraska. It applied the rule of popular sovereignty by providing that the settlers in each territory would decide whether or not to allow slavery.

The Kansas-Nebraska Act was a political disaster. Violence broke out between Northern and Southern settlers in the Kansas territory. Across the country, antislavery Northerners denounced the politicians who had supported the Kansas-Nebraska Act. Others strongly defended the act. Everywhere, attitudes toward the slavery issue hardened, and the capacity for further compromise diminished. The United States was on the road to war. See **Kansas-Nebraska Act.**

Party splits. Angered by the Kansas-Nebraska Act, antislavery Northerners formed the Republican Party in 1854. Many Democrats and Whigs who opposed slavery left their parties and became Republicans. Other Americans, disturbed by the turmoil, sought simple answers to the country's problems. They joined the Know-Nothing (or American) Party, which blamed the problems on immigrants and Roman Catholics. The stability of the two main political parties before the early 1850's had helped keep the country together. Thus, the splits in political parties deprived the country of an important unifying force.

By the mid-1850's, the Supreme Court seemed the only institution to command nationwide respect. But in 1857, the court ruled in the Dred Scott Decision that African Americans could not be citizens of the United States and that laws limiting the spread of slavery were unconstitutional. The court then lost much of its influence. More important, many Northerners came to be-

lieve that the government was controlled by a "slave power conspiracy" to expand slavery across the country, including into the North. See **Dred Scott Decision.**

The "irrepressible conflict." The dispute over slavery turned out to be an "irrepressible conflict," as Senator Seward termed it. During the 1850's, the North and South drew further and further apart over the issue. After 1854, more and more Southerners saw themselves as a separate group. In the North, abolitionists stepped up their campaign against slavery, and their message was more popular than before. Even Northerners who thought blacks were inferior to whites resented the recent proslavery actions of the federal government. They thought Southern slaveowners were violating the political rights of Northern whites as well as the human rights of black Americans. In Kansas, fighting broke out in 1856 between proslavery and antislavery settlers. Newspapers were filled with accounts of violence in "Bleeding Kansas." See **Kansas** ("Bleeding Kansas").

On Oct. 17, 1859, the abolitionist John Brown and a small band of followers seized the federal arsenal at Harpers Ferry, Virginia (now West Virginia). Brown intended the action as the first step in a general slave uprising. But federal troops easily captured him, and, after a trial, he was hanged. Brown's plan had almost no chance of success. The odds against him were so great that many people believe he was insane. Even so, many Northerners thought of him as a martyr, while many Southerners believed his attack was part of an organized movement to end slavery.

The election of 1860 reflected the nation's deep division. On paper, there were four candidates for president. But in reality, there were two separate elections. In the South, voters chose between two candidates who

The First Day at Gettysburg (1863), an oil painting on canvas by James Walker; West Point Museum, U.S. Military Academy

The American Civil War (1861-1865) ranks among the most tragic events of United States history. It pitted Northerners against Southerners in bloody battle. In the Battle of Gettysburg, *shown here,* more than 45,000 Americans were killed, wounded, captured, or missing in just three days.

The American Civil War
split the nation into two
parts—the Confederacy and
the Union. The Confederacy
was made up of 11 states that
withdrew from the Union in
1860 and 1861.

--- State or territorial boundary

Union state

Union territory

Confederate state

0   500 Miles
0   500 Kilometers

WORLD BOOK map

were defenders of "Southern rights," John Breckenridge and John Bell. In the North, voters chose between Republican Abraham Lincoln and Democrat Stephen Douglas. On Nov. 6, 1860, Lincoln won the election. He got a majority of the electoral vote even though he received no votes from Southern states.

Secession. Lincoln, a lawyer from Illinois, had earned a reputation as an opponent of slavery. His election was unacceptable to the South. Southerners feared the new president would restrict or even end slavery. Alarmed by this prospect, South Carolina seceded from the Union on Dec. 20, 1860, well before Lincoln took office. Alabama, Florida, Georgia, Louisiana, and Mississippi seceded in January 1861. The six seceded states formed the Confederate States of America in February. Later in 1861, Arkansas, North Carolina, Tennessee, Texas, and Virginia seceded and joined the Confederacy.

Lincoln took office on March 4, 1861. The new president insisted above all else on the preservation of the Union. He thought the seceded states were still part of the United States and hoped that reconciliation was possible. But a little more than a month later, the North and South went to war.

The American Civil War began on April 12, 1861, when Southern troops fired on Fort Sumter, a military post in Charleston Harbor. Both sides quickly prepared for battle after the Fort Sumter clash. The North had superior financial and industrial strength, and a larger population than the South. But the South fought strongly for its independence. The South gained the upper hand at first, but the North gradually turned the tide. Finally, Confederate resistance wore down, and Union armies swept through the South. On April 9, 1865, General Robert E. Lee, the commander of the Confederate Army, surrendered to the Union commander Ulysses S. Grant at Appomattox Court House in Virginia. The last Confederate troops surrendered on May 26.

The four years of bloody fighting between the North and South had devastating effects on the nation. About 360,000 Union troops and 260,000 Confederate troops,

Facts in brief (1850-1869)

Presidents (with political parties and dates of service)
Zachary Taylor, Whig, 1849-1850
Millard Fillmore, Whig, 1850-1853
Franklin Pierce, Democrat, 1853-1857
James Buchanan, Democrat, 1857-1861
Abraham Lincoln, Republican, 1861-1865
Andrew Johnson, National Union, 1865-1869
Ulysses S. Grant, Republican, 1869-1877

States in the Union
Number at start of period: 30
Number at end of period: 37
States added during the period:
California (1850), Minnesota (1858), Oregon (1859), Kansas (1861), West Virginia (1863), Nevada (1864), Nebraska (1867).

Important dates
1850 The Compromise of 1850 temporarily ended a national crisis over the slavery question.
1851-1852 Harriet Beecher Stowe wrote the serialized novel *Uncle Tom's Cabin* in protest about fugitive slave laws.
1854 Passage of the Kansas-Nebraska Act led to nationwide turmoil over the slavery issue.
1861-1865 The North and the South fought each other in the American Civil War.
1863 The Emancipation Proclamation declared freedom for all slaves in Confederate-held territory.
1865 The 13th Amendment outlawed slavery throughout the United States.
1865 Actor John Wilkes Booth shot and killed President Abraham Lincoln at a theater in Washington, D.C.
1867 The United States bought Alaska from Russia.
1868 The House of Representatives impeached President Andrew Johnson, but the Senate did not remove him from office.

Population growth and change

Total population, 23,191,876
1850 | Rural, 85% | Urban, 15%

Total population, 38,925,000
1869 | Rural, 75% | Urban, 25%

The South lay in ruins at the end of the Civil War. These shells of burned buildings in Richmond, Virginia, provide an example of the destruction brought on by the war.

all Americans, died in the conflict. No other war in history has taken so many American lives. Property damage was enormous, especially in the South. Southern cities, towns, plantations, and railroads lay in ruin. The war also caused deep, long-lasting feelings of bitterness and division between the victorious North and the defeated South. The Civil War was tragic in many ways, but it had two important outcomes. It led to the abolition of slavery in the United States, and it preserved the Union. For a detailed account of the war, see **Civil War, American.**

Abolition of slavery. At the start of the Civil War, Lincoln's main goal was to save the Union. But African American slaves in the South believed that the war was really about their freedom. Everywhere Union soldiers

went in the South, slaves serving for the Confederates deserted to Union lines. Thousands of slaves escaped from plantations and tried to join the Union Army. Some Union generals in the field declared slaves free, but Lincoln overturned their decisions. He worried that freeing the slaves would be unpopular and weaken support for the war in the North. But, as the battlefield casualties mounted and more African Americans escaped from slavery, Lincoln realized he had to act. He decided the huge human cost of the war could be justified only if the United States fought for freedom as well as for Union.

On Jan. 1, 1863, Lincoln issued the Emancipation Proclamation. The proclamation said that slaves in all areas of the Confederacy that were still in rebellion were "then, thenceforward, and forever free." It also invited African American men to join the Union Army. About 180,000 African Americans fought as Union soldiers. Finally, in 1865, the 13th Amendment to the Constitution abolished slavery throughout the United States. See **Emancipation Proclamation.**

Reconstruction. Toward the end of the Civil War, the North set out to establish terms under which Confederate states would be readmitted to the Union. The process through which the South returned, as well as the period following the war, was called Reconstruction.

Northerners divided into two groups over Reconstruction policy. One group, called the moderates, thought the most important task of Reconstruction was to end the bitterness between the North and South. The other group, called the radicals, thought the crucial task was to make emancipation a reality by protecting the rights of African Americans in the South.

Lincoln might have worked out a compromise. But an actor named John Wilkes Booth shot him on April 14, 1865. Lincoln died the next day, less than a week after Lee's surrender. Vice President Andrew Johnson became president. Johnson vetoed congressional bills that would protect the rights of Southern blacks. He also pardoned wealthy white Southern rebels and urged their return to power. These actions infuriated the moderates in Congress, who joined the radicals to override John-

Reconstruction measures passed by Congress after the Civil War included the creation of election boards to register African American voters. This scene shows blacks lined up to register in Macon, Georgia.

Forging the Shaft: A Welding Heat (1877), an oil painting on canvas by John Ferguson Weir;
The Metropolitan Museum of Art, New York City, Gift of Lyman G. Bloomingdale, 1901

The United States became an industrial giant during the late 1800's. The nation's factories, such as
this iron foundry, began turning out products on a much larger scale than before. Millions of rural
Americans and immigrants poured into the country's cities to work in the booming industries.

son's vetoes. Congress took charge of Reconstruction.
Johnson tried to undermine the laws Congress passed.
In 1868, the House of Representatives impeached him,
but the Senate fell short of removing him from office.
For details, see **Johnson, Andrew.**

The Reconstruction program drafted by Congress included laws to help Southern blacks make the transition
from slavery to freedom. An agency called the Freedman's Bureau distributed food, helped set up schools,
and supervised labor contracts between black workers
and white landowners. The 14th Amendment to the Constitution (1868) established the citizenship rights of African Americans. The 15th Amendment (1870) said that the
right to vote could not be denied on account of race,
color, or previous condition of servitude.

Congress stationed troops in the South. Black and
white Republicans, protected by the troops, took control of Southern state and local governments. Hundreds
of African Americans won election to office, where they
passed laws to expand school systems and protect civil
rights. White Southerners loyal to their old traditions bitterly resented the new political system. Many of them
joined the Ku Klux Klan, a secret society that used violence to keep blacks from voting and trying to achieve
equality. Klan terrorism helped drive blacks out of
Southern political life, thus bringing white Southerners
back to power. See **Ku Klux Klan.**

Congress insisted that the Confederate states ratify
the 13th, 14th, and 15th amendments to the Constitution
before being readmitted to the Union. Between 1866
and 1870, the Confederate states returned. But Reconstruction did not end formally until 1877, when the last
federal troops left the South.

Reconstruction was a period of great hope for African
Americans. They made progress toward equality and a
better life. But the old social order, based on white supremacy, returned to the South. African Americans lost
many of the rights they had gained. They were no longer
slaves, but persecution and terrorism forced them to
live in fear and poverty. The fundamental problem of
racial inequality remained to haunt future generations of
Americans. See **Reconstruction.**

Industrialization and reform (1870-1916)

After the Civil War, U.S. industry changed dramatically. Machines replaced hand labor as the main means of
manufacturing, tremendously increasing the production
capacity of industry. A new nationwide network of railroads distributed goods far and wide. Inventors developed new products the public wanted, and businesses
made them in large quantities. Investors and bankers
supplied the huge sums of money that industrial leaders
needed to expand their operations. Many big businesses grew up. They included coal mining, petroleum, and

railroad companies; and manufacturers and sellers of such products as automobiles, clothing, and steel.

The industrial growth had major effects on American life. The new business activity centered in cities, and so people moved to urban areas in record numbers. Many Americans amassed huge fortunes from the business boom, but others lived in poverty. The sharp contrast between rich and poor stirred widespread discontent. The discontent led to new reform movements, which, among other things, led to measures to aid the poor and control the size and power of big business.

The value of goods produced by U.S. industry increased almost tenfold between 1870 and 1916. Rich and varied natural resources aided the business boom. Forests provided lumber for construction and wood products. Miners took large quantities of coal and iron ore from the ground. Andrew Carnegie and other business leaders made steel from these minerals. Steel played a vital role in the industrialization process, going into machines, railroad tracks, bridges, automobiles, and skyscrapers. Other valuable minerals included copper, silver, and petroleum. Petroleum, the source of gasoline, became especially important after cars came into widespread use in the early 1900's.

Improved production methods. The use of machines in manufacturing spread throughout U.S. industry after the Civil War. With machines, workers could produce goods many times faster than they could by hand. The new large manufacturing firms hired hundreds, even thousands, of workers. Each worker was assigned a specific job in the production process. This system of organizing laborers, called the *division of labor,* sped up production. The increased production speed enabled businesses to charge lower prices for products. Lower prices, in turn, meant more people could afford the products, and so sales soared.

New products. Inventors created, and business leaders produced and sold, a variety of innovative products. In 1876, the Scottish-born inventor Alexander Graham Bell patented the telephone. Bell's invention, along with the telegraph, provided the quick communication that was vital to the smooth operation of big business. Other new products included the typewriter (1867), barbed wire (1874), the phonograph (1877), the electric light (1879), and the gasoline automobile (1885). Of these, the automobile had the greatest impact on the U.S. economy. In the early 1900's, the automotive pioneers Ransom Eli Olds and Henry Ford began turning out cars by mass production. Auto prices dropped, and sales soared. The number of automobiles owned by Americans jumped from 8,000 in 1900 to almost 3,500,000 in 1916.

A growing population. More than 25 million immigrants entered the United States between 1870 and 1916. Immigration plus natural growth caused the U.S. population to more than double during that period, rising from about 40 million to about 100 million. Population growth increased the number of consumers, and thus enlarged the market for products. It also provided the additional workers needed for the jobs created by the business boom.

Railroads. In the late 1800's, the U.S. railroad system became a nationwide transportation network. The distance of all rail lines in operation in the United States soared from about 9,000 miles (14,500 kilometers) in 1850 to almost 200,000 miles (320,000 kilometers) in 1900. A high point in rail development came in 1869, when workers laid tracks that joined the Central Pacific and Union Pacific railroads near Ogden, Utah. This event marked the completion of the world's first transcontinental railroad system. Rails linked the United States from coast to coast.

The new railroads spurred economic growth. Mining companies used them to ship raw materials to factories. Manufacturers distributed their finished products by rail to points throughout the country. The railroads became highly profitable for their owners, including Cornelius Vanderbilt and Jay Gould.

Improved sales methods also aided economic growth. Owners of big businesses sent salespeople to all parts of the country to promote their products, and

Farmers flocked to the Great Plains during the late 1800's. The Kansas farm family shown here built their house from sod. The Plains had few trees, and so lumber for building was scarce.

The world's first transcontinental rail line was completed in 1869, when lines of the Union Pacific and Central Pacific railroads met at Promontory, Utah, *shown here*. The railroads helped open the American West to settlers.

Union Pacific Railroad

company sales staffs began marketing brand-named goods. Enterprising merchants opened huge department stores in the growing cities. They included Marshall Field of Chicago, R. H. Macy of New York, and John Wanamaker of Philadelphia. The stores offered a wide variety of products at reasonable prices. Department stores also introduced set prices for goods, marking the price on the item instead of expecting customers to bargain over every sale.

Other merchants, including Montgomery Ward and Richard Sears, began mail-order companies, chiefly to serve people who lived far from stores. The companies published catalogs from which customers could order goods by mail.

Investment and banking. The business boom triggered a sharp increase in investments in the stocks and bonds of corporations. As businesses prospered, people eager to share in the profits invested heavily. Their investments provided capital that companies needed to expand their operations.

New banks sprang up throughout the country. Banks helped finance the nation's economic growth by making loans to businesses. J. P. Morgan and other bankers of the era assumed key positions in the economy because of their ability to provide huge sums of capital.

The rise of "trusts." The government did little to regulate business during the 1800's. Unrestricted, business leaders tried to wipe out competition and gain control of their industries by forming various kinds of combinations. In many industries, companies consolidated so that a few large firms dominated the industry. Many of these large firms gained *monopolies*—that is, nearly exclusive control over a product or service. Some business leaders formed *trusts*. A trust was a combination in which a group of managers controlled rival businesses without formal ownership of the businesses. Other business leaders formed *holding companies,* corporations that bought out and operated several businesses as a single firm. In the 1890's and early 1900's, Americans

Facts in brief (1870-1916)

Presidents (with political parties and dates of service)
Ulysses S. Grant, Republican, 1869-1877
Rutherford B. Hayes, Republican, 1877-1881
James A. Garfield, Republican, 1881
Chester A. Arthur, Republican, 1881-1885
Grover Cleveland, Democrat, 1885-1889
Benjamin Harrison, Republican, 1889-1893
Grover Cleveland, Democrat, 1893-1897
William McKinley, Republican, 1897-1901
Theodore Roosevelt, Republican, 1901-1909
William H. Taft, Republican, 1909-1913
Woodrow Wilson, Democrat, 1913-1921

States in the Union
Number at start of period: 37
Number at end of period: 48
States added during the period: Colorado (1876), North Dakota (1889), South Dakota (1889), Montana (1889), Washington (1889), Idaho (1890), Wyoming (1890), Utah (1896), Oklahoma (1907), New Mexico (1912), Arizona (1912).

Important dates
1876	Alexander Graham Bell patented the telephone.
1877	Thomas Edison invented the phonograph.
1879	Edison developed the first practical incandescent lamp.
1884	The world's first skyscraper was begun in Chicago.
1886	The American Federation of Labor was founded.
1898	The United States defeated Spain in the Spanish-American War.
1903	The Wright brothers made the first successful airplane flight at Kitty Hawk, North Carolina.
1913	The 16th Amendment gave the federal government the power to levy an income tax.
1914	World War I, originally called the Great War, began in Europe.

Population growth and change

Total population, 39,818,449
1870   Rural, 74%   Urban, 26%

Total population, 99,871,604
1916   Rural, 51%   Urban, 49%

Immigrants streamed into the nation by the millions in the late 1800's and early 1900's. A shipload of newcomers from Europe is shown here.

Immigration to the United States between 1870 and 1916

Over 25 million immigrants came to the United States from 1870 to 1916. The largest group came from southern and eastern Europe. Before the late 1800's, nearly all immigrants had come from northern and western Europe.

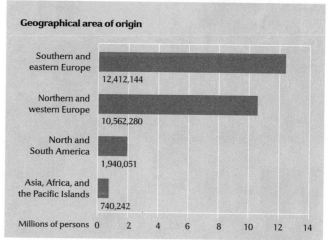

Geographical area of origin

Area	Persons
Southern and eastern Europe	12,412,144
Northern and western Europe	10,562,280
North and South America	1,940,051
Asia, Africa, and the Pacific Islands	740,242

Millions of persons 0 2 4 6 8 10 12 14

Source: U.S. Census Bureau.

often used the term "trust" to refer to all these kinds of large business combinations (see **Antitrust laws; Monopoly and competition**).

The trusts had some favorable effects on the economy. They helped make possible giant, efficient corporations that contributed greatly to economic growth. They also enabled businesses to avoid sharp fluctuations in price and output, and thus keep sales steady. On the other hand, monopolies gave some companies so much power that they could take unfair advantage of others. A company with little or no competition could demand materials from suppliers at low cost, while charging high prices for the finished product. The company could also save money by reducing a product's quality.

The rich and the poor. After the Civil War, most industry developed in the cities of the North. The industrial boom had major effects on the lives of the American people. The availability of jobs in industries drew people from farms to cities in record numbers. In 1870, only about 25 percent of the American people lived in urban areas (defined as communities with populations over 2,500 people). By 1916, the figure had reached almost 50 percent.

The lives of people in the cities contrasted sharply. A small percentage of them had wealth and enjoyed lives of luxury. Below them economically, a large middle class lived comfortably. At the bottom of the economic ladder, a huge mass of city people suffered in poverty.

The business boom opened up many opportunities. Many people established successful businesses, expanded existing ones, and profited from investments. Some business leaders and investors amassed huge fortunes. Among the millionaires were a small number who accumulated fortunes of more than $100 million each. They included Andrew Carnegie, Marshall Field, J. P. Morgan, John D. Rockefeller, and Cornelius Vanderbilt. The wealthy Americans built enormous mansions,

wore the finest clothing, ate in the best restaurants, and could afford to buy almost anything they desired. In the 1930's, during the troubled times of the Great Depression, the American historian Matthew Josephson looked back at this period and applied the disapproving term *robber barons* to Carnegie and the others.

Other city people prospered enough to live lives of comfort, if not wealth. They included owners of small businesses, and such workers as factory and office managers. They became part of the growing middle class.

The laborers who toiled in factories, mills, and mines earned only a small share of the benefits of economic growth. They usually worked about 50 hours a week for an average pay of about 20 cents an hour, and had no fringe benefits, such as paid holidays or vacations. They also had little or no job security. In slack times, unemployment was common, and the nation made almost no provision for laid-off workers.

Depressions slowed the nation's economy to a near standstill in 1873, 1884, 1893, and 1907. Unemployment soared during these depressions. Workers suffered through the periods of idleness without the unemployment benefits that are available today. Such economic hardship meant that, in many cases, every family member except young children had to seek a job.

The everyday life of the city poor was dismal and drab. They lived crowded together in slums. Much of their housing consisted of cheap apartment buildings called *tenements*. The crowded slum neighborhoods bred crime. Overwork, poor sanitation, and inadequate diet left slumdwellers vulnerable to disease. Many poor children received little or no education because they had to work to contribute to their families' support.

Despite harsh living conditions, hope made the lives of many of the poor tolerable. They knew that advancement was possible in the United States. Some families, through hard work and saving, started small businesses.

Jacob A. Riis photo; Museum of the City
of New York, Jacob A. Riis Collection

The Antique Shop, an oil painting on canvas by Louis Charles Moeller;
Collection of Mr. and Mrs. George J. Arden

The lives of the poor and the rich contrasted sharply during the industrial period. Poor city people, *left,* lived in a crowded tenement and could barely afford the necessities of life. But the wealthy, such as the well-dressed antique shoppers at the right, enjoyed lives of luxury.

Even if some workers themselves could not advance economically, they believed that their children would.

The Gilded Age. The American author Mark Twain called the era of industrialization "The Gilded Age." Twain used this term to describe the culture of the newly rich of the period. Lacking tradition, the wealthy developed a showy culture supposedly based on the customs of upper-class Europeans. The enormous mansions of the newly rich Americans imitated European palaces. The wealthy filled the mansions with European artworks, antiques, rare books, and lavish decorations. They spent their leisure time attending operas, relaxing at luxurious resorts, or engaging in other activities they believed were signs of refinement.

Most Americans, however, preferred different amusements. They enjoyed fairs that exhibited industrial machines, the latest inventions, and other evidence of material progress. The fairs included the Philadelphia Centennial Exposition of 1876, celebrating the 100th anniversary of the founding of the United States, and the Chicago World's Columbian Exposition of 1893. People eagerly attended circuses; *vaudeville* (shows consisting of songs, dances, comic skits, and other acts); and sporting events. Baseball became so popular after 1900 that it was called the national pastime. Also after 1900, a new kind of entertainment, the motion picture, began attracting audiences. Many Americans of the era enjoyed playing popular songs from sheet music on parlor pianos, or, after 1877, from records on phonographs. Readers liked illustrated magazines and *dime novels*, inexpensive books that emphasized adventure and the value of hard work and courage.

The South and white supremacy. After the Civil War, Americans in the South faced the task of rebuild-

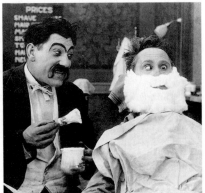

Corning-Painted Post Historical Soc., Corning, NY

Sy Seidman (WORLD BOOK photo)

Culver

Popular entertainment of the late 1800's and early 1900's included circuses, dime novels, and—after 1900—motion pictures. A circus parade through a small town, *left,* was an exciting event. A dime novel, *center,* taught the value of courage. Many movies featured slapstick comedy, *right.*

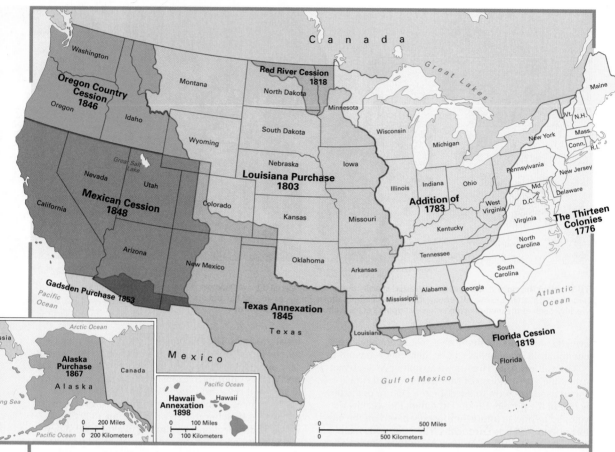

Major territorial acquisitions of the United States

The United States added territory in a number of ways. It bought vast areas, gained others by treaty, and won much land through war. Following are brief descriptions of the major territorial acquisitions of the United States from 1776 to 1898.

The Thirteen Colonies occupied what became the original area of the United States. The 13 original states and parts of Maine, Vermont, and West Virginia were formed from this area.

The Addition of 1783 extended the nation's boundaries north to the Great Lakes, south to the 31st parallel, and west to the Mississippi River. All or most of nine states were formed from this region, which more than doubled the territory of the United States.

The Louisiana Purchase of 1803 added 827,987 square miles (2,144,476 square kilometers) of land to the United States. The federal government paid France about $15 million for the territory. Part or all of 15 states were formed from the area.

The Red River Cession was included in a treaty between the United States and the United Kingdom in 1818. Parts of Minnesota, North Dakota, and South Dakota were formed from this area. The treaty also made the 49th parallel the northern boundary of the United States between the Lake of the Woods and the highland in the Rocky Mountains called the Continental Divide.

The Florida Cession of 1819 gave the United States the areas then called East Florida and West Florida. Parts of Louisiana, Mississippi, and Alabama were formed from this territory, which was ceded by Spain.

The Texas Annexation of 1845 added what was then the nation's largest state. Most of the present boundaries of Texas were established in 1850.

The Oregon Country Cession extended the western border of the United States to the Pacific Ocean in 1846. This cession also established the 49th parallel as the nation's northern boundary in the area west of the Continental Divide. Idaho, Washington, and Oregon were formed from the Oregon region.

The Mexican Cession of 1848 added more than 525,000 square miles (1,360,000 square kilometers) of land to the United States. The government paid Mexico $15 million for a region that became the states of California, Nevada, and Utah. Parts of four other states were also formed from this region.

The Gadsden Purchase of 1853 gave the United States 29,640 square miles (76,770 square kilometers) of land in what is now Arizona and New Mexico. The United States paid Mexico $10 million for the land.

The Alaska Purchase of 1867 added 586,000 square miles (1,518,000 square kilometers) of territory to the country. The government paid Russia $7,200,000 for this region.

The Hawaii Annexation of 1898 gave the United States its largest present overseas possession. The Hawaiian Islands cover 6,459 square miles (16,729 square kilometers).

ing their war-torn society. The South lagged behind the rest of the nation economically. Some industry developed in the region, but the South remained an agricultural area throughout the period of industrialization.

White Southerners tried to preserve as much of the old plantation labor system as they could. They wanted to employ newly freed blacks on their farms, paying wages but controlling the land and overseeing black laborers. The freedmen, however, insisted on control of their own labor and the opportunity to work the land by themselves. The struggle resulted in the emergence of *tenant farming,* also called *sharecropping,* an arrangement in which laborers farmed the land and paid rent in money or crops to the owner.

In the 1880's and 1890's, white Southerners controlled blacks through a series of restrictive laws. They excluded blacks from white-owned hotels and restaurants and confined them to separate libraries, hospitals, and schools. Most facilities for blacks got little funding and were inferior to those for whites. The Supreme Court of the United States upheld this racial segregation, ruling in *Plessy v. Ferguson* (1896) that the 14th Amendment did not protect the "social equality" of the races.

Beginning in 1890, all former Confederate states amended their constitutions or used other legal means to restrict black citizens' right to vote. Through a series of poll taxes and other requirements for voting, white supremacists substantially barred black Southerners from political participation. In Alabama, for example, black voter registration dropped from 100,000 in 1900 to only 3,800 in 1910.

The end of the Western frontier. The long process of settling the United States from coast to coast drew to a close after the Civil War. In 1862, Congress passed the Homestead Act, which offered public land free or at low cost to anyone who would live on it and improve it. Thousands of Americans and immigrants acquired farms in the West under the act. They settled chiefly on the Great Plains, which, contrary to earlier beliefs, included much excellent farmland. Miners flocked to the West as the demand for minerals soared. Towns sprang up near the mines. Cattle ranching spread throughout the Southwest.

After 1870, settlement became so widespread in the West that it was no longer possible to draw a continuous frontier line. The U.S. Census of 1890 officially recognized the fact that America's frontier had closed. See **Westward movement in America** (Settling the Great Plains); **Western frontier life in America.**

The settlement of the West brought an end to the American Indian way of life. Farmers occupied and fenced in much of the land. As white people moved westward, they slaughtered buffalo herds on which Indians depended for survival. Some Indians retaliated against the whites by attacking wagon trains and homes. But as in earlier days, the federal government sent soldiers to crush the Indian uprisings. In the end, the Indians were no match for the soldiers and their superior weapons. Through the years, the federal government pushed more and more Indians onto reservations. Reservation Indians suffered from poverty and illness, and could not adjust to the new way of life forced upon them. By 1900, the separate Indian way of life had become a thing of the past. For more details, see **Indian,**

American (The destruction of Indian America); **Indian reservation; Indian Territory; Indian wars.**

Government and the people. After the Civil War, the Democratic and Republican parties developed strong political organizations called *machines,* which did favors for people in return for votes. But in general, political leaders strongly supported business interests. They did little to interfere with business or to close the gap between the rich and the poor.

From the mid-1860's through the 1880's, government corruption was widespread. Ulysses S. Grant became president in 1869 and held office until 1877. Members of Grant's administration used their government positions for their own financial gain. Corruption also flourished in state and local government.

The Spanish-American War of 1898 marked a turning point in U.S. foreign policy. Spain ruled Cuba, Puerto Rico, the Philippines, and other overseas possessions. In the mid-1890's, Cubans revolted against their Spanish rulers. Many Americans demanded that the United States aid the rebels. On Feb. 15, 1898, the U.S. battleship *Maine* blew up off Havana, Cuba. No one was certain what caused the explosion, but many Americans blamed the Spaniards. Demands for action against Spain grew. "Remember the *Maine*" became a nationwide war cry.

On April 25, 1898, at the request of President William McKinley, Congress declared war on Spain. The United States quickly defeated Spain, and the Treaty of Paris of Dec. 10, 1898, officially ended the war. Under the treaty, the United States received Guam, Puerto Rico, and the Philippines from Spain. Also in 1898, the United States annexed Hawaii at the urging of sugar cane planters there. See **Spanish-American War; Hawaii** (History).

A strong spirit of reform swept through the United States during the late 1800's and early 1900's. Many Americans called for changes in the country's economic, political, and social systems. They wanted to reduce poverty, improve the living conditions of the poor, and regulate big business. They worked to end corruption in government, make government more responsive to the people, and accomplish other goals.

During the 1870's and 1880's, the reformers made relatively little progress. But after 1890, they gained much public support and influence in government. By 1917, the reformers had brought about many changes. Some reformers called themselves *progressives.* As a result, the period of U.S. history from about 1900 to about 1917 is often called the Progressive Era.

Early reform efforts included movements to organize laborers and farmers. In 1886, skilled laborers formed the American Federation of Labor (AFL), now the American Federation of Labor-Congress of Industrial Organizations (AFL-CIO). Led by Samuel Gompers, a cigar maker, this union bargained with employers and gained better wages and working conditions for its members. Farmers founded the National Grange in 1867 and Farmers' Alliances during the 1870's and 1880's. These groups helped force railroads to lower their charges for hauling farm products and aided farmers in other ways. In 1892, farmers and laborers formed the People's, or Populist, Party. The Populists called for government action to help farmers and laborers. They gained a large following, and persuaded many Democrats and Republicans to support reforms. See **Populism.**

Detail of *Battle of Manila Bay, May 1, 1898,* a lithograph by an unknown Japanese artist; Chicago History Museum

Victory in the Spanish-American War of 1898 set the United States on the road toward becoming a world power. The war lasted less than a year. In the Battle of Manila Bay, *shown here,* American ships commanded by Commodore George Dewey destroyed a Spanish fleet in the Philippines.

Unskilled laborers had less success in organizing than did skilled laborers and farmers. The Knights of Labor, a union open to both unskilled and skilled workers, gained a large membership during the 1880's. But its membership declined sharply after the Haymarket Riot of 1886. In this incident, someone threw a bomb during a meeting of workers in Haymarket Square in Chicago, and a riot erupted. At least seven police officers and one civilian died. Many Americans blamed the deaths on the labor movement.

Increasingly, unskilled workers resorted to strikes in an attempt to gain concessions from their employers. Often, violence broke out between strikers and strikebreakers hired by the employers. Socialists and others who opposed the U.S. economic system of capitalism supported the strikers and gained a large following.

The drive for woman suffrage strengthened after the Civil War. In 1869, the suffrage leaders Susan B. Anthony and Elizabeth Cady Stanton founded the National Woman Suffrage Association. The Territory of Wyoming gave women the vote the same year. Soon, a few states allowed women to vote, but only in local elections.

Government and business reforms. Reformers brought about some changes in government and introduced at least some public supervision of private business. In 1883, their efforts led to passage of the Pendleton, or Civil Service, Act. This federal law established the Civil Service Commission, an agency charged with granting some federal government jobs on the basis of merit, rather than as political favors. The commission was the first federal government regulatory agency in the nation's history.

In 1887, Congress passed the Interstate Commerce Act. The act created the Interstate Commerce Commission to eliminate unfair business practices and ensure "reasonable and just" shipping rates for interstate railroads. Three years later, the Sherman Antitrust Act prohibited business combinations that resulted in "restraint of trade." Despite the far-reaching language of these laws, the federal government seldom enforced them. In practice, it did little to regulate business before 1900.

The Progressive Era. The outcry for reform increased sharply after 1890. Members of the clergy, social workers, and others studied life in the slums and reported on the miserable living conditions there. Educators criticized the nation's school system. Concerned citizens, led by such educated middle-class women as Jane Addams and Florence Kelly, established facilities called *settlement houses* in poor neighborhoods. They tried to improve the living conditions of immigrant working-class people. A group of journalists, called *muckrakers* by their critics, wrote about such evils as corruption in government and how some businesses cheated the public. The writers included Ray Stannard Baker, Lincoln Steffens, and Ida M. Tarbell.

Many middle-class and some upper-class Americans backed reforms. The people wondered about the justice of a society that tolerated such extremes of poverty and wealth. More and more, the power of big business, corruption in government, violent strikes, and inroads by socialism seemed to threaten the American way of life.

Reformers won control of many city and some state governments. They also elected many people to Congress who favored their views. In addition, the first three presidents elected after 1900—Theodore Roosevelt, William Howard Taft, and Woodrow Wilson—supported certain reform laws. These political developments resulted in a flood of reform legislation on the local, state, and federal levels.

Goals of progressivism. Progressivism embraced many different causes and was backed by a varied and shifting group of supporters. Nonetheless, Progressives shared certain goals. Progressivism was a reform movement and did not seek revolutionary change. Instead, it sought peaceful reforms to existing institutions and improvement of social problems.

Progressivism also remained basically a political movement. Reformers believed in using government power to promote the general welfare but called for fundamental changes in how government exercised its power. Such governmental changes took many forms. On the national level, the executive branch of government expanded through the creation of independent regulatory commissions and such new agencies as the Department of Labor and the Forest Service. On the state level, three measures increased the power of voters: (1) the *initiative,* which gave voters the right to introduce new laws; (2) the *referendum,* under which laws could be submitted to a direct vote of the people; and (3) the *recall,* which enabled voters to remove public officials from office. On the local level, campaigns for efficiency and honesty led to creation of the city manager and commission forms of urban government and other efforts to reduce the power of the political machines.

Theodore Roosevelt became president in 1901. Roosevelt was a liberal Republican who called for a "square deal" for all Americans. He won fame as a "trust buster." He did not oppose monopolies altogether, but he believed they should be regulated whenever they operated against the public interest. During Roosevelt's presidency, the federal government brought lawsuits against more than 40 companies. The most famous suit, filed in 1906, broke up John D. Rockefeller's Standard Oil Company in 1911.

Roosevelt became the first president to aid laborers in a strike against employers. In 1902, the United Mine Workers struck for better wages and working conditions. Roosevelt asked the miners and the mine owners to settle their differences through arbitration, but the mine owners refused. Angered, the president threatened to have the Army take over the mines. The owners gave in and reached a compromise with the miners.

In 1906, Upton Sinclair wrote *The Jungle,* a novel about unsanitary conditions in meat packing. Roosevelt ordered an investigation of Sinclair's charges and found they were true. At Roosevelt's urging, Congress passed the Meat Inspection Act and the federal Food and Drugs Act to regulate food and drug processing.

Roosevelt expressed his foreign policy strategy with the slogan, "Speak Softly and Carry a Big Stick." He meant that the country must back up its diplomatic efforts with military strength. The United States built up its armed forces under Roosevelt. In 1902, Germany, Italy, and the United Kingdom blockaded Venezuela in an attempt to collect debts from that South American nation. Citing the Monroe Doctrine, Roosevelt forced the Europeans to withdraw. In 1903, the president used a threat of force to gain the right to dig the Panama Canal.

Taft and Wilson. Republican William Howard Taft succeeded Roosevelt in 1909. Although a conservative, Taft helped further the cause of reform. He brought twice as many suits against businesses as Roosevelt did. He also extended the civil service and called for a federal income tax.

In 1912, conservative Republicans backed Taft for their party's presidential nomination, and liberal Republicans supported Roosevelt. Taft won the nomination. The liberals then formed the Progressive, or "Bull Moose," Party and nominated Roosevelt for president. The Republican split enabled Woodrow Wilson, a Dem-

Library of Congress

The Progressive Era was marked by widespread demands for reform. Public demonstrations were common tactics among reformers of the era. Women on horseback participated in a suffrage parade in Washington, D.C., in 1914, *shown here.* Women gained the right to vote in 1920.

World War I marked the first time the United States had fought a full-scale war on foreign territory. In 1917 and 1918, troopships carried about 2 million American fighting men across the Atlantic to Europe. Called *doughboys,* the Americans helped the Allies defeat Germany.

ocrat who favored reform, to win the presidency. The Democrats also gained control of Congress.

The reform movement flourished under Wilson. Two amendments to the Constitution proposed during Taft's administration were ratified in 1913. The 16th Amendment gave the federal government the power to levy an income tax. The 17th Amendment provided for the election of U.S. senators by the people, rather than by state legislatures. In 1913, the government set up the Federal Reserve System to supervise the nation's banking and financial service industries. One year later, Wilson signed the Federal Trade Commission (FTC) Act, creating a new government agency to oversee big business. For more details on this era of reform in the United States, see **Progressive Era.**

During the 1870's and 1880's, the United States had paid relatively little attention to foreign affairs. In comparison to such European nations as France, Germany, and the United Kingdom, the United States was weak militarily and had little influence in international politics. During the 1890's and early 1900's, however, the United States developed into a world power and took a leading role in international affairs. In 1916, during Wilson's administration, U.S. troops occupied the Dominican Republic to keep order. These and other actions showed that the United States had emerged as a world power.

World War I and postwar growth (1917-1929)

In 1914, long-standing problems among European nations led to the outbreak of World War I. In this fierce, destructive struggle, the Central Powers (Germany and a few other nations) lined up against the Allies (France, Italy, Russia, the United Kingdom, and many smaller countries). Finally, events dragged the United States into the war on the side of the Allies and tested its new role as a world power. For the first time in its history, the United States mobilized for a full-scale war on foreign territory.

The United States in the war. After World War I began in 1914, the United States repeatedly stated its neutrality. But increasingly, German acts of aggression brought the United States closer to joining the Allies. In 1915, a German submarine sank the British passenger ship *Lusitania.* The attack killed 1,201 people, including 128 American passengers. Wilson and other Americans bitterly protested this killing of defenseless civilians, and Germany agreed to stop such attacks.

Wilson won reelection as president in November 1916, using the slogan, "He Kept Us Out of War." Three months later, German submarines began sinking U.S. merchant ships. These and other acts of aggression convinced Wilson and other Americans of the need to join the war against Germany to make the world "safe for democracy." The United States declared war on Germany on April 6, 1917.

The American people rallied around their government's decision to go to war. Almost 2 million men volunteered for service, and about 3 million were drafted. About 2 million U.S. fighting men crossed the Atlantic in troopships. United States troops, known as *doughboys,* fought valiantly in the trenches, forests, and fields of Belgium and France, and helped the battered Allies turn back a major German offensive.

On the home front, the spirit of patriotism grew to a fever pitch. Americans bought billions of dollars worth of Liberty Bonds to help pay the cost of the war. Fiery patriotic songs, such as George M. Cohan's "Over There" and "You're a Grand Old Flag," gave a lift to the spirits of the doughboys and the public alike. Patriotism sometimes overflowed into acts of violence against Americans of German descent and repression of radicals, pacifists, and other critics of the war.

World War I ended in an Allied victory. The two sides signed an armistice on Nov. 11, 1918. For a detailed account of the conflict, see **World War I.**

The peace treaty. In 1919, the Allies held the Paris Peace Conference to draw up the terms of the peace with Germany. Wilson viewed the conference as an opportunity to establish lasting peace among nations. He proposed a list of terms called the Fourteen Points to be used as a guide for the peace settlement. The terms included arms reductions and settlement of disputed territorial claims (see **Fourteen Points**). But the other leading Allies were chiefly interested in gaining territory and war payments from Germany. They adopted the Treaty of Versailles, which embodied many of Wilson's proposals for trade, freedom of the seas, and independence for the peoples of Central and Eastern Europe. But the treaty stripped Germany of its armed forces and much territory, and forced it to pay high war damages.

The Treaty of Versailles also made provision for Wilson's most ambitious proposal, an association of nations, later called the League of Nations, that would work to maintain peace. But Wilson suffered a final blow to his peace plans when the United States Senate failed to ratify the Treaty of Versailles. Thus, the Senate rejected U.S. participation in the League of Nations. See **League of Nations; Versailles, Treaty of; Wilson, Woodrow** (Wilson's second Administration).

The Roaring Twenties. The decade following World War I brought sweeping changes to American life. The economy entered a period of spectacular, though uneven, growth. Spurred on by the good times and a desire to be "modern," large numbers of Americans adopted new attitudes and lifestyles. The booming economy and fast-paced life of the decade gave it the nickname of the Roaring Twenties.

In many ways, the 1920's marked the point at which the United States began developing into the modern society it is today. During and after World War I, people continued to move from farms to cities in record numbers. The 1920 United States Census reported that, for the first time, a majority of Americans lived in urban areas. By the end of the Roaring Twenties, such features of modern life as the automobile, telephone, radio, and electric washing machine had become part of millions of American households.

The role of American women changed greatly in the 1920's. The 19th Amendment to the Constitution, which became law on Aug. 26, 1920, gave women the right to vote in all elections. In addition, many new opportunities for education and careers opened to women. Many women found careers outside the home and began thinking of themselves as the equal of men.

Developments of the 1920's broadened the experiences of millions of Americans. The mass movement to cities meant more people could enjoy such activities as movies, plays, and sporting events. Radio broadcasting began on a large scale during the 1920's. It brought news of the world and entertainment into millions of homes. The automobile gave people a new way to get around. In 1927, the aviation pioneer Charles A. Lindbergh helped launch the modern air age when he made the first solo flight across the Atlantic.

The new trends of the 1920's brought about problems as well as benefits. Many Americans had trouble adjusting to the impersonal, fast-paced life of cities. This led to a rise in juvenile delinquency, crime, and other antisocial behavior. City life also tended to weaken the strong family ties that had long been part of American society.

Prohibition. The 18th Amendment to the Constitution, the Prohibition amendment, caused unforeseen problems. It outlawed the sale of alcoholic beverages throughout the United States as of Jan. 16, 1920. Many otherwise law-abiding citizens considered Prohibition a

Facts in brief (1917-1929)

Presidents (with political parties and dates of service)
Woodrow Wilson, Democrat, 1913-1921
Warren G. Harding, Republican, 1921-1923
Calvin Coolidge, Republican, 1923-1929
Herbert C. Hoover, Republican, 1929-1933

States in the Union
Number at start of period: 48
States added during the period: none

Important dates

1917-1918 The United States fought in World War I.

1920 The U.S. Senate rejected American participation in the League of Nations.

1920 The U.S. Census showed that, for the first time, the majority of Americans lived in urban areas.

1920 The 18th Amendment, prohibiting the sale of alcoholic beverages nationwide, became effective; the 19th Amendment gave women complete suffrage.

1922 The government raised tariffs to the highest level ever.

1925 The Scopes Trial in Dayton, Tennessee, upheld the right of a state to ban the teaching of evolution in public schools.

c. 1925 The Golden Age of radio broadcasting began.

1927 Charles A. Lindbergh made the first solo flight across the Atlantic Ocean.

1927 *The Jazz Singer,* the first successful motion-picture "talkie," appeared.

1929 The stock market crash brought financial ruin to thousands of investors.

Population growth and change

Total population, 101,297,851

1917 Rural, 50%   Urban, 50%

Total population, 121,670,000

1929 Rural, 44%   Urban, 56%

Ford Archives, Henry Ford Museum, Dearborn, MI

Automobile ownership soared in the 1920's. During the decade, the number of automobiles in the United States nearly tripled. Cars soon crowded the streets of every U.S. city and town.

Jazzmen Photo from Ramsey Archive

A jazz band and dancers dressed in flapper costumes, *shown here,* entertained a nightclub audience. Jazz became so popular in the 1920's that the decade is sometimes called the Jazz Age.

violation of their rights. They ignored the law and bought liquor provided by underworld gangs. The supplying of illegal liquor was called *bootlegging* because smugglers sometimes hid liquor in boot legs. The profitable bootlegging business helped many gangs prosper, but competition for control of the business led to gang wars. See **Prohibition.**

The Lost Generation and Flaming Youth. A number of the nation's most prominent authors explored the discontent underlying the glamorous surface of American life. This Lost Generation of writers, many of whom went into self-imposed exile in Europe, included F. Scott Fitzgerald, whose alienated fictional characters pursued lives of empty pleasure-seeking. Another prominent author, Sinclair Lewis, won fame for novels that portrayed the "average American" as narrow-minded and dull.

In an effort to be modern, many young men and women of the Roaring Twenties adopted a lifestyle that earned them the nickname of Flaming Youth. Women began wearing new clothing styles. Short skirts, rolled-down stockings, and short "bobbed" hair replaced the full-length dresses and long hair of earlier days. Women who wore such clothes became known as *flappers.* The flappers and their escorts enjoyed such new thrills as speeding around in cars. They, along with many of their elders, visited supposedly secret nightclubs called *speakeasies.* At the speakeasies, people drank bootleg liquor; listened to jazz, the latest craze in popular music; and danced the Charleston and other modern steps.

Heroes. Americans of the Roaring Twenties developed strong admiration for individual accomplishment. Lindbergh's transatlantic flight made him a national hero. Sports superstars of the 1920's won the public's admiration for their talent. The stars included Red Grange of football, Jack Dempsey of boxing, Bobby Jones of golf, Bill Tilden and Helen Wills of tennis, and—most of all—baseball's Babe Ruth. The movies provided the public with daring fictional heroes, including good cowboys who always defeated bad Indians or outlaws.

Brown Bros.

AP/Wide World

Culver

Revival meetings attracted large numbers of people during the 1920's. At these meetings, evangelists, such as Billy Sunday, *on platform,* delivered emotional sermons.

Heroes of the 1920's included Babe Ruth and Charles A. Lindbergh. Ruth became the most famous sports star of the decade. Lindbergh made the first solo flight across the Atlantic Ocean.

Looking backward. Not all Americans saw the changes brought by the Roaring Twenties as desirable. Many people yearned for a return to old traditions, a trend reflected in many areas of life. In politics, it led to the return of a conservative federal government. In his successful presidential campaign of 1920, Warren G. Harding used the slogan "A Return to Normalcy." But, in 1923, investigators revealed widespread corruption in his administration (see **Harding, Warren G.** [Government scandals]; **Teapot Dome**). The enthusiasm for reform that marked the Progressive Era lessened after World War I. American voters elected to Congress conservatives who promised to reduce the role of government. All three presidents elected during the 1920's— Harding, Calvin Coolidge, and Herbert Hoover—were Republicans who agreed with that policy.

In religion, the trend toward tradition led to an upsurge of *revivalism* (emotional religious preaching). Revival meetings were most common in rural areas but also spread to cities. The preacher Billy Sunday drew wildly enthusiastic crowds to his revivals in big cities.

The Ku Klux Klan had died out in the 1870's, but a new Klan gained a large following during the 1920's. The new Klan had easy answers for Americans who were troubled by modern problems. It blamed the problems on "outsiders," including blacks, Jews, Roman Catholics, foreigners, and political radicals. Both Northerners and Southerners joined the Ku Klux Klan. At its height, the organization had more than 2 million members.

The fear of outsiders also led to the passage of the National Origins Act (1924), also known as the Immigration Act of 1924. The law severely restricted legal immigration to the United States and established quotas for new arrivals based on their country of origin.

The economy—boom and bust. During the 1920's, the U.S. economy soared to spectacular heights. Republicans gained control of the federal government and adopted policies that aided big business. In 1922, the government passed the Fordney-McCumber Act. The law raised tariff duties to the highest level ever to keep foreign goods from competing with American products. This and other measures did much to help American business flourish.

Technological developments contributed to economic growth. Technology enabled U.S. manufacturers to develop new products, improve existing ones, and turn out goods faster and more cheaply than ever before. Sales of such items as electric washing machines, refrigerators, and radios soared. But the manufacturing boom depended most heavily on the growth of the automobile industry. Before and during the 1920's, Henry Ford and others refined car manufacturing to a science. The cost of automobiles continued to drop, and sales soared. In just 10 years between 1920 and 1930, the number of cars registered in the United States almost tripled, from about 8 million to 23 million. The thriving auto industry triggered growth in such related industries as steel, roadbuilding, gasoline sales, and tourism.

Despite its growth and apparent strength, the economy was on shaky ground. Only one segment of the economy—manufacturing—prospered. The distribution of wealth grew lopsided. Business executives grew rich, but agriculture and labor did not share in the prosperity. A shrunken market for farm goods in war-torn Europe

and a slowdown in U.S. population growth reduced demand for farm products. As a result, farmers became worse off than before the war. Labor unions suffered major setbacks during the 1920's. A lack of government support reduced unions' power in dealing with employers, and workers in many new industries remained unorganized. Widespread poverty among farmers and laborers cut into the demand for manufactured goods, a contributing factor to the upcoming depression. For more details on the decade of the 1920's, see **Roaring Twenties.**

The stock market crash of 1929. The economic growth of the 1920's led more Americans than ever to invest in stocks. The investments, in turn, provided companies with a flood of new capital for business expansion. As investors poured money into the stock market, the value of stocks soared. The upsweep led to widespread speculation, pushing the value of stocks far beyond the level justified by earnings and dividends. Much speculation involved buying stocks *on margin*— that is, paying a fraction of the cost and borrowing the rest of the purchase price.

Finally, in 1929, wild speculation led to a stock market crash that toppled the economy. In late October, a decline in stock prices set in. Panic selling followed, lowering stock prices drastically and dragging investors to financial ruin. When the year ended, the government estimated that the crash had cost investors $40 billion.

The stock market crash sent shock waves through the financial community. Banks reduced their loans to businesses, and businesses then cut back on production. Millions of people lost their jobs because of the cutbacks. Spending dwindled, and businesses suffered even more. Factories and stores shut down, causing higher unemployment. Demand for farm products declined, and farmers became even worse off. Thousands of banks failed, and foreign trade decreased sharply. By the early 1930's, the nation's economy was paralyzed.

Wide World

The stock market crash of 1929 brought an abrupt end to the prosperity of the Roaring Twenties. Crowds of panic-stricken investors, *shown here,* gathered aimlessly on Wall Street following the dramatic drop in stock prices.

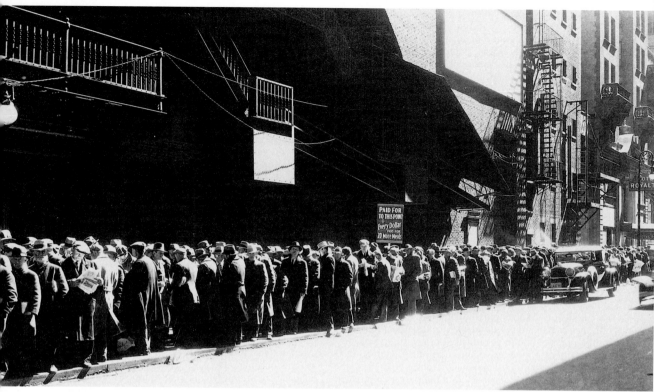

Brown Bros.

The Great Depression of the 1930's spread poverty throughout the United States. Hungry, unemployed Americans stood in long "bread lines" to receive food paid for by charitable donations. The hard times dragged on until 1942, after the United States entered World War II.

Depression and world conflict (1930-1959)

The stock market crash of 1929 combined with the other weaknesses in the nation's economy to bring on the Great Depression of the 1930's, the worst and longest depression in U.S. history. The Great Depression was not limited to the United States. It struck almost every country in the world. In some countries, the hard times helped bring to power dictators who promised to restore the economy. The dictators included Adolf Hitler in Germany and a group of military leaders in Japan. Once in power, both Hitler and the Japanese rulers began seizing neighboring lands. Their actions led to World War II, the most destructive conflict in history.

The United States in the Great Depression. The United States suffered through the Great Depression for more than 10 years. During the Depression, millions of workers lost their jobs, and large numbers of farmers were forced to abandon their farms. Poverty swept through the nation on a scale never before experienced.

Library of Congress

The Dust Bowl spread across the Great Plains and the Southwest during the 1930's, destroying much farmland. The Dust Bowl developed when windstorms carried away the topsoil after a long drought.

At the height of the Depression in 1933, about 13 million Americans were out of work, and many others had only part-time jobs. Farm income declined so sharply that more than 750,000 farmers lost their land. The Dust Bowl, the result of a terrible drought on the western Great Plains, wiped out many farmers (see **Dust Bowl**). Hundreds of thousands of people lost their life savings as a result of bank failures.

Throughout the Depression, many Americans went hungry. People stood in "bread lines" and went to "soup kitchens" to get food provided by charities. Often, two or more families lived crowded together in a small apartment. Some homeless people built shacks of tin and scraps of wood in vacant areas. They called these clumps of shacks Hoovervilles, a scornful reference to Herbert Hoover, president when the Depression struck.

Recovery and reform. Early in the Great Depression, Hoover promised that prosperity was "just around the corner." But the Depression deepened as the election of 1932 approached. The Republicans slated Hoover for re-election. The Democrats chose Franklin D. Roosevelt. In his campaign, Roosevelt promised government action to end the Great Depression and reforms to avoid future depressions. He won a landslide victory.

Roosevelt's program for recovery was called the New Deal. Its many provisions included public works projects to provide jobs, relief for farmers, aid to manufacturing firms, and regulation of banks. A solidly Democratic Congress approved almost every measure Roosevelt proposed. Many new government agencies were set up to help fight the Depression. They included the Civilian Conservation Corps and the Works Progress Administration (later the Work Projects Administration), both of which provided jobs; the Farm Credit Administration, which extended credit to farmers; and the Social Security Board, which developed the Social Security system of payments to retired workers and workers with disabilities.

The New Deal offered direct aid to the American people. It provided *subsidies* (payments) for farmers, tuition grants for needy students, public works jobs for the unemployed, pensions for the elderly, electric power for rural homes, and food for the desperate and hungry.

Roosevelt's efforts to end the Depression made him one of the most popular U.S. presidents. The voters elected him to four terms. No other president had ever won election more than twice, and, in 1951, the 22nd Amendment to the Constitution provided that no one could be elected to the presidency more than twice.

The New Deal helped relieve the hardship of many Americans. However, hard times dragged on until World War II military spending stimulated the economy. See **Great Depression; New Deal.**

World War II began on Sept. 1, 1939, when German troops overran Poland. The United Kingdom, France, and other countries (called the Allies) went to war against Germany. At first, the United States stayed out of the war. But on Dec. 7, 1941, Japanese planes bombed the U.S. military base at Pearl Harbor, Hawaii. The United States declared war on Japan on December 8. Three days later Germany and Italy, Germany's chief ally, declared war on the United States.

The American people backed the war effort with fierce dedication. About 15 million American men

served in the armed forces. They ranged from teen-agers to men well over 40. About 338,000 women served in the armed forces. At home, automobile plants and other factories were converted into defense plants where airplanes, ships, weapons, and war supplies were made. The country had a shortage of civilian men, and so thousands of women worked in the defense plants. "Rosie the Riveter," described in a popular song as "making history working for victory," became the symbol of women workers. Even children took part in the war effort. Boys and girls collected used tin cans, old tires, and other "junk" that could be recycled and used for war supplies.

On May 7, 1945, after a long, bitter struggle, the Americans and other Allies forced the mighty German empire to surrender. Vice President Harry S. Truman had become president after Roosevelt's death about a month earlier. The Allies demanded Japan's surrender, but Japan continued to fight. Truman then made one of the major decisions in history. He ordered the use of the atomic bomb, a weapon many times more destructive than any previous weapon. An American plane dropped

Facts in brief (1930-1959)

Presidents (with political parties and dates of service)
Herbert C. Hoover, Republican, 1929-1933
Franklin D. Roosevelt, Democrat, 1933-1945
Harry S. Truman, Democrat, 1945-1953
Dwight D. Eisenhower, Republican, 1953-1961

States in the Union
Number at start of period: 48
Number at end of period: 50
States added during the period:
Alaska (1959), Hawaii (1959).

Important dates

1930's The United States suffered through the Great Depression.

1933 President Franklin D. Roosevelt began the New Deal program to try to end the Depression.

1941-1945 The United States fought in World War II.

1945 An American airplane dropped the first atomic bomb used in warfare on Hiroshima, Japan.

1945 The United States became a charter member of the United Nations (UN).

1947 President Truman announced the Truman Doctrine, which pledged American aid to nations threatened by Communism.

1950's Television became part of most American homes.

1950 Senator Joseph R. McCarthy gained national fame by charging that Communists had infiltrated the federal government.

1950-1953 The United States fought in the Korean War.

1954 The Supreme Court of the United States ruled compulsory segregation in public schools unconstitutional.

1955 Martin Luther King, Jr., began organizing a movement to protest discrimination against blacks.

1957 The Soviet Union launched Sputnik 1—the first space satellite—causing the United States to place more emphasis on space research.

Population growth and change

Total population, 122,755,046

| 1930 | Rural, 44% | Urban, 56% |

Total population, 175,608,490

| 1959 | Rural, 31% | Urban, 69% |

Defense workers during World War II included many women. The women filled jobs vacated by men who entered the armed forces. The workers helped produce planes, ships, and weapons.

AP/Wide World

© Getty Images

An atomic blast fills the sky over Nagasaki. The United States dropped the first atomic bombs used in warfare on the Japanese cities of Hiroshima and Nagasaki in 1945, during World War II.

the first atomic bomb used in warfare on Hiroshima, Japan, on Aug. 6, 1945. A second atomic bomb was dropped on Nagasaki on August 9. Japan formally surrendered on September 2, and the war ended. For more details, see **World War II.**

Postwar prosperity. After World War II, the United States entered the greatest period of economic growth in its history. Periods of *inflation* (rapidly rising prices) and *recession* (business slumps) occurred. But overall, businesses and people prospered. Prosperity spread to more Americans than ever before, resulting in major changes in American life. However, not all people shared in the prosperity. Millions of Americans, including a high percentage of the nation's blacks, lived in poverty. The persistence of poverty amid prosperity brought on a period of active social protest and sparked an ambitious and controversial series of reforms.

Military spending during World War II drew the United States out of the Great Depression. Major industries, such as automobile manufacturing and housing construction, had all but stopped during the war. After the war, these industries resumed production on a much larger scale than ever. Such relatively new industries as electronics, plastics, frozen foods, and jet aircraft became booming businesses.

The shortage of goods during the war and other factors combined to create a vast market for American products. A population boom increased the number of consumers. Between 1950 and 1960 alone, the population of the United States grew by about 28 million. Labor unions became stronger than ever, and they gained high wages and other benefits for their members. Minimum wage laws and other government regulations also helped give workers a greater share of the profits of business. These developments also meant that more Americans had more money to spend on goods.

Prosperity and technological advances changed American life in other ways. Television, an experimental device before the war, became a feature of most American homes during the 1950's. This wonder of modern science brought scenes of the world into American living rooms at the flick of a switch. Fascinated, large numbers of people made watching TV one of their main leisure-time activities. New appliances made household work easier. They included automatic washers, dryers, dishwashers, and garbage disposals.

Suburban growth. After the war, millions of people needed, and could afford, new housing. Construction companies built huge clusters of houses in suburbs around the nation's cities. The suburbs attracted people for many reasons. They offered newer housing, more open space, and—usually—better schools than the central cities could provide.

The growth of suburbs also deepened racial divisions. Between 1950 and 1970, about 7 million white Americans left central cities for overwhelmingly white suburban communities. In the same period, almost 3 million blacks moved from the South to northern cities.

A rise in automobile ownership accompanied the suburban growth. The majority of suburbanites worked in the central cities and depended on cars to get to and from work. Most suburbs lacked good local transportation systems, and so families relied on cars to go shopping or almost anywhere else. By 1960, over three-fourths of all American families owned a car, and almost a fifth owned more than one. Increased automobile traffic led to the building of a nationwide network of superhighways. Increased car ownership and greater prosperity enabled more people than ever to take vacation trips. New motels, fast-service restaurants, and gas stations sprang up to serve the tourists.

Poverty and discrimination. Despite the general prosperity, millions of Americans still lived in poverty.

The poor included members of all ethnic groups, but the plight of the nation's poor blacks seemed especially bleak. Ever since emancipation, blacks in both the North and South had faced discrimination in jobs, housing, education, and other areas. A lack of education and jobs made poverty among blacks widespread.

During the early 1900's, blacks, joined by many whites, had begun a movement to extend civil rights to blacks. The movement gained momentum after World War II. Efforts of civil rights leaders resulted in several Supreme Court decisions that attacked discrimination. In the best-known case, *Brown v. Board of Education of Topeka* (1954), the court ruled compulsory segregation in public schools illegal.

Despite the gains, many civil rights leaders became dissatisfied with the slow progress of their movement. In the mid-1950's, black Southerners began organizing demonstrations protesting discrimination. In 1955, Martin Luther King, Jr., a young Baptist minister, led a successful bus boycott in Montgomery, Alabama. A supporter of nonviolent civil disobedience, King became a prominent leader of the emerging civil rights movement. Public protests soon became a major tool of Americans seeking change.

The Cold War. The United States and the Soviet Union both fought on the side of the Allies during World War II. But after the war, the two countries became bitter enemies. The Soviet Union, as a Communist country, opposed democracy. It helped Communists take over most of Eastern Europe and also aided Communists who seized control of China.

The Soviet Union and China then set out to spread

Cornell Capa, Magnum

Suburban housing developments sprang up around American cities after World War II. The postwar prosperity enabled millions of people to afford new houses in the suburbs.

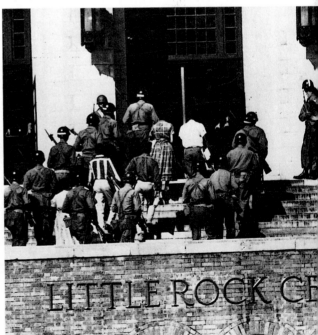

United Press Int.

A civil rights law banning compulsory school segregation led to a dramatic incident in 1957. President Eisenhower sent troops to escort black students into an all-white Arkansas school.

Communism to other lands. The United States, as the world's most powerful democratic country, took on the role of defending non-Communist nations threatened by Communist take-over. The containment of Communism became the major goal of postwar U.S. foreign policy.

The struggle between the U.S.-led non-Communist nations and the Soviet Union and its Communist allies became known as the Cold War. The conflict was so named because it did not lead to fighting, or a "hot" war, on a major scale.

Both the United States and the Soviet Union built up arsenals of nuclear weapons. The nuclear weapons made each nation capable of destroying the other, and the threat of nuclear war made both sides cautious. As a result, Cold War strategy emphasized propaganda, threats of force, and aid to weak nations. The United Nations (UN), founded in 1945, provided a forum where the nations could try to settle their Cold War disputes.

Truman and Dwight D. Eisenhower, the first two presidents of the Cold War era, pledged U.S. military support to any nation threatened by Communism. In 1949, the United States and 11 other nations established the North Atlantic Treaty Organization (NATO), a military alliance designed to discourage Soviet attack. In addition, the United States provided billions of dollars to non-Communist nations. See **Cold War.**

The Korean War resulted from the Cold War friction. On June 25, 1950, troops from Communist North Korea, equipped by the Soviet Union, invaded South Korea. The UN called on member nations to help restore peace. Truman sent U.S. troops to aid South Korea, and the UN sent a fighting force made up of troops from many nations. The war lasted three years, ending in a truce on July 27, 1953. See **Korean War.**

McCarthyism. The spread of Communism caused deep divisions within the United States. Conservatives blamed the Roosevelt and Truman administrations for allowing Communism to make its postwar gains. Sena-

tor Joseph R. McCarthy, a Wisconsin Republican, made numerous charges—usually with little evidence—that Communists had infiltrated the government, the entertainment industry, and other fields. The charges led to widespread accusations and investigations of suspected Communist activities in the United States. Conservatives believed the investigations were needed to save the country from Communist control. Liberals charged McCarthy and his followers with conducting "witch hunts"—that is, trying to fix guilt on people without evidence. See **McCarthyism.**

Protests and progress (1960-1999)

World and national events brought dramatic social changes to the United States after 1960. The space race turned the attention of Americans to new frontiers beyond their own planet. The black civil rights movement grew in intensity. Numerous other groups, including American Indians, Mexican Americans, and women, also began demanding fuller rights. Protesters of all kinds staged demonstrations seeking change. Most demonstrations were conducted peacefully, but some led to violence.

The space race. The Cold War led the United States and the Soviet Union to compete with each other in developing space programs. On April 12, 1961, the Soviet cosmonaut Yuri A. Gagarin became the first person to orbit Earth. The United States quickly matched the Soviet achievement. On May 5, 1961, astronaut Alan B. Shepard, Jr., soared into orbit from Cape Canaveral, Florida, becoming the first American in space. The United States and the Soviet Union then matched their technological skills in a race to the moon. On July 20, 1969, millions of people watched on TV as U.S. astronaut Neil A. Armstrong climbed down from his spacecraft and became the first person to set foot on the moon. The space race faded by the late 1970's, when the two countries began to pursue independent goals in space.

AP/Wide World

Civil rights for African Americans became a major issue during the 1960's. About 200,000 people, including both blacks and whites, took part in the March on Washington in 1963, *shown here.*

The civil rights movement became the main domestic issue in the nation in the early 1960's. Blacks, joined by many whites, staged demonstrations to dramatize their demands for rights and equality. One of the highlights of the movement came on Aug. 28, 1963, when more than 200,000 people took part in a civil rights march called the March on Washington in Washington, D.C.

John F. Kennedy, who became president in 1961, urged Congress to pass legislation outlawing discrimination on the basis of race. An assassin killed Kennedy on Nov. 22, 1963, and Vice President Lyndon B. Johnson became president. Johnson, a former U.S. senator skilled in dealing with legislators, persuaded Congress to pass many major civil rights laws. The Civil Rights Act of 1964 outlawed discrimination in employment, voter registration, and public accommodations. The Voting Rights Act of 1965 removed barriers to black voter registration and political participation. The Civil Rights Act of 1968 was designed to end discrimination in the sale and rental of housing. Congress, at Johnson's urging, also provided financial aid for the needy as part of a program that Johnson called the War on Poverty. For a detailed account of the black civil rights movement, see **African Americans.**

Despite government aid and a generally booming economy, poverty remained a major problem in the central cities. Discontent grew among African Americans in poor, decaying neighborhoods. In the mid-1960's, blacks rioted in the ghettos of Chicago; Cleveland, Ohio; Detroit; Los Angeles; New York City; Newark, New Jersey; and other cities. Many rioted again in 1968, following the assassination of Martin Luther King, Jr. Racial tension also erupted into riots in Miami in 1980, Los Angeles in 1992, and other cities at other times.

The drive for equality that began with African Americans spread to other minority groups. American Indians, Mexican Americans, and others organized drives for equality. In addition, large numbers of women began calling for an end to discrimination based on sex. Their activities became known as the women's rights movement. The movement helped bring about greater equality for women in employment and other areas.

Environmental and energy concerns. As the country's industry and population grew, so did the pollution of its environment. Smoke from factories and fumes from cars filled the air with dangerous gases. Wastes from factories and other sources polluted rivers and lakes. Americans began demanding government action to control environmental pollution. In response, the government passed a number of antipollution laws.

The energy crisis became another pressing problem. The nation's many industries, households, cars, and other energy users strained its limited energy supply. The energy crisis was highlighted in 1973, when an oil shortage reduced the supply of heating oil and gasoline.

The Vietnam War (1957-1975) was actually the second phase of fighting in Vietnam. The first phase had begun in 1946 as Vietnamese rebels fought for independence from France, the region's colonial ruler. The United States backed the French until they met defeat in 1954. After the French withdrew, the United States intervened even more forcefully for the non-Communist government of South Vietnam in its struggle against Communist North Vietnam and Communist rebels in the South.

In the late 1950's and early 1960's, Presidents Eisenhower and Kennedy sent military aid and advisers to support the government of South Vietnam. Soon after Johnson became president, the Communists threatened to topple the South Vietnamese government. Johnson responded by sending hundreds of thousands of U.S. combat troops to help South Vietnam fight the Communists. By the mid-1960's, the United States was deeply involved in the Vietnam War.

Public response to the Vietnam War differed from the near-unanimous support in World Wars I and II. Most Americans supported the war effort at first. But opposition to the war grew in the late 1960's. Opponents of the war argued that the United States had no right to interfere in Vietnamese affairs. Throughout the nation, college students and others demonstrated against the war.

Richard M. Nixon, who became president in 1969, planned to withdraw U.S. troops and turn the fighting over to the South Vietnamese. In the process, however, Nixon escalated the war and spread the conflict into the neighboring country of Cambodia. He did not remove the last U.S. ground forces from Vietnam until 1973. Two years later, South Vietnam fell to the Communists.

United States participation in the Vietnam War had

Facts in brief (1960-1999)

Presidents (with political parties and dates of service)
Dwight D. Eisenhower, Republican, 1953-1961
John F. Kennedy, Democrat, 1961-1963
Lyndon B. Johnson, Democrat, 1963-1969
Richard M. Nixon, Republican, 1969-1974
Gerald R. Ford, Republican, 1974-1977
Jimmy Carter, Democrat, 1977-1981
Ronald W. Reagan, Republican, 1981-1989
George H. W. Bush, Republican, 1989-1993
Bill Clinton, Democrat, 1993-2001

States in the Union

Number at start of period: 50
States added during the period: none

Important dates

1961	Astronaut Alan B. Shepard, Jr., became the first American in space.
1965	American combat troops entered the Vietnam War.
1969	Astronaut Neil A. Armstrong became the first person to set foot on the moon.
1973	The United States removed its last ground troops from Vietnam. The war ended in 1975.
1974	Richard M. Nixon became the first American president to resign from office.
1976	The United States celebrated its bicentennial.
1991	United States forces helped defeat Iraq in the Persian Gulf War of 1991.
1998-1999	The House of Representatives impeached President Bill Clinton for perjury and obstruction of justice, but the Senate found him not guilty.

Population growth and change

Total population, 179,323,175

1960 Rural, 30%   Urban, 70%

Total population, 279,040,168

1999 Rural, 21%   Urban, 79%

lasted through most of the third quarter of the 1900's. The Vietnam War was the longest war in which the United States ever took part, and the first foreign war in which the nation failed to achieve its objectives.

Political scandals in the 1970's dismayed many Americans and damaged public regard for the country's highest leaders. In 1973, Spiro T. Agnew, Nixon's vice president, came under criminal investigation. A federal grand jury began hearing charges that he had participated in graft as an officeholder in Maryland. Agnew resigned from the vice presidency on Oct. 10, 1973.

In 1972, campaign workers for President Nixon's reelection committed a burglary at the Democratic political headquarters in the Watergate building complex in Washington, D.C. Nixon was later charged with covering up the burglary and with other illegal activities. In July 1974, the Judiciary Committee of the House of Representatives adopted three articles of impeachment against the president. Evidence against Nixon mounted until it became apparent that the full House would impeach him and that the Senate would remove him from office. On Aug. 9, 1974, Nixon resigned as president. He was the only U.S. president to resign. See **Watergate.**

The hostage crisis. A revolution overthrew the government of the shah of Iran in February 1979. In November of that year, Iranian revolutionaries took over the U.S. Embassy in Tehran, Iran's capital, to protest American aid to the deposed shah. The revolutionaries held a group of U.S. diplomats as hostages and demanded that the United States return the shah to Iran for trial. The U.S. government refused to do so. The shah died in July 1980, but the revolutionaries held the hostages until January 1981. Many people thought that the United States failed to deal effectively with the crisis, particularly after an armed rescue attempt failed in April 1980.

The revival of conservatism. During the 1970's and 1980's, numerous factors led to a revival of conservatism. Many formerly Democratic voters opposed such

AP/Wide World

At the Watergate hearings, held in 1973 and 1974, former Presidential Counsel John W. Dean III testified to wrongdoing by President Richard M. Nixon. Nixon resigned in August 1974.

policies as court-ordered busing to integrate public schools; *affirmative action,* which increased opportunities for women and members of minority groups; and legalized abortion. Economic problems strengthened the appeal of lower taxes and of reduced government regulation. The hostage crisis and other setbacks in international affairs heightened fears about a decline of American power.

To convert this widespread discontent into support for their candidates and policies, conservatives organized the New Right network. Supporters of the New Right included millions of conservative Protestants called *evangelical Christians,* who previously had been disorganized and largely nonpolitical.

With the support of the New Right, Ronald Reagan won the presidency in 1980. Reagan, a conservative Republican, promised to scale back the role of government, cut taxes, rebuild the nation's military strength, and unleash the energy of the marketplace to solve economic and social problems. Although Reagan did not accomplish all of his objectives, he made conservatism a powerful force in American life.

The Information Age. The 1970's had ushered in the spread of computers to homes, schools, and businesses throughout the land. Early computers, called *mainframes,* were large machines stored in special climate-controlled rooms. These early computers had few users, chiefly large businesses and governments. Computers quickly became more compact and able to do much more than the early models could. In the mid-1970's, manufacturers introduced the personal computer (PC), and the use of computers began to soar. Schools and small businesses that could not afford big mainframes bought many of these compact machines. People throughout the country began buying PC's for home use. By the 1980's, computers were cheaper, easier to operate, and more useful than ever. The "computer revolution" had taken hold.

New methods of communication changed the way people lived and worked in the 1980's and 1990's. The first commercial cellular telephone system went into operation in 1983. Fax machines, which had been invented much earlier, became common in business. Personal computers continued to grow smaller and more affordable. Notebook computers and tiny handheld computers became popular.

A network of computers called the Internet revolutionized life in the United States and elsewhere. It enabled computer users to exchange e-mail messages and to share information in a variety of forms. The Internet and other technological marvels provided such a wealth of information that the period became known as the Information Age.

Economic changes. *High-technology industries* grew tremendously. These industries manufactured advanced technology products, such as computers and aircraft. High-tech industries themselves used the most advanced and sophisticated electronics and other modern technology. Jobs in high-tech industries generally paid more than those in traditional industries and required advanced training and skills.

Service industries, those that provided services rather than agricultural products or manufactured goods, also took on a larger role in the economy. Meanwhile, the

Computers in the mid-1900's enabled businesses and governments to perform tasks with greater speed than ever before. A programmer, like the woman shown here in 1955, could use a computer to perform thousands of mathematical calculations per minute. Computers and related advances provided such a wealth of information that the late 1900's became known as the Information Age.

© Hulton Archive/Getty Images

importance of mining, steel production, and automobile manufacturing declined. In agriculture, the family farm and tenant farming lost importance. These older systems were replaced by large, mechanized farms.

A painful adjustment followed the displacement of old forms of employment. Many people who lost their jobs in mining, manufacturing, and agriculture found it difficult to find new ones.

During the 1980's and 1990's, the economy of the Unit-

ed States became more integrated with those of other nations. The country's economic partners included not only many European nations, as in the past, but also many Asian nations, such as Japan, Singapore, South Korea, Taiwan, and Thailand.

In 1989, a trade agreement between the United States and Canada began reducing trade barriers between the two countries. The North American Free Trade Agreement (NAFTA), which took effect in 1994, built on the

© Justin Sullivan, Getty Images

Digital music players, such as Apple Computer's iPod, enable users to play a variety of music on small, portable devices. The devices store music on hard-disk drives or on memory chips. Since the mid-1900's, such advances in technology have dramatically changed how people live and work.

1989 pact. Under NAFTA, the United States, Canada, and Mexico gradually eliminated tariffs, import quotas, and other barriers to trade among the three countries. As a result of these changes, markets for United States goods and services expanded.

The end of the Cold War. The containment of Communism had dominated United States foreign policy since the mid-1940's. In the early 1970's, President Nixon took steps to reduce tensions between the United States and the two leading Communist powers, China and the Soviet Union. He visited these two countries in 1972. Jimmy Carter, who became president in 1977, also tried to improve U.S. relations with China and the Soviet Union. In early 1979, the United States and China established normal diplomatic relations. Later that year, Carter and Leonid I. Brezhnev, leader of the Soviet Communist Party, signed a treaty that limited the use of U.S. and Soviet nuclear arms.

At the request of President Reagan, the United States sharply increased military spending in the 1980's. But in 1987, Reagan and Soviet leader Mikhail Gorbachev signed a treaty to eliminate many of the ground-launched nuclear missiles of both nations. Gorbachev and George H. W. Bush, who became president in 1989, met several times and worked to increase cooperation between their countries.

Discontent in the republics that made up the Soviet Union grew in the late 1980's and early 1990's. On Dec. 25, 1991, the Soviet Union was dissolved, and its republics became independent non-Communist nations. Russia was by far the largest of the nations. During the same period, Eastern European countries that had been part of the Soviet bloc experienced changes that led to the end of Communist rule in those countries. These events marked the end of the Cold War and left the United States as the world's only superpower.

The Persian Gulf War. United States foreign policy after the Cold War made increasing use of coalitions of nations and of cooperation with the United Nations. One of the largest efforts of this type was the Persian Gulf War of 1991. In 1990, Iraq invaded Kuwait, an oil-rich Arab country between the Arab countries of Iraq and Saudi Arabia. President George H. W. Bush ordered tens of thousands of U.S. troops to Saudi Arabia, largely to help defend that country against a possible Iraqi attack. Saudi Arabia was a U.S. ally and a major source of oil for the United States and other industrialized nations.

Bush put together a coalition of nations to oppose Iraq, including Arab and Western European states. The UN authorized the United States and other UN members to "use all necessary means" to expel Iraq from Kuwait if Iraq did not withdraw. Iraq refused to withdraw. The United States and its coalition partners then drove Iraq out of Kuwait in 1991. See **Persian Gulf War of 1991.**

The Balkan conflicts. The European nation of Yugoslavia broke up in 1991, and a series of conflicts began on the Balkan Peninsula. In 1992, a civil war began in Bosnia-Herzegovina, formerly a republic of Yugoslavia. The war broke out between Bosnian Serb rebels and the country's government, which was dominated by Bosniaks (also called Bosnian Muslims). The United States attacked Serb forces to help the Bosniaks. In December 1995, representatives of Bosnia, Croatia, and Serbia signed a peace plan that included a cease-fire po-

liced by NATO. The United States sent troops to serve in the NATO peacekeeping force.

In 1999, the United States took part in NATO air strikes against Serbia. The purpose of the strikes was to halt Serbian attacks against ethnic Albanians in Serbia's province of Kosovo. After Serbian leaders agreed to withdraw from Kosovo, NATO stopped the bombing and sent an international peacekeeping force. The United States also provided troops for that NATO force.

The Clinton impeachment. Bill Clinton had taken office as president in 1993. In August 1998, he admitted to having a sexual affair with Monica Lewinsky, a White House intern, from late 1995 to 1997. In December 1998, the Judiciary Committee of the House of Representatives recommended several articles of impeachment against the president involving attempts to conceal his affair with Lewinsky. The House then impeached Clinton on charges of *perjury* (lying under oath) and obstruction of justice. In February 1999, the United States Senate held a trial on the impeachment and found Clinton not guilty. For more details, see **Clinton, Bill** (Domestic events).

The United States in the 2000's (2000-   )

In the early 2000's, the United States ranked as the most powerful country in the world. It had the world's strongest military force, the richest economy, and the most influential popular culture. Americans had one of the highest standards of living in the world. Despite its power and influence, the United States faced many challenges. In particular, U.S. leaders grappled with decisions on when and where to involve U.S. military forces in international disputes.

Election of 2000. Texas Governor George W. Bush was elected president in 2000 in one of the closest presidential elections in U.S. history. He narrowly defeated his Democratic opponent, Vice President Al Gore. The outcome was in doubt for several weeks after the vote. Delays resulted from recounts of the ballots in Florida and court challenges to the recounts.

September 11 terrorist attacks. On Sept. 11, 2001, the United States suffered the worst attack of terrorism in its history. Terrorists hijacked four commercial jets and crashed two of them into the two towers of the World Trade Center in New York City and a third into the Pentagon Building near Washington, D.C. The fourth hijacked plane crashed in Pennsylvania. The twin towers collapsed to the ground, and part of the Pentagon was destroyed. About 3,000 people were killed. President Bush called the attacks acts of war. The United States and its allies launched a military campaign against Afghanistan, the headquarters of the terrorists responsible for the attacks. The campaign overthrew the Afghan government that had sheltered and aided the terrorists. See **September 11 terrorist attacks.**

Later in 2001, Congress passed the Patriot Act to help prevent further terrorism. The act greatly expanded the powers of law enforcement officials to investigate the lives and actions of U.S. citizens and noncitizens. Supporters of the Patriot Act argued that the expanded powers were necessary to defend against terrorist threats. Opponents charged that many of its provisions unnecessarily restricted the rights of citizens of the United States. In 2003, Congress established the Cabinet-level Department of Homeland Security to improve the coun-

© Beth A. Keiser, AFP/Getty Images

The World Trade Center towers lay in ruin after terrorists crashed hijacked airplanes into the New York City buildings on Sept. 11, 2001. Both towers collapsed within hours of the crashes. Rescue and cleanup workers, *shown here,* searched through rubble in the wake of the attacks.

try's defense against future terrorist attacks.

Iraq War. Under the cease-fire agreement that ended the Persian Gulf War of 1991, Iraq had agreed to destroy its facilities for producing chemical, biological, and nuclear weapons. In 1993, Iraq formally agreed to a permanent ban on such weapons and to long-term monitoring of its weapons programs by UN inspectors. However, Iraq repeatedly clashed with the UN and refused to comply with the agreements.

In March 2003, a U.S.-led coalition of countries launched military action against Iraq. Bush said that Iraq possessed *weapons of mass destruction*—that is, biological, chemical, or nuclear weapons—and threatened the security of the United States and other countries. In April 2003, U.S.-led forces seized Baghdad, Iraq's capital, causing the fall of Saddam Hussein's government.

After major combat ended, the U.S.-led coalition forces remained in Iraq to provide security during Iraq's transition to a constitutional government. Militant groups, often called *insurgents,* attacked coalition forces and Iraqi police and civilians.

Bush faced increasing criticism as U.S. weapons inspectors failed to find weapons of mass destruction in Iraq. In 2005, a presidential commission blamed faulty gathering of intelligence for the misleading information about Iraq's weapons. Opposition to the Iraq War

Facts in brief (2000-   )

Presidents   (with political parties and dates of service)
Bill Clinton, Democrat, 1993-2001
George W. Bush, Republican, 2001-2009
Barack Obama, Democrat, 2009-

States in the Union

Number at start of period: 50
States added during the period: none

Important dates

2001   The worst terrorist attack in U.S. history destroyed the twin 110-story towers of the World Trade Center, damaged the Pentagon, and killed thousands of people.

2001   United States-led forces overthrew Afghanistan's rulers, the Taliban, who had harbored terrorists responsible for the attacks on the United States.

2003   United States-led forces ended the rule of Iraqi dictator Saddam Hussein in the Iraq War.

2005   Hurricane Katrina struck the Gulf Coast, causing more than 1,800 deaths and widespread destruction.

Population growth and change

Total population, 281,421,906

2000	Rural, 21%	Urban, 79%

Total population, 308,848,000

2008	Rural, 20%	Urban, 80%

Hurricane Katrina, in August 2005, was one of the most destructive storms ever to strike the United States. In New Orleans, *left,* floodwaters covered many streets for weeks after the storm. Along the Gulf Coast, the hurricane caused about 1,800 deaths and left thousands of people homeless.

© Chris Graythen, Getty Images

increased as the war dragged on and casualties mounted. See **Iraq War.**

Hurricane Katrina. In 2005, the United States suffered one of the worst natural disasters in its history when Hurricane Katrina struck the Gulf Coast. The hurricane caused about 1,800 deaths and widespread destruction in coastal areas from Louisiana to Florida. In New Orleans, flood defenses failed, and floodwaters covered most of the city for weeks. Officials estimated recovery costs would exceed by far those of any other disaster in U.S. history.

Immigration. During the spring of 2006, millions of immigrants and their supporters held rallies in several U.S. cities to protest a proposed federal law that would increase penalties for undocumented immigration. Experts estimated that as many as 12 million illegal immigrants lived in the United States, most from Mexico and other Latin American countries. In October, President Bush signed into law a bill that authorized the building of new fences along the United States-Mexico border.

In May 2007, tens of thousands of people in several U.S. cities participated in rallies for immigrant rights. The demonstrations, which were smaller than the immigration rallies of 2006, largely focused on the federal government's failure to pass significant immigration reform legislation.

Financial troubles. In the early 2000's, a series of corporate financial scandals severely damaged the confidence of investors in U.S. businesses and U.S. stocks. Several corporations—including Enron Corporation, a leading energy company, and WorldCom Inc., a global telecommunications firm—were found to have used dishonest accounting practices. In 2002, Bush signed into law a corporate reform bill that called for increased punishments for corporate fraud and established an in-dependent board to oversee the accounting industry.

The nation's economy took a sharp downturn in 2008. Many financial firms suffered huge losses, largely related to risky mortgages called *subprime mortgages.* In September, several large firms failed or were bailed out by the U.S. government. The stock market plunged. In October, Congress passed a law that provided up to $700 billion for the government to purchase bad debts from troubled lenders. Bush administration officials hoped the bailout would restore confidence in the financial markets and make it easier for businesses and individuals to obtain bank loans.

Historic election. Voters in the United States made history on Nov. 4, 2008, by electing Senator Barack Obama, a Democrat from Illinois, the nation's first African American president. Obama defeated Senator John McCain, a Republican from Arizona.

Robin L. Einhorn and Bruce J. Schulman

Related articles in *World Book.* See the articles on each president and the *History* section on each state. Other related articles include:

Historical periods and wars

Afghanistan War of 2001	Progressive Era
Civil War, American	Proslavery movement
Cold War	Reconstruction
Colonial life in America	Revolutionary War in America
Exploration	Roaring Twenties
French and Indian wars	Spanish-American War
Gay Nineties	Vietnam War
Great Depression	War of 1812
Indian wars	Western frontier life
Industrial Revolution	in America
Iraq War	Westward movement
Korean War	in America
Mexican War	World War I
Persian Gulf War of 1991	World War II
Pioneer life in America	

Important documents

Articles of Confederation
Atlantic Charter
Compromise of 1850
Constitution of the United States
Declaration of Independence
Emancipation Proclamation
Federalist, The
Fourteen Points
Gettysburg Address
Homestead Act
Kansas-Nebraska Act
Mayflower Compact
Missouri Compromise
Monroe Doctrine
Northwest Ordinance

Other related articles

American literature
Baby boom generation
Continental Congress
Flag
Gold rush
Immigration
Indian, American
Lewis and Clark expedition
Louisiana Purchase
Panama Canal
Political party
September 11 terrorist attacks
Slavery
States' rights
Trail of Tears
United States
United States, Government of the
United States capitals
World, History of the

Additional resources

Level I

Collier, Christopher and James L. *The Changing Face of America, 1945-2000.* Benchmark Bks., 2001.
Hakim, Joy. *A History of US.* 11 vols. 2nd ed. Oxford, 1999 .
Scott, John A. *The Story of America.* Rev. ed. National Geographic Soc., 1993.

Level II

Ambrose, Stephen E. *Americans at War.* Univ. Pr. of Miss., 1997.
Carruth, Gorton. *The Encyclopedia of American Facts and Dates.* 10th ed. HarperCollins, 1997.
Evans, Harold. *The American Century.* Knopf, 1998.
Franklin, John Hope, and Moss, A. A., Jr. *From Slavery to Freedom: A History of African-Americans.* 8th ed. Knopf, 2000.
Kennedy, David M. *Freedom from Fear: The American People in Depression and War, 1929-1945.* 1999. Reprint. Oxford, 2001.
Peavy, Linda S., and Smith, Ursula. *Frontier Children.* Univ. of Okla. Pr., 1999.
Thompson, Peter. *Dictionary of American History.* Facts on File, 2000.

United States Air Force. See Air Force, United States.

United States Air Force Academy prepares young men and women for careers as officers in the United States Air Force. It stands on an 18,000-acre (7,280-hectare) site in the foothills of the Rocky Mountains, near Colorado Springs, Colorado. The academy is an agency of the Department of the Air Force.

Students at the academy are called *Air Force Academy cadets.* Cadets take four years of academic work leading to a Bachelor of Science degree. In addition, they take professional military training to earn commissions in the U.S. Air Force. When students enter the academy, they agree to serve four years as a cadet and a minimum of five years as an Air Force officer. The United States government provides food, housing, and medical care for the cadets. Each cadet receives a monthly salary to pay for uniforms, textbooks, and their personal expenses.

Entrance requirements. Candidates for appointment to the academy must be (1) citizens of the United States, (2) at least 17 and not yet 23 years old on July 1 of the year for which they seek appointment, (3) unmarried without legal dependents, and (4) of good moral character. The academy's Web site at http://www.usafa.edu provides information on preparation and admission procedures. Students may also obtain such information from the Director of Admissions, United States Air Force Academy, CO 80840.

Nomination and selection of cadets. Candidates for the academy must be nominated by a legally established nominating source. A majority of academy vacancies are filled by nominations from government officials. At any time, each United States senator and representative, the vice president of the United States, the congressional delegate from the District of Columbia, and the resident commissioner of Puerto Rico may have five cadets attending the academy. The congressional delegates from Guam and the Virgin Islands may have two cadets each at the academy. The delegates from American Samoa and the Northern Mariana Islands and the governor of Puerto Rico may have one cadet each at the academy.

The remaining nominations are based on previous military service by the applicants or their parents. The president of the United States may appoint up to 100 candidates each year from among the children of active-duty or retired military personnel. Enlisted personnel in the regular and reserve Air Force receive 170 nominations annually. Each year, the secretary of the Air Force may nominate a combined total of 20 candidates from among the members of the Air Force Reserve Officers' Training Corps and the honor graduates of military honor schools. Up to 65 cadets may attend the academy who were nominated as children of veterans killed or disabled in action and children of prisoners of war or of personnel missing in action. An unlimited number of children of Medal of Honor winners may also attend the academy. Qualified alternates are accepted as needed to fill each class.

Candidates must pass qualifying medical examinations, a physical aptitude examination, and college entrance examinations. In addition, candidates must have demonstrated outstanding academic and leadership potential in high school to qualify for appointment.

Cadet life. Cadets live in dormitories. Their normal weekday begins with *reveille* (wake-up call) at 6:30 a.m. Before classes, cadets prepare their rooms for inspection and eat breakfast. Classes are held from 8 a.m. to noon and from 1 p.m. to 4 p.m. Most classes are held in small classrooms and laboratories. After classes, cadets participate in sports or extracurricular activities. After dinner, they study in the dormitory or academy library from 8 p.m. to 11 p.m. Taps sounds at 11 p.m.

Cadets may attend religious services of their faith in the Academy Cadet Chapel. The chapel's 17 towering aluminum spires make it an academy landmark. The chapel is divided into sections for Protestant, Roman Catholic, and Jewish religious services. Cadets may also

Air Force Academy cadets stand in formation in front of the Academy Cadet Chapel of the U.S. Air Force Academy during a graduation ceremony. The academy is located near Colorado Springs, Colorado, in the foothills of the Rocky Mountains.

attend religious services held in nearby communities.

Cadets live by an *honor code* that stresses complete integrity in word and deed. The code says, "We will not lie, steal, or cheat, nor tolerate among us anyone who does." The cadets themselves enforce the code, and violation of the code can be cause for dismissal.

Social activities are held on weekends at the academy. Privileges to leave the campus increase as the cadet progresses through the academy. Each year, all cadets receive a two-week winter *leave* (vacation), a one-week spring leave, and a three-week summer leave.

The academy curriculum consists of the academic program, military training, and physical education. The academic program includes a core curriculum of 30 courses in the basic sciences, engineering, humanities, and the social sciences. Each cadet must take certain courses that provide a general background in all subject areas. The cadet may also major in one subject or area of concentration. In addition, cadets must take a course in ethics and receive instruction in honor and ethics. Cadets may visit other Air Force or military installations to participate in various research projects. They also may compete with students from other universities for fellowships and scholarships.

The academy prepares each cadet for a role of leadership through military training. This training provides the basic military knowledge required by an Air Force officer and includes flying instruction

The Seal of the Air Force Academy

and field trips. All cadets, even those who do not plan a career in flying, must take aviation and navigation courses.

Cadets become physically fit through a varied program that includes physical education classes and athletics. Each cadet must participate in either intramural sports or intercollegiate sports while attending the academy.

History. In the 1920's, Brigadier General Billy Mitchell urged that the government set up an Air Force academy (see **Mitchell, Billy**). In 1947, the United States established the Air Force as an independent branch from the Army. The secretary of defense appointed a service academy board in 1949 to study the need for another academy. The board recommended that an academy should be established to train future Air Force officers.

Congress authorized the creation of the Air Force Academy in 1954. A committee appointed by the secretary of the Air Force chose the location for the academy. In July 1955, the first class of 306 Air Force Academy cadets began training at a temporary site at Lowry Air Force Base, near Denver, Colorado. The Air Force Academy moved to its permanent site near Colorado Springs in 1958.

In 1964, the United States government increased the size of the Air Force Academy from 2,500 cadets to its current authorized strength of 4,000 cadets. The academy began to admit women students in 1976.

Critically reviewed by the United States Air Force Academy

United States Arms Control and Disarmament Agency. See Arms Control and Disarmament Agency, United States.

United States Army. See Army, United States.

United States Army War College, in Carlisle Barracks, Pennsylvania, is the senior educational institution of the United States Army. The students consist primarily of colonels and lieutenant colonels of the Army, Navy, Air Force, Marine Corps, and the United States government agency officers and senior members of the armed forces of other nations may also train at the college. Each year, more than 300 students are selected to attend.

The curriculum of the United States Army War College focuses on national security issues, military strategy, and war operations. It emphasizes the interaction of the Army with other U.S. forces and with the forces of other nations.

The Army War College was founded in 1901 in Washington, D.C., by Secretary of War Elihu Root. Classes were suspended during World War I and from 1940 to 1950. The college moved to its present location in 1951.

Critically reviewed by the United States Army

See also **Root, Elihu.**

United States Bank. See Bank of the United States.

United States Board on Geographic Names. See Geographic Names, United States Board on.

United States Botanic Garden. See Botanic Garden, United States.

United States capitals. The U.S. government had no permanent capital until 1800, when it took up residence in Washington, D.C. Until that time, the government, in the form of its Congresses, had many different meeting places. The Continental Congress met in Philadelphia, except for brief periods during the Revolutionary War

(1775-1783), when British troops forced it to flee. The Continental Congress was succeeded in 1781 by the Congress of the Confederation, which moved several times before settling in New York City in 1785. In 1789, the Congress of the Confederation was succeeded by the Congress that was established by the Constitution of the United States. This Congress met in New York City until 1790, when it moved to Philadelphia.

The Constitution gave the new Congress power to govern a district given by the states as the site of a new capital. In 1790, the government decided to locate the capital along the Potomac River. Virginia and Maryland gave land for the new capital. In 1791, President George Washington chose the site. A commission was appointed to survey the ground and plan the city. The commission named the capital *The City of Washington* in honor of President Washington. Congress moved from Philadelphia to Washington in 1800.

The earliest American Congresses met in the cities listed below, with the dates Congress met in each city.

Philadelphia, Sept. 5, 1774, to Dec. 12, 1776.
Baltimore, Dec. 20, 1776, to March 4, 1777.
Philadelphia, March 5, 1777, to Sept. 18, 1777.
Lancaster, Pennsylvania, Sept. 27, 1777.
York, Pennsylvania, Sept. 30, 1777, to June 27, 1778.
Philadelphia, July 2, 1778, to June 21, 1783.
Princeton, New Jersey, June 30, 1783, to Nov. 4, 1783.
Annapolis, Maryland, Nov. 26, 1783, to June 3, 1784.
Trenton, New Jersey, Nov. 1, 1784, to Dec. 24, 1784.
New York City, Jan. 11, 1785, to Aug. 12, 1790.
Philadelphia, Dec. 6, 1790, to May 14, 1800.

Most scholars agree that the United States was formed when Congress issued the Declaration of Independence in 1776. Thus, the first capital of the United States was Philadelphia. Jack N. Rakove

See also **District of Columbia; United States, Government of the** (pictures: Meeting places of American Congresses); **Washington, D.C.**

United States Coast Guard. See Coast Guard, United States.

United States Coast Guard Academy prepares young men and women to serve as commissioned officers in the United States Coast Guard. The academy's campus is on the banks of the Thames River in New London, Connecticut. The academy is comparable to those of the other armed forces. However, its enrollment is smaller and entrance is by annual national competition rather than congressional appointment. Students are called *cadets.* Graduates receive bachelor of science degrees and commissions as ensigns in the United States Coast Guard.

Entrance requirements. Cadets are selected through nationwide competition based on college entrance examinations. Applicants must be U.S. citizens at least 17, but not yet 22, years of age. In addition, candidates must meet other requirements established by the commandant of the United States Coast Guard. In 1976, the academy admitted women students for the first time.

Cadets are organized as a regiment for military training. Senior cadets serve as regiment officers under the supervision of career Coast Guard officers.

The course of instruction offers a four-year program of academic, military, and physical education training. Cadets must take certain courses that provide a background in all subject areas. They also choose one of several fields for in-depth study. Such fields include marine engineering and government. Military training includes such academic courses as navigation and seamanship, plus summer training. During summers, cadets participate in Coast Guard operations aboard modern ships and the academy's training ship, the *Eagle.* Summer programs for cadets include aviation training, small arms training, and search-and-rescue training.

History. The Coast Guard cadet training system began in 1876 with the assignment of the *Dobbin* as a com-

U.S. Coast Guard Academy

Coast Guard cadets assemble on the campus parade ground as the color guard passes by. The Coast Guard Academy prepares young men and women to be commissioned officers in the United States Coast Guard. The seal of the Coast Guard Academy is shown above.

U.S. Coast Guard Academy

A summer cruise gives Coast Guard Academy cadets training in navigation and many other sailing skills.

bination training ship, classroom, and sleeping quarters. In 1890, the academy established its first land-based campus in Curtis Bay, Maryland. The campus moved to New London in 1910.

Critically reviewed by the Coast Guard Academy

See also **Coast Guard, U.S.** (Training an officer).

United States Congress. See Congress of the United States.

United States Constitution. See Constitution of the United States.

United States Department . . . . Each executive department of the U.S. government has an article in *World Book.* For a list of the departments, see United States, Government of the (Executive departments).

United States government. See United States, Government of the.

United States history. See United States, History of the.

United States Holocaust Memorial Museum. See Holocaust Memorial Museum, United States.

United States Information Agency (USIA) was an independent agency that served as the official diplomacy arm of the U.S. government from 1953 to 1999. It was established by President Dwight D. Eisenhower.

Through a wide range of activities, the USIA provided insight about the United States to people overseas. It also brought many people from other countries to the United States to experience American culture and society. The USIA's mission was to strengthen foreign understanding of and support for U.S. policies and action; to assist in establishing democratic governments and free-market economies in other countries; and to advise the president, the secretary of state, and other key officials on how public opinion in foreign countries affected U.S. policies. The USIA was known overseas as the U.S. Information Service. When the agency was dissolved, many of its responsibilities were transferred to the State Department.

The USIA maintained posts in most countries, usually in United States embassies or consulates. The director of the USIA was appointed by the president and approved by the Senate. Support for overseas posts was

organized in Washington, D.C., under (1) the Bureau of Educational and Cultural Affairs, (2) the Bureau of Policy and Programs, and (3) the International Broadcasting Bureau.

The Bureau of Educational and Cultural Affairs administered the USIA's exchange programs, including the International Visitors Program and the Fulbright scholarships (see **Fulbright scholarship**). Teachers, students, public officials, artists, and experts in various fields participated in these programs. The bureau also promoted the teaching of the English language overseas.

The Bureau of Policy and Programs operated the "Wireless File," a global computerized news service. In addition, the bureau published magazines and pamphlets that were translated into numerous languages and distributed to many countries. These publications provided news and information on U.S. policies and American culture to media, government officials, and the general public overseas. The bureau also sponsored traveling exhibits that shared U.S. culture and history with foreign audiences.

The International Broadcasting Bureau became an independent agency in 1999, when the USIA was abolished. When the bureau was part of the USIA, it carried out the same functions it does today. For example, it operated the Voice of America, a radio network that broadcasts news and entertainment in many languages worldwide (see **Voice of America**). In addition, it ran WORLDNET, a closed-circuit satellite television network that serves six continents, and Cuba Broadcasting, which consists of Radio and TV Marti.

United States International Trade Commission. See International Trade Commission, U.S.

United States Marine Corps. See Marine Corps, United States.

United States Merchant Marine Academy trains young men and women to become officers in the United States Merchant Marine. The academy, often called *Kings Point,* is on the north shore of Long Island at Kings Point, New York, approximately 20 miles (32 kilometers) northeast of New York City.

The United States Merchant Marine Cadet Corps was established in 1938. Its academy, founded in 1943, became a permanent, government-sponsored school in 1956, and received equal status with the academies of the armed forces. The United States Department of Transportation operates the academy.

U.S. Merchant Marine Academy
The academy seal

Entrance requirements. Candidates for the school must be citizens of the United States, not less than 17 and not yet 25 years of age by July 1 of the year in which they seek admission. They must be of good moral character. They must also have 16 high school credits, including 3 units in mathematics, 1 unit in science, and 4 units in English. Competitive examinations are held each year among candidates nominated to the academy by United States senators or representatives. In 1974, the

The U.S. Merchant Marine Academy color guard carries the American flag and a flag of the academy.

academy accepted its first women students.

Enrollment. Appointments to the academy are governed by a state and territory quota system that is based on population. The academy has an authorized strength of about 900 midshipmen. They represent the 50 states, the District of Columbia, Puerto Rico, Guam, American Samoa, and the Virgin Islands. In addition, the academy may admit not more than 12 candidates from Central and South America on a scholarship basis and not more than 30 students from any foreign nation on a paying basis.

The school program. The academy offers a four-year course of undergraduate study designed to prepare its graduates for the many problems that may confront merchant marine officers during their careers. Midshipmen study and gain practical experience in an atmosphere of order and discipline. Their practical experience subjects include training aboard a ship. Their academic subjects deal with marine engineering, navigation, electricity, ship construction, naval science and tactics, economics, business, languages, and history.

Midshipmen spend their first year as Fourth Classmen at the academy. During their second (Third Class) and third (Second Class) years, they spend half of each year aboard a merchant ship. The remainder of the four years is spent at the academy. All of the fourth (First Class) year is spent on campus. On completion of the program, midshipmen are examined for their original licenses as third deck, third assistant engineer, or dual license officers in the merchant marine. They may then serve on any merchant ship bearing the U.S. flag. Graduates also receive bachelor's degrees and commissions as ensigns in the naval reserve.

Critically reviewed by the United States Merchant Marine Academy

United States Military Academy at West Point, New York, is the oldest military college in the United States. It prepares young men and women to serve as officers in the United States Army. The academy is supported by the federal government and is supervised by the Department of the Army.

U.S. Army

U.S. Military Academy seal

Students at the academy are called *cadets*. After four years, they earn Bachelor of Science degrees and they receive commissions in the U.S. Army. The academy is part of a military reservation that occupies 16,000 acres (6,470 hectares) on the west bank of the Hudson River, about 50 miles (80 kilometers) north of New York City. The superintendent, an Army lieutenant general, commands the academy.

Entrance requirements. A candidate for the school must be at least 17 years old and not yet 23 years of age on July 1 of the year of admission. A candidate must be a U.S. citizen, must be unmarried, and must have no legal obligation to support a child. The academy's Web site at www.usma.edu provides information on admissions. Information can also be obtained by writing to the Director of Admissions, United States Military Academy, West Point, NY 10996.

To be considered for admission to the U.S. Military

U.S. Army

The United States Military Academy at West Point, New York, prepares young men and women to serve as officers in the United States Army. This cadet color guard is marching past a monument to George Washington that stands on the campus.

David R. Frazier

Extracurricular activities at West Point include working at the cadet radio station, *shown here.*

Academy, a candidate must obtain a nomination from an official source. Approximately three-fourths of the vacancies for the academy are filled by nominations from United States senators and representatives and certain other government officials. At any time, each United States senator and representative, the vice president of the United States, the congressional delegate from the District of Columbia, and the resident commissioner of Puerto Rico may have five cadets attending the academy. The congressional delegates from Guam and the Virgin Islands may have two cadets each at the U.S. Military Academy. The delegate from American Samoa and the governor of Puerto Rico may have one cadet each at the academy.

The United States secretary of the Army nominates candidates for about one-fourth of the cadet vacancies each year. These nominations are based on previous military service by the applicants themselves or their parents. Soldiers in the Regular Army, the Army Reserve, or the Army National Guard receive 170 nominations per year. One hundred nominations are reserved for children of career military personnel. Twenty nominations go to children of veterans killed or disabled in action and children of prisoners of war or personnel missing in action. Another 20 nominations are available for students in the Reserve Officers Training Corps. The U.S. Military Academy may enroll an unlimited number of children of Medal of Honor winners if they qualify for admission.

An admissions board at the academy examines each candidate's school records and college entrance examination scores. The board also studies the results of a candidate's medical and physical aptitude tests and other evidence of character, leadership potential, academic aptitude, and physical fitness.

Cadets are members of the Regular Army. They are paid about $6,500 a year. From this amount, they must pay for uniforms, textbooks, and personal computers. The academy provides housing, meals, and medical care for cadets.

The student body is called the Corps of Cadets. The corps is broken down into regiments, battalions, and companies. The academy's *honor code* is a cherished possession of cadets and graduates. Administered by the cadets themselves, the code states simply that a

cadet will not lie, cheat, or steal, or tolerate those who do. The code requires complete integrity in word and deed. It is strictly enforced, and any intentional violation is a cause for dismissal from the academy.

The cadet academic year extends from August to May. *Graduation Week* climaxes the year's events for the graduating *First* (senior) class. Other classes are called the *Fourth* (first-year) class; *Third* (sophomore) class; and *Second* (junior) class.

A cadet's day starts with the first call for reveille at 6:00 a.m. Cadets live in barracks, two or three to a room. They eat meals in Washington Hall. Classes and study time extend from 7:35 a.m. until 3:50 p.m. From that time until supper (5:45 to 7:25 p.m.), cadets participate in extracurricular activities, parades, or intramural and intercollegiate athletics. Taps sounds at 11:30 p.m.

Education and training. The four-year undergraduate program seeks to prepare students for service as career Army officers. It stresses academic, military, and physical fitness skills. The academic curriculum provides a basic education in engineering, mathematics, science, and the social sciences and humanities. Advanced and elective courses enable cadets to specialize in one of 25 fields of study or 22 optional majors.

Cadets receive training in military skills through participation in the Corps of Cadets, in courses taken during the academic year, and in summer training sessions. Summer training takes place at West Point, at nearby Camp Buckner, and at selected military posts around the world. It includes instruction in Army weapons and field maneuvers. A cadet also spends time as a platoon leader with a real combat unit. Students develop physical fitness skills through varsity or intramural sports and physical education courses.

History. The idea of a military academy was first proposed in the late 1700's by such early American leaders as George Washington. In March 1802, Congress established the U.S. Military Academy on an Army site at West Point, New York. The school opened officially in July of the same year.

Under Colonel Sylvanus Thayer, who served as superintendent from 1817 to 1833, the academy became a pioneer in civil engineering. Thayer also introduced many educational reforms that remain important to academy life. During the American Civil War (1861-1865), the U.S. Military Academy dropped its strict emphasis on engineering.

Today, the U.S. Military Academy provides a broad education, plus specialized and elective programs. In 1976, the academy admitted women students for the first time. In 1982, it adopted an optional majors program.

Many great American military leaders trained at West Point. They include Robert E. Lee, Ulysses S. Grant, Stonewall Jackson, Philip Sheridan, John J. Pershing, Douglas MacArthur, Dwight D. Eisenhower, George S. Patton, Jr., and H. Norman Schwarzkopf.

Critically reviewed by the United States Military Academy

See also **New York** (picture); **Thayer, Sylvanus.**

United States National Museum. See National Museum of American History; National Museum of Natural History.

United States Naval Academy at Annapolis, Maryland, is a degree-granting undergraduate college that prepares young men and women to become officers in the United States Navy and Marine Corps. The academy is supported by the federal government and is supervised by the Department of the Navy. George Bancroft, secretary of the Navy under President James K. Polk, founded the academy in 1845.

Students at the Naval Academy are called *midshipmen*. Their training takes four years. Those who complete the work are awarded a Bachelor of Science degree and are commissioned as ensigns in the Navy or as second lieutenants in the Marine Corps.

Entrance requirements. Each year, about 1,200 young men and women are selected for admission to the *plebe* (first-year) class at the Naval Academy. A candidate for the school must be at least 17 years old, and not older than 23, on July 1 of the year of admission. A candidate must be unmarried, not pregnant, of good moral character, and a U.S. citizen.

To be considered for admission to the U.S. Naval Academy, a candidate must obtain a nomination from an official source. A majority of the vacancies at the academy are filled by nominations from United States senators and representatives and certain other government officials. At any time, each United States senator and representative, the vice president of the United States, the congressional delegate from the District of Columbia, and the resident commissioner of Puerto Rico may have five midshipmen attending the academy. The congressional delegates from Guam and the Virgin Islands may have three midshipmen each at the academy. The delegate from American Samoa may have two midshipmen. The delegate from the Northern Mariana Islands and the governor of Puerto Rico may have one midshipman each.

The remaining nominations to the Naval Academy are based on previous military service by the applicants themselves or their parents. The president of the United States may nominate an unlimited number of children of career military personnel, including members of the Coast Guard. Enlisted personnel in the regular and reserve Navy and Marine Corps receive 170 nominations per year. Up to 65 midshipmen may attend the academy who were nominated as children of veterans killed or disabled in action and children of prisoners of war or personnel missing in action. Another 20 nominations are available for students in the Reserve Officers Training Corps. The academy may enroll an unlimited number of children of Medal of Honor winners.

An admissions board at the academy examines each candidate's school records and college entrance examination scores. The board also studies the results of a candidate's medical and physical aptitude tests and other evidence of character, leadership potential, academic aptitude, and physical fitness. Most young people who are accepted by the Naval Academy rank academically in the top 20 percent of their high school class.

After the midshipmen have been admitted, the U.S. government pays for their tuition, room and board, and medical and dental care. Each midshipman receives a monthly salary. From this salary, midshipmen must pay for their books, uniforms, equipment, and personal services.

The academy's Web site at http://www.usna.edu provides complete entrance information. Students can also obtain information by writing to the Dean of Admissions, United States Naval Academy, Annapolis, MD 21402.

U.S. Naval Academy

U.S. Naval Academy seal

The life of a midshipman. The program at Annapolis seeks to develop students for positions of military leadership. The academy emphasizes both academic training and the development of leadership, physical, and professional skills. During the academic year, midshipmen devote their major efforts to academic studies. However, they also must participate in a varsity sport, a club sport, or the intramural sports program. For extracurricular activity, students at the academy may choose from dozens of clubs and organizations, ranging from dramatics and glee clubs to scuba diving.

During the midshipmen's first summer, they learn the basics of military life, including how to shoot and sail. The academy requires physical tests, drills, and athletics for physical fitness. During their remaining summers, the midshipmen spend time at sea and at various naval installations. There, they learn about ships, submarines, and aircraft.

Graduates receive their diplomas and Navy or Marine Corps commissions at the end of Commissioning Week in May. They then proceed as Navy or Marine Corps officers to specialized training before reporting to their first fleet assignment.

The academic program. The academy offers a four-year undergraduate program. The curriculum includes mathematics, science, engineering, and the social sciences and humanities. It also supplies a background in leadership, navigation, weaponry, and other profession-

U.S. Naval Academy

Navigation training is provided to all midshipmen during their first summer. Additional instruction at sea ensures that they are familiar with every aspect of ship operation.

al areas. Each midshipman chooses an academic major that provides in-depth study in a field of interest. These fields consist of aerospace engineering, oceanography, political science, and a variety of other areas.

History. Midshipmen trained at sea before the academy was founded as the Naval School in 1845. George Bancroft started the school in Annapolis on the site of Fort Severn, a former U.S. Army post. In 1850 and 1851, the school was reorganized as the U.S. Naval Academy.

During the American Civil War (1861-1865), Annapolis was considered too close to the battle lines, so the midshipmen were moved to Newport, Rhode Island. In 1865, midshipmen returned to Annapolis. At about the same time, the academy began adding athletics and more recreation to the program.

The Spanish-American War, in 1898, showed the school's importance to the Navy, and the course of study was expanded. The school constructed several buildings between 1899 and 1907, and some of them are still used. Women midshipmen were first admitted to the United States Naval Academy in 1976.

Critically reviewed by the United States Naval Academy

See also **Maryland** (picture: Dress parade).

United States Naval Observatory. See Naval Observatory, United States.

United States Navy. See Navy, United States.

United States note. See Money (The rebirth of paper money).

United States Post Office. See Postal Service, United States.

United States Postal Service. See Postal Service, United States.

United States president. See President of the United States.

United States Seal. See Great Seal of the United States.

United States Steel Corporation is one of the world's largest steel producers. The company also mines iron ore and coal. United States Steel has headquarters in Pittsburgh.

United States Steel was organized in 1901, chiefly by Charles Schwab, the president of the giant Carnegie Steel Company, and J. P. Morgan, a leading American banker. Ten steel companies, including Carnegie Steel, combined to form the corporation. United States Steel was the first billion-dollar corporation in U.S. history, beginning business with assets of $1,400,000,000. Under its first chairman, Elbert H. "Judge" Gary, U.S. Steel became the world's leading steelmaker.

The corporation originally operated a number of subsidiary companies that made a variety of metal products, from tubes, wire, and sheet steel to steel bridges. Through the years, U.S. Steel gradually absorbed these companies. It purchased Marathon Oil Company in 1982. The corporation changed its name to USX Corporation in 1986. In 2001, USX changed its name to Marathon Oil Corporation and spun off U.S. Steel as an independent company.

Critically reviewed by the United States Steel Corporation

United States Supreme Court. See Supreme Court of the United States.

United States Weather Bureau. See Weather Service, National.

United Steelworkers (USW) is one of the largest labor unions in North America. It is affiliated with the American Federation of Labor and Congress of Industrial Organizations (AFL-CIO) and the Canadian Labour Congress (CLC). The USW has headquarters in Pittsburgh. Its members work mainly in the steel, aluminum, paper, forestry products, tire and rubber, mining, glass, chemical, and petroleum industries. The union also includes people working in transportation, trades, and services.

The union's official name is the United Steel, Paper and Forestry, Rubber, Manufacturing, Energy, Allied Industrial and Service Workers International Union. For the membership of the USW, see **Labor movement** (table).

The union was formed in 2005 when the United Steelworkers of America (USWA) merged with the Paper, Allied-Industrial, Chemical and Energy Workers International Union (PACE). The USWA was founded in 1936 and adopted the USWA name in 1942. PACE was formed in 1999, when the United Paperworkers International Union merged with the Oil, Chemical, and Atomic Workers. In 2008, the full union formed an alliance with the largest union in the United Kingdom and Ireland, Unite the Union, to form Workers Uniting, a global union. Workers Uniting represents workers in the steel, paper, oil, health care, and transportation industries.

Critically reviewed by the United Steel, Paper and Forestry, Rubber, Manufacturing, Energy, Allied Industrial and Service Workers International Union

United Way of America is the national service association for hundreds of independent local United Way organizations in the United States. Local United Ways are fund-raising groups that help finance community service organizations and charities. The national association provides local United Ways with programs, services, and materials in such areas as government relations, labor relations, communications, and data gathering. It collects dues from local United Way groups.

Local United Ways raise funds primarily through charitable-giving campaigns in workplaces. They rely heavily on volunteers to run such campaigns, which have raised several billion dollars in a single year. United Way of America also receives large donations from charitable foundations. These funds help thousands of organizations, including local units of the American Cancer Society and other national groups. United Ways also give financial aid to crisis hotlines, programs for abused women, and day-care centers.

In 1992, top United Way officials were accused of misusing United Way funds by drawing high salaries and spending funds lavishly. The three officials were convicted and sentenced to jail in 1995. United Way of America has since appointed new leadership, increased the representation of local United Ways on its advisory board, and adopted strict financial controls and ethical codes.

The Charity Organizations Society, the first United Way, was founded in Denver in 1887. A national office was established in 1918 as the American Association for Community Organizations. It became known as United Way of America in 1970. Headquarters are in Alexandria, Virginia.   Philip English Mackey

See also **Boys & Girls Clubs of America; Cancer Society, American; Red Cross.**

Universal Declaration of Human Rights. See Human Rights, Universal Declaration of.

Universal language. Language is the main means of communication between peoples. But so many different languages have developed that language has often been a barrier rather than an aid to understanding among peoples. For many years, people have dreamed of setting up an international, universal language that all people could speak and understand. The arguments in favor of a universal language are simple and obvious. If all peoples spoke the same tongue, cultural and economic ties might be much closer, and good will might increase between countries. But many people consider the promoters of universal languages to be impractical idealists and discourage the idea.

René Descartes, a French philosopher, is believed to have originated the idea of a universal language in the 1600's. John Comenius, a Bohemian bishop and educator of the same period, also suggested the creation of a universal language. Over 200 other languages designed for universal use have been invented since that time.

Volapük was the earliest of these languages to gain much success. The name of the language comes from two of its words meaning *world* and *speak*. Johann Martin Schleyer, a German priest, invented the suggested language in 1879. Later, Idiom Neutral, a simplified form of Volapük, was suggested. Other proposed languages include Esperanto; a revised form of Esperanto called Ido; Interglossa; Interlingua; Novial; and Spelin. However, only Esperanto is used widely.

English is close to being an international language. In the last several hundred years, it has become a second language in many countries because of economic, political, and social developments.   Robert J. Kispert

See also Esperanto; Interlingua.

Universal Postal Union. See Postal Union, Universal.

Universalist Church of America. See Unitarian Universalist Association.

Universe consists of all matter and all light and other forms of radiation and energy. It includes everything that exists anywhere in space and time.

The universe includes Earth, everything on Earth and within it, and everything in the solar system. The solar system contains the sun and the planets that orbit it along with millions of smaller bodies, such as comets, asteroids, and meteoroids.

All stars, including the sun, are part of the universe. Some other stars also have planetary systems. In addition to planets, stars, and other bodies, the universe contains gas, dust, *magnetic fields* (areas of magnetic force), and high-energy particles called *cosmic rays*.

Stars are grouped into *galaxies*. The sun is one of hundreds of billions of stars in a giant spiral galaxy called the Milky Way. This galaxy measures about 100,000 *light-years* across. A light-year is the distance that light travels in a vacuum in a year—about 5.88 trillion miles (9.46 trillion kilometers).

Galaxies tend to be grouped into *clusters*. Some clusters appear to be grouped into *superclusters*. The Milky Way is part of a cluster known as the Local Group. This cluster measures about 10 million light-years in diameter. The cluster also includes two giant spirals known as the Andromeda Galaxy and the Triangulum Galaxy and about 40 small galaxies called *dwarf galaxies*. The Local Group is part of the Local Supercluster, which has a di-

ameter of about 200 million light-years.

On an even larger scale, galaxies are grouped into huge networks made up of stringlike regions of galaxies called *filaments*. Relatively empty regions of space called *voids* surround these filaments.

Size of the universe

No one knows for sure whether the universe is *finite* (limited) or infinite in size. Scientists now know that the observable universe includes billions, possibly even trillions, of galaxies. Measurements show that the most distant galaxies observed to date are almost 13 billion light-years from Earth. They appear in every direction across the sky.

Among the most distant objects ever observed are tremendously bright objects called *quasars*. Individual quasars are as much as 1,000 times brighter than the entire Milky Way. Evidence suggests that the centers of quasars may each contain a giant *black hole*. A black hole is an object whose gravitational force is so strong that nothing—not even light—can escape from it. Matter falling into a massive black hole could produce the radiation *emitted* (given off) by quasars.

Astronomers can determine the distance to a faraway object by measuring the object's *redshift*. Redshift is a stretching of the wavelength of light or other radiation emitted by an object. Wavelength is the distance between successive crests of a wave. The stretching is called *redshift* because red light has the longest wavelength of any visible light. Objects farther away from Earth have larger redshifts.

A type of redshift known as the *cosmological redshift* occurs in the radiation emitted by cosmic objects because the universe is expanding. That is, every point in the universe is *receding* (becoming farther away) from every other point. The expansion causes distant objects to recede from one another at a rate that depends on the distance between them. More distant objects recede more rapidly and have larger redshifts.

The expansion of the universe does not cause the matter within a particular object to expand, however, because attraction among its atoms and molecules holds the object together. Similarly, the force of gravity prevents the stars in a galaxy from receding from one another. But the galaxies do recede from one another. The expansion of the universe is a basic observation that any successful theory of the universe must explain.

Changing views of the universe

In ancient times, many people thought that the heavenly bodies represented gods and spirits. Some ancient scholars thought that the sun, moon, planets, and stars revolved around Earth. But the Polish astronomer Nicolaus Copernicus suggested in 1543 that Earth and the other planets revolve around the sun. Later astronomers showed that the sun is a typical star.

Knowledge of the universe increased with the development of the telescope, the photographic plate, and the *spectroscope,* an instrument that analyzes light. Astronomers discovered that the sun is moving within a large system of stars, the Milky Way. About 1920, astronomers realized that not all of the *nebulae* (fuzzy patches of light seen in the night sky) are part of the Milky Way. Rather, many of these objects are actually other galaxies.

The discovery of the redshift of distant galaxies led to the theory of the expanding universe.

The *big bang theory* provides the best explanation of the basic observations of the universe. According to the theory, the universe began with an explosion—called the *big bang*—13 billion to 14 billion years ago. Immediately after the explosion, the universe consisted chiefly of intense radiation and hot particles. This radiation, along with various kinds of matter and energy, formed a rapidly expanding region called the *primordial fireball.* After thousands of years, the fireball cooled.

In time, the matter broke apart into huge clumps. The clumps became galaxies, many of them grouped into clusters, superclusters, and filaments. Smaller clumps within the galaxies formed stars. Part of one of these clumps became the sun and the other objects in the solar system.

Strong evidence for the big bang theory comes from observations of faint radio waves coming from all directions in space. Scientists believe this radiation, called the *cosmic microwave background* (CMB) *radiation,* is all that remains of the primordial fireball.

The *steady state theory* offers another explanation for the expansion of the universe and other observations. According to this theory, the universe has always existed in its present state. As the galaxies move apart, new matter appears between them and forms new galaxies. However, the existence of the CMB radiation and detailed studies of galaxies and *supernovae* (exploding stars) have cast strong doubts on the steady state theory.

Studies of nearby stars, distant galaxies, and the CMB radiation give scientists an idea of the types of matter and energy that make up the universe. These studies suggest that the universe consists of about 4 percent ordinary matter and radiation. The matter consists mainly of hydrogen and helium. The radiation includes light, radio, and other waves as well as cosmic rays. The rest of the universe is made up of matter and energy that scientists cannot directly observe. About 23 percent of the universe is *dark matter,* matter that does not emit, reflect, or absorb observable light or other radiation. The remaining 73 percent of the universe is composed of *dark energy.* Dark energy is a little-understood form of energy that is apparently making the universe expand more and more quickly.

Observations of supernovae and the CMB radiation suggest that the present age of the universe is about 13.7 billion years. This estimate agrees with studies of the ages of stars in groups called *globular star clusters,* which contain the oldest stars found in the Milky Way.

The future of the universe

Many studies indicate that the universe will continue to expand. Measurements of the brightness and redshift of supernovae in distant galaxies suggest that at the present time the expansion of the universe is accelerating. Observations of the CMB radiation provide evidence that the universe has the appropriate mixture of matter and energy to continue expanding. Both of these types of studies give similar predictions for the rate at which the universe is expanding.

Theories of the universe based on the German-born physicist Albert Einstein's theory of general relativity allow for the possibility that all of the matter in the universe could come back together again in a *big crunch.* This would happen if the matter's gravitational pull was strong enough to overcome its expansion. The entire universe would eventually collapse and then explode, entering a new phase that might resemble the present one. However, studies of the CMB radiation strongly suggest that the universe has an infinite mass and volume and that it will expand forever.   Kenneth Brecher

Related articles in *World Book* include:

Astronomy	Cosmology	Galaxy	Redshift
Big bang	Dark energy	Gravitation	Relativity
Black hole	Dark matter	Quasar	

Universities and colleges are schools that continue a person's education beyond high school. A university or college education helps men and women enjoy richer, more meaningful lives. It prepares many people for professional careers as doctors, engineers, lawyers, or teachers. It also gives a person a better appreciation of such fields as art, literature, history, human relations, and science. In doing so, a university or college education enables individuals to participate with greater understanding in community affairs.

Modern universities developed from the European universities of the Middle Ages. These institutions took their name from the Latin word *universitas.* This word referred to a group of people organized for a common purpose. Properly speaking, a school that is called a *university* should deal with nearly all fields of learning. Most universities provide a wide range of graduate programs and have a number of undergraduate schools. They may also have graduate professional schools or colleges. But few universities teach as many branches of learning as the word *university* implies.

The first European colleges were merely groups of students who banded together through common interests. In English universities, colleges were formed to provide living quarters and a dining room for these students. Usually they took similar studies, and so the word *college* came to refer to a specific field of learning.

Harvard University, the oldest institution of higher learning in the United States, was established chiefly to prepare men for the ministry. Today, we would call such a school a *seminary* or *theological school* (see **Seminary**). Later, schools broadened their courses to teach the liberal arts (see **Liberal arts**). These became known as *colleges of liberal arts.* The first U.S. universities divided their courses into various fields of learning, and called the departments that taught each branch *colleges* or *schools.* Thus, the word *college* has come to have two meanings in the United States. It may refer to a part of a university that teaches a special branch of knowledge, or it may designate a separate institution that specializes in a single branch of knowledge.

The type of learning available at individual colleges can often be determined from their names. Liberal-arts colleges usually call themselves simply *colleges.* Other schools may be identified by such names as *teachers colleges, agricultural colleges,* or *dental colleges.* Modern universities have many kinds of colleges or schools, from liberal arts to law, medicine, theology, dentistry, and fine arts. *Junior colleges*—also called *community colleges*—mainly offer two-year programs. Some of these programs prepare a person for a semiprofessional career or occupation. See **Community college.**

Going to college

Most high school students at some time in their studies face two questions: "Should I attend college?" and "What college will serve my purposes best?" Students should take stock of their personal abilities and desires. They must decide whether or not they will receive specific preparation in college that will help them in their future work. For example, some students may find that special vocational training, rather than a college education, will better prepare them for the careers they want (see **Vocational education**).

Decisions about attending college should be made only after serious thought about one's life goals. Individuals who enter college without being strongly motivated may find it difficult to be successful students. A person who decides against attending college must realize that such a decision does not necessarily prevent a person from increasing in earning ability or social status.

Selecting a school. Students who decide to attend college must choose the school that most nearly fits their needs, finances, and personal likes. They can discover many of the facts by talking to friends and teachers. They can learn about particular schools by writing to them for information.

There are a number of basic questions a student should ask about any school being considered.

1. Does the school offer the courses in which I am interested?

2. How well is the school equipped in general buildings, libraries, laboratories, and other property?

3. What teaching methods does the school use? What is the average size of each class?

4. What is the standing of the school? Is it accredited? What is the standing of the particular college or department of the school in which I intend to do most of my work?

5. What are the school's tuition, fees, and living expenses? Are opportunities available for earning all, or part of, my expenses while I attend school?

6. Does the school offer the *extracurricular* (nonacademic) activities in which I am interested?

7. How is the school located with regard to transportation, living quarters, and general conveniences?

Entrance requirements of the various universities and colleges may differ considerably. In general, they require satisfactory completion of a high school curriculum. Most universities and colleges require that first-year students have taken certain courses in high school. Many schools will not admit students whose high school grades are below a certain average. As more students seek to attend universities or colleges, entrance requirements tend to become higher. Many institutions require students to pass an entrance examination. Schools may also give students intelligence tests and aptitude tests for later counseling. For example, a student's adviser may use the results of the tests to guide the student's work. See **College entrance examination.**

Colleges and universities state their entrance requirements in their catalogs. They nearly always require a *transcript* (copy) of an applicant's high school credits, as well as letters of recommendation. Entrance examinations are generally given several months before the school term begins. First-year students usually take the intelligence and aptitude tests during an orientation period for newly admitted college students.

People without a high school diploma should not assume that higher education is closed to them. Many colleges and universities admit men and women who have not completed high school. This procedure allows the schools to serve an increasing number of adults seeking continuing education. It also helps extend educational opportunities to such people as military veterans and members of minority groups. Before enrolling such applicants, the university or college evaluates their work experience and reviews their scores on special tests. These tests are designed to measure whether a person's knowledge is equivalent to that of an average high school graduate.

Accrediting. A prospective college student should know the standing of the institution he or she intends to enter. Colleges and universities in the United States are accredited by six regional accrediting authorities. They are the Middle States Association of Colleges and Schools, the New England Association of Schools and Colleges, the North Central Association of Colleges and Schools, the Northwest Commission on Colleges and Universities, the Southern Association of Colleges and Schools, and the Western Association of Schools and Colleges. These authorities base their judgment on the equipment, financial status, requirements, student achievement, and teaching standards of the schools. The authorities are recognized by the Council for Higher Education Accreditation.

Professional societies accredit the various professional schools. For example, the Liaison Committee on Medical Education accredits medical schools. State boards of education also accredit schools in their states. Students may use credits from approved schools in order to obtain teaching certificates and professional licenses within the state.

For a list of the accredited, degree-granting universities and colleges in any U.S. state except Alaska, Nevada, or Wyoming, see the *Universities and colleges* table in the separate *World Book* article on the state. A similar table appears in the articles on **Washington, D.C.,** and **Puerto Rico.** For the accredited universities and colleges in Alaska, Nevada, and Wyoming, see the *Schools* section in each of the articles on those states. See also the *World Book* article on **Canada** (Education) for a discussion of higher education in Canada.

College costs vary widely. Most college catalogs list the average living costs for one year, the tuition, and other fees. In the early 2000's, the average cost of tuition, fees, room, and board at public universities was about $16,360 for all students. The cost for residents averaged less than this amount, and that for nonresidents was higher. The cost at private universities averaged about $33,300 for all students.

Working your way. Many college students earn all or part of their expenses. Many students have part-time jobs while they attend school, such as working in stores and restaurants. Most schools offer students jobs, such as waiting on tables in dormitories or working in the library. Schools often operate employment bureaus to help find part-time jobs for their students. Some students work during their summer vacations, and others drop out of college for a time to work. Many husbands or wives of students work to help their spouses pay their expenses. Sometimes both spouses are students and work part-time.

Financial help. Students may receive all or part of their college expenses through various aid programs. These programs include scholarships and fellowships; federal, state, and private loan programs; and benefits for veterans and certain other groups such as war orphans. There are so many programs of this kind that almost every college and university has a financial aid office to serve its students. A prospective student who needs financial assistance should consult this office at the schools he or she is considering. In general, there are enough financial aid programs to make it possible for any person to attend some college or university in spite of financial problems. See **Fellowship; Scholarship.**

Kinds of universities and colleges

Universities and colleges in the United States may be classified as (1) those operating under private sponsorship, and (2) those operating under public sponsorship. Private institutions may be church-related or nonsectarian. Public institutions may be sponsored by local government, state government, or the federal government. The military academies are examples of federally supported institutions. Most private liberal arts colleges are church-related, while most privately sponsored universities are not now associated with any church. Most public universities are sponsored by state governments. Most junior or community colleges are sponsored by local governments.

Income. All universities and colleges receive funds from a variety of sources. Private colleges depend primarily on student fees and on endowments and gifts for their operating income. Public institutions also have these sources, but depend mainly on state and local taxes for operating funds. Both public and private institutions may receive federal funds for research activities. The federal government distributes aid among colleges and universities according to various formulas. These formulas are based on the number of students in scholarship and loan programs, and on the enrollment of graduate students and veterans.

Both public and private institutions receive funds for construction from several sources. These sources include federal, state, and local grants or loans; gifts; student fees; and endowments.

Governing boards. Most universities and colleges are controlled by a *board of trustees* or a *board of regents.* Boards of trustees of private institutions usually elect their own members. The church body may elect the trustees of a church-related institution. The alumni association of a private institution often elects some of the trustees. The trustees of public institutions are usually appointed by the governor of the state. The voters sometimes elect the trustees or regents.

Boards of trustees or regents approve educational policies. They also appoint the chief administrative officer of the institution. In some states, coordinating committees and boards exercise supervision over those institutions financially assisted by the state.

Most church-related colleges except seminaries ad-

mit students of any religious denomination. Some of them expect all students to attend chapel exercise and to study some religious courses. But some church-related colleges apply these rules only to students of the same religious faith.

In the United States, the federal government has encouraged the development of universities and colleges since the time of the Northwest Ordinance of 1787. The Morrill Act of 1862 provided land grants to all states to support colleges that, among other subjects, would teach agriculture and the mechanical arts. In some instances, these land grants were given to existing state universities. In other cases, new institutions were established. Many are now major universities.

Seven Canadian provinces sponsor and support universities. Some provinces have also founded technical, agricultural, and junior colleges. The first provincial university was the University of Toronto. It was founded in 1827 as King's College.

School organization

Campus is the land on which a college or university stands. The main buildings on a campus usually include classroom buildings, an administration building, a library, laboratories, a gymnasium, an athletic field and stadium, and dormitories. Many institutions have a building, often called a *union,* where social gatherings, plays, and dances may be held. Many of today's universities and colleges have more than one campus.

Administration. The organization of state, province, and city-supported institutions is generally about the same as that of other universities and colleges. They usually offer about the same courses of study, although state institutions often emphasize technical and professional education more than private schools.

In most cases, a *president* or *chancellor* is the chief administrator of a university or college. Other officials handle educational programs, registration, management of funds, and collection of tuition. A *dean of students* helps direct discipline and advise students.

Each college or separate school of a university generally has an *academic dean* or *director.* He or she leads the faculty in preparing the course of study for the college or school, and takes part in university planning.

Faculty includes the teachers of a college or university. A college's faculty is divided into *departments.* Each department deals with one general course of study, such as English, mathematics, or physics. Each department has a *chairman,* who is usually a *professor.* Under the chairman are other professors, *associate professors, assistant professors,* and *instructors.* Some departments also have *teaching fellows* or *research fellows.* These are graduate students who teach or do research part-time. Some faculties include scientists or other workers whose main activity is research, not teaching. Their research is supported by the institution or by funds granted the institution by individuals or groups having specific research interests. The institutions do much research under contract with the federal government.

The student body of a university or college is divided into graduates and undergraduates. *Graduates* have already received their bachelor's degree and are working more or less independently for a master's or doctor's degree. *Undergraduates* are studying for their bachelor's degree. The undergraduates belong to one of four classes—*freshman, sophomore, junior,* and *senior—*according to year of study. Most schools also admit *special students.* These students take a number of courses, but do not work toward a degree.

Most institutions are *coeducational,* with both men and women students. Others admit students of only one sex. A *coordinate* institution generally has separate men's and women's colleges. They are controlled by the same central authority and are usually located on the same or nearby campuses. See **Coeducation.**

The calendar is the program of a school year. It is divided according to one of three systems. The most common system divides the calendar into two *semesters* of about 16 weeks each. The first semester begins in August or September. The second semester begins in January or early February. The school year ends in May or June with *commencement,* or graduation exercises (see **Graduation**). Many schools also hold a six- to eight-week summer session. By attending school all year, students may graduate in three years instead of four.

In the *quarter* system, the year is divided into four quarters of 10, 11, or 12 weeks each. The first quarter begins in the fall. Winter holidays come between the first and second quarters, and spring holidays between the second and third. Many students do not attend the fourth, or summer, quarter. The *trimester* system divides the year into three trimesters of about 15 weeks each.

Selecting courses

Curriculum. The courses given by a college or university are called the school's curriculum. The catalog of the institution outlines the complete curriculum. It gives the requirements for taking each course, as well as the credits given. Each course is designated as giving a specified number of *credits.* These usually equal the number of class hours devoted each week to the course. For example, a course that meets three times a week usually gives three credits for graduation. Schools using the semester calendar require about 120 credits for graduation. Between 30 and 40 of the required credits must be earned in the student's major subject.

Institutions vary considerably in the amount of freedom given students in selecting their courses. Almost all colleges and universities have a certain number of required subjects. Students usually can also choose non-required courses called *electives.* Liberal arts colleges usually give a student more opportunity to choose courses than do professional schools.

When college freshmen register, they usually indicate the major subject they want to study. Some students may take high-school level remedial courses before they enroll in freshman level courses. During the first two years of college, students take largely the basic required courses, such as English composition. The last two years are devoted mostly to the student's major. Many schools permit a student to have two majors.

Undergraduate study. The programs of study provided by universities and colleges are divided into undergraduate and graduate levels. Most colleges offer few, if any, graduate programs. Undergraduate programs usually require four years to complete. Some engineering programs and most architectural programs require five years. Undergraduate study may be in the arts and sciences, or in a discipline such as English, economics, or chemistry. Undergraduate programs may also be given in a professional field such as agriculture, teacher education, or business administration.

Graduate study may also be in the arts and sciences, or in a profession. It ordinarily begins only after a person has completed undergraduate study. Some professional fields will only admit a student who has completed undergraduate study. This is generally true of medicine, law, dentistry, and theology.

Graduate study is more intensive and specialized than undergraduate study. It usually involves more reading and some research experience. The time required to earn a graduate degree is usually three years in law and theology and four years in medicine. But some graduate programs may be completed in one or two years.

Degrees. The bachelor of arts or bachelor of science degree is the common degree for completing a four- or five-year program. One or two years of graduate study are usually required for the master of arts or master of science degree. A doctor's degree signifies more extensive graduate study. Many institutions also award honorary degrees for outstanding achievement in a profession or in public service. See **Degree, College.**

College life

College life gives students a welcome measure of independence. But students should realize that new responsibilities go with this independence. They must balance hard work with recreation, allow enough time and energy for social activities, and learn to use to the best advantage the opportunities their school offers.

Residence. Most colleges that offer bachelor's degrees have *residence halls* or *dormitories.* Dormitory life offers many opportunities for students to make friends. Community colleges generally do not have dormitories. Many schools also have student-run residences called *cooperatives.* In these, the students can cut expenses by doing their own housework. Students

Bob Daemmrich, Tony Stone Images

Commencement climaxes the university and college year. Graduating students receive their diplomas at commencement. A commencement speaker is addressing graduates, *above.*

may also live in private homes or apartments.

Many students live with their parents and *commute* (travel daily) between home and campus. Some colleges and universities whose campuses are in large cities provide *commuter centers,* where students who commute may spend free time while on campus.

Fraternities and sororities have houses at many schools. These groups choose their own members according to rules set up by the school. Educators do not agree on the value of the fraternity and sorority system. Some approve the social advantages of membership in these organizations. Others believe they tend to dominate college life and to become undemocratic. Some colleges prohibit social fraternities and sororities on their campuses. See **Fraternity; Sorority.**

Instruction. First-year students find they have much more time to do as they choose in college than they had in high school. Classes generally take up only about 15 hours each week, although there may be additional hours of laboratory work. The rest of the time between classes is free for study or recreation.

Most classes are lecture or discussion groups. In larger institutions, *lectures* may be given to hundreds of students at a time, sometimes with the help of closed-circuit television. *Discussion groups,* or *seminars,* are much smaller. Students often work on individual projects outside of class and report on them to the group.

Many universities and colleges offer courses known as *individualized-study* or *self-directed* courses. Such courses have no formal classroom sessions. Students work independently on assignments outlined by course materials. They complete the work at their own pace, under the guidance of a faculty member. In this kind of course, the student may use computers, individually assigned laboratory booths, and other learning aids.

For a general discussion of tests and grading, see **Grading; Testing.**

Libraries. University and college libraries are storehouses of knowledge. Some hold several million volumes. The library must be used to the fullest extent for a student to receive the greatest benefit from a course. Routine classwork can only scratch the surface of any field of knowledge. Students can round out their education only by consistent and intelligent independent reading. See **Library** (College and university libraries).

Research and laboratory work. The college teacher tries to do more than merely hand the student facts to memorize. It is far more important to develop the student's ability to find information and to learn to think intelligently. For this reason, the teacher tries to direct the student in independent study and research by recommending books for outside reading and by suggesting new avenues of study in a certain field. Students in the sciences and engineering have laboratories in which to work. World-famous scientists direct some of these laboratories. In them they have made many important discoveries, often with the help of graduate students. For example, much of the original work on the use of atomic energy was done in the laboratories of the University of Chicago and the University of California.

Extracurricular activities outside the normal routine of classes and study help develop the student's personality, and provide a proper balance for the daily routine. Athletics are one of many possible activities (see **Sports**).

Students may also work on the staffs of school newspapers and magazines. They may take part in such activities as dramatics, music, debating, religion, and student government (see **Student government**).

History

European universities. Modern universities had their origin in Europe during the 1100's. But European universities were not the first in the world. The Arabs had universities at earlier dates. Al-Azhar University, founded in Cairo in about 970, is one of the oldest universities in the world still operating.

European universities developed from the cathedral and monastery schools. Their development took place so slowly that it is difficult to know the point at which they became universities. Many scholars believe the oldest European university is the University of Bologna, Italy. It came into existence about 1100. The University of Paris developed in the late 1100's. Many other universities appeared in Europe in the 1200's and the 1300's.

These first schools were founded largely to serve the professions. They provided the first unified teaching of law, medicine, and theology. The courses of study gradually broadened. During the Renaissance in the 1400's, the universities helped direct the revival of interest in Greek and Roman learning. From this revival developed the modern concept of the liberal-arts curriculum.

First universities in the Americas. The first university in the Western Hemisphere, the University of Santo Domingo, was founded in the Dominican Republic in 1538. The University of San Marcos at Lima, Peru, was founded in 1551, as was the National Autonomous University of Mexico. Other universities appeared shortly afterward in the other Spanish colonies.

The first university planned in what is now the United States was at Henricopolis, Virginia. It was authorized in 1619, but plans were dropped after the Indian massacres of 1622. Harvard University is the oldest active school of higher education in the United States. It was founded in 1636. Canada's oldest university, Laval University, was founded as the Seminary of Quebec in 1663. It became a university in 1852. Canada's first English-speaking university was established in 1789. It was the University of King's College at Windsor, Nova Scotia.

Higher education in the United States began when knowledge was limited. The modern scientific spirit had not yet developed. The early settlers looked upon colleges chiefly as a means of training ministers.

Many small church colleges were founded during the 1700's and 1800's, particularly in the Middle West. These

The oldest U.S. universities and colleges

Name	Location	Year*
Harvard University	Cambridge, MA	1636
William and Mary, College of	Williamsburg, VA	1693
Yale University	New Haven, CT	1701
Princeton University	Princeton, NJ	1746
Columbia University	New York City	1754
University of Pennsylvania	Philadelphia	1757
Brown University	Providence, RI	1764
Rutgers, the State University of New Jersey	New Brunswick, NJ	1766
Dartmouth College	Hanover, NH	1769

*Year institution became a bachelor's degree-granting institution.

colleges were general rather than specialized. They taught liberal arts rather than technical subjects. Early in U.S. history, some leaders saw the need for education that went beyond religious concerns. The state university was one response to this need.

Another development was the granting of land in new territories for the establishment of schools. Wealthy citizens also gave gifts for the founding of nonchurch schools. A number of schools that had been established by churches also came under private control.

Growth of specialization. From the 1800's through the mid-1900's, specialization in knowledge grew. Many colleges were created to train students in such fields as agriculture, medicine, engineering, and commerce. This trend resulted in a greater emphasis on advanced study, and graduate schools were created at many larger schools. In turn, research and professional interests came to dominate all other educational interests. Education for professions overshadowed the liberal arts.

Another cause of specialization has been the increase in the number of students attending college. In the early days, universities served only a relatively limited group. But the people of the United States insisted that higher education should be available to anyone who wanted it.

Recent developments. Educators agree students need a broad education as a basis for whatever field attracts them. Some colleges stress the study of classic works of literature. Others combine campus study with practical training in factories and offices.

During the 1960's and early 1970's, programs were developed to help members of minority groups obtain a higher education. The federal government established *Upward Bound,* a project designed to encourage and prepare students from low-income homes to attend college. Some schools modified their admissions standards for members of minority groups to encourage their enrollment. Curriculum designers also fashioned new programs, such as Afro-American, American Indian, and Chicano studies. These programs were intended to broaden the student's understanding of the contributions of various ethnic groups to American society.

Another major development in American universities and colleges has been their increasing contribution to the world outside the campus. University laboratories have become important centers of experiment and discovery. College extension services, home study, correspondence courses, and radio and TV programs have spread knowledge far beyond the limits of the campus.

During the 1980's and early 1990's, the student bodies of many universities and colleges became increasingly diverse. Many campuses began offering programs that deal with such issues as gender, disability, age, and sexual preference.　　　　　　　　　　　　I. King Jordan

Related articles in *World Book.* See the separate articles on outstanding universities and colleges, such as **Harvard University.** See also the *Careers* section in the various articles on different fields of human knowledge, such as **Medicine** (Careers in medicine). Other related articles include:

Academic freedom
American Association of University Women
Careers
Coeducation
College entrance examination
Community college

Degree, College
Distance learning
Education
Extension programs
Fellowship
Fraternity
Land-grant university

Library
Scholarship

Sorority
Teaching

United Negro College Fund

Outline

I. Going to college
　A. Selecting a school
　B. Entrance requirements
　C. Accrediting
　D. College costs
　E. Working your way
　F. Financial help
II. Kinds of universities and colleges
　A. Privately controlled schools
　B. Church-controlled schools
　C. Publicly controlled schools
III. School organization
　A. Campus
　B. Administration
　C. Faculty
　D. The student body
　E. The calendar
IV. Selecting courses
　A. Curriculum
　B. Preprofessional courses
　C. Graduate study
　D. Degrees
V. College life
　A. Residence
　B. Fraternities and sororities
　C. Instruction
　D. Libraries
　E. Research and laboratory work
　F. Extracurricular activities
VI. History

Questions

What information should you get when you select a university or college?

How does a university differ from a college?

How is a university faculty usually organized?

In what three ways are school-year programs divided?

What opportunities does a university or college offer?

What is the oldest university in the United States? In Canada?

From what sources can a student obtain financial aid?

What kinds of courses did the first universities and colleges in the United States offer? Why?

Why has specialization developed in higher education?

What is the largest university in the United States? In Canada?

Additional resources

The College Board College Handbook. College Board, published annually.

Greene, Howard R. and Matthew W. *Presenting Yourself Successfully to Colleges.* Cliff Street Bks., 2001.

HEP Higher Education Directory. Higher Education Pubns., published annually.

Johnston, Julia, and Shanley, M. K. *For Parents Only: Tips for Surviving the Journey from Homeroom to Dorm Room.* Barron's, 2000.

Nourse, Kenneth A. *How to Write Your College Application Essay.* 2nd ed. VGM Career, 2001.

Schneider, Zola D. *Campus Visits and College Interviews.* Rev. ed. College Board, 2002.

University of ... See articles on universities listed under their key word, as in **Chicago, University of.**

Unknown soldier. After World War I (1914-1918), officials of the Allied countries found that the bodies of many soldiers killed in battle could not be identified. The governments of Belgium, France, Italy, the United Kingdom, and the United States decided to honor these soldiers' memory. Each country chose a symbolic unknown soldier, buried the remains near its national capital, and built a monument to the soldier. Belgium placed its unknown soldier in a tomb at the base of the Colonnade of the Congress in Brussels. The United Kingdom buried its soldier in Westminster Abbey. France buried its unknown soldier beneath the Arc de Triomphe in Paris and keeps a flame always burning over the grave. Italy's unknown soldier lies before the monument to Victor Emmanuel II, the first king of a united Italy, in Rome.

The unknown soldier of the United States was one of

four war dead taken from American cemeteries in France. An American soldier, Sergeant Edward Younger, chose the soldier from these four. The remains were brought to the U.S. Capitol to lie in state. On Armistice Day (Nov. 11), 1921, they were buried in Arlington National Cemetery in Virginia. The tomb, completed in 1931, bears the inscription, "Here rests in honored glory an American soldier known but to God."

Congress later directed that an "Unknown American" from each of three wars—World War II (1939-1945), the Korean War (1950-1953), and the Vietnam War (1957-1975)—be buried beside the Tomb of the Unknown Soldier (now called the Tomb of the Unknowns). The unknowns from World War II and the Korean War were buried in marble-capped crypts at the head of the tomb on Memorial Day in 1958. The unknown serviceman of the Vietnam War was buried between them during a Memorial Day ceremony in 1984.

The World War II unknown was chosen from two unidentified soldiers by an American sailor, Hospitalman William Charette, in a ceremony aboard the cruiser *Canberra* off Norfolk, Virginia. The Korean War unknown was chosen by an American soldier, Sergeant Ned Lyle, from the unidentified dead of that war buried in the National Memorial Cemetery of the Pacific at Honolulu. The Vietnam War unknown was the only American serviceman killed in that war whose remains could not be identified. But at the time of the ceremony, more than 2,400 servicemen were still missing. In 1998, DNA tests determined that the Vietnam War unknown was Michael Blassie, an Air Force lieutenant shot down over South Vietnam in 1972. The remains of Lieutenant Blassie were moved to a veterans cemetery near St. Louis.

An amphitheater, funded by the Grand Army of the Republic in honor of military forces killed in battle, stands near the tomb. Memorial Day services are held there each year. An honor guard from the 1st Battalion, 3rd U.S. Infantry Regiment, Fort Myer, Virginia, keeps a sentry on duty at all times. The sentry is changed every hour during the day from October 1 to March 31, and every half hour from April 1 to September 30. The sentry is changed every two hours at night.   Critically reviewed by the National Cemetery System of the Department of the Army

See also **Arc de Triomphe; Arlington National Cemetery.**

Unmanned aerial vehicle (UAV) is a type of aircraft designed to fly missions without a pilot on board. UAV's are sometimes called *drones, remotely piloted vehicles* (RPV's), or *remotely operated aircraft* (ROA's). UAV's are primarily used by the military. Advanced electronics systems enable many UAV's to collect and transmit information and to receive flight control instructions. UAV's are most commonly used for surveillance, reconnaissance, and identification of battlefield targets, and as targets for weapons tests. They typically perform dangerous missions that would put a pilot at risk, such as flying into hostile territory. Some UAV's, including those known as UCAV's (unmanned combat aerial vehicles), can fire missiles. United States forces used UAV's for this purpose in military strikes in Afghanistan in 2001 and during the Iraq War, which began in 2003.

Most UAV's are *fixed-wing craft*—that is, their design is similar to that of airplanes. However, some are *rotary-wing* UAV's similar to helicopters.

UAV's do not need many features that piloted aircraft require, such as cockpits and pilot safety systems. Thus, UAV's can be smaller and less expensive to build than similar conventional aircraft. But their additional electronic systems often make them cost about the same.

Some UAV's are programmed before a mission to follow a certain set of instructions. Others are flown manually by an operator. All UAV's today communicate with an operator—on a ship, an aircraft, or the ground—who can change the mission at any time. If communication is cut off, some UAV's can follow preprogrammed instructions to fly to a specific location and wait until communication can be reestablished.   Eric N. Johnson

See also **Aircraft, Military** (Special-mission aircraft).

Unser, Al, Sr. (1939-   ), became one of the most successful drivers in automobile racing history. He won the Indianapolis 500 race four times. In 1978, he became the third driver in racing history to win races in a single year on a paved oval track, a road course, and a dirt track. The other drivers to do it were Mario Andretti and A. J. Foyt. In 1978, Unser became the only driver in Indy car history to win three 500-mile races in one season. An Indy racing car has an open cockpit.

Alfred Unser was born in Albuquerque, New Mexico, on May 29, 1939. He began racing professionally in 1957 and made his Indy car debut in 1964. He retired as a race driver in 1994. Unser's brother Bobby has won the Indianapolis 500 race three times. Another brother, Jerry, was killed while racing at the Indianapolis 500 in 1959. Al's son Al Unser, Jr., won the Indianapolis 500 in 1992 and 1994.   Sylvia Wilkinson

Untouchable. See Caste; India (Social structure).

Untouchables. See Ness, Eliot.

Upanishads, *oo PAN uh shadz,* are a group of writings that make up the last section of the Vedas, a collection of Hindu scriptures. The Upanishads form a basic part of Hinduism and have influenced most Indian philosophy. They are sometimes called the Vedanta, which means *the summing up of the Veda.* The word *Upanishads* means *to sit close to.* It suggests that the Upanishads were originally secret. Most of them were written as dialogues between a teacher and student. The most important ones appeared between 800 and 600 B.C.

Several important Hindu schools of thought, including the sankhya and yoga schools, are based on the Upanishads. These teachings follow two basic philosophies. One states that there is a single fundamental reality, called Brahman, or God, which corresponds to Atman, the soul. Thus, there is no real distinction between the soul and God. The other philosophy states that each soul is individually eternal.   Charles S. J. White

See also **Hinduism; Vedas.**

Upas, *YOO puhs,* is a large forest tree that grows in southeastern Asia and Indonesia. Hunters mixed its poisonous milky sap with other plant poisons to poison arrows and darts. Tales about the deadliness of this poison terrified early explorers and travelers in the East Indies. Fabulous but false stories started regarding the plant. People said nothing could grow in the tree's shade and that birds that perched on or flew above the tree died. Today, botanists know that poisoning only occurs from contact with the tree's sap.   Christopher W. Dick

Scientific classification. The upas belongs to the mulberry family, Moraceae. It is *Antiaris toxicaria.*

Updike, John (1932–   ), is an American author of novels, short stories, essays, and poetry. Updike became noted for his elaborate, lyrical prose style. He served as a staff writer for *The New Yorker* magazine from 1955 to 1957 and built his literary reputation as a frequent contributor to *The New Yorker.*

Much of Updike's fiction explores the superficial but seductive materialism he sees in middle-class American life. Typical Updike characters are self-absorbed, guilt-ridden, and obsessed with their own unimportance and the prospect of their death. They relieve their anxieties through marital unfaithfulness, but this fails to help them in their search for spiritual salvation.

In the novel *Couples* (1968) and the stories collected in *Museums and Women* (1972), Updike dramatized the disintegrating morals and marriages in several suburban families. The autobiographical stories in *Too Far to Go* (1979) narrate the course of the Maple family from newlywed happiness to divorce.

Updike's first popular work, *Rabbit, Run* (1960), is a novel about Rabbit Angstrom, a former high school basketball star bewildered by family responsibilities. In *Rabbit Redux* (1971), Rabbit confronts such issues of the late 1960's as drug use, racial violence, and the Vietnam War. *Rabbit Is Rich* (1981) portrays Rabbit in middle age, wealthy but spiritually unfulfilled. *Rabbit Is Rich* won the 1982 Pulitzer Prize for fiction. Updike also won the 1991 Pulitzer Prize for *Rabbit at Rest* (1990), the fourth novel in the series, which describes Rabbit's retirement. Updike continued the story in the short novel "Rabbit Remembered," published in the collection *Licks of Love* (2000). Updike's other novels include *The Centaur* (1963), *The Coup* (1978), *The Witches of Eastwick* (1984) and a sequel called *The Widows of Eastwick* (2008), *Roger's Version* (1986), *S.* (1988), *Memories of the Ford Administration* (1992), *In the Beauty of the Lilies* (1996), *Gertrude and Claudius* (2000), *Villages* (2004), and *Terrorist* (2006).

Updike was born on March 18, 1932, in Shillington, Pennsylvania. Many of the early stories in *Pigeon Feathers* (1962) deal with the experiences of young people in a town based on Shillington. His short stories from 1953 to 1975 were collected in *John Updike: The Early Stories* (2004). Updike wrote several related stories about a novelist named Henry Bech, collected in *Bech: A Book* (1970), *Bech Is Back* (1982), and *Bech at Bay* (1998). His essays on art appeared in *Just Looking* (1989) and *Still Looking* (2005). His other essays and nonfiction were collected in *Assorted Prose* (1965), *Picked Up Pieces* (1975), *Hugging the Shore* (1983), *Odd Jobs* (1991), *More Matter* (1999), and *Due Considerations* (2007). Updike's poems were collected in *Collected Poems: 1953-1993. Self-Consciousness* (1989) is a memoir.   Arthur M. Saltzman

Upland sandpiper is a North American bird of the sandpiper family. It is usually found on wet prairies or meadows. The upland sandpiper is the only member of the tattler group that does not live near the ocean.

The upland sandpiper is sometimes called the upland plover. It is about 1 foot (30 centimeters) long and has an especially long tail for a sandpiper. Its color is blackish-brown and buff above, and buff with dark streaks on the breast and sides. Its belly is white. The bird breeds from Alaska to Montana and Maine. In fall, it migrates to southern Brazil and Argentina. There, the upland sandpiper winters on grassy plains known as the Pampas.

The upland sandpiper makes its nest in clumps of prairie grass or dry leaves on the prairie. The female lays four cream-colored or pale buff eggs, speckled with dark brown. The birds' color blends with the grass, making them hard to see. The young birds can fly by midsummer, and they start south almost at once.

Upland sandpipers destroy many harmful insects, such as locusts and cutworms. The bird is protected from hunters by law.   Fritz L. Knopf

Scientific classification. The upland sandpiper is in the family Scolopacidae. It is *Bartramia longicauda.*

WORLD BOOK illustration by Trevor Boyer, Linden Artists Ltd.
Upland sandpiper

Upper Volta. See Burkina Faso.

UPS. See United Parcel Service, Inc.

Ur, *ehr* or *oor,* a city in the ancient region of Sumer (now southeastern Iraq), was one of the world's first cities. It stood on the Euphrates River near the Persian Gulf and thrived as a commercial port as early as 3500 B.C. By about 2800 B.C., Ur had become a strong *city-state,* an independent unit consisting of the city and its surrounding villages and farmland. It had a major temple to the Sumerian moon god Nanna.

From 2400 to 2100 B.C., rival states and empires outshone Ur in political importance. About 2100 B.C., King Ur-Nammu founded Ur's third major *dynasty* (family of rulers). Under this dynasty, Ur controlled a large, well-regulated empire that extended from Assyria in the north to Elam in the east. This dynasty ended about 2000 B.C. Ur, though no longer the center of political power, remained a commercial and cultural center. Ur was abandoned by about 500 B.C.   Seth F. C. Richardson

See also **City** (picture); **Sumer; Woolley, Sir Leonard.**

Ural Mountains, *YUR uhl,* extend for about 1,500 miles (2,400 kilometers) through the western part of Russia. The mountains run south from near the Arctic Ocean to about the Kazakhstan border. Many geographers consider them to be one of the boundaries between Europe and Asia (see **Russia** [terrain map]).

The Ural Mountains have great mineral wealth. Salt mining there has been important since the 1500's. Iron and copper mining became important in the 1700's. The Ural region is famous for its gems and semiprecious stones, which include amethyst, beryl, emeralds, malachite, and topaz. Other mining products include bauxite, chromium, coal, copper, gold, iron ore, lead, nickel, platinum, potash, silver, and zinc. The Urals also have one of the world's largest asbestos reserves. Oil and natural gas are found east and west of the mountains.

The Ural Mountains supplied fuels, metals, and other materials for the armies of the Soviet Union during World War II. After the war ended in 1945, the Urals remained a major Soviet mining and industrial region. Industrialization severely polluted the air and water in the

Urals. In 1991, Russia, which had been one of the republics of the Soviet Union, became independent.

The mountains are geologically old. They were first formed about 300 million years ago. They were worn down to nearly a plain, and then formed again about 200 million years ago. Since then, they have been worn down to rounded hills, most of which rise only from 1,000 to 6,000 feet (300 to 1,800 meters). The southern range spreads as wide as about 100 miles (160 kilometers) from east to west in some places. In the north, the mountain range is narrower and less rounded. The highest peak of the Ural Mountains is Mount Narodnaya (6,217 feet, or 1,895 meters).   Craig ZumBrunnen

Ural River, *YUR uhl,* is a shallow river that rises in the southern Ural Mountains in Russia. For location, see **Russia** (terrain map). It flows south from Russia through Kazakhstan for about 1,570 miles (2,527 kilometers) and enters the Caspian Sea through several mouths. Salmon and sturgeon fisheries are along the Ural. At Orenburg and Oral railroads cross it. Magnitogorsk, a major steel center of Russia, lies on the upper Ural.   Leslie Dienes

Uranium is a silvery-white, radioactive metal. It is the source of energy used to generate electric energy at all large commercial nuclear power plants. A chunk of uranium the size of a softball can release more energy than a trainload of coal that weighs 3 million times as much. Uranium also produces the tremendous explosions of certain nuclear weapons.

Uranium is the second heaviest element found in nature. Only plutonium is heavier. Engineers put the heaviness of uranium to use in a number of applications. They use uranium in gyrocompasses for aircraft, as a counterweight for ailerons and other control surfaces of aircraft and spacecraft, and as a radiation shield. The uranium used in these applications has an extremely low level of radioactivity. Scientists also use uranium to determine the age of rocks and ground water, and of deposits of *travertine* (a form of limestone) at archaeological sites.

Uranium occurs chiefly in rocks, usually in extremely small concentrations. On average, uranium accounts for only 1.4 pounds of every million pounds of Earth's crust. Uranium occurs in even smaller concentrations in rivers, lakes, the oceans, and other bodies of water. On average, uranium accounts for only 3 pounds of every billion pounds of seawater.

In 1789, German chemist Martin H. Klaproth discovered uranium. He found it in pitchblende, a dark, bluish-black mineral. Klaproth named uranium after the planet Uranus, which had been discovered in 1781. In 1841, French chemist Eugène Péligot separated pure uranium from pitchblende.

Sources of uranium

Pitchblende, the first uranium ore discovered, is the most important variety of uraninite. Other major ores include uranophane, coffinite, and carnotite. Sandstone, shale, and phosphate may contain valuable deposits of uranium ores.

By the early 2000's, the world's mining companies had discovered about 5,100,000 tons (4,700,000 metric tons) of uranium ore that could be mined at a reasonable cost. World production of uranium is about 43,000 tons (39,000 metric tons) a year. Canada leads all countries in production. Canada's uranium comes from the Athabasca Basin of northern Saskatchewan. The chief deposits of uranium ore in the United States are in Arizona, Colorado, New Mexico, Texas, Utah, and Wyoming.

Uranium isotopes

In nature, uranium occurs in three *isotopes* (forms). Each has an *atomic number* (number of protons in the nucleus) of 92. But, each isotope has a different number of neutrons and so differs in its *atomic mass number* (total number of protons and neutrons in the nucleus). The lightest natural isotope has 92 protons and 142 neutrons, for a total of 234 nuclear particles. The name of this isotope, U-234, comes from the chemical symbol for uranium—U—and the atomic mass number. The other two natural isotopes of uranium are U-235 and U-238.

U-238 makes up about 99.28 percent of all natural uranium. U-235 accounts for approximately 0.71 percent of all natural uranium; U-234, only about 0.006 percent.

U-235 is the only natural isotope of uranium whose nucleus can easily be made to undergo *fission*—that is, to split into two nearly equal parts. Fission releases the nuclear energy used in power plants and weapons.

Properties of uranium

Uranium has a *relative atomic mass* of 238.02891. An element's relative atomic mass equals its *mass* (amount of matter) divided by $\frac{1}{12}$ of the mass of an atom of carbon 12, the most abundant form of carbon. At 25 °C, uranium's density is 19.05 grams per cubic centimeter (see **Density**). Uranium melts at 1132 °C and boils at 3818 °C. It belongs to the group of elements known as the *actinide series* (see **Element, Chemical** [Periodic table]).

Uranium combines readily with other elements. In nature, uranium always occurs in chemical compounds with oxygen. In most surface and ground waters, uranium is combined with oxygen, carbon dioxide, phosphate, fluoride, or sulfate. In addition, uranium reacts with acids to form compounds called *uranyl salts.* All uranium compounds are highly poisonous.

Radioactivity. All the isotopes of uranium are radioactive. Their nuclei *decay* (break apart), releasing particles and energy, chiefly *alpha particles, beta particles,* and *gamma rays* (see **Radiation** [diagram: Radioactive decay]). When an isotope decays, it turns into another

Leading uranium-producing countries

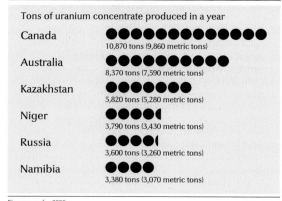

Tons of uranium concentrate produced in a year

Canada
10,870 tons (9,860 metric tons)

Australia
8,370 tons (7,590 metric tons)

Kazakhstan
5,820 tons (5,280 metric tons)

Niger
3,790 tons (3,430 metric tons)

Russia
3,600 tons (3,260 metric tons)

Namibia
3,380 tons (3,070 metric tons)

Figures are for 2006.
Source: World Nuclear Association.

isotope. A succession of decays eventually changes uranium into a lead isotope that is not radioactive.

Scientists measure the rate at which an isotope decays in terms of its *half-life*. The half-life of an isotope is the length of time after which only half the atoms of what began as a sample of that isotope would still be atoms of that isotope.

Uranium isotopes have long half-lives. The half-life of U-238 is about 4 $\frac{1}{2}$ billion years. U-235 has a half-life of about 700 million years; U-234, about 250,000 years. Much of the internal heat of the earth is thought to be a result of radiation given off by uranium.

Fissionability. A U-235 nucleus can split into two fragments when struck by a neutron. When this nucleus splits, it releases energy. It also releases two or more neutrons. These neutrons, in turn, can cause other U-235 nuclei to break apart. When the other nuclei undergo fission, they also release energy and neutrons. Under certain circumstances, this process can continue in a self-sustaining series of fission events called a *chain reaction*.

A U-238 nucleus rarely breaks apart when struck by a neutron. Usually, U-238 nuclei merely absorb neutrons that strike them.

How uranium is mined and processed

Mining uranium. Mining companies use three chief methods to remove uranium from the ground: (1) *in situ solution mining,* (2) *open-pit mining,* and (3) *underground mining.*

In situ solution mining begins with the pumping of a special solution through holes drilled into the earth. The solution dissolves oxides of uranium. The solution containing the oxides is then pumped into tanks at the surface.

In almost all cases, the holes used for in situ solution mining have already been drilled as part of an effort to locate rich deposits of uranium. During the exploratory process, prospectors lowered radiation detectors into the holes.

Open-pit mining uses explosives to break up rock and soils that cover uranium deposits near the surface of the earth. Miners dig blast holes, then fill them with the explosives. After the explosions, huge power shovels clear away the rubble. Smaller shovels then dig out the uranium ore.

Underground mining is used if the uranium ore lies far beneath the surface. Mining companies dig tunnels into the deposits. The miners drill into the tunnel walls to install explosives that loosen the ore. The miners then load the ore into buckets, which are hoisted to the surface.

Refining and processing uranium ore. The ore from the mine goes to a *mill,* where the uranium is concentrated. At the mill, workers use sulfuric acid or carbonate solutions to produce a uranium salt called *yellowcake.* The salt is purified to an oxide, also called yellowcake, which has the chemical symbol U_3O_8. At a *conversion plant,* the oxide undergoes a chemical reaction with fluorine. This reaction produces uranium hexafluoride (UF_6).

The uranium hexafluoride goes to an *enrichment plant,* where U-235 and U-238 are separated from each other. This separation produces *enriched uranium,* which has a higher percentage of U-235 than does natural uranium. Most nuclear reactors at power plants in the United States use fuel that contains about 2 to 4 percent U-235. Nuclear weapons and the reactors for nuclear-powered ships require uranium with much higher concentrations of U-235.

Enriched uranium for reactors goes to a *fuel-fabrication plant,* where the uranium hexafluoride is converted to uranium dioxide (UO_2). The uranium dioxide is compressed into cylindrical pellets that are used as fuel.

Separating uranium isotopes. Scientists have invented several methods for separating uranium isotopes. Enrichment plants use two of these methods, *gaseous diffusion* and *centrifugal enrichment.* A third method, *laser isotope separation,* is still experimental.

The gaseous diffusion method is used in the United States. In this process, a pump forces molecules of uranium hexafluoride gas through barrierlike structures. These structures have millions of tiny holes in them.

Lighter gas molecules pass through the holes in the barriers more rapidly than do heavier molecules. The lighter molecules contain U-235 atoms. As a result, gas that passes through the barrier contains a higher percentage of U-235 than did the original gas. The increase in concentration is extremely small, however. The gas must pass through the barrier several thousand times to produce enriched uranium for a power plant.

The centrifugal method is used in several plants in Europe and Japan. The centrifuge in this process consists of vertical cylinders that spin rapidly. Pumps force uranium hexafluoride gas into each cylinder through a stationary vertical tube in the center of the cylinder.

The spinning of a cylinder forces almost all the gas outward to the curved walls. In addition, a scoop connected to the bottom of the stationary tube helps create

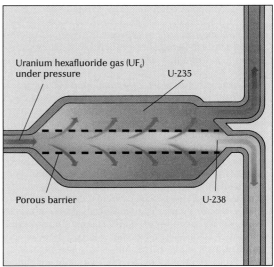

WORLD BOOK diagram by James Magine

The gaseous diffusion method of isotope separation, shown in the diagram above, uses porous barriers to separate uranium isotopes. Separation occurs because the molecules of uranium hexafluoride gas containing the isotope U-235 pass through the barriers faster than those containing U-238.

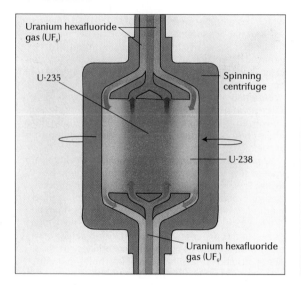

The centrifugal method of separating isotopes uses a spinning cylinder. The rotation of the cylinder forces uranium hexafluoride gas outward. Gas that contains U-238 is relatively heavy, and so it crowds against the walls. As a result, lighter gas, which contains U-235, is concentrated near the center.

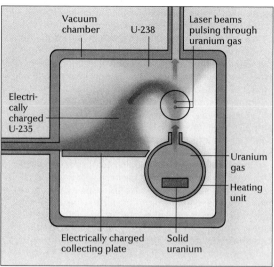

WORLD BOOK diagrams by James Magine

Laser isotope separation uses one or more beams of laser light (two beams shown here). This light causes only U-235 atoms in a uranium gas to acquire an electric charge. An oppositely charged plate attracts these atoms, but does not affect the U-238 atoms. Thus, the gas separates into two streams.

a vertical flow in the gas. Differences in temperature within the cylinder also contribute to the flow of the gas.

Due to these three influences—the spinning of the cylinder, the action of the scoop, and the temperature differences—the gas flows in a complex pattern. As a result, the gas near the bottom of the cylinder becomes more concentrated in U-238 than does the gas at the top.

The scoop at the bottom removes waste gas, which has a relatively high concentration of U-238. A scoop at the top removes enriched gas, which has a relatively high concentration of U-235. The process repeats until the desired concentration of U-235 is obtained.

Laser isotope separation uses a combination of laser light and electric charge to separate uranium isotopes. A laser produces a thin beam of light that has a very narrow range of *frequency* (rate of vibration of the light waves).

In *atomic vapor laser isotope separation* (AVLIS), a beam of electrons heats a piece of uranium at the bottom of a closed container. The heat changes the uranium into *vapor* (gas). A laser beam then pulses into the vapor. The frequency of the beam is tuned so that electrons in atoms of U-235 can absorb the light, but U-238 electrons cannot.

When a U-235 electron absorbs this light, it gains enough energy to leave the atom. This process changes the electrical balance of the atom. An electron carries a negative electric charge. A nucleus carries one or more positive charges. In a normal atom, the number of positive charges is the same as the number of negative charges. Thus, when an electron leaves an atom, the atom acquires a positive charge. Scientists say that the atom becomes a *positive ion.* Thus, the laser light ionizes U-235 atoms, but not U-238 atoms.

The hot vapor rises. Negatively charged collector plates near the top of the container attract the positive U-235 ions. Because the collector plates are cooler than

the gas, the U-235 *condenses* (changes from a gas to a liquid) on them. The U-235 liquid drips off the collector plates into special containers, forming a solid mass called a *splat.* The splats are collected, then purified and oxidized for use as nuclear fuel.

Meanwhile, the electrically neutral U-238 travels past the charged plates. It then condenses on a waste plate near the top of the container.

In another laser technique, an electric unit heats a piece of uranium, producing a vapor. Two laser beams work together to ionize U-235 atoms in the vapor. A positively charged plate collects U-235 ions, while a vapor of U-238 atoms exits through an opening in the top of the container.

Laser isotope separation uses much less electric energy than does gaseous diffusion. In addition, the separation equipment costs much less than centrifuge equipment. Government-sponsored companies in France, Japan, and the United States are experimenting with laser isotope separation.

History of the use of uranium

People have used uranium and its compounds for almost 2,000 years. Colored glass produced for a mosaic mural about A.D. 79 contains uranium oxide, and glass manufacturers continued to use this compound as a pigment until the 1800's. People who painted or glazed china also employed uranium as a pigment. In addition, the metal was used in the processing of photographs.

In 1896, French physicist Antoine Henri Becquerel discovered that uranium is radioactive. His achievement marked the first time that any element had been found to be radioactive.

In 1935, Arthur J. Dempster, a Canadian-born physicist, discovered U-235. German chemists Otto Hahn and Fritz Strassmann used uranium to produce the first artificial nuclear fission in 1938. In 1942, Italian-born physicist

Enrico Fermi and his co-workers at the University of Chicago produced the first artificial chain reaction. They used U-235 as the fissioning material. Fermi's work led to the development of the atomic bomb.

Scientific research also led to peacetime uses of uranium. In 1954, the U.S. Navy launched the *Nautilus,* the first submarine powered by nuclear fuel. In 1957, the first nuclear power plant in the United States began to operate in Shippingport, Pennsylvania, near Pittsburgh.

Since the early 1970's, uranium-fueled nuclear power plants have been an important source of energy. Approximately 30 countries now have such plants. Several of these countries continue to build uranium-fueled nuclear power plants. In the United States, however, new plants are no longer built. Reasons for the halt include public concerns over safety; government regulations relating to safety; and the high costs of building and operating new plants, relative to the costs of new plants that generate power from the burning of coal or natural gas.

Anne Lewis-Russ and Harold R. Roberts

See also **Atom** (diagram: How atoms compare); **Isotope; Nuclear energy; Nuclear weapon; Radiation** (Naturally radioactive substances).

Uranus, YUR *uh nuhs* or *yu RAY nuhs,* was the first god of the sky in Greek mythology. According to the ancient Greek poet Hesiod, Uranus was the child of Gaea, or Ge, who was the earth. Uranus had no father.

Uranus and his mother mated and produced 3 monsters called Hecatoncheires, each with 100 hands; 3 one-eyed giants called Cyclopes; and the 12 Titans, the first race of gods. Uranus feared his children, hated their violence, and tried to imprison them deep within their mother. Wracked with pain, Gaea angrily sought help from her Titan children. Only Cronus, the youngest and craftiest son, responded. Using a sickle that his mother gave him, Cronus cut off his father's sex organs. He then became king of the gods.

The goddess Aphrodite sprang full-grown from the foam that arose as Uranus's severed organs fell into the sea. From the drops of blood that fell on the earth emerged the Erinyes (Furies in Roman mythology), goddesses of vengeance; the Giants, a race of huge beings; and the Meliae, a race of nymphs.

Nancy Felson

See also **Cronus; Cyclops; Titans.**

Uranus, YUR *uh nuhs* or *yu RAY nuhs,* is the farthest planet from the sun that can be seen without a telescope. Uranus's orbit lies an average of about 1,784,860,000 miles (2,872,460,000 kilometers) from the sun. At that distance, light takes about 2 hours 40 minutes to travel from the sun to Uranus.

Uranus is a giant ball of gas and liquid. Its diameter at the equator is 31,763 miles (51,118 kilometers), over four times that of Earth. The surface of Uranus consists of blue-green clouds made up of tiny crystals of methane. Far below the visible clouds are probably thicker cloud layers made up of liquid water and crystals of ammonia ice. Deeper still—about 4,700 miles (7,500 kilometers) below the visible cloud tops—may be an ocean of liquid water containing dissolved ammonia. At the very center of the planet may be a rocky core about the size of Earth. Scientists doubt Uranus has any form of life.

Uranus was the first planet discovered since ancient times. British astronomer William Herschel discovered it in 1781. Johann E. Bode, a German astronomer, named it Uranus after a sky god in Greek mythology. Most of our information about Uranus comes from the United States spacecraft Voyager 2. In 1986, it flew within about 50,000 miles (80,000 kilometers) of the planet's cloud tops.

Orbit and rotation. Uranus travels around the sun in an *elliptical* (oval-shaped) orbit, which it completes in 30,685 Earth days, or just over 84 Earth years. As it orbits the sun, Uranus also rotates on its *axis,* an imaginary line through its center. The planet's *interior* (ocean and core) takes 17 hours 14 minutes to spin around once on its axis. However, much of the atmosphere rotates faster than that. The fastest winds on Uranus, measured about two-thirds of the way from the equator to the south pole, blow at about 450 miles per hour (720 kilometers per hour). Thus, this area toward the south pole makes one complete rotation every 14 hours.

Uranus is tilted so far on its side that its axis lies nearly level with its path around the sun. Scientists measure the tilt of a planet relative to a line at a right angle to the *orbital plane,* an imaginary surface touching all points of

Lawrence Sromovsky, University of Wisconsin-Madison, Space Science and Engineering Center

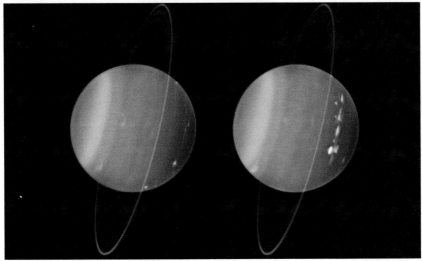

The atmosphere of Uranus features complex cloud patterns that appear in these images of the planet's opposite sides. Astronomers created the views by coloring and combining infrared images. This technique reveals differences in the clouds' altitudes and makes the planet's rings appear bright red. Seen in visible light, Uranus appears as a hazy, blue-green globe with no distinct features.

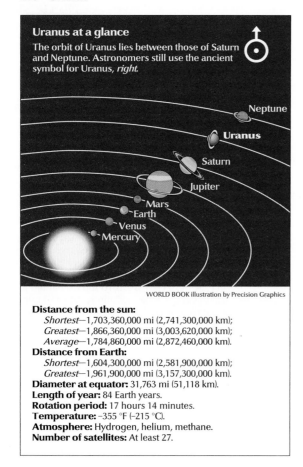

Uranus at a glance

The orbit of Uranus lies between those of Saturn and Neptune. Astronomers still use the ancient symbol for Uranus, *right.*

Neptune
Uranus
Saturn
Jupiter
Mars
Earth
Venus
Mercury

WORLD BOOK illustration by Precision Graphics

Distance from the sun:
  Shortest—1,703,360,000 mi (2,741,300,000 km);
  Greatest—1,866,360,000 mi (3,003,620,000 km);
  Average—1,784,860,000 mi (2,872,460,000 km).
Distance from Earth:
  Shortest—1,604,300,000 mi (2,581,900,000 km);
  Greatest—1,961,900,000 mi (3,157,300,000 km).
Diameter at equator: 31,763 mi (51,118 km).
Length of year: 84 Earth years.
Rotation period: 17 hours 14 minutes.
Temperature: –355 °F (–215 °C).
Atmosphere: Hydrogen, helium, methane.
Number of satellites: At least 27.

the orbit. Most planets' axes tilt less than 30°. But Uranus's axis tilts 98°, so that the axis lies almost in the orbital plane. Many astronomers think that a collision with an Earth-sized planet may have knocked Uranus on its side soon after it was formed.

Mass and density. Uranus has a *mass* (quantity of matter) 14 ½ times larger than that of Earth. However, the mass of Uranus is only about 1/20 as large as that of the largest planet, Jupiter.

Uranus has an average *density* of 1.27 grams per cubic centimeter, or about 1 ¼ times the density of water. Density is the amount of mass in a substance divided by the volume of the substance. The density of Uranus is ¼ that of Earth and is similar to that of Jupiter.

The force of gravity at the surface of Uranus is about 90 percent of that at the surface of Earth. Thus, an object that weighs 100 pounds on Earth would weigh about 90 pounds on Uranus.

The atmosphere of Uranus is composed of about 83 percent hydrogen, 15 percent helium, 2 percent methane, and tiny amounts of ethane and other gases. The *atmospheric pressure* beneath the methane cloud layer is about 19 pounds per square inch (130 kilopascals), or about 1.3 times the atmospheric pressure at the surface of Earth. Atmospheric pressure is the pressure exerted by the weight of the gases of a planet's atmosphere.

The visible clouds of Uranus are the same pale blue-green all over the planet's surface. Images of Uranus tak-

en by Voyager 2 and processed for high contrast by computers show faint bands within the clouds parallel to the equator. These bands are made up of different concentrations of smog produced as sunlight breaks down methane gas. In addition, there are a few small spots on the planet's surface. These spots probably are violently swirling masses of gas resembling a hurricane.

In 2006, astronomers using the Hubble Space Telescope discovered a large, dark spot made of whirling gases in Uranus's northern hemisphere. The spot measured 1,100 by 1,900 miles (1,700 by 3,000 kilometers)—large enough to swallow most of the United States. Scientists think that the spot formed because spring was coming to Uranus's northern hemisphere.

The temperature of the atmosphere is about –355 °F (–215 °C). In the interior, the temperature rises rapidly, reaching perhaps 4200 °F (2300 °C) in the ocean and 12,600 °F (7000 °C) in the rocky core. Uranus seems to radiate as much heat into space as it gets from the sun. Because Uranus is tilted 98° on its axis, its poles receive more sunlight during a Uranian year than does its equator. However, the weather system seems to distribute the extra heat fairly evenly over the planet.

Satellites. Astronomers have identified at least 27 satellites of Uranus, but the planet probably has more small moons that have yet to be discovered. Astronomers discovered the 5 largest satellites between 1787 and 1948. Photographs taken by Voyager 2 in 1985 and 1986 revealed 11 additional satellites. Astronomers later found more satellites by using Earth-based telescopes.

Miranda, the smallest of the five large satellites, has certain surface features that are unlike any other formation in the solar system. These are three oddly shaped regions called *ovoids.* Each ovoid is 120 to 190 miles (200 to 300 kilometers) across. The outer areas of each ovoid resemble a race track, with parallel ridges and canyons wrapped about the center. But in the center, ridges and canyons crisscross one another randomly.

Rings. Uranus has a number of rings around it. Ten of them are narrow, ranging in width from less than 3 miles (5 kilometers) to 60 miles (100 kilometers). They are no more than 33 feet (10 meters) thick. Two faint, dusty

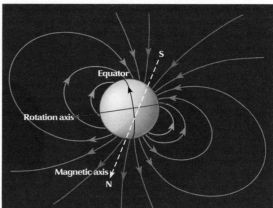

S
Equator
Rotation axis
Magnetic axis
N

WORLD BOOK illustration by Precision Graphics

The axis of rotation of Uranus is greatly offset from the planet's magnetic axis. This diagram shows how those axes are oriented when the sun is directly to the left. The curved lines indicate the direction of the magnetic field of Uranus.

Satellites of Uranus

Name	Mean distance from Uranus		Diameter of satellite		Year of discovery
	In miles	In kilometers	In miles	In kilometers	
Cordelia	30,930	49,770	25	40	1986
Ophelia	33,420	53,790	27	43	1986
Bianca	36,770	59,170	32	51	1986
Cressida	38,390	61,780	50	80	1986
Desdemona	38,950	62,680	40	64	1986
Juliet	39,990	64,350	58	94	1986
Portia	41,070	66,090	84	135	1986
Rosalind	43,460	69,940	45	72	1986
Cupid	46,480	74,800	15	24	2003
Belinda	46,760	75,260	50	81	1986
Perdita	47,490	76,420	50	80	1986
Puck	53,440	86,010	101	162	1985
Mab	60,730	97,730	20	32	2003
Miranda	80,720	129,900	293	472	1948
Ariel	118,600	190,900	720	1,158	1851
Umbriel	165,470	266,300	726	1,169	1851
Titania	271,100	436,300	981	1,578	1787
Oberon	362,580	583,520	946	1,523	1787
Francisco	2,657,000	4,276,000	7	12	2001
Caliban	4,493,000	7,231,000	61	98	1997
Stephano	4,973,000	8,004,000	12	20	1999
Trinculo	5,284,000	8,504,000	6	10	2001
Sycorax	7,568,000	12,180,000	118	190	1997
Margaret	8,917,000	14,350,000	7	11	2003
Prospero	10,100,000	16,260,000	19	30	1999
Setebos	10,820,000	17,420,000	19	30	1999
Ferdinand	12,990,000	20,900,000	7	12	2001

rings lie well outside the narrow rings. Uranus also has a broad, less-distinct ring closer to the planet than the others. The exact composition of the rings is unknown, but they probably consist of small chunks and dust-sized grains of ice coated in a material that contains carbon.

Magnetic field. Uranus has a strong magnetic field. The *axis* of the field (an imaginary line connecting its poles) is tilted 59° from the planet's axis of rotation.

The magnetic field has trapped high-energy, electri-

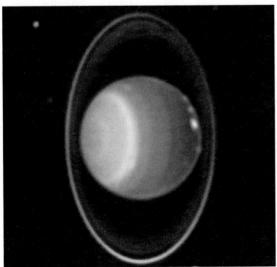

NASA/U.S. Naval Observatory

Uranus's rings and several of its moons appear in an infrared image taken by the Hubble Space Telescope. The colors in the image represent different conditions in the planet's atmosphere.

cally charged particles—mostly electrons and protons—in *radiation belts* around the planet. As these particles travel back and forth between the magnetic poles, they send out radio waves. Voyager 2 detected the waves, but they are so weak that they cannot be detected on Earth.   Peter J. Gierasch and Philip D. Nicholson

See also **Herschel, Sir William; Planet; Satellite** (Types of satellites); **Solar system; Voyager.**

Urban II (1042?-1099) was elected pope in 1088. Like the popes he followed, Urban was a vigorous reformer. He held a series of councils to promote the moral and institutional reform of the church. In 1095, Urban held a great council at Clermont, France. Although this council issued important reform decrees, it is best known for launching the call for what became the First Crusade. See **Crusades** (How the Crusades began).

Urban faced continuous opposition from the German emperor, Henry IV. Throughout the pope's reign, he had to contend with antipopes who denied him full control of Rome. But Urban was a brilliant diplomat. His manipulation of northern Italian politics prevented the emperor or the pope's other enemies from concentrating their attention on him. Urban increased the papacy's prestige by his elegant personal bearing, by his diplomatic skill, by launching the First Crusade, and by expanding papal authority into Spain. He was born in Châtillon-sur-Marne, France, near Épernay. His given name was Odo. He died on July 29, 1099.   Thomas F. X. Noble

Urban VI (1318-1389) was elected pope in 1378. Events during his reign led to the Great Schism, a controversy that divided the papacy until 1417.

Urban succeeded Pope Gregory XI, who had returned the papacy to Rome after almost 70 years in Avignon, France. Romans feared the election of another Frenchman and rioted, demanding a Roman or Italian pope. In this atmosphere, the cardinals elected Urban, an Italian. However, Urban abused the cardinals so badly that a majority concluded he was mentally unbalanced. Five months after his election, 13 cardinals declared he had been elected through intimidation. They elected Clement VII to replace Urban. England, Germany, and most of Italy gave their allegiance to Urban. Burgundy, France, Naples, Savoy, and Scotland followed Clement.

Urban was born in Naples, Italy. His given and family name was Bartolomeo Prignano. He died on Oct. 15, 1389.   Kenneth Pennington

See also **Clement VII** (antipope); **Roman Catholic Church** (The Great Schism).

Urban League is an organization that works to end racial discrimination and increase the economic and political power of blacks and other minority groups in the United States. Its full name is the National Urban League.

The league's local chapters conduct community programs that provide health care, housing and community development, job training and placement, AIDS education, and other services. The league works to influence policy by testifying before legislative bodies and by issuing reports on such matters as equal employment opportunities, income maintenance, and welfare reform. It also studies minority group problems and publishes its findings. The league was founded in 1910. It is based in New York City.   Critically reviewed by the National Urban League

See also **Jacob, John E.; Jordan, Vernon E., Jr.; Price, Hugh Bernard.**

Urban renewal is the process of removing run-down areas of a city and replacing them with new or rebuilt buildings. The new construction may include homes, stores, offices, factories, government buildings, and transportation facilities. Some renewal projects create parkland and other facilities for recreation.

The role of private investors. Private investors fund most urban renewal, also called *urban redevelopment.* When buildings age and deteriorate, they bring less return on the owners' investment. If owners demolish and replace run-down buildings, the replacements should yield enough income to cover the costs of construction loans, operating and maintaining the buildings, and taxes. The new buildings should also provide what the investors consider a reasonable profit. But racial discrimination, high crime rates, and excessive land prices can make investors wary of committing to such projects, so urban renewal often requires government help.

The role of government. City and state governments plan many urban renewal projects and provide incentives for private investors. For example, governments may encourage urban renewal by supplying part of the funding; by deferring taxes; by building streets, utilities, and parking; by easing the process of acquiring permits; and by providing special services, such as extra police and fire protection. Governments also can acquire land for urban renewal through a legal process called *condemnation* or by using the power of *eminent domain* to take private property for public use. This combination of government support and private investment is often called *public-private partnership.*

History. What may have been the first major urban renewal took place in Rome around A.D. 1. The Roman emperor Augustus thought that overcrowding due to immigration was destroying the city. He ordered the worst areas cleared for urban renewal. Workers demolished slums and replaced them with better housing.

For hundreds of years, urban renewal was done chiefly to repair districts damaged by disasters or wars. After the Great Fire of London in 1666, for example, the English architect Sir Christopher Wren rebuilt over 50 churches and several other buildings destroyed by fire.

During the late 1800's and early 1900's, many reformers became alarmed at the dreadful living conditions in large cities, such as New York City. The urban poor lived in crowded slums. Much of their housing consisted of cheap apartment buildings called *tenements.* Many social critics studied slum life and reported on the wretched living conditions there. One of the most influential reports was the book *How the Other Half Lives* (1890) by Jacob Riis. The work of Riis and others led to the first organized slum clearance efforts in North America.

The United States government became involved in clearing slums in the 1930's. Federal officials decided to demolish tenements in poor condition and replace them with public housing to provide apartments for low-income people. The federal government paid the difference between the cost of maintaining the housing and the rents that low-income families could afford. In 1949, the Urban Renewal Administration was established within the Housing and Home Finance Agency to direct slum clearance projects in hundreds of communities.

In 1965, Congress established the Department of Housing and Urban Development (HUD). The new department absorbed the Housing and Home Finance Agency and three other independent agencies involved with housing and community development.

Many large cities established urban renewal agencies, which used federal funds to buy land and demolish the old buildings on it. The cities then resold the land to local public housing authorities, who built public housing on the cleared land, or to private developers. If private developers wanted to buy the land, they usually had to submit competitive proposals. The city would choose a proposal that seemed economically sound and that met other goals. For example, the city might require that a plan include recreational and cultural land uses.

From 1978 to 1992, a program called Urban Development Action Grants gave federal funds to private developers for urban renewal. Today, the federal government funds urban renewal chiefly through a program called Community Development Block Grants. *Block grants* are fixed amounts of money given to state and local governments. State and local officials then decide where to use these funds. Another program, *urban homesteading,* offers vacant lots and abandoned houses, at low cost, to people who will build on the lots or repair the houses for their own use.   Anthony James Catanese

See also **City** (City problems); **City planning; Eminent domain; Housing; Housing and Urban Development, Department of.**

Additional resources

Rae, Douglas W. *City: Urbanism and Its End.* Yale, 2003.
Von Hoffman, Alexander. *House by House, Block by Block: The Rebirth of America's Urban Neighborhoods.* Oxford, 2003.

Urdu language is a language spoken in Pakistan and in the northern parts of India. Urdu closely resembles Hindi, the national language of India. Scholars sometimes speak of the two languages collectively as Hindi-Urdu. In the spoken form, the two languages are essentially the same. The common spoken form is sometimes called Hindustani. In the written form, Urdu and Hindi use different alphabets and different methods of writing.

Urdu belongs to the Indo-Aryan branch of the Indo-European language family. It is written from right to left and uses a Persian-Arabic alphabet with 38 basic symbols. The grammatical structures and basic vocabulary of Urdu developed from Sanskrit, an ancient Indian language. Urdu also includes many words borrowed from Persian, Arabic, Turkish, and other languages.

In the 1200's, Hindi-Urdu emerged around the city of Delhi as a *lingua franca*—that is, a common language used in trade or communication between speakers of different native languages. Urdu developed further under the Mughal Empire, which ruled most of India in the 1500's and 1600's. Early literature in Urdu appeared in Hyderabad, India, in the 1600's. In 1947, Urdu became the national language of Pakistan. However, most Pakistanis speak other regional languages, such as Baluchi, Pashto (also called Pakhto), Punjabi, or Sindhi. Urdu is also one of the official languages of India.   Afroz Taj

See also **Hindi language; Pakistan** (Cultural groups and languages); **Sanskrit language.**

Urea, *yu REE uh* or *YUR ee uh,* also called *carbamide,* is a nitrogen-rich organic compound produced by the bodies of human beings and many other animals. It is also made artificially for use in such varied products as cattle feed, fertilizers, pharmaceuticals, and plastics.

Urea is a white crystal or powder that dissolves readily in water. The human body produces urea as a means of ridding itself of excess nitrogen. Urea forms chiefly in the liver, and is eliminated mostly in the urine.

Urea was the first organic compound to be artificially produced from inorganic material. In 1828, the German chemist Friedrich Wöhler made urea by heating a water solution of ammonium cyanate, an inorganic compound. Wöhler's work helped to overthrow the belief that organic compounds could be formed only by natural forces operating within living organisms. Urea's chemical formula is $CO(NH_2)_2$. Robert J. Ouellette

Uremia, *yu REE mee uh,* is a condition that occurs when poisonous wastes build up in the blood. Such wastes normally pass out of the body in the urine, which is produced by the kidneys. Uremia results if the kidneys do not rid the body of these wastes. The word *uremia* means *urine in the blood.*

Uremia occurs mostly in adults with a kidney disease. It develops gradually as poisons accumulate because of the damaged kidneys. Doctors can successfully treat a few of the diseases that cause uremia. But in most cases, the diseased kidneys cannot be repaired, and advanced uremia occurs. Symptoms of advanced uremia include nausea, vomiting, hiccups, loss of appetite, breath that smells of urine, drowsiness, and itchy, yellowish-tan skin. Patients may also have muscular twitching, mental disturbances, and convulsions. In time, they become unconscious, a condition called *uremic coma.* Death follows in most cases.

Physicians use two methods to keep advanced uremia victims alive. A *dialysis machine* cleanses the blood in much the same way as the kidneys do. Surgeons also perform kidney transplants to replace diseased kidneys with healthy ones. Laurence H. Beck

See also **Kidney; Nephritis; Transplant.**

Urethra. See **Bladder; Kidney.**

Urey, *YOO ree,* **Harold Clayton** (1893-1981), was an American chemist who made important contributions in two main fields. During his early career, he conducted research on *isotopes.* Isotopes are atoms of the same element that differ in *mass*—that is, the amount of matter they contain. Different isotopes of an element have the same number of protons but different numbers of neutrons in their nucleus. Urey's later work centered on the history and chemical nature of the solar system. In the 1960's and 1970's, he played a key role in the interpretation of lunar samples gathered by Apollo astronauts.

Urey won the 1934 Nobel Prize in chemistry for the discovery of deuterium, a rare isotope of hydrogen (see **Deuterium**). During World War II (1939-1945), he directed a laboratory where isotopes of boron, hydrogen, and uranium were produced for use in the development of the atomic bomb. Urey's study of Earth and the solar system began after the war. He calculated the temperature of ancient oceans by determining the amount of certain isotopes in fossil shells. He also studied the chemical makeup of the sun, moon, and planets and formulated theories on the origin of the solar system.

Urey was born on April 29, 1893, in Walkerton, Indiana. He earned a Ph.D. degree from the University of California at Berkeley. He taught at Columbia University from 1929 to 1945, the University of Chicago from 1945 to 1958, and the University of California at San Diego from 1958 until his death on Jan. 5, 1981. Daniel J. Kevles

Uric acid is a nitrogen-containing chemical produced in the digestive system during the breakdown of many foods. Birds, land-dwelling reptiles, and some mammals discharge uric acid as waste matter called *guano* (see **Guano**). Some animals, including amphibians and most fishes, convert uric acid into *urea,* a compound removed mostly in the urine (see **Urea**).

Human beings normally have a small amount of uric acid in their blood, but in some cases, too much of it may accumulate. This excess of uric acid can cause a variety of diseases. For example, deposits of uric acid crystals in the kidney can result in kidney failure. Accumulations of uric acid crystals in the urine can form kidney stones. Deposits of uric acid crystals in tissues around the joints can trigger attacks of *gout* (see **Gout**). Other medical conditions associated with excess uric acid in the blood include high blood pressure, obesity, and high levels of *cholesterol* (fatty substance) in the blood.

Some babies are born with a defect in body chemistry that leads to an excess of uric acid in the body. This hereditary disorder is called *Lesch-Nyhan syndrome,* and it can result in mental retardation. John H. Lynch

Urine, *YUR uhn,* is a liquid waste product of the body produced by the kidneys. A healthy person's urine is amber-colored and slightly acid. Urine is a little heavier than water with an average specific gravity of 1.022. Urine consists mainly of water. It also contains urea, creatinine, uric acid, and such inorganic salts as sodium, potassium, ammonia, calcium, and magnesium.

Blood reaches the kidneys through the *renal* arteries. Waste matter and water removed from this blood passes from the kidneys to the urinary bladder through two small tubes, the *ureters.* Urine is stored in the bladder until *urination* occurs. The urine then is expelled to the outside through another tube, the *urethra.*

Most adults produce about $1\frac{1}{2}$ quarts (1.4 liters) of urine daily, but the amount may vary. During sleep, the amount is smaller. Less urine is produced when a person is dehydrated, and more when a person drinks large amounts of liquid. The *antidiuretic hormone,* given off by the pituitary gland, controls the amount of water held by the *nephrons* (tiny kidney tubes). Certain diseases may also change the amount and strength of urine. The condition of urine is often an index to a person's health. Sugar in the urine is a sign of diabetes. The appearance of blood in the urine may mean that the kidneys have been damaged or that an infection exists in the bladder or kidneys. Jeffrey R. Woodside

See also **Bladder; Diuretic; Incontinence; Kidney; Uremia.**

Uris, *YUR ihs,* **Leon** (1924-2003), was an American author. He became known for his best-selling novels based on modern historical events. During World War II (1939-1945), Uris served in the United States Marine Corps. He drew on his war experiences in his first novel, *Battle Cry* (1953). *Exodus* (1958) is a love story set against the founding of Israel. His other novels include *Mila 18* (1961), *Armageddon* (1964), *Topaz* (1967), *QB VII* (1970), *Trinity* (1976), *The Haj* (1984), and *A God in Ruins* (1999). Leon Marcus Uris was born on Aug. 3, 1924, in Baltimore. He died on June 21, 2003. Barbara M. Perkins

Ursa Major and Ursa Minor. See **Big and Little Dippers.**

Peter Menzel

The harbor at Montevideo, at the junction of the Atlantic Ocean and the Río de la Plata, handles most of Uruguay's international sea trade. Montevideo is the country's capital, largest city, and commercial center. About two-fifths of Uruguay's people live in the Montevideo area.

Uruguay

Uruguay, *YUR uh* GWAY *or* OO roo GWY, is a small country on the southeastern coast of South America. Among the independent nations of South America, only Suriname has a smaller area. Gently rolling grasslands cover almost all of the interior of Uruguay. Beautiful sandy beaches line the country's Atlantic coast.

Most Uruguayans are descended from Spanish settlers who came to the country in the 1600's and 1700's and Italian immigrants who arrived during the 1800's and early 1900's. Spanish is the nation's official language. Most Uruguayans live in urban areas, especially along the country's southern coast. Montevideo, the capital and largest city, has about two-fifths of the nation's total population.

Service industries, such as government, tourism, and transportation, employ more people than any other part of Uruguay's economy. But a mild climate and abundant natural pasture have made agriculture, particularly livestock raising, the base of the economy. Huge cattle and sheep ranches occupy most of the nation's interior. The leading manufacturing industries of Uruguay process meat, wool, and other livestock products.

Indians were the original inhabitants of what is now Uruguay. However, almost all of them were eventually killed by European settlers or died of diseases brought by the Europeans. Spanish and Portuguese forces fought for control of Uruguay during the 1700's, and

Richard W. Wilkie, the contributor of this article, is Professor of Geography at the University of Massachusetts at Amherst.

Brazil later tried to dominate the country. Uruguay became an independent republic in 1828. During the early 1900's, it developed into one of the most prosperous and democratic nations in South America. But an economic decline during the 1950's and 1960's brought about a period of widespread unrest and military rule. Today, Uruguay is once again ruled by an elected civilian government but remains troubled economically.

Government

National government. Since the early 1900's, democratic governments have ruled Uruguay almost continuously. But in 1973, during a time of wide urban violence,

Facts in brief

Capital: Montevideo.
Official language: Spanish.
Official name: *República Oriental del Uruguay* (Eastern Republic of Uruguay).
Area: 68,037 mi² (176,215 km²). *Greatest distances*—north-south, about 330 mi (530 km); east-west, about 280 mi (450 km). *Coastline*—about 410 mi (660 km).
Elevation: *Highest*—Mirador Nacional, 1,644 ft (501 m) above sea level. *Lowest*—sea level.
Population: *Estimated 2008 population*—3,370,000; density, 50 per mi² (19 per km²); distribution, 93 percent urban, 7 percent rural. *2004 census*—3,241,003.
Chief products: *Agriculture*—cattle, sheep, wheat, corn, sugar cane, rice. *Manufacturing*—meat products, leather goods, textiles, beer, cement. *Mining*—gravel, sand, stone.
National anthem: "Himno Nacional del Uruguay" ("National Hymn of Uruguay").
Money: *Basic unit*—Uruguayan peso. One hundred centisimos equal one peso.

military leaders seized control of the government. They suspended the country's Constitution, dissolved the national legislature, and banned all political party activities. The military ruled Uruguay until 1985, when a freely elected government once again assumed office.

Uruguay's Constitution, adopted in 1967 and restored in 1985, provides for a republican form of government. Under the Constitution, voters elect a president, the country's head, to a five-year term. The president may not be reelected until five years after leaving office. The president appoints a cabinet called the Council of Ministers to head various government divisions. Uruguay's legislature, called the General Assembly, consists of the 30-member Senate and the 99-member Chamber of Deputies. Voters elect legislators to five-year terms.

Local government. Uruguay is divided into 19 departments for purposes of local government. Voters in each department elect a governor and a legislature to handle departmental affairs.

Politics. The two largest political parties in Uruguay are the Colorado Party and the National Party, better known as the Blanco Party. The Colorados are traditionally more liberal and tend to be concerned with urban problems. The Blancos generally represent rural interests. Other political parties include the Christian Democratic Party, the Socialist Party, and the Communist Party. Segments of these parties sometimes combine in a larger group called the Broad Front Coalition. All citizens 18 years of age and older may vote.

Courts. The five-member Supreme Court of Justice serves as Uruguay's highest court. The court's justices are elected by the General Assembly to 10-year terms. The nation's judicial system also includes appeals courts, various lower courts, and justices of the peace.

Armed forces. Uruguay's army, navy, and air force have 24,700 members. Military service is voluntary.

People

Population and ancestry. Most Uruguayans live along or near the southern coast. The interior is thinly populated.

Various groups of Indians lived in what is now Uruguay long before the first Spanish settlers arrived in the 1500's. However, by the late 1700's, the country's Indian population had almost completely disappeared. During the 1800's and early 1900's, large numbers of Spanish and Italian migrant workers moved to Uruguay. Today, most Uruguayans are descended from these immigrants. Other groups with European ancestry include people of English, French, German, and Eastern European descent. Between 5 and 10 percent of Uruguay's people are *mestizos* (people of mixed European and Indian ancestry). Less than 3 percent are blacks whose ancestors were brought to Uruguay as slaves during the 1700's and early 1800's.

Languages. Nearly all Uruguayans speak Spanish, the country's official language. It is generally spoken with an Italian accent. Many Uruguayans also speak a second language, usually English, French, or Italian. Portuguese is widely spoken in the areas near the country's border with Brazil.

Way of life. Since the mid-1900's, inflation and other economic problems have created some hardships among Uruguay's people. But most Uruguayans still

David Mangurian

Uruguayan cowboys, called *gauchos,* herd cattle at a stockyard near Montevideo. Income from Uruguay's thriving livestock industry forms the basis of the country's economy.

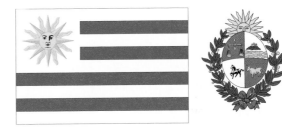

Symbols of Uruguay. The flag and the coat of arms were adopted in 1830. The sun on both is a symbol of independence. The flag's stripes represent the nine departments into which the country was originally divided after gaining independence. On the arms, the scales symbolize equality and justice; the horse and ox, liberty and plenty; and the hill of Montevideo, strength.

WORLD BOOK map

Uruguay is a small country in southeastern South America. It borders Argentina, Brazil, and the South Atlantic Ocean.

enjoy a comfortable standard of living with adequate housing and food and access to good medical care.

Montevideo, Uruguay's capital, is the country's largest city by far. It has about $1\frac{1}{3}$ million people, or about two-fifths of the country's total population. No other Uruguayan city has more than 100,000 people. Montevideo serves as a commercial, political, and intellectual center. It is a bustling city with treelined avenues, beautiful beaches and parks, impressive monuments and buildings, and a variety of cultural and recreational opportunities.

Most of the people in Montevideo and other Uruguayan cities belong to the country's large middle class. Many middle-class city dwellers hold government or professional jobs or work in business and industry. They live in apartments or in comfortable single-family houses. Business executives, government leaders, and other well-to-do city dwellers live in luxurious high-rise apartment buildings or mansions. Uruguay's urban population also includes factory workers, unskilled laborers, household servants, and other people with low-paying jobs. A small number of these working-class people live in tiny shacks on the cities' outskirts. But Uruguay has fewer urban slums than do most other Latin American countries. Electric power, running water, and sewers are available to all but the poorest city dwellers.

Many of the people who live in Uruguay's rural areas own or rent small farms. Many of them live in one-story adobe houses. Others work as wage laborers on large plantations or as *gauchos* (cowboys) on huge ranches called *estancias*. Shacks with thatch roofs and mud floors serve as housing for families of migrant laborers and ranch workers. Many wealthy landowners have homes in the cities, as well as country estates.

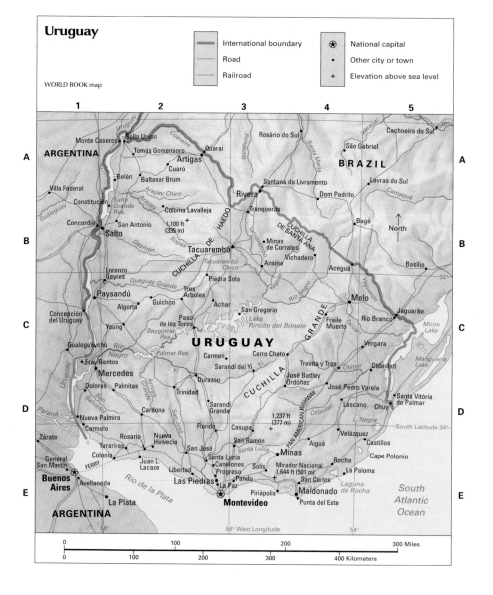

Uruguay

International boundary	⊛	National capital
Road	•	Other city or town
Railroad	+	Elevation above sea level

WORLD BOOK map

Uruguay map index

Cities

Physical features

Source: 1996 census.

Luis Villota, The Stock Market

Independence Plaza lies in the heart of Montevideo. A statue of José Artigas, Uruguay's national hero, stands in the center of the plaza. Salvo Palace, *right,* is one of the city's landmarks.

Enrique Shore, Woodfin Camp, Inc.

Beautiful sandy beaches, such as this one at Montevideo, line Uruguay's Atlantic coast. Thousands of vacationers flock to the country's many coastal resorts each year.

In general, rural Uruguayans have a lower standard of living than do urban Uruguayans. As a result, many rural people move to the cities in search of a better life.

Clothing. Most Uruguayans dress much as people do in the United States and Canada. Many gauchos still wear at least part of the traditional gaucho costume, which includes a flat, wide-brimmed hat; a blanketlike poncho; and baggy trousers tucked into boots.

Food and drink. Uruguayans eat much meat, especially beef. A favorite Uruguayan meal is a gaucho specialty called *parrillada criolla.* A typical version consists of a mixture of barbecued *chorizos* (sausages), *riñones* (kidneys), and strips of beef. Italians who immigrated to Uruguay introduced such pasta dishes as spaghetti and lasagna. Uruguay's national beverage is a kind of tea called *yerba maté* or simply *maté.* It is traditionally sipped through a silver straw from a gourd.

Recreation. Soccer is the most popular sport in Uruguay. Many Uruguayan children begin playing soccer as soon as they can walk. Soccer games draw huge crowds to stadiums in the cities. Other popular sports include basketball and rugby. Gaucho rodeos, called *domos,* attract many spectators. Uruguayans spend much time at the magnificent beaches along the country's Atlantic coast. Thousands of vacationers flock to Punta del Este and other coastal resorts each year.

Religion. About two-thirds of all Uruguayans belong to the Roman Catholic Church. However, many of them do not actively practice their religion. Uruguay also has small numbers of Protestants and Jews.

Education. Almost all Uruguayans 15 years of age or older can read and write. For Uruguay's literacy rate, see **Literacy** (table: Literacy rates for selected countries). The government provides free public schooling through the university level. Uruguay also has many private schools, which charge tuition. The law requires children from ages 6 through 14 to attend school, and almost all Uruguayan children complete the requirement. Most rural areas have elementary schools only. Rural children must go to nearby cities or towns to attend high school.

The University of the Republic in Montevideo is Uruguay's only university. It has about 35,000 students. Other higher education facilities include a teacher training institute and a nationwide system of vocational schools.

The arts. Uruguay has made major contributions to the arts in Latin America. In the 1800's, the Uruguayan painter Juan Manuel Blanes became well known for dramatic portrayals of historical events. Pedro Figari won international fame in the early 1900's for his paintings of life in Montevideo and the countryside. Uruguayan essayist José Enrique Rodó greatly influenced Latin-American thought. His best-known work, *Ariel* (1900), expresses his opposition to materialistic ways of life. The works of Horacio Quiroga, published during the early 1900's, established him as a master of the short story.

Legends of the free-spirited gaucho have inspired much of Uruguay's folk music, art, and drama. Carved maté gourds, a traditional Uruguayan handicraft, often show scenes of gaucho life.

The land

The Uruguay River forms Uruguay's western border with Argentina. Brazil lies to the north and east. The Atlantic Ocean and the Río de la Plata, an *estuary* (sea inlet) of the Atlantic, border Uruguay in the south. Uruguay can be divided into two major land regions: (1) the coastal plains and (2) the interior lowlands. The lowlands occupy about four-fifths of the country.

The coastal plains extend in a narrow arc along the Uruguay River, the Río de la Plata, and the Atlantic Ocean. They cover about a fifth of Uruguay. But most of the nation's population is concentrated in this region, especially along the southern coast. Montevideo lies on the coast near the point where the Río de la Plata and the Atlantic meet. Small family farms and large plantations occupy much of the western and southwestern coastal plains, which have Uruguay's richest and deepest soil. Beaches, sand dunes, and lagoons make up the Atlantic shore, which has many popular resorts.

The **coastal plains** of western and southwestern Uruguay have the country's richest soil. Wheat and other crops are grown on the small family farms and large plantations that occupy much of the area.

David Mangurian

The interior lowlands cover most of Uruguay. Vast, grass-covered plains and hills and numerous rivers and streams make this area an ideal place for raising livestock. Sprawling ranches occupy most of the region, and small cities and towns dot the countryside.

The Río Negro, the largest river in the interior, flows southwestward through the heart of the lowlands. A dam on the river formed Uruguay's only large lake, Lake Rincón del Bonete. A long, narrow chain of highlands curves across the interior from the Brazilian border almost to the southern coast. Uruguayans call these highlands *Cuchilla Grande* (Big Knife) because knifelike formations of rock jut through the soil on many of the ridges. The highest point in Uruguay, Mirador Nacional, also called Cerro de las Animas, rises 1,644 feet (501 meters) in the Cuchilla Grande.

Climate

Uruguay has a mild, humid climate that varies little from one area to another. The country lies south of the equator, and so its seasons are opposite those in the Northern Hemisphere. Temperatures in Montevideo average 51 °F (11 °C) in July, the coldest month, and 73 °F (23 °C) in January, the warmest month.

Uruguay receives about 40 inches (102 centimeters) of rain annually. The rain generally falls regularly throughout the year. However, Uruguay occasionally experiences droughts.

Economy

Uruguay has a developing economy based largely on agriculture. Service industries and manufacturing account for 88 percent of Uruguay's *gross domestic product* (GDP)—that is, the total value of all goods and services produced in the country yearly. But agricultural products provide Uruguay with most of its export income. Uruguay's most valuable natural resource is its land. The country's grasslands provide excellent natural pasture for livestock. Uruguay's leading manufacturing industries process beef, hides, and wool.

Most of Uruguay's businesses and industries are privately owned. However, the national government controls most utilities, much of the country's transportation industry, and some manufacturing firms.

Service industries account for 68 percent of Uruguay's GDP and employ 65 percent of the nation's work force. Government agencies have the greatest number of service industries workers. Tourism, another leading employer, thrives along Uruguay's Atlantic coast. Many Uruguayans have jobs in hotels, restaurants, and stores at seaside resorts. Others are employed by banks, health care facilities, schools, and by firms in such fields as transportation and communication.

Manufacturing accounts for 20 percent of Uruguay's GDP and employs 19 percent of all workers. Meat packing and processing is the leading industry. Other manufactured goods include leather goods, textiles, beer, cement, and tires. Most of the nation's industrial plants lie in and around Montevideo.

Agriculture accounts for 12 percent of Uruguay's GDP and employs 16 percent of the nation's workers. The raising of livestock is the leading source of farm income. Cattle and sheep estancias occupy about four-fifths of Uruguay's total land area. The larger ranches cover more than 5,000 acres (2,024 hectares).

Farmers raise such crops as corn, potatoes, sugar beets, sugar cane, and wheat in the fertile soil along the Uruguay River and the Río de la Plata. Rice is grown in irrigated fields in the east. Most farms have modern mechanical equipment. But the poorest farmers use oxen-drawn plows and old-fashioned methods.

Mining. Uruguay has few mineral resources. Construction materials, such as gravel, sand, and stone, are the leading mineral products.

Fishing. A small government-supported fishing fleet catches anchovy, croaker, hake, and weakfish off Uruguay's Atlantic coast. Most of the catch is exported.

Energy sources. Uruguay has no deposits of coal, petroleum, or natural gas, and thus must import large quantities of fuel. The country depends almost entirely on hydroelectric power for its electricity. Power plants on the Uruguay River and the Río Negro supply electricity to all parts of the country.

Trade. Beef, hides, live cattle and sheep, vegetable products, wool, and woolen textiles rank as Uruguay's leading exports. Major imports include appliances, chemical products, machinery, metal goods, and petroleum. Uruguay trades mainly with Argentina, Brazil, the

United States, and Western European nations.

Transportation and communication. Good roads link all parts of Uruguay. The country's railroad system, which is owned and operated by the government, is old and inefficient. Most Uruguayans rely on buses for transportation between cities and towns. Uruguay has an excellent government-operated bus system that serves the entire nation. A number of private companies also offer bus service.

Montevideo serves as Uruguay's major ocean port. The main international airport is located near Montevideo. The Uruguayan airline PLUNA flies within Uruguay and to some other countries.

Almost all Uruguayan families own a radio, and there is about 1 television set for every 4 people. Uruguay has about two dozen daily general interest newspapers. The largest are *El País* and *El Día* in Montevideo. The Constitution guarantees freedom of the press.

History

Early days. Indians were the first people to live in what is now Uruguay. They gathered wild fruits and seeds and hunted game for food. The Charrúa Indians, the largest group, were a warlike tribe. In 1516, the Spanish navigator Juan Díaz de Solís became the first white person to land in Uruguay. But when he and part of his crew went ashore, the Charrúa killed them. Because Uruguay lacked gold and other riches, it attracted few other Europeans until the later 1600's.

Colonial years. In 1680, Portuguese soldiers from Brazil established the town of Nova Colonia do Sacramento (now Colonia) on the Río de la Plata, across from the Spanish settlement of Buenos Aires, Argentina. Spanish colonists founded Montevideo in 1726 in an effort to check Portuguese expansion in Uruguay. Spanish and Portuguese forces battled for control of the region during the 1700's. By the 1770's, the Spaniards had settled most of Uruguay. In 1777, they attacked Colonia and drove the Portuguese out of the country. Uruguay became part of a Spanish colony called the Viceroyalty of La Plata, which also included Argentina, Paraguay, and parts of Bolivia, Brazil, and Chile (see **Argentina** [map: In 1776]). During the colonial period, almost all of Uru-

Yoram Lehmann from Peter Arnold

Textile manufacturing, especially the production of wool fabrics, is one of the leading industries in Uruguay. Most textile mills are located in and around Montevideo.

guay's Indians were killed in battles with the Europeans, died of European diseases, or fled to the interior of the continent.

Independence. During the early 1800's, a soldier named José Gervasio Artigas organized an army to fight for independence from Spain. In 1811, Artigas and his forces laid siege to Montevideo. Just when they had almost defeated the Spaniards, Portuguese troops from Brazil attacked both the Spanish and Uruguayan armies. Rather than submit to either Spanish or Portuguese rule, Artigas led his forces and thousands of Uruguayans into the countryside of neighboring Paraguay and Argentina, leaving much of Uruguay abandoned. The Spanish surrendered Montevideo to troops from Buenos Aires in 1814. This surrender permanently ended Spanish control of Uruguay. In 1815, Artigas and his forces returned to capture Montevideo for Uruguay. But, in 1816, Portuguese troops again attacked the Uruguayans. After four years of bitter warfare, the Portuguese annexed Uruguay to Brazil and forced Artigas into exile.

In 1825, a group of Uruguayan patriots called "The Immortal Thirty-Three" revolted against Brazil and renewed the struggle for independence. Within a few months, their armies held much of the countryside. Argentina supported the patriots in the war against Brazil. The United Kingdom intervened in the war because a Brazilian blockade of Montevideo and Buenos Aires interfered with British trade. In 1828, because of the British intervention, Brazil and Argentina recognized Uruguay as an independent republic. Uruguay adopted its first constitution in 1830. José Fructuoso Rivera, one of the patriot leaders, became the nation's first president.

Civil war. Manuel Oribe succeeded Rivera as president in 1835. But the next year, Rivera attempted to regain power by leading a revolt against Oribe. Most of Rivera's followers, known as the Colorados, came from the cities. Oribe's forces, the Blancos, were mainly rural landowners. The two groups, which developed into Uruguay's two major political parties, fought for control of Uruguay for 16 years. Finally, in 1852, the Colorados defeated the Blancos.

Struggles for power continued during the mid-1800's, as control of the government passed between the Colorados and Blancos. Foreign governments often interfered in Uruguay's affairs by supporting one party or the other in uprisings and rebellions. In 1865, the Colorados gained control of the government with the help of Brazil. Paraguay supported the Blancos in an attempt to regain power. Uruguay, Brazil, and Argentina then formed an alliance and fought against Paraguay. The War of the Triple Alliance ended with the defeat of Paraguay in 1870. By the end of the war, the Colorados had clearly become the dominant political party, mainly due to the rapid growth of Montevideo as Spanish and Italian immigrants poured into Uruguay. A series of Colorado leaders headed the government during the late 1800's. Some of them ruled as dictators.

Reforms in the early 1900's. In 1903, José Batlle y Ordóñez was elected president of Uruguay. Batlle believed strongly in democratic principles and social justice. Under his leadership, the ruling Colorado Party passed wide-ranging laws that established free education, minimum wages and protection of workers' rights, credit to farmers, free medical care for the poor, and

Björn Bölstad from Peter Arnold

The Spanish pioneers who settled in Uruguay during the 1700's and 1800's are honored by a life-sized bronze monument that stands in Montevideo's Batlle Park. The monument, which portrays the ox-drawn *carreta* (cart) the pioneers used, was created by the Uruguayan sculptor José Belloni.

other social welfare programs. The government took control of public utilities and many manufacturing firms, and established national banks and railroads. Batlle and his successors made Uruguay into a model of democracy, social reform, and economic stability.

National Council government. Uruguay severed diplomatic relations with Germany, Italy, and Japan in 1942 and declared war on the Axis nations three years later. But no Uruguayan troops fought in World War II. Uruguay's exports of meat and wool soared during the war, helping finance new social programs. Uruguay became a charter member of the United Nations in 1945.

In 1951, Uruguay ratified a new constitution that abolished the presidency and set up a nine-member National Council of Government. The council allowed the Colorado and Blanco parties to share power. Uruguay's economy began to decline during the early 1950's. Foreign trade decreased as a result of a loss of markets for agricultural exports. At the same time, the cost of the country's social programs rose rapidly. Inflation became a serious problem. The National Council proved inefficient in dealing with these troubles. A new constitution reestablished a presidential government in 1967.

Military government. Worsening economic problems caused wide unrest in Uruguay in the late 1960's and early 1970's. Antigovernment terrorist groups became active. One group, the Tupamaros, kidnapped and murdered Uruguayan and foreign officials. Juan Maria Bordaberry became president in 1972 and crushed the Tupamaros within a few months. In 1973, in response to growing public unrest and economic problems, military leaders took control of the government and forced President Bordaberry to dissolve the national legislature. They suspended the Constitution and formed a Council of State to rule Uruguay by decree. Bordaberry was a member of the council, but the military completely dominated the government. The military leaders removed Bordaberry from office in 1976 and named Aparicio Mendez to the presidency. General Gregorio Alvarez succeeded Mendez in 1981.

Thousands of Uruguayans participated in antigovernment protests during the early 1980's. Negotiations between the military and political parties led to democratic elections in 1984 and a return to civilian government.

Recent developments. Julio María Sanguinetti, the leader of the Colorado Party, was elected president in 1984. When he took office in 1985, he faced major economic problems. Export income had dropped sharply, and foreign debt had soared. Inflation and unemployment had increased, lowering the standard of living for many Uruguayans. In 1989, the Blanco Party won presidential and congressional elections for the first time since 1962. Luis Alberto Lacalle of the Blanco Party became president in 1990.

Lacalle focused on reducing the government's budget deficit and shrinking Uruguay's foreign debt. His economic program included smaller wage increases for government employees and the *privatization* (sale to private owners) of some state-owned companies. Labor unions opposed these policies and organized a series of strikes by all the workers in the country. In a special election in 1992, voters rejected plans to privatize several government-owned firms. In 1994, Colorado Party leader Sanguinetti was elected president again. In 1999, Jorge Batlle Ibáñez of the Colorado Party won election to the presidency. During the late 1990's and early 2000's, Uruguay experienced a severe recession.

In 2004, voters elected Tabaré Ramón Vázquez Rosas of the Socialist Party president. He was the first leftist elected president of Uruguay. Vázquez had also run in 1994 and 1999. He took office in 2005.　　Richard W. Wilkie

Related articles in *World Book* include:

Outline

IV. **Climate**
V. **Economy**
   A. Service industries
   B. Manufacturing
   C. Agriculture
   D. Mining
   E. Fishing
   F. Energy sources
   G. Trade
   H. Transportation and communication
VI. **History**

Questions

Who were the ancestors of most of today's Uruguayans?
How does the Uruguayan economy depend on agriculture?
What social reforms did President José Batlle y Ordóñez intro-
   duce in Uruguay during the early 1900's?
What are *gauchos?* How have they affected Uruguayan culture?
What are Uruguay's two major political parties? What types of
   political views do they each support?
Who were "The Immortal Thirty-Three"?
Where do most of Uruguay's people live?
What conditions led to the military take-over of Uruguay's gov-
   ernment in 1973? When was civilian rule restored?
What is Uruguay's most popular sport?
What was the National Council of Government?

Uruguay River, YUR *uh* GWAY *or* OO *roo* GWY, is part
of the great Paraná and La Plata river system of South
America. The Uruguay rises in the state of Santa Catarina
in southern Brazil and flows west, and then south for
about 1,000 miles (1,600 kilometers). It empties into the
bay of the Río de la Plata.

The Uruguay forms part of the boundary between
Brazil and Argentina, and all the boundary between
Uruguay and Argentina. Before it joins the Río de la Plata, the river becomes a lake from 4 to 7 miles (6 to 11
kilometers) wide. For the location of the Uruguay River,
see **Uruguay** (map); **Brazil** (terrain map).

Richard W. Wilkie

U.S. See United States.
U.S.A. See United States.
USA Freedom Corps is a government organization
that seeks to promote community service, volunteer activities, and responsible citizenship in the United States.
Its programs address concerns relating to education,
the environment, poverty, safety, and homeland security.
USA Freedom Corps acts in cooperation with businesses, religious organizations, schools, and other groups to
increase community participation and awareness. President George W. Bush established the organization in
2002. USA Freedom Corps is part of the White House
Office. Its headquarters are at the White House in Washington, D.C.

USA Freedom Corps works with numerous government service programs and organizations, including the
Peace Corps, AmeriCorps, Citizen Corps, and Senior
Corps. The Peace Corps is an overseas volunteer program that seeks to help people in developing countries
to improve their living conditions. AmeriCorps works
with local and national organizations to address a variety
of educational, environmental, and safety concerns. Citizen Corps coordinates volunteer efforts to make U.S.
communities safer and better prepared for emergency
situations. Senior Corps provides a network of volunteer
opportunities for older citizens.

Critically reviewed by USA Freedom Corps

See also **Peace Corps.**

USO. See United Service Organizations.
U.S.S.R. See Union of Soviet Socialist Republics.
Ustinov, Peter (1921-2004), was a popular English actor and a versatile man of letters. Besides his acting, he
was a playwright, director, screenwriter, novelist, and
producer. Ustinov was also famous for his witty conversation and his ear for dialects, which made him a popular figure on TV talk shows and in live one-man shows.

Ustinov appeared in more than 50 motion pictures,
winning Academy Awards as best supporting actor for
his performances in *Spartacus* in 1960 and *Topkapi* in
1964. He wrote several plays, most of them comedies.
He produced, directed, and acted in many of them. Ustinov's plays include *The Love of Four Colonels* (1951), *Ro-
manoff and Juliet* (1956), *Photo Finish* (1962), and *Beethoven's Tenth* (1982). He directed several motion pictures, notably *Billy Budd* (1962). Ustinov also directed
and designed scenery and costumes for several operas.
His novels include *Krumnagel* (1971) and *The Old Man
and Mr. Smith* (1990). His nonfiction includes the autobiography *Dear Me* (1977).

Peter Alexander Ustinov was born on April 16, 1921, in
London. He made his stage acting debut in 1938 and his
film acting debut in 1940. He was knighted in 1990 and
became known as Sir Peter Ustinov. He died on March
28, 2004.   Michael Seidel

Usumbura. See Bujumbura.
Usury, YOO *zhuhr ee,* is interest at a higher rate than
the law allows. The person or institution charging more
than the maximum legal rate is a *usurer.*

In Biblical times, all payments for the use of money
were regarded as usury and were forbidden. In general,
people regarded interest and usury as synonymous until
the late Middle Ages, because most of the borrowers
were poor people who needed money to obtain the necessities of life.

The Industrial Revolution brought demand for large
amounts of capital to invest in railroads, textiles, engine
works, and shipbuilding. It became accepted practice to
pay interest for the use of borrowed funds. The term
usury no longer meant interest. It came to be associated
with excessive charges.

Many financial institutions chose not to make small
loans because of high risk and cost. Some financial institutions and some illegitimate "loan sharks" filled the gap,
but they charged high, sometimes excessive interest
rates. Abuses in the United States led to passage of a
small-loan law that imposed limits on interest charges.

Ceiling rates that licensed dealers may charge have
risen over time to reflect rising interest rates. The rate
usually varies with the amount of money borrowed.
Service charges and discounts may make the real interest rate higher than the rate advertised. A U.S. law that
became effective in 1969, the federal Truth in Lending
Law, requires lenders to state clearly the actual annual
interest on loans.

The U.S. government passed the Depository Institutions and Monetary Control Act in 1980. The act allowed
higher interest rates on certain residential mortgages
and on some business and agricultural loans than some
state laws permitted.   Joanna H. Frodin

See also **Finance company; Interest; Loan company.**
USX Corporation. See United States Steel Corporation.

L. Burton, H. Armstrong Roberts

Monument Valley, in southeastern Utah, has striking formations of red sandstone that rise as high as 1,000 feet (300 meters) above the valley floor. Utah's beautiful and varied landscape includes scenic canyons, towering Rocky Mountain peaks, and vast areas of deserts.

Utah   *The Beehive State*

Utah is a state in the Rocky Mountain region of the United States. It serves as a vital link in the transportation and communications systems of the western United States. Salt Lake City is Utah's capital and largest city. In addition, it is the headquarters of the Church of Jesus Christ of Latter-day Saints. The members of this church are called *Mormons.* They make up about 70 percent of Utah's population.

Most of Utah's people live in urban areas. The state's main urban areas—including Salt Lake City—lie in the north-central part of the state in an area called the Wasatch Front. This area is named for the Wasatch Range, mountains that rise just east of it.

Utah's cities are centers of a variety of economic

activities. Service industries, such as financial institutions and medical facilities, contribute greatly to the economy. Utah's manufacturing plants turn out many products, including computer and transportation equipment, and metal products. Plants in Utah also process such farm products as fruits, grain, meat, milk, and vegetables.

Utah has rich mineral deposits. Copper, natural gas, and petroleum are the state's leading mineral products. Copper is mined near Salt Lake City. Most of the natural gas and petroleum are in the eastern part of the state. Utah has national parks, ski resorts, and other facilities that attract tourists who contribute greatly to the economy. The state is also the home of economically important military installations.

Utah has snow-covered mountains and beautifully colored canyons. The wind and rain have formed rocks into many arches and natural bridges. Great Salt Lake is the largest natural lake west of the Mississippi River. Water in the Great Salt Lake is saltier than ocean water.

The contributors of this article are Brian Q. Cannon, Professor of History at Brigham Young University; and J. Matthew Shumway, Professor of Geography at Brigham Young University.

Interesting facts about Utah

The Seagull Monument in Salt Lake City honors the sea gull, Utah's state bird. The sea gull saved crops in the region from an invasion of Mormon crickets in 1848. Two sculptured sea gulls stand atop the monument, which was unveiled in 1913.

Seagull Monument

Great Salt Lake, a closed basin in northwestern Utah, is one of the natural wonders of the world. It is a remnant of the freshwater Lake Bonneville, which existed about 25,000 years ago. The density of salt in parts of the Great Salt Lake reached 27 percent during the early 1960's. Some scientists believe that salt is carried into the lake from mountain streams. The waters of the lake do not drain away, but dry up, leaving the salt behind.

Bonneville Salt Flats International Speedway near Wendover is world famous as the site where world land speed records have frequently been set. Vehicles there have reached speeds of more than 600 miles (960 kilometers) per hour.

Bonneville Speedway

Rainbow Bridge National Monument, in the Glen Canyon National Recreation Area, is the largest known natural stone bridge in the world. The bridge reaches a height of 290 feet (88 meters) and is 275 feet (84 meters) across. It is 42 feet (13 meters) thick and 33 feet (10 meters) wide at the top.

© Dave Brown, The Stock Market

Salt Lake City is the capital of Utah and its largest city. The city ranks as one of the chief centers of culture, finance, industry, and transportation in the Rocky Mountain region.

Because the water is so salty, people can easily float in the lake. Deserts cover much of Utah, but artificially created reservoirs provide irrigation water for farmland. The largest reservoirs are Lake Powell, created by Arizona's Glen Canyon Dam, and Flaming Gorge, behind Flaming Gorge Dam.

Mormon pioneers led by Brigham Young settled the Utah region in 1847. They called the region *Deseret.* This Mormon word means *honey bee,* and it stands for hard work and industry. Utah's nickname is the *Beehive State.* The Congress of the United States organized the region as a territory in 1850 and named it *Utah* for the Ute Indian tribe that lived there. The early white settlers fought several battles against these Indians.

In 1861, the world's first transcontinental telegraph message was sent across wires that met in Salt Lake City. The first transcontinental railroad system in the world was completed at Promontory in 1869. Utah was admitted to the Union as the 45th state on Jan. 4, 1896.

Henry D. Meyer, Berg & Associates

A sheep rancher tends his flock on the dry plains of southeastern Utah. Utah is a leading wool-producing state, and a sheep-raising center of the western United States.

Utah in brief

Symbols of Utah

The state flag, adopted in 1913, bears the state seal. On the seal, adopted in 1896, the beehive on the shield stands for hard work and industry. The date 1847 is the year the Mormons came to Utah. A bald eagle, the United States national bird, perches atop the shield. A U.S. flag appears on each side.

State flag

State seal

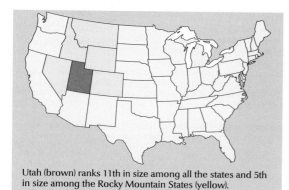

Utah (brown) ranks 11th in size among all the states and 5th in size among the Rocky Mountain States (yellow).

General information

Statehood: Jan. 4, 1896, the 45th state.
State abbreviations: Ut. (traditional); UT (postal).
State motto: *Industry.*
State song: "Utah, This Is the Place." Words by Sam and Gary Francis; music by Gary Francis.

The State Capitol is in Salt Lake City, Utah's capital since 1856. Fillmore served as capital from 1851 to 1856.

Land and climate

Area: 84,905 mi² (219,902 km²), including 2,736 mi² (7,086 km²) of inland water.
Elevation: *Highest*—Kings Peak, 13,528 ft (4,123 m) above sea level. *Lowest*—Beaverdam Creek in Washington County, 2,000 ft (610 m) above sea level.
Record high temperature: 117 °F (47 °C) at St. George on July 5, 1985.
Record low temperature: –69 °F (–56 °C) at Peter's Sink on Feb. 1, 1985.
Average July temperature: 73 °F (23 °C).
Average January temperature: 25 °F (–4 °C).
Average yearly precipitation: 12 in (30 cm).

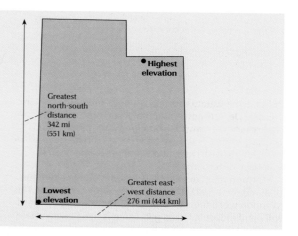

Highest elevation

Greatest north-south distance 342 mi (551 km)

Lowest elevation

Greatest east-west distance 276 mi (444 km)

Important dates

Jim Bridger probably became the first white person to see Great Salt Lake.

The United States won the Utah area from Mexico.

1776 — 1824-1825 — 1847 — 1848

Silvestre Velez de Escalante and Francisco Atanasio Domínguez made the first extensive exploration of the Utah area.

Brigham Young led the first Mormon pioneers into the Great Salt Lake region.

State bird
California sea gull

State flower
Sego lily

State tree
Blue spruce

People

Population: 2,233,169
Rank among the states: 34th
Density: 26 per mi² (10 per km²), U.S. average 78 per mi² (30 per km²)
Distribution: 88 percent urban, 12 percent rural
Largest cities in Utah

Salt Lake City	181,743
West Valley City	108,896
Provo	105,166
Sandy	88,418
Orem	84,324
Ogden	77,226

Source: 2000 census.

Population trend

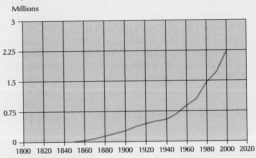

Millions

Source: U.S. Census Bureau.

Year	Population
2000	2,233,169
1990	1,722,850
1980	1,461,037
1970	1,059,273
1960	890,627
1950	688,862
1940	550,310
1930	507,847
1920	449,396
1910	373,351
1900	276,749
1890	210,779
1880	143,693
1870	86,786
1860	40,273
1850	11,380

Economy

Chief products

Agriculture: beef cattle, milk, hay, hogs, wheat.
Manufacturing: computer and electronic products, processed food and beverages, transportation equipment.
Mining: copper, natural gas, petroleum.

Gross domestic product

Value of goods and services produced in 2004: $82,546,000,000. *Services* include community, business, and personal services; finance; government; trade; and transportation and communication. *Industry* includes construction, manufacturing, mining, and utilities. *Agriculture* includes agriculture, fishing, and forestry.

Source: U.S. Bureau of Economic Analysis.

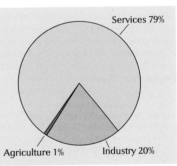

Services 79%
Agriculture 1%
Industry 20%

Government

State government

Governor: 4-year term
State senators: 29; 4-year terms
State representatives: 75; 2-year terms
Counties: 29

Federal government

United States senators: 2
United States representatives: 3
Electoral votes: 5

Sources of information

For information about tourism, write to: Utah Travel Council, Council Hall/Capitol Hill, Salt Lake City, UT 84114. The Web site at http://www.utah.com also provides information.
For information on the economy, write to: Governor's Office of Economic Development, 324 S. State Street, Suite 500, Salt Lake City, UT 84111.
The state's official Web site at http://www.utah.gov also provides a gateway to much information on Utah's economy, government, and history.

Large uranium deposits were discovered near Moab.

Utah marked the *centennial* (100th anniversary) of its statehood.

1896   **1952**   **1964**   **1996**

Utah became the 45th state on January 4.

Flaming Gorge and Glen Canyon dams were completed.

Population. The 2000 United States census reported that Utah had 2,233,169 people. The state's population had increased about 30 percent over the 1990 census figure, 1,722,850. According to the 2000 census, Utah ranks 34th in population among the 50 states.

About 90 percent of Utah's people live in the state's five metropolitan areas (see **Metropolitan area**). The Ogden-Clearfield, Provo-Orem, St. George, and Salt Lake City metropolitan areas lie entirely in the state. The Logan metropolitan area extends into Idaho. About 45 percent of Utah's people live in the Salt Lake City metropolitan area.

Salt Lake City is the capital and largest city of Utah. There are five other cities in the state with populations of more than 75,000. They are, in order of size, West Valley City, Provo, Sandy, Orem, and Ogden.

Non-Hispanic whites account for about 85 percent of Utah's population. Hispanics of any race make up about 9 percent. Utah's largest population groups include people of English, German, Danish, and Irish descent.

About 70 percent of Utah's people are Mormons. Most of the other church members are Roman Catholics or Protestants.

Utah's population ranks among the youngest in the nation. The state also has one of the nation's highest *fertility rates*—that is, the average number of children born to women of child-bearing age.

Schools. Utah's first school was a tent in the Salt Lake Valley. It was set up in 1847, the year the Mormons first settled in the region. By the mid-1850's, the Utah region had over 200 schools. Parents had to pay to send their children to these early schools because of a shortage of tax money. The region's first free public school opened in American Fork in 1866. A law passed in 1878 made all public elementary schools free. In 1884, a constitutional convention provided for the establishment and support of free public high schools in Utah. But school districts were not required to have high schools until 1911.

The State Board of Education supervises Utah's public schools. It has 15 voting members, elected to four-year terms, plus two nonvoting members appointed by a State Board of Regents. The Board of Education appoints a superintendent of public instruction as its executive officer. The State Board of Regents supervises colleges and universities in Utah.

Children in Utah must attend school from ages 6 through 17. For the number of teachers and students in Utah, see **Education** (table).

Libraries. Utah's first library was established with books hauled to the region by oxen in the 1850's. In 1897, a state law provided for free public libraries. The Salt Lake City Public Library opened the next year. The Carnegie Free Library (now Weber County Library) in Ogden was the first building in the state to be used only as a library. It opened in 1903. In 1957, the Utah State Library Commission was established.

Today, Utah has public libraries statewide. There are large collections of Mormon literature at the libraries of Brigham Young University, in Provo; and at the University of Utah, the Utah State Historical Society, and the Church of Jesus Christ of Latter-day Saints—all in Salt Lake City. The Church of Jesus Christ of Latter-day Saints library holdings also include one of the world's largest collections of genealogical records and research.

Museums. Utah has several art museums that feature regional, national, and international collections. The Utah Museum of Fine Arts in Salt Lake City has a collection representing various styles and periods. The Salt Lake Art Center exhibits contemporary art. The Brigham Young University Museum of Art and the Springville Museum of Art have works by Utah painters.

In Salt Lake City, the Utah Museum of Natural History focuses on the geology and archaeology of the Great Basin and the western United States. The Utah State Historical Society researches the histories of Utah, Mormons, and the West. In Price, the College of Eastern Utah Prehistoric Museum includes a large dinosaur display. The Anasazi State Park Museum in Boulder and the Edge of the Cedars State Park Museum in Blanding present collections and exhibits dealing with Anasazi Indian culture.

Population density

Utah is thinly populated except for a number of cities and towns in the north. Approximately 45 percent of the state's residents live in the Salt Lake City metropolitan area.

Persons per sq. mi.	Persons per km²
More than 100	More than 40
10 to 100	4 to 40
5 to 10	2 to 4
Less than 5	Less than 2

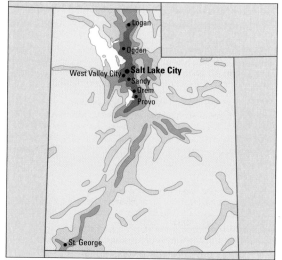

WORLD BOOK map; based on U.S. Census Bureau data.

Universities and colleges

This table lists the universities and colleges in Utah that grant bachelor's or advanced degrees and are accredited by the Northwest Commission on Colleges and Universities.

Name	Mailing address
Brigham Young University	Provo
Dixie State College of Utah	St. George
Snow College	Ephraim
Southern Utah University	Cedar City
Utah, University of	Salt Lake City
Utah State University	Logan
Utah Valley State College	Orem
Weber State University	Ogden
Western Governors University	Salt Lake City
Westminster College	Salt Lake City

Utah map index

Metropolitan areas

Logan 102,720
(91,391 in UT,
11,329 in ID)
Ogden-Clearfield 442,656
Provo-Orem 376,774
St. George 90,354
Salt Lake City 968,858

Counties

Beaver .... 6,005 .. K 3
Box Elder .... 42,745 .. C 3
Cache .... 91,391 .. C 6
Carbon .... 20,422 .. H 9
Daggett .... 921 .. E 10
Davis .... 238,994 .. D 6
Duchesne .... 14,371 .. F 9
Emery .... 10,860 .. J 8
Garfield .... 4,735 .. L 7
Grand .... 8,485 .. I 10
Iron .... 33,779 .. L 3
Juab .... 8,238 .. H 4
Kane .... 6,046 .. N 6
Millard .... 12,405 .. I 4
Morgan .... 7,129 .. D 7
Piute .... 1,435 .. K 5
Rich .... 1,961 .. C 7
Salt Lake .... 898,387 .. E 6
San Juan .... 14,413 .. M 10
Sanpete .... 22,763 .. I 6
Sevier .... 18,842 .. J 6
Summit .... 29,736 .. E 8
Tooele .... 40,735 .. F 3
Uintah .... 25,224 .. F 10
Utah .... 368,536 .. F 6
Wasatch .... 15,215 .. F 7
Washington .... 90,354 .. N 2
Wayne .... 2,509 .. K 8
Weber .... 196,533 .. D 6

Cities and towns

Abraham .... H 4
Adamsville .... K 4
Alpine .... 7,146 .. F 6
Alta .... 370 .. E 6
Altamont .... 178 .. F 9
Alton .... 134 .. M 5
Altonah .... F 9
Amalga* .... 427 .. C 6
American Fork .... 21,941 .. F 6
Aneth† .... 598 .. N 11
Angle .... K 6
Annabella .... 603 .. J 6
Antimony .... 122 .. L 5
Aurora .... 947 .. J 6
Austin .... J 5
Avon† .... 306 .. C 6
Axtell .... I 6
Ballard .... 566 .. F 10
Bauer .... F 5
Bear River City .... 750 .. C 5
Beaver○ .... 2,454 .. K 4
Benjamin .... 1,029 .. G 6
Bennion, see Taylorsville [-Bennion]
Benson† .... 1,451 .. B 6
Beryl .... L 2
Bicknell .... 353 .. K 6
Big Water .... 417 .. N 6
Bingham Canyon* .... F 6
Birdseye .... G 7
Black Rock .... J 4
Blanding .... 3,162 .. M 11
Blue Creek .... B 5
Bluebell .... F 9
Bluff† .... 320 .. N 10
Bluffdale* .... 4,700 .. F 6
Bonanza .... G 11
Boneta .... F 9
Bothwell .... C 5
Boulder .... 180 .. L 7
Bountiful .... 41,301 .. E 6
Brian Head .... 118 .. M 4
Bridgeland .... G 9
Brigham City○ .... 17,411 .. C 6
Bryce Canyon City .... M 5
Burrville .... J 6
Caineville .... K 7
Callao .... G 2
Cannonville .... 148 .. M 5
Canyon Rim*† .... 10,428 .. E 6
Carbonville .... H 8
Castle Dale○ .... 1,657 .. I 7
Castle Rock .... D 7
Castle Valley .... 349 .. J 11
Cedar .... H 8
Cedar City .... 20,527 .. M 3
Cedar Fort .... 341 .. F 5
Cedar Hills* .... 3,094 .. F 6
Centerfield .... 1,048 .. I 6
Centerville .... 14,585 .. E 6
Central .... J 5
Central .... M 2
Charleston .... 378 .. F 7
Chester .... H 6
Circleville .... 505 .. K 5
Cisco .... I 11
Clarkston .... 688 .. B 6
Clawson .... 153 .. I 7
Clear Lake .... I 4
Clear Creek .... H 7
Clearfield .... 25,974 .. D 6
Cleveland .... 508 .. I 8
Clinton .... 12,585 .. D 6
Clive .... E 3
Coalville○ .... 1,382 .. E 7
Colton .... G 7
Corinne .... 621 .. C 5
Cornish .... 259 .. B 6
Cottonwood, see Holladay [Cottonwood]
Cottonwood Heights*† .... 27,569 .. E 6
Cottonwood West*† .... 18,727 .. E 6
Cove† .... 443 .. B 6
Cove Fort .... J 4
Crescent Junction .... J 10
Croydon .... D 7
Defas Park* .... G 6
Delle .... E 4
Delta .... 3,209 .. I 4
Deseret .... I 5
Desert Mound .... M 3
Devils Slide .... D 7
Deweyville* .... 278 .. C 6
Dividend .... G 5
Dragon .... H 11
Draper .... 25,220 .. F 6
Duchesne○ .... 1,408 .. F 9
Dugway† .... 2,016 .. F 4
Dutch John .... D 11
East Carbon .... 1,393 .. H 9
East Layton* .... E 6
East Millcreek*† .... 21,385 .. F 6
Eastland .... L 11
Elberta† .... 278 .. G 6
Elgin .... I 9
Elk Ridge .... 1,838 .. G 6
Elmo .... 368 .. H 8
Elsinore .... 733 .. J 5
Elwood* .... 678 .. C 5
Emery .... 308 .. J 7
Enoch .... 3,467 .. L 3
Enterprise .... 1,285 .. M 2
Ephraim .... 4,505 .. I 6
Erda† .... 2,473 .. E 5
Escalante .... 818 .. M 6
Eskdale .... I 2
Etna .... C 2
Eureka .... 766 .. G 5
Fairfield .... F 5
Fairview .... 1,160 .. H 7
Farmington○ .... 12,081 .. D 6
Farr West* .... 3,094 .. D 6
Faust .... F 5
Fayette .... 204 .. I 6
Ferron .... 1,623 .. I 7
Fielding .... 448 .. B 5
Fillmore○ .... 2,253 .. J 5
Flowell .... J 5
Fort Duchesne† .... 621 .. F 10
Fountain Green .... 945 .. H 6
Francis .... 698 .. E 7
Freedom .... H 6
Fremont .... K 6
Fruit Heights* .... 4,701 .. E 6
Fruitland .... F 8
Gandy .... H 2
Garden City .... 357 .. B 7
Garland .... 1,943 .. B 5
Garrison .... J 2
Genola .... 965 .. G 6
Gilluly .... G 7
Glendale .... 355 .. N 4
Glenwood .... 437 .. J 6
Goshen .... 874 .. G 6
Goshute .... G 2
Granite*† .... 2,018 .. F 6
Granite Park .... F 6
Grantsville .... 6,015 .. E 5
Green River .... 973 .. I 9
Greendale .... E 10
Greenville .... K 4
Greenwich .... K 6
Grouse Creek .... B 2
Grover .... K 7
Gunlock .... N 2
Gunnison .... 2,394 .. I 6
Gusher .... F 10
Hailstone .... E 7
Hamilton Fort .... M 3
Hanksville .... K 8
Hanna .... F 8
Harrisville .... 3,645 .. D 6
Hatch .... 127 .. M 5
Hatton .... J 5
Heber City○ .... 7,291 .. F 7
Helper .... 2,025 .. H 8
Henefer .... 684 .. D 7
Henrieville .... 159 .. M 6
Herriman* .... 1,523 .. F 6
Hiawatha .... H 8
Highland .... 8,172 .. F 6
Hildale .... 1,895 .. N 3
Hinckley .... 698 .. I 4
Holden .... 400 .. I 5
Holladay [Cottonwood]† .... 14,561 .. E 6
Honeyville .... 1,214 .. C 5
Hooper† .... 3,926 .. D 5
Howell .... 221 .. B 5
Hoytsville .... E 7
Huntington .... 2,131 .. I 7
Huntsville* .... 649 .. D 6
Hurricane .... 8,250 .. N 3
Hyde Park .... 2,955 .. D 6
Hyrum .... 6,316 .. C 6
Ibapah .... G 2
Indianola .... G 7
Ioka .... F 9
Iosepa .... F 4
Iron Springs .... M 3
Ivins .... 4,450 .. N 2
Jensen .... F 11
Jericho .... H 5
Joseph .... 269 .. J 5
Junction○ .... 177 .. K 5
Kamas .... 1,274 .. E 7
Kanab○ .... 3,564 .. N 5
Kanarraville .... 311 .. M 3
Kanosh .... 485 .. J 5
Kaysville .... 20,351 .. D 6
Kearns† .... 33,659 .. E 6
Keetley .... E 7
Kelton .... B 4
Kenilworth .... H 8
Kingston .... 142 .. K 5
Knolls .... E 3
Koosharem .... 276 .. K 6
Lake Shore† .... 755 .. G 6
Lakeside .... D 4
Laketown .... 188 .. B 7
Lapoint .... F 10
La Sal† .... 339 .. K 11
La Sal Junction .... K 11
Latimer .... L 3
La Verkin .... 3,392 .. N 3
Lawrence .... I 8
Layton .... 58,474 .. D 6
Leamington .... 217 .. H 5
Leeds .... 547 .. N 3
Leeton .... F 10
Lehi .... 19,028 .. F 6
Leota .... F 10
Levan .... 688 .. H 6
Lewiston .... 1,877 .. B 6
Lindon .... 8,363 .. F 6
Little Cottonwood Creek Valley*† .... 7,221 .. E 6
Loa○ .... 525 .. K 6
Lofgreen .... G 5
Logan○ .... 42,670 .. B 6
Long Valley Junction .... M 5
Low .... E 4
Lucin .... C 2
Lund .... L 3
Lyman .... 234 .. K 6
Lynn .... B 2
Lynndyl .... 134 .. H 5
Maeser† .... 2,855 .. F 10
Magna† .... 22,770 .. E 5
Mammoth .... G 5
Manderfield .... K 4
Manila○ .... 308 .. D 10
Manti○ .... 3,040 .. I 6
Mantua .... 791 .. C 6
Mapleton .... 5,809 .. G 6
Marysvale .... 381 .. K 5
Mayfield .... 420 .. I 6
Meadow .... 254 .. J 5
Meadowville .... B 7
Mendon .... 898 .. C 6
Mexican Hat† .... 88 .. N 10
Midvale .... 27,029 .. E 6
Midway .... 2,121 .. F 7
Milburn .... H 7
Milford .... 1,451 .. K 4
Millcreek† .... 30,377 .. E 6
Mills .... H 6
Millville .... 1,507 .. C 6
Milton .... D 6
Minersville .... 817 .. K 4
Moab○ .... 4,779 .. J 10
Modena .... L 2
Mohrland .... H 7
Molen .... I 7
Mona .... 850 .. G 6
Monarch .... F 9
Monroe .... 1,845 .. J 5
Montezuma Creek† .... 507 .. N 11
Monticello○ .... 1,958 .. L 11
Moore .... J 7
Morgan○ .... 2,635 .. D 6
Moroni .... 1,280 .. H 6
Mounds .... H 8
Mount Carmel .... N 4
Mount Carmel Junction .... N 4
Mount Emmons .... F 9
Mount Olympus*† .... 7,103 .. F 6
Mount Pleasant .... 2,707 .. H 7
Mountain Green .... D 6
Murray .... 34,024 .. E 6
Myton .... 539 .. F 9
Naples .... 1,300 .. F 11
Neola† .... 533 .. F 9
Nephi○ .... 4,733 .. H 6
New Harmony .... 190 .. M 3
Newcastle .... N 2
Newton .... 699 .. B 6
Nibley .... 2,045 .. C 6
North Logan .... 6,163 .. B 6
North Ogden .... 15,026 .. D 6
North Salt Lake .... 8,749 .. E 6
Oak City .... 650 .. I 5
Oak Creek .... H 7
Oakley .... 948 .. E 7
Oasis .... I 4
Ogden○ .... 77,226 .. D 6
Ophir .... 23 .. F 5
Oquirrh*† .... 10,390 .. E 6
Orangeville .... 1,398 .. I 7
Orderville .... 596 .. N 4
Orem .... 84,324 .. F 6
Ouray .... G 10
Panguitch○ .... 1,623 .. L 5
Paradise .... 759 .. C 6
Paragonah .... 470 .. L 4
Park City .... 7,371 .. E 7
Park Valley .... B 3
Parowan○ .... 2,565 .. L 4
Partoun .... H 2
Payson .... 12,716 .. G 6
Perry .... 2,383 .. C 6
Peterson* .... E 6
Pickelville .... B 7
Pine Valley .... N 3
Pinto .... M 2
Pintura .... N 3
Plain City .... 3,489 .. D 5
Pleasant Grove .... 23,468 .. F 6
Pleasant View .... 5,632 .. D 6
Plymouth .... 328 .. B 5
Portage .... 257 .. B 5
Porterville .... D 6
Price○ .... 8,402 .. H 8
Promontory .... C 5
Providence .... 4,377 .. C 6
Provo○ .... 105,166 .. F 6
Randlett† .... 224 .. F 10
Randolph○ .... 483 .. C 7
Redmond .... 788 .. I 6
Richfield○ .... 6,847 .. J 5
Richmond .... 2,051 .. B 6
Richville .... D 6
River Heights .... 1,496 .. C 6
Riverdale .... 7,656 .. D 6
Riverside† .... 678 .. B 5
Riverton .... 25,011 .. F 6
Rockville .... 247 .. N 3
Roosevelt .... 4,299 .. F 10
Rosette .... B 3
Round Valley .... B 7
Roy .... 32,885 .. D 6
Rush Valley .... 453 .. F 5
Sage Creek Junction .... B 7
St. George○ .... 49,663 .. N 2
Salduro .... E 2
Salem .... 4,372 .. G 6
Salina .... 2,393 .. J 6
Salt Lake City○ .... 181,743 .. E 6
Sandy .... 88,418 .. F 6
Santa Clara .... 4,630 .. N 2
Santaquin .... 4,834 .. G 6
Scipio .... 290 .. I 5
Scofield .... 28 .. H 7
Sevier .... J 5
Shivwits .... N 2
Sigurd .... 430 .. J 6
Silver City .... G 5
Smithfield .... 7,261 .. B 6
Snowville .... 177 .. B 4
Soldier Summit .... G 7
South Jordan .... 29,437 .. F 6
South Ogden .... 14,377 .. D 6
South Salt Lake .... 22,038 .. E 6
South Weber* .... 4,260 .. E 6
Spanish Fork .... 20,246 .. G 6
Spring City .... 956 .. H 7
Spring Glen .... H 8
Spring Lake† .... 469 .. G 6
Springdale .... 457 .. N 4
Springville .... 20,424 .. F 6
Standrod .... B 3
Stansbury Park† .... 2,385 .. E 5
Sterling .... 235 .. I 6
Stockton .... 443 .. F 5
Sugarville .... H 4
Summit .... L 4
Summit Point .... L 11
Sunnyside .... 404 .. H 9
Sunset .... 5,204 .. D 6
Sutherland .... H 4
Syracuse .... 9,398 .. D 6
Tabiona .... 149 .. F 8
Talmage .... F 9
Taylorsville [-Bennion]† .... 57,439 .. E 6
Teasdale .... K 7
Thistle .... G 7
Thompson .... I 10
Ticaboo .... M 8
Timpie .... E 4
Tooele○ .... 22,502 .. F 5
Toquerville .... 910 .. N 3
Torrey .... 171 .. K 7
Tremonton .... 5,592 .. C 5
Trenton .... 449 .. B 6
Tridell .... F 10
Tropic .... 508 .. M 5
Trout Creek .... H 2
Tucker .... G 7
Ucolo .... L 11
Uintah* .... 1,127 .. E 6
Upalco .... F 9
Upton .... D 7
Uvada .... M 1
Venice .... J 6
Vernal○ .... 7,714 .. F 10
Vernon .... 236 .. G 5
Veyo .... N 2
Vineyard* .... 150 .. F 6
Virgin .... 394 .. N 3
Wahsatch .... D 7
Wales .... 219 .. H 6
Wallsburg .... 274 .. F 7
Washakie .... B 5
Washington .... 8,186 .. N 3
Washington Terrace .... 8,551 .. D 6
Wattis .... H 7
Wellington .... 1,666 .. H 8
Wellsville .... 2,728 .. C 6
Wendover .... 1,537 .. E 2
West Bountiful .... 4,484 .. E 6
West Jordan .... 68,336 .. E 6
West Point .... 6,033 .. D 6
West Valley City .... 108,896 .. E 6
Westwater .... I 11
Wheelon .... B 6
White City*† .... 5,998 .. F 6
Whiterocks† .... 341 .. F 10
Willard .... 1,630 .. C 6
Woodland† .... 335 .. E 7
Woodland Hills* .... 941 .. G 6
Woodruff .... 194 .. C 7
Woods Cross .... 6,419 .. E 6
Woodside .... I 9
Yost .... B 3
Zane .... L 2

*Does not appear on map; key shows general location.
†Census designated place—unincorporated, but recognized as a significant settled community by the U.S. Census Bureau.
○County seat.
Source: 2000 census. Metropolitan area figures are based on 2003 Office of Management and Budget reorganization of 2000 census data. Places without population figures are unincorporated areas.

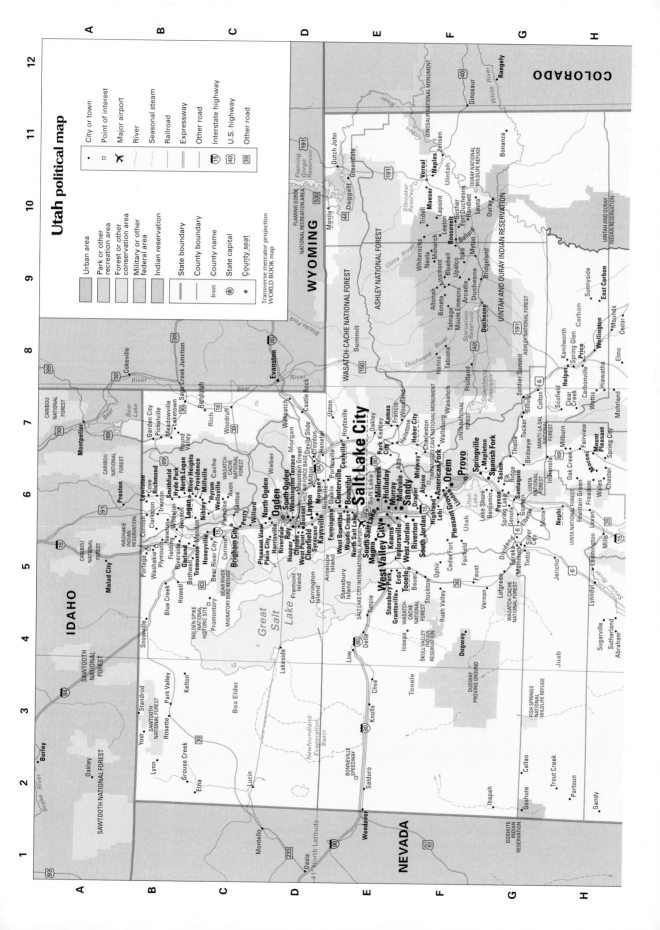

Utah political map

Legend:

- Urban area
- Park or other recreation area
- Forest or other conservation area
- Military or other federal area
- Indian reservation

- State boundary
- County boundary
- County name
- State capital
- County seat

Iron

Transverse mercator projection
WORLD BOOK map

- City or town
- Point of interest
- Major airport
- River
- Seasonal steam
- Railroad
- Expressway
- Other road
- Interstate highway
- U.S. highway
- Other road

15 40 39

IDAHO

NEVADA

WYOMING

COLORADO

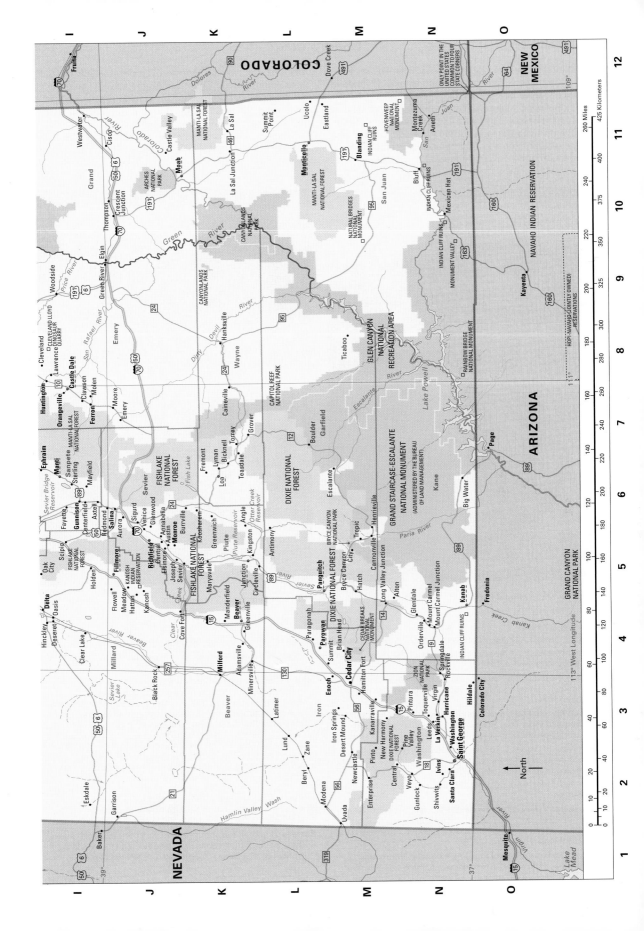

Millions of tourists visit Utah every year. The state's forests, mountains, lakes, rivers, and extensive parklands are excellent for boating, cycling, fishing, hiking, hunting, sightseeing, skiing, and swimming. Popular destinations include Great Salt Lake, the mountains of the Wasatch and Uinta ranges, and Utah's five national parks.

One of Utah's most popular places to visit is the center of Mormonism—Temple Square in Salt Lake City. It includes the majestic Mormon Temple (officially the Salt Lake Temple of the Church of Jesus Christ of Latter-day Saints) and the Tabernacle. The Mormon Tabernacle is famous for its choir and huge organ. The Mormon Temple is not open to the general public.

Each July, Utahns observe the 1847 arrival of Mormon pioneers in the Salt Lake Valley. Many Utah cities stage celebrations to commemorate the arrival.

David R. Frazier

Bryce Canyon National Park

© Mark E. Gibson, Corbis

Mormon Temple in Salt Lake City

Places to visit

Following are brief descriptions of some of Utah's many interesting places to visit:

Beehive House, in Salt Lake City, is the restored home of Brigham Young. This stately, two-story adobe house was built in the 1850's.

Bonneville Salt Flats, near Wendover, are famous for automobile speed trials. The area has about 50 square miles (130 square kilometers) of flat salt beds that are as hard as cement.

The Gateway, in Salt Lake City, includes open-air shopping, restaurants, entertainment, Olympic Legacy Plaza, a planetarium, and historic Union Pacific Depot.

Great Salt Lake, near Salt Lake City, has water saltier than that of any ocean.

Monument Valley, in southeastern Utah, has red sandstone formations that rise 1,000 feet (300 meters). In the evening, a formation called the *totem pole* casts a shadow 35 miles (56 kilometers) long.

Ruins of Indian cliff dwellings line mountain ledges near Blanding, Bluff, Kanab, Moab, Parowan, Price, and Vernal. These cliff dwellings housed Indians who lived in the Utah region hundreds of years ago.

National parks, monuments, and forests. Utah has five national parks—Arches, Bryce Canyon, Canyonlands, Capitol Reef, and Zion. The state shares Dinosaur and Hovenweep national monuments with Colorado. Other Utah national monuments are Grand Staircase-Escalante, Cedar Breaks, Natural Bridges, Rainbow Bridge, and Timpanogos Cave. The Golden Spike National Historic Site is at Promontory. Utah shares Lake Powell and the Glen Canyon National Recreation Area with Arizona. Three national forests lie entirely within Utah—Dixie, Fishlake, and Uinta. Utah shares six national forests with bordering states. Ashley and Wasatch are shared with Wyoming, Cache and Sawtooth with Idaho, Caribou with Idaho and Wyoming, and Manti-La Sal with Colorado. Lone Peak National Wilderness Area is in Uinta and Wasatch national forests.

State parks. Utah has about 40 state parks. For information on these parks, write to State Parks and Recreation, 1594 W. North Temple, Suite 116, Salt Lake City, UT 84114-6001.

Sundance Film Festival in Park City

AP/Wide World

Annual events

January-April
Sundance Film Festival in Park City (January); Bryce Canyon Winter Festival (February); Easter Jeep Safari in Moab (March or April); St. George Arts Festival (March or April); Mountain Man Rendezvous in Ogden (April and October).

May-August
Friendship Cruise in Green River (May); Reenactment of the Driving of the Golden Spike at Promontory (May 10); Strawberry Days Festival in Pleasant Grove (June); the Scottish Festival in Salt Lake City (June); Utah Arts Festival in Salt Lake City (June); the Ute Stampede, with a professional rodeo and a carnival, in Nephi (July); Mormon Miracle Pageant in Manti (July); Shakespearean Festival in Cedar City (June to August); Park City Kimball Arts Festival (August); Oktoberfest at Snowbird Resort southeast of Salt Lake City (August to October).

September-December
Utah State Fair in Salt Lake City (September); Festival of Lights Parades at Lake Powell (December); Christmas at Temple Square in Salt Lake City (December); Ballet West, *The Nutcracker,* Salt Lake City (December); Utah Oratorio Society, *The Messiah,* at Symphony Hall in Salt Lake City (Sunday before Christmas).

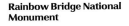
Rainbow Bridge National Monument

E. Cooper, H. Armstrong Roberts

Utah State Parks

Floating in the Great Salt Lake

Salt Lake District, Bureau of Land Management

High-speed time trials on the Bonneville Salt Flats

Land and climate

Land regions. Utah includes parts of three major land regions: (1) the Rocky Mountains, (2) the Basin and Range Region, and (3) the Colorado Plateau.

The Rocky Mountains extend generally north and south across a large part of western North America. In Utah, two ranges of the Rocky Mountains—the Uinta and the Wasatch—form an angle in the northeast corner of the state. The Uinta Range extends westward from Colorado almost to Salt Lake City. It is the only major range of the Rocky Mountains that runs east and west. Several peaks in the Uinta Range are more than 13,000 feet (3,960 meters) high. Kings Peak, the highest point in Utah, rises 13,528 feet (4,123 meters) near the center of the range. Many lakes and flat-bottomed canyons in the Uinta Range were formed by glaciers that once covered the area.

The Wasatch Range extends from Mount Nebo, near Nephi, northward into Idaho. The steep western side of this range rises 6,000 to 8,000 feet (1,800 to 2,400 meters) above the valleys that border it. The Wasatch Range also has many canyons. The canyons provide water and serve as recreation areas for the people in Utah's largest cities, just west of the mountains. Some of the canyons were *glaciated* (cut by glaciers).

The Basin and Range Region covers parts of several states, including the western part of Utah. It is one of the driest regions in the United States. Small mountain ranges and broad basins cover the center of the region. Higher ranges and plateaus border it on the east and the west. Great Salt Lake lies in the northeast part of the region. West and southwest of the lake is a barren area called the Great Salt Lake Desert. The desert has about 4,000 acres (1,600 hectares) of flat salt beds that are as hard as concrete.

The extreme southwestern corner of Utah's Basin and Range Region is the lowest and warmest area. It is known as *Utah's Dixie.* The early settlers grew cotton and grapes there.

The Colorado Plateau stretches over parts of Utah, Arizona, Colorado, and New Mexico. It covers most of the southern and eastern sections of Utah. This region consists of broad, rough uplands cut by deep canyons and valleys. High plateaus in the western part of the region include the Aquarius, Fish Lake, Markagunt, Paunsagunt, Pavant, Sanpitch, Sevier, and Tushar. These plateaus have elevations of more than 11,000 feet (3,350 meters). The famous Bryce, Cedar Breaks, and Zion

E. Cooper, H. Armstrong Roberts

Flaming Gorge National Recreation Area is located in the Rocky Mountains region of northeastern Utah. The Green River cut this spectacular gorge through the Uinta Range.

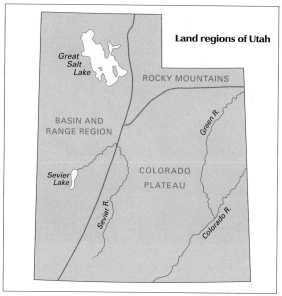

WORLD BOOK map

Map index

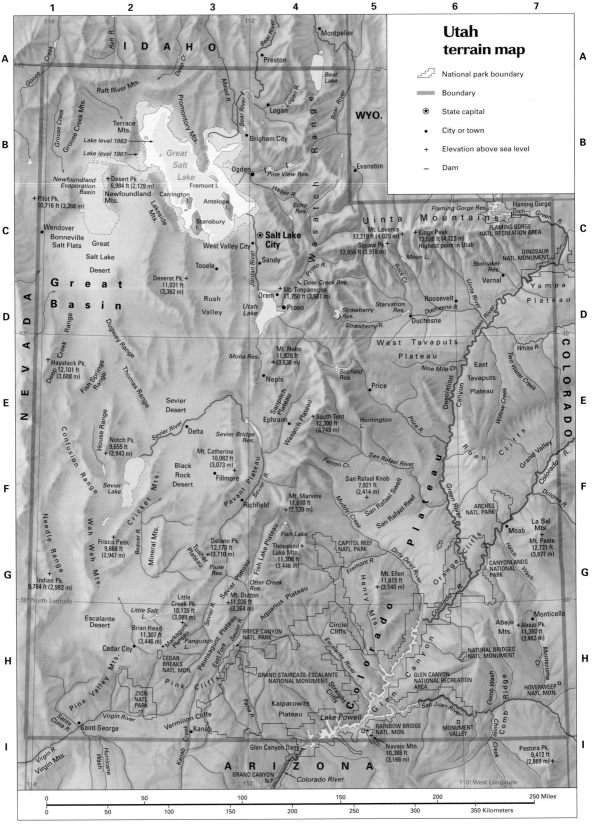

Utah
terrain map

⎍⎍⎍ National park boundary

▨▨▨ Boundary

✷ State capital

• City or town

+ Elevation above sea level

− Dam

1 2 3 4 5 6 7

A IDAHO
Raft R.
Montpelier
Preston
Bear River
Deep Cr.
Bear Lake
Malad R.
Logan R.
Logan
WYO.
Raft River Mts.
Promontory Mts.
Bear River
Grouse Creek
Goose Creek

B Terrace Mts.
Lake level 1963
Lake level 1987
Great Salt Lake
Brigham City
Ogden
Pine View Res.
Evanston
Weber R.
Echo Res.
Grouse Creek Mts.
Newfoundland Evaporation Basin
+ Desert Pk. 6,984 ft (2,129 m)
Fremont I.
Newfoundland Mts.
Carrington I.
Antelope I.
Stansbury I.
Lakeside Mts.
Wasatch Range

C + Pilot Pk. 10,716 ft (3,266 m)
Wendover
Bonneville Salt Flats
Great Salt Lake Desert
West Valley City
Salt Lake City
Sandy
Jordan River
Provo R.
Mt. Lovenia 13,219 ft (4,029 m)
+ Kings Peak 13,528 ft (4,123 m) Highest point in Utah
Squaw Pk. + 12,855 ft (3,918 m)
Uinta Mountains
Moon L.
Rock Cr.
Flaming Gorge Res.
Flaming Gorge Dam
Green R.
FLAMING GORGE NATL. RECREATION AREA
DINOSAUR NATL. MONUMENT
Steinaker Res.
Vernal
Uinta River
Yampa Plateau

D Great Basin
NEVADA
Dugway Range
Deseret Pk. + 11,031 ft (3,362 m)
Tooele
Rush Valley
Utah Lake
Orem
Provo
+ Mt. Timpanogos 11,750 ft (3,581 m)
Deer Creek Res.
Strawberry Res.
Strawberry R.
Starvation Res.
Duchesne R.
Roosevelt
Duchesne
Green River
West Tavaputs Plateau
White R.
Two Water Creek
COLORADO

E Deep Creek Range
+ Haystack Pk. 12,101 ft (3,688 m)
Fish Springs Range
Thomas Range
Sevier Desert
Sevier River
Delta
Sevier Bridge Res.
Ephraim
Sanpitch Plateau
Wasatch Plateau
+ South Tent 12,300 ft (3,749 m)
Huntington L.
Mt. Nebo 11,928 ft + (3,636 m)
Mona Res.
Nephi
Scofield Res.
Price
San Rafael River
Nine Mile Cr.
Price R.
East Tavaputs Plateau
Desolation Canyon
Willow Creek
Green River
Roan Cliffs
Grand Valley
Colorado R.

F Confusion Range
House Range
Sevier Lake
Notch Pk. 9,655 ft + (2,943 m)
Cricket Mts.
Black Rock Desert
Mt. Catherine 10,082 ft (3,073 m)
Fillmore
Pavant Plateau
Sevier R.
Mt. Marvine 11,610 ft + (3,539 m)
Richfield
Ferron Cr.
San Rafael Knob 7,921 ft (2,414 m) +
San Rafael Swell
San Rafael Reef
Muddy Creek
Orange Cliffs
Green River
Colorado Plateau
ARCHES NATL. PARK
Moab
La Sal Mts.
Mt. Peale 12,721 ft (3,877 m) +
Dolores R.
Colorado R.

G Needle Range
+ Indian Pk. 9,784 ft (2,982 m)
Wah Wah Mts.
Beaver R.
Frisco Peak 9,668 ft + (2,947 m)
Mineral Mts.
Tushar Plateau
Delano Pk. 12,173 ft + (3,710 m)
Piute Res.
Fish Lake Plateau
Fish Lake
Thousand + Lake Mtn. 11,306 ft (3,446 m)
Fremont R.
CAPITOL REEF NATL. PARK
Dirty Devil River
Mt. Ellen 11,615 ft + (3,540 m)
Henry Mts.
Colorado R.
Hatch Wash
CANYONLANDS NATIONAL PARK

H Escalante Desert
Little Salt L.
Little Creek Pk. 10,135 ft (3,089 m)
Brian Head 11,307 ft + (3,446 m)
Markagunt Plateau
Mt. Dutton + 11,036 ft (3,364 m)
Sevier Plateau
Otter Creek Res.
Aquarius Plateau
Sevier R.
Circle Cliffs
Escalante River
Colorado River
Abajo Mts.
Abajo Pk. + 11,360 ft (3,463 m)
Monticello
NATURAL BRIDGES NATL. MONUMENT
Cedar City
Pine Valley Mts.
CEDAR BREAKS NATL. MON.
Panguitch Plateau
BRYCE CANYON NATL. PARK
East Fork Sevier R.
Glen Canyon
GLEN CANYON NATIONAL RECREATION AREA
Montezuma Cr.
HOVENWEEP NATL. MON.
Comb Ridge

I Santa Clara R.
Saint George
Virgin River
Zion Natl. Park
Pink Cliffs
Paria R.
Kanab
Vermilion Cliffs
Kaiparowits Plateau
GRAND STAIRCASE-ESCALANTE NATIONAL MONUMENT
Straight Cliffs
Lake Powell
San Juan River
RAINBOW BRIDGE NATL. MON.
MONUMENT VALLEY
Comb Wash
Chinle Creek
Pastora Pk. 9,412 ft (2,869 m) +
Kanab Creek
Navajo Mtn. 10,388 ft (3,166 m)
Glen Canyon Dam
Virgin R.
Virgin Mts.
Hurricane Wash
ARIZONA
GRAND CANYON N.P.
Colorado River

114° 112° 110° West Longitude

38° North Latitude

0   50   100   150   200   250 Miles
0   50   100   150   200   250   300   350 Kilometers

WORLD BOOK map

canyons are in this area. The Henry Mountains rise west of the Colorado River, and the Abajo and La Sal mountains are east of the river. Utah's southeastern corner meets the corners of Arizona, New Mexico, and Colorado. This is the only point in the United States where four states meet (see **Arizona** [picture: Four states meet at Four Corners]).

Rivers and lakes. The uses of Utah's rivers include providing irrigation for great stretches of farmland that otherwise would be desert. The Colorado River and its main tributary, the Green River, are the largest rivers in the state. These rivers and their many branches drain the eastern half of Utah. The Snake River of Idaho and its branches drain Utah's northwest corner. The Bear, Provo, and Weber rivers begin in the Uinta Range and flow through the Wasatch Range into Great Salt Lake. The Sevier is the chief river of south-central Utah. It begins in the Paunsagunt Plateau and flows north, then bends to the southwest. Most of the Basin and Range Region, which extends across several Western states, has no outlet to the sea. It is the largest area of interior drainage in the United States.

Thousands of years ago, a huge body of fresh water covered parts of Utah. Scientists have named this ancient sea Lake Bonneville. The Bonneville Salt Flats, in the middle of the Great Salt Lake Desert, cover part of the bed of Lake Bonneville. Great Salt Lake and Utah Lake are also part of what remains of Lake Bonneville. Great Salt Lake is the largest natural lake west of the Mississippi River. The water in Great Salt Lake is saltier than ocean water. Great Salt Lake is salty because its waters are not drained by outflowing streams. Instead, some of the water evaporates and leaves salt deposits behind. When heavy precipitation occurs, the lake expands in area, often causing floods. The Jordan River drains Utah Lake and keeps its waters fresh. Utah Lake and Bear Lake, which Utah shares with Idaho, are impor-

tant reservoirs in which irrigation waters are stored. Many small lakes lie in the Boulder, Uinta, and Wasatch mountains.

Deserts cover about a third of Utah. Few plants can grow in these deserts because of the lack of rainfall. The Great Salt Lake Desert lies west and south of Great Salt Lake. Other deserts include the Sevier Desert in west-central Utah, and the Escalante Desert in the southwestern part of the state.

Plant and animal life. Forests cover about 30 percent of Utah. The forestland is found in the mountains. Common trees include aspens, firs, junipers, pines, and spruces. Many kinds of grasses, shrubs, and wildflowers grow in the mountains. The dry sections of the state have cactus, creosote bush, greasewood, mesquite, and shadscale. The state's wetter sections have grasses and sagebrush.

Common small animals in Utah include badgers,

Average monthly weather

	Salt Lake City							Milford				
	Temperatures				Days of rain or snow			Temperatures				Days of rain or snow
	°F		°C					°F		°C		
	High	Low	High	Low				High	Low	High	Low	
Jan.	37	21	3	–6	10		Jan.	41	16	5	–9	7
Feb.	43	26	6	–3	9		Feb.	47	20	8	–7	7
Mar.	53	33	12	1	10		Mar.	57	26	14	–3	8
Apr.	61	39	16	4	10		Apr.	65	32	18	0	6
May	71	47	22	8	8		May	74	39	23	4	5
June	82	56	28	13	5		June	86	47	30	8	3
July	91	63	33	17	4		July	93	55	34	13	5
Aug.	89	62	32	17	6		Aug.	91	55	33	13	6
Sept.	78	52	26	11	5		Sept.	81	45	27	7	4
Oct.	64	41	18	5	6		Oct.	68	33	20	1	4
Nov.	49	30	9	–1	8		Nov.	52	23	11	–5	5
Dec.	38	22	3	–6	9		Dec.	42	15	6	–9	6

Average January temperatures

Utah has short, mild winters. The coolest temperatures are concentrated in the northeastern part of the state.

Average July temperatures

Utah has long, warm summers. The northeast and south-central areas have the coolest summertime temperatures.

Average yearly precipitation

Utah has a dry climate. Precipitation is the lowest in the desert areas and the highest in the mountain ranges.

WORLD BOOK maps

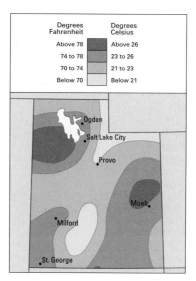

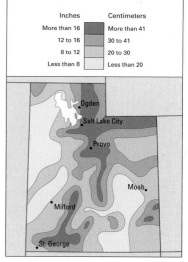

foxes, martens, muskrats, rabbits, ringtails, skunks, and weasels. Among the larger animals are black bears, bobcats, coyotes, lynxes, and mountain lions. The mule deer is the most common game animal. Buffaloes, elks, moose, and pronghorns are also found. Ducks, geese, grouse, pheasants, and quail are common game birds of Utah. The state has such reptiles as lizards, toads, tortoises, and several kinds of snakes. Trout is the state's most common fish. Other fish that are found in Utah include bass, catfish, graylings, perch, and whitefish.

Climate. Average July temperatures in Utah range from 60 °F (16 °C) in the northeast to 84 °F (29 °C) in the southwest. January temperatures average 20 °F (−7 °C) in the north part of the state and 39 °F (4 °C) in the southwest. Utah's record high temperature, 117 °F (47 °C), occurred on July 5, 1985, at St. George. The lowest temperature was −69 °F (−56 °C), recorded at Peter's Sink on Feb. 1, 1985.

Yearly precipitation varies from less than 5 inches (13 centimeters) in the Great Salt Lake Desert to up to 50 inches (130 centimeters) in the mountains of the northeast. The southwest gets little snow, but Alta, a ski area near Salt Lake City, receives more than 400 inches (1,000 centimeters) a year.

Economy

The overall structure of Utah's economy is dominated by service industries. Taken together, they account for the largest part of the *gross domestic product*—the total value of all goods and services produced in the state in a year. Services also employ about four-fifths of Utah's workers. Other important economic activities in the state include manufacturing and construction.

Natural resources of Utah include rich mineral deposits, and mountain and valley soils.

Minerals. Coal, natural gas, and petroleum are found in the Colorado Plateau. Natural gas and petroleum are also found in northeastern Utah. In addition, the state has some of the nation's richest deposits of oil shale and tar sands. Bingham Canyon, near Salt Lake City, has rich deposits of copper, gold, molybdenum, and silver. Important deposits of gold and silver lie near Utah Lake. Great Salt Lake is a source of magnesium and several salts. Utah also has clays, gemstones, gypsum, limestone, and sand and gravel.

Soils of Utah are generally poor for farming. Most of the mountain soils are poorly developed. Valley soils are often mixtures of sand, gravel, and clay carried down by mountain streams. Where water is available, these valley soils can produce good crops.

Service industries account for the greatest portion of Utah's gross domestic product. Most of the service industries are concentrated in the metropolitan areas.

Finance, insurance, and real estate forms Utah's leading service industry in terms of the gross domestic product. The real estate sector benefits from the state's rapid population growth, which has resulted in many new homes and office buildings. Salt Lake City is the state's chief financial center. Several credit card companies have large operations in Utah.

Community, business, and personal services ranks second among the service industries and is the state's leading employer. It consists of a wide variety of establishments, including engineering companies, law firms, private health care, and repair shops.

Trade, restaurants, and hotels ranks third. The wholesale trade of computers and computer equipment, food products, mined products, and motor vehicles is important in Utah. Major retail businesses include automobile dealerships, discount stores, gas stations, and grocery stores. Salt Lake City has more restaurants and hotels than any other city in Utah.

Government ranks fourth among Utah's service industries. The U.S. government owns about three-fifths of the state's land. Government services include the operation of military bases, public schools, and public hospitals. Hill Air Force Base is one of Utah's leading employers.

Transportation and communication forms the fifth-ranking service industry in Utah. Airlines, railroads, and trucking firms are the chief kinds of transportation companies in the state. Telephone companies are a major part of the communications sector. More information about this industry group appears later in this section.

Manufacturing. Goods made in Utah have a *value added by manufacture* of about $14 billion annually. Value added by manufacture represents the increase in value of raw materials after they have been turned into finished products.

Computer and electronic products are Utah's leading products in terms of value added by manufacture. Communication equipment, computer microchips, and scientific instruments are the major products of this sector. Most of Utah's electronic equipment is made in the Salt Lake City and Ogden areas.

Processed foods and beverages rank second among Utah's manufactures. These products include baked goods, dairy products, fruit and vegetable preserves, and meat products.

Production and workers by economic activities

Economic activities	Percent of GDP* produced	Employed workers Number of people	Employed workers Percent of total
Finance, insurance, & real estate	22	163,700	11
Community, business, & personal services	20	427,100	29
Trade, restaurants, & hotels	15	306,800	21
Government	14	217,400	15
Manufacturing	11	121,300	8
Transportation & communication	7	81,300	6
Construction	6	98,400	7
Mining	2	8,600	1
Agriculture	1	22,900	2
Utilities	1	4,200	†
Total‡	100	1,451,700	100

*GDP = gross domestic product, the total value of goods and services produced in a year.
†Less than one-half of 1 percent.
‡Figures may not add up to 100 percent due to rounding.
Figures are for 2004; employment figures include full- and part-time workers.
Source: *World Book* estimates based on data from U.S. Bureau of Economic Analysis.

Economy of Utah

This map shows the economic uses of land in Utah and where the state's leading farm and mineral products are produced. Major manufacturing centers are shown in red.

Grazing land with some cropland	Mostly unproductive land
Mostly shrubland	● Manufacturing center
Mostly forest land	● Mineral deposit

WORLD BOOK map

water of the Great Salt Lake is used to produce magnesium and natural salts. Utah is a top producer of molybdenum. Sand and gravel is produced throughout the state. The state's other mined products include clays, gemstones, gypsum, and phosphate rock.

Agriculture. Utah has about 15,000 farms. Farmland covers about a fifth of the state.

Livestock and livestock products provide about four-fifths of the state's total farm income. Beef cattle and milk are Utah's leading farm products. Dairy farms lie in the fertile areas east of the Great Salt Lake. Beef cattle are also raised in this region, as well as in eastern Utah. Hogs also rank among the state's leading farm products. Most of the state's hogs are raised in Beaver and Iron counties. Utah farmers also produce eggs and raise sheep. Utah ranks among the nation's leading sheep-raising states.

Crops account for about one-fourth of Utah's farm income. Most of the crops are grown in the north-central part of the state. Hay, Utah's leading crop, is used mainly as feed for the state's beef and dairy cattle. Wheat, barley, and corn rank next in importance. Fruits grown in the state include apples, cherries, and peaches. Onions are the most important vegetable grown in Utah. Greenhouse and nursery products are also an important part of Utah's agriculture. These products include such plants as potted flowers and ornamental shrubs.

Electric power and utilities. Utah's utilities provide electric, gas, and water service. About 95 percent of Utah's electric power comes from coal-fired steam plants in Emery, Millard, and Uintah counties. Most of the remaining electric power is from natural gas plants.

Transportation. The first transcontinental railroad system in the United States was completed in Utah on May 10, 1869. On that date, the Central Pacific and Union Pacific railroads were joined at Promontory.

Today, two major rail lines provide freight service, and passenger trains link major Utah cities to major cities in other states. A light rail system serves the greater Salt Lake City area. Utah has about 43,000 miles (69,000 kilometers) of roads. The largest commercial airport in Utah is in Salt Lake City.

Transportation products rank third. Many of Utah's transportation equipment plants are near Brigham City and Salt Lake City. These facilities manufacture solid rocket propulsion systems for spacecraft and weapons systems and air bags for motor vehicles.

Other products manufactured in Utah include chemicals, fabricated metal products, and primary metals. *Pharmaceuticals* (medicinal drugs) and cleaning products are the state's leading chemical products. Sheet metal and other structural metals are the leading type of fabricated metal products. Aluminum, copper, and steel are important metals produced in the state.

Mining. Utah's most valuable mined products are copper, natural gas, and petroleum. A huge copper mine lies near Salt Lake City. The eastern part of the state produces large amounts of natural gas. Most of Utah's petroleum comes from Duchesne, San Juan, and Uintah counties.

Utah is a leading producer of gold and silver. Gold and silver are mined near Salt Lake City and in other parts of the state. Utah's coal is known for its low sulfur content. Carbon, Emery, and Sevier counties supply nearly all the state's coal. Uintah County is the nation's only producer of gilsonite, a solid form of asphalt. The

Alliant Techsystems, Inc.

Manufacturing of transportation equipment is a leading industry in Utah. These workers at a plant that manufactures rocket engines oversee the mixing of *propellant* (fuel) for spacecraft.

Communication. Utah's first newspaper, *The Deseret News,* was established in Salt Lake City in 1850. Today, the state's largest newspapers are *The Deseret News* and *The Salt Lake Tribune,* both of Salt Lake City, and the *Standard-Examiner* of Ogden. The state's first radio station, KZN (now KSL), began broadcasting in Salt Lake City in 1922. Utah's first television station, KTVT (now KTVX-TV), began operating in 1948. Today, Utah has a number of radio and TV stations. Cable TV systems and Internet providers also serve many Utah communities.

Government

Constitution. Utah adopted its Constitution in 1895, the year before it became a state. Constitutional *amendments* (changes) may be proposed by the state Legislature or by a constitutional convention. An amendment proposed by the Legislature must receive the approval of two-thirds of the members of each house. The amendment must then be approved in a general election by a majority of the people voting on the issue.

Before a constitutional convention can meet, it must be approved by two-thirds of the members of each house of the Legislature. It must then be approved by a majority of the voters in a general election. Amendments proposed by a constitutional convention must receive a majority of the votes cast in a general election.

Executive. The governor of Utah is elected to a four-year term. Other executive officials—also elected to four-year terms—include the attorney general, lieutenant governor, state auditor, and state treasurer. The governor and the other elected executive officials may serve any number of terms.

The governor appoints various state officials who are not elected, including the executive directors of various state departments and members of state boards. Most of the appointments must be approved by the Senate.

Legislature of Utah consists of a 29-member Senate and a 75-member House of Representatives. Members of both houses are elected from districts drawn up according to population. State senators serve four-year terms, and state representatives serve two-year terms. They may serve any number of terms.

The Legislature meets annually on the third Monday in January. Regular sessions of the Legislature last 45 days. The governor may call special sessions of the Legislature. These sessions may not last more than 30 days.

Courts. The state's highest court is the Utah Supreme Court. This court has five justices. The state's Court of Appeals has seven judges. Utah is divided into eight judicial districts. Each district has two or more District Court judges, depending on population. Other Utah courts include justice courts, juvenile courts, and municipal courts.

The governor appoints the judges of the Supreme Court, Court of Appeals, District Court, and juvenile courts, with the advice and approval of the Senate. These judges periodically run for reelection.

Local government. Most of Utah's 29 counties are managed by a three-member board of county commissioners. Two of the members of each board are elected to four-year terms. The third member is elected for two years. The board is responsible for county affairs and for supervising county departments and officers. In most other counties, the executive and legislative responsibilities are separated. The government consists of a county executive and county council. Salt Lake County, the state's largest county, has a mayor-council government.

All other county officers are elected to four-year terms. They include an assessor, attorney, auditor, clerk, recorder, sheriff, surveyor, and treasurer. In some counties, some of these offices are combined.

Municipalities in Utah are divided into six classes, according to population. These classes are: (1) first-class cities, (2) second-class cities, (3) third-class cities, (4) fourth-class cities, (5) fifth-class cities, and (6) towns. First-class cities have 100,000 or more people. Second-class cities have between 65,000 and 99,999 people. Third-class cities have between 30,000 and 64,999 people. Fourth-class cities have between 10,000 and 29,999 people. Fifth-class cities have between 1,000 and 9,999 people. Towns have fewer than 1,000 people.

Any city or town may use a council-manager or a mayor-council form of government if it elects to do so. Otherwise, first- and second-class cities use the commissioner form of government; third-, fourth-, and fifth-class cities have a mayor-council form; and towns are governed by a town council. The state Constitution gives municipalities the right to adopt their own charters. This right is called *home rule,* but few Utah municipalities have used it.

Revenue. Taxes account for about half of the state government's *general revenue* (income). Most of the rest comes from federal grants and other U.S. government programs, and charges for government services. A general sales tax and a personal income tax make up most of the tax revenue. Taxes on motor fuels and corporate income are also important sources of tax revenue.

Politics. Through most of Utah's history, political strength was fairly evenly divided between the Democratic and Republican parties. But in the late 1900's, power shifted to the Republicans. For Utah's electoral votes and voting record in presidential elections, see **Electoral College** (table).

The governors of Utah		
	Party	**Term**
Heber M. Wells	Republican	1896-1905
John C. Cutler	Republican	1905-1909
William Spry	Republican	1909-1917
Simon Bamberger	Democratic	1917-1921
Charles R. Mabey	Republican	1921-1925
George H. Dern	Democratic	1925-1933
Henry H. Blood	Democratic	1933-1941
Herbert B. Maw	Democratic	1941-1949
J. Bracken Lee	Republican	1949-1957
George D. Clyde	Republican	1957-1965
Calvin L. Rampton	Democratic	1965-1977
Scott M. Matheson	Democratic	1977-1985
Norman H. Bangerter	Republican	1985-1993
Michael O. Leavitt	Republican	1993-2003
Olene Walker	Republican	2003-2005
Jon M. Huntsman, Jr.	Republican	2005-

Indian days. Indians probably lived in the Utah region several thousand years ago. The Anasazi, one of the early Indian groups, made their homes in pueblos and in cliff dwellings. Another early Indian group, the Fremont, lived in pit houses, dwellings dug into the ground. The Navajo arrived in the Utah region before the 1700's and now occupy large areas in southeastern Utah. White explorers who reached the Utah region in the late 1700's found four major groups of tribes—the Gosiute, Paiute, Shoshone (Snake), and Ute.

Early exploration. In 1765, a Spanish expedition led by Juan María de Rivera reached what is now southeastern Utah. In 1776, while American colonists were fighting for their independence from Britain, two Spanish Franciscan friars led an expedition into the Utah region. They were Silvestre Velez de Escalante and Francisco Atanasio Domínguez. The friars reached Utah Lake. Later, a few other Spaniards visited the region. But Spain was not interested in setting up colonies there. The first Americans to visit the region probably crossed what is now northern Utah in 1811 and 1812. They were part of a fur trading expedition.

Jim Bridger, a famous scout, was probably the first white person to see Great Salt Lake. He reached its shores during the winter of 1824-1825. Bridger tasted the salty water and thought he had found an ocean. Hundreds of fur trappers and traders soon came to the area from Taos, New Mexico; St. Louis, Missouri; and British posts in what are now Montana and Washington. By 1830, travelers were crossing central Utah to get from Santa Fe, New Mexico, to Los Angeles.

The Mormons were Utah's first permanent white settlers. This religious group belonged to the Church of Jesus Christ of Latter-day Saints. Joseph Smith established the church in Fayette, New York, in 1830. Brigham Young became leader of the Mormons after Smith's death in 1844. The Mormons were persecuted nearly everywhere they went. They traveled to Ohio, Missouri, and Illinois in search of religious freedom. In 1846, Young led a group of his people west. They reached the Great Salt Lake region in 1847, and Young settled there. He planned communities for his followers. See **Mormons**.

Many groups of Mormons settled in the valleys of north-central Utah. They irrigated the valleys and made farming productive. In the late 1840's, swarms of grasshoppers invaded the valleys and threatened to ruin the settlers' crops. But sea gulls from Great Salt Lake ate the grasshoppers. The sea gull later became the state bird, and a monument was built in Salt Lake City to honor the gulls. The kind of grasshopper that attacked the settlers' crops became known as the Mormon cricket.

In 1849, the Mormons established their Perpetual Emigrating Fund. This fund helped bring to Utah many Mormons who could not pay for the trip. The fund operated for about 40 years. It brought about 80,000 Mormons to Utah, including many from Denmark, England, Norway, Scotland, Sweden, and Wales.

Indian relations. Relations between the Mormons and the Indians were peaceful at first. But some of the Indians resented the settlers who had taken their land.

Beginning in 1853, a Ute chief named Walker led attacks against several Mormon settlements. These attacks were known as the Walker War. In 1854, Brigham Young persuaded Walker to end the attacks. For several years,

the settlers and Indians lived peacefully. But in 1865, another Ute chief, Black Hawk, led an uprising against the Mormons. The attack started the Black Hawk War. Other tribes joined in the fighting, and many Mormons and Indians were killed. The settlers suffered losses of over $1 million, and the Indians lost control of nearly all their tribal lands. Black Hawk and his followers stopped fighting in 1867 and signed a treaty in 1868. However, other Indians made occasional raids until late 1872. Most of the Ute settled on a reservation in the Uinta Basin.

Bannock and Shoshone raids in northern Utah and southern Idaho continued until 1863, when U.S. Army forces under General Patrick E. Connor defeated them in the Battle of Bear River in southeastern Idaho.

Territorial days and statehood. The Utah region belonged to Mexico when the Mormons first arrived in 1847. At the time, the United States and Mexico were fighting the Mexican War (1846-1848). The United States won the war and acquired from Mexico a large area of land, including the Utah region.

In 1849, the Mormons established the State of Deseret. They set up a temporary government with Brigham Young as governor. Church leaders filled other government offices. The settlers adopted a constitution and asked to be admitted to the Union. But Congress was engaged in a bitter debate over the question of slavery in the United States. This debate resulted in the Compromise of 1850. Part of the compromise established the Utah Territory, with Young as the first territorial governor. The territory extended far to the east and west of present-day Utah. See **Compromise of 1850**.

Between 1849 and 1895, Utah asked several more times to be admitted to the Union. But Congress refused to admit Utah because of the Mormon practice of *polygamy* (one man having more than one wife). Nearly 30 percent of Utah's families were polygamous.

President James Buchanan wanted to take control of the Utah Territory away from the Mormons. In 1857, he

Ancient cliff dwellings are preserved in Canyonlands National Park. The Anasazi Indians built many such homes in the southwestern United States between A.D. 1000 and 1300.

Historic Utah

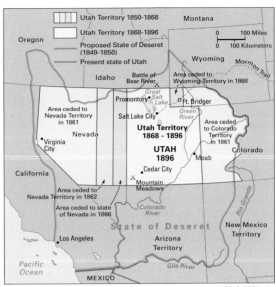

WORLD BOOK map

Brigham Young, *inset,* led a group of Mormons west in search of religious freedom. They arrived at the site of Salt Lake City (which they called Deseret) on July 24, 1847.

Utah was settled by Mormon pioneers in 1847. The area was part of the proposed State of Deseret in 1849 and 1850. Congress formed the Utah Territory in 1850. Utah became a state in 1896.

The Flaming Gorge Dam, *shown here,* the Glen Canyon Dam, and many smaller dams completed in the 1960's brought industrial growth to Utah.

WORLD BOOK illustrations by Richard Bonson, The Art Agency

Important dates in Utah

1776 Silvestre Velez de Escalante and Francisco Atanasio Domínguez made the first far-reaching exploration of the Utah region.

1824-1825 Jim Bridger probably was the first person of European descent to see Great Salt Lake.

1847 Brigham Young and the first Mormon pioneers arrived in the Great Salt Lake region.

1848 The United States won the Mexican War (1846-1848) and acquired the Utah area from Mexico.

1849 The Mormons created the State of Deseret and adopted their first constitution.

1850 Congress established the Utah Territory.

1857 A group of Mormons and their Indian allies attacked a group of travelers in an incident that became known as the Mountain Meadows Massacre.

1860-1861 The pony express crossed Utah.

1861 Telegraph lines met at Salt Lake City, providing the first transcontinental telegraph service.

1869 The first transcontinental railroad system was completed at Promontory.

1896 Utah became the 45th state on January 4.

1913 The U.S. Bureau of Reclamation completed the Strawberry River reservoir, the state's first large-scale water diversion project.

1952 Rich uranium deposits were found near Moab.

1959 Utah became an important missile-producing state.

1964 Flaming Gorge and Glen Canyon dams were completed.

1967 Construction began on the Central Utah Project, a program to provide water for major growth areas.

1996 Utah marked the *centennial* (100th anniversary) of its statehood.

2003 Lieutenant Governor Olene Walker became Utah's first woman governor after Governor Michael O. Leavitt resigned to head the U.S. Environmental Protection Agency. Walker's term ended in 2005.

appointed Alfred Cumming of Georgia as territorial governor, in place of Brigham Young. Buchanan sent federal troops to enforce the appointment. This period became known as the Utah, or Mormon, War. The soldiers marched toward Utah, stopping along the way during the winter of 1857-1858. In September 1857, a group of Mormons and their Indian allies attacked a party of about 140 travelers from Arkansas and Missouri passing through Utah. It was rumored among the Mormons that these travelers, who openly opposed Mormonism, had been responsible for the death of Joseph Smith. The attackers murdered most of the travelers. Only a few small children were permitted to live. The incident became known as the Mountain Meadows Massacre.

The federal troops arrived in Utah in the spring of 1858. The war ended shortly afterward, though the troops stayed three years. Bad feeling between the Mormons and the soldiers existed throughout this period. Brigham Young was no longer territorial governor, but he remained the real leader of the Mormons. The troops left Utah when the Civil War began in 1861.

During the 1860's, Utah's boundaries were changed several times. Parts of the territory were given to Nevada, Colorado, and Wyoming. Congress established Utah's present boundaries in 1868.

The pony express began carrying mail on April 3, 1860. Pony express riders crossed Utah on their journeys between St. Joseph, Mo., and Sacramento, Calif. On Oct. 26, 1861, the operators of the pony express announced the closing of the express. Two days earlier, telegraph lines from Washington, D.C., and from San Francisco had met in Salt Lake City. This was the nation's first transcontinental telegraph. It provided a link between the eastern and western sections of the United States, and so the pony express was no longer needed.

In 1862, Congress passed a law forbidding polygamy. That same year, federal troops were again sent to Utah, under the command of Colonel Patrick E. Conner. Conner was interested in mining, and he encouraged his troops to prospect for minerals. In 1863, gold and silver were discovered in Bingham Canyon. Conner sent out word of the discovery. He hoped that a mining boom would bring a flood of non-Mormons into Utah and reduce Mormon control of the territory. But profits from Utah's minerals were small during the 1860's, mostly because of transportation problems. Few prospectors came to the territory. By the 1870's, however, many mining companies were operating in Utah.

Plans for a transcontinental railroad had first been made during the 1850's. In 1863, the Central Pacific Railroad began building eastward from Sacramento, and the Union Pacific built westward, starting in Omaha, Neb. The two lines met at Promontory, Utah, on May 10, 1869. A railroad-building boom soon began in Utah.

During the 1880's, federal courts began enforcing federal laws against polygamy. About 1,000 Mormons were fined and sent to prison. A law passed in 1887 permitted the U.S. government to seize church property of the Mormons for use by public schools. In 1890, Wilford Woodruff, the church president, advised the Mormons to give up polygamy, which the church prohibited after 1904.

In 1895, Utah submitted a new constitution to the U.S. Congress. The Constitution outlawed polygamy and prevented control of the state by any church. Utah was admitted to the Union as the 45th state on Jan. 4, 1896.

Union Pacific Railroad

The first transcontinental railroad system in the United States was completed in 1869 in Promontory. Central Pacific and Union Pacific officials drove in the last spike.

The early 1900's brought expansion of the railroad construction that had begun after the Civil War. The railroads opened new markets for Utah's farm and mining products. Utah farmers increased livestock operations, and beef cattle and sheep became important products. Surface mining methods were introduced in Bingham Canyon in 1906. The state's copper production increased greatly. A huge federal irrigation project on the Strawberry River, completed in 1913, increased the amount of Utah's irrigated farmland.

Large smelters were built in the Salt Lake Valley during the early 1900's, and Utah's smelting industry grew. After the United States entered World War I in 1917, Utah mines supplied the Allies with large supplies of *nonferrous metals* (metals containing no iron).

Utah was hit hard by the Great Depression of the 1930's. The mining industry suffered. Farm prices dropped. Utah had one of the nation's highest percentages of unemployed workers. The state's economy improved in the late 1930's when the depression eased.

The mid-1900's. Utah's manufacturing and mining industries prospered during World War II (1939-1945). After the war, the government increased its activities in Utah. Military installations established during the war were expanded. In the 1950's, missile plants were built in Brigham City, Ogden, and Salt Lake City. By 1959, the state had become a center of missile production.

Between 1940 and 1970, Utah changed from an agricultural to an industrial state. The manufacture of steel products became an important industry. In 1952, a rich uranium deposit was discovered near Moab. Oil and gas fields were developed in eastern and southeastern Utah. In the early 1960's, the construction of Flaming Gorge Dam, Glen Canyon Dam, and many smaller dams brought further industrial growth.

Tourism became an important industry in the state during the 1950's and 1960's. An increase in the number of urban residents led to demands for more recreational facilities, and development of outdoor recreation areas in the state boomed. Ski resorts in the Wasatch Mountains attracted visitors from throughout the nation.

During the 1960's, the Utah economy suffered a series of setbacks. The need for missile parts produced in the state declined in 1963, and the value of Utah's missile industry fell. A slump in mineral prices caused the value of the state's mineral products to drop.

From the late 1940's to the early 1960's, the cost to operate Utah's schools soared. In 1963, Utah educators sought $25 ½ million more in state aid to education. The Legislature provided $11 million. Governor George D. Clyde set up a commission to examine Utah's educational needs. In 1964, the commission urged that state aid be increased by another $6 million, a request which Clyde refused as he felt it would cripple the state's economy.

The National Education Association (NEA) urged educators throughout the United States not to accept jobs in Utah until the problem was solved. Never before had U.S. teachers organized a protest against an entire state. In 1965, the Legislature increased school aid by $25 ½ million over two years. The NEA then ended its protest.

During the 1960's, environmental concerns received increased attention in Utah. In 1968, nerve gas being tested in western Utah by the U.S. Army accidentally poisoned about 6,000 sheep. Utahns demanded an end to

Alliant Techsystems, Inc.

Rocket testing is conducted at a plant in Brigham City. The huge rocket shown here is a booster for the space shuttle. The rocket burns a solid propellant.

the testing and storing of such chemicals in the state. In addition, the Utah Legislature set up a statewide program in 1969 to fight increasing air pollution.

The late 1900's. A nationwide oil shortage during the early 1970's led to increased coal production in Utah. Also, several oil companies invested millions of dollars to lease federally owned oil-shale land in Utah. But in the late 1970's, the high cost of producing oil from shale rock and concern over possible pollution problems delayed the development of Utah's oil-shale resources.

Utah's economy began to broaden its base in the 1980's. Service industries and tourism expanded, and computer software businesses developed in the state. Some industries suffered, but—overall—diversity led to economic progress in the 1980's and into the 1990's.

The early 2000's. High rates of residential and industrial growth led to increased demand for the state's limited water resources. The Central Utah Project—a system of aqueducts, canals, dams, and reservoirs—directs water to parts of the state in need. Work on the huge undertaking, which has benefited many Utah communities, began in 1967 and continued into the early 2000's. In addition to improving the state's water distribution network, Utah officials also worked to implement conservation measures to save water.

Utah also faced other challenges. Conservationists and other residents in Utah remained locked in disputes regarding land use. Conservationists argued that part of Utah's desert and mountain areas must be preserved. Other residents favored using the land for power plants, mining, and other purposes. Education costs remained a problem in Utah. Because of the Mormon emphasis on family and education, Utahns have large families and average more years in school than people in any other state, leading to high costs.

During 2002, Utah became the focus of international attention as it hosted the Winter Olympic Games. The tourist industry in the state boomed.

In 2003, President George W. Bush named the governor of Utah, Michael O. Leavitt, to head the U.S. Environmental Protection Agency. Lieutenant Governor Olene Walker replaced Leavitt. Walker became the first woman to serve as Utah's governor.

Brian Q. Cannon and J. Matthew Shumway

Related articles in *World Book* include:

Biographies

Bridger, Jim	Washakie
Browning, John M.	Young, Brigham

Cities

Ogden	Salt Lake City
Provo	

History

Anasazi	Mormons
Deseret	Ute Indians
Guadalupe Hidalgo, Treaty of	Western frontier life in
Jefferson Territory	America

National parks and monuments

Arches National Park	Rainbow Bridge National
Bryce Canyon National Park	Monument
Canyonlands National Park	Timpanogos Cave National
Capitol Reef National Park	Monument
	Zion National Park

Physical features

Colorado River	Lake Powell
Great Basin	Rocky Mountains
Great Salt Lake	Wasatch Range

Outline

I. People
　　A. Population
　　B. Schools
　　C. Libraries
　　D. Museums
II. Visitor's guide
III. Land and climate
　　A. Land regions　　　　D. Plant and animal life
　　B. Rivers and lakes　　　E. Climate
　　C. Deserts
IV. Economy
　　A. Natural resources　　E. Agriculture
　　B. Service industries　　F. Electric power and utilities
　　C. Manufacturing　　　G. Transportation
　　D. Mining　　　　　　H. Communication
V. Government
　　A. Constitution
　　B. Executive
　　C. Legislature
　　D. Courts
　　E. Local government
　　F. Revenue
　　G. Politics
VI. History

Additional resources

Level I

Heinrichs, Ann. *Utah*. Child's World, 2006.
Hirschmann, Kris. *Utah*. World Almanac Lib., 2003.
Kent, Deborah. *Utah*. Children's Pr., 2000.
Neri, P. J. *Utah*. Children's Pr., 2002.

Level II

Alexander, Thomas G. *Utah, the Right Place*. Rev. ed. Gibbs Smith, 2003.
Poll, Richard D., and others, eds. *Utah's History*. Rev. ed. Ut. State Univ. Pr., 1989.
Simmons, Virginia M. *The Ute Indians of Utah, Colorado, and New Mexico*. Univ. Pr. of Colo., 2000.

Verdoia, Ken, and Firmage, Richard. *Utah: The Struggle for Statehood*. Univ. of Ut. Pr., 1996.
Webb, Robert H., and others. *Cataract Canyon*. Univ. of Ut. Pr., 2004.
White, Jean B. *Utah State Constitution*. Greenwood, 1998.

Utah, University of, is a state-supported coeducational university in Salt Lake City. It has colleges and schools of architecture and planning, business, education, engineering, fine arts, health, humanities, law, mines and earth sciences, nursing, pharmacy, science, social and behavioral science, and social work. The University of Utah also has a school of medicine, a division of continuing education, and an honors college. Courses lead to bachelor's, master's, and doctor's degrees. The university was founded in 1850 as the University of Deseret. It received its present name in 1892.

Critically reviewed by the University of Utah

Utamaro, *oo tah mah raw,* **Kitagawa,** *kee tah gah wah,* (1753-1806), was a leading Japanese printmaker. He turned public taste in the direction of bold drawing, striking poses, and unusual color contrasts. Utamaro's beautiful women or pairs of lovers are tall and graceful. He often showed them only from the waist up, and drew faces and hands with great elegance under masses of jet-black hair. Toward the end of his life, Utamaro turned for novelty to exaggerations and distortions, which some of his followers carried even further. Utamaro was born in Kawagoe, Japan.　　　Robert A. Rorex

See also **Japanese print** (picture).

Ute Indians, *yoot,* are a tribe of the western United States. According to the 2000 U.S. census, there are about 7,000 Ute. They live on three major reservations in Utah and Colorado. The name of the state of Utah comes from the Ute Indians.

The Ute are governed by tribal councils that are elected by popular vote. Members of the tribe work in agriculture, forestry, and tourism. They are also developing the coal, gas, oil, and other mineral deposits that lie under the reservations.

The Ute once lived in the mountains and plains of Colorado and Utah and in northern New Mexico. They

Utah State Historical Society

Ute Indians traditionally made tepees of buffalo skins. This photograph was taken in the 1870's.

built cone-shaped houses of brush, reeds, and grasses and tepees of buffalo skins. The Ute assigned hunting grounds to families and hunted such animals as antelope, buffalo, and elk and other deer in annual game drives. In addition to hunting, they also gathered berries, nuts, roots, and seeds.

Each fall, the Ute traveled to New Mexico to trade with the Pueblo Indians and the Spaniards. During the 1600's, they obtained horses from the Spaniards, which increased the tribe's mobility. The Ute hunted over a wider area and developed an advanced economy that involved trading meat and hides for other goods. They became powerful warriors and fought the Arapaho, Cheyenne, Comanche, and Kiowa tribes.

The best-known chief of the Ute was Ouray, who became prominent in the 1800's. Ouray spoke Spanish, English, and several Indian languages. He settled disputes between the Ute and the white settlers and arranged the first treaty between the Ute and the United States government. The government assigned reservations to the Ute in the late 1800's.　　Travis N. Parashonts

Uterus, *YOO tuhr uhs,* or *womb,* is a hollow, muscular organ of the female reproductive system in which an unborn baby develops. The organ is near the base of the abdomen. In a woman who is not pregnant, the uterus resembles an upside-down pear in shape and is about the size of a fist. The bottom part of the uterus, called the *cervix,* contains a necklike opening that leads into the vagina. At birth, a baby passes down through the cervix and the vagina and then out of the woman's body.

Each month during a woman's childbearing years, blood vessels, glands, and cells build up in the lining of the uterus. This process prepares this organ to receive a fertilized egg. If fertilization does not occur, the built-up lining is discharged during menstruation. If fertilization takes place, the fertilized egg attaches itself to the lining of the uterus. Then the egg develops into an embryo, and tissues from the uterus and the embryo form a disk-shaped organ called the *placenta.* The placenta provides the unborn baby with food and oxygen and carries away its waste products (see **Placenta**).

The uterus expands to about 24 times its normal size during pregnancy, mainly because of an increase in the size of muscle cells in the wall of the organ. During childbirth, the muscles of the uterus contract and force the baby out of the mother's body. A second wave of contractions expels the placenta. The uterus never completely returns to its prepregnant size, and the opening of the cervix remains slightly changed in shape.

Lois Kazmier Halstead

Related articles in *World Book* include:
Cervical cancer	Menstruation
Endometriosis	Pap test
Hysterectomy	Reproduction, Human

Utica, *YOO tih kuh,* an ancient North African city, was the oldest Phoenician colony in the western Mediterranean Sea. It stood about midway between present-day Tunis and Bizerte, Tunisia. According to legend, Utica was founded in 1101 B.C. But scholars now believe it was founded in the 700's B.C. Utica was an important seaport, but its site is now about 7 miles (11 kilometers) from the sea. Some ruins of the city remain.

At first, Utica and the neighboring colony of Carthage were almost equal in power. With Motya, a colony in western Sicily, they gave Phoenicia control of the Mediterranean passage to the Straits of Gibraltar, threatening Greek sea trade. Carthage later became an independent power and began to challenge Rome by the 300's B.C. Utica fought on the side of Rome during the Third Punic War (149-146 B.C.) between Rome and Carthage. Rome won the war and made Utica capital of its new province of Africa. Utica was conquered by Arabs in the A.D. 600's.　　Louis L. Orlin

Utica, *YOO tih kuh,* New York (pop. 60,651), is an important commercial and industrial center in the Mohawk Valley along the New York State Canal System. It lies in a rich agricultural and dairy region. For location, see **New York** (political map).

Utica covers an area of about 17 square miles (44 square kilometers). With Rome, New York, the city forms part of a metropolitan area with a population of 299,896.

During the late 1800's and early 1900's, Utica ranked first among New York cities in the production of cotton cloth. In the 1940's and 1950's, a large number of textile companies moved to Southern states. Utica factories then started to produce such items as aircraft parts, electronic equipment, power tools, and processed foods. Utica is also a trading center for farmers of the Mohawk Valley.

Utica lies on the only water-level pass through the Appalachian Mountains and is a major terminal on the New York State Canal System. The city is home to several colleges, including Utica College, which is an affiliate of Syracuse University, Mohawk Valley Community College, and the State University of New York Institute of Technology at Utica/Rome.

A king's grant to British governor William Cosby and his associates in 1734 included the site of Utica. Fort Schuyler was built on the site during the French and Indian War (1754-1763). Utica was incorporated as a village in 1798. The name is that of an ancient North African town and was drawn from suggestions placed in a hat. Utica was chartered as a city in 1832. It has a mayor-council form of government and is the county seat of Oneida County.　　John Kenneth White

Utilitarianism, *yoo TIHL uh TAIR ee uh NIHZ um,* is a theory of morality that associates the rightness of an act with its consequences. It was developed in the late 1700's and 1800's by the English philosophers Jeremy Bentham, James Mill, and John Stuart Mill.

Utilitarians believe that what makes an act morally right is the fact that it leads to the best consequences. In contrast, according to most traditional codes, such as the Ten Commandments, acting morally involves following certain principles, even when doing so leads to bad effects. Utilitarians wanted to replace such a strict attachment to rules with a flexible code that allowed people to perform whatever act would have the best results.

Some Utilitarians differ in their beliefs about what makes results good or bad. Bentham believed that only pleasure or happiness is good in itself, while pain or unhappiness is the only basic evil. The right act produced the greatest happiness for the greatest number. Other Utilitarians claim that other things besides pleasure are good, such as knowledge, love, and freedom.

Bentham attempted to devise a method to measure the value of actions. He extended his theory to politics, claiming that government should promote the well-being of its citizens. His theory is an early form of cost-benefit analysis, a method now often used in politics and economics.   Stephen Nathanson

See also **Bentham, Jeremy; Ethics; Mill, James; Mill, John Stuart.**

Utility, Public. See Public utility.

Utopia, *yoo TOH pee uh,* is the name commonly given to an imaginary land where everything is supposed to be perfect. The name *utopia* comes from the Greek words meaning *no place.* The name refers particularly to a society with ideal economic and social conditions. People often apply the word *utopian* to plans of reform that they consider impractical and visionary.

The word *utopia* was used as the title of a famous book by Saint Thomas More. *Utopia* was first published in Latin in 1516 and was translated into English in 1551. It is partly in the form of a dialogue. The book gives More's views on the ideal government. But, like most writings on utopias, it also criticizes social and economic conditions of More's times.

Several other books have presented an imaginary ideal state of society. One of the first books describing a utopia was Plato's *Republic* (375 B.C.?). More recent utopias are described in Samuel Butler's *Erewhon,* which almost spells *nowhere* backwards (1872), and Edward Bellamy's *Looking Backward* (1888).   Gary A. Stringer

See also **Bellamy, Edward; Communal society; More, Saint Thomas; Plato; Wells, H. G.**

Utrecht, *YOO trehkt* (pop. 270,244; met. area 405,467), is a Dutch city that lies along the Rhine River, about 22 miles (35 kilometers) southeast of Amsterdam (see **Netherlands** [map]). Utrecht has many medieval churches and the tallest church tower in the Netherlands. The tower, called the *Domtoren,* is 367 feet (112 meters) high. The University of Utrecht is one of the country's largest universities. The city is the center of the Dutch railroad network. Its industries include metalworking, heavy construction, and food processing.

Much Dutch history centers about Utrecht. In 1579, the seven northern Protestant provinces united in this city. The nation of the Netherlands grew out of this union. A treaty that helped end the War of the Spanish Succession was signed at Utrecht in 1713.   Jan de Vries

Utrecht, *YOO trehkt,* **Peace of,** was one of the great international peace settlements of history. It ended the War of the Spanish Succession (1701–1714) and established a balance of power in Europe. The settlement consisted of the Treaty of Utrecht, the Treaty of Rastatt, and the Treaty of Baden.

The death of King Charles II of Spain in 1700 led to the War of the Spanish Succession. Charles left a will that gave the Spanish crown to a French prince, Philip of Anjou, who became Philip V of Spain. Philip was the grandson of King Louis XIV of France, and so other European nations feared that France might add Spain's empire to its own. In the war, France fought against the Grand Alliance, which included the Austrian lands, England, the United Provinces of the Netherlands, and several German states of the Holy Roman Empire. The war spread to North America, where it was called Queen Anne's War (1702-1713). In 1712, the participants met in Utrecht, the Netherlands, to discuss peace terms.

The Treaty of Utrecht, signed in 1713, marked the declining power of France and the growing worldwide strength of Britain. The treaty recognized Philip as king of Spain, but France agreed that Spain and France would never unite under one ruler. Britain gained the Spanish colonies of Gibraltar and Minorca and received a contract to supply all the Spanish colonies in America with African slaves. In North America, France gave Britain the territory around Hudson Bay, Newfoundland, and the mainland Nova Scotia region of Acadia.

Holy Roman Emperor Charles VI refused to sign the Treaty of Utrecht. He claimed that he was the heir to the Spanish throne. Fighting between France and Austria, the chief state in the Holy Roman Empire, continued until 1714. That year, the two nations signed the treaties of Rastatt and Baden, which confirmed most of the terms of the Treaty of Utrecht.   Claude C. Sturgill

See also **Acadia; French and Indian wars** (Queen Anne's War); **Succession wars.**

Utrillo, *oo TREE loh,* **Maurice,** *mow REES* (1883-1955), was a French artist known for his paintings of Paris street scenes. His favorite subject was the Montmartre district, with its steep streets and picturesque windmills. Most of Utrillo's paintings have a melancholy feeling. The long, narrow streets are empty, or a few lonely figures wander through them. New-fallen snow and leaden skies often lend a gloomy air. From 1908 to 1914, Utrillo used white and off-white colors with soft, warm ones. His later paintings incorporate brighter colors.

Utrillo was born in Paris on Dec. 26, 1883. His mother was Suzanne Valadon, a well-known painter and artists' model. She introduced him to painting, but he was essentially self-taught. He painted his scenes from memory or used picture postcards as aids.   Nancy J. Troy

Sacré Coeur de Montmartre (1937), a painting on paper mounted on canvas; Indianapolis Museum of Art, Indianapolis, Ind. Delavan Smith Fund

A typical Utrillo painting portrays lonely figures on the narrow, twisting streets of Montmartre, a district in Paris.

Uzbekistan, *OOZ behk ih STAN,* is a country in central Asia. It extends from the foothills of the Tian Shan and Pamir mountains to land just west of the Aral Sea. Its capital and largest city is Tashkent. Uzbekistan became independent in 1991, after nearly 70 years as a republic of the Soviet Union.

Government. Uzbekistan has a president, a prime minister, a Cabinet of Ministers, and a two-house legislature called the Supreme Assembly. The president is elected to a seven-year term. The Supreme Assembly consists of the Legislative Chamber, with 120 elected members, and the Senate, with 84 elected members and 16 members appointed by the president. All legislators serve five-year terms. The president is the most powerful official and appoints the prime minister, Cabinet, and governors of provinces. The prime minister and the Cabinet carry out government operations.

The dominant political party in Uzbekistan is the People's Democratic Party of Uzbekistan. It formed after the Soviet Communist Party disbanded in 1991. This party kept much of the Communist Party's membership and policies. A few other parties are allowed to exist but none that seriously challenges government policies.

People. Ethnic Uzbeks make up over 70 percent of the population. Russians, the second largest group, make up less than 10 percent. Other groups include Tatars, Kazakhs, Tajiks, and Karakalpaks. The Uzbeks are descended from Turkic tribes, Mongols, Persians, and other peoples. They live mainly in rural areas. They speak Uzbek, the country's official language, which is related to Turkish. The Russians speak Russian and live mainly in cities. Many non-Russians also speak Russian because the Soviet government encouraged people to learn the language when Uzbekistan was a Soviet republic. Russian remains part of the school curriculum.

Most people in Uzbekistan are Muslims. Islam (the Muslim religion) is an important force in Uzbek society.

Most rural dwellers are farmers. Most rural homes are made of sun-dried bricks. Many of them have no indoor plumbing or central heating. City dwellers live in single-story homes and multistory apartment buildings.

Facts in brief

Capital: Tashkent.
Official language: Uzbek.
Official name: Uzbekiston Respublikasi (Republic of Uzbekistan).
Area: 172,742 mi² (447,400 km²). *Greatest distances*—north-south, 575 mi (925 km); east-west, 900 mi (1,450 km).
Elevation: *Highest*—peak in the Gissar mountain range, 15,233 ft (4,643 m). *Lowest*—Sarykamysh Lake (seasonal salt lake bed), 65 ft (20 m) below sea level.
Population: *Estimated 2008 population*—27,890,000; population density, 161 per mi² (62 per km²); distribution, 64 percent rural, 36 percent urban. *1989 census*—19,810,077.
Chief products: *Agriculture*—cotton, eggs, grapes, livestock, milk, potatoes, rice. *Manufacturing*—agricultural machinery, chemicals, food products, paper, textiles. *Mining*—coal, copper, gold, natural gas, petroleum.
Flag: The flag has three broad horizontal bands—light blue, white, and light green (top to bottom)—separated by thin red lines. The blue band shows a white crescent and stars. See **Flag** (picture: Flags of Asia and the Pacific).
Money: *Basic unit*—Uzbek som. One hundred tijins equal one Uzbek som.

The people of Uzbekistan wear both traditional and Western-style clothing. Traditional dress for men includes long robes and black boots. Women sometimes wear bright cotton or silk dresses and silk scarves. The people often wear traditional embroidered skullcaps, both with traditional clothing and with clothing like that worn elsewhere in Europe.

Most of the families of Uzbekistan are large, and many include six or more children. In rural areas, many members of an extended family may live together in one household. Such a household might include parents, married children and their offspring, and other relatives. Because of marriage patterns, it is common for all the people in a village to be related to one another. Many marriages are arranged by the families of the bride and groom. People spend much time entertaining guests, and they have elaborate customs related to hospitality.

Foods commonly eaten include rice, vegetables, fruit, mutton, and a flat, round bread called *nan. Pilaf,* a rice dish, is also popular. Tea is the most popular drink.

Uzbekistan

	International boundary
	Road
	Railroad
⊛	National capital
•	Other city or town
+	Elevation above sea level

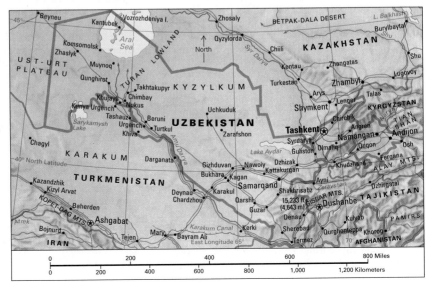

WORLD BOOK maps

Soccer is widely enjoyed in Uzbekistan. Traditional Uzbek recreational activities include wrestling and tight-rope walking. Another favorite sport is *ulaq,* a game played on horseback in which riders try to grab a dead sheep and carry it across a goal.

Uzbeks are known for their crafts. These include carpet making, embroidery, glazed pottery, jewelry making, metalwork, and woodcarving.

Children in Uzbekistan attend elementary and general secondary schools, and many young people continue their education in trade schools, institutes, or universities. The country has a number of universities and other institutes of higher education.

Land and climate. About 80 percent of Uzbekistan's land consists of plains and deserts. The vast Kyzylkum desert lies in central Uzbekistan. It is largely uninhabited except for mining towns. Plains south and east of the desert are used mostly for growing cotton. Farmers raise livestock in the plains and in irrigated desert areas. Uzbekistan's most densely populated region is the Fergana Valley, in the east. The valley receives its water from mountains of the Tian Shan range that surround it. Central Asia's two most important rivers, the Syr Darya and the Amu Darya, flow to the Aral Sea from the Tian Shan and Pamir mountains.

Summers in Uzbekistan are long, dry, and hot. Winters are cold. Summer temperatures in southern Uzbekistan may reach 113 °F (45 °C). In the north, winter temperatures may drop to –35 °F (–37 °C).

Economy. Most of Uzbekistan's economy is indirectly controlled by the government. Although many farms and small businesses are privately owned, the government controls much of the supply of raw materials and transportation. The government also regulates much of the marketing of goods, particularly exports.

Cotton is the chief agricultural product. Other important products include grapes, melons, and other fruits; milk; rice; and vegetables. Wool from the *karakul,* a breed of sheep raised in Uzbekistan, is highly prized for coats. Mining operations produce coal, copper, gold, natural gas, and petroleum. Uzbekistan's important manufactured products include agricultural machinery, chemicals, food products, and textiles.

An airport in Tashkent handles international flights. Studios in that city broadcast radio and television programs in both Uzbek and Russian. The country publishes newspapers and magazines in several languages.

History. People have lived in what is now Uzbekistan for thousands of years. Alexander the Great conquered the region in the 300's B.C. From this time through the 1400's, the area was important because of its location along the Silk Road. The Silk Road was a major trade route for caravans carrying silk and other luxury goods from China to the Middle East.

In the 600's, Arabs invaded what is now Uzbekistan and introduced Islam to the area. Turkic tribes began to arrive there in the 700's. Mongols, led by Genghis Khan, conquered the region in the early 1200's. In the late 1300's, the Mongol conqueror Timur (also known as Tamerlane) founded the capital of his vast Asian empire in Samarqand, now Uzbekistan's second largest city.

A group of Turkic tribes known as the Uzbeks invaded the region in the 1500's. Over time, states called *khanates* were created. In the 1800's, the khanates were

© Charles Lenars, The Stock Market

Farmworkers in Uzbekistan pick cotton in a large field. Cotton is the country's chief crop. Farmers grow cotton on the plains that lie south and west of the desert in central Uzbekistan.

conquered by Russia or came under Russian influence. Revolutionaries known as Bolsheviks (later called Communists) won control of Russia in 1917. In 1924, Uzbekistan became a republic of the Soviet Union, which had been formed under Russia's leadership in 1922.

The Soviets made many changes in Uzbekistan. The Soviet government built roads, schools, and modern housing, and it expanded industry. The Soviets also *collectivized* agriculture—that is, they ended private farming and transferred control of farms to the government. The Soviets strongly emphasized cotton production. Overplanting of cotton harmed the soil, and overuse of fertilizers polluted drinking water.

The Soviet government maintained strict control of all aspects of life until the late 1980's. In 1990, the Uzbek government declared that its laws overruled those of the Soviet central government. In August 1991, conservative Communist officials failed in an attempt to overthrow Soviet President Mikhail S. Gorbachev. During the upheaval that followed, Uzbekistan and several other republics declared their independence. The Soviet Union formally dissolved on December 25.

On Dec. 29, 1991, Uzbekistan held its first presidential elections following independence. Islam A. Karimov of the People's Democratic Party of Uzbekistan won. He had been the Communist party leader. The rapid changes in Uzbekistan brought economic hardships. But the government maintained political stability. However, international organizations criticized Uzbekistan's government for its failures in the area of human rights.

In 1995, a referendum extended President Karimov's term to 2000. He was reelected that year. In 2002, another referendum extended the presidential term from five years to seven.

Although Uzbekistan's Constitution sets a two-term limit for presidents, Karimov won a third term in 2007. International observers noted that he had run against three virtually unknown opponents.   William Fierman

Related articles in *World Book* include:

V is the 22nd letter of our alphabet. It came from a letter used by the Semites, who once lived in Syria and Palestine. They called the letter *waw,* their word for *hook.* They wrote the letter with a symbol borrowed from an Egyptian *hieroglyphic* (picture symbol). The Greeks borrowed the letter from the Phoenicians and gave it a Y shape. The Romans, when they adopted the letter, dropped the vertical stroke. They used it for the vowel sound, *u,* and the consonant sound, *v.* About A.D. 900, people began to write *v* at the beginning of a word and *u* in the middle.

During the Renaissance, people began using the letter *v* for the consonant and *u* for the vowel. But the change was not final for several hundred years. See **Alphabet.**

Uses. *V* or *v* is about the 21st most frequently used letter in books, newspapers, and other material printed in English. *V* is the Roman numeral for five. As an abbreviation, *V* may stand for *veteran* or *volunteer.* It is the abbreviation for *verb* in grammars and dictionaries. In music, it stands for *violin* or *voice.* It may mean *various, volt, volume,* or *versus.* In chemistry, *V* is the symbol for the element *vanadium.*

Pronunciation. A person pronounces *v* by placing the lower lip on the upper teeth, closing the *velum,* or soft palate, and forcing the breath through the teeth and lips, vibrating the vocal cords. This sound may be spelled *ph,* as in *Stephen.* In German, it may sound like the English *f.* In Spanish it may have a *b* sound. See **Pronunciation.**   Marianne Cooley

---

Development of the letter V

The ancient Egyptians drew this symbol of a supporting pole about 3000 B.C. The Semites adapted the symbol and called it *waw,* their word for *hook.*

The Phoenicians used this symbol of a hook in their alphabet about 1000 B.C.

The Greeks changed the symbol about 600 B.C. They called the letter *upsilon.*

The Romans, about A.D. 114, gave the V its capital form.

The small letter v developed during the A.D. 500's from Roman writing. It changed slightly in the 800's and, by the 1500's, had the form we use today.

A.D. 500   Today

Special ways of expressing the letter V

International Morse Code 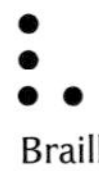   Braille

International Flag Code 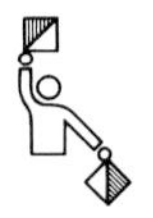   Semaphore Code    Sign Language Alphabet

---

Common forms of the letter V

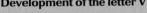

Handwritten letters vary from person to person. *Manuscript* (printed) letters, *left,* have simple curves and straight lines. Cursive letters, *right,* have flowing lines.

Roman letters have small finishing strokes called *serifs* that extend from the main strokes. The type face shown above is Baskerville. The italic form appears at the right.

Sans-serif letters are also called *gothic letters.* They have no serifs. The type face shown above is called Futura. The italic form of Futura appears at the right.

Computer letters have special shapes. Computers can "read" these letters either optically or by means of the magnetic ink with which the letters may be printed.

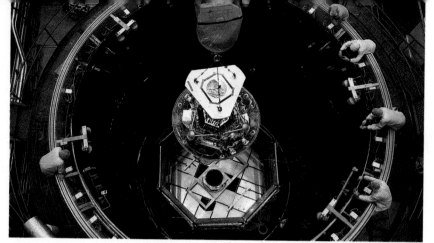

A vacuum chamber can be used to *simulate* (re-create) the airless conditions encountered in space. In this photograph, technicians lower the Phoenix probe into a large vacuum chamber for testing before its 2007 launch to Mars.

V-1, V-2. See **Guided missile** (The first guided missiles); **Rocket** (Rockets of the early 1900's).

V-E Day, which stands for Victory in Europe Day, was officially proclaimed by United States President Harry S. Truman on Tuesday, May 8, 1945. It marked the surrender of the German armed forces and the end of the fighting against Germany in World War II (1939-1945).

The German surrender was signed at the headquarters of General Dwight D. Eisenhower in Reims, France, at 2:41 a.m. on May 7. Colonel General Alfred Jodl, chief of staff of the German armed forces, signed for Germany.   Theodore A. Wilson

See also **World War II** (Victory in Europe).

V-J Day, which stands for Victory over Japan Day, marked the end of World War II. At 7 p.m. on Aug. 14, 1945, President Harry S. Truman announced that Japan had agreed to surrender. Japan had been trying to end the war, and surrender rumors had raced through the United States for the four days before August 14.

Sept. 2, 1945, has since been declared the official V-J Day. On that day, representatives of Japan signed the terms of surrender aboard the battleship U.S.S. *Missouri* in Tokyo Bay.   Theodore A. Wilson

See also **World War II** (Victory in the Pacific).

Vaca, Álvar Núñez Cabeza de. See **Cabeza de Vaca, Álvar Núñez.**

Vaccination. See **Immunization.**

Vacuum is a space that contains little matter. A vacuum holds far fewer molecules than does the same volume of air at atmospheric pressure. One cubic centimeter of air at atmospheric pressure and room temperature has roughly 25 billion billion molecules. The best artificial vacuums contain less than 1,000 molecules per cubic centimeter. *Interstellar space,* the space between the stars, has only about one atom per cubic centimeter.

Scientists measure the quality of a vacuum in terms of the pressure exerted by the matter it contains. The less matter, the lower the pressure. The international standard unit of pressure is the pascal, which equals approximately one hundred thousandth of atmospheric pressure at sea level. That is, 101,325 pascals equal 1 atmosphere. Pressure can also be measured in torr. One atmosphere equals 760 torr.

Properties of a vacuum depend on the density of molecules it contains, and thus on the pressure. In a relatively high-pressure vacuum, the molecules are more densely packed and so collide with one another frequently. Such vacuums behave in much the same way

that liquids or gases do at atmospheric pressures. Scientists describe such vacuums as having "viscous flow." In a low-pressure vacuum, molecules are less densely packed, colliding with the walls of their container more often than with one another. Such vacuums are said to have "molecular flow," with each molecule behaving independently.

Because of the low density of molecules, particles can move undisturbed for longer distances in a vacuum than they can through air. Some televisions have picture tubes that make use of this property. Within the tubes, electrons travel through a vacuum toward the screen. If the tubes contained air, the electrons would scatter, distorting the image.

In a vacuum, water and other liquids evaporate at temperatures much lower than normal. Thus, people can use a vacuum to remove moisture from a substance quickly without burning it. Workers prepare freeze-dried food in this way.

Because vacuums hold relatively few molecules, they provide clean environments for manufacturing. To help avoid contamination, they are often used in the making of such sensitive electronic devices as computer chips.

Producing a vacuum. People create artificial vacuums using seals that prevent molecules from flowing into a vacuum region. Without such boundaries, the random motions of molecules would equalize the pressure between neighboring regions, preventing the formation of a vacuum. Engineers have developed vacuum chambers made from stainless steel or other materials and sealed with metal or rubber gaskets. Such chambers are used in scientific research and in manufacturing.

The pressure of a vacuum is typically lowered by either *displacement* or *entrapment.* In displacement, also called *transfer,* a pump or other means removes molecules from the vacuum. A simple example of displacement is sucking on a straw. The sucking action removes molecules from the straw, lowering the pressure inside. The higher pressure of air outside the straw pushes fluids up the straw and into the mouth. Entrapment involves trapping molecules in an isolated region of a volume. One type of entrapment pump, called a *cryogenic pump* or *cryopump,* traps gases by freezing them onto cold surfaces.

In particle physics. Scientists have discovered that no space can ever truly be empty. This knowledge comes from *quantum mechanics,* a branch of physics that describes the behavior of atoms and *subatomic particles* (pieces of matter smaller than atoms). According to the principles of quantum mechanics, particles can appear from nowhere as long as they disappear again in a sufficiently short time. Such particles are known as *virtual particles.*

The presence of virtual particles gives even empty space some energy, called *vacuum energy.* Scientists have observed the influence of vacuum energy through an occurrence known as the Casimir effect, named for the Dutch physicist Hendrik Brugt Gerhard Casimir. The Casimir effect occurs when two parallel metal plates are separated by an extremely short distance in a vacuum. The space between the plates has a lower density of virtual particles than does the space outside the plates. This difference in density results in a pressure on the plates, pushing them together.   Tom Christensen

See also **Vacuum bottle; Vacuum cleaner; Vacuum tube.**

Vacuum bottle is a container that keeps liquids hot or cold for many hours. It is also called a *Dewar flask* or a *Thermos bottle,* which is the trademark for a brand of vacuum bottle produced by the Thermos Company. Vacuum bottles vary widely in size, ranging in capacity from 2 ounces (59 milliliters) to 15 gallons (57 liters). They are commonly used to carry coffee, juice, milk, or soup. Some types of vacuum bottles are used in scientific work to store chemicals and drugs, to transport tissues and organs, and to preserve blood plasma.

James Dewar, a Scottish chemist, invented the vacuum bottle in 1892. He developed it for storing liquefied gases. Although his flask was designed to keep heat outside the container, it worked equally well in keeping liquids hot by reducing the loss of heat from the inside.

The modern vacuum bottle has the same basic design as Dewar's flask. It blocks the three processes through which heat is transferred—*conduction, convection,* and *radiation* (see **Heat** [How heat travels]). A typical vacuum bottle has an inner container that consists of two glass or stainless steel bottles, one within the other. Glass and stainless steel do not transmit heat well, and so they reduce heat transfer by conduction. Most of the air between the bottles is removed to create a partial vacuum. This vacuum hinders heat transfer by convection because it has few air molecules to carry heat between the bottles.

The facing surfaces of glass bottles are coated with a silver solution. They act like mirrors, reflecting much of the heat coming from inside or outside the container. Thus, they prevent heat transfer by radiation. In stainless steel bottles, a layer of copper foil between the inner and outer bottles serves the same purpose.

Most vacuum bottles have a small mouth, which reduces the loss or entry of heat. The bottles are closed with a stopper made of a material that conducts heat poorly, and the vacuum chamber is encased in metal or plastic. A collar around the mouth holds the inner container in place. A rubber cushion at the base serves as a shock absorber.   Critically reviewed by the Thermos Company

Vacuum cleaner is an electric appliance that uses suction to clean. Vacuum cleaners remove dirt and other materials from carpets and bare floors. They also may be used to remove dust and dirt from furniture, woodwork, curtains, and other above-the-floor items. The first vacuum cleaning devices were developed about 1900.

A vacuum cleaner works by means of a suction fan,

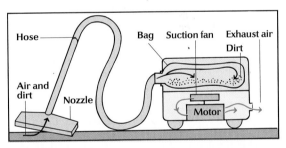

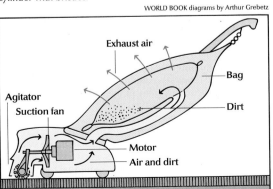

The two main kinds of vacuum cleaners are the *canister* and the *upright.* In a canister, *above,* a suction fan pulls dirt through a hose and into a bag. In an upright, *below,* a suction fan draws in waste material that has been loosened by an *agitator,* a rotating cylinder with bristles.

WORLD BOOK diagrams by Arthur Grebetz

WORLD BOOK diagram

A vacuum bottle is two bottles in one. A vacuum in the space between the inner and outer bottles helps prevent heat from passing through the bottle.

which creates a partial vacuum within the machine. Outside air, which always tries to fill a vacuum, flows rapidly into the cleaner, drawing in dirt. A bag or other filtering device traps the dirt, and the cleaned air leaves the machine. The bag must be emptied or changed regularly.

There are two main kinds of portable vacuum cleaners: (1) *canisters* and (2) *uprights*. In a canister model, a powerful suction fan pulls dirt-laden air into a bag through a hose to which a variety of nozzles can be attached. Most upright models have a small fan and an *agitator* in the base. The agitator is a rotating cylinder with bristles that loosen dirt. The airflow pulls the loosened dirt through the fan. The dirt-laden air is blown into the filtering device, which is usually attached to the machine's handle.

Other types of portable vacuum cleaners include *handheld* and *utility* vacuum cleaners. A handheld model can be held in one hand and is used primarily for above-the-floor cleaning and for stairs. A utility vacuum cleaner is a type of canister used to pick up large particles of dirt and debris, especially in home workshops. Some utility models are designed to pick up liquid.

Stationary or built-in vacuum cleaners are called *central vacuum cleaners.* They have various kinds of nozzles and a hose that connects to a special fitting on the wall. Dirt moves from the hose through a network of ducts to a remotely located dirt-collecting system.

Critically reviewed by ASTM International

Vacuum tube is a bulky device once widely used in electronic equipment to create, strengthen, combine, or separate electrical signals. Electrical signals are variations in an electric current or voltage that can be used to carry information. Radios, television sets, and computers rely on such signals for their operation. Vacuum tubes played an essential role in the development of the science and technology of electronics. Most vacuum tubes have been replaced by newer technology. Yet even today, people still use vacuum tubes for certain specialized applications.

The outer part of a vacuum tube consists of a glass or metal shell called the *envelope* or *bulb*. The envelope encloses two or more metal parts called *electrodes*. The electrodes create and control a flow of electrons within the tube. The flow of electrons creates an electrical signal. Wires passing through the base of the envelope connect the electrodes to electric circuits outside, enabling electric current to enter and leave the tube. The vacuum tube gets its name from the fact that almost all the air must be removed from the envelope for the tube to work, creating a strong *partial vacuum*. Many vacuum tubes resemble light bulbs. In fact, they were made in the same factories for many years.

From the early 1900's to the 1950's, most complex electronic equipment used vacuum tubes. Since that time, vacuum tubes have been mostly replaced by transistors. Transistors do many of the same jobs as vacuum tubes, but are smaller and more reliable and consume less power (see **Transistor**).

People today use vacuum tubes to generate microwaves in microwave ovens. Some musicians use vacuum tube amplifiers for instruments, such as the electric guitar. In addition, the screen of a traditional television set or computer monitor is one end of a large vacuum tube called a *cathode-ray tube*.

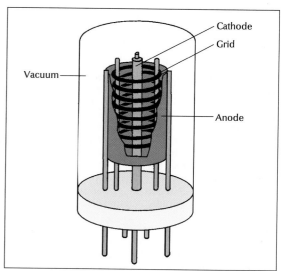

WORLD BOOK illustration by Arthur Grebetz

A triode vacuum tube creates and controls a flow of electrons in a vacuum. Electrons leave the cathode when a source of direct current is connected to the tube. The electrons flow through the grid to the anode. The voltage applied to the grid controls the number of electrons that reach the anode.

How a vacuum tube works

The two basic electrodes in a vacuum tube are the *emitter* (or *cathode*) and the *collector* (or *anode*). When connected to an outside source of current, such as a battery, the emitter has a negative electric charge and the collector has a positive charge. The emitter is a *filament* (fine wire) that gives off electrons when heated by an electric current.

The emitter's negative charge pushes away the electrons the emitter produces. This happens because electrons have a negative charge, and two negative charges (or two positive charges) always repel each other. But a negative and a positive charge always attract each other. Thus, the positively charged collector attracts the negative electrons. The electrons thus flow off the emitter, through the vacuum space, and onto the collector, forming an electric current.

The arrangement of electrodes in a vacuum tube controls the flow of current from the emitter to the collector. For example, many vacuum tubes have a third electrode called the *grid,* a wire mesh or other structure between the emitter and the collector. When a strong negative charge is placed on the grid, it repels most of the electrons, allowing only a few to reach the collector. A weak negative charge results in more electrons passing through to reach the collector. Varying the charge on the grid thus varies the flow of current from emitter to collector, creating or altering an electrical signal.

Kinds of vacuum tubes

Inventors have developed many hundreds of kinds of vacuum tubes with different sizes and functions. Electrical engineers classify all tubes into a few basic types.

Receiving tubes, once widely used to receive radio and television signals, are classified by their number of electrodes. Receiving tubes include *diodes* (two-electrode tubes) and *triodes* (three-electrode tubes).

Diodes have only an emitter and a collector. *Rectifiers* and *detectors* are the most common diodes.

Rectifiers change *alternating current* into *direct current*. Alternating current is electric current that regularly reverses its direction of flow. Direct current flows in only one direction. When an alternating current is sent to a diode, electrons flow from emitter to collector only when the emitter has a negative charge. When the current reverses, the emitter takes on a positive charge, and no electrons flow from it. Thus, the current leaving the rectifier flows in one direction and is direct current.

Detectors pick up radio waves and transfer signals carried by the waves to an electric current. Many wireless telegraph systems, the earliest radios, used detectors and rectifiers to receive messages in Morse code. The detector converted radio wave bursts into bursts of alternating current, which the rectifier changed into direct current "dots" and "dashes." Later radios used detectors to receive more complex signals that carried words or music.

Triodes have a grid between the emitter and the collector. A triode can *amplify* (strengthen) weak signals by passing them through the grid. The current passing through the grid controls the much larger current flowing from the emitter to the collector, generating a stronger copy of the signal.

A triode can also produce an alternating current if some of the large current is directed back to the grid. A triode operating in this way is called an *oscillator.*

Cathode-ray tubes, commonly called *CRT's,* are used in electronic equipment to display pictures or other information. The picture tube of a traditional television set is a CRT. In a radar display, a CRT shows tiny spots of light that locate the position of ships or airplanes.

All CRT's basically work the same way. The tube has a round or rectangular screen at one end. The tube tapers from the screen to a narrow neck at the far end. The neck contains an emitter and other electrodes arranged to form an *electron gun.* The electron gun "shoots" a focused beam of electrons toward the screen. Wherever the beam strikes the screen, it causes a special chemical coating to glow. Electrically charged metal plates inside the CRT, or electromagnets outside the CRT, quickly change the beam's shape, sending electrons to different areas of the screen. The beam thus "paints" a picture on the screen with electrons that create spots of light.

Microwave tubes produce or control radio waves of extremely high frequencies. Radar sets bounce such waves off objects to detect them. Microwave ovens use *klystrons, magnetrons,* and *traveling-wave tubes* to make waves that cook food.

History

In the mid-1800's, experimenters began working with sealed glass tubes that resembled vacuum tubes. When electric current flowed through the tubes, experimenters noticed a glow around the tubes and other unusual effects. See **Electronics** (Early experiments).

The American inventor Thomas Edison built an early diode but did not realize the importance of his invention. In the early 1880's, Edison sealed an extra electrode into one of his electric light bulbs. When the light was on, Edison found that a current flowed from the hot filament to the extra electrode, but only if this electrode was positively charged. No current flowed if the extra electrode was negatively charged. This phenomenon became known as the *Edison effect.*

The early wireless telegraph industry inspired many experiments with vacuum tubes. Historians often mention three different people when discussing the invention of *radio tubes,* vacuum tubes used in early radios. In 1904, the British scientist John Ambrose Fleming invented a diode he called a *valve.* In 1905, the American inventor Lee De Forest produced a similar device and called it an *audion.* Beginning in 1903, the German physicist Arthur Wehnelt performed many experiments using diodes. In late 1906, De Forest added a third electrode to the audion. Though it was an inefficient amplifier, this tube was the first triode.

Scientists and inventors from the United States and Europe made many advancements in vacuum tubes in the following years. These advancements included improvements in internal design and the introduction of stronger vacuums. In 1915, AT&T used vacuum tube technology in the first transcontinental telephone line.

With the growth of radio, vacuum tubes became the standard component used to build electronic devices. Researchers in many countries invented specialized vacuum tubes for different applications. These specialty tubes included the four-electrode *tetrode,* the five-electrode *pentode,* and so on, up to nine electrodes. Advances in vacuum tubes enabled the development of the first television sets in the 1920's. Some of the earliest electronic computers, built in the 1940's and 1950's, used thousands of vacuum tubes to perform calculations.

Vacuum tubes lost their central place in electronics after the development of the transistor in the 1950's and of the integrated circuit or *microchip* in the 1960's. In these *solid-state* devices, electronic signals flow through a solid material instead of a vacuum.   Thomas J. Misa

Related articles in *World Book* include:

Computer (The first electronic computers)	Fleming, Sir John
	Iconoscope
Crookes tube	Image orthicon
De Forest, Lee	Photomultiplier tube
Edison, Thomas Alva	Radar
Electronics (The vacuum tube era)	

Vaduz, *VAH doots* (pop. 5,053), is the capital and largest city of the principality of Liechtenstein. It lies in an Alpine valley on the Rhine River (see **Liechtenstein** [map]). The Vaduz castle stands on a mountain above the city. The reigning prince of Liechtenstein lives there.

Vaduz is a trade and industry center. It has many banks. The city's cultural and educational institutions include the Liechtenstein Museum of Art and the Liechtenstein University of Applied Sciences.

Vaduz was founded in the Middle Ages, probably by the mid-1100's. It was acquired by Johann-Adam Liechtenstein, a prince from Vienna, in 1712.   Janet L. Polasky

Vagina, *vuh JY nuh,* is a female reproductive organ. It consists of a tube-shaped canal that lies behind the bladder and the *urethra* (urinary canal) and in front of the rectum. The vagina extends from the *cervix* (lower part of the uterus) to an opening between the legs. During sexual intercourse, the male inserts his penis in the vagina of the female. The vagina serves as the passage through which a baby is born. It also carries blood and cells from the uterus outside the body during menstruation (see **Menstruation**).

The vagina is about 4 inches (10 centimeters) long. It has muscular walls lined with a mucous membrane that has numerous folds running across it. Normally, the walls of the vagina are collapsed so that they touch each other. In females who have not had sexual intercourse, the vaginal opening may be partially covered by a thin membrane called the *hymen.*

The mucous membrane that lines the vagina contains many nerve endings. The areas near the vaginal opening and around the *clitoris,* a small knob of tissue in front of the urethra, are especially sensitive to stimulation. Secretions from glands in the cervix moisten and lubricate the vagina's internal surface. During childbirth, the muscular walls of the vagina stretch enormously to allow the baby to pass out of the mother's body.   Lynn J. Romrell

See also **Reproduction, Human; Vaginitis.**

Vaginitis, *VAJ uh NY tihs,* is an inflammation of the vagina. Vaginitis is characterized by itching or burning, an abnormal vaginal discharge and, often, an unusual odor. The inflammation also may affect parts of the *vulva,* the external female reproductive organs. Vaginitis occurs most often during women's childbearing years.

Most cases of vaginitis result from infection by certain bacteria, fungi, or protozoans. The infectious organisms produce waste material that irritates the vagina and vulva, causing swelling and itching. One of the most common of the various bacteria that cause vaginitis is *Gardnerella vaginalis.* These bacteria cause the whitish, filmy fluid normally present in the vagina to thicken and turn gray or yellow. A fungus called *Candida,* also known as *Monilia,* turns the vaginal fluid thick and white. A protozoan called *Trichomonas* causes it to turn yellow-green or gray and become thin and foamy.

Infectious microbes may be present in the vagina without causing vaginitis. They are normally kept in balance so that none exists in harmful quantities. Vaginitis occurs when the balance is upset, allowing one or more of the organisms to reproduce in great numbers. The balance can be disturbed by many factors, including pregnancy, poor health or diet, or the use of certain drugs. A frequent cause of vaginitis is sexual contact. Cuts, scrapes, or irritation from bath or laundry products can increase the likelihood of vaginal infection.

A physician treats vaginitis by first examining the vaginal fluid to determine which organism is causing the infection. Certain antifungal drugs, antibiotics, and other medicines are used to cure vaginitis. The infections discussed in this article have no permanent effect on a woman's ability to bear children.   Timothy T. Miller

Vagrancy, *VAY gruhn see.* A person who wanders from place to place and who lives in idleness without any settled home is called a *vagrant,* or *vagabond.* Most states of the United States have laws against vagrancy, based on the idea that a vagrant has "no visible means of support" and may become a public charge.

A person arrested for vagrancy may be sentenced to a term in jail. Law enforcement officers frequently arrest beggars and criminals as vagrants. However, because many vagrancy laws do not specify the activities that make up vagrancy, many of the laws have been declared unconstitutional by state and federal courts.

George T. Felkenes

Valence, *VAY luhns,* also called *valency,* is a number that indicates the ability of a chemical element to combine with other elements. In the past, valence had several slightly different meanings. The term is gradually being replaced by more precise chemical descriptions.

Valence was first defined as the number of hydrogen atoms that can combine with each atom of an element. For example, each atom of oxygen can combine with two hydrogen atoms to form water (H_2O). Therefore, oxygen has a valence of two. A second definition of valence is based on the charges of ionized atoms. Sodium ions generally have one positive charge, so the valence of sodium is one. A third definition is based on the number of *bonds* (chemical links) that an atom forms with other atoms. Because carbon atoms usually form four bonds, carbon is said to have a valence of four. Many elements can combine in so many ways that they have several valences. For example, sulfur has common valences of 2, 4, and 6.   Mark S. Wrighton

See also **Bond (Chemical).**

Valencia, *vuh LEHN shee uh* (pop. 738,441), is the third largest city in Spain. Only Madrid and Barcelona have more people than Valencia. Valencia lies on the Turia River, 3 miles (5 kilometers) from the Mediterranean coast and its port of Villanueva del Grao (see **Spain** [political map]). Hundreds of years ago, the Romans built walls around their settlement at Valencia. These walls were torn down in 1871. A gate called Torres de Serranos was built in 1238. Two towers were added in the late 1300's and restored in 1930.

The city is a railroad center of eastern Spain and carries on a large export trade in oranges and other fruits. Valencia is noted for its silk, colored tiles, tobacco, textiles, and iron and bronze wares. Other products made in the city include cement, furniture, musical instruments, paper, toys, and perfumes and cosmetics.

Valencia was long occupied by the Moors. It has rows of white houses built in the Moorish style and many famous public buildings dating from the 1200's. However, today much of the city is modern. The University of Valencia is well known.   Stanley G. Payne

Valentine, Saint, is the name associated with two martyrs of the early Christian church. Little is known about these men. The Roman history of martyrs lists two Saints Valentine as having been martyred on February 14 by being beheaded. One supposedly died in Rome and the other at Interamna, now Terni, 60 miles (97 kilometers) from Rome. Scholars have had great difficulty in finding historical fact among Saint Valentine legends.

The Saint Valentine who died in Rome seems to have been a priest who suffered death during the persecution of Claudius the Goth about A.D. 269. A basilica was built in his honor in Rome in A.D. 350, and a catacomb containing his remains was found on this location.

Another history of martyrs mentions a Saint Valentine who was bishop of Interamna and who may have been martyred in Rome. By being remembered both in Rome and in Interamna, he may have come to be considered as two people, but this is not entirely certain.

The custom of exchanging valentines on February 14 can be traced to the English poet Geoffrey Chaucer. He mentioned that birds began to pair off on that day (see **Valentine's Day**). February 14 is also the feast day of both Saints Valentine.   Stanley K. Stowers

Valentine's Day is a special day observed on February 14. On this day, people send greeting cards called *valentines* to their sweethearts, friends, and members of their families. Many valentines have romantic verses, and others have humorous pictures and sayings. Many say, "Be my valentine."

For weeks before February 14, stores sell valentines and valentine decorations. Schoolchildren decorate their classrooms with paper hearts and lace for the occasion. On Valentine's Day, many people give candy, flowers, and other gifts to their friends.

Valentine's Day around the world

In the United States and Canada, children exchange valentines with their friends. In some schools, the children hold a classroom party and put all the valentines into a box they have decorated. At the end of the day, the teacher or one child distributes the cards. Many children make their own valentines from paper doilies, red paper, wallpaper samples, and pictures cut from magazines. Many children send their largest, fanciest cards to their parents and teachers.

Older students hold Valentine's Day dances and parties. They make candy baskets, gifts, and place cards trimmed with hearts and fat, winged children called *cupids.* Many people send flowers, a box of candy, or some other gift to their wives, husbands, or sweethearts. Most valentine candy boxes are heart-shaped and tied with red ribbon.

In Europe, people celebrate Valentine's Day in many ways. British children sing special Valentine's Day songs and receive gifts of candy, fruit, or money. In some areas of England, people bake valentine buns with caraway seeds, plums, or raisins. People in Italy hold a Valentine's Day feast.

In the United Kingdom and Italy, some unmarried women get up before sunrise on Valentine's Day. They stand by the window watching for a man to pass. They believe that the first man they see, or someone who looks like him, will marry them within a year. William Shakespeare, the English playwright, mentions this belief in *Hamlet* (1603). Ophelia, a woman in the play, sings:

> Good morrow! 'Tis St. Valentine's Day
> All in the morning betime,
> And I a maid at your window,
> To be your valentine!

In Denmark, people send pressed white flowers called *snowdrops* to their friends. Danish men also send a valentine called a *gaekkebrev* (joking letter). The sender writes a rhyme but does not sign his name. Instead, he signs the valentine with dots, one dot for each letter of his name. If the woman who gets it guesses his name, he rewards her with an Easter egg on Easter.

History

Beginnings. Different authorities believe Valentine's Day began in various ways. Some trace it to an ancient Roman festival called *Lupercalia.* Other experts connect the event with one or more saints of the early Christian church. Still others link it with an old English belief that birds choose their mates on February 14. Valentine's Day probably came from a combination of all three of those sources—plus the belief that spring is a time for lovers.

The ancient Romans held the festival of Lupercalia on February 15 to ensure protection from wolves. During this celebration, young men struck people with strips of animal hide. Women took the blows because they thought that the whipping made them more fertile. After the Romans began their conquest of Britain in A.D. 43, the British borrowed many Roman festivals. Many writers link Lupercalia with Valentine's Day because of the similar date and the connection with fertility.

The early Christian church had at least two saints named Valentine. According to one story, the Roman Emperor Claudius II in the A.D. 200's forbade young men to marry. The emperor thought single men made better soldiers. A priest named Valentine disobeyed the emperor's order and secretly married young couples.

Another story says Valentine was an early Christian who made friends with many children. The Romans imprisoned him because he refused to worship their gods. The children missed Valentine and tossed loving notes between the bars of his cell window. This tale may explain why people exchange messages on Valentine's Day.

Many stories say that Valentine was executed on February 14 about A.D. 269. In A.D. 496, Saint Pope Gelasius I named February 14 as St. Valentine's Day.

In Norman French, a language spoken in Normandy during the Middle Ages, the word *galantine* sounds like *Valentine* and means *gallant* or *lover.* This resemblance may have caused people to think of Saint Valentine as the special saint of lovers.

The earliest records of Valentine's Day in English tell that birds chose their mates on that day. People used a different calendar before 1582, and February 14 came on what is now February 24. Geoffrey Chaucer, an English poet of the 1300's, wrote in *The Parliament of Fowls,* "For this was on St. Valentine's Day, / When every fowl cometh there to choose his mate." Shakespeare also mentioned this belief in *A Midsummer Night's Dream.* A character in the play discovers two lovers in the woods and asks, "St. Valentine is past; / Begin these woodbirds but to couple now?"

Early Valentine customs. People in England probably celebrated Valentine's Day as early as the 1400's. Some historians trace the custom of sending verses on Valentine's Day to a Frenchman named Charles, Duke of Orléans. Charles was captured by the English during the Battle of Agincourt in 1415. He was taken to England and put in prison. On Valentine's Day, he sent his wife a rhymed love letter from his cell in the Tower of London.

Many Valentine's Day customs involved ways that single women could learn who their future husbands would be. Englishwomen of the 1700's wrote men's names on scraps of paper, rolled each in a little piece of clay, and dropped them all into water. The first paper that rose to the surface supposedly had the name of a woman's true love.

One description of Valentine's Day during the 1700's tells how groups of friends met to draw names. For several days, each man wore his valentine's name on his sleeve. The saying *wearing his heart on his sleeve* probably came from this practice.

The custom of sending romantic messages gradually replaced that of giving gifts. In the 1700's and 1800's, many stores sold handbooks called *valentine writers.*

Valentines through the years

The custom of sending romantic messages on Valentine's Day may have begun as early as the 1400's. At first, people made their own valentines. Commercial cards were not printed until the early 1800's. Many early valentines were blank, with space for the sender to write a message.

Unless otherwise credited, the illustrations on these two pages are from the Hallmark Historical Collection; Hallmark Cards

Smithsonian Magazine
(Charles H. Phillips)

The oldest American valentine is a handmade card from the early 1700's. It has a handwritten verse in German.

A card by Louis Prang, a famous Boston card maker, dates from the late 1800's.

A movable card from the early 1900's has a boy whose left arm moves to reveal a valentine.

Romantic valentines of the 1830's, such as this British card, featured brokenhearted lovers. Many of the verses were about love that was not returned.

Valentines by Kate Greenaway, a British artist, showed garden scenes. This card was printed in the 1880's by Marcus Ward & Company, a London greeting card company.

An American valentine from the Civil War period, which lasted from 1861 to 1865, has tent flaps that open. The photograph on the left shows the card closed. The one on the right shows the tent flaps open, revealing a Union soldier writing to his sweetheart at home.

An American valentine from the 1890's features lace, pansies, and a cupid, the symbol of love. The tiny printing above the cupid's head says, "To one I love."

Modern valentines include both humorous and romantic cards. Special ones are printed for sweethearts and for husbands, wives, and relatives. Many cards say, "Be my valentine."

These books included verses to copy and various suggestions about writing valentines.

Commercial valentines were first made in the early 1800's. Many of them were blank inside, with space for the sender to write a message. The British artist Kate Greenaway became famous for her valentines in the late 1800's. Many of her cards featured charming pictures of happy children and lovely gardens.

Esther A. Howland, of Worcester, Massachusetts, became one of the first U.S. manufacturers of valentines. In 1847, after seeing a British valentine, she decided to make her own. She made samples and took orders from stores. Then she hired a staff of women and set up an assembly line to produce the cards. Howland soon expanded her business into a $100,000-a-year enterprise.

Many valentines of the 1800's were hand painted. Some featured a cupid or showed arrows piercing a heart. Many cards had satin, ribbon, or lace trim. Others were decorated with dried flowers, feathers, imitation jewels, mother-of-pearl, sea shells, or tassels. Some cards cost as much as $10.

From the mid-1800's to the early 1900's, many people sent comic valentines called *penny dreadfuls*. These cards cost a penny and featured such insulting verses as:

'Tis all in vain your simpering looks,
You never can incline,
With all your bustles, stays, and curls,
To find a valentine.

Many penny dreadfuls and other old valentines have become collectors' items. Carol Bain

See also **Valentine, Saint.**

Additional resources

Barth, Edna. *Hearts, Cupids, and Red Roses.* 1974. Reprint. Clarion, 2001. Younger readers.
Bulla, Clyde R. *The Story of Valentine's Day.* HarperCollins, 1999. Younger readers.

Valentine's Day Massacre. See **Chicago** (The Roaring Twenties).

Valentinian I (A.D. 321-375) was Roman emperor from A.D. 364 until his death in 375. He ruled capably and with absolute power. Valentinian tried to protect the poor from dishonest government officials and powerful senators. He also allowed much religious freedom.

Valentinian was born at Cibalae, near what is now Belgrade in Serbia. He served as an officer in the Roman army. In A.D. 364, he was chosen emperor after the death of Emperor Jovian. Valentinian appointed his brother Valens co-ruler and gave him the eastern provinces to rule. Throughout Valentinian's reign, the group of German tribes in the north known as the Alemanni and the desert tribes in Africa rebelled. Valentinian spent much of his time as emperor campaigning against the Alemanni. He died on Nov. 17, 375.

Timothy David Barnes

Valentinian III (A.D. 419-455) was emperor of the West Roman Empire. He was a weak ruler, and the empire lost much territory during his reign.

Valentinian was born on July 2, 419, in Ravenna, Italy. He was the son of Emperor Constantius III and the grandson of Theodosius I. Valentinian became emperor in 425, at the age of 6. Political power rested with his mother—Galla Placidia—and various military leaders, especially Flavius Aëtius. Aëtius campaigned in Gaul (now mainly France) and in 451 won a major victory over the invading Huns, who were led by Attila. But a Germanic tribe called the Vandals conquered northern Africa during Valentinian's reign, and Roman Britain was lost to native rulers and Germanic invaders. The Visigoths and the Suevi, Germanic tribes that had settled in Gaul and Spain, also continually extended their territory. The empire's loss of provinces and the revenues they had generated produced acute political tensions. In 454, Valentinian had Aëtius murdered, and a year later, on March 16, 455, was assassinated by Aëtius's followers.

Timothy David Barnes

Valentino, Rudolph (1895-1926), was the most popular romantic star of American silent motion pictures. He won fame for his roles as a handsome, passionate lover.

Valentino's real name was Rodolfo d'Antonguolla. He was born on May 6, 1895, in Castellaneta, Italy, near Taranto. He came to New York City in 1913 and worked briefly as a gardener and laborer. Valentino then toured the country as a dancer in stage musicals. He probably began his film career in *Alimony* (1918). He became a star in *The Four Horsemen of the Apocalypse* (1921). Valentino played a desert warrior in *The Sheik* (1921) and *Son of the Sheik* (1926) and portrayed a bullfighter in

Valentino and Alice Terry in a scene from *The Four Horsemen of the Apocalypse* (1921); Culver

Rudolph Valentino was a silent motion-picture star who gained enormous fame for his roles as a handsome, passionate lover.

Blood and Sand (1922). His other films included *Camille* (1921), *Monsieur Beaucaire* (1924), *Cobra* (1925), and *The Eagle* (1925). He died at the age of 31 on Aug. 23, 1926, following surgery for peritonitis. Charles Champlin

Valera, Eamon de. See **De Valera, Eamon.**

Valerian, *vuh LIHR ee uhn,* is the name of a large family of herbs and shrubs found chiefly in the temperate regions of the Northern Hemisphere. There are more than 200 species of valerians. They include both *annuals* (plants that live one year) and *perennials* (plants that live more than two years). Some species are grown as garden or border flowers. Others are used for flavoring food or for medicinal purposes.

One group of valerians has highly fragrant roots and *rhizomes* (underground stems). The small, fragrant flowers of these valerians may be white, pink, or rose. The plants can reach a height of nearly 5 feet (1.5 meters).

The most important species in this group is the *common valerian,* also called *garden heliotrope.* Oils made from the dried roots and rhizomes of this plant are used in medicine as a sedative and in cooking as a flavoring.

Two species of annual valerians grown for their edible leaves are *corn salad* and *Italian corn salad.* Both grow about 1 foot (30 centimeters) high. Corn salad has blue flowers and Italian corn salad has pink flowers. Both are easily grown in spring and fall.   James E. Simon

Scientific classification. Valerians belong to the valerian family, Valerianaceae. The scientific name for the common valerian is *Valeriana officinalis.* Corn salad is *Valerianella locusta;* Italian corn salad is *Valerianella eriocarpa.*

Valéry, *vah lay REE,* **Paul** (1871-1945), was a French poet and critic who is often considered the greatest writer in the movement called *symbolism.* He developed a highly intellectual theory of poetry that valued calculated work and rejected chance inspiration. His writings reflect his preoccupation with the process of thinking.

Valéry's two best-known poems are *The Young Fate* (1917) and "The Cemetery by the Sea" (1920). The first poem examines the creation of ideas, and the second meditates on such philosophical problems as time and death. Valéry's collection of shorter poems, *Charms* (1922), is classical in its pure and structured form. Its symbolism is difficult but understandable.

Valéry's prose work *Introduction to Leonardo da Vinci's Method* (1895) maintains that artistic creation consists primarily in forming structures and that the artist is a kind of engineer. The fictional sketch *Evening with Mr. Teste* (1896) examines in detail the thinker observing his own mind. Valéry added to this work throughout his career. He also wrote rich and insightful literary essays. Valéry was born in Sète, France.

Edward K. Kaplan

See also **French literature** (Symbolism; The 1900's).

Valhalla, *val HAL uh,* was the great hall of the dead heroes in Scandinavian mythology. The word means *Hall of the Slain.* It was the most magnificent palace in Asgard, and Odin feasted there with his heroes.

Valhalla had walls of gold and a roof of battle shields. Huge spears held up its ceiling. They were so highly polished that the gleam from them was the only light needed. The 540 doors were so wide that 800 men could enter side by side. The guests sat at long tables. They were the dead heroes who had been brought to Valhalla by the Valkyries, or battle maidens. The Valkyries waited on the tables and served luxurious food.

The heroes rode out to the battlefield to fight every morning. They often wounded each other terribly, but their hurts were healed before they returned to Valhalla for the noonday feast.   C. Scott Littleton

See also **Odin.**

Vallandigham, *vuh LAN dih guhm,* **Clement Laird** (1820-1871), an Ohio politician, criticized President Abraham Lincoln's Civil War policies. Vallandigham was one of the best known of the northern Copperheads or Peace Democrats. He favored compromise with the South, and was arrested and convicted of treason in 1863. President Lincoln banished him to the Confederacy, but he escaped to Canada.

Vallandigham was born in New Lisbon, Ohio. He served in the Ohio state legislature in 1845 and 1846, and in the United States Congress from 1858 to 1863.

During his exile in 1863, Ohio Democrats nominated him for governor, but he lost the election. Vallandigham returned to the United States in 1864, but he never regained political prominence.   James M. McPherson

Valle, *VAH yay,* **José Cecilio Del** (1780-1834), a Central American patriot and statesman, wrote the Central American Declaration of Independence, proclaiming freedom from Spain on Sept. 15, 1821. He became a leader of Guatemala's independence movement in 1821. Mexico annexed Guatemala in 1822, and imprisoned Valle briefly. He was elected vice president of the Central American Confederation in 1823, but refused to serve. Valle was born in Honduras.   John A. Booth

Valletta, *vahl LEHT tah* (pop. 9,239), is the capital and chief seaport of Malta. It lies on a narrow peninsula between two deep harbors on Malta's northeast coast. Valletta is the administrative, cultural, and commercial center of Malta. It is the home of the Royal Malta Library. The Royal University of Malta is in Msida, just outside Valletta. The Cathedral of Saint John and the Palace of the Grand Masters (now the governor general's residence) are among the city's sights.

Valletta became the capital of Malta in 1571. It had been founded about five years earlier. Valletta was named for Jean Parisot de la Vallette, grand master of the Knights Hospitallers, also known as the Knights of Malta. The British maintained a naval base at Valletta from the early 1800's until 1979.   David I. Kertzer

See also **Malta** (map; picture).

Valley is a natural trough in the earth's surface. Systems of valleys extend through plains, hills, and mountains. Rivers and streams flowing through valleys drain interior land regions to the ocean. The bottoms of many valleys have fertile soil, which makes excellent farmland.

All valleys are similar in shape. The bottom of a valley is called its *floor.* Most floors slope downstream. Mountain valleys usually have narrow floors. But in low-lying plains, a floor may be several miles or kilometers wide. The part of the floor along riverbanks is called the *flood plain.* When the river overflows its banks, it floods the flood plain. In some cases, flooding is helpful because it adds *nutrients* (nourishing substances) to the soil. But severe flooding can damage crops and buildings and even kill people. A valley's sides are called *valley walls* or *valley slopes.* The ridge formed where the walls of neighboring valleys meet is a *divide.*

Kinds of valleys. Various kinds of valleys are named according to their appearance. A deep valley with steep walls is called a *canyon.* One of the most famous canyons is Grand Canyon in Arizona. Along coastlines, valleys flooded by the ocean are called *drowned valleys.* Chesapeake Bay and Delaware Bay are drowned valleys.

Where a valley joins a larger valley from the side, the two floors usually meet at the same level. But sometimes the floor of the side valley is higher than that of the main valley. The side valley is then called a *hanging* valley. A river flowing through a hanging valley may form a waterfall where the water enters the main valley.

Not all valleys are on land. Many deep *submarine* canyons are found on the slopes leading up from the ocean floor to the edge of the continental shelf. Hudson Canyon is a submarine canyon. It extends southeastward down the continental shelf to the Atlantic Ocean floor from a point near New York City.

How valleys are formed. Most valleys on dry land are formed by the running water of streams and rivers, and by the erosion of slopes leading to them. Erosion moves material down the slopes to the valley floor, where the stream carries it to a lake or to the ocean. In addition, the stream may erode its channel deeper. Hanging valleys are usually formed when erosion is greater in the main valley than in the side valley.

A *rift valley* may form when a long, narrow section of Earth's crust sinks. One system of rift valleys extends from the Sea of Galilee south through the Red Sea, and into southeastern Africa.

Glaciated valleys are valleys enlarged by the action of glaciers. They are often found high in mountains and are U-shaped rather than V-shaped.

H. J. McPherson

Related articles in *World Book* include:

Canyon	Imperial Valley
Death Valley	Ocean (map: The land beneath the oceans)
Delaware Water Gap	
Erosion	Shenandoah Valley
Ice age (Extent of the Pleistocene Glaciers)	Valley of the Kings
	Wyoming Valley

Valley Forge, Pennsylvania, is an area along the Schuylkill River, about 25 miles (40 kilometers) northwest of Philadelphia. General George Washington and his troops camped there in the winter of 1777 and 1778, during the American Revolution. These months were discouraging for the Americans. The Continental Army endured months of suffering.

Conditions at Valley Forge. Washington led his troops to Valley Forge after his defeats at Brandywine and Germantown, Pennsylvania. These defeats left Philadelphia under British control. Washington's soldiers had little food and too little clothing to protect themselves from the cold. The Continental Congress could not provide more supplies for them. The army of about 10,000 lived in crude log huts that they built themselves. On Dec. 23, 1777, Washington wrote: "We have this day no less than 2,873 men in camp unfit for duty because they are barefooted and otherwise naked."

An estimated 2,500 soldiers died during this period. Many others were either too weak or too sick to fight because of a smallpox epidemic. But the people around Valley Forge enjoyed all the comforts of a rich countryside because little fighting took place at this time. The British lived a carefree life in Philadelphia.

The winter at Valley Forge tested the loyalty of the American troops. Only dedicated patriots stayed with the Continental Army. Many people criticized Washington, but he held his position at Valley Forge throughout the winter and spring. He improved his troops with the help of Baron von Steuben, a former Prussian soldier. Steuben drilled the soldiers in a system of field formations. By spring, Washington had a disciplined, well-trained army. The news of the alliance between France and the United States reached Valley Forge on May 6, 1778. It cheered Washington and helped him move successfully against the British in June.

Valley Forge National Historical Park covers the campsite. For area, see **National Park System** (table: National historical parks). The park's buildings and monuments were built in memory of Washington's Continental Army. The old stone house he used as headquarters still stands there. Other structures in the park include the Washington Memorial Chapel and the National Memorial Arch.   William Morgan Fowler, Jr.

See also **Revolutionary War in America; Washington, George; Steuben, Baron von.**

Valley of the Kings is a rocky, narrow gorge, which was used as a cemetery by the *pharaohs* (kings) of ancient Egypt between 1550 and 1100 B.C. The Valley, sometimes called the Valley of the Tombs of the Kings, lies on the west bank of the Nile River across from Luxor. More than 60 tombs have been discovered in the Valley of the Kings and in the adjoining Western Valley.

The tombs are in the form of corridors and chambers cut into rock. Carved and painted religious scenes and hieroglyphic texts cover the walls of many tombs. The art work depicts mainly the dead king and the gods in the hereafter. The tomb that archaeologists believe held the remains of about 50 sons of Ramses II, discovered in 1995, is the largest tomb. That of Seti I is the most ornate. Other tombs include those of Tutankhamun, Thutmose III, Ramses II, and Ramses III.   Richard H. Wilkinson

Valois, *vah LWAH,* was the family name of a line of kings who ruled France from 1328 to 1589. The Valois line was a branch of the Capetian family, which had begun to rule France in 987. The Valois kings were followed by rulers from the Bourbon family, another branch of the Capetians. The Valois line presided over such events as the Hundred Years' War (1337-1453) be-

Granger Collection

Valley Forge served as a campsite for General George Washington and his troops in the winter of 1777 and 1778 during the American Revolution. The American soldiers were cold, hungry, and sick. They endured what has often been called the "Winter of Despair."

tween France and England and most of the Renaissance and Reformation in France.

In 1328, the last king from the main branch of the Capetian family, Charles IV, died without a son. His closest male heir was his nephew Edward III of England. To prevent the succession of an English king, the French gave the crown to Charles's cousin Philip of Valois, who became Philip VI. In putting Philip on the throne, the French applied a principle derived from an ancient law code called the *Salic law*. Under this principle, French rulers had to be male and could claim succession only through male ancestors. Edward III could claim succession only through his mother.

The last Valois king, Henry III, died in 1589 without an immediate male heir. As a result, the French used the Salic law to identify Henry IV, France's first Bourbon king, as the country's next monarch.   Donald A. Bailey

Related articles in *World Book* include:

Charles VIII (of France)	Henry III (of France)
Francis I	Louis XII
Henry II (of France)	Philip VI (of France)

Valparaíso, VAHL *pah rah EE soh* or VAL *puh RY soh* (pop. 275,982), is the principal seaport and one of the largest cities of Chile. Valparaíso lies on a wide inlet of the Pacific Ocean about 70 miles (110 kilometers) northwest of Santiago. For location, see **Chile** (political map). *Valparaíso* is Spanish for *Valley of Paradise.*

Valparaíso is a modern city and an important manufacturing center. The chief products include cotton goods, liquor, machinery, refined sugar, and tobacco. The National Congress of Chile moved to Valparaíso from Santiago in 1990. The city has many fine public buildings and schools. An electric railroad joins Valparaíso with Santiago, and another line joins the city with the mining section of inland Chile. In 1906, a severe earthquake destroyed parts of the city.   Jerry R. Williams

Value, in economics, means the power of a commodity to command other commodities in exchange. Value relates to the terms upon which one commodity exchanges for others. It must not be confused with price. A commodity's *price* means its exchange power in terms of money (see **Price**). Its *value* means its exchange power in terms of other commodities.

Value and utility. To possess value, an article must have *utility*—that is, it must have the power to satisfy a want. For example, farm products always have value because everyone desires them. So farmers can usually find a market for their products. The desire for articles must be backed by purchasing power. No article will have any value if those who want it have no money or commodities to offer in exchange for it.

A thing may have great value and still be used in ways that harm humanity. For example, drugs and alcohol possess great utility and are beneficial when used properly. But they become harmful when people misuse them or become addicted to them.

Value and scarcity. To possess value, an article must be scarce. That is, it must be so limited in quantity that those who have it can get something else in exchange for it. Air, which has great utility, seldom has any value. There is so much of it that ordinarily everyone can have any quantity without paying for it. But under certain conditions, air does have value. A good illustration is compressed air, which is bought and sold.   Irving Morrissett

Value, in color. See **Color** (The Munsell color system; illustration).

Value added by manufacture is a statistic used to measure and compare the value of manufacturing activity. For example, if a state had a total value added by manufacture of $10 billion in 1990 and $20 billion in 2000, its manufacturing activity doubled. The statistic is one of the chief measures of economic activity that is used by the United States government.

Value added by manufacture is the increase in value of raw material after it becomes a finished product. It represents the effect of manufacturing in terms of money. To compute this value, economists subtract the cost of materials, supplies, containers, fuel, electric power, and contract work from the value of manufactured products as they leave the factory. The value added by a firm is the difference between the firm's sales revenue and its purchases from other firms.   Thomas F. Dernburg

Value-added tax is a tax imposed by a government at each stage in the production of a good or service. The tax is paid by every company that handles a product during its transformation from raw materials to finished goods. The amount of the tax is determined by the amount of the value that a company adds to the materials and services it buys from other firms.

Suppose that a company making scratch pads buys paper, cardboard, and glue worth $1,000. The company adds $500 in labor costs, profits, and depreciation, and sells the scratch pads for $1,500. The value-added tax is calculated on the $500. The companies that had sold the paper, cardboard, and glue to the scratch pads company would also pay a tax on their value added. In this way, the total value added taxed at each stage of production adds to the total value of the final product.

Most firms that pay a value-added tax try to pass this expense on to the next buyer. As a result, most of the burden of this tax in time falls on the consumer. In this sense, the final effect is equal to that of a retail sales tax. The tax is levied at a fixed percentage rate and applies to all goods and services. However, many nations use different rates. In these nations, the less necessary a product is, the higher the rate will be.

In 1954, France became the first nation to adopt a value-added tax. This tax has grown in popularity, and Canada and more than 100 nations now use it. It is not used by the United States on the federal level. But most of the other large industrial nations use it.   Vito Tanzi

Values. See **Moral education**.

Valve. See **Heart** (Chambers, valves, and inner lining; Valve disease); **Mitral valve prolapse**.

Valve is a term used for various mechanical devices that open and close to control the flow of fluids in pipes and vessels. The term also is used in physiology for natural growths in the body, which serve much the same purpose as mechanical valves. Among these are the valves of the heart, which open and close to control the flow of blood through the chambers of the heart.

Mechanical valves include *check valves, relief valves, manual valves,* and *automatic control valves.* Check valves and relief valves allow flow in one direction only. In a check valve, a gate or disk covers an opening called the *seat.* Gravity or a spring holds the disk in place. Pressure on one side of the disk forces the valve open. But pressure on the other side pushes the disk into the seat,

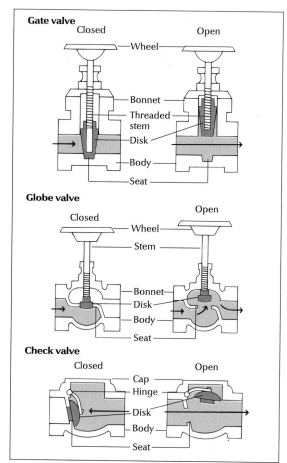

Gate valve

Closed   Open

Wheel

Bonnet

Threaded stem

Disk

Body

Seat

Globe valve

Closed   Open

Wheel

Stem

Bonnet
Disk
Body
Seat

Check valve

Closed   Open

Cap
Hinge
Disk
Body
Seat

WORLD BOOK illustration by William Graham

Principal types of valves. The manual gate and globe valves are used to turn on or shut off the flow of liquids. The check valve allows a liquid to flow in one direction, but it closes shut to stop flow in the opposite direction.

preventing flow. In a relief valve, the disk is held closed by a compressed spring on one side. It opens only when pressure against the other side of the disk is greater than that of the spring.

Manual valves are controlled by hand. The common water faucet is a manual valve. Automatic control valves are controlled by some external power source, such as electricity or compressed air. These valves have become important in industry because hundreds of them can be operated from a central location by a computer or a device called a *controller.*   Alan H. Glenn

See also **Carburetor; Gasoline engine; Safety valve.**

Vampire is a corpse that supposedly returns to life at night to suck people's blood. Stories of similar creatures come from many parts of the world. But most vampire tales originated in Eastern European and Balkan countries, such as Albania, Greece, Hungary, and Romania.

There are many superstitions about vampires. People who commit suicide, die violently, or are condemned by their church supposedly become vampires. According to folklore, a vampire can be destroyed in several ways—for example, by driving a wooden stake through its heart or by cutting off its head. In Europe, from the

late 1600's to the early 1800's, people dug up graves looking for vampires. In literature, a vampire must have a constant supply of fresh blood obtained by biting the neck of sleeping victims. After being bitten, the victims lose strength, die, and become vampires themselves.

The horror novel *Dracula* (1897), by the Irish author Bram Stoker, is the most famous vampire story. The fictional character of Dracula is based on Vlad Tepes, a cruel prince from Walachia (now part of Romania). Vlad was nicknamed Dracula, which in Romanian means *son of the devil* or *son of a dragon.* Many motion pictures have been based on Stoker's *Dracula.*   Heide A. Crawford

See also **Dracula; Stoker, Bram.**

Vampire bat is the name given to three species of blood-eating bats in Central and South America. The bats feed on such warm-blooded animals as cattle, fowl, and horses. The best known is the *common vampire bat,* a small reddish-brown animal about 3 inches (8 centimeters) long. It has sharp, triangular-shaped front teeth, which cut like a razor. Its esophagus is short and narrow and will let nothing but fluids pass.

Vampire bats sometimes attack people who are sleeping. The bite itself is harmless and soon heals, but vampire bats may carry rabies. Vampire bats have destroyed livestock and other animals in some localities and have also infected human beings.

Weird stories have been told about the viciousness of these mammals. Their peculiar name comes from

© Stephen Dalton, Photo Researchers
Vampire bat

the superstitious legends about the vampire, an imaginary being that sucks people's blood.   Frank B. Golley

Scientific classification. Vampire bats belong to the New World leaf-nosed bat family, Phyllostomidae. The common vampire bat is *Desmodus rotundus.*

See also **Bat; Stoker, Bram; Vampire.**

Vanadium, a silvery-white metallic element, occurs throughout Earth's crust in extremely small quantities. Traces of vanadium also have been found in meteorites.

Vanadium is used chiefly by steel manufacturers, who combine it with iron in an *alloy* (metal mixture) called *ferrovanadium.* Vanadium improves steel's hardness at high temperatures and its ability to withstand shock. It also makes *alloy steel* (steel that contains nickel, chromium, and molybdenum) resistant to corrosion. Manufacturers use alloy steel to make axles, gears, and springs for airplanes, automobiles, and locomotives. High-speed cutting tools also are made of alloy steel containing vanadium. Engineers use vanadium to make some parts for nuclear reactors because it resists attack by many chemicals but allows neutrons to penetrate readily.

Vanadium compounds have many uses. *Vanadium pentoxide* and *vanadium oxytrichloride* serve as *catalysts* (substances that speed up chemical reactions) in the production of synthetic materials and industrial chemicals. Vanadium pentoxide and many other vanadium compounds are used in dyes, glazes, and glass coloring.

Vanadium has the chemical symbol V. Its *atomic number* (number of protons in its nucleus) is 23. Its *relative atomic mass* is 50.9415. An element's relative atomic mass equals its *mass* (amount of matter) divided by ½₂ of the mass of carbon 12, the most abundant form of carbon. Vanadium has a density of 6.1 grams per cubic centimeter at 20 °C. It melts at 1890 ± 10 °C and boils at 3380 °C. Andrés Manuel del Río, a Mexican mineralogist, first recognized it as a new element in 1801. But del Río later thought it was impure chromium. Nils Sefström, a Swedish chemist, rediscovered it in 1830 and named it after Vanadis, the Scandinavian goddess of beauty.

Vanadium never occurs alone in nature. It is found combined with other elements in over 60 minerals. A major commercial source is titaniferous magnetite, found mainly in Finland, Russia, and South Africa.

Vanadium is considered an essential trace element in the human body. Some vanadium salts and complexes can mimic the effects of the hormone insulin, which regulates glucose levels in the blood.   Vincent L. Pecoraro

Van Allen, James Alfred (1914-2006), a physicist, discovered the Van Allen belts, two zones of electrically charged particles that surround Earth. His team of scientists used data from the United States Explorer 1 satellite to make the discovery in 1958. Van Allen was born on Sept. 7, 1914, in Mount Pleasant, Iowa, and graduated from Iowa Wesleyan College and the University of Iowa. He headed the University of Iowa's department of physics and astronomy from 1951 to 1985. Van Allen died on Aug. 9, 2006.   Roger H. Stuewer

Van Allen belts, also called *radiation belts,* are two zones of electrically charged particles that surround Earth high above its surface. The belts were named for James A. Van Allen, an American physicist, who discovered them in 1958. He based his discovery on data from the Explorer 1 satellite. The belts surround Earth somewhat like doughnuts. The inner belt extends from about 600 to 3,000 miles (1,000 to 5,000 kilometers) above Earth. The outer belt reaches from about 9,300 to 15,500 miles (15,000 to 25,000 kilometers).

The radiation in the belts consists of high concentrations of charged particles, such as protons and electrons. Earth's magnetic field traps such particles and directs them toward the magnetic poles. The trapped particles spiral along a system of imaginary lines of the magnetic field. These *field lines* curve from the north magnetic pole to the south magnetic pole. As particles approach either pole, the converging field lines reflect them back toward the opposite pole. This effect keeps particles in the belts bouncing between the poles.

The inner belt traps particles set free from Earth's atmosphere by *cosmic rays,* high-energy particles from outer space. The outer belt acquires particles from the *solar wind,* a continuous stream of charged particles from the sun, and from *solar flares,* violent eruptions on the sun's surface. Intense solar activity disrupts the belts and leads to *magnetic storms.* Disruptions of the belts also interfere with radio reception, cause surges in power transmission lines, and produce auroras.

Jupiter, Saturn, Uranus, and Neptune—like Earth—are surrounded by magnetic fields. In the 1970's and 1980's, the Voyager space probes found evidence that these planets also have radiation belts.   Jay M. Pasachoff

Related articles in *World Book* include:

Aurora
Cosmic rays
Magnetic storm
Solar wind
Van Allen, James A.
Voyager

Van Allsburg, Chris (1949-   ), is an American author and illustrator of children's books. His style is a dreamlike combination of fantasy and reality. Van Allsburg won Caldecott Medals for his illustrations for *Jumanji* (1981) and *The Polar Express* (1985). In 1993, Van Allsburg won the Regina Medal, which honored his lifetime contribution to children's literature.

Van Allsburg was born on June 18, 1949, in Grand Rapids, Michigan. He graduated from the University of Michigan in 1972 and received a Master of Fine Arts degree from the Rhode Island School of Design in 1975. For many years, he taught illustration there.

Van Allsburg wrote and illustrated his first book, *The Garden of Abdul Gasazi,* in 1979. He also wrote and illustrated *Ben's Dream* (1982), *The Wreck of the Zephyr* (1983), *The Mysteries of Harris Burdick* (1984), *Just a Dream* (1990), *The Sweetest Fig* (1993), *Zathura* (2002), and *Probuditi!* (2006). He illustrated Mark Helprin's adaptation of *Swan Lake* (1989), based on the ballet composed by Peter Ilich Tchaikovsky.   Kathryn Pierson Jennings

See also **Literature for children** (picture: *Jumanji).*

Vanbrugh, *van BROO* or *VAN bruh,* **Sir John** (1664?-1726), was an English playwright and architect. His plays lightly satirize London high society, but they sometimes seriously criticize social values and institutions. Vanbrugh's first and most famous comedy, *The Relapse* (1696), ridicules sentimental comedies in which villains suddenly reform at the end. It also shows how mistreatment can tempt good people to act badly. *The Provoked Wife* (1697) deals with an unhappy marriage. His other plays are adaptations from French writers.

The buildings Vanbrugh designed are large, ornate, and almost overpowering in the fashion of his time. His most famous building is Blenheim Palace near Oxford (see **Churchill, Sir Winston** [picture: Blenheim Palace]). Vanbrugh also designed Castle Howard in Yorkshire and the Queen's Theatre in London. He was born in London. He died on March 26, 1726.   Gerald M. Berkowitz

Van Buren, Abigail (1918-   ), was the pen name of Pauline Phillips, who wrote a newspaper advice column called *Dear Abby.* The column, which Pauline's daughter Jeanne Phillips writes today under the same pen name, is published in over 1,200 newspapers in the United States and other countries. It largely consists of responses to reader questions.

Pauline Esther Friedman was born on July 4, 1918, in Sioux City, Iowa. In 1939, she married Morton Phillips, a businessman. In 1956, she became an advice columnist for the *San Francisco Chronicle.* She

Harry Langdon

Abigail Van Buren

began co-writing *Dear Abby* with Jeanne Phillips in 1987 and retired from the column in 2002. Her twin sister, Esther Pauline Lederer, wrote a popular advice column called *Ann Landers* (see **Landers, Ann**).   William McKeen

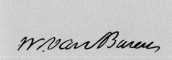

8th President of the United States 1837-1841

Jackson
7th President
1829-1837
Democrat

Van Buren
8th President
1837-1841
Democrat

W. H. Harrison
9th President
1841
Whig

Richard M. Johnson
Vice President
1837-1841

Oil painting on canvas (1864) by George Peter Alexander Healy; © White House Historical Association (National Geographic Society)

Van Buren, Martin (1782-1862), ran for President three times but won only the first time. He served during the nation's first great depression, the Panic of 1837. The panic brought financial ruin and misery to millions. Many turned to the government for aid, but Van Buren refused to help. He believed in Thomas Jefferson's idea that government should play the smallest possible role in American life. "The less government interferes," Van Buren explained, "the better for general prosperity."

Van Buren's erect bearing and high, broad forehead gave him a dignified appearance. He had served as Vice President under Andrew Jackson, and, as President, Van Buren inherited much of Jackson's popularity. But during the three years of the panic, Van Buren bore the anger of a disappointed people. His enemies accused him of being a sly, scheming politician. They called Van Buren "The Little Magician" and "The Fox of Kinderhook." They ridiculed his courteous manners. When he continued to deal politely with his political rivals, his enemies said this approach showed his lack of deep convictions.

By defending his Jeffersonian ideals, Van Buren demonstrated that actually he had both deep convictions and courage. Partly because he refused to compromise, he was defeated for reelection in 1840 by William Henry Harrison, whom he had beaten in 1836. Van Buren ran again for President in 1848 but finished a poor third.

In Van Buren's time, Washington, D.C., was still a city of muddy streets and few trees. One traveler said: "It looks as if it had rained naked buildings upon an open plain." But life in the capital reflected the excitement of a growing country. The first railroad into Washington was completed in time to bring visitors from New York City and Philadelphia to Van Buren's inauguration. Frontiersmen such as Sam Houston mingled with courtly Southerners and proper New Englanders. Washington host-

esses sought out the popular author Washington Irving for their dinner parties. Out West, the frontier town of Chicago became an incorporated city, and the Republic of Texas began its fight for statehood.

Early life

Childhood and education. Martin Van Buren was born in the Dutch community of Kinderhook, N.Y., on Dec. 5, 1782. He was the third of the five children of Abraham and Maria Hoes Van Buren. Martin had an older brother and sister, and two younger brothers. His mother was the widow of Johannes Van Alen, and had three other children by her first marriage. Abraham Van Buren ran a truck farm and a tavern. As a child, Martin enjoyed listening to the tavern patrons as they argued politics in the Dutch language.

Martin attended the village school. At the age of 14, he began to study law under Francis Sylvester, a local attorney. He showed great talent, and Sylvester soon let him work in court. Martin first took part in a court trial at the age of 15. Another lawyer from Sylvester's office had tried the case. As he was about to sum up his arguments, he turned to Martin and said: "Here, Mat, sum up. You may as well begin early." The boy was rewarded

Important dates in Van Buren's life

1782	(Dec. 5) Born in Kinderhook, N.Y.
1812	Elected to the New York Senate.
1821	Elected to the United States Senate.
1828	Elected governor of New York.
1829	Appointed secretary of state.
1832	Elected Vice President of the United States.
1836	Elected President of the United States.
1840	Defeated for reelection by William H. Harrison.
1848	Nominated for President by the Free Soil Party.
1862	(July 24) Died in Kinderhook, N.Y.

Iowa became a territory in 1838. This new territory included all of present-day Iowa, most of Minnesota, and two-thirds of North and South Dakota.

The U.S. flag had 26 stars during most of Van Buren's term of office. The 26th star was added on July 4, 1837, to represent Michigan, which had become a state in January.

The world of President Van Buren

Economic depression struck the United States in 1837 and caused widespread hardship.

The first steel plow that could easily turn the heavy sod of the American prairie was invented by John Deere in 1837.

Queen Victoria began her 63-year reign over the United Kingdom of Great Britain and Ireland in 1837.

The first popular method of photography, invented in 1837 by Louis Daguerre of France, produced images on copper plates called *daguerreotypes.*

Samuel F. B. Morse gave his first demonstration of the telegraph in 1837 and patented his device in 1840.

Revolts in Upper and Lower Canada began in 1837. In 1840, the British Parliament voted to unite the two colonies into the Province of Canada.

Thousands of Indians were forced to move from their homelands in the Southeastern United States to what is now Oklahoma in the 1830's and early 1840's. The Indians included the Cherokee, who called their forced march the *Trail of Tears.* This term is sometimes used to refer to the removal of the other tribes as well.

A U.S. Navy expedition to Antarctica was led by Lieutenant Charles Wilkes between 1838 and 1842. He sighted land in 1840 and sailed along 1,500 miles (2,410 kilometers) of the Antarctic coast. He was the first person to recognize that Antarctica was a continent and not just a huge field of ice.

The first teacher-training school in the United States opened in Lexington, Massachusetts, in 1839. Only women were admitted to the school.

WORLD BOOK map

that day with a silver half dollar. He soon became a familiar sight in the village court.

In 1801, Van Buren moved to New York City to continue his studies. He was admitted to the bar in 1803 and opened a law office in Kinderhook with his half brother, James I. Van Alen.

Van Buren's family. On Feb. 21, 1807, Martin Van Buren married his distant cousin and childhood sweetheart, Hannah Hoes (March 8, 1783-Feb. 5, 1819). Mrs. Van Buren died 18 years before her husband became president. The couple had four sons. Abraham, the eldest, was his father's White House secretary, and later served on the staff of General Zachary Taylor during the Mexican War (1846-1848). John, the second son, became attorney general of New York.

Political and public career

Van Buren's enthusiasm for the ideas of Thomas Jefferson took him into politics as a Democratic-Republican (see **Democratic-Republican Party**). He was elected to the New York Senate in 1812. Shortly after his reelection to the Senate in 1816, Van Buren was appointed attorney general of New York. In this post, Van Buren helped form the first modern political *machine,* an organization that does favors for citizens in return for votes. His machine was known as the Albany Regency.

U.S. senator. In 1820, a split in the Democratic-Republican Party of New York gave Van Buren a chance to display his new political power. Governor De Witt Clinton tried to get John C. Spencer into the U.S. Senate through a special election. Van Buren opposed Clinton and successfully managed the election of Rufus King, an independent Federalist. A year later, when the other Senate seat was vacated, Van Buren's standing had so increased that the legislature elected him.

Van Buren took his seat in the Senate on Dec. 3, 1821. He became a leader in the fight against imprisonment for debt, a great social evil of the time. In 1828, Congress passed a law abolishing such imprisonment. Van Buren also tried to stop the extension of the slave trade. He introduced a bill forbidding the importation of slaves into Florida unless they were owned by settlers. This bill was defeated. Van Buren won reelection to the Senate in 1827. That year, he created an alliance between the Albany Regency and Virginia's powerful Democratic machine, the Richmond Junto. The two organizations backed Andrew Jackson for president because they thought he was most likely to preserve states' rights.

Secretary of state. Late in 1828, Van Buren resigned from the Senate after being elected governor of New York. He served as governor only two months then re-

From *A History of Old Kinderhook* by Edward A. Collier, G. P. Putnam's Sons, 1914

Van Buren's birthplace was in Kinderhook, New York. The house has been torn down. The only record of what it looked like comes from drawings made during Van Buren's lifetime.

signed to become secretary of state under President Jackson. Van Buren successfully pressed claims for damages to American shipping by French and Danish warships during the Napoleonic Wars. Under his leadership, the United States reestablished trade with the British West Indies. The British had closed West Indian ports to American shipping in 1826 in retaliation for high American tariffs on British goods.

Vice President. In 1831, Jackson appointed Van Buren U.S. minister to Britain. But the Senate, by one vote, refused to confirm the appointment. By this act, Van Buren's enemies thought they had destroyed his career. Jackson took the Senate's action as a personal insult. In 1832, he supported Van Buren's nomination to the vice presidency. Jackson also made it clear that Van Buren was his choice to be the next President. As Vice President, Van Buren reluctantly backed Jackson's decision to withdraw federal deposits from the Bank of the United States (see **Bank of the United States**). Van Buren also hesitated to support Jackson's actions to enforce federal authority after South Carolina declared a federal law unconstitutional (see **Nullification**).

Election of 1836. In spite of Van Buren's political beliefs, he retained Jackson's support and easily won the Democratic nomination for President in 1836. He defeated William Henry Harrison, the main Whig candidate, by 97 electoral votes. In the vice presidential race, no candidate won a majority of the electoral votes. The United States Senate then chose Van Buren's running mate, Representative Richard M. Johnson of Kentucky. No other Vice President has ever been elected by the Senate.

Van Buren's Administration (1837-1841)

The Panic of 1837. Van Buren owed the presidency to Jackson. But many of the problems that faced him as President had developed during Jackson's Administration. Congress had failed to limit the sales of public lands to actual settlers, even though Jackson urged such action during his last year in office. Everyone was speculating in public lands, even clerks and shoeshine boys. State banks and branches of the Bank of the United States had joined the speculative splurge. They made vast loans without security in gold or silver. Unable to limit land sales, Jackson had issued his *Specie Circular* of July 11, 1836. It required the government to accept only gold and silver in payment for public lands. Banks could no longer make loans without security, and the speculation ended. A financial crash was inevitable. It came on May 10, 1837, just 67 days after Van Buren took office. Banks in Philadelphia and New York City closed, and soon every bank in the country did likewise. The first great depression in U.S. history had begun.

Van Buren's election

Place of nominating convention	.....Baltimore
Ballot on which nominated	.........1st
Whig opponent	.....................William Henry Harrison
Electoral vote*	.....................170 (Van Buren) to 73 (Harrison)
Popular vote	.........................764,176 (Van Buren) to 550,816 (Harrison)
Age at inauguration	54

* For votes by states, see **Electoral College** (table).

© White House Historical Association (National Geographic Society)
Angelica Singleton Van Buren, the widowed President's daughter-in-law, served as his White House hostess. She married his oldest son, Abraham, in November 1838.

The independent treasury. The Panic of 1837 placed Van Buren in a politically dangerous situation. Although he had pledged to limit the use of federal power, he acted decisively to protect government funds, which were on deposit in private banks. He called Congress into special session and proposed that a treasury be created to hold government money. A bill putting this plan gradually into effect was defeated twice but finally passed Congress on July 4, 1840. The battle over the treasury cost Van Buren the support of many bankers and bank stockholders, especially in the strong Democratic states of New York and Virginia. This loss crippled his bid for reelection.

Life in the White House. Van Buren avoided extravagant White House parties because of the depression. He limited his entertaining to simple dinners. Many visitors to the Executive Mansion found the atmosphere formal and austere, even with Van Buren's four sons present. The people of Washington admired the modesty and personal charm of the youths, all in their 20's. But many, especially Dolley Madison, regretted the lack of a woman in the household. She introduced the President's eldest son, Abraham, to Angelica Singleton of South Carolina. A romance soon developed, and the young people were married in late 1838. Angelica Van Buren assumed the role of White House hostess.

Growing unpopularity. The depression was only one of many disturbances during Van Buren's Administration. Border disputes developed with Canada. In 1839, a boundary dispute between Maine and New Brunswick nearly resulted in open warfare. Van Buren handled the problem with tact, and the dispute was settled peacefully. However, he received little credit for his efforts. See **New Brunswick** (The Aroostook War).

Antislavery leaders blamed Van Buren for the expensive war to drive the Seminole Indians from Florida. They feared the region might become a new slave state. Proslavery leaders attacked the President for not working to annex Texas. The proslavery people believed that

Vice president and Cabinet

Vice president	* Richard M. Johnson
Secretary of state	John Forsyth
Secretary of the treasury	Levi Woodbury
Secretary of war	Joel R. Poinsett
Attorney general	Benjamin F. Butler Felix Grundy (1838) Henry D. Gilpin (1840)
Postmaster general	Amos Kendall John M. Niles (1840)
Secretary of the Navy	Mahlon Dickerson James Paulding (1838)

*Has a separate biography in *World Book.*

Van Buren did not want to admit a new slave state into the Union.

Election of 1840. The Democrats nominated Van Buren for reelection in 1840 in spite of his unpopularity. Vice President Johnson had so many enemies that he failed to gain renomination. The Democrats could not agree on any vice presidential candidate. As a result, Van Buren became the only presidential candidate in American history to seek election without a running mate. The Whigs again nominated William Henry Harrison for president and chose former Senator John Tyler of Virginia as his running mate.

Harrison launched a boisterous campaign in which he attacked Van Buren as an aristocrat who had no interest in the unemployment caused by the depression. Using the slogan "Tippecanoe and Tyler too," Harrison campaigned on the basis of his colorful military career. Few people were surprised when Van Buren lost by an electoral vote of 234 to 60. But many were amazed by the close popular vote. Of 2,400,000 votes cast, Van Buren lost by fewer than 150,000. See **Harrison, William Henry** (Elections of 1836 and 1840).

Later years

Van Buren retired to his country estate, Lindenwald, near his birthplace. He remained active in politics for more than 20 years. In 1848, the antislavery Free Soil Party nominated him for president (see **Free Soil Party**). He lost the election but took so many New York votes from Democrat Lewis Cass that the Whig candidate, Zachary Taylor, was elected.

As the slavery disputes grew hotter, Van Buren made his antislavery position clear. But he remained a loyal Democrat, supporting Franklin Pierce in 1852 and James Buchanan in 1856. Van Buren died at Lindenwald on July 24, 1862, and was buried beside his wife in Kinderhook. The Lindenwald estate became the Martin Van Buren National Historic Site in 1974. James C. Curtis

Related articles in *World Book* include:

Free Soil Party
Harrison, William Henry
Jackson, Andrew
Johnson, Richard Mentor
President of the United States
Vice president of the U.S.

Outline

I. Early life
- A. Childhood and education
- B. Van Buren's family

II. Political and public career
- A. U.S. senator
- B. Secretary of state
- C. Vice President
- D. Election of 1836

III. Van Buren's Administration (1837-1841)
- A. The Panic of 1837
- B. The independent treasury
- C. Life in the White House
- D. Growing unpopularity
- E. Election of 1840

IV. Later years

Questions

Whose support assured Van Buren's nomination for president?
What events caused Van Buren to lose popularity?
What social evil did Van Buren oppose while serving as a United States senator?
What political organization did Van Buren help found in New York state?
Why was Van Buren called "The Fox of Kinderhook"?
What was Van Buren's plan to protect federal funds from the effects of a depression?
What caused the Panic of 1837?
Why was Van Buren the only person ever to run for president without a vice presidential running mate?

Additional resources

Favor, Lesli J. *Martin Van Buren.* Children's Pr., 2003. Younger readers.
Ferry, Steven. *Martin Van Buren.* Child's World, 2002. Younger readers.
Niven, John. *Martin Van Buren.* 1983. Reprint. Am. Political Biography Pr., 2000.
Widmer, Ted. *Martin Van Buren.* Times Bks., 2005.

Vance, Cyrus Roberts (1917-2002), served as secretary of state from 1977 to 1980 under President Jimmy Carter. Vance, a lawyer and former official in the Department of Defense, came to the Department of State as an experienced diplomat. In 1967, he settled a dispute between Greece and Turkey over Cyprus. In 1968 and 1969, he served as deputy United States negotiator at the Paris peace talks on the Vietnam War.

As secretary of state, Vance played a major role in establishing full diplomatic ties between the United States and China. He also helped negotiate a peace treaty between Egypt and Israel. He resigned because he could not support a plan by the Carter administration to rescue American hostages held in Iran (see **Carter, Jimmy**).

In late 1991, the United Nations asked Vance to help end fighting between Croats and Serbs in Croatia. His efforts led to a cease-fire there in 1992.

Vance was born on March 27, 1917, in Clarksburg, West Virginia. He graduated from Yale University and from Yale Law School. He enlisted in the Navy in 1942, during World War II. In 1947, he joined a New York City law firm.

In 1961, President John F. Kennedy named Vance general counsel of the Department of Defense. Vance became secretary of the Army in 1962, and President Lyndon B. Johnson appointed him deputy secretary of defense in 1964. Vance died on Jan. 12, 2002.

Nancy Dickerson Whitehead

Vance, Zebulon Baird (1830-1894), was a Confederate governor of North Carolina and a Democratic United States senator. Vance opposed secession, but he served in the Confederate Army during the American Civil War (1861-1865). He became governor of North Carolina in 1862 and devoted himself to supplying North Carolina soldiers. He was elected to the U.S. Senate in 1870, but was refused his seat. He was elected governor again in 1876 and served in the U.S. Senate from 1879 until his death.

Vance was born on May 13, 1830, in Buncombe County, North Carolina, and died on April 14, 1894. He represents North Carolina in Statuary Hall. Thomas L. Connelly

Vancouver is Canada's busiest port. It is also the largest city and the major cultural and industrial center of British Columbia. Skyscrapers rise near Vancouver's harbor. The Coast Mountains tower in the background.

Barry Rowland, Tony Stone Images

Vancouver, *van KOO vuhr,* is the largest city in British Columbia and the busiest port in Canada. It also ranks as one of the largest cities in Canada. The people who live in the Vancouver metropolitan area make up about half the entire population of British Columbia. The city is the province's major center of commerce, culture, industry, and transportation.

Vancouver lies in southwestern British Columbia, about 25 miles (40 kilometers) north of the Canadian-United States border. The city's chief asset is its natural harbor in Burrard Inlet. The harbor is connected with the Pacific Ocean by English Bay, the Strait of Georgia, and Juan de Fuca Strait. Ships can use the port the year around because the harbor's waters never freeze. The port handles nearly all of Canada's trade with Japan and other Asian nations. Vancouver is often called *Canada's Gateway to the Pacific.*

The first permanent European settlement on the site of what is now Vancouver grew up near a sawmill built in 1865. Rich timber resources helped the settlement become a bustling lumber town. In 1884, the Canadian Pacific Railway chose the site as the western terminal of Canada's first transcontinental railroad. William Van Horne, the railroad's general manager, named the town for Captain George Vancouver, a British explorer who had sailed into Burrard Inlet in 1792.

Greater Vancouver

Vancouver covers 44 square miles (115 square kilometers) on the southern shore of Burrard Inlet. The city lies in a beautiful setting, near the Coast Mountains and the ocean. The protective mountains and warm winds blowing in from the Pacific help provide a mild climate for a city so far north.

The Vancouver metropolitan area, called Greater Vancouver, occupies 1,111 square miles (2,877 square kilometers). Greater Vancouver is Canada's third-largest metropolitan area. Only the Montreal and Toronto metropolitan areas have larger populations.

The city lies on two ridges separated partly by a shallow inlet called False Creek. Stanley Park, the main recreational area, is on the shorter, northern ridge. Farther south and east on this ridge are downtown Vancouver

and rows of high-rise apartment buildings in an area called the West End. The southern ridge includes Vancouver's East End, a large residential section of mostly single-family homes.

The intersection of Granville and Georgia streets is the heart of downtown Vancouver. The 30-story Toronto Dominion Bank Tower rises over the intersection. It stands in Pacific Centre, a complex that also has a department store and an underground shopping center. Royal Centre, a development that includes a 33-story office tower, hotel, and shopping mall, stands nearby at Georgia and Burrard streets.

Several other downtown streets have special characteristics. Robson Street, also known to Vancouver residents as Robsonstrasse, its name in German, is a fascinating center of European import stores. Restaurants that specialize in French, German, Greek, Italian, and other types of cooking help give the street an international charm. Most of Vancouver's Chinatown, one of the

Vancouver's coat of arms, adopted in 1969, includes a lumberman and a fisherman. They represent two industries that have contributed much to the city's growth.

Facts in brief

Population: 578,041. *Metropolitan area population*—2,116,581.
Area: 44 mi² (115 km²). *Metropolitan area*—1,111 mi² (2,877 km²).
Altitude: 38 feet (11.6 m) above sea level.
Climate: *Average temperature*—January, 37 °F (3 °C); July, 64 °F (18 °C). *Average annual precipitation* (rainfall, melted snow, and other forms of moisture)—47 inches (120 cm). For the monthly weather in Vancouver, see **British Columbia** (Climate).
Government: Council-manager. *Terms*—3 years for the mayor and the 10 other council members.
Founded: 1865. Incorporated as a city in 1886.

largest Chinese communities in North America, is on Pender Street. Thousands of people of Chinese descent live on or near Pender Street, which is lined by restaurants, gift shops, and nightclubs.

Gastown, the original center of Vancouver, consists of a few redeveloped blocks just north of Chinatown. Gastown's old brick buildings and cobblestone streets recall the city's early days. This area has several antique shops and art galleries.

The False Creek waterfront, once Vancouver's center of industry, has been redeveloped into a pleasant residential area. A community of town houses and apartments lines the south shore of False Creek. Nearby is Granville Island, a popular tourist shopping destination that features markets, boutiques, and restaurants.

The metropolitan area. The Coast Mountains, including two snow-capped peaks called the Lions, rise majestically north of Vancouver. Point Grey, a peninsula, juts into the Strait of Georgia at the west end of the city. The flat, green delta lands of the Fraser River basin spread south of Vancouver.

The suburb of Surrey ranks as British Columbia's second largest city, after Vancouver. Other suburbs include Burnaby, Coquitlam, Richmond, Delta, North Vancouver, and West Vancouver.

People

About half of Vancouver's people were born in Canada. People of British ancestry make up the largest group.

Other large groups include those of Asian (mainly Chinese) and western European descent.

The mild climate in Vancouver has helped to make the city a popular retirement center. In addition, the city's climate attracts large numbers of young people from other parts of Canada. However, many of them lack job skills and cannot find work. As a result, they contribute to the relatively high rate of unemployment in the city. Poverty is another major problem in Vancouver. Most of the poor people live in run-down buildings just east of the downtown section and in parts of the East End.

Economy

Trade and finance. Vancouver is Canada's busiest port. Vancouver's port handles millions of tons of cargo annually. It serves as the main center for the distribution of goods shipped between Canada and Asia. The port is also the center of an important northern coastal trade. Numerous steamship lines serve Vancouver.

Vancouver is the largest wholesale and retail trading center of western Canada. Tens of thousands of workers in Greater Vancouver are employed by wholesale and retail companies. Almost every large business in British Columbia has its headquarters in the city. The tourist industry ranks among Vancouver's fastest-growing sources of employment. Vancouver has more banks, loan companies, and other financial institutions than any other city in western Canada.

City of Vancouver

BRITISH COLUMBIA

Vancouver

Vancouver, the largest city in British Columbia, is the busiest port in Canada. The map shows the city and its major points of interest.

—— City boundary

===== Expressway

—— Other road or street

—— Railroad

----- SkyTrain (rapid transit)

▪ Point of interest

▨ Park

▨ Indian reserve

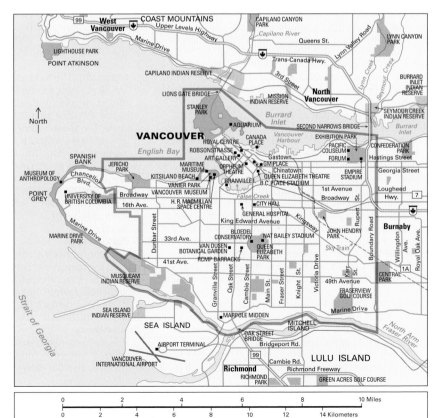

WORLD BOOK map

© Al Harvey, The Slide Farm

Colorful totem poles stand in Vancouver's Stanley Park. Stanley Park is the city's main recreational area and one of the largest city parks in Canada. The park covers 1,000 acres (400 hectares).

Transportation. Vancouver serves as the western terminal of Canada's two transcontinental railroads, the Canadian National Railway and the Canadian Pacific Railway. The British Columbia Railway Company, which is owned by the provincial government, has its general offices in North Vancouver. The BNSF (Burlington Northern Santa Fe) Railway connects Vancouver with United States cities.

Vancouver International Airport is Canada's second busiest airport. Only the airport at Toronto serves more passengers. Major Canadian, Asian, European, and U.S. airlines use Vancouver's airport.

Local transportation facilities include a bus system. An elevated rapid transit system, SkyTrain, connects downtown Vancouver with the suburb of Surrey to the southeast. Ferry lines connect Vancouver and nearby Vancouver Island. The Lions Gate Bridge spans Burrard Inlet. It is 1,550 feet (472 meters) long and links Stanley Park and West Vancouver. A commuter rail line extends about 42 miles (68 kilometers) between downtown Vancouver and the municipality of Mission to the east. The Trans-Canada Highway connects Vancouver and other Canadian cities.

Industry. Greater Vancouver ranks as the most important Canadian industrial center west of Ontario. There are hundreds of factories in Greater Vancouver, employing tens of thousands of workers.

The area's leading industries are food processing and the manufacture of wood and wood products. Fish processing and meat packing rank as the chief activities of the food products industry. Vast evergreen forests in British Columbia provide the raw materials for the area's sawmills, pulp and paper mills, and veneer and plywood plants. Other activities include metal fabricating, the making of paper and related products, and the manufacture of petroleum and coal products.

Industry plays a key role in Vancouver's economy. However, many of the city's industries have caused environmental damage to the area. The waters of Burrard Inlet, for example, have become heavily polluted.

Communication. Vancouver has two major daily newspapers, *The Province* and *The Vancouver Sun.* Several television and radio stations serve the city. The Canadian Broadcasting Corporation has its regional headquarters in Vancouver.

Education

Schools. A nine-member school board supervises Vancouver's public schools. In addition, Vancouver has a number of church-supported schools and private schools.

The University of British Columbia, on Point Grey, is one of the largest universities in Canada. Simon Fraser University is in Burnaby.

Libraries. The Vancouver Public Library system includes a central library in the downtown area and branches throughout the city. The University of British Columbia Library has special collections of materials relating to the development of the Canadian Pacific Railway and Chinese immigration to Canada.

Cultural life and recreation

The arts. The Vancouver Opera performs in the Queen Elizabeth Theatre. Major stage attractions are presented by the Arts Club Theatre Company and the Playhouse Theatre Company. The Vancouver Symphony Orchestra performs at the Orpheum Theatre. The Vancouver Art Gallery features paintings by European and Canadian artists.

Museums. The Vancouver Museum and the H. R. MacMillan Space Centre form part of a modern cultural center at the mouth of False Creek in Vancouver. The museum features exhibits on the settlement of western Canada. The space center includes simulated space flights and a planetarium. Nearby on the waterfront, the Vancouver Maritime Museum displays the Arctic exploring ship *St. Roch.* This vessel was the first to sail through the Northwest Passage from both the west and the east. The *St. Roch* made the voyages between 1940 and 1944. The Museum of Anthropology, one of the finest museums of its kind, is at the University of British Columbia.

Parks. Vancouver has more than 200 parks. Stanley Park occupies 1,000 acres (400 hectares) and ranks among the largest city parks in Canada. It includes the Vancouver Aquarium, which is one of the finest marine centers in the world and the largest in Canada. Stanley Park is also known for its flower gardens. Queen Elizabeth Park includes an arboretum and the Bloedel Floral Conservatory.

Vancouver's mild climate makes it attractive for many outdoor activities, including fishing, golfing, and tennis. Vancouver also has many fine beaches. The Pacific National Exhibition, western Canada's largest fair, attracts many tourists to Vancouver in late August and early September every year. It includes agricultural and industrial displays and many kinds of entertainment.

Sports. The city is the home of two major professional sports teams. The British Columbia Lions play in the Canadian Football League. The Vancouver Canucks compete in the National Hockey League.

Government

Vancouver has a mayor-council form of government. The voters elect the mayor and the 10 other members of the City Council to three-year terms. Property taxes furnish most of the city government's revenue. But these and other taxes do not provide enough money to pay for public services and needed improvements. As a result, Vancouver depends on funds from the federal and provincial governments to meet its expenses.

Other problems in Vancouver include air and water pollution and a shortage of low-rent housing. City leaders are also concerned about the increasing rate of construction on land that may be needed for parks or for other recreational use.

History

Salish Indians lived in what is now the Vancouver area for more than 2,000 years before white explorers arrived. In 1791, José María Narváez, a Spanish explorer, became the first European to see the area. Captain George Vancouver sailed into Burrard Inlet in 1792.

The settlement that became Vancouver was founded in 1865, when a sawmill company built Hastings Mill on the site. In 1867, John Deighton, a former English sailor, built a saloon nearby to serve the loggers. He had the nickname "Gassy Jack" because he was so talkative, and the community soon became known as Gastown.

Early growth. In 1884, the Canadian Pacific Railway chose the site of Vancouver as its western terminal. The young lumber town was incorporated as the city of Vancouver in April 1886. At that time, about 2,000 people lived there. A fire destroyed most of Vancouver two months later, but the city was quickly rebuilt.

The Canadian Pacific Railway reached Vancouver from eastern Canada in 1887. The city's population rose to 8,000 in 1889. In 1891, ships of the Canadian Pacific Steamship Company began to sail between the city and Asia. By 1901, the population of Vancouver was 42,000.

The great boom. Between 1900 and 1910, job opportunities made Vancouver the fastest-growing city in Canada. The salmon-canning and wood-processing industries created many of these jobs. Immigrants poured into the city from China, India, Japan, the United Kingdom, and the United States. In 1904, the Great Northern Railway linked Vancouver with Seattle and other U.S. cities. By 1911, about 86,000 people lived in Vancouver.

The opening of the Panama Canal in 1914 greatly increased business for Vancouver's port. The canal provided a cheaper way to ship fish, grain, and lumber from western Canada to eastern Canada, Europe, and the eastern United States. By 1921, Vancouver had 163,220 people. In 1929, the neighboring communities of Point Grey and South Vancouver became part of Vancouver. In 1931, nearly 250,000 people lived in the city.

The mid-1900's. Vancouver suffered severely during the Great Depression of the 1930's. Thousands of unemployed and homeless people moved to the city from other parts of Canada to seek jobs and relief from the cold winters. Many of these people found no work and

took part in several demonstrations against the provincial and federal governments.

World War II (1939-1945) brought prosperity to the city as shipbuilding and other industries expanded. During the war, Vancouver served as headquarters of the coastal defense staffs of the Canadian Army.

The city changed rapidly after the war. Tall apartment buildings appeared in the West End, and modern office towers replaced old structures downtown. Shopping centers were built near many residential areas.

Vancouver's seaport grew in importance in the 1960's because of a rapid growth of trade between Canada and Japan. In 1970, a coal-loading terminal equipped to handle the world's largest cargo ships opened just south of Vancouver at Roberts Bank.

During the 1960's and 1970's, private developers erected more tall apartment buildings in the West End and office towers in the downtown area. The downtown developments included Pacific Centre and Royal Centre. In 1974, the city prohibited automobile traffic on part of Granville Street and turned this section into a mall.

Recent events. Canada Place was constructed on the Vancouver waterfront in the mid-1980's. The complex includes the World Trade Centre office building, a hotel, a convention center with an unusual saillike roof, and docking facilities for cruise ships. Expo 86, an exposition of communication and transportation technologies, attracted over 22 million visitors to Vancouver in 1986.

Four major construction projects were completed in Vancouver in 1995. They were Library Square, a new public library; General Motors Place, a sports arena; Ford Centre, a theater; and a new terminal for Vancouver International Airport. The Ford Centre was later renamed the Centre in Vancouver for Performing Arts.

In 2003, the International Olympic Committee selected Vancouver to host the 2010 Winter Olympic Games. The ski resort of Whistler, British Columbia, will be the site of many of the events.   Stephen Hume

See also **British Columbia** (pictures); **Canada** (picture); **Park** (picture: Urban parks).

Vancouver (pop. 143,560) is a port city on the Columbia River in southwestern Washington. It lies across the river from Portland, Oregon (see **Washington** [political map]). Vancouver is also an important banking and railroad center for southwestern Washington.

Nearby Bonneville Dam, a large federal power project on the Columbia River, helps provide electric power for the region. The area's main industries include a paper mill and electronics companies.

Vancouver is the oldest continuously occupied settlement in the state of Washington. The city grew up around Fort Vancouver, which was completed in 1825 by the Hudson's Bay Company, a British trading firm. The fort was named for Captain George Vancouver, a British explorer who had sailed along the coast of Washington in 1792. Vancouver was incorporated as a city in 1857. It is the seat of Clark County and has a council-manager form of government.   Thomas Hardy Ryll

Vancouver, George (1757-1798), was a British explorer. Vancouver Island and cities in Washington and in British Columbia, Canada, are named after him.

He was born at King's Lynn, Norfolk, England, on June 22, 1757. He entered the Navy as an able seaman at the age of 13. His early experiences were on Captain James

Cook's two last voyages (see **Cook, James**). Vancouver served as a midshipman on the last voyage.

An incident concerning Nootka Sound, off the west coast of Vancouver Island, threatened war between Britain and Spain. Vancouver was ordered there, and he sailed in April 1791. He went by way of the Cape of Good Hope, Australia, and New Zealand, after Cook's example.

Brown Bros.

George Vancouver

He made valuable charts of the coasts of these areas. He reached the American continent in 1792. Vancouver participated in certain formalities involving Nootka Sound, and then sailed through Juan de Fuca Strait and around Vancouver Island. His surveys of the west coast of North America from San Diego to southern Alaska were pioneering achievements. He returned to England via Cape Horn in 1795. His book, *A Voyage of Discovery to the North Pacific Ocean and Round the World in the Years 1790-1795,* was published in 1798. Vancouver died on May 12, 1798.   Barry M. Gough

Vancouver Foundation is an institution that collects donations and distributes funds to various charitable organizations in British Columbia. The foundation's central goal is to enhance the quality of life for people and animals throughout British Columbia. A board of private citizens governs the foundation. The Vancouver Foundation is one of the largest private foundations in Canada.

The policies and programs of the Vancouver Foundation seek to promote human growth and dignity, inclusiveness, fairness, and equality for all people. The foundation provides funds for programs in seven primary *fields of interest.* The fields are (1) animal welfare; (2) arts and culture; (3) children, youth, and families; (4) education; (5) environment; (6) health and social development; and (7) youth philanthropy. The foundation also administers the BC Medical Services Foundation (BCMSF) and the Disability Supports for Employment Fund (DSEF). The BCMSF supports medical research and health education. The DSEF helps people with disabilities obtain assistance in the workplace.

The origins of the Vancouver Foundation date back to the early 1940's. Alice G. MacKay, a Canadian secretary, and W. J. VanDusen, a Canadian businessman and philanthropist, started the organization. The foundation was formally established by the Vancouver Foundation Act, passed by the British Columbia legislature in 1950. For assets, see **Foundation** (table).   Bruce Cronin

Vancouver Island is the largest island on the Pacific Coast of North America, and an important part of the Canadian province of British Columbia. Vancouver Island extends for 285 miles (459 kilometers) along the southwestern coast of Canada and is from 40 to 80 miles (64 to 130 kilometers) wide. Victoria, the largest city on the island, is the capital of British Columbia. The other chief cities are Nanaimo and Port Alberni. About 700,000 people live on the island.

Location, size, and features. Vancouver Island is separated from the British Columbia mainland by Queen

WORLD BOOK map

Location of Vancouver Island

Charlotte Strait, Johnstone Strait, and the Strait of Georgia. The Strait of Juan de Fuca lies south of the island.

Vancouver Island covers 12,079 square miles (31,284 square kilometers). It is the southern end of a partly sunken mountain chain called the Island, or Vancouver, Range. The tops of the range rise sharply from the Pacific Ocean to heights of 5,000 to 7,000 feet (1,500 to 2,100 meters). Dangerous reefs and small, rocky islands are common along the western shore. The valleys of the sunken range form many winding, fiordlike bays. Quatsino, Nootka, and Barkley sounds reach into the heart of the island. Pacific Rim National Park is on the western coast. The eastern shore is less rugged and broken.

Vancouver Island has the mildest climate in Canada because of the Kuroshio (Japan Current). But in the northern and western mountains, the winters are often severe. The western coast receives heavy rainfall.

The island's resources. The slopes of the mountains on Vancouver Island are covered with fir, cedar, and hemlock forests. Lumbering is the chief industry. The island has several large pulp mills, sawmills, and plywood plants. Farms are cultivated in the eastern lowlands. The southeast coast produces many berries and flower bulbs. Excellent game fishing attracts many tourists.

History. Tribes of Indians probably lived on Vancouver Island more than 10,000 years ago. In 1774, the Spanish explorer Juan Perez became the first European to sight the island. In 1778, the British navigator James Cook became the first European to land on Vancouver Island. George Vancouver, a member of Cook's expedition, returned to the island in 1792 and sailed around it. The island is named for him. See **Vancouver, George.**

During the 1800's, the United States claimed the island and nearby territory on the mainland. But the United States surrendered these claims to the United Kingdom in 1846. The first European settlement on the island was made in 1843, when the Hudson's Bay Company built Fort Victoria. In 1849, Vancouver Island became a British colony. In 1866, it was united with mainland settlements to form British Columbia, which became a Canadian province in 1871.   Graeme Wynn

See also **Nootka Indians; Victoria** (B.C.).

Vandalism is criminal damage to property. It includes breaking the windows of public or privately owned buildings, painting slogans on the walls of public places, breaking furniture or machinery, and many other forms of damage. Vandalism may be an act of revenge or a way of expressing a political opinion. Both young people and adults sometimes commit the crime just for "fun." For example, football fans may tear down the goal posts after an important game.

In the United States, the damage caused by vandalism totals millions of dollars yearly. In most cases, the costs are paid by the business, school, or government that has been vandalized, or by individual victims.

Vandalism is punishable by fine or imprisonment. A number of local governments have laws that hold parents responsible for vandalism committed by their children. But most acts of vandalism are not punished. Law enforcement is difficult, and the expense of repairing most individual acts of damage is not large enough to make legal action worthwhile.   George T. Felkenes

Vandals were a Germanic tribe that invaded the West Roman Empire during the early A.D. 400's. The Vandals invaded the empire along with other Germanic peoples and helped bring about its decline. The Vandals were no more destructive than other invaders, but the word *vandal* has come to mean someone who destroys or damages valuable things.

The Vandals probably originated in what is now southern Scandinavia. By A.D. 100, they had settled in what are today the regions of Silesia and Galicia in eastern Europe. The Vandals moved west from this area in the late A.D. 300's, partly because they were threatened by the Huns and other peoples from the east. In 406, the Vandals crossed the Rhine River and looted Gaul (now mainly France), an area controlled by Rome. In 409, they crossed the Pyrenees Mountains and entered Spain, where they became a major power.

The Vandals reached the peak of their power under the Vandal king Gaiseric (or Genseric), who ruled from 428 to 477. In 429, the Vandals invaded northern Africa, where they quickly conquered a number of Roman provinces and established a strong kingdom. From their base in northern Africa, the Vandals dominated the western Mediterranean Sea. They looted Rome in 455. An army from the Byzantine Empire conquered the Vandal kingdom in northern Africa in 533 and 534.

Malcolm Todd

Van de Graaff, *VAN duh GRAF,* **Robert Jemison** (1901-1967), an American physicist, invented the electrostatic generator named after him. This device builds up a high-voltage electric charge whose field can accelerate charged particles. Scientists use Van de Graaff generators for studying atomic nuclei.

Van de Graaff was born on Dec. 20, 1901, in Tuscaloosa, Alabama. He graduated from the University of Alabama in 1922 and earned a doctor's degree from Oxford University in 1928. Van de Graaff built his first high-energy generator in 1931, while a researcher at Princeton University. That same year, he went to the Massachusetts Institute of Technology, where he continued to develop the generator. In 1946, Van de Graaff helped found the High Voltage Engineering Corporation for producing advanced generator models. He died on Jan. 16, 1967.   Roger H. Stuewer

Vandenberg Air Force Base, California, is the United States Air Force's rocket-launching site on the Pacific Coast. The Air Force Space Command tests missiles

on the Western Range, which stretches across the Pacific Ocean to the Indian Ocean. The Air Combat Command has a headquarters at Vandenberg for intercontinental ballistic missile forces. Vandenberg Air Force Base covers about 98,400 acres (39,800 hectares) northwest of Los Angeles. It was established in 1957 on an Army training post and named after General Hoyt S. Vandenberg, the second chief of staff of the U.S. Air Force.   Wayne Thompson

Vanderbilt, Cornelius (1794-1877), was the most successful and powerful American businessman of his time. He made his fortune in steamship lines and railroads but also had investments in manufacturing and banking. Vanderbilt was often called "Commodore" because of his steamship interests.

Vanderbilt was born on May 27, 1794, in Port Richmond on Staten Island, New York. At the age of 16, he bought a small sailboat, which he used to ferry freight and passengers. During the War of 1812, Vanderbilt transported supplies to forts along New York Harbor. He formed a steamship company in 1829 and soon dominated shipping along the Atlantic coast and on the Hudson River. After the California gold rush began in 1849, Vanderbilt established a steamship line that carried prospectors from New York City to San Francisco. The route included an overland crossing through Nicaragua. By the mid-1850's, Vanderbilt's ships made regular trips to and from Europe, and he had become the leading American steamship owner.

During the 1840's, Vanderbilt began buying shares in railroads in New York and New Jersey. In the mid-1860's, he gained control of the Hudson River Railroad. Shortly afterward, he merged this line with the New York Central Railroad to form a network that ran from New York City to Buffalo, New York. By 1873, he owned rail lines that extended as far west as Chicago.

Vanderbilt helped build the nation's transportation system. But he also was a fierce competitor who often cut freight rates to force competing businesses to sell out to him. Vanderbilt did not support charities. But late in life, he gave $1 million to Vanderbilt University in Nashville and $50,000 to the Church of the Strangers in New York City. At his death on Jan. 4, 1877, Vanderbilt left a fortune of over $105 million, the largest in U.S. history up to that time.   W. Bernard Carlson

See also **Gould, Jay; Hunt, Richard Morris** (picture: The Breakers).

Additional resources

Auchincloss, Louis. *The Vanderbilt Era.* 1989. Reprint. Macmillan, 1990.
Patterson, Jerry E. *The Vanderbilts.* Abrams, 1989.
Vanderbilt, Arthur T. *Fortune's Children: The Fall of the House of Vanderbilt.* 1989. Reprint. Quill Paperbacks, 1991.

Vanderbilt University is a coeducational, privately controlled research university in Nashville. It has a college of arts and science; professional schools of divinity, education, engineering, law, management, medicine, music, and nursing; and a graduate school. Courses lead to bachelor's, master's, and doctor's degrees. Vanderbilt offers many educational opportunities, including extracurricular research projects, community service, and seven overseas study programs.

Vanderbilt University was endowed in 1873 after Cornelius Vanderbilt, an American businessman, gave

$1 million to build and support the school.

Critically reviewed by Vanderbilt University

Van der Goes, *van duhr GOOS,* **Hugo** (1440?-1482), was the leading Flemish painter of religious subjects and portraits of his generation. His pictures reflect the influence of the Flemish painters Jan van Eyck in their rich detail and Rogier van der Weyden in their dramatic poses. Van der Goes' paintings, however, communicate a more emotional, intense feeling through the individu-

Death of the Virgin (about 1481), an oil painting on wood panel; Groeninge-Museum, Bruges, Belgium (Art Resource)

A Van der Goes painting shows the artist's skill at portraying emotional subjects through gestures, posture, and expressions.

alized posture, gestures, and expressions of his solidly formed figures. These figures range from earthy peasants to the Holy Family. Van der Goes painted many large-scale religious works, frequently emphasizing such highly emotional subjects as the death of the Virgin Mary. One of his famous paintings is a *triptych* (three-paneled painting), the Portinari Altarpiece.

Little is known of Van der Goes' early life. In 1467, he was accepted as a master in the artists' guild in Ghent, in what is now Belgium. About 1475, he entered a monastery near Brussels as a lay brother. His complex personality was marked by periods of melancholy, which may account for expressionistic aspects of his paintings.

Linda Stone-Ferrier

Van der Weyden, *van duhr VYD uhn,* **Rogier,** *roh GEER* (1399?-1464), was a Flemish painter of portraits and religious subjects. In his religious paintings, van der Weyden focused attention on the emotional responses of elegant and graceful groups of figures. But the artist also distanced the viewer from the intensity and immediacy of the religious experience in a variety of ways. For example, he sometimes placed his figures against a gold

Painting on wood panel (1464); the Louvre, Paris

Van der Weyden's *Saint Mary Magdalene* shows his skill at portraying dignified figures and realistic landscapes.

background, as in *The Descent from the Cross* (about 1435), which is reproduced in the **Painting** article. In some paintings, he deliberately avoided integrating the figures into the detailed setting, often arranging them to create a rhythmic surface pattern. Some paintings include painted sculptural archways that function as frames for the subject matter.

Van der Weyden was born in Tournai, in what is now Belgium. In the 1430's he moved to Brussels, where he was appointed "painter of the town." His workshop included many apprentices and his style influenced Flemish, German, and French art for many years. His portraits for the court of Burgundy preserve the haughty manner and proud bearing of the Burgundian nobles.

Linda Stone-Ferrier

See also **Painting** (The northern Renaissance).

Van Dine, S. S. (1888-1939), is the pen name of Willard Huntington Wright, an American author of detective fiction. Van Dine's novels featured the scholarly and snobbish amateur detective Philo Vance. Van Dine introduced Vance in *The Benson Murder Case* (1926). Vance also appears in 11 other novels, including *The Canary Murder Case* (1927) and *The Bishop Murder Case* (1929). In the Philo Vance stories, the murderers use unusual methods to commit crimes. Under his own name, Wright wrote books on literary criticism and art, as well as a study of German philosopher Friedrich Nietzsche. Wright was born in Charlottesville, Virginia.

David Geherin

Van Doren, Carl (1885-1950), was an American biographer and critic. He won the 1939 Pulitzer Prize for biography for his book *Benjamin Franklin* (1938). Van

Doren also wrote *Swift* (1930), a biography of the English author Jonathan Swift.

Van Doren wrote many critical essays about American authors. Much of his literary criticism was collected in *The Roving Critic* (1923) and *Many Minds* (1924). Van Doren wrote a number of books about the Revolutionary War in America (1775-1783). They include the *Secret History of the American Revolution* (1941) and *Mutiny in January* (1943). He also wrote an autobiography, *Three Worlds* (1936). Carl Clinton Van Doren was born in Hope, Ill., near Urbana. His younger brother, Mark Van Doren, was also a noted author.   Samuel Chase Coale

Van Doren, Mark (1894-1972), was an American poet, critic, and educator. He wrote more than 50 works of prose and poetry and won a Pulitzer Prize in 1940 for his *Collected Poems* (1939).

Many of Van Doren's poems describe the beauty of nature and New England's changing seasons. Others are based on American legends and show his love for the nation's cultural heritage. Some poems that Van Doren wrote in the 1940's reflect his somber thoughts about World War II (1939-1945). These poems are included in *Collected and New Poems: 1924-1963* (1963). In *Good Morning: Last Poems* (published in 1973 after his death), he expressed calm acceptance of the prospect of death.

Van Doren's career as a critic began with *Henry David Thoreau* (1916), a study of Thoreau's writings. He also wrote essays on the works of other writers, including John Dryden, Nathaniel Hawthorne, and William Shakespeare. His major critical writings appear in *Private Reader* (1942) and *The Happy Critic* (1961). He also wrote novels, plays, short stories, and *Autobiography* (1958).

Mark Albert Van Doren was born in Hope, Ill., near Urbana. From 1920 to 1959, he taught English at Columbia University. His older brother, Carl Clinton Van Doren, was also a noted writer.   Elmer W. Borklund

Van Druten, *van DROOT uhn,* **John William** (1901-1957), was a playwright who became known for his polished comedies. His plays are noted for their sophisticated dialogue and strong portrayals of women. Van Druten's comedies include *Old Acquaintance* (1940), *The Voice of the Turtle* (1943), *I Remember Mama* (1944), and *Bell, Book and Candle* (1950). He adapted his best-known serious play, *I Am a Camera* (1951), from Christopher Isherwood's stories, *Goodbye to Berlin,* about life in Germany as the Nazis were coming to power.

Van Druten was born in London and taught at University College, Wales. He turned to literature as a career after *Young Woodley* (1925), his second play, succeeded in New York City. The play had been banned in England as an exposé of its public school system. He moved to the United States in 1926.   Thomas P. Adler

Van Dyck, *van DYK,* **Sir Anthony** (1599-1641), was one of the most popular portrait painters of his time. He is sometimes known as Anton Van Dyck. The artist was sought after by the royalty, aristocracy, and upper-middle class of Flanders, Italy, and especially England. Van Dyck also painted religious and mythological pictures, and was a fine engraver and etcher.

Van Dyck's style of portrait painting typically emphasized the elegance and wealth of his subjects. He often slightly exaggerated the height of the figure, and lengthened the outline of the hands to suggest greater refinement and stature. Many of Van Dyck's figures are

Robert Rich, Earl of Warwick (about 1635), an oil painting on canvas; the Metropolitan Museum of Art, New York City, the Jules S. Bache Collection, 1949 (WORLD BOOK photo by Malcolm Varon)

A typical Van Dyck portrait shows a full-length figure posed against a landscape background. The portrait above illustrates Van Dyck's drawing skill and his ability to paint rich fabrics.

dressed in luxurious clothing painted in rich color. The settings characteristically include elegant furniture, draped tapestries, imported rugs, and large architectural elements such as columns. He also used landscape as background for his portraits.

Van Dyck was born in Antwerp, in what is now Belgium. He showed great talent as a boy and had his own studio and pupils at the age of about 16. From about 1618 to 1620, he worked with the famous Antwerp painter Peter Paul Rubens. Van Dyck visited England briefly in 1620 and lived in Italy from 1621 to about 1627. Van Dyck's portraits of the nobles of Genoa and their children rank among his finest works. His Italian paintings reflect the influence of the warm colors and loose brushwork of the Venetian Renaissance painter Titian.

After leaving Italy, Van Dyck returned to Antwerp. He went to England in 1632, where King Charles I made him court painter. Van Dyck painted about 350 portraits while in England, including about 40 of the king. His famous *Portrait of Charles I Hunting* (about 1635) appears in the **Painting** article. The portrait cleverly combines flattering aspects of the aristocratic hunt and references to Charles's authority as king. Van Dyck's portraits of the English court established a tradition followed by Thomas Gainsborough and Sir Joshua Reynolds, English portrait painters of the 1700's.   Linda Stone-Ferrier

See also **Clothing** (pictures: The Ruff; Clothing of the 1600's).

Additional resources

Brown, Christopher, and Vlieghe, Hans, eds. *Van Dyck, 1599-1641.* Rizzoli, 1999.
Moir, Alfred. *Anthony Van Dyck.* Abrams, 1994.

Van Eyck, *van EYEK,* **Jan,** *yahn* (1380?-1441), was one of the greatest and most influential Flemish painters of altarpieces and portraits of the 1400's. His work typically portrays the subjects in minute realistic detail and bright colors. Although van Eyck did not invent oil painting, as has been previously thought, he achieved stunning effects with oil paint. He applied layer after layer of the paint to achieve the effect of shimmering jewels or rich textures. *The Annunciation,* an example of the artist's precise style, appears in the **Painting** article.

Many of van Eyck's paintings include what has been called *disguised symbolism.* The realistic objects in the pictures often have a deeper meaning related to the religious nature of the image. Examples of hidden symbolism appear in his painting *Portrait of Giovanni Arnolfini and His Wife* (also known as *The Arnolfini Wedding*).

Oil painting on wood (1435); Städelsches
Kunstinstitut, Frankfurt (am Main), Germany (Kunst-Dias Blauel)

Van Eyck's *Lucca Madonna* shows the artist's skillful handling of light and his ability to paint fabrics and jewels in precise detail. Van Eyck's realistic style influenced many painters.

Scholars generally believe that the painting depicts an Italian merchant and his bride. They have removed their shoes to indicate they stand on holy ground as they exchange wedding vows. The single burning candle in the chandelier symbolizes both the presence of Jesus Christ and the "marriage candle" that was part of the ceremony. The dog may symbolize fidelity in marriage. Van Eyck and another person, who served as the two required witnesses, are reflected in a mirror on the back wall.

According to tradition, van Eyck was born in the province of Limburg, in the border region between the Netherlands and what is now Belgium. He worked for wealthy and sometimes powerful patrons. Van Eyck collaborated with Hubert van Eyck, probably his brother, on the large multipanel painting called the *Ghent Altarpiece* (1432). Jan van Eyck died on June 22 or 23, 1441.
          Linda Stone-Ferrier

See also **Jerome, Saint** (picture); **Painting** (The northern Renaissance); **Renaissance** (picture: A northern Renaissance painting).

Van Gogh, *van GOH* or *van GAWKH,* **Vincent** (1853-1890), was a Dutch painter. He is one of the most famous painters in modern art. But during his lifetime, he received little recognition and sold only one painting.

Van Gogh was born on March 30, 1853, in Groot-Zundert, near Breda, the Netherlands. When he was 16, he went to The Hague to work for his uncle, an art dealer. Vincent's brother Theo, to whom he was devoted, stayed in the family art business and eventually became his dealer. In 1876, Vincent tried to become a minister but failed his theology exams. Although he was not ordained, in 1878 he became a preacher in a poor coal-mining district in what is now southwestern Belgium.

In 1880, van Gogh turned to painting as a profession. His early works were still lifes and scenes of peasant life done in dark colors. For an example of van Gogh's work from this period, see **Letter writing** (picture).

In 1886, van Gogh went to Paris. He became part of the intellectual excitement of the Paris art scene through contact with such French painters as Camille Pissarro, Emile Bernard, Paul Gauguin, and Georges Seurat. He experimented with Impressionism and other modern art styles and painted scenes of suburban and city life. He also started to collect Japanese prints, which profoundly influenced his work.

In 1888, van Gogh moved to Arles in southern France. There, the influence of the sunlight and landscape inspired him to use even more vivid colors. His commitment to God and to showing the beauty of God's natural world became a strong theme in his painting. In his works, nature vibrates with energy, motivated by the presence of God that van Gogh perceived in all living things. Van Gogh's *Self-Portrait,* reproduced in this article, shows a man of intensity and vision. The circular motion of the brushstrokes in the green background gives the effect of a shimmering halo. In his painting *The Night Café* (1888), van Gogh used a steep perspective, strong colors, and gaslights with rings of light around them to express what he called "the terrible passions of humanity." *The Starry Night,* an example of the artist's Arles period, appears in the **Painting** article.

In 1888, Gauguin visited van Gogh in Arles. The visit ended when van Gogh threatened Gauguin with a razor and cut off his own earlobe. Van Gogh spent the last 19

Oil painting on canvas; courtesy of the Fogg Art Museum, Harvard University, Cambridge, Massachusetts, Bequest—Collection of Maurice Wertheim

Van Gogh painted this self-portrait in 1888.

Vanilla is the name of a group of climbing orchids. The vanilla extract that is used to flavor chocolate, ice cream, pastry, and candy comes from these plants. The vanilla vine has been cultivated in Mexico for hundreds of years. This type of vanilla has been introduced into other tropical areas. Comoros, Indonesia, Madagascar, and Reunion produce much of the world's supply. Another species grows on the island of Tahiti in the South Pacific.

The vanilla vine has little rootlets by which the plant attaches itself to trees. The cultivated plant lives about 10 years. It produces its first crop after three years.

The plant produces a fruit in the shape of a cylindrical *pod* (bean) from 5 to 10 inches (13 to 25 centimeters) long. The fruit has an oily black pulp that holds many tiny black seeds. The pods are gathered when they are a yellow-green color. Then the curing, or drying, process takes place. This process shrinks the bean and turns it a rich, chocolate-brown color. The process also gives the bean the flavor and aroma of vanilla as we know it.

Vanilla extract is prepared by a complicated, expensive process. The beans are chopped and percolated with alcohol and water. Food scientists have developed artificial vanilla flavors that cost less. David S. Seigler

Scientific classification. Vanilla is in the orchid family, Orchidaceae. The scientific name for the vine of Mexico and Madagascar is *Vanilla planifolia*.

Van Lawick-Goodall, Jane. See Goodall, Jane.
Van Leeuwenhoek, Anton. See Leeuwenhoek, Anton van.
Van Leyden, *vahn LY duhn,* **Lucas** (1494?-1533), was a Dutch graphic artist and painter best known for his en-

months of his life fighting a mental illness that has never been firmly diagnosed. In this time, periods of deep depression alternated with periods of great productivity. Realizing that his mental condition would not improve, he committed suicide on July 29, 1890. Ann Friedman

See also **Expressionism; Painting** (Postimpressionism; picture: The Starry Night); **Postimpressionism.**

Additional resources

Greenberg, Jan, and Jordan, Sandra. *Vincent van Gogh.* Delacorte, 2001. Younger readers.
Homburg, Cornelia, and others. *Vincent van Gogh and the Painters of the Petit Boulevard.* Rizzoli, 2001.

Vanier, *va NYAY,* **Georges-Philias,** *zhawrzh FIHL ee uhs* (1888-1967), served as governor general of Canada from 1959 to 1967. He was the first French Canadian and the first Roman Catholic to hold the office, which represents the British monarch in Canada.

During Vanier's term as governor general, an independence movement in Quebec gained strength. Vanier worked for national unity and respect for Canadians' diverse ethnic backgrounds. His name is also spelled Georges-Philéas Vanier.

Vanier was born on April 23, 1888, in Montreal, Quebec. He earned his law degree at Laval University in Quebec, and then practiced law for a few years before joining the Army. He served in Europe during World War I (1914-1918), where he lost a leg fighting in France. During World War II (1939-1945), Vanier held several posts in the Canadian government and military. He reached the rank of major general. From 1944 to 1953, he was Canada's ambassador to France. Vanier died on March 5, 1967. J. L. Granatstein

Abraham and Isaac (early 1500's); The Metropolitan Museum of Art, New York City, Harris Brisbane Dick Fund, 1925

A woodcut by Lucas Van Leyden shows the landscape setting and skillful use of perspective that are typical of his work.

gravings. He became one of the first artists to design compositions in which the main character is not necessarily the largest or most central figure. Lucas's engravings have been praised for their richly detailed landscape settings. He knew and admired the work of German engravers, especially Albrecht Dürer. However, his engraving style is less ornamental than theirs, using fine and precise strokes of the *burin* (engraver's cutting tool). This technique tended to create effects of light and shadow, rather than contour.

Lucas was born in Leiden, the Netherlands. The engravings he made between the ages of about 16 and 26 are considered his best and most original, including *Ecce Homo* and *The Milkmaid* (both 1510). He died on Aug. 8, 1533.   Jane Campbell Hutchison

Van Rensselaer, *van REHN suh luhr,* **Kiliaen** (1585?-1643), was one of the leading Dutch colonizers of the territory that later became New York. In 1629, the Dutch West India Company authorized large grants of land in New Netherland to company shareholders who promised to colonize their lands. The land grants were called *patroonships.* Van Rensselaer and four other wealthy and prominent shareholders founded patroonships, but only Van Rensselaer's colony succeeded. His colony of Rensselaerswyck included two counties and part of a third on both banks of the Hudson River south of Albany. Van Rensselaer invested most of his fortune earned as a diamond merchant in the colony, but he had great difficulty recruiting settlers.

Van Rensselaer was born in Hasselt, north of Zwolle, in the Netherlands. He died in Amsterdam and was buried there on Oct. 7, 1643.   Oliver A. Rink

Vanuatu, *VAH noo AH too,* is an island country in the southwest Pacific Ocean. It consists of 80 islands that cover about 4,700 square miles (12,200 square kilometers) of land. The country's largest islands are, in order of size, Espiritu Santo, Malakula, Efate, Erromango, and Tanna. Vanuatu has about 223,000 people. Port-Vila, on Efate, is the the nation's capital and largest urban community. It has a population of about 30,000. From 1906 to 1980, the French and British jointly governed the islands, then called the New Hebrides. In 1980, the islands became the independent nation of Vanuatu.

Government. Vanuatu is a republic. A Parliament, whose members are elected by the people to four-year terms, makes the country's laws. A prime minister, who heads the majority party in Parliament, runs the government with the aid of a Council of Ministers. Village, regional, and island councils handle local government affairs. The Parliament and the regional council presidents elect a president to a five-year term. The president's role is chiefly ceremonial.

People. More than 90 percent of Vanuatu's people are Melanesians. Asians, Europeans, and Polynesians make up the rest of the population. About 75 percent of the people live in rural villages. Many village houses are made of wood, bamboo, and palm leaves. Port-Vila and Luganville—on Espiritu Santo—are the only urban communities. More than 100 languages are spoken in Vanuatu. Bislama, a type of Pidgin English that combines mainly English words and Melanesian grammar, is commonly used throughout the country (see **Pidgin English**). Vanuatu has about 300 elementary schools and several high schools. About 85 percent of the people are Chris-

tians, and most of the rest practice local religions.

Land and climate. The islands of Vanuatu form a Y-shaped chain that extends about 500 miles (800 kilometers) from north to south. Most of the islands have narrow coastal plains and mountainous interiors. Several have active volcanoes. The northern islands have a hot, rainy climate, with a year-round temperature of about 80 °F (27 °C) and annual rainfall of about 120 inches (305 centimeters). Temperatures in the southern islands range from about 67 to 88 °F (19 to 31 °C), and the yearly rainfall totals about 90 inches (230 centimeters). Vanuatu lies in an area where cyclones occur.

Economy of Vanuatu is based on agriculture. Farmers grow fruits and vegetables; raise cattle, chickens, and hogs; and catch fish. Beef, cacao, and *copra* (dried coconut meat) are among the leading exports. Manufacturing centers on the processing of agricultural and fishing products. Tourism and offshore banking are also important to the economy. Small ships and airplanes serve as the main means of transportation among the islands. Vanuatu has few good roads and no railroads.

History. Melanesians have lived in what is now Vanuatu for at least 3,000 years. In 1606, Pedro Fernandez de Quirós, the commander of a Spanish expedition from Peru, became the first European to see the islands. The British explorer James Cook mapped the region in 1774 and named the islands the New Hebrides after the Hebrides islands of Scotland.

British and French traders, missionaries, and settlers began coming to the islands during the 1840's. In 1887, the United Kingdom and France set up a joint naval

Vanuatu

▬▬	International boundary
✪	National capital
✈	Airport
•	Town
+	Elevation above sea level

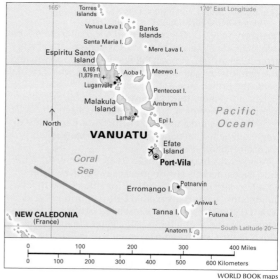

WORLD BOOK maps

Vanuatu Tourist Information Bureau

Vanuatu consists of 80 islands in the southwest Pacific Ocean. People enjoy boating on sparkling blue water near the sandy shore of one of the islands, *shown here.*

commission to oversee the area. In 1906, the commission was replaced by a joint British and French government called a condominium.

After the United States entered World War II in 1941, the New Hebrides became a major Allied military base. United States troops built roads, bridges, and airstrips there. A movement for independence began in the islands during the 1960's. The New Hebrides became the independent nation of Vanuatu on July 30, 1980.

In 1987, a cyclone struck Vanuatu. It caused a number of deaths and much damage.   Lamont Lindstrom

Van Winkle, Rip. See Rip Van Winkle.

Vanzetti, Bartolomeo. See Sacco-Vanzetti case.

Vapor is the gaseous state into which solids and liquids pass when heated. In a technical sense, both oxygen and steam are vapors. But a distinction can be made between gases and vapors. Gases, such as oxygen, remain gases when compressed at ordinary temperatures. Vapors, such as steam, resume their liquid or solid state under high pressure at ordinary temperatures. The process of converting a substance from liquid into vapor is called *vaporization. Evaporation* and *boiling* of liquids are forms of vaporization. In evaporation, the change to a vaporous form happens slowly. In boiling, it occurs rapidly. The formation of vapor directly from a solid state is called *sublimation.* Vaporization in connection with atmospheric conditions bears an important relation to climate. Water vapor is always present in the air. When condensed under varying conditions, water vapor forms clouds, dew, rain, or snow. See also **Boiling point; Evaporation; Gas.**   Richard A. Martin

Vapor lock occurs in a gasoline engine when some of the gasoline boils in the fuel-supply system. Excessive heating of the engine may cause boiling, or *vaporization,* of the fuel. This reduces the amount of fuel pumped to the engine, because vapor takes up more space than liquid. The engine then runs erratically or stops until the vaporized gasoline cools and turns to liquid. Vapor locks occur most often during long, steep climbs on hot days, or when slowing suddenly after a hard drive. See also **Fuel injection.**   David E. Cole

Vapor trail. See Contrail.

Varanasi, *vuh RAH nuh see* (pop. 1,100,748), is an ancient holy city of the Hindus in northern India. It is sometimes called the cultural capital of India. The city, also known as Banaras, Benares, or Kashi, lies along a sandy ridge on the west bank of the Ganges River (see **India** [political map]).

Varanasi is one of the largest cities in the state of Uttar Pradesh. Products of the city include shawls, saris, gold-embroidered cloth, hand-hammered brassware, heavy gold and silver jewelry, and fine silk fabrics.

The Ganges River, considered sacred by the Hindus, is one of Varanasi's greatest attractions. Each year, about 2 million Hindus make pilgrimages from all parts of India to bathe in the Ganges. They can enter the river from over 80 *ghats* (stairways along the river) before saying their daily prayers. The city also has thousands of temples, shrines, monasteries, and palaces. Varanasi, known as a seat of learning, is the site of Banaras Hindu University and many other universities and colleges.

Rana P. B. Singh

See also **Asia** (picture: Hindus bathe in the Ganges River).

Varennes, Pierre Gaultier de. See La Vérendrye, Sieur de.

Varèse, *vah REHZ,* **Edgard,** *ehd GAIR* (1883-1965), was a leading composer of the early 1900's. He refused to follow any school or system of musical composition and did not even consider himself a composer in the traditional sense. Varèse declared he was merely an "organizer of sounds." His works influenced many American and European composers of the mid-1900's.

Varèse composed almost all of his important works from 1921 to 1935. He was one of the first to write for percussion instruments only. His most famous composition, *Ionisation* (1931), requires 13 performers who play 39 percussion instruments, including an assortment of drums, a piano, gongs, and chimes. The work also includes two sirens and a "lion's roar." These compositions are mostly played by traditional instruments, but they reflect Varèse's early interest in the unusual sounds and precise ability to control them that he later found in electronic music (see **Electronic music**).

Varèse was born on Dec. 22, 1883, in Paris and settled in the United States in 1915. He became a U.S. citizen in 1926. Varèse founded the New Symphony Orchestra in 1919 and helped establish the International Composers Guild in 1921. Both organizations were dedicated to promoting modern music. Varèse died on Nov. 6, 1965.

Stephen Jaffe

Vargas Llosa, *VAHR gahs YOH sah,* **Mario** (1936-   ), is the first Peruvian novelist to win international renown. Vargas Llosa often deals with the issues of violence and political corruption in Peruvian society. He uses experimental techniques, including intermingled plotlines, shifting time frames, and multiple points of view, to express his themes. Much of his fiction also reveals his skill as a storyteller.

Vargas Llosa's first novel, *The Time of the Hero* (1963), explores the theme of injustice through a tale of theft and murder in a military academy. *The Green House* (1966) examines conflicts among Peru's economic classes and its ethnic and regional groups. In *Conversation in the Cathedral* (1969), Vargas Llosa explores hypocrisy and corruption in Peruvian business and politics. *The War of the End of the World* (1981) is a historical novel about a rebellion in Brazil. Vargas Llosa's other novels include the humorous *Captain Pantoja and the Special Service* (1973) and *Aunt Julia and the Scriptwriter* (1977); *The Real Life of Alejandro Mayta* (1984); *In Praise of the Stepmother* (1990); *The Notebooks of Don Rigoberto* (1998); *The Feast of the Goat* (2001); *The Way to Paradise* (2003); and *The Bad Girl* (2007). His essays on culture, government, and society were collected in *Making Waves* (1997) and *The Language of Passion* (2003).

Vargas Llosa was born on March 28, 1936, in Arequipa. He campaigned for president of Peru but lost a run-off election in 1990. Vargas Llosa has also written drama, short stories, and the autobiography *A Fish in the Water* (1994).   Naomi Lindstrom

See also **Latin American literature** (The "Boom").

Variation, in music, is the technique of adding to or changing some element of a composition. The technique is often called *theme and variations.* Composers take a theme—either their own or that of another composer—and write a set of variations on that theme.

The number of variations that can be written on a theme is limited only by the composer's imagination. The main types are *melodic variation* and *harmonic variation.* In melodic variation, the melody is altered but remains recognizable. For example, it may be speeded up or slowed down, or played in different meters. In harmonic variation, the composer may completely change the melody, but the basic harmony is preserved.

Spanish and English composers originated the theme and variations form in the 1500's. Since that time, most composers have used the form, either for independent pieces or as sections of sonatas, symphonies, and other large-scale instrumental works.   Stewart L. Ross

Varicella. See Chickenpox.

Varicose vein, *VAIR uh kohs,* is a swollen vein caused by some body condition that interferes with the flow of blood toward the heart. Veins in the legs often become varicose, especially when a person stands a great deal. Heart and liver diseases, gout, pregnancy, abdominal tumors, and tight garters may also cause varicose veins.

In advanced cases of varicose veins, bluish knotty lumps form along the vein. The patient feels considerable pain in the leg. The chief dangers are that blood will clot in the vein or that the vein will burst, and cause hemorrhage. The diseased veins can also keep the tissues from getting enough nourishment. Water may collect under the skin and cause swelling. Then the leg is likely to develop ulcers.

Physicians suggest wearing an elastic stocking or bandage, which will support the varicose vein with steady pressure. Physicians often inject the varicose veins with drugs that tend to shrink them. They may also remove the veins by surgery. A disorder known as *hemorrhoids* is varicose veins of the rectum.   Richard H. Dean

See also **Hemorrhoids.**

Varnish is a transparent liquid used to protect wood, metal, and other materials from air and moisture, and to improve their appearance. A varnish leaves a hard, glossy film when it dries.

Clear varnishes protect the surface of wood while allowing the natural grain of the wood to show through.

Varnish stains contain dyes that change the color of the wood but still bring out the grain. Varnishes used on metal are sometimes called *lacquers.* Lacquers help prevent corrosion without dulling the metallic appearance. Varnishes are also used to protect insulating wires, masonry, and paper from moisture.

Varnishes can be baked on objects in ovens at temperatures of 150 to 400 °F (66 to 200 °C). This improves the wearing quality of the varnished object.

Types of varnish. There are two main classes of varnishes, spirit and oleoresinous. *Spirit varnishes* are made of chemicals called *resins.* The resins are dissolved in a quickly evaporating solvent such as alcohol. These varnishes dry when the solvent evaporates. Shellac is a common spirit varnish. Other spirit varnishes include Japan, dammar, and pyroxylin lacquers.

Oleoresinous varnishes are mixtures of resins and drying oils that are heated and dissolved in turpentine or petroleum products. These varnishes dry in two ways, by evaporation of the solvent, and by the hardening of the resin-oil mixture when it combines with oxygen. Oleoresinous varnishes withstand outdoor conditions well. Spar varnish, used on the wood exterior of boats, is an oleoresinous varnish.

Making varnish. Both natural and synthetic resins are used to make varnish. *Natural resins* come from living plants and fossil plants. Shellac, dammar, and rosin are natural resins. *Synthetic resins* include such chemical compounds as phenol-formaldehyde, urea-formaldehyde, alkyd (glyceryl phthalate), and cumar.

In making spirit varnishes, the resin is dissolved by churning it with the solvent. Small amounts of heat are sometimes used to speed the dissolving process. After the resin is dissolved, the varnish is refined by filtering and is then ready for use.

In making oleoresinous varnishes, the oil and resin are cooked in closed kettles that hold 5,000 gallons (19,000 liters) or more. The mixture is kept at a temperature of 450 to 700 °F (230 to 370 °C) until it reaches the desired *body* (thickness). Then the mixture is cooled, and thinners are added. Some natural resins will not dissolve easily in oils. These resins are heated to temperatures of 482 to 662 °F (250 to 350 °C) to break them down into smaller, more soluble molecules. This process is called *pyrolysis.*

Drying oils are added to the varnish to hasten the drying time. Linseed oil was probably the first oil to be used in varnishes. Many other drying oils, such as perilla, tung, dehydrated castor, soybean, and fish oils, are used today. Compounds of lead, cobalt, or manganese are often added to quicken drying.

Varnishes are named by giving the number of gallons of oil that have been mixed with 100 pounds of resin. For example, a 30-gallon tung-oil kauri varnish is made with 30 gallons of tung oil and 100 pounds of kauri resin. Varnishes used on outdoor surfaces contain more oil than those used indoors.   Roger D. Barry

See also **Airbrush; Lacquer; Resin; Shellac.**

Vasco Da Gama. See Da Gama, Vasco.

Vase is a general term for a decorative or ornamental hollow vessel that is usually used to hold flowers. For illustrations of vases, see **Art Nouveau; China** (The arts); **Delft; Flower** (Flower arranging); **Furies; Islamic art; Painting** (Greek painting); **Porcelain; Pottery.**

Vasectomy is a surgical procedure performed to permanently prevent a man from fathering children. In adult males, sperm cells are produced in a pair of sex glands called *testicles*. The sperm travel through two tubes called the *vas deferens* to a gland called the *prostate*. In the prostate, the vas deferens meet the ducts of two fluid-producing glands called *seminal vesicles*. Fluids produced by the prostate and seminal vesicles mix with sperm to form a thick liquid called *semen*. Semen supports sperm and helps carry them out of the body through the penis. A vasectomy blocks the sperm flow in the vas deferens, so the semen will carry no sperm.

Vasectomy is performed through a small incision or puncture in the *scrotum,* the pouch behind the penis that contains the testicles. The surgeon exposes the vas deferens and then removes sections of them, ties or burns the ends, or uses a combination of these methods. After a vasectomy, the testicles continue to produce sperm, but they cannot enter the semen and so are reabsorbed by the body. It may take one to six months, however, to completely eliminate sperm from the vas deferens. During this time, the man remains fertile. A vasectomy does not affect a man's sexual function.

A vasectomy is safer, easier to perform, and less expensive than female surgical sterilization. It is a voluntary procedure, and men who choose to have it done must be certain they wish to become permanently sterile. Surgical techniques to reverse a vasectomy and restore fertility have success rates of less than 50 to 70 percent.   Richard E. Berger

See also **Birth control; Reproduction, Human.**

Vaseline. See Petrolatum.

Vásquez de Coronado, Francisco. See Coronado, Francisco Vásquez de.

Vassar, Matthew (1792-1868), was an American brewer who founded Vassar College. He was born on April 29, 1792, in East Tuddingham, England, and was brought to the United States in 1796. He established a successful brewery in Poughkeepsie, New York, and made a large fortune. He also owned a whaling dock in Poughkeepsie and was part owner of a whaling fleet. Vassar became interested in higher education for women, and in 1861 gave a large sum of money to found Vassar College. The wide publicity given to the venture created interest in college education for women throughout the world. Gifts by Vassar to the college during his life totaled more than $800,000. Matthew Vassar died on June 23, 1868.   Peter A. Coclanis

Vassar College is a coeducational liberal arts college at Poughkeepsie, New York. It is privately controlled and offers courses in languages and literature, arts, physical sciences, and social sciences. Vassar students live in residence houses on a 1,000-acre (400-hectare) campus. Vassar was founded as a school for women in 1861. It was the first women's college to have equipment and resources equal to those of men's colleges. Vassar became coeducational in 1969. See also **Vassar, Matthew.**

Critically reviewed by Vassar College

Vatican City, *VAT ih kuhn* (pop. 1,000), is the smallest independent country in the world. It serves as the spiritual and governmental center of the Roman Catholic Church, the largest Christian church in the world. Vatican City covers only 109 acres (44 hectares), but it exercises spiritual influence over millions of Roman Catholics. Its ruler is the pope. Vatican City lies entirely within the city of Rome, Italy. But it is foreign soil to Italian citizens. Vatican City has been an independent country since 1929. For the location of Vatican City, see **Italy** (political map); **Rome** (map: Central Rome).

The official name of Vatican City in Italian is Stato della Città del Vaticano (The State of Vatican City). *The Vatican* is a short name for the country and for the city that makes up the country. People often use the term *Vatican* to refer to the pope and the government of Vatican City.

Description

Vatican City is about as large as an average city park. It lies on Vatican Hill in northwestern Rome, just west of the Tiber River. High stone walls surround most of the city. The irregularly shaped area within these walls contains picturesque buildings in several architectural styles. It also contains many courtyards, landscaped gardens, and quiet streets. The huge St. Peter's Basilica, with its giant dome, dominates the entire city.

St. Peter's Basilica is one of the world's largest Christian churches. A basilica is a church that is given certain ceremonial privileges by the pope. St. Peter's is not a cathedral, which is the principal church of a bishop's diocese and contains his official throne. The pope is the bishop of Rome, and his cathedral church is the Basilica of St. John Lateran. See **Saint Peter's Basilica.**

Vatican Palace is a group of connected buildings with well over 1,000 rooms. The palace's various apartments, chapels, museums, and other areas cluster around several open courts. The pope's apartment, the offices of the Secretariate of State, and reception rooms and halls occupy one part of the palace. The remainder is devoted largely to the Vatican Museums, the Vatican Archive, and the Vatican Library.

Vatican Museums have a priceless collection of statuary, including the famous *Apollo Belvedere* and the *Laocoön* (see **Laocoön** [picture]). The museums also have large sections devoted to pagan and Christian inscriptions, to Egyptian and Etruscan antiquities, and to modern religious art. The many rooms and chapels within the museums are decorated by the works of such master artists as Fra Angelico, Leonardo da Vinci, Pinturicchio, Raphael, and Titian. Some of Michelangelo's greatest paintings decorate the ceiling and one large wall of the Sistine Chapel (see **Michelangelo; Sistine Chapel**).

Vatican Archive contains important religious and historical documents. Pope Paul V organized the archive in 1612. It houses such important documents as the request of the English Parliament for the annulment of the marriage of Henry VIII to Catherine of Aragon (1530), the original report on the trial of Galileo (1633), and the concordat of Napoleon (1801). Pope Leo XIII opened the archive to scholars in 1881. Since then, many European nations have created historical institutes to search the archives for information on their particular countries.

Vatican Library has one of the world's largest and most valuable collections of early manuscripts and books.

Other buildings belonging to Vatican City but located outside the city walls include the basilicas of St. John Lateran, St. Paul's-outside-the-Walls, and St. Mary Major, all in Rome; and the pope's summer villa and the Vatican observatory at Castel Gandolfo.

Vatican City covers an area of only 109 acres (44 hectares) in northwestern Rome. This picture shows a portion of the gardens to the left of St. Peter's Basilica, with its famous dome. St. Peter's Square extends from the church entrance to the right.

Administration

The pope, as absolute ruler of Vatican City, heads all government branches. But, since he devotes his time primarily to religious and ecclesiastical matters, he delegates most of his temporal authority to other officials.

The internal domestic affairs of Vatican City are the responsibility of the Pontifical Commission for the State of Vatican City, which is appointed by the pope. The president of the commission, whose duties resemble those of a mayor, directs Vatican City's administration. Foreign affairs are handled by the Cardinal Secretary of State, who also coordinates ecclesiastical and political affairs. The Vatican has civil law courts in addition to the Tribunal of the Roman Rota, which handles religious cases. But most civil criminal cases are prosecuted by the Italian government. The office of the Master of Papal Ceremonies directs all ceremonies in which the pope takes part. The Prefecture of the Papal Household arranges audiences with the pope and also handles matters of protocol and etiquette. Vatican finances are controlled by a number of administrations, or departments.

Vatican City issues its own coins, license plates, and postage stamps. The pope's yellow-and-white banner is the official state flag of Vatican City (see **Flag** [picture: Flags of Europe]).

Public works. The Vatican maintains its own lighting and street-cleaning services, mail system, telephone and telegraph systems, and water supply. It also has its own bank, a large printing plant, and a rarely occupied jail. Although the state has its own railroad station, no one has ever bought a ticket to Vatican City. The 300 yards (270 meters) of track that connect the station in Vatican City with an Italian railroad carry only freight.

Armed forces. Vatican City has no army or navy. It depends on the Italian military for defense. However, the Vatican does have a military corps known as the Swiss Guard. The Swiss Guard maintains a constant watch over the pope and his personal residence (see **Swiss Guard**). In addition, the Central Office of Vigilance guards Vatican City. The St. Peter and Paul Association provides Vatican City with everyday police services.

Diplomatic corps of Vatican City includes *legates* (ambassadors) and other diplomatic personnel. The pope maintains diplomatic relations with most of the countries of the world through the corps. The highest-ranking legates of the corps, the papal ambassadors, are called the *nuncios*. The nuncios serve as representatives to governments and religious groups of various nations, including Canada, the United Kingdom, and the United States. Legates of lesser rank are called *pro-nuncios*. Papal representatives in countries that have no formal diplomatic relations with the Vatican are called *apostolic delegates.*

Communications. The Vatican publishes *L'Osservatore Romano,* one of the most influential daily newspapers in the world. The Vatican also has a press office that reports news daily. Vatican Radio, a broadcasting station devoted to serving the pope's ministry, was founded in 1931 with the assistance of the Italian scientist Guglielmo Marconi. The network broadcasts news and programming in numerous languages. The Vatican Television Center produces live programming of papal events.

History

Vatican Hill was once the site of the Roman Emperor Nero's public gardens and circus. Many early Christians suffered martyrdom there. According to tradition, Saint Peter was crucified in Nero's circus and buried in a nearby tomb. In the A.D. 100's, a shrine was erected on the site, and it became a place for Christian pilgrimages.

In the A.D. 300's, the Christian emperor Constantine the Great built a basilica over the tomb in which Saint Peter was believed to be buried. The basilica was one of the largest building projects undertaken in ancient Rome. The basilica endured for over 1,000 years. The Vatican Palace and other structures were gradually built around the basilica. But the main residence of the popes during the Middle Ages was the Lateran Palace in Rome, not the Vatican. In the early 1500's, construction began on the current St. Peter's Basilica, which was built on the site of the first basilica.

For hundreds of years, popes ruled an area in central Italy called the Papal States. With the unification of Italy in 1861, the Kingdom of Italy took over the Papal States. Rome became the capital of Italy in 1871. In protest, Pope Pius IX and his successors withdrew inside the Vatican and refused to deal with the Italian government. In 1929, the Lateran Treaty was signed. By the terms of the treaty, the pope gave up all claim to the Papal States, and Italy agreed to the establishment of the independent State of Vatican City. For the provisions of this treaty, see **Papal States.**

In 1939, Pope Pius XII initiated a series of excavations beneath St. Peter's Basilica. Archaeologists uncovered a tomb thought to be that of Saint Peter, as well as parts of a Roman *necropolis* (cemetery).   Michael Keating

See also **Pope; Roman Catholic Church.**

Additional resources

McDowell, Bart. *Inside the Vatican.* 1991. Reprint. National Geographic Soc., 2005.
Scotti, R. A. *Basilica: The Splendor and the Scandal: Building St. Peter's.* Viking, 2006.
Tronzo, William, ed. *St. Peter's in the Vatican.* Cambridge, 2005.

Vatican Council I was the 20th *ecumenical* (general) council of the Roman Catholic Church. Pope Pius IX summoned the council, which met in Rome from December 1869 to September 1870. It was the first ecumenical council since the Council of Trent ended in 1563. About 800 bishops and other churchmen participated in the council, and it gathered for the first time bishops from throughout the world. See **Pius IX.**

Vatican I took a stand against many of the *secular* (nonreligious) trends of the age. It promoted a centralized church extending beyond national boundaries with supreme authority residing in the pope. The council proclaimed the *infallibility* of the pope's teaching authority in the constitution *Pastor Aeternus (The Eternal Shepherd).* The constitution stated that the pope cannot commit error when he speaks as head of the church to define solemnly, in matters of faith and morals, what is to be accepted by all Roman Catholics as the revelation coming from Jesus Christ and his apostles.

The council ended after the new Kingdom of Italy annexed Rome, causing the pope to withdraw to the Vatican Palace. Thus, the period of Vatican I witnessed both the peak of the pope's religious authority and the disappearance of his civil power.   Robert P. Imbelli

Vatican Council II was the 21st *ecumenical* (general) council of the Roman Catholic Church. Pope John XXIII called the council, which met in four sessions in Rome. The first session ran from Oct. 11 to Dec. 8, 1962; the second session from Sept. 29 to Dec. 4, 1963; the third

session from Sept. 14 to Nov. 21, 1964; and the final session from Sept. 14 to Dec. 8, 1965. Vatican Council II was the first ecumenical council held by the church since the suspension of Vatican Council I in 1870.

John XXIII was elected pope in 1958 at the age of 76. On Jan. 25, 1959—less than three months after his election—John surprised the world by announcing his intention to summon an ecumenical council of the Catholic Church. After three years of preparation, the council opened on Oct. 12, 1962, with about 2,500 participants and many non-Catholic observers. It was the largest church council in history, far surpassing the approximately 800 churchmen who attended Vatican Council I.

The work of the council. Commissions directed by the Roman Curia, the pope's administrative arm, prepared draft documents on a variety of subjects for council consideration. However, many bishops in the council found the drafts insufficiently pastoral and too conservative in tone. The council rejected the drafts and began, with the support of the pope, to chart its own course, which led to many progressive and reforming actions.

John XXIII died on June 3, 1963, and Paul VI was elected the next pope. Paul had been a leading progressive in the first session of the council. He reconvened the council and guided it to its conclusion.

Vatican Council II issued 16 documents—four *constitutions,* three *declarations,* and nine *decrees.* The most important were the constitutions, which dealt with the liturgy, divine revelation, and the church.

The Constitution on the Liturgy (called *Sacrosanctum Concilium* in Latin) started a number of reforms. The constitution led to the celebration of the Mass in the *vernacular*—a congregation's native language—instead of in the traditional Latin. This constitution was one of the council's most far-reaching accomplishments. It brought the central act of Catholic worship closer to the people and made it clear that the celebration was one in which the entire Catholic community played a part.

The Constitution of Divine Revelation (Dei Verbum) restored the Bible to a central place in Catholic thought and practice. It insisted that the church's teaching authority must always be submissive to the word of God. The constitution stressed that revelation itself is not found primarily in verbal statements, but in the person of Jesus Christ who is the fullness of revelation. However, the whole community, under the leadership of its bishops, lives out the revelation it has received and transmits it from generation to generation. For centuries, Catholic theologians had treated revelation in a philosophical and abstract fashion. In contrast, Vatican Council II adopted a more Biblical language and perspective. It presented revelation as the concrete personal encounter of men and women in history with the living God who calls them to salvation.

The Dogmatic Constitution on the Church (Lumen Gentium) described the church as the visible sign or sacrament of humanity's union with God and with one another. This constitution's favorite image of the church was that of "the people of God." By emphasizing this image, the council underscored the church's involvement in human history and its close spiritual ties with the people of Israel. This focus on the church as the whole people of God enabled the council to break with the one-sided emphasis of preceding centuries on the power of the clergy. The constitution gave lay people specific responsibilities and rights within the church.

One key feature of this constitution was its teaching on the "collegiality of bishops." According to the document, the bishops and the pope form one body. This teaching complemented Vatican Council I's teaching on papal primacy and infallibility (see **Vatican Council I**). It also supported the view of the church as a communion of local churches with the pope as its head. The constitution thus returned to the bishops some of the authority the papacy had absorbed over the centuries.

The Pastoral Constitution on the Church in the Modern World (Gaudium et Spes) promoted a dialogue between the Catholic Church and the modern world. Since the French Revolution (1789-1799), much of the church opposed modern attitudes in non-Catholic society, some of which were considered hostile to Christianity. The constitution recognized that the church exists in the world and must proclaim its message in terms the world can understand. The constitution also acknowledged that the church has much to learn from the authentic values of modern life. The constitution altered the isolation from the non-Catholic world that had characterized previous church councils. In the document, John's *aggiornamento* (modernization) found practical expression in establishing a new relationship with non-Catholics.

Other documents. The council issued two notable declarations. One, called *Declaration on the Relation of the Church to non-Christian Religions (Nostra Aetate)*, celebrated the special spiritual ties binding Christians and Jews. It denounced all forms of anti-Semitism and laid the basis for a new understanding and respect between Christians and Jews. The *Declaration on Religious Liberty (Dignitatis Humanae)* owed much to the efforts of bishops and theologians in the United States, especially the Jesuit theologian John Courtney Murray. The declaration broke with the idea that "error has no rights." It stressed that individual conscience demands respect, especially in matters of religious faith and observance.

The influence of the council. Vatican Council II started the most far-reaching reforms within the Catholic church in 1,000 years. Probably few participants in the council fully realized the magnitude of the changes they had set in motion. The council helped transform the church from a European-centered institution into a more genuinely worldwide church.

These striking transformations also created tensions. From the beginning of the council, there were conflicts between conservative and progressive views. Some Catholics believed the council actions resulted in too much change. They opposed Catholic reformers who wanted to vigorously update worship, doctrine, and the church's view of its place in the world. As one legacy of the council, Catholics have tried to emphasize the importance of the local or regional church united around its own bishop. They have also attempted to affirm a common faith while encouraging different cultural expressions of that faith.   Robert P. Imbelli

See also **Religious life** (Religious life in the 1900's); **Roman Catholic Church** (Vatican Council II; picture).

Vaudeville, *VAW duh vihl* or *VOHD vihl,* is a kind of theatrical entertainment that features a wide variety of acts. It was the most popular form of entertainment in the United States from the 1880's to the early 1930's.

Vaudeville developed many stars who later gained great success in other types of entertainment, especially motion pictures and radio. These stars included Jack Benny, George Burns, Eddie Cantor, W. C. Fields, Al Jolson, Sophie Tucker, and Ed Wynn.

Some vaudeville theaters presented 20 or more acts in a single *bill* (performance). But the standard pattern was 8 to 10 acts. A vaudeville show presented jugglers, animal acts, skits, recitations, celebrities of the day, singers, and, most popular of all, comics and magicians.

Because of the efforts of powerful producers and theater owners, vaudeville became a highly organized nationwide big business. A number of individuals controlled large *circuits* (chains) of theaters. The best known of these circuits were operated by E. F. Albee, Martin Beck, Willie Hammerstein, B. F. Keith, Marcus Loew, William Morris, Alexander Pantages, and F. F. Proctor. All vaudeville performers wanted to star in "big-time" theaters that presented only two shows a day. But most appeared in "small-time" theaters that offered 3 to 12 shows a day. Some theaters presented shows that began about 9:30 a.m. and lasted until about 10:30 p.m.

The term *vaudeville* comes from a French word for a light play with music that was popular in France during the 1800's. The American form grew out of attempts by saloon owners to attract more customers by offering free shows. These shows were known as *variety.* At first, variety had a bad reputation because it took place in saloons and often included vulgar material. But by the 1890's, it had achieved respectability under the more elegant French name of *vaudeville.* Soon vaudeville had become the major form of live entertainment for family audiences. Showman Tony Pastor is credited with converting vaudeville into family entertainment by prohibiting drinks and upgrading the quality of the performers. He presented many famous vaudeville stars at Tony Pastor's Opera House in New York City.

Vaudeville's popularity declined with the development of sound motion pictures in the late 1920's. But vaudeville-style acts are still presented in some nightclubs and on television.   Don B. Wilmeth

See also **Williams, Bert.**

Additional resources

Slide, Anthony. *The Encyclopedia of Vaudeville.* Greenwood, 1994.
Trav S. D. *No Applause—Just Throw Money, or, The Book That Made Vaudeville Famous.* Faber & Faber, 2005.

Vaughan, Sarah (1924-1990), was a famous jazz singer who also achieved great success in popular music. She sang in a rich contralto voice with a three-octave range. Her sensitivity to harmony and her skill in improvising singled her out as one of the great musical performers of the 1900's. Vaughan was nicknamed "Sassy" because of her personality and "The Divine One" because of the respect other musicians had for her voice and musicianship.

Sarah Lois Vaughan

Magnum Photos

Sarah Vaughan

was born on March 27, 1924, in Newark, New Jersey. She began her career by winning a talent contest in New York City at age 18. From 1943 to 1946, she sang with several bands. Later, she worked with many important jazz musicians, including Count Basie, Dizzy Gillespie, Miles Davis, and Charlie Parker. From 1947 through the 1980's, she led several combos, touring and recording with the groups. Her first hit recordings were "Lover Man" (1945) and "Tenderly," "I Cover the Waterfront," and "It's Magic" (all 1947). Vaughan's other popular records included "Mean to Me" (1950), "Lullaby of Birdland" (1954), and "Broken-Hearted Melody" and "Misty" (both 1958). She died on April 3, 1990.   Frank Tirro

Vaughan Williams, *vawn WIHL yuhmz,* **Ralph,** *rayf,* (1872-1958), was one of the United Kingdom's foremost composers. His music mingles the flavors of English folk songs and Tudor church music, both of which he studied intensively. His major works include nine symphonies and six operas. He also composed music for the coronation of Queen Elizabeth II in 1953.

Vaughan Williams was born on Oct. 12, 1872, in the parish of Down Ampney, Gloucestershire. He began composing comparatively late in life. His notable earlier works include the song cycle *On Wenlock Edge* (1909) to poems by A. E. Housman; *A Sea Symphony* (1909) for orchestra and voices; *Fantasia on a Theme by Thomas Tallis* (1910) for strings; *A London Symphony* (1914); and an opera on folk themes, *Hugh the Drover* (completed in 1914, first performed in 1924).

Vaughan Williams became more productive as he grew older. His music also turned more somber and more abstract. His Piano Concerto (1931), later revised for two pianos and orchestra, pointed the way toward his final period. This period included his last four symphonies and the opera *The Pilgrim's Progress* (1951). His *Concerto for Bass Tuba* (1954) demonstrates his interest in less popular instruments, such as the harmonica, vibraphone, and flugelhorn. Vaughan Williams died on Aug. 26, 1958.   Stewart L. Ross

Vault is an architectural term for an arched roof or ceiling. Vaults are most commonly made of brick, concrete, or stone. The main kinds are (1) the barrel vault, (2) the groined vault, (3) the ribbed vault, and (4) the dome.

The barrel vault, the simplest type, is a single continuous unbroken arch in the form of a tunnel. The groined vault is formed by joining two barrel vaults of the same shape at right angles. The lines at which the two vaults meet are called *groins.* In the ribbed vault, projecting ribs cover the groins, or are placed in decorative patterns elsewhere on the vault's surface. The dome is a vault in the form of a *hemisphere* (half sphere) built on a circular base.   William J. Hennessey

See also **Architecture** (table; pictures: A vault; Gothic cathedrals); **Rome, Ancient** (Arts and sciences).

VCR. See **Videotape recorder.**

Veal is the flesh of cattle that are too young and small to be sold as beef. These cattle are divided into *vealers* and *calves.* Vealers are animals less than 14 weeks old that are fed with milk. Although calves eat grass or grain like older cattle, calf flesh is not as tasty as beef.

In the United States, vealers and calves are sold by weight and according to five grades set up by the federal government. The U.S. grades are *prime, choice, good, standard,* and *utility.* The best grades of veal are plump

and range in color from light pink to light gray. The flesh of lower grades is generally thin and watery.

Calf flesh is darker and has more definite grain than vealer flesh. In addition, most calves have more fat covering than vealers. The meat of both calves and vealers has little trimming waste when sold in stores.

Veal contains more water than beef, but it has less fat. Veal is more tender than beef, but the older age of beef makes it tastier than veal.   Donald H. Beermann

See also **Beef; Cattle** (Beef cattle); **Meat.**

Veblen, *VEHB luhn,* **Thorstein Bunde** (1857-1929), an American economist, was one of the most original and creative thinkers in the history of American economic thought. His first book, *The Theory of the Leisure Class* (1899), is a scholarly and satirical protest against the false values and social waste of the upper classes. *The Theory of Business Enterprise* (1904) criticizes capitalism and predicts it will drift into fascism or socialism. In *The Engineers and the Price System* (1921), Veblen assigned to scientists and engineers a major role in building a new planned economic society. Veblen was born on June 30, 1857, in Cato, Wisconsin. He died on Aug. 3, 1929.   Dudley Dillard

Vecellio, Tiziano. See **Titian.**

Vedas, *VAY duhz,* are the oldest sacred books of Hinduism. They were probably composed beginning about 1400 B.C. The Vedas include the basis of the doctrines about Hindu divinities. They also present philosophical ideas about the nature of Brahman, Hinduism's supreme divine being. The word *veda* means *knowledge.*

There are four Vedas. They are, in order of age beginning with the oldest, Rigveda, Samaveda, Yajurveda, and Atharvaveda. The Vedas are also called Samhitas. They are collections of chiefly verse texts that provided the liturgies of the holiest rites of the early religion. Attached to the Vedas are two important later texts. The Brahmanas are long prose essays that explain the mythological and theological significance of the rites. After the Brahmanas came highly speculative works called the Upanishads. The inward reflection of the Upanishads and their search for unity in existence gave rise to the development of Indian philosophy.

Hindu law permitted only certain persons to hear the Vedas recited, and so the works became surrounded by mystery. Nevertheless, ideas presented in the Vedas spread throughout Indian culture.   Stanley Insler

See also **Brahman; Hinduism; Sanskrit literature; Upanishads.**

Vega, also known as Alpha Lyrae, ranks as the sixth brightest star in the sky. As seen from Earth, only the sun and four other stars shine more brightly. Vega is the brightest star in the constellation Lyra, the Harp. The star appears in Earth's northern sky.

Vega is a *main-sequence* star. Main-sequence stars produce most of their energy by *fusing* (combining) hydrogen nuclei in their cores. Vega's *mass* (amount of matter) measures about 2.3 times that of the sun. It produces roughly 35 times as much power as does the sun.

Astronomers group Vega in the A *spectral class* (see **Star** [Spectral classes]). Stars in this class typically appear white or bluish-white. Vega and two other bright A stars, Altair and Deneb, form the Summer Triangle. It appears on summer evenings in the Northern Hemisphere.

In 2006, astronomers announced that Vega is rotating

at speeds nearly high enough to cause it to break apart. The rotation causes Vega to swell at its equator, where its diameter is about 25 percent greater than the distance between its poles. The rotation also causes Vega's temperature to rise toward its poles, which are about 30 percent hotter than its equator. Deane Peterson

See also **Lyra; North Star; Star** (table: The 10 brightest stars as seen from Earth).

Vega, *VAY gah,* **Lope de,** *LOH pay day* (1562-1635), was the most productive playwright of Spain's Golden Age. He is credited with creating a Spanish national drama. Lope wrote more plays than any other author. Scholars generally agree that he wrote more than 400 plays. The two largest categories are "cloak-and-sword" plays of intrigue, and historical plays, such as *The Best Mayor, the King* (1616?) and *Fuenteovejuna* (1619?).

Lope described his theory of drama in *The New Art of Writing Plays* (1609). He rejected the dramatic unities that restricted action to a single place during a specific length of time. He believed that the best themes were conflicts of passion and the Spanish honor code. His characters usually lack individuality, but his style is poetic, and his situations are exciting.

Lope Félix de Vega Carpio was born on Nov. 25, 1562, in Madrid. He led an adventurous and troubled life. Several of his love affairs ended sadly, particularly one with Marta de Nevares, whom he met after becoming a priest in 1614. Lope died on Aug. 27, 1635. Harry Sieber

See also **Drama** (The Golden Age of Spanish drama); **Spanish literature** (The 1600's).

Vegetable commonly refers to an edible part of a nonwoody plant. Such edible parts include leaves, roots, seeds, stems, or even fruits. Vegetables rank among the most healthful of all foods. They contain many key *nutrients* (nourishing substances). People eat raw or cooked vegetables as a dish in a main meal, as part of a salad or soup, or as a snack. Vegetable growing forms a major branch of *horticulture,* a field of study that also includes fruit production, flower production, and landscaping.

Most vegetables come from plants called *annuals,* which live for one growing season. They include muskmelons, watermelons, and other foods often thought of as fruits. Such vegetables as carrots and onions come from *biennials,* plants that require two growing seasons to produce seed. Asparagus, Jerusalem artichokes, and a few other vegetables grow as *perennials.* These plants live for more than two growing seasons.

Vegetables form a vital part of the human diet. They provide good sources of vitamins A, B, and C and such minerals as iron and potassium. Vegetables also yield fiber, which helps people digest food properly. In addition, vegetables contain compounds called *phytonutrients,* many of which may help prevent certain cancers.

People eat vegetables fresh or processed. Leading vegetables sold fresh to consumers include potatoes, the most widely grown vegetable, as well as lettuce and carrots. Food processing companies handle more tomatoes than any other vegetable. Processed tomatoes occur in cans—both whole or diced—as well as in tomato paste, ketchup, and salsas. *Pureed* tomatoes are cooked until soft and then processed in a blender or pushed through a strainer or sieve. Major processed frozen vegetables include broccoli, peas, and sweet corn.

China ranks as the leading producer of several major vegetable crops. Other key vegetable-growing countries include India, Nigeria, and the United States.

This article deals primarily with the commercial production of vegetables. For information on home vegetable growing, see **Gardening.**

Kinds of vegetables

Vegetables are often grouped according to the part of the plant from which they come. Plant parts used as vegetables include bulbs, flower buds, fruits, leaves, roots, seeds, stems, and tubers.

Bulbs are underground organs consisting of several layers of fleshy leaves that surround a short or flattened stem. Bulb crops include garlic, onions, and shallots.

Flower buds. Broccoli ranks as the most common flower bud used as a vegetable. It has a head composed of densely packed flower buds on a thick, fleshy flower stalk. Globe artichokes, another flower bud vegetable, consist of edible bases and leafy scales.

Fruits are ripened *ovaries*—that is, the parts of flowering plants that contain the seeds. Vegetables from fruits include eggplants, muskmelons, okra, peppers, pumpkins, snap beans, snap peas, squash, and tomatoes.

Leaves eaten as vegetables include Brussels sprouts, cabbage, kale, lettuce, and spinach. In two leaf vegetables, celery and rhubarb, *petioles* (leaf stalks) make up the edible parts instead of the leaf blades.

Roots form vegetables in such plants as beets, carrots, parsnips, radishes, and turnips. Most root vegetables occur as enlarged main roots called *taproots.* Sweet potatoes develop from enlarged *fibrous roots* on stem cuttings used to *propagate* (reproduce) the plants.

Seeds. Horticulturists usually classify seeds eaten in immature form as vegetables. Cowpeas, kidney beans, and sweet corn rank among the major seed vegetables.

Stems support the branches, leaves, and fruits of plants. For one stem vegetable, kohlrabi, people eat only the main stem's swollen base. For another type, aspara-

© Janine Wiedel Photolibrary/Alamy Images

Colorful vegetables at an outdoor market include beans, lettuce, peppers, and tomatoes. This market, in the city of Muğla in southwestern Turkey, also sells bananas and various other fruits.

Plant parts used as vegetables

Vegetables are healthful foods that come from various parts of plants. People may consume bulbs, flower buds, fruits, leaves, roots, seeds, stems, and tubers as vegetables.

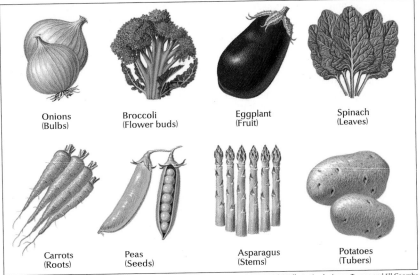

Onions (Bulbs)   Broccoli (Flower buds)   Eggplant (Fruit)   Spinach (Leaves)

Carrots (Roots)   Peas (Seeds)   Asparagus (Stems)   Potatoes (Tubers)

WORLD BOOK illustration by James Teason and Jill Coombs

gus, people eat both the stem and the young shoot.

Tubers grow from *stolons* (specialized underground stems) that develop into enlarged, fleshy organs. Tuber vegetables include potatoes and Jerusalem artichokes.

Growing vegetables

Growers use the term *vegetable culture* to describe the various practices for growing vegetables. Vegetable culture involves four primary steps: (1) field preparation, (2) planting, (3) irrigation, and (4) pest control.

Field preparation. Growers initially prepare fields for planting by plowing deep layers of soil. They then spread chemical fertilizer or manure on the land to provide nutrients for the coming crop. They mix the fertilizer into the soil and break up large soil particles to form a flat, uniform seed bed. Some growers create raised beds to provide better drainage and help warm the soil.

Planting. Growers plant vegetables in rows, either by *direct seeding* or by *transplanting.* In direct seeding, specialized machines called *seeders* make a small furrow in the soil, drop the seeds into the furrow, cover the seeds, and press the soil firmly over them. Seeds may be *coated* with coloring and protective chemicals or *pelleted* with clay or other materials to make them more uniform and easier to plant. Some seeders deposit bands of additional fertilizer beside the seeds.

In transplanting, growers cultivate vegetables from small seedlings called *transplants.* They grow transplants on *flats* (small trays) in temperature-controlled greenhouses. Workers plant the seeds in the flats either by hand or by specialized machines. They then place the flats on greenhouse benches and moisten them to germinate the seeds and grow the seedlings. Once the seedlings reach an acceptable size, farmers transport them to the field for hand or machine transplanting. Many transplanting machines also inject water or fertilizer into the transplant holes to help the plants grow.

Irrigation. Most vegetables need extra irrigation to maintain strong, uniform growth. There are three major types of irrigation: (1) *furrow irrigation,* (2) *sprinkler irrigation,* and (3) *drip irrigation.*

In furrow irrigation, workers make deep furrows between the rows of the planted crop. Tubes divert water from irrigation canals to the crop through these furrows.

In sprinkler irrigation, wide pipes transport water from a pond or well to sprinklers in the field. This system enables farmers to deliver water evenly to crops.

In drip irrigation, hoses move water from wells or other sources to plastic pipes and tubes that run above the surface of the field. Small, regularly spaced holes in the tubing enable water to drop slowly onto the planted rows. Farmers prefer drip irrigation to other methods because it delivers water directly to the plants and conserves the water supply.

Pest control. Harmful crop pests include weeds, insects, and diseases. Weeds reduce crop yields by competing with them for nutrients, water, and sunlight. Several weed-controlling methods exist. Many farmers spray the soil with *selective herbicides,* chemicals that kill weeds but not crops. For such warm-season vegetables as tomatoes and cucumbers, farmers cultivate the plants on beds covered with thin, porous sheets of black plastic. This practice not only helps control the weeds, which grow only in uncovered parts, but also conserves water and nutrients.

Various insects consume the leaves or juices of vegetable plants, thus reducing crop yields and often damaging the edible portions of crops. Other insects called *vectors* transfer diseases to plants that affect the leaves, roots, or fruits. Bacteria, fungi, or viruses also may spread such diseases. Many growers kill pests by spraying pesticide chemicals on crops. Yet overuse of pesticides can damage the environment, and farmers must use caution to avoid possible pesticide residues on food crops. To avoid these potential problems, many farmers now control pests by using pest-resistant vegetable varieties. Scientists have created many such varieties by altering the plants' *genes* (units of heredity).

Some farmers combat crop damage by using a practice known as *organic farming.* Organic farmers usually avoid chemical fertilizers and genetically engineered vegetable varieties. Instead, they employ natural soil-improving techniques to minimize the harmful effects of weeds, insects, and diseases.

Harvesting and marketing vegetables

Farmers must harvest vegetables at the correct stage of maturity. In many cases, they immediately cool the harvested crop to prevent loss of water and wilting. Some vegetables, such as tomatoes and melons, will not achieve acceptable eating quality if picked when they are immature. If picked when overripe, most vegetables will lose eating quality or spoil during shipment.

Growers with small plots often market their vegetables locally at a farm stand or farmers' market. They harvest ripe crops so that the vegetables will be ready for consumption when they reach the local markets.

Growers with large farms usually sell their vegetables to brokers or distribution companies. They typically harvest crops at a slightly immature stage to allow for longer-term storage and shipping. Such growers must grade fresh-market vegetables for size and quality, trim the outer leaves, and sometimes cool and wash the produce before packing. For some crops, farmers may grade and pack the vegetables in the field using machines. For crops that need washing or special sorting, grading, or cooling, growers use large packing sheds.

Distribution companies typically ship vegetables by refrigerated trucks, railroad cars, and planes to regional warehouses. There, they store the produce at cool temperatures for a brief period before shipping them to various markets.

J. Brent Loy

Related articles in *World Book.* See the state, province, and country articles for a discussion of vegetables grown there, such as **Arkansas** (Agriculture). Additional related articles include:

Vegetables

Artichoke	Corn	Lettuce	Rutabaga
Asparagus	Cowpea	Lima bean	Salsify
Bean	Cress	Muskmelon	Shallot
Beet	Cucumber	Mustard	Sorrel
Broccoli	Eggplant	Okra	Soybean
Brussels	Endive	Onion	Spinach
sprouts	Garlic	Parsley	Squash
Cabbage	Horseradish	Parsnip	Sweet potato
Carrot	Jerusalem	Pea	Swiss chard
Cauliflower	artichoke	Peanut	Taro
Celery	Jicama	Pepper	Tomato
Chayote	Kale	Potato	Turnip
Chinese	Kohlrabi	Pumpkin	Watermelon
cabbage	Leek	Radish	Yam
Chive	Lentil	Rhubarb	Zucchini
Collards			

Other related articles

Agriculture	Gardening	Plant
Farm and farming	Horticulture	Truck farming
Food	Nutrition	Vegetable oil
Food, Frozen	(illustration: The	Vegetarianism
Food preservation	food pyramid)	

Vegetable oil is a fatty substance obtained from certain plants. Manufacturers obtain most vegetable oils from seeds and fruits. Most of these oils are liquids, but a few, including cocoa butter, coconut oil, and palm oil, are solids at room temperature. Vegetable oils consist almost entirely of fat, an essential part of a healthy diet. For information on their food value and chemical composition, see **Fat.** One of the most commonly used vegetable oils is soybean oil. Other important oils include canola, corn, olive, peanut, safflower, and sunflower oil.

Uses. Many people use vegetable oils to fry foods and as salad oil. Manufacturers make most margarine and salad dressings with such oils as soybean or sunflower oil. Cocoa butter or coconut oil is a chief ingredient in various candies.

Many nonfood products also contain vegetable oils. For example, manufacturers make certain cosmetics and soaps from coconut or palm oil. Many paints and varnishes contain a drying oil, such as linseed, soybean, or tung oil. Drying oils combine with oxygen from the air to form a tough coating. See **Oil** (Fixed oils).

Production. Manufacturers use various methods to extract oil from plants. One common process, called *solvent extraction,* involves soaking the seeds or fruit in a liquid known as a *solvent.* The solvent draws the oil out of the plant material. Machines then remove the plant material from the resulting mixture and evaporate the solvent, leaving only the crude oil.

Another method, called *expeller pressing,* uses a high-pressure press to squeeze out the oil. However, the high pressure heats the oil, causing it to develop a dark color and undesirable flavor. The oil also loses some of its nutritional value. A similar process, known as *prepress solvent extraction,* uses less pressure than does expeller pressing and extracts only some of the oil. A solvent is used to obtain the remaining oil.

Oils obtained by solvent extraction, expeller pressing, or prepress solvent extraction require further processing to make them suitable for use in foods. Machines refine, bleach, and deodorize the oils to create a clear, mild-tasting product. Oils obtained by a method called *cold pressing* do not require such processing. Cold pressing, which uses low pressure to squeeze out the oil, generates little heat. As a result, the oil retains its original flavor, color, and nutritional value. But cold pressing removes less oil than do the other processes.

Daniel R. Sullivan

Related articles in *World Book* include:

Canola oil	Cottonseed oil	Palm oil	Soybean
Castor oil	Linseed oil	Peanut	Sunflower
Chocolate	Margarine	Rape	Tung oil
Copra	Olive oil	Safflower	Varnish
Corn oil			

Vegetarianism is the practice of not eating meat. Strict vegetarians regard the flesh of all animals, including that of fish and poultry, as meat. Many vegetarians avoid eating meat for moral or religious reasons. They believe it is wrong to kill animals for food. Other vegetarians consider eating meat unhealthy.

Vegetarians vary in the kinds of foods they consider acceptable. For example, *lacto-ovo-vegetarians* include milk and eggs in their diet. *Lacto-vegetarians* do not eat eggs, but they do eat dairy products. *Vegans* avoid all foods derived from animals, including gelatin and honey. Some vegetarians eat the flesh of certain animals, a practice sometimes called *semivegetarianism. Pesco-vegetarians,* for example, eat fish but no meat or poultry.

Daily meals for vegetarians should include appropriate servings of grains, vegetables, fruits, and protein. Nonvegetarians get much protein from meat, fish, and poultry. Vegetarians, on the other hand, get much of their protein from legumes, beans, eggs, nuts, and seeds. Protein from individual plant sources contains only some of the *amino acids* (building blocks of proteins) required by the body. But a mixed and varied vegetarian diet that includes many nutritious foods will supply enough protein to grow and repair the body.

Vegans must be especially careful to ensure that their diets provide sufficient protein, calcium, and vitamins D, riboflavin, and B_{12}. Dairy alternatives, such as soy milk, often replace the nutrients from dairy products, especially calcium. Food manufacturers may fortify cereals, dairy alternatives, or meat alternatives with vitamin B_{12}. Plant foods do not provide any of this important vitamin, though they may be rich in other B vitamins. Vegans, especially teenagers and nursing mothers, must take a vitamin B_{12} supplement.

A well-balanced vegetarian diet offers certain health benefits over a diet that includes meat. For example, vegetarians generally consume less saturated fat and cholesterol. A high level of cholesterol in the blood is associated with heart disease. Studies have shown that vegetarians in many parts of the world often have less risk of developing certain diseases, such as heart disease and high blood pressure. Some studies suggest that a vegetarian diet can help people live longer. Such longevity may result in part from *antioxidants,* chemicals that protect cells against certain types of damage and other healthy *phytochemicals* (plant-derived compounds) in vegetarian diets. Most vegetarian diets also contain fewer calories than diets that include meat.

Some religious groups call on their members to follow vegetarian diets, especially the Buddhists, Hindus, and Seventh-day Adventists. Other people choose vegetarian diets because they believe that consumption of meat, especially beef, reduces the world food supply. They think that grain used to fatten cattle would nourish more people if eaten directly. Other vegetarians judge that meat production creates unnecessary pollution and wastes resources, particularly water.   Georgia E. Hodgkin

Vegetation. See **Desert; Forest; Grassland; Plant.**

Vein. See **Leaf** (The parts of a leaf).

Vein is a blood vessel that carries blood toward the heart. The blood circulates in the body through a system of tubes called blood vessels. The three kinds of vessels are arteries, capillaries, and veins. Most veins return blood to the heart after it has given out nourishment to the tissues and taken up waste products and poisons. Blood in veins is called *venous* blood. See the Trans-Vision three-dimensional picture with **Human body.**

The blood returning from the body cells has lost much of its oxygen, and is dull brownish-red. It circulates through the right side of the heart and then goes to the lungs. Here it gives off its waste carbon dioxide and takes on a new supply of oxygen. Bright red blood from the lungs returns to the heart through the pulmonary veins. Then it begins its trip through the body.

The veins begin at the capillaries. At first, they are tiny and are called *venules.* Small veins join to form larger ones. Finally, all the venous blood of the body pours into two large veins that open into the heart. One of these, the *superior vena cava,* carries blood from the head and arms. The other, the *inferior vena cava,* carries it from the trunk and legs.

Veins, like arteries, have walls made of three layers. But the vein walls are thinner, less elastic, and less muscular than those of the arteries. The lining membrane of the veins is the *intima.* In many of the larger veins, the in-

tima has folds that serve as valves. These folds lie against the wall when the blood is flowing freely. Several things can cause the blood to slow down or stop—the weight of blood above the vessel, effects of gravity, pressure on a vein, or low fluid pressure. Then the valves open out and stop the blood from flowing backward. The valves are usually just above the place where two veins join. There are no valves in the veins of the abdomen, brain, and lungs, or in the smaller veins.

Veins that are swollen, stretched, or coiled on themselves are *varicose* veins. *Phlebitis* is inflammation of a vein. Phlebitis may produce redness, tenderness, swelling, and pain in the area of the vein.   Dominick Sabatino

Related articles in *World Book* include:

Aneurysm	Artery	Heart	Phlebitis
Angiogenesis	Bloodletting	Jugular vein	Varicose vein

Velázquez, *vuh LAHS kuhs,* **Diego,** *DYAY goh* (1599-1660), was an important Spanish Baroque painter. Many characteristics of his style can be seen in one of his masterpieces, *Las Meninas,* which is reproduced in the **Painting** article. *Las Meninas* shows Velázquez's use of realism, rich colors, and light and shadow. In addition, it shows the painter's ability to place his subjects in space. Velázquez stands beside the huge canvas on which he is painting a portrait of the king and queen, whom we see reflected in a mirror on the back wall. Princess Margarita has entered with her maids and entertainers to watch while a courtier stands in the still-open door. Velázquez created an illusion of space both within and beyond the painting. By including the reflection of the king and queen, who would be standing about where the viewers stand, Velázquez includes the space in front of the

Oil painting on canvas (about 1650); Metropolitan Museum of Art, New York City, Fletcher Fund, Rogers Fund, and Bequest of Miss Adelaide Milton de Groot, by exchange, supplemented by gifts from friends of the Museum

Velázquez's portrait of Juan de Pareja shows how well the Spanish painter captured the personality of his subjects.

canvas as part of the composition. See **Baroque** (Baroque painting).

Diego Rodriquez de Silva y Velázquez was born in Seville, probably in June 1599. As a youth, he studied with Francisco Pacheco. Pacheco taught him the style of the Italian artist Michelangelo Caravaggio, characterized by its realism and use of somber light and dark tones. In 1623, Velázquez became official painter for King Philip IV. He became an important courtier as well as a successful court painter for the rest of his life.

In 1629, Velázquez went to Italy, where he studied the art of ancient Rome and perfected his ability to paint nudes. After his return to Spain in 1631, he produced a series of great royal portraits as well as *The Surrender of Breda (The Lances),* one of the world's finest historical paintings. He again visited Italy from 1649 to 1651. While in Rome, Velázquez did a penetrating portrait of Pope Innocent X and also painted his only pure landscapes. After his return to Spain, Velázquez painted some of his greatest pictures. These include his most dazzling court portraits; *Venus with a Mirror,* one of the few nudes in Spanish art; and *Las Meninas.* He died in Madrid on Aug. 6 or 7, 1660.   Marilyn Stokstad

Velcro is the trade name for a fastening device made up of tiny hooks that mesh with tiny loops. Such fasteners are used in clothing, athletic and medical equipment, and automobile and airplane interiors. Velcro is a trademark of Velcro Industries, but many people use the word to refer to any hook-and-loop fastener. The name *Velcro* is a combination of *velvet* and *crochet. Crochet* is the French word for *hook.*

A Velcro fastener consists of two strips that are glued or sewed to the fabrics or other objects to be joined. Flexible hooks made of strong nylon or polyester thread cover one of the strips. A fuzzy mat of loops made of thinner threads covers the other. When pressed together, the hooks attach to the loops and form a strong bond. The strips can be easily separated by peeling them apart, and they can be joined and separated thousands of times.

Georges de Mestral, a Swiss engineer, got the idea for Velcro in the 1940's while pulling burs from his trousers and his dog's fur. He helped found Velcro Industries, which exclusively sold the fasteners until 1978, when the patent for Velcro expired.   Valerie Steele

Velikiy Novgorod, *vyih LEE kee yuh NAWV guh ruht* (pop. 216,856), is an important industrial center and one of the oldest cities in Russia. It lies on both banks of the Volkhov River. For location, see **Russia** (political map). The city was once known as Novgorod.

Velikiy Novgorod has numerous architectural monuments built between the 1000's and 1600's, including many churches. These sites attract many tourists. Velikiy Novgorod's industries include the production of chemicals, china, furniture, and machinery.

The city probably existed as early as the A.D. 600's. In the 900's, it became an important city in Kievan Rus—the first East Slavic state. Between the 1200's and 1500's, the city was a financial and commercial center. In the early 1600's, invading Swedish forces caused much destruction. After the Russian Revolution of 1917, the government established factories in the region. German forces destroyed much of Novgorod during World War II (1939-1945). The city was rebuilt as an industrial center, and historic landmarks were restored. In 1998, the city reclaimed its historic name, Velikiy Novgorod, which means *Novgorod the Great.*   Zvi Gitelman

Velociraptor, *vuh LAHS uh RAP tuhr,* was a quick, fierce meat-eating dinosaur. It lived about 80 million years ago in what is now Mongolia and northern China. This dinosaur grew to about 20 inches (50 centimeters) tall at the hips and 6 feet (1.8 meters) long.

Velociraptor used a variety of natural weapons to kill prey. It had a large mouth full of sharp, bladelike teeth. Its grasping hands ended in three long, slender fingers with large claws. Powerful legs enabled *Velociraptor* to run swiftly. On the second toe of each hind foot, the animal had a large curved, razor-sharp claw. These two claws probably were *Velociraptor's* main weapons.

Velociraptor normally ate small dinosaurs and mammals. It used its quickness to catch such prey. Once it held the victim in its grasp, *Velociraptor* may have kicked the animal's unprotected belly with its giant toe claws. These swift, powerful kicks would have killed the prey and torn it apart.

When *Velociraptor* walked, it probably raised its huge toe claws off the ground to protect their sharp points. *Velociraptor's* rigid tail may have balanced the animal when it was running or making sudden turns.

Scientists first described *Velociraptor* in 1924. In

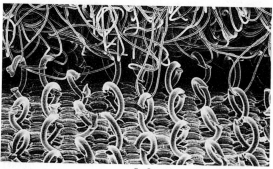

Dee Breger, Lamont-Doherty Earth Observatory

A Velcro fastening device is made up of tiny loops and hooks that fit together. The loops appear in the top part of this view through a microscope, and the thicker hooks are at the bottom.

WORLD BOOK illustration by Alex Ebel

Velociraptor was a meat-eating dinosaur that used several natural weapons to kill prey. These weapons included sharp teeth, grasping hands, and a large claw on the second toe of each foot.

1971, a remarkable fossil skeleton of this dinosaur was found in the Gobi desert of Mongolia. The skeleton's arms still clutched the skull of its prey, another dinosaur. The two creatures may have been buried alive as they fought with each other during a sandstorm.

Hans-Dieter Sues

Velocity, *vuh LAHS uh tee,* is the rate at which a body moves in space in a given direction. Velocity is expressed in distance and time, such as miles per hour or meters per second.

There is an important difference between speed and velocity. *Speed* indicates the rate of motion, but it does not indicate anything about the direction of motion. When a body is said to have a speed of 40 miles per hour, the direction is unknown. To specify the *velocity,* it is necessary to indicate both the rate and the direction of motion. For example, a body may have a velocity of 40 miles per hour toward the north. Mathematically, velocity is a *vector* quantity, because it has both speed and direction.

Types of velocity. Velocity may be *uniform,* which means the distances and the direction traveled during a given unit of time are the same throughout the motion. To find the uniform velocity of a body, we need only divide the distance traveled by the time. This could be stated in the formula $v = \dfrac{d}{t}$ where v is equal to velocity, d is equal to distance, and t is equal to time.

Velocity may be *variable.* This means that the distances traveled in a given unit of time are not equal throughout the motion, or that the direction changes, or both. For example, a moving object could have a velocity of 30 meters per second at a certain instant and then speed up to 60 meters per second. If the object gained speed uniformly, its average velocity would equal its initial velocity plus its final velocity divided by two. This could be written Av. $v = \dfrac{v_1 + v_2}{2}$ where Av. v represents the average velocity, v_1 is equal to the initial velocity and v_2 is equal to the final velocity.

Acceleration is a change in the velocity of a moving body. *Positive acceleration* means that, during each portion of time, the body moves through a greater distance than during the preceding portion of time. A falling body has a positive acceleration. In *negative acceleration,* such as a train stopping, a smaller space is traveled in each successive unit of time. *Centripetal acceleration* occurs when the rate of motion stays the same, but the direction changes. Lucille B. Garmon

See also **Motion; Falling bodies, Law of; Calculus.**

Velvet is a handsome fabric with a soft and luxurious feel. It may be made of silk, rayon, nylon, polyester, acetate, or a combination of these fibers. Weavers make many weights and types of velvet. Some are lightweight and almost transparent, and others are thick and heavy. Lightweight velvet is generally made into clothing when a dressy effect is wanted. Heavier weights are used for upholstery and draperies.

The softness and rich appearance of velvet result from its construction. Two sets of yarns—called the *warp*—run the length of the fabric, and another set—called the *filling*—is placed in a crosswise direction. One warp is tightly interlaced with the filling. The other is held more loosely to form a series of closely spaced loops that stand on top of the fabric. These loops are cut open at the top to form the pile, a short, thick, furry surface on the fabric. The pile consists of threads that reflect a good amount of light. The reflection of light from the surface of the pile gives velvet its attractive appearance.

Phyllis Tortora

Velvetleaf is a weed that has velvety, heart-shaped leaves. It is a member of the mallow family (see **Mallow**). The plant is native to India. It is also called *Indian mallow, butterprint,* and *stamp weed.* Velvetleaf was once used to stamp designs on hand-churned butter.

Velvetleaf grows from about 2 feet (60 centimeters) to over 6 feet (1.8 meters) tall, depending on the fertility of the soil. The plant has attractive yellow flowers and fruits with 10 to 15 seed-containing beaks radiating from the center. Velvetleaf was introduced into the New World as a potential fiber crop. It has become a troublesome weed and is a special pest in corn and soybean fields.

Walter S. Judd

Scientific classification. Velvetleaf belongs to the mallow family, Malvaceae. The scientific name of the velvetleaf is *Abutilon theophrasti.*

Vending machine is a self-service device that dispenses a product or provides a service when money or a token, card, or key is inserted into it. Vending machines dispense such items as candy, cigarettes, coffee, newspapers, postage stamps, and soft drinks. Some vending machines dispense frozen foods, soups, salads, sandwiches, fruits and desserts, and complete meals. Service machines include coin-operated washing machines, pay telephones, and subway fare-card machines. In some airports, vending machines rent cellular telephones and carrying carts. Vending machines sell billions of dollars worth of goods and services each year.

How vending machines work. Most vending machines accept coins. With some types, the user must insert the exact change before the machine will operate. With others, the user can insert a coin or paper money larger than the purchase price. The machine will dispense the item and refund the proper amount of change. A special vending machine called a *currency changer* accepts paper money and makes change in coins that can then be used in other vending machines. Currency changers can distinguish between bills of different denominations and return the proper amount of change for each denomination that they can accept.

The vending machine industry is composed of manufacturing companies, operating companies, and companies that supply the products that are sold in the machines. Operating companies usually pay a fee, called a *commission,* to the owner of the location where a machine is placed for the use of the space. The commission is based on the sales made through the vending machines at that location.

History. A device that dispensed holy water in a Greek temple in Alexandria, Egypt, in 215 B.C. is the earliest known vending machine. The first vending machines in the United States began dispensing chewing gum on New York City train platforms in 1888. Candy and cigarette vending machines first appeared during the 1920's. The first coffee machine was introduced in 1946. Larry M. Eils

Venerable Bede, The. See **Bede, Saint.**
Venereal disease. See **Sexually transmitted disease.**

WORLD BOOK photo by Milt and Joan Mann

A residential area in Caracas, Venezuela's capital and largest city, has many high-rise apartment buildings. In most Venezuelan cities, modern apartment buildings like these are rapidly replacing traditional Spanish-style houses, which have one story and center on a courtyard.

Venezuela

Venezuela, *VEHN ih ZWAY luh,* is a South American country that ranks as one of the world's leading producers and exporters of petroleum. Before its petroleum industry began to grow rapidly during the 1920's, Venezuela was one of the poorer countries in South America. Its economy was based on such agricultural products as cacao and coffee. Since the 1920's, however, Venezuela has become one of the wealthiest and most rapidly changing countries on the continent. Income from petroleum exports enabled Venezuela to carry out huge industrial development and modernization programs.

Venezuela lies on the north coast of South America along the Caribbean Sea. Mountain ranges extend across much of northern Venezuela, which is the most densely populated region of the country. Caracas, the capital and largest city, lies in this region. Vast plains called the Llanos spread across central Venezuela. High plateaus and low mountains cover the south.

Most of Venezuela's people live in cities and towns. Nearly all Venezuelans speak Spanish. Most of the people are descendants of Europeans, American Indians, and Africans who intermarried.

The famous explorer Christopher Columbus landed in what is now Venezuela in 1498 on his third voyage to the New World. It was his first landing on the mainland of the Americas. Later, European explorers in northwestern Venezuela found Indian villages where the houses were built on poles over the waters of the Gulf of Venezuela and Lake Maracaibo. Some of the explorers were reminded of the Italian city of Venice, where buildings stood along the water. They named the area *Venezuela,* which is Spanish for *Little Venice.* Later, the name Venezuela was applied to a large area of northern South America. Spain ruled Venezuela for about 300 years. In 1811, Venezuela declared its independence.

Government

Venezuela is a federal republic. Citizens 18 years old and older may vote. Venezuela has had 27 constitutions since 1811. Its present Constitution was adopted in 1999.

Facts in brief

Capital: Caracas.
Official language: Spanish.
Official name: República Bolivariana de Venezuela (Bolivarian Republic of Venezuela).
Area: 352,145 mi^2 (912,050 km^2). *Greatest distances*—north-south, 790 mi (1,271 km); east-west, 925 mi (1,489 km). *Coastline*—1,750 mi (2,816 km).
Elevation: *Highest*—Pico Bolívar, 16,411 ft (5,002 m) above sea level. *Lowest*—sea level along the coast.
Population: *Estimated 2008 population*—28,112,000; density, 80 per mi^2 (31 per km^2); distribution, 88 percent urban, 12 percent rural. *2001 census*—23,054,210.
Chief products: *Agriculture*—bananas, beef cattle, chickens and eggs, coffee, hogs, milk. *Manufacturing*—aluminum, petrochemicals, pig iron, processed foods, refined petroleum, steel. *Mining*—bauxite, coal, iron ore, natural gas, petroleum.
National anthem: "Gloria al Bravo Pueblo" ("Glory to the Brave People").
Money: *Basic unit*—bolívar fuerte. One hundred céntimos equal one bolívar fuerte.

Jennifer L. McCoy, the contributor of this article, is Professor of Political Science at Georgia State University.

National government. According to the Constitution, the president is head of state and head of the executive branch. The president is elected by the people to a six-year term and can serve no more than two consecutive terms. The National Assembly is Venezuela's legislature. The people elect its members to five-year terms. The Supreme Court of Justice is the highest court.

Local government. Venezuela is divided into 23 states and the Federal District. Each state and the Federal District have governors and legislatures elected by the people. The country also has many islands in the Caribbean that are federal dependencies.

Armed forces. About 82,000 people serve actively in Venezuela's army, navy, air force, and national guard. In addition, the army has about 8,000 reservists. Men may be drafted for 30 months of military service after reaching 18 years of age.

People

Ancestry. Many Indian tribes lived in what is now Venezuela before Spaniards colonized the area in the 1500's. The Spaniards conquered many of these tribes. They also imported Africans to work as slaves. Many of the Indians, Spaniards, and Africans intermarried. Today, about two-thirds of the people are of mixed ancestry. People of unmixed European, African, or *indigenous* (native) ancestry make up the rest of the population.

After 1945, and especially in the 1950's, many Europeans and Colombians moved to Venezuela to seek jobs. Most of the Europeans came from Spain, Italy, and Portugal. Many Colombians entered Venezuela illegally in the 1970's and early 1980's. At that time, a sharp jump in oil prices caused a dramatic increase in Venezuela's wealth, and the government started a number of projects that created jobs.

Languages. Almost all Venezuelans speak Spanish, the country's official language. Indians in remote areas speak various tribal languages.

Ways of life. Compared with some other Latin American countries, Venezuela has an open society. In general, the people are not rigidly segregated on the basis of ethnic or class differences.

Since the 1940's, many Venezuelans have moved from rural areas to cities. Today, most of the people live in urban centers. As cities have grown, so has the middle class, which includes business people, government workers, and doctors, lawyers, teachers, and other professionals. Most middle-class Venezuelans live comfortably. They dress well, own a car, and take vacations. Some families live in one-story, Spanish-style houses that center on a courtyard. But in most cities, high-rise apartment buildings are rapidly replacing such houses.

Venezuela's economy expanded from the 1950's to the 1970's. But a drop in oil prices in the 1980's and 1990's led to a steep rise in poverty. Housing is scarce, and many Venezuelans live in crowded squatter settlements on the outskirts of cities. Many of them live in small shacks called *ranchos,* which sit dangerously on mountainsides without good roads or sanitation. But they often have televisions and refrigerators and access to electricity. Thousands of ranchos cover large areas in and around many cities.

Since the 1960's, the Venezuelan government has carried out massive programs to improve the living condi-

WORLD BOOK photo by Milt and Joan Mann

The Venezuelan Capitol in Caracas houses the National Assembly. This view of the Capitol shows part of its large courtyard. The building was completed in 1872.

Venezuela's state flag, used by the government, was adopted in 1954. The civil flag has no coat of arms.

Coat of arms. The running horse symbolizes liberty; the wheat sheaf, unity; and the swords, independence.

WORLD BOOK map

Venezuela lies on the north coast of South America along the Caribbean Sea. It borders Colombia, Brazil, and Guyana.

WORLD BOOK map

Venezuela map index

*Not shown on map; key indicates general location.
Sources: 2001 census for states and other divisions; 2000 official estimates for cities with populations greater than 150,000; 1988 official estimates for other cities.

tions of the poor. For example, it has furnished building materials, electricity, water, and sewerage facilities for some rancho dwellers. Large public housing units also have been built in many cities. In addition, the government has taken steps to improve rural life so that people will stay on farms rather than move to crowded cities. In many rural areas, for example, the government has built paved roads, extended electrical service, and set up educational and health facilities. In the early 2000's, the government began a new program to bring health clinics, adult education programs, and subsidized food markets to people living in poor neighborhoods.

Food. Traditional Venezuelan foods include black beans, a type of banana called *plantains,* and rice, which are usually eaten with beef, pork, poultry, or fish. The traditional bread is a round corn-meal cake called *arepa.* However, Venezuelans also buy prepared foods in supermarkets and commonly eat wheat bread.

The national dish of Venezuela is the *hallaca,* which is served mainly at Christmas. Hallacas consist of corn-meal dough filled with a variety of foods and cooked in wrappers made of a type of banana leaf.

Recreation. Baseball and soccer are the most popular spectator sports in Venezuela. Professional teams play before large crowds in city stadiums. Several cities have bullfights, but they do not attract as many people as competitive sports events do.

Venezuelans enjoy music and dancing. Popular dances include the exciting, rhythmic *salsa* and such fast, lively Caribbean dances as the *merengue* and *guaracha.* The national folk dance of Venezuela is the *joropo.* This stamping dance is performed to the music of *cuatros* (four-stringed guitars), the harp, and *maracas* (rattles made of gourds). Rock music is also popular among young Venezuelans.

Religion. Roman Catholicism has long been the traditional religion in Venezuela, and most people are baptized Catholics. However, the Constitution guarantees freedom of worship. Protestantism is growing. About 10 percent of Venezuelans are Protestants.

Education. Most Venezuelans 15 years of age or older can read and write. For the country's literacy rate, see Literacy (table).

The law requires children from ages 7 through 13 to attend school. Venezuelans can receive a free public education from kindergarten through university graduate school. The country has about 50 public and private universities. The largest and most important is the Central University of Venezuela, a public university in Caracas.

The arts. Several Venezuelan writers and artists have won international fame. The novelist Teresa de la Parra and the poet Andrés Eloy Blanco were among the most important writers of the 1900's. But probably the best-known writer was Rómulo Gallegos, who also served as president of the country in 1948. Gallegos portrayed the distinctive character of different regions of Venezuela in such novels as *Doña Bárbara* (1929), *Canaima* (1935), and *Pobre Negro* (1937). Leading artists have included the abstract painters Alejandro Otero and Jesús Soto.

Venezuela also has produced some spectacular modern architecture. Outstanding examples can be found on the campus of the Central University of Venezuela, where boldly designed buildings have been brought together with imaginative murals and sculptures.

WORLD BOOK photo by Milt and Joan Mann

Crowded squatter settlements cover large areas in and around many Venezuelan cities. In Caracas, almost a third of the people live in *ranchos* (small shacks) like those shown here.

WORLD BOOK photo by Milt and Joan Mann

A sunny sidewalk cafe provides a pleasant place to relax in Caracas. The cafe is on a street in the Sabana Grande, one of the city's main shopping and business districts.

WORLD BOOK photo by Milt and Joan Mann

A rodeo, held near the city of Barinas, attracts many young Venezuelans. Barinas is the capital of the state of Barinas, a cattle-raising area in the western part of the country.

Land regions

Venezuela has four major land regions. They are
(1) the Maracaibo Basin, (2) the Andean Highlands, (3) the
Llanos, and (4) the Guiana Highlands.

The Maracaibo Basin lies in northwestern Venezuela and consists of Lake Maracaibo and the lowlands
around it. Lake Maracaibo is the largest lake in South
America. It covers 5,217 square miles (13,512 square
kilometers). The continent's largest known petroleum
deposits lie in the Maracaibo Basin.

The Andean Highlands begin southwest of the Maracaibo Basin and extend across northern Venezuela.
Most of Venezuela's people live in this region. The region has three sections. They are, from west to east:
(1) the Mérida Range, (2) the Central Highlands, and (3)
the Northeastern Highlands.

The Mérida Range consists of mountain ranges and
high plateaus. Pico Bolívar, the highest point in Venezuela, rises 16,411 feet (5,002 meters) above sea level.

The Central Highlands consist of two parallel mountain ranges along the Caribbean coast. Fertile valleys lie
between these ranges. This area has more people and
more industries than any other area in Venezuela.

The Northeastern Highlands consist of low mountains

WORLD BOOK photo by Milt and Joan Mann

The Andean Highlands begin southwest of the Maracaibo
Basin and extend across northern Venezuela. Many small farms
and towns lie in the mountains. This farmer is tending carrots.

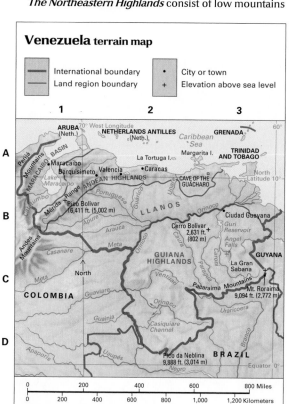

WORLD BOOK map

and hilly land. A famous natural feature of this area is the
Cave of the Guácharo, near the town of Caripe. Thousands of large birds called *guácharos* live in the cave.
These birds are found only in northern South America
and chiefly in this cave.

The Llanos lie between the Andean Highlands and
the Guiana Highlands. The Orinoco River, which begins
in the Guiana Highlands, flows from west to east along
the southern border of the Llanos. The river and its tributaries drain most of Venezuela. The Orinoco extends
1,284 miles (2,066 kilometers) and is the longest river in
the country. Large cattle ranches cover much of the
Llanos. The cowhands on these ranches are called
llaneros. The Llanos also have farmland. But the region
has a long dry season, and irrigation is needed to grow
such crops as rice and sesame. Important oil fields lie in
the eastern part of the Llanos.

The Guiana Highlands rise south of the Llanos and
cover nearly half of Venezuela. Swift-flowing rivers have
deeply eroded the region's high plateaus. Angel Falls,
the world's highest waterfall, plunges 3,212 feet (979 meters) in the Guiana Highlands. Tropical forests cover
much of the southern part of the region. See **South
America** (picture: Spectacular Angel Falls).

Scattered tribes of Indians live in the Guiana Highlands, but many areas have no inhabitants. The region
has valuable deposits of bauxite, iron ore, and gold.
Some of the rivers near Ciudad Guayana have been
dammed and provide large amounts of electricity.

Climate

Venezuela lies entirely within the tropics. But the average temperatures vary throughout the country, depending chiefly on altitude. Lowland areas are warm all year.
The highest average annual temperature, 83 °F (28 °C),
occurs in the central part of the Llanos and in the northern Maracaibo Basin. At higher elevations, the weather

Physical features

Andean Highlands	B	2	Lake Maracaibo	B	1
Angel Falls	C	3	Llanos (plains)	B	2
Apure River	B	2	Maracaibo Basin	A	1
Casiquiare			Margarita Island	A	2
Channel	D	2	Mérida Range	B	1
Guiana Highlands	C	2	Orinoco River	B	3
Guri Reservoir	B	3	Pacaraima		
La Gran Sabana			Mountains	C	3
(plateau)	C	3	Pico Bolívar (peak)	B	1

The Llanos consist of gently sloping plains that stretch across central Venezuela. The region has many large ranches, like the one shown here, on which cowhands called *llaneros* herd cattle on horseback.

WORLD BOOK photo by Milt and Joan Mann

is much cooler. In the Andean Highlands at Mérida, the annual temperature averages 67 °F (19 °C).

The amount of rainfall varies greatly in different parts of Venezuela. Annual rainfall averages about 120 inches (305 centimeters) in the Perijá Mountains, which are west of Lake Maracaibo, and in the southern Guiana Highlands. In contrast, much of the Caribbean coast is dry, and some areas receive only 16 inches (41 centimeters) of rainfall yearly. Most of the rest of the country has alternate wet and dry seasons. In the eastern Llanos, annual rainfall averages about 40 inches (100 centimeters).

Economy

Venezuelans have a high standard of living in relation to the rest of Latin America. This is mainly because of the country's large petroleum production. But Venezuela's wealth is not distributed evenly among the people, and poverty and unemployment are major problems in some areas. Another difficulty is the economic instability created by changes in the price of petroleum.

Natural resources. Petroleum is Venezuela's most important natural resource. The most productive oil fields lie in the Maracaibo Basin and in the eastern Llanos. Large amounts of natural gas occur in the oil fields. Venezuela also has huge deposits of bauxite, coal, diamonds, gold, and phosphate rock. The Guri Dam on the Caroni River in the Guiana Highlands is one of the world's largest dams.

Service industries employ about three-fourths of Venezuela's workers. Service industries include such economic activities as education and health care, wholesale and retail trade, and the operation of hotels and transportation companies. Tourism is an important source of income for several service industries in Venezuela. Another major service activity in the country is the wholesale trade of food and mineral products.

Manufacturing has grown rapidly in Venezuela since 1970. About 10 percent of the country's workers are employed in manufacturing. Petroleum processing is the leading manufacturing activity. Venezuela's petroleum refineries produce large amounts of fuels and petrochemicals. Maracaibo is the country's leading center of petroleum refining. Venezuela also manufactures aluminum, cement, motor vehicles, pig iron, processed foods, steel, and textiles. Ciudad Guayana is a major producer of aluminum and steel. A variety of products are made in Caracas, Barquisimeto, and Valencia.

Agriculture. About 10 percent of Venezuela's workers are farmers. The main crops include bananas, coffee, corn, rice, and sorghum. Farmers also raise beef and dairy cattle, hogs, and poultry. Large farms and ranches raise most of Venezuela's commercial farm products.

Most Venezuelan farms are operated by their owners, though a small percentage of them are rented. Some Venezuelans farm land that they do not own or rent. Most of these people live in isolated areas where they cultivate small plots called *conucos.* They produce only enough food to support themselves. In the 1960's, the government began programs that provided farmland for many landless rural families. A law passed in 2001 called for the redistribution of private farmland that was not being used productively to families without land.

Mining. Natural gas ranks second to petroleum among Venezuela's leading mineral products. Other important mineral products in the country include bauxite, coal, diamonds, gold, iron ore, and phosphate rock.

International trade. Petroleum is by far Venezuela's leading export. Venezuela is one of the world's largest exporters of petroleum. Other exports include aluminum, chemicals, and iron and steel. Venezuela's main imports include chemicals, industrial machinery, and transportation equipment. Colombia, Germany, Japan, Mexico, and the United States are among Venezuela's chief trading partners.

Transportation and communication. Modern highways link Caracas with other large cities in Venezuela, including Maracaibo, Valencia, and Ciudad Guayana. Most of the roads in rural areas are unpaved. The country has few railroads. Maiquetía International Airport, near Caracas, is Venezuela's busiest airport. The leading seaports are La Guaira, Maracaibo, and Puerto Cabello.

Leading newspapers include *El Nacional, El Universal,* and *Ultimas Noticias,* all published in Caracas; and *Panorama,* published in Maracaibo. Both the government and commercial broadcasters operate the country's television and radio stations.

WORLD BOOK photo by Milt and Joan Mann

The petroleum industry provides the great majority of Venezuela's export earnings. Much of the oil comes from the Maracaibo Basin. Many wells are in Lake Maracaibo, *shown here.*

WORLD BOOK photo by Milt and Joan Mann

Iron-ore mining is one of Venezuela's major industries. Cerro Bolívar, *shown here,* and other mountains of high-grade ore lie in the Guiana Highlands of southern Venezuela.

WORLD BOOK photo by Milt and Joan Mann

Modern expressways link the major Venezuelan cities. This expressway interchange in Caracas is popularly called the *araña,* which is a Spanish word meaning *spider.*

History

Early inhabitants. Many American Indian tribes lived in what is now Venezuela before European settlers arrived. The chief tribes belonged to two groups—the Carib and the Arawak. The Carib lived in the eastern part of Venezuela, and the Arawak lived in the west. Both groups lived by farming, hunting, fishing, and gathering wild plants. Diseases brought to the Americas by the Europeans killed large numbers of Indians. Many other Indians starved or were killed in warfare.

European exploration and settlement. Christopher Columbus was the first European to reach Venezuela. In 1498, he landed on the Paria Peninsula. In 1498 and 1499, Spaniards explored most of South America's Caribbean coast. Spanish settlers soon followed the explorers.

During the early 1500's, the Spaniards came to Venezuela to collect pearls from oyster beds around the islands of Margarita and Cubagua. They called the area from the Araya Peninsula to Cape Codera the Pearl Coast. The Spaniards also worked the extensive salt ponds on the Araya Peninsula. These ponds produced salt for several centuries. From 1528 to 1546, King Charles I of Spain leased Venezuela to a group of German bankers to pay off his debts to them. The Germans did little to advance the economy of the colony.

By the 1700's, Venezuela was one of Spain's poorest South American colonies. To increase trade and develop the economy, Spain gave the Royal Guipuzcoana Company of Caracas, a private trading company, the right to control all trade in Venezuela. The company began to operate in 1730. It expanded the colony's economy, which was based on cacao, indigo, and hides. But the colonists resented the company's rigid control over trade. The firm eventually lost much of its power and went out of business in 1784.

The struggle for independence. During the early 1800's, Spain's South American colonies began to fight for independence. The chief leaders in the independence movement included the Venezuelans Simón Bolívar, Francisco de Miranda, and Antonio José de Sucre. They and their followers fought for many years to free all of northern South America from Spanish rule.

Venezuela was the first Spanish colony in South America to demand its independence. The colony declared its freedom on July 5, 1811, though Spanish forces still occupied much of the country. Venezuela did not become truly independent until 1821, when Bolívar won a great victory against the Spaniards at Carabobo (near Valencia). Meanwhile, in 1819, Bolívar had set up and become president of Gran Colombia, a republic that eventually included what are now Venezuela, Colombia, Ecuador, and Panama. Venezuela broke away from Gran Colombia in 1829 and drafted a separate constitution in 1830. General José Antonio Páez, a leader in Venezuela's independence movement, became the first president of the new Venezuelan republic in 1831.

Rule by dictatorships. After achieving independence, Venezuela had many periods of civil unrest. A series of dictators known as *caudillos* ruled the country until the mid-1900's. Two of these caudillos, Generals Antonio Guzmán Blanco and Juan Vicente Gómez, greatly influenced Venezuela's development.

Guzmán Blanco ruled Venezuela from 1870 to 1888.

Before 1870, civil wars and political instability had torn the country apart. Guzmán Blanco established order. He built roads and communication systems, and foreign firms began to invest in the country. Gómez ruled Venezuela from 1908 to 1935. He crushed all opposition to his rule. During his administration, the petroleum industry began to grow. With the oil profits, Gómez paid off the country's huge debt and created a strong army. But he also used some of the profits for personal benefit.

The road to democracy. After 1935, opposition to dictatorship increased greatly among Venezuelans. New, reformist political parties were organized. A party called Acción Democrática (AD), supported by the army, seized power in 1945. In 1947, the people elected Rómulo Gallegos of the AD as president. But in 1948, the army overthrew him. A military trio ruled Venezuela until 1950, when Marcos Pérez Jiménez became dictator. A revolt against Pérez Jiménez broke out in 1958, and he went into exile. Later that year, the voters chose Rómulo Betancourt of the AD as president. Since 1958, Venezuelan presidents have been democratically elected.

The late 1900's. In the early 1980's, the worldwide demand for petroleum decreased, causing oil prices to drop. As a result, Venezuela's economy suffered greatly. Venezuela's government sought to reduce the country's dependence on petroleum. It increased other economic activities, such as the production of petrochemicals and of a fuel called liquefied petroleum gas. The aluminum and steel industries were also developed.

In 1989, Carlos Andrés Pérez, who had served as president from 1974 to 1979, again became president. Pérez tried to open up the economy and cut government debt. But hardships caused by his economic plan resulted in much social unrest. In 1992, military officers led by Hugo Chávez Frías tried to overthrow Pérez but failed. In May 1993, the Senate removed Pérez from office on charges of misuse of government funds. The Supreme Court of Justice convicted him on some of these charges in 1996.

In 1993, Rafael Caldera was elected president. He had served as president from 1969 to 1974. In his 1993 campaign, Caldera promised to fight corruption and help the poor. Soon after he took office, the country suffered a severe banking crisis. The government then took steps to tighten control over the country's banking system. In 1998, Hugo Chávez was elected president. He promised to reform the nation's political system. In a 1999 referendum, voters approved a new constitution that allowed for the reelection of the president for a second term.

In late 1999, floods and mudslides caused by heavy rains in northern Venezuela killed about 30,000 people.

Recent developments. In 2000, Chávez was reconfirmed as president under the new Constitution. His attempts to increase his control of Venezuela's state-run oil company led business and labor leaders to organize protests in April 2002. Violence broke out during the protests, and military leaders removed Chávez from office. International disapproval and popular support for Chávez led the military to return him to power two days later. In late 2002 and early 2003, business, labor, and political opposition leaders held a national strike to protest Chávez's rule. The strike interfered with oil production and caused the economy to shrink significantly.

In late 2003, opponents of Chávez collected signatures demanding a referendum on whether he should

remain president. After an extended and controversial signature verification process, the national electoral council scheduled a referendum for Aug. 15, 2004. A majority of Venezuelans voted to let Chávez remain in office. The opposition claimed that the referendum had been fraudulent, but international observers found no evidence of fraud. In 2005, Chávez's opponents refused to take part in elections for the National Assembly, and government supporters won control of the legislature.

Chávez was reelected president in a landslide election in December 2006. In January 2007, the legislature gave him permission to rule by decree for 18 months. Chávez promoted his plan to create a "21st-century Socialism" and took steps to put important Venezuelan industries under public control. He also renewed efforts to redistribute large, private estates to poor people.

In mid-2007, Chávez introduced reforms to the Constitution that would have eliminated presidential term limits, reorganized the nation's territorial divisions, ended the independence of the Central Bank, and provided more benefits for workers. The reforms were defeated in a close referendum in December.   Jennifer L. McCoy

Related articles in *World Book* include:

Biographies

Bolívar, Simón
Chávez Frías, Hugo

Miranda, Francisco de
Sucre, Antonio José de

Cities

Barquisimeto
Caracas

Ciudad Bolívar
Maracaibo

Other related articles

Andes Mountains
Angel Falls
Caribbean Sea
Cleveland, Grover (Foreign affairs)
Cuquenán Falls
Lake Maracaibo

Organization of the Petroleum Exporting Countries
Orinoco River
Petroleum (map)
Roosevelt, Theodore (Foreign policy)
Spanish Main
Yanomami Indians

Outline

I. Government
A. National government
B. Local government
C. Armed forces

II. People
A. Ancestry
B. Languages
C. Ways of life
D. Food
E. Recreation
F. Religion
G. Education
H. The arts

III. Land regions
A. The Maracaibo Basin
B. The Andean Highlands
C. The Llanos
D. The Guiana Highlands

IV. Climate

V. Economy
A. Natural resources
B. Service industries
C. Manufacturing
D. Agriculture
E. Mining
F. International trade
G. Transportation and communication

VI. History

Additional resources

Dinneen, Mark. *Culture and Customs of Venezuela*. Greenwood, 2001.
McCoy, Jennifer L., and Myers, D. J. *The Unraveling of Representative Democracy in Venezuela*. Johns Hopkins, 2004.
Winter, Jane K., and Baguley, Kitt. *Venezuela*. 2nd ed. Benchmark Bks., 2002.
Wardrope, William. *Venezuela*. Gareth Stevens, 2003. Younger readers.

Venice occupies about 120 islands off the northeast coast of Italy. In Saint Mark's Square, the heart of the city, a bell tower called the Campanile, *center,* rises above the domed roof of the Basilica of Saint Mark. The Doges' Palace stands next to the basilica.

Venice, *VEHN ihs,* Italy (pop. 309,422), is one of the world's most famous and unusual cities. Venice lies on about 120 islands in the Adriatic Sea and has canals instead of streets. Its people use boats instead of automobiles, buses, taxis, and trucks. Venice also includes part of the Italian mainland.

Fine architecture and priceless works of art have long helped make Venice a major tourist center. The city also ranks as one of Italy's largest ports. Venice is the capital of Venetia (Veneto), one of the 20 political regions of Italy. The city's name in Italian is Venezia.

Venice lies at the north end of the Adriatic Sea, $2\frac{1}{2}$ miles (4 kilometers) off the coast of Italy. For location, see Italy (political map).

The city's location on the Adriatic made it an important trading center as early as the A.D. 800's. Venice became a strong sea power and gradually built a colonial empire that extended throughout much of the eastern Mediterranean area. At the height of its power, Venice was known as the "Queen of the Adriatic."

Through the centuries, Venice lost much of its economic and political strength. But the city's art treasures helped it keep its place as a cultural center of the world. Today, floods and polluted air and water threaten to slowly destroy the city. People from many parts of the world have joined various campaigns to save Venice.

The city forms a governmental unit of Italy called a *commune.* The islands of Venice make up the historic center of the city. The modern industrial centers of Marghera and Mestre on the mainland are part of the commune of Venice. See Italy (Local government).

A lagoon separates the islands of Venice from the mainland. A roadway over the lagoon carries traffic between the mainland and two of the islands. Automobiles, buses, and trains use terminals on those islands. More than 150 canals take the place of streets on all the islands of Venice, and boats provide transportation. Black, flat-bottomed boats called *gondolas* once served as the chief means of transportation on the islands. Today, motorboats have replaced most of the gondolas (see **Gondola**). More than 400 bridges cross the canals and link the main islands of Venice. Narrow alleyways called *calli* run between the buildings on the islands.

The Grand Canal, the city's main canal, winds through the heart of Venice. Marble and stone palaces built between the 1100's and 1800's stand along both sides of the Grand Canal. The Rialto Bridge crosses the canal in the heart of the city. Venice's chief shopping district lies along the Merceria, a narrow street that runs from the Rialto Bridge to Saint Mark's Square.

Saint Mark's Square is the center of activity in Venice. The Basilica of Saint Mark, on the east side of the square, ranks as one of the world's outstanding examples of Byzantine architecture (see **Saint Mark, Basilica of**). A bell tower called the Campanile stands nearby. Buildings in the Renaissance style of architecture rise along the other three sides of the square. Cafes in front of these buildings are favorite meeting places for tourists and for residents of the city. The Doges' Palace, just off the square, was built as a residence for early Venetian rulers called *doges* (see **Doge**).

Priceless artworks may be seen in buildings throughout Venice. The Academy of Fine Arts has an outstanding collection of famous paintings, including works by such Venetian masters as Titian, Tintoretto, and Paolo Veronese. Hundreds of students attend Venice's schools of architecture, art, and music. The University of Venice has about 15,000 students.

Venice has few parks or gardens. But the Lido, a narrow sandbar that borders the islands on the east, is one of Europe's most popular beach resorts.

Venice's location gives the city unique characteristics, but it has also caused serious problems. For example, during winter storms, floodwaters sweep through the islands, covering public squares and walkways and damaging buildings. The constant exposure to water is also weakening the foundations of Venice's buildings. In addition, air pollution is eroding the buildings, as well as many of the city's outdoor art treasures. The islands of Venice were sinking an average of about ⅕ inch (5 millimeters) yearly until the mid-1970's. A number of scientists believe that the sinking resulted partly from the removal of underground water for use by industries. The Italian government restricted the use of water from the city's underground wells. Water pressure then built up under the islands, and the city stopped sinking.

The people of Venice's islands are continually affected by the water that surrounds them. The water influences their food and housing as well as their transportation. For example, seafood is the main course of a typical Venetian lunch or dinner. Houses and other buildings do not stand on solid ground but on wooden *piles* (posts) driven into the mud.

Almost all Venetians are Roman Catholics. Several annual events, in addition to religious holidays, attract large crowds to the city. One of these events, the Feast of the Redeemer, commemorates the end of a plague that struck Venice in 1575. During this all-night festival in July, musicians perform in lighted boats along the canals. A *regatta* (gondola race) is held each September.

Since about 1950, thousands of Venetians have left the islands to live in the mainland communities of Marghera and Mestre. The majority of Venice's people now live in Mestre. Many people have moved off the islands because the mainland offers greater job opportunities and a lower cost of living. The modern apartment buildings in Marghera and Mestre also attract many Venetians. Most of the buildings on the islands were erected hundreds of years ago, and there is no room to build new housing.

Economy. Tourism is the chief economic activity of the islands of Venice. Each year, millions of tourists visit

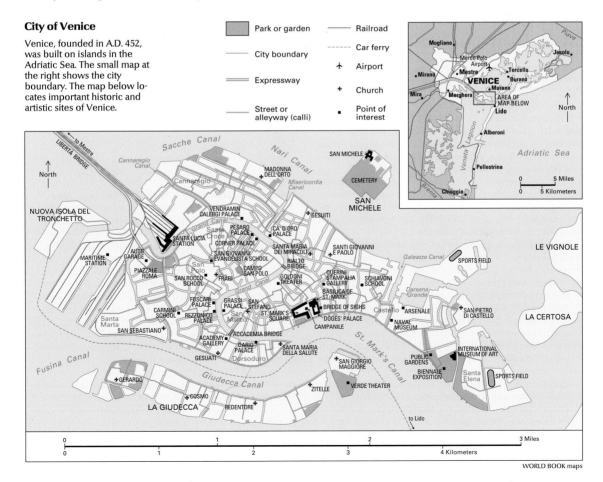

City of Venice

Venice, founded in A.D. 452, was built on islands in the Adriatic Sea. The small map at the right shows the city boundary. The map below locates important historic and artistic sites of Venice.

	Park or garden	Railroad
	City boundary	Car ferry
	Expressway	✈ Airport
	Street or alleyway (calli)	✚ Church
		Point of interest

WORLD BOOK maps

Bullaty/Lomeo, Rapho Guillumette

Canals take the place of streets in Venice, and boats are used for transportation. Most of the buildings that line the canals are hundreds of years old. Bridges link the city's main islands.

the historic center of the city. They make up an important market for goods produced by craftworkers who live on the various islands. The islands of Murano have won fame for fine crystal and glassware. Lace and embroidered work come from Burano.

The industrial and trade activities of Venice center in Marghera and Mestre. Factories in these communities produce aluminum, chemicals, coke, fertilizer, paint, petroleum products, steel, and other goods. Venice's port facilities are centered at Marghera.

Industrial development in the mainland portion of Venice has created thousands of jobs for Venetians. But it has also been a major cause of the serious air and water pollution that threaten the city.

History. The first settlers of Venice fled to the islands during the A.D. 400's to escape Germanic peoples who were invading Italy from northern Europe. The early Venetian economy was based on fishing and trading. The Venetians traveled along the Adriatic coasts to find new markets. By the 800's, Venice was trading with Constantinople (now Istanbul) and cities on the Italian mainland and northern coast of Africa. Venice developed into a nearly independent city-state, ruled by nobles.

Venetian ships provided the transportation for the Fourth Crusade, which lasted from 1202 to 1204. The Venetians joined the crusaders in battle and conquered the Byzantine Empire, including Constantinople (see **Crusades** [The Fourth Crusade]). The growing strength

of Venice led the city into a series of wars with Genoa, a rival sea power. Venice finally defeated Genoa in 1380 and gained control over trade in the eastern Mediterranean Sea. Venice became one of the largest cities in Europe. It reached the height of its power in the 1400's, when its colonial empire included Crete, Cyprus, the Dalmatian coast (now part of Croatia), and part of northeastern Italy. Venetian ships carried almost all the silks, spices, and other luxury items that reached Europe from Asia. Venice became a leading center of Renaissance art in the late 1400's and 1500's (see **Renaissance**).

In the late 1400's, Christopher Columbus journeyed to America and Vasco da Gama found a sea route to India. The center of trade in Europe then shifted to the Atlantic Ocean, and Venice's power declined. The city gradually lost its eastern colonies to the Ottoman Empire.

In 1797, French forces led by Napoleon Bonaparte occupied Venice. Napoleon divided what was left of the Venetian empire between France and Austria. The city itself came under Austrian control. In 1866, Venice became part of the independent Kingdom of Italy.

The industrialization of Marghera and Mestre began in the early 1900's. During World War II (1939-1945), German troops took over the city. Allied planes bombed the port at Marghera but spared Venice's islands.

In 1966, a disastrous flood that struck much of Italy caused extensive damage in Venice. The flood badly damaged or destroyed many of the city's paintings and statues. International organizations and private citizens gave money to help the Italian government pay for repairs. After the flood, government committees and private researchers began studies on pollution control. In the late 1980's, the government approved funds for public-works projects to protect the city from flooding and from erosion caused by pollution.   John A. Davis

Related articles in *World Book* include:

Bridge of Sighs	Glass (The Middle Ages)
Campanile	Gondola
Doge	Italy (picture: Tourism)
Europe (picture: Canals and rivers)	World, History of the (picture: The Basilica of St. Mark)

Venison. See Deer.

Venizelos, VEH nee ZEH laws, **Eleutherios,** EH lehf THEH ryaws (1864-1936), was the dominant figure in Greek politics from 1910 to 1935. He served as prime minister of Greece six times between 1910 and 1933, and he helped Greece acquire many Aegean islands, Crete, and other territories. In opposition to Greek King Constantine I, Venizelos brought Greece into World War I in 1917 on the side of the Allies (France, Britain, and Russia). During the early 1920's, he helped prepare Greece for war against the Ottoman Empire. Greece lost this war in 1922. Venizelos also helped persuade the Greeks to establish a republic in 1924. He was born on Crete on Aug. 23, 1864. He died on March 18, 1936. See also **Greece** (George I).   John A. Koumoulides

Venom, VEHN uhm, is a poisonous substance produced by many kinds of animals. These animals, which include certain species of snakes, bees, fish, marine snails, scorpions, and spiders, use venom to kill and digest prey. The poison is manufactured by a venom gland and is injected into the victim in various ways.

Venom contains many toxic substances that act together to poison a victim. These substances differ among the species of animals that produce venom. Some venoms include poisons that block the transmission of nerve impulses to muscle cells, causing numbness and paralysis. Certain substances in venom slow or stop the heart. Many venoms also break down the walls of blood capillaries, causing swelling and massive bleeding. Some venoms contain poisons that cause the victim's blood to clot. Others contain substances that prevent clotting.

Animals that produce venom use various body parts to inject the poison into their victims. Snakes have fangs through which the poison passes into a victim's body. Many kinds of fish use sharp, bony spines to inject venom. Bees, hornets, and wasps have stingers for poisoning their prey. Most kinds of spiders inject venom by biting a victim. Scorpions use stings on their tail to shoot venom into prey.

Venom has many uses in the treatment of illness. For example, physicians use the venom of the Malayan pit viper to treat certain types of heart attacks. Cobra venom is used to relieve some cases of severe pain, and bee venom helps in the treatment of arthritis. Venoms are also used in biological research. For instance, venoms that block the transmission of nerve impulses serve as a tool in the study of nerve function.   Anthony T. Tu

Related articles in *World Book* include:

Bee (Sting)	Snake (Fangs and venom
Hornet	glands)
Scorpion	Snakebite
	Wasp

Ventilation supplies fresh air to indoor places and removes stale air from these places. For people to feel comfortable, they need fresh air free from dust, soot, and odors. The air must not be too warm or too cool, and it must have the right amount of moisture.

Even if the air in a room is fresh to begin with, important changes take place when people come into the room. The air becomes warmer because the human body gives off heat. The amount of moisture in the air increases because of the water vapor given off as people breathe and perspire. Also, the air becomes stale because of perspiration and the oily matter given off from people's skins, noses, throats, and clothing. Smoking especially makes the air stale.

People remove the gas oxygen from the air they inhale, and give off another gas, called *carbon dioxide,* to the air they exhale. Many people once thought that the carbon dioxide gas breathed out was harmful to anyone who breathed it in again. Although breathing increases the carbon dioxide and decreases the oxygen in a room, these changes are so slight that they have little or no effect on a person's health.

The more people there are in a room, or the harder they work, the faster the air becomes stale. Stale air must be removed and replaced with fresh air. If the air outside is fresh, simply opening a window and perhaps turning on a fan will ventilate the room. However, if the outside air is not fresh or the room is on the inside of a building, special equipment is needed to clean the air, cool or heat it, and remove or add moisture. This equipment is called *air conditioning* (see **Air conditioning**).

James E. Hill

See also **Humidity; Air cleaner.**

Ventricle. See Heart.

AP/Wide World

Ventriloquist Edgar Bergen gained fame on radio and in the movies in the mid-1900's. He performed with his dummy Charlie McCarthy, *above,* who wore a tuxedo and had a monocle.

Ventriloquism is the illusion of making the voice appear to come from somewhere other than its source. It takes long and steady practice to develop the ability to imitate near and distant sounds. The sounds are produced in the usual method, but the lips are held as nearly motionless as possible. The tongue is drawn well back and only the tip is moved. A deep breath is taken in and exhaled very slowly. Sounds are modified, or changed, by the muscles of the throat and the palate. The ventriloquist often changes consonants to avoid moving the lips. For example, the letter *p* becomes a *k,* and *b* is quickly slurred into a *g* or *k.* Lack of facial expression by the performer helps to fool the audience. The performer also constantly directs the attention of the audience to the place from which the sound is supposed to come. Theatrical ventriloquists often use a *dummy* or a puppet with whom they pretend to carry on a conversation (see **Puppet** [Dummies]).

Ventriloquism is an ancient art. The Greeks thought it was the work of demons. They believed the voice came from the abdominal region. The word ventriloquism comes from the Latin *venter,* meaning *belly,* and *loqui,* meaning *to speak.* During the 1700's and 1800's, ventriloquism emerged as a form of entertainment. Today, it is also recognized as an art.   Don B. Wilmeth

Ventris, *VEHN trihs,* **Michael George Francis** (1922-1956), a British architect, solved one of the great mysteries of archaeology. He deciphered *Linear B,* a system of writing used by the ancient Greeks about 3,500 years ago. Inscriptions in Linear B were first found on clay tablets discovered at Knossos, Crete, about 1900. But all efforts to decipher them failed until Ventris, an amateur cryptographer, succeeded in 1953. He proved that Linear B was Greek written in the form of writing used by the Minoans, the people of ancient Crete. As a result, scholars changed their views about the early history of ancient Greece. Ventris was born at Wheathampstead, England. See also **Greece, Ancient** (Beginnings); **Aegean civilization.**

Venturi, Robert (1925-   ), is an American architect whose theories and designs helped establish Postmodernism as an important architectural movement. Venturi discussed his theories in his influential book *Complexity and Contradiction in Architecture* (1966). Venturi advocated mixing symbols from classical architecture, particularly Italian Renaissance and Roman architecture with modern architectural forms and ideas from such *vernacular* (common) buildings as fire stations.

Venturi wrote that he wanted to achieve an architecture of "messy vitality." Venturi wrote a second significant book, *Learning from Las Vegas* (1972), with Steven

Matt Wargo, Venturi, Scott Brown and Associates, Inc.

Venturi's Seattle Art Museum has an exterior of limestone. The windows at ground level are framed in red granite and colorful terra-cotta tiles. The building opened in 1991.

Izenour and Denise Scott Brown, Venturi's wife. The book criticizes modern American architecture and urban planning through a favorable analysis of the spontaneous commercial architecture of Las Vegas, Nevada.

Venturi was born on June 25, 1925, in Philadelphia. He demonstrated his theories in two early designs in the city, the Vanna Venturi House (1963) and Guild House (1965). Critics viewed the designs as attacks on modern architecture, particularly works of Frank Lloyd Wright and Mies Van der Rohe. His later projects include the Seattle Art Museum and the Sainsbury Wing of the National Gallery in London (both 1991).   Dennis Domer

See also **Architecture** (Architecture today); **Postmodernism.**

Venus, *VEE nuhs,* was a major goddess in Roman mythology. She originally was a protector of gardens. Later, she took on the myths and qualities of Aphrodite, the goddess of fertility, love, and beauty in Greek mythology. Venus symbolized the creative force that sustains all life. Cupid, the Roman god of love, was her son.

Venus was also mother of Aeneas, a Trojan ancestor of the legendary founders of Rome. The Romans worshiped her because of her association with the city's early history. They believed the family of the ruler Julius Caesar descended from Venus through Aeneas.

Venus was born full-grown from the foam of the Mediterranean Sea and came to land on the island of Cyprus. She married Vulcan, the lame and ugly blacksmith god. Venus had a love affair with Mars, the god of war, and she also fell in love with Adonis, a mortal.

Venus plays a part in a famous myth called the *Judgment of Paris.* Venus and the goddesses Juno and Minerva all claimed a golden apple, a prize reserved for the most beautiful goddess. The god Jupiter ordered Paris, the son of King Priam of Troy, to choose the most beautiful of the three. Paris awarded the apple to Venus. In revenge, Juno and Minerva made certain that Troy was destroyed during the Trojan War.

Venus has been a popular subject of painters and sculptors. Many works show her admiring herself in a mirror. Others portray the Judgment of Paris or show Venus with Mars or Adonis.   E. N. Genovese

Related articles in *World Book* include:
Adonis
Aphrodite
Painting (picture: *Birth of
  Venus)*
Paris (in mythology)
Venus de Milo
Vulcan

Venus is known as Earth's "twin" because the two planets are so similar in size. The diameter of Venus is about 7,520 miles (12,100 kilometers), approximately 400 miles (644 kilometers) smaller than that of Earth. No other planet comes nearer to Earth than Venus. At its closest approach, it is about 23.7 million miles (38.2 million kilometers) away.

As seen from Earth, Venus is brighter than any other planet or even any star. At certain times of the year, Venus is the first planet or star that can be seen in the western sky in the evening. At other times, it is the last planet or star that can be seen in the eastern sky in the morning. When Venus is near its brightest point, it can be seen in daylight.

Ancient astronomers called the object that appeared in the morning Phosphorus, and the object that appeared in the evening Hesperus (see **Evening star**). Later, they realized these objects were the same planet. They named Venus in honor of the Roman goddess of love and beauty.

Orbit. Venus is closer to the sun than any other planet except Mercury. Its *mean* (average) distance from the sun is about 67.2 million miles (108.2 million kilometers), compared with about 93 million miles (150 million kilometers) for Earth and about 36 million miles (57.9 million kilometers) for Mercury.

Venus travels around the sun in a nearly circular orbit. The planet's distance from the sun varies from about 67.7 million miles (108.9 million kilometers) at its farthest point to about 66.8 million miles (107.5 million kilometers) at its closest. The orbits of all the other planets are more *elliptical* (oval-shaped). Venus takes about 225 Earth days, or about $7\frac{1}{2}$ months, to go around the sun once, compared with 365 days, or one year, for Earth.

Phases. Viewed through a telescope, Venus seems to go through "changes" in shape and size. These apparent changes are called *phases,* and they resemble those of the moon. They result from different parts of Venus's sunlit areas being visible from Earth at different times.

As Venus and Earth travel around the sun, Venus

NASA

Thick clouds of sulfuric acid cover Venus. Because visible light cannot penetrate the clouds, astronomers cannot see the planet's surface with even the most powerful optical telescopes.

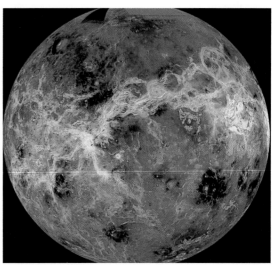

NASA

The surface of Venus was scanned with radar waves beamed from orbiting space probes to produce this image. The colors are based on photos taken by probes that landed on Venus.

can be seen near the opposite side of the sun about every 584 days. At this point, almost all of its sunlit area is visible. As Venus moves around the sun toward Earth, its sunlit area appears to decrease and its size seems to increase. After about 221 days, only half the planet is visible. After another 71 days, Venus nears the same side of the sun as Earth, and only a thin sunlit area of Venus can be seen.

When Venus is moving toward Earth, the planet can be seen in the early evening. When moving away from Earth, Venus is visible in the early morning.

Rotation. As Venus travels around the sun, it rotates very slowly on its axis, an imaginary line drawn through its center. Venus's axis is not *perpendicular* (at an angle of 90°) to the planet's path around the sun. The axis tilts at an angle of approximately 178° from the perpendicular position. For an illustration of the tilt of Venus, see **Planet** (The axes of the planets). Unlike Earth, Venus does not rotate in the same direction in which it travels around the sun. Rather, Venus rotates in the *retrograde* (opposite) direction and spins around once every 243 Earth days.

Surface and atmosphere. Although Venus is called Earth's "twin," its surface conditions appear to be very different from those of Earth. Geologists have had difficulty learning about the surface of Venus because the planet is always surrounded by thick clouds of sulfuric acid. They have used radar, radio astronomy equipment, and space probes to "explore" Venus.

Until recently, much of what geologists knew about the surface of Venus came from ground-based radar observations, the Soviet Union's Venera space probes, and United States Pioneer probes. In 1990, the U.S. space probe Magellan began orbiting Venus, using radar to map the planet's surface.

The surface of Venus is extremely hot and dry. There is no liquid water on the planet's surface because the high temperature would cause any liquid to boil away.

Venus has a variety of surface features, including

Venus at a glance

Venus is the second closest planet to the sun. Astronomers sometimes use the ancient symbol for Venus, *right.*

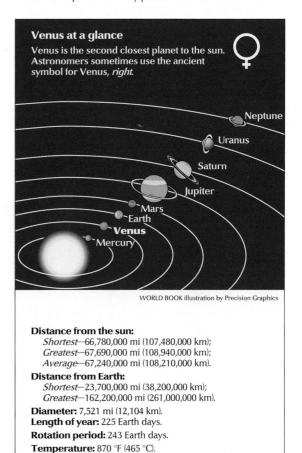

WORLD BOOK illustration by Precision Graphics

Distance from the sun:
Shortest—66,780,000 mi (107,480,000 km);
Greatest—67,690,000 mi (108,940,000 km);
Average—67,240,000 mi (108,210,000 km).

Distance from Earth:
Shortest—23,700,000 mi (38,200,000 km);
Greatest—162,200,000 mi (261,000,000 km).

Diameter: 7,521 mi (12,104 km).
Length of year: 225 Earth days.
Rotation period: 243 Earth days.
Temperature: 870 °F (465 °C).
Atmosphere: Carbon dioxide, nitrogen, water vapor, argon, carbon monoxide, neon, sulfur dioxide.
Number of satellites: 0.

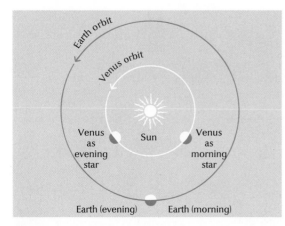

Venus appears in the evening sky when moving toward the earth. It is in the morning sky after it has passed between the sun and the earth and begins moving away from the earth.

level ground, mountains, canyons, and valleys. About 65 percent of the surface is covered by flat, smooth plains. On these plains are thousands of volcanoes, ranging from about 0.5 to 150 miles (0.8 to 240 kilometers) in diameter. Six mountainous regions make up about 35 percent of the surface of Venus. One mountain range, called Maxwell, is about 7 miles (11.3 kilometers) high and about 540 miles (870 kilometers) long. It is the highest feature on the planet. In an area called *Beta Regio* is a canyon that is 0.6 mile (1.0 kilometer) deep.

There are also *impact craters* on the surface of Venus. Impact craters form when a planet and asteroid collide. The moon, Mars, and Mercury are covered with impact craters, but Venus has substantially fewer craters. The scarcity of impact craters on Venus has led geologists to conclude that the present surface is less than 1 billion years old.

A number of surface features on Venus are unlike anything on the earth. For example, Venus has *coronae* (crowns), ringlike structures that range from about 95 to 360 miles (155 to 580 kilometers) in diameter. Scientists believe that coronae form when hot material inside the planet rises to the surface. Also on Venus are *tesserae* (tiles), raised areas in which many ridges and valleys have formed in different directions.

The atmosphere of Venus is heavier than that of any other planet. It consists primarily of carbon dioxide, with small amounts of nitrogen and water vapor. The planet's atmosphere also contains minute traces of argon, carbon monoxide, neon, and sulfur dioxide. The *atmospheric pressure* (pressure exerted by the weight of the gases) on Venus is estimated at 1,323 pounds per square inch (9,122 kilopascals). This is about 90 times greater than the atmospheric pressure on the earth, which is about 14.7 pounds per square inch (101 kilopascals).

Temperature. The temperature of the uppermost layer of Venus's clouds averages about 55 °F (13 °C). However, the temperature of the planet's surface is about 870 °F (465 °C)—higher than that of any other planet and hotter than most ovens.

The plants and animals that live on the earth could not live on the surface of Venus, because of the high temperature. Astronomers do not know whether any form of life exists on Venus, but they doubt that it does.

Most astronomers believe that Venus's high surface temperature can be explained by what is known as the *greenhouse effect.* A greenhouse lets in radiant energy from the sun, but it prevents much of the heat from escaping. The thick clouds and dense atmosphere of Venus work in much the same way. The sun's radiant energy readily filters into the planet's atmosphere. But the large droplets of sulfuric acid present in Venus's clouds—and the great quantity of carbon dioxide in the atmosphere—seem to trap much of the solar energy at the planet's surface.

NASA

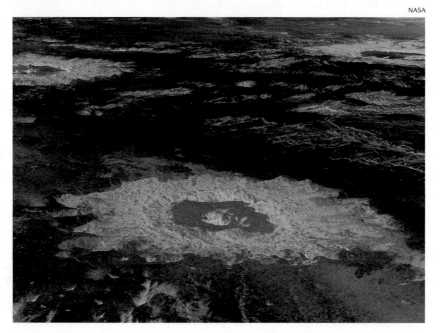

An impact crater on Venus measures about 23 miles (37 kilometers) across the depression in its center. A computer produced this image in 1991, using information from a radar scan by the U.S. space probe Magellan.

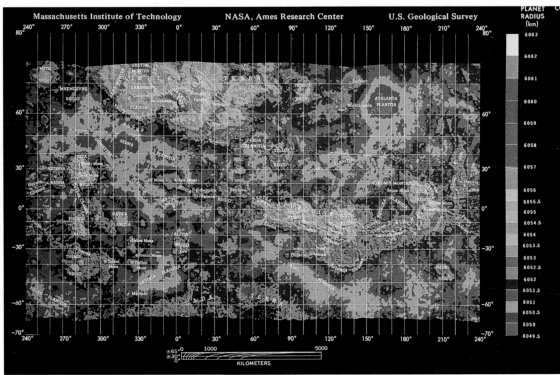

This map of Venus is based on a radar survey taken by the U.S. Pioneer Venus 1 space probe. The radius scale, *right,* uses colors to indicate distances from the planet's center to the top of its surface features. Venus's highest mountain range appears as a red mass at 0° longitude and about 65° north latitude. It rises about 7 miles (11.3 kilometers) above the plains, which appear as blue areas.

Mass and density. The *mass* of Venus is about four-fifths that of Earth (see **Mass**). The force of gravity on Venus is slightly less than on Earth. For this reason, an object weighing 100 pounds on Earth would weigh about 91 pounds on Venus. Venus is also slightly less *dense* than Earth (see **Density**). A portion of Venus would weigh a little less than an equal-sized portion of Earth.

Flights to Venus. Venus was the first planet to be observed by a passing spacecraft. The unmanned U.S. spacecraft Mariner 2 passed within 21,600 miles (34,760 kilometers) of Venus on Dec. 14, 1962. It measured various conditions on and near Venus. For example, instruments carried by the spacecraft measured the high temperatures of the planet.

Two unmanned Soviet spacecraft "explored" Venus in 1966. Venera 2 passed within 15,000 miles (24,000 kilometers) of the planet, and Venera 3 crashed into Venus.

In 1967, spacecraft from both the United States and the Soviet Union reached Venus. The Soviet spacecraft Venera 4 dropped a capsule of instruments into Venus's atmosphere by parachute. The U.S. spacecraft Mariner 5 passed within 2,480 miles (3,990 kilometers) of Venus. It did not detect a magnetic field. Both probes reported large amounts of carbon dioxide in the planet's atmosphere. In 1970, the Soviet spacecraft Venera 7 landed on Venus. The U.S. planetary probe Mariner 10 flew near Venus in 1974. The probe transmitted the first close-up photographs of the planet.

In 1975, the unmanned Soviet spacecraft Venera 9 landed on Venus and provided the first close-up photograph on the planet's surface. Three days later, another Soviet craft, Venera 10, reached Venus. It photographed Venus's surface, measured its atmospheric pressure, and determined the composition of rocks on its surface.

Four unmanned spacecraft reached Venus in 1978. The U.S. craft Pioneer Venus 1 orbited the planet. This craft transmitted radar images of Venus, produced a map of its surface, and measured temperatures at the top of the planet's clouds. The U.S. craft Pioneer Venus 2 entered the planet's atmosphere and measured its density and chemical composition. The Soviet craft Venera 12 landed on Venus. A second Soviet lander, Venera 11, reached the planet's surface soon after. Both probes sent back data on the lower atmosphere.

Two more Soviet spacecraft landed on Venus in 1982—Venera 13 and Venera 14. Both probes transmitted photographs of Venus and analyzed soil samples. Beginning in 1983, two additional Soviet spacecraft mapped the region of Venus north of 30° north latitude using radar. These spacecraft, Venera 15 and Venera 16, finished their mapping in 1984. The two probes provided clear images of features as small as 0.9 mile (1.5 kilometers) across.

The U.S. spacecraft Magellan began orbiting Venus in 1990. Radar images received from Magellan show details of features on Venus that are as small as 330 feet (100 meters) across. On Oct. 11, 1994, controllers purposely lowered the altitude of Magellan's orbit, enabling the craft to take measurements inside Venus's atmosphere before crashing into the planet.

In 2005, the European Space Agency launched the Venus Express probe. The probe was designed to study Venus's atmosphere in detail and to scan the planet's surface for signs of ongoing volcanic activity. The craft went into orbit around Venus in 2006. In 2007, scientists reported that the probe had confirmed earlier evidence indicating that Venus once had more water vapor in its atmosphere. The craft's instruments also found evidence of present-day lightning in the planet's clouds.

James W. Head III

See also **Mountain** (On Venus); **Planet; Solar system; Space exploration.**

Additional resources

Grinspoon, David H. *Venus Revealed.* Addison-Wesley, 1997.
Spangenburg, Ray, and Moser, Kit. *A Look at Venus.* Watts, 2001.

Venus de Milo, *VEE nuhs duh MEE loh,* is a famous ancient Greek statue. The marble sculpture represents Aphrodite, the Greek goddess of love and beauty (Venus in Roman mythology). It stands 6 feet 8 inches (203 centimeters) tall. It was created by an unknown sculptor, perhaps about 130 B.C. The statue has broad hips and breasts in contrast to a fine-boned, serene head. Drapery seems to be slipping off her hips.

The statue was named *Venus de Milo (Venus of Milos)* because a peasant found it on the Greek island of Milos in 1820. It was broken into two parts. Other fragments were found, including pieces of arms and a pedestal with an inscription. These fragments later disappeared and have never been recovered. It was one of many statues of Aphrodite inspired by the Aphrodite of Knidos by the Greek sculptor Praxiteles (see **Praxiteles**).

The Marquis de Rivière, French ambassador to Turkey, bought the statue. After it was repaired, he gave it to King Louis XVIII of France. Louis presented the statue to the Louvre museum in Paris, where it is now exhibited.   Marjorie S. Venit

Venus's-flytrap, *VEE nuhs sihz,* is a plant found in a small area of the coastal regions of North and South Carolina. It is also called *Dionaea (DY uh NEE uh).* This plant traps insects in its leaves and digests them. Because of this habit, it is called a *carnivorous* (meat-eating) plant. Venus's-flytrap grows in bogs where the soil has little nitrogen or phosphorus. The insects provide these nutrients in the plant's diet. The plant grows best in a damp atmosphere but requires sunshine.

Runk/Schoenberger from Grant Heilman
Venus's-flytrap

Venus's-flytrap grows about 1 foot (30 centimeters) high. It bears a cluster of small, white blossoms at the top of the flower stalk. The blossoms rise from a tuft of oddly shaped leaves. The leaves have a lower bladelike portion and an upper part with two lobes hinged to a rib. The surface of each lobe has three sensitive hairlike parts, and the edges of each lobe are fringed with sharp bristles. When an insect lights on one of the hairlike parts, the lobes close and

trap the insect. The insect's soft parts are digested by a fluid secreted by special glands of the leaf. After the plant has taken in the food, the trap opens, and the leaf can capture another victim. When a leaf has caught several insects, it withers and dies.   Norman L. Christensen, Jr.

Scientific classification. The Venus's-flytrap is in the family Droseraceae. Its scientific name is *Dionaea muscipula.*

Veracruz, *VEHR uh KROOZ* (pop. 457,119), is the chief port of Mexico. Its official name is Veracruz Llave (pronounced *YAH vay).* The city overlooks a harbor on the Gulf of Mexico, 200 miles (320 kilometers) east of Mexico City. Its products include chocolate, cigars, shoes, and textiles. Veracruz is a railroad center. The city is the site of the fortress of San Juan de Ulúa, built by the Spanish in the 1500's. For location, see **Mexico** (political map).

Hernán Cortés founded Veracruz in 1519 (see **Cortés, Hernán**). The city was the first Spanish settlement in Mexico. United States Marines occupied Veracruz for a time in 1914, after a dispute with Mexico over the arrest of some U.S. sailors.   Roderic A. Camp

Verb is a part of speech that expresses an action or a state of being. A verb may consist of one word, such as *send,* or a group of words, such as *has been sending.* Verbs occupy characteristic positions in a sentence. For example, only a verb makes sense in the blank spaces in the following sentences:

She _____ the letter. (sent, began)
He _____ my father. (is, answered)
Did they _____? (go, begin)

Some words, such as *theft* and *loneliness,* express an action or a state of being but are not verbs. These words are nouns. They cannot be used in the verb position of a sentence. In addition, they do not possess other features of verbs called *formal characteristics.*

Formal characteristics of verbs can be illustrated by the forms of the verb *fall.* These forms are *fall, falls, fell, fallen,* and *falling. Fall* is the base form, or infinitive, with or without the preceding particle *to. Fall* is also the form of the first and second person singular and plural, as in *I fall, you fall, we fall. Falls* is the form of the third person singular, used with a noun or a pronoun subject. *Fell* is the past tense form. *Fallen* is the past participle. It is used after an auxiliary verb, such as *be* and its forms *(am, is, are, was,* and *were).* It is used alone when the verb is used as a modifier, as in Fallen *leaves covered it. Falling* is the present participle, used as a modifier, as in *The* falling *snow blinded him,* and after forms of *be,* as in *He was* falling.

Auxiliary verbs, such as *do, be,* and *have,* serve a double function. They may be used as independent verbs *(He has it. He did his homework)* or as auxiliary verbs *(She has tried it. She did not finish her report).*

Modal verbs, such as *can, may, should, might,* and *must,* do not have the same characteristics as other verbs. They cannot be preceded by *to.* They cannot follow other verbs (We cannot say *She will can do it).* They are usually followed by the base form of a verb, as in *John* can *go, but Peter* must *stay.*

Regular and irregular verbs are classified according to the way they form the past tense and past participle. A verb's base form, past tense form, and past participle are called its *principal parts.*

Most English verbs are regular. The past tense form and the past participle of a regular verb are created by adding -*ed* to the base form, as in *happen, happened, happened*. The principal parts of all verbs of recent origin are formed by adding -*ed* to the base form, as in *computerize, computerized, computerized*.

Irregular verbs change in other ways to form the past tense and past participle. One kind of irregular verb changes in the past tense and then keeps that same form in the past participle. Examples include *feed, fed, fed;* and *win, won, won.* Another kind adds an -*n* or -*en* to the base form or to the past tense form to make the past participle. Examples include *know, knew, known;* and *speak, spoke, spoken.* Other verbs have irregular changes in spelling for each principal part, as in *slay, slew, slain.* Still others, called *invariables,* use the same form for all parts. They include *cost, cut, set,* and *shut.*

A large group of irregular verbs shows a change of vowel in both the past tense and past participle: *begin, began, begun; swim, swam, swum.* Through usage, many verbs of this type are gradually changing into regular verbs with -*ed* endings. For example, the verb *strive* has the irregular forms *strive, strove, striven* and also has the regular forms *strive, strived, strived.*

Transitive and intransitive verbs. Verbs may be classified as either transitive or intransitive. A transitive verb has an object, as in *He found the money.* The object of *found* is *money.* An intransitive verb has no object, as in *She is speaking.* Many verbs may be transitive in one sentence and intransitive in another. For example, *The chorus sang a popular song* (transitive); *The chorus sang well* (intransitive). Also, *The chef is cooking the potatoes* (transitive); *The potatoes are cooking* (intransitive).

Linking, or copulative, verbs occur in two general structures. In one, the verb is followed by an adjective, as in *He is good* or *It smelled good.* Such verbs as *seemed, looked, tasted, smelled, became, sounded,* and *turned* can be used as linking verbs. In the other linking-verb structure, a noun following the verb refers to the subject, as in *She is my mother;* and *He became mayor.*

Finite and nonfinite verbs. A finite verb, together with a subject, can form a grammatically complete sentence: *She drives; She is driving.* A nonfinite verb, or *verbal,* is derived from a verb but acts as another part of speech. There are three forms of verbals: *gerunds, participles,* and *infinitives.* A gerund is used as a noun: *Swimming is fun.* Participles serve as adjectives: *Susan held the winning ticket.* Infinitives can be used as nouns, adjectives, or adverbs. In the sentence *To run a mile is difficult,* the infinitive *to run* serves as a noun. In the sentence *I have reading to do,* the infinitive *to do* is used as an adjective. In *Alice practiced to become a better singer,* the infinitive *to become* serves as an adverb.

Multiple-word verbs. In English, many verbs have the form of two (or sometimes three) words, of which the first word is a verb and the second word is an adverb (sometimes called a particle). For example, the two-word verb *phone up* is similar in meaning to the verb *telephone: Mary* phoned *her* up *and told her the good news* and *Mary* telephoned *her and told her the good news.* See **Adverb.**   Susan M. Gass

Related articles in *World Book* include:

Conjuga- tion	Inflection Mood	Number Participle	Person Sentence	Tense Voice

Verbena, *ver BEE nuh,* is the name of a large group of plants, almost all of which are native to North and South America. Most wild verbenas grow in tropical and subtropical regions. A species native to Europe was once thought to be an effective remedy for blockages in the bladder and bowel, vision disorders, and many other ailments. Only a few species of verbenas are cultivated.

Most wild verbenas have spikes of small flowers that are not showy. These verbenas are often called *vervains.* Cultivated verbenas have clusters of showy flowers in a

WORLD BOOK illustration by Lorraine Epstein

The garden verbena produces clusters of blossoms on a slender stem. The blossoms may be red, pink, or other colors.

great variety of colors, including pink, red, white, and purple. The flowers of all verbenas have a tubelike shape, and they flare into five petals at the tip.

Wild verbenas grow in prairies and meadows. They are also found along roads as weeds. Cultivated verbena plants are usually started from seed indoors and are later transplanted outdoors. They may also be started from cuttings.   Donna M. Eggers Ware

Scientific classification. Verbenas belong to the vervain family, Verbenaceae. The most commonly cultivated variety is *Verbena hybrida.*

Verchères, *vehr SHAIR,* **Marie Madeleine Jarret de** (1678-1747), was a French-Canadian heroine who led the defense of her family's fort against an attack by Iroquois Indians. Madeleine de Verchères, as she is usually called, was only 14 years old at the time. The fort stood on her father's land at Verchères, her birthplace, in what is now the province of Quebec. She was born there on March 3, 1678.

On Oct. 22, 1692, a group of Iroquois attacked the fort. The main account of the event is a letter that Madeleine wrote in 1699. She claimed that she had barely outrun an Iroquois warrior, entered the fort, and disguised herself as a soldier. She then fired the cannon, frightening away the Iroquois and warning nearby settlements of their presence. Some 30 years later, Madeleine wrote a more dramatic version of her story. In it, she stated that she had stopped a frightened soldier from exploding the fort's military supplies; bravely ventured out of the fort alone during the siege; and managed the fort's defense for eight days, until a French lieutenant arrived. In recognition of her heroism, Madeleine received a pension from the French king. Madeleine de Verchères died on Aug. 8, 1747.   Colin M. Coates

Verdi, *VAIR dee,* **Giuseppe,** *joo ZEHP peh* (1813-1901), was an Italian composer whose operas are performed more often today than those of any other composer. Between 1851 and 1871, Verdi produced a series of masterpieces, including *Rigoletto* (1851), *Il Trovatore* (1853), *La Traviata* (1853), *The Sicilian Vespers* (1855), *Simon Boccanegra* (1857, revised 1881), *A Masked Ball* (1859), *La Forza del Destino* (1862), *Don Carlos* (1867), and *Aida* (1871). Verdi wrote 26 operas. He composed all to Italian *librettos* (texts) except the *Sicilian Vespers* and *Don Carlos,* which he wrote to French librettos.

Verdi gained fame for his mastery of theatrical effect and for the stirring melodic quality of his operas. He took several of his plots from the plays of such great dramatists as Victor Hugo of France, Friedrich Schiller of Germany, and William Shakespeare of England. Verdi wrote many melodies for soloists and small groups of singers. His operatic choruses remain familiar throughout the world.

Verdi, a fiery Italian patriot, became a symbol of Italy's struggle for independence from Austria during the mid-1800's. He had frequent conflicts with Austrian authorities, who felt that his operas encouraged Italian nationalism. Much of the music of his early operas, particularly of *Nabucco* (1842) and *I Lombardi* (1843), became identified with the Italian nationalist movement.

Verdi was born on Oct. 10, 1813, in Le Roncole, near Parma. He studied music as a boy in Busseto, a nearby town. He tried to enter the Milan Conservatory in 1832 but was rejected because he was too old and lacked sufficient formal training. Verdi began taking private music lessons in Milan.

In 1839, Verdi's first opera, *Oberto,* was a success at its première at La Scala, the leading opera house in Milan. Between 1838 and 1840, his first wife and two small children died. The grief-stricken composer finished a comic opera, *Un Giorno di Regno,* which was a failure when presented in 1840. But his third opera, *Nabucco* (1842), made him the foremost Italian composer of his time. After completing *Aida* in 1871, Verdi apparently decided to end his career because of illness and age. During the next 16 years, his only important composition was a *Requiem Mass* (1874), written in memory of the Italian author Alessandro Manzoni.

Verdi returned to opera composing in the mid-1880's through the urging of his friend Arrigo Boito, a noted Italian poet and composer. Boito contributed librettos for Verdi's *Otello* (1887) and *Falstaff* (1893). Some critics regard Verdi's *Otello* as the greatest of all Italian operas. *Falstaff* was only Verdi's second comic opera, but it ranks as one of the greatest comic operas ever written.

Verdi's only works after *Falstaff* were four beautiful religious compositions for voices called *Quattro Pezzi Sacri* (1898). A period of national mourning was declared in Italy following Verdi's death on Jan. 27, 1901. *The Complete Operas of Verdi* (1970) by Charles Osborne analyzes the historical, literary, and musical elements of the operas composed by Verdi.   Charles H. Webb

See also **Opera** (Giuseppe Verdi); **Boito, Arrigo.**

Verdin, *VUR duhn,* is a small, yellow-headed bird that lives in the arid portions of the southwestern United States and of Mexico. It is about 4 ¼ inches (11 centime-

M. P. L. Fogden, Bruce Coleman Inc.

The verdin builds its nest of twigs in a thorny tree. The scratchy thorns protect the eggs and young birds from enemies.

ters) long. Its body is ash-colored, and the breast is lighter. The nest is ball-shaped with a small entrance on the side. It is made of twigs and built in a thorny tree. It protects the bird from enemies and harsh weather. The female typically lays four or five eggs, which are greenish-blue with brown specks. Verdins often raise a new family twice during a breeding season. The birds primarily feed on insects and spiders. They also sometimes eat fruit and flower nectar.   Glenn E. Walsberg

Scientific classification. The verdin is in the subfamily Polioptilinae of the family Certhiidae. Its scientific name is *Auriparus flaviceps.*

Verdun, *vehr DUHN* or *vur DUHN,* **Battles of.** Verdun, one of the oldest cities of France, has been a battleground since Attila the Hun ravaged it in A.D. 450. This city on the Meuse River in northern France is about 50 miles (80 kilometers) from the German border. It often played a key role in resisting enemy invasion.

The most famous battle occurred during World War I (1914-1918). On Feb. 21, 1916, German troops launched a surprise attack. The Germans believed that the French would defend Verdun to the last soldier. They hoped that French losses would be so great that France would drop out of the war. The French, led by General Henri Philippe Pétain, defended the area stubbornly (see **Pétain, Henri Philippe**). In July 1916, after both sides had suffered large losses, the Germans reduced their efforts at Verdun. The French regained their two key forts, one in October and the other in November. The battle ended in December, but fighting resumed at Verdun in March 1917 and continued until the end of the war.

In 1940, during World War II (1939-1945), German forces easily captured Verdun. United States forces recaptured it in 1944.   Robert A. Doughty

Verdun, *vehr DUHN* or *vur DUHN,* **Treaty of,** divided Charlemagne's empire into three parts. Charlemagne's grandsons fought for control of the empire, especially after their father, Louis I, died in 840. They finally signed the treaty in 843. Charles the Bald received most of what is now France. Louis the German took almost all the land east of the Rhine, which became modern Germany. Lothair kept the title of emperor, and ruled a strip of land in the middle, from the North Sea to central Italy.

As a result of the treaty, the lands that became France and Germany were divided. The section in between remained a battleground for a thousand years. Northern Italy soon fell away from Lothair's kingdom and became part of the German empire, later called the Holy Roman Empire. Part of Lothair's kingdom became known as *Lotharingia* or, later, Lorraine.   Thomas F. Madden

Vérendrye, Sieur de la. See La Vérendrye, Sieur de.

Verga, *VAYR gah,* **Giovanni,** *joh VAHN nee* (1840-1922), was an Italian novelist, playwright, and short-story writer. His style—objective and impersonal, yet highly effective—influenced many later Italian writers.

Verga was born on Sept. 2, 1840, in Catania, Sicily, and his best work deals with Sicily and the poverty of its people. In *The House by the Medlar Tree* (1881), Verga described the struggle of a fishing family to keep their home and integrity despite tragedy. Verga planned it as the first of five novels describing people's unsuccessful efforts to improve their lives. The project ended with the second novel, *Mastro Don Gesualdo* (1889).

Verga's literary success began in 1866 with the publication of the first of several romantic novels of middle-class life. He also wrote several short stories set in Sicily. His collection *Life in the Fields* (1880) includes "Cavalleria rusticana," the basis of an opera by Pietro Mascagni. Verga died on Jan. 27, 1922.   Richard H. Lansing

Vergil. See Virgil.

Verlaine, *vair LEN,* **Paul** (1844-1896), was a French poet who became a leader of the poetic movement called Symbolism. His poem "On the Nature of Poetry" (written 1871-1873) defines the technical innovations he made famous. They include lines of odd-numbered syllables, vagueness of imagery, the mixture of literary and colloquial vocabulary, and the quest for pure musicality.

Verlaine's volume of verse *Fêtes galantes* (1869) both celebrates and satirizes the sentimental paintings of Antoine Watteau, a French artist of the 1700's. Verlaine's remarkable ability to evoke delicate emotional states came to perfection in *Songs Without Words* (1874). His biographical and critical study *Accursed Poets* (1884) helped establish the reputations of several French poets.

Verlaine was born in Metz, France, on March 30, 1844. In the early 1870's, he became involved in a stormy homosexual love affair with poet Arthur Rimbaud. In 1873, Verlaine, in a drunken rage, shot Rimbaud in the wrist and was imprisoned for two years. He converted to the Roman Catholic Church in 1874. During his last years, Verlaine suffered from alcoholism and poverty. He died on Jan. 8, 1896.   Edward K. Kaplan

See also **French literature** (Symbolism); **Symbolism.**

Vermeer, *vuhr MEER,* **Jan,** *yahn* (1632-1675), was a Dutch painter skilled at painting domestic interiors. In many of his paintings, middle-class men and women talk, drink, or play musical instruments. Vermeer is also known for paintings of individual female figures quietly performing simple tasks before a mirror or a window, such as reading a letter or holding a pitcher. He placed his figures close to the viewer in relatively simplified composition. Many of his subjects appear caught in tranquil moments of concentration. Vermeer's *Young Woman Reading a Letter* appears in the **Painting** article.

Officer and Laughing Girl (about 1660), an oil painting on canvas; © The Frick Collection, New York City

A typical Vermeer painting shows a quiet scene of middle-class domestic life illuminated by sunlight from a window.

Vermeer employed the *pointillist* or *stippling* method, in which the painter uses small dots or points of unmixed color that blend in the eye of the viewer. In such paintings as *The Lacemaker* and *The Milk Maid,* he used this technique to suggest the illusion of soft light playing fleetingly over textured surfaces. Vermeer's conception of soft light results in slightly blurred outlines.

Vermeer's two outdoor scenes, *The View of Delft* and *Street in Delft,* rank among the finest landscape paintings of the 1600's. Vermeer was born in Delft on Oct. 31, 1632. He spent his entire life there, working primarily as an art dealer and innkeeper. He died on Dec. 15, 1675.   Linda Stone-Ferrier

Vermiculite, *vur MIHK yuh lyt,* is a mineral that occurs as layered flakes. It resembles the mineral *mica.* Vermiculite consists mainly of the chemical elements aluminum, iron, magnesium, oxygen, and silicon. It may be brown or yellow. When expanded by heat, vermiculite becomes a lightweight, fireproof substance with good heat insulating properties. It is used chiefly in building materials for insulation and soundproofing. It is also used as a soil conditioner and potting material. The United States produces and consumes more vermiculite than any other nation.   Ray E. Ferrell, Jr.

See also **Mica.**

Vermilion, *vuhr MIHL yuhn,* is a bright, scarlet pigment used to color inks, paints, and other substances. Chemical companies make vermilion from deposits of mercuric sulfide called *cinnabar.* They also prepare it by heating mercury and sulfur to form mercuric sulfide, then purifying that material. The name *vermilion* comes from a Latin word meaning *little worm,* and refers to the dried bodies of insects from which *carmine,* another red dye, was once obtained.   George J. Danker

See also **Cinnabar.**

Paul O. Boisvert

Camels Hump, near Huntington, rises in the Green Mountains, which run the length of central Vermont. Vermont's mountains attract many skiers, hikers, and other outdoor enthusiasts.

Vermont *The Green Mountain State*

Vermont, a New England state of the United States, is famous for its Green Mountains. These tree-covered peaks run the entire length of central Vermont. They divide the state into eastern and western sections. The beauty of the Green Mountains helps make Vermont one of the most scenic states. Every year, the mountains attract millions of skiers and other tourists. Montpelier is the capital of Vermont, and Burlington is the state's largest city.

The many tourists who visit Vermont help benefit the state's service industries. Service industries, such as retail trade and finance, combine to employ about three-fourths of Vermont's workers. Manufacturing is also important to Vermont. Computer components are the state's leading manufactured product.

Vermont has the lowest percentage of city dwellers of any state in the United States. Only three Vermont cities have more than 15,000 people. They are Burlington, Rut-

land, and South Burlington. Vermont has the smallest population of any state that lies east of the Mississippi River. The state ranks 49th among all the states in population. The only state that has fewer people than Vermont is Wyoming.

Forests cover about four-fifths of Vermont, and a variety of mineral deposits lie under the ground. These natural resources provide the raw materials for two of the state's manufacturing industries—wood processing and stone processing. Trees from Vermont's forests supply maple syrup and wood for making paper, furniture, and many other products. Vermont granite and marble are used in buildings, memorials, and tombs. Slate is used for roofing and for other purposes.

Vermont is the only New England state without a coastline on the Atlantic Ocean. However, water forms the boundary for more than half the state. The Connecticut River forms Vermont's entire eastern border. Lake Champlain extends along the northern half of the western border of Vermont. In addition to the Green Mountains, Vermont has many other mountainous and hilly areas. These include the Northeast Highlands and the Taconic Mountains.

The contributors of this article are John McCardell, Professor of History and President of Middlebury College; and Harold A. Meeks, Professor of Geography at the University of Vermont.

Downtown Burlington includes the Church Street Marketplace, which offers a variety of shops and restaurants, and an indoor mall.

Paul O. Boisvert

Interesting facts about Vermont

WORLD BOOK illustrations by Kevin Chadwick

The Concord Academy was the first school established solely for the purpose of training teachers. The academy was opened in 1823 by Reverend Samuel Read Hall.

The first patent issued by the United States government was granted to Samuel Hopkins of Vermont on July 31, 1790, for his method of making potash and pearl ash out of wood ash. Thomas Jefferson, the secretary of state at the time, signed the patent.

Concord Academy

Vermont has the lowest percentage of urban residents in the United States. More than three-fifths of the state's citizens live in rural areas. In addition, Montpelier, the capital of Vermont, has the lowest population of any state capital.

Vermont was the first state to forbid involuntary slavery. The issue of emancipation was included in one of the articles of the state's constitution, signed on July 2, 1777.

Vermont is the largest producer of maple syrup in the United States. Factories in Vermont bottle the syrup or use it to make such products as maple cream, maple sugar cakes, granulated maple sugar, and maple taffy. The syrup is also used in other products, such as salad dressing and barbecue sauce.

Maple syrup

Early in the Revolutionary War, Vermont's Green Mountain Boys, led by Ethan Allen, gained fame for their capture of Fort Ticonderoga from the British. But Vermont was not admitted to the newly formed United States after the war. It remained an independent republic until about 10 years after the last battle. Then, on March 4, 1791, Vermont entered the Union as the 14th state. It was the first state admitted to the Union after the 13 original colonies.

During the 1850's, Vermont began a voting record unequaled by any other state. From then until the 1960's, the voters of Vermont chose only Republicans in elections for president and governor. They also chose Republicans in all elections for the United States Senate and House of Representatives between the mid-1800's and the mid-1900's. No other state has voted so many times in a row for major candidates of the same political party. Two Vermont Republicans, Chester A. Arthur and Calvin Coolidge, served as president of the United States.

The word *Vermont* comes from *Vert Mont,* the French words for *Green Mountain.* Vermont's nickname is the *Green Mountain State.*

Hanson Carroll

A town meeting enables Vermont citizens to take a direct part in their government. All town voters may attend the annual meetings to elect officials and decide other local matters.

Vermont in brief

Symbols of Vermont

The state flag, adopted in 1923, bears the Vermont coat of arms. It shows a large pine tree, three sheaves of grain, and a cow. Mountains rise in the background. On the state seal, adopted in 1779, a pine tree with 14 branches represents the 13 original states and Vermont. A row of wooded hills cuts across the center. Wavy lines at the top and bottom represent sky and water. Sheaves of grain and a cow symbolize agriculture.

State flag

State seal

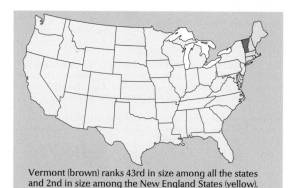

Vermont (brown) ranks 43rd in size among all the states and 2nd in size among the New England States (yellow).

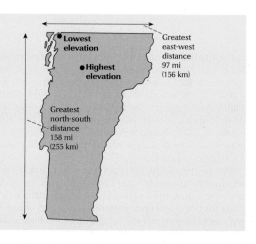

The State House is in Montpelier, the capital of Vermont since 1805. Many towns served as temporary capitals between 1777 and 1805.

General information

Statehood: March 4, 1791, the 14th state.
State abbreviations: Vt. (traditional); VT (postal).
State motto: *Freedom and Unity.*
State song: "These Green Mountains." Words and music by Diane Martin.

Land and climate

Area: 9,615 mi² (24,903 km²), including 366 mi² (947 km²) of inland water.
Elevation: *Highest*—Mount Mansfield, 4,393 ft (1,339 m) above sea level. *Lowest*—Lake Champlain in Franklin County, 95 ft (29 m) above sea level.
Record high temperature: 105 °F (41 °C) at Vernon on July 4, 1911.
Record low temperature: –50 °F (–46 °C) at Bloomfield on Dec. 30, 1933.
Average July temperature: 68 °F (20 °C).
Average January temperature: 17 °F (–8 °C).
Average yearly precipitation: 39 in (99 cm).

Lowest elevation

Highest elevation

Greatest east-west distance 97 mi (156 km)

Greatest north-south distance 158 mi (255 km)

Important dates

Massachusetts established Fort Dummer, the first permanent white settlement in the Vermont region.

Vermont became the 14th state on March 4.

| 1609 | 1724 | 1777 | 1791 |

Samuel de Champlain, probably the first white person to explore Vermont, arrived at Lake Champlain.

Vermont declared itself an independent republic.

State bird
Hermit thrush

State flower
Red clover

State tree
Sugar maple

People

Population: 608,827
Rank among the states: 49th
Density: 63 per mi² (24 per km²), U.S. average 78 per mi² (30 per km²)
Distribution: 62 percent rural, 38 percent urban
Largest cities in Vermont

Burlington	38,889
Essex†	18,626
Rutland	17,292
Colchester†	16,986
South Burlington	15,814
Bennington†	15,737

†Unincorporated place.
Source: 2000 census.

Population trend

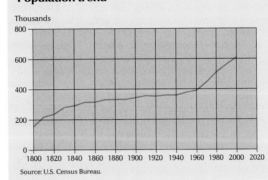

Thousands

Source: U.S. Census Bureau.

Year	Population
2000	608,827
1990	562,758
1980	511,456
1970	444,732
1960	389,881
1950	377,747
1940	359,231
1930	359,611
1920	352,428
1910	355,956
1900	343,641
1890	332,422
1880	332,286
1870	330,551
1860	315,098
1850	314,120
1840	291,948
1830	280,652
1820	235,981
1810	217,895
1800	154,465
1790	85,425

Economy

Chief products

Agriculture: apples, beef cattle, greenhouse and nursery products, hay, maple syrup, milk.
Manufacturing: electronic equipment, fabricated metal products, food products, machinery, nonmetallic mineral products.
Mining: granite, limestone, marble, talc.

Gross domestic product

Value of goods and services produced in 2004: $21,992,000,000. *Services* include community, business, and personal services; finance; government; trade; and transportation and communication. *Industry* includes construction, manufacturing, mining, and utilities. *Agriculture* includes agriculture, fishing, and forestry.

Source: U.S. Bureau of Economic Analysis.

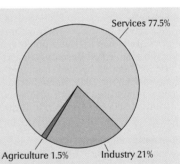

Services 77.5%
Agriculture 1.5%
Industry 21%

Government

State government

Governor: 2-year term
State senators: 30; 2-year terms
State representatives: 150; 2-year terms
Towns: 237 (towns, rather than counties, are the main units of local government in Vermont).

Federal government

United States senators: 2
United States representatives: 1
Electoral votes: 3

Sources of information

For information about tourism, write to: Vermont Department of Tourism and Marketing, 6 Baldwin Street, Drawer 33, Montpelier, VT 05633-1301. The Web site at http://www.vermontvacation.com also provides information.
For information on the economy, write to: Agency of Commerce and Community Development, National Life Building, Drawer 20, Montpelier, VT 05620-0501.
The state's official Web site at http://www.vermont.gov also provides a gateway to much information on Vermont's economy, government, and history.

Philip H. Hoff became the first Democrat to win election as governor of Vermont since 1853.

Vermont became the first state to allow a *civil union,* similar to marriage, for two people of the same sex.

1864 — **1962** — **1970** — **2000**

Confederate soldiers raided St. Albans in the northernmost land action of the Civil War.

The Environmental Control Law, permitting the state to limit major developments that might harm the environment, was passed.

Population. The 2000 United States census reported that Vermont had 608,827 people. The state's population had increased 8 percent over the 1990 census figure, 562,758. According to the 2000 census, Vermont ranks 49th in population among the 50 states.

Fewer people live in Vermont than in any other state east of the Mississippi River. West of the Mississippi, only Wyoming has fewer people.

More than three-fifths of Vermont's people live in rural areas—a greater percentage than in any other state. The Burlington-South Burlington metropolitan area is Vermont's only metropolitan area (see **Metropolitan area**). About one-third of the state's population lives in this metropolitan area. Burlington is the largest city in the state. It has a population of less than 40,000, but more than twice as many people as Rutland, the second largest city. Vermont's seven other cities, in order of size, are South Burlington, Barre, Montpelier, St. Albans, Winooski, Newport, and Vergennes. Essex, the largest unincorporated place in Vermont, has more people than any city except Burlington. Vermont has approximately 40 villages and 240 towns.

About 96 of every 100 Vermonters were born in the United States. Vermont's largest population groups include people of English, Irish, French, German and French-Canadian descent. Like other New Englanders, the people of Vermont have long been called *Yankees.* This word is used to refer to people considered to have such traits as thrift, conservative manners, reserved speech, and respect for individual rights.

Schools. The town of Guilford voted funds for a free public school in 1761. Vermont's Constitution of 1777 required each town to have a public school. In 1780, Bennington established Vermont's first secondary school. Vermont's first statewide school fund was approved by the Legislature in 1825. Samuel Read Hall, a pioneer educator, established the first teacher-training school in the United States at Concord in 1823.

A state commissioner of education and a 10-member State Board of Education supervise Vermont's public schools. The governor appoints the board members to six-year terms. The board, with the governor's approval, appoints the state commissioner for an indefinite term.

Local boards of directors administer Vermont's city and town school districts. All districts belong to administrative units called *supervisory unions.* Some unions consist of only one large school district, but others are comprised of several smaller districts. A superintendent heads each union. Vermont law requires children between the ages of 6 and 16 to attend school. For the number of students and teachers in Vermont, see **Education** (table).

Libraries. Vermont's oldest continually operating library opened in Brookfield in 1791. The Department of Libraries, in Montpelier, specializes in historical and legal research and reference works, and has the state's best collection of early Vermont newspapers. The Bailey/Howe Library of the University of Vermont is the largest library in the state. The Vermont Automated Libraries System is an online service that provides information on library holdings and state government.

Museums. The Vermont History Museum in Montpelier features exhibits on local history from prehistoric times to the present. It owns one of the oldest globes made in the United States. James Wilson made the globe in the early 1800's. The museum also has one of the first printing presses used in the nation.

The Bennington Museum has early American glassware, pottery, Vermont art, and historic flags. The University of Vermont's Robert Hull Fleming Museum in Burlington is the state's leading museum of art and anthropology. The Saint Johnsbury Athenaeum has fine paintings. The Henry Sheldon Museum of Vermont History, in Middlebury, houses early Vermont documents, household furnishings, portraits, and tools.

Population density

Vermont's population is scattered around its many mountainous areas. About one-third of the state's people live in the Burlington metropolitan area. More than three-fifths live in rural areas.

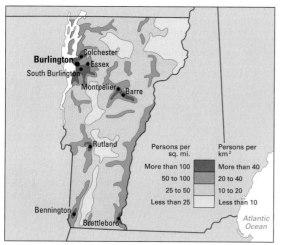

Universities and colleges

This table lists the universities and colleges in Vermont that grant bachelor's or advanced degrees and are accredited by the New England Association of Schools and Colleges.

Name	Mailing address
Bennington College	Bennington
Burlington College	Burlington
Castleton State College	Castleton
Champlain College	Burlington
Goddard College	Plainfield
Green Mountain College	Poultney
International Training, School for	Brattleboro
Johnson State College	Johnson
Lyndon State College	Lyndonville
Marlboro College	Marlboro
Middlebury College	Middlebury
Norwich University	Northfield
St. Joseph, College of	Rutland
St. Michael's College	Colchester
Southern Vermont College	Bennington
Sterling College	Craftsbury Common
Vermont, University of	Burlington
Vermont Law School	South Royalton
Vermont Technical College	Randolph Center
Woodbury College	Montpelier

Vermont map index

Metropolitan area

Burlington-South Burlington 198,889

Counties

Addison 35,974 F 4
Bennington 36,994 N 4
Caledonia 29,702 E 8
Chittenden 146,571 E 5
Essex 6,459 C 10
Franklin 45,417 C 5
Grand Isle 6,901 C 3
Lamoille 23,233 D 6
Orange 28,226 H 7
Orleans 26,277 C 8
Rutland 63,400 J 4
Washington 58,039 F 6
Windham 44,216 M 5
Windsor 57,418 J 6

Cities, towns, and villages

Adamant E 7
Addison▲ 1,393 G 3
Albany 165 ▲840 C 7
Alburg 488 ▲1,952 B 3
Alburg Springs B 4
Amsden K 7
Andover▲ 496 L 6
Arlington† 1,199 ▲2,397 M 4
Ascutney K 7
Athens▲ 340 M 6
Averill 8 B 10
Averys Gore* B 10
Bakersfield▲ 1,215 C 5
Baltimore*▲ 250 K 6
Barnard▲ 958 I 6
Barnet▲ 1,690 F 8
Barnumville L 4
Barre*▲ 7,602 F 7
Barre 9,291 F 7
Barton 742 ▲2,780 C 8
Bartonsville L 6
Beebe Plain B 8
Beecher Falls B 11
Bellows Falls 3,165 M 7
Belmont K 5
Belvidere*▲ 294 C 6
Bennington†○ 9,168 ▲15,737 N 4
Benson▲ 1,039 I 3
Berkshire▲ 1,388 B 5
Berlin▲ 2,864 F 6
Bethel▲ 1,968 H 6
Blissville J 3
Bloomfield▲ 261 C 10
Bolton▲ 971 E 5
Bomoseen J 4
Bondville L 5
Bowlsville K 5
Bradford 815 ▲2,619 H 8
Braintree*▲ 1,194 H 6
Brandon† 1,684 ▲3,917 I 4
Brattleboro† 8,289 ▲12,005 N 6
Bridgewater▲ 980 J 6
Bridport▲ 1,235 H 3
Brighton*▲ 1,260 C 9
Bristol▲ 3,788 G 4
Brookfield▲ 1,222 G 6
Brookline▲ 467 M 6
Brownington▲ 885 C 8
Brownsville K 7
Brunswick*▲ 107 C 10
Buel's Gore* 12 F 5
Burke*▲ 1,571 D 9
Burke Hollow D 9
Burlington○ 38,889 E 4
Cabot 239 ▲1,213 E 7
Cadys Falls D 6
Calais▲ 1,529 E 7
Cambridge 235 ▲3,186 D 5
Cambridgeport L 6
Canaan▲ 1,078 B 11
Castleton▲ 4,367 J 4
Cavendish▲ 1,470 K 6
Centerville D 6
Charleston*▲ 895 B 9
Charlotte▲ 3,569 F 3
Chelsea○▲ 1,250 H 7
Chester▲ 3,044 L 6
Chester [-Chester Depot]† 999 L 6
Chippenhook J 4
Chittenden▲ 1,182 I 5
Clarendon▲ 2,811 J 5
Clarendon Springs J 4
Colbyville E 6
Colchester▲ 16,986 D 4
Concord▲ 1,196 E 9
Cookville G 7
Corinth*▲ 1,461 G 8
Corinth Center G 8
Cornwall▲ 1,136 H 4
Coventry▲ 1,014 C 8
Craftsbury▲ 1,136 D 7
Cuttingsville J 5
Danby▲ 1,292 K 4
Danby Four Corners K 4
Danville▲ 2,211 E 8
Derby*▲ 4,604 B 8
Derby Center 670 B 8
Derby Line 776 B 8
Dorset▲ 2,036 L 4
Dover▲ 1,410 N 5
Dummerston*▲ 1,915 N 6
Duxbury▲ 1,289 F 6
East Barnard I 6
East Barre, see Graniteville [-East Barre]
East Burke D 9
East Calais E 7
East Charleston C 9
East Charlotte F 4
East Concord E 10
East Corinth G 8
East Dorset L 4
East Dover N 5
East Dummerston N 6
East Franklin B 5
East Granville G 5
East Hardwick D 7
East Haven▲ 301 D 9
East Johnson D 6
East Lyndon D 9
East Middlebury H 4
East Montpelier▲ 2,578 F 7
East Orange G 7
East Peacham F 8
East Poultney J 4
East Putney M 7
East Randolph H 6
East Richford B 6
East Rupert L 4
East Ryegate F 8
East St. Johnsbury E 9
East Thetford I 8
East Topsham G 8
East Wallingford K 5
Eden▲ 1,152 C 6
Eden Mills C 7
Elmore*▲ 849 E 7
Ely H 8
Enosburg*▲ 2,788 B 5
Enosburg Falls 1,473 B 5
Essex*▲ 18,626 E 4
Essex Junction 8,591 E 4
Evansville C 8
Ewells Mill E 8
Fair Haven† 2,435 ▲2,928 J 3
Fairfax▲ 3,765 D 4
Fairfield▲ 1,800 C 5
Fairlee▲ 967 H 8
Fayston*▲ 1,141 F 5
Felchville K 6
Ferdinand* 33 C 10
Ferrisburgh▲ 2,657 F 3
Fletcher▲ 1,179 D 5
Florence I 4
Forest Dale H 4
Foxville G 7
Franklin▲ 1,268 B 5
Gallup Mills D 10
Gassetts K 6
Gaysville I 6
Georgia*▲ 4,375 C 4
Georgia Plains C 4
Gilman E 10
Glastenbury* 16 M 4
Glover▲ 966 C 8
Goshen▲ 227 H 4
Grafton▲ 649 L 6
Granby▲ 86 D 10
Grand Isle▲ 1,955 C 3
Graniteville [-East Barre]† 2,136 G 7
Granville▲ 303 H 5
Green River O 6
Greensboro▲ 770 D 8
Greensboro Bend D 8
Groton▲ 876 F 8
Guildhall○▲ 268 D 10
Guilford▲ 2,046 N 6
Halifax▲ 782 O 6
Hancock▲ 382 H 5
Hanksville F 5
Hardwick▲ 3,174 E 7
Harmonyville M 6
Hartford▲ 10,367 I 7
Hartland▲ 3,223 J 7
Healdville K 5
Heartwellville N 5
Highgate*▲ 3,397 B 4
Highgate Center B 4
Highgate Falls B 4
Highgate Springs B 4
Hinesburg▲ 4,340 F 4
Holden I 5
Holland▲ 588 B 9
Hortonia I 3
Hubbardton▲ 752 I 4
Huntington▲ 1,861 F 5
Hyde Park○ 415 ▲2,847 D 6
Hydeville J 4
Irasburg▲ 1,077 C 8
Irasville F 5
Island Pond† 849 C 9
Isle La Motte▲ 488 B 3
Jacksonville 237 N 5
Jamaica▲ 946 M 5
Jay▲ 426 B 7
Jeffersonville 568 D 5
Jericho† 1,457 ▲5,015 E 5
Johnson 1,420 ▲3,274 D 6
Jonesville E 5
Keeler Bay D 3
Kirby*▲ 456 E 9
Lake Dunmore H 4
Lake Elmore D 7
Landgrove*▲ 144 L 5
Leicester▲ 974 H 4
Lemington▲ 107 C 11
Lewis* B 10
Lincoln▲ 1,214 G 4
Londonderry▲ 1,709 L 5
Lowell▲ 738 C 7
Lower Granville H 5
Lower Village E 6
Lower Waterford E 9
Ludlow 958 ▲2,449 K 6
Lunenburg▲ 1,328 E 10
Lyndon▲ 5,448 D 9
Lyndon Center D 9
Lyndonville 1,227 D 9
Maidstone▲ 105 D 10
Manchester○ 602 ▲4,180 L 4
Manchester Center† 2,065 L 4
Manchester Depot L 4
Marlboro▲ 978 N 6
Marshfield 262 ▲1,496 E 7
McIndoe Falls F 8
Mechanicsville E 4
Mendon▲ 1,028 J 5
Middlebury†○ 6,252 ▲8,183 G 4
Middlesex▲ 1,729 F 6
Middletown Springs▲ 823 J 4
Mill Village D 7
Milton 1,537 ▲9,479 D 4
Monkton▲ 1,759 F 4
Monkton Ridge F 4
Montgomery▲ 992 B 6
Montpelier○ 8,035 F 6
Moretown▲ 1,653 F 5
Morgan▲ 669 B 9
Morristown▲ 5,139 D 6
Morrisville 2,009 D 6
Morses Line B 5
Moscow E 6
Mount Holly▲ 1,241 K 5
Mount Tabor▲ 203 K 5
New Haven▲ 1,666 G 4
Newark▲ 470 D 9
Newbury 396 ▲1,955 G 9
Newfane○ 116 ▲1,680 M 6
Newport*▲ 1,511 B 7
Newport○ 5,005 B 8
North Bennington 1,428 N 3
North Concord E 9
North Danville E 8
North Dorset L 4
North Fairfax C 4
North Fayston F 5
North Ferrisburgh F 4
North Hero○▲ 810 C 3
North Landgrove L 5
North Montpelier F 7
North Pomfret I 7
North Pownal N 3
North Randolph H 6
North Sheldon B 5
North Springfield K 6
North Troy 593 B 7
North Tunbridge H 7
North Westminster 271 M 7
Northfield 3,208 ▲5,791 G 6
Norton▲ 214 B 10
Norwich▲ 3,544 I 7
Old Bennington 232 N 4
Orange▲ 965 G 7
Orleans 826 C 8
Orwell▲ 1,185 I 3
Panton▲ 682 G 3
Passumpsic E 9
Pawlet▲ 1,394 K 4
Peacham▲ 665 F 8
Perkinsville 142 K 6
Peru▲ 416 L 5
Pittsfield▲ 427 I 5
Pittsford▲ 3,140 I 4
Pittsford Mills I 4
Plainfield▲ 1,286 F 7
Plymouth▲ 555 J 6
Pomfret▲ 997 I 6
Pompanoosuc I 8
Post Mills H 8
Poultney 1,575 ▲3,633 J 4
Pownal▲ 3,560 O 3
Proctor▲ 1,877 I 4
Proctorsville K 6
Putnamville F 6
Putney▲ 2,634 M 7
Quechee I 7
Randolph▲ 4,853 H 6
Rawsonville L 5
Reading*▲ 707 J 6
Readsboro▲ 809 O 5
Richford▲ 2,321 B 6
Richmond▲ 4,090 E 4
Ripton▲ 556 H 4
Rochester▲ 1,171 H 5
Rockingham▲ 5,309 L 7
Roxbury▲ 576 G 6
Royalton▲ 2,603 I 6
Rupert▲ 704 L 4
Rutland*▲ 4,038 J 4
Rutland○ 17,292 J 5
Ryegate*▲ 1,150 F 8
St. Albans*▲ 5,086 C 4
St. Albans○ 7,650 C 4
St. Albans Bay C 4
St. George*▲ 698 E 4
St. Johnsbury†○ 6,319 ▲7,571 E 9
Salisbury▲ 1,090 H 4
Sandgate▲ 353 L 4
Saxtons River 519 L 7
Searsburg▲ 96 N 5
Shaftsbury▲ 3,767 M 4
Sharon▲ 1,411 I 7
Sheffield▲ 727 D 8
Shelburne▲ 6,944 E 4
Shelburne Road Section* E 4
Sheldon▲ 1,990 B 5
Sherburne*▲ I 5
Shoreham▲ 1,222 H 3
Shrewsbury▲ 1,108 J 5
Simonsville L 6
Somerset* 5 M 5
South Alburg B 3
South Barre† 1,242 G 7
South Burlington 15,814 E 4
South Cambridge D 5
South Duxbury F 5
South Hero▲ 1,696 D 3
South Lincoln G 5
South Londonderry L 5
South Lunenburg E 10
South Newfane N 6
South Peacham F 8
South Pomfret I 6
South Randolph H 6
South Royalton I 6
South Ryegate F 8
South Wallingford K 4
South Wardsboro M 5
South Windham M 6
South Woodbury E 7
Springfield† 3,938 ▲9,078 L 7
Stamford▲ 813 O 4
Stannard▲ 185 D 8
Starksboro▲ 1,898 F 4
Stevens Mills B 6
Stockbridge▲ 674 I 5
Stowe ▲4,339 E 6
Strafford▲ 1,045 H 7
Stratton▲ 136 M 5
Sudbury▲ 583 I 4
Sunderland▲ 850 M 4
Sutton▲ 1,001 D 9
Swanton 2,548 ▲6,203 B 4
Taftsville J 7
Talcville H 5
Thetford*▲ 2,617 I 8
Tinmouth▲ 567 K 4
Topsham*▲ 1,142 G 8
Townshend▲ 1,149 M 6
Troy▲ 1,564 B 7
Tunbridge▲ 1,309 H 7
Tyson K 6
Underhill▲ 2,980 D 5
Union Village I 8
Vergennes 2,741 F 3
Vernon▲ 2,141 O 7
Vershire▲ 629 H 7
Victory▲ 97 E 9
Waits River G 8
Waitsfield▲ 1,659 F 5
Walden▲ 782 E 8
Wallace Pond B 10
Wallingford† 948 ▲2,274 K 5
Waltham*▲ 479 G 4
Wardsboro▲ 854 M 5
Warners Grant* B 9
Warren▲ 1,681 G 5
Warrens Gore* 10 B 9
Washington▲ 1,047 G 7
Waterbury 1,706 ▲4,915 F 6
Waterford*▲ 1,104 E 9
Waterville▲ 697 C 6
Weathersfield* ▲2,788 K 7
Weathersfield Bow K 7
Websterville G 7
Wells▲ 1,121 K 4
Wells River 325 G 8
West Berkshire B 5
West Berlin F 6
West Braintree H 6
West Brattleboro† 3,222 N 6
West Burke 364 D 9
West Castleton J 3
West Charleston B 8
West Corinth G 7
West Danville E 8
West Dover N 5
West Fairlee▲ 726 H 8
West Glover C 8
West Hartford I 7
West Haven▲ 278 I 3
West Lincoln G 4
West Milton D 4
West Newbury G 8
West Norwich I 7
West Pawlet K 3
West Rupert L 4
West Rutland† 2,263 ▲2,535 J 4
West Salisbury H 4
West Topsham G 7
West Townshend M 6
West Windsor*▲ 1,067 J 7
Westfield▲ 503 B 7
Westford▲ 2,086 D 4
Westminster 276 ▲3,210 M 7
Westminster West M 6
Westmore▲ 306 C 8
Weston▲ 630 L 5
Weybridge▲ 824 G 4
Wheelock▲ 621 D 8
White River Junction† 2,569 J 7
Whiting▲ 380 H 4
Whitingham▲ 1,298 O 5
Wilder† 1,636 I 7
Williamstown▲ 3,225 G 6
Williamsville N 6
Williston▲ 7,650 E 4
Williston Road Section* E 4
Wilmington▲ 2,225 N 5
Windham▲ 328 L 6
Windsor▲ 3,756 K 7
Winhall*▲ 702 L 5
Winooski 6,561 E 4
Wolcott▲ 1,456 D 7
Woodbury▲ 809 E 7
Woodford▲ 414 N 4
Woodstock○ 977 ▲3,232 J 6
Worcester▲ 902 E 6

*Does not appear on map; key shows general location.
†Census designated place—unincorporated, but recognized as a significant settled community by the U.S. Census Bureau.
○County seat.
▲Entire town (township), including rural area.
Source: 2000 census. Metropolitan area figure is based on 2003 Office of Management and Budget reorganization of 2000 census data. Places without population figures are unincorporated areas.

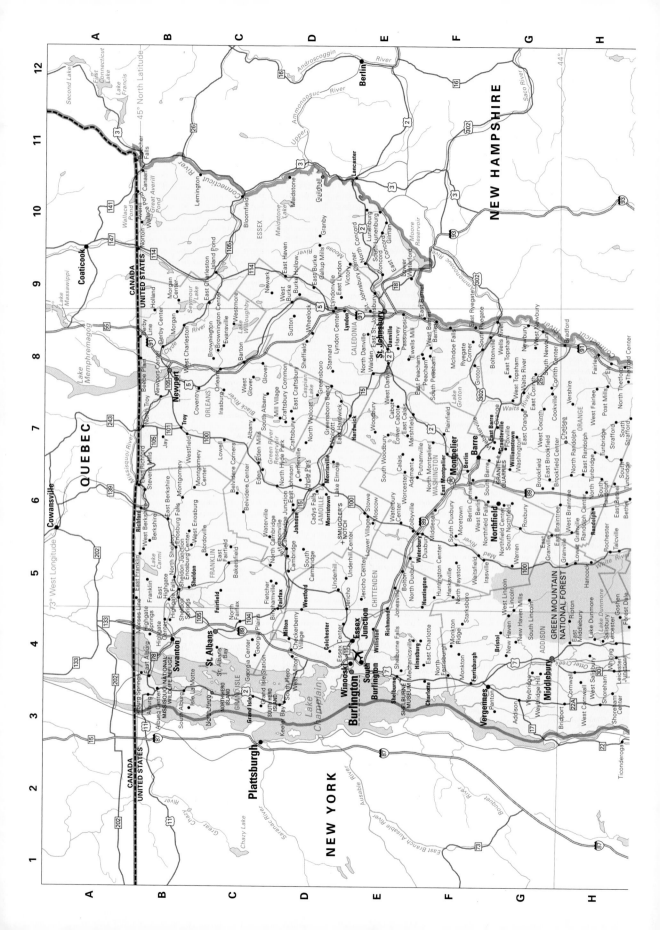

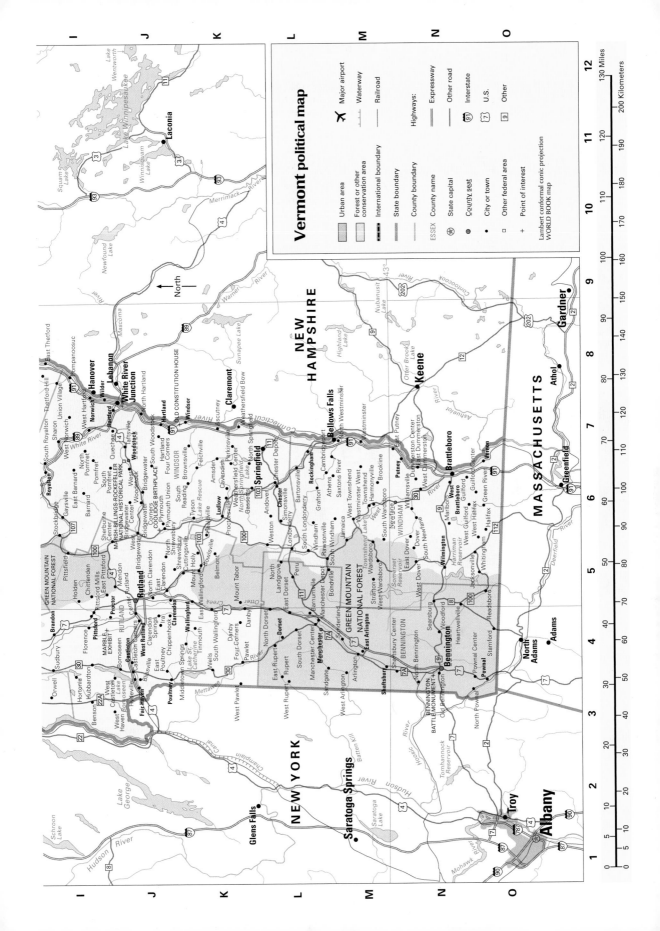

Vermont political map

Vermont's mountains, lakes, and streams offer a variety of recreational activities. Visitors to the Green Mountains can hike on the Long Trail. This footpath winds through the mountains from Massachusetts to Canada. Overnight camps lie along the trail every 6 to 8 miles (10 to 13 kilometers). In winter, tourists flock to ski resorts in the Green Mountains and other ranges. The largest ski resorts are near Jay, Manchester, Rutland, Stowe, Waitsfield, and Wilmington. The skiing season usually lasts from mid-December to mid-April. Visitors also enjoy summer boating on the larger lakes and fishing in the state's many streams.

Many vacationers go to Vermont just for the beautiful scenery. In the fall, the state is ablaze with the orange, purple, red, and yellow colors of turning leaves. Vermont's quiet towns and villages are other favorite scenes. They are noted for their white churches.

Skiing contests rank among the most popular annual events and take place in many areas during the winter. The maple sugar season begins when the winter snows start melting, usually in March. Many people gather at maple sugarhouses to watch syrup being made from maple sap. Craft fairs, antique shows, and summer theater programs are held throughout the summer. The best time to see the brilliant colors of Vermont's autumn leaves is from mid-September through mid-October.

Paul O. Boisvert

An autumn scene in West Townshend

Bennington College

The Bennington Battle Monument

Places to visit

Following are brief descriptions of some of Vermont's many interesting places to visit:

Bennington Battle Monument, in Bennington, is a limestone tower that rises 306 feet (93 meters) high. The monument honors the colonists who defeated the British in the Battle of Bennington in 1777. The tower is one of the highest battle monuments in the world.

Granite Quarries cut deeply into Millstone Hill (known locally as Quarry Hill) in Barre. Visitors can watch large granite blocks being quarried, and see granite being sawed, polished, and carved in the world's largest stone-finishing plant.

Old Constitution House, in Windsor, is the building in which Vermont's first Constitution was adopted. This two-story frame house, which was originally a tavern, was built in 1772.

Plymouth Notch Historic District includes the birthplace of President Calvin Coolidge, the family home where he took the oath of office, a general store, and a visitor's center. Coolidge's grave is marked by a single gravestone in a nearby cemetery.

Shelburne Museum, in Shelburne, is a reconstruction of an early American village. The museum includes more than 30 historic buildings with such items as carriages, china, dolls, furniture, glass, paintings, pewter, rugs, textiles, and toys. The side-wheeler steamship *Ticonderoga* is part of the museum.

Smuggler's Notch, near Stowe, is a wide gap between Mount Mansfield and the Sterling Mountains. The notch got its name during the War of 1812 (1812-1815), when smugglers brought goods through the notch from Canada to Boston.

Vermont Marble Museum, in Proctor, deals with the long history of marble quarrying and finishing in Vermont. It features the world's largest collection of various kinds of marble.

National forest. Green Mountain National Forest, established in 1932, is in southern and central Vermont.

State parks and forests. There are 52 state parks and 36 state forests in Vermont. For information, write to the Department of Forests, Parks & Recreation, 103 S. Main Street, Waterbury, VT 05676, or go to the department's Web site at http://www.vtfpr.org.

Annual events

January-June
Stowe Winter Carnival (January); Town Meeting Day, state-wide (first Tuesday in March); Vermont Maple Festival in St. Albans (April); Vermont Dairy Festival in Enosburg Falls (June); Antique Gas and Steam Engine Show in Brownington (June).

July-November
Vermont Quilt Festival in Northfield (July); Arts Festival on the Green in Middlebury (July); Vermont Mozart Festival in Burlington and other locations in northern and central Vermont (July-August); fairs in Barton, Bradford, Essex Junction, Lyndonville, Rutland, Tunbridge, and other towns (July to September); Foliage Festivals, statewide (September to October).

Eric Sanford

George Rockwin, Bruce Coleman Inc.

Winter Carnival in Stowe

Gathering maple sap in Dummerston

Hanson Carroll

Skiing on Killington Mountain

Land regions. Vermont has six main land regions. They are (1) the Northeast Highlands, (2) the Western New England Upland, (3) the Green Mountains, (4) the Vermont Valley, (5) the Taconic Mountains, and (6) the Champlain Valley.

The Northeast Highlands cover the northeastern corner of Vermont and parts of New Hampshire and Maine. This region is an area of granite similar to New Hampshire's White Mountains. The Northeast Highlands have granite mountains that rise 2,700 to 3,300 feet (823 to 1,010 meters) above sea level. The highest are Gore Mountain (3,330 feet, or 1,015 meters), Burke Mountain (3,267 feet, or 996 meters), and Mount Monadnock (3,140 feet, or 957 meters). Swift streams cut between the mountains and flow into the Connecticut and other rivers.

The Western New England Upland covers most of eastern Vermont. It also extends into Massachusetts and Connecticut. This region is sometimes called the *Vermont Piedmont.* In the east, it consists of the broad, fertile lowlands of the Connecticut River Valley. Farmers in the valley raise dairy cattle and grow apples and strawberries. The lowlands rise gradually to hills in the west. The granite hills near Barre include 1,700-foot (518-meter) Millstone Hill, also called Quarry Hill. Many lakes lie among hills in the northern part of the Western New England Upland.

The Green Mountains region covers central Vermont. The famous Green Mountains make up all but the northeastern corner of the region. In the northeast, the Green Mountains taper off into the Northfield, Worcester, and several other low mountain ranges.

Mount Mansfield, one of the Green Mountains, is the highest peak in Vermont. It rises 4,393 feet (1,339 meters) above sea level. Killington Mountain (4,241 feet, or 1,293 meters), Mount Ellen (4,083 feet, or 1,244 meters), and Camels Hump (4,083 feet, or 1,244 meters)—all in the Green Mountains—are Vermont's next tallest peaks. The Green Mountains region is the center of Vermont's tourist industry. It is also an important source of minerals.

The Vermont Valley is a narrow region that stretches about halfway up western Vermont from the Massachusetts border. The region includes the valleys of several small rivers, including the Batten Kill and the Walloomsac. Many people passed through the valley before settling in Vermont.

The Taconic Mountains region covers a narrow strip in southwestern Vermont. The region also extends into Massachusetts. In Vermont, it includes many mountains.

The highest ones are Equinox Mountain (3,816 feet, or 1,163 meters), Dorset Peak (3,770 feet, or 1,149 meters), Little Equinox Mountain (3,320 feet, or 1,012 meters), Mother Myrick Mountain (3,290 feet, or 1,003 meters), and Bear Mountain (3,260 feet, or 994 meters). Swift streams cut through the mountains, and the mountains surround many scenic lakes.

The Champlain Valley, also called the *Vermont Lowland,* borders Lake Champlain. This region includes Burlington, the state's largest city; and some of Vermont's best farmland. The valley has many dairy farms and apple orchards. Farmers in the region also raise corn, hay, oats, and wheat on rolling hills and broad fertile lowlands. Lake Champlain has a series of islands, including Grand Isle and Isle La Motte. These islands are part of Vermont.

Rivers and lakes. The Connecticut River forms Vermont's entire eastern border. In 1934, a ruling by the Supreme Court of the United States gave control of the river to New Hampshire. Its western border is the low water mark on the Vermont side of the river. Otter Creek is the longest river within Vermont. It rises near East Dorset, flows 100 miles (160 kilometers) north, and emp-

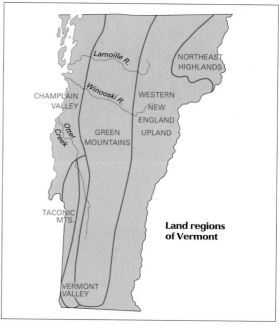

Land regions of Vermont

WORLD BOOK map

Map index

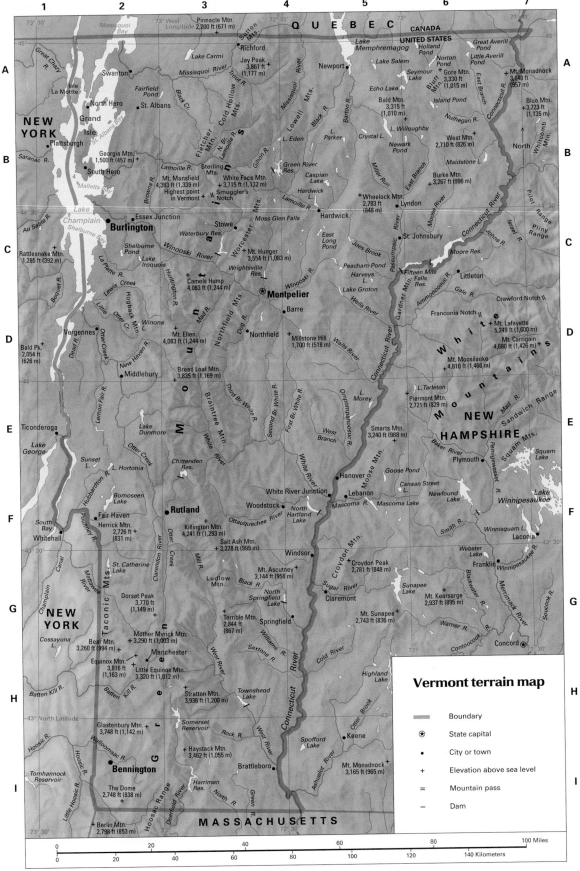

Vermont terrain map

Legend:
- ▬ Boundary
- ✪ State capital
- • City or town
- + Elevation above sea level
- = Mountain pass
- — Dam

WORLD BOOK map

Map labels (top border, columns): 1 2 3 4 5 6 7

Map labels (side borders, rows): A B C D E F G H I

QUEBEC CANADA
UNITED STATES
NEW YORK
NEW HAMPSHIRE
MASSACHUSETTS

Pinnacle Mtn. 2,200 ft (671 m)
Missisquoi Bay
73° West Longitude
72°
71° 30'
Sutton Mts.
Richford
Jay Peak 3,861 ft (1,177 m)
Lake Memphremagog
Newport
Lake Salem
Holland Pond
Great Averill Pond
Little Averill Pond
Mt. Monadnock 3,140 ft (957 m)
Norton Pond
Gore Mtn. 3,330 ft (1,015 m)
Blue Mtn. +3,723 ft (1,135 m)
Great Chazy R.
Lake Carmi
Missisquoi River
Trout R.
Cold Hollow Mts.
Lowell Mts.
Missisquoi River
Black R.
Seymour Lake
Echo Lake
Island Pond
Bluff Mtn.
Swanton
Fairfield Pond
Bald Mtn. 3,315 ft (1,010 m)
Isle La Motte
North Hero
St. Albans
L. Parker
Crystal L.
L. Willoughby
Newark Pond
Nulhegan R.
West Mtn. 2,710 ft (826 m)
Whitcomb Mtn.
NEW YORK
Grand Isle
St. Albans Bay
Georgia Mtn. 1,500 ft (457 m)
Lamoille R.
Fletcher Mtn.
N. Br. Lamoille R.
Gihon R.
Green River Res.
Miller Run
Maidstone L.
North
Pilot Range
Plattsburgh
Saranac R.
Browns R.
Sterling Mts.
White Face Mtn. +3,715 ft (1,132 m)
Smuggler's Notch
L. Eden
Hardwick L.
East Branch
Burke Mtn. +3,267 ft (996 m)
Israel R.
Pliny Range
South Hero
Mt. Mansfield 4,393 ft (1,339 m) Highest point in Vermont
Caspian Lake
Lamoille R.
Wheelock Mtn. 2,783 ft (848 m)
Lyndon
Connecticut River
Lake Champlain
Shelburne Bay
Au Sable R.
Essex Junction
Stowe
Moss Glen Falls
Hardwick
East Long Pond
Joes Brook
St. Johnsbury
Moore Res.
Littleton
Crawford Notch
Burlington
Worcester Mts.
Mt. Hunger 3,554 ft (1,083 m)
Winooski River
Waterbury Res.
Peacham Pond
Passumpsic River
Fifteen Mile Falls Res.
Moore Res.
Rattlesnake Mtn. 1,285 ft (392 m)
Shelburne Pond
Lake Iroquois
Wrightsville Res.
Winooski R.
Harveys L.
Gardner Mtn.
Ammonoosuc R.
Gale R.
Camels Hump 4,083 ft (1,244 m)
Lake Groton
Franconia Notch
Winona L.
Montpelier
Wells River
Mt. Lafayette 5,249 ft (1,600 m)
La Platte R.
Hogback Mtn.
Huntington R.
Barre
Mt. Carrigain 4,680 ft (1,426 m)
Little Otter Cr.
Mt. Ellen 4,083 ft (1,244 m)
Northfield
Mt. Moosilauke +4,810 ft (1,466 m)
Vergennes
Mad R.
Dog R.
Northfield Mts.
Millstone Hill 1,700 ft (518 m)
Waits River
Connecticut River
Bald Pk. 2,054 ft (626 m)
Dead R.
New Haven R.
Bread Loaf Mtn. 3,835 ft (1,169 m)
White Mountains
Middlebury
Braintree Mtn.
Third Br. White R.
Second Br. White R.
First Br. White R.
Ompompanoosuc R.
L. Morey
Piermont Mtn. 2,721 ft (829 m)
Mad R.
Sandwich Range
Lemon Fair R.
White River
Ticonderoga
Lake Dunmore
West Branch
Smarts Mtn. 3,240 ft (988 m)
NEW HAMPSHIRE
Lake George
Sunset L.
Otter Creek
Moose Mtn.
Baker River
Pemigewasset R.
Squam Mts.
Squam Lake
Hubbardton R.
L. Hortonia
Chittenden Res.
Hanover
Goose Pond
Plymouth
South Bay
Bomoseen Lake
White River
Canaan Street L.
Newfound Lake
Lake Winnipesaukee
Fair Haven
Herrick Mtn. 2,726 ft (831 m)
Rutland
White River Junction
Lebanon
Mascoma R.
Mascoma Lake
Whitehall
Poultney R.
Killington Mtn. 4,241 ft (1,293 m)
Woodstock
North Hartland Lake
Smith R.
Winnisquam L.
Canal
Salt Ash Mtn. +3,278 ft (999 m)
Ottauquechee River
Laconia
St. Catherine Lake
Mill R.
Windsor
Webster Lake
Metawee River
Clarendon R.
Mt. Ascutney 3,144 ft (958 m)
Croydon Mtn.
Croydon Peak 2,781 ft (848 m)
Franklin
Winnipesaukee R.
Taconic Mts.
Dorset Peak 3,770 ft (1,149 m)
Ludlow Mtn.
Black R.
Sugar River
Claremont
Sunapee Lake
Mt. Kearsarge 2,937 ft (895 m)
Blackwater R.
Merrimack River
Soucook R.
NEW YORK
Cossayuna L.
Mother Myrick Mtn. +3,290 ft (1,003 m)
North Springfield Lake
Mt. Sunapee 2,743 ft (836 m)
Warner R.
Bear Mtn. 3,260 ft (994 m)
Otter Creek
Terrible Mtn. 2,844 ft (867 m)
Springfield
Williams R.
Equinox Mtn. 3,816 ft (1,163 m)
Manchester
Little Equinox Mtn. 3,320 ft (1,012 m)
West River
Saxtons R.
Cold River
Highland Lake
Contoocook R.
Concord
Green Mtns.
Batten Kill R.
Batten Kill R.
Stratton Mtn. 3,936 ft (1,200 m)
Townshend Lake
Connecticut River
Glastenbury Mtn. 3,748 ft (1,142 m)
Somerset Reservoir
Rock R.
Spofford Lake
Otter Brook
Keene
Hoosic R.
Walloomsac R.
Haystack Mtn. 3,462 ft (1,055 m)
West River
Ashuelot River
Mt. Monadnock 3,165 ft (965 m)
Tomhannock Reservoir
Bennington
Harriman Res.
Brattleboro
Little Hoosic R.
Hoosic R.
The Dome 2,748 ft (838 m)
Hoosic Range
Deerfield River
North R.
Green R.
Berlin Mtn. 2,798 ft (853 m)
MASSACHUSETTS

73° 30'
73°
72° 30'
72°
45°
44° 30'
44°
43° 30'
43° North Latitude

Scale:
0 20 40 60 80 100 Miles
0 20 40 60 80 100 120 140 Kilometers

ties into Lake Champlain. The Batten Kill River also rises near East Dorset. It flows south into New York.

Most other Vermont rivers run down the slopes of the Green Mountains. Some flow down the eastern slopes and empty into the Connecticut River. Others wind down the western slopes and empty into Lake Champlain. Three large rivers—the Missisquoi, the Lamoille, and the Winooski—rise east of the Green Mountains and pass through them. The rivers empty into Lake Champlain.

Vermont has about 430 lakes and ponds. Most are in the northeast. Lake Champlain, the largest lake in New England, covers 322 square miles (834 square kilometers) in northwest Vermont. The rest of the 490-square-mile (1,270-square-kilometer) lake lies in New York and Quebec. Vermont's second largest lake is Lake Memphremagog. About one-third of it, or 10 square miles (26 square kilometers), lies in the state, and the rest is in Quebec. Bomoseen Lake, west of Rutland, is the largest lake entirely in Vermont. It covers about 4 square miles (10 square kilometers).

Plant and animal life. Forests cover about three-fourths of the state. Common trees include ashes, basswoods, beeches, birches, cedars, hemlocks, maples, pines, poplars, and spruces. Many kinds of ferns grow in the mountain regions of Vermont. Several types of grasses and sedges grow in the forests and lowlands. Anemones, arbutuses, buttercups, daisies, gentians, goldenrods, lilacs, pussy willows, and violets grow throughout the state.

The white-tailed deer is Vermont's most common game animal. Fur-bearing animals found in the state include bears, beavers, bobcats, foxes, minks, moose, muskrats, raccoons, and skunks. Porcupines, rabbits, squirrels, and woodchucks live in the forests.

Climate. Summers in Vermont are short, with few hot days. Summer nights are cool and crisp, especially in the mountains. Vermont has an average July temperature of 68 °F (20 °C). Vernon had the highest temperature that was ever recorded in the state, 105 °F (41 °C) on July 4, 1911.

Vermont winters are long and cold, with an average January temperature of 17 °F (–8 °C). Bloomfield had the record low temperature, –50 °F (–46 °C) on Dec. 30, 1933. Snowfall in the Connecticut River Valley and the Champlain Valley ranges from 60 to 80 inches (250 to 200 centimeters) yearly. The mountains receive from 80 to 120 inches (200 to 305 centimeters) a year. Snow is important to Vermont's economy. The deep snows on mountains attract thousands of skiers. Yearly *precipitation* (rain, melted snow, and other forms of moisture) averages about 39 inches (99 centimeters).

Average monthly weather

Burlington					
	Temperatures				Days of
	°F		°C		rain or
	High	Low	High	Low	snow
Jan.	27	9	–3	–13	14
Feb.	29	11	–2	–12	11
Mar.	40	22	4	–6	13
Apr.	53	34	12	1	12
May	68	45	20	7	14
June	77	55	25	13	13
July	81	60	27	16	12
Aug.	78	58	26	14	12
Sept.	69	50	21	10	12
Oct.	56	39	13	4	12
Nov.	44	30	7	–1	14
Dec.	32	17	0	–8	15

Average January temperatures

Vermont has long, cold winters. Snowfall is heavy throughout the state. The northern section has the lowest temperatures.

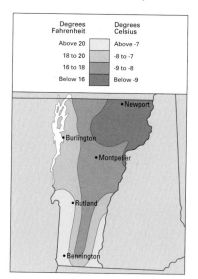

Degrees Fahrenheit	Degrees Celsius
Above 20	Above -7
18 to 20	-8 to -7
16 to 18	-9 to -8
Below 16	Below -9

Average July temperatures

Vermont summers are mild, with crisp, cool evenings, especially in the mountains. The south is the warmest section.

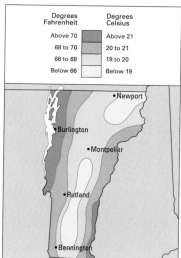

Degrees Fahrenheit	Degrees Celsius
Above 70	Above 21
68 to 70	20 to 21
66 to 68	19 to 20
Below 66	Below 19

Average yearly precipitation

Much of the state's precipitation comes in the form of snow, especially in the mountainous regions.

WORLD BOOK maps

Inches	Centimeters
More than 46	More than 117
42 to 46	107 to 117
38 to 42	97 to 107
Less than 38	Less than 97

Millions of tourists visit Vermont for its tree-covered mountains and picture-postcard villages, benefiting the state's service industries. This economic activity is also important in Vermont's larger cities, where most of the service industries are concentrated. Manufacturing is also a major economic activity in Vermont. Computer machinery and components are the state's most valuable products from this sector. Milk is Vermont's leading farm product, and granite is the leading mined product.

Natural resources of Vermont include valuable mineral deposits, forests, and fertile soil.

Soil. Vermont's most fertile areas are its river valleys. Some parts of the state are rocky with little or no soil.

Forests cover about four-fifths of Vermont. The state's hardwood trees include ashes, birches, beeches, maples, and oaks. Softwood trees include cedars, hemlocks, red and white pines, and spruces.

Minerals. Large granite, marble, slate, and talc deposits make the Green Mountains region Vermont's chief mining area. Valuable marble deposits are also found in the Vermont Valley and the Taconic Mountains. Much of Vermont's slate comes from the Taconic Mountains. Granite is found in eastern Vermont.

Service industries, taken together, account for the greatest portion of Vermont's *gross domestic product—* the total value of goods and services produced in the state in a year. Most of the service industries are concentrated in Burlington and Rutland, which are the state's largest incorporated cities, and in popular tourist centers.

Community, business, and personal services ranks as Vermont's leading service industry group in terms of the gross domestic product. This industry group employs more people than any other group in the state. It consists of a variety of businesses, including private health care, law firms, theaters, and repair shops.

Vermont's second leading service industry groups are (1) trade, restaurants, and hotels and (2) finance, insurance, and real estate. These groups each account for a

Economy of Vermont

This map shows the economic uses of land in Vermont and where the state's leading farm, mineral, and forest products are produced. Major manufacturing centers are shown in red.

WORLD BOOK map

roughly equal share of the gross domestic product.

Wholesale trade consists of buying goods from producers and selling the goods to other businesses. The wholesale trade of food products, petroleum and petroleum products, and wood products is important in Vermont. Retail trade involves selling goods directly to consumers. Major types of retail businesses include car dealerships, food stores, hardware stores, and service stations. This sector also includes hotels, restaurants, and most ski resorts. Many popular ski resorts lie in the Green Mountains.

The buying and selling of homes and other property is a significant part of Vermont's economy. Many people in New York and Massachusetts have vacation homes in Vermont. Burlington is the chief financial center of the state.

Government ranks fourth among service industry groups in Vermont. Government services include the operation of public schools and hospitals. The public school system is one of the state's major employers.

Transportation and communication ranks fifth among service industry groups in terms of the gross domestic product. Railroads and trucking companies transport much of the freight in Vermont. Telecommunications and publishing companies are the leading part of the communications sector. More about transportation and communication appears later in this section.

Manufacturing. Goods made in Vermont have a *value added by manufacture* of about $5 billion yearly. This figure represents the increase in value of raw materials after they have become finished products.

Production and workers by economic activities

Economic activities	Percent of GDP* produced	Employed workers Number of people	Percent of total
Community, business, & personal services	22	139,400	33
Trade, restaurants, & hotels	18	93,600	22
Finance, insurance, & real estate	18	25,500	6
Government	13	55,100	13
Manufacturing	13	40,100	10
Transportation & communication	6	16,800	4
Construction	5	31,300	8
Agriculture, forestry, & fishing	2	12,400	3
Utilities	2	1,800	†
Mining	†	1,000	†
Total‡	100	417,000	100

*GDP = gross domestic product, the total value of goods and services produced in a year.
†Less than one-half of 1 percent.
‡Figures do not add up to 100 percent due to rounding.
Figures are for 2004; employment figures include full- and part-time workers.
Source: *World Book* estimates based on data from U.S. Bureau of Economic Analysis.

The production of electronic equipment is Vermont's leading manufacturing activity by far. The most important products of this industry are semiconductors and other electronic components. IBM, one of the world's largest electronics companies, has a large plant in the Burlington area that makes computer components.

Fabricated metal products rank second among the state's manufactures. Vermont's fabricated metal products include guns, hand tools, industrial valves, machine shop products, and structural metals.

Food products rank third in terms of value added by manufacture. Dairy products provide about half of the income for Vermont's food-processing industries. Bakery goods, chocolate products, and meat products are also produced in the state.

Machinery ranks fourth among Vermont's manufactures. Machines for making machine tools and semiconductors are the main types of this product made in the state.

Nonmetallic mineral products rank fifth in terms of value added by manufacture. These products include glass items, concrete, and abrasive products such as grinding wheels. Vermont's other manufactures include furniture, paper products, plastic products, printed materials, transportation equipment, and wood products.

Arnold Kaplan, Berg & Associates

Granite is quarried from a pit near Barre, *shown here*. Granite ranks as Vermont's leading mined product. The Barre area is a major United States granite-producing region.

Agriculture. Farmland covers about a fifth of Vermont's land area. The state has about 6,300 farms.

Dairy farming accounts for about three-fourths of Vermont's annual farm income. Most of the state's dairy farms lie in the Champlain Valley of northwestern Vermont. Farmers also raise beef cattle, sheep, and other livestock throughout the state.

Vermont is the leading state in producing maple syrup. Specialty food products, such as cheese, ice cream, and sauces, contribute significantly to Vermont's agricultural economy. Sweet corn ranks as the leading vegetable, and apples as the leading fruit. Corn, hay, and oats are grown as animal feed. Greenhouse and nursery products are an important source of income.

Mining. Granite is Vermont's leading mined product. Large granite quarries are in the Barre area. Granite is used for buildings, memorials, monuments, tombs, and other purposes. Other products mined in Vermont include dolomite, limestone, marble, sand and gravel, slate, and talc. Most of the marble comes from the west-central part of the state. Many parts of the state produce sand and gravel.

Electric power and utilities. Vermont's utilities provide electric, gas, and water service. Nuclear power plants provide about two-thirds of Vermont's electric power. The major nuclear facility serving the state is the Vermont Yankee Nuclear Power Plant in Vernon. Hydroelectric plants generate most of the remaining electric power in Vermont.

Transportation. Vermont has about 14,000 miles (23,000 kilometers) of roads and highways. Interstate 89 and Interstate 91 are the chief highways. Interstate 89 extends northwest from White River Junction to the Canadian border at Highgate. Interstate 91 runs north and south between Guilford and Derby Line. The historic, scenic Ethan Allen Highway, also known as U.S. Route 7, is popular with tourists. It extends between Bennington in the south and the Canadian border, near Lake Champlain, in the north. Vermont's chief airport is at Burlington. Eight rail lines provide freight service in the state.

Communication. Vermont has about 65 newspapers, including 10 dailies. *The Vermont Gazette* was published in Westminster for a brief period, beginning in 1780. The *Rutland Herald* is Vermont's oldest continuously published newspaper. It was begun as a weekly in 1794 and is now a daily. *The Burlington Free Press* and the *Rutland Herald* are the state's largest dailies.

Vermont's first radio station, WSYB, opened in Rutland in 1930. The first television station, WCAX-TV, began broadcasting from Burlington in 1954. Vermont has about 80 radio stations and 7 television stations. Many communities have access to cable TV and the Internet.

Government

Constitution of Vermont was adopted in 1793. Vermont had two earlier constitutions, adopted in 1777 and 1786. The Constitution of 1777 was the most liberal of its time. It gave all adult male citizens the right to vote, without regard to their race or religion, or whether they owned property. It also forbade slavery.

Amendments (changes) to the Constitution may be proposed every four years by a two-thirds vote of the state Senate. The proposed amendments must be approved by a majority vote in the state House of Representatives. At the next legislative session two years later, the amendments require approval by a majority of both the House and the Senate. Finally, to become law, amendments need the approval of a majority of the people who vote on the proposals in an election.

Executive. The governor is elected to a two-year

term. The governor may be reelected any number of times. Voters also elect the lieutenant governor, attorney general, auditor, secretary of state, and treasurer to two-year terms. The governor appoints most other top officials, with Senate approval.

Legislature of Vermont, called the General Assembly, consists of a 150-member House of Representatives and a 30-member Senate. Depending on total population, voters in each of 13 senatorial districts elect from one to six senators. Voters in each of 108 representative districts and subdistricts elect one or two representatives, depending on voter population. Senators and representatives serve two-year terms. The legislature is scheduled to meet in odd-numbered years but usually also meets in even-numbered years. Sessions begin on the first Wednesday after the first Monday in January.

Courts. The Supreme Court, Vermont's highest court, has a chief justice and four associate justices. The General Assembly elects the Supreme Court justices to six-year terms. It also elects Superior Court judges to six-year terms. Each county has one or two Probate Courts, whose judges are elected to four-year terms. The governor appoints the District Court judges to six-year terms.

Local government in Vermont is centered in towns. Vermont towns are similar to townships in other states. That is, they are geographic areas that may include several communities and large rural districts under one government. In Vermont, there are 237 towns with local governments. Five towns—Averill, Ferdinand, Glastenbury, Lewis, and Somerset—do not have enough inhabitants to have governments. They range in population from no people in Lewis to 33 in Ferdinand. Each of Vermont's nine cities also has a local government.

Vermont towns use the *town meeting* form of government, the purest type of democracy, in which citizens take a direct part in government. Each March, town voters assemble to elect officials, approve budgets, pass laws, and decide other local business. Vermont cities operate under council-manager or mayor-council governments. Cities, towns, villages, and special districts must submit changes in their charters to the Vermont General Assembly for approval. The powers of county

The governors of Vermont

	Party	Term		Party	Term
			Roswell Farnham	Republican	1880-1882
			John L. Barstow	Republican	1882-1884
As an independent republic			Samuel E. Pingree	Republican	1884-1886
			Ebenezer J. Ormsbee	Republican	1886-1888
Thomas Chittenden	None	1778-1789	William P. Dillingham	Republican	1888-1890
Moses Robinson	None	1789-1790	Carroll S. Page	Republican	1890-1892
Thomas Chittenden	None	1790-1791	Levi K. Fuller	Republican	1892-1894
			Urban A. Woodbury	Republican	1894-1896
As a state			Josiah Grout	Republican	1896-1898
			Edward C. Smith	Republican	1898-1900
Thomas Chittenden	None	1791-1797	William W. Stickney	Republican	1900-1902
Paul Brigham	None	1797	John G. McCullough	Republican	1902-1904
Isaac Tichenor	Federalist	1797-1807	Charles J. Bell	Republican	1904-1906
Israel Smith	* Dem.-Rep.	1807-1808	Fletcher D. Proctor	Republican	1906-1908
Isaac Tichenor	Federalist	1808-1809	George H. Prouty	Republican	1908-1910
Jonas Galusha	* Dem.-Rep.	1809-1813	John A. Mead	Republican	1910-1912
Martin Chittenden	Federalist	1813-1815	Allen M. Fletcher	Republican	1912-1915
Jonas Galusha	* Dem.-Rep.	1815-1820	Charles W. Gates	Republican	1915-1917
Richard Skinner	* Dem.-Rep.	1820-1823	Horace F. Graham	Republican	1917-1919
Cornelius P. Van Ness	* Dem.-Rep.	1823-1826	Percival W. Clement	Republican	1919-1921
Ezra Butler	† Nat. Rep.	1826-1828	James Hartness	Republican	1921-1923
Samuel C. Crafts	† Nat. Rep.	1828-1831	Redfield Proctor	Republican	1923-1925
William A. Palmer	Anti-Masonic	1831-1835	Franklin S. Billings	Republican	1925-1927
Silas H. Jennison	Whig	1835-1841	John E. Weeks	Republican	1927-1931
Charles Paine	Whig	1841-1843	Stanley C. Wilson	Republican	1931-1935
John Mattocks	Whig	1843-1844	Charles M. Smith	Republican	1935-1937
William Slade	Whig	1844-1846	George D. Aiken	Republican	1937-1941
Horace Eaton	Whig	1846-1848	William H. Wills	Republican	1941-1945
Carlos Coolidge	Whig	1848-1850	Mortimer R. Proctor	Republican	1945-1947
Charles K. Williams	Whig	1850-1852	Ernest W. Gibson	Republican	1947-1950
Erastus Fairbanks	Whig	1852-1853	Harold J. Arthur	Republican	1950-1951
John S. Robinson	Democratic	1853-1854	Lee E. Emerson	Republican	1951-1955
Stephen Royce	Republican	1854-1856	Joseph B. Johnson	Republican	1955-1959
Ryland Fletcher	Republican	1856-1858	Robert T. Stafford	Republican	1959-1961
Hiland Hall	Republican	1858-1860	F. Ray Keyser, Jr.	Republican	1961-1963
Erastus Fairbanks	Republican	1860-1861	Philip H. Hoff	Democratic	1963-1969
Frederick Holbrook	Republican	1861-1863	Deane C. Davis	Republican	1969-1973
J. Gregory Smith	Republican	1863-1865	Thomas P. Salmon	Democratic	1973-1977
Paul Dillingham	Republican	1865-1867	Richard A. Snelling	Republican	1977-1985
John B. Page	Republican	1867-1869	Madeleine M. Kunin	Democratic	1985-1991
Peter T. Washburn	Republican	1869-1870	Richard A. Snelling	Republican	1991
George W. Hendee	Republican	1870	Howard Dean	Democratic	1991-2003
John W. Stewart	Republican	1870-1872	Jim Douglas	Republican	2003-
Julius Converse	Republican	1872-1874			
Asahel Peck	Republican	1874-1876			
Horace Fairbanks	Republican	1876-1878			
Redfield Proctor	Republican	1878-1880			

*Democratic-Republican   †National Republican

The Vermont House of Representatives meets in the House chambers in the State Capitol in Montpelier. The members are elected to two-year terms.

governments are limited mainly to judicial affairs.

Revenue. Taxes account for about half of the state government's *general revenue* (income). Most of the rest comes from federal grants and other programs of the United States government, and from charges for government services.

A personal property tax accounts for the greatest portion of the tax revenue. Other important sources of tax revenue include a personal income tax, general sales tax, and taxes on motor fuels, motor vehicle licenses, corporate income, and insurance premiums.

Politics. Vermont's electoral votes went to the Republican candidate in every presidential election from 1860 through 1960. Since then, however, the state has voted for the Democratic candidate in several presidential elections. For Vermont's voting record in presidential elections, see **Electoral College** (table).

All of Vermont's governors from 1854 until 1963 were Republicans. Since then, both Democrats and Republicans have won the office several times. In 1974, Patrick J. Leahy became the first Democrat to be elected to the U.S. Senate from Vermont since the early 1800's.

History

Indian days. Vermont was chiefly an Indian hunting ground before white settlers came. The Abenaki, Mahican, and Penacook tribes of the Algonquian Indian family first claimed the region. Powerful New York Iroquois Indians drove the Algonquian out. The Algonquian returned during the early 1600's. With help from the French, they defeated the Iroquois.

Exploration and settlement. Samuel de Champlain of France was probably the first white person to explore what is now Vermont. He arrived at Lake Champlain in 1609 and claimed the Vermont region for France. In 1666, the French built a fort dedicated to Saint Anne on Isle La Motte in Lake Champlain. In 1690, Jacobus de Warm led British soldiers from Albany, New York, to a point near the site of present-day Middlebury, Vermont. De Warm founded a fort at Chimney Point, west of Middlebury. Vermont's first permanent white settlement was made at Fort Dummer, in what is now Brattleboro. Fort Dummer was built by Massachusetts settlers in 1724 to protect that colony's western settlements from raids by the French and Indians.

The Lake Champlain region became a major battleground during the French and Indian War (1754-1763). In this war, Britain gained from France the control of Vermont and much of the rest of North America. See **French and Indian wars.**

Land disputes. Benning Wentworth, the royal governor of New Hampshire, made 131 grants of Vermont land between 1749 and 1763. This land was called the *New Hampshire Grants.* But New York claimed the same land and granted it to other settlers. In 1764, Britain recognized the grants made by New York. Britain ordered settlers who held New Hampshire Grants to surrender their land or pay New York for it. In 1770, these settlers organized a military force called the *Green Mountain Boys* to defend their land. The Green Mountain Boys attacked many New York settlers and drove them from Vermont. See **Green Mountain Boys.**

The Revolutionary War in America began in Massachusetts in 1775, before the Vermont land disputes were settled. Vermonters united to fight the British. Ethan Allen, Benedict Arnold, and more than 80 Green Mountain Boys captured Fort Ticonderoga from the British in May 1775. Colonial troops held the fort until 1777, when the British drove them out. The troops retreated south from Fort Ticonderoga, with the British in pursuit. In Hubbardton, a rear guard led by Seth Warner stopped the retreat and fought the British. The rear guard was defeated. But the fighting delayed the British long enough to allow the rest of the colonists to escape.

The Battle of Bennington, on Aug. 16, 1777, was a major Revolutionary War conflict. It is often thought of as a Vermont battle. But it was actually fought just west of Vermont, in New York. The battle of Bennington and the British surrender at Saratoga (also in New York) marked the end of British land operations in the Northern Colonies.

Independent republic. On Jan. 15, 1777, Vermont settlers declared their territory an independent republic. They named it *New Connecticut.* In July 1777, Vermont adopted its first constitution and its present name.

New Hampshire and New York still claimed parts of Vermont. But Vermont ignored the claims. In 1783, George Washington wrote that he believed it would be necessary to send troops to overthrow the Vermont government. But this never happened, and Vermont remained an independent republic for 14 years. In 1790, Vermont settled its dispute with New York by paying it $30,000. New Hampshire also gave up its claim to Vermont. Such improved relations helped clear the way for Vermont's admission to the Union. On March 4, 1791, Vermont became the 14th state.

The 1800's. During the War of 1812, Vermont volunteers fought the British in the battles of Chippewa, Lundy's Lane, and Plattsburgh. But the war was unpopular in Vermont, because trade with British-controlled

Historic Vermont

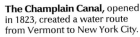

Fort Dummer

Fort Dummer became Vermont's first permanent white settlement. It was built in 1724 by Massachusetts pioneers to protect that colony's western settlements from raids by the French and by Indians.

The Lake Champlain region was a major battleground during the French and Indian War (1754-1763). The English gained control of Vermont and much of the rest of North America as a result of the war.

Vermont joined the Union in 1791. It was the first territory after the original 13 colonies to become part of the United States.

The Green Mountain Boys of Vermont, led by Ethan Allen, captured Fort Ticonderoga from the British in 1775.

The Champlain Canal, opened in 1823, created a water route from Vermont to New York City.

WORLD BOOK illustrations by Kevin Chadwick

Important dates in Vermont

1609 Samuel de Champlain claimed the Vermont region for France.

1724 Massachusetts established Fort Dummer, the first permanent white settlement in the Vermont region.

1763 England gained control of Vermont.

1775 Ethan Allen and the Green Mountain Boys captured Fort Ticonderoga in the Revolutionary War.

1777 Vermont declared itself an independent republic.

1791 Vermont became the 14th state on March 4.

1823 The opening of the Champlain Canal created a water route from Vermont to New York City.

1881 Chester A. Arthur, born in Fairfield, became the 21st president of the United States.

1923 Calvin Coolidge, born in Plymouth Notch, became the 30th president of the United States.

1962 Philip H. Hoff became the first Democrat to win election as governor of Vermont since 1853.

1970 The state legislature passed the Environmental Control Law. This law permitted Vermont to limit major developments that could harm the state's environment.

1984 Madeleine M. Kunin became the first woman to be elected governor of Vermont.

2000 Vermont became the first state to allow a *civil union,* similar to marriage, for two people of the same sex.

The Battle of Bennington, on Aug. 16, 1777, was a major Revolutionary War victory for American forces. The victory helped end British land operations in the Northern Colonies.

Oil painting on canvas (1938) by LeRoy Williams; Bennington Museum, Vermont (A. Blake Gardner)

Canada had become important to the state's economy. In 1817, after a harsh winter, many people began to move from Vermont to the growing Midwest. Some feared future economic hardships in Vermont. Others were attracted by the great opportunities to the west.

The Champlain Canal, which opened in 1823, connected Lake Champlain and New York's Hudson River. The canal allowed Vermont farmers to ship their goods by water all the way to New York City, a major market. Farmers in the Champlain Valley prospered, especially those who raised Spanish Merino sheep for wool. By 1840, Vermont had six times as many sheep as people. Many small, water-powered mills were built in Vermont to process the wool from the sheep. During the mid-1800's, competition from Western states and other countries made wool prices drop. By 1860, Vermont farmers had sold half their sheep to be used as meat. This crisis caused Vermont to change from a sheep-raising state to a dairy-farming state.

During the American Civil War (1861-1865), about 34,000 Vermonters served with the Union forces. The northernmost land action of the war took place in Vermont in 1864. A group of 22 Confederate soldiers raided banks in St. Albans and fled to Canada with over $20,000.

Agriculture declined in Vermont after the Civil War. More and more Vermont farmers left the state for cities or for better farmland in the Midwest and elsewhere. Most of the French Canadians and Europeans who moved to Vermont settled in cities to work in factories. The late 1800's brought great growth to Vermont's wood-processing and cheese-making industries. Burlington grew rapidly as a port city that processed lumber from Canada and shipped it to other cities in the United States. The granite industry boomed in Barre. Vermont's once important textile industry declined during the late 1800's. Many textile mills moved to the South, where labor costs were lower.

The early 1900's. The value of Vermont's manufactured products more than tripled between 1900 and 1920. Manufacturing replaced agriculture as Vermont's most important economic activity.

Vermont's tourist industry also grew rapidly during the early 1900's. Many large resort hotels and vacation camps were built. In 1911, Vermont became the first state with an official publicity bureau to attract tourists.

In 1923, Calvin Coolidge, born in Vermont, became the 30th president of the United States. He had been elected vice president under President Warren G. Harding, who died in office. Coolidge was a shy man who was quiet in public. To many people, he seemed to be a "typical Vermont conservative."

The nationwide Great Depression of the 1930's brought severe hardship to Vermont. Many small factories and lumber mills closed. Vermont farmers were hurt by falling prices and reduced sales. Vermont's economy improved during the late 1930's.

The worst flood in Vermont history occurred in November 1927. Waters from the Winooski River and branches of the Connecticut River swept away entire sections of towns. The flood caused 60 deaths and millions of dollars in damage.

The mid-1900's. During World War II (1939-1945), Vermont factories produced war materials. After the war, the state increased its efforts to attract new industries. The Vermont Development Department, established in 1949, promoted industrial development and tourism. The state's Municipal Bond Act of 1955 gave Vermont communities permission to issue revenue bonds. Money from the bonds financed industrial construction programs.

In the 1960's, a few large corporations built factories in Vermont. But most of the industry attracted to Vermont would be considered small in many other states. An interstate highway from Massachusetts to the Canadian border, developed during the 1960's, contributed to the growth of industry and tourism in Vermont.

As Vermont manufacturing grew, agriculture became less important to the state's economy. Farms decreased in number and increased in size, and the population began to shift from rural to urban areas.

Politically, Vermont remained a Republican center of strength. Republicans held such control that the election of a few Democrats in the 1950's and 1960's made national news. William H. Meyer, elected to the U.S. House of Representatives in 1958, became the state's first Democratic member of Congress since 1853. Philip H. Hoff, who served as governor of Vermont from 1963 until 1969, was the first Democrat to hold that office since 1854. From 1856 through 1960, Vermont gave its electoral votes to the Republican nominee in every presidential election. In 1964, the state gave its electoral votes to the Democratic nominee, Lyndon B. Johnson.

The late 1900's. The Democratic Party steadily continued to gain strength in Vermont. In 1974, Patrick J. Leahy became the first Democrat to be elected to the U.S. Senate from Vermont since the early 1880's. Following Hoff, other Democrats won election as governor. In 1984, Madeleine M. Kunin became the first woman to be elected governor of Vermont. In the 1992 and 1996 presidential elections, the state's electoral votes were given to the Democratic nominee for only the second and third times. Bill Clinton carried the state then.

Manufacturing and tourism continued to contribute greatly to Vermont's economy. The tourist industry, centered in the Green Mountains, brought large sums of money to the state. But some manufacturing and tourist activities were a concern to Vermonters who strongly supported maintaining the state's rural environment. In 1970, the legislature passed the Environmental Control Law. This law, one of the strictest of its kind, allows the state to limit major developments that could harm the environment. It has been used to prevent potentially damaging projects.

Recent developments. The greatest challenge facing Vermont lies in balancing the competing expectations between the people who favor development and their opponents. The economic benefits of development regularly clash with the desire to maintain Vermont's rural character and natural beauty.

In 1999, in a landmark decision, the Vermont Supreme Court ordered the state government to offer homosexual couples the same rights and benefits as heterosexual couples. In 2000, the Vermont legislature approved a bill that allows couples of the same sex to enter into a civil union, a legal relationship similar to a marriage. Partners in civil unions are entitled to many of the rights and benefits of married couples. Vermont was the first state to enact such a law.

John McCardell and Harold A. Meeks

Related articles in *World Book* include:

Biographies

Allen, Ethan
Arthur, Chester A.
Champlain, Samuel de
Coolidge, Calvin
Jeffords, James Merrill
Morrill, Justin S.
Warner, Seth

Cities

Burlington Montpelier Rutland

Physical features

Connecticut River Green Mountains Lake Champlain

Other related articles

Green Mountain Boys Revolutionary War in America

Outline

I. People
  A. Population
  B. School
  C. Libraries
  D. Museums
II. Visitor's guide
  A. Places to visit
  B. Annual events
III. Land and climate
  A. Land regions
  B. Rivers and lakes
  C. Plant and animal life
  D. Climate
IV. Economy
  A. Natural resources
  B. Service industries
  C. Manufacturing
  D. Agriculture
  E. Mining
  F. Electric power and utilities
  G. Transportation
  H. Communication
V. Government
  A. Constitution
  B. Executive
  C. Legislature
  D. Courts
  E. Local government
  F. Revenue
  G. Politics
VI. History

Questions

How long was Vermont an independent republic?
Who were the Green Mountain Boys?
Which U.S. presidents were born in Vermont?
What is Vermont's single most important economic activity?
How many Vermont towns have no local government? Why do they not have their own government?
Where did the northernmost land action of the Civil War take place?
Why was the War of 1812 unpopular with Vermonters?

Additional resources

Level I
Czech, Jan M. *Vermont.* Children's Pr., 2002.
Flocker, Michael. *Vermont.* World Almanac, 2002.
Heinrichs, Ann. *Vermont.* Children's Pr., 2001.
Pelta, Kathy. *Vermont.* 2nd ed. Lerner, 2002.

Level II
Aiken, Kenneth. *Touring Vermont's Scenic Roads.* Down East, 1999.
Bellesiles, Michael A. *Revolutionary Outlaws: Ethan Allen and the Struggle for Independence on the Early American Frontier.* 1993. Reprint. Univ. Pr. of Va., 1995.
Coffin, Howard. *Full Duty: Vermonters in the Civil War.* Countryman, 1994.
Haviland, William A., and Power, M. W. *The Original Vermonters: Native Inhabitants, Past and Present.* Rev. ed. Univ. Pr. of New England, 1994.
Morrissey, Charles T. *Vermont.* Norton, 1981.

Vermont, University of, is a state-supported coeducational school in Burlington, Vermont. Its official name is the University of Vermont and State Agricultural College. It has colleges of agriculture and life sciences; arts and sciences; education and social services; engineering and mathematical sciences; medicine; and nursing and health sciences. It also has a school of business administration, a school of environment and natural resources, a graduate college, and an honors program. The university grants bachelor's, master's, and doctor's degrees. It was the first United States university to admit women to the national honor society Phi Beta Kappa.

The University of Vermont was chartered in 1791. The Vermont Agricultural College was chartered in 1864, and joined with the university in 1865 to form the University of Vermont and State Agricultural College.

Critically reviewed by the University of Vermont

Vernal equinox. See Equinox.

Verne, *vurn,* **Jules** (1828-1905), a French novelist, wrote some of the first science-fiction stories. Although his books were written before the invention of the airplane, they have remained popular in the space age. Verne forecast the invention of airplanes, television, guided missiles, and space satellites. Verne even predicted their uses accurately.

Verne cleverly used realistic detail and believable explanations to support incredible tales of adventure. His fantastic plots took advantage of the widespread interest in science in the 1800's. Verne's *Twenty Thousand Leagues Under the Sea,* published in 1870, tells about Captain Nemo, a mad sea captain who cruises beneath the oceans in a submarine. In *Around the World in Eighty Days* (1873), Phileas Fogg travels around the world in the then un-heard-of time of 80 days, just to win a bet. Other thrillers include *A Journey to the Center of the Earth* (1864), *From the Earth to the Moon* (1865), and *Around the Moon* (1870).

Brown Bros.

Jules Verne

Verne knew a great deal about geography and used his knowledge to make his stories realistic. He also wrote several historical novels, including *North Against South* (1887), a story about the American Civil War (1861-1865).

Verne was born on Feb. 8, 1828, in Nantes. He studied law in Paris but decided to become a writer. His first works were plays and the words for operas. Verne's first novel, *Five Weeks in a Balloon* (1863), brought him immediate success. It was based on an essay he wrote describing the exploration of Africa in a balloon. The essay was rejected several times before one publisher suggested that Verne rewrite it as a novel of imagination. The popularity of the book encouraged Verne to continue writing on science-fiction themes. Verne died on March 24, 1905.   Thomas H. Goetz

Vernier, *VUR nee uhr,* is an instrument used in measuring lengths and angles. It is named for Pierre Vernier, a French mathematician who invented it in the 1600's.

The most common vernier has a short, graduated scale, or "ruler," which slides along a longer scale. The subdivisions on the short rule are nine-tenths as long as the subdivisions on the long scale. Nine small divisions on the large scale are equal to 10 on the small scale.

A vernier scale measures lengths and angles.

In using the vernier, the large scale is laid along the object to be measured. The small scale is slid until it reaches the end of the object. In the picture, the object's length is somewhere between 20 and 21 on the large scale. By noting which division on the small scale lines up most closely with a division on the large scale, a more exact measurement can be derived. In the picture, the 5 on the small scale lines up perfectly with a division on the large scale. This means the object's length is exactly 0.5 longer than 20 on the large scale.

Engineers often use calipers with a vernier attachment (see **Caliper**). Some read to $\frac{1}{1000}$ inch (0.0254 millimeter) without a magnifier. The caliper's beam is divided into inches and tenths, and each tenth is divided into fourths. The vernier is divided into 25 parts. The beam may be divided into fiftieths of an inch. The vernier has 20 divisions to each of its 19.   Daniel V. De Simone

Vernon, Mount. See Mount Vernon (Virginia).

Verny. See Almaty.

Veronese, *VAY roh NAY say,* **Paolo,** *PAH oh loh* (1528-1588), painted in and around Venice at the end of the Italian Renaissance. His real name was Paolo Cagliari, but he was called Veronese because he was born in Verona. His art is typically Venetian in its dependence on the poetic effects of color. Veronese became most popular for paintings of historical subjects and myths, and for representations of the life of Venetian aristocracy. He also painted religious subjects and portraits. His figures are robust and handsome, splendidly costumed, and theatrically posed in rich settings. His major works include *Marriage at Cana* in the Louvre in Paris and *Mars and Venus* in the Metropolitan Museum of Art in New York City. Veronese died on April 9, 1588.

Vernon Hyde Minor

See also **Painting** (picture: *Feast in the House of Levi*).

Verrazzano, *VEHR uh ZAH noh,* **Giovanni da,** *joh VAHN ee dah* (1485?-1528?), an Italian navigator in the service of France, sailed to North America in 1524. On the voyage, he sought the Northwest Passage to China. He did not find the passage. But he explored the eastern coast of North America from the Carolinas to Newfoundland. Verrazzano later made two more voyages to the New World. Historians believe that during the second of these voyages, he was killed by Indians in the Caribbean region.

Verrazzano was born near Florence. His family name is sometimes spelled *Verrazano.*   Helen Delpar

See also **Great-circle route; New York** (Exploration and early settlement); **North Carolina** (Exploration and settlement); **Rhode Island** (Exploration).

Verrocchio, *vuh ROH kee OH,* **Andrea del,** *ahn DREH uh dehl* (about 1435-1488), was an Italian sculptor and painter. One of his great works is a standing figure

The Baptism of Christ (about 1472), a tempera painting on wood; Uffizi Gallery, Florence (Scala/Art Resource)

John the Baptist's baptism of Jesus was portrayed in this painting by Andrea del Verrocchio and Leonardo da Vinci.

of David with the head of Goliath at his feet. The work shows how Verrocchio, with his knowledge of anatomy, controlled the muscles of David's body and face to enrich the meaning of his subject. The bronze group *Christ and Saint Thomas* demonstrates his mastery of psychology in the hesitancy of Saint Thomas's stride and gesture in contrast to the calm and poise of Christ.

Verrocchio's large bronze of Bartolommeo Colleoni is sometimes called the world's finest *equestrian statue* (statue of a man on a horse). His one unquestioned painting is *The Baptism of Christ.* The angel on the left was probably painted by his pupil Leonardo da Vinci.

Roger Ward

Versailles, *vehr SY* or *vehr SAYLZ,* **Palace of,** is a magnificent palace in northern France. It was built by King Louis XIV during the 1600's and was the royal residence for more than 100 years. It is now a national museum. The palace stands in the western part of the city of Versailles, southwest of Paris (see **France** [political map]). The palace and the beautiful grounds around it make up one of the most visited sites in France.

The palace is more than ¼ mile (0.4 kilometer) long and has about 1,300 rooms. Many of the rooms have been restored and refurnished to look as they did when royalty lived in them. The palace also has paintings and sculptures by famous European artists.

Versailles was originally the site of a hunting lodge built in 1624 by Louis XIII. After he died, his son Louis XIV ordered that a palace be constructed on the same site. Work began in 1661 under the direction of Louis Le Vau, a French architect. The palace took more than 40 years to complete. Through the years, later kings added more rooms to the building.

The interior of the palace is richly decorated. The most famous rooms include the living quarters of the king and queen, the Room of Hercules, and the Hall of Mirrors. The Hall of Mirrors, designed by Charles Le Brun, was begun in 1678. It is a long hallway lined with mirrors that runs along the front of the palace. The ceiling is decorated with paintings glorifying the achievements of Louis XIV. The palace also contains a magnificent royal chapel and a private theater.

The palace gardens were first laid out by landscape designer André Le Nôtre in the 1660's. They were enlarged several times and now cover nearly 250 acres (101 hectares). Plantings, fountains, and statues are arranged in geometric patterns. The park also includes two small palaces called the Grand Trianon, designed by J. H. Mansard in 1687, and the Petit Trianon. Nearby are stables; an *orangery* (greenhouse for growing orange trees); and the picturesque *hameau,* a miniature farm designed for Queen Marie Antoinette.

The French Revolution of 1789-1799 led to the overthrow of the French king. Mobs invaded the palace during the revolution and removed or destroyed a majority of the furniture and art. Little was done to maintain the building until the early 1900's, when restoration work began. This project is still going on. William J. Hennessey

See also **Fountain** (picture: A fountain at the Palace of Versailles); **Le Nôtre, André.**

Versailles, *vehr SY* or *vehr SAYLZ,* **Treaty of,** officially ended military actions against Germany in World War I. The treaty was signed at the Palace of Versailles, near Paris, on June 28, 1919, and went into effect on Jan. 10, 1920. Actual combat had ended when Germany accepted an armistice on Nov. 11, 1918.

The treaty provided an official peace between Germany and nearly all the 32 victorious Allied and associated nations, including France, Italy, Japan, and the United Kingdom. China never signed the treaty. The United States would make a separate peace with Germany in 1921 because the U.S. Senate did not ratify the treaty.

The treaty provided a reorganization of the boundaries and certain territories of European nations and areas they controlled in Africa, Asia, and Pacific Ocean islands. It also created several new international organizations, including the League of Nations and the Permanent Court of International Justice. In addition, the treaty provided a system for administering the former colonies of the defeated countries.

United States President Woodrow Wilson, British Prime Minister David Lloyd George, French Premier Georges Clemenceau, and Italian Prime Minister Vittorio Orlando played the main roles in drafting the treaty. They were called the Big Four. Orlando temporarily left the conference in protest when the Allies refused Italy's

© Alain Perceval, Photographic Aerienne

The Palace of Versailles and its grounds make up one of the most beautiful sights in France. The palace was built during the 1600's as the royal residence of France, but today it is a museum. The building has about 1,300 rooms, many of which have been restored and refurnished.

claims to the port of Fiume in Yugoslavia and to former Austrian territories.

Background of the treaty. Preparations for peace began well before the armistice. Beginning in 1915, a number of the Allied governments, including Italy and Japan, adopted secret treaties intended to divide among them certain parts of Germany, the Ottoman Empire (now Turkey), and other enemies in the war. German colonial territories in Africa, Asia, and the Pacific Ocean also were to be annexed. Italy joined the Allied war effort as a result of such promises.

President Wilson presented his ideas for peace in his famous Fourteen Points address on Jan. 8, 1918. He opposed carrying out terms of any secret treaties. The president hoped to apply the principle of *ethnic self-determination,* under which no ethnic group would have to be governed by a nation or state that it opposed. Wilson also called for moderate punishment, both economic and territorial, for Germany. He believed this approach would encourage Germany to establish a democratic government, to help rebuild Europe, and to refrain from waging war in the future out of bitterness.

Wilson's chief goal was to have the treaty provide for the formation of a League of Nations (see **League of Nations**). He hoped that the threat of economic or military punishment from League members, including Germany, would prevent future wars.

The other major Allies, however, had little interest in honoring either Wilson's Fourteen Points or all his goals for the League of Nations. Clemenceau sought to cripple Germany economically, militarily, and territorially. He also sought security against any future German aggression through creation of special military alliances with the United Kingdom and the United States. Lloyd George wanted to leave Germany with enough resources for trade but not enough for waging war. Other Allies, especially Italy and Japan, were chiefly concerned with obtaining more land.

Provisions. At the Paris Peace Conference of 1919, representatives of the 32 Allied nations met to draw up terms of peace with Germany and its allies. German representatives were not allowed to take part. The main provisions of the treaty set up the League of Nations, revised boundaries, disarmed Germany, and called for *reparations.* Reparations consisted of money and other resources Germany would have to give the Allies for severe losses they suffered in the war.

To win support for certain changes concerning the League of Nations, Wilson compromised on the ideals he had set forth in the Fourteen Points. For example, he accepted terms made in secret treaties. Thus, Italy received the South Tyrol region of Austria-Hungary, and Japan obtained German colonies in the North Pacific Ocean and German holdings in China's Shantung province. Wilson also compromised on reparations, agreeing to much more than Germany could afford. Germany had to give the Allies coal, livestock, ships, timber, and other resources, plus cash payments.

Germany lost all its overseas colonies. From its homeland, Germany lost the provinces of Alsace and Lorraine to France; small areas of Eupen, Malmédy, Moresnet, and St. Vith to Belgium; and another small border area near Troppau (now Opava) to Czechoslovakia. As a result of a *plebiscite* (popular vote), Germany also lost North-

ern Schleswig to Denmark. France gained possession of the coal mines in Germany's Saar region for 15 years. Danzig (now Gdańsk, Poland) was taken from Germany and became a "free city" under protection of the League of Nations. Poland gained most of West Prussia and much of the province of Posen (now Poznan). Germany's Rhineland was to be demilitarized. But the Allies were to occupy parts of it for 15 years. See **Europe** (Europe between the world wars; maps).

Ratification. In early May 1919, the treaty was presented to Germany. German officials strongly objected, but they had to accept the terms and sign the treaty. The treaty was ratified by Germany's new republican government and all the major Allied powers except China and the United States. It took effect early in 1920.

Strong opposition to the treaty developed in the United States. Many Americans disagreed with Wilson's generous approach to war-torn Europe. Republicans objected to U.S. commitments to the League of Nations. In March 1920, the U.S. Senate refused to approve the treaty. The United States never joined the League of Nations or the Permanent Court of International Justice. In August 1921, however, Germany and the United States concluded a separate peace in the Treaty of Berlin.

Effects. The lost land and huge reparations angered many Germans, who also felt bitter about a "war guilt" clause in the treaty that declared Germany solely responsible for the war. These factors, aggravated by poor economic conditions in the 1930's, may have aided the rise of German dictator Adolf Hitler. Geoffrey Wawro

See also **World War I** (The peace settlement); **World War II** (The Peace of Paris).

Vertebra. See Spine.

Vertebrate, *VUR tuh briht* or *VUR tuh brayt,* is an animal with a *spinal column* (backbone) and a *cranium* (brain case). There are about 40,000 species of vertebrates. They may be divided into eight classes: (1) hagfishes (Myxini); (2) lampreys (Cephalaspidomorphi); (3) sharks and other cartilaginous fish (Chondrichthyes); (4) bony fish (Osteichthyes); (5) frogs and other amphibians (Amphibia); (6) reptiles (Reptilia); (7) birds (Aves); and (8) mammals (Mammalia).

Most vertebrates have a spinal column made of bones called *vertebrae* (see **Spine**). But some, such as the shark, do not have a bony spinal column. Sharks have vertebrae made of *cartilage* (waxy tissue).

All vertebrates are *bilaterally symmetrical*—the left and right sides of the body are alike. The body is usually divided into a head and a trunk. The more advanced land vertebrates have a neck. In mammals (animals with milk glands for feeding their young), the trunk is divided into a thorax (chest) and abdomen. Vertebrates never have more than two pairs of limbs. Lawrence C. Wit

Scientific classification. Vertebrates are classified in the phylum Chordata and make up the subphylum Vertebrata.

Related articles in *World Book* include:

Amphibian	Mammal	Reptile
Amphioxus	Nervous system	Shark
Bird	(In vertebrates)	Skate
Chordate	Prehistoric animal	Tail
Fish	(The first	
Invertebrate	animals with	
Lamprey	backbones)	

Vertical take-off aircraft. See V/STOL; Helicopter.

Vertigo. See Dizziness.

Verwoerd, *fuhr VOORT,* **Hendrik,** *HEHN drihk* (1901-1966), was prime minister of South Africa from 1958 to 1966. He was the main architect of South Africa's policy of racial segregation called *apartheid*. This policy was officially in effect from 1948 to 1991.

Hendrik Frensch Verwoerd was born on Sept. 8, 1901, in Amsterdam, the Netherlands. He came with his family to South Africa in 1903. He studied at the University of Stellenbosch in South Africa and at universities in Europe and the United States. From 1927 to 1937, he taught at the University of Stellenbosch.

While at the university, Verwoerd joined the National Party. The party sought to unify Afrikaners (whites of mainly Dutch ancestry) as a nation and protect their interests. In 1937, Verwoerd became editor of the party newspaper, *Die Transvaler*. After the party won elections in 1948, Verwoerd was appointed to the Senate. As minister of native affairs from 1950 to 1958, he worked hard to further develop the apartheid policy. After Verwoerd became prime minister, the police and military received extensive powers to enforce racial segregation. Verwoerd also oversaw the creation of separate black African homelands, which were granted limited self-rule. Verwoerd survived an assassination attempt in 1960, but on Sept. 6, 1966, he was stabbed to death by a mentally ill parliamentary messenger. Nancy L. Clark

See also **Apartheid; South Africa** (History).

Vesalius, *vih SAY lee uhs,* **Andreas,** *ahn DREH ahs* (1514-1564), a Flemish physician, made important contributions to the study of human anatomy. His book *On the Structure of the Human Body,* or *Fabrica* (1543), was the first manual of anatomy with clear, detailed illustrations. Vesalius is often called the founder of human anatomy.

Vesalius was born on Dec. 31, 1514, in Brussels, in what is now Belgium. At age 23, he became a professor of anatomy and surgery at the University of Padua in Padua, Italy. An innovative teacher, Vesalius performed dissections on human corpses as he taught. The traditional method of instruction had been for the teacher to read from a prepared text while an assistant did the dissection. Vesalius also popularized the use of drawings to help make anatomy lectures more easily understood.

He was trained in anatomy from the widely accepted writings of Galen, a physician who practiced medicine in the A.D. 100's. But, through his many dissections, Vesalius found errors in Galen's theories, and corrected many of them in *Fabrica*. The book has the first accurate descriptions of the small bones of the head and ear, and excellent illustrations of the muscles and skeleton. *Fabrica* is the model for modern anatomy textbooks. Later in his career, Vesalius served as physician to Holy Roman Emperor Charles V and Philip II of Spain. Vesalius died in a shipwreck on Oct. 15, 1564. John Scarborough

See also **Biology** (picture: The human muscular system); **Medicine** (The Renaissance; picture: Scientific study of anatomy).

Vesey, *VEE zee,* **Denmark** (1767?-1822), a black freedman, planned a slave revolt in the state of South Carolina that involved more blacks than any other uprising in United States history. The revolt never took place. But the threat of it caused South Carolina to pass restrictive laws against black literacy and religion.

In 1822, Vesey recruited hundreds of slaves and free blacks in South Carolina's coastal counties for a July 14 assault on Charleston. As many as 5,000 slaves may have known of the plot, and two slaves informed their owners. Charleston officials arrested several leading rebels and whipped them until they gave information leading to the arrest of Vesey and his chief lieutenant. After a trial by a special *tribunal* (court), Vesey and 34 others were hanged. The tribunal ordered 37 conspirators, including Vesey's son Sandy, to be sold to Spanish-ruled Cuba.

Vesey was probably born in St. Thomas, in what are now the U.S. Virgin Islands. In 1781, he was purchased by Captain Joseph Vesey to serve as a cabin boy and domestic slave. He bought his freedom in 1799 with lottery winnings, then worked as a carpenter and a lay preacher until his death on July 2, 1822. Douglas R. Egerton

Vespasian, *veh SPAY zhee uhn* (A.D. 9-79), was a Roman emperor. Rome prospered under his rule. He set up new taxes and supervised their collection, thereby restoring the empire's financial condition. He built a forum and the Temple of Peace, the Colosseum, and other buildings (see **Forum, Roman; Colosseum**). He also founded professorships to encourage education.

Vespasian was born on Nov. 17, A.D. 9, northeast of Rome, near Reate. His full name was Titus Flavius Vespasianus. He became a senator and, during A.D. 43 and 44, commanded troops in the conquest of Britain. In A.D. 67, Emperor Nero sent him to put down a Jewish revolt in Judea. After Nero died in A.D. 68, Galba, Otho, and Vitellius followed one another as emperor. But in A.D. 69, Vespasian's troops occupied Rome and proclaimed him emperor. In Rome, the Senate enacted the *Lex de imperio Vespasiani,* the first known written statement of a Roman emperor's powers. Vespasian died in June A.D. 79 and was succeeded by his son Titus. F. G. B. Millar

Vespucci, *veh SPOO chee,* **Amerigo,** *uh MEHR uh GOH* (1451?-1512), was an Italian-born explorer for whom America was named. He claimed to have explored the American mainland in 1497 and thought he had reached a "New World." Christopher Columbus had sailed to this area in 1492. But Columbus thought he had arrived at islands off Asia and may never have realized his error.

Martin Waldseemüller, a German mapmaker, believed that Vespucci was the first European to reach the New World. In 1507, he suggested that the land be named *America*. Soon, this name was used throughout Europe. Today, however, many scholars doubt Vespucci's importance in the exploration of America.

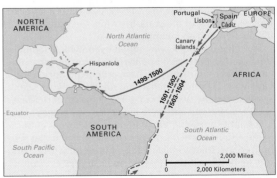

WORLD BOOK map

Amerigo Vespucci made three known voyages to America, the first one in 1499. He reported that he also reached America in 1497, but most historians now question this claim.

Life and expeditions. Vespucci was born in Florence, probably on March 9, 1451. He studied navigation as a youth and spent his early career in the banking firm of Lorenzo di Pier Francesco de' Medici of Florence. In 1491, he moved to Seville, Spain, and became connected with a company that equipped ships for long trips.

Vespucci later claimed that he made four voyages to the New World. After what he called his first voyage, in 1497, he said he had sighted a vast continent (South America). In 1499 and 1500, Vespucci took part in an expedition led by the Spanish explorer Alonso de Ojeda. During this voyage, Vespucci's ship traveled along the coast of Venezuela. In 1501 and 1502, and again in 1503 and 1504, Vespucci sailed with the fleet of Gonçalo Coelho, a Portuguese captain. Both of these expeditions explored the southern coast of Brazil.

Vespucci's reputation came largely from a letter he wrote to Lorenzo di Pier Francesco de' Medici in 1502 or 1503. In it, Vespucci told of his discovery of a new continent and vividly described it. The letter was published in 1503, and again in 1504, under the title of *Mundus Novus (New World)*. It became extremely popular and later was published in several editions and translations. The letter established Vespucci as a famous explorer. He published another letter about his travels in 1505.

Vespucci became a Spanish citizen in 1505 and went to work for a government agency that regulated commerce with the New World. He served as the agency's chief navigator from 1508 until he died on Feb. 22, 1512.

The controversy. Soon after Vespucci died, scholars began to question his claims of discovery. They found little evidence to support his own reports of making a voyage in 1497. Vespucci also claimed to have led all the expeditions, but he actually had been only a navigator or commander of a single ship. In time, Christopher Columbus became known as the European discoverer of the New World. But it was Vespucci who publicized its discovery.   Ann E. Moyer

Vessel, Blood. See Blood; Artery; Vein.

Vesta was a household goddess in Roman mythology. The hearth was the center of family life in ancient Rome, and Vesta's symbol was the fire in the hearth. Every Roman home had a shrine honoring Vesta and the household gods called the *lares* and the *penates.*

Vesta came to be identified with the Greek hearth goddess Hestia. As such, she was a daughter of Saturn, the god of fertility and planting, and Ops, the goddess of the plentiful harvest. In addition, Vesta was a sister of Jupiter, the king of the gods. In myths, she was portrayed as young and unmarried.

In addition to being worshiped by individual families, Vesta had an important public role as a protector of the city of Rome. This role may have originated during the early days of Rome, when a king ruled the city. Vesta safeguarded the welfare of the king's hearth and household, a matter of concern to the entire community.

A temple honoring Vesta stood in the Forum of Rome. In the temple burned a perpetual sacred flame that symbolized the Roman belief in the city's eternity. The flame was tended by six priestesses known as *Vestal Virgins.* The Romans considered it a great honor to serve as a Vestal Virgin. The priestesses often had much power and influence in Roman political life.   Daniel P. Harmon

See also **Hestia; Lares and penates.**

Vesuvius, *vuh SOO vee uhs,* is the only active volcano on the mainland of Europe. It is probably the most famous volcano in the world. It rises on the Bay of Naples, about 7 miles (11 kilometers) southeast of the city of Naples, Italy. Vesuvius has been studied by scientists more than any other volcano because it erupts frequently and is easy to reach. Vesuvius is a cone within the rim of Mount Somma, a big crater formed when the top of the mountain collapsed in the eruption of A.D. 79. The height of the cone changes with each eruption. In 1900, it was 4,275 feet (1,303 meters) high. But after several eruptions since then, its height has dropped to 4,190 feet (1,277 meters). The top of the cone is a cup-shaped crater, ranging from 50 to 400 feet (15 to 120 meters) across. Vesuvius spouts columns of steam, cinders, and sometimes small amounts of lava into the air.

In spite of Vesuvius's history of eruptions, many people live on the lower slopes of the mountain and on the plains at its foot. The volcanic soil is extremely fertile, and the area is famous for its vineyards of wine grapes.

Early eruptions. Prehistoric people probably saw Vesuvius in eruption. Roman legends say that the gods had once used the mountain as a battleground, but at the time of Christ it had been dormant for hundreds of years. A large earthquake that probably occurred in A.D. 62 alarmed the people who lived in the neighborhood of Vesuvius. Some smaller quakes occurred in the following years. The first recorded eruption of Vesuvius occurred on Aug. 24, A.D. 79, when the cities of Herculaneum, Pompeii, and Stabiae were covered by ashes and lava. An eyewitness account of the disaster was written by a Roman author, Pliny the Younger. His uncle, Pliny the Elder, was killed during the eruption.

In 472, ashes poured from the crater in such great amounts that they were carried by the wind as far as Constantinople (now Istanbul). Streams of lava and boiling water fell on the villages at the foot of the mountain in 1631. About 4,000 people were said to have died.

Later eruptions. Other destructive eruptions came in 1794, 1822, 1855, 1872, 1880, 1895, 1906, 1929, and 1944. The greatest destruction in the 1900's occurred in April 1906, when several towns were destroyed. The eruption that took place in March 1944, during World War II, destroyed the village of San Sebastiano. Soldiers of the Al-

© Jonathan Blair, Woodfin Camp, Inc.

Mount Vesuvius towers over the city of Naples, Italy. Despite the volcano's frequent eruptions, many people farm the nearby land. The ash from Vesuvius has made the soil extremely fertile.

lied armies helped the people of nearby towns escape the lava and volcanic dust.

Before the eruption of 1944, thousands of visitors came to Vesuvius every year. They could go down into the crater for some distance and see a crimson stream of lava flow from the cone and turn into a bed of cold stone. A cable railway which took visitors to within 450 feet (137 meters) of the edge of the crater was destroyed in this eruption. Many people still visit the area.

A Royal Observatory was established on the slopes of the mountain in 1844. Since that time, scientists have kept a constant watch over the volcano during and between eruptions. One observer lost his life standing by his post.   David I. Kertzer

See also **Herculaneum; Mountain** (diagram: Major mountains); **Naples; Pompeii; Volcano** (Stratovolcanoes).

Vetch is a type of vine that is grown chiefly as feed for cattle and sheep. A form of vetch called *horse bean* or *broad bean* is grown for its seed, which is eaten as a vegetable. Vetches are also used as fertilizer.

The leaves of vetches have many leaflets. Vetches have *tendrils* (threadlike structures) that attach themselves to other plants for support. Vetches have weak stems that grow 2 to 5 feet (60 to 150 centimeters) long or more. Most vetches require a cool growing season.

Farmers worldwide grow vetch to make such animal feed as hay, pasturage, and silage. In the United States, vetch is most widely grown in the southern half of the country and in the Pacific Coast States. Because of the mild winters in these areas, vetch can be planted in the fall. It grows in the winter and is plowed in the spring. This process fertilizes the soil.   Vern L. Marble

Scientific classification. Vetch is in the pea family, Fabaceae or Leguminosae. It is genus *Vicia.* There are about 150 species of vetch. The most common are hairy vetch, *V. villosa,* common vetch, *V. sativa,* and purple vetch, *V. atropurpurea.*

See also **Broad bean.**

Veterans Administration. See Veterans Affairs, Department of.

Veterans Affairs, Department of, also called the VA, is an executive department of the United States government. It administers benefits to veterans of U.S. military service, their dependents, and the dependents of deceased veterans. The secretary of veterans affairs, a member of the president's Cabinet, heads the department. The secretary is appointed by the president, subject to U.S. Senate approval.

The benefits administered by the department include health care, disability and death compensation, education assistance, burial assistance, and help in getting home loans. Veterans apply at VA health care facilities to get health care benefits. Veterans and their dependents apply at the department's regional offices to receive all other benefits. The dependents of veterans are not eligible for health care benefits.

The Department of Veterans Affairs has at least one regional office in each U.S. state. It also has regional offices in Puerto Rico, the

The seal of the Department of Veterans Affairs

Secretaries of veterans affairs

Name	Took office	Under president
Edward J. Derwinski	1989	G. H. W. Bush
*Jesse Brown	1993	Clinton
Togo West	1998	Clinton
Anthony J. Principi	2001	G. W. Bush
Jim Nicholson	2005	G. W. Bush
James B. Peake	2007	G. W. Bush

*Has a separate biography in *World Book.*

Philippines, and Washington, D.C. In addition, the department operates veterans' hospitals in all U.S. states, Puerto Rico, and Washington, D.C. The Department of Veterans Affairs administers national cemeteries for deceased veterans and for their spouses and children. The department's Web site at http://www.va.gov presents information on its activities.

Benefits and other services. The VA pays disability or death compensation or pensions to millions of veterans and dependents of deceased veterans. The department also treats veterans in its hospitals and operates clinics for veterans. Millions of veterans and members of the military service hold insurance policies administered by the department. The VA also guarantees home loans to veterans and their dependents.

The Department of Veterans Affairs administers an educational training program authorized by a series of laws popularly referred to as GI Bills. Veterans and their dependents have received GI Bill training since 1944. That year, Congress passed the first GI Bill, the Servicemen's Readjustment Act, for veterans of World War II (1939-1945). The second GI Bill, the Veterans' Readjustment Assistance Act of 1952, aided veterans of the Korean War (1950-1953). The Veterans' Readjustment Act of 1966 was intended for people who served in the armed forces after the Korean War. The act provided educational benefits for those who served between Feb. 1, 1955, and Jan. 1, 1977.

Men and women entering military service between Jan. 1, 1977, and July 1, 1985, qualified for the Post-Vietnam Era Veterans' Educational Assistance Program. To get benefits, members of the military service must deposit part of their pay in a special savings fund. The government deducts contributions from each person's monthly pay and adds a certain extra amount to the fund, depending on how much the person invests.

The Montgomery GI Bill, which became effective July 1, 1985, established two educational benefits programs. The first program benefits men and women who began active duty after June 30, 1985. Participants in this program have their military pay reduced for a certain period of their active duty. In return, they receive a larger amount of money for full-time training.

The second program under the Montgomery GI Bill provides educational benefits for members of the Reserves and the Army and Air National Guard. The program is available to members who enlist, reenlist, or extend an enlistment for six years after June 30, 1985. Participants receive money while attending an institution of higher learning as full-time students. Veterans covered by the Montgomery GI Bill include those who took part in the Persian Gulf War of 1991 and the Iraq War, which began in 2003.

History. Veterans of the Revolutionary War in America (1775-1783) received pensions under a series of laws adopted in the late 1700's and early 1800's. Temporary help had been given to these veterans in the form of cash bonuses and land grants. The office of the commissioner of pensions was set up in 1849 to administer all military pension laws under the direction of the secretary of the interior. The first U.S. Soldiers' Home was established in 1851 in Washington, D.C., to provide a home for invalid or disabled soldiers.

Today, the Department of Veterans Affairs operates *domiciliaries* for veterans who do not need hospital care but who are unable to earn a living and lack means of support. There are also nursing home units associated with the hospitals operated by the VA.

During World War I (1914-1918), the Bureau of War Risk Insurance was created under the War Risk Insurance Act. The bureau administered insurance against death or disability of members of the armed forces. The act also set up the Federal Board for Vocational Education to provide vocational rehabilitation for disabled veterans. Five government agencies were then serving veterans. To eliminate the duplication, Congress created the Veterans Bureau in 1920. In 1930, the Veterans Administration (VA) was created by combining the Veterans Bureau with the National Home for Disabled Volunteer Soldiers and the Bureau of Pensions.

In 1988, Congress passed a bill that made the Veterans Administration an executive department of the U.S. government. The bill renamed the VA the Department of Veterans Affairs. The changes went into effect in 1989. Edward J. Derwinski became the first secretary of veterans affairs.   Critically reviewed by the Department of Veterans Affairs

See also **Agent Orange; Pension** (Federal pension plans).

Veterans Day honors men and women who have served in the United States armed services. Veterans Day is a legal federal holiday in the United States. It is celebrated on November 11, the anniversary of the end of World War I (1914-1918). Canada, Australia, and New Zealand observe November 11 as Remembrance Day to honor people who have died in war. The United Kingdom celebrates Remembrance Day on the Sunday closest to November 11. Veterans Day celebrations in the United States include parades and speeches. Special services are held at the Tomb of the Unknowns in Arlington National Cemetery in Arlington, Virginia.

In 1919, President Woodrow Wilson proclaimed November 11 as Armistice Day to remind Americans of the tragedies of war. A 1938 law made the day a federal holiday. In 1954, Congress changed the holiday's name to Veterans Day to honor all U.S. veterans.   Sharron G. Uhler

Veterans of Foreign Wars of the United States (VFW) is one of the largest veterans' organizations in the United States. The organization seeks to develop comradeship among its members, assist needy veterans and their families, and organize memorial services for deceased veterans. It also promotes patriotism and community and legislative activities.

Any officer or enlisted man or woman, either on active duty or honorably discharged, who fought in any foreign military campaign of the United States may join the VFW. VFW membership includes veterans of World War I (1914-1918), World War II (1939-1945), the Korean War (1950-1953), the Vietnam War (1957-1975), the Persian Gulf War of 1991, and the Iraq War, which began in 2003. The VFW has admitted women since 1978.

National Headquarters, VFW
VFW emblem

The Ladies Auxiliary to the VFW is a woman's organization devoted to community service and patriotism. It assists the VFW with many of its programs. Any woman with a close relative who is eligible to join the VFW may join the VFW Auxiliary. Any woman who herself fought in a foreign war may also join.

The first attempts to organize veterans of foreign wars began in the late 1890's. Three organizations combined in 1913 to form the VFW. Its headquarters are in Kansas City, Missouri.   Critically reviewed by the VFW

Veterans' organizations include former members of a nation's armed services. The organizations may limit membership to veterans who served during a particular war or military campaign. Or they may accept only veterans who fought overseas or were disabled.

Veterans' organizations have been chiefly patriotic and social in purpose. They promote the comradeship formed during war and work to support the laws and government of the nation. They also provide care for the spouses and children of deceased veterans. Veterans' organizations conduct memorial services and take care of the graves of deceased veterans.

These groups usually have significant political influence because of their large membership. They use this power to obtain legislation that will benefit veterans, such as pensions, and care for disabled veterans.

In the United States, the Society of the Cincinnati was the first veterans' organization. Major General Henry Knox suggested establishment of a society of veterans who fought in the Revolutionary War in America (1775-1783). The Society of the Cincinnati began in 1783, with George Washington as its first president.

The veterans' organizations formed after the War of 1812 and the Mexican War (1846-1848) were not large. After the American Civil War (1861-1865), which had large armies, strong veterans' organizations came into existence. The Grand Army of the Republic (G.A.R.), an organization of veterans of the Union Army, began its work in 1866. It had enough influence to control the Republican Party for almost 40 years. It reached its highest membership in 1890. The support of the G.A.R. often meant the difference between victory and defeat for candidates in the North. The United Confederate Veterans held a similar position in the South.

The Jewish War Veterans of the United States was established in 1896. Other attempts to organize the veterans of foreign military campaigns began in the late 1890's. The United Spanish War Veterans, founded in 1898, included soldiers who had fought in the Spanish-American War, which took place earlier that year. Three organizations of veterans of foreign wars joined in 1913 to form the Veterans of Foreign Wars (VFW). In 1919, following World War I (1914-1918), veterans who fought in France formed a veterans' organization called the American Legion. The Disabled American Veterans was established in 1920.

After World War II (1939-1945), veterans formed new organizations. The American Veterans of World War II (now called simply American Veterans or AMVETS) was founded in 1944. Vietnam Veterans of America was created in 1978.

In Canada, the Royal Canadian Legion is the country's largest veterans' organization. It was founded in 1926. The Army, Navy, and Air Force Veterans in Canada is the country's oldest veterans' group. It was founded in 1837. Other Canadian veterans' organizations include the Armed Forces Pensioners'/Annuitants' Association of Canada, the Canadian Corps Association, the Canadian Paraplegic Association, and the War Amputations of Canada.   Thomas M. DeFrank

Related articles in *World Book* include:

Veterinarian. See **Veterinary medicine** (Careers in veterinary medicine).

Veterinary medicine is the branch of medicine that deals with the diseases of animals. Doctors who treat animals are called *veterinarians.* Veterinarians are trained to prevent, diagnose, and treat illness in large and small animals. Their work is especially valuable because many animal diseases can be transmitted to human beings. Such diseases, called *zoonoses,* include anthrax, brucellosis, plague, *psittacosis* (parrot fever), Q-fever, rabies, tuberculosis, and *tularemia* (rabbit fever).

In cities, most veterinarians care for dogs, cats, and other household pets. Veterinarians in cities primarily work in animal hospitals. These hospitals contain equipment much like that used in hospitals for human beings.

There, animals may be cared for during illnesses, and surgery may be performed to treat an illness or injury.

An important part of the duties of a veterinarian is the control of rabies. Proper vaccination of dogs, cats, and ferrets against rabies contributes to the prevention of this deadly disease. In addition, veterinarians vaccinate pets against distemper and other diseases. See **Distemper; Rabies.**

Veterinarians also are associated with the public health services of cities, states, and the federal government. These doctors investigate outbreaks of human and animal diseases such as food-borne diseases, influenza, Lyme disease, rabies, and West Nile virus. Veterinarians may inspect meat and meat products in slaughtering and packing houses and help ensure the safety of food in restaurants. They may also work in laboratories testing milk or other dairy products, preparing serums and vaccines, or conducting research. Veterinarians working in environmental health study the effects of pesticides and pollution on animals and people.

On farms and ranches, veterinarians are concerned chiefly with the care and treatment of livestock. Veterinarians help keep farm animals in good health and work to prevent outbreaks of animal diseases. Epidemics of animal diseases, or *epizootics,* may be extremely dangerous, not only to animals, but also to human beings. Modern vaccines have made it possible for veterinarians to protect farm animals against many diseases.

Veterinarians have played an important role in controlling bovine tuberculosis, a form of tuberculosis that can be passed from cows to human beings. In 1917, the federal government began a program to wipe out this disease. A cooperative plan set up by the federal and state governments allows veterinarians to test dairy cattle for tuberculosis. Another project works to control and eradicate bovine brucellosis. This disease also can be transferred from cattle to human beings. Brucellosis and tuberculosis have been nearly eliminated from cattle in the United States by veterinarians (see **Brucellosis**).

WORLD BOOK photo by Dan Miller

Veterinary practice in cities chiefly involves caring for pets. Veterinarians examine and treat sick and injured animals, and also provide vaccinations and other preventive care.

Cameramann International, Ltd.

Rural veterinarians help keep livestock and other farm animals in good health. The veterinarian shown here is putting a powdered antibiotic into the throat of a cow.

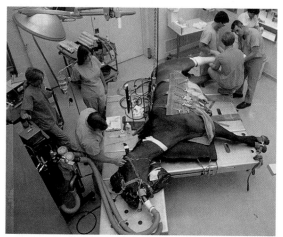

Cary Wolinsky, Stock, Boston

A college of veterinary medicine has modern operating rooms and equipment. This photograph shows faculty veterinarians teaching students how to fit a cast on a horse's rear leg.

Careers in veterinary medicine. People who want to become veterinarians must have at least two years of preveterinary college work, followed by four years of study in a college of veterinary medicine. In veterinary school, students study such subjects as anatomy, physiology, microbiology, pathology, and surgery.

There are 27 colleges of veterinary medicine in the United States, 4 colleges in Canada, and 8 colleges in various other countries that are fully accredited by the American Veterinary Medical Association. These schools offer courses of study that lead to the Doctor of Veterinary Medicine (D.V.M. or V.M.D.) or equivalent degree. After earning a degree, the graduate must comply with the license regulations of the state in which he or she plans to practice.

After receiving a license, a veterinarian may go into private or institutional clinical practice. Veterinarians may also be employed in government service, including the military. A veterinarian interested in research may want to work at the U.S. Department of Health and Human Services, the U.S. Department of Agriculture, an agricultural experiment station, a college, or a private company. Some veterinarians teach at colleges of veterinary or human medicine or work in commercial laboratories. Other career opportunities for veterinarians include working at animal shelters, race tracks, zoos, aquariums, or wildlife refuges, or serving in programs sponsored by such agencies as the U.S. Peace Corps and the World Health Organization (WHO).

The American Veterinary Medical Association works to maintain the professional standards of veterinary medicine. The association's headquarters are in Schaumburg, Illinois.

Critically reviewed by the American Veterinary Medical Association

Veto is a Latin word that means *I forbid.* In American government, the word *veto* usually refers to the president's power to kill a law that the legislative branch has already passed.

The president of the United States has a *limited* veto power. It is not absolute. A vote of a two-thirds majority of the members present in each house of Congress can override it. The sovereign of the United Kingdom still holds the power of *absolute* veto. But no British king or queen has used this power since 1707.

Vetoing a bill. When the two houses of the U.S. Congress pass a bill or joint resolution, it is sent to the president. Then one of four things must happen:

(1) The president may approve the bill. If so, the president signs it, and it becomes law.

(2) The president may allow the bill to become law without signing it. This can take place under the clause in the Constitution which provides that "if any bill shall not be returned by the president within 10 days (Sundays excepted) after it shall have been presented to him, the same shall be a law in like manner as if he had signed it, unless the Congress by their adjournment prevent its return, in which case it shall not be a law."

(3) The president may retain the bill, expecting that Congress will adjourn within 10 days—not including Sundays—and thus the bill will be defeated. This method, called the *pocket veto,* is used by presidents who oppose a bill but do not want to veto it openly.

(4) The president may veto the bill. In that case, the president must send a message to Congress stating the reasons for the veto. Vetoing a bill defeats all parts of it. All provisions and "riders" attached to the bill are vetoed with it.

Line-item veto. In 1996, Congress approved a law that gave the president a *line-item veto* power. In a line-item veto, the president could veto individual items in spending bills without vetoing the whole bill. To override a line-item veto, Congress first had to pass a bill against it. If the president vetoed that bill and Congress overrode that bill's veto, the item in the spending bill took effect. In 1998, however, the Supreme Court ruled that the law was unconstitutional. Nevertheless, many members of government continue to support the idea. They believe that presidents should be able to use the line-item veto to block unneeded spending that Congress, under pressure from local groups, might include in legislation.

Presidents' use of the veto. When the Constitution was adopted, Alexander Hamilton declared that presidents would veto bills only with great caution. Several presidents did not veto any bills. Franklin D. Roosevelt, who served as president longer than any other person, vetoed the most bills. He used 372 regular vetoes and 263 pocket vetoes. Grover Cleveland ranks second, with 346 regular vetoes and 238 pocket vetoes.

Congress has overridden only about 4 percent of all presidential vetoes of bills. Some of the presidents who vetoed bills had no vetoes overridden by Congress. Congress reversed only 9 of Roosevelt's 372 regular vetoes and only 2 of the 36 issued by Dwight D. Eisenhower. But it overrode 15 of Andrew Johnson's 21 regular vetoes. Presidential veto power serves as a major check on Congress (see **Checks and balances**).

The line-item veto was used, by President Bill Clinton, to kill 82 spending items in 11 laws. Congress restored 38 of those items by overriding some of Clinton's vetoes. The Supreme Court decision against the line-item veto restored the rest of the 82 items.

Governors' veto power. All state governors have a power to veto bills. But in some states, the governor's veto may be overridden by a simple majority of the members present in the houses of the legislature rather than by a required two-thirds majority. Most governors also can veto parts of spending bills.   Peter Woll

See also **President of the United States** (Legislative leader); **United Nations** (Voting); **United States, Government of the** (diagram: How a bill becomes law); **Washington, George** (First veto).

VFW. See Veterans of Foreign Wars of the United States.

Viacom Inc. is a major media and communications company. It owns a number of popular cable television channels, including BET (Black Entertainment Television), CMT (Country Music Television), Comedy Central, MTV, Nickelodeon, Spike TV, TV Land, and VH1. Viacom produces and distributes feature films through its motion-picture division, Paramount Pictures Corporation. It also owns Paramount Home Entertainment Inc., a distributor of films on DVD and via digital download from the Internet. In 2006 and 2007, Viacom struck digital distribution deals with several large digital outlets. These outlets include Yahoo!, Microsoft, AOL, and Bebo. In addition, the company negotiated an agreement with the Chinese online-search leader Baidu to provide video over the Internet. The deal with Baidu gave Viacom access to the world's fastest-growing Internet market.

In 1971, a United States Federal Communications Commission (FCC) ruling forced the Columbia Broadcasting System (CBS), Inc., to spin off some cable TV and syndication operations, forming Viacom. In the 1990's, many entertainment companies began to consolidate. Viacom purchased Paramount in 1994 and CBS in 2000. At the end of 2005, Viacom split itself into two separate media companies, one called Viacom and the other called CBS Corporation. Both companies have headquarters in New York City.

CBS Corporation owns the U.S. national broadcast network CBS and many local TV and radio stations. With Warner Bros. Entertainment, CBS Corporation jointly owns another national broadcast network, the CW. CBS Corporation's other operations include TV programming, book publishing, and outdoor advertising.
    Critically reviewed by Viacom Inc.

Viaduct, *VY uh duhkt,* is like a bridge, except that it crosses over dry land instead of water. Some viaducts do cross water, but they also cross dry land instead of merely extending from one land bank to the other.

Most viaducts have a series of supports under beam-and-slab or arch construction. Viaducts carry railroad tracks over valleys and gorges. Some are built higher than the general level of the land to carry railroads over highways or to make a safe crossing for highways over railroads. The ancient Romans built the first viaducts to carry water to cities. They often also served as roadways.

Today, the main part of the pier viaduct over the mouth of the River Tay in Scotland has 84 steel spans and is more than 2 miles (3.2 kilometers) long. The Tunkhannock Viaduct, a railroad bridge crossing Tunkhannock Creek in northeastern Pennsylvania, is one of the largest steel and concrete viaducts in the world. It is 2,375 feet (724 meters) long and includes 10 spans of 180 feet (55 meters) each. Other well-known viaducts are the Pecos River viaduct in Texas; the Landwasser viaduct across Albula Pass, in the canton of Graubünden, Switz-

erland; and the Pulaski Skyway between Newark and Jersey City in New Jersey.   Boyd C. Paulson, Jr.

Vibraphone is a percussion instrument with a number of aluminum bars arranged on a frame like the keys of a piano. Most vibraphones have 37 bars with a range of three octaves. A player strikes the bars with mallets. Variations in tone quality can be produced by mallets with heads of soft or hard yarn. A hollow metal tube called a *resonator* lies beneath each bar of a vibraphone. An electric motor operates a revolving valve inside each resonator. The valve creates a vibrating sound called a *vibrato.* The vibraphone also has a *sustaining pedal* that can lengthen or muffle each note. The vibraphone has a harplike sound. The vibraphone was invented in 1921 by Hermann Winterhoff, an American executive, and engineers of a United States instrument manufacturer. It has become especially popular in jazz.   John H. Beck

See also **Music** (picture: Percussion Instruments).

Vibration, in mechanics, is the rapid "to-and-fro" motion of an object. Almost everything vibrates, though the vibrations may be too weak, too fast, or too slow for us to detect. Vibration occurs during earthquakes and when the oceans move up and down, causing the tides. An automobile vibrates as a result of repeated explosions in the cylinders of its engine. Many sounds are produced by vibrating objects.

Vibrations can be used to perform many useful tasks. When we tap a salt shaker, for example, we use vibrations to make the salt flow. Workers use devices that produce vibrations to pack down soil under roadways. In medicine, vibrators are used to treat sore muscles.

Vibrations can also cause problems for people and machines. Vibrations at certain rates and intensities cause discomfort. Too much vibration can cause people to lose their ability to concentrate. In machines, vibrations can cause noise, wear, and breakage.

Engineers have developed ways of correcting vibration problems. They may use elastic materials or springs to reduce the effects of vibration. For example, automobiles are equipped with pneumatic tires and shock absorbers to absorb the vibrations caused by traveling over rough roads.

Vibrations can be described by their *amplitude* and their *frequency.* Amplitude is the distance the vibrating object travels from a position of rest. Frequency is the number of complete vibrations during a certain period, usually one second. Frequency is measured in a unit called the *hertz.* Most people can hear vibrations with frequencies from 20 to 20,000 hertz.

Vibrations can be classified as *free* or *forced,* depending on whether an outside force keeps the vibration going. A guitar string, for example, vibrates freely after it is plucked. However, the vibration of a violin string is forced while the bow is drawn over it.   James D. Chalupnik

See also **Sound; Waves.**

Vice admiral. See Rank, Military.

Vice president is the second highest executive officer in the government of some nations. In many countries, the vice president assumes the presidency if the president dies, resigns, is removed from office, or becomes disabled. In some nations, including Argentina and the United States, the vice president also serves as the presiding officer of the national senate.

See also **Vice president of the United States.**

Office of the Vice President

The seal of the vice president of the United States includes an eagle holding arrows and an olive branch. The olive branch symbolizes the desire for peace, and the arrows represent the ability to wage war. The Latin words *E Pluribus Unum* mean *Out of Many, One* and refer to the unity of the United States.

Portrait gallery of the vice presidents

The term of each vice president, as well as the name of the president under whom the vice president served, is listed under each picture. The asterisks identify those who later served as president.

Vice president of the United States

Vice president of the United States is only a heartbeat away from the most powerful elective office in the world. The vice president must be ready to become president or acting president at a moment's notice if the president dies, resigns, is removed from office, or becomes unable to perform the duties of office.

Fourteen vice presidents have become president, eight because of the death of a president. These eight so-called "accidental presidents" were John Tyler, Millard Fillmore, Andrew Johnson, Chester A. Arthur, Theodore Roosevelt, Calvin Coolidge, Harry S. Truman, and Lyndon B. Johnson. The other vice presidents who became president were John Adams, Thomas Jefferson, Martin Van Buren, Richard M. Nixon, Gerald R. Ford, and George H. W. Bush. Ford was the only vice president to take office because of a president's resignation.

The United States Constitution also provides that the vice president shall become acting president if the president is disabled. In 1967, the 25th Amendment to the Constitution was ratified. It spelled out procedures in case of presidential disability and provided for vice

*John Adams 1789-1797 *Washington* | *Thomas Jefferson 1797-1801 *J. Adams* | Aaron Burr 1801-1805 *Jefferson* | George Clinton 1805-1812 *Jefferson-Madison* | Elbridge Gerry 1813-1814 *Madison* | Daniel D. Tompkins 1817-1825 *Monroe*

John C. Calhoun 1825-1832 *J. Q. Adams-Jackson* | *Martin Van Buren 1833-1837 *Jackson* | Richard M. Johnson 1837-1841 *Van Buren* | *John Tyler 1841 *W. H. Harrison* | George M. Dallas 1845-1849 *Polk* | *Millard Fillmore 1849-1850 *Taylor*

William R. D. King 1853 *Pierce* | John C. Breckinridge 1857-1861 *Buchanan* | Hannibal Hamlin 1861-1865 *Lincoln* | *Andrew Johnson 1865 *Lincoln* | Schuyler Colfax 1869-1873 *Grant* | Henry Wilson 1873-1875 *Grant*

William A. Wheeler 1877-1881 *Hayes* | *Chester A. Arthur 1881 *Garfield* | Thomas A. Hendricks 1885 *Cleveland* | Levi P. Morton 1889-1893 *B. Harrison* | Adlai E. Stevenson 1893-1897 *Cleveland* | Garret A. Hobart 1897-1899 *McKinley*

presidential succession (see **Constitution of the United States** [Amendment 25]). Presidents James A. Garfield, Woodrow Wilson, and Dwight D. Eisenhower all had serious illnesses. But their vice presidents carefully avoided assuming the duties of the president. In 1985, George H. W. Bush became the first vice president to serve as acting president. He held the office for about eight hours. President Ronald Reagan had designated Bush as acting president when Reagan had surgery.

The vice president serves as the presiding officer of the United States Senate and has the title of *president of the Senate*. The Constitution gives the vice president no

other official duty. For more than 100 years, the job's lack of political importance caused it to be treated as somewhat of a joke. Some people had humorously suggested that the vice president be addressed as "Your Superfluous Excellency."

Yet the Founding Fathers had high hopes for the office of the vice presidency. James Iredell of North Carolina, who later served on the Supreme Court of the United States, explained that there would be "two men … in office at the same time; the president, who will possess, in the highest degree, the confidence of the country, and the vice president, who is thought to be

Facts in brief about the vice president

Qualifications: The Constitution provides that a candidate must be a "natural-born" U.S. citizen and must have lived in the United States for at least 14 years. The candidate must be at least 35 years old and must be eligible under the Constitution for the office of president. No law or court decision has defined the exact meaning of the term *natural-born*. Authorities assume that the term applies to all citizens born in the United States and its territories. But they are not certain if the term also includes children born to U.S. citizens in other countries.

How nominated: By a national political convention. If a vacancy in the vice presidency exists, the president nominates a new vice president, who takes office upon confirmation by a majority vote of both houses of Congress.

How elected: By a majority vote of the Electoral College, held in December after the general election held on the first Tuesday after the first Monday in November of every fourth year.

Inauguration: Held at noon, January 20, after election by the Electoral College. If the date falls on Sunday, the ceremony is held on Monday, January 21.

Term: The vice president is elected for four years and can serve any number of terms.

Income: $221,100 annual salary, $20,000 expense allowance, and an allowance for staff support.

Removal from office: Impeachment by a majority vote of the House of Representatives, and trial and conviction by a two-thirds vote of those present in the Senate.

---

*Theodore Roosevelt
1901
McKinley

Charles W. Fairbanks
1905-1909
T. Roosevelt

James S. Sherman
1909-1912
Taft

Thomas R. Marshall
1913-1921
Wilson

*Calvin Coolidge
1921-1923
Harding

Charles G. Dawes
1925-1929
Coolidge

Charles Curtis
1929-1933
Hoover

John N. Garner
1933-1941
F. Roosevelt

Henry A. Wallace
1941-1945
F. Roosevelt

*Harry S. Truman
1945
F. Roosevelt

Alben W. Barkley
1949-1953
Truman

*Richard M. Nixon
1953-1961
Eisenhower

*Lyndon B. Johnson
1961-1963
Kennedy

Hubert H. Humphrey
1965-1969
L Johnson

Spiro T. Agnew
1969-1973
Nixon

*Gerald R. Ford
1973-1974
Nixon

Nelson A. Rockefeller
1974-1977
Ford

Walter F. Mondale
1977-1981
Carter

*George H. W. Bush
1981-1989
Reagan

Dan Quayle
1989-1993
G. H. W. Bush

Al Gore
1993-2001
Clinton

Richard B. Cheney
2001-2009
G. W. Bush

Joe Biden
2009-
Obama

the next person in the Union most fit to perform this trust."

The prestige of the vice presidency has gradually increased since the early 1920's. Beginning in 1933 with the presidency of Franklin D. Roosevelt, vice presidents have regularly attended meetings of the president's Cabinet. Dwight D. Eisenhower and John F. Kennedy did more than any other presidents to establish the importance of the office of vice president. Eisenhower's vice president, Richard M. Nixon, and Kennedy's vice president, Lyndon B. Johnson, had important duties and responsibilities. When Kennedy was assassinated in 1963, many experts believed that Johnson was the best-prepared "accidental president."

The vice president has offices in the Capitol, the Richard B. Russell Office Building of the U.S. Senate, and the Executive Office Building. All these offices are in Washington, D.C. In 1974, Congress established a 33-room mansion on the grounds of Washington's Naval Observatory as the vice president's official residence. Secret Service agents guard the vice president.

Choosing a vice president

Nomination of the vice presidential candidate occurs at the party's national convention. The convention delegates usually nominate the person preferred by the presidential nominee. A contest develops only if the presidential nominee makes no choice. The vice presidential candidate is often called the presidential nominee's *running mate.*

Many factors may influence the selection of a vice presidential nominee. After a bitter campaign for the presidential nomination, the nominee may want a running mate who can help restore party harmony. The choice for vice president may be one of the losing candidates for the presidential nomination, or a supporter of one of the losers. In 1844, the Democrats nominated Senator Silas Wright of New York for vice president. They did this to appease former President Martin Van Buren, who had failed to win the Democratic presidential nomination. But Wright, a close friend of Van Buren, refused. In 1972, the Democratic vice presidential nominee, Senator Thomas F. Eagleton, became the only person ever to withdraw after having accepted a party's nomination at a national convention. He did so following the disclosure that he had received psychiatric treatment. See **Eagleton, Thomas F.**

Often the vice president comes from one of the states considered to be especially important in the election. This may be a state in which the election outcome is expected to be very close, or it may simply be a state with a large electoral vote. By appealing to local loyalties, the vice presidential candidate may strengthen the party's vote in this "home" state.

Sometimes the vice presidential candidate is chosen because the person is thought to appeal to a large bloc of voters. In 1984, the Democrats nominated Representative Geraldine A. Ferraro of New York for vice president. She was the first woman and the first person of Italian descent ever chosen as the vice presidential candidate by a major American political party.

The vice presidential choice often is made to *balance the ticket.* If an older candidate is nominated for president, a younger person may be chosen for vice presi-

dent. A presidential nominee from the East may be balanced with a vice presidential nominee from the West. If the presidential nominee is known as a conservative, the vice presidential nominee may be a liberal. By balancing the ticket, party leaders hope to win the support of the largest possible number of voters.

The system of selecting a vice president helps the party win the election. It does not necessarily produce the person best qualified to serve as vice president. The custom of balancing the ticket with people of conflicting political beliefs has often been criticized. Theodore Roosevelt said early in his political career: "It is an unhealthy thing to have a vice president and president represented by principles so far apart that the succession of one to the place of the other means a change as radical as any party overturn." This occurred when John Tyler succeeded William Henry Harrison and when Roosevelt later succeeded William McKinley.

The campaign. The vice presidential candidate plays an active role in the election campaign. The vice presidential and presidential candidates usually map out separate campaign routes for maximum coverage of the country. They may later change places to cover all strategic areas with repeated campaigning.

Election. Voters select the same electors for the vice president when they choose presidential electors. They cannot split the ticket. That is, a person cannot vote for electors of the presidential candidate of the Republican Party and for electors of the vice presidential candidate of the Democratic Party. Citizens must vote for a slate of electors pledged to one party's candidates.

The Electoral College elects the president and vice president on separate ballots (see **Electoral College**). If the Electoral College fails to choose the vice president by a majority vote, the Senate elects one of the two leading candidates. At least two-thirds of the Senate must be present at the voting, and the winner must receive a majority vote of the entire membership.

The Senate has elected a vice president only once. In 1837, the Senate elected Richard M. Johnson, a Democrat, by a vote of 33 to 16 over Francis Granger, a Whig. Johnson had fallen one vote short in the Electoral College. He became so controversial that the Democrats refused to renominate him in 1840. In fact, they failed to nominate any vice presidential candidate—the only time any convention has done so.

Inauguration. Until 1933, the vice president took the oath of office in the Senate. Today, both president and vice president are inaugurated in the same ceremony in January after their election. The vice president is sworn into office immediately before the president is inaugurated. The vice president's oath may be administered by the retiring vice president, by a member of Congress, or by some other government official, such as a justice of the Supreme Court. In the early days, the vice president made an inaugural address. This custom has disappeared with the adoption of the combined ceremony in which the president gives the inaugural address.

The 25th Amendment spells out procedures for filling a vacancy in the vice presidency. The office becomes vacant if the vice president dies, resigns, or is unable to carry out the duties of office. Then the president appoints a new vice president. The appointment is subject to the approval of a majority of both the Senate and the

The vice presidents of the United States

Name	Birthplace	Occupation or profession	Political party	Age at inauguration	Served	President
1. Adams, John (a)	Braintree, MA	Lawyer	Federalist	53	1789-1797	Washington
2. Jefferson, Thomas (a)	Albemarle County, VA	Planter	Democratic-Republican	53	1797-1801	J. Adams
3. Burr, Aaron	Newark, NJ	Lawyer	Democratic-Republican	45	1801-1805	Jefferson
4. Clinton, George (c)	Little Britain, NY	Soldier	Democratic-Republican	65	1805-1809	Jefferson
				69	1809-1812	Madison
5. Gerry, Elbridge (c)	Marblehead, MA	Businessman	Democratic-Republican	68	1813-1814	Madison
6. Tompkins, Daniel D.	Fox Meadows, NY	Lawyer	Democratic-Republican	42	1817-1825	Monroe
7. Calhoun, John C. (d)	Abbeville District, SC	Lawyer	Democratic-Republican	42	1825-1829	J. Q. Adams
			Democratic	46	1829-1832	Jackson
8. Van Buren, Martin (a)	Kinderhook, NY	Lawyer	Democratic	50	1833-1837	Jackson
9. Johnson, Richard M.	Beargrass, KY	Lawyer	Democratic	56	1837-1841	Van Buren
10. Tyler, John (b)	Charles City County, VA	Lawyer	Whig	50	1841	W. H. Harrison
11. Dallas, George M.	Philadelphia	Lawyer	Democratic	52	1845-1849	Polk
12. Fillmore, Millard (b)	Locke, NY	Lawyer	Whig	49	1849-1850	Taylor
13. King, William R. D. (c)	Sampson County, NC	Lawyer	Democratic	66	1853	Pierce
14. Breckinridge, John C.	near Lexington, KY	Lawyer	Democratic	36	1857-1861	Buchanan
15. Hamlin, Hannibal	Paris, ME	Lawyer	Republican	51	1861-1865	Lincoln
16. Johnson, Andrew (b)	Raleigh, NC	Tailor	Union (e)	56	1865	Lincoln
17. Colfax, Schuyler	New York City	Auditor	Republican	45	1869-1873	Grant
18. Wilson, Henry (c)	Farmington, NH	Businessman	Republican	61	1873-1875	Grant
19. Wheeler, William A.	Malone, NY	Lawyer	Republican	57	1877-1881	Hayes
20. Arthur, Chester A. (b)	Fairfield, VT	Lawyer	Republican	51	1881	Garfield
21. Hendricks, Thomas A. (c)	near Zanesville, OH	Lawyer	Democratic	65	1885	Cleveland
22. Morton, Levi P.	Shoreham, VT	Banker	Republican	64	1889-1893	B. Harrison
23. Stevenson, Adlai E.	Christian County, KY	Lawyer	Democratic	57	1893-1897	Cleveland
24. Hobart, Garret A. (c)	Long Branch, NJ	Lawyer	Republican	52	1897-1899	McKinley
25. Roosevelt, Theodore (b) (a)	New York City	Author	Republican	42	1901	McKinley
26. Fairbanks, Charles W.	near Unionville Center, OH	Lawyer	Republican	52	1905-1909	T. Roosevelt
27. Sherman, James S. (c)	Utica, NY	Lawyer	Republican	53	1909-1912	Taft
28. Marshall, Thomas R.	North Manchester, IN	Lawyer	Democratic	58	1913-1921	Wilson
29. Coolidge, Calvin (b) (a)	Plymouth Notch, VT	Lawyer	Republican	48	1921-1923	Harding
30. Dawes, Charles G.	Marietta, OH	Lawyer	Republican	59	1925-1929	Coolidge
31. Curtis, Charles	Topeka, KS	Lawyer	Republican	69	1929-1933	Hoover
32. Garner, John N.	Red River County, TX	Lawyer	Democratic	64	1933-1941	F. Roosevelt
33. Wallace, Henry A.	Adair County, IA	Farmer	Democratic	52	1941-1945	F. Roosevelt
34. Truman, Harry S. (b) (a)	Lamar, MO	Businessman	Democratic	60	1945	F. Roosevelt
35. Barkley, Alben W.	Graves County, KY	Lawyer	Democratic	71	1949-1953	Truman
36. Nixon, Richard M. (a)	Yorba Linda, CA	Lawyer	Republican	40	1953-1961	Eisenhower
37. Johnson, Lyndon B. (b) (a)	near Stonewall, TX	Teacher	Democratic	52	1961-1963	Kennedy
38. Humphrey, Hubert H.	Wallace, SD	Pharmacist	Democratic	53	1965-1969	L. Johnson
39. Agnew, Spiro T. (d)	Towson, MD	Lawyer	Republican	50	1969-1973	Nixon
40. Ford, Gerald R. (f) (g)	Omaha, NE	Lawyer	Republican	60	1973-1974	Nixon
41. Rockefeller, Nelson A. (f)	Bar Harbor, ME	Businessman	Republican	66	1974-1977	Ford
42. Mondale, Walter F.	Ceylon, MN	Lawyer	Democratic	49	1977-1981	Carter
43. Bush, George H. W. (a)	Milton, MA	Businessman	Republican	56	1981-1989	Reagan
44. Quayle, Dan	Indianapolis	Lawyer	Republican	41	1989-1993	G. H. W. Bush
45. Gore, Al	Washington, D.C.	Journalist	Democratic	44	1993-2001	Clinton
46. Cheney, Richard B.	Lincoln, NE	Businessman	Republican	59	2001-2009	G. W. Bush
47. Biden, Joe	Scranton, PA	Lawyer	Democratic	66	2009-	Obama

(a) Elected to the presidency. (b) Succeeded to the presidency upon the death of the president. (c) Died in office. (d) Resigned. (e) The Union Party consisted of Republicans and War Democrats. Johnson was a War Democrat. (f) Became vice president by filling a vacancy. (g) Succeeded to the presidency on resignation of the president. Each vice president has a separate biography in *World Book*.

House of Representatives. In 1973, House Minority Leader Gerald R. Ford became the first vice president under the terms of the 25th Amendment. Ford succeeded Vice President Spiro T. Agnew, who resigned (see Ford, Gerald R.). Before the 25th Amendment, vacancies in the vice presidency remained unfilled until the next election.

Roles of the vice president

The vice president can be only as important as the president chooses. The vice president has almost no political power, unless the president asks for advice about party policy and political appointments. Even the vice president's role as a Cabinet member depends on the president's wishes. But with the president's support, the vice president can exert a great amount of influence. The vice president's attendance at conferences between the president and congressional leaders strengthens the vice president's power with the legislative branch. If the president gives the vice president diplomatic missions, the vice president can help shape U.S. foreign policy.

A typical day for the vice president might begin with a breakfast conference called by the president. A legislative meeting might follow. The two officials confer with their party's congressional leaders about legislation being debated by the Senate and the House of Representatives. The vice president may then work at an office in the White House, the Executive Office Building, or the Senate wing of the Capitol. The vice president reads and answers mail and sees callers who have appointments. Tourists or unexpected visitors on emergency matters also may arrive. If the Senate is meeting that day, the vice president enters about noon to preside at the opening of the session. The vice president may remain at the session, depending on the nature of the day's business and the vice president's own schedule. If the vice president leaves, the president *pro tempore* or another senator takes over.

The vice president spends many evenings away from home. The vice president must make various kinds of public appearances, many of which require speeches. The vice president may go to the airport to greet dignitaries from other nations. Ceremonial duties may require the vice president to dedicate a public-works project, open an athletic tournament, or present an award to the winner of a contest.

President of the Senate. When presiding over the Senate, the vice president performs the duties of chairperson and cannot take part in any Senate debates. Nor can the vice president vote, except in the rare case of a tie. John Adams cast a deciding vote 29 times, more than did any other vice president.

The vice president enforces the rules established by the Senate for its own guidance. Senators can speak only after being recognized by the vice president or the president *pro tempore.* By using this power of recognition, the vice president can either aid or hold back legislation by permitting only certain senators to speak. The vice president also has the power to make rulings in disputes over procedure by interpreting the rules of the Senate. But the Senate can reject such rulings by a majority vote. In 1919, Vice President Thomas R. Marshall ruled three times in one day on a certain point. He was fighting to save the controversial Versailles Treaty and

U.S. membership in the League of Nations. The Senate overruled Marshall three times and defeated the treaty.

The president of the Senate also directs the counting of electoral votes for president and vice president. Early vice presidents could decide whether to count or disallow disputed votes. Congress has since assumed this power, leaving the vice president only formally in charge of counting electoral votes.

Administration and policymaking. The vice president attends meetings of the president's Cabinet and is a member of the National Security Council (NSC). The NSC is the highest advisory body to the president on matters of foreign and defense policies. The vice president also is a member of the Board of Regents of the Smithsonian Institution.

The president may assign the vice president general counseling and liaison activities. Such duties may involve trips abroad to spread good will, exchange information, and learn about the attitudes of various nations toward the United States. The vice president may also act as an intermediary between the president and their political party. The vice president attempts to build party support for the president's program.

Social duties. One of the oldest functions of the vice president is to serve as ceremonial assistant to the president. For example, the vice president attends many receptions and other social events at which the president cannot be present. The vice president often plays host to dignitaries from other countries.

Some vice presidents have enjoyed their ceremonial and social duties, but others have not. Calvin Coolidge took a characteristically philosophic approach. When his hostess at a dinner once remarked to him how annoying it must be to have to dine out so often, Coolidge replied: "Have to eat somewhere." John Nance Garner drew the line on social life. He went to bed early and refused to receive calls from 6 p.m. to 7 a.m., saying these hours "are my own."

History of the vice presidency

Early days. Most historians believe that Alexander Hamilton first proposed the office of vice president. Not all the delegates to the Constitutional Convention sup-

---

Interesting facts about the vice presidents

Who was the youngest vice president to be inaugurated? Breckinridge, 36. **The oldest?** Barkley, 71.
Which vice presidents were chosen under provisions of the 25th Amendment? Ford, Rockefeller.
Who was the first vice president to attend meetings of the Cabinet regularly? Coolidge.
Who was the first vice president to become a regular member of the National Security Council? Barkley.
Who was the first vice president to officially serve as acting president? G. H. W. Bush, for about eight hours during President Ronald Reagan's cancer surgery in 1985.
What vice president-elect died without ever performing the duties of office? King.
Who was the first vice president to succeed to the presidency, then win the office by election? T. Roosevelt.
Who was the first vice president to be assigned administrative duties by the president? Wallace.
Who was the only vice president to succeed to the presidency upon the resignation of the president? Ford.
Which vice presidents resigned? Calhoun, Agnew.

What vice president was selected by the Senate because the Electoral College failed to agree? R. Johnson.
Who was the first vice president nominated at a national political convention? Van Buren.
What state has produced the most vice presidents? New York.
What vice presidents died while in office? G. Clinton, Gerry, King, H. Wilson, Hendricks, Hobart, Sherman.
Who was the youngest vice president to succeed to the presidency upon the death of the president? T. Roosevelt, 42. **The oldest?** Truman, 60.
What teams of president and vice president were reelected to a second term? Washington and J. Adams, Monroe and Tompkins, W. Wilson and Marshall, F. Roosevelt and Garner, Eisenhower and Nixon, Nixon and Agnew, Reagan and G. H. W. Bush, Bill Clinton and Gore, G. W. Bush and Cheney.
What vice presidents served under two different presidents? G. Clinton, Calhoun.
What vice president took the oath of office in another country? King, in Havana, Cuba.

ported the idea. However, on Sept. 6, 1787, the convention approved Hamilton's proposal. The Founding Fathers originally provided that the person who received the second highest electoral vote for president should become vice president. Electors had two votes, which they cast for the two people they considered best qualified for the presidency. Under this system, John Adams became the first vice president and Thomas Jefferson the second.

Adams and Jefferson developed different views of the vice presidency. Adams wrote his wife: "My country has in its wisdom contrived for me the most insignificant office that ever the invention of man contrived or his imagination conceived." Jefferson declared that "the second office in the government is honorable and easy; the first is but a splendid misery."

The rise of political parties caused the breakdown of this election system. In 1796, the Electoral College gave the greatest number of votes to Adams, a Federalist. Jefferson, a Democratic-Republican, received the next largest number of votes, and became vice president. The conflicting party loyalties of the two men created discord in the administration.

In 1800, Jefferson and Aaron Burr both ran as Democratic-Republicans. They tied with 73 electoral votes each, and the election was given to the House of Representatives, where each state has one vote in a presidential election. Burr hoped for Federalist support, and tried to be elected president instead of vice president. But he failed. After 36 ballots, Jefferson won a majority of the votes, and Burr became vice president. The system's weakness became apparent during this election. In 1804, Congress adopted Amendment 12 to the Constitution, which provided for separate ballots for president and vice president. This solved the immediate problem, but it also lessened the prestige of the vice presidency. The vice president was no longer elected as the second choice for the presidency.

In 1832, John C. Calhoun became the first vice president to resign. He resigned after being elected to fill a U.S. Senate seat from South Carolina.

Tyler takes over. The Constitution provides that in case of the death or disability of the president, "the powers and duties" of the office shall transfer to the vice president. How this would work remained uncertain until 1841, when William Henry Harrison died in office, the first president to do so. His vice president was John Tyler. Former President John Quincy Adams and other leaders believed Tyler should be called *acting president,* not president. They opposed Tyler's receiving the full presidential salary and even his occupying the White House. Tyler ignored them. He took the oath and title of *president,* occupied the White House, and asserted full presidential powers. His action was not challenged legally, and he thereby established the right of the vice president to full succession.

Vice presidents have responded in many ways when a president has become disabled. Vice President Chester A. Arthur did not see James A. Garfield from the day Garfield was shot until he died 80 days later. Arthur got reports of Garfield's condition from Secretary of State James G. Blaine. He refused to assume Garfield's duties for fear he would be doing wrong. Vice President Thomas R. Marshall also declined to take up the presi-

dent's duties during Woodrow Wilson's six-month illness. During Dwight D. Eisenhower's illnesses in 1955 and 1956, Vice President Richard M. Nixon presided at Cabinet and National Security Council meetings. He kept in close touch with the president. These experiences, and the 1963 assassination of President John F. Kennedy, led to the 25th Amendment to the Constitution. This amendment, ratified in 1967, sets procedures for presidential and vice presidential succession.

Growth of the vice presidency. In 1791, Vice President John Adams attended a Cabinet meeting. No other vice president did so until 1918. That year, President Wilson asked Vice President Marshall to preside over the Cabinet while Wilson attended the Paris Peace Conference that followed World War I. After Wilson returned home, Marshall was again excluded.

President Warren G. Harding invited Vice President Calvin Coolidge to attend all Cabinet meetings. Coolidge did so until he became president after Harding's death. Vice President Charles G. Dawes declared that he would not attend Cabinet sessions, because if he did so "the precedent might prove injurious to the country." Therefore, Coolidge did not ask him to participate. Nor did President Herbert Hoover invite Vice President Charles Curtis to take part in Cabinet meetings.

Since the first term of President Franklin D. Roosevelt, all vice presidents have regularly attended Cabinet meetings. President Eisenhower strengthened the vice presidency further by directing that Vice President Nixon should preside at Cabinet meetings in the president's absence. Previously, the secretary of state had presided at such times. Congress made the vice president a member of the National Security Council in 1949. Eisenhower directed in 1954 that the vice president should preside over council meetings when the president was absent.

President John F. Kennedy further extended the duties of his vice president, Lyndon B. Johnson. Johnson was chairman of the National Aeronautics and Space Council and headed the President's Committee on Equal Employment Opportunity. After he became president, Johnson continued to upgrade the vice presidency. Vice President Hubert H. Humphrey helped unify the Johnson administration's antipoverty and civil rights programs.

President Richard M. Nixon also gave important duties to his vice president, Spiro T. Agnew. Agnew promoted the administration's domestic programs among state and local officials. His outspoken defense of Nixon's policies against criticism by liberals and the news media made Agnew a controversial figure.

In 1973, Agnew became the second vice president to resign. He left office when a federal grand jury began to investigate charges that he had participated in widespread graft as an officeholder in Maryland. Nixon nominated House Minority Leader Gerald R. Ford to succeed Agnew. Ford became the first vice president chosen under terms of the 25th Amendment. In 1974, Nixon resigned. Ford then became the first vice president to succeed to the presidency because of a president's resignation. Former New York Governor Nelson A. Rockefeller became vice president. For the first time, three vice presidents and two presidents had held office during one four-year term. Also for the first time, neither the president nor the vice president had been elected.

President Jimmy Carter continued the trend of giving

The White House

The vice president's official residence is a 33-room mansion on the grounds of the United States Naval Observatory in Washington, D.C. Congress established this mansion as the official residence in 1974.

Outline

I. Choosing a vice president
  A. Nomination   D. Inauguration
  B. The campaign   E. The 25th Amendment
  C. Election
II. Roles of the vice president
  A. A typical day
  B. President of the Senate
  C. Administration and policymaking
  D. Social duties
III. History of the vice presidency

Questions

What is meant by "balancing a ticket"?
What are the legal qualifications for a vice presidential candidate?
What are the official duties of the vice president?
In what various ways have vice presidents responded when a president has become disabled?
What happened in 1800 to bring about a change in the method of electing the vice president?
How did the vice presidency change after 1804?
How has the vice presidency grown in importance since World War I?
How can a vice president be removed from office?
How is the vice president elected if the Electoral College fails to select one by majority vote?

Additional resources

Level I
Anderson, Marilyn D. *The Vice Presidency.* Chelsea Hse., 2001.
Ingram, Scott. *The Vice President of the United States.* Blackbirch Pr., 2002.

Level II
Purcell, L. Edward, ed. *The Vice Presidents.* 2nd ed. Facts on File, 2001.
Walch, Timothy, ed. *At the President's Side: The Vice Presidency in the Twentieth Century.* Univ. of Mo. Pr., 1997.

the vice president important assignments. His vice president, Walter F. Mondale, helped develop U.S. policy on southern Africa and helped draft a plan to reorganize U.S. intelligence agencies.

Vice President George H. W. Bush headed a group of advisers that provided President Ronald Reagan with proposals on how to respond to foreign crises. Bush became the first vice president to serve as acting president. He held the position for only about eight hours on July 13, 1985, when Reagan had cancer surgery.

During Bush's term as president, Vice President Dan Quayle traveled throughout the United States and to other countries to promote the administration's policies. Quayle also headed the National Space Council and a council to evaluate the effect of government regulations on the economic competitiveness of the United States.

Vice President Al Gore exercised considerable influence in the administration of President Bill Clinton. Gore played a leading role in foreign affairs, environmental protection, and efforts to improve U.S. communications technology. In 1993, he headed a federal panel called the National Performance Review, which recommended ways to increase the federal government's efficiency and reduce its costs.

During the presidency of George W. Bush, Vice President Richard B. Cheney had a substantial influence on many of the administration's major policy decisions. He served as a chief adviser to the president and was actively involved in decisions relating to national security, energy policy, and foreign affairs.   *Marie D. Natoli*

Related articles in *World Book.* See the biography of each vice president listed in the *table* in this article. See also:

Address, Forms of
Cabinet
Constitution of the U.S. (Amendment 12; Amendment 20; Amendment 25)
Electoral College
Flag (picture: Flags of the U.S. government)

Franking and penalty privileges
National Security Council
Political convention
President of the United States
Presidential succession
Senate

Viceroy is an official who rules a province or colony in the name of a king. The British governor general of India was a viceroy. After World War II ended in 1945, opposition to colonialism grew worldwide. As a result, the term viceroy fell in general disfavor and is seldom used today.   *Anthony D'Amato*

Vichy, *VIHSH ee* or *vee SHEE* (pop. 26,915), is a resort town on the Allier River in central France (see **France** [political map]). People have bathed in the town's hot mineral springs since Roman times. Vichy became a famous *spa* (health resort) in the 1800's. The sparkling water from local springs, known as Vichy water, is sold throughout the world.

During World War II, Vichy served as the capital of unoccupied France from July 1940 until November 1942. Marshal Henri Philippe Pétain headed the Vichy government. In November 1942, German troops occupied all of France, and Vichy became the seat of the German-controlled French government. French officials in Vichy cooperated with the Germans, and the name *Vichy* came to represent collaboration with Germany. In 1944, Allied troops freed the city.   *William M. Reddy*

Vicksburg, Mississippi (pop. 26,407), is a Mississippi River port on the west border of the state (see **Mississippi** [political map]). Its products include chemicals, fabricated metals, and wood products. The French and then the Spaniards founded outposts in the area in the 1700's. In 1825, the town was incorporated. During the American Civil War (1861-1865), Vicksburg fell to the Union Army after a 47-day siege (see **Civil War, American**

[The Vicksburg campaign]). Vicksburg National Military Park is in the city. Vicksburg is the seat of Warren County and has a mayor-council form of government. See also **Mississippi** (pictures). Charlie Mitchell

Victor Emmanuel II (1820-1878) was king of the Kingdom of Sardinia from 1849 to 1861 and the first king of Italy from 1861 to 1878. He helped lead the effort to unite Italy into one country.

Victor Emmanuel was born in Turin, Italy, on March 14, 1820. He became king of Sardinia after his father, King Charles Albert, gave up the throne. In his efforts to unite Italy, Victor Emmanuel drew his main support from Piedmont, a region at the base of the Alps that was part of the Kingdom of Sardinia. His first step was to expel the Austrians from Italy. His prime minister, Count di Cavour, made an alliance with France, and in 1859 the two countries defeated Austria. As a result, Victor Emmanuel gained the region of Lombardy. In 1861, central Italy (except for Rome) and the Kingdom of the Two Sicilies in southern Italy joined the Kingdom of Sardinia to form a united kingdom of Italy. Victor Emmanuel became king. The region of Venetia was added in 1866 and Rome in 1870. Victor Emmanuel died in Rome on Jan. 9, 1878. Philip V. Cannistraro

See also **Cavour, Count di; Garibaldi, Giuseppe; Italy** (History); **Papal States; Sardinia, Kingdom of.**

Victor Emmanuel III (1869-1947) was king of Italy from 1900 to 1946. He became unpopular because of his cooperation with the fascist dictator Benito Mussolini.

Victor Emmanuel III was born in Naples, Italy, on Nov. 11, 1869. He became king after the assassination of his father, King Humbert I. In 1922, Victor Emmanuel refused to proclaim martial law to stop Mussolini's march on Rome. Under pressure from Mussolini's supporters, the king made Mussolini prime minister and in 1925 allowed Italy to become a dictatorship. He approved all of Mussolini's laws, including those that discriminated against Jews.

Italy entered World War II in 1940 on the side of Nazi Germany. In 1943, members of the Italian government overthrew Mussolini and restored Victor Emmanuel's authority. In 1946, Victor Emmanuel abdicated in favor of his son, Prince Humbert. But later that year, the Italian people voted to abolish the monarchy. The former king died on Dec. 28, 1947. Philip V. Cannistraro

See also **Fascism; Italy** (History); **Mussolini, Benito.**

Victoria (1819-1901) was queen of the United Kingdom of Great Britain and Ireland from 1837 to 1901. Her 63-year reign was the longest in British history. The United Kingdom reached the height of its power during this period. It built a colonial empire that stretched around the world and achieved tremendous industrial expansion at home. The time of Victoria's reign is often called the Victorian Age.

Early years. Victoria was born at Kensington Palace in London on May 24, 1819. She was the only child of Edward, Duke of Kent, fourth son of George III, and of Victoria Maria Louisa, daughter of Francis, Duke of Saxe-Coburg and Saalfeld. Victoria's father died before she was a year old, and she was reared by her mother.

Victoria's uncle King William IV died on June 20, 1837. He had no heirs, and so she succeeded to the throne. Victoria was crowned queen at Westminster Abbey on June 28, 1838. Lord Melbourne served as her first prime

WALERY PHOTOGRAPHER TO THE QUEEN   COPYRIGHT   V R   164 REGENT STREET, LONDON

Bridgeman/Art Resource

Victoria was queen of the United Kingdom for 63 years. During her reign, often called the Victorian Age, the United Kingdom built a huge empire and became the world's richest country.

minister and educated her in politics and government.

Events of her reign. Many important events took place during Victoria's reign. The United Kingdom acquired the island of Hong Kong after fighting China in the First Anglo-Chinese War (1839-1842), also known as the First Opium War. The country also fought in the Crimean War (1853-1856) against Russia, and in the Anglo-Boer War of 1899-1902 to protect its interests in southern Africa.

In 1858, control of India was transferred from the British East India Company, a trading firm, to the British government. Victoria was proclaimed empress of India in 1876. The United Kingdom seized control of Egypt and many other areas. British colonies united in Australia and Canada, and these countries became important members of the growing British Empire.

British industries benefited from the expanding empire and made the United Kingdom the richest country in the world. The United Kingdom ended restrictions on foreign trade, and its colonies became both sources of raw materials and markets for its manufactured goods. The United Kingdom was called the *workshop of the world*. The British Empire included a fourth of the world's land and a fourth of its people.

The population of the United Kingdom itself increased 50 percent during Victoria's reign, and the United Kingdom changed from mainly an agricultural to mainly an industrial nation. More people won the right to vote, and local government became increasingly democratic. The British Parliament passed acts that improved labor

Growth of the British Empire under Queen Victoria

During Victoria's reign (1837-1901), the British Empire grew enormously. Additions included major territories in Africa and southern Asia and smaller territories in the Pacific and Indian oceans.

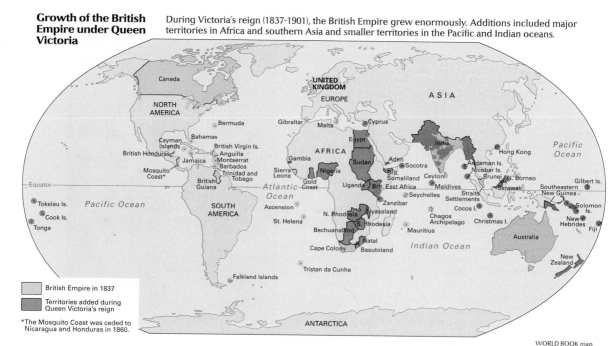

British Empire in 1837

Territories added during Queen Victoria's reign

*The Mosquito Coast was ceded to Nicaragua and Honduras in 1860.

WORLD BOOK map

conditions, required all children to attend school, and reformed the civil service. In Ireland, the Protestant Church of Ireland was separated from the government, and the land system was reformed.

Achievements. The British people had lost respect for the throne when Victoria became queen. But she gained their affection and admiration as a hard-working monarch concerned with the welfare of her people.

Victoria was a wise and capable monarch. But the success of the United Kingdom was due chiefly to her able prime ministers, including Lord Melbourne, Sir Robert Peel, Viscount Palmerston, Benjamin Disraeli, William Gladstone, and the Marquess of Salisbury. Gradually the queen had to accept that the monarchy would not survive unless its powers were reduced and her ministers in Parliament were allowed to rule the nation. Victoria accepted the switch from political to symbolic ruler.

Personal life. In February 1840, Queen Victoria married a cousin, Prince Albert of Saxe-Coburg and Gotha. They had four sons and five daughters. The prince was a scholar, philanthropist, and businessman. He actively assisted his wife in her royal duties. Albert died in 1861, and Victoria never recovered from her grief at his loss. She withdrew from social activities and dressed in black for many years. Victoria died on Jan. 22, 1901, and her eldest son became King Edward VII.   James J. Sack

Related articles in *World Book* include:

Albert, Prince
Connaught and Strathearn,
 Duke of
Edward VII

English literature (Victorian literature)
United Kingdom (History)
Windsor

Additional resources

Arnstein, Walter L. *Queen Victoria.* 2003. Reprint. Palgrave, 2005.
De-la-Noy, Michael. *Queen Victoria at Home.* Carroll & Graf, 2003.
Rappaport, Helen. *Queen Victoria: A Biographical Companion.* ABC-CLIO, 2003.

Victoria is the smallest state on the Australian mainland. Among the Australian states, only the island of Tasmania covers a smaller area. People of British descent make up the largest ethnic group. Many immigrants from other European countries settled in Victoria after World War II ended in 1945. During the 1980's, numerous immigrants came from Southeast Asia, particularly Vietnam.

Victoria is one of Australia's chief farming regions. The state also has important manufacturing industries. Melbourne, on Port Phillip Bay, is Victoria's capital and largest city (see **Melbourne**).

Land and climate. Victoria lies at the southeastern tip of Australia. For detailed maps, see **Australia.** Mountains cover much of the eastern and central parts of the state. Extensive areas of plains are in the north. In the south, plains lie between hilly areas along the coast and the highlands farther to the north. The Murray River, Australia's longest permanently flowing river, rises in the mountains in the east and flows northwestward to form much of the boundary between Victoria and New South Wales. Port Phillip Bay is Victoria's largest natural harbor. It opens into Bass Strait.

Victoria's hottest month is January, with an average maximum temperature in Melbourne of 79 °F (26 °C) and a minimum of 56 °F (13 °C). In July, the Melbourne average maximum temperature falls to 56 °F (13 °C) and the minimum to 41 °F (5 °C). The northwest part of the state has hotter, drier weather

WORLD BOOK map

Location of Victoria

© iofoto/Shutterstock

The Twelve Apostles are one of the most popular attractions in the Australian state of Victoria. These rock formations stand along Victoria's southern coast, in Port Campbell National Park.

than the coastal southeast, with maximum temperatures over 90 °F (32 °C) in January. Rainfall in Victoria ranges from an annual average of 12 inches (31 centimeters) in the northwest to 35 inches (89 centimeters) in the southeast. Annual rainfalls of more than 70 inches (178 centimeters) have been recorded in northeastern Victoria. In winter and spring, snow falls on the mountains in the middle of the state.

People. The 2006 Australian census reported that Victoria had 4,932,422 people. Education for children ages 6 to 15 is compulsory. About two-thirds of the students attend state schools, and one-third attend private schools. Victoria has nine universities. The oldest is the University of Melbourne, opened in 1855.

Economy. Victoria's chief crops include wheat, oats, barley, potatoes, and many kinds of fruit. Dairy farming and the raising of sheep and beef cattle are widespread. Manufactured products include agricultural machinery, automobiles, chemicals, dyes, leather products, metal products, paints, paper, plastics, rubber products, tex-

tiles and clothing, tobacco, and wines. *Lignite* (brown coal), petroleum, and natural gas are the state's chief mineral products. Petroleum and natural gas come from offshore wells in the Bass Strait.

Victoria is connected by highway and railroad to the neighboring states of New South Wales and South Australia. Melbourne Airport handles almost all of the state's interstate commercial traffic and all of the state's international flights. The Port of Melbourne is a major handler of import and export container freight for national and international trade.

Government. The British Crown appoints a governor for Victoria, on the advice of the Victorian government. However, the governor's post is largely ceremonial. A premier actually heads the government. The premier is assisted by a Cabinet of ministers. Victoria's legislature is made up of a 40-member upper house and an 88-member lower house.

History. George Bass, a British naval surgeon and navigator, explored the eastern coast of Victoria in 1797. However, colonists did not settle permanently until 1834. The territory formed part of New South Wales until 1851, when it became a separate colony. The colony was named for Queen Victoria.

Gold was discovered in Victoria in 1851. A series of gold rushes attracted thousands of settlers. Many miners later became farmers. The settlers won self-government in 1855. Victoria joined the Commonwealth of Australia in 1901.   Murray Mottram

Victoria (pop. 78,057; met. area pop. 330,088) is the capital of British Columbia. Victoria lies along a picturesque harbor at the southeastern tip of Vancouver Island. See **British Columbia** (political map).

Victoria's attractions include its scenic surroundings and pleasant climate. Its narrow streets and neat gardens resemble those of England. Victoria has a milder climate than any other Canadian city. Its temperatures average 40 °F (4 °C) in January and 60 °F (16 °C) in July.

The buildings of the British Columbia Legislature overlook Victoria Harbour. The nearby Empress Hotel is famous for its elegance. An outstanding collection of totem poles can be seen in the Royal British Columbia Museum and adjoining Thunderbird Park. Victoria's City Hall borders Centennial Square downtown. Butchart Gardens, which has beautiful flowers, lawns, ponds,

© Eric Neurath, Stock, Boston

Victoria is the capital of British Columbia. The city lies along a picturesque harbor at the southeastern tip of Vancouver Island. The green-domed buildings shown house the British Columbia Legislature.

shrubs, and trees, lies north of Victoria at Brentwood Bay. The University of Victoria lies just outside the city.

About a third of the workers of the Victoria metropolitan area have jobs related to the tourist industry. About a fifth are employed by the federal, provincial, or local government. Canada's chief naval base on the west coast is at nearby Esquimalt Harbour. Boatbuilding, fishing, forestry, and research and technology are important industries in the Victoria area. Retired people make up nearly a fourth of Victoria's population.

Coast Salish Indians lived in what is now the Victoria area before white settlers arrived there. The Hudson's Bay Company of London, a fur-trading organization, founded Victoria in 1843. The settlement was named for Queen Victoria of the United Kingdom. It was the capital of the crown colony of Vancouver Island from 1849 to 1866, when the island became part of the colony of British Columbia. Victoria became the capital of colonial British Columbia in 1868. It has been the capital of the province since British Columbia joined Canada in 1871.

The British Royal Navy established the naval base at nearby Esquimalt Harbour in 1865. Tourism became important to the city after the Canadian Pacific Railway opened the Empress Hotel in 1908. Ferry lines linked the city with railroad terminals on the mainland. Victoria Harbour and Esquimalt Harbour were key Canadian shipbuilding centers during World War I (1914-1918) and World War II (1939-1945).

During the 1960's and 1970's, Victoria completed several projects that beautified the city and preserved its older areas. These projects included renewal of a historic downtown residential district and construction of new docks and walkways for the harbor. Today, the city has a growing industry in research and technology. It has a council-manager government.   Lon Wood

See also **British Columbia** (pictures); **Christmas** (picture: Outdoor decorations).

Victoria, Guadalupe, GWAHD uhl OOP or GWAHD hah LOO pay (1789?-1843), was the first president of Mexico. He held office from 1824 to 1829. Before he became president, Victoria had been a military leader in Mexico's struggle for independence from Spain.

Victoria was born Miguel Fernández y Félix in Tamazula, Durango. He studied law in Mexico City. He joined the struggle for independence in 1812. During the war, he changed his name to Guadalupe Victoria. He took the name *Guadalupe* to honor Mexico's patron saint, Our Lady of Guadalupe (often called the Virgin of Guadalupe). He chose *Victoria* to demonstrate his belief in Mexico's eventual victory in the war.

Victoria later led rebel forces in the state of Veracruz but was defeated by the Spaniards in 1818. He then hid in the mountains of Veracruz for 30 months and became a legendary hero to many Mexicans. In 1821, Victoria rejoined the rebels, who won independence later that year. In 1823, he helped overthrow Agustín de Iturbide, the emperor of Mexico. Victoria was elected president in 1824. He died on March 21, 1843.   Ward S. Albro

Victoria, Lake. See Lake Victoria.

Victoria and Albert Museum, in London, houses one of the world's most important collections of decorative art and fine art. The museum is named for Queen Victoria, queen of Great Britain and Ireland from 1837 to 1901, and her husband, Prince Albert.

The huge museum has more than 150 galleries. Some are organized to give an overview of a particular civilization or historical period, such as the Tudor era in England. Other galleries are devoted to a single material, such as glass, silver, or textiles. Many galleries display British decorative arts, including ceramics, embroidery, and furniture. Others specialize in the art of other European countries as well as China, Japan, Korea, and the Middle East. The museum also has a major collection of European fashionable clothing from 1600 to today.

The Victoria and Albert Museum displays many masterpieces of fine art, including an important collection of the works of the English painter John Constable. The museum is also the home of the National Art Library.

The museum's collections originated from works purchased during the Great Exhibition of 1851, a world's fair held in London. The permanent museum building was completed in 1909. The principal museum designer was the English architect Sir Aston Webb.

Critically reviewed by the Victoria and Albert Museum

Victoria Day commemorates the birthday of Queen Victoria on May 24, 1819. The people of the Commonwealth of Nations have always celebrated the birthday of the ruling British monarch as a patriotic holiday. During the long lifetime of Queen Victoria, her birthday came to have a special meaning. After Victoria's death, people continued to celebrate her birthday to express their loyalty to the British Empire. In the early 1900's, the people of Canada celebrated Victoria's birthday as Empire Day. The name became Commonwealth Day in 1947. Canadians now celebrate Victoria Day and the official birthday of the reigning monarch as a legal holiday on the Monday before May 25.   Richard W. Davis

Victoria Desert. See Great Victoria Desert.

Victoria Falls is a spectacular waterfall in southern Africa. It lies between Zambia and Zimbabwe, about halfway between the mouth and the source of the Zambezi River. The British explorer David Livingstone sighted Victoria Falls in 1855. He named it in honor of Queen Victoria of the United Kingdom.

The Zambezi River is about 1 mile (1.6 kilometers) wide at the falls and drops suddenly into a deep, narrow chasm. A canyon about 40 miles (64 kilometers) long permits the water to flow out. The height of the falls varies from 256 feet (78 meters) at the right bank to 355 feet (108 meters) in the center.

The mist and spray created by the falls can be seen for a great distance. This cloud and the constant roar caused the people of the area to name the falls *Mosi oa Tunya* (smoke that thunders). A hydroelectric plant produces a small amount of power at the falls. A railway bridge crosses the river just below the point where the waters rush out of the chasm.   Hartmut S. Walter

See also **Seven Natural Wonders of the World; Waterfall** (table; picture).

Victorian Age. See English literature (Victorian literature); United Kingdom (History); Victoria (queen).

Vicuña, *vih KOON yuh,* is the smallest member of the camel family. It lives in the Andes Mountains of Bolivia, Chile, and Peru, in areas from 12,000 to 18,000 feet (3,660 to 5,490 meters) above sea level. Its home is generally near the snowline. The vicuña and guanaco are the wild members of the camel family in South America. The alpaca and llama are domesticated. None has a hump.

© Sullivan & Rogers from Bruce Coleman Inc.

The vicuña lives in the Andes Mountains of South America. The fleece of the vicuña is used in making fine woolen fabrics.

The vicuña measures 2 ¼ to 3 feet (70 to 90 centimeters) high at the shoulder and weighs from 75 to 140 pounds (35 to 65 kilograms). It has a reddish-yellow to deep tan or reddish-brown upper body. Its belly and lower legs are white. Vicuñas eat grass and other vegetation. They usually live in herds that have one male and several females. The male defends a *territory* (area of ground) from other males.

Vicuñas have an extremely fine fleece used to make high-grade cloth. A vicuña produces about 4 ounces (113 grams) of fleece a year. The fleece grows until it hangs below the flanks and knees. Only the inner fleece is used to make cloth.

The ancient Inca protected vicuñas and hunted them only once in four years. Only royalty could use the fleece. In the early 1900's, so many vicuñas were killed for their wool that the animal became endangered by the 1960's. Since then, conservation efforts have increased vicuña populations. Kenneth J. Raedeke

Scientific classification. The vicuña is in the camel family, Camelidae. It is *Vicugna vicugna.*

See also **Alpaca; Animal** (picture: Animals of the mountains); **Guanaco; Llama.**

Vidal, vee DAHL, **Gore,** gawr (1925-   ), is an American author best known for his novels. Some have historical themes, and others satirize American society. Vidal has also written essays, short stories, and plays.

Many of Vidal's novels feature historical figures. *Julian* (1964) portrays the Roman emperor of the A.D. 300's who fought against Christianity. *Creation* (1981) is set in the

400's B.C. Its characters include the Chinese philosopher Confucius and Persian rulers Darius I and Xerxes I. *The Smithsonian Institution* (1998) is a historical fantasy set in Washington, D.C., in 1939. Vidal wrote a series of novels dealing with American history. They are, in the order of the periods they describe, *Burr* (1973), *Lincoln* (1984), *1876* (1976), *Empire* (1987), *Hollywood* (1990), *Washington, D.C.* (1967), and *The Golden Age* (2000). He satirized modern life in *Myra Breckenridge* (1968) and its sequel, *Myron* (1974). He satirized feminism in *Kalki* (1978).

Vidal's short stories were collected in *A Thirsty Evil* (1956) and *Head of a Sad Angel* (1990). Some of his essays were published in *United States: Essays 1952-1992* (1993) and *Perpetual War for Perpetual Peace* (2002). During the 1950's, Vidal wrote three detective novels under the name Edgar Box. His best-known play, *The Best Man* (1960), deals with a presidential convention. He also wrote two memoirs, *Palimpsest* (1995) and *Point to Point Navigation* (2006). More essays appeared in *The Last Empire: Essays 1992-2000* (2001). Vidal was born on Oct. 3, 1925, in West Point, New York.   Barbara M. Perkins

Video. See Television; Videotape recorder.

Video art uses video technology to create visual art through one or more television monitors. Video art is named for videotape, which video artists used to record images from the 1960's through the 1980's. Today, video artists often work with DVD's or other technology.

Video art may tell a running story or consist of still images. Much video art combines images with sound, such as music, spoken dialogue, or narration. A work of video art may last a few seconds or many hours and be repeated without interruption. The subject matter is almost limitless, including familiar objects, a performance by one or more actors, or animation. The work may be abstract or realistic.

Some video art uses elements of popular culture, such as advertisements or familiar TV shows. Many video artists use the form to make political or satirical statements. A live camera can be focused on the viewers, incorporating the public into the artwork.

Video artists may exhibit their work on a single monitor or as "installations" of massed monitors. The artist might group several monitors into free-standing shapes, arrange them against a wall, or scatter them. Each monitor might show a different image or set of images. An installation can re-create a specific environment, such as a supermarket, with several monitors showing different views around the environment. The spectator may view the monitors in a sequence or at random, depending on the effect the artist seeks.

Video art can be combined with other art forms. For example, video cameras and monitors can be included in or with a sculpture to create a multimedia work. Video art may also be incorporated into a live stage performance, such as dance or a play.

Video art emerged during the 1960's and 1970's with the advancement of video technology. The first widely known video artist was Nam June Paik, a composer, sculptor, and performance artist. He was born in what is now South Korea and settled in New York City in 1964. Paik began his career in video art in 1965, using a portable video recorder and magnets to distort TV images.

Rebecca Jeffrey Easby

Video camera. See Camcorder.

Video game. See Electronic game.

Videocassette recorder. See Videotape recorder.

Videophone is a telephonelike device or combination of devices that sends and receives both images and sound. Videophone systems enable users to see each other while talking. To participate fully, each person in a videophone conversation must have a videophone.

Videophones have at least four parts. They are: (1) a camera to capture images or video, (2) a screen to display images or video, (3) a microphone to capture sound, and (4) a speaker to re-create sound.

A videophone user sits or stands in front of the screen. The camera records the user's image, much as a video camera would. The microphone picks up the user's speech. The videophone converts the sound and image into a continuously varying *analog* signal or, more commonly, a *digital* (numeric) code. The signal or code is then sent to the receiving videophone, which converts it back into sound and image.

Early videophones had a camera, screen, microphone, and speaker built into a single specialized device. These expensive videophones connected to one another through telephone lines. Later videophones connected through radio waves and satellite transmission. Today, computers with cameras and camera-equipped cell phones serve many of the same functions as more traditional videophones. These modern videophones connect to one another through cellular phone networks or the Internet.

People have envisioned videophones since the early 1900's. The American Telephone and Telegraph Company (AT&T) displayed a videophone at the New York World's Fair in 1964 and introduced Picturephone, a videophone service in public phone booths. None of the early videophone systems achieved widespread use, in part because they were too expensive. Also, many people do not want to be concerned about their appearance when talking on the telephone.   Paul Levinson

Videotape recorder is a device that records visual images and sound on magnetic tape. Videotape recorders, also known as VTR's or simply *video recorders,* also play back the recorded *video* (picture) and *audio* (sound) information on television sets.

Videotape recorders were first used by the television broadcasting industry during the 1950's. Since then, they have become essential equipment to record and replay commercials, regular TV series, and many other telecasts. VTR's allow programmers to plan and organize TV schedules. They also enable broadcasters to show reruns of programs and to replay commercials. Most television newscasts feature reports recorded on tape.

Videotape has a number of advantages over motion-picture photographic film. For example, videotape can be played back immediately after being recorded on, but film must be developed before it can be viewed. For this reason, camera operators who use videotape can determine right away whether a scene needs to be re-recorded. In addition, videotape can be erased and recorded over, but film cannot.

Types of videotape recorders

In addition to the professional models used by TV broadcasters, there are also several other types of VTR's. Some schools and businesses use *semiprofessional*

videotape recorders to record educational programs and employee training films. Consumers can record TV programs and play back prerecorded cassettes of movies on *home videotape recorders,* also called *videocassette recorders* (VCR's). The various types of video recorders differ in the size of the tape they use and the quality of the pictures they produce. Most types are designed to use tape cassettes.

People commonly use portable *camcorders* to make home movies. These devices combine a camera and a VTR in a single unit powered by batteries. The camera and a microphone send video and audio signals to the recorder. See **Camcorder.**

How videotape recorders work

Videotape consists of a long plastic strip coated with particles of iron oxide, a material that is readily magnetized. Videotape recorders record television signals by translating them into magnetic fields. These fields create patterns of magnetization in the coating. The process is reversed during playback, when the magnetic patterns are translated into television signals for viewing on TV sets. For information about where television signals come from and how they are made into a TV picture, see **Television** (Video entertainment systems).

Videotape recorders store visual images and sound as either (1) *analog signals* or (2) *digital signals.* In an analog recording, the magnetic patterns are *analogous* (similar) to those of the original television signals. Most home video recorders use analog signals. In a digital recording, the recorder translates the television signals into a numerical code. Digital recording produces better picture and sound quality than analog recording does. Many professional videotape recorders and many camcorders use digital technology.

Most home recorders can record at more than one speed. The fastest speed, *standard play* (SP), yields the highest quality picture and sound. The slowest speed normally available on home recorders, called *extended play* (EP) or *super long play* (SLP), produces lower quality picture and sound, but it provides three times the recording time on a tape that SP does.

The television industry uses professional videotape recorders to record and edit TV programs. This television station employee is preparing taped segments for a news broadcast.

Recording. The recorder converts the TV signal into electric current, which travels through wire coils of small electromagnets called *heads.* A head is a ring of metal that has a narrow cut called a *gap.* Opposite the gap, a coil of wire is wrapped around the ring. This coil conducts the current corresponding to the TV signal. The current produces a strong magnetic field in the ring and in the gap. When videotape passes over the gap, the field creates the patterns of magnetization. The patterns remain until they are recorded over or they are removed by an *erase head,* which demagnetizes the tape.

The patterns recorded on many types of analog videotape consist of three types of *tracks* (lines of magnetized particles): (1) video tracks, (2) audio tracks, and (3) control tracks.

Video tracks contain signals that represent visual images. The tracks are recorded *helically* (diagonally) and take up most of the tape. Video tracks are recorded by video heads mounted on a rotating metal cylinder called a *drum.* The heads *scan* (pass over) the tape at high speed while recording or playing back video signals.

Analog audio tracks contain sound signals. Control tracks contain signals that keep a tape playing back at the proper speed and the video heads aligned with the video tracks. Analog audio tracks and control tracks are recorded by separate, stationary heads. Audio tracks run along one edge of the tape, and control tracks along the other. Not all recorders use control tracks.

In professional digital videotape recorders, both the video and audio signals are recorded in helical scan tracks. In most digital recorders, both the video and audio signals can be recorded and edited separately. Digital recorders have error correction systems that ensure the playback of signals without visual or audible defects.

Playback. As tape passes over the heads during playback, the tape's magnetic patterns create a varying magnetic field in the head. When the magnetic field reaches the wire coil, it is converted into electric voltage. The varying voltage, which contains the audio and video signals, is sent to a television set, which transforms it into sounds and pictures.

History

The development of videotape recorders began during the 1940's. However, the first videotape recorder that was capable of recording a television picture of broadcasting quality on magnetic tape was not invented until 1956. This reel-to-reel machine, produced by the Ampex Corporation of California, featured four heads mounted on a rotating wheel.

In 1959, the Toshiba Corporation of Japan introduced the first single-head helical recorder. This VTR, which was smaller and less expensive than previous recorders, helped videotape recording spread outside the television industry. By the mid-1980's, two main types of home VCR systems, called Beta and VHS (Video Home System), had been developed. Today, home VCR's use VHS systems. In 1985, Sony Corporation of Japan introduced the 8 mm VCR system. This system uses 8-millimeter tapes in camcorders. In 1995, manufacturers introduced the first digital camcorder for home use. It uses 6.35-millimeter tapes called DV's or MiniDV's.

Since the late 1990's, manufacturers have introduced other recording devices to compete with VCR's. These

Analog videotape recording

Videotape recorders record video signals in *helical* (diagonal) tracks on the tape. The video heads are mounted on a rotating cylinder called a *drum.* Separate, stationary heads record control tracks and analog audio tracks.

WORLD BOOK diagram by Sarah Figlio

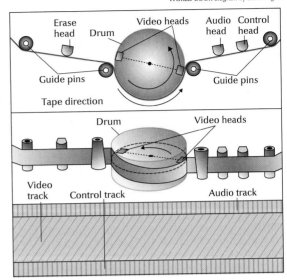

devices include *digital video recorders* (DVR's), also called *personal video recorders* (PVR's) (see **Digital video recorder**). DVR's can record and store 100 or more hours of television programs as a digital file, on a hard drive similar to that of a computer. Manufacturers have also developed systems that record programs on special DVD's, discs of the same size as compact discs, but which can hold much more information. Today, some camcorders also record on hard drives or special DVD's.   Ken C. Pohlmann

Vienna, *vee EHN uh* (pop. 1,550,123), is the capital and largest city of Austria. The city lies in northeastern Austria, on the south bank of the Danube River. For the location of Vienna, see **Austria** (political map). Vienna is Austria's leading cultural, economic, and political center. The city's name in German is *Wien.*

Vienna became the capital of the *duchy* (territory ruled by a duke) of Austria in 1150, under the Babenberg dynasty. The Habsburg (or Hapsburg) family acquired the Babenberg lands in 1278. Vienna was the base for the Habsburgs for most of the years until 1918. In the 1700's and 1800's, Vienna won fame as a center of medicine, music, and theater. The Habsburg dynasty collapsed at the end of World War I (1914-1918), and Vienna lost much of its political importance. Between 1938 and 1945, the murder of most of Vienna's Jewish population under Nazi rule devastated the city's cultural life. In 1979, Vienna became an official United Nations (UN) seat. Many UN offices are housed there. Several other international organizations also have offices in Vienna.

The city covers about 160 square miles (415 square kilometers) at the eastern end of a narrow plain between the Carpathian Mountains and the Alps. An important mountain gap through the Carpathians is just east of Vienna. The city's location at this transportation crossroads played an important role in its growth and economic development.

The old "Inner City" forms the center of Vienna. This area includes many of the city's historical buildings and landmarks, as well as its most fashionable shopping districts. The famous St. Stephen's Cathedral stands at the heart of the Inner City. Several blocks west is the Hofburg, a palace that consists of both modern buildings and medieval structures. The palace includes the royal apartments, now occupied by the president of Austria; the National Library; several museums; and the Spanish Riding School. Nearby lie two of Vienna's most beautiful parks, the Burggarten and the Volksgarten.

A band of streets called the Ringstrasse encircles the Inner City. Some of Vienna's most impressive public buildings line these streets. They include City Hall, the Museum of Art History, the Opera House, the Parliament Building, and the Stock Exchange. These buildings date from the second half of the 1800's.

The older suburban districts of the city lie outside the Ringstrasse. They became part of Vienna in the 1800's. Several important buildings are in the suburbs, including the Karlskirche (Church of St. Charles) and the Belvedere Palace. These structures rank among the finest existing examples of Baroque architecture, a highly decorative style that developed in the 1600's and 1700's.

The noted Austrian architect Johann Bernhard Fischer von Erlach designed several Viennese buildings, includ-

ing the Karlskirche and the Schönbrunn Palace. The palace stands at the city's southwestern edge. The Schönbrunn Zoo lies on the palace grounds. Built in 1752, it is the world's oldest zoo. A long park called the Prater is north of Vienna along the Danube. The Vienna Woods line the western edge of the city.

The people. Most Viennese are German-speaking Austrians. Some of Vienna's people have roots in the other European lands that the Habsburgs ruled. Viennese people wear clothing similar to that worn in the United States. People in Vienna often dress up, especially during *Fasching,* the Austrian carnival season that includes many formal dances. Some Viennese wear Austrian folk costumes on special occasions.

Viennese foods reflect the mixture of nationalities in the city. A favorite Viennese pastime is to gather at a coffee house or at a *Konditorei* (pastry shop). People also enjoy visiting the wine houses north and west of the city to drink freshly made wine, called *Heurigen.*

Most Viennese own or rent apartments in four- or five-story buildings. Some suburban families live in their own homes. The city has built apartment complexes to replace residences that were destroyed during World War II (1939-1945).

Education and cultural life. Vienna is the home of many fine institutions of higher learning. They include the Academy of Fine Arts Vienna, the University of Music and Performing Arts Vienna, the University of Vienna, and the Vienna University of Technology.

Vienna has many famous museums and art galleries, including the Albertina, the Belvedere, and the Museum of Art History. It has several libraries, including the National Library. Musical venues include the Konzerthaus, the Musikverein, the State Opera House, and the Volksoper. The Vienna Boys' Choir sings every Sunday in the Hofburgkapelle (Hofburg Chapel). Major theaters include the Burgtheater and the Theater in der Josefstadt.

Many famous artists, scholars, scientists, and writers have lived in Vienna. Such composers as Ludwig van Beethoven, Johannes Brahms, Joseph Haydn, Wolfgang Amadeus Mozart, and Franz Schubert resided there.

Economy. Vienna is Austria's chief industrial city. Its industries manufacture chemicals, clothing, leatherware, and medicine. The city is also Austria's administrative, communications, and financial center. Vienna has an excellent system of public transportation, with buses, streetcars, and a subway train system. Most people use public transportation, but automobile use has grown.

History. People have lived in what is now Vienna since prehistoric times. In 15 B.C., the Romans set up a frontier post there named Vindobona. They ruled the area until Germanic tribes took over in the late A.D. 400's. During the late 800's, the Magyars, who founded Hungary, gained control of Vienna. German forces conquered the city in the late 900's. In 1150, Vienna became the main residence for the ruling Babenberg family.

In 1273, Rudolf I of the Habsburg family became Holy Roman emperor. In 1278, he acquired the Austrian lands for the Habsburgs. Vienna prospered as the seat of the Habsburg dynasty. Armies of the Ottoman Empire besieged Vienna in 1529 and again in 1683, but they failed to capture the city. Some of the city's beautiful Baroque palaces and churches were built in the early 1700's.

French forces seized Vienna twice during the Napole-

Joachim Messerschmidt, Bruce Coleman Inc.

Vienna, the capital of Austria, is a leading cultural center of Europe. It is famous for its art galleries, churches, and theaters. The Burgtheater, *shown here,* is one of Vienna's many landmarks.

© Wenzel Fischer, FPG

The old "Inner City" of Vienna has many sidewalk cafes and beautiful buildings. People enjoy gathering at the cafes to eat and drink and to observe life around them.

onic Wars (1793-1815). The Habsburg defeat in World War I reduced Vienna to capital of the small Austrian republic. German troops occupied the city from 1938 to the end of World War II in 1945. Allied bombing badly damaged Vienna during the war. From 1945 to 1955, the city was under the joint control of the Allied powers.

Austria's postwar economic boom helped restore Vienna's prosperity. The city rebuilt most of its destroyed or damaged landmarks. In 1965, Vienna became the headquarters of the Organization of the Petroleum Exporting Countries (OPEC). Beginning in the 1970's, new hotels and an expanded subway system were built. A center for UN agencies opened in 1979.   Steven Beller

See also **Architecture** (Early modern architecture in Europe; pictures); **Austria** (pictures).

Vienna, *vee EHN uh,* **Congress of,** was a series of meetings held from late 1814 through early 1815 to settle the issues arising from almost 25 years of war between France and the rest of Europe. The congress decided how Europe would be ruled after the imminent defeat of the French emperor and military leader Napoleon I. The workable settlements made in Vienna, Austria, won credit for helping avoid any wide European conflict for 100 years afterward. See **Napoleon I.**

The chief decisions were made by representatives of the victorious Quadruple Alliance—Austria, Prussia, Russia, and the United Kingdom—and of France. The congress restored many European kings and princes forced from power by Napoleon or by forces associated with the French Revolution (1789-1799). See **French Revolution.** The restored rulers included the monarchs of Spain and of what is now southern Italy and the rulers of a number of states in Germany and northern Italy.

The congress also ratified several allied conquests. The United Kingdom retained a number of colonies it had seized during the fighting. Russia kept Finland and Bessarabia and won most of Poland. Austria and Prussia regained control of the remaining parts of Poland.

In addition, the congress attempted to limit the power of France by placing strong countries on France's bor-

ders. For example, it created the Kingdom of the Netherlands on the northeastern border of France by joining together Belgium, Holland, and Luxembourg. Prussia received German territories that bordered eastern France, and Austria gained major provinces in northern Italy.

The Congress of Vienna was bitterly criticized for many years because it ignored the strong democratic and nationalistic sentiments of many Europeans. These sentiments contributed to democratic revolutions in numerous European countries in 1830 and 1848 and to nationalistic movements in Germany and Italy. But some historians have praised the Congress of Vienna for creating a balance of power in Europe and for not treating defeated France too harshly.   Peter N. Stearns

See also **Austria** (Metternich and revolution); **Germany** (The Congress of Vienna); **International relations** (History); **Italy** (The French Revolution and Napoleon).

Vientiane, *vyehn TYAHN* (pop. 420,000), is the capital and largest city of Laos. It is also the country's chief commercial center. Vientiane lies on the Mekong River, which forms the border between Laos and Thailand (see **Laos** [map]). River, road, and air transportation link Vientiane to other parts of Laos and to neighboring countries. A bridge across the Mekong connects the city with a railroad line in Thailand.

Vientiane was the capital of the kingdom of Lan Xang from the mid-1500's until the early 1700's, when the kingdom divided into three parts. Vientiane became the capital of one of the smaller kingdoms. In 1828, Siam (now Thailand) destroyed the city and took over the kingdom. The city was later rebuilt. France took control of Laos in the late 1800's and made Vientiane the country's administrative capital. Laos became an independent nation in 1953.   Charles Keyes and Jane Keyes

See also **Laos** (History; picture: A Buddhist festival).

Viet Cong were South Vietnamese guerrillas who fought South Vietnamese and United States military forces during the Vietnam War (1957-1975). The Communist government of North Vietnam supported the Viet Cong. The guerrillas sought to overthrow South Vietnam's government and unite North and South Vietnam.

In 1957, South Vietnamese President Ngo Dinh Diem began to crack down on Communists and other political groups in his country. Diem described anyone who resisted his rule as Viet Cong, whether they were Communists or not. The term *cong* is scornful slang for *Communists.* Diem's actions increased opposition to his rule and drove many non-Communists into an alliance with the Communists.

In 1960, various anti-Diem groups formed the National Liberation Front (NLF). The NLF's military wing, called the People's Liberation Armed Forces, was labeled the Viet Cong by its opponents. With North Vietnamese backing, the Viet Cong waged a successful guerrilla war against Diem's army. The United States, which wanted to stop the spread of Communism, responded by sending thousands of troops to South Vietnam in 1965. North Vietnam, in turn, sent thousands of its troops. In the late 1960's, Viet Cong casualties began to mount, and North Vietnam switched its focus to conventional warfare. As a result, the Viet Cong played a lesser role in the rest of the war. In 1975, the war ended, and the two Vietnams were united under Communist rule.   Marc Jason Gilbert

Vietminh. See **Vietnam** (History).

© Steve Raymer, CORBIS

The rice fields of Vietnam provide one of the primary foods of the Vietnamese people. Most of the people in Vietnam are farmers, and rice is the chief crop.

Vietnam

Vietnam, *VEE eht NAHM* or *VEE eht NAM,* is a country in Southeast Asia with its eastern coast on the South China Sea. Vietnam is bordered by China to the north and Laos and Cambodia to the west. The Gulf of Thailand lies to the southwest. Hanoi is the capital of Vietnam. Ho Chi Minh City, formerly named Saigon, is the largest city.

The population of Vietnam is concentrated in the Red River Delta in the north and the Mekong River Delta in the south. Central Vietnam is less heavily populated than either the north or the south because it has mountainous terrain. Although Vietnam has a number of ethnic groups, most of the people are classified as Kinh—that is, ethnic Vietnamese.

Most Vietnamese are farmers who live in small villages. Rice is the main crop. But manufacturing has become an increasingly important economic activity.

People have lived in what is now Vietnam since prehistoric times. Ethnic Vietnamese developed a culture in the Red River Delta 4,000 to 5,000 years ago. Through the centuries, this group expanded its control of what is now Vietnam. At the same time, the Vietnamese fought many foreign invaders, frequently the Chinese.

The French governed Vietnam from the mid-1800's until Japan occupied it during World War II. After Japan's defeat in 1945, France tried to regain control of Vietnam. But the Vietminh, a group headquartered in the north and headed by Vietnamese patriot and Communist leader Ho Chi Minh, resisted the French. In 1954, fighting between the French and the Vietminh ended

with a French defeat in the Battle of Dien Bien Phu.

An international peace conference, held in Geneva, Switzerland, decided to divide Vietnam temporarily into two zones—Communist North Vietnam and non-Communist South Vietnam. Elections were supposed to be held to reunite the country, but they were continually postponed and never took place. In 1957, fighting broke out between revolutionaries in the South and the South Vietnamese government. The fighting eventually developed into the Vietnam War, which the Vietnamese call the American War. The United States became the chief ally of the South. It backed the South's war effort with supplies and hundreds of thousands of troops.

In 1973, the participants in the war agreed to a cease-fire, and the United States withdrew its last combat troops. But the fighting soon resumed. In April 1975, the Communists defeated South Vietnam. In 1976, they unified North and South Vietnam into a single nation, which they named the Socialist Republic of Vietnam.

Facts in brief

Capital: Hanoi.
Official language: Vietnamese.
Area: 128,066 mi² (331,689 km²). *Greatest distances*—north-south, 1,030 mi (1,658 km); east-west, 380 mi (612 km). *Coastline*—2,140 mi (3,444 km).
Elevation: *Highest*—Fan Si Pan, 10,312 ft (3,143 m) above sea level. *Lowest*—sea level along the coast.
Population: *Estimated 2008 population*—87,009,000; density, 679 per mi² (262 per km²); distribution, 74 percent rural, 26 percent urban. *1999 census*—76,323,173.
Chief products: *Agriculture*—rice. *Manufacturing*—cement, fertilizer, shoes, steel, textiles. *Mining*—coal.
Money: *Basic unit*—dong.

Patricia M. Pelley, the contributor of this article, is Assistant Professor of History at Texas Tech University.

Government

According to the Vietnamese Constitution, which was adopted in 1980 and extensively revised in 1992, Vietnam is a socialist nation. It is governed by a single political party—the Communist Party of Vietnam (CPV). The party is the leading force in the state and society. Political power in Vietnam is based on the principle of *democratic centralism*. Under this principle, authority and power originate at the highest levels of the CPV and flow downward through a rigid political structure.

National level. The National Assembly is the highest legislative body in Vietnam. The 498 delegates to the Assembly are elected by the people to a maximum term of five years. No candidate can run for the Assembly without the approval of the Communist Party. All Vietnamese 18 years of age or older are allowed to vote.

Vietnam's highest government officials are the president and the prime minister. The National Assembly elects one of its own members to serve as president. The president directs members of the Assembly to appoint the vice president, prime minister, chief justice of the Supreme People's Court, and head of the Supreme People's Organ of Control. As head of state, the president acts as official representative of Vietnam, has overall command of the armed forces, and chairs the National Defense and Security Council. As chief executive, the prime minister manages the government, assisted by deputy prime ministers and cabinet ministers.

Local level. Vietnam is divided into 57 *tinh* (provinces) and four municipalities—Da Nang, Haiphong, Hanoi, and Ho Chi Minh City. Each tinh and municipality has a legislature called a People's Council and an executive body known as a People's Committee. The people elect the members of each People's Council, who then elect the members of the People's Committee.

Courts. The judicial system of Vietnam consists of two main divisions: the People's Courts and the People's Organs of Control. The People's Courts include the Supreme People's Court, local courts, and Military Tribunals. The People's Organs of Control monitor the bodies of government.

Armed forces of Vietnam consist of a *main force* and *paramilitary forces*. The main force includes an army of about 412,000 members and a small navy and air force. The paramilitary forces include local urban and rural militias and border defense forces. About 40,000 people serve in the paramilitary forces.

People

Ancestry. Vietnam has 54 ethnic groups. Over 85 percent of the people of Vietnam are Kinh—that is, ethnic Vietnamese—who are spread throughout the country. Minority ethnic groups live mainly in the mountain areas of the country. The largest groups are the Tay, who live to the north and northeast of the Red River Delta; and the Tai, who live in scattered villages in valleys of the Red and Black rivers, in the northwest and north-central interior. Other large minority groups include the Hmong, the Khmer, the Muong, and the Nung. A number of ethnic Chinese people, known as the Hoa, live mainly in the cities.

Language. Vietnamese is the most widely spoken language in Vietnam. However, minority peoples speak their own language and may have only limited knowledge of Vietnamese. In urban areas, English is the most widely spoken foreign language, but Chinese, French, and Russian are also spoken.

Way of life

Rural life. Most Vietnamese live in small villages in the countryside. Most rural Vietnamese are farmers who organize their lives around the cultivation of crops, especially rice. In general, the family and the village are the centers of social life in rural areas.

Houses in the villages vary. Some have tile roofs and walls made of clay or brick. Others have thatched roofs and walls made of woven bamboo. In the mountains and in areas that flood, many houses stand on stilts.

City life. Many villagers have migrated to the cities in search of jobs and a higher standard of living. However, urban development has not kept pace with immigration from the countryside. As a result, the cities of Vietnam are densely packed and face serious housing shortages. In many cases, two or three generations of a family share a one-room apartment.

Vietnam's cities bustle with traffic. Bicycles are a popular means of transportation. Cities also have numerous motor scooters and *cyclo taxis*—three-wheeled, pedaled

Vietnam's flag and coat of arms feature a star that stands for Communism. The rice and the cogwheel on the coat of arms represent the importance of agriculture and industry to Vietnam. The flag was first officially adopted by Vietnamese Communists when they declared independence in 1945. The shape of the star was modified slightly in 1955.

WORLD BOOK map

Vietnam is in Southeast Asia, with its eastern coast on the South China Sea. It is also bordered by Cambodia, Laos, and China.

cycles with a seat in front for carrying passengers. Cafes, food stands, and stalls that sell craftworks, books, clothing, and other items line many urban streets. Architecture in the cities ranges from simple wooden dwellings to elegant colonial villas built by the French to modern high-rise office and apartment buildings.

Urban Vietnamese work in a variety of occupations. For example, some are employed as public officials or work in factories, hotels, or restaurants. Others are merchants who own their own business.

Clothing. The Vietnamese typically wear lightweight clothing. Rural women wear loose-fitting dark pants and blouses that are often embroidered in brilliant colors. Conical hats called *non la* shield their faces from the sun. In cities, many girls and women wear the traditional *ao dai,* a long tunic worn with loose-fitting pants. However, a growing number of urban women now wear dresses and skirts. Rural and working-class men typically wear simple shirts and trousers. City men generally wear clothing similar to that worn by North Americans and Europeans.

Members of minority groups often dress in traditional costumes. For example, Hmong women wear blouses and skirts or baggy shorts, with embroidered belts and aprons or long vests. Some roll their hair into a turban, but most wrap their heads with a cloth. Hmong men wear skullcaps, loose trousers, shirts, and a long vest.

Food and drink. The national dish of Vietnam is a noodle soup called *pho.* This dish consists of long rice noodles and fresh vegetables in a broth with meat or seafood. Many Vietnamese also eat boiled rice with vegetables, *tofu* (soybean curd), seafood, chicken, pork, or duck. A fish sauce called *nuoc mam* is used as a seasoning in many dishes. People in central Vietnam often eat beans, corn, cassava, sweet potatoes, or other starchy foods instead of rice.

Green tea is the most popular beverage. Fruit and sugar cane juices, coconut milk, and soft drinks are widely available. In urban areas, cafes and restaurants serve local and imported beer, wine, and liquor. Coffee and long loaves of bread called *baguettes,* which were both favorites of the French, are still popular in Vietnam.

Recreation. The Vietnamese, especially children, enjoy swimming in the country's many lakes and rivers, and in the sea. Vietnamese children also engage in lively games of soccer. Many people play chess or tennis. Competitions involving judo and the martial arts of tae

kwon do and kung fu are also popular. Families who can afford to do so vacation at seaside resorts.

Religion. Most Vietnamese practice a combination of the Three Teachings—that is, Mahayana Buddhism, Confucianism, and Taoism. The country also has a small number of Christians and Muslims. In the south, a religion known as Cao Dai and the Hoa Hao Buddhist sect, both of which originated in Vietnam, have numerous followers. Some people, especially in villages, worship the spirits of animals, plants, and other parts of nature.

Education. Nearly all Vietnamese 15 years of age or older can read and write. For the literacy rate, see **Literacy** (table: Literacy rates). Children ages 6 through 10 are required to attend school. Schools of higher education in Vietnam include universities, agricultural colleges, technical institutes, and private business academies. The largest are Hanoi University of Technology, Vietnam National University, and Can Tho University. Vocational training is available to adults.

The arts. Traditional Vietnamese forms of art include woodblock printing, woodcarving, lacquerware, ceramics, jade carving, silk painting, and basketry. The Vietnamese are also known for their fine embroidery.

In 1925, the French opened the École des Beaux-Arts de l'Indochine (School of Fine Arts of Indochina) in Hanoi, and Vietnamese artists began to study European-style painting. They started using such materials as oil paints and canvas, painting portraits and scenes of everyday life, and adopting such styles as Cubism and Impressionism. In the late 1940's and early 1950's, a number of artists created works that focused on the resistance to French colonial rule. From the mid-1950's to the 1970's, Socialist Realist artists in the North created paintings that celebrated combat and glorified work.

After the reunification of Vietnam in the mid-1970's to the mid-1980's, art continued to serve mainly a social and political purpose. Since the mid-1980's, however, Vietnamese art has become more open, and paintings now include a variety of styles and subjects. The country's best-known artists include Bui Xuan Phai, known for his Hanoi street scenes; Nguyen Tu Nghiem, whose subjects come from mythology and folklore; Nguyen Sang, who creates paintings of village people; and Do Quang Em, noted for his realistic still lifes and portraits.

Traditional Vietnamese musical instruments include a variety of string, wind, and percussion instruments. Among them are the *dan nhi,* a two-stringed fiddle; the

Vietnam map index

*Does not appear on map; key shows general location.

Sources: 1999 census (provinces); 1992 United Nations estimates (indicated by †); 1989 and earlier census and official estimates for other places.

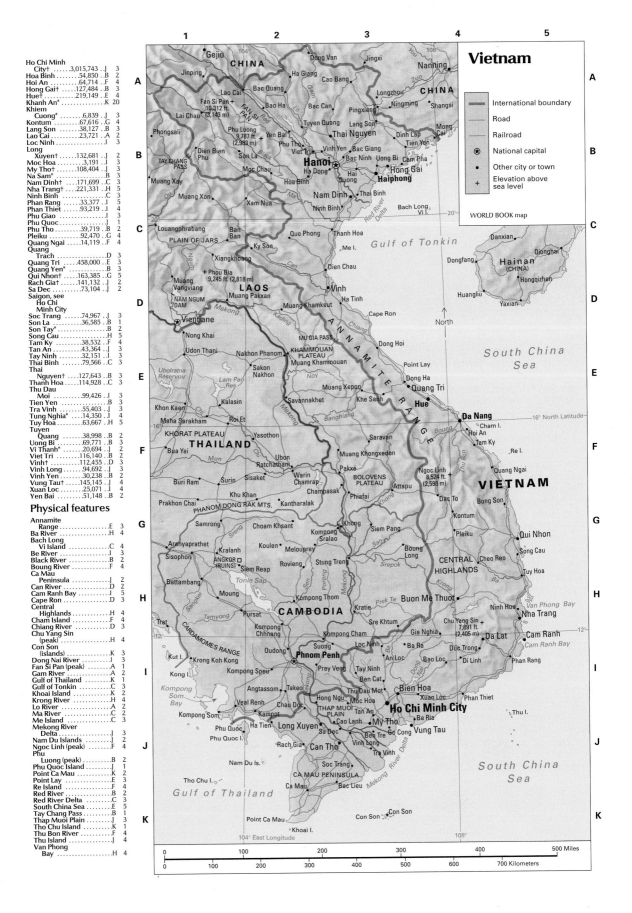

Traffic in Vietnam's cities fills the streets with many kinds of vehicles. This street in Ho Chi Minh City is crowded with bicycles, motor scooters, and cars. Two pedal-driven cyclo taxis, *foreground,* carry their passengers through the traffic.

© Catherine Karnow, CORBIS

dan tranh, a 16-string zither; the *dan nguyet,* a long-necked lute; the *dan ty ba,* a pear-shaped lute; the *dan tam,* a three-stringed banjo; the *sao,* a bamboo flute; the *trong com,* a barrel-shaped drum; and the *chieng,* a gong.

Vietnam has a long tradition of oral literature. The nation's first great writer was Nguyen Trai, who lived in the late 1300's and early 1400's. He became famous as a pioneer of *chu nom*—a form of Vietnamese written in modified Chinese characters. Literature written in Vietnamese began to appear around the 1600's. *Truyen Kieu (The Tale of Kieu),* a long poem by Nguyen Du from the early 1800's, ranks as one of the greatest works in the Vietnamese language. Although a love story, the poem also reflects society's struggles during Nguyen Du's time.

Authors of the late 1900's and early 2000's include Duong Thu Huong, known for her novels *Paradise of the Blind* (1988) and *Novel Without a Name* (1991); Bao Ninh, whose most famous work is the novel *The Sorrow of War* (1991); and the short-story writer Nguyen Huy Thiep, some of whose works have been collected in *The General Retires and Other Stories* (1988).

The land

Vietnam occupies an S-shaped stretch of the rugged eastern Indochinese Peninsula. Four-fifths of the country is covered by hills, plateaus, and mountains. The coastline borders on the South China Sea and extends more than 2,100 miles (3,400 kilometers) from the Gulf of Tonkin to the Gulf of Thailand. Geographers divide Vietnam into three regions: northern, central, and southern.

Northern Vietnam extends from the border with China in the north to about Thanh Hoa in the south. This region is dominated by the Red River Delta, the most densely populated center of agricultural production in Vietnam. The triangular delta is the heartland of Vietnamese civilization, and the capital city of Hanoi is there.

Northern Vietnam also includes the mountains of the north and northwest. Vietnam's highest mountain is Fan Si Pan, also spelled Phan Xi Pang. It rises to 10,312 feet

(3,143 meters) in northwestern Vietnam.

Central Vietnam is the most mountainous of the country's three regions. The Annamite Range, also known as the Truong Son mountains, dominates this area. The Central Highlands lie to the south. Poor soil makes farming difficult in central Vietnam. However, rich soil is available in the lowlands along the coast and on a few plateaus in the Central Highlands.

Southern Vietnam. The Mekong River in the southern part of Vietnam forms the country's largest network of agricultural plains. As a result, the Mekong Delta is often referred to as the "rice bowl" of Vietnam. Ho Chi Minh City, formerly named Saigon, is the region's major urban center and the country's economic hub.

Climate

Vietnam has a tropical climate with high humidity. Most of Vietnam has two seasons—a wet, hot summer and a drier, slightly cooler winter. *Monsoons* (seasonal winds) affect the weather throughout the year. The summer monsoon brings heavy rains from the southwest. The winter monsoon brings lighter rainfall from the northeast.

In Hanoi, in northern Vietnam, the average temperature is about 63 °F (17 °C) in January and about 85 °F (29 °C) in June. From May to October, the Red River Delta has high temperatures, heavy rains, and some typhoons, which sweep across the Gulf of Tonkin. Hanoi receives about 68 inches (173 centimeters) of rainfall a year.

In southern Vietnam, most rain falls in summer. The Ho Chi Minh City area receives about 70 inches (180 centimeters) of rain between May and October. From November through February, the weather is cooler with little rain. Average temperatures there range from about 79 °F (26 °C) in December to about 86 °F (30 °C) in April.

Central Vietnam has the greatest temperature range and includes the driest and the wettest regions of the country. Typhoons often strike the central coast. Mountain areas generally have lower temperatures and less rainfall than the delta regions and the coastal lowlands.

Economy

From 1976 to 1986, the state owned all banks and factories in Vietnam and controlled nearly every sector of the economy. During that period, the economy steadily declined. In 1986, however, Vietnamese leaders began adopting a series of far-reaching economic changes known as *doi moi* (renovation). These changes were designed to restore some economic power to the private sector. Under doi moi, for example, farmers who had satisfied their obligations to the state were allowed to produce for the market. Some state-run industries that had operated at a loss for a decade or more were dismantled. Vietnam also began to welcome foreign investment in the form of direct loans and joint ventures.

Agriculture is the leading economic activity in Vietnam. Rice is the chief crop. Most Vietnamese farmers practice wet-rice agriculture, in which rice is grown on irrigated paddies. This farming method requires much labor but produces high yields. Vietnamese farmers also cultivate cashews, a root crop called cassava, corn, peanuts, and sweet potatoes. Bananas, coconuts, melons, and other fruits are also grown. Many farmers raise animals, especially chickens, ducks, and hogs. Industrial crops, such as coffee, rubber, sugar cane, tea, and tobacco, are cultivated on large plantations.

Manufacturing. Textile production is the leading manufacturing industry in Vietnam. The country also produces cement, chemical fertilizers, glass, shoes, steel, and tires. Factories manufacture various household goods, including bicycles and televisions. Most of Vietnam's industrial development is in the south. Ho Chi Minh City has a number of high-tech industries.

Mining. Vietnam is rich in mineral resources. Its coal fields, most of which are in the north, have tremendous reserves. The country also has large deposits of chromite, copper, gold, iron ore, lead, phosphate, tin, and zinc. Bauxite, the basic ingredient of aluminum, is also mined. An abundance of limestone contributes to a thriving cement industry. Vast deposits of silica supply the basis for the manufacture of glass. The country also has extensive reserves of petroleum and natural gas, mainly offshore.

Fishing industry. With Vietnam's long coastline and many lakes and rivers, fishing has always played an important role in the economy. Vietnamese fishing crews catch a variety of fish and shellfish. Vietnam is rapidly becoming one of the world's leading producers of processed shrimp.

Service industries are those industries that provide services rather than produce manufactured goods or agricultural products. Many Vietnamese work in service industries as barbers, clerks, computer technicians, construction workers, drivers of cyclo taxis, hairdressers, housekeepers in hotels, and waiters in restaurants.

International trade. Vietnam's chief exports include clothing and textiles, coffee, fish and shellfish, petroleum, rice, rubber, shoes, and tea. Its main imports include cotton, fertilizer, machinery and equipment, motorcycles, petroleum products, and steel products. Vietnam's chief trading partners are Japan, Singapore, South Korea, and Taiwan.

Transportation and communication. Bicycles and motorcycles are popular forms of transportation in Vietnam. Many people also ride buses. The nation's rivers are widely used to transport goods and people. Vietnam has about 62,000 miles (100,000 kilometers) of roads, though only about a fourth of them are paved.

A railroad network connects the major cities of the Red River and Mekong deltas and cities along the coast. However, much of the system was damaged by bombs during the Vietnam War and remains in disrepair. Vietnam's chief ports include Da Nang, Haiphong, and Ho Chi Minh City. Hanoi and Ho Chi Minh City have international airports.

Several daily newspapers are published in Vietnam. The government controls all newspapers, magazines, and television and radio broadcasts.

History

People have lived in what is now Vietnam since prehistoric times. Archaeologists have discovered remains of a stone age culture dating back about 500,000 years in the province of Thanh Hoa. Agriculture developed in northern Vietnam more than 7,000 years ago.

About 5,000 years ago, a kingdom called Van Lang emerged in the Black and Red river valleys under the rule of the Hung kings. One of the most important cultures of Van Lang, the Dong Son civilization, flourished in the valleys of the Red and Ma rivers from about 800 to 300 B.C. This civilization is known mainly for its elaborately decorated bronze drums.

Nam Viet. In 258 B.C., a leader named An Duong founded the kingdom of Au Lac. In 207 B.C., an official of China's Qin dynasty named Zhao Tuo (Trieu Da in Vietnamese) founded the kingdom of Nam Viet. Nam Viet included Au Lac and several other kingdoms in what is now northern Vietnam. In 111 B.C., the Chinese Han dynasty conquered Nam Viet. Through the centuries, many Vietnamese resisted Chinese rule. But not until A.D. 939, as a result of a rebellion led by Ngo Quyen, did the Vietnamese gain independence.

Despite the centuries of Chinese occupation, many aspects of Vietnamese culture remained in place, but new patterns also emerged. Specifically, the rise of a mixed Chinese and Vietnamese ruling class ensured the lasting importance of Chinese writing, even though the Viet-

Important dates in Vietnam

111 B.C. The Chinese conquered Nam Viet, a kingdom in what is now northern Vietnam.

A.D. 939 China ended its rule over the Vietnamese, who then set up an independent state.

1802 Nguyen Anh united the country and called it Vietnam.

1860's-1880's France took control of Vietnam.

1940-1945 Japan controlled Vietnam during World War II.

1946 War began between France and the Vietminh.

1954 The Vietminh defeated the French. The Geneva Conference temporarily divided Vietnam into two zones.

1957 The Vietnam War began, as Communist-supported rebels began a revolt against the South Vietnamese government.

1973 United States participation in the Vietnam War ended.

1975 The Vietnam War ended on April 30 with the surrender of South Vietnam.

1976 The Communists unified North and South Vietnam into the Socialist Republic of Vietnam.

1986 Vietnam's Communist government introduced some free-market economic reforms.

1995 Vietnam joined the Association of Southeast Asian Nations.

The Indochina Peninsula in 1900

This map shows French Indochina, which included Cambodia, Laos, and Vietnam. France divided Vietnam into Tonkin, Annam, and Cochin China. Present-day Vietnam is shown in yellow.

WORLD BOOK map

namese continued to speak their own language. Chinese ideas of historical writing also had an enormous impact on how Vietnamese historians represented their past. Vietnamese officials sometimes adopted Chinese administrative practices. The Three Teachings—Mahayana Buddhism, Confucianism, and Taoism—are another legacy of Chinese rule.

Independence. After Ngo Quyen's death in 944, Vietnam was troubled by succession disputes and the competition of war lords. These troubles ended with the establishment of the Dinh dynasty in 968, though the dynasty lasted only 12 years. The succeeding dynasty, established in 980, lasted only until 1009. Two long-lasting dynasties, the Ly (1009-1225) and the Tran (1225-1400), stabilized politics.

In 1400, Ho Quy Ly seized the Vietnamese throne, and in 1407, the Ming Chinese invaded the country and took control. In 1428, Le Loi drove out the Chinese rulers and established the Le dynasty. Under the Le rulers, the Vietnamese empire continued the process of Nam Tien (Advance to the South). During the 1400's, for example, the Vietnamese conquered Champa, a rival kingdom in what is now central Vietnam.

In 1527, the Mac dynasty overthrew the Le dynasty, and, in 1540, was formally recognized by the Ming Chinese. Le forces regained control over central Vietnam in 1545 and northern Vietnam in 1592. However, Mac forces continued to fight against the Le for more than 35 years.

During the mid-1500's, Vietnamese politics became further fragmented as the Trinh and Nguyen families, the two clans closest to the Le court, drifted apart. By 1600, the country was effectively divided, and the Le kept control in name only. Even though the Ming Chinese had recognized the Le dynasty as ruler of Vietnam, the Trinh lords actually governed the north and the Nguyen lords were in charge of the south. In the 1600's,

the rivalry between these two clans occasionally erupted into armed conflict.

The Nguyen lords continued their expansion to the south until 1771. That year, three brothers from the region of Tay Son in central Vietnam began a series of successful attacks against Nguyen rule. This upheaval, known as the Tay Son Rebellion, resulted in the collapse of Nguyen power in the south, Trinh power in the north, and, in 1788, the end of the Le dynasty. After defending Vietnam against an invasion of Qing Chinese troops in 1789, the Tay Son dynasty tried to consolidate its rule over all of what is now Vietnam.

In 1802, Nguyen Anh became the first emperor of the Nguyen dynasty. He took the reign name of Gia Long. He united the country and called it Vietnam. The Nguyen dynasty, Vietnam's last, established its capital in Hue. It formally ended in 1945.

French rule. In 1858, French warships captured the city of Da Nang. The French claimed that they were protecting Jesuit missionaries and Vietnamese who had converted to Roman Catholicism. By continuing the armed attacks and through diplomatic pressure, France succeeded in taking control of the southern part of Vietnam, known then as Cochin China, in the 1860's. In the 1880's, France took control of the northern (Tonkin) and central (Annam) parts of Vietnam. With the conquest of Cambodia in the 1860's and of Laos in the 1890's, French control of Indochina was complete.

The French were principally interested in Vietnam and the surrounding area as a base for trading with China. They also hoped to exploit the mineral wealth of Vietnam and to establish plantations for coffee, rubber, and tea. To help carry out these plans, the French built roads and railways linking the lowlands, the midlands, and the mountains. They also expanded port facilities.

Under French rule, the traditional Vietnamese ruling class withdrew from public life, and a new French-Vietnamese ruling class emerged. The romanized written version of Vietnamese known as *quoc ngu* also became more prominent in private and public affairs.

Through the years, Vietnamese resistance to French rule grew. Various nationalist associations and societies emerged, as did a number of political parties. These parties included the Vietnamese Nationalist Party, Indochinese Communist Party, and the New Vietnamese Revolutionary Party.

The August Revolution of 1945. In August 1940, during World War II (1939-1945), France's wartime Vichy government granted Japan permission to use northern Vietnam for military operations. When Japanese troops advanced into other Southeast Asian colonies of European powers, they took control over the colonial governments. In Vietnam, the Japanese at first allowed French officials to continue to carry out their administrative duties. In March 1945, however, the Japanese ousted the French officials.

Initially, most Vietnamese had welcomed the Japanese, expecting that they would free Vietnam from French rule. When it seemed that Japan was also a threat to their independence, however, many Vietnamese reconsidered their plans to join with the Japanese to fight the French. One result of such reconsideration was the creation of an organization called the Vietminh in 1941. Established by Ho Chi Minh and other leaders of the Indochinese Communist Party, the Vietminh was designed to encourage national unity and independence.

Japan agreed to surrender on Aug. 14, 1945. Within days, anticolonial activists in Vietnam staged the August Revolution. On September 2, Ho recited Vietnam's declaration of independence, in which he quoted directly from the American Declaration of Independence. Ho and other revolutionary leaders expected that the United States would support the new state—the Democratic Republic of Vietnam (DRV)—for a number of reasons. For instance, the United States had gained its own independence through a revolution. The United States had also criticized European colonialism for most of the 1900's. In addition, the Vietminh had cooperated with U.S. diplomatic and military personnel during World War II. However, the DRV never received U.S. support, mainly because of U.S. opposition to Communism.

The First Indochina War. After World War II, France tried to reclaim its former colonies in Southeast Asia. In 1946, war broke out between France and the Vietminh. Throughout the war, the French controlled cities in north and south Vietnam. The revolutionaries, based in the mountains of the north and northwest, controlled most of the countryside. Many southern Vietnamese rejected the idea of a Communist-dominated government and sided with the French. By mid-1949, the French had formed the Associated State of Vietnam to oppose the Vietminh. Bao Dai, the last of the Nguyen emperors, headed the government of the Associated State. The fighting in Vietnam ended in May 1954, when the Vietminh defeated the French garrison at Dien Bien Phu.

Fearing the growth of Communism, the United States began in 1948 to channel aid to the countries of Western Europe to help them rebuild after the devastation of World War II. The assistance provided by the Marshall Plan made it possible for France to rebuild and to continue fighting the war in Vietnam. Further expressing its support for the French attempt to reconquer Vietnam, the United States formally recognized the Associated State of Vietnam in 1950.

During the final stages of the First Indochina War, negotiators representing nine countries—Cambodia, China, France, Laos, the United Kingdom, the United States, the Soviet Union, the Democratic Republic of Vietnam, and the Associated State of Vietnam—assembled in Geneva, Switzerland. In July 1954, the representatives produced a series of agreements known as the Geneva Accords. One of these agreements provided that Vietnam be temporarily divided into northern and southern zones at the 17th parallel. Another agreement called for an election in 1956 to unify the country. Fearing that Ho Chi Minh would win such an election, however, southern Vietnamese, with U.S. support, refused to participate. The election was never held.

The Vietnam War began in 1957. It is sometimes called the Second Indochina War, and the Vietnamese know it as the American War. Communist-supported rebels in the South began a revolt against the government of Ngo Dinh Diem, who was backed by the United States. United States military and civilian advisers then rushed to aid South Vietnam. Through the years, South Vietnam received extensive assistance from the United States, including cash, military equipment, and more than 500,000 troops. Despite this aid, South Vietnam

© Hulton/Archive

Vietnamese refugees flee fighting during the Vietnam War (1957-1975). The war caused enormous destruction and resulted in millions of deaths. Millions of Vietnamese became refugees.

failed to shape itself into a popularly supported, non-Communist state. In April 1975, the People's Army of North Vietnam launched an offensive that resulted in the complete collapse of Southern power.

The Vietnam War caused enormous destruction. The United States dropped tons of chemicals on central Vietnam designed to clear the jungles and forests. Parts of the country remained barren of vegetation for many years afterwards. The U.S. forces also destroyed many rice fields and villages. The Vietnam War resulted in the deaths of millions of Vietnamese, many of them civilians. More than 58,000 American military personnel also lost their lives. For a detailed discussion of the war, see **Vietnam War.**

Postwar Vietnam. In April 1976, national elections determined the nearly 500 members of the new National Assembly for a reunited Vietnam. In July, the Socialist Republic of Vietnam was officially proclaimed. In the process of establishing a single state, leaders of the new government sought out supporters of the former South Vietnamese government. According to official sources, more than 1 million southerners were subjected to some form of "reeducation" in the political culture of the North. For most of these people, this process took several days or weeks. But thousands of others, viewed as greater threats, spent a decade or more in labor camps.

Following reunification, thousands of northerners resettled in the south. As a consequence, the northern dialect of Vietnamese is now regarded officially as standard Vietnamese. In addition, the government has taken thousands of Kinh from the deltas and relocated them in the highlands and mountains.

With the collapse of the Southern regime, many Vietnamese fled the country. They settled in the United States, Canada, and Australia, or joined earlier generations of exiles in Belgium and France. Following the government's nationalization of industries, tens of thousands of ethnic Chinese also left the country.

Many refugees left Vietnam in boats, risking drowning and pirate attacks in the South China Sea. These refugees became known as *boat people*. They went to other countries in Southeast Asia, where they stayed in refugee camps until they could be relocated. Many later moved to the United States. In the mid-1990's, the United Nations and countries that housed or helped pay for the camps closed nearly all of them. Most of the remaining refugees were sent back to Vietnam.

Invasion of Cambodia. In 1978, Vietnam invaded Cambodia. It replaced Cambodia's Khmer Rouge Communist government with a pro-Vietnamese Communist government. The Khmer Rouge and non-Communist groups then fought against the government and the Vietnamese forces in Cambodia. Vietnam gradually withdrew its troops in the 1980's, and the war ended in 1991.

Recent developments. In the late 1980's, the Vietnamese government began a program of economic restructuring known as *doi moi*. This program encouraged some forms of private enterprise and competition as well as foreign investment. In early July 1995, Vietnam and the United States established diplomatic ties. Later that month, Vietnam became a member of the Association of Southeast Asian Nations (ASEAN), a regional organization that promotes political, economic, cultural, and social cooperation among its members. In 2006, the U.S. Congress passed a bill establishing normal trade relations with Vietnam for the first time since the Vietnam War.

Patricia M. Pelley

Related articles in *World Book* include:

Association of Southeast Asian Nations
Da Nang
Dien Bien Phu, Battle of
Geneva Accords
Haiphong
Hanoi
Ho Chi Minh
Ho Chi Minh City
Hue
Indochina
Mekong River
My Lai Massacre
Ngo Dinh Diem
Southeast Asia
Southeast Asia Treaty Organization
Viet Cong
Vietnam War

Outline

- **I. Government**
  - A. National level
  - B. Local level
  - C. Courts
  - D. Armed forces
- **II. People**
  - A. Ancestry
  - B. Language
- **III. Way of life**
  - A. Rural life
  - B. City life
  - C. Clothing
  - D. Food and drink
  - E. Recreation
  - F. Religion
  - G. Education
  - H. The arts
- **IV. The land**
  - A. Northern Vietnam
  - B. Central Vietnam
  - C. Southern Vietnam
- **V. Climate**
- **VI. Economy**
  - A. Agriculture
  - B. Manufacturing
  - C. Mining
  - D. Fishing industry
  - E. Service industries
  - F. International trade
  - G. Transportation and communication
- **VII. History**

Questions

What area is the heartland of Vietnamese civilization?
What is considered the leading force in the state and society in Vietnam?
What are the Three Teachings?
What nation controlled Vietnam during World War II?
What was the importance of the Battle of Dien Bien Phu?
What is the chief crop of Vietnam?
What are the largest minority groups in Vietnam?
Why did Ho Chi Minh and other Vietnamese leaders expect the United States government to support the Democratic Republic of Vietnam?

Additional resources

McLeod, Mark W., and Nguyen, T. C. *Culture and Customs of Vietnam*. Greenwood, 2001.
Pelley, Patricia M. *Postcolonial Vietnam: New Histories of the National Past*. Duke Univ. Pr., 2002.
Willis, Terri. *Vietnam*. Children's Pr., 2002. Younger readers.
Woods, L. Shelton. *Vietnam: A Global Studies Handbook*. ABC-CLIO, 2002.

Vietnam Veterans Memorial is a monument in Washington, D.C., that honors the Americans who served in the Vietnam War. The memorial, which stands on the National Mall, features two black granite walls that meet at an angle. The names of more than 58,000 Americans who died in the war, or who remained classified as missing in action when the walls were built in 1982, are inscribed on the walls.

Maya Ying Lin, a student at Yale University, designed the two walls. The memorial also includes a large bronze sculpture of three servicemen, which was added in 1984, and one of three servicewomen, which was added in 1993. In 2004, officials dedicated a plaque that honors service members who died after the war from injuries suffered in Vietnam. For pictures of the memorial, see **Washington, D.C.** (The Mall).

Critically reviewed by the National Park Service

Vietnam War was the longest war in which the United States took part. It began in 1957 and ended in 1975. Vietnam, a small country in Southeast Asia, was divided at the time into the Communist Democratic Republic of Vietnam, commonly called North Vietnam, and the non-Communist Republic of Vietnam, commonly called South Vietnam. North Vietnamese and Communist-trained South Vietnamese rebels sought to overthrow the government of South Vietnam and to eventually reunite the country. The United States and the South Vietnamese army tried to stop them, but failed.

The Vietnam War was actually the second phase of fighting in Vietnam. During the first phase, which began in 1946, the Vietnamese fought France for control of Vietnam. At that time, Vietnam was part of the French colonial empire in Indochina. The United States sent France military equipment, but the Vietnamese defeated the French in 1954. Vietnam was then split into North and South Vietnam.

United States aid to France and later to non-Communist South Vietnam was based on a Cold War policy of President Harry S. Truman. The Cold War was an intense rivalry between Communist and non-Communist nations. Truman had declared that the United States must help any nation challenged by Communism. The Truman Doctrine was at first directed at Europe and the Middle East. But it was also adopted by the next three presidents, Dwight D. Eisenhower, John F. Kennedy, and

The Vietnam War was the longest war in which the United States took part. It lasted from 1957 to 1975. In the war, U.S. and South Vietnamese forces battled against Communist-trained South Vietnamese rebels and North Vietnamese troops. Helicopters often ferried U.S. soldiers, such as these Marines, from one site to another.

Hulton Getty from Liaison Agency

Lyndon B. Johnson, and applied to Indochina. They feared that if one Southeast Asian nation joined the Communist camp, the others would also "fall," one after the other, like what Eisenhower called "a row of dominoes."

The Vietnamese Communists and their allies called the Vietnam War a war of national liberation. They saw the Vietnam War as an extension of the struggle with France and as another attempt by a foreign power to rule Vietnam. North Vietnam wanted to end U.S. support of South Vietnam and to reunite the north and south into a single nation. China and the Soviet Union, at that time the two largest Communist nations, gave the Vietnamese Communists war materials but not troops.

The Vietnam War had several stages. From 1957 to 1963, North Vietnam aided rebels opposed to the government of South Vietnam, which fought the rebels with U.S. aid and advisory personnel. From 1964 to 1969, North Vietnam and the United States did much of the fighting. Australia, New Zealand, the Philippines, South Korea, and Thailand also helped South Vietnam. By April 1969, the number of U.S. forces in South Vietnam had reached its peak of more than 543,000 troops. By July, the United States had slowly begun to withdraw its forces from the region.

In January 1973, a cease-fire was arranged. The last American ground troops left Vietnam two months later. The fighting began again soon afterward, but U.S. troops did not return to Vietnam. South Vietnam surrendered on April 30, 1975, as North Vietnamese troops entered its capital, Saigon (now Ho Chi Minh City).

The Vietnam War was enormously destructive. Military deaths reached about 1.3 million, and the war left much of Vietnam in ruins.

Just before the war ended, North Vietnam helped rebels overthrow the U.S.-backed government in nearby Cambodia. After the war, North Vietnam united Vietnam and helped set up a new government in nearby Laos. The U.S. role in the war became one of the most debated issues in the nation's history. Many Americans felt

U.S. involvement was necessary and noble. But many others called it cruel, unnecessary, and wrong. Today, many Americans still disagree on the goals, conduct, and lessons of U.S. participation in the Vietnam War.

Background to the war

The Indochina War. In the late 1800's, France gained control of Indochina—that is, Vietnam, Laos, and Cambodia. Japan occupied Indochina during most of World War II (1939-1945). After Japan's defeat in 1945, Ho Chi Minh, a Vietnamese nationalist and Communist, and his Vietminh (Revolutionary League for the Independence of Vietnam) declared Vietnam to be independent. But France was determined to reclaim its former colonial possessions in Indochina. In 1946, war broke out between France and the Vietminh. It finally ended in 1954, following the conquest of the French garrison of Dien Bien Phu by Vietminh forces in May. In July, the two sides signed peace agreements in Geneva, Switzerland.

The Geneva Accords provided that Vietnam be temporarily divided into northern and southern zones at the 17th parallel. The accords also called for national elections in 1956 to reunify the country.

The United States had provided aid to the French in Indochina since 1950. President Harry S. Truman had been convinced that such assistance was necessary in part because of the Communist take-over of China in 1949. Truman feared a Vietminh victory in Vietnam would lead to a Communist take-over of Indochina as part of a larger Communist plan to dominate Asia. This fear was so great that Truman ignored pleas by Ho for U.S. aid against French colonialism and for an alliance with the United States.

The divided country. After 1954, Ho strengthened the rule of his Communist government in the Democratic Republic of Vietnam, which became known as North Vietnam. He suppressed non-Communist political parties. He also enacted land reforms and established legal equality between men and women. Ho hoped the elections of 1956 would provide him with the means with

Important dates in the Vietnam War

1957	The Viet Cong began to rebel against the South Vietnamese government headed by President Ngo Dinh Diem.
1963	(Nov. 1) South Vietnamese generals overthrew the Diem government, and Diem was killed the next day.
1964	(Aug. 7) Congress passed the Tonkin Gulf Resolution, which gave the president power to take "all necessary measures" and "to prevent further aggression."
1965	(March 6) President Lyndon B. Johnson sent U.S. Marines to Da Nang, South Vietnam. The Marines were the first U.S. ground troops in the war.
1968	(Jan. 30) North Vietnam and the Viet Cong launched a major campaign against South Vietnamese cities.
1969	(June 8) President Richard M. Nixon announced that U.S. troops would begin to withdraw from Vietnam.
1973	(Jan. 27) The United States, North and South Vietnam, and the Viet Cong signed a cease-fire agreement.
1973	(March 29) The last U.S. ground troops left Vietnam.
1975	(April 30) South Vietnam surrendered.

which to peacefully reunify the country under his revolutionary government. These elections never occurred.

The United States moved to make the division of Vietnam permanent by helping leaders in the southern half to form a non-Communist Republic of Vietnam, also known as South Vietnam. Ngo Dinh Diem, who had once refused a place in Ho's government and vigorously opposed any Communist influence in his country, became president of South Vietnam in 1955. With the approval of the United States, he refused to go along with the proposed nationwide elections scheduled for the following year. He argued that the Communists would not permit fair elections in North Vietnam. Most experts believe, however, that Ho was so popular that he would have won the elections under any circumstances. President Dwight D. Eisenhower provided economic aid and sent several hundred U.S. civilian and military advisers to assist Diem.

Early stages of the war

The Viet Cong rebellion. Diem suppressed all rival political groups in his effort to strengthen his government. But his government never achieved widespread popularity, especially in rural areas, where his administration did little to ease the hard life of the peasants. Diem became increasingly unpopular in 1956, when he ended local elections and appointed his own officials down to the village level, where self-government was an ancient and honored tradition. From 1957 to 1959, he sought to eliminate members of the Vietminh who had joined other South Vietnamese in rebelling against his rule. Diem called these rebels the Viet Cong, meaning *Vietnamese Communists*. These rebels were largely trained by the Communists, but many were not Communist Party members.

Although North Vietnam had hoped to achieve its goals without a military conflict against the United States or the South Vietnamese government, it supported the revolt against Diem from its early stages. In 1959, as U.S. advisers rushed aid to South Vietnam by sea, North Vietnam developed a supply route to South Vietnam through Laos and Cambodia. This system of roads and trails became known as the Ho Chi Minh Trail. Also, in 1959, two U.S. military advisers were killed during a battle. They were the first American casualties of the war.

By 1960, discontent with the Diem government was widespread, and the Viet Cong had about 10,000 troops. In 1961, they threatened to overthrow Diem's unpopular government. In response, President John F. Kennedy greatly expanded economic and military aid to South Vietnam. From 1961 to 1963, he increased the number of U.S. military advisers in Vietnam from about 900 to over 16,000.

The Buddhist crisis. In May 1963, widespread unrest broke out among Buddhists in South Vietnam's major cities. The Buddhists, who formed a majority of the country's population, complained that the government restricted their religious practices. Buddhist leaders accused Diem, a Roman Catholic, of religious discrimination. They claimed that he favored Catholics with lands and offices at the expense of local Buddhists. The government responded to the Buddhist protests with mass arrests, and Diem's brother Ngo Dinh Nhu ordered raids against Buddhist temples. Several Buddhist monks then set themselves on fire as a form of protest.

The Buddhist protests aroused great concern in the United States. Kennedy urged Diem to improve his dealings with the Buddhists, but Diem ignored the advice.

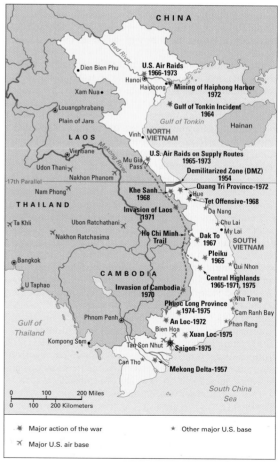

WORLD BOOK map

The Vietnam War was fought mainly in North and South Vietnam from 1957 to 1975. Troops also battled in Laos and Cambodia, and U.S. pilots flew missions from bases in Thailand.

Kennedy then supported a group of South Vietnamese generals who opposed Diem's policies. On Nov. 1, 1963, the generals overthrew the Diem government. Diem and Nhu were murdered.

The fall of the Diem government set off a period of political disorder in South Vietnam. New governments rapidly succeeded one another. During this period, North Vietnam stepped up its supply of war materials and began to send units of its own army into the south. By late 1964, the Viet Cong controlled up to 75 percent of South Vietnam's population.

The Gulf of Tonkin incident. In 1964, President Lyndon B. Johnson approved secret South Vietnamese naval raids against North Vietnam. Just after one of these raids, on Aug 2, 1964, North Vietnamese torpedo boats attacked the U.S. destroyer *Maddox,* which was monitoring the impact of the raid off the coast of North Vietnam in the Gulf of Tonkin. Johnson warned the North Vietnamese that another such attack would bring "grave consequences." On August 4, he announced that North Vietnamese boats had again launched an attack in the gulf, this time against the *Maddox* and another U.S. destroyer, the *C. Turner Joy.*

Some Americans doubted that the August 4 attack had occurred, and it has never been confirmed. Nevertheless, Johnson ordered immediate air strikes against North Vietnam. He also asked Congress for power to take "all necessary measures to repel any armed attack against the forces of the United States and to prevent further aggression." On August 7, Congress approved these powers in the Tonkin Gulf Resolution. The United States did not declare war on North Vietnam. But Johnson used the resolution as the legal basis for increased U.S. involvement. In March 1965, he sent a group of U.S. Marines to South Vietnam, the first American ground combat forces to enter the war.

The fighting intensifies

The opposing forces. The war soon became an international conflict. United States forces rose from about 60,000 in mid-1965 to a peak of over 543,000 in 1969. They joined about 800,000 South Vietnamese troops and a total of about 69,000 troops from Australia, New Zealand, the Philippines, South Korea, and Thailand. The North Vietnamese and the Viet Cong had over 300,000 troops, but the exact number is unknown.

The two sides developed strategies to take advantage of their strengths. The United States had the finest modern weapons and a highly professional military force. Its field commanders were General William C. Westmoreland from 1964 to 1968 and, afterward, Generals Creighton Abrams and Frederick Weyand. The United States did not try to conquer North Vietnam. Instead, American leaders hoped superior U.S. firepower would force the enemy to stop fighting. The United States relied mainly on the bombing of North Vietnam and "search and destroy" ground missions in South Vietnam.

The United States used giant B-52 bombers as well as smaller planes for the main air strikes against the enemy. American pilots used helicopters to seek out Viet Cong troops in the jungles and mountains. Helicopters also carried the wounded to hospitals and brought supplies to troops in the field.

In contrast, Viet Cong and North Vietnamese leaders

AP/Wide World

Antiwar demonstrations took place throughout the United States in the late 1960's and early 1970's. Thousands of protesters gathered for this demonstration in Washington, D.C., in 1971.

adopted a defensive strategy. Their more lightly armed troops relied on surprise and mobility. They tried to avoid major battles in the open, where heavy U.S. firepower could be decisive. The Viet Cong and North Vietnamese preferred guerrilla tactics, including ambushes and hand-laid bombs. Their advantages included knowledge of the terrain and large amounts of war materials from the Soviet Union and China.

Course of the war. From 1965 to 1967, the two sides fought to a highly destructive draw. The U.S. bombing caused tremendous damage, but it did not affect the enemy's willingness or ability to continue fighting. North Vietnam concealed its most vital resources, and the Soviet Union and China helped make up the losses.

American victories in ground battles in South Vietnam also failed to sharply reduce the number of enemy troops there. The U.S. Army and Marines usually won whenever they fought the enemy. But North Vietnam replaced its losses with new troops. Its forces often avoided defeat by retreating into Laos and Cambodia.

Reactions in the United States. As the war dragged on, it divided many Americans into so-called *hawks* and *doves.* The hawks supported the nation's fight against Communism. But they disliked Johnson's policy of slow, gradual troop increases and urged a decisive defeat of North Vietnam. The doves opposed U.S. involvement and held mass protests. Many doves believed that U.S. security was not at risk. Others charged that the nation was supporting corrupt, undemocratic, and unpopular governments in South Vietnam.

The growing costs of the war, however, probably did more to arouse public uneasiness in the United States than the antiwar movement did. By late 1967, increased casualties and Johnson's request for new taxes helped produce a sharp drop in public support for the war.

The Tet Offensive. North Vietnam and the Viet Cong opened a new phase of the war on Jan. 30, 1968, when they started to attack military bases and major cities in South Vietnam. The fighting was especially fierce in the city of Saigon, South Vietnam's capital, and in Hue. This campaign began the day before Tet, the Vietnamese New Year celebration. North Vietnam and the Viet Cong hoped the offensive would deal a serious blow to U.S. forces and make the South Vietnamese people lose faith in their government and rise against South Vietnamese leaders. They also hoped that the offensive would persuade U.S. officials to enter into peace negotiations with North Vietnamese leaders.

The plan failed to achieve many of its objectives. No widespread uprising of the population occurred in South Vietnam. Also, the United States and South Vietnam quickly recovered their early losses, and the enemy suffered a huge number of casualties. But the Tet attacks stunned the American people and demoralized their war managers. Shortly before the offensive, the U.S. commander in the field, General Westmoreland, had assured the nation that the enemy had already been largely beaten. But the Tet offensive seemed to contradict this statement. As a result of the offensive, Johnson made a number of basic changes in his policies. He cut back the bombing of North Vietnam and rejected Westmoreland's request for 206,000 more troops. He also called for peace negotiations and declared that he would not seek reelection. Peace talks opened in Paris in May.

Vietnamization

The U.S. withdrawal begins. The peace talks failed to produce agreement, and more and more Americans became impatient for the war to end. President Richard M. Nixon felt he had to reduce United States involvement in the conflict. On June 8, 1969, he announced a new policy known as Vietnamization. This policy called for stepped-up training programs for South Vietnamese forces and the gradual withdrawal of United States troops from South Vietnam. The U.S. troop withdrawal began in July 1969.

The invasion of Cambodia. In April 1970, Nixon ordered U.S. and South Vietnamese troops to clear out military supply centers that North Vietnam had set up in Cambodia. Large stocks of weapons were captured, and the invasion may have delayed a major enemy attack. But many Americans felt the campaign widened the war. The invasion aroused a storm of protest in the United States, especially on college and university campuses.

The nation was shocked on May 4, 1970, when National Guard units fired into a group of demonstrators at Kent State University in Ohio. The shots killed four students and wounded nine others. Antiwar demonstrations and riots occurred on hundreds of other campuses throughout May. A move began in Congress to force the removal of the troops from Cambodia. On June 3, Nixon announced the completion of troop withdrawals from Cambodia. That same day, the Senate voted to repeal the Tonkin Gulf Resolution. These actions ended the Cambodian campaign.

Growing protest. Opposition to the war in the United States grew rapidly during Nixon's presidency. Many people claimed that this increased opposition was due to the news media, particularly television coverage, which brought scenes of the war into millions of homes. Most scholars have concluded, however, that media coverage reflected, rather than brought about, America's growing opposition to the war.

In March 1971, the conviction of Lieutenant William L. Calley, Jr., for war crimes raised some of the main moral issues of the conflict. Calley's unit was part of the Army company that massacred hundreds of civilians in 1968 in My Lai, a hamlet in South Vietnam. All of those killed were unarmed women, children, and old men. None had given any resistance to United States forces. Calley was found guilty of the murder of at least 22 Vietnamese and was sentenced to prison. He was paroled in 1974.

Some war critics used Calley's trial to call attention to the large numbers of civilians killed by U.S. bombing and ground operations in South Vietnam. Others pointed to the vast stretches of countryside that had been destroyed by bombing and by spraying of chemicals. United States forces used such weedkillers as Agent Orange to reveal enemy hiding places in the jungle and to destroy enemy food crops (see **Agent Orange**).

Public distrust of the U.S. government deepened in June 1971, when newspapers published a secret government study of the war called *The Pentagon Papers.* This study raised questions about decisions and secret actions of government leaders regarding the war.

Invasion of the south. In March 1972, North Vietnam began a major invasion of South Vietnam. Nixon then renewed the bombing of North Vietnam and used American airpower against the exposed formations of regular enemy troops and tanks. He also ordered the placing of explosives in the harbor of Haiphong, North Vietnam's major port for importing military supplies. These moves helped stop the invasion, which had nearly reached Saigon by August 1972.

The high cost paid by both sides during the 1972 fighting led to a new round of peace negotiations. The talks were conducted by Henry A. Kissinger, Nixon's chief foreign policy adviser, and Le Duc Tho of North Vietnam. On Jan. 27, 1973, a cease-fire agreement was signed in Paris by the United States, South Vietnam, North Vietnam, and the Viet Cong. The pact provided for the withdrawal of all U.S. and allied forces from Vietnam and for the return of all prisoners—both within 60 days. It also permitted North Vietnam and the Viet Cong to leave their troops in the south. In addition, it called for internationally supervised elections that would let the South Vietnamese decide their political future.

The end of the war. On March 29, 1973, the last U.S. ground forces left Vietnam. But the peace talks soon broke down, and the war resumed. Congress, responding to voters who wished to see an end to the war, opposed further U.S. involvement. As a result, American troops did not return to the war. In mid-1973, Congress began to reduce military aid to South Vietnam.

In late 1974, North Vietnamese and Viet Cong troops attacked Phuoc Long, northeast of Saigon, and won an easy victory. In March 1975, the North Vietnamese forced South Vietnamese troops into a retreat from a region known as the Central Highlands. Thousands of civilians—many of them families of the South Vietnamese soldiers—also fled and died in the gunfire or from starvation. This retreat became known as the Convoy of Tears. Although some South Vietnamese army units fought on, few soldiers or civilians rallied in support of the failing South Vietnamese government.

Early in April, President Gerald R. Ford asked Congress for $722 million in military aid for South Vietnam. But Congress, believing defeat was now inevitable, pro-

AP/Wide World

Fleeing from advancing North Vietnamese troops, South Vietnamese civilians scrambled to get aboard a United States evacuation helicopter near the end of the war in April 1975.

vided only $300 million in emergency aid. The money was mainly for the evacuation of Americans from Saigon, which was threatened by rapidly advancing enemy troops. The war ended on April 30, 1975, when these troops entered Saigon and the South Vietnamese government formally surrendered to them. Saigon was then renamed Ho Chi Minh City.

Results of the war

Casualties and destruction. About 58,000 American military personnel died in the war, and about 300,000 were wounded. South Vietnamese military losses were approximately 224,000 killed and 1 million wounded. North Vietnamese and Viet Cong losses totaled about 1 million dead and 600,000 wounded. Countless numbers of civilians in North and South Vietnam also perished.

The U.S. bombing in the conflict was more than three times as great as the combined U.S.-British bombing of Germany in World War II. The American air strikes destroyed much of North Vietnam's industrial and transportation systems. But South Vietnam, where most of the fighting took place, suffered the most damage. The war made refugees of as many as 10 million South Vietnamese. The bombing and the use of chemicals to clear forests scarred the landscape and may have permanently damaged much of South Vietnam's cropland and plant and animal life.

Other effects in Southeast Asia. In 1976, North and South Vietnam were united into a single nation, which was renamed the Socialist Republic of Vietnam. North Vietnamese leaders then forced their own rigid political culture on people of the south. They imprisoned thousands who had held positions of responsibility in the South Vietnamese army or government. They also waged a campaign against independent businesses, run mainly by Vietnamese merchants of Chinese descent. As a result, over 1 million Vietnamese fled Vietnam between 1975 and the early 1990's, and the economy stagnated. But the harsh social divisions between rich and poor were ended, and literacy rates soared.

North Vietnam had helped establish Communist governments in Laos and Cambodia in 1975. However, the anti-Vietnamese policies of the pro-Chinese Communist Khmer Rouge movement in Cambodia forced Vietnam into a lengthy and costly campaign in that country. China reacted to this evidence of Vietnam's growing influence in the region by briefly invading Vietnam in 1979.

Effects in the United States. The Vietnam War also had far-reaching effects in the United States. The United States spent about $200 billion on the war. Many experts believe that this high cost of the war damaged the U.S. economy for years after the war's conclusion.

The Vietnam War was the first foreign war in which U.S. combat forces failed to achieve their goals. This failure hurt the pride of many Americans and left bitter and painful memories. The Americans most immediately affected included the approximately 2,600,000 men and women who had served in the war, and their families. Most veterans adjusted smoothly to civilian life. But others, particularly those with psychological problems associated with combat stress, encountered difficulties in making the adjustment to postwar American society. These veterans suffered from high rates of divorce, drug abuse, unemployment, and homelessness.

After World Wars I and II, the country viewed its soldiers as heroes. Americans who opposed the U.S. role in Vietnam had embraced those veterans who joined the antiwar movement upon their return from the battlefield, but some criticized or shunned those veterans who felt the war was justified. Many Americans who supported the war came to regard Vietnam veterans as symbols of America's defeat. Some leading hawks opposed expanding benefits to Vietnam veterans to match those given to veterans of earlier wars. These reactions shocked the veterans. Many of them felt that the nation neither recognized nor appreciated their sacrifices.

After the war, Congress and the public became more willing to challenge the president on military and foreign policy. The war also became a standard of comparison in situations that might involve U.S. troops abroad.

Today, Americans still disagree on the main issues and lessons of the war. Some believe U.S. participation was necessary and just. Many of these people say the war was lost because the United States did not use its full military power and because opposition at home weakened the war effort. Others point to the failure of the South Vietnamese government to develop popular support and to its overreliance on the United States. Still others view U.S. involvement as immoral and unwise. Some of them feel U.S. leaders made the war a test of the nation's power and leadership. Some view the conflict as a civil war that had no importance to U.S. security. Since Vietnam, many Americans have argued that the nation should stay out of wars that do not directly threaten its safety or vital interests.   Marc Jason Gilbert

Related articles in *World Book* include:

War (table)

Westmoreland, William C.

War crime (The Vietnam War)

Additional resources

Dowswell, Paul. *The Vietnam War.* World Almanac Lib., 2002. Younger readers.

Hillstrom, Kevin and Laurie C. *Vietnam War.* 4 vols. UXL, 2001.

Tucker, Spencer C., ed. *Encyclopedia of the Vietnam War.* 3 vols. ABC-CLIO, 1998.

Young, Marilyn B., and Buzzanco, Robert, eds. *A Companion to the Vietnam War.* Blackwell, 2002.

Vigée-Lebrun, *vee zhay luh BRUHN,* **Elisabeth,** *ay lee za BEHT* (1755-1842), was one of the most fashionable portrait painters in France before the French Revolution (1789-1799). Vigée-Lebrun was a friend of Marie Antoinette, the French queen, and painted the royal family as well as most notable members of French society. The artist produced over 800 paintings. Vigée-Lebrun had a graceful style. She devoted much attention to rich fabrics and fine clothes. Her portraits flattered her subjects.

Elisabeth Vigée was born on April 16, 1755, in Paris. She received some training in art from her father, Louis Vigée, who was a minor portrait painter. At the age of 15, Elisabeth was already an established portrait painter. In 1776, she married Jean-Baptiste Lebrun, a leading art dealer. Because of her connections with the royal family, Vigée-Lebrun had to flee France at the outbreak of the revolution. For the next 12 years, she successfully continued her career painting portraits of nobility in Austria, Germany, Italy, and Russia. She returned to Paris in the early 1800's and wrote *Souvenirs,* an informative but biased autobiography. She died on March 30, 1842.

Eric M. Zafran

Vigilante, *VIHJ uh LAN tee,* is a member of a self-appointed citizen group called a vigilance committee. Such groups help fight criminal activity or other unruly behavior in their communities. Vigilante groups often form where people believe that regular law enforcement is inadequate.

Before 1900, many vigilante groups formed in frontier areas of the United States. Most of these groups consisted of law-abiding citizens who were generally considered heroes in their communities for their work in preserving law and order. But some frontier vigilantism involved mob action and excessive violence.

The growth of drug abuse and other crime in United States cities after 1960 led to the formation of modern urban vigilance committees. These committees include anticrime patrols as well as neighborhood watch groups.   Peter Woll

Vigny, *vee NYEE,* **Alfred de** (1797-1863), a French author, was a leading figure in the Romantic movement. He is best known for his lyric and descriptive poetry. From his *Antique and Modern Poems* (1826) to *Les Destinées* (1864), Vigny's themes include the solitude of individuals of genius, the alienation of God from humanity, the search for greatness through suffering and resignation, and the nobility of thought as expressed in philosophical poetry. Vigny's other writings include the play *Chatterton* (1835) and the novel *Cinq-Mars* (1826).

Vigny was born on March 27, 1797, in Loches. He spent much of his life living in isolation. An unhappy love affair and his failure to win political office intensified his sense of loneliness. Vigny died on Sept. 17, 1863.

Thomas H. Goetz

Vikings were fierce pirates and warriors who terrorized Europe from the late 700's to about 1100. During this period, daring Viking sailors also explored the North Atlantic Ocean and even reached America. Such deeds have given this period of European history the name *the Viking Age.*

The Vikings lived in Scandinavia, a region of Europe that includes what are now Denmark, Norway, and Sweden. The Vikings conquered or looted parts of England, France, Germany, Ireland, Italy, Russia, Scotland, and Spain. At first, they raided these areas to obtain loot. Later, they set up trading centers and trade routes. Viking ships carried settlers to Iceland and to Greenland, which had been unknown to Europeans until then. Leif Ericson (also spelled Ericson, Ericsson, or Eiriksson), a Viking explorer, landed in North America around 1000, about 500 years before Christopher Columbus arrived there in 1492. The Vikings established a settlement in North America, but it lasted only a few years.

The name *Viking* did not come into use until after the Viking Age. It probably came from *Vik,* the name of a pirate center in southern Norway during Viking times. Among the Scandinavians, the expression *to go a-viking* meant *to fight as a pirate or warrior.* Other Europeans called the Scandinavians *Norsemen, Northmen,* or *Danes.* Swedish Vikings settled in eastern Europe, including part of what became Russia. Many historians believe that the Swedes became known there as the *Rus,* and that Russia was named for them.

Few Scandinavians of the Viking Age spent all their time going a-viking. The majority worked most of the time as farmers or in other peaceful occupations. These skills allowed the Vikings to establish outposts in places such as Iceland where there were few other people.

The Viking Age began during a period of rapid population growth in Scandinavia. Historians speculate that this growth reduced the amount of available farmland, leading many Vikings to seek wealth or a new place to live outside of Scandinavia. At the same time, Scandinavians developed new shipbuilding techniques that enabled their ships to travel farther than ever before.

The Vikings had no direct effect on the history of America. But their conquests in Europe influenced relations between England and France for hundreds of years after the Viking Age.

Viking life

Ancestry and population. The ancestors of the Vikings were Germanic peoples who once lived in northwestern Europe. Beginning about 2000 B.C., these peoples moved to what are now Denmark, Norway, and Sweden. A separate group of Vikings developed in each of these areas, but the three groups shared the same general culture.

The Vikings spoke a Germanic language that had two major dialects. All the Vikings understood both dialects. The Vikings used an alphabet made up of characters called *runes.* Each rune consisted chiefly of straight lines arranged singly or in combinations of two or more. See **Rune.**

James A. Graham-Campbell, the contributor of this article, is Professor of Medieval Archaeology at University College London and the author of The Viking World.

WORLD BOOK illustration by H. Charles McBarron, Jr.

Fierce Viking warriors terrorized many seaside and riverside towns in Europe. Their swift, light warships sailed well in rough seas or shallow rivers and could be rowed when the wind was not favorable. These ships made possible the Vikings' surprise attacks and quick retreats.

The Vikings lived on farms or in villages. A king or chief ruled each Viking community. The people were divided into three social classes—nobles, free men and women, and slaves. The nobles included the kings, chiefs, and other people who had great wealth or were descendants of highly honored ancestors. The free men and women included farmers, merchants, and others who served the ruler or worked for themselves. Many of the slaves were Scandinavians whose ancestors had been enslaved. Others were Europeans who had been captured in Viking raids and battles. The majority of Vikings stayed in one class for life.

Each Viking community had a governing council called a *Thing.* This council, made up of the community's nobles and free men, made laws, decided whether the community would go to war, and held trials to judge criminals. Its decisions were more important than rulings of the king or chief.

Economic activities. The great majority of Vikings were farmers. They grew barley, oats, rye, and a variety of fruits and vegetables. They also raised cattle, goats, pigs, and sheep. Other Vikings worked in fishing, metalworking, shipbuilding, and woodcarving. In the largest communities, many people made their living as merchants. Those who were interested mainly in trade traveled widely. They sailed to most parts of the known world and traded farm products, furs, various other goods, and slaves for such products as gold, silk, silver, and weapons.

Daily life. Parents arranged most Viking marriages. The husband ruled the Viking family, but Viking women had more rights than did the women of other European societies of that time. For example, any Viking woman could own land or other property, and a wife had a right to share in the wealth that her husband gained. Viking law permitted a married woman to get a divorce whenever she wished.

Three or more generations of a Viking family lived together. The family was bound together by honor. If one member of the family was disgraced, the entire family, including its ancestors, was disgraced. Conflicts between individuals of different families often turned into feuds between the families.

The Vikings became known for burial customs that involved great ceremony. In what is known as *boat burial,* Vikings were laid to rest in a rowing or fishing boat that was then buried. Some wealthy Viking men and women were buried in full-sized ships. Many of the dead person's possessions, including beds, jewelry, and weapons, were placed in the ship. In some cases, the person's dogs and even slaves were buried alive in the grave.

Food. The Vikings ate two meals daily, one in the morning and the other in the evening. They used spoons and knives, but had no forks. Most of the food, including beef, bread, cheese, eggs, and milk, came from their farms.

The Vikings also hunted and fished for food. Hunters supplied meat from deer, elks, seals, whales, and wild birds. The fish catch included cod, herring, salmon, and trout.

Clothing. Most Viking men wore two basic garments—trousers that reached to the knee or ankle, and a long-sleeved pullover shirt that reached below the waist. Viking women wore loose-fitting dresses that were made of linen or wool and hung almost to the ankles. All the Vikings wore leather shoes.

Housing. Most Viking houses were one-story structures with slanted roofs. Some houses had only one room. Others had three or more. Builders made the walls mainly out of wood or stone, and covered the roof with shingles, sod, or straw. Each home included a hearth that provided heat and light as well as a place to cook. Viking houses had few or no windows. The husband used a chair called the *high seat.* The rest of the family sat on benches. Raised platforms on either side of the hearth served as beds.

Religion played an important role in Viking life. The Vikings worshiped a number of gods. The most impor-

Viking houses typically were one-story structures. They had walls built of stone or wood and slanted roofs made of shingles, sod, or straw. In this photograph, actors pose outside a reconstructed Viking home at L'Anse Aux Meadows National Historic Site in Newfoundland and Labrador, Canada.

tant ones were Odin, Thor, Frey, and Freyja.

Odin, also known as Woden, was chief among the Norse gods and goddesses. He was the father of Thor and other gods. Odin lived in *Asgard,* the home of the gods. The Vikings believed that if they died fighting, they would go to a hall in Asgard called *Valhalla.* There, they could fight all day and dine all night. *Wednesday* was named in honor of Odin. See **Odin.**

Thor, ruler of the sky, was the god of thunder and lightning. He was the most popular Viking god because his life reflected the values of Viking warriors. *Thursday* was named after Thor. See **Thor.**

Frey was the god of agriculture and fertility. His twin sister, Freyja, was the goddess of love and fertility. Frey ensured the success of a harvest, and Freyja blessed a marriage. See **Frey** and **Freyja.**

Contact between the Vikings and European Christians led to the end of the Norse religion. English and German missionaries helped make Christianity the chief religion in Scandinavia by the early 1100's.

Viking artifacts

Woodcarving of a horse's head decorated part of a Viking tent. This carving was done in the 800's.

A picture stone was carved on a monument in the 700's. It shows a warrior on horseback and magic symbols.

The sword was a prized weapon among the Vikings. A sword maker of the 1000's fashioned this handle out of silver.

Cultural life and recreation. Poetry and storytelling were popular among the Vikings. Favorite subjects included the gods and Viking battles. Court poets called *skalds* entertained Viking kings and their guests. Their verses often praised the kings for such qualities as generosity or bravery.

Many Viking artists used a style in which animals were portrayed with twisted bodies. A favorite subject was the *gripping beast,* which was pictured wildly gripping its throat, sides, or other parts of its body. Some Swedish artists carved animals, *interlace* (weaving patterns), and other figures on limestone slabs known as *picture stones.*

The Scandinavians worked skillfully at many crafts, especially metalworking and woodcarving. They produced attractive bracelets, necklaces, pins, and other kinds of jewelry, much of it from silver. Viking woodcarvers decorated homes, ships, and wagons with elegant, detailed carvings of beasts and warriors.

For recreation, the Vikings especially liked rowing, skiing, swimming, and wrestling. They also enjoyed watching horse races and playing board games.

Shipbuilding and navigation

The sea almost surrounded the Vikings' Scandinavian homelands. In addition, hundreds of *fiords* (inlets to the sea) cut into the coastline. As a result, water travel was the main form of transportation in the region, and the Vikings became a seafaring people.

The Vikings as shipbuilders. The Vikings ranked among the best shipbuilders of their time. They built

© Universitetets Oldsaksamling, Oslo, Norway

This Viking ship was found buried in a grave in Norway. It is about 75 feet (23 meters) long and was built mostly of oak.

their ships out of wood that they cut from the vast Scandinavian forests. Viking shipbuilders greatly improved the sailing ability of Scandinavian ships by adding a *keel,* a long, narrow piece of wood which formed the backbone of a ship. It extended down into the water along the center of the entire length of the ship. The keel reduced a ship's rolling motion. By doing so, it greatly improved the ship's speed and thus the distance it could travel without stopping for supplies. The keel also made it easier to steer the ship.

The size of a Viking ship varied, depending on whether the ship was used for trade or for battle. Trading ships, called *knorrs,* were about 50 feet (15 meters) long. Warships, also known as *long ships,* ranged in length from about 65 to 95 feet (20 to 29 meters) and were about 17 feet (5 meters) wide.

A Viking warship sailed well in either rough seas or calm waters. It was light enough to enter shallow rivers. At sea, the Vikings depended mainly on the wind and the ship's large woolen sail for power. On a river, rowers powered the ship. A warship had from 15 to over 30 pairs of oars. The *prow* (front end) of a Viking warship curved gracefully upward and sometimes ended with a carving of the head of a dragon or snake. See **Ship** (Viking ships; pictures).

The Vikings as navigators. Early Viking navigators depended primarily on sightings of the sun and the stars to determine direction and approximate location at sea. By the late 900's, however, the Vikings had developed a system that enabled them to determine the latitude in which they were sailing. They made a table of figures that showed the sun's midday height for each week of the year. By using a measuring stick and this table, a navigator could make a sighting and estimate the latitude of the ship's location.

Viking navigators also relied on landmarks. The Vikings sailed from Norway to Greenland using sightings of the Shetland and Faroe islands and Iceland as landmarks.

Scholars do not know all the methods Viking sailors used to navigate. They may have used certain crystals to locate the sun on overcast days. They may have found their directions with the help of ravens, other types of birds, or whales. Whatever methods they employed, the Vikings' impressive navigation skills enabled them to travel throughout Europe and the North Atlantic.

Warfare

Viking warriors enjoyed fighting. They were bold and adventurous, but they were also brutal and fearsome. They murdered women and children as well as men. What they did not steal, they burned. The Vikings created such terror in the hearts of other Europeans that one French church created a special prayer for protection: "God, deliver us from the fury of the Northmen."

The cruelest and most feared Viking warrior was called a *berserker* or *berserk.* Some historians believe berserkers were raging madmen. Others think they were normal people who became wild and fearless after eating certain mushrooms or other foods that contained drugs. The term *berserk* is still used to describe a person who acts wildly.

Battle strategy and tactics. When the Vikings invaded a territory, they launched a fleet of several hundred

WORLD BOOK illustration by H. Charles McBarron, Jr.

A Viking warrior fought with a sword that had a broad two-edged blade made of iron or steel. For protection, he carried a round wooden shield and wore a leather helmet.

warships, each probably carrying about 30 warriors. Thousands of fighters landed, overpowered the defenders, and overran the land. In this way, the Vikings conquered land in England and France. Most Viking warfare, however, was waged by small raiding parties. Such forces consisted of from 2 to 10 ships, also with about 30 raiders on each ship.

Targets of Viking raids included small, poorly defended towns and isolated farms. The main bounty of these raids was cattle, horses, and food. Churches and monasteries were also favorite targets because they contained much treasure and were largely defenseless. Many held such richly ornamented articles as beautiful ivory *croziers* (ornamental staffs) and books covered with gold and precious stones. High-ranking church officials could be captured and ransomed. Other captured monks could be sold into slavery.

The Vikings became known for surprise attacks and quick retreats. They could row their light, swift ships into shallow rivers and then easily drag them ashore. They often struck so fast that their victims had no time to defend themselves.

Weapons and armor. The Vikings fought mainly with axes, bows and arrows, spears, and swords. The *broad axe* had a long handle and a large flat blade with a curved cutting edge. The Viking warrior used two hands to swing the broad axe at an opponent. The Viking sword had a broad two-edged blade that was made of iron or steel. The fighter swung the sword with a chopping or hacking motion, aiming at an opponent's arms or legs.

Most Viking warriors carried round wooden shields for protection. Many raiders also wore a sort of armor made from thick layers of animal hides, perhaps with

bone sewn into them for added protection. Viking warriors also wore cone-shaped helmets made of leather. Only Viking leaders wore metal helmets and coats of *mail* (metal armor). Artists have often pictured Viking warriors wearing helmets with cattle horns on the sides, but the Vikings never had such helmets.

Exploration and conquest

Scholars link the start of the Viking rampage with several conditions in Scandinavia at the time. Perhaps the most important was a rapidly growing population, which led to overcrowding and a shortage of farmland. In addition, family feuds and local wars made life in Scandinavia difficult for many Vikings. Many other Vikings, especially those who were young, poor, or without land of their own, saw in raiding and conquering a means to obtain wealth and honor.

The Norwegian Vikings began the Viking reign of terror. In June 793, Norwegian raiders attacked and looted the monastery of Lindisfarne on an island off the east coast of England. A wave of Norwegian raids against England, Ireland, the Isle of Man, and Scotland followed.

Ireland's many fertile farms and rich churches and monasteries made it an especially attractive target. The Irish city of Dublin was established as a winter base for Viking raiders in 841. It later became an important Viking seaport. Turgeis, a Norwegian pirate chief, led raids throughout eastern Ireland and along the River Shannon.

During the mid-800's, Norwegian raiders struck targets farther from their homeland. They looted and burned towns in France, Italy, and Spain. In the late 800's, many of the Norwegians turned their attention from Europe to the North Atlantic. Norwegian settlers began to migrate to Iceland about 870. About 25,000 Vikings had settled in Iceland by the mid-900's.

About 982, Erik the Red, a Norwegian who had been living in Iceland, sailed with his family to Greenland. About 985, he persuaded several hundred Icelanders to settle in Greenland (see **Erik the Red**). Soon afterward, Bjarni Herjolfsson, a Viking sea captain, became the first known European to see the mainland of North America. He made the sighting after sailing off course during a voyage from Iceland to Greenland. After Bjarni reached Greenland, he told the settlers there about the territory he had passed. Having just arrived in Greenland, the settlers were not interested in exploring other lands at that time.

About 10 years later, after all the good cropland in Greenland had been taken, interest began to grow in the land Bjarni had sighted. About 1000, Leif Eriksson, a son of Erik the Red, led an expedition westward from Greenland to find the new territory. He and his crew landed somewhere on the east coast of North America and spent the winter there. The Vikings made wine from the plentiful supply of grapes they found, and Leif called the area *Vinland,* or *Wineland.* See **Leif Eriksson; Vinland.**

The Vikings soon established a colony in Vinland. In time, however, they were driven away by Indians and did not return. Some historians believe that Vinland was located in what is now Maine or Massachusetts. Others think Vinland was on the present-day Canadian island of Newfoundland. According to the *sagas* (stories of heroic deeds) written by Icelanders long after Viking times, a number of settlements were established in Vinland over a period of about 20 years.

The main evidence of the Vikings' presence on the mainland of North America comes from remains of a Viking settlement found at L'Anse aux Meadows, Newfoundland, in 1960. There, scientists discovered house foundations like those of Vikings in Iceland and Greenland, as well as several small Viking objects.

The Danish Vikings began their raids in the early 800's. They looted and burned towns on the coasts of what are now Belgium, France, and the Netherlands. In 865, the Danes invaded England. They conquered all the English kingdoms except Wessex and settled in the eastern half of the country. Alfred the Great, king of Wessex, won major victories against the Vikings in 878 and 886 and forced the Vikings to withdraw to the eastern third of England (see **Alfred the Great**). This area became known as the *Danelaw.*

In the late 800's, Danish Vikings began to raid French towns again. In 886, King Charles the Fat of France paid the Vikings a huge treasure to end their yearlong siege of Paris. In 911, King Charles III of France and a Viking chieftain named Rollo agreed to what became known as the treaty of St. Clair-sur-Epte. According to the treaty, Rollo accepted Christianity and pledged to support the French king. In turn, Charles granted the Vikings control of much of the area in France now known as *Normandy* (Land of the Northmen). See **Normans.**

In the late 900's, the Danish Vikings renewed their interest in England. Ethelred II had become king of England in 978, when he was only about 10 years old. The English nobility refused to support Ethelred, and so England's defense against invasion was much weakened. In 994, Danes led by Sweyn Forkbeard, a son of King Harald Bluetooth of Denmark, went to war against England. In 1016, Sweyn's son Canute finally brought England under Danish control. The Danes ruled England until 1042.

The Swedish Vikings began to raid towns along rivers in eastern Europe during the early 800's. They set up trade centers in this region, which included what are now western Russia, eastern Belarus, and eastern Ukraine. The people of that area were mostly Slavs. The Slavs called the Swedish Vikings the *Rus.*

The Swedes gained control of the key trade routes between the Baltic Sea and the Black Sea. By the late 800's, the East Slavic towns of Novgorod (now Velikiy Novgorod) and Kiev had become Swedish strongholds. In time, Kiev became the center of Kievan Rus, the first state of the East Slavs.

By the mid-900's, the Rus had adopted many of the customs of the East Slavic peoples. About 988, the Rus prince Vladimir I (also known as Volodymyr) destroyed all the symbols of the Viking religion in Kiev and made Christianity the official religion of the Rus.

Viking influence

The most important influence of the Viking period was its effect on Scandinavia, the homeland of the Vikings. The creation of three strong Viking kingdoms in Scandinavia led to the development of three nations— Denmark, Norway, and Sweden. When the Vikings adopted Christianity, they then brought Scandinavia into the mainstream of European civilization.

The Norsemen also influenced developments in England and France. Viking invasions in the 800's and 900's led to the unification of England under a single king. The establishment of Normandy in France in 911 was the source of years of conflict between France and England. William the Conqueror, a Norman descendant of the Viking chieftain Rollo, led a Norman army to victory over the English and became king of England in 1066. England and France later fought for control of Normandy during the Hundred Years' War (1337-1453). See **William I, the Conqueror; Hundred Years' War.**

The Vikings had a lasting effect on Iceland, where they established a permanent settlement that reflects some elements of Viking culture to this day. Although

The Vikings sailed from Scandinavia in three main directions from the A.D. 700's to the 1000's. The Danes went south and raided Germany, France, England, Spain, and the Mediterranean coast. The Norwegians traveled to North America. The Swedes went to eastern Europe.

WORLD BOOK map

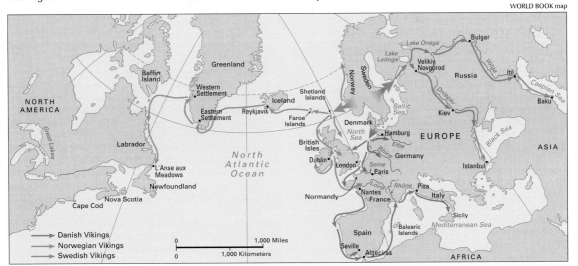

the Vikings established Vinland in North America, they did not influence later European exploration of the New World. Vinland remained unknown to the rest of Europe until long after the famous explorer Christopher Columbus gained credit as the European discoverer of America.   James A. Graham-Campbell

Related articles in *World Book* include:

Outline

I. **Viking life**
   A. Ancestry and
      population
   B. Economic activities
   C. Daily life
   D. Religion
   E. Cultural life and recreation
II. **Shipbuilding and navigation**
   A. The Vikings as shipbuilders
   B. The Vikings as navigators
III. **Warfare**
   A. Battle strategy and tactics
   B. Weapons and armor
IV. **Exploration and conquest**
   A. The Norwegian Vikings
   B. The Danish Vikings
   C. The Swedish Vikings
V. **Viking influence**

Questions

Why were Viking ships well suited to surprise raids?
What were the three classes of Viking society?
What was a *berserker?*
Why did the Vikings come to North America?
What was a *boat burial?*
What was the occupation of most Vikings?
How did the establishment of Normandy by the Vikings affect the history of France and England?
Why did the Vikings raid churches and monasteries?
Who were the four most important Viking gods?
What were some of the conditions that led to the Viking movement out of Scandinavia?

Additional resources

Level I
Berger, Melvin and Gilda. *The Real Vikings: Craftsmen, Traders, and Fearsome Raiders.* National Geographic Soc., 2003.
Gallagher, Jim. *Viking Explorers.* Chelsea Hse., 2001.
Hopkins, Andrea. *The Viking Library.* 6 vols. PowerKids Pr., 2002.
   Each volume focuses on an aspect of Viking life, such as their explorations, their way of farming, and their shipbuilding.

Level II
Graham-Campbell, James A. *The Viking World.* 3rd ed. Francis Lincoln, 2001.
Haywood, John. *Encyclopaedia of the Viking Age.* Thames & Hudson, 2000.
Konstam, Angus. *Historical Atlas of the Viking World.* Checkmark, 2002.

Villa, *VEE yah,* **Pancho,** *PAHN choh* (1878-1923), was a Mexican rebel general during the Mexican Revolution (1910-1920). He sought to control Mexico after the fall of President Porfírio Díaz in 1911. After the murder of President Francisco Madero in 1913, Victoriano Huerta became president. Villa supported him briefly. When Venustiano Carranza moved to gain control of Mexico in 1914, Villa attacked him. Álvaro Obregón, who supported Carranza, defeated Villa and helped Carranza be-

United Press Int.

Pancho Villa, *right,* and Álvaro Obregón are shown at a meeting near El Paso, Texas, in 1914. They later became enemies.

come acting chief of Mexico (see **Mexico** [The constitution of 1917]; **Obregón, Álvaro**).

The United States encouraged Villa at first, but President Woodrow Wilson turned to Carranza after Obregón defeated Villa at the Battle of Celaya in 1915. Villa retaliated against Americans in Mexico by stopping trains and shooting any Americans on board. In 1916, his troops raided Columbus, New Mexico. They burned the town and killed 18 people. President Wilson sent thousands of U.S. soldiers under the command of General John J. Pershing into Mexico in pursuit of Villa, but Pershing failed to capture him. All Mexicans, including President Carranza, resented Pershing's expedition. They considered it an attempt to intervene in Mexico's revolution. Wilson withdrew the expedition from Mexico in 1917 (see **Wilson, Woodrow** [Crisis in Mexico]).

Obregón drove Carranza from power in 1920 and pacified Villa by a grant of land. Villa was shot and killed from ambush by enemies on July 20, 1923. He was born Doroteo Arango in the Mexican state of Durango. He changed his name to Francisco Villa and was called Pancho Villa.   W. Dirk Raat

Villa-Lobos, *VEE lah LOH bohs,* **Heitor,** *AY tur* (1887-1959), was a Brazilian composer who played a crucial role in developing a Brazilian national style of music. Villa-Lobos composed nine *Bachianas Brasileiras* (1930-1944) that blend Brazilian folk tunes with the style of the German composer Johann Sebastian Bach. Villa-Lobos wrote 16 *Chôros* (1920-1928), primarily for large orchestra. These works were named for Brazilian bands of street musicians whose style was based on improvisation. Villa-Lobos also composed 12 symphonies and 16 string quartets, as well as ballets, operas, and oratorios.

Villa-Lobos was born in Rio de Janeiro on March 5, 1887. He died on Nov. 17, 1959.   Vincent McDermott

Village is any small group or community of houses and dwellings. It is often the trade and social center of a township. In local government, the term *village* refers to a community that the state has chartered as a municipality. Such a village is governed by a village president and a board of trustees. The village usually has its own clerk, treasurer, and police official. See also **Charter; Local government.**   Susan H. Ambler

Villein, *VIHL uhn,* was an agricultural worker whose status was between that of freedom and slavery during the Middle Ages in England. Villeins differed from slaves because villeins were not the property of a master. They differed from free people because they were bound to a plot of land that they did not own. In return for the use of this land and protection on it, villeins were required to render certain manual and other services to the lord of the manor. The children of villeins were born into the same bondage as their parents.

Lands held in villeinage often passed from father to son until the family acquired a right to them by *prescription* (long use). But the villein still had to serve a master. Villeinage began to decline in the 1100's, when villeins began to trade labor services for money. In time, villeins became free tenants who paid rent for land. By the 1500's, few were left in England.   Bryce Lyon

See also **Manorialism; Serf.**

Villella, *vihl EHL uh,* **Edward Joseph** (1936-   ), an American dancer, gained fame while performing with the New York City Ballet. Villella became known for his style of dancing called *bravura,* which means *brilliant* and *daring.* He also won recognition for his comic acting in such ballets as *Pulcinella.*

Villella was born on Oct. 1, 1936, in Bayside, New York, near Great Neck. He began training at the School of American Ballet when he was 10 years old and joined the New York City Ballet in 1957. During his years with that company, he won praise for his performance in the title role of *Prodigal Son.* He also created roles in *Tarantella, Harlequinade,* and *Dances at a Gathering.*

About 1979, Villella began to perform less, though he did not officially retire. Since then, he has served as artistic adviser to several regional ballet companies. In 1986, he became the founding artistic director of the Miami City Ballet in Florida.   Katy Matheson

Villiers, George. See Buckingham, Duke of.

Villiers de l'Isle-Adam, *vee lee AY duh LEEL ah DAH,* **Comte de** (1838-1889), a French writer, was a leading figure in the Symbolist movement. Villiers became known for his short stories. Collections include *Cruel Tales* (1883) and *New Cruel Tales* (1888). Many of the stories emphasize supernatural, Gothic, or fantastic elements. Often, it is unclear whether what a character sees is real or a hallucination.

In Villiers's novel *The Future Eve* (1885-1886), the main character is a fictionalized version of the American inventor Thomas A. Edison, whom the French greatly admired. In the novel, Edison creates a robot in the image of a beautiful woman who appears perfectly human. Villiers's use of existing technology and his anticipation of future inventions makes *The Future Eve* a pioneer work of science fiction. Villiers's other major work is the unfinished long poetic drama *Axël.* Villiers was born in St-Brieuc, France, on Nov. 7, 1838. He spent most of his life living in extreme poverty in Paris. He died there on Aug. 19, 1889.   Esther Rashkin

See also **Symbolism.**

Villon, *vee YAWN,* **François,** *frahn SWAH* (1431- ?), was a great French poet. His principal works are *Le Petit Testament* and *Grand Testament.* Villon's fast-moving verses bring to life a vivid and colorful description of the sights, sounds, and smells of Paris.

Villon ridiculed the great and the powerful. He poked fun at lawyers, churchmen, and merchants, and laughed at the tricks, shady dealings, and bawdy jokes of the sharpsters, thieves, prostitutes, and rowdy students who were his acquaintances. But Villon also wrote poetry of great tenderness, charm, and melancholy. He was sin-

cerely religious, and his deepest themes include brotherhood and love for humanity.

Villon was born in Paris and studied for the clergy at the University of Paris. But he became involved in murder, theft, and street brawls. He was sentenced to be hanged in 1463, but his sentence was reduced to banishment from Paris. Nothing is known of his life after this date.   Robert B. Griffin

Vilnius, *VIHL nee uhs* (pop. 542,287), is the capital and largest city of Lithuania. It lies in southeastern Lithuania, on the Neris (Vilija) River (see **Lithuania** [map]).

Vilnius is an important industrial, transportation, and cultural and educational center. Its products include chemicals, computers, food products, furniture, industrial machinery, and textiles. Railroads pass through the city, and an airport is nearby. The State University was founded in Vilnius in 1579.

Vilnius is best known for its many old churches and other buildings that date from between the 1400's and 1800's. The city also has many modern buildings that were built after World War II ended in 1945.

Vilnius was founded about 1323 by Lithuanian Grand Duke Gediminas. The city was controlled by Russia from 1795 to 1918. Lithuania became an independent nation in 1918, but Vilnius was controlled by Poland from 1920 to 1939. In 1939, the city was returned to Lithuania. In 1940, Lithuania was seized by the Soviet Union and forced to become part of that country. In 1991, Lithuania broke away from the Soviet Union and became an independent nation again.   Jaroslaw Bilocerkowycz

See also **Lithuania** (picture).

Vimy Ridge, *VIHM ee* or *VEE mee,* **Battle of,** was a World War I battle in which Canadian forces won an important victory over the Germans. In the battle, the Canadians captured Vimy Ridge, a strategically located hill near Arras, in northern France. The battle began April 9, 1917. The Canadian Corps was part of the British Army, and the battle was part of a British offensive. The British attacked Arras, while the Canadians attacked the ridge. The chief goal was to draw German troops away from Aisne, a town to the south that the French were to attack a week later. Another goal was to win Arras and Vimy Ridge. The Canadians took the ridge on April 14. Of the 100,000 Canadians who fought in the battle, 3,598 were killed and 7,004 wounded. The British offensive succeeded, but the French offensive failed. Nevertheless, Canadian possession of Vimy Ridge complicated German operations for the rest of the war.   Geoffrey Wawro

Viña del Mar, *VEEN yuh dehl MAHR* (pop. 286,931), is one of the largest cities in Chile and the country's leading seaside resort city. Viña del Mar lies on the Pacific coast, about 4 miles (6 kilometers) north of Valparaíso. For location, see **Chile** (political map). The city's mild climate, beaches, hotels, nightclubs, and race tracks make it one of the most popular vacation spots in South America. Viña del Mar has several food-processing plants. Oil refineries lie near the city.   Jerry R. Williams

Vincennes, *vihn SEHNZ* (pop. 18,701), was the first permanent settlement in what is now Indiana. The city lies along the Wabash River in southwestern Indiana (see **Indiana** [political map]). French settlers chose the site for a waterfront trading post in the early 1700's. In 1732, the French founded a permanent settlement there. The settlement was named after its founder, François

Marie Bissot, Sieur de Vincennes.

Today, Vincennes is a center for agriculture, industry, services, and tourism. The area's major crops include corn, soybeans, wheat, potatoes, melons, apples, and grapes. Its chief industries produce automobile frames, steel products, magnetic wire, glass products, and powdered milk. Coal is the area's leading mined product. Two major highways, two railroads, and the Wabash River link Vincennes with other cities in the Midwest and Southeast. Good Samaritan Hospital helps make Vincennes a regional medical center. The city is the home of Vincennes University, a community college founded in 1812. The city's newspaper, the *Vincennes Sun-Commercial,* began as the *Indiana Gazette* in 1804.

The city has many historical buildings and memorials. These include George Rogers Clark National Historical Park, which honors Clark's victories in the Revolutionary War in America (1775-1783). Also in the city are the Territorial Capitol, used by William Henry Harrison while he served as the first governor of the Indiana Territory; Grouseland, a mansion built by Harrison; and the Old Cathedral, Indiana's oldest Roman Catholic church, built in 1732.

The community established by the French settlers came under British control in 1763 as a result of the French and Indian War. The British built Fort Sackville at Vincennes in 1777, during the Revolutionary War. In 1778, Virginia troops and local French volunteers commanded by George Rogers Clark occupied Fort Sackville. The British recaptured the fort, but Clark attacked again and gained control of Vincennes in 1779. Clark's efforts in the West helped the United States win a huge area of land between the Appalachian Mountains and the Mississippi River called the Northwest Territory.

The Indiana Territory, established in 1800, was formed from part of the Northwest Territory. Vincennes served as its capital from 1800 to 1813. The city was incorporated in 1856. Vincennes is the seat of Knox County and has a mayor-council form of government.   Bruce Bigelow

Vincent de Paul, Saint (1581-1660), a Roman Catholic leader, founded two important religious orders. In 1633, he and Saint Louise de Marillac established the Daughters of Charity (now often called the Sisters of Charity), the largest Catholic order for women worldwide. Vincent de Paul founded the Congregation of the Mission for men in 1625. Its members are called *Lazarists* or *Vincentians.* The early Vincentians directed seminaries and organized conferences and retreats to train priests. They also traveled to villages as missionaries. Today, Vincentians staff many Catholic schools and universities.

Vincent de Paul was born on April 24, 1581, in southwestern France to peasant parents. He was ordained a priest in 1600 and served as pastor and chaplain in Paris and Lyon, where he organized help for the poor. The Saint Vincent de Paul Society was founded in Paris in 1833 to carry on his work for the poor. Today, there are society members in many countries. Members visit the poor and work to supply them with food, clothing, and other necessities. Saint Vincent de Paul died on Sept. 27, 1660. His feast day is September 27.   John Patrick Donnelly

Vincent's infection. See Trench mouth.

Vine usually means a plant that has a weak and flexible stem requiring some kind of support. Some vines can climb walls, trellises, or other plants. Other vines creep along the ground. Some vines have tendrils, which wind around their support. Other vines have disks that cling to the object they are climbing. There are two important kinds of vines—*woody vines,* also called *lianas,* and *herbaceous vines.* Grapes are woody vines. Sometimes the woody vine is fairly short and can support itself. Then it is somewhat like a shrub. It is often difficult to tell the difference between such a vine and a shrub. Common kinds of herbaceous vines include cucumbers, garden peas, and beans.   David S. Seigler

Related articles in *World Book* include:

Bean	Cranberry	Jicama	Pelican
Betel	Gourd	Liana	flower
Bignonia	Grape	Loosestrife	Philodendron
Bittersweet	Greenbrier	Moonflower	Smilax
Bramble	Honeysuckle	Morning-	Virginia
Chayote	Hop	glory	creeper
Clematis	Ivy	Pea	Wisteria
Cowpea			

Vinegar is a sour liquid used for seasoning and for preserving foods. The name *vinegar* comes from a French word meaning *sour wine.* But many kinds of vinegar are made from substances other than wine. Vinegar is produced by the action of yeast and bacteria on agricultural products, including fruits, grains, and such sugar solutions as honey and molasses. Different kinds of vinegar take their names from the material used. For example, wine vinegar comes from grapes, cider vinegar from apples, and malt vinegar from malted barley.

Making vinegar involves several steps. First, the raw material is made liquid and its sugar content is adjusted to the level desired by the producer. Fruits are crushed. Grains are soaked in water in a process called *malting,* which releases their sugars. Water is added to honey or molasses to *dilute* (weaken) the sugar concentration.

In the second step, the sugars in the liquid are turned into alcohol. This process is called *fermentation.* The liquid undergoes fermentation in a barrel or tank that air cannot enter. Yeast added to the liquid begins the fermentation process, which lasts two or three days.

In the third step, the alcohol is converted to *acetic acid* and water in a process called *acetification.* Acetic acid gives vinegar its sour taste and its preservative quality. Bacteria of a variety called *acetobacter* in combination with air causes acetification to occur. The speed of the acetification process depends largely on the rate at which the alcohol is exposed to air. The method of acetification used today allows the alcohol rapid exposure to the air and usually requires only one or two days. In this method, the alcohol trickles through a bed of wood shavings, corncobs, or other coarse material that has been packed into a vessel called a *generator.* Air pumped up from the bottom of the generator comes into contact with the liquid as it trickles through the bed. The liquid may flow through the generator several times before all the alcohol has turned into acid. After acetification, the vinegar is filtered to remove impurities. It is then pasteurized and bottled for sale.

In the traditional method of acetification, the alcohol partly filled an open vessel such as a barrel. Only the liquid's surface came into contact with the air. Acetification took weeks or months to complete by this method.

Uses of vinegar. Vinegar is sold for use both at home and by commercial food processors. It is used mainly as a flavoring agent, especially in salad dressings and sauces and on vegetables and meats. Vinegar is also used to preserve fruits, vegetables, and other foods in a process called *pickling* (see **Pickle**).

Kinds of vinegar. In the United States, vinegar sold for use at home typically contains from 4 to 5 percent acetic acid. Most vinegar used in commercial food processing contains from 12 to 20 percent acetic acid.

A kind of vinegar called *distilled alcoholic vinegar* or *spirit vinegar* is commonly used by commercial food processors. It is produced by boiling the fermented liquid and then condensing and collecting the vapor that forms. The distilled liquid can be shipped economically in a concentrated form to commercial users, who then acetify it. This kind of vinegar loses much of its flavor in the distilling process.   Henry P. Fleming

See also **Acetic acid; Cider; Fermentation.**

Vinegar eel is a tiny roundworm that lives in vinegar. Vinegar eels are usually found in barrels or jars of non-pasteurized cider vinegar. They feed on fruit pulp and the bacteria that produce the vinegar from the cider. Vinegar eels are harmless when swallowed. The vinegar eel is slender and threadlike and about 1/16 inch (1.6 millimeters) long. There are separate males and females. Most female vinegar eels live about 10 months and produce as many as 45 tiny larvae, which are about 1/100 inch (0.25 millimeter) long.   David F. Oetinger

Scientific classification. The vinegar eel belongs to the roundworm phylum, Nematoda. It is *Turbatrix aceti.*

See also **Roundworm.**

Vinland is the name early Scandinavian explorers gave to a region on the east coast of North America. Many historians believe that Norwegian Vikings visited this coastal area almost 500 years before Christopher Columbus sailed to America in 1492. Some historians believe Vinland was probably in the region of Cape Cod, Massachusetts. Other historians believe it was in what is now the Canadian province of Newfoundland and Labrador. In 1961, archaeologists found the remains of a Viking settlement at L'Anse aux Meadows, near St. Lunaire, Newfoundland and Labrador.

Early Norse *sagas* (stories of heroic deeds) tell of the explorers' voyages. Many historians do not consider these stories as completely reliable. These tales describe a fertile land with a mild climate. The Norsemen called the region *Vinland* (also spelled *Vineland* or *Wineland)* because of the grapes that grew there or because it was a fine land of meadows. The sagas tell that Leif Eriksson (also spelled *Ericson, Ericsson,* or *Eiriksson),* son of Erik the Red, wintered in Vinland about A.D. 1000. Historians believe the Norsemen had to abandon Vinland because they could not defend their settlements against Indians.   Barry M. Gough

Vinson, *VIHN suhn,* **Frederick Moore** (1890-1953), was chief justice of the United States from 1946 to 1953. He served as a Democratic member of the U.S. House of Representatives from Kentucky from 1923 to 1929, and again from 1931 to 1938. He then served until 1943 as a judge on the U.S. Court of Appeals for the District of Columbia. He became director of the Office of Economic Stabilization in 1943. He then served as federal loan administrator before becoming director of the Office of War Mobilization and Reconversion. President Harry S. Truman named him secretary of the treasury in 1945.

Vinson served as treasury secretary for about a year and had an important part in arranging financial settlements at the close of World War II.

Vinson was born on Jan. 22, 1890, in Louisa, Kentucky. He died on Sept. 8, 1953.   Bruce Allen Murphy

Vinyl. See Polyvinyl chloride.

Viol, *VY uhl,* is the name of a class of stringed instruments played with a bow. Viols were popular during the 1500's and 1600's. By about 1750, they had been largely replaced by other stringed instruments, including the viola and the cello. Interest in viol playing revived in the early 1900's as part of a renewed interest in early music.

Viols resemble instruments of the violin family. But unlike violins, viols have a flat back and sloping shoulders. Bows and the way in which a viol player holds the bow also differ. Most viols have six strings that are thinner than violin strings. Viols are made in several sizes, ranging from soprano—the smallest—to bass—the largest. Players hold smaller viols upright on the lap and larger ones between the knees.   André P. Larson

See also **Bass; Cello; Viola; Violin.**

Viola, *vee OH luh* or *vy OH luh,* is a stringed musical instrument that resembles a large violin. The viola serves as the tenor voice in the violin family, with the violins taking the higher parts and the cello and bass taking the lower parts. Like the other members of the violin

Northwestern University (WORLD BOOK photo by Ted Nielsen)

The viola looks like a large violin, and the musician holds and plays it like a violin. But the viola has a full, rich tone and a pitch lower than that of a violin.

family, the viola has four strings and is played with a bow. The instrument has a range of more than three octaves, and produces a distinctive rich, velvety sound.

The viola originated in the 1500's. Since the late 1700's, it has had a prominent role in symphonic music and chamber music. Composers such as Hector Berlioz, Richard Strauss, and Sir William Walton have written for the viola as a solo instrument.   Abram Loft

Violence. See Crime; Domestic violence; Revolution; Riot; Terrorism.

The **bird's-foot violet** gets its name from its leaves, which resemble birds' feet. This violet often bears purple flowers.

Violet is the common name of a group of flowering plants. Their blossoms are among the most attractive of all flowers. Violets grow throughout most of the world. They bloom in groups in early spring. Their leaves partly conceal the five-petaled flowers. Each flower grows on a slender stalk. There are more than 500 species. About 100 of these grow in the United States. Some varieties bear white and yellow flowers, but the blue and purple violets are world favorites.

Northwestern University (WORLD BOOK photos by Ted Nielsen)

To play the violin properly, tuck the instrument under your chin and rest it on your shoulder. Keep your chin in a straight line with the scroll. Keep your left elbow in close to the body. Cup your fingers over the strings, and place the thumb against the side of the finger board.

Purple violets include the common *meadow,* or *hooded, violet,* and the *bird's-foot violet,* whose blue and purple flowers often bloom twice a year, in spring and summer. The bird's-foot violet received its name because its leaves are shaped like birds' feet.

The *dog violet* is so called by the English because it lacks fragrance. The word *dog* is a term of contempt. It is quite different from *dogtooth violet,* a member of the lily family. The pansy is a cultivated kind of violet.

The violet was adopted as state flower by Illinois, New Jersey, Rhode Island, and Wisconsin. The violet is also the flower for the month of March.   James S. Miller

Scientific classification. Violets belong to the violet family, Violaceae. They are in the genus *Viola.* The blue violet is *Viola sororia;* the bird's-foot, *V. pedata;* the dog, *V. canina.* The wild form of the cultivated pansy is *V. tricolor.*

See also **Flower** (picture: Garden perennials); **Pansy.**

Violin is a stringed instrument that is played with a bow. It is probably the best known and most widely used of all orchestral instruments. Some of the greatest music in the world owes much of its beauty to the violin. Such music may be the sound of a mighty orchestra, with dozens of violins playing together. Or it may be the music produced by one great master playing alone on a violin to a hushed audience.

Several other instruments are similar to the violin in construction and in method of playing. These include the cello and viola. They are considered members of the *violin family.*

Parts of a violin

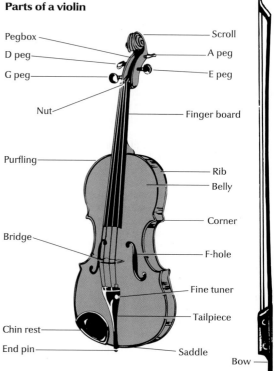

WORLD BOOK illustration

Music for the violin covers a wide range. Some composers, such as Johann Sebastian Bach, Eugene Ysäye, and Béla Bartók, have written music for the violin alone. Many composers have written pieces for the violin with piano or orchestral accompaniment. The violin also has an important role as part of a group of instruments, as in an orchestra or in a string quartet.

Parts of the violin. A violin is a special kind of box that *amplifies* (makes louder) the sound of the strings stretched across it. If you stretch a piece of string tightly and then pluck it, you will hear a faint note. If you stretch it across a wooden box, you will hear a much louder note. A violin maker uses soft pine or spruce for the *belly* (front) of the violin, and maple or sycamore for the *back* and the *ribs* (sides). The *head* (scroll and pegbox) and *neck* are made of maple. The graceful shapes of the back and belly are carved out of solid pieces of wood. The violin maker cuts two *f-holes* in the belly to allow the sound to escape, and makes the *finger board* and the *tailpiece* (string-holder) of ebony. Ebony is a hard wood that will be long lasting. The violin maker glues the violin parts together, using no nails or screws.

The violin has four *strings,* which are tuned in the interval of a fifth from each other. The first (*E*) string is generally made of steel. The second (10*A*) string and the third (*D*) string are sometimes made of plain *catgut,* a material made from the intestines of sheep. But most players prefer to use *A* or *D* strings made of a thinner gut overwound with fine aluminum wire. Synthetic materials such as nylon are also used. The fourth (*G*) string is generally made of gut covered with silver or copper wire. The strings are attached to pegs set in the head. The player tightens the strings with these pegs to tune them to the correct notes.

There are two other important parts of the violin that are not permanently glued to the body. The *bridge* stands on the belly, midway between the two *f*-holes. It supports the strings. A pattern of holes is cut into the bridge to give it greater flexibility. The *sound-post,* a thin rod of pine, is wedged between the back and the belly underneath the bridge, inside the violin. The sound-post conducts the sound from the front to the back of the violin. It also supports the belly against the pressure of the strings. The sound-post is slightly behind one foot of the bridge. The *bass-bar,* a bar of pine that is glued on the underside of the belly, gives further support for the belly. It runs lengthwise underneath the other foot of the bridge.

The bow is a curved, springy stick about 27 inches (69 centimeters) long that has a flat ribbon of hair attached to it. This ribbon consists of more than 150 horsehairs. The hair is attached to the point of the bow and to a sliding wood block called a *frog* or *nut* at the other end, near the point at which the violinist holds the bow. By turning a screw set into the end of the bow, the player can move the frog back and forth to tighten the hair against the spring of the bow. The bow is made of *Pernambuco wood,* a light, springy wood from a tree that grows in Brazil.

Playing the violin. The player tucks the end of the violin between the chin and the left shoulder. To obtain a good grip, the player uses a *chin-rest* clamped to the top of the violin, and a *shoulder-rest* or a *pad* between the back of the violin and the shoulder. The violin should be supported entirely without the aid of the player's left hand. The bow is held in the player's right hand.

The player makes the strings of the violin vibrate by drawing the hair of the bow across them. Each of the separate strands of hair on the bow is rough, with minute projections. These projections make the strings vibrate as the bow slides over them. The player can vary the loudness of the tone and get other special effects by the way in which the bow is drawn across the strings. The player can also pluck the strings with the fingers, a

Historic violins

The first reference to stringed instruments appears in Persian and Chinese writings from the 800's. Developments over the next 800 years led to the superb violins of Stradivari.

WORLD BOOK illustrations by Oxford Illustrators Limited

The kemantche, an ancient Persian instrument, consisted of a stick extending through half of a coconut.

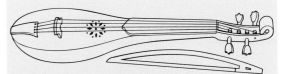

The European rebec was popular in medieval times. It resembled a long, slender pear.

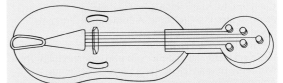

The vielle ranked as the most important stringed instrument in the 1100's and 1200's. It had five strings.

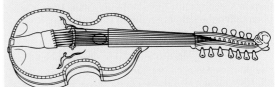

The viola d'amore was held and played like the violin of today. It was used in Europe in the 1500's and 1600's.

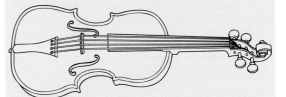

Violins made by Antonio Stradivari in the late 1600's and early 1700's are famous for their tone and power.

form of violin playing that is known as *pizzicato*.

Violinists practice for years to perfect their skills, but little strength is required to play the violin well. In fact, improvement is usually the result of using less tension in the hands, arms, and body. The finest violinists make playing look easy, with a minimum of muscle activity.

The strings of the violin give the player four notes. To obtain other notes, the player shortens the vibrating length of the strings by pressing them down on the finger board with the fingers of the left hand. Flutelike tones called *harmonics* can be produced by touching the strings lightly in certain places.

History. Musicians have used many kinds of stringed instruments, such as harps and lyres, for thousands of years. But no one knows when players began to use bows, instead of just plucking the strings. Chinese players used bowed instruments in the A.D. 900's. A hundred years later, musicians used forms of bowed instruments in many countries of Asia, Europe, and northern Africa. In the 1400's, players started using bows to play instruments of the guitar family. These bowed guitars developed into the instruments called viols.

Violins date from the 1500's. They were developed from the early bowed instruments. For many years, viols and violins developed side by side, each influencing the other. But by the late 1600's, most musicians favored the violin family, and the viols dropped out of use.

The little Italian town of Cremona became the most important center of violin making. Members of the Amati family made fine instruments there in the late 1500's and early 1600's. In the 1600's, Antonio Stradivari, a pupil of the Amatis, perfected the design of the violin and produced some of the finest violins ever made. Another great family was that of Guarneri. The violins of Giuseppe Guarneri, known as Guarneri del Gesù, rival those of Stradivari for tone. A Frenchman, François Tourte, perfected the bow in the late 1700's.

From the 1600's to the early 1800's, many outstanding violinists were also the main composers for violin. Their works led to developments in playing technique. Among the most important of these composers were Arcangelo Corelli, Niccolò Paganini, Giuseppe Tartini, and Giovanni Viotti and Antonio Vivaldi of Italy and Rodolphe Kreutzer and Pierre Rode of France. Viotti has been called the father of modern violin playing. He greatly improved and extended the use of the violin bow.

There is much interest today in performing violin music composed in the 1700's on instruments of that period. Their thinner wood, the lighter bows, and the gut strings then widely used result in a more gentle sound, especially when accompanied by a harpsichord rather than a modern piano. In the 1900's the violin also became a significant instrument in nonclassical music. For example, it is a major solo instrument in country music, where it is often called a *fiddle*. There have also been a number of skillful violinists in jazz.   Stephen Clapp

Related articles in *World Book* include:

Violinists

Corelli, Arcangelo	Oistrakh, David	Tartini, Giuseppe
Heifetz, Jascha	Paganini, Niccolò	Vivaldi, Antonio
Kreisler, Fritz	Perlman, Itzhak	Zukerman,
Menuhin, Yehudi	Stern, Isaac	Pinchas
Milstein, Nathan		

Other related articles

Amati family	Music (Stringed	Suzuki method
Bass	instruments)	Viol
Cello	Stradivari, Antonio	Viola
Guarneri		

Additional resources

Bacon, Tony, ed. *The Violin Book.* Backbeat Bks., 1999.
Kolneder, Walter. *The Amadeus Book of the Violin.* Amadeus Pr., 1998.
Roth, Henry. *Violin Virtuosos: From Paganini to the 21st Century.* Calif. Classics, 1997.
Scott, Heather K., ed. *Violin Owner's Manual.* String Letter, 2001.

Violoncello. See Cello.

Viper is any of a large group of poisonous snakes that have a pair of long, hollow fangs in the upper jaw. Many vipers possess a deep hollow in the side of the head, a little lower than the eye and in front of it. Snakes with this hollow, or pit, are called *pit vipers.* Those without the pit are known as *true vipers.*

True vipers live in Africa, Europe, and Asia. Pit vipers live in North and South America, Asia, and Europe east of the lower Volga River. Of the approximately 230 *species* (kinds) of vipers, more than half have pits. Most vipers live in dry places, including deserts.

Vipers have a head much broader than the neck, and eyes with catlike pupils. Many other snakes, however, also possess these features, and vipers cannot be recognized clearly by the shape of the head and pupils. A majority of vipers have thick bodies and rather short tails.

A viper's poison is formed in special glands. The hollow fangs inject the poison into an animal's body the way a hypodermic needle injects liquid. Vipers use their poison to kill prey and to defend themselves. All vipers can be dangerous to people, but many of the small kinds rarely, if ever, kill anyone with their bite. Certain kinds of large vipers are so harmless that they will not bite unless someone teases or annoys them.

WORLD BOOK illustration by Richard Lewington, The Garden Studio
A viper is a poisonous snake with two long, movable fangs. Russell's viper, *shown here,* lives in southern and southeastern Asia.

A pit viper's facial pit is a sense organ that is highly sensitive to heat. It helps the pit viper to locate its warm-blooded prey. Vipers eat mostly small mammals, but they also will feed on small birds and lizards. After biting their prey and injecting venom, vipers let the prey go and track it down later to eat it.

Familiar North and South American pit vipers include *rattlesnakes* and *bushmasters,* and the *water moccasin, copperhead,* and *fer-de-lance.* Bushmasters and the fer-de-lance live only in tropical climates. All these snakes bear their young alive except the bushmasters, which lay eggs.

The *common viper,* or *adder,* is the only poisonous reptile of the United Kingdom. Other familiar true vipers include the *Gaboon viper* and *puff adder* of Africa, and *Russell's viper* of southern and southeastern Asia. Most true vipers bear their young alive.   Albert F. Bennett

Scientific classification. Vipers make up the viper family, Viperidae. True vipers belong to the subfamily Viperinae. The common European viper, or adder, is *Vipera berus.* Other true vipers include the Gaboon viper, *Bitis gabonica;* the puff adder, *B. arietans;* and Russell's viper, *Daboia russellii.* Pit vipers belong to the subfamily Crotalinae. They include the rattlesnakes, which are genera *Crotalus* and *Sistrurus;* the bushmasters, genus *Lachesis;* the copperhead, *Agkistrodon contortrix;* the water moccasin, *A. piscivorus;* and the fer-de-lance, *Bothrops atrox.*

Related articles in *World Book* include:

Adder	Fer-de-lance	Snake
Bushmaster	Rattlesnake	Water moccasin
Copperhead		

Viper's bugloss, BYOO glahs, also known as *blue thistle,* is a plant with a spotted stem and showy blue flowers. The Viper's bugloss is a *biennial,* which means that seeds planted one year will not produce flowers until the next year. The flowers of the Viper's bugloss are reddish when they are budding but turn blue when they open. Viper's bugloss grows widely in the dry pastures of the eastern United States. People once thought that viper's bugloss cured viper bites.   Peter H. Raven

Scientific classification. Viper's bugloss belongs to the borage family, Boraginaceae. It is classified as *Echium vulgare.*

Virchow, FIHR koh, **Rudolf** (1821-1902), was a prominent German physician, scientist, and statesman. He helped develop *pathology* (the study of diseased body tissue). Virchow believed that the cell is the basic unit of human life and that disease results from disturbances in the function of cells. He showed that the effects of disease could be detected by observing cells through a microscope. Virchow described his findings in his book *Cellular Pathology* (1858).

Virchow believed that some diseases were caused by bad living conditions, and he devoted his political career to promoting social reform and public health. He participated in the Revolution of 1848, a series of European uprisings for greater political freedom. In 1859, Virchow was elected to the Berlin City Council, where he argued that every citizen had a constitutional right to health. In 1861, Virchow was elected to the Prussian National Assembly. From 1871 to 1893, he served in the Reichstag (parliament) of Germany. Virchow was born on Oct. 13, 1821, in Schivelbein (now Świdwin, Poland). He died on Sept. 5, 1902.   Matthew Ramsey

Vireo, VIHR ee oh, is the name of a group of small birds found in forests and thickets of the Americas. Vireos are greenish or grayish above and white or yellow

WORLD BOOK illustration by Trevor Boyer, Linden Artists Ltd.
The yellow-throated vireo has bright yellow underparts.

below. Most live in tropical regions. But several species nest in the United States and Canada.

The most familiar vireo in eastern North America is the *red-eyed vireo.* The bird's red eyes can only be seen when it is close. People can recognize this vireo by the white stripe bordered by black above the eyes. The bird's song sounds conversational. It is also called *preacher bird* because it repeats its song continually during the spring and summer. The *yellow-throated vireo* has bright yellow underparts. In summer, this bird migrates from tropical regions to the eastern half of the United States and Canada.

Vireos build cup-shaped nests that hang from forked branches in the trees. The female vireo lays two to four white eggs, which are marked with dark specks near the large end. Vireos eat mainly insects.   David M. Niles

Scientific classification. Vireos make up the subfamily Vireoninae of the vireo family, Vireonidae. The red-eyed vireo is *Vireo olivaceus,* and the yellow-throated vireo is *V. flavifrons.*

Virgil (70-19 B.C.), also spelled *Vergil,* was the greatest poet of ancient Rome and one of the outstanding poets in world literature. His masterpiece was the *Aeneid,* the national epic of Rome.

His life. Virgil was born on Oct. 15, 70 B.C., in Andes, a tiny village near Mantua in northern Italy. His full name was Publius Vergilius Maro. Virgil attended school in Cremona and Milan and then studied rhetoric in Rome and philosophy in Naples. He prepared for a career as a lawyer, but he was too shy and preferred the private life of a poet. His first poems won him the patronage of Maecenas, a wealthy lover of the arts and political adviser to the future Emperor Augustus. Maecenas gave Virgil a house near Naples and encouraged him to write poems about Italy and its history.

Virgil died on Sept. 21, 19 B.C., before he could finish the *Aeneid.* He left instructions to destroy it because he did not think it was good enough. But Augustus refused to permit the poem's destruction and appointed two of Virgil's friends to prepare the epic for publication.

His works. The first poems definitely attributed to Virgil are the *Eclogues,* or *Bucolics,* composed between 42 and 35 B.C. These 10 poems are *pastorals*—that is, they portray scenes from the lives of shepherds. In writing the *Eclogues,* Virgil imitated the Greek pastoral poems of Theocritus, but Virgil adapted their settings and themes to the Italian countryside. The fourth eclogue prophesies the birth of a wonderful child who will bring in a new age. After Rome became Christian under the emperor Constantine the Great in the early A.D. 300's, many people thought the prophecy referred to the birth of Jesus.

Virgil spent about seven years writing the *Georgics,* a poem in four books, which was published in 29 B.C. On one level, the *Georgics* is a poem of advice to farmers. The first book deals with crops, the second with vines and olive trees, the third with breeding cattle and horses, and the fourth with keeping bees. But the *Georgics* goes beyond practical instruction to show the origin of civilization in the endless work of farming and to celebrate the beauty of Italy and its country life. The books on animals suggest the weaknesses and strengths of human beings and their sufferings in love, war, and sickness. Similarly, the world of the beehive is a model for the life of a human city under its ruler.

For the story of the *Aeneid,* Virgil used many sources. The most important were the *Iliad* and the *Odyssey,* the two great Greek epics attributed to Homer. Virgil based the first six books of the *Aeneid* on the *Odyssey* and the last six on the *Iliad.* The *Aeneid* describes the adventures of Aeneas, the legendary Trojan hero who survived the fall of Troy to the Greeks. Aeneas sailed westward to Italy. There he formed a new nation where his descendants founded the city of Rome. The poem, however, is not just the story of Aeneas. It also shows Rome as the fulfillment of a divine plan and mentions the greatest achievements of Roman history up to Virgil's time.

Virgil treats Aeneas as the ancestor of Augustus. He showed that just as the gods appointed Aeneas to create the people of Rome, so they appointed his descendant Augustus to save Rome and re-create the city after the Roman civil wars of the 40's and 30's B.C. In this way, Virgil glorified both Augustus and his country, but also reminded Romans that power must be used to benefit others and to bring peace to the world.

His influence. Roman schools began to use Virgil's works as textbooks soon after his death. Copies of the *Aeneid* were kept in Roman temples, and people practiced prophecy by opening the poem at random and interpreting the first words that they saw. Later, Christian writers used verses from Virgil's poems to express Christian beliefs. During the Middle Ages (from about the A.D. 400's through the 1400's), people thought of Virgil as a prophet who had foreseen the coming of Jesus. Some believed Virgil had been a sorcerer.

The Italian poet Dante Alighieri based his great epic *The Divine Comedy* (1321) on the sixth book of the *Aeneid.* In Dante's poem, it is Virgil who guides the poet on his journey through hell and Purgatory.

During the Renaissance, Virgil's *Eclogues* influenced the pastoral poetry of such writers as Petrarch in Italy, Joachim du Bellay in France, and Sir Philip Sidney in England. In the 1500's and 1600's, English writers regarded Virgil as the ideal poet. The poet John Milton imitated Virgil in his own works, especially *Paradise Lost* (1667). The poet John Dryden translated the *Aeneid* into English verse in the late 1600's. Virgil also influenced many poets of the 1800's, including William Wordsworth and Lord Tennyson. In the 1900's, the poet T. S. Eliot admired and imitated Virgil's poetry, and there are fine modern translations of the *Aeneid* by American and British poets.   Elaine Fantham

See also **Aeneid; Latin literature** (The Augustan Age).

Virgin Islands are an island group in the West Indies, about 40 miles (64 kilometers) east of Puerto Rico. They form the western end of the Lesser Antilles island chain. The islands are divided into two political units, each with territorial status. The British Virgin Islands are a territory of the United Kingdom. The rest of the islands comprise the United States Virgin Islands. The Virgin Islands have a total land area of about 190 square miles (490 square kilometers). The North Atlantic Ocean lies to the north of the islands, and the Caribbean Sea lies to the south.

The main populated islands in the British territory are Jost Van Dyke, Tortola, and Virgin Gorda. The chief islands of the U.S. territory are St. Croix, St. John, and St. Thomas. The Virgin Islands group also has many islets and reefs, most of which are uninhabited.

About 132,000 people live on the Virgin Islands. A large majority of the population is of African descent. English and Spanish are the main languages spoken. Tourism is a major source of employment for islanders. Other important economic activities include manufacturing and financial services.

The Virgin Islands have a mild, subtropical climate. Temperatures range from about 70 to 90 °F (20 to 32 °C). The islands receive from 40 to 60 inches (100 to 150 centimeters) of rainfall annually. Many of the islands are rugged and hilly. Mount Sage, on Tortola, is the highest point, at 1,709 feet (521 meters).

Virgin Islands

Boundary
Road
Capital
Town
Elevation above sea level

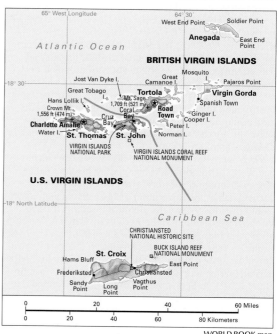

WORLD BOOK map

Fossils show that the ocean once covered the Virgin Islands. The composition of the rocks that form much of the land is evidence that volcanoes pushed the islands up from the ocean floor.

Arawak, Carib, and Ciboney Indians lived on the Virgin Islands before Europeans settled there. In 1493, Christopher Columbus, an Italian navigator employed by Spain, sighted the islands and claimed them for Spain. But Spain did not settle the islands. Beginning in the 1600's, Denmark, the Dutch Republic (now the Netherlands), England (now part of the United Kingdom), and France established settlements. England annexed the British Virgin Islands in 1672, and the United States took control of the U.S. Virgin Islands from Denmark in 1917.

Kathryn R. Dungy

See also **Virgin Islands, British; Virgin Islands, United States.**

Virgin Islands, British, are an overseas territory of the United Kingdom in the West Indies. They lie near the western end of the Lesser Antilles island group. A channel called *the Narrows* separates them from the United States Virgin Islands (see **Virgin Islands** [map]). The territory has a land area of 59 square miles (153 square kilometers). It consists of 16 inhabited islands and more than 40 uninhabited islands and *cays* (reefs). The largest populated islands are Anegada, Jost Van Dyke, Tortola, and Virgin Gorda. Road Town (pop. 9,400), on Tortola, is the capital.

The islands have a subtropical climate. Trade winds blow for most of the year. Temperatures range from 70 to 90 °F (21 to 32 °C). The islands receive about 59 inches (130 centimeters) of rainfall annually. Mount Sage, on Tortola, is the islands' highest point. It rises 1,709 feet (521 meters).

About 24,000 people live on the islands. Over 80 percent are of African descent. The rest are of Asian, European, or mixed ancestry. English is the official language.

Tourism generates nearly half the territory's income. Other major economic activities on the British Virgin Islands include construction, light industry, financial services, and the distillation of rum.

The Dutch settled on Tortola, in what are now called the British Virgin Islands, in 1648. England annexed the islands in 1672.   Kathryn R. Dungy

See also **British West Indies; West Indies.**

Virgin Islands, United States, are a group of small islands east of Puerto Rico and west of the British Virgin Islands. They lie south of the Atlantic Ocean and north of the Caribbean Sea. St. Croix, St. John, and St. Thomas islands, as well as many nearby islets, make up the U.S. Virgin Islands. They are a territory of the United States and the easternmost U.S. possession.

The U.S. Virgin Islands have a mild, subtropical climate, and tourism dominates their economy. A few good harbors make the territory an important center of trade. Refined petroleum products are the islands' chief exports. Except for St. Croix, the Virgin Islands are rugged and hilly. Agriculture is limited, and the islanders must import much of their food.

Virgin Islanders are mainly of African descent. Many are descendants of slaves who worked on plantations in colonial times. About half the people are native-born. Immigrants include other West Indians, Americans from the continental United States, and Puerto Ricans.

Facts in brief on the U.S. Virgin Islands

Capital: Charlotte Amalie (since 1917).
Government: *U.S. Congress*—one delegate in the House of Representatives who votes only in committees. *Territorial legislature*—a one-house legislature of 15 senators.
Area: 134 mi² (347 km²). *Coastline*—117 mi (188 km).
Elevation: *Highest*—Crown Mountain on St. Thomas, 1,556 ft (474 m) above sea level; *Lowest*—sea level along the coasts.
Population: *Estimated 2008 population*—108,000; density, 806 per mi² (311 per km²); distribution (2000 census), 93 percent urban, 7 percent rural. *2000 census*—108,612.
Chief products: *Agriculture*—beef cattle, chickens, eggs, fruits, goats, hogs, milk, nuts, vegetables. *Manufacturing*—alumina, concrete products, electronics, petroleum products, pharmaceuticals, rum, textiles, and watches.

The Italian explorer Christopher Columbus sighted the islands in 1493. Their fresh beauty and untouched appearance charmed him. Columbus named them the Virgin Islands in honor of Saint Ursula, a British Christian of the A.D. 300's or 400's. According to legend, an Asian people called the Huns, because they opposed Christianity, killed Ursula and 11,000 other young women traveling with her. Columbus claimed the islands for Spain, but the Spanish did not settle there. About 1672, Denmark established a permanent settlement on St. Thomas. The Danes took possession of St. John in 1717 and bought St. Croix from France in 1733. Danish colonists developed a profitable sugar industry that supported the islands' growth. In 1917, the United States purchased the islands from Denmark. Today, they are a popular travel destination.

Government

The Virgin Islands are an *unincorporated territory* of the United States—that is, an area under U.S. jurisdiction where Congress has determined that not all provisions of the U.S. Constitution apply. For example, Virgin Islanders are U.S. citizens, but they may not vote in U.S. presidential elections.

The Revised Organic Act of the Virgin Islands, passed by the U.S. Congress in 1954, provides for the government of the territory. The president of the United States serves as chief of state of the Virgin Islands. A governor and lieutenant governor elected by Virgin Islanders for four-year terms head the local government. They may serve up to two consecutive terms.

The territory has a *unicameral* (one-house) legislature, which consists of a 15-member Senate. The people elect

The territorial flag and seal. The flag, adopted in 1917, features a modified version of the Great Seal of the United States. The islands' seal, adopted in 1991, shows the yellow breast, the official bird, on a branch of the yellow cedar, the official tree.

The city of Charlotte Amalie, on St. Thomas, is the capital of the U.S. Virgin Islands. Ocean liners, like the one shown in the distance, transport thousands of tourists to the islands each year.

the senators to two-year terms. The governor may veto any bills. The governor can also apply a *line-item veto* on funding measures, rejecting individual items in a bill without vetoing the whole bill. A two-thirds majority of the Senate may override either type of veto. The Senate meets at Charlotte Amalie, the territorial capital. The islands have three major political parties—the Democratic Party, the Independent Citizens Movement, and the Republican Party.

The U.S. Federal District Court of the Virgin Islands hears federal cases. The president of the United States appoints its judges with the advice and consent of the U.S. Senate. The Superior Court of the Virgin Islands handles local affairs. The Supreme Court of the Virgin Islands hears appeals of decisions made by the Superior Court. The governor appoints judges to both the Superior Court and the Supreme Court.

All residents who are 18 years of age or older and are U.S. citizens may vote in local elections. The residents elect a delegate to the U.S. House of Representatives for a two-year term. The delegate has voting powers only in House committees, not in the full House.

People

Population and ancestry. About 75 percent of Virgin Islanders are black people of African descent, and nearly 15 percent are white. The rest are of mixed ances-

try or belong to other population groups. Nearly half of all islanders were born in the Virgin Islands. Most other residents moved to the islands from other West Indian islands, including Puerto Rico, and the continental United States.

The official language is English. On St. Croix, many people speak Spanish. Some people also speak Creole, a dialect that combines West African grammar and speech patterns with colonial Danish, Dutch, English, and French.

Religion. A majority of Virgin Islanders are Protestants, especially Baptists. About one-third of the people, many of whom are immigrants from the Dominican Republic and Puerto Rico, are Roman Catholics. Some islanders also practice *obeah,* a traditional African religion with elements of sorcery and witchcraft.

Food. Cooking in the Virgin Islands reflects a mixture of African, Asian, European, and *indigenous* (native) influences. Virgin Islanders eat many soups and stews, including *callaloo* (also spelled *kallaloo),* a soup made with the leaves of the taro plant. Many meats are barbecued with tangy spices or made into a spicy stew called *curry.* Islanders eat a variety of local fish as well. *Johnnycakes* are a popular traditional type of deep-fried bread. Root vegetables provide much of the starch in islanders' diets, as does *fungi* (pronounced *FOON gee),* a dish made from cooked cornmeal.

Virgin Islanders shop at a local produce market. About three-fourths of the people are of African descent. Nearly half the population was born on the islands. Other residents are immigrants who moved to the Virgin Islands from other West Indian islands and the U.S. mainland.

Clothing and architecture. Virgin Islanders wear clothing much like that worn elsewhere in North and South America. In general, they dress modestly when out in public.

The cities of Charlotte Amalie and Christiansted have many examples of traditional West Indian architecture from the 1700's. Many houses there are two or three stories tall and have exterior staircases, window shutters, and low roofs with sloping ends and sides. The houses are built of brick, *rubble* (coarse pieces of stone and coral), and wood, and often have pastel exteriors. The city of Frederiksted has many Victorian-style buildings from the 1800's.

Education. The Virgin Islands' public school system provides free education from kindergarten through high school. A commissioner of education and a nine-member board of education supervise the system. Board members are elected to four-year terms. Children must start kindergarten during the year when they turn 5 and attend school until the end of the school year closest to their 16th birthday. The University of the Virgin Islands is the only accredited institution of higher education in the islands. It has campuses on St. Thomas and St. Croix.

Land and climate

Location. The United States Virgin Islands lie about 40 miles (64 kilometers) east of Puerto Rico, just west of the British Virgin Islands. The island group forms the westernmost part of a chain of West Indian islands called the Lesser Antilles. Miami, Florida, lies about 1,100 miles (1,770 kilometers) to the northwest, and Panama is about 1,200 miles (1,930 kilometers) to the southwest. The U.S. Virgin Islands have a general coastline of 117 miles (188 kilometers) and a *tidal shoreline,* including bays, creeks, offshore islands, rivers, and sounds, of 175 miles (282 kilometers).

Islands. All of the U.S. Virgin Islands except St. Croix are rugged and hilly. St. Croix has less mountainous terrain. The islands have many bays and inlets that shelter a variety of animal and plant life. Tropical flowers and trees flourish, including bougainvillea, poinciana (also known as flame trees), and hibiscus. Fossils of ancient animals show that the sea once covered the islands. The composition of the rocks that form much of the land suggests that volcanoes pushed the islands up from the ocean floor. Only St. Croix, St. John, St. Thomas, and Water Island have permanent populations.

St. Croix—pronounced *saynt kroy*—(pop. 53,234) is the largest of the islands. It lies about 40 miles (64 kilometers) south of St. Thomas. St. Croix covers 82 square miles (212 square kilometers) and makes up about two-thirds of the island group's land mass. Christiansted (pop. 2,637) is St. Croix's local government center. Frederiksted (pop. 732) is a center for trade. People also live in small towns and on estates throughout the island.

St. John (pop. 4,197) lies 2 miles (3 kilometers) east of St. Thomas and less than 1 mile (1.6 kilometers) from British Tortola. It covers 19 square miles (49 square kilometers). The Virgin Islands National Park takes up about two-thirds of the island. The majority of islanders live in the Cruz Bay community. There is also a large tourist development at Caneel Bay. Many islanders live on small plots of land and raise their own produce and poultry.

St. Thomas (pop. 51,181) covers 27 square miles (70

square kilometers). Its central range of hills offers lovely ocean views. Crown Mountain, the islands' highest point, rises 1,556 feet (474 meters) above sea level. Charlotte Amalie (pop. 11,004), the territorial capital, is the largest town in the Virgin Islands. Its excellent harbor makes it the islands' chief center of trade. The harbor is also a popular destination for cruise ships.

Water Island (pop. 161) covers less than 1 square mile (2.6 square kilometers). It lies southwest of Hassel Island, at the outer edge of St. Thomas Harbor. During World War II (1939-1945), the U.S. government began construction of fortifications, including underground bunkers, on the island. For several years after the war, the United States used Water Island to test chemical weapons. Today, most buildings on the island are private homes.

Climate. The Virgin Islands have a delightful subtropical climate all year long. Steady breezes called *trade winds* blow most of the year, and there are no extremes of heat or cold. The temperature ranges from 70 to 90 °F (21 to 32 °C) and averages 80 °F (27 °C). The islands receive from 40 to 60 inches (100 to 150 centimeters) of rainfall a year. The amount of rainfall varies widely from island to island, and higher elevations may get from 50 to 60 inches (130 to 150 centimeters) a year. The heaviest showers generally occur from September to November.

Economy

Services, mainly those related to tourism, employ a large majority of the Virgin Islands' work force. Construction and manufacturing are other important sectors of the economy. International business and financial services are a growing economic activity. The islands are not suited to large-scale farming, and islanders must import most of their food. The United States and Puerto Rico are the islands' chief trading partners.

Tourism is the U.S. Virgin Islands' chief industry. It accounts for about 70 percent of the islands' *gross domestic product*—that is, the total value of goods and services produced in the islands in one year. Hundreds of thousands of tourists visit the islands annually to enjoy the pleasant climate, excellent beaches, and lovely scenery. Historic buildings and plantations, the Virgin Islands National Park, and coral reefs attract many visitors. A carnival held every spring on St. Thomas is a popular event.

Manufacturing. St. Croix has a large petroleum refinery, and refined petroleum products are a chief export. Factories on the islands produce electronics, *pharmaceuticals* (medicinal drugs), watches, and textiles. The distillation of rum, made from sugar cane, is one of the Virgin Islands' oldest industries.

Agriculture and mining. Less than 1 percent of Virgin Islanders are farmers. Farm products include vegetables, tropical fruits, eggs, and nuts. Farmers also cultivate grain sorghum to feed livestock. Beef cattle and dairy herds produce some revenue. Islanders also raise chickens, goats, sheep, and pigs. Basalt, used in road building or in the manufacture of concrete, and bauxite, used to make aluminum, are the islands' chief minerals.

Transportation. Airlines carry people from all over the world to the U.S. Virgin Islands. Airports on St. Croix and St. Thomas handle commercial flights. Small planes and ferries carry people from one island to another. Over 1,000 cruise ships, freighters, and naval vessels dock at the territory's ports each year. All the inhabited

© Steve Simonsen

Traditional West Indian architecture can be seen in Charlotte Amalie, *shown,* and Christiansted. Multistory buildings with window shutters, pastel exteriors, and low, sloping roofs are typical.

islands have paved roads. As in many other West Indian islands, motorists drive on the left side of the road.

Communication. Newspapers published in the Virgin Islands include *The Virgin Islands Daily News,* on St. Thomas, and the *St. Croix Avis.* The islands have daily airmail service and a local telephone system. Long-distance telephone service links the islands with Puerto Rico and the United States mainland. Many islanders also use the Internet and cellular telephones. Radio-telegraph service connects the islands to all parts of the world. Radio and television stations broadcast on St. Croix and St. Thomas.

History

Exploration. Several groups of Indians lived in the Virgin Islands before Europeans arrived. They included the Ciboney, Igneri, Taíno, and Carib. Christopher Columbus sighted the Virgin Islands in 1493, on his sec-

ond voyage to the Americas, and claimed them for Spain. The Carib Indians attacked members of Columbus's crew at Salt River Bay on St. Croix. During the 1500's, the Spanish killed many of the Indians or enslaved them and took them to work on other islands. Many other Indians fled to escape the Spanish. All the Indians had died or left the islands by about the time England and the Dutch Republic (now the Netherlands) established settlements in the mid-1600's.

Early settlement. The Spanish used the Virgin Islands as a place to hide their treasure ships from pirates but never settled there. During the late 1500's and the 1600's, European pirates and *privateers* (private ships licensed to attack enemy vessels) often visited the islands. In 1607, a group of English travelers stopped at the islands on their way to establish a colony in Jamestown, Virginia. Dutch and English settlers landed on St. Croix in 1625. The Dutch abandoned their colony following quarrels with the English and the murder of their governor in 1645. In 1650, a group of Spaniards from Puerto Rico drove the English from their settlement. By 1651, France had driven the Spaniards from the island. The French controlled St. Croix until 1733, when they sold it to Denmark for $150,000.

Danish rule. In 1666, Denmark established a settlement on St. Thomas and formally claimed the island. Erik Smit served as the island's first governor, but his colony failed. The Danes made no successful settlement on St. Thomas until 1672. In 1717, they also settled on St. John. The Danish West Indies, including St. Croix, St. John, and St. Thomas, remained under Denmark's authority during most of the years until 1917.

The Danish West India and Guinea Company, under a royal charter, directed the islands' commercial development in the late 1600's and early 1700's. A plantation system of agriculture developed, and the company imported thousands of slaves from Africa to work the land. Cotton and sugar crops sold to Europe became the basis of the islands' economic growth. Plantation owners came from several countries, including Denmark, England, the Dutch Republic, and France. In 1724, the company tried to boost trade by allowing St. Thomas to trade directly with countries besides Denmark.

A bloody slave uprising on St. John in 1733 destroyed the island's economic prospects. The uprising caused Denmark to increase its military authority in the Danish West Indies. In 1754, the islands became a colony of the Danish Crown.

© Steve Simonsen

Virgin Islands National Park covers much of the island of St. John. These hikers on the park's Reef Bay trail are looking at the ruins of a sugar plantation built in the 1700's, during the period of Danish colonial rule.

The British occupied the Virgin Islands from 1801 to 1802 and from 1807 to 1815, during the Napoleonic Wars in Europe. Use of the English language on the islands increased in the years during and after the second British occupation.

Another slave revolt began on St. Croix on July 2, 1848. On July 3, Peter von Scholten, the Danish governor general, proclaimed an end to slavery. Without slavery, efforts to develop the islands proved unsuccessful, and the colony became a financial burden to Denmark.

United States rule. On Aug. 4, 1916, the governments of Denmark and the United States signed a treaty transferring control of the Virgin Islands to the United States. The treaty was formally ratified on Jan. 17, 1917. Actual control of the islands passed to the United States on March 31, 1917. The United States government paid Denmark $25 million for the islands, or about $295 an acre (0.4 hectare). James H. Oliver served as the territory's first governor.

In 1927, the U.S. Congress passed a law making the people of the Virgin Islands citizens of the United States. In 1936, islanders who could read and write English received the right to vote in local elections.

During World War II (1939-1945), the Virgin Islands served as a U.S. military outpost. In 1954, the U.S. Congress provided for a territorial legislature in the Virgin Islands. Congress created the Virgin Islands National Park in 1956.

John D. Merwin, the first native-born governor of the islands, served from 1958 to 1961. In 1968, Congress passed a law that gave Virgin Islanders the right to elect their own governor, beginning in 1970. In 1969, Melvin H. Evans was appointed the first native-born black governor. The next year, voters chose Evans as the islands' first elected governor. He served until 1975.

Recent developments. Hurricane Hugo lashed the Virgin Islands in 1989, resulting in three deaths and $500 million in damage. In 1995, Hurricane Marilyn killed eight people and damaged more than three-fourths of the houses on St. Thomas. In 1996, the United States Department of the Interior began to transfer control of Water Island to the territorial government of the Virgin Islands. It completed the transfer in 2005.

In 2005, the Self Government Committee of St. Croix submitted a petition, signed by approximately one-fourth of the island's registered voters, asking the United States Congress to make the island a separate territory of the United States. Supporters of the petition hoped that seceding from the rest of the Virgin Islands would bring St. Croix more United States funds. St. Croix has higher unemployment and more poverty than St. Thomas or St. John.   Kathryn R. Dungy

Related articles in *World Book* include:

Buck Island Reef National Monument
Carib Indians
Caribbean Sea
Charlotte Amalie
Virgin Islands
Virgin Islands, British
Virgin Islands National Park
West Indies

Outline

I. Government
II. People
   A. Population and ancestry
   B. Religion
   C. Food
   D. Clothing and architecture
   E. Education
III. Land and climate
   A. Location
   B. Islands
   C. Climate
IV. Economy
   A. Tourism
   B. Manufacturing
   C. Agriculture and mining
   D. Transportation
   E. Communication
V. History

Questions

Who lived in the Virgin Islands before Europeans settled there?
What role did the Virgin Islands play in World War II?
Who was the first European to see the Virgin Islands?
How did the Virgin Islands get their name?
Which island has the largest area? Which is the smallest inhabited island?
What is *callaloo*?
When did Virgin Islanders acquire U.S. citizenship?
What is the Virgin Islands' chief industry?
When did Denmark establish its first successful colony in the Virgin Islands? Where?
What languages are spoken in the Virgin Islands?

Virgin Islands National Park lies chiefly on the island of St. John in the Caribbean Sea. St. John is part of the United States Virgin Islands. For the location of the park, see **Virgin Islands** (map). The U.S. Congress authorized the creation of the park on Aug. 2, 1956. Laurance S. Rockefeller, an American conservationist, donated over 5,000 acres (2,000 hectares) for the park.

Virgin Islands National Park occupies about two-fifths of St. John, 15 acres (6 hectares) on St. Thomas Island, and 5,700 acres (2,300 hectares) of waters and smaller islands. For the park's area, see **National Park System** (table: National parks). Lush tropical vegetation grows in the park. The land rises to 1,277 feet (389 meters) at Bordeaux Peak.

Mules and jeeps provide the chief methods of transportation. The park is reached by a 2 ½-mile (4-kilometer) ferry trip from eastern St. Thomas Island across Pillsbury Sound to Cruz Bay, the main village on St. John. Tourist facilities are limited, but campgrounds, hotels, and cottage colonies are planned.

Virgin Islands National Park has many reminders of the Danish occupation of St. John, which lasted from the 1700's to 1917. Remains of Danish sugar mills and lavish plantations can be found. See **Virgin Islands, United States** (picture: Virgin Islands National Park).

Critically reviewed by the National Park Service

Virgin Mary. See Mary.
Virgin of Guadalupe. See Guadalupe Day.
Virginal is a keyboard instrument that resembles a harpsichord. A virginal has a rectangular case, and the keyboard is on one of the longer sides. When a player presses the keys down, small pieces of quill or leather pluck the metal strings. The virginal has a light, clear, and somewhat tinkling tone.

The virginal was especially popular as a solo instrument in England during the 1500's and early 1600's. The English *Fitzwilliam Virginal Book* (about 1625) contains nearly 300 compositions and is the principal collection of music for virginals.   F. E. Kirby

Gene Ahrens, Bruce Coleman Inc.

Shenandoah National Park lies in the forest-covered Blue Ridge Mountains. Virginia's beautiful scenery and wealth of historic sites attract tourists from all over the United States.

Virginia *Old Dominion*

Virginia, a Southern State of the United States, was the site of some of the most important events in American history. The first permanent English settlement in America was made at Jamestown in 1607. In 1619, the Jamestown colonists established the first representative legislature in America. Some of the greatest battles of the Revolutionary War in America and the American Civil War were fought in Virginia. American independence from Britain was assured when George Washington forced Lord Cornwallis to surrender at Yorktown, Virginia, in 1781. The Civil War ended when Confederate forces surrendered at Appomattox, Virginia, in 1865.

Virginia was named for Queen Elizabeth I of England, who was known as the *Virgin Queen.* Historians think the English adventurer Sir Walter Raleigh suggested the name about 1584. That year, Elizabeth gave Raleigh permission to colonize the Virginia region.

Virginia is also known as the *Old Dominion.* King Charles II gave it this name because it remained loyal to

the crown during the English Civil War of the mid-1600's. Virginia is one of four states officially called *commonwealths.* The others are Kentucky, Massachusetts, and Pennsylvania.

Virginia has the nickname *Mother of Presidents* because eight U.S. presidents were born there. They include four of the first five presidents—George Washington, Thomas Jefferson, James Madison, and James Monroe. Other presidents born in Virginia were William Henry Harrison, John Tyler, Zachary Taylor, and Woodrow Wilson.

Virginia also has the nickname *Mother of States.* All or part of eight other states were formed from western territory once claimed by Virginia. These states are Illinois, Indiana, Kentucky, Michigan, Minnesota, Ohio, West Virginia, and Wisconsin.

Tourists from all parts of the United States come to Virginia to see its battlefields, famous old churches, colonial homes, and other historic sites. Famous homes include George Washington's Mount Vernon, Thomas Jefferson's Monticello, and George Mason's Gunston Hall. Mason was a Virginia statesman who wrote the Virginia Declaration of Rights, the first American bill of rights. The Tomb of the Unknowns and the grave of President John F. Kennedy are in Arlington National

The contributors of this article are Ted Tunnell, Associate Professor of History at Virginia Commonwealth University, and Susan L. Woodward, Professor of Geography at Radford University.

Melissa Grimes-Guy, Photo Researchers

Downtown Richmond rises beyond the Federal Reserve Plaza, *shown here.* Richmond is Virginia's capital.

Interesting facts about Virginia

WORLD BOOK illustrations by Kevin Chadwick

The only full-length statue of George Washington made from life stands in the rotunda of the Virginia State Capitol in Richmond. Jean Antoine Houdon, a famous French sculptor, created the marble statue. It is said to be a near-perfect likeness of Washington. Houdon took measurements for the statue at Mount Vernon, Washington's home, in 1785. The sculpture, completed in 1791, was placed in the Capitol in 1796.

George Washington statue

Northrop Grumman Newport News, formerly known as Newport News Shipbuilding, is one of the world's largest privately owned shipyards. Founded in 1886, the Newport News-based company has produced many famous ships. These include the *Enterprise,* the world's first nuclear-powered aircraft carrier, launched in 1960. The company also built two passenger ships that were the largest ever constructed in the United States when they were launched—the *America* (1939) and the *United States* (1951).

Phi Beta Kappa, the first American Greek-letter society, was founded at the College of William and Mary in Williamsburg on Dec. 5, 1776. Phi Beta Kappa is now a well-known college and university honor society for men and women that encourages scholarship in the liberal arts and sciences.

Phi Beta Kappa

Cemetery. The cemetery surrounds the mansion of Civil War General Robert E. Lee and his wife, Mary Custis Lee. Williamsburg, Virginia's second colonial capital, has been restored to look as it did in the 1700's.

Many tourists also come to see Virginia's beautiful scenery. The Skyline Drive along the top of the Blue Ridge offers spectacular views of the Shenandoah Valley. In this fertile valley, General Stonewall Jackson won victories over Union armies during the Civil War. Virginia's natural wonders include the Natural Bridge, Natural Chimneys, Natural Tunnel, and many large caves.

Many agencies of the federal government have offices in northeastern Virginia, which lies next to Washington, D.C. These offices include the Pentagon and the headquarters of the Central Intelligence Agency. Virginia also has several military bases.

Factories in Virginia make chemicals, processed foods, tobacco products, transportation equipment, and many other products. Shipyards in the Hampton Roads area build ships for the U.S. Navy and for commercial use. *Broilers* (young, tender chickens) are Virginia's leading farm product. Coal is the leading mineral product.

Richmond, the capital of the Confederacy from May 1861 to April 1865, is Virginia's capital. According to the 2000 census, Virginia Beach is the state's largest city.

David Forbert, Shostal

The University of Virginia in Charlottesville was founded in 1819 by Thomas Jefferson. Jefferson designed the Rotunda, *shown here,* modeling it after the Pantheon of ancient Rome.

Virginia in brief

Symbols of Virginia

Virginia officially adopted its state flag in 1861. The flag bears the front of the state seal. The seal of the Commonwealth was adopted on July 5, 1776. The front side shows the Roman goddess Virtus representing the spirit of the Commonwealth, dressed as an Amazon, triumphant over Tyranny. She holds a spear and a sheathed sword. The back of the seal displays the Roman goddesses of eternity, liberty, and fruitfulness.

State flag

State seal

Virginia (brown) ranks 36th in size among all the states and 9th in size among the Southern States (yellow).

General information

Statehood: June 25, 1788, the 10th state.
State abbreviations: Va. (traditional); VA (postal).
State motto: *Sic Semper Tyrannis* (Thus Always to Tyrants).
State song: none.

*In its 1997 regular session, the legislature retired the state song "Carry Me Back to Old Virginia."

The State Capitol is in Richmond, Virginia's capital since 1780. Earlier capitals were Jamestown (1607-1699) and Williamsburg (1699-1780).

Land and climate

Area: 40,598 mi² (105,149 km²), including 1,000 mi² (2,591 km²) of inland water but excluding 1,728 mi² (4,476 km²) of coastal water.
Elevation: *Highest*—Mount Rogers, 5,729 ft (1,746 m) above sea level. *Lowest*—sea level.
Coastline: 112 mi (180 km).
Record high temperature: 110 °F (43 °C) at Columbia on July 5, 1900, and at Balcony Falls, near Glasgow, on July 15, 1954.
Record low temperature: −30 °F (−34 °C) at Mountain Lake Biological Station on Jan. 22, 1985.
Average July temperature: 75 °F (24 °C).
Average January temperature: 36 °F (2 °C).
Average yearly precipitation: 43 in (109 cm).

Greatest north-south distance 201 mi (323 km)

Lowest elevation along coast

Highest elevation

Greatest east-west distance 462 mi (744 km)

Important dates

America's first representative legislature, the House of Burgesses, met in Jamestown.

Virginia gave up its western land claims to the United States.

1607 — 1619 — 1776 — 1784 — 1788

The Virginia Company of London established the colony of Jamestown.

Virginia adopted its first constitution. It included a declaration of rights.

Virginia became the 10th state on June 25.

State bird
Northern cardinal

State flower
American dogwood

State tree
American dogwood

People

Population: 7,078,515
Rank among the states: 12th
Population density: 174 per mi² (67 per km²), U.S. average 78 per mi² (30 per km²)
Distribution: 73 percent urban, 27 percent rural

Largest cities in Virginia

Virginia Beach	425,257
Norfolk	234,403
Chesapeake	199,184
Richmond	197,790
Arlington†	189,453
Newport News	180,150

†Unincorporated place.
Source: 2000 census.

Population trend

Millions

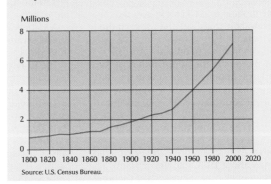

Source: U.S. Census Bureau.

Year	Population
2000	7,078,515
1990	6,187,358
1980	5,346,797
1970	4,651,448
1960	3,966,949
1950	3,318,680
1940	2,677,773
1930	2,421,851
1920	2,309,187
1910	2,061,612
1900	1,854,184
1890	1,655,980
1880	1,512,565
1870	1,225,163
1860	1,219,630
1850	1,119,348
1840	1,025,277
1830	1,044,054
1820	938,261
1810	877,683
1800	807,557
1790	691,737

Economy

Chief products

Agriculture: beef cattle, broilers, corn, hogs, milk, soybeans, tobacco, tomatoes, turkeys.
Manufacturing: chemicals, computer and electronic products, food products, tobacco products, transportation equipment.
Mining: coal, crushed stone, natural gas.

Gross domestic product

Value of goods and services produced in 2004: $327,032,000,000. *Services* include community, business, and personal services; finance; government; trade; and transportation and communication. *Industry* includes construction, manufacturing, mining, and utilities. *Agriculture* includes agriculture, fishing, and forestry.

Source: U.S. Bureau of Economic Analysis.

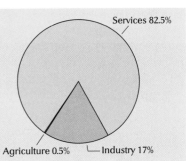

Services 82.5%

Agriculture 0.5%   Industry 17%

Government

State government

Governor: 4-year term
State senators: 40; 4-year terms
State representatives: 100; 2-year terms
Counties: 95

Federal government

United States senators: 2
United States representatives: 11
Electoral votes: 13

Sources of information

For information about tourism or the state's economy, write to: Virginia Tourism Corporation, 901 E. Byrd Street, Richmond, VA 23219. The Web site at http://www.virginia.org also provides tourist information.
The state's official Web site at http://www.virginia.gov provides a gateway to much information on Virginia's economy, government, and history.

Virginia was the major battleground of the Civil War.

The Chesapeake Bay Bridge-Tunnel, connecting the mainland and the Eastern Shore, was opened.

L. Douglas Wilder, the nation's first elected African American governor, held office.

1861-1865   **1940-1945**   **1964**   **1971**   **1990-1994**

New industries began during World War II, adding to the state's industrial growth.

A new state constitution went into effect.

Population. The 2000 United States census reported that Virginia had 7,078,515 people. The state's population had increased 14 ½ percent over the 1990 census figure, 6,187,358. According to the 2000 census, Virginia ranks 12th in population among the 50 states.

About 85 percent of the people in Virginia live in the state's 11 metropolitan areas (see **Metropolitan area**). These metropolitan areas are Blacksburg-Christiansburg-Radford; Charlottesville; Danville; Harrisonburg; Kingsport (Tennessee)-Bristol (Tennessee)-Bristol (Virginia); Lynchburg; Richmond; Roanoke; Virginia Beach-Norfolk-Newport News; Washington, D.C.-Arlington-Alexandria; and Winchester. More than 65 percent of Virginia's people live in the Richmond; Virginia Beach-Norfolk-Newport News; and Washington, D.C.-Arlington-Alexandria metropolitan areas. For the population of each of the metropolitan areas, see the *Index* to the political map of Virginia.

About 20 percent of Virginia's people are African Americans. About 5 percent of the population is of Hispanic origin. Other large population groups in the state include people of German, English, and Irish descent. Many immigrants from Southeast Asia live in northern Virginia.

Schools. The Syms Free School was founded in Hampton about 1635. It was the first free school in the United States. Another early free school, the Eaton Free School, was begun by about 1659, also in Hampton. Some Virginia communities established private schools called *Old Field schools*. They built these schools in open fields. Beginning in the mid-1700's, many private academies were founded in Virginia. In 1810, the General Assembly created a literary fund to help poor children receive an education.

Virginia's statewide public school system began in 1870. Today, the state Board of Education supervises Virginia's public school system. The board's nine members are appointed by the governor, subject to the approval of the legislature. The board elects one of its members to serve a two-year term as president.

The state Department of Education administers the public school system of Virginia, carrying out state laws and Board of Education regulations. The Department of Education is headed by the superintendent of public instruction. This official is appointed by the governor, subject to the approval of the legislature. The superintendent serves during the governor's term of office.

A state law requires children from age 5 through 17 to attend school. For the number of students and teachers in Virginia, see **Education** (table).

The College of William and Mary, founded in Williamsburg in 1693, is the second oldest institution of higher learning in the United States. Harvard University is the oldest. Phi Beta Kappa, the honorary scholastic society, was founded at William and Mary in 1776 (see **Phi Beta Kappa**).

Libraries and museums. Virginia's first public library was established in Alexandria in 1794. Today, public libraries serve Virginia's cities, towns, and counties. The Library of Virginia in Richmond, founded in 1823, houses state and local government records and a special collection of works by Virginian authors.

Robert Llewellyn

Fox hunting is a sport that was brought to the colony of Virginia by English settlers. Many Virginians are of English ancestry.

Population density

Most of Virginia's people live in the eastern part of the state—in and around Arlington, Richmond, Norfolk, and Virginia Beach. Most of the thinly populated areas lie in the central part of the state.

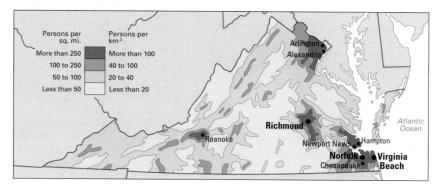

Persons per sq. mi.	Persons per km²
More than 250	More than 100
100 to 250	40 to 100
50 to 100	20 to 40
Less than 50	Less than 20

WORLD BOOK map;
based on U.S. Census Bureau data.

The Museum of the Confederacy, in Richmond, has many items relating to the Confederacy and the South of the 1800's. The White House of the Confederacy, where Jefferson Davis lived as president of the Confederate States of America, stands beside the museum. The American Civil War Center, also in Richmond, has exhibits that explain the perspectives of the Union, the Confederacy, and African Americans. The Virginia Historical Society in Richmond maintains a library and museum that cover four centuries of Virginia history.

The Virginia Museum of Fine Arts in Richmond owns many valuable works of art. Valentine Richmond History Center in Richmond has exhibits on Richmond's history. Also in Richmond, the Science Museum of Virginia has many interactive exhibits. The Edgar Allan Poe Museum in Richmond has exhibits on the poet's stay in that city. The Mariners' Museum in Newport News displays models and paintings of ships and has other items that show the development of the shipping industry. The Virginia Museum of Natural History in Martinsville has exhibits and educational programs. The National Museum of the Marine Corps in Triangle, near the Marine Corps base in Quantico, features galleries and exhibits that trace the history of the Marines from 1775 to the present.

Universities and colleges

This table lists the universities and colleges in Virginia that grant bachelor's or advanced degrees and are accredited by the Southern Association of Colleges and Schools.

Name	Mailing address	Name	Mailing address	Name	Mailing address
Argosy University	Arlington	Hampton University	Hampton	Saint Paul's College	Lawrenceville
Averett University	Danville	Hollins University	Roanoke		
Bluefield College	Bluefield	Institute for the		Shenandoah University	Winchester
Bridgewater College	Bridgewater	Psychological Sciences	Arlington	Sweet Briar College	Sweet Briar
Bryant & Stratton College	*	James Madison University	Harrisonburg	Union Theological Seminary	
Christendom College	Front Royal	Jefferson College of		and Presbyterian School	
Christopher Newport		Health Sciences	Roanoke	of Christian Education	Richmond
University	Newport News	Liberty University	Lynchburg	Virginia, University of	Charlottesville
College at Wise, University		Longwood University	Farmville		
of Virginia's	Wise	Lynchburg College	Lynchburg	Virginia Commonwealth	
DeVry University	†	Marine Corps University	Quantico	University	Richmond
Eastern Mennonite		Mary Baldwin College	Staunton	Virginia Intermont	
University	Harrisonburg	Mary Washington,		College	Bristol
Eastern Virginia Medical		University of	Fredericksburg	Virginia Military Institute	Lexington
School	Norfolk			Virginia Polytechnic Institute	
ECPI College of		Marymount University	Arlington	and State University	Blacksburg
Technology	Virginia Beach	Norfolk State University	Norfolk	Virginia State University	Petersburg
Emory & Henry College	Emory	Old Dominion University	Norfolk	Virginia Union University	Richmond
Ferrum College	Ferrum	Radford University	Radford	Virginia Wesleyan	
George Mason		Randolph College	Lynchburg	College	Norfolk
University	Fairfax	Randolph-Macon College	Ashland	Washington and Lee	
Hampden-Sydney		Regent University	Virginia Beach	University	Lexington
College	Hampden-Sydney			William and Mary,	
		Richmond, University of	Richmond	College of	Williamsburg
		Roanoke College	Salem		

*Campuses at Richmond and Virginia Beach.   †Campuses at Arlington and McLean.

Van Bucher, Photo Researchers

The Virginia Museum of Fine Arts in Richmond is the nation's oldest state-supported art museum. Visitors may relax in the museum's beautiful sculpture garden, *shown here.*

Van Bucher, Photo Researchers

The Museum of the Confederacy has about 15,000 items from the American Civil War. The museum stands beside the original Richmond home of Confederacy President Jefferson Davis.

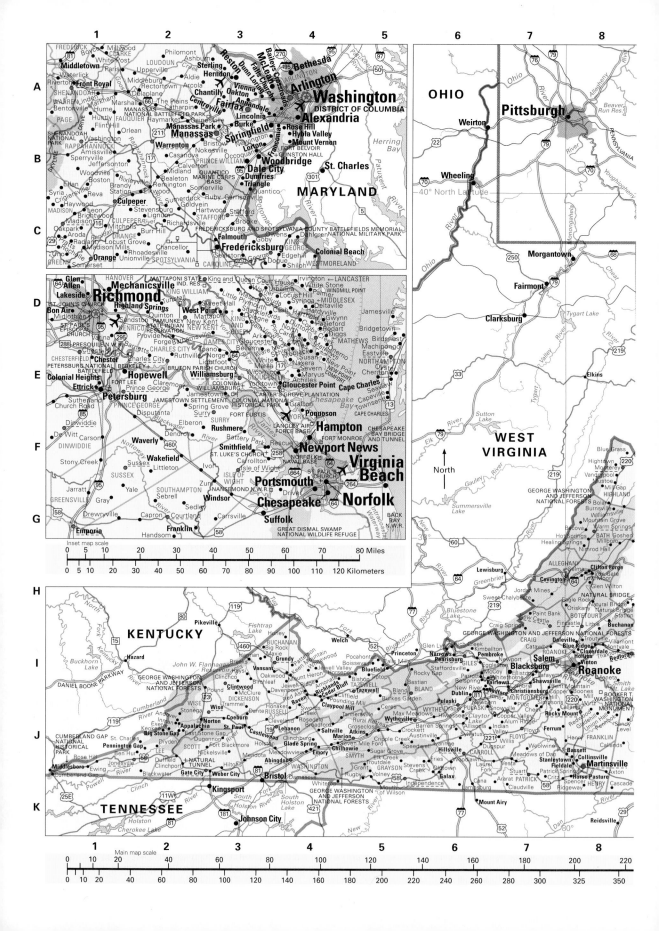

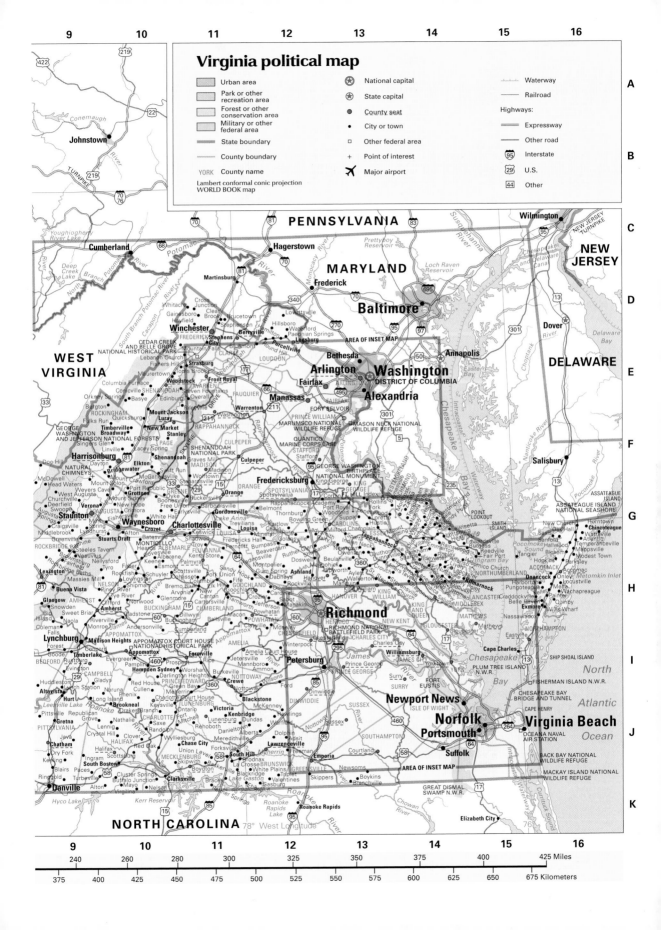

Virginia political map

Virginia map index

Place	Population	Key
Inman		J 2
Iron Gate	404	H 8
Irvington	673	D 4
Isle of Wight○		F 3
Ivanhoe		J 6
Ivor	320	F 3
Jamaica		H 14
Jamestown		E 3
Jamesville		D 5
Jarratt	589	G 1
Java		J 9
Jefferson*‡	27,422	A 3
Jeffersonton		B 1
Jetersville		I 11
Jewell Ridge		I 4
Jewell Valley		I 4
Jonesville○	995	J 2
Jordan Mines		H 7
Keeling		J 9
Keen Mountain		I 4
Keene		H 10
Keller	173	H 15
Kenbridge	1,253	J 11
Kents Store		H 11
Keokee‡	316	J 2
Keswick		G 11
Keysville	817	J 10
Kilmarnock	1,244	H 14
Kimballton		I 6
King and Queen Court House○		D 3
King George○		G 13
King William○		H 13
Kinsale		G 14
Lacey Spring		F 10
La Crosse	618	J 11
Ladysmith		G 12
Lafayette, see Elliston [-Lafayette]		
Lake Barcroft*‡	8,906	E 13
Lake Ridge*‡	30,404	F 12
Lakeside‡	11,157	D 1
Lambsburg		K 6
Lancaster○		H 14
Laneview		H 14
Laurel*‡	14,875	H 12
Laurel Fork		J 7
Lawrenceville○	1,275	J 12
Lebanon○	3,273	J 4
Lebanon Church		E 11
Leesburg○	28,311	E 12
Lennig		J 10
Leon		C 1
Lewisetta		G 14
Lexington†○	6,867	H 9
Lightfoot		E 3
Lignum		C 2
Lincolnia‡	15,788	A 3
Lincolnia Heights*		A 3
Linden		A 1
Linville		F 10
Lithia		I 8
Little Plymouth		D 3
Lively		H 14
Loch Lomond*‡	3,411	F 12
Locust Grove		C 2
Locust Hill		D 4
Locustville		H 16
Long Branch*		E 13
Long Island		I 9
Loretto		G 13
Lorton‡	17,786	B 3
Lottsburg		G 14
Louisa○	1,401	G 11
Lovettsville	853	D 12
Lovingston○		H 10
Low Moor‡	367	H 8
Lunenburg○		J 11
Luray○	4,871	F 10
Lynch Station		I 9
Lynchburg†	65,269	I 9
Lyndhurst‡	1,527	G 9
Machipongo		E 5
Macon		H 11
Madison○	210	F 11
Madison Heights‡	11,584	I 9
Madison Mills		C 1
Manakin		H 12
Manassas†○	35,135	E 12
Manassas Park†	10,290	B 3
Mangohick		H 13
Mannboro		I 12
Manquin		H 13
Mantua*‡	7,485	E 12
Mappsville		H 16
Marion○	6,349	J 5
Markham		A 1
Marshall		A 2
Martinsville†○	15,416	J 8
Maryus		E 4
Mascot		D 3
Massies Mill		H 9
Mathews○		I 14
Mattaponi		D 3
Mattaponi State Indian Reservation	58	D 3
Maurertown		E 10
Max Meadows‡	512	J 6
Maxie		I 4
Mayo		K 10
McClure		I 3
McCoy		I 6
McDowell		F 9
McGaheysville		F 10
McKenney	441	J 12
McLean‡	38,929	A 3
Meadow View, see Emory [-Meadow View]		
Meadows of Dan		J 7
Mechanicsville‡	30,464	D 1
Meherrin		I 11
Melfa	450	H 15
Mendota		J 3
Meredithville		J 11
Merrifield*‡	11,170	E 13
Merry Point		H 14
Middlebrook		G 9
Middleburg	632	A 2
Middletown	1,015	A 1
Midland		B 2
Midlothian		D 1
Miles		E 4
Milford		G 13
Mill Gap		G 8
Millboro		G 8
Millers Tavern		H 13
Millwood		A 1
Mineral	424	G 12
Mint Spring		G 9
Mitchells		C 1
Mobjack		E 4
Modest Town		H 16
Mollusk		H 14
Moneta		I 8
Monroe		H 9
Monterey○	158	F 8
Montclair‡	15,728	B 3
Montpelier		H 12
Montrose*‡	7,018	H 12
Montross○	315	G 14
Montvale		I 8
Morattico		H 14
Moseley		I 12
Mount Crawford	254	G 10
Mount Heron		I 4
Mount Jackson	1,664	F 10
Mount Landing		G 13
Mount Sidney		G 10
Mount Solon		F 9
Mount Vernon‡	28,582	B 4
Mountain Falls		E 10
Mountain Grove		G 8
Mouth of Wilson		K 5
Mundy Point		G 14
Mustoe		F 8
Naola		H 9
Narrows	2,111	I 6
Naruna		I 9
Nassawadox	572	H 15
Nathalie		J 10
Natural Bridge		H 8
Naxera		E 4
Nellysford		H 10
Nelson		K 10
New Canton		H 11
New Castle○	179	H 7
New Church		G 16
New Hope		G 10
New Kent○		D 2
New Market	1,637	F 10
New Point		E 4
New River		I 6
Newbern		I 6
Newington‡	19,784	B 3
Newport		I 7
Newport News†	180,150	J 14
Newsoms	282	J 13
Newtown		G 13
Nickelsville	448	J 3
Nimrod Hall		G 8
Nokesville‡	1,236	B 2
Nomini Grove		G 14
Norfolk†	234,403	J 15
Norge		E 3
North		D 4
North Springfield*‡	9,173	E 13
Norton	3,904	J 3
Norwood		H 10
Nottoway○		I 11
Nuttsville		H 14
Oak Hall		G 16
Oakpark		C 1
Oakton‡	29,348	A 3
Oakwood		I 4
Occoquan	759	B 3
Oilville		H 12
Oldhams		G 14
Oldtown		J 6
Onancock	1,525	H 15
Onemo		E 4
Onley	496	H 15
Ontario		J 10
Orange○	4,123	G 11
Oriskany		H 8
Orkney Springs		E 10
Orlean		B 1
Ottoman		H 14
Overall		E 11
Owens		C 4
Owenton		H 13
Oyster		E 5
Paces		J 9
Paint Bank		H 7
Painter	246	H 15
Palmer		D 4
Palmer Springs		K 11
Palmyra○		H 11
Pamplin	199	I 10
Pamunkey State Indian Reservation	58	D 2
Paris		A 1
Parksley	837	H 16
Parkview*		F 10
Parrott		I 6
Partlow		G 12
Patrick Springs‡	2,068	K 7
Patterson		I 4
Pearisburg○	2,729	I 6
Pembroke	1,134	I 6
Penhook‡	726	J 8
Pennington Gap	1,781	J 2
Petersburg†	33,740	I 12
Phenix	200	I 10
Philomont		A 2
Pilot		J 7
Pimmit Hills*‡	6,152	E 13
Pinero		D 4
Piney River		H 9
Pittsville		J 9
Plain View		D 3
Plains, The	266	A 2
Pocahontas	441	I 5
Poquoson†	11,566	F 4
Port Republic		G 10
Port Royal	170	G 13
Portsmouth†	100,565	J 14
Pound	1,089	I 3
Pounding Mill		I 4
Powhatan○		H 11
Pratts		C 1
Prince George○		I 13
Prospect		I 10
Providence Forge		D 2
Pulaski○	9,473	J 6
Pungoteague		H 15
Purcellville	3,584	E 12
Quantico	561	B 3
Quantico Station*‡	6,571	F 12
Quicksburg		F 10
Quinby		H 15
Quinton		D 2
Radford†	15,859	I 7
Radiant		C 1
Rainswood		G 14
Randolph		J 10
Raphine		G 9
Rappahannock Academy		G 13
Raven‡	2,593	I 4
Rawlings		J 12
Rectortown		A 2
Red Ash		I 4
Red House		I 10
Red Oak		J 10
Redart		D 4
Redwood		J 8
Reedville		H 14
Rehoboth		J 11
Remington	624	B 2
Republican Grove		J 9
Rescue		F 3
Reston‡	56,407	A 3
Reva		C 1
Rhoadesville		C 1
Rice		I 11
Rich Creek	665	I 6
Richardsville		C 2
Richlands	4,144	I 4
Richmond†	197,790	H 12
Ridgeway	775	K 8
Rileyville		E 11
Riner		I 7
Ringgold		K 9
Riverton		A 1
Riverville		H 10
Rixeyville		B 1
Roanoke†	94,911	I 8
Robley		H 14
Rochelle		C 1
Rockbridge Baths		H 9
Rockfish		H 10
Rockville		H 12
Rocky Gap		I 6
Rocky Mount○	4,066	J 8
Rollins Fork		G 13
Rose Hill‡	15,058	B 4
Rosedale		J 4
Round Hill	500	E 12
Ruby		B 3
Ruckersville		G 11
Rugby		K 5
Rural Retreat	1,350	J 5
Rushmere‡	1,083	F 3
Rustburg‡○	1,271	I 9
Ruther Glen		G 12
Ruthville		E 2
Sabot		H 12
St. Charles	159	J 2
St. Paul	1,000	J 3
St. Stephens Church		H 13
Salem†○	24,747	I 7
Saltville	2,204	J 4
Saluda○		H 14
Sandston		D 1
Sandy Hook		H 11
Sandy Level‡	689	J 8
Sanford		G 16
Saxe		J 10
Saxis	337	G 16
Schley		E 4
Schuyler		H 10
Scottsburg	145	J 10
Scottsville	555	H 10
Sealston		C 3
Seaview		E 5
Sebrell		G 2
Sedley		G 2
Selma‡	485	H 8
Seven Corners*‡	8,701	E 13
Seven Fountains		E 11
Seven Mile Ford		J 5
Severn		E 4
Shacklefords		D 3
Sharps		H 14
Shawsville‡	1,029	I 7
Shenandoah	1,878	F 10
Shiloh		C 4
Shipman		H 10
Shumansville		G 13
Simpsons		J 7
Singers Glen		F 10
Skippers		K 12
Skipwith		J 10
Smithfield	6,324	F 3
Snowden		H 9
Snowville		J 7
Somerset		C 1
Somerville		B 2
South Boston	8,491	J 10
South Hill	4,403	J 11
Sparta		G 13
Speedwell		J 5
Spencer		K 8
Sperryville		B 1
Spotsylvania○		G 12
Spring Grove		E 2
Springfield‡	30,417	B 3
Stafford○		F 12
Staffordsville		I 6
Stanardsville○	476	G 11
Stanley	1,326	F 10
Stanleytown‡	1,515	J 8
Staunton†○	23,853	G 9
Steeles Tavern		G 9
Stephens City	1,146	D 11
Stephenson		D 11
Sterling		A 3
Stevens Creek		J 6
Stevensburg		C 2
Stonega		J 2
Stony Creek	202	F 1
Strasburg	4,017	E 11
Stuart○	961	J 7
Stuarts Draft‡	8,367	G 9
Suffolk†	63,677	J 14
Sugar Grove‡	741	J 5
Sugarland Run*		E 12
Sumerduck		C 2
Supply		G 13
Surry○	262	I 13
Susan		E 4
Sussex○		J 13
Sutherland		E 1
Sweet Briar		H 9
Sweet Chalybeate		H 7
Sweet Hall		D 3
Swift Run		F 10
Swoope		G 9
Swords Creek		J 4
Sylvatus		J 6
Syria		C 1
Syringa		D 4
Tamworth		H 11
Tangier	604	H 15
Tannersville		J 5
Tappahannock○	2,068	G 13
Tazewell○	4,206	I 5
Temperanceville		G 16
Templeman		G 14
Thaxton		I 8
Thornburg		G 12
Tidewater		H 14
Timberlake‡	10,683	I 9
Timberville	1,739	F 10
Tiptop		I 5
Toano		E 3
Toms Brook	255	E 10
Townsend		E 5
Trammel		J 3
Trevilians		G 11
Triangle‡	5,500	B 3
Triplet		J 12
Troutdale	1,230	J 5
Troutville	432	I 8
Troy		G 11
Tuckahoe*‡	43,242	H 12
Tunstall		D 2
Turbeville		K 9
Tye River		H 10
Tyro		H 9
Tysons Corner*‡	18,540	E 13
Union Hall‡	957	J 8
Union Level		J 11
Unionville		C 1
Uno		C 1
Upperville		A 2
Urbanna	543	D 3
Valentines		K 12
Vanderpool		F 8
Vansant‡	989	I 3
Varina		D 1
Verona‡	3,638	G 9
Vesta		J 7
Vesuvius		H 9
Victoria	1,821	J 11
Vienna	14,453	A 3
Villa Heights*‡	845	J 8
Village		G 14
Villamont		I 8
Vinton	7,782	I 8
Virgilina	159	K 10
Virginia Beach†	425,257	J 15
Volney		K 5
Wachapreague	236	H 16
Wakefield	1,038	G 2
Walkerton		H 13
Ware Neck		E 4
Warfield		J 12
Warm Springs○		G 8
Warner		D 3
Warrenton○	6,670	F 12
Warsaw○	1,375	G 14
Washington○	183	F 11
Water View		H 14
Waterford		D 12
Wattsville		G 16
Waverly	2,309	F 2
Waynesboro†	19,520	G 10
Weber City	1,333	J 3
West Augusta		G 9
West Gate*‡	7,493	F 12
West Point	2,866	D 3
West Springfield*‡	28,378	E 13
Westmoreland		G 14
Weyers Cave‡	1,225	G 10
Whitacre		D 11
White Hall		G 10
White Marsh		E 3
White Plains		J 11
White Post		A 1
White Stone	358	D 4
Whitetop		K 5
Whitewood		I 4
Wicomico		E 4
Wicomico Church		H 14
Williamsburg†○	11,998	I 14
Williamsville		G 8
Willis		J 7
Willis Wharf		H 15
Wilsons		I 11
Winchester†○	23,585	D 11
Windsor	916	G 3
Winterpock		I 12
Wirtz		I 8
Wise○	3,255	J 3
Wolf Trap*‡	14,001	E 13
Wolftown		F 11
Woodbridge‡	31,941	B 3
Woodford		G 12
Woodlawn‡	2,249	J 6
Woodstock○	3,952	E 10
Woodville		B 1
Woolwine		J 7
Worsham		I 10
Wylliesburg		J 10
Wytheville○	7,804	J 6
Yale		G 1
Yorkshire*‡	6,732	E 12
Yorktown‡○	203	I 14
Zacata		G 14
Zuni		F 3

*Does not appear on map; key shows general location.
†Independent city, not part of any county.
‡Census designated place—unincorporated, but recognized as a significant settled community by the U.S. Census Bureau.
§Corrected count from 2000 census.

○County seat. Some of Virginia's independent cities serve as county seats, though they are not officially part of the counties that surround them.
Source: 2000 census. Metropolitan area and metropolitan division figures are based on 2003 Office of Management and Budget reorganization of 2000 census data. Places without population figures are unincorporated areas.

Virginia is known for its stately old homes and other historic sites. The most popular homes include George Washington's Mount Vernon near Alexandria, and Thomas Jefferson's Monticello near Charlottesville. Williamsburg, Virginia's second colonial capital, has been restored to look as it did in the 1700's. See **Monticello; Mount Vernon; Williamsburg.**

Many visitors drive along the crest of the Blue Ridge Mountains. They travel on the Skyline Drive in the north, and on the Blue Ridge Parkway in the south. In spring, azaleas, dogwoods, and laurels bloom on the mountain slopes. In autumn, the leaves of hardwood trees and shrubs turn bright red, orange, and yellow.

The Atlantic Ocean, Chesapeake Bay, and tidal rivers offer boating activities, fishing, and beach sports. Virginia Beach is an especially popular ocean resort. Virginia's mountains offer hiking, camping, and hunting. Virginia has many resort and public golf courses.

Many of Virginia's most beautiful homes and gardens are open to the public during Historic Garden Week. This event takes place late in April. Another popular event is Pony Penning on Chincoteague Island, held on the last Wednesday and Thursday in July. The wild ponies live on nearby Assateague Island. But at Pony Penning time they are driven across the shallow channel to Chincoteague, where some of them are auctioned off.

Mount Vernon, George Washington's home

Rick Buettner, Bruce Coleman Inc.

Places to visit

Following are brief descriptions of some of Virginia's many interesting places to visit:

Churches. Bruton Parish Church (built from 1712 to 1715) in Williamsburg is one of the nation's oldest Episcopal churches. George Washington worshiped at Christ Church (1767-1773) in Alexandria. The Second Virginia Convention met in 1775 at St. John's Church (1739-1741) in Richmond. There, Patrick Henry gave his famous call for liberty. St. Luke's Church (1682) near Smithfield is an excellent example of Gothic architecture in the United States. St. Paul's Church (1739) in Norfolk was the city's only building to survive a British bombardment during the Revolutionary War. Robert E. Lee and Jefferson Davis worshiped in Richmond's St. Paul's Episcopal Church (1845), the "Church of the Confederacy."

Family entertainment centers. Paramount's Kings Dominion, near Richmond, has roller coasters and other rides. Busch Gardens Williamsburg has rides and areas that reflect the culture of a number of European countries.

Homes. Berkeley (1726), near Richmond, was the birthplace of President William Henry Harrison. Carter's Grove (1750-1755) is among the most beautiful of the old plantations along the James River. Gunston Hall (1755), near Lorton, was the home of George Mason, the author of the Virginia Declaration of Rights. The John Marshall House (about 1790) in Richmond was long the home of the great chief justice of the United States. Stratford Hall (about 1730), near Montross, was the birthplace of Robert E. Lee.

Jamestown Settlement, on the James River, has reproductions of the three ships that brought the first permanent English settlers to America in 1607. Nearby at Jamestown Island stands Old Church Tower, the ruined tower of a brick church from the settlement of the 1600's.

Natural Bridge is a landmark south of Lexington. Water carved away softer rock and left the hard rock that forms the bridge.

Natural Chimneys are seven rock towers. They rise over 100 feet (30 meters) near Mount Solon.

Natural Tunnel, near Gate City, is a giant passageway cut through the Purchase Ridge by the waters of Stock Creek. A railroad runs through it, and it has a path for visitors.

National parklands. The National Park Service administers a variety of areas in Virginia. They include battlefields, cemeteries, historic sites, memorials, monuments, national parks, and scenic trails.

Shenandoah National Park in the Blue Ridge Mountains, George Washington Birthplace National Monument in Westmoreland County, and Booker T. Washington National Monument near Roanoke are described under their own names in *World Book.* The Blue Ridge Parkway is a scenic drive that connects Shenandoah and Great Smoky Mountains national parks. Colonial National Historical Park includes Jamestown—the first permanent English settlement in North America—and Yorktown Battlefield, where the final major battle of the Revolutionary War in America took place. Appomattox Court House National Historical Park includes McLean House, the site of the agreement on the terms of surrender in the American Civil War. Manassas National Battlefield Park is the site of the Civil War Battles of Manassas, or Bull Run. See **National Park System** (table).

The U.S. Forest Service administers George Washington and Jefferson national forests, which occupy a long stretch of land in western and northern Virginia. Small parts extend into West Virginia and Kentucky.

State forests and parks. Virginia has 49 state parks, natural areas, and natural area preserves; an interstate park; and several other historical and recreational areas. For more information on Virginia's state forests and parks, write to Virginia Department of Conservation and Recreation, 203 Governor Street, Suite 302, Richmond, VA 23219.

Michael Ventura, Bruce Coleman Inc.

Pony Penning on Chincoteague Island

Colonial National Historical Park

Old Church Tower at Jamestown Island

Photri

Natural Bridge near Lexington

Van Bucher, Photo Researchers

St. John's Church in Richmond

Annual events

January-June

Highland County Maple Sugar Festival in Monterey (March); Garden Symposium in Williamsburg (late March or early April); International Azalea Festival in Norfolk (late April); Virginia Gold Cup in The Plains (early May); Shenandoah Apple Blossom Festival in Winchester (early May); Harborfest in Norfolk (early June); Boardwalk Art Show in Virginia Beach (late June); Hampton Jazz Festival (late June).

July-December

Scottish Games and Gathering of the Clans in Alexandria (July); The Big Gig in Richmond (July); Highlands Arts and Crafts Festival in Abingdon (first two weeks in August); Old Fiddlers' Convention in Galax (August); Olde Towne Ghost Walk in Portsmouth (late October); The Grand Illumination in Colonial Williamsburg (early December).

Land regions. Virginia has five main land regions: (1) the Appalachian Plateau, (2) the Ridge and Valley Region, (3) the Blue Ridge, (4) the Piedmont Plateau, and (5) the Atlantic Coastal Plain.

The Appalachian Plateau is a rugged region in the southwestern part of the state. It has an average elevation of 2,000 feet (610 meters). Many streams flow west through the region. In some places, they have cut deep gorges. The plateau is covered with forests and has valuable coal fields.

The Ridge and Valley Region consists of a series of parallel mountain ridges that extend northeast and southwest along most of the state's western border. The Great Valley, or Valley of Virginia, lies in the eastern part of this region. The Great Valley is a series of separate river valleys. The largest is the Shenandoah Valley in the north. A prominent mountain ridge, the Massanutten, divides the Shenandoah Valley into two parts for much of its length. The Ridge and Valley Region has many caves and other formations created by the action of water on limestone.

The Blue Ridge borders the Ridge and Valley Region on the east. This outstanding feature of Virginia is the main eastern range of the Appalachian Mountain System. Northeast of Roanoke, the ridge is narrow and rises sharply from the lower land east and west of it. South of Roanoke, the Blue Ridge broadens into a plateau with mountain peaks, valleys, and deep ravines. The highest

peaks in Virginia—Mount Rogers (5,729 feet, or 1,746 meters) and Whitetop Mountain (5,520 feet, or 1,682 meters)—are in the southern part of the Blue Ridge.

The Piedmont Plateau, in central Virginia, is the state's largest land region. It is an elevated, gently rolling plain, about 40 miles (64 kilometers) wide in the northeast and widening to about 140 miles (225 kilometers) at the North Carolina border. The Piedmont Plateau has an average elevation of 800 to 900 feet (240 to 270 meters) in the west. It slopes gradually to an average elevation of 200 to 300 feet (61 to 91 meters) in the east. Many rivers and streams flow southeast across the Piedmont Plateau. They break into low waterfalls at the eastern edge of the region, known as the *fall line* (see **Fall line**).

The Atlantic Coastal Plain is a lowland region about 100 miles (160 kilometers) wide that extends north and south along the Atlantic Ocean. It is often called the *Tidewater,* because tidal water flows up its bays, inlets, and rivers. Chesapeake Bay divides the region into a western mainland section and a peninsula called the *Eastern Shore.* The region has salt marshes and swamps. The largest is Great Dismal Swamp, in the southeastern part of the state.

Coastline. Virginia has a general coastline of 112 miles (180 kilometers). The *tidal shoreline* (including small bays and inlets) is 3,315 miles (5,335 kilometers). Sand bars and islands along the coast have created several lagoons. A long, sandy beach stretches south from

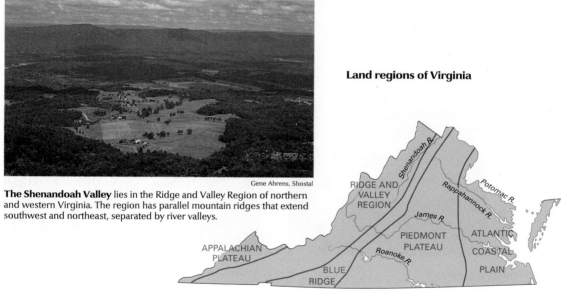

Gene Ahrens, Shostal

The Shenandoah Valley lies in the Ridge and Valley Region of northern and western Virginia. The region has parallel mountain ridges that extend southwest and northeast, separated by river valleys.

Land regions of Virginia

WORLD BOOK map

Map index

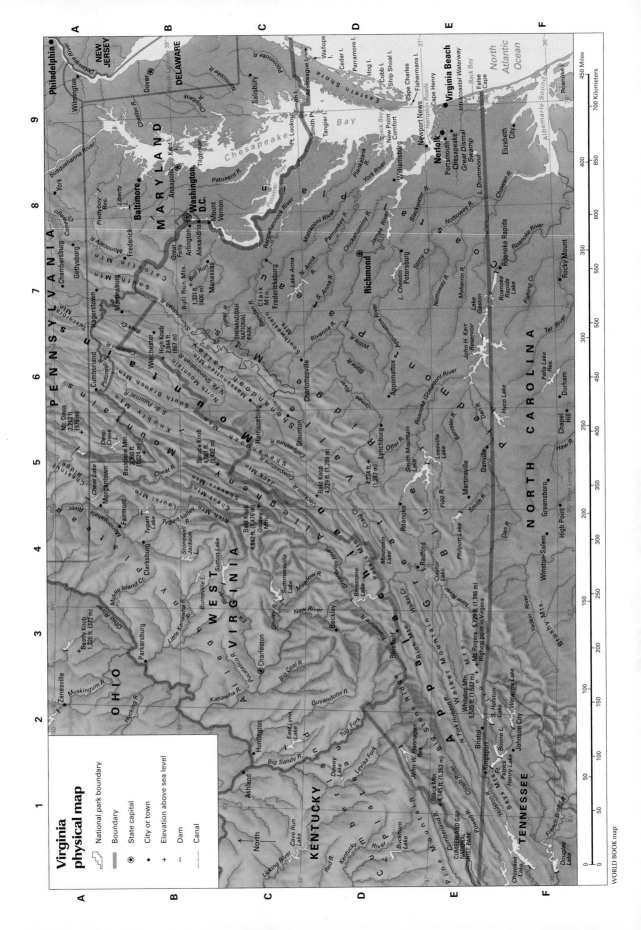

Virginia physical map

National park boundary

Boundary

⊛ State capital

• City or town

+ Elevation above sea level

– Dam

Canal

WORLD BOOK map

The Rappahannock River flows through northern Virginia from the western mountains into Chesapeake Bay. Several rivers in the state flow southeast into the bay, dividing the Atlantic Coastal Plain into a series of peninsulas.

Robert Llewellyn

the Norfolk area. Ocean waves have *eroded* (worn away) much of the shoreline.

Rivers and lakes. Several rivers flow from the western mountains and the Piedmont Plateau into Chesapeake Bay. These rivers include the Rappahannock, James, and York. They divide the Tidewater area into a series of peninsulas. The Potomac River forms Virginia's northeastern border. It is an important transportation route between Alexandria and Chesapeake Bay. The Shenandoah River flows north through the Great Valley and empties into the Potomac.

The Roanoke River flows southeast across the Piedmont Plateau into North Carolina. The New River begins in North Carolina and flows north and west through southwestern Virginia into West Virginia. Several rivers in the southwestern corner of the state, including the

Average monthly weather

	Norfolk						Roanoke					
	Temperatures				Days of rain or snow			Temperatures				Days of rain or snow
	°F		°C					°F		°C		
	High	Low	High	Low				High	Low	High	Low	
Jan.	48	32	9	0	11		Jan.	45	27	7	–3	10
Feb.	50	34	10	1	10		Feb.	49	29	9	–2	10
Mar.	58	40	14	4	11		Mar.	58	37	14	3	11
Apr.	67	48	19	9	10		Apr.	68	44	20	7	10
May	75	58	24	14	10		May	76	52	24	11	12
June	83	66	28	19	9		June	83	60	28	16	10
July	87	71	31	22	11		July	88	65	31	18	12
Aug.	85	70	29	21	10		Aug.	86	63	30	17	10
Sept.	79	65	26	18	8		Sept.	79	57	26	14	9
Oct.	69	53	21	12	8		Oct.	69	45	21	7	8
Nov.	61	44	16	7	8		Nov.	58	37	14	3	9
Dec.	52	36	11	2	9		Dec.	49	30	9	–1	9

Average yearly precipitation

Precipitation is lightest along the northern border of Virginia. The state receives its heaviest precipitation in the Tidewater region and in the southwestern corner.

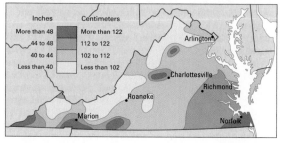

Inches	Centimeters
More than 48	More than 122
44 to 48	112 to 122
40 to 44	102 to 112
Less than 40	Less than 102

WORLD BOOK map

Average January temperatures

Virginia has mild winters. The Tidewater area along the Atlantic Coast has the mildest temperatures. The mountainous Blue Ridge area to the west generally has the coldest winters.

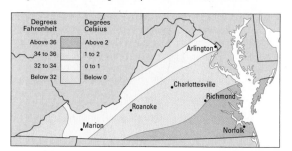

Degrees Fahrenheit	Degrees Celsius
Above 36	Above 2
34 to 36	1 to 2
32 to 34	0 to 1
Below 32	Below 0

Average July temperatures

Virginia is warm with little variation in temperature during the summertime. The eastern portion of the state generally is a few degrees warmer than the higher elevations in the interior.

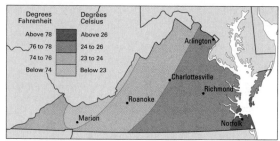

Degrees Fahrenheit	Degrees Celsius
Above 78	Above 26
76 to 78	24 to 26
74 to 76	23 to 24
Below 74	Below 23

Clinch, Holston, and Powell, flow southwest toward the Tennessee Valley.

Virginia has two natural lakes—Lake Drummond (3,200 acres, or 1,290 hectares), which lies in Great Dismal Swamp, and small Mountain Lake, near the top of Salt Pond Mountain in southwestern Virginia. Many artificial lakes have been formed by damming rivers for hydroelectric power, recreation, or other purposes. The largest of these is Kerr Reservoir on the Virginia-North Carolina border. About 36,140 acres (14,625 hectares) of this lake are in Virginia.

Plant and animal life. Forests cover more than 60 percent of Virginia. Common trees include ashes, beeches, birches, black tupelos, hemlocks, hickories, locusts, maples, redcedars, sweet gums, and yellow-poplars. Red spruces can be found on the highest peaks. Flowering dogwood, the state flower, blooms in early spring. Wild azaleas, mountain laurels, redbuds, rhododendrons, and other flowering plants grow in mountain areas. Wildflowers include bloodroots, mayapples, violets, and Virginia bluebells.

Deer roam the wooded areas. Black bears and wildcats live in the mountains and in Great Dismal Swamp. Small animals include foxes, muskrats, opossums, rabbits, and raccoons. Ducks, geese, quails, ruffed grouse, and turkeys live in the state. Freshwater fishes include alewife, bass, carp, perch, pickerel, pike, and trout. Drum, flounder, mackerel, menhaden, and shad swim in the Atlantic Ocean, in Chesapeake Bay, and in Virginia's many inlets. Clams, crabs, oysters, and scallops live in Chesapeake Bay and in shallow coastal waters.

Climate. The climate of Virginia is mild. Temperatures vary from east to west as the elevation of the land and the distance from the ocean increase. In January, temperatures average 41 °F (5 °C) in the Tidewater area, and about 32 °F (0 °C) in parts of the Blue Ridge. July temperatures average 78 °F (26 °C) in the Tidewater and about 68 °F (20 °C) in the mountains. The state's highest temperature, 110 °F (43 °C), occurred at Columbia on July 5, 1900, and at Balcony Falls, near Glasgow, on July 15, 1954. The record low, –30 °F (–34 °C), occurred at Mountain Lake Biological Station on Jan. 22, 1985.

Virginia's precipitation is lightest in the Shenandoah and New River valleys, where it averages about 36 inches (91 centimeters) a year. In the south, it averages about 44 inches (112 centimeters). Snowfall ranges from 5 to 10 inches (13 to 25 centimeters) in the Tidewater to 25 to 30 inches (64 to 76 centimeters) in the western mountains.

Economy

Throughout its early history, Virginia had an agricultural economy based on tobacco and other plantation crops. Government activities and manufacturing industries grew rapidly after about 1940. Today, service industries, taken together, account for the largest portion of Virginia's *gross domestic product*—the total value of all goods and services produced in the state in a year. Many federal government agencies operate in northern Virginia, near Washington, D.C. Virginia also benefits from military bases in the state.

Virginia's location near the highly populated Northeast and the rapidly growing Southeast is favorable for manufacturing and trade. Plentiful natural resources, good transportation by land and water, and a growing population also favor these industries. Virginia's historic sites, beaches, and other attractions draw tens of millions of tourists each year.

Natural resources of Virginia include varied soils and many mineral deposits.

Soil. Most of the western, mountainous part of Virginia has shallow, rocky soils. The valley soils are stony and not fertile, except in parts of the Shenandoah Valley and other areas where the soil contains much lime. Soils are stony and shallow in the northern part of the Blue Ridge but deeper and darker in the southwest. Piedmont soils are generally light in color and have a loamy texture. Most soils in the Atlantic Coastal Plain are sandier than those in other parts of Virginia. The sandy soils are generally deep and easily cultivated.

Minerals. Coal is Virginia's most important mined resource. Most of the coal comes from the southwestern part of the state. *Bituminous* (soft) coal makes up most of the state's reserves. The famous Pocahontas coal of Buchanan and Tazewell counties is among the bituminous deposits.

Virginia stones include basalt, dolostone, gneiss, granite, limestone, marble, sandstone, shale, slate, soapstone, and traprock. Most of the limestone is found in the Ridge and Valley Region. The Atlantic Coastal Plain has large deposits of clay and sand and gravel. Some manganese and iron ore occur in mountainous areas. Other mined products include kyanite, natural gas, petroleum, and vermiculite.

Service industries account for the largest part of Virginia's gross domestic product. Service industries are concentrated in the state's largest cities.

Ranking first among Virginia's service industry groups

Production and workers by economic activities

Economic activities	Percent of GDP* produced	Employed workers Number of people	Employed workers Percent of total
Community, business, & personal services	22	1,466,900	32
Finance, insurance, & real estate	22	417,000	9
Government	17	841,000	18
Trade, restaurants, & hotels	13	919,000	20
Manufacturing	9	309,000	7
Transportation & communication	8	244,400	5
Construction	5	320,400	7
Utilities	2	11,600	†
Agriculture	1	73,200	2
Mining	†	10,800	†
Total‡	100	4,613,300	100

*GDP = gross domestic product, the total value of goods and services produced in a year.
†Less than one-half of 1 percent.
‡Figures may not add up to 100 percent due to rounding.
Figures are for 2004; employment figures include full- and part-time workers.
Source: *World Book* estimates based on data from U.S. Bureau of Economic Analysis.

Tobacco is one of Virginia's most valuable crops. Products made from tobacco rank as the state's most valuable type of manufactured product. These workers are stringing tobacco leaves for curing.

Wendell Metzen, Bruce Coleman Inc.

are (1) community, business, and personal services and (2) finance, insurance, and real estate. Each group contributes roughly the same amount to Virginia's gross domestic product.

Community, business, and personal services employs more people than any other group in the state. These services consist of a variety of economic activities, including computer programming and engineering companies, private health care, repair shops, and telephone call centers. Much of the growth in this service industry comes from the state's technology sector. Computer programmers, consultants, engineers, and researchers receive much business from federal government agencies. Several companies have their telemarketing or mail-order operations based in Virginia.

Falls Church and Richmond are the leading banking centers in the state. Richmond is the headquarters of the Fifth Federal Reserve District Bank, one of the 12 federal banks established by Congress. Real estate is an important part of this sector. The rapid growth in Virginia's population has resulted in the construction of many homes, shopping centers, and other properties.

Government ranks third. This sector includes the operation of public schools, public hospitals, and military bases. Federal government agencies have many offices in northeastern Virginia. The Pentagon is in Arlington, and the headquarters of the Central Intelligence Agency is near McLean. The state's military bases include Naval Station Norfolk and Marine Corps Base Quantico. Most state government offices are in Richmond.

Ranking next among Virginia's service industries is trade, restaurants, and hotels. Wholesale trade consists of buying goods from producers and selling them to other businesses. The wholesale trade of automobiles, groceries, and petroleum is important in Virginia. Retail trade involves selling goods directly to consumers. Retail businesses include automobile dealerships, department stores, and grocery stores. Tourists visiting Virginia's coastal, mountain, and urban areas provide much income for the state's hotels, resorts, and restaurants.

The transportation and communication group ranks

fifth. Norfolk Southern, one of the nation's largest railroad companies, is headquartered in Virginia. Internet service providers, publishers, and telephone companies are important parts of the communications sector. More information about transportation and communication can be found later in this section.

Manufacturing. Goods manufactured in Virginia have a *value added by manufacture* of about $50 billion yearly. This figure represents the increase in value of raw materials after they become finished products.

Beverage and tobacco products are Virginia's leading type of manufactured products in terms of value added by manufacture. Tobacco products are the most valuable part of this sector by far. Most of the state's tobacco industry income comes from cigarette factories in Richmond. Soft drinks and beer are made in several parts of the state.

Computer and electronic equipment ranks second. Computers and computer equipment, scientific instruments, and semiconductors are the leading types of computer and electronic equipment made in Virginia.

Transportation equipment ranks third in terms of value added by manufacture. The industry's chief products are boats and ships, motor vehicle parts, and trucks. Northrop Grumman Newport News is one of the world's largest privately owned shipbuilding yards. Norfolk and Portsmouth also have shipbuilding and repair yards.

Food processing ranks fourth. Virginia's chief food products include baked goods, dairy products, and meat products. Smithfield is famous for hams. The Shenandoah Valley has many large poultry processing plants. Baked goods are produced in many parts of the state. Candy and seafood products also rank among Virginia's leading food products.

Chemicals rank fifth among goods manufactured in Virginia. *Pharmaceuticals* (medicinal drugs) are the leading chemical product. Elkton, Petersburg, and Richmond have pharmaceutical plants. Other important chemical products include paints and synthetic fibers.

Virginia's other manufactured products include paper products, plastics and rubber products, and printed

Economy of Virginia

This map shows the economic uses of land in Virginia and where the state's leading farm and mineral products are produced. Major manufacturing centers, which are in the state's urban areas, are shown in red.

WORLD BOOK map

☐ Mostly cropland		▨ Urban area	
▨ Woodland mixed with cropland and grazing		• Manufacturing or service industry center	
▨ Mostly forest land		• Mineral deposit	

Limestone · Fruit · Stone · Arlington · Cement · Beef cattle · Horses · Stone · Turkeys · Granite · Milk · Poultry · Corn · Corn · Milk · Stone · Clay · Sand, Gravel · Vegetables · Milk · Vermiculite · Vegetables · Soapstone · Corn · Soybeans · Oysters · Vegetables · Beef cattle · Slate · Richmond · Clay · Crabs · Cement · Kyanite · Fish · Fruit · Poultry · Poultry · Sand, Gravel · Fish · Limestone · Roanoke · Milk · Petersburg · Hogs · Newport News · Coal · Coal · Coal · Clay · Beef cattle · Tobacco · Corn · Norfolk · Coal · Natural gas · Soybeans · Portsmouth · Virginia Beach · Coal · Beef cattle · Milk · Milk · Clay · Vegetables · Hogs · Sand, Gravel · Petroleum · Stone · Clay · Beef cattle · Stone · Poultry · Tobacco · Vegetables · Clay · Tobacco

materials. Tires are manufactured in the Danville and Roanoke areas. Many paper products are made in the Richmond area. Valuable printed materials include books, business forms, and newspapers.

Agriculture. Virginia has about 47,000 farms. Farmland covers about a third of the state's land area.

Livestock and livestock products provide about 70 percent of Virginia's farm income. *Broilers* (young, tender chickens) are the state's most valuable farm product. Beef cattle rank next among Virginia's farm products. Other main livestock products include milk and turkeys. Rockingham County in northwestern Virginia is a lead-

ing producer of beef cattle, broilers, milk, and turkeys. Virginia ranks as a leading state in raising turkeys. Farmers also raise hogs, mainly in eastern Virginia.

Tobacco, once the basis of Virginia's economy, remains one of the state's most valuable cash crops. Farmers grow tobacco on only a small part of Virginia's cropland. Most tobacco is grown in the Piedmont region south of the James River and in the far western part of the state. Other leading field crops in Virginia are corn and soybeans.

Most commercial production of vegetables takes place near Chesapeake Bay. Virginia's leading vegetable crops include cucumbers, potatoes, and tomatoes. The state has large apple orchards. Most of the apples are grown in the Shenandoah Valley.

Mining. Coal is Virginia's chief mined product. Most of it comes from Buchanan and Wise counties in the southwestern part of the state. Most of Virginia's mines are underground and produce bituminous coal.

Among Virginia's other mined products, crushed stone and natural gas are the most valuable. Most Virginia counties produce crushed stone. Natural gas comes mainly from wells in western Virginia. The state's other mined products include cement, clay, kyanite, lime, and sand and gravel.

Fishing industry. Virginia's yearly fish catch is worth about $150 million. Virginia is a leading state in crab and scallop production. Other important fish catches include Atlantic croaker, menhaden, summer flounder, spot, and striped bass. The Hampton Roads area has the state's leading fishing port.

Electric power and utilities. Virginia's utilities provide electric, gas, and water service. Dominion Virginia Power is the state's biggest utility. Plants that burn coal supply about half of the electric power generated in Virginia. Nuclear power plants provide about one-third. Most of the remaining electric power comes from plants that burn petroleum or natural gas.

Transportation. Virginia has more than 71,000 miles (114,000 kilometers) of roads and highways. Long

AP/Wide World

A huge shipyard in Newport News has built hundreds of vessels for military and commercial purposes. The city is one of the nation's largest centers for shipbuilding and ship repair.

bridges cross the Tidewater rivers. The Chesapeake Bay Bridge Tunnel, 18 miles (29 kilometers) long, connects the mainland with the Eastern Shore. Ferries provide transportation across some bay inlets.

The first Virginia railroad began operating in 1831. The wooden track, 13 miles (21 kilometers) long, linked the coal mines of Chesterfield County with Richmond. Today, nine rail lines provide freight service on about 3,400 miles (5,500 kilometers) of rail track in the state.

Virginia is home to two of the nation's busiest airports. Washington Dulles International Airport, one of the nation's largest in area, is in Herndon. Ronald Reagan Washington National Airport is near Alexandria. Virginia's other main airports are at Norfolk and Richmond.

Large ships can travel on Chesapeake Bay and some distance up the James and Potomac rivers. Hampton Roads, at the junction of the James, Nansemond, and Elizabeth rivers, is an important harbor area. Norfolk, on Hampton Roads, is one of the leading ports in the United States. Other ports include Newport News on Hampton Roads, Alexandria on the Potomac, and Hopewell and Richmond on the James. The Dismal Swamp Canal and the Albemarle and Chesapeake Canal form part of the Atlantic Intracoastal Waterway (see **Atlantic Intracoastal Waterway**).

Communication. In 1736, William Parks, Virginia's public printer, founded the *Virginia Gazette,* the first newspaper in the colony. Today, the *Richmond Times-Dispatch* and *The Virginian-Pilot* of Norfolk are among the most widely read dailies in the state. *USA Today,* a national newspaper, is based in the state. Publishers in Virginia produce about 210 newspapers, about 25 of which are dailies.

Virginia's first commercial radio station, WTAR, began in Norfolk in 1923. The state's first television station, WTVR, started in Richmond in 1948. Virginia has about 360 radio stations and 25 television stations. Cable TV systems and Internet providers serve most communities.

Government

Constitution of Virginia became effective in 1971. The state had five earlier constitutions, which went into effect in 1776, 1830, 1851, 1869, and 1902.

Constitutional amendments may be proposed in either house of the state legislature. To become law, the proposed amendments must be approved by a majority of both houses in two successive sessions. Then they must be approved by a majority of people who vote on the issue. The Constitution may also be amended by a constitutional convention. Such a convention is called by a majority of the legislature with the approval of a majority of Virginia's voters.

Executive. The governor of Virginia is elected to a four-year term and cannot serve two terms in a row. The lieutenant governor also is elected to a four-year term. The governor appoints most top state officials, including the secretary of the commonwealth, adjutant general, treasurer, and comptroller. The people of Virginia elect the attorney general to a four-year term. The legislature elects the auditor, who also serves a four-year term.

Legislature of Virginia is called the General Assembly. It is the oldest representative legislature in America. It traces its history to the House of Burgesses, formed in 1619 (see **House of Burgesses**).

The General Assembly consists of a 40-member Senate and a 100-member House of Delegates. The Senate and the House of Delegates are apportioned into single-member districts. Voters in each senatorial district elect one senator, and voters in each delegate district elect one delegate. Senators serve four-year terms, and delegates serve two-year terms.

The General Assembly holds regular sessions every year. Sessions begin on the second Wednesday in January. They last up to 60 days in even-numbered years and up to 30 days in odd-numbered years. The General Assembly may extend a session by up to 30 days. The governor may call special sessions.

By law, the legislature must *reapportion* (redivide) itself the year after each U.S. census. The redistricting is designed to provide equal representation based on population.

Courts. The state's highest court is the Supreme Court of Virginia. It has seven justices, who are elected by the General Assembly to 12-year terms. The chief justice is chosen by a majority vote of the seven justices. The next highest court is the Court of Appeals of Virginia. It hears criminal cases, workers' compensation cases, domestic relations cases, and appeals from the Circuit Court, the next highest court in Virginia. Judges on the Court of Appeals and the Circuit Court serve eight-year terms. Lower courts in Virginia include juvenile and domestic relations courts and general district courts. The General Assembly elects the judges of these courts to six-year terms.

Local government. Virginia has 95 counties. Each county, except Arlington, is governed by a board of supervisors. Arlington has a county board. In most counties, voters elect other officials, including a commissioner of revenue, treasurer, sheriff, commonwealth's attorney, and county clerk. The clerk has an eight-year term. The other officials serve four-year terms. A few counties have a county-manager or county-executive government. In these counties, a county manager or the board of supervisors appoints executive officials.

Any Virginia town with 5,000 or more people may become an independent city if the people so wish. Virginia has 40 independent cities. Unlike the cities of most other states, these 40 cities are legally separate from the counties in which they sit. One of the first forms of council-manager government in a U.S. city was established in Staunton in 1908. Today, all Virginia cities have council-manager governments. Some towns in Virginia have council-manager governments, and the others have mayor-council governments.

Revenue. Taxes account for approximately half of the state government's *general revenue* (income). Most of the rest comes from federal grants and charges for state government services. A state lottery also contributes to the general revenue. The largest source of state tax revenue in Virginia is a personal income tax. The state's second largest source of tax revenue is a general sales tax. Other important tax revenue sources include taxes on al-

The **Virginia Senate** meets in chambers in the State Capitol in Richmond. The 40 members are elected to four-year terms.

Everett C. Johnson, StockFile

The state governors of Virginia

	Party	Term		Party	Term
Patrick Henry	None	1776-1779	William Smith	Democratic	1864-1865
Thomas Jefferson	None	1779-1781	Francis H. Pierpont	Republican	1865-1868
William Fleming	None	1781	Henry H. Wells	Republican	1868-1869
Thomas Nelson, Jr.	None	1781	Gilbert C. Walker	Republican	1869-1874
Benjamin Harrison	None	1781-1784	James L. Kemper	Democratic	1874-1878
Patrick Henry	None	1784-1786	Frederick W. M. Holliday	Democratic	1878-1882
Edmund Randolph	None	1786-1788	William E. Cameron	R.-Rep.†	1882-1886
Beverley Randolph	None	1788-1791	Fitzhugh Lee	Democratic	1886-1890
Henry Lee	Federalist	1791-1794	Philip W. McKinney	Democratic	1890-1894
Robert Brooke	Dem.-Rep.*	1794-1796	Charles T. O'Ferrall	Democratic	1894-1898
James Wood	Dem.-Rep.	1796-1799	James Hoge Tyler	Democratic	1898-1902
James Monroe	Dem.-Rep.	1799-1802	Andrew Jackson Montague	Democratic	1902-1906
John Page	Dem.-Rep.	1802-1805	Claude A. Swanson	Democratic	1906-1910
William H. Cabell	Dem.-Rep.	1805-1808	William Hodges Mann	Democratic	1910-1914
John Tyler, Sr.	Dem.-Rep.	1808-1811	Henry Carter Stuart	Democratic	1914-1918
James Monroe	Dem.-Rep.	1811	Westmoreland Davis	Democratic	1918-1922
George William Smith	Dem.-Rep.	1811	Elbert Lee Trinkle	Democratic	1922-1926
Peyton Randolph	Dem.-Rep.	1811-1812	Harry Flood Byrd	Democratic	1926-1930
James Barbour	Dem.-Rep.	1812-1814	John Garland Pollard	Democratic	1930-1934
Wilson Cary Nicholas	Dem.-Rep.	1814-1816	George C. Peery	Democratic	1934-1938
James Patton Preston	Dem.-Rep.	1816-1819	James H. Price	Democratic	1938-1942
Thomas Mann Randolph	Dem.-Rep.	1819-1822	Colgate W. Darden, Jr.	Democratic	1942-1946
James Pleasants	Dem.-Rep.	1822-1825	William M. Tuck	Democratic	1946-1950
John Tyler, Jr.	Dem.-Rep.	1825-1827	John S. Battle	Democratic	1950-1954
William Branch Giles	Democratic	1827-1830	Thomas B. Stanley	Democratic	1954-1958
John Floyd	Democratic	1830-1834	J. Lindsay Almond, Jr.	Democratic	1958-1962
Littleton Waller Tazewell	Whig	1834-1836	Albertis S. Harrison, Jr.	Democratic	1962-1966
Wyndham Robertson	Whig	1836-1837	Mills E. Godwin, Jr.	Democratic	1966-1970
David Campbell	Democratic	1837-1840	A. Linwood Holton, Jr.	Republican	1970-1974
Thomas Walker Gilmer	Whig	1840-1841	Mills E. Godwin, Jr.	Republican	1974-1978
John Mercer Patton	Whig	1841	John N. Dalton	Republican	1978-1982
John Rutherford	Whig	1841-1842	Charles S. Robb	Democratic	1982-1986
John Munford Gregory	Whig	1842-1843	Gerald L. Baliles	Democratic	1986-1990
James McDowell	Democratic	1843-1846	L. Douglas Wilder	Democratic	1990-1994
William Smith	Democratic	1846-1849	George Allen	Republican	1994-1998
John Buchanan Floyd	Democratic	1849-1852	James S. Gilmore III	Republican	1998-2002
Joseph Johnson	Democratic	1852-1856	Mark R. Warner	Democratic	2002-2006
Henry A. Wise	Democratic	1856-1860	Timothy M. Kaine	Democratic	2006-
John Letcher	Democratic	1860-1864			

*Democratic-Republican   †Readjuster-Republican

coholic beverages, corporate profits, insurance premiums, motor fuels, motor vehicle licenses, and public utilities.

Politics. The Democratic Party controlled state politics throughout most of Virginia's history. However, Republican Party strength increased during the last half of the 1900's. In 1969, A. Linwood Holton, Jr., became the first Republican to be elected governor of Virginia since 1869. By the end of the 1990's, the Republican Party had become the dominant party in the state. However, Democrats won governor's races in 2001 and 2005 and a U.S. Senate seat in 2006.

Until the 1950's, Virginia voted for the Democratic candidate in presidential elections most of the time. Since then, the state's voters have usually supported the Republican candidate (see **Electoral College** [table]).

History

Early days. When the first English colonists arrived in the Virginia region, American Indian tribes of three major language groups lived there. The Powhatan, who were members of the Algonquian language group, lived in the coastal area. The Monacan and Manahoac, who spoke the Siouan language, occupied the Piedmont Plateau. Other Siouan tribes included the Nahyssan along the James River and the Occaneechi along the Roanoke River. The Susquehanna near the upper Chesapeake Bay, the Cherokee in the southwest, and the Nottoway in the southeast spoke the Iroquoian language.

The first Europeans who settled in Virginia were a group of Spanish Jesuits. In 1570, the group established a mission, perhaps on the York River. However, Indians wiped out the settlement a few months later.

In 1584, Queen Elizabeth I of England gave the English adventurer Sir Walter Raleigh permission to establish colonies in America. Raleigh and others soon sent expeditions there. These expeditions failed because they had too few supplies. Historians think it was Raleigh who gave the name *Virginia* to what is now the Eastern United States. The name honored Elizabeth, who was known as the *Virgin Queen.*

The Jamestown settlement. In 1606, King James I chartered the Virginia Company of London (later shortened to Virginia Company) for colonization purposes (see **London Company**). In May 1607, colonists sent by the company established the first permanent English settlement in America, at Jamestown. The colony, led by Captain John Smith, survived many hardships. In 1609, Smith was injured and had to return to England. The following winter, so many settlers died from lack of food that the period became known as the *starving time.* In the spring, the discouraged colonists started to leave Jamestown. But they returned after they met the ships of Governor Thomas West, Lord De La Warr, at Hampton Roads. The ships brought supplies and new colonists. After Lord De La Warr returned to England, Thomas Gates and Thomas Dale served as deputy governors.

Progress of the colony. John Rolfe, one of the colonists, began to raise tobacco in 1612. Rolfe improved the method of curing tobacco. Rolfe also proved that tobacco could be successfully exported. Tobacco exporting helped save the colony. In 1614, Rolfe married Pocahontas, a daughter of Powhatan, chief of the Indian confederation around Jamestown. Their marriage brought a period of peace between the Indians and the colonists.

By 1619, all free colonists had been granted land of their own. That year, the Virginia Company made plans to send young women to the colony to become wives of the lonely settlers. Also in 1619, the first Africans were brought to Jamestown by Dutch traders.

The first representative legislature in America, the House of Burgesses, was formed in 1619. Its first meeting was called by Governor George Yeardley, who acted on instructions from the Virginia Company. The House of Burgesses met with the governor and his council to make laws for the colony. This combined lawmaking body was called the General Assembly of Virginia.

Chief Powhatan died in 1618. In 1622, his successor, Chief Opechancanough, led an attack on the colonists. The Indians killed more than 300 colonists.

Royal governors and Cromwell. In 1624, King James I revoked the Virginia Company's charter and made Virginia a royal colony. The colonists often quarreled with the royal governors sent by England. Sir William Berkeley, who served as governor from 1642 to 1652, had good relations with the colonists. But in 1652, Berkeley was forced to surrender Virginia to the rule of Oliver Cromwell, who had overthrown King Charles I.

From 1652 until Charles II became king in 1660, the Virginia colonists were allowed to take almost complete charge of their own government. In spite of the political freedom they enjoyed under Cromwell, most of the colonists remained loyal to the English royalists. Some English supporters of the future King Charles II, called Cavaliers, sought refuge in Virginia.

In 1660, after Berkeley had been elected by the royalist Virginia assembly, Charles II reappointed him governor. Berkeley's new term brought widespread discontent. The governor kept the same members of the House of Burgesses in office for 14 years. Berkeley also allowed a *Tidewater aristocracy* to rule the colony. This group included the heads of the wealthy eastern families.

Westward expansion. By the mid-1600's, many small farmers had pushed westward to the eastern edge of the Piedmont Plateau. This area is known as the *fall line.* The interests of the western farmers differed from those of the Tidewater aristocracy. The westerners wanted protection from the Indians and fewer political and economic regulations. They resented the English government's navigation acts, which greatly restricted colonial trade (see **Navigation Acts**). A group of discontented colonists rebelled against the government in 1676. They were led by Nathaniel Bacon, a young planter (see **Bacon's Rebellion**). In 1699, the capital was moved from Jamestown to Williamsburg.

By 1700, Virginia had a population of about 58,000 and was the largest North American colony. The growing population took up all the land along the tidal rivers and creeks. Therefore, many pioneers moved westward into the Piedmont Plateau, the Great Valley, and the mountains. Germans and Scotch-Irish from Pennsylvania also settled in the Great Valley. The westward expansion of

Historic Virginia

Jamestown was the first permanent English settlement in America. Captain John Smith and a group of English colonists established the settlement in May 1607.

WORLD BOOK map

Virginia was settled by English colonists in the early 1600's. Virginia became a U.S. state in 1788. In 1863, during the American Civil War, West Virginia was formed from northwestern Virginia.

Lee surrendered to Grant at Appomattox Court House on April 9, 1865. Within the next two months, all remaining Confederate forces also surrendered, ending the American Civil War.

WORLD BOOK illustrations by Richard Bonson, The Art Agency

Important dates in Virginia

1607 The Virginia Company of London established the colony of Jamestown.

1612 John Rolfe helped save the colony by introducing tobacco growing and exporting.

1619 America's first representative legislature, the House of Burgesses, met in Jamestown. Dutch traders brought the first blacks to Jamestown.

1624 Virginia became a royal colony.

1676 Nathaniel Bacon led a rebellion against the government.

1693 The College of William and Mary was founded.

1775 George Washington, a Virginian, became commander in chief of the Continental Army.

1776 Virginia declared its independence and adopted its first constitution, which included a declaration of rights. Thomas Jefferson of Virginia wrote the Declaration of Independence.

1781 Lord Cornwallis surrendered to George Washington at Yorktown in the last major battle of the American Revolution.

1788 Virginia became the 10th state on June 25.

1789 George Washington became the first president of the United States.

1792 Kentucky was formed from Virginia's westernmost counties.

1801-1825 Three Virginians served as president: Thomas Jefferson (1801-1809), James Madison (1809-1817), and James Monroe (1817-1825).

1831 Nat Turner led a famous slave revolt.

1841 William Henry Harrison, born in Virginia, became president. Harrison died a month later. Vice President John Tyler, also a Virginian, became president.

1849 Zachary Taylor, another Virginian, became president.

1861-1865 Virginia seceded from the Union and became the major battleground of the American Civil War.

1863 West Virginia was formed from northwestern Virginia.

1870 Virginia was readmitted to the Union.

1912 Woodrow Wilson became the eighth Virginian to be elected president.

1940-1945 New industries opened during World War II.

1969 A. Linwood Holton, Jr., became the first Republican to be elected Virginia's governor since 1869.

1971 A new state constitution went into effect.

1990-1994 L. Douglas Wilder served as Virginia's governor. Wilder was the first African American to be elected governor of a U.S. state.

2007 Virginia Polytechnic Institute and State University (Virginia Tech) became the site of the deadliest school shooting in U.S. history on April 16.

Nathaniel Bacon, *right,* led a rebellion against Virginia governor William Berkeley, *left,* in 1676. Bacon, a prosperous planter, and other farmers in western Virginia wanted protection from Indians and fewer economic regulations.

National Park Service, Jamestown

the British colonists conflicted with the interests of the French and led to the French and Indian War of 1754-1763 (see **French and Indian wars**).

During the early 1770's, frequent Indian raids spread terror along the western frontier. In 1774, these attacks led to a campaign against the Indians called Lord Dunmore's War, after Virginia's governor, John Murray, Earl of Dunmore. A group of Virginia soldiers led by Andrew Lewis defeated the Shawnee Indians at Point Pleasant (now in West Virginia) on Oct. 10, 1774. Indian attacks then decreased in western Virginia.

The course toward independence. Like many other colonists, Virginia's leaders were disturbed by the laws passed by the British Parliament without the consent of the colonies (see **Revolutionary War in America** [British policy changes]). Although most Virginians were loyal to the king, they favored liberty and wanted to govern their own affairs. Virginia's leaders, including Patrick Henry and Thomas Jefferson, led the way in voicing the complaints of the colonists. Patrick Henry's resolutions helped arouse the colonists against the Stamp Act in 1765 (see **Stamp Act**).

In 1774, the British Parliament ordered the port of Boston closed, following the Boston Tea Party in 1773 (see **Boston Tea Party**). The House of Burgesses, in sympathy with the Boston colonists, made the day of the port closing a day of fasting and prayer. This action angered Lord Dunmore, and he dissolved the House of Burgesses. Its members then met without official permission on Aug. 1, 1774, in Williamsburg. They called themselves the First Virginia Convention. The members elected delegates to the First Continental Congress (see **Continental Congress**). A Virginia delegate, Peyton Randolph, was chosen president of the congress.

At the Second Virginia Convention, on March 23, 1775, at St. John's Church in Richmond, Patrick Henry made his plea for the colonial cause. According to tradition, his speech included the famous words, "Give me liberty or give me death!"

Independence and statehood. In 1775, the Second Continental Congress elected George Washington, a Virginian, as commander in chief of the Continental Army. Virginia became an independent commonwealth in June 1776, when it adopted its first constitution. The constitution included a declaration of rights written by Virginia statesman George Mason. This declaration was the first bill of rights in an American constitution. Patrick Henry was elected as the commonwealth's first governor. The capital of the commonwealth was moved from Williamsburg to Richmond in 1780.

Virginia militiamen drove Lord Dunmore from the colony after several skirmishes in 1776. Also in 1776, the colony submitted to the Continental Congress a resolution calling for American independence (see **Declaration of Independence**).

During the Revolutionary War (1775-1783), a larger proportion of people in Virginia opposed the British than in any other southern colony. The Declaration of Independence was written by Thomas Jefferson, who later served as the state's second governor. Virginia also contributed the great cavalry leader "Light-Horse Harry" Lee and Daniel Morgan, the hero of the battles of Freeman's Farm and Cowpens. In 1778 and 1779, George Rogers Clark won victories in the Northwest Territory. His forces took from the British Kaskaskia and Cahokia in what is now Illinois, and Vincennes in present-day Indiana. This territory had long been claimed by Virginia. In 1781, the last major battle of the war was fought on Virginia soil, at Yorktown. In the battle, Lord Cornwallis surrendered to George Washington.

Until 1789, the 13 former colonies were loosely joined under the Articles of Confederation (see **Articles of Confederation**). Virginia had *ratified* (approved) the Articles on July 9, 1778. In order to persuade Maryland to accept the Articles, Virginia promised in 1781 to give up its claim to the Northwest Territory. Virginia did so in 1784 (see **Northwest Territory**).

The Articles of Confederation soon proved ineffective. James Madison and other Virginians led in creating the Constitution of the United States to replace the Articles. Virginia ratified the Constitution on June 25, 1788, and became the 10th state of the Union.

The *Mother of Presidents*. Virginia furnished the United States with four of its first five presidents— George Washington, Thomas Jefferson, James Madison, and James Monroe. Washington was elected as the first president in 1789. He appointed Jefferson as the first secretary of state and Edmund Randolph as the first attorney general. In 1792, the westernmost counties of Virginia became the state of Kentucky.

Thomas Jefferson, James Madison, and James Monroe were often called the *Virginia Dynasty.* During their presidential terms, they strengthened the new nation and added new territory to it. Another Virginian, John Marshall, served as chief justice of the United States from 1801 to 1835.

In 1830, Virginia adopted a new constitution, chiefly as a result of growing discontent in the western counties. The new constitution gave the westerners more representation in the General Assembly. But eastern leaders kept control of the government.

In 1831, Nat Turner, a black slave and preacher from Southampton County, led a famous slave rebellion. About 60 whites were killed—more than in any other slave revolt in United States history. After the rebellion, the Virginia legislature tentatively discussed the abolition of slavery. But all measures promoting an end to slavery were defeated.

In 1841, two more Virginians became president. William Henry Harrison and John Tyler had been born in the same Virginia county. Harrison died a month after his inauguration, and Tyler became president. During the Mexican War (1846-1848), Virginia furnished many of the chief military leaders, including Generals Winfield Scott and Zachary Taylor. Largely because of his military fame, Taylor was elected president in 1848.

The western counties continued to press for reforms in government. Their demands were incorporated into the Constitution of 1851. This constitution gave all white men the right to vote. It also provided for the election of the governor and other officials by popular vote. Until that time, only landowners could vote, and the General Assembly had elected the governor.

The Civil War and Reconstruction. South Carolina and six other Southern states withdrew from the Union during the winter of 1860-1861. But Virginia remained in the Union. Most Virginians hoped that compromise could save the Union and prevent war. President Abraham Lincoln called for troops on April 15, 1861. Two days later, a Virginia convention voted to *secede* (withdraw) from the Union.

Many westerners in Virginia would not agree to secede. They set up an independent government in northwestern Virginia that stayed loyal to the Union. On June 20, 1863, 48 counties of northwestern Virginia became the state of West Virginia. Two other counties joined them in November 1863.

Richmond was the capital of the Confederacy from May 1861 to April 1865, when it surrendered to Union troops. Danville served briefly as the last headquarters of the Confederacy. Virginia's Robert E. Lee gained lasting fame as the South's outstanding military leader. The state contributed other leading Confederate generals, including Stonewall Jackson, Joseph E. Johnston, John S. Mosby, George E. Pickett, and Jeb Stuart.

The South won its greatest victories on Virginia battlefields—the first and second battles of Bull Run (also called Manassas), Jackson's Valley Campaign, and the battles of Fredericksburg and Chancellorsville. More battles were fought in Virginia than in any other state. Union armies repeatedly tried to seize Richmond and the Shenandoah Valley. This fertile valley was called the *Granary of the Confederacy.* The 1862 battle between the *Monitor* and the *Merrimack* (which was renamed the *Virginia* by the Confederate Navy) at Hampton Roads was the first fight between ironclad warships. This battle marked a turning point in naval warfare.

The Civil War, like the Revolutionary War, ended in Virginia. Lee surrendered to General Ulysses S. Grant at Appomattox on April 9, 1865.

After the war, the federal government passed the Reconstruction Act of 1867, which placed Virginia under army rule as Military District No. 1. This act also provided for a state constitutional convention to draw up a new constitution for Virginia. The constitutional convention, headed by Judge John C. Underwood, met in December 1867. It was controlled by Radical Republicans, and nearly a fourth of its members were blacks. A constitution was adopted in 1869. It gave blacks the right to vote and provided for a statewide system of public

Bettmann Archive

Richmond lay in ruins after the Civil War ended in 1865. Richmond was the Confederate capital during most of the war. Warehouse fires, set by fleeing Confederates, were whipped out of control by strong winds and burned much of the city.

schools. Virginia was readmitted to the Union on Jan. 26, 1870. See **Reconstruction.**

A major problem facing Virginia after the war was its debt of about $45 million. The state became divided between the "funders," who wanted to pay the debt, and the "readjusters," who wanted to pay only part of it. The Readjuster Party finally triumphed by bringing about passage of the Riddleberger Act of 1882. The act reduced the state's share of the debt to about $21 million. Later court decisions assigned $14 million to West Virginia. That state had been part of Virginia when the debt was acquired (see **West Virginia** [Civil War and statehood]). After the settlement of the debt issue, the Readjuster Party soon dissolved.

Progress in government and industry. Modern industry in Virginia began during the early 1880's, when cigarette factories, cotton textile plants, and shipbuilding plants were built. In 1912, another man born in Virginia, Woodrow Wilson, was elected president. Carter Glass of Lynchburg, then a congressman, became the "father" of the Federal Reserve banking system.

During the early 1900's, many Virginians moved to other states in search of better job opportunities. More than 400,000 people left the state in the 1920's.

Harry F. Byrd, Sr., was governor from 1926 to 1930. He used the recommendations of a study commission to reorganize the state government and make it more efficient. In 1933, Byrd was appointed to the U.S. Senate, where he served more than 30 years. Throughout this period, Byrd played a leading role in Virginia politics.

The 1930's were an important period of change in Virginia. Federal government activities in the state during the Great Depression created jobs and helped stop the flow of population leaving the state. Synthetic textile industries were established in many parts of Virginia.

World War II (1939-1945) brought thousands of servicemen and servicewomen to the Virginia suburbs of Washington, D.C., and to the Norfolk area. Many of these people returned to Virginia to live after the war. During the 1940's and 1950's, the state also attracted many other new residents, including federal employees and employees of new industries. By 1955, it had more urban than rural dwellers.

School integration. Many Virginia communities built new schools during the 1950's. In the late 1950's, the issue of school integration became critical.

In 1954, the Supreme Court of the United States ruled that compulsory segregation in public schools was unconstitutional. In 1956, the Virginia legislature passed so-called "massive resistance" laws to close any public school that the federal courts ordered integrated. In 1959, federal and state courts declared these laws invalid. That same year, public schools in Arlington County and Norfolk became the first in Virginia to integrate. But Prince Edward County closed its public schools in 1959 to avoid integration. It reopened the schools in 1964. In the late 1960's, a series of court decisions speeded up integration in the state.

Continued industrial growth. Industry continued to expand in Virginia during the 1960's. The greatest growth occurred in the manufacture of chemicals, clothing, electrical equipment, furniture, and transportation equipment. In 1964, the General Assembly reduced certain taxes to attract new industry.

The $200-million Chesapeake Bay Bridge-Tunnel was completed in 1964. This series of bridges, tunnels, and causeways extends 23 miles (37 kilometers) and links the Norfolk area with the Eastern Shore.

Political changes. Virginia's political life changed during the 1960's. Conservative Democrats, led by U.S. Senator Harry F. Byrd, Sr., had long controlled Virginia politics. But Byrd retired in 1965, and elections became more competitive. In 1966, Virginia voters elected William B. Spong, Jr., a moderate Democrat, to the U.S. Senate. In 1967, William F. Reid became the first African American elected to the state legislature since 1891. The Republican Party also gained strength during the 1960's. In 1969, A. Linwood Holton, Jr., became the first Republican to be elected governor since 1869. In 1970, voters approved a new state constitution. It took effect in 1971.

Pollution problems. During the 1970's and 1980's, urban settlement and the location of industries along Chesapeake Bay caused pollution and some damage to plants and wildlife. Efforts to clean the water and to protect the threatened plants and animals were begun.

Virginia, a leading coal-producing state, also was challenged by the reduced use of coal in the United States. This situation developed because of widespread concern over air pollution caused by the burning of coal. Scientists sought ways to reduce the pollution hazard so more coal could be used.

Recent developments. In 1989, Virginia's voters elected L. Douglas Wilder governor. Wilder became the first African American ever elected governor of a U.S. state. He served one term, from 1990 to 1994.

Virginia maintained a strong economy through the end of the 1900's and into the 2000's. This is largely because the state's economy has a broad base. Manufacturing, agriculture, tourism, and activities of the federal government all contribute much to the economy.

In April 2007, Virginia Polytechnic Institute and State University (Virginia Tech) in Blacksburg was the site of the deadliest shooting in U.S. history. A student gunman killed 32 people, including 27 fellow students and 5 teachers, and wounded many more before taking his own life.   Ted Tunnell and Susan L. Woodward

Related articles in *World Book* include:

Biographies

Bacon, Nathaniel	Mosby, John S.
Berkeley, Sir William	Nelson, Thomas, Jr.
Blair, John	Newport, Christopher
Braxton, Carter	Pickett, George E.
Byrd, Richard E.	Powhatan
Byrd, William, II	Randolph, Edmund
Gabriel	Randolph, John
Glass, Carter	Randolph, Peyton
Harrison, Benjamin	Rolfe, John
(1726-1791)	Ruffin, Edmund
Harrison, William H.	Seddon, James A.
Henry, Patrick	Smith, John
Jefferson, Thomas	Spotswood, Alexander
Johnston, Joseph E.	Stuart, Jeb
Lee, Francis L.	Taylor, Zachary
Lee, Henry	Turner, Nat
Lee, Richard H.	Tyler, John
Lee, Robert E.	Washington, Booker T.
Madison, James	Washington, George
Marshall, John	Washington, Martha Custis
Mason, George	Wilder, L. Douglas
Mason, James Murray	Wilson, Woodrow
Monroe, James	Wythe, George

Cities

Alexandria	Petersburg
Charlottesville	Richmond
Fredericksburg	Roanoke
Hampton	Virginia Beach
Newport News	Williamsburg
Norfolk	Yorktown

History

Annapolis Convention
Civil War, American
Colonial life in America
Harpers Ferry
House of Burgesses
Jamestown
Kentucky and Virginia resolutions
London Company
Revolutionary War in America

Military installations

Fort Belvoir	Fort Monroe
Fort Eustis	Langley Air Force Base
Fort Lee	

Physical features

Allegheny Mountains	James River
Appalachian Mountains	Luray Caverns
Blue Ridge Mountains	Piedmont Region
Chesapeake Bay	Potomac River
Cumberland Gap	Rappahannock River
Dismal Swamp	Shenandoah River
Fall line	Shenandoah Valley
Hampton Roads	

Other related articles

Appomattox Court House
Arlington National Cemetery
Booker T. Washington National Monument
George Washington Birthplace National Monument
Monticello
Mount Vernon
Pentagon Building
Shenandoah National Park

Outline

I. **People**
  A. Population
  B. Schools
  C. Libraries and museums
II. **Visitor's guide**
  A. Places to visit
  B. Annual events
III. **Land and climate**
  A. Land regions   D. Plant and animal life
  B. Coastline   E. Climate
  C. Rivers and lakes
IV. **Economy**
  A. Natural resources   F. Fishing industry
  B. Service industries   G. Electric power and utilities
  C. Manufacturing   H. Transportation
  D. Agriculture   I. Communication
  E. Mining
V. **Government**
  A. Constitution   E. Local government
  B. Executive   F. Revenue
  C. Legislature   G. Politics
  D. Courts
VI. **History**

Questions

When and where was Virginia's first public library established?
What was the Granary of the Confederacy?
Where are Virginia's highest peaks?
Why did discontent spread throughout the Virginia colony after King Charles II reappointed William Berkeley governor?

What are Virginia's chief manufactured products?
Why is Virginia's General Assembly notable?
What is Virginia's most important mineral resource?
What Virginia college is the second oldest institution of higher learning in the United States?
Why is Virginia called the *Old Dominion?* The *Mother of Presidents?* The *Mother of States?*
Why did northwestern Virginia separate from the rest of the state in the 1860's?
What conditions in Virginia favor manufacturing and trade?

Additional resources

Level I
Barrett, Tracy. *Virginia.* 2nd ed. Benchmark Bks., 2004.
Blashfield, Jean F. *Virginia.* Children's Pr., 1999.
DeAngelis, Gina. *Virginia.* Children's Pr., 2001.
Pobst, Sandy. *Virginia, 1607-1776.* Children's Pr., 2004.
Pollack, Pamela. *Virginia.* World Almanac Lib., 2002.

Level II
Abramson, Rudy. *Hallowed Ground.* Lickle Pub., 1996. History of the development of the Piedmont region of Virginia.
Barnes, Brooks M., and Truitt, B. R., eds. *Seashore Chronicles: Three Centuries of the Virginia Barrier Islands.* Univ. Pr. of Va., 1997.
Billings, Warren M., and others. *Colonial Virginia.* KTO Pr., 1988.
Blair, William A. *Virginia's Private War: Feeding Body and Soul in the Confederacy, 1861-1865.* 1998. Reprint. Oxford, 2000.
Dabney, Virginius. *Virginia.* 1971. Reprint. Univ. Pr., of Va., 1983.
Ely, Melvin P. *Israel on the Appomattox: A Southern Experiment in Black Freedom from the 1790s Through the Civil War.* Knopf, 2004.
Selby, John E. *The Revolution in Virginia, 1775-1783.* Colonial Williamsburg, 1988.
Sturtz, Linda L. *Within Her Power: Propertied Women in Colonial Virginia.* Routledge, 2002.

Virginia, University of, is a state-controlled coeducational school in Charlottesville, Virginia. The university has a college of arts and sciences; schools of architecture, commerce, education, engineering and applied science, law, medicine, and nursing; and graduate schools of arts and sciences and business administration. Courses lead to bachelor's, master's, and doctor's degrees. The University of Virginia's College at Wise in Wise, Virginia, grants the bachelor's degree. Thomas Jefferson founded the University of Virginia in 1819. See also **Virginia** (picture).

Critically reviewed by the University of Virginia

Virginia Beach (pop. 425,257) is the largest city in Virginia. It is a resort as well as a busy urban center. Virginia Beach lies in the southeast corner of Virginia, bordering the Atlantic Ocean and Chesapeake Bay. For the city's location, see **Virginia** (political map).

Virginia Beach covers 310 square miles (803 square kilometers). It is part of the Virginia Beach-Norfolk-Newport News metropolitan area, which has a population of 1,576,370.

Virginia Beach is a popular resort city. It has a mild climate and 28 miles (45 kilometers) of public beaches. Inlets, streams, lakes, and the ocean coast of Virginia Beach offer opportunities for swimming, boating, and fishing. More than 2 ½ million tourists visit the city each year, greatly aiding the economy.

Virginia Beach is also a commercial center. A number of manufacturing, distributing, and service companies have headquarters in the city. The Christian Broadcasting Network is also headquartered there. Agriculture also contributes to the city's economy. Farmers raise fruits and vegetables in the rural southern part of Vir-

Virginia Beach Convention and Visitors Bureau

Virginia Beach has many sandy ocean beaches. Tall, modern buildings stand along a beach, *shown here.* Both a resort and busy urban center, Virginia Beach is Virginia's largest city.

ginia Beach. In addition, thousands of Virginia Beach residents work at one of the four military bases in the city or at nearby bases.

The cultural facilities of Virginia Beach include the Virginia Aquarium & Marine Science Center, the Contemporary Art Center of Virginia, and the Sandler Center for the Performing Arts. The city's historical sites include Adam Thoroughgood House, built in 1680, and Lynnhaven House, which dates from approximately 1725.

In 1607, the first permanent English settlers in America landed at Cape Henry in what is now Virginia Beach before establishing Jamestown nearby. Cape Henry Lighthouse, authorized and funded by the first Congress of the United States, was built on the cape in 1791. Permanent settlement began in what is now Virginia Beach in about 1621.

In the late 1800's, a small resort town began on the site of what is now Virginia Beach. It was incorporated as the town of Virginia Beach in 1906.

The community was still a small resort of about 8,000 people in 1960. In 1963, the town merged with Princess Anne County, increasing the community's population to about 100,000. Rapid population increases were soon accompanied by the growth of businesses. During the 1980's, Virginia Beach became the state's largest city. Virginia Beach has a council-manager form of government.
Elizabeth Thiel

Virginia City, Nevada, is one of the most celebrated and best-preserved old mining towns in the West. The American author Mark Twain, an early resident, wrote about its turbulent first years in his book *Roughing It* (1872). The town lies in the Virginia Range, 23 miles (37 kilometers) southeast of Reno. For its location, see **Nevada** (political map).

Virginia City was founded in 1859, after the discovery of rich gold and silver deposits in nearby canyons. Its population may have reached 25,000 in 1876, at the peak

of the Comstock Lode's producing power.

Today, the Virginia City area has only about 3,000 permanent residents. But tens of thousands of tourists visit the town each week during the summer. Virginia City serves as the seat of Storey County.   William D. Rowley

See also **Comstock Lode; Nevada** (picture).

Virginia creeper is a creeping and high-climbing woody plant. It is native to North America and grows in many other parts of the world. Virginia creeper is also called *woodbine, American ivy,* and *five-leaved ivy.*

Virginia creeper's strong but slender *tendrils* (specialized leaves) have long branches that end in tiny, sticky disks. The disks stick to surfaces on which the plant grows. A single tendril with five branches bearing these disks may hold up a weight of 10 pounds (4.5 kilograms).

Virginia creeper looks somewhat like poison ivy. But

Michael P. Gadomski, Earth Scenes

Virginia creeper adds brilliant color to its surroundings in autumn when its leaves turn flaming red.

the leaves of Virginia creeper have five leaflets, and those of poison ivy have three. In autumn, Virginia creeper has brilliant red leaves and bunches of dark blue berries.   Theodore R. Dudley

Scientific classification. Virginia creeper belongs to the family Vitaceae. Its scientific name is *Parthenocissus quinquefolia.*

See also **Ivy.**

Virginia Plan. See **Randolph, Edmund; Constitution of the United States** (The compromises).

Virginia Resolutions. See **Kentucky and Virginia Resolutions.**

Virginium. See **Francium.**

Virginius Affair was an incident in 1873 that almost started a war between the United States and Spain. During a Cuban revolt against Spanish rule called the Ten Years' War (1868-1878), the Spanish gunboat *Tornado* captured the ship *Virginius* off Jamaica. The Spanish claimed the ship was aiding the Cuban rebels. The *Virginius* was registered in New York and flew the American flag. Its captain, Joseph Fry, was an American.

Spanish authorities in Cuba executed Fry, 36 crew, and 16 passengers. United States President Ulysses S. Grant then demanded the release of the ship and the surviving passengers, threatening military action. Later, however, an investigation showed that the *Virginius* was illegally registered, had no right to fly the American flag, and was owned by Cubans. Nevertheless, Spain surrendered the ship and the survivors. It also made payments as compensation for the deaths of American and British citizens killed in the incident.   Michael Perman

Virgo is the sixth sign of the zodiac. Virgo, an earth sign, is symbolized by a virgin. Astrologers believe Virgo is ruled by the planet Mercury, which was named for the messenger of the ancient Roman gods. Among the ancient Greeks, Virgo was a symbol of fertility and the life cycle of birth, growth, and death.

According to astrologers, people born under the sign of Virgo, from August 23 to September 22, have characteristics typical of an earth sign. They are intelligent, practical, and sensible and like order and tidiness in all things. Virgoans are good at concentrating on details

Virgo—The Virgin

Symbol

Birth dates: Aug. 23–Sept. 22.
Group: Earth.
Characteristics: Careful, efficient, modest, orderly, practical, tidy.

Signs of the Zodiac

Aries
Mar. 21–Apr. 19
Taurus
Apr. 20–May 20
Gemini
May 21–June 20
Cancer
June 21–July 22
Leo
July 23–Aug. 22
**Virgo
Aug. 23–Sept. 22**
Libra
Sept. 23–Oct. 22
Scorpio
Oct. 23–Nov. 21
Sagittarius
Nov. 22–Dec. 21
Capricorn
Dec. 22–Jan. 19
Aquarius
Jan. 20–Feb. 18
Pisces
Feb. 19–Mar. 20

WORLD BOOK illustration by Robert Keys

and tend to find fault with things that other people consider unimportant.

Virgoans often rely on reason rather than emotion, and they may seem unsympathetic and proud. Virgoans succeed at jobs that require them to be orderly and pay attention to details. They are also successful at skilled crafts. Virgoans have an interest in health, which leads many into the medical professions.   Charles W. Clark

See also **Astrology; Horoscope; Zodiac.**

Viroid, *VY royd,* is one of the smallest known agents of infectious disease. All known viroids are highly structured molecules of *RNA* (ribonucleic acid) that cause disease in certain plants. There are no known animal or human viroids.

Like viruses, viroids can reproduce only within living cells. But viruses typically consist of a core of a nucleic acid surrounded by a coat of protein (see **Virus** [The structure of a virus]). Viroids lack a protein coat. Also, viroids are at least 10 times as small as the smallest viruses.

Scientists have identified about a dozen viroid diseases of higher plants. These diseases affect such diverse crops as potatoes, citrus fruits, tomatoes, palms, cucumbers, hops, chrysanthemums, and avocados. Many of these diseases cause significant economic

damage. For example, a disease that later proved to be caused by viroids nearly destroyed the chrysanthemum industry in the United States in the early 1950's.

The Swiss-born scientist Theodor O. Diener is credited with the discovery of viroids. In 1971, Diener published evidence that a particle that infected potatoes differed structurally from viruses. Diener proposed the term *viroid* to describe this submicroscopic particle.
           Robert A. Owens

Virtual reality, also known as *VR,* is an artificial, three-dimensional environment created by a computer. A VR experience replaces what a person normally sees and hears with computer-generated images and sounds, making the user feel as if he or she has entered another place.

In most VR systems, the user wears a head-mounted display (HMD), which contains two small display screens and stereo headphones. The HMD can be a helmet, goggles, or lightweight glasses. When wearing an HMD, the user sees a three-dimensional view, because the computer sends slightly different pictures to each eye.

In VR systems, sensors enable the computer to track the user's head and body movements. When the head is turned in a particular direction, the computer determines what the user sees and hears when looking in that direction. VR systems also feature special gloves that the user wears, or handheld devices. The computer uses signals from this equipment to track movements of the hands and to generate the illusion that the user is touching objects. This illusion is typically provided by visual and sound feedback given in response to the user's movements. But current virtual reality systems cannot mimic weight or resistance. A user who picks up a ball in a virtual environment, for example, does not feel the weight of the ball. In most VR systems, a wire runs from the headset and gloves to the computer. But some systems transmit signals wirelessly. Some VR systems allow a user to walk throughout a large room.

Along with *virtual reality,* the terms *virtual environment* and *synthetic environment* are sometimes used to

© Randy Pausch

A virtual reality system can help a user to quickly experiment with interior design. A head-mounted display enables this user to see in three dimensions the room that is projected on the screen. Sensors in the gloves enable her to "move" the furniture and other objects with the displayed hands.

describe room-sized devices. One such device, a CAVE (Cave Automatic Virtual Environment) system, projects images on the floor and any of three walls of a room, depending on the position of the user. Sometimes the term *VR* is also used to describe an interactive experience displayed on a single screen, such as a video game.

None of the current types of VR can duplicate the detail and complexity of the real world, but the illusion is good enough for use in various applications, particularly in training. The National Aeronautics and Space Administration (NASA) has used virtual reality to prepare astronauts and their ground crews for space shuttle missions. VR also has applications in architecture, education, engineering, and medicine.

The term *virtual reality* was coined by the artist and scientist Jaron Lanier in the late 1980's. But early research on VR began in the 1960's, most notably by the computer scientist Ivan Sutherland. VR games first appeared in stores and arcades in the early 1990's.

Randy Pausch

See also **Computer graphics.**

Virus is a microscopic organism that lives in a cell of another living thing. Although viruses are extremely small and simple, they are a major cause of disease. Some viruses infect human beings with such diseases as measles, influenza, and the common cold. Others infect animals or plants, and still others attack bacteria. Viruses produce disease in an organism by damaging some of its cells. However, viruses sometimes live in cells without harming them.

Viruses are so primitive that many scientists consider them to be both living and nonliving things. By itself, a virus is a lifeless particle that cannot reproduce. But inside a living cell, a virus becomes an active organism that can multiply hundreds of times.

Viruses are shaped like rods or spheres and range in size from about 0.01 to 0.3 micron. A micron is 0.001 millimeter or $\frac{1}{25,400}$ inch. Most viruses can be seen only with an electron microscope, which magnifies them by thousands of times. The largest virus is about $\frac{1}{10}$ as big as a bacterium of average size.

The study of viruses began in 1898, when a Dutch botanist named Martinus Beijerinck realized that something smaller than bacteria could cause disease. He named this particle a *virus,* a Latin word meaning *poison.* In 1935, Wendell M. Stanley, an American biochemist, showed that viruses contain protein and can be crystallized. This research and other studies led to the development, in the 1950's, of vaccines for measles, poliomyelitis, and other diseases. *Virologists* (scientists who study viruses) demonstrated in the early 1900's that viruses can cause cancer in animals. Late in the 1900's, research linked viruses to a few cancers in humans.

The structure of a virus. Viruses, unlike other organisms, are not made up of cells. Therefore, they lack some of the substances needed to live on their own. To obtain these substances, a virus must enter a cell of another living thing. It then can use the cell's materials to live and reproduce.

A typical virus has two basic parts, a core of a nucleic acid and an outer coat of protein. The core consists of either *DNA* (deoxyribonucleic acid) or *RNA* (ribonucleic acid). The DNA or RNA enables the virus to reproduce after it has entered a cell (see **DNA; RNA**). Some RNA viruses contain an enzyme called *reverse transcriptase,* which converts virus RNA to a DNA copy inside cells. Such viruses are called *retroviruses.* The virus that causes AIDS (acquired *i*mmuno*d*eficiency *s*yndrome) is a retrovirus. The coat of a virus consists of individual proteins that give the virus its shape. This coat protects the nucleic acid and helps the DNA or RNA get inside a cell. Some viruses have an additional outer membrane that provides further protection.

How a virus infects an organism. Most viruses reproduce in specific cells of certain organisms. For example, viruses that cause colds reproduce in cells of the human respiratory tract. Viruses cannot reproduce outside their particular cells. They must be carried into the organism by air currents or some other means, and then transported by body fluids to the cells.

When a virus comes into contact with a cell that it can enter, it attaches itself to the cell at areas called *receptors.* Chemicals in the receptors bind the virus to the cell and help bring it or its nucleic acid inside. The nucleic acid then takes control of the cell's protein-making process. Previously, the cell made only the proteins specified by its own *genes.* The genes are the cell's hereditary structures, and they consist of nucleic acid. A cell that has been infected by a virus begins to produce the proteins that are called for by the nucleic acid of the virus. These proteins enable the virus to reproduce itself hundreds or thousands of times.

As new viruses are produced, they are released from the cell and infect other cells. The new viruses lose their ability to reproduce as soon as they are released. But when the viruses enter another cell, they start to reproduce again and thus spread infection to more cells.

When a virus reproduces, it changes a cell's chemical makeup. This change usually damages or kills the cell, and disease results if many cells are affected. Some viruses change a cell only slightly because they do not reproduce. The DNA copy of a retrovirus may hide inside a cell on cell DNA. Such a virus may cause no immediate symptoms but might later damage the cell.

Virus diseases in human beings include AIDS; chickenpox; colds; cold sores; hepatitis; influenza; measles; mumps; poliomyelitis; rabies; rotavirus; and yellow fever. The nature of the disease caused by a particular type of virus is determined by which cells and tissues in the body the virus tends to invade.

The body protects itself from viruses and other harmful substances by several methods, all of which together are called the *immune system.* For example, white blood cells called *lymphocytes* provide protection in two ways. Some lymphocytes produce substances called *antibodies,* which cover a virus's protein coat and prevent the virus from attaching itself to the receptors of a cell. Other lymphocytes destroy cells that have been infected by viruses and thus kill the viruses before they can reproduce. However, some viruses are able to suppress the functioning of the immune system and thus enable themselves to reproduce more easily. Such viruses include those that cause measles, influenza, and AIDS.

Lymphocytes do not start to produce antibodies until several days after a virus has entered the body. However, the body has additional methods of fighting virus infections. For example, the body produces a high fever to combat such virus diseases as influenza and measles. The high fever limits the ability of the viruses to reproduce. To fight colds, the body forms large amounts of mucus in the nose and throat. The mucus traps many cold viruses, which are expelled from the body by sneezing, coughing, and blowing one's nose. The body also makes protein substances called *interferons* that provide some protection against many types of viruses.

The treatment of a virus disease consists mainly of controlling its symptoms. For example, physicians prescribe a drug called *acetaminophen* to bring down a high fever. In most cases, doctors cannot attack the cause of the disease because most drugs able to kill or damage a virus also damage healthy cells. The U.S. Food and Drug Administration has approved a few drugs—including zidovudine (formerly called azidothymidine and commonly known as AZT), adenine arabinoside (ara-A), and acyclovir—for limited use against certain virus diseases. Researchers have found other potential antiviral drugs, including interferons. But these drugs must undergo further testing before their safety and effectiveness are known. Until then, the best way to deal with viruses is immunization before a virus disease strikes. Immunization with vaccines causes the immune system to produce antibodies that will resist a virus when it enters the body. Doctors use vaccines to prevent such virus diseases as influenza, measles, and polio.

A few viruses are called *slow viruses* because they reproduce more slowly than the others. Some researchers believe a slow virus causes multiple sclerosis, a disease of the brain and spinal cord (see **Multiple sclerosis**). Other viruses, such as the herpesviruses, can remain dormant in cells for years and then become reactivated and cause sporadic outbreaks of symptoms. Still other viruses, including HIV, the virus that causes AIDS, can cause prolonged, persistent infections in which the virus multiplies continuously. Some viruses have been linked to human cancer. For example, hepatitis B virus is linked to *hepatoma,* a type of liver cancer. *Burkitt's lymphoma,* a cancer of the lymph tissues, may be caused by the Epstein-Barr virus. In addition, some leukemias are caused by human retroviruses.

Virus diseases in animals. Viruses cause hundreds of diseases in animals. These diseases include distemper in dogs and foot-and-mouth disease in cattle. Most virus diseases in animals occur in certain species. But some of the diseases spread to other species, and a few of them infect human beings. For example, dogs can

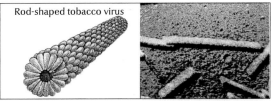

Rod-shaped tobacco virus

Alfred Pasieka, Taurus

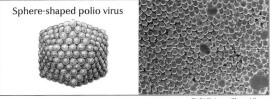

Sphere-shaped polio virus

CNRI/Science Photo Library

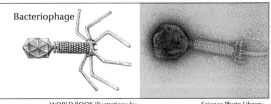

Bacteriophage

WORLD BOOK illustrations by   Science Photo Library
Margaret Ann Moran   from Photo Researchers

Viruses have two basic shapes. Some, such as tobacco viruses, look like rods. Others, such as polio viruses, resemble spheres. A bacteriophage is a virus with a tail.

give people rabies, which destroys nerve cells.

Certain viruses can cause cancer in animals. These viruses do not destroy all the cells they infect. Some of the infected cells have their chemical makeup altered, which causes them to behave abnormally. These altered cells reproduce in an uncontrolled manner, forming masses of tissue called tumors. Cancerous tumors invade and damage surrounding healthy tissue. Researchers have discovered a similarity between some viruses that cause cancer in animals and certain viruses that infect human beings.

Virus diseases in plants. Viruses infect all kinds of plants and can cause serious damage to crops. Plant cells have tough walls that a virus cannot penetrate. But insects penetrate the cell walls while feeding on a plant and thus enable viruses to enter. Plant viruses may infect

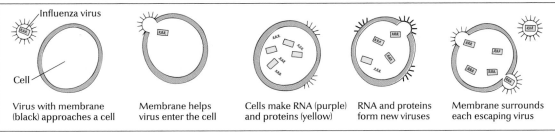

Influenza virus

Cell

Virus with membrane (black) approaches a cell

Membrane helps virus enter the cell

Cells make RNA (purple) and proteins (yellow)

RNA and proteins form new viruses

Membrane surrounds each escaping virus

WORLD BOOK diagram by David Cunningham

Viruses reproduce rapidly inside cells. An influenza virus multiplies almost immediately after infecting a cell, *above.* Such rapid reproduction by a virus can lead to disease. Newly formed viruses escape from a cell and infect other cells before the body can stop the process.

one or two leaves or an entire plant. They produce billions of viruses, which are carried to other plants by insects or air currents. Common viral diseases of plants include tobacco mosaic and turnip yellows mosaic.

Viruses that attack bacteria are called *bacteriophages.* The word *bacteriophage* means *bacteria eater.* Bacteria, like plants, have tough cell walls. To penetrate these walls, most bacteriophages have a structure that works like a hypodermic needle. This structure consists of a sphere-shaped head that contains a nucleic acid, and a hollow, rod-shaped tail made of protein. When a bacteriophage enters a bacterium, the tail first penetrates the cell wall. Then the nucleic acid in the head moves through the tail and into the cell.

How viruses are used. Virologists study viruses chiefly to learn how they cause disease and how to control these organisms. Scientists also use viruses for such purposes as (1) insect control, (2) cell research, and (3) development of vaccines and other drugs.

Insect control. Certain viruses cause fatal diseases in insects. Virologists are seeking ways to use these viruses to kill insects that damage crops. The use of such viruses may someday replace insecticides, which kill insects but also may harm plants as well as other animals.

Cell research. Viruses are such simple organisms that scientists can easily study them to gain more knowledge about life itself. Research on bacteriophages has helped biologists understand genes, DNA, and other basic cell structures. Future research may provide further knowledge of how cells function and reproduce.

Development of vaccines and other drugs. Scientists produce vaccines from either dead or live viruses. Those used in dead-virus vaccines are killed by chemicals and injected into the body. They cause the body to produce antibodies and other substances that resist viruses. For live-virus vaccines, virologists select very mild forms of living viruses that stimulate the body's immune system but cause no serious harm. In addition, scientists can genetically engineer bacteria to produce interferons that fight virus infections (see **Genetic engineering**). This technique, called *gene-splicing* or *recombinant DNA,* is also used to make new types of virus vaccines and drugs.   Neil R. Blacklow

Related articles in *World Book* include:

Some virus diseases

AIDS	Foot-and-mouth	Mumps
Canine parvovirus	disease	Pneumonia
Chickenpox	Hantavirus	Poliomyelitis
Cold, Common	Hepatitis	Rabies
Dengue	Herpesvirus	SARS
Distemper	Influenza	Shingles
Ebola virus	Kawasaki disease	Smallpox
Encephalitis	Measles	West Nile virus
Epstein-Barr virus	Mosaic disease	Yellow fever

Other related articles

Antiviral drug	Immunization	Rous, Francis
Bacteria	Interferon	Salk, Jonas E.
Disease	Prion	Viroid
Gnotobiotics		

Additional resources

Crawford, Dorothy H. *The Invisible Enemy: A Natural History of Viruses.* Oxford, 2000.
Wagner, Edward K., and Hewlett, Martin. *Basic Virology.* 2nd ed. Blackwell, 2003.

Visa, *VEE zuh,* is an endorsement that government officials place on a passport to show the passport is valid (see **Passport**). Officials of the country a traveler is entering grant the visa. The visa certifies that the traveler's passport has been examined and approved. Immigration officers then permit the bearer to enter the country. A government that does not want a person to enter the country can refuse to grant that person a visa.

Robert J. Pranger

Viscosity, *vihs KAHS uh tee,* is a measure of the resistance of a *fluid* (liquid or gas) to flow. Fluids with *high viscosity,* such as molasses, flow more slowly than those with *low viscosity,* such as water.

For a fluid to flow, the mobile molecules that make up the fluid must move past one another. Two actions oppose this movement, giving rise to viscosity: (1) Molecules collide with one another, and (2) molecules are drawn toward one another due, for example, to attractive forces between opposite electric charges that they carry.

Changes in temperature affect the viscosity of both liquids and gases. The molecules of liquids are close to-

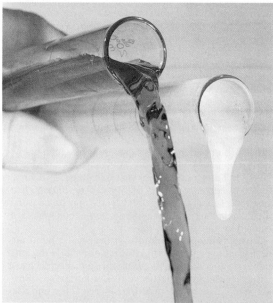

Larry Stepanowicz, Panographics

The viscosity of liquids is a measure of the degree to which they resist flowing. A liquid with low viscosity, *left,* flows much faster than a liquid that has high viscosity, *right.*

gether. As a result, the attractive forces between the molecules are strong. When a liquid is heated, its molecules move apart, reducing the attraction between them. Raising the temperature of a liquid thus decreases its viscosity.

In gases, however, molecules are widely separated. Viscosity therefore results chiefly from collisions. Heating a gas makes its molecules move more rapidly and collide more often. Hot gases are thus more viscous than cold ones.

A liquid may be made more viscous by dissolving *polymers* (long-chain molecules) in it. The polymers interfere with the movement of the liquid's molecules past one another. The amount of interference increases with temperature. Polymers are added to motor oils to ensure that the oil will not be too thin when the engine is hot.   R. Hogg

Viscount, *VY kownt,* is a title held by certain British noblemen. A viscount ranks below an earl and above a baron. The title was adopted from the French nobility. John Beaumont, an officer and deputy to an earl, was the first to receive the title in 1440. It is usually given to men that the ruler wishes to honor.   Joel J. Rosenthal

Vishnu, *VIHSH noo,* is one of the two main gods of Hinduism. The other is Shiva. Vishnu has a kindly nature, and Hindus call him *the Preserver.* They believe he tries to ensure the welfare of humanity.

Vishnu sometimes descends from heaven to the earth in one of his *avatars* (physical forms). He does so when a

Stone statue (A.D. 900's to 1100's) by an unknown Indian sculptor; the Art Institute of Chicago, Gift of Mr. and Mrs. Robert Andrew Brown

Vishnu is an important Hindu god. Hindus believe he someday will descend from heaven to the earth and destroy all evil.

catastrophe faces the universe or if humanity needs comfort and guidance. According to Hindu belief, Vishnu has already appeared in nine principal avatars. The two most important ones were the Indian prince Rama and the god Krishna. As Rama, Vishnu was the hero of the Ramayana, a Hindu epic. As Krishna, Vishnu took part in the Bhagavad-Gita, a philosophical dialogue that forms part of the Mahabharata, another epic. Hindus believe that Vishnu will return to the earth someday to destroy all evil and begin a new Golden Age of humanity.   Charles S. J. White

Related articles in *World Book* include:
Bhagavad-Gita   Hinduism (Deities)   Rama
Gupta dynasty   Holi   Ramayana
    (picture)   Krishna

Visigoths. See Goths.
Vision. See Eye.
Vistula River, *VIHS choo luh,* is an important waterway of east-central Europe. It carries much of Poland's river traffic. The Vistula rises in the Carpathian Mountains in southern Poland and then takes a circular course northward. The river runs through the city of Warsaw. It empties by several branches into the Baltic Sea. Gdańsk lies at the mouth of the Nogat, the westernmost branch. The river's name in Polish is *Wisła* (pronounced *VEE swah).* For location, see **Poland** (terrain map).

Light boats sail up the river as far as Kraków. The Vistula is frozen two to three months of the year.

Canals link the Vistula with the Oder, the Dnieper, and the Neman, all navigable rivers. The Vistula is 678 miles (1,091 kilometers) long and drains about 74,000 square miles (192,000 square kilometers).   Janusz Bugajski

Vital statistics are a record of the most basic human events, including birth, marriage, divorce, sickness, and death. They indicate some of the changes occurring in the population of a country, state, province, or local community. They are gathered from birth and death certificates, marriage licenses and divorce records, disease reports, and other official records. Government officials collect reports of the individual events, tabulate and analyze them, and publish vital statistics reports.

Using vital statistics. Business people, government workers, social scientists, and others use vital statistics for many purposes. Total numbers of births, marriages, divorces, illnesses of a specific type, and deaths that occur during a period of time are useful statistics. For example, the total number of deaths in the United States in a given year may be subtracted from the total number of live births to obtain the natural increase of population during that year. In addition, public health agencies study the number of cases of certain diseases to plan immunization and prevention campaigns.

The rate at which events happen is often more informative than the total number of events. A *crude rate* is the number of events happening during a period of time, measured in proportion to the size of the total population. For example, the crude birth rate in the United States in the early 1990's was about 16 births for every 1,000 people. The rate was about 10 in Germany, 14 in Canada, and 45 in Nigeria.

Another kind of rate, called a *specific rate,* is the number of events in a certain part of the population. The part may be defined according to such factors as age, gender, and ethnicity. Statisticians often combine information from vital statistics and other sources to figure specific rates. For example, they may use death certificates, census data, and special sample surveys to determine the specific rate for lung cancer deaths among white female cigarette smokers between the ages of 45 and 64.

Collecting and publishing vital statistics. In the United States, state laws regulate registration of most vital events. Physicians or hospital attendants file birth certificates with local *registrars* (official recorders). Physicians or coroners return death certificates to funeral directors, who file them with local registrars. The local registrars send birth and death certificates to a county or state registrar. After a marriage ceremony, the presiding official sends the record certifying the marriage to the license clerk. The licensing office then sends the record to the state registrar. Attorneys file divorce records with the clerk of the court that grants the divorce. The court clerk reports the divorce to the state registrar. Doctors must report certain diseases to local or state health departments.

Vital statistics are tabulated at the state and federal levels. The national Vital Statistics Division of the National Center for Health Statistics tabulates, analyzes, and publishes national data. The division is an agency of the U.S. Department of Health and Human Services.

In Canada, vital statistics are collected by the health division of Statistics Canada, an agency of the federal government. In other countries, police departments, churches, government offices, or other agencies may collect and keep vital records. These statistics are then tabulated and published at the national level.

Karl Taeuber

Related articles in *World Book* include:

Birth and death rates — Divorce
Birth certificate — Marriage
Census — Population

Vitamin is an organic chemical compound that the body needs in small amounts. Vitamins make up one of the major groups of *nutrients,* food substances necessary for growth and health. Vitamins regulate chemical reactions by which the body converts food into energy and living tissues.

Some vitamins that the human body needs are produced within the body itself. These vitamins are biotin, choline, niacin, pantothenic acid, vitamin D, and vitamin K. Bacteria in the human intestine make biotin, pantothenic acid, and vitamin K, but not always in sufficient quantities to meet the body's needs. Sunlight shining on the skin produces vitamin D. But the rest of the vitamins a person needs must come from the person's diet or from a vitamin supplement.

Each vitamin has such specific uses that one vitamin cannot replace, or act for, another. Sometimes the lack of one vitamin can interfere with the function of another. Over time, continued lack of one vitamin can result in a *vitamin deficiency disease.* Such diseases include beriberi, pellagra, rickets, and scurvy. Investigators first discovered vitamins while searching for the causes of such diseases. To be considered a vitamin, a substance must be required to prevent a deficiency disease.

The best way for a healthy individual to obtain vitamins is to eat a balanced diet. A daily diet that includes a variety of foods from each of the basic food groups—including grains, fruit, vegetables, dairy, and meat and beans—provides an adequate supply of all the vitamins. Nutrition experts have established a *Recommended Dietary Allowance* (RDA) for most vitamins. To provide a margin of safety, the RDA is considerably greater than the amount of a vitamin needed daily for good health. The RDA is established by the Food and Nutrition Board of the United States National Academy of Sciences Institute of Medicine.

People who do not eat a well-balanced diet every day may not obtain the RDA of all vitamins from the food they eat. In addition, people who are elderly, pregnant, or ill have an increased risk of vitamin deficiency. Some people can benefit by taking a daily vitamin supplement, in the form of a multivitamin tablet. Such supplements contain doses of vitamins in the range of their RDA's.

Treating a vitamin deficiency disease sometimes involves taking one or more preparations that contain large doses of a certain vitamin or combination of vitamins. But people should use such preparations only under the care of a physician. Taking *megadoses* of vitamins—doses many times larger than the RDA—without proper medical supervision can be dangerous.

Kinds of vitamins

Scientists divide vitamins into two general groups. *Fat-soluble* vitamins dissolve in fats, while *water-soluble* vitamins dissolve more readily in water.

Fat-soluble vitamins are the vitamins A, D, E, and K. The body can store these vitamins in the liver and fatty tissues.

Vitamin A, also known as *retinol,* occurs naturally only in animal foods. Eggs, liver, and milk provide much vitamin A. Some plants contain substances called *carotenes,* or *provitamins A,* that the body converts into vitamin A. Such plants include dark green leafy vegetables and deep orange vegetables, such as carrots and pumpkins.

Vitamin A is essential for the development of babies before birth and for the growth of children. It is especially needed for the growth of bones and teeth. Vitamin A keeps the skin healthy and helps produce mucous secretions that build resistance to infection. People who do not get enough vitamin A may develop *xerophthalmia,* a condition in which the surface of the eye becomes dry and likely to develop infection. Vitamin A also forms part of the two pigments that help the eyes to function normally in different amounts of light. Night blindness is an early symptom of a vitamin A deficiency.

Vitamin D helps prevent the bone disease rickets (see **Rickets**). The vitamin exists in several forms. One form, *calciferol* or *vitamin D_2,* develops in plants upon exposure to ultraviolet light. Another form, *cholecalciferol,* or *vitamin D_3,* occurs in the tissues of animals, including human beings. It is called the "sunshine vitamin" because it forms in the skin when the body is exposed to sunlight. Fish-liver oils contain much vitamin D_3. Food producers often fortify milk and other products by adding vitamin D.

Vitamin E, or *tocopherol,* helps prevent compounds called *polyunsaturated fatty acids* from *oxidizing* (combining with oxygen). Vitamin E thus plays an important role in maintaining cell membranes, which contain substantial amounts of polyunsaturated fatty acids. Sources of vitamin E include seed oils, vegetable oils, wheat germ, and whole grains.

Vitamin K is essential for blood clotting. Cauliflower and green leafy vegetables, such as cabbage, kale, and spinach, are rich in vitamin K. Intestinal bacteria manufacture vitamin K in the body, so severe deficiencies of this vitamin are rare. Doctors sometimes give women vitamin K before childbirth to prevent bleeding in the newborn baby. Babies do not have enough intestinal bacteria to produce adequate amounts of the vitamin until they are about 2 weeks old.

Water-soluble vitamins dissolve more readily in water and other fluids, including blood and urine. These vitamins are less easily stored by the body and individuals should eat foods that contain them daily. The water-soluble vitamins include vitamin C, and others that are often collectively called the *B complex* or *B vitamins.*

Vitamins essential for human health

Vitamin	What it does	Sources	Recommended dietary allowance	
			Children (ages 1-10)	Adolescents and adults
A	Helps maintain skin, eyes, urinary tract, and lining of the nervous, respiratory, and digestive systems.	Butter, carrots, dark green leafy vegetables, eggs, fish liver oil, liver, milk, deep orange fruits and vegetables.	300-600 µg RE	600-900 µg RE (males) 600-700 µg RE (females)
D	Essential for calcium and phosphorus metabolism.	Eggs, fish liver oils, salmon, tuna, fortified milk, sunlight.	5 µg*	5-15 µg*
E	Helps prevent the oxidation of polyunsaturated fatty acids in cell membranes and other body structures.	Almost all foods, vegetable oils; margarine; olives.	6-11 mg TE	11-15 mg TE
K	Needed for normal blood clotting.	Leafy vegetables; made by intestinal bacteria	30-60 µg*	60-120 µg* (males) 60-90 µg* (females)
Niacin	Essential for cell metabolism and absorption of carbohydrates.	Fish, liver, enriched breads, lean meat, whole grains.	6-12 mg NE	12-16 mg NE (males) 12-14 mg NE(females)
Riboflavin (B_2)	Helps body cells use oxygen. Promotes tissue repair and healthy skin.	Milk, fish, green vegetables, liver, poultry.	0.5-0.9 mg	0.9-1.3 mg (males) 0.9-1.1 mg (females)
Thiamine (B_1)	Needed for carbohydrate metabolism. Helps heart and nervous system function properly.	Legumes, nuts, organ meats, pork, grains, vegetables.	0.5-0.9 mg	0.9-1.2 mg (males) 0.9-1.1 mg (females)
B_6	Needed for carbohydrate, fat, and protein metabolism.	Eggs, fish, nuts, organ meats, poultry, whole grains.	0.5-1.0 mg	1.0-1.7 mg (males) 1.0-1.5 mg (females)
Pantothenic acid	Helps the body convert carbohydrates, fats, and proteins into energy.	Almost all foods; made by intestinal bacteria.	2-4 mg*	4-5 mg*
Biotin	Helps the body form fatty acids. Maintains healthy skin.	Egg yolk, kidney, liver, nuts; made by intestinal bacteria.	8-20 µg*	20-30 µg*
B_{12}	Essential for proper development of red blood cells. Helps proper function of nervous system.	Eggs, fish, meat, milk, milk products, poultry.	0.9-1.8 µg	1.8-2.4 µg
Folic acid	Needed for production of red blood cells.	Fruit, legumes, liver, green leafy vegetables.	150-300 µg	300-400 µg
Choline	Needed for proper function of brain and nervous system.	Egg yolks, organ meats, beans.	250-375 mg*	550 mg* (males) 400-425 mg* (females)
C	Essential for sound bones and teeth. Needed for tissue metabolism.	Cantaloupe, citrus fruits, potatoes, cabbage, tomatoes.	15-45 mg	45-90 mg (males) 45-75 mg (females)

µg=micrograms; mg=milligrams; RE=retinol equivalents; NE=niacin equivalents; TE= tocopherol equivalents
*Adequate Intake (AI). The AI is a value based on experimentally derived intake levels or approximations of observed mean nutrient intakes by a group or groups of healthy people. Because there is less information on which to base allowances, these figures are not classified as RDA's.
Source: The National Academy of Sciences. Courtesy of the National Academy Press, 2000, 2001, 2004.

Niacin helps prevent the disease pellagra (see **Pellagra**). The best sources of niacin include fish, lean meat, and whole grains. Milk and eggs, though they have little niacin, help prevent pellagra. They contain *tryptophan,* a compound that the body can convert into niacin.

Niacin is essential for growth, for healthy tissues, and for the conversion of nutrients called *carbohydrates* into energy. It also helps produce fats in the body. Without niacin, the vitamins thiamine and riboflavin cannot function properly. Lack of niacin may cause ailments of the skin and of the digestive and nervous systems.

Riboflavin, or *vitamin B_2* is found in such foods as fish, liver, milk, poultry, and leafy green vegetables. Direct sunlight destroys riboflavin in milk. This vitamin is needed for growth and for healthy skin and eyes. It promotes the body's use of oxygen in converting food into energy. If a person does not get enough riboflavin, cracks may develop in the skin at the corners of the mouth. The person also may have inflamed lips, a sore tongue, and scaly skin around the nose and ears. The eyes may become overly sensitive to light.

Thiamine, also spelled *thiamin,* or *vitamin B_1,* prevents and cures the nervous disease beriberi (see **Beriberi**). Sources of thiamine include *legumes* (members of the pea family), nuts, organ meats, pork, whole grains, and most vegetables. This vitamin is needed for growth and helps change carbohydrates into energy.

Vitamin B_6, pantothenic acid, and biotin. A deficiency of these vitamins has never been reported in people who eat a balanced diet. Vitamin B_6 helps the body use *amino acids,* the chemical units that make up proteins. Lack of this vitamin damages the skin and nervous system. The body converts pantothenic acid into *coenzyme A,* a vital substance that helps produce energy from food. Biotin helps the body change fats into fatty acids, which also aid in producing energy.

Vitamin B_{12}, folic acid, and choline. Vitamin B_{12}, also known as *cobalamin,* contains cobalt and is essential for the normal functioning of folic acid, also called *folate.* Vitamin B_{12} and folic acid are needed to produce *deoxyribonucleic acid* (DNA) in the body's cells. DNA is the molecule that governs each cell's activities. A deficiency of either of these two vitamins produces anemia (see **Anemia**). Lack of vitamin B_{12} also damages the nervous system. Eggs, fish, meat, milk, and poultry all supply vitamin B_{12}. Strict vegetarians sometimes lack this vitamin.

Physicians advise all women who may become pregnant to take folic acid or eat foods fortified with it daily to reduce the risk of the serious birth defect *spina bifida* (see **Spina bifida**). Folic acid is found in all food groups, especially fruits and vegetables. In the United States, food manufacturers fortify bread, many cereals, and other foods with folic acid.

Choline works with folic acid and vitamin B_{12} to help cells maintain their structure and to manufacture other important compounds. The brain and other organs may not function as well without sufficient choline.

Vitamin C, or *ascorbic acid,* prevents and cures *scurvy,* a disease marked by sore gums and bleeding under the skin (see **Scurvy**). The body stores some vitamin C, but it is best to eat foods containing it daily. Such foods include cantaloupe, citrus fruits, raw cabbage, strawberries, and tomatoes. Vitamin C is essential for healthy blood vessels, bones, and teeth. It also helps form *collagen,* a protein that holds tissues together.

How vitamins work

Vitamins function as *catalysts* in the body. A catalyst is a substance that increases the speed of a chemical reaction without being consumed by the reaction. Vitamins help accelerate certain reactions that occur in the body and are essential for health. Without vitamins, these reactions would occur much more slowly or not at all. Most vitamins act as *coenzymes*—that is, they attach to and assist in the function of biological catalysts called *enzymes* (see **Enzyme**).

Some vitamins occur in food and pills in inactive forms. The body converts them into their active forms. Vitamin D is unique because it functions not only as a vitamin but also as a "chemical messenger," or *hormone.*

History

Such diseases as beriberi, pellagra, rickets, and scurvy have been known for centuries. But the idea that they might result from a dietary deficiency is comparatively new. James Lind, a Scottish physician, became one of the first people to study the effect of diet on human health. As early as the 1740's, Lind used lemons and oranges to cure scurvy in sailors, who rarely ate fresh fruit on long voyages. In 1882, the Japanese physician Kanehiro Takaki cured beriberi among naval crews by adding meat and vegetables to their diet of rice. Christiaan Eijkman, a Dutch scientist, studied beriberi in the Dutch East Indies, now Indonesia. About 1900, he showed that peo-

ple who ate *polished* rice—that is, rice with the hulls and bran layers removed—developed the disease. Those who ate unpolished rice did not. Eijkman concluded that rice polishings contained a beriberi-fighting substance that was essential for health.

In 1912, the Polish biochemist Casimir Funk tried but failed to extract the pure beriberi-fighting substance from rice polishings. Funk thought the substance belonged to a group of chemical compounds called *amines,* and he named it *vitamine,* meaning *amine essential to life.* Meanwhile, the British biochemist Frederick Hopkins conducted research on the effect of diet on the growth of rats. His work, published in 1906, demonstrated that certain foods contain substances that are vital for the growth and development of the body. Hopkins called these substances "accessory food factors" to distinguish them from the well-established "basic food factors"—carbohydrates, fats, proteins, minerals, and water. Later, the word *vitamin* was used for all such accessory substances. Together, Hopkins and Funk developed the vitamin theory of deficiency disease.

At first, scientists thought there were only two vitamins, a fat-soluble one and a water-soluble one. By 1922, the American biochemist Elmer V. McCollum had proved that the fat-soluble vitamin was a mixture of vitamins. About that time, Joseph Goldberger, an American physician, showed that the water-soluble vitamin also was a mixture. Since then, at least 14 vitamins have been recognized, and more may be found.   Susan Nitzke

Related articles in *World Book* include:
Antioxidant
Diet (Normal diet)
Dietary supplement
Folic acid
Food additive (Nutrients)
Goldberger, Joseph
Health food
Hodgkin, Dorothy Crowfoot
Nutrition (Vitamins)
Wald, George

Additional resources

Cooperman, Tod, and others, eds. *ConsumerLab.com's Guide to Buying Vitamins and Supplements.* ConsumerLab.com, 2003.
Lieberman, Shari, and Bruning, Nancy. *The Real Vitamin and Mineral Book.* 3rd ed. Avery Pub., 2003.
Navarra, Tova. *The Encyclopedia of Vitamins, Minerals, and Supplements.* 2nd ed. Facts on File, 2004.
Royston, Angela. *Vitamins and Minerals for a Healthy Body.* Heinemann Lib., 2003. Younger readers.

Vitiligo, *VIHT uh LY goh,* is a noninfectious disease in which people develop white spots on the skin. The spots vary in size and location. They occur where skin cells called *melanocytes* have been destroyed. These cells normally produce *melanin,* a brown-black pigment that determines the color of skin and hair.

Vitiligo affects about 2 percent of all people, regardless of skin color or age. The white spots often appear on exposed areas of skin, such as the hands, face, and upper part of the chest. The spots do not cause pain, itching, or burning, but they burn easily when exposed to sunlight. The course of the disease is unpredictable. The spots can get larger or stay the same size. Vitiligo can also turn hair white.

No one knows the exact cause of vitiligo. Researchers believe some people are born with a tendency to develop the disease. The melanocytes of people with vitiligo are thought to interact with the immune and nervous systems to bring about their own destruction. An injury, such as a burn or cut, can trigger vitiligo. The start of the disease is sometimes linked to emotional stress.

There is no cure for vitiligo. Many patients use cosmetics to cover the spots. A treatment that combines use of the drug psoralen with exposure to sunlight or artificial ultraviolet light can bring back some or all skin color. Such treatment can increase the number of healthy melanocytes in affected areas.   Rebat M. Halder

Vivaldi, *vih VAHL dee,* **Antonio** (1678-1741), was an Italian composer. He was one of the most productive composers in the Baroque style, which was marked by regular rhythm and elaborate melody.

Vivaldi helped develop the Baroque concerto, which influenced the German composer Johann Sebastian Bach and the early symphony composers. Bach admired Vivaldi's concertos and arranged 10 of these works for the harpsichord and the organ.

Vivaldi was an accomplished violinist and composed his most important works for the violin. Four violin concertos known as *The Four Seasons* (1725) are his best-known compositions. They are an important example of *program music*—that is, music that tells a story or depicts a landscape. He also composed operas, cantatas, oratorios, and solo and trio sonatas. His best-known sacred choral work is the *Gloria in D Major* (1708).

Vivaldi was born on March 4, 1678, in Venice. He was ordained a priest but devoted his life to music. In 1703, he became a violin teacher at the Venetian Ospedale della Pietà, a girls' orphanage with a noted chorus and orchestra. He composed many of his works for the orphanage musicians, writing concertos for almost every instrument then known in Europe. Vivaldi died on July 28, 1741.   Joscelyn Godwin

Viviparous animal, *vy VIHP uhr uhs,* is an animal that reproduces by means of eggs that are fertilized and develop inside of the mother's body. The offspring of viviparous animals look like the adult animals but are smaller. Most types of mammals, many reptiles, and some fish are viviparous.   George B. Johnson

Vixen. See Fox (The life of a fox).

Vizier, *vih ZIHR* or *VIHZ yuhr,* is the title some Muslim countries give to certain high officials, such as ministers of state. The word *vizier* comes from the Arabic word *wazir,* which means a *bearer of burdens.* In the Ottoman Empire, viziers were the chief advisers and deputies of the Ottoman *sultan* (ruler). In the 1800's, heads of Ottoman government departments were called viziers. The top administrator was the Grand Vizier.   Justin McCarthy

Vizsla, *VEEZ lah,* is a short-haired hunting dog also known as the *Hungarian pointer.* Vizslas resemble other short-haired pointing breeds except that they have deep, rusty-gold coats. The dog weighs about 50 pounds (23 kilograms) when full-grown. Its tail is sometimes *docked* (cut). Dog experts believe the breed is descended from dogs that were brought into central Europe by the Magyars about 1,000 years ago (see **Magyars**). Central Europeans first used the dogs to hunt with falcons, and later to point and retrieve game birds.

Critically reviewed by the Vizsla Club of America

Vladimir I, *VLAD uh mihr* or *vlah DEE mihr* (956?-1015), was a Grand Prince of Kiev, in what is now Ukraine. He also ruled the principality of Novgorod, which included

what is now the city of Velikiy Novgorod in Russia. As the ruler of Kiev and Novgorod, Vladimir built up the powerful state of Kievan Rus, which extended from the Baltic Sea to near the Black Sea. In Ukrainian, his name is spelled *Volodymyr* (pronounced *vahl uh DEE mihr).*

Vladimir was probably born in or near Kiev. He became prince of Novgorod about 969 and Grand Prince of Kiev and All Rus in 980. He converted to Christianity about 988. He married Anna, sister of the Byzantine Emperor Basil II, and made Christianity the state religion. During Vladimir's rule, agriculture and trade flourished, and Kiev became famous for its rich cultural life.

Vladimir established relations with the pope and European leaders. He defended and expanded Kievan Rus by fighting neighboring Lithuanians, Bulgars, Poles, and Pechenegs. Vladimir died on July 15, 1015. He is recognized as a saint by all Catholic and Orthodox churches. His feast day is July 15.   James Cracraft

See also **Slavs** (East Slavs).

Vladivostok, *vlad uh vahs TAHK* (pop. 594,701), is Russia's most important port on the Pacific Ocean. It lies in southeastern Siberia, near the North Korean and Chinese borders. See **Russia** (political map).

Vladivostok serves as headquarters of the Russian Pacific Fleet. It is a major international trading port. Many fishing fleets and fish canneries also are based there. The harbor is usually frozen between January and March, but icebreakers keep it open. Vladivostok marks the eastern end of the railroad line that crosses Siberia (see **Trans-Siberian Railroad**).

Russia founded Vladivostok in 1860 on territory annexed from China. In the 1870's, the city became an imperial naval base. In 1958, during the period when Russia was part of the Soviet Union, Vladivostok was closed to foreigners. It reopened to foreign ships and visitors at the start of 1992.   Richard H. Bidlack

Vlaminck, *vlah MANK,* **Maurice de,** *moh REES duh* (1876-1958), was a French artist. With André Derain and Henri Matisse, he led the Fauve movement in the early 1900's. Vlaminck was influenced by the Dutch artist Vincent van Gogh. Like van Gogh, he used slashing brushstrokes and brilliant colors to convey dramatic impact. However, the exuberance of Vlaminck's work contrasted

WORLD BOOK photo by E. F. Hoppe
The Vizsla is a powerful hunting dog.

with the feeling of suffering associated with certain of van Gogh's paintings.

From about 1908 to 1914, Vlaminck painted under the influence of the French artist Paul Cézanne and of Cubism. About 1915, he began painting gloomy landscapes that emphasized dark colors and the illusion of deep space. Vlaminck also created etchings and lithographs in this style. He was born in Paris on April 4, 1876, and died on Oct. 11, 1958. Nancy J. Troy

See also **Fauves.**

Vocabulary is the total number of words in a language. It is also the collection of words a person knows and uses in speaking or writing.

The vocabulary of a language is always changing and growing. As life becomes more complex, people devise or borrow new words to describe human activity, and they change the meanings of existing words to fit new circumstances. No one knows the exact number of English words today, but there are probably about 1 million.

A person has two kinds of vocabularies. The *active* or *use* vocabulary is made up of words used in speaking or writing. The *passive* or *recognition* vocabulary consists of words a person understands when listening or reading. Many people have a recognition vocabulary several times larger than their use vocabulary. This means that they understand words they hear or read but do not habitually use in speaking or writing. For Americans, the average use vocabulary is 10,000 words, but the average recognition vocabulary is 30,000 to 40,000 words.

A person continually builds a vocabulary. Studies have shown that a child entering school may know from 8,000 to 15,000 words. But by the completion of college, he or she may know 50,000 words or more.

The range of a person's vocabulary is a clue to the person's culture and education. Control over words is often the same as control over the ideas the words represent. The dictionary is an important tool for increasing vocabulary. If you encounter a word you do not know, look it up and find out what it means and how it is used.

Marianne Cooley

See also **Dictionary; Reading; Shakespeare, William** (Vocabulary).

Vocal cords. See **Voice.**

Vocation. See **Careers.**

Vocational education prepares people for an occupation that does not require a bachelor's degree. It is designed mainly to help meet society's need for workers and to give students more educational options. Courses are taught in such subject areas as agriculture, business, trades and industry, health services, family and consumer sciences, and technical fields. Courses are classified as either *exploratory* or *occupational.* Exploratory courses provide an introduction to an occupation or to a number of similar jobs. Occupational courses teach entry-level skills necessary for specific semiskilled, skilled, or technical occupations.

Vocational education forms a part of the process of *career education,* which helps students choose and prepare for a career. In kindergarten and elementary school, career education provides information about various jobs and helps children determine their own abilities and interests. In middle school or junior high school, students begin to explore the careers that interest them most. In high school, most students who plan to get a job immediately after graduation take some type of vocational education. About 75 percent of all high school graduates take at least one course designed to provide preparation for a specific occupation.

Sources of vocational education

The chief sources of vocational education are (1) public high schools, (2) proprietary schools, and (3) community and junior colleges. Many businesses, labor unions, the armed forces, and other organizations also provide job training.

Public high schools are supported by taxes and provide vocational training at little or no charge. They prepare students for careers in agriculture, carpentry, cosmetology, drafting, family and consumer sciences, secretarial work, and other fields. Many high schools, called *comprehensive high schools,* offer both vocational training and college preparatory programs. Other institutions, known as *vocational high schools,* specialize in job training. *Technical high schools* are vocational schools that are specially equipped to teach technical subjects, such as automobile repairing and electronics. Many public high schools offer adult-education programs for people who want to learn new job skills.

Proprietary schools include private business colleges, technical institutes, and trade schools. Such schools are owned by individuals or businesses and operate to make a profit. These institutions charge tuition and fees, but they may offer a greater variety of educational opportunities than public schools. Proprietary schools teach clerical skills, data processing, television repairing, and many other subjects. Some schools specialize in training such workers as barbers, dental assistants, truck drivers, or pilots.

Community and junior colleges provide advanced training in engineering, health services, and many other semiprofessional and technical fields. Students learn such jobs as those of computer specialist, laboratory technician, pollution control specialist, and medical assistant. Most community and junior colleges receive funds from the local or state government. Therefore, the tuition the students must pay is considerably less than the cost of the instruction.

Other sources. Labor unions in such skilled trades as bricklaying and printing offer apprenticeship programs for their members. Apprenticeships combine on-the-job experience with individual or classroom instruction. Many businesses and industries also conduct training programs for their employees.

Men and women in the armed forces may be trained in a variety of technical jobs. Many of these people later find a market for their skills in civilian life.

The Job Corps program of the federal government provides work training for disadvantaged youths. Another source of vocational education is a revenue-sharing program established by the Workforce Investment Act of 1998. Under this law, state and local governments receive federal funds to furnish job training for unskilled, disadvantaged youths and for needy adults.

Vocational teaching methods

Vocational education emphasizes a teaching method known as *learning by doing* or *hands-on practice.* Under this method, students learn job skills by practicing them with actual machines or tools. Instruction may take place in a laboratory or in a special classroom called a *shop* that duplicates a real workplace. For example, students in the automotive department of a high school work on automobiles with the same tools used in repair shops. Such equipment makes vocational education one of the most expensive types of education.

Most vocational schools offer individualized instruction, which enables an individual to study the material at his or her own pace. Students work independently with tape recordings, devices called *teaching machines,* computer-assisted instruction, and other materials. The teacher gives individual help.

Another method of vocational education combines classroom studies with work experience. In such *cooperative education,* students attend school part-time and work part-time, usually in a paying job. Business firms and other organizations cooperate with schools in employing the students. A faculty member called a *teacher-coordinator* helps students obtain jobs that match their field of study. See **Cooperative education.**

Challenges to vocational education

Some people oppose specialized job training at the high school level. They believe that such instruction takes too much time away from academic education. But some educators argue that many students who have difficulty with academic work become more interested in their studies after they begin vocational education. The students realize that mathematics, reading, and other skills are necessary in their working life.

Some members of minority groups charge that vocational education teaches minority students to aim only for what they consider low-level jobs. Leaders of the women's rights movement have also demanded reform of vocational programs, which they claim pressure female students into "women's jobs." Most female students in vocational training take secretarial or consumer and homemaking subjects rather than industrial and trade courses.

During the mid-1980's, a national study commission indicated that vocational education experienced challenges that needed to be overcome in 10 areas. It pointed to the need for improvement in the perception of vocational education; access; equity; curriculum; teacher education and recruitment; standards and accountability; articulation; leadership; business, labor, and community involvement; and field-based learning, including cooperative education.

History

Vocational education began in ancient times. Parents and other adults taught children how to provide food, build a shelter, and perform other jobs. Through the centuries, the apprenticeship system of training developed. Under this system, a young person learned a craft or trade by working under a skilled master.

Early vocational education in schools. During the 1800's, schools began to offer vocational education under such names as *manual training* and *mechanical arts.* The Morrill Act of 1862 provided for the establishment of certain colleges and universities to teach agriculture and mechanical arts (see **Land-grant university**).

In 1868, a Russian educator named Victor Della Vos

designed several courses by which schools could teach skilled trades formerly learned through apprenticeships. Della Vos, the director of the Imperial Technical School in Moscow, established blacksmithing, carpentry, and metal-turning shops there.

Della Vos's methods spread to the United States in 1876 at the Philadelphia Centennial Exposition. Two American educators, Calvin M. Woodward and John D. Runkle, saw an exhibition of products made by Russian students. In 1880, Woodward opened the Manual Training School in St. Louis, the first school of its kind in the United States. Runkle, the president of the Massachusetts Institute of Technology, established shop courses there modeled on Della Vos's system.

The 1900's. During the early 1900's, the U.S. government officially recognized the need for vocational education. For example, the Smith-Hughes Act of 1917 financed job training in high schools. During the Great Depression of the 1930's, the federal Civilian Conservation Corps provided on-the-job training for unemployed young men.

During World War II (1939-1945), vocational schools operated around the clock to train the millions of workers needed for war production. After the war, a government program called the GI Bill of Rights provided funds for veterans to attend various types of educational institutions. It created a boom for proprietary schools, where veterans learned a variety of skills.

High unemployment during much of the 1960's and 1970's brought further government support for vocational education. The Manpower Development and Training Act of 1962 furnished federal funds to train unemployed adults. The Vocational Education Act of 1963 provided money for new buildings, programs, and teacher training. The Economic Opportunity Act of 1964 established the Job Corps. The Vocational Education Amendments of 1968 expanded training opportunities for disabled people and the disadvantaged. The Education Amendments of 1976 required schools receiving federal funds to avoid sex discrimination in vocational education. As a result, many automotive, metalworking, plumbing, and other courses became coeducational for the first time.

Two federal acts passed during the 1980's, the Job Training Partnership Act of 1982 and the Carl D. Perkins Vocational Education Act of 1985, again stressed the importance of overcoming sex bias in vocational education classes. Both of these acts expanded the vocational training opportunities for disadvantaged students.

Edwin L. Herr

Related articles in *World Book* include:

Adult education	Disability
Agricultural education	Education (Vocational education)
Apprentice	
Career education	FFA
Careers (Preparing for a career)	Industrial arts
	Job Corps
Cooperative education	

Vocational guidance. See **Careers.**

Vocational rehabilitation is a program or service designed to help disabled people become fit for jobs. Vocational rehabilitation programs generally are designed for people age 16 and older who have physical or mental disabilities. Services are also available for alcoholics and people who have been released from jail or prison. There are three primary activities in vocational rehabilitation: (1) rehabilitation counseling, (2) vocational evaluation, and (3) job placement.

Specialists in each of the three main areas of vocational rehabilitation usually work as a team. A rehabilitation counselor advises disabled people about the type of work or training they may need to support themselves financially. A vocational evaluator determines the most suitable specific job or field of training for each person seeking help. This decision is made after the disabled person takes written examinations and is tested on samples. The written examinations measure the person's scholastic achievement and vocational aptitude. The work samples imitate specific job skills and compare the person's performance to standards in that career. A job-placement specialist helps disabled people schedule job interviews and obtain work suited to their vocational interests and skills.

Vocational rehabilitation programs in the United States developed during the late 1800's, when various government agencies tried to help disabled veterans find jobs. But little else was done until Congress passed the Civilian Vocational Rehabilitation Act of 1920. Since then, numerous federal laws have helped establish vocational rehabilitation as a profession.

In Canada, the Vocational Rehabilitation of Disabled Persons Act of 1961 sets guidelines in the field of vocational rehabilitation. This law encourages Canada's provinces to develop complete vocational rehabilitation programs. Federal and provincial governments split the cost of the programs.

Today, the demand for qualified vocational rehabilitation specialists exceeds the supply. Careers in vocational rehabilitation generally require at least a bachelor's degree, and most require a master's degree. College students who wish to enter the profession major in rehabilitation, and their courses include counseling, human relations, industrial psychology, statistics, and testing. An internship also is part of the course work.

Vocational rehabilitation specialists may work for public or private agencies. The public agencies consist chiefly of state-operated vocational rehabilitation programs and those serving disabled veterans. Private agencies include nonprofit hospitals and rehabilitation centers and for-profit companies that work with insur-ance firms representing clients who were injured in industrial accidents.   Ray V. Sakalas

Additional resources

Rubin, Stanford E., and Roessler, R. T. *Foundations of the Vocational Rehabilitation Process.* 5th ed. Pro-Ed, 2001.
Wehman, Paul. *Life Beyond the Classroom: Transition Strategies for Young People with Disabilities.* 3rd ed. Paul H. Brookes, 2001.

Vocations. See Careers.

Voice. Almost all animals have voices. A few animals, like the giraffe, rarely use their voices. But most higher animals can bark, cry, howl, groan, growl, chirp, or make some other noise. Many of the animals use their voices to communicate with one another. Birds can make music with their voices. Dogs can express several feelings with their voices. They whimper when begging or when they feel guilty, they growl when angry, and bark eagerly when they are happy. Several of the zoo animals, such as the chimpanzee, also make various sounds to show different feelings. However, no animal's voice is as highly developed as the voice of a human being.

The human voice can express ideas through a variety of arrangements of consonant and vowel sounds. It can also be used for singing. The human voice can combine speech with music, and sing words. Because the human voice is so highly developed, people have been able to create elaborate languages. These languages allow people to tell one another their detailed thoughts and actions.

The vocal cords are the main sound producers in human beings. These two small folds of tissue stretch across the *larynx* (voice box). One fold stretches on each side of an opening in the *trachea* (windpipe). Muscles in the larynx stretch and relax the vocal cords.

When we breathe, we relax our vocal cords so they form a V-shaped opening that lets air through. When we speak, we pull the vocal cords by the attached muscles, narrowing the opening. Then, as we drive air from the lungs through the larynx, the air vibrates the tightened vocal cords and sound results.

Varying the sound. The voice mechanism is so well organized that we use our vocal cords, muscles, and lungs in many combinations without thinking about it. The more tightly the vocal cords are stretched, the

How the vocal cords produce sounds

In human beings, sounds of the voice are made chiefly by the *vocal cords,* small bands of tissue that stretch across the larynx. Muscles in the larynx stretch and relax the vocal cords on each side of an opening in the trachea. When we speak, the larynx muscles pull on the cords, narrowing the opening. Air forced from the lungs vibrates the tensed cords, producing sound.

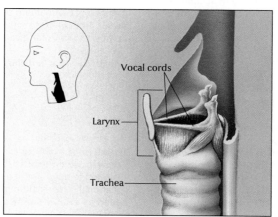

Vocal cords

Larynx

Trachea

Relaxed vocal cords for breathing

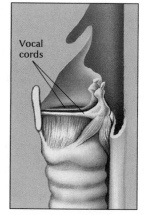

Vocal cords

Tensed vocal cords

higher are the sounds produced. The more relaxed the cords, the lower the sounds. Even in normal speech we stretch and relax the vocal cords to many degrees. This stretching and relaxing produces variations in the sounds of our voice.

The pitch of the voice is determined by the size of the larynx. Women's voices are usually pitched higher than men's because their vocal cords are shorter. Boys and girls have vocal cords of about the same size until boys reach puberty. At puberty, the voice boxes of the boys grow larger. As a result, the boys' voices become lower.

The tongue, lips, and teeth also help shape the sounds of the voice. In addition, the nasal cavity gives resonance and color to the voice. When a person becomes ill with a cold and the nasal passages stop up, the person's voice changes.

Straining the voice affects the vocal cords. So does a general muscular tension caused by nervousness. In the disease called *laryngitis* the larynx is inflamed, irritated, or infected. Sometimes the sick person cannot speak at all for a day or two. Charles W. Cummings

Related articles in *World Book* include:

Laryngitis	Singing	Trachea
Larynx	Stuttering	Voiceprint

Voice, in grammar, is a feature of *transitive* verbs. A transitive verb is a verb that takes a direct object. Voice tells whether the subject of the verb acts or is acted upon. English has two voices, *active* and *passive.*

A verb is in the active voice when its subject is the doer of the action. For example, the verb is in the active voice in the sentence *John sees the picture,* because the subject *(John)* performs the action *(sees).*

A verb is in the passive voice when its subject receives the action. In *The picture was seen by John,* the subject *(picture)* receives the action *(was seen).* The verb is therefore passive. In English, the passive voice consists of some form of the verb *be* (such as *is, was, were,* or *been*), plus the past participle of the main verb (such as *seen*). Passive forms of *see* include *is seen, was seen, were seen, will be seen, have been seen, is being seen,* and *was being seen.* Only transitive verbs can be changed to passive voice. Sara Garnes

See also **Conjugation; Verb.**

Voice of America (VOA) is the primary official worldwide broadcasting service of the United States. Its chief aims are to (1) present accurate information and news; (2) reflect the values, institutions, and way of life of the United States and its people; and (3) express policies of the U.S. government. VOA also seeks to support democratic ideals.

VOA began in 1942—during World War II—as a news service of the Office of War Information. Today, VOA reaches millions of people in Africa, Asia, Europe, Latin America, and the Pacific Islands. A special unit called *Radio Marti* broadcasts to Cuba. All broadcasts originate in the United States. Some programs are in English, but most are in other languages.

The nature of VOA programs has changed over the years. In early years, Voice of America broadcast largely to Communist countries, and much of the programming dealt with Cold War issues. Over the years, VOA has broadened its programming to include such subjects as American science, sports, and music. It has also expanded its service to reach a wider world audience.

From 1953 to 1999, it was part of the United States Information Agency (USIA). In 1994, the International Broadcasting Bureau (IBB) was created within the USIA to oversee VOA and other world broadcasting networks. In 1998, Congress voted to abolish the USIA and to make the IBB an independent agency. The IBB continued to oversee VOA. Taylor Stults

See also **United States Information Agency.**

Voiceprint, also called *speech spectrogram,* is a visual record of the sound waves of a human voice. Voiceprints and tape recordings of voices of several people are sometimes compared to identify a certain person's voice. But some scientists question the reliability of this method as a means of identification. Voiceprints are also

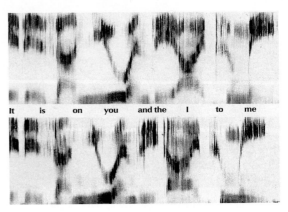

Voiceprints, like fingerprints, can be used as a means of identification. The two voiceprints shown above were made by the same person saying the same words at different times.

used in the study of speech and hearing disorders.

Several police departments in the United States use voiceprint evidence in criminal cases. They believe the voiceprint method is reliable as a method of identification when used with tape recordings. Voiceprints often have been used to clear of wrongdoing people who have been suspected of such crimes as extortion and the making of obscene telephone calls. Voiceprint evidence has been admitted in many criminal cases. But some experts believe voiceprints are difficult to interpret and are not accurate enough for use in court.

Voiceprints are made by running a tape recording of a voice through an instrument called a *sound spectrograph.* A voiceprint shows the duration of spoken words and the loudness, pitch, and quality of the recorded voice.

Three American scientists at the Bell Research Laboratories first developed the sound spectrograph in the 1940's. The American physicist Lawrence G. Kersta and the American audiologist Oscar I. Tosi later contributed to the development of voiceprints as a means of identification. Jack M. Kress

Voile, *voil,* is a thin, open cloth made of silk, cotton, polyester, rayon, or nylon. It gets its name from the French word *voiler,* which means *to veil.* Voile has a plain weave. Voiles are used in making dresses, curtains, and trimmings. Keith Slater

Vojvodina. See Serbia.

A **volcanic eruption** at Kilauea, in Hawaii, shoots fountains of glowing lava into the air. As a volcano erupts, ash, gases, and molten rock from deep underground pour from an opening called a *vent.* Erupted rock and ash can build up around the vent to form the body of the volcano.

© Greg Vaugh, Tom Stack & Associates

Volcano

Volcano is a place where ash, gases, and molten rock from deep underground erupt onto the surface. The word *volcano* also refers to the mountain of erupted rock and ash that often accumulates at such a place.

Volcanic eruptions result from *magma* (molten rock below the ground). Magma usually forms 30 to 120 miles (50 to 200 kilometers) beneath Earth's surface. It rises because it is less dense than the surrounding rock. Rising magma can collect below or inside a volcano in a region called a *magma chamber.* As the magma accumulates, the pressure inside the chamber increases. When the pressure becomes too great, the chamber breaks open, and magma rises in the volcano. If magma reaches the surface, an eruption occurs. The hole through which the magma erupts is called a *vent.*

If magma accumulates at a high enough rate, the volcano erupts almost continuously. With magma that accumulates more slowly, the eruption may halt for periods while new magma replaces that which has erupted.

The violence of an eruption depends largely on the amount of gas dissolved in the magma and the magma's *viscosity* (resistance to flow). Magmas with little gas produce relatively calm eruptions in which lava flows quiet-

Scott K. Rowland, the contributor of this article, is Associate Professor of Geology and Geophysics at the University of Hawaii in Honolulu.

ly onto the surface. Magmas with much gas can shoot violent jets of gas and ash high into the air. *Viscous* (thick and sticky) magmas tend to erupt more violently than runnier, more fluid magmas. Water mixing with the erupting magma can make any eruption more explosive.

Volcanoes can create many dangers. Hot ash, gas, lava, and mud can bury or burn people and buildings near an erupting volcano. The most violent eruptions launch large clouds of ash and gas high into the atmosphere, causing problems far from the volcano itself.

Volcanoes also provide benefits. Erupted materials contain many nutrients and can break down to form fertile soils. Volcanic activity provides an important source of *geothermal energy,* energy from Earth's interior heat. Geothermal energy can power electric generators and heat water and buildings. Undersea volcanoes have built up over time to form islands on which millions of people live. Volcanoes also have inspired myths and legends in many cultures. The word *volcano* comes from Vulcan, the Roman god of fire. Scientists who study volcanoes are called *volcanologists.*

This article discusses volcanic eruptions, the dangers of volcanoes, where volcanoes form, the types of volcanoes, and how scientists study volcanoes. Most of the article deals with volcanoes on Earth. For information on volcanoes elsewhere, see the section *Volcanoes in the solar system* at the end of this article.

Volcanic eruptions

Volcanic eruptions differ in their violence and in the

materials they produce. Some eruptions involve calm outpourings of lava. Other eruptions produce powerful explosions and large volumes of rock, ash, and gas.

Products of eruption. During an eruption, a variety of materials can come from a volcanic vent. These include lava, *pyroclasts* (rock fragments), and gases.

Lava is magma that flows onto Earth's surface. As lava spreads from a vent, parts of it begin to cool and harden. The resulting stream of lava and rock is called a *lava flow.* Lava flows vary greatly in appearance depending on their viscosity, temperature, and rate of advance.

Fluid lava flows spread easily from the vent. Two common types of fluid lava flows are *pahoehoe* (pronounced *PAH hoy hoy* or *pah HOY hoy)* and *aa* (pronounced *ah AH* or *ah ah).* Pahoehoe flows have smooth, glassy surfaces and wavy, ropelike ridges. They form when hot, fluid lava advances relatively slowly. Aa flows have rough, broken surfaces. They form when less fluid lava advances rapidly. *Pahoehoe* and *aa* are Hawaiian terms adopted by most volcanologists.

Highly viscous lavas cannot flow easily. They pile up around the vent to form thick mounds called *lava domes* or short, stubby flows with rugged surfaces. These domes and flows advance extremely slowly.

Pyroclasts, also called *pyroclastics,* form when fragments of magma are thrown into the air by expanding gas. More explosive eruptions tend to produce finer pyroclasts. Pyroclasts that settle to the ground can cement together to form a rock called *tuff.*

Volcanologists often classify pyroclasts by their size. The finest pyroclasts, dust-sized and sand-sized grains, make up *volcanic ash.* Volcanologists call pebble-sized pyroclasts *lapilli.* Rock-sized and boulder-sized fragments are known as *volcanic bombs.*

Volcanologists also classify pyroclasts by texture. *Pumice,* a lightweight pyroclast, contains many tiny cavities left behind by gas bubbles in the magma. The cavities trap air, enabling some pumice to float on water. *Scoria* (cinder), another pyroclast, also has many tiny cavities, but it does not float on water. Pumice and scoria come from vigorous eruptions that hurl magma fragments high into the air. They solidify before landing, often forming a loose pile around the vent called a *scoria cone* or *pumice cone.*

Spatter, a fluid pyroclast, comes from less vigorous eruptions. Blobs of spatter do not fly high, and they land while still molten. Spatter collects around vents in steep structures called *spatter cones* and *spatter ramparts.*

Gases from volcanic eruptions include water vapor, carbon dioxide, and sulfur dioxide. Deep underground, the gases are dissolved in the magma. As magma rises, the pressure it is under decreases. The gases come out of solution to form bubbles and may eventually escape.

The violence of an eruption depends on the amount of gas dissolved in the magma and the magma's viscosity. Magmas rich in gas develop many bubbles as they rise to the vent. The bubbles increase the pressure in the vent, causing a more explosive eruption. Viscous magmas resist the expansion of bubbles, leading to a buildup of pressure in the magma. When the pressure of the bubbles finally overcomes the magma's viscosity, an explosive eruption occurs. In more fluid magmas, the bubbles expand without building up excess pressure. The resulting eruptions are relatively mild.

When external water, such as groundwater or sea water, mixes with magma, the water rapidly turns to steam, expanding in the process. This increases the violence of an eruption. Some volcanologists call eruptions involving external water *hydromagmatic eruptions.*

As gases and pyroclasts erupt from a volcano, they draw in and heat some of the surrounding air. The heated air, gases, and pyroclasts form an *eruption column.* If an eruption draws in enough air and heats it sufficiently, the eruption column becomes lighter than the surrounding air. As a result, the column floats upward in a process called *convective rise.* Convective rise can carry erupted gas and ash high into the atmosphere. Some eruptions do not draw in enough air or heat it sufficiently to produce convective rise. In these eruptions, erupted materials remain closer to the ground.

The dangers of volcanoes

Volcanoes can endanger people, wildlife, and property. Volcanic disasters are much more difficult to avoid once an eruption begins. Instead, volcanologists and disaster planners strive to identify and evacuate dangerous areas before eruptions occur. Most damage results from (1) lava flows, (2) pyroclastic hazards, (3) lahars, (4) dangerous gases, (5) avalanches and landslides, and (6) tsunamis.

Volcano terms

Caldera is a depression that forms when part of the ground above a magma chamber collapses.
Divergent boundary is a line where two plates pull apart.
Flood basalt is a huge deposit of hardened lava that covers hundreds of thousands of square miles.
Hot spot is an area where hot rock rises through the mantle far from the boundaries between plates.
Lahar is a volcanic mudflow.
Lava is molten rock that flows onto Earth's surface.
Lava flow is a moving stream of lava and rock.
Magma is molten rock beneath the ground.
Magma chamber is an area below or inside a volcano where magma collects.
Mantle is the rocky layer beneath Earth's crust where magma forms.
Mid-ocean ridge is a place on the ocean floor where magma erupts as two plates pull apart.
Monogenetic field is a large field of separate volcanic vents

that share a common magma chamber.
Plates are the rigid pieces that make up Earth's rocky outer shell.
Pyroclastic flows and surges are clouds of hot ash and gas that move rapidly along the ground.
Pyroclasts are fragments of magma tossed into the air by expanding gas.
Shield volcano is a broad, gently sloping volcano composed of hardened lava flows.
Silicic caldera complex is a volcano that consists of a vast caldera above a huge magma chamber.
Stratovolcano is a steep-sided volcano made up of layers of pyroclasts and hardened lava.
Subduction zone is a boundary where two plates collide, forcing one plate to sink beneath the other.
Vent is an opening through which magma erupts along with the material that builds up around it.

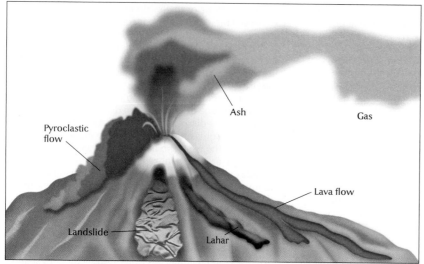

Ash

Gas

Pyroclastic flow

Lava flow

Landslide

Lahar

WORLD BOOK illustration by Adam Weiskind

Volcanic hazards can harm people, wildlife, and property. The greatest danger is posed by *pyroclastic flows,* fast-moving clouds of hot gas and ash that can burn, bury, choke, or poison. Lava flows can damage property but usually move too slowly to threaten people. Landslides and *lahars* (volcanic mudflows) can devastate areas near an erupting volcano. Ash and gas can travel great distances on the wind, causing problems far from the eruption.

Lava flows. Many people fear being buried by lava, but lava flows rank as the least dangerous volcanic hazard. Lava usually advances at less than 6 miles (10 kilometers) per hour, slow enough for people and animals to escape. Unusually fluid lavas can flow fast enough to be dangerous, but this rarely occurs. However, lava flows can burn and bury buildings, roads, and other structures. Because lava hardens into solid rock, repairing buried areas can prove slow and costly.

Pyroclastic hazards. Flying volcanic bombs pose relatively little danger because they usually fall near the vent. Ash and lapilli, however, can travel on the wind for tens or even hundreds of miles or kilometers. Falling ash and lapilli can contaminate water supplies, damage crops, and collect in great masses on roofs, causing them to collapse. Falling ash also blocks sunlight and reduces visibility, complicating evacuations. Ash can clog the engines of jet aircraft and parts of other machines, causing them to fail. Dispersed ash can remain in the

AP/Wide World

Volcanic ash can travel on the wind and fall to the ground far from the erupting volcano. This man works to remove a crust of ash that accumulated on his automobile following an eruption.

stratosphere for years, where it can cool the atmosphere by blocking some sunlight.

The most dangerous volcanic hazards are *pyroclastic flows and surges,* clouds of hot ash and gas that travel mostly along the ground. They can choke or poison people with gases, bury people with debris, and burn them with temperatures of up to 1100 °F (600° C). They advance tens or hundreds of feet or meters per second and can even cross such natural barriers as rivers and ridges. People and animals cannot outrun pyroclastic flows and surges. In 1902, pyroclastic flows and surges from Mount Pelée on the island of Martinique swept through the city of St. Pierre, killing about 28,000 people.

Some pyroclastic flows occur when the column of ash and gas rising from a vent becomes too heavy to be supported by rising air. The column collapses and flows away from the vent. Other pyroclastic flows occur when the edge of a steep-sided lava dome or flow collapses, releasing pressurized gases mixed with lava fragments.

Lahars are mudflows that occur when loose ash on a steep volcano mixes with rain or melting snow. Eruptions or earthquakes, which often accompany volcanic activity, can dislodge the resulting mud. As lahars travel downhill, they pick up trees, boulders, and other debris. They usually follow river and stream valleys, where there may be many towns. Lahars leave a thick layer of mud that can harden like cement. Lahars from Nevado del Ruiz volcano in Colombia destroyed the town of Armero in 1985, killing more than 23,000 people.

Dangerous gases may be nearly invisible. Carbon dioxide, the most dangerous volcanic gas, causes suffocation in high concentrations. Where air circulation is poor, carbon dioxide can collect in low areas. People in these areas can be overcome before they realize the danger. Clouds of erupted gas can occasionally descend into populated areas, causing widespread suffocation.

Avalanches and landslides often occur on volcanoes because many are steep-sided and covered with loose ash and fractured lava flows. Many volcanoes also produce tremors or explosions that can dislodge snow and rubble. A landslide or avalanche may stem from an eruption or may happen when no eruption is occurring.

Tsunamis. A tsunami is a series of large ocean waves that can devastate coastal areas. Volcanic tsunamis can begin when a pyroclastic flow or avalanche enters the ocean, when a volcano in or near the ocean collapses, or when an underwater volcano erupts. During the 1883 eruption of Krakatau in Indonesia, the summit of the volcano collapsed, causing a tsunami that killed more than 30,000 people on nearby coasts.

Where volcanoes form

Volcanoes form above regions where magma is produced in the *mantle,* the rocky layer beneath Earth's crust. The theory of *plate tectonics* helps explain why volcanoes form where they do. According to the theory, Earth's outer shell consists of rigid pieces called *plates* that slowly move against one another. Nearly all volcanoes form along the edges of plates at *subduction zones* and *divergent boundaries.* Some volcanoes appear above locations called *hot spots* that can be far from plate boundaries.

Subduction zones are boundaries where two plates push up against each other, forcing an oceanic plate to *subduct* (sink) beneath another plate. The subducting plate moves downward, carrying water trapped in sediments and rock into the mantle. When the plate reaches a depth of about 60 to 90 miles (100 to 150 kilometers), Earth's heat causes the water to boil. The boiling water rises into the overlying mantle. There, the water lowers the melting point of the rock, which turns to magma in a process called *hydration melting.* The magma can then rise through the overlying plate to erupt at the surface.

Subduction zones produce viscous magmas that contain much water vapor and other gases. For this reason, subduction zone volcanoes tend to erupt explosively.

Bands of subduction zone volcanoes often form along the edges of continents where an oceanic plate subducts beneath a continental plate. These include the volcanoes of the Andes Mountains in South America and the Cascade Range in North America. Other bands of volcanoes occur where two oceanic plates meet and one subducts beneath the other. These include the volcanoes of Japan and Indonesia. Subduction zones border most of the Pacific Ocean, creating a region of volcano and earthquake activity called the *Ring of Fire.*

Divergent boundaries are areas where two plates are pulling apart. As the plates separate, hot rock from the mantle rises to fill the space between them. The pressure on the rock decreases as the rock rises, causing it to melt in a process called *decompression melting.* The resulting magma erupts along the fracture between the plates and cools to form new plate material.

Divergent boundaries usually produce fluid magmas that contain few gases. Accordingly, eruptions at divergent boundaries tend to be less violent than eruptions at subduction zones. Most divergent boundaries involve two oceanic plates. For this reason, most eruptions at divergent boundaries occur underwater.

Hot spots are areas where columns of hot, solid rock rise slowly through the mantle. At the top of the column, decompression melting turns the rock into relatively fluid magma with little gas. This magma rises to erupt through the overlying plate. Many hot spot volcanoes, such as those of the Hawaiian Islands, occur far from plate boundaries. However, some hot spot volcanoes, such as those of Iceland, lie on or near plate boundaries.

Types of volcanoes

Many schemes exist for classifying volcanoes. Most volcanoes fit into one of these types: (1) shield volcanoes, (2) stratovolcanoes, (3) silicic caldera complexes, (4) monogenetic fields, (5) mid-ocean ridges, and (6) flood basalts.

Where volcanoes occur This map shows the location of many volcanoes. It also shows the large, rigid plates that make up Earth's rocky outer shell. Volcanoes usually occur along the boundaries between plates.

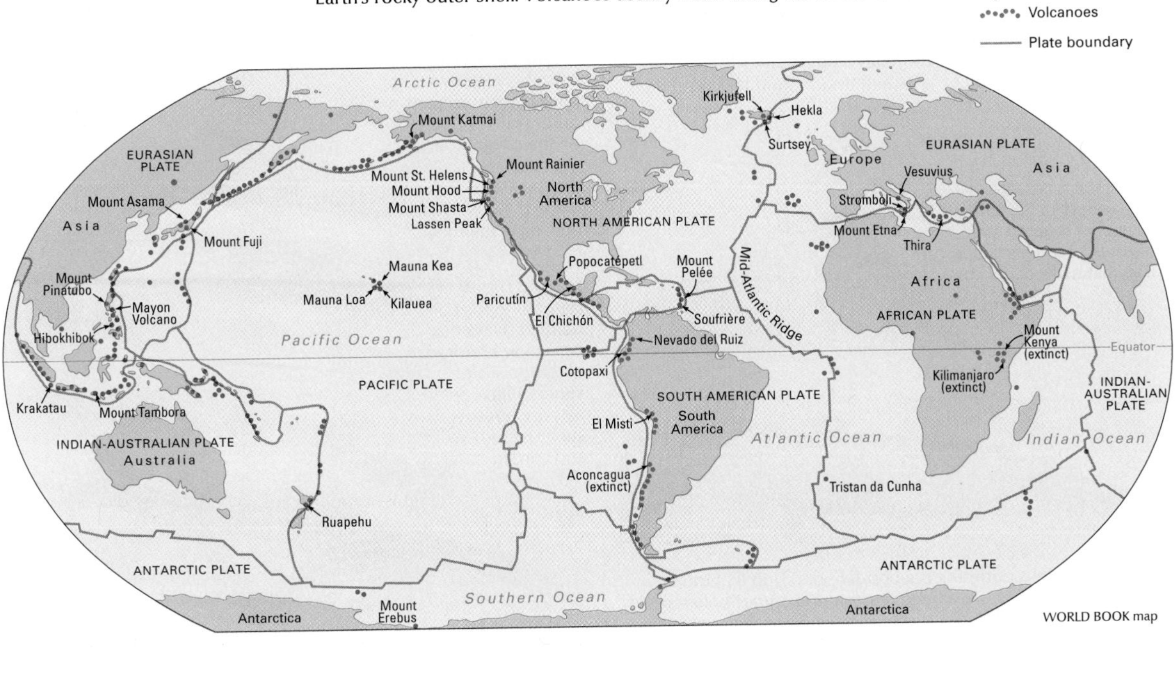

•·•·•·• Volcanoes

—— Plate boundary

WORLD BOOK map

Shield volcanoes build up over time from hundreds of thousands of lava flows. They erupt large volumes of fluid lava and few pyroclasts. The lava spreads far from the vent, creating a broad volcano with gently sloping sides. The word *shield* refers to the volcano's profile, which resembles the shallow curve of a warrior's shield.

Shield volcanoes include some of the largest volcanoes on Earth. Mauna Loa, a shield volcano on the island of Hawaii, rises about 30,000 feet (9,000 meters) from the ocean floor to its summit.

Most shield volcanoes form at hot spots. These include the volcanoes of Comoros, the Galapagos Islands, Hawaii, and many volcanoes in Iceland. Some of them, such as Westdahl Peak in Alaska, occur at subduction zones. Other shield volcanoes, including Erta Ale in Ethiopia and Nyamuragira in Congo (Kinshasa), appear at divergent boundaries between continental plates.

Stratovolcanoes form from explosive eruptions that produce viscous lava and a large volume of pyroclasts. These materials pile up around the vent to form a steep-sided volcano. Most stratovolcanoes are smaller than shield volcanoes and erupt less often. The name *stratovolcano* refers to the *strata* (layers) of pyroclasts and hardened lava that make up the volcano's cone.

Stratovolcanoes are among the most common volcanoes on Earth. They include many famous historical volcanoes, such as Krakatau in Indonesia, Mount Pinatubo in the Philippines, and Vesuvius in Italy.

Most stratovolcanoes occur along subduction zones.

Nyiragongo in Congo (Kinshasa), however, is a stratovolcano that lies on a divergent continental boundary.

Silicic caldera complexes produce the most violent volcanic eruptions. A silicic caldera complex can be difficult to recognize as a volcano because it consists of a broad, low-lying depression rather than a mountain.

Silicic caldera complexes form when a huge volume of magma collects below the surface in a giant magma chamber. The magma eventually erupts explosively, throwing ash high into the atmosphere and producing pyroclastic flows that damage vast areas. During the eruption, the ground above the chamber usually collapses, producing a large depression called a *caldera*.

A caldera can also form when part of a shield volcano or stratovolcano collapses into an opening left behind by erupting magma. These calderas are much smaller than silicic caldera complexes and are considered part of the larger volcano.

No silicic caldera complex has produced a major eruption in recent history. However, geologists have found evidence of such eruptions in Earth's past. These eruptions occur rarely because the large volume of magma they require takes a long time to accumulate. For example, a huge silicic caldera complex at what is now Yellowstone National Park in Wyoming produced three massive eruptions roughly 600,000 years apart.

Silicic caldera complexes are sometimes called *resurgent calderas*. This is because scientists think the caldera floor can *resurge* (rise again) as magma accumulates in

Kinds of volcanoes   Most volcanoes fit into one of the following groups: (1) shield volcanoes, (2) stratovolcanoes, (3) silicic caldera complexes, (4) monogenetic fields, (5) mid-ocean ridges, and (6) flood basalts.

WORLD BOOK illustrations by Adam Weiskind

A shield volcano has a broad profile that resembles the shallow curve of a warrior's shield. Its gently sloping sides build up over time from the eruption of large amounts of fluid lava.

A monogenetic field is an area where magma from one source erupts through many vents. What appear to be individual volcanoes are actually vents in the larger field.

A stratovolcano is a steep-sided volcano formed by violent eruptions. The word *stratovolcano* refers to the *strata* (layers) of erupted rock fragments and hardened lava that make up its cone.

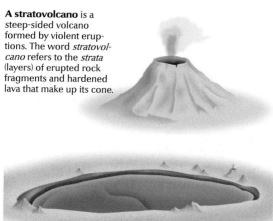

A mid-ocean ridge develops where two *plates* (rocky pieces of Earth's outer shell) spread apart on the ocean floor. As the plates separate, magma erupts between them and cools to form new plate material.

A flood basalt is a layered deposit of hardened lava that can cover hundreds of thousands of square miles. Scientists are not sure how such lavas erupted and spread so far.

A silicic caldera complex is a broad depression that forms when the ground above a huge deposit of *magma* (molten rock) collapses. These volcanoes produce the most violent eruptions.

the magma chamber before an eruption.

Silicic caldera complexes usually form on land near a hot spot or subduction zone. Famous examples include La Primavera in Mexico, Taupo in New Zealand, Toba in Indonesia, and the Yellowstone caldera.

Monogenetic fields form when magma from a single source flows to the surface through many different vents. Each vent forms during a single eruption. The word *monogenetic* means *of one origin.* Casual observers may not realize that what appears to be a single volcano is actually one vent in a large monogenetic field.

Monogenetic fields usually occur near subduction zones and hot spots. The best known is the Michoacan-Guanajuato field in Mexico. The field's newest vent, a large cone called Paricutín, formed in a thinly populated area during an eruption that lasted from 1943 to 1952. Monogenetic fields also occur in and around the cities of Auckland, New Zealand, and Flagstaff, Arizona.

Mid-ocean ridges are places at divergent boundaries where erupting magma creates new oceanic plate material. The mid-ocean ridge system forms the longest mountain chain on Earth. Estimates of its total length range from 30,000 to 50,000 miles (50,000 to 80,000 kilometers). Many geologists consider smaller segments of the ridge system to be individual volcanoes. At mid-ocean ridges, the material built up by eruptions spreads out as the plates pull apart. Ridges that spread rapidly, such as the East Pacific Rise, are broad and low. Ridges that spread slowly, such as the Mid-Atlantic Ridge, are narrow and steep.

Flood basalts, also known as *plateau basalts,* consist of layers of a dark volcanic rock called *basalt* that can cover hundreds of thousands of square miles. No flood basalt has erupted in recorded history, and geologists are still debating how they form. They once thought that the expanses of basalt resulted from rapid "floods" of lava because slow-moving lava would solidify before flowing so far. However, more recent research has shown that slow-moving lava can flow long distances if it develops an insulating skin or crust of rock. Flood basalts include the Columbia River basalts in Washington, Oregon, and Idaho, the Deccan Traps in India, and the Paraná basalts in Brazil.

Studying volcanoes

The study of volcanoes offers many benefits. Erupting magma can carry material from deep underground to the surface, providing scientists with samples from Earth's interior. Hardened lava and ash deposits preserve evidence of major changes in Earth's history. Studying ancient volcanoes also helps scientists find new deposits of ores. The fluids moving through volcanoes can concentrate valuable metals in deposits called *veins.*

Perhaps most importantly, scientists study volcanoes to learn how to predict eruptions. This information can help reduce the damage and loss of life eruptions cause.

Predicting eruptions. To determine whether or when a particular volcano will erupt, volcanologists monitor *seismic activity* (earthquakes) near the volcano. They also watch for changes in the volcano's shape caused by pressure from magma below. They analyze the types and amounts of gases coming from vents. Changes may signal that an eruption is coming.

Modern volcanologists can state fairly confidently the probability that a particular volcano will erupt sometime in the next tens, hundreds, or thousands of years. With enough information, they can occasionally provide warnings a few days to a few hours before an eruption. Volcanologists are working to develop the ability to forecast an eruption a few years to a few months before it occurs. Warnings on this time scale would prove most

How a volcano erupts

Magma (molten rock) forms deep underground and rises toward the surface, *left,* collecting in a *magma chamber.* As pressure builds, the chamber breaks open and magma rises through a *conduit, right.* At openings called *vents,* the magma erupts as gas, lava, and *pyroclasts* (rock and ash). Layers of erupted lava and pyroclasts make up the body of a *stratovolcano, shown here.*

WORLD BOOK diagrams by Jay Bensen

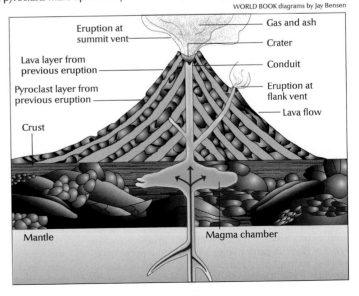

Some famous volcanoes

Name	Location	Height above sea level in feet	in meters	Interesting facts
*Aconcagua	Argentina	22,835	6,960	Highest mountain in Western Hemisphere; volcano extinct.
*Cotopaxi	Ecuador	19,347	5,897	Eruption in 1877 produced *lahar* (mudflow) that traveled about 150 miles (241 kilometers) and killed about 1,000 people.
El Chichón	Mexico	3,478	1,060	Eruption in 1982 killed 187 people and released a cloud of dust and sulfur dioxide gas high into the atmosphere.
*Krakatau	Indonesia	2,667	813	Great eruption in 1883 heard about 3,000 miles (4,800 kilometers) away; produced sea waves almost 130 feet (40 meters) high that drowned over 30,000 people on nearby coasts.
*Lassen Peak	California	10,457	3,187	One of several volcanoes in the Cascade Range; last erupted in 1921.
*Mauna Loa	Hawaii	13,677	4,169	World's largest volcano; rises about 30,000 feet (9,100 meters) from ocean floor.
*Mount Etna	Sicily	10,902	3,323	About 20,000 people killed in 1669 eruption.
*Mount Pelée	Martinique	4,583	1,397	*Pyroclastic flows and surges* (rushing clouds of hot ash and gas) from 1902 eruption destroyed city of St.-Pierre, killing about 28,000 people in minutes.
*Mount Pinatubo	Philippines	4,875	1,486	Eruption in 1991, perhaps the largest of the 1900's, spewed about 20 million tons (18 million metric tons) of sulfur dioxide gas into the atmosphere.
*Mount St. Helens	Washington	8,364	2,549	In 1980, violent eruptions released large amounts of molten rock and hot ash; killed 57 people.
Mount Tambora	Indonesia	9,350	2,850	In 1815, eruption released 6 million times more energy than the explosion of an atomic bomb; killed about 92,000 people.
Nevado del Ruiz	Colombia	17,717	5,400	Eruption in 1985 triggered lahars and floods; destroyed city of Armero and killed over 23,000 people.
*Paricutín	Mexico	9,213	2,808	Newest volcanic mountain in the Western Hemisphere. Began in farmer's field in 1943; built cinder cone over 500 feet (150 meters) high in six days.
*Stromboli	Mediterranean Sea	3,031	924	Active since ancient times; erupts constantly for months or even years.
Surtsey	North Atlantic Ocean	568	173	In 1963, underwater eruption began forming island of Surtsey; after last eruption of lava in 1967, island covered more than 1 square mile (2.6 square kilometers).
Thera†	Mediterranean Sea	1,850	564	Eruption in about 1500 B.C. may have destroyed Minoan civilization on Crete; legend of lost continent of Atlantis may be based on this eruption.
*Vesuvius	Italy	4,190	1,277	In A.D. 79, produced history's most famous eruption, which destroyed towns of Herculaneum, Pompeii, and Stabiae.

*Has a separate article in *World Book.*   †Name in ancient times. Now called Thira, or Santorini.

useful to disaster planners.

Most volcanologists consider any volcano that has erupted in the last 10,000 years or so to be *active.* Some of them use the term *dormant* to describe an active volcano that is not currently erupting or showing signs of a coming eruption. Volcanologists label a volcano *extinct* if there is strong evidence it will never erupt again.

Describing eruptions. Volcanologists sometimes rate the explosive power of an eruption using a scale called the Volcanic Explosivity Index (VEI). The index ranks eruptions according to the volume of magma erupted, the amount of energy released, and the height of the eruption cloud. Most eruptions have VEI ratings from 0, for nonexplosive, to 8, for extremely explosive. Each number on the index represents a tenfold increase in explosive power or the volume of material erupted. For example, a VEI rating of 5 represents 10 times more power or eruption volume than a rating of 4.

Another common method for describing eruptions is based on how they produce pyroclasts. In this system, both *Plinian* and *Hawaiian* eruptions produce pyroclasts almost continuously. Plinian eruptions produce convective rise that can carry huge plumes of fine pyroclasts into the atmosphere. Hawaiian eruptions do not cause convective rise. Their pyroclasts are larger and stay closer to the ground, often landing while still molten. *Vulcanian* and *Strombolian* eruptions produce pyroclasts in bursts separated by periods of relative calm. Vulcanian eruptions produce convective rise, but Strombolian eruptions do not. Some volcanologists use classification schemes that have additional categories of eruptions.

Volcanoes in the solar system

Beyond Earth, planetary scientists have identified evidence of volcanic activity on the moon and on Mars, Venus, and Io, a large satellite of Jupiter. Much of the activity on these planets resembles volcanic activity on Earth. Scientists have identified basalt, a rock commonly erupted on Earth, in samples retrieved from the moon and in space probe observations of Mars. Many volcanoes on Mars and Venus resemble giant versions of shield volcanoes found on Earth. The shield volcano Olympus Mons on Mars ranks as the largest volcano in the solar system. It measures more than 370 miles (600 kilometers) in diameter and rises about 16 miles (25 kilometers) above the surrounding plain.

Io ranks as by far the most volcanically active body in the solar system. Space probes and telescopes have identified hundreds of volcanoes on Io, many of them active. Some eruptions on Io measure at least 350

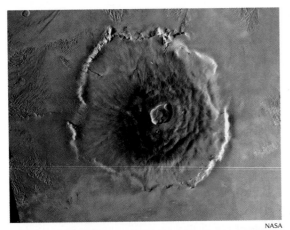

NASA

Olympus Mons on Mars is the largest volcano in the solar system. It measures more than 370 miles (600 kilometers) wide and rises about 16 miles (25 kilometers) above the surrounding plain.

Fahrenheit degrees (175 Celsius degrees) higher than the hottest eruptions on Earth. Other eruptions on Io involve sulfur rather than molten rock. Probes have recorded eruptions shooting sulfur as high as 310 miles (500 kilometers) above Io's surface.

Scientists studying Neptune's moon Triton have found evidence of a process called *cryovolcanism*. Cryovolcanism resembles volcanic activity but is driven by melted ice rather than magma. Volcanolike vents on Triton erupt liquid nitrogen far above the moon's frigid surface. Scientists think cryovolcanism may occur on other cold bodies in the outer solar system.   Scott K. Rowland

Related articles in *World Book* include:

Volcanoes

See the articles on the volcanoes marked by an asterisk in the table *Some famous volcanoes* in this article. See also:

Chimborazo	Kilauea	Mount Fuji	Orizaba, Pico
El Misti	Kilimanjaro	Mount Kenya	de
Hekla	Mauna Kea	Mount Rainier	Pichincha
Ixtacihuatl	Mount Ararat	Mount Shasta	Popocatépetl

Other related articles

Climate (Volcanic eruptions)	Katmai National Park
Crater	Lava
Crater Lake	Mountain (Volcanic mountains)
Earthquake	
Fumarole	Pumice
Geyser	Ring of Fire
Hot spot	Rock (Igneous rock)
Hot springs	Seamount
Igneous rock	Tsunami
Island (Kinds of islands)	

Outline

I. **Volcanic eruptions**
  A. Products of eruption
  B. The violence of an eruption
II. **The dangers of volcanoes**
  A. Lava flows
  B. Pyroclastic hazards
  C. Lahars
  D. Dangerous gases
  E. Avalanches and landslides
  F. Tsunamis
III. **Where volcanoes form**
  A. Subduction zones

  B. Divergent boundaries
  C. Hot spots
IV. **Types of volcanoes**
  A. Shield volcanoes
  B. Stratovolcanoes
  C. Silicic caldera complexes
  D. Monogenetic fields
  E. Mid-ocean ridges
  F. Flood basalts
V. **Studying volcanoes**
  A. Predicting eruptions
  B. Describing eruptions
VI. **Volcanoes in the solar system**

Questions

What is *magma?* What is a *magma chamber?*
What kind of volcano produces the most violent eruptions known?
Where does the word *volcano* come from?
What three basic kinds of materials may erupt from a volcano?
Where is the Ring of Fire?
How does a caldera form?
What is a *hot spot?*
What is the largest volcano in the solar system?
What scale do volcanologists use to rate the explosive power of an eruption?
Where does hydration melting occur?

Additional resources

Level I
Bunce, Vincent J. *Volcanoes*. Raintree Steck-Vaughn, 2000.
Rogers, Daniel. *Volcanoes*. Raintree Steck-Vaughn, 1999.
Trueit, Trudi S. *Volcanoes.* Watts, 2003.

Level II
Lopes, Rosaly M. C., and Gregg, T. K. P. *Volcanic Worlds: Exploring the Solar System's Volcanoes.* Springer-Praxis, 2004.
Sigurdsson, Haraldur, and others, eds. *Encyclopedia of Volcanoes.* Academic Pr., 2000.
Simkin, Tom, and others. *Volcanoes of the World.* 2nd ed. Geoscience Pr., 1994.

Volcanology. See Volcano (Studying volcanoes).

Volcker, *VOHL kur,* **Paul Adolph** (1927-   ), served as chairman of the Board of Governors of the Federal Reserve System (FRS) from 1979 to 1987. The FRS is an independent federal agency that directs the United States banking system and helps manage the nation's economy. Volcker was appointed chairman by President Jimmy Carter and was reappointed to the position by President Ronald Reagan in 1983.

The United States faced a high rate of inflation when Volcker first became chairman. Under Volcker's leadership, the FRS helped slow down inflation by curbing the growth of the nation's money supply. But many economists believe that Volcker's policy also contributed to the highest unemployment rates since 1941.

Volcker was born on Sept. 5, 1927, in Cape May, New Jersey. He graduated from Princeton University in 1949 and earned a master's degree from Harvard University in 1951. During his career, Volcker worked for the Chase Manhattan Bank and the United States Department of the Treasury. From 1975 to 1979, Volcker served as president of the Federal Reserve Bank of New York.

Lee Thornton

Vole is a mouselike animal. Voles have plump bodies about 5 inches (13 centimeters) long. They have short or medium-length tails, short legs, and tiny ears. Most have gray fur. The many species are usually named for their habitats. *Meadow voles* are the most common North American species. They live in grassy fields and eat

Rod Planck, Tom Stack & Assoc.

A vole has a plump, furry body and tiny ears. The meadow vole, *shown here,* lives in grassy fields of North America.

grass, roots, and seeds. *Water voles* live near water. *Tundra voles* live in cold, swampy plains called *tundra.*

Voles are closely related to lemmings. The vole population changes greatly every three to seven years, as does that of lemmings (see **Lemming**). The number of voles may increase by 20 times in this period. Then, probably because of enemies, diseases, and lack of food, it drops sharply to its original level. Clyde Jones

Scientific classification. Voles belong to the family Muridae. Meadow voles are genus *Microtus.* The scientific name for one of the most common species is *M. pennsylvanicus.*

Volga, *VOHL guh,* **River** is the most important river in Russia and the longest river in Europe. It flows 2,300 miles (3,700 kilometers) through western Russia (see **Russia** [terrain map]). The Volga begins in the Valdai Hills northwest of Moscow and flows southeastward into the Caspian Sea near the city of Astrakhan.

The Volga has about 200 tributaries, the most important of which are the Kama, the Oka, the Vetluga, and the Sura rivers. Almost half of Russia's population lives in the area drained by the Volga and its tributaries.

Although all parts of the Volga are frozen for at least three months of each year, the river is a major artery for transporting passengers and freight. More than 900 ports line its banks. Canals link the Volga with the Baltic Sea and the White Sea, as well as with the Black Sea through the Sea of Azov. A canal connects Moscow to the Volga.

Volgograd and Nizhniy Novgorod (formerly Gorki) are important manufacturing cities on the banks of the Volga River. A number of hydroelectric power stations and several large artificial lakes formed by dams lie along the Volga. The largest lakes are, from north to south, the Rybinsk, Nizhniy Novgorod, Samara, and Volgograd reservoirs.

The Volga River contains many kinds of fish, including most of Russia's sturgeon. Sturgeon eggs are used to make the well-known delicacy caviar. However, dams built along the river prevented many fish from swimming upstream to spawn. Industrial pollution, agricultural runoff, and logging during the period when Russia was part of the Soviet Union severely damaged the river. After the collapse of the Soviet Union in 1991, environmental groups drew attention to the Volga's decline, and the Russian government made efforts to revive the river. But high pollution levels and overfishing remain serious problems.

In the 100's A.D., the scholar Ptolemy mentioned the Volga in his *Geography.* A powerful Bulgarian empire once flourished where the Kama River joins the Volga. Volgograd was the scene of the Battle of Stalingrad, the major victory of the Soviet Union over Germany in World War II (1939-1945). Richard H. Bidlack

Volgograd, *vohl guh GRAD* (pop. 1,011,417), is an important manufacturing city, river port, and transportation hub in southwestern Russia. It lies along the west bank of the Volga River (see **Russia** [political map]). The city's industries include oil refining, steel and cement production, shipbuilding, and food processing.

Volgograd was founded in 1589 as Tsaritsyn to defend Russia's colonized territory along the Volga. In 1925, as the Soviet leader Joseph Stalin was acquiring dictatorial power, the city was renamed Stalingrad for him. From August 1942 to February 1943, the Stalingrad area was the site of a battle that marked a turning point in World War II (see **Stalingrad, Battle of**). In the battle, the Soviet Red Army destroyed Germany's Sixth Army and ended the German advance into the Soviet Union.

Stalingrad was rebuilt after World War II. A dam and a hydroelectric plant were constructed north of the city on the Volga. The city's name was changed to Volgograd in 1961, after Stalin was denounced by Nikita S. Khrushchev, the Soviet leader who succeeded him. Richard H. Bidlack

Volkswagen AG, *VOHKS WAG uhn* or *FOHLKS vah guhn,* a German automobile manufacturer, is one of the world's leading producers of passenger cars. The German word *Volkswagen* means *people's car. AG* is the abbreviation for a German word meaning *corporation.*

Volkswagen manufactures automobiles in a number of countries throughout the world. Subsidiary companies of Volkswagen include Audi of Germany, Bentley Motors of the United Kingdom, Bugatti of France, and Lamborghini of Italy. Volkswagen also manufactures automotive parts and electronic products. Volkswagen's headquarters are in Wolfsburg, Germany.

The German government established Volkswagen in 1937. The German dictator Adolf Hitler wanted a compact, durable car that most people could afford. Hitler contacted Ferdinand Porsche, an Austrian engineer, who designed the car that would evolve into the Beetle. Only a few Beetles were built before World War II (1939-1945) began. Volkswagen shifted to building vehicles for the German army during the war.

From 1945 until the mid-1960's, Volkswagen produced chiefly Beetles. Also known as the "Bug," the Beetle became one of the most popular cars ever built. The company stopped production of Beetles at its German plants in the late 1970's and altogether in 2003. In 1998, Volkswagen began selling the New Beetle. Other popular Volkswagen models have been the Golf—called the Rabbit in the United States and Canada—and the Jetta. The company is publicly owned. More than 30 percent is held by Porsche AG, the car company founded by Ferdinand Porsche in 1931. Barry Winfield

See also **Manufacturing** (table: World's leading manufacturers).

Volleyball is a game in which the players hit a ball back and forth across a net with their hands, arms, or feet. It is one of the world's most popular team sports.

There are two main forms of volleyball. Indoor volleyball is played on a court with a wooden or synthetic surface. It has six players on a team. Outdoor volleyball is played on a sand or grass court. It may have two, three, four, or six players on a team. The two forms have similar rules. This article discusses indoor volleyball.

William G. Morgan, a physical education instructor at the YMCA in Holyoke, Massachusetts, invented volleyball in 1895. Indoor volleyball became an official sport of the Olympic Games in 1964. About 220 national federations belong to the Fédération Internationale de Volleyball (FIVB). This organization sponsors various world tournaments, most notably the men's and women's World Championships, held every four years.

The ball is round and has a leather cover. It measures about 25 to 26 inches (65 to 67 centimeters) in circumference and weighs about 9 ½ ounces (270 grams).

The court measures 59 feet (18 meters) long and 29 ½ feet (9 meters) wide. A net suspended across the center of the court divides the court in half. The net is 7 feet 11 ⅝ inches (2.43 meters) high for men's games and 7 feet 4 ¼ inches (2.24 meters) high for women. An *attack line* is placed 9 feet 9 inches (3 meters) from the net and runs on either side of the net. The back row of players must attack the ball from behind this line, though they may jump from behind the line and land in front of it.

Tony Duffy, All-Sport

Volleyball games provide spirited fun and exercise for young people and adults. The players bat a ball back and forth across a high net, and often leap high to *spike* a ball, or drive it downward. Volleyball can be played on both indoor and outdoor courts and by mixed teams of boys and girls. The diagram with this picture shows the positions for teams of six players.

← 29 ½ ft. →			29 ½ ft. →		Service area
Left back	Left forward		Right forward	Right back	29 ½ ft.
Center back	Center forward		Center forward	Center back	
Right back	Right forward	Net	Left forward	Left back	
		Attack lines			

There are six positions—right back, center back, left back, left forward, center forward, and right forward. Until the ball has been served to start each play, players must assume a position on the court according to the order in which they serve. Two referees and two or four linespersons serve as officials for the game.

The game starts with the right back of the serving team serving from the service area. The right back player serves the ball by hitting it with an arm or a hand. The serve must pass over the net into the receiving team's court. If the serve grazes the net, the receiving team must still play it. Players must return the ball by cleanly hitting it with their hands or arms. They cannot catch, lift, scoop, or throw the ball. A team may hit the ball no more than three times before sending it back over the net. If the ball is touched on a blocking attempt, that touch does not count as one of the three permitted hits.

The players on each team try to hit the ball to the floor of the other team's court. The players leap and dive to prevent the ball from touching their floor. They also try to make it hard for the other team to return the ball. A player may try to spike the ball—that is, hit it sharply downward over the net into the opponents' court. No player may touch the ball twice in a row unless the first touch was made in blocking an opponent's spike.

In scoring, the *rally point* system usually is used. A point is awarded after each serve. When the serving team commits a fault, the receiving team scores a point and gains the serve. A team scores a point each time the ball touches the opposing team's floor or that team hits the ball more than three times. A team also scores a point if the opposing team hits the ball out of bounds or commits a foul. Some matches in the United States use *side out* scoring, in which only the serving team can score a point.

After the serving team loses a point, the opposing team serves. But first, each of its players rotates clockwise one position. The right forward moves to the right back position, the right back becomes the center back, and so on.

Volleyball competitions are played as three- or five-game matches. The games in a match are usually called *sets*. In a three-set match, the first team to win two sets wins the match. In a five-set match, the first team to win three sets wins the match. In each set, the first team to score 25 points wins, except that the deciding set (the third or fifth set) is played to 15 points. A team must win a set by at least 2 points.   Critically reviewed by USA Volleyball

See also **Beach volleyball**.

Volstead Act, *VAHL stehd,* provided for the enforcing of national prohibition of the use of intoxicating liquors. It was passed by the Congress of the United States in 1919, over the veto of President Woodrow Wilson. The 18th Amendment to the Constitution prohibited the manufacture, sale, or transportation of intoxicating liquors within the United States. It also banned the import or export of such beverages. The Volstead Act provided the means to investigate and punish violators of the amendment. The act took its name from that of Representative Andrew J. Volstead of Minnesota, who introduced it. The act defined intoxicating liquors as beverages that contain "one-half of one per centum or more of alcohol by volume." After the ratification of Amendment 21, which repealed prohibition, the Volstead Act expired automatically, except in the Territories. See also **Prohibition.** David E. Kyvig

Volt is a unit of electrical measurement. The volt measures the ability of an *electric field* to give energy to electric charges. An electric field is the influence that an electric charge creates in the region around it. The field exerts forces on other charges in the region.

An electric field supplies energy to a charge if the charge moves between two points. The amount of energy divided by the charge is known as the *potential difference,* or *voltage,* between the two points. The volt is used to measure this quantity. The potential difference is 1 volt when the field supplies 1 joule of energy to 1 *coulomb* of charge. One coulomb is the charge that flows through a wire in 1 second when the electric current is 1 ampere. A potential difference of 1 volt supplies enough energy to push 1 ampere of current through an electrical resistance of 1 ohm. A 1.5-volt flashlight battery, for example, supplies 1.5 joules of energy to each coulomb of charge that flows through an electric circuit.

The volt was named for the Italian scientist Alessandro Volta. Its symbol is V. Richard Wolfson

See also **Ampere; Volta, Alessandro.**

Volta, *VAHL tah* or *VOHL tuh,* **Alessandro** (1745-1827), won fame as the inventor of the *voltaic pile,* an early type of electric battery. He made several discoveries in electrostatics, meteorology, and pneumatics. He invented an electrical device called an *electrophore,* a forerunner of the capacitor. The *volt,* a unit of electrical measurement, is named for him (see **Volt**). Volta was born in Como, Italy, into a noble family. In the early 1800's, the French leader Napoleon I made Volta a count. His full name was Alessandro Giuseppe Antonio Anastasio Volta. See also **Battery; Electricity** (Experiments with electric charge). Ronald R. Kline

Voltaire, *vahl TAIR* or *vohl TAIR* (1694-1778), was the pen name of François Marie Arouet, a French author and philosopher. Voltaire's clear style, sparkling wit, keen intelligence, and strong sense of justice made him one of France's most famous writers.

Candide (1759), Voltaire's best-known work, is a brilliant philosophical tale. On the surface, the work describes the adventures of an inexperienced young man as he wanders around the world. Philosophically, *Candide* is recognized as a complex inquiry into the nature of good and evil.

Voltaire was born in Paris. He received an excellent education at a Jesuit school. He showed little inclination to study law, and his schooling ended at the age of 16. He soon joined a group of sophisticated aristocrats. Paris society sought Voltaire's company because of his cleverness, his remarkable ability to write verses, and his gift for making people laugh.

There are several theories about the origin of Voltaire's pen name, which he adopted in 1718. The most widely accepted one is that *Voltaire* comes from an imperfect arrangement of the letters making up the French equivalent of *Arouet the Younger.*

Imprisonment and early success. In 1717, Voltaire was imprisoned in the Bastille for satirical verses that he may or may not have written ridiculing the government. During his 11 months in prison, he finished his tragedy *Oedipe.* The success of the play in 1718 made Voltaire the greatest French playwright of his time. He main-

tained this reputation—with more than 50 plays—for the rest of his life. While in prison, Voltaire also worked on *La Henriade,* an epic poem about King Henry IV.

Voltaire became independently wealthy in his early 30's through an inheritance and wise investments. He was also a celebrity who had three plays performed in 1725 to help celebrate the wedding of King Louis XV. Royal pensions and other honors followed. But all this success ended abruptly in 1726 when the Chevalier de Rohan, a powerful young nobleman, scornfully asked: "What is your name anyway? Monsieur de Voltaire or Monsieur Arouet?" His question implied that Voltaire was claiming to be a nobleman while he was in fact of common origin. Voltaire supposedly replied that whatever his name was, he was bringing it honor, which was more than Rohan could say for himself. This answer cost Voltaire a beating by Rohan's men. Challenged to a duel by Voltaire, Rohan had him thrown into the Bastille again. A few days later, Voltaire was allowed to choose between continued imprisonment and exile.

Exile and return to France. Voltaire chose exile. From 1726 to 1729, he lived in England, for him a land of political and religious freedom. There, he met the writers Alexander Pope and Jonathan Swift and was attracted to the ideas of the philosopher John Locke and the scientist Sir Isaac Newton. It has been said that Voltaire went into exile a poet and came back a philosopher.

Voltaire returned to France in 1729, and published several works. The most important ones were *History of Charles XII* (1731) and his best-known play, *Zaïre* (1732). In 1733, his *Letters Concerning the English Nation* appeared in England. This book appeared in France the next year in an unauthorized edition called *Philosophical Letters.* Voltaire's praise of English customs, institutions, and style of thought was an indirect criticism of their French counterparts. French authorities condemned the book, and he fled from Paris.

Detail of a pastel (1736) by Maurice Quentin de La Tour; Palais de Versailles, Versailles, France

Voltaire

Voltaire found a home with the Marquise du Châtelet, one of the most cultured and intelligent women of the day. From 1734 to 1749, he lived in her chateau at Cirey in Lorraine. During this period, he wrote several plays, an essay on metaphysics, two works on Sir Isaac Newton, and some poetry. He also wrote two notable philosophical tales. One of them, *Zadig* (1747), explores the problem of human destiny. The other, *Micromégas,* was started at Cirey and was published in 1752. In it, Voltaire used giant visitors from a distant star and from the planet Saturn to discuss the relative insignificance of human pretensions in answering religious questions. In this work, Voltaire also encouraged the use of human reason for the development of science.

Later years. Following du Châtelet's death in 1749, Voltaire accepted the invitation of Frederick the Great to settle in Berlin. After three years of living under the social and intellectual tyranny of the "Philosopher King," as

Voltaire called him, Voltaire settled in Switzerland. A severe earthquake in Portugal in 1755 inspired Voltaire to write an important philosophical poem, *The Lisbon Disaster.* This work was published with his *Poem on Natural Law* in 1756.

In 1759, Voltaire purchased an estate called Ferney on the French-Swiss border. Ferney soon became the intellectual capital of Europe. There Voltaire wrote *Candide,* added to his *Philosophical Dictionary,* and completed his *Universal History,* also called *Essay on the Manners and Spirit of Nations* (1759-1766). He fought religious intolerance and aided victims of religious persecution. His rallying cry was "Écrasez l'infâme" ("Crush the evil thing"), referring to religious superstition.

Voltaire returned to Paris at the age of 83 and was enthusiastically received. There he saw his last play, *Irène* (1778), warmly applauded. But the excitement of the trip was too much for him, and he died in Paris.

The Roman Catholic Church, because of much criticism by Voltaire, refused to allow him to be buried in church ground. However, his body was finally taken to an abbey in Champagne. In 1791, Voltaire's remains were transferred to the Panthéon in Paris, where many of France's greatest are buried.   Carol L. Sherman

See also **Châtelet, Marquise du; Peace** (From the 1400's to the 1700's).

Additional resources

Gray, John. *Voltaire.* 1997. Reprint. Routledge, 1999.
Knapp, Bettina L. *Voltaire Revisited.* Twayne, 2000.
Mason, Haydn T. *Candide: Optimism Demolished.* Twayne, 1992.
        Voltaire. Johns Hopkins, 1981.

Volume of a body is the amount of space it occupies. The unit of measurement for volume is the cube, whose edges are of equal length. The volume of a box may be measured in either cubic feet or cubic meters.

There are several ways of measuring the volume of a substance, depending upon the shape of the substance and whether it is a solid or liquid. The volume of a rectangular solid, such as a box, is found by multiplying the length by the width by the depth (or height). This could be stated in the formula $v = lwd$ (or lwh). A cubic foot equals 1,728 cubic inches, and a cubic meter equals 1,000,000 cubic centimeters.

The volume of a cylinder is determined by multiplying the area of the base by the height, or $v = \pi r^2 h$. The area of the base is obtained by multiplying π (or about 3.1416) by the square of its radius. The volume of a sphere is computed by the formula $v = \frac{4}{3}\pi r^3$ (or about $4.189 r^3$).

Liquids are usually measured by special glass devices having a graduated scale. In the inch-pound system of measurement customarily used in the United States, the main units are the gallon, quart, pint, and fluid ounce. A gallon equals 4 quarts, a quart equals 2 pints, and a pint equals 16 fluid ounces. In the metric system, liquids are measured mainly in milliliters and liters. One liter is equal to 1,000 milliliters.   Leland F. Webb

Related articles in *World Book* include:

Barrel	Gallon	Pint	Weights and
Bushel	Liter	Quart	measures
Density	Peck		

Volunteers of America is a Christian human service organization that provides spiritual and material services to the needy. It has more than 700 program centers throughout the United States.

Volunteers of America operates maternity homes and child placement services, summer camps, homes and clubs for the aged, nursing homes and special care facilities, rehabilitation services for disabled people, emergency shelters for the homeless, and day-care centers. It sponsors low-cost housing for the poor and the elderly, and has helped establish such housing in many communities. The Volunteers gather clothing and household goods for the needy and assist prisoners and parolees and their families. The organization's spiritual services include missions, Sunday schools, Bible study groups, and spiritual counseling and guidance.

Ballington Booth and his wife, Maud Ballington Booth, founded Volunteers of America in New York City in 1896. The organization's headquarters are in Alexandria, Virginia.   Critically reviewed by the Volunteers of America

Volvox. See Protozoan (Flagellates).

Vomiting, *VAHM uh tihng,* is the action that expels the contents of the stomach through the mouth. It may indicate something as minor as overeating or as serious as approaching death. Vomiting can result from a wide variety of causes, including anxiety, bacterial infections, chemical irritation of the stomach, pregnancy, radiation, ulcers, unusual motion, or severe pain. Vomiting is usually preceded by *nausea,* an unpleasant sensation in the stomach area (see **Nausea**).

Vomiting can cause death by suffocation in people who accidentally breathe in the *vomitus* (vomited material). This often occurs in intoxicated or unconscious people who vomit while lying on their backs. Repeated vomiting over many hours can cause death by dehydration, especially in infants (see **Dehydration**). Vomiting after a head injury may indicate damage to the brain stem, and the person should receive treatment immediately.

When a person vomits, the stomach contents are expelled by pressure created by the abdominal muscles and the *diaphragm,* a large muscle at the bottom of the ribs. This muscular activity is called *retching.* Retching involves movement of the diaphragm downward, contraction of the abdominal muscles, and squeezing of the stomach contents upward. A person vomits when retching becomes intense enough to force the stomach contents through the *esophagus*—the tube connecting the stomach and throat.   K. E. Money

Von Braun, *vahn BROWN,* **Wernher,** *VAIR nuhr* (1912-1977), was one of the world's foremost rocket engineers and a leading authority on space travel. Von Braun directed teams that built the rockets that sent the first American into space and landed the first astronauts on the moon.

Von Braun was born on March 23, 1912, in Wirsitz, Germany (now Wyrzysk, Poland). In 1932, he became an adviser in Germany's rocket program. He played a major role in developing the V-2 rocket, with which Germany bombed Allied cities during World War II (1939-1945). In 1944, Heinrich Himmler, chief of the Nazi secret police, tried to take over the German rocket program. He jailed von Braun, who refused to cooperate. Adolf Hitler, the Nazi dictator, freed von Braun later that year.

In 1945, von Braun led a group of German scientists who surrendered to the United States Army. Von Braun and 116 others were sent to the United States to work on guided missile systems. In 1950, the Army assigned von Braun and his team to the Redstone Arsenal in

Huntsville, Alabama, to develop the first large U.S. ballistic missile. Von Braun became a United States citizen in 1955.

Von Braun's team developed the four-stage Jupiter rocket that launched Explorer 1, the first United States Earth satellite. Another of the group's rockets, the Redstone, launched America's first astronaut, Alan B. Shepard, Jr., in 1961. Other von Braun projects included the Saturn rockets. In 1969, a Saturn 5 rocket launched the astronauts who made the first landing on the moon.

In 1960, the Army transferred von Braun and his team to Huntsville's new George C. Marshall Space Flight Center, operated by the National Aeronautics and Space Administration (NASA). In 1970, NASA appointed von Braun deputy associate administrator for planning. In 1972, von Braun resigned from NASA and became an executive of Fairchild Industries, a major aerospace company. From 1975 to 1977, he was president of the National Space Institute, an organization that seeks to promote better public understanding of the U.S. space program. Von Braun died on June 16, 1977.

William J. Cromie

Vonnegut, *VAHN uh guht,* **Kurt** (1922-2007), was an American author who used many devices of science-fiction writing in his works, including space travel and fantastic inventions. Although the tone of his fiction is often playful, he was admittedly a moralizing writer with a gloomy view of humanity.

Vonnegut portrayed a universe that is essentially without purpose in such novels as *Player Piano* (1952), *Cat's Cradle* (1963), and *Breakfast of Champions* (1973). In these works, all absolute systems for organizing human activity—whether political, religious, or scientific—are inevitably destructive. Vonnegut's moralizing consists of advice to be kind, to have pity, to seek companionship, and to enjoy the simple human pleasures.

Vonnegut's experiences in World War II (1939-1945) particularly affected his attitudes. While serving in the United States Army, he was captured by the Germans and imprisoned in Dresden, Germany. He saw that city's destruction by British and American bombing in 1945. His response to that event is reflected throughout his fiction, but dealt with directly only in *Slaughterhouse-Five* (1969), generally considered his most significant work. In that novel, he confronted and accepted what he saw as humanity's tendency to inflict catastrophe on itself. He suggested that our only hope for survival lies in a despairingly comic awareness of human folly.

Vonnegut's other novels include *The Sirens of Titan* (1959), *Mother Night* (1962), *God Bless You, Mr. Rosewater* (1965), *Slapstick* (1976), *Jailbird* (1979), *Deadeye Dick* (1982), *Galápagos* (1985), *Bluebeard* (1987), and *Hocus Pocus* (1990). Vonnegut blended fiction and nonfiction in *Timequake* (1997).

Several of Vonnegut's short stories were collected in *Welcome to the Monkey House* (1968). Many of his nonfiction pieces were collected in *Wampeters, Foma and Granfalloons* (1974), *Palm Sunday* (1981), *Fates Worse Than Death* (1991), *Bagombo Snuff Box* (1999), and *A Man Without a Country* (2005). Vonnegut was born on Nov. 11, 1922, in Indianapolis. He died on April 11, 2007.

Arthur M. Saltzman

Von Neumann, *vahn NOY mahn,* **John** (1903-1957), was a notable mathematician. He wrote *The Mathemati-*

cal Foundations of Quantum Mechanics (1932). Quantum mechanics is a field of physics that describes the structure of the atom and the motion of atomic particles.

Von Neumann also founded *game theory,* a mathematical method for studying competitions. This method is used to investigate complex problems in economics, political science, and sociology. Perhaps von Neumann's best-known book is *The Theory of Games and Economic Behavior* (1944), written with Oskar Morgenstern. See **Game theory.**

Von Neumann made important contributions to the design of high-speed electronic computers. Several generations of computers have been based on his concepts. Von Neumann was born on Dec. 28, 1903, in Budapest, Hungary. In 1937, he became an American citizen. He died on Feb. 8, 1957.

Arthur Gittleman

Von Recklinghausen's disease. See **Neurofibromatosis.**

Von Sternberg, Josef (1894-1969), was an American motion-picture director. He became famous for directing films that starred the German-born actress Marlene Dietrich. These movies feature the vivid, unusual settings and lighting that characterize his major films.

Von Sternberg first directed Dietrich in *The Blue Angel,* which was made in Germany in 1930. The success of this movie led to six more Von Sternberg-Dietrich films, all produced in Hollywood. They were *Morocco* (1930), *Dishonored* (1931), *Shanghai Express* (1932), *Blonde Venus* (1932), *The Scarlet Empress* (1934), and *The Devil Is a Woman* (1935).

Von Sternberg, whose real name was Jonas Sternberg, was born on May 29, 1894, in Vienna, Austria. His family moved to the United States when he was 7 years old. He made his debut as a director in *The Salvation Hunters* (1925). Von Sternberg directed three of the earliest gangster films—*Underworld* (1927), *The Drag Net* (1928), and *The Docks of New York* (1928). He died on Dec. 22, 1969.

John F. Mariani

Von Willebrand's disease, *vahn WIHL uh brandz,* is a hereditary disease in which blood fails to clot properly. For clotting to occur, blood must contain various substances called *clotting factors.* Von Willebrand's disease is caused by a deficiency of one such factor, called the *von Willebrand factor.* It is similar to a more serious blood disorder called *hemophilia,* which causes severe internal bleeding (see **Hemophilia**). Most von Willebrand's patients experience mild bleeding, often from the nose. But some patients bleed severely, especially after having a tooth extracted or following surgery or childbirth. Blood products containing the von Willebrand factor are given intravenously to treat the disease. A drug called *desmopressin acetate* also helps some patients.

Alan David Gilman

Voodoo, also spelled *vodou,* is a term used for a variety of beliefs, traditions, and practices that are derived largely from traditional African religions and from Christianity. The word *voodoo* comes from an African word that means *god, spirit,* or *sacred object.* Various forms of voodoo are practiced in Haiti and other Caribbean countries, in Brazil, in Benin and other West African countries, and in parts of the United States.

Followers of voodoo, or *voodooists,* believe in the existence of one supreme being and of strong and weak spirits. Each person has a protector spirit who rewards

R. Rowan, FPG

A voodoo ceremony in Haiti centers around a chalk diagram and includes special prayers. West African slaves introduced voodoo to Haiti.

the individual with wealth and punishes with illness. Voodooists also believe that when people die, they go to a place called *Nan Guinin,* which means *Africa but located under the sea.* Each voodoo temple is headed by a *houngan* (priest), also spelled *oungan,* or a *manbo* (priestess) who performs occasional or yearly ceremonies for the benefit of a *pitit kay* (congregation). Assistants called *laplas* and *onsi* help the houngan or manbo. Sometimes, voodoo temples are part of a network of militarylike secret societies established to protect the congregations against abuses from outsiders.

Voodoo originated in Benin and surrounding areas, then spread to the West Indies, especially Haiti. When the first West African slaves arrived in colonial Haiti, they did not have much contact with one another. But as the slaves developed extended families and communities, they began to share beliefs and practices. Many of these traditions came from other faiths, including African religions, Roman Catholicism, and Native American religions. After the Haitian revolution against French colonial rule ended in 1803, traditions were combined, and centers of worship established. In 2003, the Haitian government officially recognized voodoo as a religion in Haiti.   Michel S. Laguerre

See also **Haiti** (People); **Magic** (Contagious magic).

Additional resources

Galembo, Phyllis. *Vodou.* Rev. ed. Ten Speed, 2005.
Ward, Martha. *Voodoo Queen: The Spirited Lives of Marie Laveau.* Univ. Pr. of Miss., 2004.

Vorster, *FAWR stuhr,* **Balthazar Johannes,** *BAHL ta sahr yoh HAHN uhs* (1915-1983), was prime minister of South Africa from 1966 to 1978. Before becoming prime minister, Vorster served as minister of justice. In this position, he vigorously enforced *apartheid,* the nation's racial segregation policy. Police were given broad powers to crush opposition to apartheid. As prime minister, he relaxed some apartheid practices but still maintained the overall policy. He enforced territorial segregation, declaring several black African areas to be self-governing. Police control remained strict. In 1976, violent riots erupted in response to his government's policies.

Vorster resigned as prime minister in 1978. He was then appointed to the ceremonial post of state presi-

dent. But he resigned in 1979 after a government commission revealed his involvement in a financial scandal. Vorster died on Sept. 10, 1983.

Vorster was born on Dec. 13, 1915, in Jamestown, in what is now Eastern Cape province. From 1942 to 1944, during World War II, he was imprisoned for his connection with a pro-Nazi political movement. In 1953, he was elected to Parliament as a member of the National Party. He became minister of justice in 1961.   John Lambert

Voting is a method by which groups of people make decisions. In most countries, people vote to choose government officials and to decide public issues. People also vote to make decisions in such groups as juries, labor unions, corporations, and social clubs. This article deals with voting in political elections.

The right of citizens to select their leaders in open elections is a key feature of democracy. Specific election rules vary. In *direct elections,* the citizens themselves vote for the officials. In *indirect elections,* the citizens elect representatives, who then choose the officials. For instance, the president of the United States is elected indirectly. The voters of each state select electors, who make up the Electoral College. The Electoral College, in turn, chooses the president.

Many voting decisions are based on *majority rule.* Under majority rule, a candidate must receive more than half the votes in order to win. A decision by *plurality* may be used when there are more than two candidates. A candidate with a plurality receives more votes than any other candidate, but does not necessarily have a majority of the votes. In some countries, elections are conducted according to *proportional representation.* Under such systems, a political party is represented in government in proportion to its share of the total vote.

People can vote on a variety of issues. For example, they may vote on whether the government should build a school, expand the police force, or impose a tax. Under some systems, voters may approve or reject proposed laws through elections called *referendums.* A *recall election* allows voters to remove elected officials from office before the end of their term.

Who may vote. Governments usually require that citizens reach a certain age before they have the right to vote. In most countries, the minimum voting age for national elections is 18. Governments also usually require that people live in the country for a certain number of years before they can vote.

All democracies limit the right to vote in certain cases. In many countries, for example, people who are serving prison sentences for certain crimes are not allowed to vote. Some countries deny the voting rights of people with certain types of mental disabilities.

Democratic nations have extended *suffrage* (the right to vote) to many people who were once denied that right. For instance, women could not vote in many countries until the early 1900's. In South Africa, a policy of *apartheid* (racial segregation) denied black citizens the vote for many years. The policy ended in 1991.

The Constitution of the United States has been amended several times to extend voting rights. The 15th Amendment, adopted in 1870, prohibited states from denying a citizen the right to vote because of race. The 19th Amendment, adopted in 1920, protected the voting rights of women.

In the United States, even after the adoption of the 15th Amendment, several states sought to deprive African Americans of their voting rights. Certain states required citizens to pay a *poll tax* to gain the right to vote. Officials in some states applied the poll tax laws only to African Americans and poor whites. In 1965, Congress passed the Voting Rights Act to prevent these and other methods of depriving people of their rights.

Registration is the process by which a person's name is added to an official list of qualified voters. On election day in many countries, officials check each person's name against the registration list before they let the person vote. In some countries, the voter receives a voter registration card. In the United States, voters can usually register in person or by mail. In most states, voters remain permanently registered unless they move.

Many governments do not require formal registration prior to an election. Instead, they require people to show proof of citizenship or residence—such as a passport or identification card—before voting.

Voting districts. Many countries, states, and provinces are divided into areas called *districts* for election purposes. The smallest voting areas in the United States are *precincts*. In the United Kingdom and several other countries, voting districts are called *constituencies*. Citizens usually vote at a *polling place* in their district.

In most countries, each district has about the same number of inhabitants and equal representation in government. The boundaries of voting districts must sometimes be changed to reflect changes in population. The redrawing of district boundaries is called *redistricting*. In some countries, members of government have sought to use redistricting to favor one political party over another. This process is called *gerrymandering*.

Since 1962, the Supreme Court of the United States has issued several rulings concerning redistricting. The rulings have sought to ensure that each voter has equal power in the election process.

Methods of voting. Until the 1800's, voting was usually conducted orally and in public. But as more people gained the vote, many countries began using written ballots. For many years, the ballots of different political parties had distinct features that made it easy for onlookers to see what party a voter supported. But under this system, some citizens faced pressure to vote in certain ways, and bribery was common. As a result, many countries began using secret ballots. Today, most countries use a system in which each voter marks a ballot while alone in a booth.

Many countries use *voting machines*—that is, mechanical devices or computerized systems for recording and counting votes. In a *lever machine,* the oldest type of voting machine, voters use a pointer to select candidates and then pull a lever to enter their votes.

Voting methods have changed as technology has advanced. Since the late 1900's, computerized voting systems have become increasingly popular. With *punch card* systems, voters select candidates by punching holes in computer cards. The cards are then fed into a card reader, and a computer totals all valid votes. With *optical scanning* systems, voters mark ballots that are then fed into a computerized scanning device. Other computerized systems allow voters to make selections by pushing buttons or by touching boxes on a computer screen. Oregon has conducted elections entirely by mail since 1998, and other U.S. states have begun using the same method. Some governments have experimented with allowing voters to cast ballots over the Internet.

Most governments allow *absentee voting* for citizens who are unable to vote in person. Absentee voters send their ballots by mail. Absentee voters may include people in the armed forces, college students, people with disabilities, and travelers who are abroad on business or vacation. In some countries, a voter may authorize another person to cast a vote for him or her. Such a vote is called a *proxy* vote. Another nontraditional voting method is *early voting*. Early voting allows people to vote in special polling places before the election.

If a voting machine system is used, votes are counted automatically. But in some elections, paper ballots must be counted by hand. If the result of an election is close, one or more *recounts* may be held.

Voting behavior. Many people do not exercise their right to vote. *Voter turnout* is the percentage of people qualified to vote who actually vote. Since the 1970's, voter turnout in U.S. presidential elections has usually been between 50 and 55 percent. In many other democracies, voter turnout is 80 percent or higher. Turnout is usually higher for national elections than it is for state, provincial, and local elections.

Social scientists in many countries have examined the voting patterns of various groups. In most countries, men have traditionally been more likely to vote than women. But the number of women voters has increased significantly since the 1970's. In some countries, such as the United States and Japan, women are now more likely to vote than men. Studies have also shown that people between the ages of 55 and 75 are more likely to vote than people of other ages.

Many voters consistently support one political party over another. Others, called *independents,* do not have loyalty to a party. Family and social background can greatly influence how people vote. For example, many people adopt the same political party identification as their parents. Dramatic national or world events may also affect voting patterns. For instance, during the Great Depression of the 1930's, United States voters increasingly favored the Democratic Party, which emphasized government aid for the needy.   Thomas R. Palfrey III

Related articles in *World Book* include:

Apportionment	Democracy	Parliamentary pro-
Ballot	Election	cedure (Voting
Civil rights	Election campaign	on motions)
Colonial life in	Fifteenth	Plebiscite
America (Gov-	Amendment	Poll tax
ernment and	Gerrymander	Recall
law enforce-	Grandfather clause	United Nations
ment)	Initiative and	(Meetings and
Congress of the	referendum	voting; Voting)
United States	Logrolling	Voting machine
(Passing a bill)		Woman suffrage

Voting machine is a mechanical device or computerized system for recording and counting votes. Voters in the United States and other countries use voting machines when choosing candidates for government office. They also use such machines when voting on various issues, such as proposals to raise property taxes or issue municipal bonds. Certain kinds of voting machines, called legislative voting machines, record votes

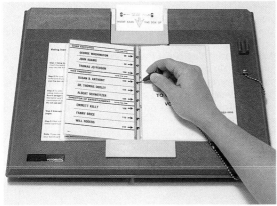

Larry Korb, Business Records Corporation

A punch-card voting system uses a computer card. The voter punches holes in the card, as shown with this mock ballot. A computer later counts the votes and prints the results.

in a number of lawmaking bodies, including the U.S. House of Representatives and many state legislatures. This article discusses voting machines used in elections.

Kinds of electoral voting machines. Lever machines were the earliest voting machines used in elections. To use a lever machine, the voter moves a master lever that closes a set of curtains around the voter and unlocks the voting machine. In front of the voter are the names of all the candidates, arranged in rows according to the office they are seeking and their political party. The voter turns a pointer next to the name of each candidate he or she chooses. After selecting the candidates, the voter pulls the master lever back to the starting position, and the votes are recorded in the machine.

Computerized voting systems are the most widely used voting method in many countries. There are three main categories of these voting systems: (1) direct-recording electronic (DRE) systems, (2) punch-card systems, and (3) optically scanned paper ballots. The DRE technology is similar to the lever machine. But, instead of pulling a lever, the voter makes selections by pushing a button or by touching boxes on a computer screen. The votes are counted electronically, not mechanically.

With punch-card systems, the voter punches a hole in a computer card. The small piece of paper that is punched out of the card is called a *chad.* The punch cards are fed into a card reader, and a computer totals all valid votes for each candidate. With optically scanned paper ballots, voters make choices either by filling ovals or boxes with a pencil or by completing arrows to the candidates' names. A computer then scans the ballot and records the votes.

Advantages and disadvantages. Properly designed voting machines provide a fast, accurate, impartial, and secret count of election results. Machines with effective safeguards make it hard to tamper with ballots or "stuff" a ballot box with illegal ballots. Well-designed systems can also reduce the likelihood of *overvotes* and *undervotes.* An overvote results from a voter accidentally voting for too many candidates for a particular office. An undervote occurs when no vote is recorded. This can occur when a ballot is improperly marked or misread.

On the other hand, confusing ballot layouts and tech-

nical problems can lead to large numbers of overvotes and undervotes. Many punch-card systems may not properly count votes if the chads have not been completely punched out from the cards. Debates regarding partially punched ballots and complaints about confusing ballot layouts were largely responsible for a delay in the decision of the U.S. presidential election of 2000. See **Election of 2000.**

History. The first use of voting machines in an election was in Lockport, New York, in 1892. Manufacture and distribution of the machines continued steadily through the mid-1900's. In the late 1900's, computerized voting systems gradually replaced lever machines. By the 1990's, they had become the most popular method of voting in the United States. Several other countries use computerized voting systems for national or local elections. Thomas R. Palfrey III

Voting Rights Act of 1965. See African Americans (Political gains).

Voucher, in education, is a certificate that a family can use to pay for a child's schooling. Under a *voucher plan* or *voucher system,* a government or organization provides a family with a voucher worth a fixed amount of money to be spent on the education of each child. Families may then use the funds for education at a school that accepts vouchers and that will admit their child. The voucher system usually applies to children's education at the elementary school level. But, in some cases, it may also apply to high school students. Vouchers usually take the form of checks made out to parents. The checks must be endorsed over to the schools.

A number of countries use voucher plans, or similar arrangements, in their primary and secondary school systems. In some countries—including Chile, the Netherlands, and Sweden—school funding provided by the government can be used at public or private institutions.

In the United States, voucher plans have been the subject of much debate. Supporters of vouchers believe that families should be able to choose from among several options when deciding where to send their children to school. They also argue that voucher systems increase competition among schools, which leads to improved instruction. Opponents of voucher plans argue that the programs mainly benefit families that have the resources to learn about school options and to send their children outside local neighborhoods. They also argue that voucher programs may weaken public education and increase segregation. Many feel that public funds should not be used to fund education offered by religious groups, which operate many private schools.

Because of the controversy surrounding voucher systems, their use in the United States has been limited. Some cities, including Milwaukee and Cleveland, have issued publicly funded vouchers for low-income children to attend private schools. A number of private foundations have also provided vouchers to poor children in large cities. In 2004, the U.S. Congress passed a law to create a federally funded voucher system for students in Washington, D.C. The law allows the vouchers to be used at private schools.

Outside the field of education, a voucher can be a receipt or certificate that provides evidence of a payment, or is *redeemable* (able to be exchanged) for goods and services. Such vouchers are commonly used by businesses and other organizations.   Lawrence O. Picus

See also **Education** (Who should choose a child's school?).

Vowel. When a person says "ah" for the doctor, an open sound is made with free passage of breath. This sound is a vowel, as are all the other open and freely breathed sounds in speech. In English, the vowel sounds are represented by the letters, *a, e, i, o, u,* and sometimes *w* and *y* (as in *now, city).* But each letter stands for several sounds. The open quality of vowels distinguishes them from *consonants.* Consonants are formed with the organs of speech more or less closed. A vowel may be a syllable in itself, or it may be joined with one or more consonants to produce a syllable. See also **Consonant; Pronunciation.**   Susan M. Gass

Voyager is either of two United States space probes launched in 1977 to Jupiter and beyond. The two craft continue to provide valuable information.

Information gathered by the Voyager probes forms the basis of the modern study of Jupiter, Saturn, Uranus, Neptune, and their satellites, rings, and *magnetic fields* (regions where magnetic force can be detected). The probes discovered nearly two dozen natural satellites. They also found evidence of geologic activity on two previously known moons—volcanoes on Jupiter's moon Io and icy geysers on Neptune's moon Triton. The mission also discovered craters on most of the satellites, an ancient record of intense bombardment by meteoroids and comets. Scientists used Voyager data to calculate the density of 17 satellites and to determine the composition of the atmosphere of Saturn's moon Titan.

The National Aeronautics and Space Administration (NASA) launched Voyager 1 on Sept. 5, 1977. The probe made its closest approach to Jupiter on March 5, 1979, encountered Saturn on Nov. 12, 1980, then headed toward *interstellar space* (the space between the stars). Voyager 2, launched on Aug. 20, 1977, made its closest approach to Jupiter on July 9, 1979, Saturn on Aug. 25, 1981, Uranus on Jan. 24, 1986, and Neptune on Aug. 25, 1989, then traveled toward interstellar space.

The Voyagers carried identical sets of scientific instruments. One instrument measured the strength, shape, and direction of the planets' magnetic fields. Another studied waves traveling through *plasma* trapped within the fields. Plasma consists of electrically charged atoms, as well as electrons that are not parts of atoms.

Three devices measured the quantities and speeds of these charged particles. Five instruments measured ultraviolet rays, visible light, infrared rays, and radio waves given off by the planets and their satellites, rings, and plasma. Also, as the two craft moved behind each planet, the planet's atmosphere and rings blocked the radio signals transmitted by the Voyagers in ways that revealed details of their structure.

The Voyagers' radio receivers and their particle and magnetism detectors were still operating in the early 2000's. Scientists monitored their data in hope of detecting the *heliopause,* where interstellar space begins. In late 2004, Voyager 1 crossed a shock wave called the *termination shock,* becoming the first craft to reach the region of space that lies just inside the heliopause. The crossing occurred at a distance of about 8.7 billion miles (14 billion kilometers) from the sun. In 2007, Voyager 2 crossed the shock in a different area and at a distance of

about 7.8 billion miles (12.6 billion kilometers) from the sun. By detecting the shock at different distances from the sun, the two craft confirmed scientists' belief that the solar system is not perfectly round.   Carolyn C. Porco

Voyageurs National Park, *VWAH yah ZHURZ,* lies in northern Minnesota at the United States-Canadian border. Early French-Canadian traders and pioneers known as *voyageurs* traveled the area's scenic waterways. The park was approved by Congress in 1971 and established in 1975. It contains many lakes. Waterways are the main means of travel in the park. The major lakes include Kabetogama, Namakan, and Rainy. Moose, black bears, deer, timber wolves, wildfowl—including golden eagles—and other animals live in the park. For the park's area, see **National Park System** (table: National parks).
    Critically reviewed by the National Park Service

V/STOL is a type of aircraft that can take off and land vertically or on a short runway. The term *V/STOL* stands for Vertical/Short Take-Off and Landing.

A V/STOL plane can take off from or land on a runway less than 500 feet (150 meters) long. Large conventional planes may need more than 5,000 feet (1,500 meters) of runway. V/STOL's have great military value because they can land on small airstrips near battlefields and take off from and land on ships that do not have big flight decks.

Although helicopters can take off and land vertically, they are not considered V/STOL's. A helicopter has one or two rotors, or *rotary wings.* But a V/STOL aircraft has *fixed wings,* like those of a conventional airplane, that provide lift during forward flight. This feature enables a V/STOL to fly much faster than a helicopter can. V/STOL aircraft can slow to a hover in the air. But they operate less efficiently than helicopters when hovering.

V/STOL's can be classified into five main groups, depending on their lift-propulsion system. (1) Tilt-wing aircraft have engines mounted on their wings. The wings can be tilted to change the direction of the engine thrust. (2) Tilt-engine aircraft have engines that can be moved to direct the engine thrust. (3) Variable-thrust aircraft have special nozzles attached to their engines. The nozzles can be moved to change the direction of the engine thrust. (4) Lift-and-thrust aircraft have two sets of engines. One provides forward thrust, and the other provides lift. (5) Lift-fan aircraft have horizontally mounted *ducted propellers* that provide vertical thrust for hovering, take-off, and landing (see **Ducted propeller**).

The United States tested the first modern V/STOL's in 1954. These aircraft included the Navy's Convair XFY-1 "Pogo." It took off and landed in a vertical position, with its tail touching the ground (see **Airplane** [picture: The Convair XFY-1]). But it was too difficult to land to be practical. The other V/STOL tested in 1954 was the Transcendental Model 1G. A tilting rotor at the end of each wing let it take off vertically. The first widely used V/STOL, the Harrier, entered service with Britain's Royal Air Force in 1969 and with the U.S. Marine Corps in 1971. British and U.S. forces have used Harriers frequently. In the 1970's, the Soviet Navy developed a V/STOL called the Yak-38 Forger. After the Soviet Union broke up in 1991, Russia withdrew the Yak-38's from service.   William A. Crossley

See also **Airplane** (picture: V/STOL's).

Vuillard, *vwee YAHR,* **Édouard,** *ay DWAR* (1868-1940), was a French painter. His pictures portray his private world—a view from a window, or corners of his studio and living room enclosed by walls and furniture. In his interior scenes, he showed figures reading, relaxing, or concentrating on common tasks. Many show women engaged in sewing or dressmaking, the profession of his mother, with whom Vuillard lived for much of his career. He painted his environment both as a place of quiet and rest and as a disturbing situation where even the walls appear menacing. Vuillard was influenced by Japanese art, which can be seen in the brilliantly colored flat patterns of his paintings.

Vuillard was born on Nov. 11, 1868, in Cuiseaux, near Chalon. He moved to Paris in 1877, and he became associated with the *Nabis* group of artists. Nancy J. Troy

Vulcan, *VUHL kuhn,* in Roman mythology, was the god of fire, metalworking, and skilled craftwork in general. He also served as the blacksmith of the gods. Vulcan produced armor, weapons, and many other works. All were perfectly made, and some had magic qualities. Roman metalworkers and other craftworkers worshiped Vulcan as their patron.

Vulcan was originally a god of fire, especially fire as a destructive force. The English word *volcano* comes from the Italian form of Vulcan's name. Vulcan came to be identified with the Greek god Hephaestus and thus became associated with metalworking and craftwork. Many of the myths about Vulcan are identical with myths about Hephaestus.

Vulcan was believed to be a son of Jupiter and Juno, the king and queen of the gods. One myth describes Vulcan as being the son of Juno alone, with no father. Vulcan was lame—the only major Roman god who was physically imperfect. Some myths say he was born lame, and others say he became lame from a fall. Although Vulcan was the least attractive of the gods, he married Venus, the goddess of love and beauty. Venus was unfaithful to Vulcan with both gods and mortal men. Many myths tell of Vulcan's jealousy over his wife's love affairs.

Daniel P. Harmon

See also **Hephaestus; Venus.**

Vulgate, *VUHL gayt,* is the name of a Latin translation of the Bible, which was largely the work of Saint Jerome. Jerome's contribution to the Vulgate was completed in A.D. 405. The Vulgate replaced earlier Latin versions and eventually became the standard Bible of the Western Church. The word *vulgate* comes from a Latin word that means *common* or *popular.*

The Council of Trent made the Vulgate the standard Roman Catholic translation in 1546. The official text consisted of a revised edition that was not issued until the 1590's. The traditional English translation of the Vulgate is called the Douay-Rheims, or Douay, Bible. It was named after Douay, France, where the Old Testament was published in 1609 and 1610; and Rheims, France, where the New Testament was published in 1582. Richard Challoner, an English bishop, revised the Douay Bible from 1749 to 1763. Challoner's edition was the standard Bible of English-speaking Catholics until about 1943. In that year, Pope Pius XII encouraged Catholic Biblical scholars to base modern translations on the original Greek and Hebrew texts. A number of English translations of the Bible are now approved for Catholic use. But only a few of these are based on the Vulgate.

The Vulgate differs from the original Hebrew and Greek texts of the Bible in the names of some of the books and in the way some of the chapters and verses have been divided. The Vulgate Old Testament, like the Greek Old Testament, also contains some books that Protestants consider to be part of the Apocrypha.

From 1969 to 1977, a commission appointed by Pope Paul VI prepared a new Latin translation of the Bible. This translation reflects modern advances in Biblical scholarship but keeps the style and much of the language of the Vulgate. Terrance D. Callan

See also **Bible** (The first translations).

Vulture is a common name for various large birds of prey. Vultures feed chiefly on *carrion* (dead and decaying animal flesh). Most vultures have weak feet and a bare head and neck. All have a slightly hooked beak. Their feathers generally are uniform in color and are brownish, black, or white. Vultures live on all continents except Australia and Antarctica, usually in open country. They have keen eyesight and are excellent soaring birds.

Vultures tend to live in groups. During the breeding season, males pair off with females and nest on the ground under overhanging cliffs, in logs, and in caves. The female lays from one to three light-colored eggs. Both parents share in caring for the young.

There are two distantly related families of vultures— *New World vultures* and *Old World vultures.* New World vultures are native to North and South America. Old World vultures are native to Europe, Asia, and Africa.

New World vultures consist of seven species, five of which are native to North America. All New World vultures have a unique *nostril hole* in their beak. When the bird is viewed from the side, a person can see through its beak by looking into the nostril hole.

The *black vulture* is the most common North American vulture. It ranges from the southern United States to central Chile and Argentina and measures about 24 inches (61 centimeters) long. The *turkey vulture* is found from southern Canada to Argentina. It has dark brown to olive-gray feathers. In some areas, black vultures, turkey vultures, and *lesser yellow-headed vultures* soar together in flocks of thousands of birds. These flocks resemble columns of smoke in the sky.

Norman Myers

Egyptian vultures use rocks to break open ostrich eggs. The bird hurls the rock from its beak with a snap of the neck.

Turkey vulture
Cathartes aura
Found from southern Canada
to southern South America
Body length: 26 to 32 inches
(66 to 81 centimeters)

Black vulture
Coragyps atratus
Found from southern United States
to southern South America
Body length: 23 to 27 inches
(58 to 69 centimeters)

WORLD BOOK illustrations by Guy Tudor

The *king vulture* is one of the most striking vultures. Its head is deeply furrowed and brilliantly colored, with fleshy growths of rich orange. This bird ranges from southern Mexico to northern Argentina and grows to a length of about 27 inches (69 centimeters).

A New World vulture called the *California condor* is one of the most endangered birds. During the mid-1980's, scientists captured all remaining wild California condors. Since then, some California condors have been bred in captivity and then released in California. The California condor measures up to 55 inches (139 centimeters) long and has a wingspread of up to 9 $\frac{1}{2}$ feet (2.9 meters). Its relative, South America's *Andean condor,* has a slightly larger wingspread. It is the world's largest bird of prey. See **Condor.**

Old World vultures form a family of 15 species. The largest is the *cinereous vulture,* or the *European black vulture.* This bird lives chiefly in mountains of the Mediterranean region and central Asia, including the Himalaya. It grows to 39 inches (99 centimeters) long. Its wingspread reaches about 9 feet (2.7 meters). This species often drives off other vultures to feed on carrion.

The large, powerful *lammergeier* occurs in about the same range as the European black vulture. It is also called the *bearded vulture* because it has a "beard" of black bristles on its chin. Occasionally, it breaks bones by dropping them on rocks from high in the air. It then eats the exposed marrow. See **Lammergeier.**

The *Egyptian vulture* is found from Africa to India. It often eats ostrich eggs, which it breaks by hurling small stones with its beak. The *white-headed vulture* and the *palm nut vulture* live in Africa south of the Sahara. The white-headed vulture sometimes hunts small antelope, lizards, and flamingos. The palm nut vulture feeds mainly on oil from the nuts of palm trees.

Thomas G. Balgooyen

Scientific classification. New World vultures are in the family Cathartidae. The king vulture is *Sarcoramphus papa;* the California condor, *Gymnogyps californianus;* and the Andean condor, *Vultur gryphus.* Old World vultures are in the family Accipitridae. The cinereous vulture is *Aegypius monachus;* the lammergeier, *Gypaetus barbatus;* the Egyptian vulture, *Neophron percnopterus;* the white-headed vulture, *Trigonoceps occipitalis;* and the palm nut vulture is *Gypohierax angolensis.*

See also **Buzzard.**